NETWORKING THE LEARNER

Computers in Education

IFIP - The International Federation for Information Processing

IFIP was founded in 1960 under the auspices of UNESCO, following the First World Computer Congress held in Paris the previous year. An umbrella organization for societies working in information processing, IFIP's aim is two-fold: to support information processing within its member countries and to encourage technology transfer to developing nations. As its mission statement clearly states,

IFIP's mission is to be the leading, truly international, apolitical organization which encourages and assists in the development, exploitation and application of information technology for the benefit of all people.

IFIP is a non-profitmaking organization, run almost solely by 2500 volunteers. It operates through a number of technical committees, which organize events and publications. IFIP's events range from an international congress to local seminars, but the most important are:

- The IFIP World Computer Congress, held every second year;
- open conferences;
- working conferences.

The flagship event is the IFIP World Computer Congress, at which both invited and contributed papers are presented. Contributed papers are rigorously refereed and the rejection rate is high.

As with the Congress, participation in the open conferences is open to all and papers may be invited or submitted. Again, submitted papers are stringently refereed.

The working conferences are structured differently. They are usually run by a working group and attendance is small and by invitation only. Their purpose is to create an atmosphere conducive to innovation and development. Refereeing is less rigorous and papers are subjected to extensive group discussion.

Publications arising from IFIP events vary. The papers presented at the IFIP World Computer Congress and at open conferences are published as conference proceedings, while the results of the working conferences are often published as collections of selected and edited papers.

Any national society whose primary activity is in information may apply to become a full member of IFIP, although full membership is restricted to one society per country. Full members are entitled to vote at the annual General Assembly, National societies preferring a less committed involvement may apply for associate or corresponding membership. Associate members enjoy the same benefits as full members, but without voting rights. Corresponding members are not represented in IFIP bodies. Affiliated membership is open to non-national societies, and individual and honorary membership schemes are also offered.

NETWORKING THE LEARNER

Computers in Education

IFIP TC3
Seventh IFIP World Conference on Computers in Education
WCCE 2001
July 29–August 3, 2001, Copenhagen, Denmark

Edited by

Deryn Watson
King's College London
United Kingdom

Jane Andersen
IT University of Copenhagen
Denmark

KLUWER ACADEMIC PUBLISHERS
BOSTON / DORDRECHT / LONDON

Distributors for North, Central and South America:
Kluwer Academic Publishers
101 Philip Drive
Assinippi Park
Norwell, Massachusetts 02061 USA
Telephone (781) 871-6600
Fax (781) 681-9045
E-Mail <kluwer@wkap.com>

Distributors for all other countries:
Kluwer Academic Publishers Group
Post Office Box 322
3300 AH Dordrecht, THE NETHERLANDS
Telephone 31 786 576 000
Fax 31 786 576 474
E-Mail <services@wkap.nl>

Electronic Services <http://www.wkap.nl>

Library of Congress Cataloging-in-Publication Data

IFIP World Conference on Computers in Education (7th : 2001 : Copenhagen, Denmark)
Networking the learner : computers in education : Seventh IFIP World Conference on Computers in Education, WCCE 2001, July 29–August 3, 2001, Copenhagen, Denmark / IFIP TC3 ; edited by Deryn Watson, Jane Andersen.
p. cm. — (International Federation for Information Processing; 89)
Includes bibliographical references and index.
ISBN 1-4020-7132-9 / 1-4020-7133-7 (pbk.)
1. Computer-assisted instruction—Congresses. 2. Education—Computer network resources—Congresses. 3. Distance education—Congresses. I. Watson, Deryn. II. Andersen, Jane, 1952–. III. IFIP Technical Committee on Education. IV. Title. V. International Federation for Information Processing (Series); 89.

LB1028.5 .I35 2002
371.33'4—dc21 2002-069498

Printed on acid-free paper.
Printed in the United States of America.

Contents

PART EIGHT

PART NINE

PART XI

Preface

Deryn Watson and Jane Andersen
Editors

INTRODUCTION

The role of a Preface is to introduce the nature of the publication. The book that emerges from an IFIP Technical Committee World Conference on Computers in Education is complex, and this complexity lies in the nature of the event from which it emerges. Unlike a number of other major international conferences, those organised within the IFIP education community are active events. A WCCE is unique among major international conferences for the structure that deliberately ensures that all attendees are active participants in the development of the debate. In addition to the major paper presentations and discussion, from international authors, there are panel sessions and professional working groups who debate particular themes throughout the event.

There is no doubt that this was not a dry academic conference – teachers, lecturers and experts, policy makers and researchers, learners and manufacturers mingled and worked together to explore, reflect, discuss and plan for the future. The added value of this event was that we know that it will have an impact on future practice; networks will be formed, both virtual and real - ideas will change and new ones will emerge.

Capturing the essence of this event is a challenge – this post-conference book has three parts. The first is the substantial number of theme papers. These represent a proportion of the total number of papers presented at WCCE 2001. All conference presentations are selected after an international refereeing panel has reviewed their value. A further review then takes place to select those papers that should be identified as *theme papers* for the conference and publication in this book. So this book is not a full conference proceedings, but rather a selection to capture the range, essence and excellence. In addition there are two further parts. The *reports from the discussion panels,* from which the flavour of the debates and active issues emerge. And then the substantial *Professional Group reports*. These cover key topics of current interest within our community, and report the deliberations, ideas and key issues that emerged.

Keynotes hold a particular place in all major conferences, and they are no exception in WCCE 2001. But true to the nature of our field, no keynote address has a printed paper version, as they all were interactive presentations using the full facilities of the media. A synopsis of their content will however be referred to in the Editorial which follows. But this preface does contain the Welcoming and Opening addresses. Firstly because in the IFIP education community we feel that our post-conference books should reflect as many aspects of the nature of the event itself – and the tone and content of the welcoming addresses contribute to this. And secondly, we are always privileged to attract serious Opening Speakers, whose thoughts and ideas set the tone for the complex issues that we will be discussing for the week. The Danish Minister for Education Margrethe Vestager and Deputy Assistant Director-General for Education, UNESCO, Aicha Bah Diallo presented the formal opening speeches. Not only their presence but also the content of their speeches are evidence that this conference is not just an issue for educators and students. IT, Informations Technology is just as much a political project in both the western world and in the developing countries. And so we are proud to include our opening addresses in the Preface. And finally this is where we can acknowledge the contribution of so many colleagues who made the event, and thus this book, possible.

Six years since the last World Conference on Computers in Education, this IFIP meeting, entitled Networking the Learner, promises to be another milestone in the on-going development, progress and reflection on the relationship between Information Technologies and Education.

WELCOME FROM THE CONFERENCE CHAIR

Peter Bollerslev
President of the International Federation of Information Processing, IFIP, and WCCE 2001 Conference Chair

Welcome to WCCE 2001, the Seventh World Conference on Computers in Education – Networking the Learner. In essence this conference has been in preparation since 1993 when the Annual Meeting of the IFIP Technical Committee in Education decided to charge me with organising the event – and this was before the sixth WCCE, in 1995 in Birmingham UK, had occurred! While the preparations have not been intense right from the beginning, activity has built up, and since UNI•C, the Danish Centre for Education and Research, undertook the role as conference host at the beginning of 2001, a group of people have worked hard to prepare for the event. Some have dedicated their full-time work to WCCE 2001 for the last six months.

Perusal of the conference programme indicates that such effort has been worthwhile. Experts from the field of Education and Information Technologies from all parts of the world, over 38 countries, will present in paper sessions, in demonstrations, in workshops, in poster sessions, and in panel sessions – 324 in total. From their content, it is impressive how Information Technology has penetrated education in so many different ways. Participants, currently over 1200 from 60 different countries, will have the opportunity over the week to exchange ideas, to learn from one another's experiences, to make new contacts, to renew old friendships and make new ones.

To arrange a WCCE is a costly affair. The conference fee paid by participants covers a fair part of the total costs, but far from all, and therefore I am grateful to the financial sponsors of the conference: The City of Copenhagen, The Ministry of Education, Gyldendal Education, Lego Dacta, UNI•C, SUN microsystems, TDC (TeleDanmark), Cisco Systems, NetOp, Danware Data, Centr*i*nity, Lærerstandens Brandforsikring, and Learning Lab Denmark. They have supported us with help and assistance, as well as money. The attachment of their logos to conference materials and rooms is an acknowledgement of their support.

I wish to express my thanks to all the people who have worked so hard, most of them on a voluntary basis; the International Programme Committee, the National Organising Committee, Submissions Refereeing Panel, the sub-committees and groups, and all the people behind the scenes. It has been a pleasure to be involved in the preparatory stage; now we have the greater pleasure in joining with all the attendees in the event itself. And we will share this event with others, unable to be here, through the publication of the Post-conference book.

I am proud to welcome every individual participant to the Seventh World Conference of Computers in Education in Wonderful, Wonderful Copenhagen.

WELCOME FROM THE HOST – UNI•C

Dorte Olesen
Managing Director, UNI•C, The Danish IT Centre for Research and Education

On behalf of the National Organizing Committee it is my pleasure to welcome all of you to Copenhagen. I hope you will enjoy your stay here, and benefit from attending this conference. Much effort has been put into creating the programme for the days to come, but in the end the success of this event depends on you – all of you. IFIP Conferences on Computers in Education have been going on since 1970. Much has happened on the IT scene during these 31 years. Most notably, the network has improved tremendously, and with it the communication possibilities between people wanting to learn something new. So the overall theme of the conference 'Networking the Learner' could not be timed better.

When UNI-C took up the challenge of organising this event, it was very much in the hope that we could turn it into a really interactive and dynamic conference. A real networking conference where the input from the presenters would be enhanced by the response from the rest of the participants. So the programme contains many different types of activities, and the opening here with a large audience and a few speakers is not the model for most of the programme – as I am sure you have already noticed looking at the many activities for the days to come. So even though we have speeches in the traditional sense, we also do have a lot of much more directly interactive sessions at WCCE 2001. And I hope you will take this opportunity to be really active here, and hence make the conference an event where you as participants contribute just as much as the speakers. Because most of us learn from doing things ourselves, not from just listening, trying to absorb what is presented and prepared beforehand.

This is a basic learning experience that I believe we all share – and for which IT is such a very suitable tool. With IT, everybody has the chance to be active also during lessons. In this conference we mounted a number of activities that will underpin and enhance this – such as the LEGO Team Challenge where you actually can build you own robot, or the exhibition where pupils will show up and be creative in the virtual classroom on the spot. Pupils from one Copenhagen school will work with animations of cartoons in the exhibition area every morning Monday-Wednesday. I stress this because it is a good example of the ways in which IT can enhance creativity, not demolish it, as is sometimes claimed by people who get scared that modern technology will limit on old fashioned creativity and the use of imagination. And this fear is not totally unjust, but should be coped with in a creative fashion – which is, I believe, what really goes on today in many Danish schools.

Staff at UNI•C and many people from other Danish institutions have worked hard to bring this Conference about. I hope we can all join together to make this Conference a really interactive event.

AN INTERNATIONAL DIALOGUE IN DENMARK

Margrethe Vestager
The Danish Minister of Education

I am pleased and proud that Denmark is hosting the Seventh World Conference on Computers in Education. And I would like to thank the organisers for inviting me to officially open this conference. The title of the conference, Networking the Learner seems most appropriate. It emphasises the learner as the centre of integrating ICT, or IT as I will refer to it.

With some 60 participating countries I am convinced that the conference will offer an excellent opportunity to develop truly international dialogue on the ways and means to direct focus away from the machines and cables and towards content and collaborative learning styles. The conference title also makes a fine point of reference for informing you about the Danish initiatives and the Danish approach to IT in education. In the same way, we definitely look forward to hearing about the ideas and experiences from your home countries.

The Danish government is working hard on the development of IT in society as a whole. Many initiatives have already been taken and right now the government is developing strategies and plans in many sectors. I am sure that your experiences are important to us in this process.

Internationalisation and globalisation

In a world of rapid and profound changes in almost all aspects of life the educational system has become a key agent in the development of society. It must endow the citizens with skills for meeting the challenges caused by all the changes. Our lives no longer follow a beaten track. We have made a virtue of constant change. We change jobs and move from place to place and abroad more than ever. We increasingly tailor our lives according to out personal needs and abilities. The rapid changes require skills for adjustment, adaptation and updating in all fields of life – and throughout life – for everyone who will – or shall – play an active part in society.

Values are discussed most seriously when society changes and traditions change. This is happening, as we are approaching a new order of society based on informatics, networks, knowledge – 'the creative knowledge society' – as you may call it. This implies general acceptance of knowledge as the obvious way to a fuller life. The ever-increasing and exhaustive political co-operation between the states also creates completely new conditions for both the national and the local political work and challenges the traditional comprehension of democracy. Education for all, lifelong learning and life-wide learning are seen as the main driving forces behind society's development .

The educational system can contribute decisively in meeting these challenges. It can and must provide citizens with the necessary pre-requisites in the form of know-how, creativity, language or cultural skills to the awareness of values that constitutes the society and the community. Education is crucial to our ability to live and act in the global community and in the creative knowledge-society, but education must be supported by other pillars of society: family, local society, the workplace – and the global society. In all these spheres, IT can play an important role - especially in education. IT can enhance the quality of education, sustain different learning styles, and give more flexible access to learning resources for all learners in a networked lifelong learning environment.

I therefore welcome the integration of IT in education. We perceive IT – not as an end in itself but as a means to pursue educational goals – such as creating an inclusive education system with equal educational opportunities for all, offering high quality courses and using the most suitable pedagogic methods. Of course, IT is a 'must' in modern education – in the sense that everybody must know about and learn to use IT in an effectual way. But even more, I perceive IT as a valuable tool in the learning process itself – especially in the context of individual learning, interdisciplinary and collaborative learning methods, accessing top quality learning resources and relating education to the world outside the class and lecture rooms. It should be used as a fun and interesting tool when learning. Focus should therefore be shifted form the handling of the technology towards the use if uts pedagogic possibilities.

Danish Strategies for education, learning and IT

At the end of August the Danish government will publish a new strategy for education learning and IT. Over the last few years we have formed a basis in which the support of IT, in my view, enables us to reach our educational goals even better. This is in accordance with our present plan of action. The aim until now has been concentrated on establishing and extending

- The technical IT network for educational institutuions

- The in-service training of teachers
- The provision of tools for organisational change.

Allow me to say a few words about each of these initiatives.

The Sektornet

The Ministry of Education launched an educational network in 1994 for all Danish educational institutions, the Sektornet. Most are now connected; via the Sektornet, they have access, not only to the internet but also to a wide range of added resources – all tailor made for education. These include email and discussion areas, databases with subject-based and qualified links, project and partner finding tools, and a wealth of other services.

The physical network infrastructure at the various educational levels now supports new educational methods, including team working, both among teachers and students. Many institutions even establish their own intranet to encourage information exchange and support collaboration, and to develop the school as a learning organisation.

Teacher training – Skole-IT

It is a fact that children and young people have grown up with computers, and many are far better technically skilled that their teachers, who have not had the same lifetime experience. Like most other professions, most teachers of today have had to learn to use computers as more than just an advanced typewriter. But for educators the requirements are even bigger than for other professions. Not only must they cope with the technicalities and the networks. They must also gain deep insight in how to integrate IT pedagogically. And accordingly they must practice individually in their own teaching and in teams with their colleagues.

Therefore the Pedagogical Driving Licence has been developed. It is named the Skole-IT. The experiences gained so far are very positive. Pedagogic issues and IT meet and interact. A sound base for a new educational practice is created. By the end of 2001 more than 50% of primary and secondary school teachers in Denmark have either carried through, or are attending Skole-IT. And we are supporting the enrolment of even more teachers. The concept has also been developed for other educational levels and Teacher Colleges of Education. For instance the upper secondary level which has just completed an initial phase of in-service training for teachers and now is ready to implement IT.

Changing organisation

To provide tools for changing the organisation, the Ministry of Education has initiated the Poseidon project, which focused on development of strategies for IT integration at local level. A general 'toolbox' named Poseidon has been developed and put in the internet as a free offer to all educational institutions wanting to develop a local IT strategy or action plan. The toolbox is also available in English and is being offered through the European Schoolnet's Innovation area.

From 'learning about' to 'learning with IT'

The ground now seems to be ready for a new level of integrating IT in education. While much effort and energy has been spent on learning about technology – the computers, the software, the internet – a new tendency now emerges. Some learners are now able to take the step from 'learning about IT' to 'learning by the use of IT'. This is an important step, as focus thereby is shifting from perceiving IT as a tool for the teacher, to a personal tool for the pupils and students in a lifelong learning process.

However, to further this development, two things are required – tools and content. IT integration is a dynamic process. The technological development in itself requires that institutions evaluate and consider whether and when they must invest in new equipment and whether the teachers' qualifications are current. These considerations are a local responsibility, but from a government perspective we can still do a lot to suppport the process. Our focus will accordingly move form the machines and networks tom tolls and content.

Networking – sharing information, building knowledge together

Networking the learner is the headline of this conference. The overall objective of our IT strategy in education is to enable people in the education area to find what they are searching for, to share information and build knowledge together – in other words to network. Allow me to mention a Danish inititaitve – SkoleKom, short for school communication. In SkoleKom, Danish schools have an electronic forum for communication that is quite unique. It's a conference system on the Sektor-net, providing teachers and students at all educational levels with a wide selection of open and closed electronic conferences.

Though SkoleKom is divided according to educational level, it also encourages interaction and collaboration between different levels of education. SkoleKom is the largest system world-wide of its kind, with currently around 300,000 users and 20,000 online conferences all on educational topics.

Other initiatives

During the conference you will have the opportunity to hear more about our expereinces in the Danish Way sessions. So today I will, only briefly mention that in the e-learning area we are presently developing virtual offers at different educational levels. At the Folkskole primary and lower secondary schools, we have launched a comprehensive programme where schools throughout the country will take part in developing content of the teachinhg through IT. At the upper secondary level, we have initiated an analysis and investigation, which aims at presenting a comprehensive view on vocational, pedagogical, organisational and IT related issues and possibilities, such as a virtual gymnasium.

Similar initiatives are generated at other levels. Two IT universities were established in 1999. They are both teaching and research based tertiary institutions concerned with IT and the opportunity it offers. Both are funded to undertake both theoretical and applied research into the growing importance of IT to society and industry.

And an example from one institution - the library of the Aarhus School of Business is a virtual library. The library has established a learning resource centre with the aim of increasing the integration between virtual services and the library and lecture rooms. And finally I shall mention the Learning Lab Denmark (LLD), which is an independent research-based experimental centre at the Danish University of Education Science. A core task for the LLD is to expand our understanding of how knowledge is used, spread and shared by the reflective practitioner by the use of IT.

Conclusion

The development of IT raises many questions – not only in relation to education, but also to the development of society as a whole. In a world perspective, I see it as an important challenge to consider how IT can contribute to a development with less inequality between the richer and the poorer parts of the world. In relation to education it is important that we always have in mind the crucial question: how can IT be of assistance to make our educational goals, dreams and visions come true?

I am sure that the conference will offer excellent opportunities for everybody to share ideas about this and the nature of innovations, and also to discuss, collaborate and develop an international dialogue in the increasingly important field of networking the learner.

We have been looking forward to seeing you here in Denmark. A country where almost three out of four of the population have access to the internet, at home or at work. A country where more than 70% of all households have a computer. A country where more than half of the households are already on-line – on the internet.

I wish you good days in Copenhagen, a warm welcome to Denmark, and declare the conference open.

BRIDGING THE DIGITAL DIVIDE

Aicha Bah Diallo
Deputy Assistant Director-General for Education, UNESCO

It is a great pleasure for me to attend this meeting and to extend to you a warm salutation on behalf of the Director General of UNESCO. UNESCO is pleased to be part of this event that touches on one of the central challenges of our time: building networks and bridges of co-operation and knowledge sharing for all individuals, across highly diverse national, cultural and linguistic settings, in an ever increasing inter-connected world.

Bridging the digital divide between developing and developed countries by ensuring the free flow of and equitable access to knowledge, information for all is one of the major concerns of UNESCO. Today, the process of globalisation coincides with a fundamental transformation to knowledge-based societies – largely driven by information and communication technologies (ICTs).

Knowledge – the key to capacity building – has become a principal force of economic and social transformation. Building human capacities and technical skills and developing content necessary to translate knowledge and information into assets of empowerment and production are global issues that need to be addressed by the international community at large: governments, educational authorities, civil societies and the private sector.

UNESCO's specific contribution stems from the particular expertise it brings together in its main fields of competence, all of which are recognised as the top-of-the-agenda priorities by Member States. In the light of the ongoing and new global challenges, UNESCO's mandate during the medium term period 2002-2007 will be to contribute to peace and human development in an era of globalisation by pursuing three main strategic thrusts.

- Developing universal principles and norms, based on shared values, in order to meet the emerging challenges in education, science, culture and communication and to strengthen the 'common public good'.
- Promoting pluralism, through recognition and enhancement of diversity together with the observance of human rights.

- Promoting empowerment and participation in the emerging knowledge society through equitable access, capacity-building and sharing of knowledge.

UNESCO's mission to promote education is central to all its tasks for its international standing. To provide quality education for all represents a paramount challenge for all countries. The right to education, which is a basic human right, must be transformed from ideal to reality as today over 100 million children still do not attend school and 150 million drop out without learning to read, write and use numbers. The illiteracy of almost 9000 million adults limits their individual growth and the social development of their communities.

We know that there can be no information for all without education for all. The World Education Forum (Dakar, Senegal, April 2000) confirmed UNESCO as the co-ordinator of the Education For All (EFA) partners and charged it with the task of maintaining their collective momentum. The realisation that of the six goals of the Dakar Framework for Action is the overriding priority for UNESCO's education strategy, covering both formal and non-formal education.

From among these six goals, I would like to mention only three, which are of direct relevance to the topic of the conference.

- Ensuring that the learning needs of all young people and adults are met through equitable access to appropriate learning and life-skills programmes.
- Achieving a 50% improvement in levels of access to basic and continuing education for all.
- Improving all aspects of the quality of education and ensuring excellence of all so that recognised and measurable learning outcomes are achieved by all, especially in literacy, numeracy and essential life skills.

The Dakar Framework for Action, adopted at this Forum, states that everyone has the 'human right to benefit from an education that will meet their basic learning needs in the best and fullest sense of the term, an education that includes learning to know, to do, to live together and to be'.

These four pillars of education, first mentioned in the Delors report to UNESCO of the International Commission on Education for the Twenty-first Century, entitled *Learning: the treasure within*, break down the traditional distinction between diverse fields and sectors of education. They underline lifelong learning as necessary in the present day globalisation and knowledge-rich world where individuals, throughout their lives, must learn

- to accumulate knowledge and aptitudes,
- to adapt to the requirements of the world of work,
- to understand and tolerate others, and
- to develop their personality, critical faculty and ability to act.

Concerned that the growing digital divide may actually lead to greater inequalities in development, UNESCO formulated a new cross-cutting strategy with regard to the contribution of ICTs to the development of education, science and culture and the construction of a knowledge society. The goal of this cross-cutting strategy is to show how the Organisation intends to provide a co-ordinated response, based on an interdisciplinary approach. Four strategic objectives will be pursued.

- Agreeing on common principles for the construction of knowledge societies, enhancing learning opportunities through access to diversified contents and delivery systems.
- Strengthening capacities for scientific research, information sharing and cultural exchanges.
- Promoting the use of ICTs for capacity building, empowerment, governance and social participation.

UNESCO is committed to promoting ICT-for-education for all. ICTs offer the potential to expand the scope of learning, breaking through traditional constraints of space and time as well as boundaries of current education systems. The international community is faced with a new challenge – to define the best use of ICTs for improving the quality of teaching and learning, introducing a higher degree of flexibility in response to societal needs, lowering the cost of education. Computer literacy is a basic skill for performing in the knowledge society.

UNESCO will promote the judicious use of ICTs as innovative and experimental tools to renew education. It will also explore their potential as new delivery mechanisms and for system-wide expansion and by focusing on non-formal education. As a result of these actions, the following outcomes are expected.

- A wide dissemination of knowledge and best practices related to the impact of ICTs on education through an online clearing-house, knowledge base and multimedia resource centre.
- A broader base by governments of ICT-based delivery systems in formal ands non-formal education, using both new and traditional media and appropriate methodologies.
- Dissemination of research results on the impact of ICTs on the teaching-learning process, on content and teacher-learner interaction, in particular as regards distance education and teacher training and development.
- Promotion of international debate and reflection in favour of developing internationally compatible standards for e-learning courseware and for e-learning institutions.

UNESCO will not be acting alone. It will be joining forces with many institutions – intergovernmental organisations of the United Nations system, the World Bank, non-governmental organisations, private and public sector partners, which are competent to act in these fields. UNESCO undertakes to use its links with its professional partners to reach those who are unreached by ICTs and specifically those who are under the greatest risk of being left out of the knowledge revolution: the rural populations, the urban poor, the illiterate and the marginalised.

Co-operation between UNESCO and the International Federation of Information Processing (IFIP) has been steadily developing over many years now for the mutual benefit of both organisations. In particular, I would like to mention the significant contribution IFIP made to the successful organsiation of UNESCO's Second International Congress on Education and Informatics (Moscow 1996), in which four of IFIPs former and present Presidents participated – Academician Blagovest Sendov (Bulgaria), Dr Sylvia Charp (USA), Professor Kurt Bauknecht (Switzerland) and Dr Peter Bollerslev (Denmark).

Documnents elaborated by IFIP experts have enjoyed wide dissemination and audience among UNESCO Member States. I am pleased to mention a few names: Professors Jacques Hebenstreit and Bernard Cornu (France), Professors Bernard Levrat and Raymond Morel (Switzerland), Professors Tom van Weert and Betty Collis (The Netherlands), Professor Sandra Wills (Australia), Professors Ivan Stanchev and Roumen Nikolov (Bulgaria), and Professor Alexei Semenov (Russia Federation).

At the present conference UNESCO and IFIP will organise a joint session focussing on the discussion of ongoing projects in primary, secondary and higher education. The high-level meeting between Koichiro Matsuura, Director-General of UNESCO and Peter Bollerslev, IFIP current President, and Robert Aiken, IFIP President elect, held in January 2001, gave a fresh impetus and opportunity of outlining a future framework for more joint projects and initiatives in the field of ICTs-for-education for all. To achieve our common goals, knowledge and capability will be the key. Both UNESCO and IFIP should join forces in transforming all countries into learning economies and knowledge societies. We should seek to create a truly inclusive knowledge society for all.

I wish your conference every success. After so many years of such work and success, UNESCO is proud of IFIP.

A GUIDE TO THE CONFERENCE STRUCTURE

Brian Samways
Chair of IFIP Technical Committee on Education, and Chair of the International Programme Committee

WCCE 2001 will be stimulating and interesting – but it is also complex. How can participants get the best and most out of the week, with so many presentations, events, streams, activities, facilities and people? We have planned a structure that should be flexible enough to enable individuals to chart different routes through the event. This structure also represents a number of features of IFIP Education events.

- Guided tours – where participants new to this style of conference meet with a guide for the first day over breakfast, and then plan together which sessions they will attend according to their interests in different themes and style of activities. By the end of their first day, a new network will have been formed amongst those who may have arrived at the conference knowing no-one.
- Panels where the discussions that develop will be reported and published.
- Active Poster sessions where the poster presenters can engage with participants in the implications of their material.
- Professional Group discussions, which take place over the week. These are hosted by the seven Working Groups of the Technical Committee on education. Stimulated by briefing papers circulated beforehand, participants bring their expertise and information gleaned during the conference to prepare a reflective document on the topic. They share this with all participants on the last day of the conference, and the reports are also published afterwards.

The seven working groups will be both organising the professional groups, and also holding the Annual General meetings during the week. Attendees are invited to approach the Working Group chairs if they are interested in becoming involved further with their work. And so a final welcome to the conference, and let the activities now begin.

CONFERENCE ORGANISERS

All conferences take a substantial amount of organisation, and those for the IFIP educational community are no exception. The quinquennial World Conference on Computers in Education takes many years of work, from initial planning to the event. All is done by voluntary members of the local organising and international programme committees. A particular feature is the strong and friendly working relationship that develops between these communities; without them the conferences would not occur. This book records with thanks the work of those who ensured the conference, and thus this publication happened. Thanks are also due to the Organising Institutions and Conference Sponsors, without whose financial and other support, the conference could not have taken place.

International Programme committee

Peter Bollerslev (DK) Conference Chairman and IFIP President
Brian Samways (UK) IPC chair and TC3 Chair
Robert Aiken (US) WG 3.6 member
Bernard Cornu (FR) WG 3.1 member and recent chair
Raymond Morel (CH) TC3 Vice-chair
Deryn Watson (UK) Managing Editor and WG 3.1 chair
Tom van Weert (NL) Chair WG 3.2

Working Group Chairs

WG 3.1 (Secondary)	Deryn Watson
WG 3.2 (University)	Tom van Weert
WG 3.3 (Research)	Jari Multisilta
WG 3.4 (Vocational)	Mikko Ruohonen
WG 3.5 (Primary)	Sindre Rosvik
WG 3.6 (Distance)	Gordon Davies
WG 3.7 (Management)	Alex Fung

National Organising Committee

Dorte Olesen	Uni•C, The Danish IT Centre for Education and Research
Jane Andersen	IT University of Copenhagen
Bent. B. Andresen	The Danish University of Education
Peter Bollerslev	Gyldendal Education
Lone Dirkinck-Holmfeld	University of Aalborg
Christian Gram	
Leo Hojsholt-Poulsen	Uni•C, The Danish IT Centre for Education and Research
Aage Melbye	
Ole Windelov	DR Education
with	
Christine Mohr	Uni•C, The Danish IT Centre for Education and Research
Charlotte Solovej	Uni•C, The Danish IT Centre for Education and Research

Acknowledgements

The editors would like to thank Anton Knierzinger at Pädagogische Akademie of Diôzese, Linz, Austria for technical help with the paper reviewing process, and Christine Mohr and Lene Wiencke at Uni•C, Denmark for their substandial help and support in the preparation of the book.

EDITORS BIOGRAPHIES

Deryn Watson is Professor of Information Technologies and Education at King's College London. Her interests include the use of computers in social sciences and the humanities, the impact of ICT on learning and professional development. She is currently researching the impact of public policy and the reality of use of ICT in education. She is Chair of IFIP Working Group 3.1, ICT and Informatics in secondary education.

Jane Andersen is Head of Development at The IT University of Copenhagen. Her interests include the impact of ICT on learning in particular distance education. She is currently developing the platform and concepts for distance education at the IT University. She is member of IFIP Working Group 3.4, IT-professional and vocational education in information technology.

CONFERENCE ORGANISERS

SPONSORS/PARTNERS

A special thank to all the sponsors. The Danish Ministry of Education has especially given contributions for the printing of the conference book.

Editorial

Networking the Learner

Promises, Complexities, Opportunities, and Issues

Deryn Watson
Department of Education and Professional Studies, King's College London, London SE1 9NN, UK.
deryn.watson@kcl.ac.uk

Keywords: professionals, collaborative learning, students, communication

Abstract: This editorial presents the structure of the book through a matrix of main themes and keywords. Thus the reader may select a particular theme, such as *open and distance learning*, or *national initiatives*, or select keywords such as *object oriented modelling* or *virtual learning*. Throughout a picture emerges of both the potentials and problematics of harnessing new information technologies in education for networking the learner.

1. INTRODUCTION

The papers, panel discussions and professional group reports that form chapters in this book provide a powerful analysis on the role that Information and Communication Technologies (ICT) can have in teaching and learning. In particular, with the focus on networking the learner, there is an emphasis on how the growth of communication capability has opened up new avenues for perceiving the nature of the teacher/learner interface itself, just as much as the learner/technology interface.

The perspectives presented here provide us with a range of insights that enable this volume to do justice to this important topic. Thus this is not about simple matters or making unsupported claims. The authors draw upon experience and research to probe the use they and others are making of the complexity of networking capabilities – the internet, world wide web, chat rooms, asynchronous communications and multimedia. Such use is inevitably both exciting and problematic. There can be little doubt that most of those engaged in this work are themselves convinced of the substantial advantages that ICT can have for education, and in particular for the nature and style of learning which it can stimulate and support. But equally, the writings of these individuals and groups presented here carefully explore not simply the possibilities and myths, but also the reality and problematics of use. The reader will find here reports of experiments and case studies, the probing through large questionnaires or detailed interviews of the perceptions of various groups involved - software designers, administrators, teachers and learners – at all levels of education. This reflects a mature community concerned to look beyond the surface.

This community has for some time been engaged in exploring the integration of new information and communication technologies into education, and in re-thinking the purposes and forms of education in ways that harness the potential ICT presents. Each new wave of technologies, or enthusiasm for particular aspects, can lure us into thinking that this time there will be a definite advance towards substantive change. And this may be the case, though not necessarily in the direction that was anticipated. This is now the seventh book associated with the (roughly) quinquennial World Conferences on Computers in Education, an international event organised by the IFIP Technical Committee on Education. Because of its scale, and the time period, the refereed selected contributions here provide a perspective on changes to the ICT environment, and what we educationalists have made of it, over a period of time.

Thus perusal of these chapters indicates how far ideas and initiatives about networks and the learner have moved since the last conference in 1995. The tentative ideas then about the potential of using communications technologies have firmed up into a strong series of chapters that reflect teaching and researching the use of the internet and web as networks to support learners in a range of settings. A focus on liberating the learner though networks has grown into concern for the nature of user interactions and the related styles of learning and pedagogy. New themes are emerging, such as schools of the future, relationships between distance learning and virtual environments, synchronous and asynchronous communication, and equity. All provide frameworks for the testing of new and important ideas. Thus the chapters in this book display a heady mix of foreseeing and practical reporting, of planning for the future but at the same time respecting the problems we already have with networking technologies.

The richness of the book stems in part from the range of experience of the international authors – from academics, administrators and policy makers, to teachers and curriculum and software designers. This mix ensures that the central questions that are addressed are considered not simply from a variety of personal perspectives, but also from different cultural and environmental experiences. And yet interest must also lie in the commonality of reporting and discussion-based reflections of activity in the field. All contributions draw heavily on research and experience in a range of educational settings, both formal and informal, virtual and real, and with all ages – from pupils in the kindergarten to adults in the community. The opinions and discussions are thus grounded in knowledge gained from work embedded in the reality of today's use of networks for learning. This must be the only sound base upon which to reflect on the promises for the future.

And it is here that the reporting of panel discussions and professional groups provides a unique opportunity for readers to engage with the current reflections of this community. These reports provide a window on their perspectives on future issues that need to be addressed – from social and ethical concerns, virtual universities, and the next generation of programming languages, to the interface between virtuality and reality in schools, and the role of large multinational projects to stimulate change. This book is therefore not simply a passive collection of papers from a conference; and although it has emerged from a particular event, it is far more than a simple proceedings. It deliberately attempts to present ongoing agendas, to reflect the concerns and dynamism of community, and the growing contribution it is making to the ongoing debates about the nature of education itself.

In this chapter it is my intention to present the variety of promises, complexities, opportunities, and issues associated with networking the learner, through the themes and cross-cutting keywords around which this book has been structured. I have argued above that the substance and value of this book lies in its complexity. And yet such complexity needs to be framed in such a way that there are signposts of content. The themes and keywords provide the equivalence of a matrix that readers may chose to use according to their interests. My purpose is to enable the reader to engage enough for other conceptual themes to also emerge.

2. THEMES

Contributions in the book are grouped into a sequence of sections or themes into which the material falls: open and distance learning, ICT in learning, new pedagogic ideas, teaching mathematics, teaching computer science, forms of assessment, management and resource, teacher education, and national initiatives. Each theme has a form of coherence, and a linear structure which loosely relates chapters with their neighbours. Thus readers may select themes to suit themselves, and use the abstracts for each chapter to provide further detail. An alternative strategy could be to select a keyword from the list at the end, such as secondary education, multimedia, distance education or video-conferencing, to identify those chapters that include this area. Others may search by author, or simply dip in from place to place. And so this book should be seen not simply as a linear text, but a complex resource.

2.1 Open and distance learning

The chapters within this theme focus on different experiences that students and teachers have had with open and distance learning environments – from university students in the Netherlands (Lam and Markenhof) to teachers in Brazil (Vidal et al) and adults in France (Nodenot). Perspectives include concerns that the potential of virtual learning processes does not mean that they will necessarily be fully used (Takle et al), a conviction that virtual schooling can only occur with a complete cultural shift (Jo and Russell), and an affirmation that only through conceptual understanding of the processes of higher order thinking can instructional programs promote effective and interactive online learning (Nicholson and White). Notions such the social presence online (Stacey) and three interlocking facets of online education environments (Nodenot) illustrate the range covered in this theme. Here Schrum provides an illustration of concerns.

> Development of an online educational environment is a complex task. Faculty members have had an especially difficult time changing the ways in which they teach, regardless of these educators' own personal use of electronic media (Candiotti and Clarke 1998). In an electronic environment the role of faculty changes in many ways, and in particular, each instructor must give up some control of the classroom environment. Faculty members are forced to develop and design their activities and interactions in new ways, and may be frustrated without the ability to recognise when students are puzzled (Schrum and Berge 1998). Kember (1995) urged designers to work toward deep learning, which requires moving away from excessive assignments and shallow assessments, and toward some individual freedom in activities. These challenges go far beyond the need to be comfortable with the reliance on technology to support their courses. Wiesenberg and Hutton (1996) identified three major challenges for the designer to consider: increased time for delivery of the course (they estimate two or three times what is necessary for a traditional course), creating a sense of online community, and encouraging students to become independent learners. They also reported fewer interactions than expected from participants of an online course.

These issues all have implications for faculty members and students in an online environment.

2.2 ICT in learning

The chapters in this theme focus on a range of different learning issues, from a problem-based learning in Hong Kong (Yip), technology mediated interactions in Australia (Geer and Barnes) to encouraging students to make oral presentations in Turkey (Inelman) and new approaches to design education (Sagun). Authors focus on topics such as lessons learnt through trans-national analysis of research on teachers in training, indicating gender differences (Knezek and Christensen), secondary students scaffolding learning in a technology rich environment (McDougall and Boyle), and the role of intelligent computer programs to act as agents to mediate learning (Dowling). Iding et al remind us of some additional advantages the technologies may bring.

> Machine interviewing technologies like the Past Recorder and Automatic Interviewer have great potential as formative and summative assessment tools for students in all content areas, especially when linked to electronic portfolios and even to content performance standards. These technologies are particularly appealing for recording changes in individuals' understandings over time, and for capturing important verbal interchanges and performances that might not as easily be expressed in written form.

2.3 New pedagogic ideas

Chapters in this theme remind us of the stimulation that ICT can have through generating new ideas for pedagogy. From details of primary teachers using software about mini-beasts such as insects and arachnids (Masters and Yelland), cross-sectional teaching for media literacy (Hauf-Tulodziecki and Weber), to the use of Encarta to influence learning retrieval skills (Drenoyianni et al), and the develoment of a web-based project to enable students to encounter the biodiversity of the natural world (Hawkey), authors provide a subject or area context for the pedagogy they discuss. Cautionary notes on the use of the web (Le and Le) contrast the positive reports on the effects on the learning of disadvantaged students. Dimitriadi, writing about new technological environments to support children with learning difficulties, reports the following.

The preliminary findings have indicated that the children's work included all the elements and the responsibilities involved in authorship. They took ownership of the product, and they negotiated meaning. The effect of mastery in the use of the tool led on from a sensory-motor activity to a conscious and structured task where respect towards varied needs of different types of audience became part of the context. One of the children's responses to those needs was to create a guessing 'Game' card as the people who were going to use the project 'must have fun'. As indicated by their teachers and samples of their schoolwork, the children demonstrated an active role in the process quite different to their previous authoring attempts with more traditional media. They were willing to revisit their work and redraft it, discuss the choice of language, the style and content of their presentations.

2.4 Teaching mathematics

It is inevitable that in the search for new ideas in pedagogy, there will be a particular place for mathematics. Chapters here include substantial initiatives to support mathematics teaching in the USA (Bitter and Pryor) and Germany (Weber and Frankhanel) and cover such topics as automatic differentiation for graphing (Katkov and Novosselova) and discrete mathematics for computation (Mendes et al). Vincent reports on the role of software for learning geometry.

While there are certain restrictions imposed on modelling with dynamic geometry software and constructions of many linkages may prove too difficult for the majority of students, these limitations do not diminish the usefulness of the computer models in exploring geometric properties and relationships. Whether the students construct the computer models of the linkages themselves or are provided with constructions, the unique features of dynamic geometry software and the curiosity aroused by the operation of the linkages create a visually rich and motivating environment for students to explore, conjecture and construct geometric proofs.

2.5 Teaching computer science

These chapters cover themes of object oriented modelling (Brinda and Schubert), simulations (Gabbert and Tru), systems engineering (Ohnari) and programming environments (Henri and Dore). Topics include accreditation of computer science course for undergraduates in the USA (Lu et al), teaching microcomputer interfacing and real time computing in Australia

(Fulcher), and using simulators to teach theory of computation in a new way in Brazil (Tiaraju). Ohnari reflects on the need for students to use and build something in which they are interested.

> Education of the computer is usually aimed to make students able to use computers up to a limited level. The theme of this conference is Computers in Education. I think this theme urges teachers to create an environment to students who freely use computers for their interesting field and chances to cultivate their abilities of finding issues and solving problems by computers. For these purposes it is important to maintain computer environments and to prepare useful application software for their use. As a result these environments strengthen their insights into issues, user's requirements and selection of software in views of problem solving and raise the level of their abilities for IT.

2.6 Forms of assessment

Chapters here cover work on adult education and assessment in Denmark (Witfelt et al), assessing performance quality in Australia (Summons), assessment through electronic portfolios in the USA (Barrett), and web-based student profiling in Australia (Fountain and Allison). This hitherto little discussed area appears now to be attracting more attention. Witfelt et al reflect on the issues associated with change.

> To many people, chatting suggests the notion of non-serious, very light discussions, often without deeper meaning. However, our experiences as teachers from other flexible courses and education was that chat can be used for discussing serious issues as well - with very good results. But in order to turn chat into a valuable tool, the users need to develop a special language, as is the case with any other media. We wanted to stimulate the students to do this and to test chat as a media for serious discussions by using chat as a media for exams.

2.7 Management and resource

Chapters in this theme include work on computerised school management systems in The Netherlands, Hong Kong and the United Kingdom (Fung et al), portal technology as a means to establishing the effective management of resource in Malaysia (Abdullah and Udin), visions on the value of mobile technologies as a resource for primary learning in Finland (Ketamo et al), and a perception that wireless is nearly the total solution for resourcing (Newhouse). While diverse in content the relationship between the nature of the resources that the technology now offers and management of the learning potential and administration is becoming clearer. In the comparative study between three countries, Fung et al explore school information systems (SIS), and conclude that as with other applications, implementation is only as effective as the design of an application and training in its use.

> Overall, the research indicates that although there is room for improvement SISs are a useful, if not indispensable tool for school administration. However, school staff should benefit much more from the possibilities of SISs to support their higher order management work. To achieve the latter we first of all need better SISs, systems that have been designed from the perspective of school management work. The results clearly highlight the impact of the implementation process, particularly the role played by training.

2.8 Teacher education

Chapters in this theme reflect the opportunities for distance education that networking provides for trainee teachers. Using the internet is a common thread, from reducing stress (White and le Cornu), disseminating examples of practice through video case studies (Cannings and Talley), to virtual tutoring and electronic conferencing between the institution and schools (Albion), and using virtual reality to improve kindergarten teachers awareness of children's emotional experiences (Passig and Noyman). All suggest that various aspects of networking changes the nature of the education experience, for teachers as much as students. Nevertheless, Albion points to one of the residual inhibitors of uptake.

> Although computers are widely available in schools and their use is supported by public policy, their uptake by teachers is not universal. There is evidence that, even where teachers have access and essential skills, they lack confidence in their ability to integrate computers in their teaching. Multimedia cases have been developed for the purpose of increasing teachers' self-efficacy beliefs (confidence) for teaching with computers. It was important to understand what factors might influence such beliefs.

2.9 National initiatives

The importance which governments attach to ICT, and in particular the growth of communications capabilities, cannot be overemphasised. The chapters under this theme report and analyse a range of national initiatives, including Brazil (Notare et al), Jamaica (Abernethy et al), Gemany (Hense et al), Oman (Naqvi) and New Zealand (Lamont). Reports cover phases or stages that are considered essential to successful development (Notare et al, and Callegrin and Cortesi), and also describe the impact of policy in different levels (Rohs). Throughout there is a sense of policies in the process of implementation, and the significance placed on the web as a source for consolidating coverage. Most of all, there is a sense of substantial difference in progress in different parts of any one system. Here Notare et al emphasis this differential.

> With the identification of the phases of computer usage in education we can notice that there are in Brazil schools in all levels of evolution, in other words, there are schools that have not started the use of computer not even in their administrative activities and, at the same time, there are schools that use the Internet in order to promote research, communication and co-operative work among students. It is known that the computerisation process of education is slow if compared to the computerisation of other activity areas. And this is because it involves a change of mind concerning the society's concepts and values, as new ways of thinking and acting come up with this revolution.

3. COMPLEXITIES AND ISSUES

All the chapters raise a variety of issues, but these concerns are specifically articulated in the last two sections of the book.

3.1 Professional concerns

A variety of issues were raised by the professional groups, each organised by one of the seven working groups (WGs) that make up the Education Committee of IFIP. The significant contribution of these group reports is that they reflect not a single voice, but the considered perspective of a number of individuals, who met at the event for possibly the first time, and used the opportunity to probe an issue in depth over four separate meetings. These chapters, reporting their deliberations and concerns, are a means of capturing some of the problematics with which we are still grappling.

Chapters here report a range of concerns: that pupils leave education with little understanding of the basic concepts of informatics/ICT, and even less of associated social and ethical issues; that schools of the future will involve a radical re-think of structural and organisational matters to support new conceptions of the role of school; and that teachers and students need to develop critical understandings about the nature and use of virtual reality. Here also professionals debated the nature of indicators of success, the challenges of teacher co-operation, the problems facing implementing ICT in higher education, and need to author meaningful content for learning with networks. Research offers agendas to understand more fully the nature of knowledge transmission and the ongoing debate about professional development strategies most likely to succeed; tools for concept mapping alert us to different forms of perception and articulation; the impact of learning at a distance and virtual universities force us to probe the nature of learning and teaching to be expected with such change. The concerns for cultural change and the dangers of networking increasing social division force us to ask if we care about the less beneficial affects of the internet.

Readers who want to focus on the issues and problematics may chose to read these reports of the professional groups first.

3.2 Panel reports

Panels were an opportunity for attendees to debate points raised at the start of the session by the panellists. Arguments ranged across the rooms, and reflect the diverse options and opinions in each topic. Programming as an engineering discipline, using robotics to engineer change, can research that can lead to practical outcomes, and can ICT improve teaching and learning – such topics indicate the vibrancy of the discussions.

Experiments in tele-learning, setting national standards, setting up a new project on the rainforest, and attempts to provoke new approaches to learning and integrating ICT at a curriculum level, all report work ongoing. The history of the Nordic countries initiatives, and the international PLANIT project findings point to a long trajectory for such work, and the enduring nature if some of the questions probed.

What these panel discussions indicate is that many face similar problems in implementation, and as we become closer to understanding them, we often expose further issues to be considered. And all while the technology advances and enables us to have greater visions for change.

4. KEYNOTE ADDRESSES

A contrast to the concerns expressed in other chapters and sections, the keynote speakers presented views focussed on the opportunities and displayed substantial optimism for the field. A synopsis of their presentations indicates the basis of such a perspective.

4.1 The landscape for education is changing in Europe

Mike Couzens, Managing Director Corporate Communications and Training, Cisco Systems, Europe, Middle East and Africa, invited us to imagine 200,000 students attending one education institution – impossible? No, not when the courses are available and continuously updated via the Internet. This is what Cisco Networking Academy Programme has developed, and always is expanding. A programme that can be followed in 6,706 educational establishments world-wide. Cisco helps the education centres' networking by providing them with an online up-to-date curriculum that matches needs within the industry. The programme is a result of public-private partnership launched to meet the demand for people who can design, build and maintain computer networks.

Couzens believes the traditional education systems are not able to adapt quickly enough to the changes in skills and the scales for technology used in the field of education. In several countries the public sector is merely in the process of discussing pros and cons of integrating ITC in education. The private sector, however, is experienced in developing and changing technology rapidly and efficiently - and in educating their staff at a rapid pace. If we want efficient and up-to-date education that meets the need of labour manpower, a public-private partnership is an evident option in the achievement of this goal.

4.2 The power of knowledge

Hans Appel, Chief Technology Officer at Sun Microsystems, subtitled his presentation The Disappearing of the Internet. What he meant this was that the tools we use for communication and sharing information are going to be more and more invisible. Computers are going to be ubiquitous and yet invisible. A tool we use for work, communication, sharing information without having to think about how to use it. Like a telephone. We can use it without any understanding of how the software or hardware works. We will not need to know how the appliances work, but how to use them. We do not have to be software experts to write an email. At the same time the actual web is going to be split up in six interconnected webs.

The six webs are the pocket communicator web, the entertainment web, the e-business web, the voice-activated web, the pervasive computing web, and of course the traditional web. The pocket computer web is the personal web for connecting mobile phones and DPA's, and follows you around. The entertainment web is for video games, storytelling and other kinds of entertainment brought instantly to you on the couch. The e-business web is a marketplace for consumers and businesses. The voice-activated web is the web that understands what we are saying and also a web that responds in an intelligent way. The pervasive computing web is the web of machines talking to each other so that the information we give to one machine will be handed over to the machines that need that information to respond adequately to our demands.

Appel believes we are going to prepare our children for a market of e-communities, where conversations, loyalty, empathy and fascination are keywords and an employee is an entrepreneur in a networked community. A society where the human imaginative power and intellectual capital is vital and adaptation to the constant development is crucial for individual person.

4.3 Go ahead – give your mind a hand

Robert Kramer Rasmussen, Director for Product and Research Development in Lego Dacta, is a former schoolteacher and, as he puts it, representative of the children. The network in our brain is essential to learning. We need to connect the 125 billions neurons in our brain in order to learn; the better connected the more learning will take place. We need to facilitate creativity, learning (creating knowledge) and thinking (using knowledge) with a fundamental aspect: motivation.

Rasmussen asserts that learning has to be enjoyable, because in that way we can make the children remember and share what they have learned. Enjoyable learning happens when the learning environment offers hard fun and learning by making. And when you do something you care about the learning becomes richer, because the motivation is there. Emotions combined with motivation will then be the engine of useful and creative learning.

Hard fun is finding the challenges for the children and is placed somewhere between challenge and skills, between "can do" and "have to do". In this interaction between our skills, the challenges we meet and our emotions can be used to reach the highest level of learning. Learning is not just about thinking, but just as much emotions; a combination of cognitive and evolutionary psychology. Learning by making is about making learning tangible and letting the motivation push the learning forward and up. Lego is trying to combine IT and children's fascination of IT with their need for building and creating. By building and creating children can make their ideas tangible and that is, as Rasmussen says, fuel for the urge to learn.

4.4 How to increase the level of communication between schools and communities

As 'Chief Evangelist of Centrinity', Scott Welsh perceives himself as the bringer of good tidings, and the tidings he brings are about First Class. Complex technology lies behind the systems and facilities we use today. And yet applications designs are often invasive and affect how the user perceives the functions of the tool. The challenge is to design around the functionality of the tool a user needs, and not the technology used to build it.

First Class was the result of collaboration between three authors, including Welsh, challenged to build a tool to bring together and then establish educational communities built upon collaboration and communication using simply email. Education is fundamentally a different world than that of business and corporations. First class was designed to account for these differences - it is fast, complex and reliable; it enables you to work on your individual machine safe in the knowledge that all the information you need is at your fingertips; it is designed with the needs of education in mind.

So Welsh believes that First Class supports the nature of education as a community, with different players all with the same goals. Collaboration has enabled educational communities to move forwards for years before it became the goals of businesses. There is strength in communities – the class, school, business country, parents and children. First Class supports project based learning, drawing on the different strengths in each community to provide a collaborative product. And all this supports rather than replaces face-to-face learning, though the face to face encounters may not always be in a classroom..

5. ALTERNATIVE SLICES

5.1 Keywords

Keywords are of course pointers that enable readers to take different slices across all the chapters. They enable the reader to trace through which chapters may be of particular interest to them – whether a level, such as primary or higher education, or an approach, such as distance education of object oriented modelling. Any reader could probably produce a valid alternative structure to the one used here, based in these levels and foci.

Keywords however also provide and opportunity to look at different conceptual slices. A selection of certain words, such as collaboration, problem solving, interactions, and cognition will take you to a range of contexts and levels, but where the conceptual concerns are fundamentally the same, although how they are interpreted may be different. And what these keywords also indicate is that this book represents work which has moved well beyond reporting into a level of analysis that often uses fundamental constructs, drawn from theories of the sociology and psychology of learning, in our attempts to come to terms ICT and education. Chapters about problem-solving curriculum design, learners scaffolding knowledge, social interaction, and the role of modelling environments frequently draw on theoretical frames as a basis, for instance, for developing software, structuring the learning, and analysing teacher and learner behaviour.

My search through one keyword may illustrate the point about alternative slices and thus construction of meaning from the book.

5.2 Collaborative learning

The interactive nature of the new technologies has for long been seen as a contributor to the development of collaborative learning around the keyboard. Networks have brought the use of collaboration as a valuable process to the fore. This could be perceived as fundamental plank upon which much discussion about the new learning is based.

A search through these chapters using the keywords collaboration and collaborative learning will produce around 19 different 'hits'. Many stress the importance of collaborative learning; Geer and Barnes reflect that collaboration can be perceived as providing the highest level of meaningful interaction and engagement – it implies not simply working with each other, but also challenging and critiquing each other's ideas. But in this book we also learn though direct experience and research that providing the networks for learners results in neither automatic collaboration, nor an even spread of its use. The panel chaired by Bruillard comments in particular on differences in culture and learning style as problems affecting collaborating groups. Both Lockhorst et al and Schrum outline a number of variables that appear to be needed to ensure effective collaboration.

Absence of some variables will create disadvantage for some. For instance Schrum reports that some students, despite plenty of access to the technology, felt they never had enough time to complete the [open-ended] work. Other students had no place to study at home; some had families who made fun of their efforts to learn on-line. Stacey reports that the socio-effective support provided by the collaborative group environment was of major importance to the success of the students. Here the role of the teacher was crucial to helping students project their on-line social presence, and thus establishing an environment for learning in computer conferences.

Naruse, reporting on the video conferencing between Northern Ireland and Japan, found that the availability of the facility was not enough to facilitate meaningful use. It was only when collaborative assignments were set that two communities were forced to work collaboratively, rather than simply report to each other, that the students began to develop the skills that enabled them to communicate effectively. The effect of the task, its style and design purpose is also significant; Lockhorst et al report that group and task behaviour differs according to task and design elements. And not all members of the group are collaborating; as Geer and Barnes also report, non-participating students deserve and may need considerable individual attention from a diligent educator to get them to engage and then contribute.

Groups collaborating open up real considerations of assessment of group as well as individual efforts, and matters of privacy security. But mostly effective collaborative learning appears to demand substantial amounts of teacher/educator time and input to ensure it is effective. Here the real meaning of 'a facilitator for learning' emerges.

6. CONCLUSION

And so the networking technologies - aiding communication and collaboration though the exciting advent of email, the web and electronic fora - enable us to overcome previous physical and time constraints, and probe the new opportunities these creates. Harnessing ICT effectively demands a re-consideration of the nature and style of teaching, learning, and educational institutions (virtual or real), a reconsideration that is already underway in educational thinking in general. But just as critically an exploration of the means to encompass such change exposes both shifts in perception and a recognition of enduring issues that remain.

It is my hope that this book leaves the reader in no doubt that WCCE 2001 was not a dry academic conference – teachers, lecturers and informatics experts, policy makers and researchers, learners and manufacturers mingled and worked together to explore, reflect, discuss and plan for the future. We know the added value of networking in conference is that that it will have an impact on future practice; networks have been formed, both virtual and real - ideas will change and new ones will emerge. It is our intention that this book will have a similar effect. Networking the Learner encapsulates the promises and opportunities of an innovation, while forcing us to come to terms with the issues and complexities of change.

6.1 A Coda

An interesting coda to the concerns explored here is provided by some reflections of three students who addressed the conference during the closing session. They study at Elizabeth Vale School in South Australia, a Discovery Schools in the Learning Technologies Project.

Samantha Burge stated that in the five days they had learnt a lot about how grownups behave at conferences......... They have heard a lot of adults talking a lot about using technology. But what they had not heard is a lot of people talking a lot about learning; it would be good next time to hear more about the education in computers. She really liked the presenter in one session who said "You should fit the computer into the curriculum, not the curriculum into the computer".

Chloe Worden is on the Learning Technology Committee at their school, and appreciated the opportunity to hear what other countries are doing. In her opinion they have a pretty good deal with the technology in their school and what they can do. But one of the things that had puzzled them was that presenters kept talking about kids using easy software first. They think adults should trust students, because using simple software can be a waste of their learning time. They would rather use the best software to do the job; so maybe adults should ask kids what they would like to do.

Rebecca Maher recognised that it had been a real privilege to come to the 7th World Conference; they would like to thank the Education Department of South Australia for making it happen. In particular they were going back to challenge themselves more in some areas like animation and Robolab. They hoped that adult participants would take what they have learnt back and make a difference for their learners.

Such a coda is a timely reminder that the views and experiences of learners need to be incorporated into educational frames of reference.

PART ONE

OPEN AND DISTANCE LEARNING

1

Dimensions of Student Success in Online Learning

Lynne Schrum
Department of Instructional Technology, University of Georgia USA
lschrum@coe.uga.edu

Keywords: learner-centred learning, open flexible learning, electronic communication, collaborative learning

Abstract: Online learning has become a popular method of education. This transition is not a trivial matter, and while faculty members may have support in making this transition in their teaching style and methods, they may know little about how to assist students in succeeding in a new learning environment. Similarly, students may not be prepared to tackle the new demands put upon them. This research sought to identify the characteristics and qualifications of successful online learners, by examining primary screening documents from institutions, mapping these dimensions to the literature base, and weaving personal research projects through the resulting information.

1. INTRODUCTION

Online learning has undergone rapid development. We know the stated reasons for growth in this area: public media have raised individuals' expectations, the digital economy has created a demand for technical expertise, and adults are demanding greater flexibility and control over their learning. Moreover, business and industry have begun to challenge the traditional models of learning and teaching, through corporate universities, for-profit institutions, and other less formal opportunities.

Educational institutions are responding rapidly to learners' demands for 'anytime and anywhere' education by devoting substantial resources to the development of online distance learning. Throughout the world, traditional and non-traditional individuals are taking advantage of these offerings. However, the transition to this online environment is not a trivial matter, and the challenge is to understand the relationships between the user and the technology, the instructor and the participants, and the relationships among the participants (Gibbs 1998, Palloff and Pratt 1999, Schrum 1998). Faculty members may have support in recreating their courses for digital media, yet they may know little about how to assist students in succeeding in a new learning environment and to adapting their teaching style and methods.

In an effort to provide information to assist faculty members to understand the demands their students face in online learning, and to design effective online environments to support these new challenges, this research sought to first identify characteristics and qualifications of successful online learners. Next, data were collected from successful online teachers to investigate strategies they have found useful to ensure student success.

2. PERSPECTIVES

Traditional distance learning environments were based on correspondence through passive media (paper, audio and video broadcast) and were most often conducted as independent experiences, with each learner corresponding only with the instructor. Recent developments in technology and access have offered organisations and universities the opportunity to improve these environments through increased communication, interactivity among participants, and incorporation of collaborative pedagogical models, specifically through electronic networks and groupware (Gerencher 1998, Gibbs 1998, Schrum 1998). Other advantages to using this type of distance learning are the potential combination of instantaneous (synchronous) and delayed (asynchronous) communication, access to and from geographically isolated communities, multiple participation within activities, and cultural sharing of diversity and recognition of similarities among the people of our world.

In this transformed model of distance learning, learners expect interactivity and close to 'traditional' classroom based education. The demand for online courses, enhanced by the ease of access, media attention, and interest from the private sector, has accelerated the rush toward online learning activities. Some of the courses are traditional subject matter courses, often undergraduate, while others are geared more to ongoing professional work activity. These include informal courses, professional development tutorials, and even full degree programs; however, much uncertainty exists about the conditions that are essential to create a successful experience for educators and learners.

Development of an online educational environment is a complex task. Faculty members have had an especially difficult time changing the ways in which they teach, regardless of these educators' own personal use of electronic media (Candiotti and Clarke 1998). In an electronic environment the role of faculty changes in many ways, and in particular, each instructor must give up some control of the classroom environment. Faculty members are forced to develop and design their activities and interactions in new ways, and may be frustrated without the ability to recognise when students are puzzled (Schrum and Berge 1998). Kember (1995) urged designers to work toward deep learning, which requires moving away from excessive assignments and shallow assessments, and toward some individual freedom in activities. These challenges go far beyond the need to be comfortable with the reliance on technology to support their courses. Wiesenberg and Hutton (1996) identified three major challenges for the designer to consider: increased time for delivery of the course (they estimate two or three times what is necessary for a traditional course), creating a sense of online community, and encouraging students to become independent learners. They also reported fewer interactions than expected from participants of an online course. These issues all have implications for faculty members and students in an online environment.

3. METHODS

These data derived from a variety of sources. To begin, an examination was made of over seventy institutions from around the globe that currently offer online learning opportunities. While many more institutions do offer online courses, only those that appeared to have an educational focus, and other components that seem essential for post-secondary education (library facilities, student support personnel, etc.) were considered. The original group was narrowed again, so that only those that provided potential students the opportunity to investigate their own suitability for this environment, through a substantive needs-assessment, which included advanced organisers, surveys, or other materials designed to provide potential students with necessary information were ultimately included.

A document analysis was then completed on those needs assessment or pre-enrolment instruments. Standard document analysis techniques were employed to compare the similarities, distinguish the areas of divergence, and identify the various functions of presentation, scoring, feedback, and supporting documentation (Miles and Huberman 1984). After the analysis was completed, a substantial literature review was undertaken, to verify the practical field analysis and to identify areas or characteristics that were missing from that analysis. The literature was thus woven through the resulting characteristics of successful students.

In addition, the author has completed several research studies that investigated various perspectives of online learning (Schrum 1992, Schrum 1998, Schrum 2000, Schrum and Berge 1998). In each study, completed primarily at the author's institution, an ongoing focus of investigation was the identification of factors that influenced student success, gathered from students' perspectives. These experiences were analysed through constant comparative methods, and were woven into the material presented in this paper.

Finally, this information was aggregated and presented to experienced online educators. These individuals verified these seven characteristics, and provided rich descriptions of the ways in which they ensure student success, as related to these dimensions. These data were also analysed using constant comparative methods (Lincoln and Guba 1985).

4. DIMENSIONS

Seven dimensions were found to impact the success of adults who enroll in distance learning courses and degree programs. Of course, not all dimensions are significant for each student, and only the individual will be able to determine those that are most pertinent and essential in his or her life. Moreover, while these dimensions are presented separately, in reality they do not function independently. Rather, they are interconnected, as are the pieces of a puzzle, and work together to support or challenge the online learner. The seven significant dimensions that emerged from the data included:

4.1 Access to tools

The first dimension concerns tools that students must have readily available. Research has demonstrated that easy access to technology, at home and perhaps at work, is one of the most significant contributors to success in online learning environments (Bonk and Dennen 1999, Schrum 1998). Access to all these tools is essential in a convenient and timely fashion, however, any discussion of specific tools is subject to revision almost immediately. Yet it is worthwhile to create a minimum standard for hardware and software, plus peripherals. An institution can provide a highly successful way of testing the equipment by offering potential students a free mini-course to experiment with the components and also to demonstrate exactly what an online learning experience might be like.

4.2 Technology experience

While having convenient access to the tools is the first step, experience using the tools for personal or work related activities is also important. More than one study has suggested that students who have little technological experience would delay learning new content while they learned the tools (Schrum 1998, Yakimovicz and Murphy 1995). Important experiences for new online learners include the ability to write documents using a word processor, printing, sending email on a regular basis, sending and receiving files via email, conducting searches through the World Wide Web, and accessing online information.

Students who are comfortable and adept at these tools will be able to solve small technical problems, such as rebooting their machine, installing software, resolving printer questions and cartridge changes, and answering simple configuration issues. They will also be able to distinguish between the problems they can solve and those problems that are not related to their individual hardware and software, and thus know when to contact the system administrator or institution to report difficulties and request assistance.

4.3 Learning preferences

Students may be concerned that they might miss traditional face to face instruction. It is true that each person learns in a unique way – in general, people know the ways in which they are best able to remember a phone number or address. Some people will write it down, others will say it several times, and still others will make a rhyme out of it. Each is appropriate for the individual who uses it. It is important to recognise that when one learns off campus, individual strengths and weaknesses may be amplified (Bonk and Dennen 1999).

4.4 Study habits and skills

One of the greatest benefits of learning at a distance is also one of its greatest challenges. Learners appear to appreciate the greater control over their learning, yet with that control comes substantial responsibility for completing assignments and being prepared. It may be more difficult to stay focused on those assignments so it is essential that students adopt a model of self-directed learning.

An individual's study habits play an important role in the success of that student. Learners must be able to turn off the television and concentrate on their work in a timely fashion, in order to stay on track in turning in assignments. It is fairly clear that those students who do not keep up with the class and the work are in greater danger of dropping out. A student may need to assess his/her basic academic proficiencies, such as skimming for information, and then reading the important portions more carefully. Students also find that the act of writing demands greater reflection than speaking, and reading a textbook presents more of a challenge than reading a novel. Students will also need to be able to organise and analyse complex ideas, and be able to communicate those ideas to others.

4.5 Goals and purpose

Adults have a variety of reasons for seeking educational experiences, and these may include a mandated upgrade of skills, requirement for additional credits to maintain licensure, need to change careers, or a simple desire to gain knowledge. Realisation of these goals, however, is often subject to the strength of the motivation that drives these desires (Schrum and Benson 2000). Motivation describes the internal and external conditions that influence behaviour and is one of the most significant factors in persistence in online learning (Schrum 1998). A non-motivated student may experience difficulty in completing an online course.

4.6 Lifestyle factors

Today we all lead extremely busy lives – and many adults have obligations beyond work. Students must determine if they have 10-20 hours a week to devote to studying. They must also ascertain if they have flexibility in their schedules, or if little room exists for rearrangement. It is vital that potential learners have the full support of their family, friends, and employer. When competing demands put stress on a student, they often feel they must give up or minimise their studying to keep peace in the family (Schrum and Benson 2000). It may also be helpful for the student to find someone who has taken distance courses to act as a mentor for support and advice.

4.7 Personal traits and characteristics

A few of the dimensions have touched on the ways in which individuals study and learn, but this dimension offers a perspective on fundamental ways in which individuals actually handle their daily activities, and patterns of behavior that go far beyond school related issues. This includes questions about the way one completes daily tasks. For example, is the individual always on time for appointments, or do simple tasks get forgotten in the midst of daily activities? Looking at our personal qualities can be somewhat difficult but it is an important step toward successful online learning. For example, Eastmond (1995) found students must be instructed in ways to take personal responsibility for becoming involved in the interactions and with their colleagues.

5. RESULTS OF FACULTY RESPONSE

Recognition of the complexities of taking an online course is important, but it is not enough. One goal of distance education has always been to encourage lifelong learning, especially among those who may not fit the traditional model of a university student. If success is the goal, steps toward it must be found; therefore it was essential to identify a small group of educators who were experienced in online learning to gather suggestions to support students in online experiences.

The first task was to gather input on the seven characteristics, and ascertain if any other characteristics belonged in this group. An international group of experienced online educators, all at the post-secondary level, was contacted and invited to respond to a web-based survey. The dimensions were explained, and their input was invited. Additionally, each faculty member was invited to provide his/her own strategies and ideas of teaching in the online environment. Overwhelmingly, the responses supported the idea that the identified characteristics were indeed the ones that were essential to student success. The respondents all had stories of students surrounding those same characteristics. Some students had thought they had enough access at work, but could never get their work done, or who had no place in their home to study, or even those whose families made fun of their efforts to learn 'online'.

The responding educators suggested ways in which they alerted students to the challenges of online learning. For example, one educator mentioned the way in which assignments were broken up into smaller chunks of work, each with a deadline, criteria, and feedback. Another spoke about the way in which she puts students into virtual teams to support and provide information to each other. One professor described the way he provides clear directions for how a virtual team operates and what he means by collaboration. Others tried to let students understand that working alone can create feelings of isolation, and how to overcome that feeling.

It is important that students become self-motivated and to help them become immersed into the online community. This might require more time exploring and participating in the various components of the education site, and instructors offered that they work hard to make that site attractive and friendly. An overwhelming amount of information can also intimidate students, so an intuitive organisation is important. Similarly, because of a lack of immediate feedback in asynchronous communication, students may feel frustrated, so educators worked hard to provide rapid response, and also to encourage all students to communicate with each other. Protocols for appropriate behaviour in online communications were often created and shared with learners.

All of the respondents described their concerns, uncertainty, and frustration when students drop out of an online program. Many took this as a personal failure, rather than as simply an individual student's decision. Although educators were aware that a students' needs analysis should precede any design of instruction, it is not always possible. One way to deal with this is to have benchmarks throughout the course to assess and accommodate the class's idiosyncrasies.

Evaluation was another challenge in the online environment, and again, these experts provided excellent suggestions. Some of them tried to have short weekly assignments so that they kept the students involved, and many of these assignments were components of a larger assignment. The goals of the evaluation were to examine the process and progress that the learners were making, rather than just examining the end products.

6. CONCLUSION

Currently, many institutions of higher education are creating and promoting online education for traditional and non-traditional students, and yet little is known about how to ensure success in this environment. Faculty members are under incredible pressure to put their courses online, so it is vital that information be shared about the rewards, challenges, and impact of online learning among faculty members.

This research investigated the characteristics of successful online learners, and verified them with expert online educators. It looked carefully at the strategies these educators use to ensure success for their students, prepare them for the unique challenges of this educational environment, and make the experience as meaningful as possible. This paper presented those characteristics and strategies, as a first step in explicating the complexities of this transition, so that the pedagogy and content might drive the process instead of the technology. Only through sharing our experiences will we truly be able to encourage successful lifelong learning for all citizens.

REFERENCES

Bonk, C. J. and Dennen, V. (1999) Learner issues with WWW-based systems. *International Journal of Educational Telecommunications*, 5 (4), pp. 401-417.
Candiotti, A. and Clarke, N. (1998) Combining universal access with faculty development and academic facilities. *Communications of the ACM*, 41 (1), pp. 36-41.
Eastmond, D. V. (1995) *Alone but together: Adult distance study through computer conferencing*. Cresskill, NJ: Hampton Press, Inc.
Gerencher, K. (1998, December 21) MBA programs go online. *InfoWorld*, 20, pp. 71-72.
Gibbs, W. J. (1998) Implementing online learning environments. *Journal of Computers in Higher Education*, 10 (1), pp. 16-37.
Kember, D. (1995) *Open learning courses for adults: A model of student progress*. Englewood Cliffs, N.J.: Educational Technology Publications.
Lincoln, Y. S. and Guba, E. G. (1985) *Naturalistic inquiry*. Newbury Park, CA: SAGE Publications.
Miles, M. B. and Huberman, A. M. (1984) *Qualitative data analysis*. Newbury Park, CA.: Sage Publications.
Palloff, R. M. and Pratt, K. (1999) *Building learning communities in cyberspace: Effective strategies for the online classroom*. San Francisco: Jossey-Bass Publishers.
Schrum, L. (1992) Professional development in the information age: An on-line experience. *Educational Technology*, 32 (12), pp. 49-53.
Schrum, L. (1998) On-line education: A study of emerging pedagogy. In *Adult Learning and the Internet*, B. Cahoon (eds.), Vol. 78, San Francisco: Jossey-Bass Publishers, pp. 53-61.
Schrum, L. (2000) Online teaching and learning: Essential conditions for success! In *Online teaching and learning*, L. Lau (eds), Hershey, PA: Idea Group Publishing, pp. 91-106.
Schrum, L. and Benson, A. (2000) Online professional education: A case study of an MBA program through its transition to an online model. *Journal of Asynchronous Learning Environments*, (4) 1. [http://www.aln.org/alnweb/journal/Vol4_issue1/schrum.htm].
Schrum, L. and Berge, Z. L. (1998) Creating student interaction within the educational experience: A challenge for online teachers. *Canadian Journal of Educational Communication*, 26 (3), pp. 133-144.
Wiesenberg, F. and Hutton, S. (1996) Teaching a graduate program using computer-mediated conferencing software. *Journal of Distance Education*, 11 (1), pp. 83-100.
Yakimovicz, A. D. and Murphy, K. L. (1995) Constructivism and collaboration on the Internet: Case study of a graduate class experience. *Computers and Education*, 24 (3), pp. 203-209.

BIOGRAPHY

Lynne Schrum is an Associate Professor; her research and teaching are focused on on-line teaching and learning, educator professional development, and the appropriate integration of information technology in primary and secondary school settings.

2

Student-centred Learning in a Telematic Learning Environment

Ineke Lam and Angela Markenhof
Institute of Education, Utrecht University, PO BOX 80127, 3508 TC Utrecht, The Netherlands
i.lam@ivlos.uu.nl

Keywords: learner-centred learning, integration of ICT, didactics, distance learning, higher education

Abstract: Due to an increasing number of part-time and adult students and new visions of the learning process, a need has arisen for a more flexible and student-centred form of education. The Internet offers a useful setting. The Institute of Education, Utrecht University, transformed an existing teacher-oriented course on 'designing a research problem' into a student-centred telematic learning environment, called PreScriptum. In this environment students can arrange their own learning process. They can choose their own path between and within the different modules. The teacher provides the students with individual written feedback on their assignments. Research shows that students do in fact follow different educational routes through PreScriptum. We conclude that this is possible through an effective use of hypertext, different functionalities and a non-linear design (content) in the learning environment.

1. INTRODUCTION

For over 15 years, the Institute of Education (IVLOS) a department of Utrecht University has given numerous successful courses geared to the acquisition of academic skills, such as writing and defining a research problem. University students from all grades and disciplines can follow these courses on a voluntary basis. Until recently, these courses were teacher-oriented with students attending classes located at the university.

Due to societal changes such as the shift to an information society, an increasing number of part-time and adult students, and new visions on the learning process, a need arose for alternative forms of education (Plomp et al. 2000). Learners have to become more active and more responsible for arranging their own learning process. Thus, education needs to be more flexible and learner-centred. Modern technological opportunities, like the Internet, make it possible to meet these needs.

However, most of the current ICT-applications are used to facilitate teacher-oriented arrangements of the learning process (Veen et al. 1999). IVLOS took up the challenge to develop a student-centred telematic learning environment (TLE) on 'defining a research problem' as the basis for a research plan (outline). The starting point was an existing course which was already running quite successfully. In our TLE, we wanted to keep the successful parts of this course and expand it with the new possibilities which the Internet offers.

In this paper, we focus on the following question: which characteristics of a TLE transform an existing, teacher-oriented course into a student-centred learning environment? We will start with a description of the existing course. Afterwards, we will describe the design and evaluation of the TLE, called 'PreScriptum'. We will end the paper with conclusions and a discussion.

2. EXISTING COURSE ON DESIGNING A RESEARCH PROBLEM

In this paragraph, we will describe the educational format of the existing course. Students, PhD or other, can sign up for this course if they have an approved research topic and a subject matter coach at their faculty. The essence of the course is that it deals with the formal aspects of a research problem and not the content. More specifically, students learn an approach. They learn how to define their research problem and draw an outline of their research paper or thesis, before they actually to start to collect the data and to write eventually.

This course has been successful for 15 years. It is given several times a year and approximately 10 to 15 students participate each time. In sum, approximately 250 students attend the course each year and by now, IVLOS has given this course to over 3,000 students.

2.1 Educational design

The organisation of the learning process can be characterised as 'teacher-oriented', despite the use of various instructional formats, such as individual assignments and exchange between students. The sequence of the subjects to discuss is preformatted and the teacher determines the agenda for the meetings.

Before going into more detail on the course, we will first describe a few basic principles (Oost and De Jong 1996).

1. Students work with their own material during the course. Thus, in this course on designing a research problem, students work on their own research project.
2. The course is very structured. It consists of six sessions which take place in a class setting at the university. Each session has the same structure.
3. A third principle is the exchange between students. Students discuss each others assignments and provide each other with oral feedback.
4. Finally, the course can be followed by students from different disciplines. The course is about generic skills and not subject matter knowledge.

The first session is an introductory one in which the purpose and method of the course are described. In the remaining five sessions, the five key components of the course are discussed in a fixed order; that is: (1) disciplinary embedding, (2) research question, method and answer, (3) research sub-questions, (4) objective, and (5) chapter order and work plan.

In the first hour and a half of each session, the teacher describes, explains and discusses the theory and students work on general assignments. During the remaining hour, students work on a specific assignment involving their own research. Thus, students apply the things they have learned to their own material. At the end of each session, the students hand in their assignment. The following week, the teacher returns the individual assignments with written feedback.

Students work with a syllabus, in which the theory is described and with a preformatted workbook, in which they work out their assignments.

The existing course on defining a research problem has mainly been teacher-oriented. Students can take an active role to a certain extent and they work with their own material, but they do not have the freedom to follow the course at their own time and pace. Furthermore, all students have to follow the same preformatted programme in which individual wishes and differences between students are not taken into account.

3. STUDENT-CENTRED EDUCATION AND THE INTERNET

Nowadays, a need exists for more flexible and learner-centred education. For instance, with the need for 'life-long learning', education has to deal with different types of learners with different educational backgrounds and baggage. Learner-centred education offers an optimal educational setting for these different types of learners, where traditional teacher-oriented education fails to do so.

What is learner-centred education? In learner- or student-centred education the learner or student not only takes an active role, but they are also responsible for the arrangement of the majority of activities belonging to the learning process. In a 'traditional' arrangement of the learning process, the teachers control these activities (Plomp et al. 2000). It is assumed that ICT can facilitate the shift from a more teacher-oriented towards a more learner or student-centred education (Montgomery 1995, Plomp et al. 2000).

At IVLOS, we experienced an increasing demand for a more student-centred education (we prefer to use the term student-centred instead of learner-centred because IVLOS mainly deals with students in higher education). Furthermore, we already had experience with ICT in education. Thus, it seemed logical to integrate the two. We decided to take up the challenge to rebuild the existing course on designing a research problem into an on-line learning environment.

The fact that a PhD-thesis on this subject appeared at the end of 1999, was an extra impulse to develop the TLE. In his thesis about the quality of research problems in dissertations, Oost (1999) introduces a model of the structure of a research question, i.e. a standard defining and clarifying the criteria a research problem should meet. The structure model consists of five elements: question, discipline, reason, strategy, and answer. The model in itself is non-linear, which means that there is no sequential order in handling the elements. After all, all elements should fit together logically.

The Internet, with its hypertext structure fits perfectly with the non-linear structure model. Hypertext is the organisation of information units into connected associations that a user can choose to make. An instance of such an association is called a link or hypertext link (http://whatis.com). "These links may be represented textually or graphically and provide information users with an ability to control the sequence of information as well as to 'navigate' within a rich information environment" (Jaffe 1995). In other words, users are able to construct their own way by chunking and linking from topic to topic rapidly and non-sequentially through the material presented on the Internet.

4. DESIGNING A RESEARCH PROBLEM

The TLE on designing a research problem was developed in WebCT (http://www.webct.com) and received the name PreScriptum. We chose WebCT because this software contains the three main categories of functionalities of a TLE which we wanted to integrate into the course, that is: information, communication and interactivity.

4.1 Something old, something new

With PreScriptum, we wanted to rebuild the existing course into a student-centred TLE. In order to do so, we had to evaluate the basic principles of the course. Three of the four basic principles of the existing course (see paragraph 2.1) remained starting points of PreScriptum as well. (1) Students work with their own material, they complete an assignment and they receive written feedback individually from the teacher. (2) PreScriptum is about generic skills instead of subject matter knowledge. (3) The nature of PreScriptum is still very structured. These principles made the existing course a success and, as such, we wanted to keep them in the new set-up. In contrast with the existing course, exchanges between students are optional in PreScriptum.

To develop a more student-centred TLE, we had to rewrite the existing course for two reasons. In the first place, the new theoretical insights of the non-linear structure model lead to new content. A second reason was the nature of this new medium. Writing for the Web is completely different than writing for a printed publication due to the hypertext structure: "....proper hypertext structure is not a single flow 'continued on page 2'; instead, split the information into coherent chunks that each focus on a certain topic. The guiding principle should be to allow readers to select those topics they care about and only download those pages" (Nielsen 2000, p.112). One also has to take into account how people read web pages. Reading from a computer screen is about 25% slower than reading from paper. Thus, the text we wrote for the TLE had to be succinct. Furthermore, we wrote for scannability. Users do not want to read long continuous blocks of texts; therefore, one needs to write short paragraphs and make use of subheadings and bulleted lists (Nielsen 2000, p. 101).

4.2 The new educational design

Because PreScriptum is based on a non-linear model and because hypertext provides for non-linear learning and thinking (Jonassen et al.

1999), we wanted to deliberately develop PreScriptum in a non-linear way, not only at the level of the modules, but also within each single module.

PreScriptum consists of five modules: disciplinary embedding, relevancy, precision, methodical functionality and consistency. These modules can be found as buttons on the Homepage of PreScriptum, along with the calendar, bulletin board and e-mail.

The non-linear nature of PreScriptum makes it possible for each individual student to decide where to start in the programme. We developed it in such a way that each single module can function as a starting module. All modules have the same set-up (see Figure 1) but a different colour, which facilitates navigation through the site.

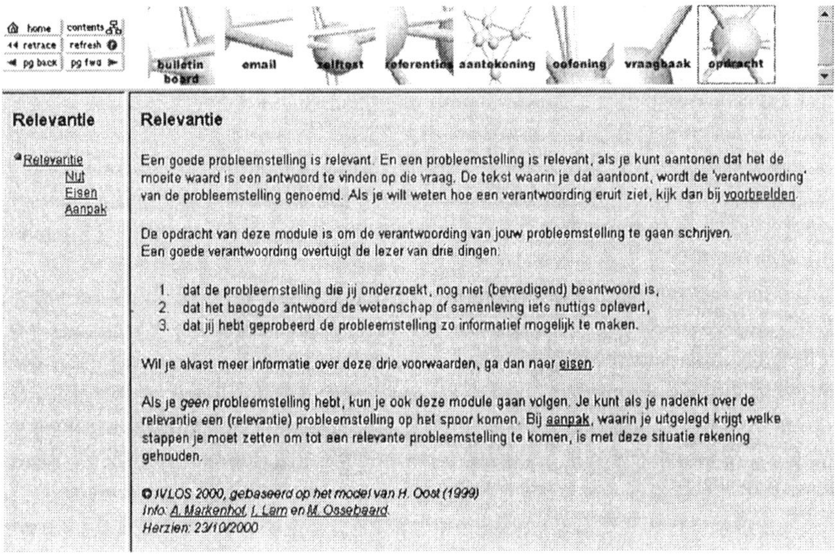

Figure 1. Example – in Dutch – of the set-up of a module (i.c. 'Relevancy')

PreScriptum is also non-linear within each individual module. We made use of hypertext in such a way that students can also decide what to start with in each module; that is, students can start with an exercise (interactivity), first study the theory (information) or do a self-test (interactivity). Depending on the concern of the individual student, he or she can choose the appropriate starting point. In the end, all the students have to complete an assignment and place this on the bulletin board on time. Thus, in fact "multiple versions of the materials can be developed by (……) the learners themselves, while the instructional product can be maintained in its original version" (Bevilacqua referred to in Ambrose 1991).

PreScriptum is a complete on-line learning environment except for the plenary starting and closing sessions which take place at the university. From former experiences (Veen et al. 1998), we learned to integrate an on-line experience with at least one plenary face-to-face starting meeting. We integrated the plenary face-to-face closing session in the design to really mark the end of the course. During the starting session, the method of work is explained and students practice with submitting a message to the bulletin board in PreScriptum. At the closing session, students reflect on their experiences and they fill in an evaluation questionnaire. During the five weeks between those sessions, students complete an assignment each week, which they place on the bulletin board before the stipulated time and date. There is no syllabus or workbook, the whole learning takes place within the TLE.

Thus, in contrast with the existing course, the organisation of the learning process in PreScriptum is meant to be student-centred. The teacher creates the structure and limits the learning environment, but the student is in control of their own learning within this environment. Students can follow PreScriptum at their own chosen time, pace and place. They can also determine for themselves which route they want to follow in the course, not only with regards to the whole module, but within each module as well. In other words, students can follow their own learning styles, something that can hardly be achieved in large classes. The teacher's role is to provide the students with individual written feedback on their five assignments and to be available for (e-mail) questions.

To conclude, from the instructional designers point of view, PreScriptum is created in such a way that students can use it in a non-linear manner. Do students actually choose a non-linear educational route through the course? In the next paragraph we will go into some more detail on this aspect.

5. DO STUDENTS USE A NON-LINEAR ROUTE?

Three pilots took place during Spring 2000. In total, 15 regular students and 10 PhD students worked in PreScriptum. Every pilot was evaluated through a questionnaire. Overall, PreScriptum received a positive evaluation. In the context of this paper, we particularly want to know whether the students did indeed choose a non-linear route throughout PreScriptum, both between the modules as well as within the modules. We make a distinction between regular students and PhD-students because the latter group had a slightly different instruction: they were not supposed to work on the Consistency module during the pilot.

Table 1. Students (N=15) and PhD-students educational route (N=10)

Regular students educational route through the modules of PreScriptum →				
Discip.	Relevancy	Precision	Meth.funct.	Consistency
Discip.	Precision	Relevancy	Meth.funct.	Consistency
Discip.	Precision	Consistency		
Discip.	Relevancy			
Relevancy	Discip.	Meth.funct.		
Relevancy	Discip.	Precision	Meth.funct.	Consistency
Relevancy	Precision	Meth.funct.	Discip.	Consistency
Relevancy	Precision	Discip.	Meth.funct.	Consistency
Relevancy	Precision	Discip.		
Relevancy	Meth.funct.	Precision	Discip.	Consistency
Relevancy	Meth.funct.	Precision	Discip.	
Meth.funct.	Discip.	Precision	Relevancy	
Meth.funct.	Relevancy	Precision	Discip.	Consistency
Meth.funct.	Relevancy	Discip.	Precision	
Meth.funct.	Relevancy	Discip.	Precision	
PhD-students educational route through the modules of PreScriptum →				
Discip.	Relevancy	Precision	Meth.funct. (3x)	
Discip.	Precision	Relevancy	Meth.funct.	
Discip.	Precision	Meth.funct.	Relevancy	
Relevancy	Discip.	Precision	Meth.funct. (3x)	
Relevancy	Precision	Discip.	Meth.funct.	
Meth.funct.	Discip.	Precision	Relevancy	

Table 1 indicates that with respect to the module level, both regular students and PhD students did, in fact, start with different modules in PreScriptum. Half of the group of regular students started with the 'Relevancy', while half of the group of PhD students started with the 'Disciplinary' embedding. As these were the modules we demonstrated during the two starting sessions, there might be a relationship between those two aspects. Interestingly enough, no one started with the 'Precision' module.

Furthermore, it is remarkable that both groups of students do not continue their educational route in a similar way, even when they share the same starting module. For instance, Table 1 indicates that the seven regular students who started with the module Relevancy, all – except for two – continued in a different way through PreScriptum. The 10 PhD students chose six different routes, two of which proved to be quite popular. Three PhD students followed the route starting with the module Disciplinary embedding. The route starting with the module Relevancy was chosen by three other PhD-students, two of whom collaborated throughout the course.

With respect to the students' route within the modules, we do not have detailed information. What we do know is that the majority of both regular and PhD students start each module by studying the theory. Afterwards, they generally do the exercises and self-tests, that is, the interactive functionalities. The least used functionalities are the frequently asked questions (faq's), references and notes.

6. CONCLUSION AND DISCUSSION

We have focused on the question: which characteristics of a TLE transform an existing, teacher-oriented course into a student-centred learning environment? To answer this we described the design and development of PreScriptum, a TLE on designing a research problem. New to PreScriptum, compared to the existing course, was the introduction of non-linearity at the level of the module as a whole as well as within each module.

PreScriptum turned out to be at least as successful as the existing course. Both, regular students and PhD students gave the on-line learning environment a positive evaluation on various aspects, such as the content, pedagogy and techniques. At the module level we noticed that most students follow different educational routes through PreScriptum. Furthermore, within each module, the results showed that most students prefer to begin by studying the theory. They differed in the functionalities they subsequently prefer, although the exercises and self-tests are most frequently used.

Considering the variety of educational routes, we can conclude that students took advantage of the opportunity to arrange their own learning process. As such, PreScriptum can be considered an example of a student-centred TLE. The effective use of hypertext, different functionalities and a non-linear design (content) are the main characteristics which make the development of such a student-centred TLE possible.

In this paper, we have shown that students follow their own chosen route through PreScriptum. However, we have not, investigated if each student chose the most optimal route for his or her learning process. Therefore, our next step will be to experiment with a so-called diagnostic module. With the integration of such a module in PreScriptum we want to find out if it is possible to give individual students a personal advice on the 'optimal route to follow through PreScriptum'.

REFERENCES

Ambrose, D. W. (1991) The effects of Hypermedia on Learning. A Literature Review. *Educational Technology*, 31, pp. 51-55.

Jaffe, J. M. (1995) *Media Interactivity, Cognitive Flexibility, and Self-efficacy.* [http://research.haifa.ac.il/~jmjaffe/Dissert/] 15.11.1999.

Jonassen, D. H., Peck, K. L. and Wilson, B. G. (1999) *Learning with technology. A constructivistic perspective.* Prentice Hall, New York.

Montgomery, S. M. (1995) *Addressing Diverse Learning Styles Through the Use of Multimedia.* [http://fie.engrng.pitt.edu/fie95/3a2/3a22/3a22.htm] 23.2.2000.

Nielsen, J. (2000) *Designing Web Usability. The practice of simplicity.* New Riders publishing, Indianapolis.

Oost, H. and De Jong, J. (1996) Cursus scriptie schrijven. In *Leren leren in didactisch perspectief,* J. Kaldeway, J. Haenen, S.Wils and G.Westhoff (eds.), Wolters-Noordhoff, Groningen, pp.214-231.

Oost, H. (1999) *De kwaliteit van probleemstellingen in dissertaties. Een evaluatie van de wijze waarop vormtechnische aspecten van probleemstellingen worden uitgewerkt.* [The quality of research problems in dissertations. An evaluation of the elaboration of formal aspects of research problems]. W.C.C., Utrecht.

Plomp, T., Brummelhuis, A. ten and Drent, M. (2000) *Integrating Information and Communication Technology in teacher education: the case of the Netherlands.* Paper presented at the European Conference on Educational Research 2000, Edinburgh, UK.

Veen, W., Lam, I. and Taconis, R. (1998) A virtual workshop as a tool for collaboration: towards a model of telematic learning environments. *Computers and Education,* 30, pp. 31-39.

Veen, W., Tartwijk, J.van, Lam, I., Pilot, A., Geloven, M. van, Moonen, J. and Peters, E. (1999) *Flexibel en open hoger onderwijs met ICT. Een inventarisatie van ICT gebruik, meningen en verwachtingen.* [Flexible and open higher education with ICT. An inventory of the use, opinions and expectations of ICT in Higher Education in the Netherlands]. IVLOS: Utrecht. [To be downlaoded at http://www.ivlos.uu.nl/ictho.htm]

BIOGRAPHY

Ineke Lam, a qualified consultant and researcher, has worked since 1994 at IVLOS, Utrecht University. She works with ICT-projects such as T3-project (Telematics for Teacher Training), ICT in Higher Education, and PreScriptum: a WebCT telematic learning environment. She is especially interested in telematic learning environments,didactics and fascinated by non-linear learning

Angela Markenhof, also at IVLOS, Utrecht University specialises in research planning and the pedagogy of academic skills. She has lectured extensively in these fields. She teaches degreee and postdegree students how to construct and formulate a well-defined, relevant research problem. In conjunction with Ineke Lam she designed PreScriptum.

3

Social Presence Online: Networking Learners at a Distance

Elizabeth Stacey
Faculty of Education, Deakin University, 221 Burwood Highway, Burwood, Victoria 3125, Australia
estacey@deakin.edu.au

Keywords: collaborative learning, distance learning, pedagogy, higher education

Abstract This paper draws on two studies which researched the use of online small group environments where collaborative learning is a central structure for learning. The establishment of social presence is facilitated through the socio-affective aspect of small group interaction which contributed to the effectiveness of learning online. Social presence, the ability of online learners to project themselves into a textual environment which has few visual or contextual cues, will be explored as an important element in facilitating effective online learning. The teacher's role in helping students project their online social presence and in establishing an environment for learning within the larger group computer conference will also be discussed.

1. INTRODUCTION

"Sometimes we just talked about things not connected to the course at all like the weather, books we were reading and wine we were drinking while studying. These are some of the bonuses of working with computer conferencing. You can develop a good professional and personal rapport with fellow students and facilitators."

"The success of online conferencing seems to lie in the hands of the teacher who 'facilitates' discussions along the way-keeping the momentum going when needed." *Students learning online.*

This paper explores the findings of two research studies which focus on the use of small group online environments for collaborative learning. The first study found that the socio-affective support provided by the collaborative group environment was of major importance to the success of the students and provided the basis for the second study which researched the development of this social support system by analysing the establishment of social presence in the course computer conferences. The importance of the teacher's role in helping students project their online social presence and in establishing an environment for learning in a computer conference is also explained.

2. BACKGROUND OF THE STUDY

As the online environment becomes more widely used for teaching courses and networking learners, the process of participants establishing social presence in an online environment is beginning to be explored. Social presence, defined by Garrison (1997a) as "the degree to which participants are able to project themselves affectively within the medium", is a growing area of focus for research as teachers and researchers find that for cognitive presence to be sustained, social presence must be established first. In the field of communications technology, which studies social presence as the degree to which communicating participants are able to project their presence through the technology, social presence can be projected best when the verbal and non verbal cues and the context can be also be communicated (Rice 1993). By these criteria, computer mediated communication (CMC) would be judged low on social presence (Lindlif and Shatzer 1998) and the role of the participants in compensating for lack of cues becomes more important.

Walther (1996), writing from the field of communication research, reflected that early empirical studies into CMC use had concluded that participants would be less sociable and more task oriented and he challenged the notion that CMC was a depersonalised medium. The results of the studies had been explained theoretically as an effect of the lack of non verbal cues, a perspective called 'cues-filtered-out' (Culnan and Markus 1987). However since this early research, field research has shown that with unconstrained interaction time, participants with high levels of social interaction through email, listserves, internet chat etc. (e.g. Parks and Floyd 1996) provide outcomes which counter the empirical data, though without explaining its results. Walther drew on a social information processing perspective that suggested that as communicators in CMC are as driven as any participants to develop social relationships, the longer time factor of an ongoing computer conference can provide the opportunity for the accrual of interpersonal impressions and the gathering of social information through text messages. In this way relationships can still develop despite fewer cues and the earlier time -limited empirical research results were explained.

Walther tested this theory (Walther 1993, Walther and Burgeon 1992) and found that though interpersonal impressions were formed more slowly with CMC, relationships developed in the same way as in face to face situations, even becoming more socially oriented in the online context.

Though Gunawardena and Zittle (1997) claim that social presence in a CMC context focus on the group members' reactions to one another because the teacher acts as 'more of a facilitator than the main source of information', this paper describes a proactive role the teacher plays in developing a socially responsive discourse that models a combination of social encouragement with content discussion. Garrison has called this aspect of the teacher's successful conference moderation 'contextualising' where the teacher provides the communication model as well as organising and focusing the online discussion (1997b). The criteria analysing social presence involves extending an analysis framework developed for the first study to include social presence factors developed in a study by Rourke, Anderson, Garrison and Archer (1999), which measured social presence. Their work in defining the 'community of inquiry' model that holds the teaching presence as an important factor in structuring learning and facilitating active learning is extended here.

3. CONTEXT OF THE RESEARCH

The first study into online collaborative learning of students within a Masters of Business Administration Program (Stacey 1999) found that interactive online group discussion was central to the learners' effective construction of new conceptual understandings. Through the social context of group interaction, the collaborative groups developed a consensus of knowledge through communicating different perspectives, receiving feedback from other students and teachers and discussing ideas, until a final negotiation of understanding was reached. The social nature of cognition as theorised by Vygotsky (1978) and developed through neo-Vygotskian research (Forman and McPhail 1993) was seen as influential to a person's construction of knowledge. The provision of dialogue within a community of learners was of major importance as knowledge construction is perceived as a dialectic process in which individuals test their constructed views on others and negotiate their ideas. Drawing on Vygotsky's theory that conceptual understandings are developed through verbal interaction, this research found that a socially constructed learning environment is essential for effective learning. The social conversation provided the learner with a context and stimulus for thought construction and learning which was the means by which the group contributes more to each learners' understanding than they are able to do individually.

The groups were based in a diverse range of workplaces and geographical locations in three states of Australia remote from the delivering university location. The gender balance of the groups represented the overall course population with more males (21) than females (10). The socio-affective support provided by the collaborative group environment was found to be important to the success of the students who established social support systems through their online groups. This support system was particularly vital to them as distance learners who may otherwise be isolated from other students. The posting of supportive comments and sharing of personal anecdotes and information provided a network of social interaction that underlay the mutual respect and trust needed for successful collaborative learning.

Each small group's message content analysis revealed more than 50% of messages sent online were social in nature, intended to maintain the cohesion of the group and support and encourage the groups' individual members. The social messages gave the students the friendship and sense of belonging that helped to motivate them to apply themselves to their study when they were finding it hard to manage, particularly because of the conditions of studying at a distance. Their accountability and responsibility to the other members of the group for their participation in online collaborative tasks were strong motivators for their persistence and such a sense of a strong group network depended on their establishment of social presence online.

4. SOCIAL PRESENCE RESEARCH

The second study was designed to explore these findings and was developed within the content area of an Open and Distance Education specialism of a Masters degree program. This paper focuses on one course called *Teaching and Learning with Computer Mediated Communication* which was developed in response to students' growing interest in the theory and practice of teaching and learning in a virtual medium. Online conferencing has been used in this program since 1993 with all units having conferences established through the communication software FirstClass, for electronic discussion of ongoing tasks and activities with the aim of engaging students in learning interactively. The small group collaborative learning environment was researched to explore how the collaborative learning environment affects the students' learning and within this context, how social presence factors were established online particularly focusing on the role of teacher in modeling techniques of social interaction.

5. RESEARCH METHODS

Data were gathered electronically using qualitative methods through archiving and analysing the online interaction of the students and by gathering students' perceptions and reflections. Quantitative data were collected through analysis of the frequency and type of messages on the conferences as well as through content analysis of the computer conferences. The participant group had 20 members.

1. Through the FirstClass unit conferences, a voluntary focus group was set up within a course conference area where questions were posted at the beginning and at the end of the semester. These asked about the students' experience studying online.
2. Another interactive FirstClass conference was established three months later to discuss the early analysis of results and further encourage student reflections on the effect conferencing had on their learning.
3. The main data gathering process used for identifying social presence factors was through retrospectively analysing the archived conference messages to categorise and measure frequency of communication and learning processes. This process involved calculating the frequency of messaging, and analysis of conference message content.

In the first study, the main purpose of the messages had been categorised into a simple three way framework which was extended to include the social presence factors. The analysis framework used a categorisation similar to the first study, but which labelled units of meaning within each message for its primary purpose and content into:

- *Cognitive/content*, discussion and commentary on the course content
- *System messages* (relating to learning the FirstClass software, or access issues) and administrative messages and
- *Social content analysed into social presence factors using the multiscale.*

Social Presence categories developed by Rourke et al. (1999) for defining and measuring social presence in a computer conference These are:

- *Interactive responses*, threaded responses of socially appreciative nature,
- *Affective responses* expressing emotion, feeling and mood which are expressed by emoticons, humour and self disclosure and
- *Cohesive responses* which are group activities which build a cohesive group environment. These are measured by factors such as salutations,

addressing participants by name and addressing the group as 'we', 'our' or 'us'.

6. FINDINGS OF THE STUDY

6.1 The teacher's role in facilitating social presence

In the early stages, the teacher had an important role helping students establish social presence. In the first weeks, students were required to introduce themselves to the group with specific points of discussion such as professional role, purpose for course choice and previous conferencing experience. Though most students were comfortable with the internet for email and as an information source (76.5%), computer conferencing was new to many. Students talked about their feelings of inadequacy entering a space with no visual cues about the other students.

The course was structured so that the teacher modeled social presence factors in the first week of semester. Each introductory message sent by students was responded to encouragingly by the teacher who used that period to teach the students social practice and use of the software elements. Such factors as use of reply and quoting in messages rose in frequency in response to both the teacher's model and the specific directions given about these aspects of the software. Similarly the 'affective' behaviour category of humour, emotion and self disclosure were a style of communication used by the teacher from an early stage and quickly emulated by many students.

By the second week the group began to welcome one another and to practise the social presence factors modelled by the teacher (shown below).

Table 1. Social Presence Factors

Social Presence	Affective units	Interactive units	Cohesive units	Total
Week 1Students	31	29	33	93
Teacher	4	13	18	35
Total	35	42	51	128
Week 2 Students	55	117	57	229
Teacher	2	14	3	19
Total	57	131	60	248
Week 3 Students	15	20	16	51
Teacher	1	6	4	10
Total	16	26	20	113

6.2 Social presence in small group structure

The structure of the course required task based small group discussions be established in the early stages of the semester. After the introduction phase, students communicated in conference spaces with fewer participants who shared a content focus they had both suggested or chosen. Moving into a small group collaborative environment meant that students could establish small group relationships in a more informal space and this was conducive to social presence comments included in most content messages whatever their complexity. The course required the students to break into subgroups by choice of issue for discussion and then if common issues showed a grouping pattern, the issues discussion groups were used as the basis of forming small collaborative groups for the second collaborative assessment task.

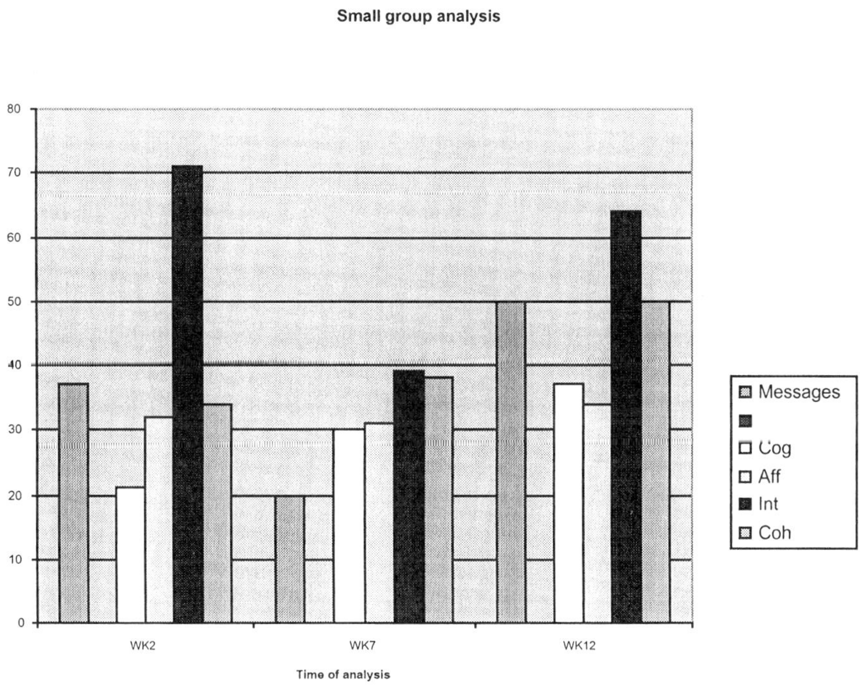

Figure 1. Total of small group factors compared over 3 analysis periods

Their comments continued to project a social presence and group cohesiveness as the groups interacted and the predictions of Walther (1996)

that groups would work even harder to establish personal relationships online over a long period of time were shown to occur in the analysis of one representative small group shown in Figure 1. Cognitive content also rose over several weeks, reflecting the cognitive focus and purpose of the discussions, but this was accompanied by a continued high level of social presence factors.

These results do not agree with those of Rourke et al. (1999) and Hara, Bonk and Angeli (2000), who found that purely social interaction, not focused on the content of the course, declined as the conference progressed, which they concluded was because students got to know one another better. The conclusions from the analysis of this research study support the argument that social relationships require continuation of social presence factors through a much longer period, as one semester is only the beginning of group formation online.

6.3 Monitoring small groups and providing multiple layers of communication

Again, the teacher played an active role in monitoring progress and social cohesion of small groups through the small group discussions. There was some need for multiple layers of communication for effective social presence to be established in some groups and the teacher can organise and suggest communication through phone calls, meetings or synchronous chat as well as through the computer conference. This helped the group to establish the trust and ease of communication for cognitive development to occur. One of the small collaborative groups laboured under misinterpreted social presence until they talked their issues over by phone with the teacher's guidance.

6.4 Collaborative learning

As with the first study, collaborative learning was reported as an enhancement of learning. The students described working harder than in other distance subjects because of their accountability to the group and because they engaged more with reading and reflection on a wider range of resources than they would have consulted alone, particularly as they had to contribute to an ongoing discussion. Many described the motivation for learning that group communication provided as the group developed and they described their enjoyment of the interaction which reduced their usual isolation in distance learning or in fact any adult study. The different perspectives provided by the different students was particularly seen as an advantage to their learning as it took them out of their own limited view of the subject.

7. CONCLUSIONS

Walther's (1996) proposition that relationships require longer to develop in an electronic medium was supported by the study into social presence where even at the end of the semester, members of the groups were motivated to continue their social interaction and their social relationships. Establishing social presence is an important aspect for effective online interaction and learning where the high rate of cognitive analysis of units within messages showed the active engagement students maintained with the cognitive learning of the course. This was accompanied by a continuing high rate of social presence factors establishing the interrelationship of cognitive and social presence online. The teacher's role developing a secure learning environment and modelling social presence factors and continuing to monitor and facilitate conference interaction was a major factor in the success of this interactive process in online learning.

REFERENCES

Culnan, M. J. and Markus, M. L. (1987) Information technologies. In *Handbook of organisational communication: An interdisciplinary perspective*, F. M. Jablin, L. Putnam, K. H. Roberts and L. W. Porter (eds.), Newbury Park, CA. (Sage cited in Walther (1996)).

Forman, E. A. and McPhail, J. (1993) Vygotskian perspective on children's collaborative problem-solving activities. In *Contexts for Learning: Sociocultural Dynamics in Children's Development*, E. A. Forman, N. Minick and C. A. Stone (eds.), Oxford University Press, New York, pp. 213-229.

Garrison, D. R. (1997a) Computer conferencing and distance education: cognitive and social presence issues. In *The new learning environment: A global perspective*, Proceedings of the ICDE World Conference, Pennsylvania State University.

Garrison, D. R (1997b) Computer conferencing: the post-industrial age of distance education. *Open Learning*, June, pp. 3-11.

Gunawardena, C. N. and Zittle, F. (1997) Social presence as a predictor of satisfaction within a computer-mediated conferencing environment. *American Journal of Distance Education*, 11, 3, pp. 8-26.

Hara, N., Bonk, C. J. and Angeli, C. (2000) Content Analysis of Online Discussion in an Applied Educational Psychology. *Instructional Science*, 28 (2), pp. 115-152.

Lindlif, T. R. and Shatzer, M. J. (1998) Media ethnography in virtual space: strategies, limits, and possibilities. *Journal of Broadcasting and Electronic Media*, Spring, 42, 2, pp. 170-189.

Parks, M. R. and Floyd, K. (1996) Making friends in cyberspace. *Journal of communication*, 46 (1), pp. 80-90.

Rice, R. E. (1993) Media appropriateness: Using social presence theory to compare traditional and new organisational media. *Human Communication Research*, 19, pp. 451-484. (Quoted in Lindlif and Shatzer (1998)).
Rourke, L., Anderson T., Garrison, D. R. and Archer, W. (1999) Assessing social presence in asynchronous text-based computer conferencing. *Canadian Journal of Distance Education,* 14, 2, pp. 50-71.
Stacey, E. (1999) Collaborative learning in an online environment. *Canadian Journal of Distance Education,* 14, 2, pp. 14-33.
Vygotsky, L. S. (1978) *Mind in Society: The Development of Higher Psychological Processes.* (Cole, M. M., Lopez-Morillas, Luria, A. R and Wertsch, J. (trans.)), Harvard University Press, Cambridge, MA.
Walther, J. B. (1993) Impression development in computer mediated interaction. *Western Journal of Communication*, 57, pp. 381-398.
Walther, J. B. (1996) Computer-mediated communication: Impersonal, interpersonal, and hyperpersonal interaction. *Communication Research,* 23 (1), pp. 3-41.
Walther, J. B. and Burgeon, J. K. (1992) Relational communication in computer mediated interaction. *Human Communication Research*, 19, pp. 50-88.

BIOGRAPHY

Dr. Elizabeth Stacey is a Senior Lecturer in the Education Faculty at Deakin University. She teaches pre-service teacher education studies, postgraduate distance education coursework and supervises students researching flexible learning and computer and communication technologies. Her research and publications are focused on these areas including learning with computers, and the use of interactive technologies, particularly audiographics, interactive television and computer conferencing.

4

Teaching for Quality Learning Online

A Layered Design Model for Higher-order Thinking

Paul Nicholson and Geoff White
School of Scientific and Developmental Studies, Deakin University, Burwood, 3125, Australia
pauln@deakin.edu.au

Keywords: learning models, learner-centred learning, thinking, internet, electronic communication

Abstract: The majority of online instructional programs are transmissive, viewing learning as passive, rather than as interactive and engaging – important attributes for the promotion of higher order learning. We argue that the lack of clear pedagogical models for online learning is a critical limiting factor in the development of quality teaching online. We present a model for designing online learning environments for facilitating higher-order thinking in traditional and 'fuzzy' contexts. Conceptualising user interaction with the instructional system under the categories of 'Interaction and 'Expertise Development' greatly facilitates the incorporation of effective pedagogical approaches in the instructional design process.

1. INTRODUCTION

The majority of online instructional programs are transmissive, viewing learning as passive, rather than as interactive and engaging – important attributes for the promotion of higher order learning. Why do online course designers routinely ignore such well-known pedagogical approaches to facilitating effective learning? Presumably, this neglect is a consequence of a focus on developing lower-order thinking or skills, sharing with the traditional classroom a passive and transmissive pedagogy as the default design model. However, in this paper we argue that the lack of clear pedagogical models for online learning, particularly for supporting the development of higher-order thinking, is a critical limiting factor in the development of quality teaching online. As a step towards overcoming this barrier, we present a design model that we have developed and refined over the past ten years, and which we believe provides significant advantages for designing online learning environments for facilitating higher-order thinking.

2. WHY HIGHER ORDER THINKING AND LEARNING?

The constant change that characterises contemporary workplaces is nowhere more apparent than in the dynamic organisations that value and utilise their employees' capacities for strategic and responsive thinking. For such organisations, learning is their central and strategic focus (Zuboff 1988). The 'knowledge era' organisation generates its own knowledge and understandings and anticipates, defines and understands its own strategic opportunities. Such organisations place significant learning demands upon its employees as they operate within workplaces described by Barnett (1999) as characterised by 'supercomplexity'. Contrasting with these 'knowledge era' organisations are those which are reactive to change, preferring instead to focus upon the maintenance of traditional practices.

But what exactly is required of those who work in supercomplex contexts? Despres and Hiltrop (1995) identify the following attributes of a knowledge-era workplace: knowledge and skills are specialised and deep; groups and projects provide the locus of activity; skill obsolescence is rapid; performance measures value process effectiveness; customers, problems and issues are the focus of work activity; employee loyalty is to the profession, networks and peers. Finally, the individual worker's impact on organisational performance is infrequent but strategic.

Within the context of online training and development, what design models will help people efficiently develop and refine their capacities to contribute to organisational survival in the new economies – to think and learn in higher order ways? The cognitive competencies involved in such thinking include the ability to:

1. analyse claims, opinions and complex situations
2. make critical judgements of alternative views
3. evaluate and synthesise a variety of positions into a coherent whole
4. apply their knowledge and understanding in productive and defensible ways
5. meet strategic challenges facing their organisation.

3. DEVELOPING ONLINE ENVIRONMENTS FOR TRADITIONAL CONTEXTS

Traditional education and training contexts are those that focus on developing clearly defined knowledge and skills, and which constitute a bounded knowledge system (Nicholson and Johnson 1999). These contexts usually require the incisive and expert transfer and application of existing knowledge to new, but predictable, situations. In such cases, there is a well-defined knowledge base of content, rules and practices to guide the development of both traditional and on-line training programs (e.g., Murray 1996), the majority of which focus on developing low-level skills and knowledge. Such programs are often characterised by:

1. A transmissive instructional model
2. Direct trainer-to-learner delivery
3. Clearly specified and delineated content – skills, software, procedures
4. Little long-term retention unless in a workplace context.

Such knowledge bases commonly contain both declarative and procedural knowledge – a structure that simplifies the development of software-based training packages by providing functional decomposition of the knowledge base for a particular area into knowledge and process components. This fragmentation is critical to the success of program designers who attempt to recreate expert knowledge in adaptive software environments that require precisely articulated knowledge structures at their core. In this instructional-design paradigm, incorrect or misunderstood knowledge is referred to as 'buggy knowledge' because it introduces 'errors' into the self-consistent data model that commonly underpins such software. Dealing with buggy knowledge is a major design problem in both traditional and on-line programs, both in terms of identifying the strategies that could begin to address it, and in terms of the time and resources needed to be devoted to it's inclusion in an otherwise clearly articulated instructional sequence. This is particularly so in situations that are trying to change, or to build on, long established workplace practices where the persistence and resilience of deeply held situative beliefs and practices are well documented (e.g., Anderson, Greeno, Reder, and Simon 2000, Putnam and Borko 2000).

Adult learning theories such as Mezirow's Transformational Learning Theory, Knox's Proficiency Theory, Self-directed Learning, and Knowle's Androgyny, while widely discussed and employed in varying ways and degrees in face-to-face training, have little impact on the design of traditional on-line learning environments (DeMartino 1999). This appears to be a consequence of the perceived conflict between the instructional design paradigms (as above) and the requirements of the learning theories. For example, the following aspects of adult learning theories (DeMartino 1999, p.786) raise serious, but not insurmountable, challenges to instructional designers intent on developing an instructional sequence predicated on the transfer of a fixed body of knowledge and skills:

1. Individual experience of the world is important to learning
2. Learning is not the discovery of independent, pre-existing knowledge but the construction of meaning through experience
3. Learning is more subjective than objective
4. The emphasis is on the individual learner's interpretation, integration and transformation of knowledge
5. Knowledge is actively constructed by the learner, not passively received from the environment.

This perceived mismatch, however, disappears when the focus of 'instruction' shifts from delivering content to developing higher-order thinking as naive assumptions about the passive learning of content have to be replaced by a more sophisticated understanding of the requirements of person-centred, active-learning models. This reconceptualisation is necessary because higher-order thinking results from information and information stored in memory being interrelated and/or rearranged to achieve a purpose or find possible answers to complex problems. (Lewis and Smith 1993). Cognitive complexity is the hallmark of such learning contexts and demands the use of an active learning sequence as in Figure 1 for the achievement of the necessary higher order learning.

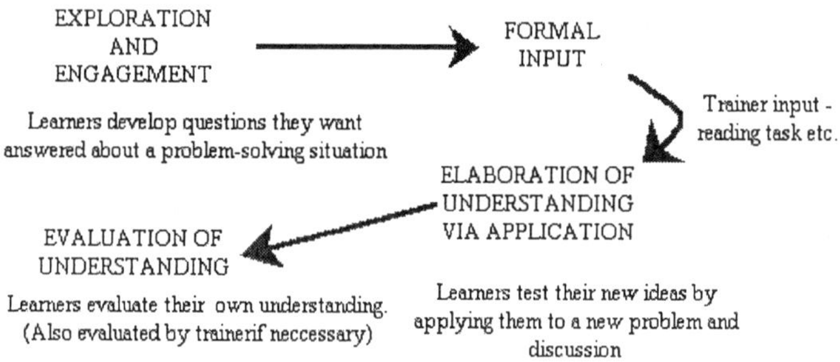

Figure 1. Essential components of an active learning sequence (Nicholson and White 2000)

Initial exploration and engagement are key aspects of an active learning sequence, as this is the part of the learning sequence that engages and contextualises issues by providing learners with the opportunity to locate the issue or content in their own context. Contextualisation requires the learners to bring their prior knowledge, experiences, and interpretations into an authentic learning sequence. Formal instructor input into the sequence is also required, as simply engaging with the issues does not guarantee higher order learning will occur. This stage, of course, is one that dominates many passive learning models.

Subsequent stages in the active learning sequence have the learners testing their own understandings by applying them to new problems and, in some cases, evaluating their own understandings. This combination of a focus on higher-order thinking, active learning, and a situative approach has been described as comprising a Rich Environment for Active Learning (REAL) (e.g. Dunlap 1999). The most important aspect of a REAL is the engagement and interaction of participants between themselves, external mentors, and the course content. Online technologies are able to support such interaction, and can be used in many ways to structure interactions amongst the participants of a REAL.

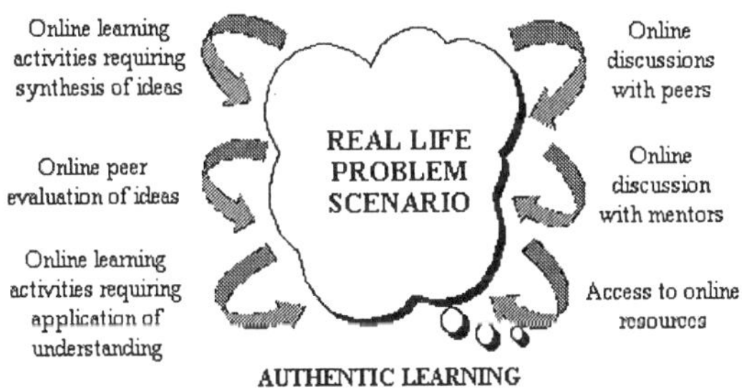

Figure 2. Conceptual design of a generic online REAL (Nicholson and White 2000)

Figure 2 depicts a conceptual design for an online REAL that is based on our work over the past 10 years in developing online adult learning environments for facilitating higher-order thinking. It was used as the basis of a state-wide professional development program for the Victorian Department of Employment, Education and Training. This was to assist teachers in adopting successful planning, teaching and classroom management strategies that would help to provide a better environment for their children's learning in the Middle Years of Schooling (MYS). The design required the development of an online learning environment that would eventually replace an effective face-to-face professional development program. The program was not particularly focused on higher-order thinking about the embedded issues, but rather, about the transfer of existing knowledge and skills to new contexts – in this case a 'traditional' context. The initial stage provides the participants with an overview of the nature and content of the course, and provides the participants with the opportunity to meet with other course participants – an aspect we suspect is due largely to the demographics of the teacher workforce and their lack of experience in, and confidence with, online learning.

We fitted our REAL design to an apprentice-based learning model (Guzdial and Kehoe 1998) as this is a proven approach to adult online learning in this context. Figure 3 shows how our generic conceptual design for a REAL was implemented in this particular case. Due to teacher resistance to working solely in an online mode, the initial and final phases of the program are conducted face-to-face. The role of technology in the MYS program is simply to facilitate participants' access to people and resources; there is no inherent cognitive scaffolding, other than that provided by the mentors. The outcome of the course is the production of an action plan for implementing MYS strategies in each participant's school – an instance of the peer-evaluation aspect of the REAL design in Figure 1.

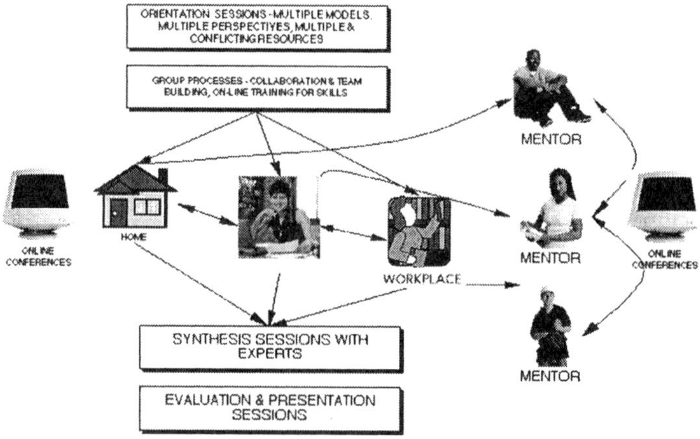

Figure 3. The Middle Years of Schooling REAL structure

4. FUZZY CONTEXTS AND HIGHER-ORDER THINKING

There is no argument that development of a REAL, either face-to-face or online, is a reasonable approach for traditional contexts. However, it is problematic for developing higher order thinking and understanding when the issue or content is 'fuzzy' and does not comprise a bounded knowledge system (as in the MYS project above). This means there is an absence of key factors such as a well-articulated (or perhaps cohesive) knowledge base, a clear solution, or an obvious basis for decision making.

Because unbounded knowledge systems lack ready-made answers to be 'learned', fuzzy environments need a design that accommodates uncertainty as a key feature, and one that is focused upon higher-order thinking. In such designs, the learner has to develop an answer meaningful within the context of the learning experiences provided by the teacher or course. Examples of contemporary fuzzy problems in a 'real-world' business context include issues such as deciding on strategic e-commerce structures and processes, and meeting the challenges of globalisation. Within the education context, coping with the 'threat' of virtual schooling or the commercialisation and internationalisation of education present similar levels of conceptual complexity characteristic of fuzziness. Such fuzzy problems intersect with both knowledge and value domains, and are not amenable to simple solutions. The challenge for designers trying to develop courses for such fuzzy contexts then becomes a matter of responding to a set of difficult questions that include:

1. How to facilitate higher-order learning & knowledge growth?
2. How to structure and sequence tasks with 'fuzzy' outcomes and unbounded knowledge bases?
3. How to build on existing expertise and 'intellectual capital'?
4. How to evaluate 'fuzzy' program outcomes?

In general, traditional instructional design paradigms cannot cope with the nature, scope, and incorporation of uncertainty and values that fuzzy contexts contain. We argue that any instructional design model that purports to address fuzzy contexts must include aspects that deal with the following (cf. Dunlap 1999) as basic design requirements:

1. Uncertainty ('fuzziness')
2. Decisions on a path of action
3. Judgement & interpretation
4. Multiple perspectives
5. Imposing meaning, effortful thinking and multiple solutions
6. Self-regulation of thinking.

In order to accommodate these features, the traditional instructional design process of creating a predetermined learning *sequence* needs to be replaced with one that creates a set of *loosely structured learning* pathways, as the notion of sequential learning is problematic in fuzzy contexts. There is a clear need for a range of new design paradigms that can be adapted to suit a wide range of fuzzy contexts. The layered-design model in Figure 4 is one such approach to developing higher-order thinking in fuzzy contexts that has proven its value in this regard.

5. A DESIGN FOR FUZZY ENVIRONMENTS

We developed the layered-design model (Figure 4) over time, as it became clear that in designing for fuzzy contexts, at least four separate design processes had to be undertaken.

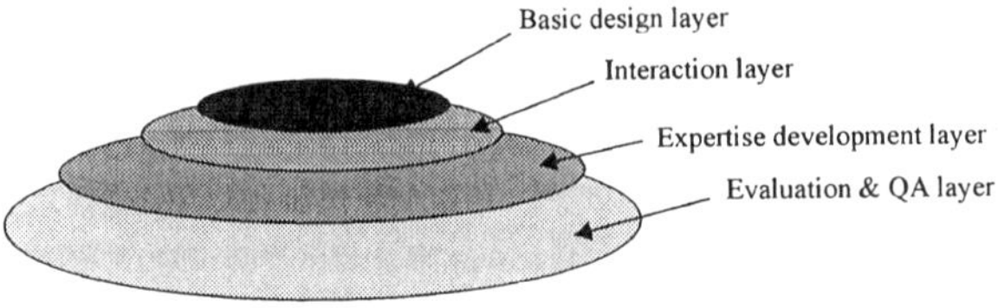

Figure 4. A layered-design model for fuzzy environments

These focus on (a) technical aspects of the design; (b) the nature and purposes of the ways in which learners will interact with the course content, other participants, and external individuals; (c) the pedagogical structures and processes that will build upon the interactions to develop expertise in the particular fuzzy context; and (d) the authentic assessment processes that need to be developed to ensure the attainment of expertise can be evaluated in a meaningful, as opposed to simplistic, manner. While these might seem to be straightforward, in our experience it is not an easy task to develop the content and processes with the same level of certainty as in a traditional design context. Indeed, the design task becomes more of a 'crafting' of the learning environment than one of technical construction.

The first design task examines the basic design layer – the choice of platform, software, and other essentially technical considerations. These are often seen as precursors to the design process, however we believe they have to be integrated because of the implications of such decisions for the rest of the design process. In other words, learning needs, not the platform or software, should dictate the design (cf. Alexander 1999).

Figure 4 is an abstraction of aspects of Figure 2, focusing on ensuring that specific aspects of the online discussions and engagement with content and resources are properly structured to achieve the desired learning outcomes. Content, while critical, is no more important than the discussions and arguments associated with its analysis. We have found it is important to differentiate between interaction and the development of expertise, as the two are fundamentally distinct, a point often overlooked in traditional contexts. Simply planning structures and processes such as learning sequences, discussions and online seminars etc. to engage learners with content is insufficient for the facilitation of higher order learning. These components must be supplemented by the purposeful development of expertise arising from such interactions.

The expertise development stage is also affected by the situative nature of fuzzy contexts. For example, in the case of a business trying to address the challenges of globalisation, the required expertise is not only that of understanding the issues (which might be amenable to a traditional design context), but also includes an understanding of situative aspects such as strategies for the development of a management-team approach, the sharing of understandings and the leveraging of group intellectual capital in the pursuit of corporate goals. In Education, it could relate to university students developing a real (as opposed to mathematical) appreciation of the basis of non-deterministic chaos theory. In both cases the desired outcomes include personal and group aspects that have to be developed along with the content knowledge needed to support them.

Similar issues also affect the assessment process. The notion of peer and self-assessment was raised in Figure 2, and it is relevant here. For example, how should the evaluation of the business case (above) be conducted, and by whom? There is no 'correct' answer to assess, other than that the participants' ability to perform the desired tasks has improved, an issue best determined in the workplace. In such cases, the assessment layer design would include a large element of employer evaluation of performance over time, a distinguishing feature relative to the all too common 'end of course' competency assessment which is axiomatically unsuited to fuzzy contexts.

6. CONCLUSION

Being grounded in notions of active learning and authentic contextualised settings, the layered design model we have outlined in this paper stands in stark contrast to many of the mastery-learning based online environments currently available for knowledge and procedural competency training. Our model has been used for a range of higher order learning purposes, and through this experience we have learned the significant dependence of the model upon detailed knowledge of the learning theories literature, an understanding of the dynamics of learning, and expertise in the delivery of instruction designed to facilitate higher order thinking and learning. Our experience affirms the importance of these understandings and competencies, rather than technical imperatives, as the primary driver of design for higher order learning online. After all, online technologies are a medium, not a training solution, most particularly so when the desired training outcome is the higher order strategic thinking valued by today's knowledge era organisations.

REFERENCES

Alexander, S. (1999) Selection, dissemination, and evaluation of the TopClass WWW-based course support tool. *International Journal of Educational Telecommunications, 5* (4), pp. 271-283.

Anderson, J., Greeno, J., Reder, L. and Simon, H. (2000) Perspectives on learning, thinking and activity. *Educational Researcher, 29* (4), pp. 11-13.

Barnett, R. (1999) Learning to work and working to learn. In *Understanding learning at work,* D. Boud (ed.), Routledge, London, pp. 29-44.

DeMartino, D. J. (1999) Employing adult education principles in instructional design. In *Proceedings of SITE'99,* J. Price, J. Willis and D. Willis et al. (eds.), San Antonio, February, pp. 783-788.

Despres, C. and Hiltrop, J. (1995) Human resource management in the knowledge age: current practice and perspectives on the future. *Employee Relations,* 17 (1), pp. 9-23.

Dunlap, J. (1999) Rich environments for active learning on the web: guidelines and examples. In *Proceedings of WebNet 99 – World Conference on the WWW and Internet,* P. de Bra and J. Leggett (eds.), Honolulu, October, pp.313-318.

Guzdial, M. and Kehoe, C. (1998) Apprenticeship-based learning environments: A principled approach to providing software-realized scaffolding through hypermedia. *Journal of Interactive Learning Research, 9* (3/4), pp. 289-336.

Lewis, A. and Smith, D. (1993) Defining higher-order thinking. *Theory into Practice, 32*(3), pp. 131.

Murray, T. (1996) Special purpose ontologies and the representation of knowledge. In *Proceedings of the International Conference on the Learning Sciences, 1996,* D. Edelson and E. Domeshek (eds.), Evanston IL., July, pp. 235-242.

Nicholson, P. and Johnson, R. (1999) MetaMaps: Assessing understanding of large, complex or distributed knowledge domains. *Education and Information Technologies, 4* (3), pp. 297-312.

Nicholson, P. and White, G. (2000) *Rich Environments for Active Learning.* Paper presented at the Australian Institute of Training and Development seminar on Adult Learning, Melbourne.

Putnam, R. and Borko, H. (2000) What do new views of knowledge and thinking have to say about research on teacher learning? *Educational Researcher, 29* (1), pp. 4-15.

Zuboff, S. (1988) *In the age of the smart machine: the future of work and power.* New York, Basic Books.

BIOGRAPHY

Paul Nicholson and Geoff White both have current research interests in the design and use of online environments for developing higher-order thinking and the development of ICT-based tools to support effective online teaching. Paul has undertaken a number of projects in researching and evaluating the role of ICT in education and adult training. Geoff has undertaken a number of major evaluation projects in adult learning, quality teaching, and national policy impact studies.

5

Distance Learning by Video Conference System

Electric Teaching Materials by Ultra High Voltage Generator for Science Subject in Lower Secondary School

Toshinori Yamasaki*, Yukihiro Matsubara*, Fumio Matsushita**, Hiroo Hizume*** and Syun-ji Akaguma***

**Faculty of Engineering, **Faculty of Education, ***Takamatsu Lower Secondary School, Attached to Faculty of Education, Kagawa University, Takamatsu, Kagawa 761-0396, Japan*
yamasaki@eng.kagawa-u.ac.jp

Keywords: distance learning, video conference system, electricity, thunderbolt experiment, faraday cage

Abstract: Learning through the experimental experience is a helpful way for students to master the science subject. However, it is difficult to do experiments in electrical learning as the high voltage and large electric current are dangerous. This paper presents a new teaching style of science experiments through a video conference system via an ISDN line connected between the research laboratory of an electric power company and the experimental room in a lower secondary school. At first, students do electric experiments using a Faraday cage and study electric current, the electric shock and the function of earth line. After the experiments, the students try to understand electricity and ask the researcher details of electricity through the video conference system. They can also confirm their knowledge about electricity through observing the thunderbolt experiment with a high voltage generator in the research laboratory. This system is useful for students to learn about real electric phenomenon.

1. INTRODUCTION

As the electronic communication high-technology such as the Internet and personal computer recently and developed rapidly, new education systems which use these latest techniques are proposed and reported

(Sakamoto 1997). We know the examples of the new distance education systems have provided for the following generation. On Line University (OLU), a project which links distance universities by a high-speed multimedia network, were done for advanced remote lectures. Space Collaboration System (SCS) which uses a communications satellite, spread mainly through the national university in Japan. We can undertake a new style of lectures with audio visual media exchanging.

On the other hand, because LAN environments are serviced widely, the distance education by Internet became popular too. Now, we can study a social subject through observing various museums from the remote place (Okamura et al. 1997). Another interesting example reported is science learning by operating a telescope at the observatory via the Internet (Soga et al. 1998). The students can learn impressively by repeating a valuable experience through the use of advanced equipment. Recently, with the spread of the ISDN digital line, we can use a videophone, a personal computer or a video conference system easily. Therefore, the development of the new education systems can be expected by using these new tools (Yamasaki and Akaguma 1999).

In this paper, we report the new distance educational system for science in a lower secondary school using a video conference system. We linked a research laboratory in the electric power company and a lower secondary school by the video conference system, and developed a new style lesson. In science learning of a lower secondary school, learning through experience is useful for the students. The impressive experience promotes a learning motivation. The student can learn actively from this experimental lesson. However, for the high voltage and the large electric current of the electric materials such as the thunderbolt, it is not possible to do an experiment in a school, because of the danger.

In such a case, we use audio-visual teaching materials by VTR. However, with the VTR teaching materials, students only ascertain the result, which was already experimented. They have no longing for unknown strange phenomena. Also, we cannot design attractive learning that introduces flexible questions and answers. In this case, it is helpful to observe real experiments done at a research laboratory in a remote place using a video conference system.

In our lesson, the students do a Faraday cage experiment in the science room. They also observe the thunderbolt experiment in the research laboratory via a video conference system. The students can ask the researcher details about the experiment and confirm their question through the remote system.

2. VIDEO CONFERENCE SYSTEM AND THUNDERBOLT EXPERIMENT

2.1 The system configuration

We connect a science room in lower secondary school and the ultra high voltage research laboratory in the electric power company by the video conference system via the ISDN line. Figure 1 shows the outline of our system.

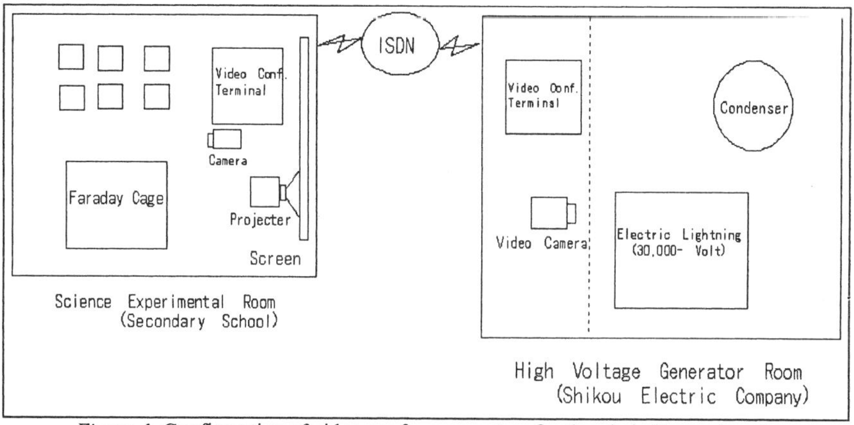

Figure 1. Configuration of video-conference system for thunderbolt experiment

The video conference system is FM-A71 (NTT) attached a communication board (NTT:h.320/ISDN extension card, CODEC). Ultra high voltage laboratory is the room where the electric insulate ability and the thunder protect of the power transmission facilities were examined. This equipment can generate more than 100,000 volts using large sized condenser piled more than 4 meters height. This equipment is unique and uncommon in Japan.

The students do Faraday cage experiment at the science laboratory in lower secondary school. They carry forward the learning of voltage, an electric current, a resistance and the function of the electric ground through this experiment. They also ask the researcher various question via ISDN line. Finally, they deepen their understanding by observing the thunderbolt experiment of the high voltage occurrence equipment in the research laboratory.

2.2 Faraday Cage and Thunderbolt Experiment

We prepare the wire netting box (Faraday cage, electric sealed room) into which a teacher can enter and do an experiment for electric current. The students observe the flowing electric current around the Faraday cage using the Tesla induction coil, which generates high voltage. They consider a voltage, electric current, resistance and the function of electric ground through this experiment.

Ultra high voltage equipment in the electric power laboratory is used for high voltage insulation efficiency and defense against a thunderbolt. This consists of large sized condenser and can generate more than 100,000 volts. We device this learning to give stronger impression by this experiment. That is, the thunderbolt experiments are designed for showing strong flashlight of the spatial discharge and the burst experiment of an apple. The students observe the thunderbolt experiment by video-conference system through the ISDN line. After that, they can proceed the learning to ask researcher their questions.

3. CONSIDERATION OF THE LESSON PRACTICE

3.1 Trial lesson

At first, the students act the high voltage of the Tesla induction coil on the paper. They can observe the burning of the paper by the electric current. Next, they begin to do the Faraday cage experiment. After a teacher enters into the Faraday cage, the students give high voltage shown in Figure 2. They estimate the dangerous situation of a teacher from the former burning experiment. But actually, they confirm a safe of a teacher. From this experiment, they consider a voltage, an electric current, resistance and an electric ground action. After these learning through the Faraday cage experiment, the students develop the check experiment on the electric sealed way. By this learning, the students can expand their idea to the thunderbolt experiment in the research laboratory.

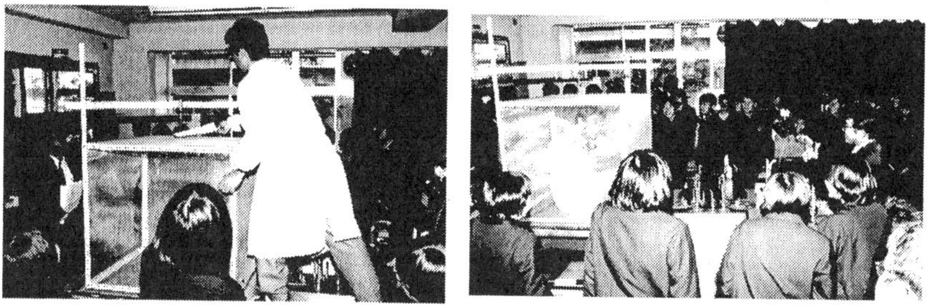

Figure 2. Faraday cage (science room in lower secondary school)

After the learning in the above-mentioned science room, the students observe the huge scale experiment in the research laboratory. The experimental equipment has a large condenser piled as high as 4 meters, and generates more than 100,000 volts. The experiment is designed for fruit (apple) burst by thunder in addition to the flash-light observation between the electrode space. We stick the wire electrodes of 3 [cm] top and bottom to assist breaking apple. Apple-burst experiment by thunder gives a big sound and strong flash light and the apple burst. The students are surprised by this phenomena and get a strong impression. After these experiments, the students ask various questions to the researcher in the laboratory and confirm their understanding shown in Figure 3.

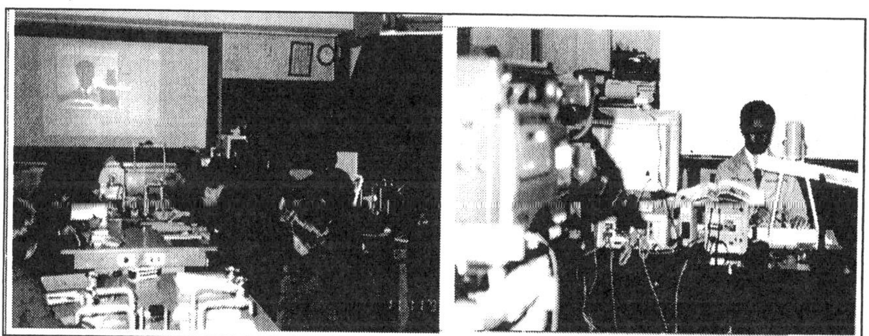

Figure 3. Students ask questions to the researcher via ISDN line

3.2 Evaluation of the picture, the sound via ISDN line and the lesson

In our experiment, it is important that the students can observe the electric lightning really through the ISDN line. It emits blare sound and intense flashlight. The system must send this situation as faithfully as possible. The blare sound was the one when we narrowed down the speaker volume at the science room. The students can recognise the wildness of this sound sufficiently. On the other hand, as the luminous time of the lightning was very short, the system cannot convey the lightning enough. We can monitor the lightning only once in the four times experiments.

Figures 4 and 5 show the post investigation results of the students about the picture and sound from ISDN line in the experiment. These results tell us that the students do not seem to fit in with moving pictures and the delaying sound in this system.

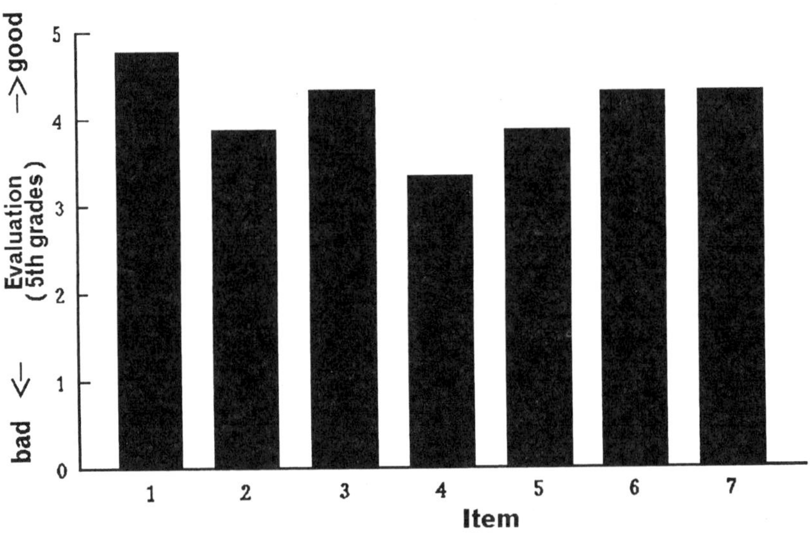

Figure 4. Evaluation of picture via ISDN

The opinions of the students about this lesson are as follows. They have a familiar feeling as if they participate in this experiment in the research laboratory. They were moved to observe the large-scale experiments, which they could not do by themselves. The professional researcher answered a question immediately. They hope to do this lesson again, because it is an attractive lesson. The above-mentioned reports of the students show the affirmative opinion about this lesson.

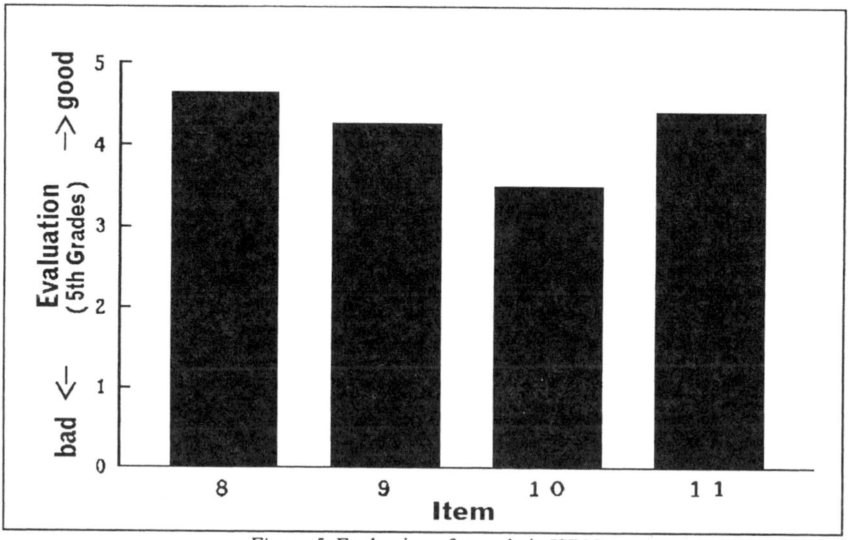

Figure 5. Evaluation of sound via ISDN

4. CONCLUSIONS

We proposed and carried out a new style of the science subject lesson in a lower secondary school using a video-conference system. We linked the science room in the lower secondary school and the research laboratory in the Shikoku Electric Power Company with ISDN digital line. The students do a Faraday cage experiment in the science room. After that, they observe the thunderbolt experiment done at the research laboratory via ISDN line. The students carry forward the learning about the voltage, electric current, resistance and the function of the electric ground through observing the experiment and ask questions to the researcher. This learning system is useful for the learning of science empirically.

On the other hand, the system could not transmit the blare sound and strong flush light enough. For this purpose, we must use a high-speed camera. Through this experiment, we must arrange the system adjustment and personnel arrangement for support when performing this lesson. These are the problems still to be resolved in the future.

ACKNOWLEDGMENT

We would like to thank the members of Shikoku Power Electric Company for accomplishing the thunderbolt experiment.

REFERENCES

Sakamoto, T. (1997) Communication Technologies: The Present State and Tasks for Research and Development. *IEICE Transactions*, vol. J80-D-II, no. 4, pp. 829-834.

Okamura, K., Tsuru, M. and Fujiki, T. (1997) Study on Making Remote Class on Internet Practicable. *JSISE Transactions*, vol.14, no. 3, pp. 84-94.

Soga, M., Watanabe, K. and Okyudo, M. (1998) Design of Global Observation Based Learning Environment with Remote Equipment – In Case of a Remote Telescope – In *Proceedings of JSISE Conference 1998*, D4-5, pp. 347-350.

Yamasaki, T. and Akaguma, S. (1999) Electric Lightning Experiment Learning for Science Subject in Lower Secondary School using Video Conference System. *JSISE Transactions*, Vol. 15, No.4, pp. 323-327.

BIOGRAPHY

Toshinori Yamasaki is professor of Kagawa University, Faculty of education. He has a Ph.D. degree from Osaka University, Japan. His research interests are pattern analysis, human-computer interaction and network-based learning systems. Yukihiro Matsubara is associate professor of Kagawa University, Faculty of Engineering. He has a Ph.D. degree from Hiroshima University, Japan. His research interests are intelligent tutoring system, Kansei engineering and human interface. Fumio Matsushita is professor of Kagawa University, Faculty of Education. His research interests are educational technology, mainly the video conference system and it's application to education. Hiroo Hizume is vice principal of Takamatsu junior high school, attached to faculty of education, Kagawa University. He has worked as a teacher of social subject and interested in networked-based teaching materials. Syun-ji Akaguma is teacher of Takamatsu junior high school, attached to faculty of education, Kagawa University. He has worked as a teacher of science subject and interested in developing new science teaching materials.

6

Desktop Video Conferencing

How to Avoid Teacher and Student Frustration

Paula F. Furr and Ronald G. Ragsdale
Northwestern State University, Natchitoches, Louisiana, USA
furrp@nsula.edu

Keywords: distance learning, higher education, tele-teaching, video-conferencing

Abstract: As a relatively new delivery medium, desktop video conferencing (DVC) promises to bring traditional face-to-face teaching to computer screens. Although ample literature covers incorporating technology into classrooms, little documents the experiences and perceptions of participants in DVC courses and DVC's effects on teaching and learning. A recent ethnographic study that examined incidental learning in five DVC courses offered at an American university found that incidental learning often overshadowed the planned curriculum and found a high level of participant frustration. The study's results reaffirmed the importance of incidental learning in a DVC course and of developing an environment that reduces faculty and student frustrations.

1. INTRODUCTION

The steady growth of distance education relies on technology, with the International Data Corporation (DESIEN 1999) predicting a $5 billion market for multimedia applications in Internet or intranet training by 2003. Desktop video conferencing (DVC), a new addition to content delivery systems, has been hailed as a 'dynamic, synchronous environment which can give a high degree of interaction between students and instructor' (Mize 1996). The system uses the personal computer with special hardware and software to code and decode audio and video signals, the Internet, and existing telephone infrastructure. From their desks or a classroom, students can interact with a remote instructor by audio, video, and keyboard in a synchronous environment. Unlike content delivery to large groups of students by compressed video and satellite TV technologies, DVC is considered most appropriate for individual or small-group use (Woodruff and Mosby 1996, Chute et al. 1999). Bivens and Chute (2000) found the use of DVC becoming increasingly important for training and educational applications, as bandwidths increase, technology improves, and costs decline.

However, Green (1999) noted that in the steady evolution of distance learning, technology remains "a black boks" and "the largest unknown". Ehrmann (1998) stated, "We sell faculty on the technology and teach the rudiments, but we don't prepare them for problems they might encounter as part of the teaching activity". Although Cuban (1986) noted the "powerful tug that the machine has in capturing student interest", he also noted that computers, like all machines, are subject to problems, from maintenance to logistics to adequate teaching training. Such problems have and can affect student and teacher perceptions of a machine's educational merit and its ultimate widespread adoption.

Ever since McLuhan popularised *The medium is the message* in the 1960s, that aphorism has been at the vortex of the continuing debate about technology's effects on learning, both anticipated and unanticipated consequences. Technology's non-neutrality has been discussed by many, from Ellul (1964) to Ehrmann (1999), who noted that technologies, whether paper or computer, do not have predetermined outcomes. Ragsdale (1988) stated that proponents of computer technology tend to focus on "what they would like to have computers do" and not on what computers can or cannot do nor on what they should or should not do. However, because "human intentions and media outcomes interact continuously", unanticipated outcomes result. These unplanned side effects, whether good or bad, often supersede original intentions. Postman (1993) stated succinctly, "Unforeseen consequences stand in the way of all those who think they see clearly the direction in which a new technology will take us".

What is known is that teaching students at distant sites is intensive work (Moore 1995), and as Collis (1998) stated: "Good teaching is never easy nor is the handling of new technologies". Consider these demands for a desktop video conferencing class. An instructor must design or redesign and deliver content tailored to the medium; listen to students and stimulate and encourage their critical thinking; control class discussion and manage student behaviours among and within remote sites; attend to administrative matters like attendance; and handle the technology and unexpected problems. Nevertheless, expectations remain for faculty to transition seamlessly from lectern to computer console and for students to learn in technology-mediated environments with "no significant differences" (Russell 1997).

Many researchers, including Brown and Wack (1999), Diaz (2000), Phipps and Merisotis (1999) and Saba (1998), have questioned the efficacy of media comparison studies and Clark's (1985) claim that "computers make no more contribution to learning than the truck which delivers groceries to markets contributes to improved nutrition in a community." Lias (1982) contended that each medium biases or distorts the message it carries in significant ways and that new media cause underlying social values to change. Further, Kozma (1994) suggested that any particular technology is not irrelevant, as it may be well or poorly suited to support a particular learning or teaching method. Lockee et al. (1999) proposed that distance education research has largely been biased to show positive results because "stakeholders desire to prove that participants in distance-delivered courses receive the same quality of instruction off-campus as those involved in the 'traditional classroom setting'".

Ehrmann (1998) stated that evaluation policies commonly have been framed to report achievement rather than being "forced to look at and talk about failure". Hara and Kling (1999) found potentially critical issues like student frustration a 'taboo topic' because the major body of literature favours distance education and "once consensus is reached, it tends not to be disturbed by a dissonant ideas". They also attributed the lack of 'socially realistic' studies about student attitudes to the few qualitative research studies conducted and to the lack of opportunities for students to express their frustrations. Student frustration is a serious problem in distance education, according to Hara and Kling, because it interferes with pursuing goals (Reber 1985), impedes cognitive and affective learning (Jonassen and Grabowski 1993), and hampers motivation (Jonassen and Grabowski 1993). Motivation strongly influences student learning (Alexander and Murphy 1998, Stage 1996), especially in a distance education, which requires that students be regulated (Abrahamson 1998). Acknowledging that the research of those who extol the virtues of computer-mediated distance education (Yakimovicz and Murphy 1995, Harasim et al. 1996, Barnard 1997) has helped to propel the field forward, Hara and Kling said it is "time to seriously consider the actual experiences among students in distance education and to critically discuss the phenomena of distance education".

Ehrmann (1999) called for changing assessment strategies that emphasize local evaluative studies charged to detect problems in order to improve programs. Similarly, Scriven (1991) suggested goal-free evaluations, which focus on "finding out what the program is actually doing" and not on a program's stated goals and objectives. He warned, however, that such evaluations are not without risk because "the client may get a nasty shock when the report comes in". Ragsdale (1997) also favoured a goal-free approach, calling for intensive observations in natural settings to detect side effects. He stated the "main advantage of goal-free evaluation is the removal of blinders which focusing on the 'intended' results can put on the observer". Other recent notable researchers who have promoted the importance of such 'naturalistic inquiry' include Lincoln and Guba (1985), Patton (1990), Wolcott (1994, 1997), and Bogdan and Biklen (1998).

2. RECENT DVC STUDY AND FINDINGS

Furr (2000) completed an ethnographic study at a mid-sized American university in the rural South that examined and described through thick description the incidental learning activities of students and instructors in DVC classes in a higher education setting. The researcher defined incidental learning as planned, unplanned, and unanticipated learning outcomes not identified as part of the formal curriculum. The study was limited to observing two of six teacher education courses offered by the university in spring 2000 via DVC to eight remote sites; three other DVC classes were purposefully sampled to triangulate data from observed classes. Each remote site was equipped with 10 computers, and two classes were offered simultaneously.

Of the 113 adult students ranging in age from 19 to 51, 60 volunteered to participate in the study. Twenty-five were undergraduates and 35 were graduate students pursuing a master's degree; 80% (N=48) were female. The five instructors observed were all veterans of higher education teaching, with the instructors of the two observed courses having taught pilot courses for the university's DVC initiative the previous semester. The other three instructors were novices with the new delivery system, although one had extensive experience with incorporating technology into the classroom. The university's support staff consisted of three full-time employees and part-time student workers; during spring 2000, the staff supported 59 electronic courses with a student enrolment of 2,012. Of the 13 proctors assigned to monitor courses, nine volunteered to participate. Eight of these proctors were also students in the courses they proctored.

The researcher observed 35 DVC class sessions and became an observer participant on two occasions as a guest lecturer. The researcher triangulated data by analysing observations, interviews, student and instructor journals, e-mail correspondence, class documents, and official documents. The trustworthiness of the investigator was enhanced by prolonged engagement with participants, checks by participants, thick description, and the researcher's reflective journal entries. By the end of the study, the researcher was considered 'one of the group,' whether that group was faculty, students, or support staff. As a result, comments were candid and flowing. The resulting more than 800 typed pages of collected field notes provided the researcher with a substantial pool of data from which to render an accurate and plausible account of participants' experiences. Although the study's results can be generalized only to these particular courses, they nonetheless add to the body of research on DVC's effects on teaching and learning and its potential and limitations as an educational technology.

General findings included the following.

- Technical problems, ranging from audio and video delays of a few seconds to several minutes to a largely untested system with eight remote sites, led to faculty and student frustration and degraded the overall learning and teaching experience. One student wrote in a journal entry: "The problem is the 30 second delay of audio signals. I can see your mouth moving but it takes too long for the sound to come over the head set. Both parties end up speaking at the same time, resulting in poor information flow."
- Although technical problems diminished greatly midway through the semester after the software maker provided needed audio and video 'patches,' negative attitudes and distinct behaviour patterns among students at remote sites were already established and less easily correctable. As one instructor noted: "I don't believe we ever established an on-line classroom culture. Even at individual sites they didn't seem to bond. I didn't get to know my students, and I wouldn't recognize them if they walked up to my door." One student, a high school math teacher, commented. "Being behind this camera is like having a mask on. No one really knows you. It's easy for me to tune out and weed through information I don't need. I can then do other things during class, so I'm not really wasting my time here."
- The average faculty training time of 4.2 hours on the equipment was woefully inadequate to prepare them to troubleshoot an unfamiliar system while simultaneously delivering complex content and managing the interaction and participation of students at remote sites. Faculty and students both noted the result was lessened academic rigor and quality of instructional delivery. No faculty development on the pedagogy of teaching at a distance and specific applications to DVC was offered. One instructor observed that technicians fail to appreciate the added intensity, focus, and concentration for instructors to deliver the course and for students to receive and process that delivery. He described the results as 'fatigue' and 'going mentally off-line.'
- An overstretched technical support staff could not adequately assist faculty or students before, during, or after class sessions, compounding

frustrations and overall teaching and learning satisfaction. Instructors noted that without the presence and reassurance of technical support during class, they felt isolated, and all considered technology problems and lack of support the greatest barrier to teaching and learning success.

- Given the nature of this DVC initiative, which was to reach students in economically depressed rural areas, those students without access to a computer or the Internet at their home or at their work site were more disadvantaged in completing coursework and in improving their technical computer skills. A few 'slow' students literally held learning hostage as an instructor devoted time to their technical questions and problems. On the other hand, some students with the most computer knowledge used it to their learning disadvantage by playing around during class. Throughout the semester, the researcher observed students surfing the Internet, playing games on the computer, sending and reading e-mail, inserting personal CD's to listen to music, word-processing documents for other classes or work, coming and leaving class at will, napping, chatting with peers, and making rude comments about instructors and students at other sites.
- No overall administrative system was established for instructors, students, and proctors to exchange materials reliably and predictably. No program was established for students to contact instructors outside of class or via e-mail. These factors contributed to the overall student perception of inadequate feedback.
- A credible proctoring system for instructor liaison, academic integrity, and classroom management did not exist, resulting in a diminished environment for academic quality and allowing negative student behaviour to go unchecked.
- Because no student evaluations and no student or faculty focus groups or feedback were sought, the university had no documented evidence for assessment and evaluation to plan and implement program improvements.
- Smaller classes work best for DVC. Student participation and instructor control declined noticeably when total enrolment for a course exceeded 15 to 20 students. The course rated best for student-teacher interaction and overall learning had 14 graduate students and an instructor with more than 20 years' experience in incorporating technology in the classroom.

In sum, the semester's learning was frustrated by technology issues and their consequences. For example, of the 208 student journal entries collected for the semester, 72.5% focused on technology problems. A student submitted this entry during the fourth week of class.

> "I'm sorry that we didn't make it through the whole class today. Our system shut down on us 5 times. The last time we were unable to reconnect. It was very frustrating. The other class had a speaker hooked up to one computer so that the entire class could hear. They were trying not to overload the system, but in turn we could barely hear what was going on in our class. I tell you, it is definitely frustrating."

Of the 2,520 'chat box' entries students wrote during classes, 48% focused on technology problems. During the last month of the semester, technology-related comments dropped to 25%, a still sizable percentage. During the fifth week of class, student comments included: "we are having serious trouble please help" and "I lost contact for about 20 minutes so I WILL NEED TO CATCH UP."

Of the 35 instructor journal entries collected during the semester, 80% addressed technology problems encountered while teaching. One wrote: "No video again tonight, only audio. This system is dysfunctional; it's a challenge to teach this way and I'm physically exhausted after class." During 19 exit interviews with student participants, technology was cited most frequently as the barrier to course success. One graduate student who rated her success as a 6 on a scale of 10 said the following.

> "I rated my accomplishment level a 6 because there were too many technical glitches, and we had to spend so much time to make the technology work that it got in the way of learning. For example, we spent three classes trying to get one student's presentation to work. In the meantime, the rest of us didn't have much to do. Some students would grade papers and sometimes we could work on other things, so we weren't wasting all the time. I don't think there was enough time to practice the skills, and I think it would be especially hard for someone who had a low computer use level."

Frustrating was the word most frequently used by participants to describe their teaching and learning experiences. Nearly half (46%) of the 52 students who answered surveys at the end of the semester and all five instructors rated student-teacher interaction and student participation worse in a DVC course than a face-to-face course with similar content. Still, however, nearly half (48%) said they would take another DVC course because they believed technical glitches would be fixed and they liked the convenience of not driving to campus; 17% said 'no' to another DVC course; 21% were undecided; the remaining percentage of students did not answer, most indicating they were graduating. Ninety percent remained optimistic about the future of distance education in general. As one student said: "It's a good program, and I don't want to be too critical because I don't want them to get rid of the classes. If I can take classes this way or over the Internet, that saves me from driving. Plus, technology is the future."

3. CONCLUSIONS AND RECOMMENDATIONS

Furr (2000) found two types of incidental learning not identified as part of the formal curriculum: learning to use technology and individual and group attitudes and behavioural patterns. Factors that afforded positive experiences and perceptions were convenience and reduced driving time, informal class atmosphere, small classes, prior computer skills, access to a computer and the Internet, internal student traits, and instructor facility with technology and distance education pedagogy. Factors that diminished a positive experience were technical problems, insufficient administrative support, inadequate training, weak proctor system, and negative student behaviours. The study illustrated the importance of developing a learning environment that fosters positive outcomes and highlighted the need for ongoing local evaluative studies to gauge program progress and to monitor participants' experiences and perceptions.

Only two instructors offered courses via DVC the following semester and no courses are being offered for fall 2001. Such a cycle of initial enthusiasm for a new technology followed by unrealised potential and unused equipment need not continue or happen in other settings if those in charge understand that distance education and DVC in particular require extensive training, practice, technical support, and reflection. Local evaluations and longitudinal studies that can document patterns and changes and guide policy decisions are critical for program success and survival.

REFERENCES

Abrahamson, C. E. (1998) Issues in interactive communication in distance education. *College Student Journal,* 32(1), pp. 33-43.

Alexander, P. A. and Murphy, P. K. (1998) The research base for APA's learner-centered psychological principles. In *Issues in School Reform: A Sampler of Psychological Perspectives on Learner-Centered Schools,* N. Lambert and B. McCombs (eds.), American Psychological Association, Washington, DC, pp. 33-60.

Barnard, J. (1997) The World Wide Web and higher education: The promise of virtual universities and online libraries. *Educational Technology,* 37 (3), pp. 30-35.

Bivens, H. L. and Chute, A. (2000) *Distance learning futures: Creating new learning environments and developing new pedagogical skills.* [www.lucent.com/cedl/icdeenv2.html] 5.5.2001.

Bogdan, R. C. and Biklen, S. K. (1998) *Qualitative Research for Education: An Introduction to Theory and Methods* (3rd ed.). Allyn and Bacon, Boston.

Brown, G. and Wack, M. (1999 May) The difference frenzy and matching buckshot with buckshot. *The Technology Source.* [http://horizon.unc.edu/ts/reading/1999-05.asp] 5.5.2001.

Chute, A. G. et al. (1999) *The McGraw-Hill Handbook of Distance Learning.* McGraw-Hill, NewYork.

Clark, R. E. (1985) Evidence for confounding in computer-based instruction studies: Analyzing the meta-analyses. *Educational Communication and Technology,* 33 (4), pp. 249-262.

Collis, B. (1998) New didactics for university instruction: Why and how? *Computers & Education,* 31 (4), pp. 373-393.

Cuban, L. (1986) *Teachers and Machines: The Classroom Use of Technology since 1920.* Teachers College Press, New York.

DESIEN Newsletter (1999 October) *IT Spending Boom Forecast for Colleges.* [http://uwex.edu:80/disted/desien/1999/9909/ibtext.htm] 6.10.2000.

Diaz, D. P. (2000 March/April) Carving a new path for distance education research. *Horizon.* [http://horizon.unc.edu/TS/commentary/2000-03a.asp] 5.5.2001.

Ehrmann, S. (1998 June) *What outcomes assessment misses.* Speech delivered at the 1998 AAHE Assessment Conference. [http://www.tltgroup.org/programs/outcomes.html] 6.15.2000.

Ehrmann, S. (1999 January) *What do we need to learn about technology use in education?* [http://tltgroup.org/resources/fquestions.html] 7.6.2000.

Ellul, J. (1964) *The Technological Society.* Alfred A. Knopf, New York.

Furr, P. (2000) *The occurrence of incidental learning in higher education desktop video conferencing courses: An ethnographic study.* Ed. D. thesis, Northwestern State University.

Green, K. C. (1999 March/April) When wishes come true: Colleges, and the convergence of access, lifelong learning, and technology. *Change.* [http://www.campuscomputing.net/] 5.5.2001.

Hara, N. and Kling, R. (1999) *Students' frustrations with a web-based distance education course: A taboo topic in the discourse.* Working paper. [http://www.slis.indiana.edu/CSI/wp99-01.html] 9.8.2000.

Hara, N. and Kling, R. (2000) Students' distress with a web-based distance education course. Article accepted for publication in *Information, Communication & Society.* [http://www.slis.indiana.edu/CSI/wp00-01.html] 5.7.2001.

Harasim, L. et al. (1996) *Learning Networks.* MIT Press, Cambridge, MA.

Jonassen, D. H. and Grabowski, B. L. (1993) *Handbook of Individual Differences, Learning, and Instruction.* Lawrence Erlbaum, Hillsdale, NY.

Kozma, R. B. (1994) Will media influence learning? Reframing the debate. *Educational Technology Research and Development,* 42 (2), pp. 7-19.

Lias, E. J. (1982) *Future Mind.* Little, Brown, and Company, Boston.

Lincoln, Y. S. and Guba, E. G. (1985) *Naturalistic Inquiry.* Sage, Thousand Oaks, CA.

Lockee, B. et al. (1999) No comparison: Distance education finds a new use for 'no significant difference.' *Educational Technology Research and Development,* 47 (3), pp. 33-42.

Mize, C. D. (1996, November/December) Desktop video communication: A primer. *TechTrends,* 41 (6), pp. 44-47.

Moore, M. G. (1995) Editorial: The death of distance. *American Journal of Distance Education,* 9 (3). [http://www.ed.psu.edu/acsde/ajde/ed93.asp] 5.5.2001.

Patton, M. C. (1990) *Qualitative Evaluation and Research Methods* (2nd ed.). Sage, London.

Phipps, R. A. and Merisotis, J. P. (1999 April) *What's the difference? A review of contemporary research on the effectiveness of distance learning in higher education.* Institute for Higher Education Policy. [http://www.smcccd.cc.ca.us/smcccd/faculty/confer/Hittle1.html] 5.5.2001.

Postman, N. (1993) *Technopoly: The Surrender of Culture to Technology.* Vintage Books, New York.

Ragsdale, R. G. (1988) *Permissible Computing in Education: Values, Assumptions, and Needs.* Prager, New York.

Ragsdale, R. G. (1997 March) *Surprised by technology: Unanticipated outcomes.* Paper presented at the annual meeting of the American Educational Research Association, Chicago, IL. [http://alpha.nsula.edu/~ragsdale/papers.html] 6.4.200.

Reber, A. S. (1985) *The Penguin Dictionary of Psychology.* Penguin, Books London.

Saba, F. (1998) Is distance education comparable to "traditional education"? *Distance Education Report*, sample issue, 3.

Scriven, M. (1991) *Evaluation Thesaurus.* (4th ed.). Sage, London.

Stage, F. K. (1996) Setting the context: Psychological theories of learning. *Journal of College Student Development,* 37 (2), pp. 227-235.

Wolcott, H. F. (1994) *Transforming Qualitative Data: Description, Analysis, and Interpretation.* London: Sage.

Wolcott, H. F. (1997) Ethnographic research in education. In *Complementary Methods for Research in Education,* R. M. Jaeger (ed.), American Educational Research Association, Washington, DC, pp. 327-398.

Woodruff, M. and Mosby, J. (1996) *Videoconferencing in the classroom & library* [http://www.kn.pacbell.com/wired/vidconf/intro.html] 5.5.2001

Yakimovicz, A. D. and Murphy, K. L. (1995) Constructivism and collaboration on the Internet: Case study of a graduate class experience. *Computers and Education,* 24 (3), pp. 203-209.

BIOGRAPHIES

Paula Furr recently completed her doctorate in educational technology at Northwestern State University in Natchitoches, Louisiana. She is currently an assistant professor of journalism at NSU and continuing her interest in online education as an extension of communications studies.

Ronald Ragsdale recently retired from educational technology at Northwestern State University. He is also Professor Emeritus at the Ontario Institute for Studies in Education, University of Toronto (OISE/UT).

7

Effective Collaborative Work Utilising Videoconferencing

Northern Ireland – Toyama Videoconference Link Project

Yoshinori Naruse, David Farrell and Jun-ichi Yamanishi
Toyama National College of Maritime Technology, 1-2 Ebie-Neriya Shinminato, Toyama 933-0293, Japan
naruse@toyama-cmt.ac.jp
Ballyclare Secondary School, Doagh Road, Newtownabbey, N Ireland BT39 9BG, U.K
Faculty of Education, Toyama University, 3190 Gofuku, Toyama 930-8555, Japan

Keywords: collaborative learning, electronic communication, motivation, video-conferencing

Abstract: Since September 1991 the Japanese Studies Project has linked twenty schools in Northern Ireland with schools in Japan. The videoconference links proved to be interesting and extremely motivating for the students involved, but it was recognised that a more structured approach would be required in order for all parties to obtain maximum benefit from the links. After considerable discussion it was decided that we should create a collaborative assignment which would require students in both countries to utilise as many skills as they could, in order to communicate effectively and to learn something about each other's culture.

1. INTRODUCTION

At present most schools in Northern Ireland and Japan are connected to the Internet and with the introduction of the cross-curricular studies module in Japan there is the necessity to have effective examples of international links. In both countries it has been decided to incorporate the use of ICT into the subjects being taught rather than as an appendix to the educational system. In other words we seek to educate using ICT rather than educate about ICT (Lynch et al. 2000).

Since September 1991 the Japanese Studies Project has linked twenty schools in Northern Ireland with schools in Japan. As a result of the Project, students in schools in Northern Ireland have been introduced to the Japanese language, electronic mail links with partners in Toyama and access to the World Wide Web. Japanese students have also had the opportunity to develop language skills and have been introduced to developing information communication infrastructure. Early links were heavily dependant upon the use of email to exchange information about themselves, their schools and their towns. While this was very effective in the early 1990's it became increasingly obvious that as the technology advanced the opportunity was being created for collaborative work between the students (Naruse 1993).

As a result of considerable discussion between us, by email and reciprocal visits to Japan and Northern Ireland, it was decided the time had come to expand the opportunity for by utilising videoconferencing.

Early experiments in videoconferencing between Toyama and Northern Ireland in 1996-1997 had clearly shown that it was a viable means of communication between students in Japan and Northern Ireland but the major obstacle was the connection cost. Videoconferencing requires the use of two ISDN lines to Japan therefore each call is double the normal rate to Japan.

In the spring of 1998 we decided to pursue funding for this type of link. In 1998 we were provided the funds to allow videoconference links between Toyama University and a school in Northern Ireland to commence. These initial links took place once or twice a month. Another school was in Japan was provided with funds to allow videoconference links which would commence in September 1999.

The video-conference links in the academic year 1998-1999 proved to be interesting and extremely motivating for the students involved, but it was recognised at the end of the academic year, that a more structured approach would be required in order for all parties to obtain maximum benefit from the links (Figure 1).

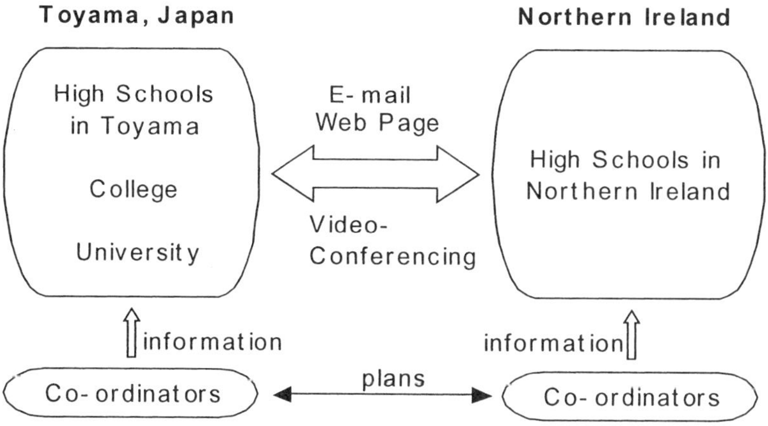

Figure 1. Northern Ireland – Toyama Videoconference Link Project

2. RECENT DEVELOPMENTS

In August 1999, we agreed to establish a more structured project between schools in Toyama and schools in Northern Ireland. After considerable discussion it was decided that we should create a collaborative assignment that would require students in both countries to utilise as many skills as they could, in order to communicate effectively and to learn something about each other's culture.

Many educational projects using computer mediated communication have been attempted, linking classes together to work on pre-arranged collaborative work. Some projects have adopted the joint problem solving style where students could share ideas and experiences about issues presented to them (Robinson 1998).

Such a collaborative piece of work which would allow students an opportunity to examine the culture and language of their respective partner countries was required and also provide them with the opportunity to develop their ICT skills as required by the curriculum in each country.

In September 1999 Japanese co-ordinators visited Northern Ireland for their research. During this visit, time was taken out to arrange a meeting with three local schools and an officer of the North Eastern Education and Library Board (NEELB) to discuss an assignment which could last from October 1999 to January 2000 and which could be incorporated into their Japanese Studies classes. During the meeting the details were presented to the teachers from the three other schools and after minor modifications it was accepted by all and the structure and timing of the exercise was agreed.

The Project co-ordinators have recognised the importance of using the synchronous communications in collaborative studies between students. The synchronous communications, such as face to face communication, have immediacy in exchanging ideas (Ingram et al. 2000). As for situations when students cannot communicate face-to-face, equivalent communications have been achieved on the Internet and using video conferencing equipment. But because of the problem of the line fee and the time difference (8-9 hours) students are not allowed to use video conferencing equipment with any degree of frequency.

This type of communication was held for the following purpose:

- To establish friendship between students
- To motivate the student to take part in the study of each other's community
- To make students report back on the outcome of their studies with each other.

3. ASSIGNMENT DETAILS

3.1 Objectives

To raise awareness of the language, geography and culture of each other's country.

To raise awareness in the use of information technology, including:

- Electronic mail
- Internet Access
- Word Processing
- Spreadsheets
- Web Page Creation
- Video Conferencing.

To improve communication skills.

3.2 Task

Using a budget of $1500 students are to plan a visit to each other's country. Using this budget they are to book flights, find accommodation, visit places of interest and travel in Japan or the United Kingdom.

3.3 Rules

1. Students from Northern Ireland must spend at least three days in Toyama and students from Japan must spend at least three days in Northern Ireland
2. Students must only use the Internet, email and video-conferencing to get information about their respective countries
3. Students must not write to agencies, travel agents or embassies to gain information
4. Students should keep all data as evidence to be used when they are compiling their final report. The task must be completed by 31 December 1999.

3.4 Procedure

Students should use the Internet:

- to find out information about the geography of the country they intend to visit
- to investigate the costs of flights to that country
- to create an itinerary for the main areas of interest they wish to visit
- to find out the details of the cost of transportation around the country
- to find details of hotels/hostels etc.
- to work out a daily budget for their stay in each country
- to decide what time of the year they wish to visit the country.

They may wish to engage in sporting activities or participate in festivals.

3.5 Guidelines

Each school can enter one team. All participating schools can access the mailing list set up to answer queries about Japan or Northern Ireland. Students can access the mailing list as often as they wish to ask questions or to seek help with their proposed trip. Their mailing list is their 'tour guide' and we will promise to answer all email enquiries within 48 hours.

Students can also have a personal link with a student in their partner school. This information will not be regulated and can be on a one to one basis.

3.6 Timescale

PHASE 1	
October 1999	NI students email Japan asking questions about a potential trip to Japan. Emails must be brief and contain no more than three questions.
PHASE 2	
November 1999	Japanese schools email NI asking questions about their trip
PHASE 3	
December 31	Schools can communicate with each other without restriction, asking questions and making final plans. Final presentation forwarded to Toyama University to be placed on the home-page

3.7 Video conference

Every three weeks a videoconference lasting 20 minutes was to be held in each school. This would allow students an opportunity to discuss each other's culture and should have been active and creative. Role-play was recommended. For example students in Northern Ireland may be shown how to enter a Japanese house and what they should say or students in Japan may wish to know how to ask directions from a person on the street. This can be demonstrated by videoconference. The videoconference could also discuss areas of possible cultural interest or examples of food.

3.8 Final report

Students must create a web page detailing their trip. All costs must be clearly given. It must be a detailed account of how they will spend their 1500 or the equivalent in Japanese yen. Key places of interest should be identified and students should simply state why they would like to visit the location they have chosen.

4. EVALUATION

To date, the assignment has worked very well between Ballyclare Secondary and Toyama Maritime College and has made a major contribution to Japanese Studies within the school. The other three schools involved had a mixed experience. One school faced major technical problems that prevented effective videoconferencing to take place. Due to the fact that the other schools had no previous experience of videoconferencing with Japan, it was no surprise that teething problems were identified. These problems are part of the learning experience and the lessons will be incorporated into next year's plans.

It was intended to complete the assignment by December 1999 but this date was completely unrealistic. The deadline was subsequently extended to the end of April.

It was hoped that schools would be able to submit a completed home page by this date. However, not all schools could manage to submit the final page as planned, however all are in agreement that the exercise has been very beneficial in promoting each other's culture and lifestyle and developing ICT skills. The students have had regular email contact with their partners, access to web pages created by their partners in Toyama, a bulletin board/discussion area and videoconferencing.

For all schools involved it has been a learning experience which will be built upon in the next academic year, but an experience which has effectively introduced participating students to each others culture. Negotiations have already commenced between schools in Northern Ireland, Toyama University and Toyama Maritime College as to how the project could be improved during the next academic year and how we could consolidate the work which has been commenced.

5. CONCLUSIONS

To date the link has been successful but what are the lessons to be learnt?

- In order to have effective communication and to establish collaborative work between schools it is essential for close liaison between the teachers and co-ordinators of the Project before the links commence.
- Financial implications must be considered and agreed before links commence.
- The collaborative work to be undertaken must be clearly understood by all parties involved.
- The teachers involved must have the basic ICT skills however as Cifuentes and Murphy (2000) report a result of the links which have been established is that teachers who have become involved in collaborative work have also sought to master their ICT skills.
- Student motivation increases with the use of video-conferencing in collaborative work. Students wish to learn more of their partner's language so that simple communication can be established before the collaborative work commences.

REFERENCES

Cifuentes, L. and Murphy, K. L. (2000) Promoting multicultural understanding and positive self-concept through a distance learning community: Cultural connections. *Educational Technology Research and Development*, 48, 1, pp. 69-83.

Ingram, A. L., Hathorn, L. G. and Evans, H. (2000) Beyond chat on the internet. *Computer & Education*, 35, pp. 21-35.

Lynch, W., Hobbs, B. and Hollanders, H. (2000) Dancing on quicksand, The role of the ICT co-ordinator in the primary school, *Research in Education*, 62, pp. 32-40.

Naruse, Y. (1993) Educational projects making use of international tele-communication. *Research Studies of Toyama National College of Maritime Technology*, 26, pp. 95-102.

Robinson, D. (1998) Student portfolios in mathematics. *The Mathematics Teacher*, 91, 4, pp. 318-325.

BIOGRAPHY

Yoshinori Naruse is an Associate Professor of Mathematics. His current research interest is the assessment utilising ICT. He has researched on CAI and collaborative studies using the Internet and videoconferencing. He is leading schools in the Province of Toyama which are linked with Northern Ireland and working with teachers of k-12 to promote students' motivation for their studies with ICT.

David Farrell is Vice Principal of Ballyclare Secondary School in Northern Ireland and Consultant to the Education and Library Boards in Northern Ireland for Japanese Studies. During the 1991 Japan Festival in the United Kingdom, he established one of the earliest ICT links between schools in the United Kingdom and Japan. This link is still going and recently it has incorporated the use of video conferencing with schools in Japan.

Jun-ichi Yamanishi is a Professor of the Department of Computer and Instructional Sciences in Toyama University. He has been researching ICT and Integrated Studies using the Internet in k-12 in Japan and recently developed a Web-based instruction for lifelong education. He is working for on an educational link between US and Toyama in addition to a link with Northern Ireland.

8

Teleconsulting

An Extension of Netbased Distance Learning

Odd Rudjord
RealKompetanse as (Oslo, Norway), Hosleveien 84, N-1357 Bekkestua, Norway
odd.rudjord@realkompetanse.no

Keywords: competencies, distance learning, future, learner-centred learning, support services

Abstract: In the same way that the use of consultants may be seen as an extreme type of ad hoc, one-on-one arrangement to further learning, teleconsulting may be viewed as an extension of distance education. When solutions for net-based distance education are adapted for teleconsulting, new opportunities open up to establish systems for cost-effective and high quality customer care. All types of organisations that are engaged in contacts with customers – or with the public at large – may find teleconsulting on the net a viable supplement and/or alternative, both to face-to-face contacts, to mail-based correspondence and to telephone call centres. Teleconsulting also offers exciting opportunities to create virtual organisations.

1. TEACHING VS CONSULTING

Teaching and consulting is traditionally seen as two separate fields, with no or very little overlap. It is, of course, easy to observe that most of the practicioners, ie the teachers and the consultants, have rather different public images and work conditions. Whilst teachers' salaries, social standing, and reputation on the whole has been declining for many decades, consultants have, as a group, become both well paid and well respected. These two professions are, nevertheless, destined to wage turf-wars in the near future. The arena in which these fights will take place is the internet. And the main weapons of the opposing forces will be *teleconsulting* and *distance education*.

1.1 Who controls education?

From the moment most young children enter schools and untill well into their university studies, they have very little control over what they are taught. The curricula are set, decided either by political or educational authorities. Even the way they are taught is given, as most courses come with no options or alternatives as to methodology. With respect to control over education we have not come very far, just like in the 19th century it is the providers who decide, not the recipients.

This situation is, however, changing at an increasing speed. The main force behind this change is modern society's need for constantly up-dated and ever more specialised skills and knowledge.

This is reflected in the not so new diversification of course contents at the level of secondary and higher education. Courses with optional modules and components give the participants a certain degree of freedom to choose the contents of their education.

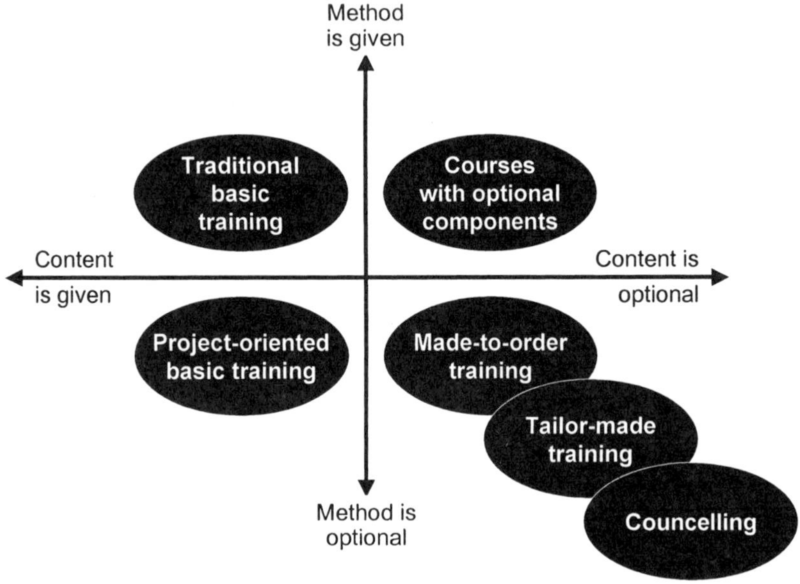

Figure 1: The development of flexibility in the contents and methods of education

The trend towards project-oriented learning is noticable, not least in Scandinavia. It signifies a movement towards participant control even when methodoly is concerned, as learners – again within certain limits – are given the choice as to which learning activities are to be performed.

Educators usually cater for the needs of pupils and students. Most schools had, untill rather recently, not much experience with customers. This is certainly true in Scandinavia, where almost all education has been financed by the governments. I suspect it may be true even in countries where a larger proportion of schools have been privately financed: The individual student has not beed seen as – nor treated as – a proper, commercial customer. To the educators the governments, and in some cases the sponsors, have been the real, but usually very remote customers. It goes without saying that the lack of paying customers have done little to promote service attitudes or willingness to change within the established educational systems.

As private companies have to invest more money more frequently in the training of a greater proportion of their workforces, providers of made-to-order and tailor-made courses are in demand. Since this demand has not been met to a satisfactory degree by the established schools, colleges and universities, a number of new and more flexible training providers has emerged. Even though the established institutions usually are the only ones that can provide academic degrees and certificates signifying formal competence, the newcomers have an ace up their sleeves: They claim that they can deliver the real competence that is needed in the workplaces.

The real picture is, of course, a bit more complicated than this. Universities, colleges and even secondary schools set up departments or 'competence centres' to provide adaptaions of their existing courses for commercial clients. And some of the up-starts in the business seek various ways of recognition from governments and established institutions in order to obtain the right to hand out degrees to their students. The combined effect is that the players in the field of education more and more have to cater for the needs of paying customers. Neither the contents nor the methodology are any longer given – they will to a larger extent than in the past have to be adapted to suit each customers needs, ie satisfy the actual learning needs of the actual course participants.

Figure 2. Men on horses – opposing styles in riding

When a company approaches a training provider and place a commission for a tailor-made course, the similarity to the commissioning of ordinany consultancy work is evident. The course deginer/teacher and the consultant are both agents of change. The teacher promotes learning which, by definition, is change of aptitude and attitude. The consultant also deals in change – if their work does not result in the solution to a problem or the realisation of an opportunity, the effort is surely wasted.

Among educators the traditional grade school teachers and the consultants are placed at opposing sides of the continuum. The old school master's challenge was, to a great extent, to perform the same task, over and over again, preferrably without unnecessary deviations. The consultant, on the other hand, ideally has to rethink his or her approach each time a new customer wants the consultants assistance. The old schoolmaster and the consultant are both educators, much in the same way the participants in a dressage and a rodeo competition are both riders on horses.

1.2 Teaching and consulting on the internet

There is almost no end to the hype that is being produced about the internet's ability to provide learning. An alarmingly large proportion of journalists (and even a few educators) seems to belive that anyone with a PC and a modem is at risk of becoming a qualified expert of almost anything. I suggest that these people – and the rest of us, for that matter – first try to sort out some of the basic questions about ways to learn. If we do, we may find and build on some very simple truths:

- *There is no learning without activity*, ie in order to learn anyone needs to be exposed to, percieve and mentally elaborate on the effects of stimuli. It is possible to learn on one's own, and all types of learning include self-study as a prerequisite. The internet is not a syringe filled with predigested knowledge, at best it can be molded into an arena for learning activities.
- *Peer-learning is an extension of self-studies*, as it signifies individuals' non-guided, collaborative efforts to learn.
- *Education is organised and assisted learning*, providing the learners with assistance from persons who either are knowledgable in the subject at hand, or act as study facilitators, or both.
- *The main difference between teaching and consulting* is found in the degree of ad hoc adaptations to the recepients' needs and abilites to learn. There is a continuum of educational approaches, streching from basic and traditional training of huge numbers of students – to individual, one-on-one councelling.

The internet should, in this context, be seen as a new and challenging medium which provides all kinds of educators with exciting opportunities:

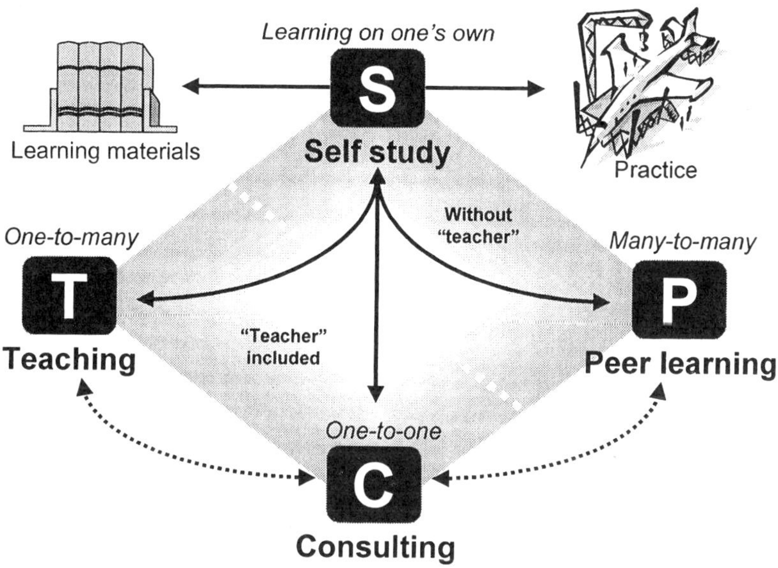

Figure 3. A basic taxonomy of ways to learn. Self-study forms the basis for all types of learning, with or without the assistance from a 'teacher'

- *The internet is a distribution medium for learning materials*. One may store texts and other types of computer files on servers and allow learner to download and utilise these in their studies. Interactive learning materials, such as simulations and quizzes, can easily be published. One may even organise the complete contents of the net as reference materials for students, using anything from simple indexes to advanced artificial intelligence software.
- *The internet is a communication medium* which can facilitate both interaction between learners, and between learners and their 'teachers'. To traditional, mail-based correspondence studies the internet represents a modest revolution. Not only does the student-teacher interaction become faster (and possibly more frequent), one may even set up systems for organised peer-learning and establish project groups on the internet. 'Virtual' campuses, emulating all main function of an ordinary campus, would not have been possible without the internet.
- *The internet can facilitate tests and exams* at a distance. Students' assignments, term-papers and (proctored) examinations can be arranged by use of the web and other internet services.

- *The internet is an administrative tool* which, by use of specially adapted software, can sustain large-scale systems for distance education. Such operations include not only vast amounts of formal and informal communication (much of which must be registered and stored in a retrievable form), but also high numbers of participants, teachers, and facilitators of many kinds.
- *The internet is a medium for marketing.* Any provider of competence building measures can market his or her services on the net. Ordinary indexes and search engines allow internet users to find well-tagged websites, whilst specialised services, clearing-houses and intelligent searchware will track down even the not-so-well tagged offers.

The many new options provided by the internet, the ever increasing rate of technological change and the need for better qualified and constantly updated workforces, they all form the background for the often expressed need for more 'flexible learning'.

Flexible learning signifies a long overdue change towards learner-centred education, to the extent that it implies that the learner is a customer, a person or an institution that is entitled to get what it orders. Flexible learning represents the break-through of commercialism in the field of education. This, in effect, makes the similarities between the teachers and the consultants much easier to see.

Figure 4. Flexible learning demands a customer-oriented approach to education, whether it be in the form of training courses or consultants' services

In order to provide truely flexible learning, the providers must have access to and know how to best employ all means of education. As one tries to satisfy customers' needs, the question is not whether or not any particular approch or favoured method is the correct one. It very soon becomes a question of which mix of means and measures will best serve the customer. The internet may be ideal for interaction among students, but proximity education will still be needed for, say, chemical experiments or training of brain surgeons. And, even though hypertext can be very convenient for many purposes, regular textbooks have some important advantages over texts on screens.

In other words, the successful providers of education (consultants included) must in the future have access to a complete set of educational tools. The ability to combine many specialised forms of presentation and interaction may soon become the prime factor of success.

2. TOOLS FOR TELECONSULTING

2.1 KnowledgeStreamer

At the present there are not much software around for internet consulting. In the following I will be referring to KnowledgeStreamer, a server application for teleconsulting. It was first designed and developed by ObjectPlanet and RealKompetanse, two small companies based in Oslo (Norway), during last year.

The users, ie the customers, access an installation of KnowledgeStreamer through the web, using any recent browser.

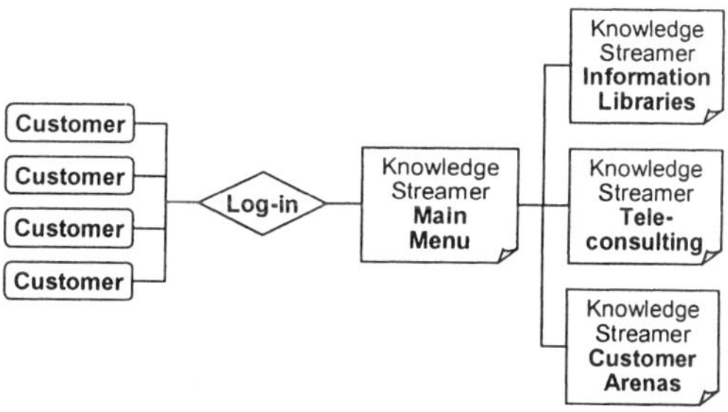

Figure 5. *KowledgeStreamer's main functions, as seen from the users point of view*

If the log-in function is activated, the users will have to submit their personal IDs and passwords in order to get to the system's main menu. From this menu the users may select one of three options: (1) The information libraries, (2) the teleconsulting interface, or (3) the customer arenas.

The information library may contain any number of useful materials and references. KnowledgeStreamer comes with tools for creating, organising and editing FAQ-files and best practices-documentation. In addition it is, of course, possible to include hyperlinks to one own's and other's existing materials on the internet. An indication as to which types of resources that may be interesting is shown in Figure 6.

The teleconsulting interface provides the users with an opportunity to pose questions and to make requests to the owner of the teleconsulting site. These messages are typed into a simple webform, and are tagged by the users so that it is clear which subject area they refer to and how urgently a response is needed.

KnowledgeStreamer allows the owner/operator of the site to route messages of certain contents and urgency to the particular employees that are assigned to handle them. From the owner's point of view this allows him or her the freedom of not only assigning the regular 'proximity consultants' to such tasks, but also the option of including any employee with access to the net to teleconsulting responsibilities.

Most organisations have employees who usually do only in-house work and, since teleconsulting is an in-house task, these may be among the assigned specialists. One may also act as a teleconsultant when on travel, as long as one can access the web. One may not even be an employee to be recruited, freelancers and stringers may well be included in the teleconsulting staff.

The customer arenas are user forums, set up to facilitate peer interaction among the users of the teleconsulting service. As all managers of user forums know from experience – such services depend heavily on the intended target groups' enthusiasm and level of interest. So, a customer arena should only be established as a result of a manifest request from customers.

KnowledgeStreamer nevertheless includes tools for administration of customer arenas. The rationale for this is twofold: (1) By providing customer interaction facilities, the owner of the site will make his or her area on the web a central resource for the customer and the market in general, and (2) by allowing free peer interaction, the owner may easily observe what his or her customers' problems are, what they are thrilled by, and what does not meet with their approval. Customer arenas will in effect enhance the website's market appeal and, simultaneuosly, collect valuable market intelligence.

In order to deliver its services, KnowledgeStreamer includes a set of administrative tools. There are, as already mentioned, access control, editors for FAQs and best practices-documentation, a 'switchboard' that routes customer inqueries to the assigned consultants, and tools for moderating customer arenas. KnowledgeStreamer's built-in alarms will sound if a customer does not receive a response within the time-limits set for the relevant type of inquiery.

2.2 KnowledgeExchange

KnowledgeExchange is based on KnowledgeStreamer. It will provide application service providers (ASPs) with a platform for multi-user teleconsulting. KnowledgeExchanged will also incorporate new functionality, such as a marketplace for consultants ('hire-a-consultant') and benchmarking tools for the services of consultants. The release of this new software is planned for mid-2002.

2.3 NORSK

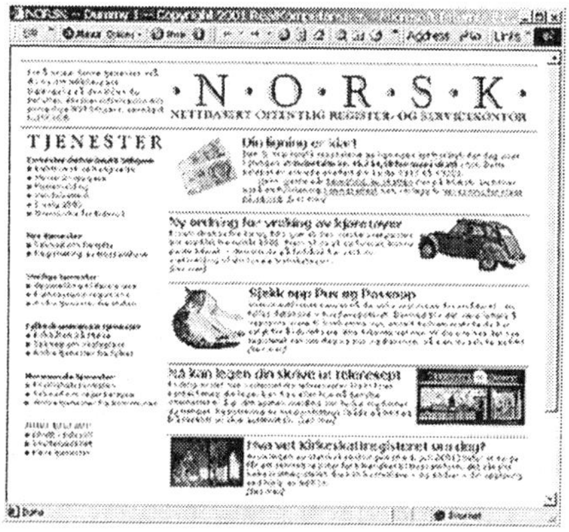

NORSK is a Norwegian acronym which stands for 'Net-based Governmental Register- and Service-bureau'. It is an initiative to establish a national service that will allow each individual citizen to securely interact with the government's many agencies, sharing whatever information they may have that is relevant to the individual user of the service.

This project takes teleconsulting to the extreme. In addition to the security-issues that have to be solved (encryption of communications with millions of potential users, as well as secure retrievial, storage and distribution of highly sensitive data from central databases), it requires a major shift in the way governmental agencies work. New skills and new attitudes towards the public will also be needed in order to reap the potentially vast benefits of teleconsulting.

3. THE FUTURE ROLE OF TELECONSULTING

Just as consulting represents the high-end of the market for learning (and change in general), teleconsulting will be the most expensive and exclusive type of net based learning. This is a logical consequence of the nature of teleconsulting: Customers will typically want quick and meaningful answers to non-standard questions, from a set of consultants who more or less will be standing by, waiting to serve any in-coming customer requests. Unlike simple net-based distance education, where the teachers mostly will evaluate and comment upon responses to standard tasks, teleconsulting will always deal with special and concrete problems. And, in contrast to distance education where responses usually are due within days, teleconsulting can be set up to respond to customers queries within hours – or even minutes.

To an established consultancy firm, teleconsulting may provide a welcomed addition to its established repertoire of services. By providing an internet service, the consultants are establishing themselves on their computers own computer screens, easily accessible and only a few keystrokes away. The lower limit on the size of acceptable commissions may be lowered, as teleconsulting may be more cost-efficient than on-site visits and work.

Teleconsulting may, indeed, be of interest to any company that provides services and products. A server software packages, as for instance KnowledgeStreamer, can be used to facilitate an extended helpdesk function, taking care of customers who have problems in their use of whatever service or product they have purchased.

And, last but not least, teleconsulting may be employed by traditional educators (teachers, trainers, coaches, mentors, or professors) to break into the markets that have traditionally been serviced by consultants. Access to a website for teleconsulting will make it possible for anyone who has expertice – for which there is a commercial market – to set up shop on the internet.

There will be obstacles, of course, since it is hard to become visible on the net, since there are language barriers, and since new businesses do not come free of charge. On the other hand, teleconsulting can be combined with any dayjob, as long as one does not promise customers immediate responses. Teleconsulting may become a tempting proposition, especially for teachers and academics with a certain standing in a given environment.

BIOGRAPHY

Odd Rudjord is vice president at RealKompetanse as. His main areas of responsibility are concept design and internet-related business development. In previous positions he has developed and designed distance education courses. He initiated the ETUE-net programme (sponsored by the European Commission's Fourth framework programme), and served as *rektor* for the Norwegian National Institute of Technology's Distance education college.

9

A Virtual Environment for Distance Learning

Creto Augusto Vidal, Antonio José Melo Leite Júnior, Camilo Camilo Almendra, Emanuele Marques dos Santos, Joaquim Pedro Carvalho de Oliveira and João Carlos Silveira Costa Filho

Department of Computing,, Universidade Federal do Ceará, Fortaleza, Ceará, Bloco 910 - Caixa Postal 12.166 - 60.455-760, Brazil

cvidal@lia.ufc.br

Keywords: collaborative learning, distance learning, virtual reality

Abstract: Brazil, such as many other countries, does not have the capacity to train enough teachers to attend the educational needs of the growing population of children. This has a direct impact on the quality of education that the students receive. The low cost and ease of use of semi-immersive virtual reality environments have recently resulted in a rapid expansion of this technology across the world. In this work, we present a low cost distributed virtual reality system for the education of students from grades K to 12. The proposed system is based on an architecture that allows efficient data distribution in low bandwidth networks. We believe that virtual schools, based on the proposed virtual reality system, where remote teachers and students can exchange ideas and propose activities, may be an important part of the solution to this problem.

1. INTRODUCTION

The State of Ceará in North-eastern Brazil has a serious problem of low-level academic and pedagogic formal education of a large portion of its board of teachers. This causes a direct impact on the quality of education that the students receive. The situation is very dramatic in the public school system and even worse in small towns in the countryside of the State. The two main causes for this situation are the low salaries and the poor living standards offered by the urban centres in the countryside of Ceará. Considering that the socio-economic development of those cities may take decades to occur, it is very unlikely that, in the short run, the students will be taught by well-prepared teachers, using up to date teaching methodologies.

In order to explore the most recent advances in computer technology and telecommunication, a new distance education program was recently proposed. Its main purpose is to provide the opportunity for continuous education of teachers, especially those from small cities far from the state's capital; and it relies heavily on the use of videoconference. Nine videoconference rooms were specified in the initial phase of the program, one located in the state's capital and the others located in eight urban centres in the countryside of the state. Besides short duration courses or discussions about new teaching methodologies, several licensing degree programs and graduate programs are also being prepared for this project. The implementation of these programs needs a telecommunication infrastructure which will be provided by the State Telecommunication Network, the so-called 'information highways', through which will be transmitted text, sound and image data (Pequeno 1998). Many other applications, based on the Internet protocols, can take advantage of the state's 'information highways'. Thus, other distance education initiatives are being proposed since the connection to the Internet opens up the door to access a wide variety of information resources in the whole world.

In this work, we present a distributed virtual reality system, which relies on the State Telecommunication Network, for the education of students from grades K to 12. Our system is well aligned with the UNESCO recommendations for the period from 2002 to 2007 (UNESCO 2000), which encourage the creation of virtual educational communities, of virtual schools and of virtual universities in developing countries. It can be adapted to other regions and countries of the world that can benefit from the ICT (Information and Communication Technologies) potentials for education.

This work is organised as follows: in section 2, we present basic concepts of virtual reality systems; in section 3, we describe the available resources in the proposed virtual environment; in section 4, we discuss the components of the architecture used in our system; and in section 5, we draw some conclusions.

2. VIRTUAL REALITY

The ideal virtual reality model considers virtual reality as the ultimate navigation tool through which one can visualise, manipulate and interact with computers and complex data sets. Thus, virtual reality can be understood as the most advanced type of human-computer interface available nowadays (Çapin et al. 1999). This technology relies in the artificial construction of the so-called virtual world where all the elements with which one wants to interact are embodied in a creative representation defined by the virtual world designer. Once the virtual environment is created, the users, or their representations, can start exploring it and interacting with its elements. The form of interaction in the virtual world tries to mimic, as close as possible, the form of interaction one has in the real world, where the five human senses play a major role.

If the virtual environment is designed in such a way that the users actually feel themselves to be a part of it, we say that the system provides the sense of immersion. In order for a system to provide the sense of total immersion, it would have to stimulate vision, hearing, touch, smell and taste. Is it really possible to achieve total immersion? Could someone, for example, sit on the shade of a virtual tree, feel the freshness of the virtual breeze, see the virtual birds flying and listen to them singing, sense the smell of a virtual apple, take a bite of it and appreciate its flavour? Even if it were possible to use a number of specialised hardware to try to reproduce this simple scene, how useful would this hardware be in reproducing other situations from the real world? Is it really worth the effort to strive for transforming a virtual world into the real world?

For a number of important applications it is enough to be in the middle ground. Thus, a lot of research effort was put into developing specialised hardware and the corresponding software to improve the sense of immersion without using all of the human senses. As a consequence of the research and development effort in special hardware for virtual reality, a great number of equipment is offered in the market today. Also, the computer power had to increase in order to perform complex computations in real time.

Considering the other end of the spectrum, there are virtual reality systems where the screen of a video monitor provides only one sensorial stimulus, the visual stimulus. These types of systems rely essentially on computer graphics to model the virtual world and the user representations, the so-called avatars or virtual humans. The real user interacts with the virtual world from, what some authors call, a 'fish tank' point-of-view. These systems are considered to provide no sense of immersion or just a partial sense of immersion. However, the low cost and ease of use of these systems made them experience a very rapid expansion all over the world. These advantages are stimulating more and more people to devise applications for this type of virtual reality technology. Another very important factor for the growth of this 'fish tank' type of virtual reality is the ease of integration of virtual worlds and users over a network. Now, many applications can be hooked together in a distributed system's approach and the complexity and usefulness of the virtual environments are limitless. The users, now, can easily share these complex distributed virtual worlds with other remote users and interact with them in this virtual environment. This type of interaction and socialisation among users brings about an emotional content that is a very important fact to be exploited in many areas.

3. AVAILABLE RESOURCES

In this virtual environment, there are important resources available to make it possible for the users to interact with each other. They can use voice communication, which is the most natural form of communication, or exchange text messages, which is the most suitable form of communication over low bandwidth networks.

Sometimes, in a virtual classroom, the students and the teachers want to expose some ideas combining text, 3D graphics, images, and sound. This can be achieved by using Web pages with all these resources embedded. Another option is to prepare the presentation as three-dimensional panels of text, images, sound and animation that can be arranged in the virtual environment and inspected with a VRML browser.

Another important resource that allows sharing of information is the so-called Whiteboard. It simulates a classroom whiteboard by displaying all the drafts or annotations, written on a small tablet, on a whiteboard in the virtual environment. All the students and teachers logged in the system can work cooperatively using this tool.

The virtual environment can be accessed twenty-four hours a day and, even if none of their classmates or teachers is around to interact with, the student can still interact with simuloids (autonomous virtual humans). These simuloids can help the students to accomplish tasks requested by the teacher during class. The users can have access to information available outside the virtual environment by asking some specialised simuloids, which integrate the virtual world with the Web and with other external resources (Vidal et al. 2000). The simuloids can also assume the role of reproduction avatars. For example, if students miss a mathematics class and later logs into the virtual system, they will be informed that the missed class is available in playback mode in the mathematics virtual classroom. There, a simuloid can be asked to reproduce all the discussion that took place during the class.

Although our virtual system represents a virtual school, it is composed of several specialised virtual worlds, which represent specialised rooms. For example, they can represent study rooms for specific subjects. They can represent training classrooms for continuous education of the schoolteachers, functioning as an alternative to the videoconference based training rooms implemented by the Ceará State's Government. They can also represent rooms for simulation of a teacher's office hours, where the student can clear doubts or exchange opinions with the teacher about common interest subjects. The number of specialised virtual worlds that can be incorporated into the system is constrained only by the limits of our imagination and, of course, by the limits of the available hardware.

4. THE ÁRVORE ARCHITECTURE

ÁRVORE is a generic architecture, developed so that multi-user virtual reality environments and multimedia resources can be made available even over low bandwidth computer networks. Several client applications provide the necessary means for the user to interact with characters controlled by other users or by computers inside the virtual reality environment. One of the main characteristics of this architecture is the low cost distribution of virtual reality and multimedia elements through specialised replication structures. These types of structures send the elements, upon demand, to be stored locally and in a persistent manner in several predefined components.

Since this is an open architecture, it is possible for the final system to be implemented over several distinct platforms, which are defined according to the specific needs of each provided service. The system is composed of several specialised components, which can be independently implemented. This makes the development of the distributed system easier and, later, its maintenance. The components of the system are divided into two main groups: the server components and the client components.

4.1 Servers

The routing server is the basic integration element of the architecture. It controls the information flow among the several components of the virtual environment. The message routing criterion is based upon the service being requested. This defines the way a message is conducted to one or more destinations. The information about the available services is stored, in the routing server, as a persistent list relating the services and their respective locations in the distributed system. The adoption of this routing strategy is essential in warranting the extensibility of the architecture, since the growth of the system occurs by the inclusion of elements followed by a reconfiguration of the list of services. Thus, the functions of these new elements can be rapidly incorporated into the system and made available to all the other components of the distributed system.

The environment server is responsible for the behaviour control of the virtual reality elements of the virtual world, and maintains the state of all relevant virtual structures, i.e., those that present some type of pre-programmed reaction – characters and tri-dimensional objects. In the virtual world, the interaction between a character and an object triggers events, according to a pre-specified behaviour, which are treated by the environment server.

The replication server is responsible for the distribution upon demand of multimedia and virtual reality elements to the clients of the ÁRVORE architecture. In this architecture, however, video and audio streams are not considered as distribution elements, since they would necessarily require communication channels with high bandwidth. In any case, continuous media can still be made available to the set of clients through a simple transfer of its files. The replication server can be considered one of the main responsible for the low cost of the ÁRVORE architecture. It allows for the distribution of multimedia and virtual reality elements in low speed networks, which, until then, were not able to support such an intense traffic using classical solutions (Sgouros 1999).

The validation server provides session management for the virtual environment, controlling the users' access to the several available resources. The log server is responsible for the documentation of the overall functioning of the distributed system.

4.2 Clients

The users, through the interaction client, access the set of available services in the virtual reality environment. This client is a virtual reality user interface that renders the tri-dimensional structures of the system, taking into consideration the avatars' characteristics and their positions in the virtual environment. Hence, a certain user can interact with other users as well as with objects of the virtual world in which he is immersed.

Simuloids can be implemented as computer-controlled clients, which integrate external applications with the virtual reality environment. Thus, avatars and other simuloids can interact with a given simuloid in order to use, implicitly, the external applications' services that it makes available. To make these interactions as close as possible to those of a human being, it is necessary to establish a pre-programmed behaviour for the simuloid (Çapin et al. 1999).

The management client interacts with certain components of the ÁRVORE architecture. One of its responsibilities is the configuration of the following services: maintenance of the list of services provided by the routing server, maintenance of the access policies contained in the validation server, and inclusion of new elements in the replication server. The management client also collects information from several components of the architecture, including the log server, and then generates summaries about the overall functioning of the distributed system. These summaries are dynamically requested and processed in accordance with the system administrators' needs.

4.3 Model

The model considered in the ÁRVORE architecture can easily be extended so that multiple virtual worlds run simultaneously. Several instances of the components foreseen in this architecture can be executed in a number of inexpensive microcomputers connected through the Internet. Thus, this architecture provides efficient communication and interaction in shared virtual reality environments to a great number of users. Each virtual world has its own set of server applications. In order to warrant reliability and availability of the system, it is possible to replicate some of the components or even a complete virtual world.

Despite the intensive use of the Internet as a data transmission medium, the proposed ÁRVORE architecture is a low cost solution to the problem just posed, since, from its conception, it does not rely in high-speed networks.

In order to allow the integration and management of the participants' accesses to the whole set of available virtual worlds, it is necessary to include a central structure that is responsible for the storage of the access privileges of all the users of this integrated virtual reality system. The access to the information contained in this central structure can be carried out directly by the Routing Server of each virtual world. However, a much more interesting solution to this access problem is provided by the partitioned replication process (Singhal and Zyda 1999), which is capable of individually updating each validation server used in the virtual environments. Such replications can be made at specific times when the network traffic is less intense, preventing possible congestion.

4.4 Access

The users of the system can be organised in access groups, according to the specific needs of a class in a real school's classroom. There are situations where the access to a specific part of the complete virtual environment might be restricted to certain special groups of users. The access rights information is stored in the central structure. In the ÁRVORE architecture, it seems to be natural that the central structure be integrated with the student's record office of an educational institution, which maintains a database with all the information about a student's history (class schedules, courses taken, grades obtained, courses' pre-requisites, etc.). The information contained in this database may determine certain access privileges in the virtual environment.

The user can access the virtual system in three ways. First, the user can connect to any of the available virtual worlds. Second, the user directly logs into the central structure. After the user's identification (username and password), the client application is automatically connected to a particular virtual world according to certain predefined access policies. For example, if the user logs into the system at ten o'clock and, according to the user's schedule, she should be attending a biology class, then the user will be directly connected to the corresponding virtual world. Finally, when the user is already connected to a virtual world, she can automatically move to another virtual world, if permission is granted, by just passing through a specific region of the world. This technique is called Portal (Singhal and Zyda 1999).

5. CONCLUSION

Virtual reality in Brazil has experienced a considerable growth in recent years and a number of new ideas are being proposed, implemented and tested by research groups in universities and in research institutes. A very promising area of application for virtual reality in Brazil is distance education. Recently the Brazilian government financed a number of research projects on distance education and an expressive part of those projects involved virtual reality applications.

It is a fact that the network infrastructure of Brazil is growing in a faster pace than the capacity of the country to train enough teachers to attend the educational needs of the growing population of children. Therefore, we can dream of virtual schools, those schools with virtual laboratories, fully equipped with virtual instruments available for cooperative virtual experiments. They will also have virtual classrooms, where remote teachers and students can exchange ideas and propose activities. Such a dream is not only for children of small communities in remote areas of the country, but, perhaps, also the only hope for social justice and a way forward for those currently excluded from society.

REFERENCES

Çapin, T., Pandzic, I., Magnenat-Thalmann, N. and Thalmann, D. (1999) *Avatars in Networked Virtual Environments*. John Wiley & Sons, USA.

Pequeno, M. (1998) *Infra-estrutura física e tecnológica para Rede de Videoconferência do Estado do Ceará.* Project sponsored by FINEP (Financiadora de Estudos e Projetos), Brazil. [www.sct.ce.gov.br/fr-infovia.htm].

Sgouros, N. M. (1999) Involving the Audience in Distributed, Interactive Entertainment Systems. In *Proceedings of EG Multimedia '99 Workshop*, Italy.

Singhal, S. and Zyda, M. (1999) *Networked Virtual Environments – Design and Implementation*. Addison-Wesley, USA.

UNESCO (2000) *Hundred and sixtieth Session of Executive Board*, 160 EX/17. United Nations Educational, Scientific and Cultural Organization., pp. 11-12. [unesdoc.unesco.org/ulis]

Vidal, C., Leite Jr, A., Almendra, C., Santos, E. and Oliveira, J. (2000) *Uma Proposta de Integração de Ferramentas Externas a Ambientes Virtuais através Aplicações Mediadoras e Simulóides*. In Proceedings of 3rd Workshop on Virtual Reality, Brazilian Computer Society, Gramado – Brazil, October, pp. 131-142.

BIOGRAPHY

Creto Vidal is a professor of computer science; his current research interests are computer graphics and virtual reality applications to distance education. He is currently the coordinator of three government-sponsored projects investigating the use of networked virtual environments for training and education (www.lcg.dc.ufc.br/projects).

Melo Leite Júnior is a professor of computer graphics; his current research focus on the applications of networked virtual environments in education and training.

Camilo Almendra, Emanuele Marques, Joaquim Oliveira and João Costa Filho are research assistants in computer graphics and networked virtual reality.

10

Development and Future of Flexible Distance Learning in Denmark

Susanne Tellerup and Niels Henrik Helms
The Dabish Institute for Educational Training of VocationalTteachers, Noerrehus, Thomas B. Thrigesgade 48 B, DK-5000 Odense, Denmark
susanne.tellerup@delud.dk

Keywords: distance learning, didactics, compentencies, lifelong learning

Abstract: The way we have thought about and worked with education and teaching is changing and therefore new challenges, opportunities and problems are raised. The new focus on distance learning and interpretation of the concept can be explained by various interrelated factors like. We will try to describe the situation and development from different angles. Focusing on the pedagogical, technological and organising perspectives.

1. DISTANCE LEARNING

Distance Learning (DL) was never a ‘big thing’ in Denmark. Geographic distance is not a problem in this country as such, therefore DL was often considered a second-rate form of learning for people who were unable to attend ‘real’ education. But this has changed profoundly within a short span of years. A lot of Danes have attended especially the so-called ECDL-courses as distance learning and now e-learning is on everybody’s lips as an important part of the national strategy for learning, especially relating to companies’ strategies for learning. The new focus on distance learning and interpretation of the concept can be explained by various interrelated factors.

- The growth of accessibility through the spreading of the Internet
- The potentials in and also confidence in ICT in general

- The demand for continuous learning related to globalisation and change to a knowledge-society
- The individual interest in lifelong learning.

Distance Learning has developed over the last decade – and today it plays a major role in the Danish educational system. How come? One of the answers we may seek lie in the development of ICT. It has given us new possibilities for delivering and organising learning and for access to education.

On an individual level the development of competencies in the knowledge society means that the each and everybody of us face the challenge of constantly improving our competencies and acquiring new ones. If we are talking about Lifelong Learning, the answer is not traditionally organised education. The way we have thought about and worked with education and teaching is changing and therefore new challenges, opportunities and problems are raised.

1.1 Moving to flexible and distance learning

In many countries distance education has a long history. But often it has been seen as a kind of 'emergency teaching' and offered to people who could not participate in what was considered 'proper' education..

The establishment of the Open University, its success and the establishment of corresponding institutions gave notion to another dimension, that education could be open. More people gained access to education, which was much in line with the thinking in the 60s and 70s. Education was seen as a vital resource to create a democratic and equal society. In the 80s and especially in the 90s the development of competencies was in focus. Now education was seen as an investment made by the individual or the company.

At the same time the enhancement of learning was in focus. The problem of organising learning and learning processes as integrated parts of and combined with the work processes and the production in the companies was prominent. And FDL was put on the agenda instead of the former discussion about Open and Distance Education.

1.2 Changes in the educational landscape

According to the American Professor James D. Duderstadt, the educational landscape has changed. It has developed from 'education-just-in-case' over 'education-just-in-time' to 'education-just-for-me'.

At the same time the real synchronous learning spaces are replaced by asynchronous network learning, and learning can take place everywhere at any time. Therefore it is difficult to find your bearings with the old pedagogical theories and methods. New and innovative thinking is needed within the pedagogical field, because the field extends and changes.

To understand the pedagogical needs we first of all must define FDL. With reference to Keegan, we can point out that Distance Learning is characterised by:

- Teacher and learner are quasi-separated
- The existence of an institution scaffolding the learning processes
- Contrary to private studies
- Use of technological media to connect teacher, learner and the subjects
- Dialogue between the teacher and the learner – contrary to the 'teach-your-self' media.

Furthermore Keegan points out the absence of a learning group. But on this point we do not agree with Keegan, a fact that illustrates the differences and difficulties in the definitions of FDL. Contrary to Keegan we find that the social dimension in the learning process can be vital and important. And this point of view is supported by the improvement of the theories about collaborative learning.

The infinite access to information provided by the internet makes it possible to 'learn about', but not to 'learn to be', as Bruner points out. 'Learning to be' depends upon social interactions and the competent combination of different kinds of teaching and learning processes in 'Learning Communities', which can also be virtual.

In our definition of FDL:

- Teacher and learner are separated in time and space
- Subjects and interaction are mediated by technology
- Collaboration and personal communication are both scaffolding the learning processes and establishing a social practice
- An educational institution delivers (the learning package).

And how does FDL differ from Distance Education? Sometimes it does not! It depends upon the individual learning possibilities. Some concepts for Distance Education are very flexible and give room for a variety of learning styles and collaborative processes.

The vital questions are:

- Does the teacher-learner separation enhance the possibilities for the learner both to learn and to complete the course?
- Does the chosen technology enhance flexibility and collaborative learning?
- Are the learning processes designed in the best possible way in relation to the learner's needs and potentials?

1.3 From the learner's point of view

The conference system can be a key-point in FDL. When you choose a conference system, you should consider the folowing.

- Speed – How quickly can the learner get access, both to begin with and during the course?
- Cost – How much does it cost the learner to use the system?
- Interaction – How and with whom can you interact within this conference system?
- Total experience – How do speed, cost, interaction, goals, skills, subject and use relate?

It is important that the technology is not too advanced and complicated. Otherwise the technology can be the inflexible factor that blocks the essential: the enhancement of learning. Again you must consider:

- The learner's needs, conditions and working tasks
- The wanted and expected learning process.

Some very simple rules are important, when you organise and construct e-learning courses and resources:

- Keep it simple
- Show it
- Enhance transparency
- Consider the learner's point of view – over and over again.

You have to structure virtual learning spaces, which scaffold the perception, the survey and personal task of constructing meaning and knowledge.

1.4 Pedagogy and teachers' competencies

The competencies of the teachers are another key to FDL. Working with FDL is a didactic challenge rather than a technological challenge. The teacher must use the new learning spaces and design new teaching and learning strategies corresponding with FDL. This means that the teacher must improve many competencies:

- ICT-competence. To use the technology and give advise about common problems.
- Facilitator-competence. To guide in a way so that the learner feels motivated to go on. To use different kinds of guidance-strategies – based on both written and oral communication.
- Internet-communication-competence. To communicate concretely, clearly and constructively in an attentive way without being without taking over.

- Structural competence. To create structure. In the traditional school the structure is made up by the timetable, the classrooms, the architecture etc. A structure pointing out very clearly what school is all about. With FDL there also are some the signs – but the teacher plays a major part structuring and connecting things.
- Search and navigation competence. To search and navigate on the Internet and to assess material found on the Internet.
- Organisational competence. To organise and inspire. The teacher has to establish and improve the collaborative learning communities.
- Moderator competence. To moderate different kinds of e-discussions and to let the learners be in charge playing different roles.
- Meta-communication-competence. To be above the situation. The teacher should provoke the learner's thinking and acting.

1.5 The didactic competencies

The teacher should be able to understand learners in flexible learning. The learners' needs, interests and also their lives and situations. The distinct problems compared to their classroom counterpart call for different competencies but also emphasise some of the competencies of the traditional teacher. First of all teachers of flexible learning must do much of their work before they know the specific students on the course. The content must be well structured and prepared beforehand, learning objectives clearly stated. It is important to create courses, which are open to being structured in a traditional flow, but also leaves room for a more holistic cyclic process.

1.6 Resources for learning

The learning resources should be easily accessible first of all. The materials should be developed considering demands like transparency and easy navigation. – And should also be simple in design and language. The important thing is to avoid that the learner feels confused or even stupid. Among other things that means that:

- The learner should know how and when assignments should be posted
- The learner should be sure which parts give credit in the assignments
- The learner should know where and when things are being discussed
- Which parts are optional
- What kind of learning is to be expected from participating in an activity.

1.7 Future dialogue and learning environments

The first problem most developers and providers of FDL face is very often the lack of activity. The participants don't do anything. But when this has been solved other problems arise. Here the question of qualified net-dialogue seems extremely important. The dialogue is the core of collaborative learning in a virtual context. – And a new generation of web-literate learners have competencies in using new ways of communication such as chat. But chat is used to establish social contact, becoming members of communities and probably also to define and try out your own identity. Where as net dialogue is about comprehending, developing analytical understanding and seeing the perspectives. Therefore an important part of the FDL-agenda is to develop a flexible learning environment which accommodates the needs and interests of the individual learner and supports the development of communities of practise. Furthermore is it important to construct these environments in a way so that they leave possibilities for the learner to actively play a part in constructing the environments. Taking into account the differences between learners, the developers need to find the right balance here between structure, involvement and room for creativity.

1.8 Organisation – formulating a strategy

The logic, structure and also culture relating to FDL are very different from traditional teaching. The development of FDL as the important activity for an organisation therefore calls for:

- Developing a vision for FDL in the organisation
- Establishing competency-units relating to FDL
- Formulating plans, indicators etc. for the development of FDL.

The vision is important because the different individuals in the organisation should be able to develop understanding of their own role in this change. Very many teachers are against FDL because they feel that it endangers their identity as teachers and they are very often correct in that assumption. This should not be hidden but brought out into the open. Emphasising the changing role of the teacher means that in the future the teacher should be able to handle different roles such as developer, facilitator and mediator. The fact that there will still be a need for more traditional teachers might overcome at least some of the resistance.

Competency-units are a way of describing what is needed. There must be different supporting competencies available to the team and a competency unit needs to have access to the necessary infrastructure, resources and be organised and placed in the setup in a way which is beneficial to the development and delivery of FDL.

1.9 Networking

As stated above each organisation has to find its identity in this development. But working with FDL means that you work in a national and sometimes global context and furthermore it means that you have to focus on your key-competencies. All in all this calls for different types of models and co-operation. One way is to establish networks where one organisation takes care of the technology and delivery and another deals with the content and learning.

Another form is to establish co-operation between institutions, which share interests and benefits from a closer co-operation when developing FDL-courses We have seen this in the area of higher and academic education and also in further education. The important issues for these co-operations and networks seem to be as follows.

- Understanding and developing the core-competencies of your own organisation and seeing how they can interact in a mutually beneficial way with the competencies of other organisations
- Developing dialogue between the participating organisations.

2. CONCLUDING REMARKS

The Danish tradition in education emphasising co-operation and dialogue has an important role to play in the further development of FDL. Small is supposed to be beautiful but in the development and in the delivery of traditional distance education that is not necessarily the case. Developing major distance learning programmes based on a concept of broadcasting calls for big industrial organisations with a high degree of specialisation. But in a modern post-industrial world we also need other forms of FDL that emphasise collaboration, co-operation and dialogue. And in this area the Danish tradition of co-operation and also capacity for change will be important. The central issue will be how to develop the relationship between organisation, learning and technology in order to develop learning which can cope with the challenges of 'Learning just in time' and 'learning just for me'.

On the major conference on Distance Learning in Copenhagen in the spring 2000 the Canadian practitioner and theorist Terry Andersson introduced the concepts of 'Big' and 'Small Distance Learning'. He sees Big Distance Learning as the major programmes developed and delivered by big providers for a big market, very often for the whole world. But according to Terry Andersson there is and will be a growing demand for 'Small Distance Learning' where specific needs are in focus. These two forms should probably not be seen as contradictions to each other but rather as supplements. We have tried to describe the development from different angles. Focusing on the pedagogical, technological and organising perspectives.

In a somewhat reduced form we can see a relationship between these different angles as illustrated in the model below (Figure 1)

The nucleus of the model shows the traditional distance learning which aims at distributing and providing access to information for a (large) number of learners. The technology should be designed for smooth delivery, which means that it could be radio, traditional mail or the Internet. This mode demands a high degree of division of labour between developers, experts in the subject matter, delivery and control. The best known example of these organisations is the Open University in UK.

At the next level we focus on skills. It could be language, math or vocational skills. Together they share the need for practise and training, and multimedia is often a good way to do that. Developing quality multimedia is however a very expensive task. Therefore the market is often left to major commercial enterprises focusing more on mainstream accessible edutainment than on quality learning. Networks between colleges and private enterprises and European co-operation can be ways of overcoming this problem.

Collaborative virtual and real learning processes are the most important form of learning in the network society.

The individual learner constructs his or her own learning-portfolio (Learning just for me) but the collaborative processes opens up for developing competencies. Now we are at level three in the model. That kind of learning calls for a more flexible, simple and open technology than for advanced solutions. In this perspective the logic of the model might transform! The nucleus would then be that the individual learner develops his or her competency in learning groups working in collaborative GroupWare.

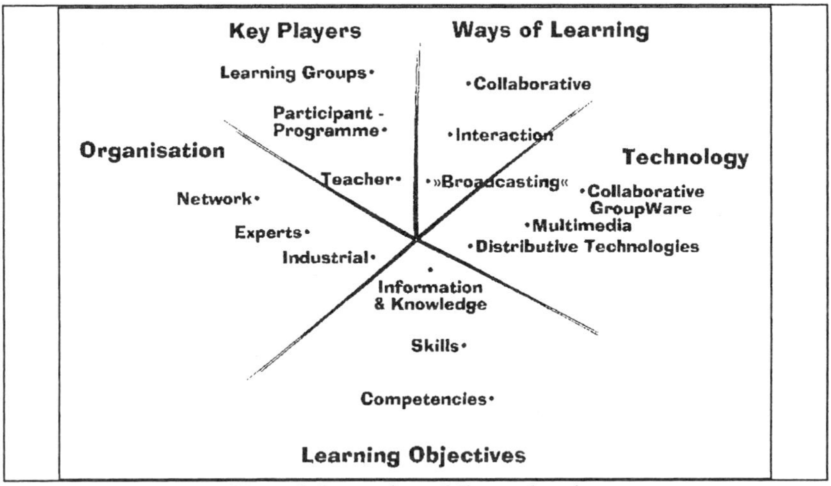

Figure 1. Perspectives of distance learning

And from there identifies the need for training skills or for getting a more formalised education. We are already now in the middle of such a development where individuals create their own learning portfolio related to worklife and personal development and seek the most relevant learning resources on a global market. That means that the learning environment becomes more local (combinations of work and private life) and more global (access to providers of education all over the world).

This is a development where the Danish tradition in general (working in networks on a small scale but with a global market) and also in learning and education (dialogue and co-operation) has much to offer. But if this is to happen the institutions should be focusing on developing virtual dialogue, flexible learning together with the learners and especially combining the potentials of big – and small – distance learning.

REFERENCES

Andersson, T. (1998) *Networked Learning.* McGrawHill, Montreal.

Helms, H. Jørgensen, J. J. and Tellerup, S. (1999) *Fjernundervisning.* Erhvervsskolernes Forlag Odense, Denmark.

Jarvis, P., Holford, J. and Griffin, C. (1998) *Theory and Practice of Learning.* Kogan Page, London.

Katz, R. N. (1999) *Dancing with the Devil.* Jossey Bass, San Francisco.

Keegan, D. (1993) *Distance Education: New Perspectives.* Routledge, London.

Paloff, R. M. (1999) *Building Learning Communities in Cyberspace.* Jossey Bass, San Francisco.

Peters, O. (1998) *Learning and Teaching in Distance Education.* Kogan Page, London.

11

A Case for an Adult Educational Technology

Thierry Nodenot
Laboratoire d'Informatique de l'Université de Pau et des Pays de l'Adour (LIUPPA) IUT de Bayonne, 3 avenue J. Darrigrand, 64115, Bayonne, France
Thierry.Nodenot@iutbayonne.univ-pau.fr

Keywords: integration, ICT and change, innovative pedagogical methods

Abstract: The paper addresses role-oriented aspects of Open Distance Learning identifying specific components like system, co-operation and organisational facets used in the interaction-oriented learning process. We envisage the design and the operation of educational environments in which the actors (pupils, groups of pupils, instructors, ...) can interact via computerised media in the accomplishment of an activity constructed to drive learning. These interactions are educationally regulated (in an automated fashion or monitored by the teacher) from the specifications previously established by the designer of the educational activity. After presenting the principles, we describe the technological platform capable of supporting such an environment.

1. INTRODUCTION

Open Distance Learning (ODL) Systems have the wind in their sails. Carried by the tide of the Internet, they are pushed forward by big business in order to train their clients and colleagues and also by several universities (mainly in the United States) for whom their Web Site advertises more and more modules available on line.

In this paper, we claim a focus on educational environments based on interactions. We consider that the teacher must hold a central role even in ODL; so, rather than removing the teacher from his/her role of regulating the relationship between the learner and knowledge, we envisage a model allowing the exploitation of new Information Technologies:

- in order to make the relationship between the learner, the knowledge and the teacher more efficient,
- in order that the teachers adhere to new technologies and profit from them at an educational level.

The suggested model works on the principal that for the teacher, a class is a system in which the interactions between actors are at least as significant as their individual performances (Tardif 1997, Mucchielli 2000, George and Leroux 2001). A detailed study of this system allows one to envisage the design (and the operation) of educational environments in which the actors (pupils, groups of pupils, instructors, teachers) are going to be able to interact via computerised media/mediums in the accomplishment of an activity constructed to drive learning. These interactions are educationally regulated (in an automated fashion or monitored by the teacher) from the specifications previously established by the designer.

After justifying our approach, we present the principals of such an environment. We end by describing the platform capable of supporting such an environment: it relies on XML, object based systems and distributed computing.

2. OPEN DISTANCE LEARNING – INTERACTION-BASED E-LEARNING

What is good and bad is never certain. Down the years, work and research in Computer-Aided Learning (CAL) has remained restricted to small groups of researchers. But now, as a result of new Information and Communication Technologies, we have witnessed an explosion of advertising and material for open distance learning from retailers of platforms (WebCT, Lotus Learning Space) and also from those who develop (and commercialise) educational material from this kind of platforms. Even within educational institutions, people say that very soon, on-line courses are going to compete with our lessons and for near enough same costs, the students will thus have access to individual training that is more efficient and better adapted to their needs (Lotus 1998).

Considering the challenge for our institutions, and taking into consideration the power of these firms or universities, we think it both pointless and unnecessary to fight on the same ground:

- *pointless* because the developers of ODL solutions have indisputable assets: a significant production capacity, a capacity to tap into a huge market-place via the Web (cheap courses but to a very large potential audience/courses at a higher cost but sufficiently in depth to interest people on a world-wide scale), a capacity to offer training on the same wavelength as the market and technology advance (because they are capable of mobilising, on demand, numerous human resources for the production of just in time courseware).

- *unnecessary* because the educational environments developed for the majority of ODL platforms on the market are very limited as to the educational dialogue they offer to the student. These are teaching aids accompanied by a methodological guide and a range of exercises allowing self-learning and self-evaluation. And this package has a user-interface with communication functions (mails, chats, video-conferencing) in order to allow the student to contact other students or an instructor during a learning session. It would be very surprising that such solutions that have been largely and justifiably criticised ten years ago for the weak educational dialogue that they provided would find public approval today only because they are circulated en masse via the web. Such solutions can probably, in the context of further education be justified but we think that other ways have to be found to ensure quality initial education aided by technology within our institutions (or in liaison with them).

We think on the other hand that it is desirable and possible to produce educational environments by using ICT which, because they are based on a model where the teacher retains a central role, will mean that these new technologies will not have the effect of removing students from our system of learning. It is therefore a question of integrating the use of new Information Technologies into every day educational practice and of finding some protocols which will entail an increase in the educational dialogue between students and teachers and consequently the educational return of our teaching (Dillenbourg 1999, Soller et al. 1999).

This education centering on interactions (Tardif 1997, Mucchielli 2000, George and Leroux 2001) that we strongly advise is complementary to education through problem-situations which are taught in teacher training colleges in France:

- the problem-situation defines the context of the interaction which is going to be established between actors (between students; between the students and instructors): it consists of presenting not only the proposed activity to the students, but also the activity objectives and problems that the students must overcome, the material they can require, the criteria to be met (both functional and formal), ...
- the study of interactions allows one to define the rules (Taveter 1999) that actors must conform to in solving the problem-situation, the modes of intervention for each actor and the dynamics of these interventions.

In earlier works, we have dealt with methods and tools for the specification of teachings based on problem-situations (Nodenot 1995,

Marquesuzaa 1998). Here, we are going to present the characteristics of the interactive educational environment which is currently being developed in our Laboratory. It is a system of specification and regulation of co-operative activities which allows:

- The educational designer (a teacher) to define the interactions that can be established between actors (students, groups of students, human and system instructors) in the course of a problem-situation activity.
- The activities of the different actors to be monitored by the environment on the basis of the established specifications.

3. STUDY OF A SYSTEM OF SPECIFICATION AND REGULATION OF COOPERATIVE ACTIVITIES

This system is complex to analyse because it is an environment spread throughout space and time:

1. *In space* because actors whether they are students, instructors or teachers use a specific computer equipped with software dedicated to the tasks they have to achieve:
   - To perform the tasks they are assigned, the learners have at their disposal tools that can be quite standard (spreadsheets, word-processors, programming environments, ...) or specific-purpose tools (e.g. an editor allowing the learner to know instantly the tasks that remain for him to accomplish in order to succeed). Among these tools there will also be facilities of communication which allow them to exchange information with other actors in the context of the task (the possibilities for communication are limited only to the actors with which the learner has a right to communicate in the script defined by the educational designer).
   - The teachers or instructors (that intervene at the discretion of the designer) will also use dedicated tools allowing them to follow the tasks undertaken by the learners to evaluate results and to intervene in the learners activities. Our objective is to empower these actors to take decisions and to help them prioritise the need to intervene.
2. *In time* because all the constraints that are going to be imposed on the actors as regards the activity (via a semi-automatic regulation) are the result of an initial specification work (that is the preparation phase). At this stage, the educational designer must define the roles played by different actors, the grouping of actors, the possibilities for communication and the tools offered to different actors, the synchronisation of activities between one another with regard to information sharing and shared processes.

To develop such an environment, we suggest an approach that would allow us to take into account all of these constraints. We explore:

- *a Tool-based approach* that we can summarise as such: What platform could support the activity of the user during the phases of preparation and regulation of the educational activity? What user-interfaces should be proposed to the actors to facilitate their co-operative activities?
- *an Interaction-based approach* to master the co-operative activities that the educational environment must promote,
- *a Method-based approach* whose objective is chiefly to help the designer describe the key elements of a protocol that the educational environment will enforce during the regulation phase.

We consider that these three approaches cannot be studied and implemented in a dissociated manner and incidentally, we agree with current thinking in the field of Co-operative Information Systems (an Information System is co-operative "if it shares goals with other agents in its environment, such as other information systems, human agents and the organisation itself, and contributes positively towards the fulfilment of these common goals... " (De Michelis et al. 1998)). The educational environment that we promote is a co-operative Information System that is composed of:

- *A System facet* whose focus is "how information will be processed and put at the disposal of actors (or at the disposal of the organisation, in general)". In our context, this facet must promote interoperability between the tools put at the disposal of the students or of the instructors whose job is to monitor the educational activity. This is based on sharing Information representing the educational specifications established during the preparation phase.
- *a Co-operation facet* which focuses on the actors involved in the common activity (or process) (Boloni and Marinescu 2000, Bourguin 2000, Lee et al. 2000), how they coordinate their activities to be able to adapt to unforeseen circumstances and modify their methods of work accordingly:
- *An Organisational facet* whose focus is to maintain consistency with regard to its educational objectives, its conditions of interaction, ... In general this facet is defined through the system specifications but in our context, such a facet must be satisfied and enforced during the regulation of the activity; consequently, this facet is largely dependent on the capacity of technology to implement and regulate such a cooperative Information system. The principal questions concerning this facet are:
    1. Which description language should be used (vocabulary and level of expression of this educational language) to represent the actors, their roles in the activity, the resources they dispose to achieve their goals, the methods of co-operation that are imagined by the educational designer)?

2. How to express the educational rules that govern the regulation of such an environment (Taveter 1999)?

Figure 1. The three facets of an educational environment

At the moment, we try to answer both questions, from the study of the following problem-situation:

1. The educational objective for the learners is to understand the benefits of using styles with Word and to learn how to manage them,
2. The problem-situation consists of producing a Word document composed of several chapters and a table of contents. This document must be produced through the co-operation of several groups and the document must conform to a pre-defined format. These groups must coordinate their activities, exchange productions, ...
3. The obstacle that must be overcome consists of dealing with different levels of title, to associate styles with titles in a style-sheet and to generate the table of contents from these titles.
4. Three groups of students participate in this activity, helped in their tasks by the educational environment (through integrated teaching functions) and a human instructor.
5. The computerised environment is responsible for enforcing the established rules of communication,
6. The computerised environment and the human instructor if necessary can help the students in their consultation of resources (centered on formatting paragraphs, formatting styles, designing style-sheets, generating tables of contents). They must also consolidate the learning of students by undertaking consolidation exercises.

From this we highlight three facets of the educational environment.

3.1 Aspects of organisation/co-operation

The objective is to provide an organisation that allows control of the interactions to be established between the different groups of learners in order to satisfy the educational objectives. The organisation specified by the designer must describe:

- the actors, their roles, their tasks
- the rules that govern the exchange of documents between actors (i.e. the document that group C may send to group A and its format, the fact that group C cannot modify the documents distributed by groups A and B)
- the interaction protocols between the actors (services provided by each actor, actors involved in each interaction, steps to achieve a task).

The organisation must then enforce these specifications of interaction and co-operation and this leads us to deal with the System facet.

3.2 Aspects of organisation/system

The educational designer must be able to describe this organisation in a declarative fashion via a simple language that is precise enough in order that, during the regulation phase, computers are able to enforce the defined rules.

Our current works are focused on the definition of such a language in order to allow a designer to express the rules of interaction between actors (information and resources that can be exchanged). These rules or Educational Partner Agreements (cf. the Trading Partner Agreements that exist to express the rules of interaction with regard to e-business trade (Sachs and Ibbotson 2000) define all the characteristics of possible interactions between actors during the educational activity (including the assistance given by the system or the human instructor). These rules can be expressed at the design level as specifications using a language like the Unified Modeling Language, or at the implementation stage as XML specifications (works in progress in our lab). We have not yet studied how to exploit these XML specifications to control the environment at the regulation stage. Yet, we know from experience that XML is well suited to automatic processing and work led on tpaML and ebxml (Grangard et al. 2000) have shown that these specifications can be used to control interactions, i.e. in e-trade environments.

3.3 Aspects of co-operation/system

In order to support cooperation between actors at the regulation stage, we suggest to use an Object Oriented Database Management System (OODBMS) serving the community with shared information and resources:

- the XML specifications corresponding to EPAs defined by the designer,
- the shared educational resources which are often structured, multimedia and put at the disposal of the actors in order to aid their learning (in our example, the resources are about style sheets, generation of tables of contents, exercises for practice and consolidation).

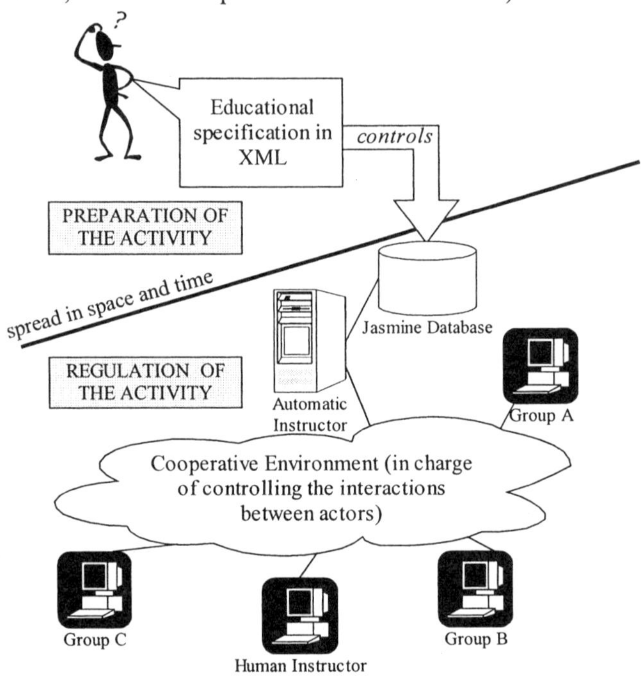

Figure 2. The topology of the system

The OODBMS that we use is Jasmine ('Computer Associates' Trade Mark). One of its advantages is to implement interfaces for different technologies (Corba, COM, ...) useful in our context. One of these interfaces is the XML provider: the XML data is thus seen through the OODBMS just like other resources stored in the database. Then, these data is accessed via a powerful query language that we exploit through Java (McCarthy 1999).

4. CONCLUSION

In this article, we have started to explain that there are educational and technical alternatives to the current Open Distance Learning platforms. We intended to show that it is possible to promote New Information Technology to enhance an educational dialogue:

- in allowing the educational designer to specify the interactions that can be established between actors (learners, groups of learners, instructors, teachers, ...) during an educational activity based on a problem-situation
- in developing a methodological infrastructure and techniques that allow the enforcement of these specifications during the interactions between actors.

In 1991, N. Balacheff questioned himself about the role of computing in education and concluded with his hope that computers could play the role of an educational partner. He wrote (Balacheff 1991): "*the problem of the explanation of a tutor to the teachers, whose subject would be the nature of the apprenticeship and the types of interactions with the learner has not been, until now, studied. Yet, the pedagogues will not accept any partnership with a machine unless such a machine can communicate through a didactic language*". We hope that our infrastructure will contribute, when completely implemented, to consolidate this strong idea of N. Balacheff.

REFERENCES

Balacheff, N. (1991) *Contribution de la didactique et de l'épistémologie aux recherches en EIAO*. 13èmes journées francophones sur la Formation Intelligemment Assistée par Ordinateur (FIAO), Genève.

Boloni, D. and Marinescu, D. C. (2000) *An Object-Oriented Framework for Building Collaborative Network Agents Intelligent Systems and Interfaces*. A. Kandel, K. Hoffmann, D. Mlynek, and N. H. Teodorescu (eds.), Kluewer Publishing House.

Bourguin, G. (2000) *Un support informatique à l'activité coopérative fondé sur la Théorie de l'Activité: le projet DARE*. Doctorat de l'Université de Lille, (n° ordre: 2753).

McCarthy, B. and Cassady-Dorion, L. (1999) *Java Distributed Objects: the Authoritative Solution*. SAMS Publishing.

De Michelis, G. et al. (1998) Cooperative Information Systems: a manifesto. In *Cooperative Information Systems: Trends & Directions*, M. P. Papazoglou and G. Schlageter (eds.), Academic-Press, New York, pp. 315-363.

Dillenbourg, P. (1999) *What do you mean by Collaborative Learning?* Collaborative Learning: Cognitive and Computational approaches. Elsevier Science, Oxford.

George, S. and Leroux, P. (2001) *Splach: Project Based Learning as a Basis for a CSCL Environment: an example in Educational Robotics*. European Conference on Computer-Supported Collaborative Learning Euro-CSCL2001, Maastricht, Netherlands.

Grangard, J. A. et al. (2000) *Electronic Business XML (ebXML)*. Technical Architecture Specification.

Lee, F. L., Liang, S. and Chan, T.-W. (2000) An attempt to design Synchronous Collaborative Learning Environments for Dyad Peers on the World Wide Web. *Journal of Educational Research*, vol. 21 (2), pp. 221-253.

Lotus (1998) *Learning Space: solutions for anytime learning*. Lotus Development Corporation Strategic White Paper.

Marquesuzaa, C. (1998*) OMAGE: Outils et Méthode pour la spécification des connaissances au sein d'un Atelier de Génie Educatif.* Thèse de Doctorat de l'Université de Pau et des Pays de l'Adour (n° ordre: 412).

Mucchielli, R. (2000*) La dynamique des groupes: processus d'influence et de changement dans la vie affective des groupes.* ESF Editeur.

Nodenot, T. (1995) What if the pedagogues specified Educational Software? In *Conference Proceedings WCCE'95: sixth IFIP World Conference on Computers in Education*, J. D. Tinsley and T. J. van Weert (eds.), North Holland Publications, Birmingham, UK.

Sachs, M. and Ibbotson, J. (2000) *Electronic Trading-Partner Agreement for E-Commerce (tpaML).* Pre-submission Draft, version 1.0.3, IBM corporation.

Soller, A., Linton, F., Goodman, B. and Lesgold, A. (1999) Toward Intelligent Analysis and Support of Collaborative Learning Interaction. In *Proceedings of the Ninth International Conference on Artificial Intelligence in Education*, Le Mans, France.

Tardif, J. (1997) *Pour un enseignement stratégique: l'apport de la psychologie cognitive.* Les éditions LOGIQUES.

Taveter, K. (1999) *Business Rules approach to the Modelling, Design and Implementation of Agent Oriented Information Systems.* CaiSE Workshop on Agent Oriented Information Systems (AOIS'99), Heidelberg.

BIOGRAPHY

Thierry Nodenot is senior lecturer in computer science at the Institute of Technology of Bayonne (France) and responsible of a master of science in Multimedia Applications Engineering. He carries out his research at the Liuppa Laboratory in a group called Information Systems and Learning. His works dedicated to the Educational Technology focus Methods and Tools to promote and operate Problem-based (co-operative) Learning and Teaching.

12

Towards Interoperable and Reusable Learning Environments

Luis Anido, Martin Llamas and Mancel J. Fernández
Área de Ingeniería Telemática, Depto. Tecnologías de las Comunicaciones, ETSI Telecomunicación, University of Vigo, Campus Universitario s/n, E-36200 Vigo, Spain
lanido@ait.uvigo.es

Keywords: authoring tools, courseware, lab-ware, CBT, ODL

Abstract: Learning technology standardisation is one of the key activities in the field of computer-based education. Eventually, this standardisation process will support resource sharing and interoperability. This paper presents an up-to-date survey on this process, and then discusses our contribution to it. We have defined a distributed software architecture built on the CORBA middleware platform. The provided functionality is made available through software interfaces defined according to existing recommendations and standards on e-learning. The architecture discussed can be implemented using traditional CORBA objects or CORBA Component Model (CCM) components.

1. INTRODUCTION

Computer-based learning platforms are usually developed *ad-hoc* to meet the requirements of a particular institution. Heterogeneous systems appear with no interoperability mechanism among them. Courses developed for a particular system cannot be reused by a different one. The students' performance profiles, as stored by a specific system, cannot be read or managed by a different educational platform. An evident interoperability problem exists in learning technology. A learning technology standardisation process has been started to overcome this heterogeneity problem.

Most computer-based learning systems share some common functionality usually implemented from the scratch by each of them. The existence of reusable software elements to implement that functionality in a generic way would drastically reduce the time needed to develop a new computer-based educational system. The open definition of the interfaces provided by each component contributes to the interoperability among different systems and the standardisation process of learning technologies. Our work is mainly focused on this field. The first part of this paper is outlines the current trends in learning technology standardisation. The second part presents a CORBA (OMG 2001) architecture to develop scalable learning platforms making use of agreed recommendations on learning resources

2. INTEROPERABILITY

The main contributors to the learning technology standardisation are the following: IEEE's Learning Technology Standardisation Committee (LTSC 2001); IMS Global Learning Consortium (IMS 2001); Aviation Industry CBT Committee (AICC 2001); US Department of Defense's Advanced Distributed Learning initiative (ADL 2001); Alliance of Remote Instructional Authoring and Distribution Networks for Europe project (ARIADNE 2001); Getting Educational Systems Talking Across Leading Edge Technologies (GESTALT 2001); PROmoting Multimedia access to Education and Training in EUropean Society (PROMETEUS 2001); European Committee for Standardization Information Society Standardization System, Learning Technologies Workshop (CEN/ISSS/LT) (CEN 2001); and, Gateway to Educational Materials project (GEM 2001).

The IEEE's LTSC is the institution that is actually gathering recommendations and proposals from other learning standardisation institutions and projects. Specifications that have been approved by the IEEE go through a more rigorous process to become ANSI or ISO standards. In fact, a new ISO/IEC JTC1 Standards Committee for Learning Technologies, SC36 (JTC1 2001), was approved in November 1999. Below we present the main outcomes of these standardisation efforts obtained so far.

2.1 Metadata for learning resources

The learning metadata definition area has been one of the main activities for the learning standardisation community during the last few years. Metadata is just data about data, in this case, data about educational data and resources. The purposes of these definitions are, among others: to allow humans to search, evaluate, acquire and use learning objects, to enable sharing and exchanging of learning objects across any technology-supported learning system, let computer agents to automatically and dynamically compose personalised lessons for an individual learner, to enable educational institutions to express educational content and performance standards in a standardised format that is independent of the content itself. In short, it aims at the standardisation of learning resource description.

Important outcomes have been already delivered. One of the main contributors to this effort is the IEEE LTSC's (LTSC 2001) Learning Objects Metadata (LOM) working group. The LOM specification describes learning content cataloguing information. Relevant properties of learning objects include type of object, author, owner, terms of distribution, format, teaching or interaction style, grade, level, mastery level and prerequisites. The structured approach to metadata definition implies that the actual data elements of a learning resource are grouped into meaningful categories. The base LOM scheme consists of nine such categories: General, Lifecycle, Meta-metadata, Technical, Educational, Rights, Relation, Annotation and Classification.

LOM metadata is becoming a *de-facto* standard among the e-learning community. However, this specification is the result of the effort of many contributors, among them, the European ARIADNE project (ARIADNE 2001) and the IMS project (IMS 2001) stand out. ARIADNE uses LOM version 3.8, to which it contributed significantly, to index and exploit its network of interconnected knowledge pools (KPS). The IMS Learning Resources Metadata Specifications (August 1999) is directly based on the IEEE's LOM with some changes based on implementation testing and detailed document reviews by the IMS Technical Board, which will probably be incorporated into the IEEE specifications. The IMS metadata specification identifies a minimum set of IEEE metadata elements called the IMS core (19 out of 86 LOM elements). The remaining IEEE metadata elements form the IMS Standard Extension Library, SEL, (67 out of 86 LOM elements). The IMS has also completed a survey to identify taxonomies and vocabularies, which can be used as *values* for the defined metadata elements.

The DoD's ADL (ADL 2001) Sharable Courseware Object Reference Model, applies the IEEE/IMS definitions to the three components of the SCORM model: raw media, content and courses. Other system that has extended the LOM definition is (GESTALT 2001), which delivered its own metadata specification: GEMSTONES. The main extensions of LOM include external rights management and the improvement of the quality of service description. GEMSTONES are used by the GESTALT brokerage service to locate learning resources. The Gateway to Educational Materials

(GEM 2001) system also provides a brokerage service based on extensions of Dublin Core (DC 2001).

2.2 Learner records and profiles

Description of learner's profiles and records has also been studied in order to deliver recommendations on standards that allow the exchange of student data. The IEEE LTSC's (LTSC 2001) Public and Private Information (PAPI) specification describes portable and implementation-independent learner records. Learner records are organised into six major categories: personal, preference, performance, portfolio information, relations and security. They describe information about learners, about their technical, learning and physical preferences, about learners history and about their current works. Based on PAPI, the IMS (IMS 2001) Enterprise Data Model Specification (January 2000) is aimed at administrative services that need to share data about learners, courses, performance, etc., across platforms, Operating Systems, user interfaces and so on. This data model is supported through the use of three data objects: *person*, *group* and *group membership*.

2.3 Course structure formats

The US Department of Defense ADL initiative (ADL 2001), as part of its SCORM model, has identified an XML-based representation of a course structure format (CSF) that can be used to define all course elements, structure and external references necessary to move a course from one system to another. It is not course packaging, as the course structure format is just one (albeit very important) of the elements needed to move a course from a given system to another one. CSF describes a course using three groups of information. The first group, called *globalProperties*, is the data about the overall course. The second, called *block*, defines the structure of the course, and the third group, *objectives*, defines a separate structure for learning objectives with references to course elements within the assignment structure. Course sequencing is defined using prerequisites and completion requirements for *blocks*, *assignable units* and *objectives*. ADL's CSF is derived from the AICC (AICC 2001) file-based content model for course structures, properties, and objectives.

2.4 Course packaging

The IMS project (IMS 2001) is leading the standardisation process in this particular field. The IMS Content & Packaging Specification (March 2000) makes it easier to create reusable learning resources. The key element is the package: an abstract description of a unit of reusable content. A package must provide all files and data needed to transfer the learning resources it embodies from one system to another. It is also possible to aggregate a package into a higher level one. The two components of a package are the *manifest* file and the *physical resources*. The *manifest* contains a metadata description of the package as a whole, one or more ways of organisation of the content, and can include or reference sub-manifests which describe the packages that have been included or referenced. The *physical resources* are a collection of resources physically included within a package.

2.5 Questions and tests interoperability

In February 2000, the IMS project has delivered the first specification on questions and test interoperability. It addresses the need to share test items and other assessment tools across different systems, and describes the data structures needed to provide interoperability between questions and test systems, particularly those that are Internet-based. The specification also defines a taxonomy that describes a set of response types and different forms for each of them.

2.6 Learning run time environments

Regarding the specification of concrete run time environments, the work by the AICC (AICC 2001) and the DoD's ADL (ADL 2001) stand out. The AICC guidelines for interoperability of Computer-Managed Instruction (CMI) systems and the ADL's SCORM based on the AICC specifications, deal with a common problem: in the past, authoring systems made the customer a captive of his own CMI system. In order to avoid this dependence between CMIs and CBTs (contents), a standard approach is defined to allow a single CMI system to initiate lessons from different CBT vendors. To accomplish this function, CMI and CBT must communicate by means of standard types of data: data from CMI to CBT to start the lesson, data from a CBT system to CMI needed to record student performance and assign the next learning unit, and data needed for evaluation of a lesson such as item response data, simulation performance data, etc.

Additionally, the GESTALT project (GESTALT 2001) identifies a run time architecture made up of components from previous ACTS projects: GAIA, Renaissance and Prospect. Business objects comprising the interfaces among the various software components within the GESTALT architecture are identified. Middleware solutions were used for this purpose: DCOM (DCOM 2001) for interfaces among systems to be run in the same institution and CORBA (CEN 2001) for those interfaces among systems from different institutions.

3. A CORBA-BASED FRAMEWORK

So far, the most outstanding results in the learning technologies standardisation area are from learning metadata, definitions of learner records and models, and course structure formats. Standardisation of the software that supports Computer-Managed Instruction or Learning Management Systems is more difficult to cope with. The next step should be to provide software that could be easily reused. Open interfaces would also allow interoperability at run time, even among systems from different institutions, to share not only learning resources, but also learning services. The AICC/ADL run time environments provide a clear and precise definition for the interfaces needed to manage educational resources. However, their interfaces do not describe a complete learning environment. GESTALT copes with the whole learning environment. They compose such kind of environment from the outcomes of three previous projects. Therefore, they only define interfaces between those elements belonging to different former projects. A greater level of detail and interfaces among objects from the same project are required. We need an interface definition as precise and detailed as the provided by AICC/ADL run time environments. But we also need to cover the whole learning spectrum, from the interaction between the learning contents and their management systems to a suitable location and brokerage tool for learning resources. We intend to define those interfaces using the CORBA (OMG 2001) technology.

We have defined a prospective CORBA domain interface to develop distributed learning environments using reusable elements instead of starting from scratch. These components have open interfaces that allow other objects, even from different systems, to access their services. In addition, the learning resources managed and delivered could be easily reused and localised as international format and metadata standards are used. Thus, interoperability both at business-logic and data level is achieved.

3.1 CORBA Middleware

CORBA (OMG 2001) is an object-based distributed architecture that allows distributed and heterogeneous applications to interoperate on a network. CORBA is a standard defined by more than 800 institutions that form the Object Management Group (OMG). Nowadays, the hot topic for the OMG is the definition of high level services, clearly oriented to a particular business domain. Examples of already existing domain interfaces are in the areas of Telecommunications, Manufacturing, Finance and Healthcare. They identify the objects needed, and their interfaces, in those domains to cover the needs of a wide range of requirements. Different vendors may change the implementation but the functionality is the same thanks to the agreed interface. Thus, CORBA domain interfaces contribute to the interoperability among systems. In addition, the OMG is an open consortium with no ties with particular software platforms or programming languages. Therefore, we chose CORBA as our middleware framework among other available options (e.g. DCOM (DCOM 2001)).

3.2 Distributed architecture for learning environments

The CORBA-based architecture for interoperable learning environments that we propose is outlined in Figure 1. Object interfaces are used as the basis for a computer-based education domain interface. Clients access learning services, through standard CORBA communication mechanisms, using the interfaces provided by *Learning Server Objects*. Two different interfaces have been defined: an AICC/ADL run time compliant interface and our Standard Run-time Interface (SRI). The latter defines standard mechanisms to interact with a learning environment (e.g. login, course index, next unit, previous unit, next assignment, etc.) and advanced features like predictive navigation (the object evaluates which learning resources are more likely to be requested next and sends them to the client side if their prerequisites were already fulfilled).

Navigation Manager objects could impose particular navigation sequences based on designer criteria and/or students' performance. So far, we defined interfaces for the AICC/ADL Course Structure Format (CSF) and a basic hierarchical structure with no prerequisites. *Learning Server Objects* use these interfaces to evaluate the next learning unit to be sent to a student, to check the prerequisites to access a unit or to resume student status in a particular course from stored data about previous learning sessions.

Students' performance tracking is done by Student Trackers who receive information from Learning Server Objects through Student Tracking channels based on the CORBA event service. Trackers are responsible for storing tracking information and providing later access to it. AICC-compliant and PAPI-compliant interfaces have been already defined. Performance Information at a higher level becomes grading information. Trackers report Administration objects whenever they detect students have fulfilled all needed requisites to pass a course. A CORBA event channel, Student Grading, is used to send this information from Trackers to Administration Objects, which update students' records. So far, administrative data are stored, accessed and managed using a PAPI-compliant interface. Learning Server Objects may use PAPI preference information to fit their behaviour to each student.

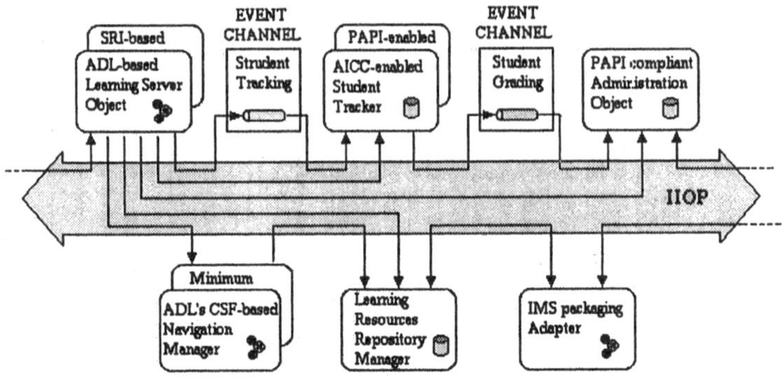

Figure 1. A CORBA-based architecture for Interoperable Learning Environments

The Learning Resources Repository Manager is responsible for making transparent for the rest of the system the particular storage mechanism. Both learning contents and metadata is stored by this object and accessed through it. The IMS Packaging Adapter defines through its interface operations to create and aggregate learning packages using the IMS packaging specification. It also provides operations to extract packaged data. These services are accessed following CORBA standard mechanisms. Defined objects do not impose restrictions regarding their physical location. They may run all of them in the same computer or distributed over a local network or over the Internet. Communication mechanisms are based on IIOP protocol that relies on TCP/IP standard protocol.

3.3 Definition using the CORBA components model

Defined objects could be implemented following the forthcoming CORBA Components Model (CCM) (OMG 2001), which is part of the CORBA 3.0 specification. The CCM extends the traditional CORBA object model by defining features and services that allow application programmers to implement, manage, configure and deploy software components that integrate commonly used CORBA services. The CCM standard not only enables greater software reuse but it also provides greater flexibility for dynamic configuration of CORBA applications. A component is a basic CORBA meta-type that can be referenced by multiple object references. Components can also interact with external entities through a rich set of port mechanisms. The architecture presented in Figure 1 can be implemented through a components model as shown in Figure 2 (the figure uses the CCM graphic symbols (OMG 2001)).

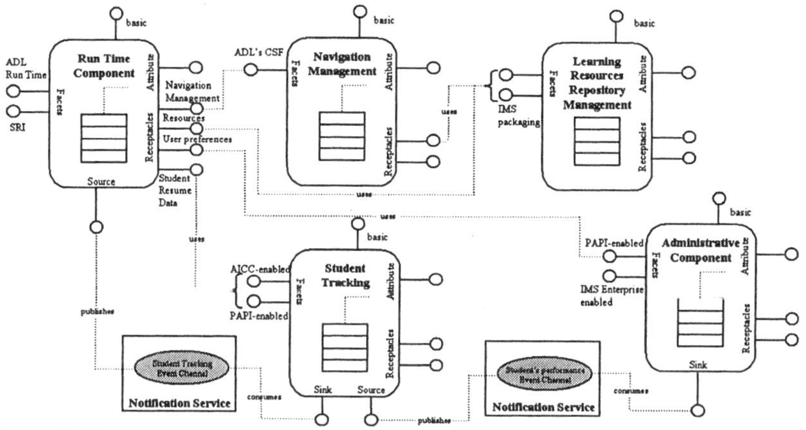

Figure 2. CORBA Components Model for the interoperable and reusable learning architecture

In this case, the same component offers different facets to provide the same functionality that was implemented by different objects in the traditional CORBA model. Communication among components is directly carried out through receptacles and event sources/sinks. These features, together with the deployment capabilities offered by the CCM, seems to make it a suitable framework to develop this kind of distributed systems. Unfortunately, at the time of this writing no CORBA implementation supports the CCM.

4. CONCLUSIONS

The CORBA architecture for computer-based learning allows the development and the deployment of distributed learning systems using reusable software elements. Scalability is fully provided because objects can be installed individually and later connected to other components to provide a more refined functionality (e.g. simple or performance-based navigation, single or federated searches, etc.). Developers do not need to start from scratch because defined objects are reusable. Therefore, the development and deployment process is improved and can be carry out quicker. The use of the CCM will notably improve the reusability of the defined objects (components). We present object interfaces as open definitions for object behaviours that, together with the use of internationally agreed formats for learning data and metadata (an up-to-date survey on this area appears in the first part of this paper) make our model a full interoperable framework for distributed computer-based learning systems. This leads to the possibility of using these interfaces as a new CORBA domain interface. Currently, we are also defining the interfaces for a learning brokerage system. This CORBA-based search tool allows one to locate, evaluate and retrieve educational resources.

REFERENCES

ADL (2001) DoD's Advanced Distributed Learning. [http://www.adlnet.org] 23.4.2001.
AICC (2001) Aviation Industry CBT Committee. [http://www.aicc.org] 23.4.2001.
ARIADNE (2001) ARIADNE. [http://ariadne.unil.ch] 23.4.2001.
CEN (2001) CEN/ISSS/LT. [http://www.cenorm.be/isss/Workshop/lt/] 23.4.2001.
DC (2001) Dublin Core metadata. [http://purl.org/dc/] 23.4.2001.
DCOM (2001) Microsoft's Distributed COM (DCOM). [http://www.microsoft.com/com/tech/dcom.asp] 23.4.2001.
GEM (2001) GEM project. [http://www.geminfo.org] 23.4.2001.
GESTALT (2001) GESTALT. [http://www.fdgroup.co.uk/gestalt] 23.4.2001.
IMS (2001) IMS Global Learning Consortium. [http://www.imsproject.org] 23.4.2001.
JTC1 (2001) ISO-IEC JTC1 SC36. [http://www.jtc1sc36.org] 23.4.2001.
LTSC (2001) IEEE's LTSC. [http://ltsc.ieee.org] 23.4.2001.
OMG (2001) OMG's CORBA. [http://www.omg.org] 23.4.2001.
PROMETEUS (2001) PROMETEUS. [http://prometeus.org] 23.4.2001.

BIOGRAPHY

Luis Anido works at the Telecommunication Engineering Faculty of the University of Vigo where he is working towards his PhD. His main areas of interest are the standardisation of learning technologies and distributed computing.

13

Virtual Portfolios

Lessons Learned from Four Years of Implementation

Eugene S. Takle, Elsebeth K. Sorensen, Michael R. Taber and Douglas Fils
Department of Agronomy and Department of Geological and Atmospheric Sciences, Iowa State University, Ames, Iowa 50011, USA
gstakle@iastate.edu
Department of Communication, Aalborg University, Kroghstraede 3, DK-9220 Aalborg Oest, Denmark.
Department of Earth Sciences, University of Northern Colorado, Greeley, CO 80631, USA
Department of Physics, Iowa State University, Ames, Iowa, 50011, USA

Keywords: pedagogy, collaborative learning, higher education, self-assessment, communication

Abstract: We have developed virtual portfolios as structures that help students organise knowledge and the knowledge-building process in virtual environments. These online portfolios allow learners to easily navigate their virtual learning space, collaborate at many levels, and acquire a heightened level of awareness of (inter)actions in the virtual learning environment. We report our experiences over the last 4 years in using virtual portfolios for enhancing the learning process in an American university course in global environmental change. Examples are given of how students respond to different functional capabilities offered within the virtual portfolio and to different requirements for evaluating student performance.

1. INTRODUCTION

The Internet is being used more frequently for educational support, not only in continuous and lifelong learning, but also as an alternative method in higher education (Bates 1999, Harasim 1999). The obvious advantages of this platform include enhanced flexibility and time and space independent organization of the learning process within higher education (Harasim 1999).

The availability of this promising and flexible potential as a platform for design and management of virtual learning processes, does not, however, guarantee that it will be used, – or the quality of its use. The need for a significantly enlarged range of design and delivery structures has become evident (Kaye 1993, Collis 1996). Implementation structures that support learners' navigation, interaction and collaboration at many levels in the virtual world (Sorensen 1997) are both possible and essential. The virtual portfolio is an example of one such structure that helps the organisation of knowledge and knowledge building (Stahl 1999) for the learner in supporting the process of awareness and the processes of (inter)-actions in the virtual learning space (Sorensen et al. 2000).

This paper addresses the structuring potential of virtual portfolios for web-based learning. It reports on 4 years of experience in using this tool in a web-based American course on global environmental change, as a means of creating and structuring collaborative and individual spaces throughout the learning process.

In section 2 the virtual portfolio and its potential for supporting web-based learning are described. We also provide a brief summary of the course context in which we have implemented the portfolio. Section 3 provides a description of the various types of portfolios we have used, and section 4 gives some quantitative results documenting student performance characteristics under different implementations. We summarise our experiences in section 5.

2. CONTEXT FOR IMPEMENTING PORTFOLIOS

We first provide our definition of an online portfolio and give a brief outline of the context in which it is implemented.

2.1 Definition

A general short definition of an online portfolio is: A structured image over time of a process of development (Sorensen et al. 2000). In more specific terms, an online learning portfolio may be viewed as a structured collection of items and functionalities developed under a reflective process that represents and demonstrates knowledge, skill, abilities, personality, processes, and learning experiences that may be used to serve various learning and professional purposes.

A virtual portfolio, therefore, may serve as a structuring tool for managing a growing multitude of components of the learning processes. It may have the form of an individual portfolio, built and functioning from the perspective of the individual learner or the learning assistant (instructor, teacher, mentor, curriculum advisor). Or it may be deployed as a group portfolio for structuring the collaborative activities of a group of learners (collaborating students in a course or team of researchers). Any instructional approach in learning can be implemented in the portfolio. Consequently, the extent to which an online portfolio enhances learning is, to a large extent, dependent on the implemented instructional approach and its assumed criteria of quality in the learning process.

2.2 Context of experience: 'Global Change'

The Global Change (GC) course has been taught for 12 years at Iowa State University and has been on the web with interactive dialog since 1995. The course addresses environmental changes of global and regional scale that threaten to disturb and degrade natural and managed ecosystems and ultimately human health and welfare. Although presently an on-campus course, GC was established with the vision that ultimately it should be delivered globally to address environmental problems that span national and continental borders. This would require engaging students asynchronously over the web from a wide range of cultures, languages, and educational traditions, to search for multi-national solutions to global environmental problems. Therefore, the course was structured from its onset with a vision toward virtual interactions in support of learning environments.

Student virtual portfolios (see Figure 1), introduced into the course in 1997 (Taber et al. 1997), allowed students to better manage their interaction in and through the course. An instructor portfolio introduced the same year allows the instructor to more intensively interact with the student as guide in the learning process. The course, including materials entered by the instructor and materials and public discussion entered by students, was structured to be an organically growing database (much of which is contributed by students) that offers students an increasingly rich body of learning resources for each subsequent offering of the course.

3. USE OF PORTFOLIOS IN GLOBAL CHANGE

Students register for both individual and group portfolios in support of their interactions in the course.

3.1 Individual student portfolios

Students manage their interaction with the course through their personal portfolios. The portfolio has a calendar function that gives students the assignments that are due each day and a record of their assignments submitted. Quizzes they are required to take with each learning unit are accessed from the portfolio. Students use personal portfolios to archive all their electronic submissions, instructor's grades and comments, and responses of other students, faculty, or others to electronic dialog comments. Students' reviews of research papers are posted on the web and linked where appropriate to learning narratives. A 'message of the day' allows the instructor to quickly communicate with all students through their personal portfolios. From their individual portfolios, students manage their interactions (a) publicly in the general dialog, (b) privately with other students in group portfolios they share with other members of small groups, and (c) privately with the instructor through which they submit their self assessments and dialog with the instructor on the evaluation and assessment processes.

The course was divided into three five-week blocks with each block having nearly identical elements to be assessed (e.g., quizzes, response to ethical question, response to a broad-topic question, self assessment of writing quality, etc.). By observing student performance on three successive and identical assessment blocks, the instructor can observe the student's learning *process* as well as individual learning *products*. The individual portfolio structure is replicated for each block to provide the student with a "new slate" from which to begin anew after having reflected over and having been assessed by the instructor on the previous block.

3.2 Group portfolios

The Global Change course has used two implementations of group portfolios, serving two different purposes.

3.2.1 Group portfolio for collaborative knowledge building

The first type of group portfolio provides workspaces for small groups of students to interact privately and write a common document summarizing various elements of a particular learning unit (e.g., lecture and its supporting online materials and student discussion on the topic). Teams of 3-4 students were established to take notes of class discussion and instructor comments during the regular 50-minute class meetings. These students met electronically through a group portfolio and produced a document summarizing all materials relevant to that topic. This document is subsequently was posted on the web, with contributing group members as authors, as a contribution to the growing database for that particular topic. Group portfolios were private to the group and even the instructor did not have access to them. Only those students of the group that participated in the construction of the online document are acknowledged on the web as co-authors.

3.2.2 Group portfolio as laboratory for collaborative experiments

A second type of portfolio was used in conjunction with an experimental laboratory for the course. This portfolio provided an electronic workspace from which teams of students could collectively design and run experiments, archive results and develop reports summarizing results from numerical experiments of authentic simulation of plants interacting with atmospheric and soil environments. For this implementation, teams of 3-4 students were assigned portfolios for sharing results of numerical experiments and collectively (albeit asynchronously) analysing, interpreting, and reporting results. In this way, students act in roles of professional researchers working as a research team, a time-honoured method for creating new knowledge. The students met physically to get started on the experiments and then managed their interaction remotely. Interpretation and report writing were done as a team effort and submitted electronically.

3.2.3 Instructor portfolio

An instructor portfolio was designed to enable the instructor to view student records of quiz scores and dialog submitted under various topics. The instructor had the option to view entries of all students for a given assignment or chronological entries of a single student for all assigned tasks. The latter form of display was particularly useful for two reasons: an overview scan of the entire record gives a complete picture of a particular student's contribution over the evaluation period. This allows the instructor to see the range of topics on which the student had written and gives a general overview of the student's writing capabilities and interests. Secondly, the concatenation of all writing for the evaluation period allows the instructor to observe progress in achieving stated goals for the online dialog. The instructor can observe the impact of recommendations to the student by having permanent and shared access to 'before' and 'after' products of the student. Space also was provided for instructor-student dialog on student self assessment and instructor evaluation thereof.

4. IMPACT OF IMPLEMENTION

Student online dialogue is a very important element of the GC course as discussed in section 2. Virtual portfolios facilitate implementation of alternative pedagogical strategies for the use of dialog. For instance, when the GC course was first established on the web in 1995 with dialog encouraged but only voluntary, the volume of comments was relatively low and the quality rather superficial (with some notable exceptions). When virtual portfolios were introduced in 1997 we began to put requirements on the dialog such as a minimum number of entries and eventually a demonstration of higher-order reasoning. Although new topics have been added over time, a sufficiently large common set of topics provides a useful database of student-generated materials for analysis of how students respond to different learning opportunities and imposed conditions. Table 1 shows how the number of comments per student in the second 5-week period of the course changed over the years in response to these changes in pedagogy. Evidently the more stringent requirements stimulated a substantially higher volume of comments.

Table 1. Number of on-campus students (A) enrolled in the Global Change course since 1995, mean number of comments per student (B) in each learning unit (covering material equivalent to one lecture), and mean number of comments per student (C) in one assessment cycle (covering 15 learning units)

Year	1995	1996	1997	1998	1999	2000
A	32	31	32	33	26	45
B	0.069	0.106	0.350	0.390	0.320	0.480
C	1.0	1.6	5.3	5.9	4.8	7.2

In the first two 5-week periods (assessment cycles) of the 2000 offering of the course, students were struggling to learn to use the higher-order reasoning requirements in their online dialog. By the third assessment cycle, students had fully grasped the intent and characteristics of these requirements and posted more and substantially higher quality comments. We took a random sample of 10 comments from dialog for three different years and made a subjective judgement of the quality of the comments and also did a word count on each comment. Mean values shown in Table 2 indicate an increase in quality and an increase by a factor of 26 in the size of each comment. The use of three assessment cycles within the virtual portfolio with all materials archived allows the instructor in online counselling of individual students to point to specific deficiencies and improvements or lack thereof from cycle to cycle.

Table 2. Mean subjective evaluation of comment quality and mean number of words per comment in 10 comments randomly drawn from dialog in three different years in the Global Change course

Year	Quality (0-10)	Number words/comment
1995	4.4	88
1997	3.2	93
2000	5.3	2,505

For the course offered in 2000, students were required to post 5 comments per cycle, including 3 responses to other student comments. Additionally, they were required to elicit 3 comments from other students to receive full credit. Table 3 shows that students went far beyond minimum requirements on number of comments and somewhat above the minimum on other categories.

Table 3. Number of comments made per student, number of comments in response to other student comments, and number of comments received from other students in the third assessment cycle for the course offered in 2000

Comment type	Number
Mean total comments per student	9.3
Mean number responses to others	3.2
Mean number responses received	3.2

From these experiences we assert that the portfolio facilitates direct implementation of desired pedagogies and adds pedagological value to conventional teaching tools. It can be used to implement assessment cycles to allow assessment of learning *process* as well as learning *products* and promote pedagological goals such as good writing and higher-level critical thinking skills.

5. SUMMARY

The personal portfolio provides the student with an electronic home from which to link to web course material, to archive their own learning products, to link privately to other students in collaborative learning experiences and to the instructor for assessment and feedback in the learning process. Careful structuring through virtual portfolios supports and adds quality to both virtual learning and virtual instruction through enhanced overview of the learning process and content, increased clarity of learning expectations, and individual and collaborative spaces for learning activities and self-reflection (Sorensen et al. 2000). It also helps support smooth flow and contextual organisation of ideas, despite separate and distinctly different historical educational traditions of participants.

From our experience we have gained insight on how students respond to different functional capabilities offered within the virtual portfolio and to different requirements for evaluating student performance. As a result of our aim at supporting collaborative learning among students, we have explored the challenges implied in the establishment and maintenance of peer discussion and interaction, as well as the instructional aspects of judging the quality of such group interaction and dialogue as components of the collaborative knowledge building process.

REFERENCES

Bates, A. W. (1999) *Managing Technological Change: Strategies for Academic Leaders*. Jossey Bass, San Francisco.

Collis, B. (1996) *Tele-learning in a Digital World*. International Thomson Computer Press, London.

Harasim, L. (1999) *The Virtual-U Field Trials*. Lessons about Teaching and Learning Online.

Kaye, A. R. (1992) Learning Together Apart. In *Collaborative Learning Through Computer Conferencing*, A. R. Kaye (ed.), NATO ASI Series, Volume 90, Springer-Verlag, pp. 1-24.

Sorensen. E. K. (1997) *Learning in Virtual Contexts. Navigation, Interaction, and Collaboration*. Ph.d. Thesis, Aalborg University, Danmark.

Sorensen, E. K., Takle, E. S., Taber, M. R. and Fils, D. (2000) CSCL: Structuring the past, present and future through virtual portfolios. In *Learning in Virtual Environments*. L. Dirckinck-Holmfeld and B. Fibiger (eds.), Samfundslitteratur, Copenhagen.

Stahl, G. (1999) Reflections on WebGuide: Seven issues for the next generation of collaborative knowledge-building environments. In *Proceedings of the Computer Support for Collaborative Learning (CSCL) 1999 Conference*. C. M. Hoadley and J. Roschelle (eds.), Stanford University, Palo Alto, CA, pp. 600-610. (Available from Lawrence Erlbaum Associates, Mahwah, NJ), [http://kn.cilt.org/cscl99/A73/A73.HTM].

Taber, M. R., Takle, E. S. and Fils, D. (1997) Use of the internet for student self-managed learning. In *Preprints, Sixth Symposium on Education*. Long Beach, CA. American Meteorological Society, Boston, MA.

BIOGRAPHY

Eugene S. Takle is professor of atmospheric science and professor of agricultural meteorology. His research focuses on numerical simulation of regional climate change and turbulent flow through vegetation in heterogeneous agroecosystems. He is interested in bridging the gap between scientific research using numerical simulation tools and use of authentic simulation models as tools for learning. His collaboration with Professor Sorensen focuses on carrying these interests into the virtual learning environment.

14

Virtual Schools
Revolution in Pedagogy and Technology

Jun Jo and Neil Russell
Griffith University, Gold Coast Campus, PMB 50 Gold Coast Mail Centre, Queensland 9726, Australia
J.Jo@mailbox.gu.edu.au

Keywords: virtual school, future, catalyst for change, learner-centred learning, pedagogy

Abstract: This paper explores the question of whether 'virtual' schooling is a realistic concept and faces the challenging question of whether computers will replace teachers. A possible scenario of future school education is described, and economic, technological and social factors that might encourage or hinder such a change are considered. Recent developments in video streaming technology are reviewed and the use of video streaming technology related to the viability of virtual schools concepts. Implications are drawn for students, teachers and teacher educators relating to the concept of virtual schools.

1. A SCENARIO OF SCHOOL EDUCATION IN 2010

Jenny, who is 15, attends classes at a secondary school for two days a week. This morning, she will have lessons in English, Mathematics and Japanese, and in the afternoon she will participate in sport. The morning lessons all involve networked computers. The school has purchased complete curriculum packages from a private commercial supplier, and these are delivered over the World Wide Web using real time video streaming technology. The curriculum package is directly related to the State Education Department outcomes based syllabus. Completed work is sent electronically to a computer service supply company, and forwarded to casual 'fee for service' tutors in the State capital for assessment and return. Work will be assessed in terms of outcomes achieved.

For the other three days of the week, Jenny works from home. The school has offered a computer-based curriculum program to students in exchange for discounted school fees, and Jenny's mother has arranged her part-time work so that she can monitor her daughter's work. An inexpensive internet-capable computer with a desktop video-conferencing camera enables Jenny to complete her schoolwork without leaving the house. Jenny receives lessons prepared and presented by experienced teachers using video-streaming technology.

2. PREDICTING WAYS COMPUTERS WILL BE USED

Attempts to predict the ways in which computers will be used in the future have been notoriously bad, as Denning and Metcalfe (1997) point out. In the application of computers to education, it is likely that those who in an earlier era considered the question of whether computers could replace teachers did so when the connectivity of the 21st century was as yet undeveloped. In the pre-World Wide Web era of the 1980's, when computers were less common in schools and homes, it is not surprising that writers such as Hilbun (1983) and Pheasant (1989) would believe that it was unlikely that computers would replace teachers.

During the 1990's, however, as networked computers became common, two groups could be identified with opposing views. While some teachers defended their role and argued that computers could be seen as a vital component of the teaching process, some critics saw traditional school education as flawed, inefficient and dated. In this understanding of schooling, schools and teachers are seen as redundant because they belong to an inefficient industrial age. Tiffin and Rajasingham (1995) argue that schools are currently designed for an industrial society rather than one based on information, while Perelman maintains that "the classroom and the teacher have as much place in tomorrow's learning enterprise as the horse and buggy have in modern transportation." (1992, p.19). While the debate between traditional educators and their critics is necessarily constrained by the technology and the context in which they live, it is also affected by broader events over time. A historical overview of workers' opposition to machines that threatened to displace them provides a useful perspective.

3. IMPROVEMENTS IN THE MECHANISM: HISTORICAL ANTECEDENTS

It is clear that there are a number of reasons why a new technology might be opposed. In the early stages, the innovation may be seen as impractical, expensive, or unsafe. However, a continuing theme is that of resistance by groups who see new technology as an economic threat to their livelihood. Sometimes, those who saw themselves as threatened ran a program which reminded the public of the disadvantages of the new technology, as the telegraph companies did in the USA when they opposed the introduction of the telephone in the early Twentieth Century (Technological Trends 1937, p. 50).

Historical precedents suggest that, in school education, arguments opposing the replacement of teachers by computers on educational grounds may mask a justifiable fear related to the loss of employment. While educators may advance convincing arguments about the poor quality of computer-delivered education, or the inability of computers to replace key human functions, the issue can be interpreted in terms of two opposing vested interest groups.

The school education sector is one of these interest groups, and it represents a significant number of people who earn their living from traditional schooling, either directly or indirectly. A change involving the replacement of some teachers with computers could mean the end of school as we know it, and in addition to teachers, groups such as clerical and maintenance workers, administrators, and textbook suppliers would have to diversify or accept changed employment conditions.

Opposed to traditional employees in education and related occupations are those who would benefit from technologies which might replace teachers. Principally, this involves those in the IT industry such as hardware and software manufacturers and retailers, providers of online services and curriculum packages, and members of the advertising and media industries.

Reappraisal of school functions, in the context of changing societal expectations, suggests that in addition to the pressures for replacement of teachers by computers, there may be significant changes to teachers' tasks. Those who continue their involvement with children's education may still be referred to as teachers, but what they do in future may be very different from those who have taught in previous eras.

4. REPLACEMENT, DE-SKILLING OR RE-SKILLING?

The discourse arising from the question of teachers being replaced by computers can be seen in terms of a threat to teachers' jobs, and in changes to customary teaching practices, involving both de-skilling and re-skilling. The Luddites had seen themselves as skilled, and were proud of the quality of their work. When they were forced to change their traditional mode of textile work at home for factory life, some traditional skills were lost. Similarly, teachers' change in role from expert to facilitator (ACT Department of Education 1996) could result in the loss of traditional skills central to self-esteem and social and economic value.

Didactic teaching which follows a traditional information transmission model, or networked computers threaten the 'banking' model criticised by Friere (1995). When teachers expertise is based on their knowledge of subject matter, competition from information sources such as the World Wide Web, CD-ROMS and the availability of computers at home may mean that students no longer rely on teachers as their chief information source.

In addition to losing their status as the main providers of information, teachers can also find that the curriculum has been prescribed and provided by an educational authority, and as a consequence, their skills of curriculum design are redundant. Apple and Jungck (1998) provide an example of a computer literacy unit, which did not require a skilled teacher to teach it. The concept of a 'canned curriculum' can be traced back to at least the Sputnik era of the 1950's (Apple 1982), when perceived inadequacies in the American educational system in the Sputnik era led to a perception that teachers could not be trusted with curriculum. As a result, there was an identifiable trend in which curriculum was specified in detail, and textbooks were prescribed which limited teachers' ability to respond to students' needs.

The Internet has created a new and different culture with the 'Computer/Net' generation thinking differently to older generations. It creates the new 'Web life style' (Gates 1999), such as Internet marketing, banking, billing mortgaging, and paying accounts via a credit card. In education, the Internet has the potential to help with different learning styles.

> Some people learn better by reading, some by listening, some by watching someone else do a task, some by doing the task. Most of us learn from some combination of all these methods. And all people have different levels of aptitude and different personalities and life experiences that may motivate them to learn or de-motivate them. A highly motivated student can learn from difficult reading materials, where a poorly motivated student needs accessible materials such as a video to learn.

New software is helping students learn regardless of learning style or pace (Gates 1999, p. 399)

There is also some evidence that students learn many computer applications at home rather than at school, even though some applications are taught in regular classes. In Australia, the Real Time Report (Detya 1999) reported a survey of computer skills of 6213 students in schools across all educational sectors. Although some individual skills had been mostly learned at school, students indicated that a majority of their computer skills had been learned at home.

While computer skills are only a small part of what students are expected to learn at school, it is likely that continuing proliferation of sophisticated software, and the availability of networked computers from home will change what teachers do in classrooms. Although many teachers will remain within the instructional loop, their function will gradually become more of a manager and supervisor. There will still be discussion and assistance with students' learning, but student interaction will increasingly be with a computer rather than a teacher. Consequently, the traditional feedback between teacher and student will be reduced. Administrators who realise that different skills are now required of teachers may consider employing tutors or even using parents or volunteers to supervise the students' learning.

Yet despite concerns that the increased use of computers on schools will lead to the deskilling of teachers, there is also a strong argument in favour of their re-skilling. Students who encounter information overload from the World Wide Web will still need skilled assistance to analyse and synthesise data, and to detect bias and irrelevance. There may be more of a need for differently skilled teachers in the classroom rather than less. Calls by politicians and educators for teachers to undergo professional development in learning technology so that their pedagogy will be more appropriate for the information age reflect a continuing dissatisfaction with teaching practices.

5. TECHNOLOGICAL CHANGE AND TEACHERS

The possibility that computers will replace teachers is also related to the effectiveness with which computers are able to carry out teachers' tasks, although there are certainly other factors to be considered. If extrapolations of existing trends continue uninterrupted, Bell and Gray (1997) predict that by 2047 computers will be at least one hundred thousand times more powerful than they are today, and the factor may indeed be in the billions. Future students are likely to have access to a version of the World Wide

Web, which will be used by many people as part of their everyday life. There should be few problems with accessing interactive websites with full-motion video at home, at school, or from an internet-capable mobile phone. Those elements of teaching practice which are related to the dissemination of information, and even interactivity, is likely to be challenged with such developments as a consequence.

In addition to preparing teaching materials, teachers developing activities for students enrolled in the virtual school will need to understand and deal with various aspects of technology to prepare the computer based learning materials effectively. They will need to develop skills in:

- how to use various formats of multimedia data such as bitmap/vector graphics, 2D images/3D objects, animation/movie, and sound/music
- evaluating options to compress large amounts of data into a file of manageable size without losing its original quality
- deciding what is the best option among all the new technologies to efficiently deliver information to students seamlessly
- managing and analysing an Internet database, to observe students' progress
- tracing and analysing patterns of students' navigation methods and use of teaching materials.

Demands for this new teaching environment have implications for the content and pedagogy of teacher education programs. New approaches for preparing teachers for work in virtual schools could include majors in areas such as multimedia data management in education, Internet Technology in Education, and integrating the use of the Internet across the curriculum.

The use of IT in Education can be segmented into three major parts:

- Authoring
- Delivery of teaching materials
- Developing the Student-computer Interface.

Teachers will need to prepare teaching materials in quite different formats to traditional schooling situations. This change will need to provide students with more flexible and interactive teaching programs. (Perez and Jo 2000). This current research into the preparation of teaching materials for use in virtual schools has indicated that the time taken to prepare useful materials for students to work on is very extensive, particularly when dynamic media such as audio/video are used. In the near future, the authoring environment will become much easier to use, with educators being able to use authoring software in similar ways to the way a word processing program is used currently.

Two crucial limitations in delivering educational materials are the large size of multimedia files and the slow speed of data transmission over the

Internet. To overcome these problems approaches are being developed to deliver multimedia information seamlessly.

In the software development area, various international compression standards in multi-media information, such as MPEG1, MPEG2, and MPEG4 have been developed. Recently a number of multimedia companies such as, Real Networks, Windows and Media Technologies and Apple QuickTime have developed various forms of audio/video streaming technology.

Another approach to improve online delivery is in the hardware area. High bandwidth equipment that is currently available includes ADSL, ISDN, Cable TV line using HFC networks and Satellites using a satellite dish. These high bandwidth options are currently expensive and not practical for most student learning applications. However, these access methods will be more readily available and cost-effective in the near future (Jones et al. 2000). Teachers in the future virtual school should possess enough understanding of the new and evolving technologies therefore, to be able to choose one or a combination of appropriate delivery methods for specific subjects or courses.

Although the User Interface (UI) seems to have evolved at a slower rate compared with the authoring and delivery aspects of the virtual learning environment, the user interface procedure is very important to provide students with efficient and realistic interactions.

One interesting development of UI is the so-called 'Intelligent Interface' Woern (1997). Intelligence in UI means that the interface software, hardware or system can understand the user's behaviours and expectation and helps guide his/her uses. One early example of intelligent interface is the 'auto correction tool' in word processing programs others include speech recognition and techniques that allow the user – system interaction to be adapted to different users.

The types of UI that are available to the students will affect the navigation patterns. Educators will need to be familiar with the new UI technologies and develop teaching materials for them.

6. CUSTODIAL FUNCTION OF SCHOOLS: CHANGING EXPECTATIONS OF EDUCATION

The future may see students using computers from home while their parents supervise them, but this notion runs counter to the expectation that the state or an educational authority supervises students during the day while parents earn a living elsewhere. For this reason, it is likely that the non-compulsory sector of school education, senior high school, will be among the first to trial off-site schooling as an alternative for students. As this mode of learning slowly gains acceptance, it will increasingly become available to other high school students whose parents are prepared to accept it, and finally to primary school students.

Although the movement from traditional classroom-based education may be initially slow, the pace is likely to be accelerated both by the models provided by higher education and the changing nature of societal understandings of schooling.

While primary schools would initially seen to be apart from such considerations, schooling will continue to be changed by their use of computers both at school and at home. The school, which is not connected to the Internet in industrialised countries, is becoming the exception. In the USA, 95% of public schools are connected to the Internet (NCES 2000), and home access to the Internet is also increasing in many countries. As connectivity increases, schools will increasingly place homework and whole units of work on the World Wide Web, where parents can monitor their child's progress and assist with the work. Some parents who accept that networked learning is a valid learning mode may be willing to consider the next step, which is to supervise their child themselves at home.

7. THE VIRTUAL SCHOOL AND THE LATE AGE OF TRADITIONAL SCHOOLING

In Australia, Education Queensland has established a Virtual School concept to enable additional curriculum choice to small, rural and remote schools. (Ewing and Smith 2000). Students can log into the Virtual School via a web page on the State Education Department network and participate in both real time links to their teachers or use online delivery methods. During Virtual School classes, students can interact with teachers using voice communication, sharing documents and accessing resource materials using a Virtual school web site. As students can access the Virtual School from home as well as at school this Virtual School will become a viable option for those parents who want to home school their children. In addition, schools can consider a timetable, which may include several days a week of students working from home.

Additional examples of Virtual Schools can be located without difficulty on the World Wide Web. (Phillips 1998). As virtual schools become more common, the resulting challenge to assumptions about teachers' roles in conventional school classrooms may result in the present era being seen as the Late Age of Schooling. Teachers face turbulent times as they are forced to both re-skill and deskill, while concurrently, a modest increase in computer-related home schooling may lead to some teachers effectively being replaced by computers. A complex mix of economic, technological and social factors will help to determine the future shape of school education.

8. CONCLUSION

The concept of teaching in a virtual school may need a totally different culture to be established compared with those of a traditional school. Multimedia designers can assist teachers to develop activities for students enrolled in the virtual school, but teachers still need to understand and decide on the best options to deliver the curriculum effectively. Hence in order to prepare curriculum materials, teachers will need to understand and decide on the best options to author and deliver the curriculum effectively and the best way for students to interact with it. Fortunately, the rapid development of multimedia authoring tools will enable this aspect of a teacher's professional development to be achieved, without burying the teacher in technological detail.

We have argued in this paper that there is a need to re-skill teachers to work in virtual school settings if this concept of a virtual school is to be realised. This re-skilling will need to involve establishing benchmarks or standards in both the technology and pedagogy areas for graduating teachers if they are to contribute to the development of the virtual school.

REFERENCES

ACT Department of Education and Training and Children's Youth and family Services Bureau (1996) *Gateways – Information technology in the learning process.* Author, Tuggeranong.

Apple, M. W. (1982) *Education and Power.* Routledge & Kegan Paul, London.

Apple, M. W. and Jungck, S. (1998) "You don't have to be a teacher to teach this unit": Teaching, Technology and Control in the Classroom. In *Education/Technology/Power: Educational Computing as a Social Practice*, H. Bromley and W. M. Apple (eds.), State University of New York Press, Albany, pp. 133-154.

Bell, G. and Gray, J. N. (1997) The Revolution yet to happen. In *Beyond Calculation: The Next fifty Years of Computing*, P. J. Denning, and R. M Metcalfe (Eds.), Springer-Verlag, New York, pp. 5-32.

Denning, R. J. and Metcalfe, R. M. (1997) Preface. In *Beyond Calculation: The Next fifty Years of Computing,* P. J. Denning and R. M. Metcalfe (eds.), Springer-Verlag, New York, pp. xiii-xvi.

DETYA (1999) *Real Time: Computers, Change and Schooling – National sample study of the information technology skills of Australian school students.* Australian Key Centre for Cultural and Media Policy. [http://www.detya.gov.au/schools/publicat.htm] 19/01/2000.

Ewing, R. A. and Smith, D. L. (2000) Curriculum Issues Raised by Technology. *Curriculum Perspectives,* 20 (3), p. 65.

Freire, P. (1995) *Pedagogy of the Oppressed.* Continuum, New York.

Gates, B. (1999) *Business @ The Speed of Thought.* Viking Books, U.K.

Hilbun, J. and Maxcy, S. J. (1983) If computers can think, do we need teachers? *Focus on Learning,* 9 (2), pp. 40-45.

Jones, V., Cranitch, G. and Jo, J. H. (2000) Hyweb: A hybrid-web system for delivery and enhancement of web-based and traditional teaching. To appear in *Proceedings of AusWeb 2001*, Coffs Harbour.

Perelman. L. J, (1992) *School's Out: Hyperlearning, the New Technology and the End of Education.* William Morrow and Company, New York.

Perez, M. and Jo, J. H. (2000) Learning Sequence controlled by Learners and Educators, within a CBI System. In *Proceedings of CAP's3: Third International Conference on Human-Learning System,* Paris.

Pheasant, M. F. W. (1989) Computers as surrogate teachers: A study of potential legal barriers in four western states. *DAI*, 50, no. 05A, 1165.

Phillips, V. (1998) *Virtual Classrooms, real education.* [http://geteducated.com/articles/genb.htm].

Technological Trends (1937) *Technological Trends and National Policy, including the Social Implications of New Inventions.* Report of the Subcommittee on Technology to the National Resources Committee, June 1937, United States Government Printing Office, Washington.

Tiffin, J. and Rajasingham, L. (1995) *In search of the virtual class: Education in an information society.* Routedge, London.

Woern, A. (1997) *What is an Intelligent Interface.* [http://www.sics.se/~annika/papers/intint.html].

BIOGRAPHY

Dr Jun Jo has developed and implemented an online teaching system for one of his subjects since 1999. He is conducting the 'Intelligent Multimedia Research (IMR) Laboratory' and e-learning is one of his research interests.

Professor Neil Russell is currently researching the computing skills of very young children and the development of 'virtual' schools and universities.

PART TWO

ICT IN LEARNING

15

Students' Perceptions of the Technological Supports for Problem-based Learning

Willie Yip
The Hong Kong Polytechnic University, Department of Computing, Hung Ham, Hong Kong, China
cswiyip@comp.polyu.edu.hk

Keywords: problem-based learning, support tools, students' perceptions, technological supports

Abstract: This paper reports students' perceptions of the technological supports that assist problem-based learning (PBL). There are a number of tasks in the PBL processes, which can be supported by technological advances. A Web-based system has been developed to support the problem-based learning strategy. The system provides facilities to both teacher and students to facilitate learning and teaching. These include on line teaching materials retrieval, a discussion area for problem analysis and brainstorming, a facility for project planning and monitoring, a private group area for the purposes of discussion, a facility for the submission of development work and learning resources, and a posting area to display good work to motivate students. The progress of the students can be monitored and feedback can be given to them. This paper presents a pilot study of student views of and preferences for various technological supports used to enhance learning effectiveness.

1. INTRODUCTION

The author undertook a learning and teaching project in the autumn of 1999, with the aim of promoting problem-based learning in the subject Information Systems Analysis. The PBL approach was introduced for the first time to teach Information Systems Analysis to second year students in the Higher Diploma in Information Systems programme. It was the only subject in the programme that used the PBL approach, with which students had no prior experience. However, it was envisaged that students would learn better with the PBL approach, which is facilitated by technological advances.

Problem-based learning is a promising recent development in tertiary education, which recognises the need to develop problem-solving skills as well as the necessity of helping students to acquire necessary knowledge and skills (Boud and Feletti 1997). The amount of direct instruction is reduced in problem-based learning, as students assume greater responsibility for their own learning. Students are given ill-structured problems through which they develop high-order thinking and problem-solving skills. The shift in the teaching and learning process is more student-centred than teacher-centred. The teacher as knowledge provider becomes less important as students learn from other students, the World Wide Web (WWW), and from other information resources. The role of the teacher is to encourage student participation, provide guidance to students, offer timely feedback, and also assume the role of learner (Roblyer et al. 1997). A problem case, unlike a case study, provides less information to students and requires them to do more information searching. There can be alternative solutions to a problem, through which students learn to make evaluations and justifications. Problem cases, which require students to tackle ill-structured problems, not only develop interpersonal communication and social skills, but also stimulate critical thinking, creativity, and problem-solving skills.

Many universities around the world are using the WWW in direct support of teaching and learning, as both a primary means of information delivery and a supplement to classroom teaching (Harasim 1999). The use of the Web as a teaching resource can benefit students (Milheim and Harley 1998, Sloan 1997). Students can learn better when the pedagogical process of PBL is supported by technology to foster teaching and learning. Learning and teaching courseware is available (Blumenstyke 1999, Frederickson 1999) and the author's university has been using WebCT as the teaching platform since September 1999. Nevertheless, WebCT features are unable to support the various PBL processes, in particular project planning and controlling, and private discussion facilities for collaborative learning, which are important processes within PBL. Thus, a Web-based system has been developed to support PBL instead. The technology provides facilities for both teacher and students to facilitate learning and teaching. This paper presents a pilot study of student perceptions of the technological supports used to enhance learning effectiveness.

2. HYBRID PBL APPROACH TO EFFECTIVE LEARNING

The introduction of a hybrid approach to PBL may be more appropriate for undergraduates. A full PBL approach with less lecturing, more students working in small groups, and more self-direct learning, may not be appropriate initially for two reasons. First, most undergraduate students are accustomed to teacher-centred learning and they may need a short period to get used to the PBL setting. Another consideration is that their academic achievements may not be the best. Expecting students to be able to read well and provide answers to ill-structured problems initially may not be workable. Second, every subject is time-tabled and designated with both lecture and tutorial hours. As such, this is an institutional constraint, because teaching activities need to follow these patterns. However, there follows a gradual reduction in formal lectures for knowledge dissemination, with the replacement of more discussion activities that take place during lecture hours.

A number of PBL strategies have been tried in learning and teaching (Tang et al. 1997). The author used the hybrid problem-based learning strategy, with students working in teams of six, as follows.

- Teaching materials can be accessed on the Web and students prepare for classes
- Students are given problem cases that simulate real-life situations
- Brainstorming sessions are held to identify learning issues
- A group project plan is formulated
- Students undertake self-directed and collaborative learning
- Each group of students presents their findings (report writing and presentation)
- Exemplary work is posted on the Web for experience sharing
- Students reflect on what they have learnt through feedback.

The Web-based system provides functionalities to support the various PBL processes are shown below.

PBL processes	Technological supports in the Web-based system
Problem cases	Posted on problem case area
Identifying learning issues	Problem analysis
Group project planning	Group project plan
Self-directed learning	Reading – Teaching materials are posted on the Web (Teaching materials area)
	Searching – Information search through the WWW
	Understanding – Individual work submission

Collaborative learning	Group discussion
Report writing and presentation	Teamwork submission
Reflection	Feedback, posting area (showing good student work), bulletin board

3. STUDENTS' PREFERRED TECHNOLOGICAL SUPPORTS FOR PBL

Table 1 . Students' preferred facilities on the Web site

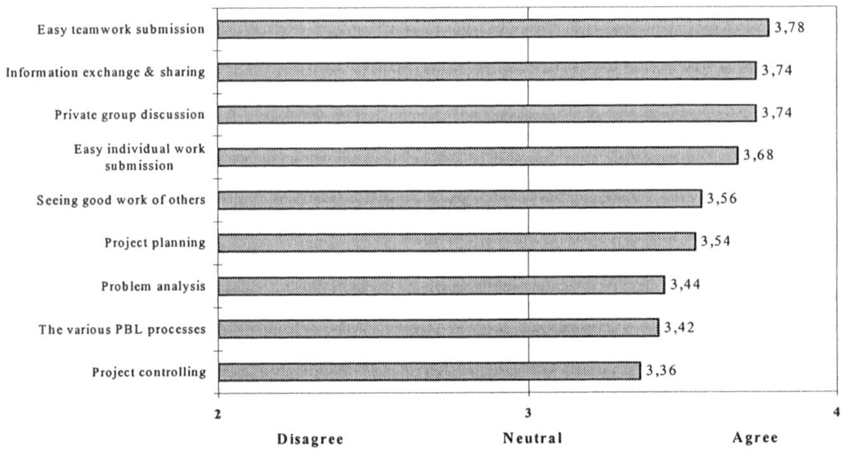

Student learning can be enhanced when the pedagogical process of PBL is supported by technology. A Web-based system provides functionalities to support the various PBL processes. Teaching materials, problem cases and PBL guidelines are posted on the Web. Facilities such as private group area for discussion and brainstorming, a problem analysis area for identifying learning issues, a simple table for group project planning, individual work and teamwork submission facility for on-line work submission, and a posting area for displaying the exemplary student work – are all intended to enhance better learning and teaching. Students were requested to rate their preferred facilities on a scale of 1 to 5, with 5 being the highest score and 1 the lowest. Table 1 presents students preferred facilities on the Web site. The following sections describe in detail the students' perceptions of the technological supports.

3.1 The author's views on posting teaching materials on the Web

Students are interested in receiving the teaching materials available on a course Web site (Holmes 1999, Weible 1999). They can download subject information (subject syllabus, teaching plan) and teaching materials (lecture notes, review questions, references, problem cases and problem-based learning guidelines). Students are encouraged to develop the habit of making preparations for lectures. They are also encouraged to raise questions for discussion in class and there is little doubt that they will understand the subject better. As students participate more in class discussion, the atmosphere of a lecture session is enhanced. The usual one-way method of communication that most teachers use is dull and uninteresting. Since the teaching materials are stored in PDF format with four pages of materials printed on a page, the content is legible but paper is saved in printing. Teaching materials are useful to students and can be updated easily. The Web-based system also solves the problem of photocopying overhead projector transparencies in the production of handouts.

3.2 Students' perceptions of receiving teaching resources on the Web

Despite the tremendous efforts that have been used in preparing the teaching materials and posting them on the Web at the beginning of the semester, it is surprising to find that students do not, in general, use this facility to its best potential. Table 2 presents the students' views of receiving teaching resources on the Web. With the teaching materials available on the Web, students do not make use of the resources in making preparation for lectures. They download the lecture notes for lectures without much preparation. As such, they fail to learn how to prepare for lectures. The number of questions raised in class is the same as with the traditional teaching approach. However, some students do make preparation for lectures and posting teaching resources on the Web can improve their learning style, as they need to print the lecture handouts for lectures. They also find the supplied references useful for obtaining more information.

Table 2. Students' perceptions of receiving teaching resources on the Web

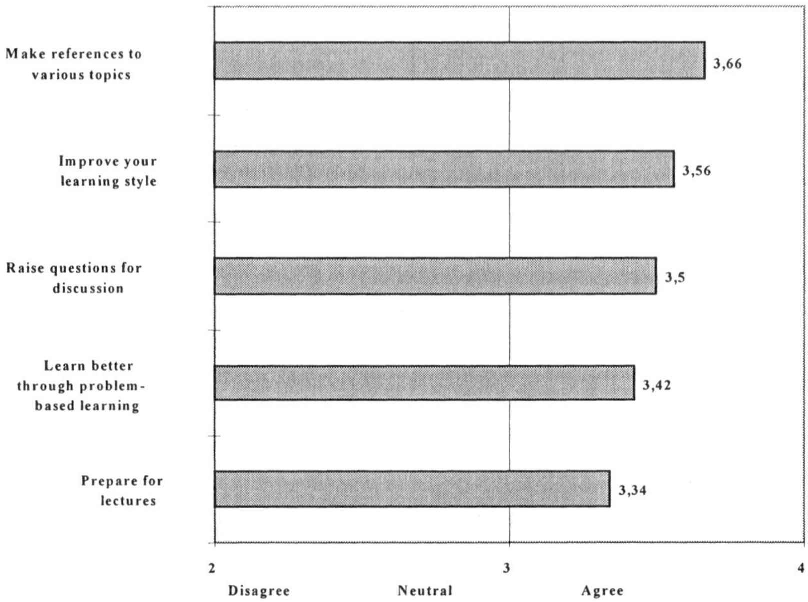

3.3 Self-directed learning and easy individual work submission

When students undertake self-directed learning, they use the WWW, which is an excellent tool for searching, containing a number of search engines. To ensure that students read and understand the information that they locate from a number of sites, they are required to write a short paragraph or two summarising their impressions of the information presented at the site. This enables the students to understand the topic, to practice their writing skills, and also to reflect on the work done. The student work can be shared among the team members. When the work is to be submitted electronically, it need not be during office hours, and this provides more flexibility to students. Students in the process of searching for information often encounter two problems. First, some initially do not know how to search for information on the Web. Second, they encounter an information overload problem. However, students have been reminded to select the relevant information rather than all the information. They should also learn how to make group decisions based on the information available. More importantly, they should have skills and knowledge in the use of the various WWW search engines and in employing efficient search strategies in information-seeking.

Each student is encouraged to prepare some individual work before they meet as a group. He/she should develop the habit of self-learning and accumulate experience and skills in problem-solving through teamwork situations. A student can contribute towards teamwork in two ways: first, the student takes an active approach to participating in discussion, offers creative ideas, and either proposes a good plan or revises others to arrive at an even better plan. With the Web-based system, the discussion records of each student can be seen and the performance of each individual can be identified. Second, the individual student undertakes the assigned tasks and produces quality work on time. The individual work submission function facilitates the sharing and exchanging of information. There are two ways for students to submit their work. The first way allows a student to present his/her work on their Web site and submit the URL of the page. The other is using the online editor provided by the Web-based system.

3.4 Public and private Web areas for information exchange and sharing

Students need a mechanism to share their individual work and the results of their teamwork. The Web-based system is an automatic development environment through which students' work can be accessed, commented on and refined by team members electronically. It enables students to create knowledge and to share among themselves. Two areas, both public and private, are for the posting and sharing of information: a public area for the whole class and a private area for each team. The public area serves as a bulletin board, which is for information dissemination and also for posting the best work in the class. Another important use of this public area is for questions and answers that can clarify misunderstandings of materials. One of the important teaching and learning issues is to motivate students to learn better and to work harder. It has been found that the quality of student work has been declining in recent years and teaching efforts can be maximised to produce better results if students are motivated to learn. The purpose of having an electronic display facility is to create a co-operative learning environment where students benefit from the activities of their peers. At the same time, the posting of good work by students will provide higher motivation for them to perform well. The private area contains communication, the work plan, the individual work and the teamwork. The teacher is permitted to access this area for monitoring work and also to provide feedback and guidelines. Other students can benefit by reading the teacher's comments before viewing the information.

3.5 Collaborative learning and videotaped presentations for feedback

Students need to practise teamwork and understand that they learn more from people than working as individuals. Group work and team-building skills are essential in organisations (EI-Shinnawyn 1998). Collaborative learning enables students to share and exchange information to arrive at group decision-making and develop a more comprehensive understanding of the subject. A good team generally produces better results, and poor team morale and conflicts between students often lead to poor team performance. In mixed ability groups, the stronger students tend to encourage and motivate the weaker students to achieve better performance levels. At the same time, the stronger students can practise leadership skills and can serve as consultants for their team-mates (Buffington 1998). However, each student should have the opportunity to develop leadership skills. Students should be adaptable to a new team situation, with people having different personalities and experiences. The performance of each team was videotaped at the beginning and at the end of the semester for review feedback. Table 3 presents their views on videotaping their presentation. They valued the opportunity for self-evaluation and assessed how they could improve themselves in presentations.

Table 3. Video-taped presentations for feedback

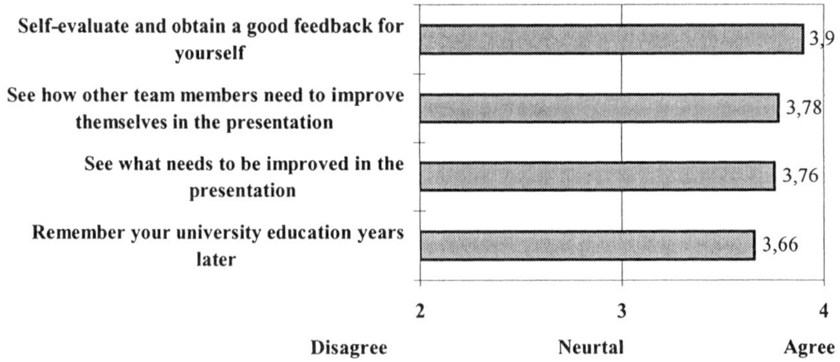

The progress of the tutorial sessions can be more effective and productive since both students and teacher can review the work done by each individual in each team via the Web before the tutorials. Students have increased time for reflection on the problem. Shorter meetings and higher learning productivity are to be achieved. However, teamwork was enhanced with the Web technology, which provided an extra communication facility, and students make use of the Web for sharing and exchanging information.

3.6 Peer evaluation as part of assessment

When students are working in a team situation, each student is expected to contribute to teamwork. Students are responsible for completing a project but have no authority to 'tell' other team members to be co-operative. Team learning can only be fruitful when each team member is committed and contributes to the teamwork. The assessment of this subject is continuous, without examinations. There are three components in the formal assessment of each student. They include individual contribution, group work as a whole and peer evaluation by students themselves. Students are assessed by a peer review system, with the intention that every student should contribute positively in a teamwork situation. Peer-grading is performed after each problem case has been completed, and the individual performance such as presentation, tutorial contribution, individual work and team contribution can be measured. Table 4 presents students' view on having peer evaluation of team members. They feel that they can express their satisfaction or dissatisfaction openly. Individual assessment is based on the work produced individually and also on the individual contribution to team work discussions. Individual and group marks are given equal weight. On the other hand, good students should not be penalised if they have been assigned to work with other less hard-working students. Students should be allowed to assess other team members' efforts as this encourages each team member to contribute to the teamwork situation and the team leaders and/or good students deserve higher weighting. Each student is requested to assess his/her members for their relative percentage of contribution to the problem case, and also on the quality of work submitted. The peer evaluation of students relies on the judgment and honesty of the students in making such evaluations. In general, students have been fair in their peer evaluation assessments.

Table 4. Having peer evaluation of the team members

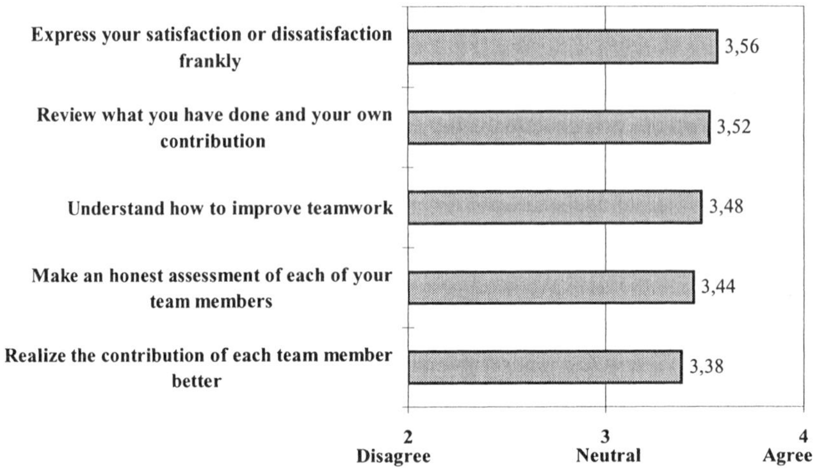

3.7 Posting board to motivate students

The purpose of having a posting facility is to create a co-operative learning environment where students benefit from the activities of their peers. At the same time, the posting of good work (reports and presentation files) by students will provide higher motivation for them to perform well. The motivation factor may not be a monetary reward, but recognition by their peers is important. This also facilitates the experience of sharing 'excellent' work in the specified subject, and enables students to learn from good quality work. Other students can benefit by seeing how other teams tackle the same problem, and this can further enrich the knowledge of the students. One of the important learning and teaching issues is to motivate students to learn better and to work harder. Table 5 presents the students' views of having a posting board to exemplify good work. It is evident that the posting facility motivates them to perform better.

4. FEEDBACK FROM STUDENTS AND DIFFICULTIES ENCOUNTERED

Students had the experience of using three different types of courseware, and they rated this Web-based system as the best, as it is well designed and

Table 5 . Viewing good work of other teams

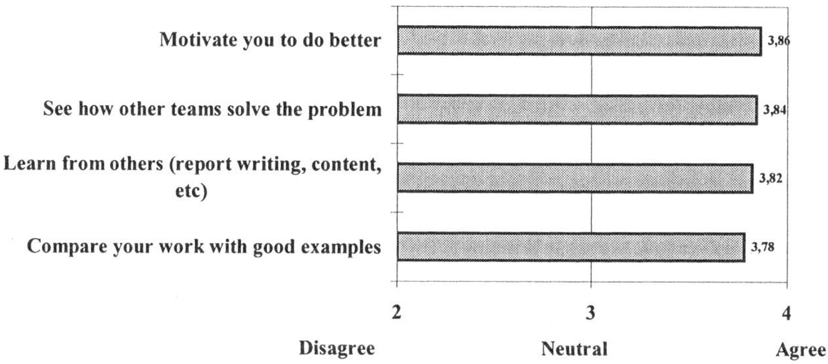

easy to use. The facilities they like include: easy on-line work submission, private area for group discussion, the facility for information exchange and sharing, and the posting board for seeing the good work of other teams. Students tended to spend more time than necessary on searching for information, despite having been guided to look for relevant information rather than all the information. Some students reported that they could search for information on the Web more systematically than before. The learning outcome has been found to be positive, in that students spent more time on the subject.

The workload for the author has increased when compared with traditional teaching without technological support. The progress of the students must be monitored, as there is a need to ensure that each student participates and contributes in teamwork situations. There were also problems of computer virus attacks when students submitted group reports which were found to contain viruses.

4.1 Problems encountered with using technology

When asked about problems encountered with using technology to enhance learning, students commented that the discussion board (thread discussion) is not quite as useful as ICQ, e-mail and face-to-face communication. Students tend to like formal meetings better. If their home computer has a problem, they cannot do anything and therefore learning is technology- dependent. Information searching requires a lot of time. They have difficulty in summarising information that is found on the Web, and the Web site does not allow them to submit diagrams. Sometimes, they had difficulty connecting to the university's Internet connection. This may affect their discussions with their teammates and also submission of their work. They prefer that the website be designed so that they can make reference to the problem case that they tackled previously.

5. CONCLUSION

This paper has described an approach to enhance the teaching of Information Systems Analysis to undergraduate students through PBL with the aid of technological advances. Students have been found to do more reading and engage themselves in problem-solving with problem cases. They realise that teamwork is more important than individual work in problem-solving. The author takes the view that a practical and cost-effective technological solution should be adopted to facilitate PBL. The application of the Web-based system to the various stages of the proposed problem-based learning /teaching strategy benefits students. The system allows students to download teaching materials. A private Web area is designed for each team of students to enhance collaborative learning. It can be used for the purposes of communication, project planning, development work, and learning resources for a project team. The public Web site can serve as a bulletin board for information dissemination. A posting area allows the display of students' good work to motivate them to work better. Students have remarked favorably on what they learnt, including: better problem analysis, understanding of how to formulate a project plan and subsequent control of their work, better written and oral communication, teamwork, practicing leadership skills, and better information search via the Internet.

ACKNOWLEDGMENT

I would like to express my gratitude to the Learning and Teaching Development Committee of The Hong Kong Polytechnic University for providing funding for this project.

REFERENCES

Blumenstyk, G. (1999) The Marketing Intensifies in Distance Learning. *The Chronicle of Higher Education*, pp. 27-30.

Boud, D. and Feletti, G. I. (1997) *The challenge of problem-based learning.* Kogan Page, London.

Buffington, J. R. (1998) Self-directed teams in the introductory information systems course: Lessons learned. In *International Academy for Information Management Proceedings 13th Annual Conference*, pp. 76-82.
El-Shinnawy, M. and Vinze, A. S. (1998) Polarization and Persuasive Argumentation: A Study of Decision Making in Group Settings. *Management Information Systems Quarterly*, 22, (2), pp. 165-198.
Frederickon, S. (1999) Web-based Instruction: A Comparison of Ten Programs. In *Proceeding of the 15th Annual Conference in Distance Teaching and Learning*, Madison, WI.
Harasim, L. (Sept. 1999) A Framework for Online Learning: The Virtual U. *IEEE Computer*, 32:9, pp. 44-49.
Holmes, W. N. (Sept 1999) The Myth of the Educational Computer. *IEEE Computer*, 32:9, pp 36-42.
Milheim, W. D. and Harvey, D. M. (Feb 1998) Design and Development of a World Wide Web Resource Site. *Educational Technology the magazine for managers of change in education*, Volume 38, No. 1, pp. 53-56.
Roblyer, M. D., Edwards, J. and Havriluk, M. A. (1997) *Integrating educational technology into teaching.* Prentice-Hall Upper, Saddle River, NJ.
Sloan, A. (1997) Learning with the Web: Experience of using the World Wide Web in a learning environment. *Computers and Education*, Vol. 28, No. 4, pp. 207-212.
Tang, C., Lai, P., Tang, W., Davies, H., Frankland, S., Oldfield, K.,Walters, M., Mei Leung, N. G., Taylor, G., Tiwai, A., Yim, M. and Yuen, E. (1997) Developing a context based PBL model. *Research and Development in Problem Based Learning*, Vol 4, Newcastle: Australian Problem Based Learning Network, pp. 579-595.
Weible, R. (1999), Course Web site: Student preferences and good examples. *International Academy for Information Management Proceedings 14th Annual Conference*, pp. 203-207.

BIOGRAPHY

Willie Yip has undertaken a number of funded learning and teaching projects in the past few years. He has the experience of running virtual teams for Hong Kong and US students for problem-based learning. Recently, he has introduced problem-based learning with technical support to his teaching in Information Systems Analysis with great success.

16

Impact of New Information Technologies on Teachers and Students

Gerald Knezek and Rhonda Christensen
Department of Technology and Cognition, University of North Texas, Denton, TX, USA
gknezek@tenet.edu

Keywords: ICT integration, teacher training, primary and secondary education, research

Abstract: This paper summarises findings from several commissioned studies, doctoral dissertations, and federally funded technology in education projects coordinated by the authors in conjunction with international colleagues over the past five years. It features evidence regarding the impact of information technologies on teacher training and student achievement, and spotlights trans-national trend analysis through common instrumentation as the technique believed to be the most promising research avenue for the future.

1. INTRODUCTION

Quantitative assessments conducted since 1995 in several school systems in the USA and other parts of the world have yielded consistent and encouraging results regarding the influence of new information technologies on teacher and student attitudes, skills, and the use of technology tools. This paper summarises findings from several commissioned studies, doctoral dissertations, and federally-funded technology in education projects coordinated by the authors in conjunction with international colleagues over the past five years. It concludes with discussion of the evidence gathered to date regarding the impact of new information technologies on student achievement, and spotlights trans-national trend analysis as the technique believed to be the most promising research avenue for the future.

2. FUNDED INSTRUMENTATION RESEARCH

During 1995-97 the authors were awarded research support from a University of North Texas endowed fund to construct instruments for assessing teachers' attitudes toward new information technologies. The result was the Teachers' Attitudes Toward Computers (TAC) questionnaire (Christensen and Knezek 1996) and the Teachers Attitudes Toward Information Technology (TAT) Questionnaire (Knezek and Christensen 1998). This development effort, which involved selecting and revalidating items from 15 separate computer attitude instruments, received recognition in its early stages in the form of a Best Quantitative Studies Award by the Society of Information Technology in Teacher Education (1997). During the ensuing years one or both of these instruments has been translated into Arabic, Chinese, Dutch, Japanese, Korean, Portuguese, Spanish, and Thai.

TAC and TAT development work was founded in earlier work funded by the Fulbright Foundation of Washington D.C., the Japan Society for the Promotion of Science, and the Texas Center for Educational Technology, concerning the measurement of student attitudes toward information technology at the elementary and secondary education level. Two instruments, the Young Children's Computer Inventory (YCCI) and the Computer Attitude Questionnaire (CAQ) were developed during the first half of the 1990s as part of this initiative. Findings regarding the impact of computer use by young children in Mexico, Japan, and the USA were reported at the Fifth World Conference on Computers in Education, in Birmingham, England (Knezek, Miyashita, and Sakamoto 1995). These were later merged with complementary findings from the Information Technology in Education and Children Project (ITEC) and the International Association for the Assessment of Educational Achievement Computers in Education Project (IEA-CompEd) in a book entitled *Children and Computers in School* (Collis, Knezek, Lai, Miyashita, Pelgrum, Plomp, and Sakamoto 1996). An instruments book featuring the YCCI, CAQ, TAC and TAT was released during the year 2000 (Knezek, Christensen, Miyashita and Ropp 2000b) and a book of multi-national findings based on this set of instruments was published in the year 2000 as well (Morales, Knezek, Christensen and Avila 2000).

3. MAJOR FINDINGS ACROSS CULTURES

Several major cross-cultural findings related to information technology and education emerged from studies completed during the 1990s:

1. Early initial exposure to computers in school increases computer enjoyment by approximately 2/3 of a standard deviation. (Collis et al. 1996).
2. No gender differences were found in attitudes toward computers at the first grade level in Mexico, Japan, or the USA (Collis et al. 1996).
3. The only area where consistent gender differences were found at the first grade level was empathy (a caring concern for the thoughts and feelings of others) (Collis, et al. 1996). Females were found to have higher empathy than males for Japan, Mexico, and the USA. Empathy findings were also later replicated for older children in the USA and Mexico (Knezek and Christensen 2000, Morales et al. 2000).
4. Girls in the fourth through sixth year of school in selected populations may enjoy computers more than boys (Alamhaboub 2000, Knezek and Christensen 2000).
5. By approximately the seventh year in school and continuing throughout secondary education, boys appear to enjoy computers more than girls (Collis et al. 1996, Knezek and Christensen 2000).
6. Psychological impacts of appropriate technology integration appear to emerge within a relatively short time frame in students at the primary school level. For example, positive impacts on the perceived enjoyment and importance of computers appear to occur within the first three months of exposure to computers in school (Collis et al. 1996), and may possibly occur within the first six weeks of school (Knezek and Christensen 2000).
7. Measurable impacts related to achievement may take much longer to emerge. For example, evidence has been found of measurable positive impact ($p < .03$) of high- versus low-integrating teachers on student vocabulary, reading, and writing scores as measured by the Iowa Test of Basic Skills at the end of the fifth grade school year in the USA (Knezek and Christensen 2000), and measurable positive influence ($p < .01$) on motivation and study habits was found to emerge in Japanese primary school children in grades 1-3 after four years of school computer use (Collis, et al., 1996). In addition, significant associations have been found ($r = .34$, $p < .05$) in a study involving 100 Texas school districts, predicting average school district standardised achievement test score based on level of technology expenditures (Knezek, Christensen, Hancock and Shoho 2000a).
8. Teacher competence and confidence with Information and Communication Technology (ICT) is the principal determinant of effective classroom use by students (Collis et al. 1996).

9. Successful technology integration in a classroom environment appears to require will, skill, and access to technology tools on the part of the teacher (Knezek et al. 2000a).
10. Teacher advances in technology integration appears to proceed through a set of well defined stages, where the highest stages require changes in attitude more so than skills (Knezek and Christensen 2000).
11. Self-appraisal of level of technology integration can be effective in prescribing training for an educational professional (Knezek and Christensen 2000).

4. FOCUSED DOCTORAL RESEARCH

Several doctoral dissertations have provided detailed analysis of selected topics in the area of ICT in education over the past five years. Some of those in which the authors have been directly involved include:

1. Christensen, R. (1997) Effect of technology integration education on the attitudes of teachers and their students. This doctoral dissertation featured three time-sequenced administrations of the TAC and YCCI in a large public elementary school in northern Texas, in order to assess the impact of needs-based technology integration education. The treatment of intensive summer start-up activities followed by monthly visitations by the lead trainer was found to be effective in enhancing the attitudes and skills of teachers. A unique feature of this dissertation was that it demonstrated that the impact of effective teacher training could be measured in terms of changes in attitudes on the part of the teachers and their students.
2. Gilmore, E. (1998) Impact of Training on the Information Technology Attitudes of University Faculty. This dissertation employed the Faculty Attitudes Toward Information Technology questionnaire (Knezek et al. 2000b) which was produced by extracting selected scales from the TAC. Major findings based on surveys completed by 218 university faculty were that a university whose faculty participated in a semester-long ICT professional development initiative showed positive, broad-based gains in their attitudes toward information technology, while peers in comparable university without the training program did not.
3. Hopson, M. H. (1998) Effects of a Technology Enriched Learning Environment on Student Development of Higher Order Thinking Skills. This dissertation employed the CAQ and Ross Test of Higher Cognitive Processes to assess the impact of technology enriched learning on 166 fifth and sixth grade students in a public middle school in Texas. The study demonstrated that a Technology Enhanced Learning Environment

significantly and positively impacted the development of the higher order thinking skill of 'Evaluation' for fifth grade students. The study also determined that exposure to technology is associated with positive student attitudes in the areas of computer importance, motivation, and self-reported creative tendencies.

4. Alamhaboub, S. F. (2000) Attitudes Toward Computer Use and Gender Differences among Kuwaiti Sixth Grade Students. The CAQ was used in this dissertation to survey 562 students from 10 public schools in Kuwait. Kuwaiti girls were found to be more positive than boys in their attitudes toward computers as well as in empathy. The study also verified that students who had computers at home had more positive attitudes toward computers than those who had access to computers only in school. In addition, the study found a significant correlation between Attitudes Toward Computers and Motivation, Study habits, Creative Tendencies, and achievement in the field of informatics.
5. Moonen, B. (2001) Teacher Learning in INservice Networks on Internet Use in Secondary Education. This dissertation focused on the integration of the Internet into foreign language teaching, and included TAC measurements gathered from all teacher network participants at four time periods. A key finding was that ongoing inservice training is effective in reducing anxiety and increasing productivity in trainees. A major conclusion was that support in the form of coaching activities is important to solidify effective instructional utilisation. This work also pointed out that groups of trainees with different initial ICT skill levels may require different lengths of intensive support before their attitudes change, and that attitudes change in phases, by type. Specifically anxiety reduction took place relatively quickly during the initial year of the project while a reduction in avoidance and a positive change in the perception of usefulness of ICT for professional productivity did not occur until after the project had been in place for two years.

5. FINDINGS FROM FEDERALLY-FUNDED PROJECTS

Since 1999, the authors have participated in two large projects funded by the U.S. national government related to technology, teaching and learning. One is a five-year, $9.2 million U.S. Department of Education Technology Innovation Challenge Fund grant for which they are serving as external evaluators. The other is a four-year, $940,000 U.S. Department of Education Preparing Tomorrow's Teachers to Use Technology (PT3) grant for which they are Principal Investigator and Internal Evaluator, respectively. First year findings from each of these projects have produced many interesting results.

6. FINDINGS REGARDING TEACHERS

Teachers' proficiency with technology. Findings from data analysis gathered from more than 500 teachers in a Texas school district using a technology proficiency questionnaire (Ropp 1999) indicate that the professional development activities carried out with these teachers during the 1999-2000 school year were highly effective in advancing the skills of teachers. The impact was strong in all four areas selected as relevant to teaching with technology: E-mail skills, WWW skills, classroom use of Integrated Applications, and incorporating methods of Teaching with Technology.

Stages of Adoption of technology. In the study cited in the previous paragraph, teachers also completed the one-item Stages of Adoption (Christensen 1997) survey. Findings from the survey indicate that these teachers advanced as a group throughout the 1999-2000 school year approximately one stage of adoption on a six-stage scale, moving from: *Stage 4: Familiarity and confidence* (I am gaining a sense of confidence in using the computer for specific tasks. I am starting to feel comfortable using the computer.) and moving toward: *Stage 5: Adaptation to other contexts* (I think about the computer as a tool to help me and am no longer concerned about it as technology. I can use it in many applications and as an instructional aid.) Teacher profiles for attitudes at various stages of adoption of technology clearly delineate different levels of enthusiasm and anxiety with respect to integrating technology into the classroom.

Needs and beliefs. Teachers in the 1999-2000 Texas study reported a sizable gain in expertise in several of the skill areas identified as important to the project goals and objectives. Teachers' general beliefs and needs fell into four major categories, and remained reasonably stable from the beginning to the end of the school year. Specific item level needs that changed to a great extent from the fall to the spring were: 1) a lesser need for training in how to use the computer and 2) a greater need to be trained in teaching techniques and strategies to integrate technology into the curriculum.

7. FINDINGS REGARDING STUDENTS

Computers vs. television. YCCI data gathered from 1737 K-6 students during the fall of 1999 and spring of 2000 from the eight elementary schools in Texas indicate that high technology-integrating teachers at the first grade level rapidly influence the preference of their students toward using computers over the more passive medium of watching television.

High vs. low integration classrooms. Across grades 1-3, looking at the classroom environment from a pre-post perspective, we find that among teachers who were low integrators of technology, student Attitudes Toward Computers ($p<.001$), Attitude Toward School ($p<.05$), Computer Importance ($p<.01$) and Computer Enjoyment ($p<.02$) declined significantly from the first to the last six-weeks of school. The students of the teachers who had been previously identified by their principals as high integrators of technology also had a significant decline in Attitudes Toward School ($p<.02$) but yet increased significantly for Computer Enjoyment ($p<.02$).

Lack of home computer access. The general impact of technology integrating teachers over several months, across grades 1-6, appears to have been the greatest in the area of Attitudes Toward Computers on students without computers at home. This is evidenced by significant ($p < .01$) declines in student attitudes toward computers, from fall to spring, among those students without home access to computers who also had low integrating teachers in school.

Changes across grade levels. Student dispositions as a whole tended to decline from the younger grade levels to older grades (grade 1 to grade 6). This is similar to trends found in past studies (Knezek et al. 1995, Christensen 1997). Although all measured attitudes declined, the three indices related to computers declined less across grade levels than other learning-related dispositions.

Gender differences. With respect to student dispositions by gender, girls in north Texas were significantly higher than boys in Empathy, Computer Enjoyment, Attitude Toward School, Motivation to Study, and Study Habits as of fall 1999. During spring 2000, the girls remained significantly higher than boys in Attitudes Toward School and Empathy, while boys became significantly higher on the Motivation subscale.

Skills and attitudes among secondary students. Based on CAQ information gathered from 1507 grade 7-12 Texas students during 1999-2000, secondary school students appear to have positive attitudes toward information technology and most learning-related dispositions. Their information technology skills showed healthy growth during the 1999-2000 school year, to a point where they approached the level of their teachers (Knezek and Christensen 2000). Their relatively low (and declining with increasing age) ratings on attitudes toward school are consistent with studies conducted at the elementary school level and findings from earlier studies using the same scales (Christensen 1997, Knezek et al. 1995). This data, even with its senior year positive spike, may be more of an indictment of our modern system of education in general, rather than of the policies and/or teaching methods found in these district schools.

8. ADVANTAGES OF INTERNATIONAL COLLABORATION

Great benefits have been found to accrue from international collaboration in the study of ICT in education. The most obvious is the rich exchange of ideas and the opportunity for consensus identification of research topics believed to be important worldwide. Less obvious but equally important is the ability to use common instruments to identify trends that hold true in several nations and cultures (and some that do not). For example, international collaboration between Mexico and the USA has allowed researchers to conclude that even though the level of access to information technology is very different in these two nations, teachers' beliefs about the usefulness of ICT for improving teaching and learning are very similar in Mexico and the USA.

International collaboration can also be useful for proving that trends thought to be universal may not necessarily hold true for every nation or culture in the world. For example, after several years of studies confirming that females are generally measurably higher in empathy than males, even if no other gender differences are found on a battery of instruments, preliminary results have emerged from Colombia indicating that the opposite may be true in that nation. Further research is needed to determine if these findings can be replicated, and, if they are replicated, why the trend in this nation is different from what appears to be the norm in most of the world. Only though international comparisons was special attention called to this finding in Colombia. These and other comparisons can benefit researchers from any nation who are attempting to answer similar questions about the impact of technology on teaching and learning.

9. SUMMARY AND REFLECTIONS

Over the past ten years, trans-national research based on universally agreed upon ICT instruments has yielded a number of enlightening findings regarding students and teachers. The only consistent gender difference observed in students at the first grade level is in the area of empathy, where females are already more empathetic than males. This difference between males and females seems to persist throughout elementary and secondary education. Past research has revealed that ICT attitudes are not generally differentiated based on gender until around grade four. Historically, males' attitudes toward ICT have become more positive than females as they progress through their schooling. However, there is emerging evidence at the 4th through 6th grade level that females may be evolving toward a greater enjoyment of computers than their male counterparts in this age range.

Teachers' attitudes toward ICT are clearly multi-faceted (with at least seven underlying dimensions) and tend to become more positive due to ongoing, needs-based training across attitudinal types. Anxiety tends to be reduced rather quickly with meaningful exposure to ICT. On the other hand, enthusiasm/acceptance of ICT and belief in the utility of ICT for professional productivity is slower to evolve. It appears that other types of attitudes take longer to change, in the time frame of years rather than months.

Teachers' beliefs regarding the usefulness of ICT in education appear to be surprisingly consistent as of the year 2000 across several nations and cultures. This is true in spite of widely varying levels of connectivity and access to other ICT resources. Conversely, teachers' perceived needs are strongly dependent on level of access to ICT resources and current stage of adoption of technology in education. As teachers progress from lower level, simple applications toward full integration of technology in the classroom in support of higher cognitive functions, attitudes progress in predictable patterns along with changes in their needs. The highest stage of integration involves a change in perception of teaching with technology rather than additional training or resources. While many of these findings have been replicated in multiple studies and in multi-national contexts, research in almost every area is far from conclusive and is still ongoing.

REFERENCES

Alamhaboub, S. F. (2000) *Attitudes Toward Computer Use and Gender Differences among Kuwaiti Sixth Grade Students*. Doctoral dissertation, University of North Texas.

Christensen, R. (1997) *Effect of technology integration education on the attitudes of teachers and their students*. Doctoral dissertation, University of North Texas. [http://courseweb.tac.unt.edu/rhondac].

Christensen, R. and Knezek, G. (1996) *Constructing the Teachers' Attitudes Toward Computers (TAC) Questionnaire*. ERIC Document Reproduction Service No. ED398244.

Collis, B., Knezek, G., Lai, K., Miyashita, K., Pelgrum, W., Plomp, T. and Sakamoto, T. (1996). *Children and Computers in School*. Lawrence Erlbaum, Mahwah, NJ.

Gilmore, E. (1998) *Impact of Training on the Information Technology Attitudes of University Faculty*. Doctoral dissertation, University of North Texas.

Hopson, M. H. (1998) *Effects of a Technology Enriched Learning Environment on Student Development of Higher Order Thinking Skills*. Doctoral dissertation, University of North Texas.

Knezek, G. and Christensen, R. (1998) Internal consistency reliability for the Teachers' Attitudes Toward Information Technology (TAT) questionnaire. *In Technology and Teacher Education Annual 1998*, J. Willis, J. Price, S. McNeil, B. Robin and D. Willis (eds.), Association for the Advancement of Computing in Education, Charlottesville, VA, pp. 853-856.

Knezek, G. and Christensen, R. (2000) *Refining Best Teaching Practices for Technology Integration: KIDS Project Findings for 1999-2000.* University of North Texas, Denton, TX.

Knezek, G., Christensen, R., Hancock, R. and Shoho, A. (2000a) Toward A Structural Model of Technology Integration. In *Proceedings of the Annual Hawaii Educational Research Association*, Honolulu, February.

Knezek, G., Christensen, R., Miyashita, K. and Ropp, M. (2000b) *Instruments for Assessing Educator Progress in Information Technology*. Institute for the Integration of Technology into Teaching and Learning, Denton, TX.

Knezek, G. A., Miyashita, K. T. and Sakamoto, T. (1995) Findings from the Young Children's Computer Inventory Project. In *World Conference on Computers in Education VI*, J. D. Tinsley and T. J. van Weert (eds.), Birmingham, London, pp. 909-920.

Moonen, B. (2001) *Teacher Learning in INservice Networks on Internet Use in Secondary Education.* Doctoral Dissertation, University of Twente, NL.

Morales, C., Knezek, G., Christensen, R. and Avila, P. (Eds.) (2000) *Impact of New Technologies on Teaching and Learning*. Instituto Latinamericano de la Comunicacion Educativa (ILCE), Mexico City, Mexico.

Ropp, M. M. (1999) Exploring individual characteristics associated with learning to use computers in preservice teacher preparation. *Journal of Research on Computing in Education*, 31 (4), pp. 402-424.

BIOGRAPHY

Gerald Knezek is Professor of Technology and Cognition with a primary research interest in measurement of the impacts of ICT in education. He has taught teacher preparation courses for the past 19 years. Rhonda Christensen is a Research Scientist and evaluator for several ICT-related projects. She is lead instructor for courses featuring technology integration in preservice teacher education.

17

Curriculum Focused ICT – the Critical Resource

Robert Munro
Department of Business and Cumputer Education, University of Strathclyde, Glasgow G13 1PP, Scotland
r.k.munro@strath.ac.uk

Keywords: classroom teaching, integration of ICT, teaching materials, multimedia/hypermedia, development

Abstract: While ICT has assumed considerable importance in education its contribution to teaching and learning is frequently questioned. Educationalists focus solely on the latest technology and strongly hyped 'killer' applications, ignoring valuable software that develops skills, competences and conceptual understanding. In this paper the contribution of curriculum-oriented CD-ROMs to teaching and learning is exemplified through an exploration of one sophisticated resource which allows pupils to investigate differing urban environments and social history characteristics of Victorian Scotland. The paper acknowledges the many factors that inhibit the development of such CD-ROMs and argues that national initiatives are essential to effectively exploit the potential of this valuable educational resource.

1. A CONFLICT OF IMPERATIVES

The penetration and use of Information and Communications Technology (ICT) in education have been considerable since the early nineteen eighties when microcomputers were first introduced into schools. In the twenty intervening years ICT has assumed tremendous importance in the educational process. However, many educationalists have expressed concern as to whether ICT has significantly enhanced teaching and learning (Oppenheimer 1997).

The penetration and use of ICT have been driven by a number of imperatives – not least the political imperative. This initially focused on the alleged need to create a skilled workforce and to try to create and exploit a market for computer equipment. More recently the political attention of many countries has centred on the dream of creating a knowledge society (Blair 1997). The members of this interconnected society will have ubiquitous access to ICT, be confident and competent in all aspects of its use and will exploit it to fulfil their everyday work and leisure demands. Not surprisingly, to achieve this dream, the political argument demands all school pupils gain ICT confidence and competence so they might make a smooth transition into, and an effective contribution to, the adult sector of the knowledge society.

Sadly the variations on the political imperative theme have prevailed over the key educational imperative – that of integrating ICT so that it might facilitate and support teaching and learning. Since the heady days of the nineteen eighties, many educational decision-makers have appeared more anxious to chase the technology, equip the schools with ever more advanced (yet in reality ever more rapidly obsolescent) hardware, and inculcate knowledge of how the technology and the software packages work – rather than harnessing ICT to transform the teaching and learning process.

Regrettably, they have largely neglected to consider how best this innovative, powerful and sophisticated hardware resource might be deployed and supported – by using and creating educationally relevant and significant software and courseware materials and offering appropriate programmes of teacher education – to advance pupil understanding and the development of pupil knowledge.

Over the last twenty years a welter of software innovation, much with tremendous untapped potential for transforming aspects of the educational process, has been briefly flirted with and then unceremoniously dumped as the next killer application swept in. Education is presently fixated on the Web. This is the current killer application – the salvation for education. Most administrators, parents, teachers and pupils exhibit an obsessive desire to see this ICT resource incorporated into every facet of education in every classroom.

The hype behind the selling of the Web has resulted in its public acceptance as the catalyst of the knowledge revolution – the engine of the knowledge society – the Holy Grail for ICT where all the data, information and, indeed, answers and solutions to any issue resides. Many in education sincerely believe that all learners, no matter the context, can and will turn to the Web for data on any issue or topic, transform the data they instantly unearth into information and spin these threads of information into cloths of rich knowledge. Unfortunately this idealised scenario reflects the increasing expectation held by all sectors of society.

The Web is a fantastic resource. It is the ultimate multimedia/hypermedia delivery system for education. Ironically, it is an educational resource that most teachers are still struggling to effectively exploit. They find it difficult to handle, difficult to search, difficult to locate data which matches their demands and very difficult to usefully incorporate into their teaching strategies and their pupils' learning. Their pupils, often more technologically adept, would rather use the Web for social interaction in chat rooms than slake their thirst for knowledge with a search engine.

The Web may well prove to be the Holy Grail of education but current over-reliance on it, and an unquestioning commitment to it, really does teaching and learning a disservice. I am convinced that the multimedia/hypermedia delivery system is the most effective and valuable use of ICT in education. However, until the Web is more available and accessible, is easier to search and also to integrate into classroom activity, I contend that CD-ROM delivery of educational resources is more valuable to teachers and learners.

The aforementioned difficulties associated with the Web, the sheer size and range of data which is available and the bewildering choice and complexity of multifarious search engines and directories are instantly obviated by presenting material on CD-ROM. The teacher is presented with a focused resource where all content is easily accessible and all the extraneous noise of the Web is stripped away.

Given the current plethora of CD-ROMs on the education market it may appear strange to argue for even more development. However, the resources I envisage that would be of most benefit are not the comprehensive encyclopaedias like Encarta and Grolier or many of the topic-oriented products that are frequently written at a high academic level and contain but a small volume of content applicable to the curriculum. Teachers need CD-ROMs with a particular and precise curriculum focus. These should encapsulate the entire gamut of media resources woven together and specially structured to assist the teacher to help all pupils in their class to find relevant data, identify significant information, use software tools to manipulate the data and arrive at meaningful conclusions on trends, relationships and results. Varied interaction with the resource should enhance understanding of concepts, issues, events and actions.

2. THE STRATHCLYDE CONTRIBUTION

While such a resource can be successfully deployed across the curriculum it has proved of particular benefit in Art, Geography, History and Modern Studies. Initiatives at the University of Strathclyde have resulted in the production of curriculum-oriented CD-ROMs for all these areas.

Some are aimed at the teacher training student e.g. The Language of Art (Ewing 1997) which was designed to foster the understanding of, and the classroom use of, specific art techniques. Most, however, have been developed to address a particular curriculum topic and have been specifically targeted at pupils aged between 10 and 16 (in Scotland this represents the last two years of Primary school education and the first four years of Secondary education). These resources are all underpinned by the desire to enhance children's understanding of a specific curriculum area and to offer opportunities to explore and research this area.

Looking at Art, Coutts and Hart (1998) and Scanning the City (Coutts et al. 1999) attempt to stimulate discussion of Art and Design issues and encourage pupils to experiment with particular art techniques. Scotland's Weather (Munro 1998) runs under a Web browser and offers students a comprehensive resource on weather data and conditions for an entire year, including dynamic spreadsheets and a stunning set of almost 400 European satellite photographs. There is a growing suite of resources in History which comprises Moving House, Glasgow: A Tale of Two Cities, Tiree: Famine and Clearance 1840-1900, Doon The Watter, and Auld Reekie and the Dear Green Place (Hillis and Calderhead 1993-2001).

While all of these products encompass a common aim their design and development has been quite different – reflecting the different teaching styles adopted in these subject/curricular areas. A brief examination of the structure and content of one such package will illustrate the important contribution they can make to enhancing teaching and learning.

The quaintly named Auld Reekie and the Dear Green Place gives little indication of the content – unless you are Scottish! This history resource deals with life in the two major Scottish cities of Edinburgh (Auld Reekie – or the old smoky town) and Glasgow (The Dear Green Place – so called because of the remarkably large areas given over to parkland and gardens) during Victorian times – 1850-1900. This is the most recent in a series of electronic courseware resources which have addressed historical concepts associated with change over time, differing societal groupings, varied conditions of urban life, disparities in and between different areas of similar urban environments and general lifestyle problems experienced by people in the past.

In order to provide pupils with a comprehensive picture of life in Victorian times, to enable them to compare and contrast situations both within and between the two major urban centres of Scotland, and to help them to assess past scenarios with life of the present, the advantages afforded by multimedia/hypermedia to make available an eclectic set of resources were used to their fullest. Teachers would have found it incredibly difficult to gain access to many of the rich and diverse resources that were gathered together for this CD-ROM – let alone collect these resources together and present them to their pupils for exploration and analysis. It has always been a paradox that, while History has such a vast media resource base, teachers frequently find their knowledge of it to be incomplete, their access to it inhibited and their ability to acquire much of severely constrained (often financially).

On this CD-ROM all facets of different mediums are represented:

- Historical maps of different areas of the two cities
- Detailed maps/plans of Sandyford Place and the Gorbals areas of Glasgow and Royal Terrace and the Cowgate areas of Edinburgh
- Population Census data for the years 1851 and 1891 for these four areas held in a database of over 2000 records
- Textual detail of many of the families who lived in the affluent areas of Sandyford Place and Royal Terrace
- Pictures/photographs of many of the heads of these families – manufacturers, industrialists and professionals – who often held important social positions
- Archive photographs and film illustrating environmental conditions and issues
- Local press cuttings and newspaper advertisements from the nineteenth century
- Old plans of houses
- Textual extracts/transcripts from books and articles – notably on the bodysnatchers 'Burke and Hare', suitably embellished with sound effects!
- Interviews – text, audio and video
- Modern day photographs and video film of the areas and of house interiors
- Songs and music of Victorian times – plus theatre bills/programmes
- Sketches and drawings.

This rich set of resources was selected to provide pupils with a full and detailed picture of contrasts in urban life during Victorian times. It was then organised into selected groupings or topics – illustrated in Figure 1.

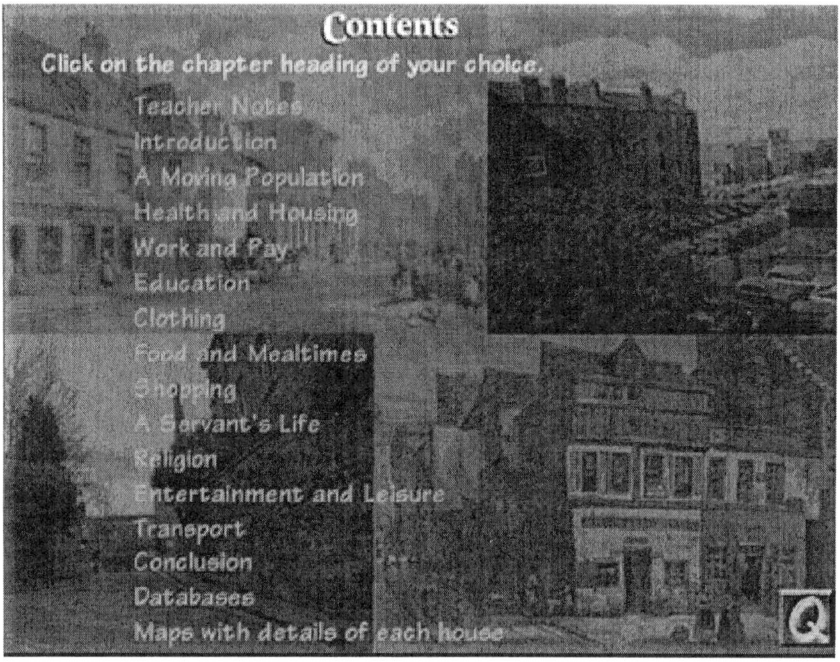

Figure 1. Auld Reekie and the Dear Green Place – main topics

These were carefully chosen to afford pupils the scope, within the general thrust of exploring contrasting lifestyles, to investigate independently or collaboratively a particular issue or area of interest. They can examine a particular urban area over a period of time or they could compare and contrast one area with another. They are encouraged to share their findings and conclusions on any issue or topic they investigate, with other groups. It is therefore possible to build up class profiles of certain areas, social classes or particular socio-economic and environmental issues.

To help pupils investigate or research in a purposeful way and to focus their attention on specific topics and important elements of these topics, a range of tasks were incorporated into the CD-ROM framework. These tasks lead the pupils to many key conclusions and help them grasp major historical concepts – secure foundations for further development. The tasks provide effective scaffolding and are differentiated to ensure the different abilities of learners are accommodated. The inclusion of structured tasks reflects a genuine attempt to help pupils learn, and indeed learn *how* to learn. These tasks are not prescriptive – the Teachers Notes clearly state that 'Each chapter contains suggested pupil tasks which should be supplemented depending on the use of the program'.

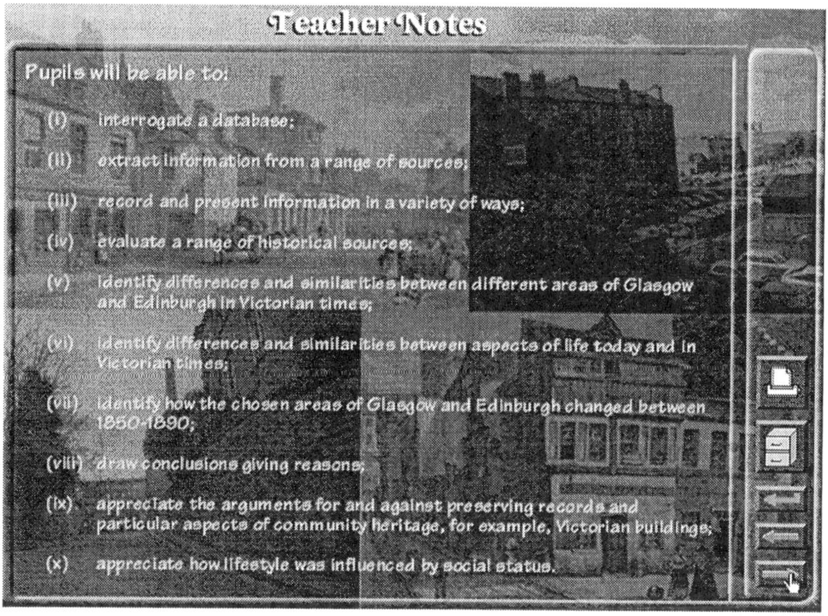

Figure 2. General skills developed using Auld Reekie and the Dear Green Place

The Teacher Notes (Figure 2) are extremely important. The development of the CD-ROM took into account the problems that teachers had reported in using ICT in the classroom and the difficulties they had experienced in teaching aspects of this topic in the past. This coloured the selection of resources and the topics selected for investigation. It also influenced the writing of the tasks and investigative activities for the pupils.

In Scotland primary school teachers and secondary school teachers of History have to teach within the parameters of the document Environmental Studies 5-14 (SOED 1993) which lays down skills pupils must acquire and levels of competence they should attain. Teachers are reassured to find that both the general 5-14 skills which may be achieved through activities associated with this CD-ROM (see Figure 2), as well as the detailed skills which should result from coverage of specific topics, are clearly listed.

Aware of the problems which pupils experience when interrogating databases, a simple user-friendly (and to date foolproof) search facility was created. For pupils who experience difficulties in reading text, audio commentaries were provided on longer text passages and a mouse click displays a pop-up definition of difficult words or phrases. The user can 'blow-up' pictures, plans, maps and advertisements and then scrolls the enlarged image. This technique allows the user to scroll detailed street maps, click on properties and access pictures of individual houses and associated census detail (Figure 3). For example, if 10 Royal Terrace is accessed, the user can discover that, in 1851, this property was owned by David Marshall, a retired sea captain who had worked for the East India Company. He lived with his wife, two sons, daughter and three servants. In 1891 his widow Christina, aged 75, was still living in the house with one of the sons but had five servants to attend to their needs.

Figure 3. A rather splendid property – 10 Royal Terrace, Edinburgh

The program enhancements were implemented to reduce the frustrations which are often experienced by users of ICT in classrooms – both teachers and pupils – and to ensure the learning process is enhanced, not inhibited, by technology! All the resources were knitted together using MacroMind Director and the resultant CD-ROM is a seamless, comprehensive resource which teachers can deploy in myriad ways in classrooms – with every pupil! They can do so confident that all the learning is related to a specific area of the curriculum or syllabus. There are detailed teaching notes and suggestions for use for any teacher unsure as to how this resource might be integrated into their teaching strategy.

Through independent and collaborative investigation of these resources pupils will develop greater awareness of events and the social fabric of the past. They will be able to explain and account for problems and issues and reflect on how life today varied from or resembled life in the past

3. THE RESOURCING DILEMMA

The beauty of this form of ICT is that it eases access to and integration of the many different and diverse resources and media formats which together can afford a vivid illustration of, and spark an explanation of, the past. One small disc can bring to classrooms a set of resources that would be impossible to provide in their primary or raw form. This richness and versatility is not deliverable in any other acceptable format.

Unfortunately few examples of this type of valuable curriculum resource have been created for teachers to use in schools. Most CD-ROM resources are of the encyclopaedic variety – valuable but daunting in their content and frequently lacking a curricular focus. Those targeted at specific curriculum areas are desirable but are expensive to produce and often are not commercially viable. CD-ROM resources are also expensive in terms of development time – time to identify and collect together resources, to examine and organise resources into a usable framework, to create learning tasks which realise the teaching potential of the resources and to mount the composite resource electronically in a structured, integrated, accessible and user-friendly multimedia format. This last task demands the input of skilled educators married with the input of skilled courseware developers who have developed particular expertise with specialist authoring software.

Consequently, few national educational organisations are prepared to underwrite the development of curriculum-oriented resources on CD-ROM. Many teachers are therefore turning to the Web for help There are curriculum specific resources here, often courtesy of educators in the USA, which, because of different curricular foci and teaching strategies/formats have to be significantly modified for classroom use. Similar modification is usually necessary for topic-oriented Web resources created by commercial organisations or charities. Few teachers can afford the time to trawl for resources which require extensive modification or identify what appear to be potential resources but turn out to be yet another listing of resources. Bad experiences just result in opportunities to foster ICT integration being wasted.

We have had twenty years of politically led and directed ICT development. Surely it is time to reappraise the role of ICT in education and focus our activity on the enhancement of the teaching and learning process. This can only be sustained if the software/courseware resource base is widened, users are freed from the many constraints and difficulties currently posed by ICT and teachers are supported through the provision of curriculum relevant resources and pedagogical training. The establishment of national initiatives designed to create a pool of curriculum-oriented electronic multimedia/hypermedia resources which teachers can access and obtain for use in their classrooms would represent a major contribution to the realignment of ICT in education. These resources could be progressively mounted on the Web so that they could be deployed as, and when, the Web becomes an ubiquitous educational resource.

REFERENCES

Blair, A. (1997) *Connecting the Learning Society*. HMSO, London.
Coutts, G. and Hart, D. (1997) *Looking at Art*. CD-ROM, University of Strathclyde, Glasgow.
Coutts, G. et al. (1999) *Scanning the City*. CD-ROM, University of Strathclyde, Glasgow.
Ewing, S. (1997) *The Language of Art*. CD-ROM, University of Strathclyde, Glasgow.
Hillis, P. and Calderhead, D. (1993) *Moving House*. CD-ROM, University of Strathclyde, Glasgow.
Hillis, P. and Calderhead, D. (1994) *Glasgow: A Tale of Two Cities*. CD-ROM, University of Strathclyde, Glasgow.
Hillis, P. and Calderhead, D. (1996) *Tiree: Famine and Clearance 1840-1900*. CD-ROM, University of Strathclyde, Glasgow.
Hillis, P. and Calderhead, D. (1998) *Doon The Watter*. CD-ROM, University of Strathclyde, Glasgow.
Hillis, P. and Calderhead, D. (2001) *Auld Reekie and the Dear Green Place*. CD-ROM, University of Strathclyde, Glasgow.
Munro, R. (1997) *Scotland's Weather*. CD-ROM, SCET/Scottish Office, Edinburgh.
Oppenheimer, T. (1997) The Computer Delusion. *The Atlantic Monthly*, Vol. 280, No. 1, pp. 45-62.
SOED (Scottish Office Education Department) (1993) *Environmental Studies 5-14*. Edinburgh.

BIOGRAPHY

Robert Munro is a senior lecturer in the Department of Business and Computer Education who has been involved in developing the ICT skills of teachers for over fifteen years. He has directed numerous ICT research projects and helped create a range of educational software, particularly for History and Geography teaching.

18

Tracking Technology and Literacy Practices

Looking for Common Ground

Katina Zammit and Toni Downes

School of Education and Early Childhood Studies, University of Western Sydney, Penrith South, 1797, Australia

k.zammit@uws.edu.au

Keywords: literacy, curriculum changes, classroom teaching, integration of ICT, primary

Abstract: Technology standards, such as the National Educational Technology Standards (NETS) (ISTE 1999) have been developed to assist teachers achieve technology outcomes. However, these standards do not take into consideration the literacy demands of the technology, and literacy frameworks tend to ignore the place of technology. This paper reports on an exploration of how a technology-focused framework (ISTE 1999) and a literacy-focused framework (Downes and Zammit 2000) can be blended in a way that is useful to teachers. The outcome was the development of a single revised literacy curriculum framework which unites the two areas of technology and literacy.

1. INTRODUCTION

Education systems, professional organisations and researchers have responded to the ever increasing use of new information and communications technologies in classrooms by developing new curriculum frameworks and standards for student learning to support teachers' plans for effective use of technology. Generally, these guidelines or standards focus on technology as a separate area of the classroom curriculum. For example, the International Society for Technology in Education (ISTE) has developed the National Education Technology Standards for students (ISTE 1999); and the UK has developed Schemes of Work for Information Technology as part of their Standards Site (DfEE 2000). Similarly, in Australia, there is now a separate technology goal in the Adelaide Declaration on National Goals for Schooling in the 21st Century (MCEETYA 1999).

While this approach provides classroom teachers with guidance about the nature of the technology outcomes, it leaves them with the task of aligning these outcomes against those in traditional subjects and of making judgements about how the two areas fit together for effective learning. Teachers generally ask: "How can I use the new technologies to enhance the teaching of English or Mathematics?" Such a question implies a one way process: technology enhancing the subject area. This denies the possibility that the use of the new technologies might demand different literacy and or mathematics learning outcomes or that the careful focus of literacy and numeracy within technology use might in fact enhance technology use.

Downes and Zammit (2000) reviewed the nature of the tasks that students undertook when communicating, handling information and researching with new technologies and found that there and novel literacy demands being placed on students. When using the new technologies, the students were interacting with different types of texts and modes of representation from those they would normally work with in traditional literacy classrooms. These texts required different or additional skills and abilities. So Downes and Zammit (2000) redefined literacy to encompass new modes, mediums and types of text and a broader range of processes. This broader definition generated an expanded curriculum framework with new texts and technologies.

Although there were many advantages to the framework, teachers still had to work out where the technology outcomes fitted into this curriculum framework. Thus they were still asking: "How does the technology fit into this framework"? "This framework still required the teacher to blend the two different sets of outcomes and to generate a framework for integrating the learning experiences. This paper explores how the two perspectives can be blended to be useful to teachers. The methodology included critically evaluating both approaches together. The National Educational Technology Standards developed by ISTE was used as an example of the approach technology focused. Our existing literacies curriculum framework as the literacy focused framework.

1.1 A Literacies curriculum framework

The literacies framework, Figure 1, addresses the demands placed on learners that use traditional and new types of texts for learning about and engaging with their global and digital world. The outcome is of a multiliterate individual, able to be literate in several modes of representation, and to apply their skills and understandings to new learning environments and other modes of representation. The essential skills of the multiliterate individual are locating, comprehending, using, critiquing and creating texts within personal, social, educational, historical, cultural and workplace contexts.

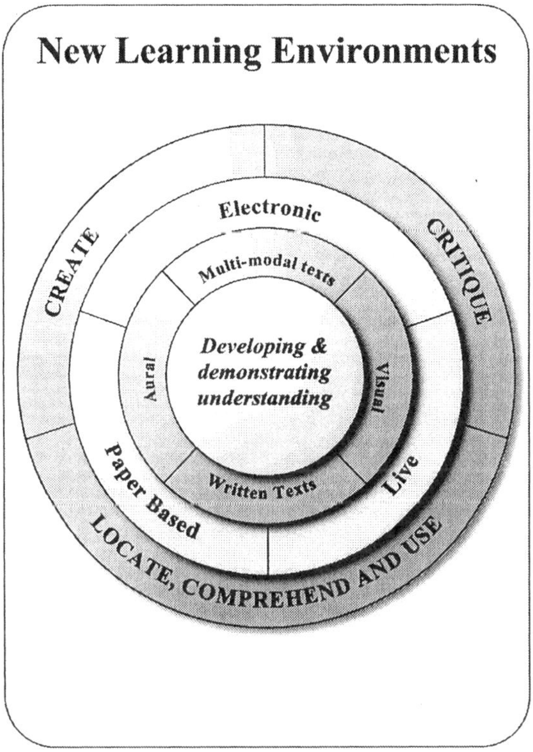

Figure 1. A literacies curriculum model for new learning environments

The actual diagram presents the intersection of the texts, medias and processes required within new learning environments, whatever the subject area. The inner circle is 'Developing and demonstrating understandings'. This emphasises that all teachers and all classrooms are literacy classrooms, where the teaching of literacy is in the service of a deeper engagement with the content of the subject area. The next two layers represent the range of texts and medias with which students engage. They include visual, aural and multimodal texts as well as written texts. The medium of these texts can be live (as in speeches and dramatic performances), paper-based or electronic. The framework recognises that these texts are part of social practices, that they may be part of a collection of texts, and not just individual items.

The outer circle focuses on the processes of teaching and learning, as teachers and students work with texts. Equal emphasis is placed on three sets of processes: 'locate, comprehend and use', 'critique', and 'create'. For many years the emphasis has been on the comprehension and use of texts. Locating texts has become a more strategic skill and is intertwined with 'comprehending and using' as learners move from accessing limited, moderated and ordered collections such as those found in school libraries to accessing the chaotic, anarchic and almost boundless collection of texts in the Internet. Critiquing texts has been a common feature of literary and media studies for many years but not a focus in other more general areas of study.

Teachers can use the framework to map their classroom practices. The mapping can then provide information about the types of texts, medias and processes that students are engaging with regularly and those that need more attention. Teachers can then incorporate those less used texts, medias and/or processes.

1.2 The national standards for educational technology

The National Standards for Educational Technology (Table 1)are designed to provide guidelines for teachers who are "planning technology-based activities in which students achieve success in learning, communication, and life skills" (ISTE 1999). Accompanying the Standards are performance indicators within grade-based profiles and some classroom examples. These indicators and examples help to clarify the six identified foci of the standards. They focus on the students having the necessary technical skills and understandings to use the technology as a tool for enhancing productivity, communicating, undertaking research, solving problems and making decisions and to make appropriate social and ethical decisions about its use.

Table 1. Technology Foundation Standards for Students (ISTE 1999)

1. Basic operations and concepts
• Students demonstrate a sound understanding of the nature and operation of technology systems.
• Students are proficient in the use of technology.
2. Social, ethical, and human issues
• Students understand the ethical, cultural, and societal issues related to technology.
• Students practice responsible use of technology systems, information, and software.
• Students develop positive attitudes toward technology uses that support lifelong learning, collaboration, personal pursuits, and productivity.
3. Technology productivity tools
• Students use technology tools to enhance learning, increase productivity, and promote

creativity.
- Students use productivity tools to collaborate in constructing technology-enhanced models, prepare publications, and produce other creative works.

4. Technology communications tools
- Students use telecommunications to collaborate, publish, and interact with peers, experts, and other audiences.
- Students use a variety of media and formats to communicate information and ideas effectively to multiple audiences.

5. Technology research tools
- Students use technology to locate, evaluate, and collect information from a variety of sources.
- Students use technology tools to process data and report results.
- Students evaluate and select new information resources and technological innovations based on the appropriateness for specific tasks.

6. Technology problem-solving and decision-making tools
- Students use technology resources for solving problems and making informed decisions.
- Students employ technology in the development of strategies for solving problems in the real world.

Recurring themes across the profiles are collaborative activity; personal, literary and informational uses; use of technology to convey information to a range of audiences; use of a variety of resources and tools; problem solving using technology; and the consideration of social and ethical use of technology. There are implicit references to what Downes and Zammit (2000) refer to as medias, modes of representations and texts. While the term 'text' itself does not appear, there are various references to students creating, using, collecting, evaluating such artefacts as products, publications, works and resources – a set of terms that seem to be used interchangeably. There is also in Standard 4, a reference to 'a variety of media and formats'. In this instance the variety of formats could refer to the written, visual, aural and multimodal modes of representation. However, the grade-based profiles and examples do not refer to the different media and formats. In general, the age-based profiles continue to use relatively ill-defined terms such as 'knowledge' or 'multimedia products' or 'information sources'.

Where the standards and profiles do provide greater guidance is in deconstructing for the teacher what are appropriate examples of information systems, hardware and software for the various age groups. As a result there is a progression from skills in using input devices (K-2), to input and output devises (3-5) and troubleshooting across common hardware and software problems (6-8). Similarly, a progression is evident in software use. The K-2 focus is on using developmentally appropriate multimedia resources such as interactive books, educational software and multimedia encyclopaedias, puzzles, and digital cameras. The 3-5 focus on general-purpose productivity tools and a range of others, such as multimedia authoring tools, web tools, digital cameras, email, and online discussions. In the 6-8 profiles, in addition to the productivity and multimedia tools, is the inclusion of content-specific tools and software, and simulations.

1.3 Technology standards from a literacy perspective

When reflecting on the ISTE standards from a literacy perspective, a number of issues come to the fore. These include the role of hierarchies of technology use, the lack of a strong socio-cultural framework and the need for recognition of the diversity of texts used in concert with the various technology tools. Across the profiles is a hierarchy from personal use to information-based (subject area/concept) use. It is only in the 6-8 level that technology begins to be situated within subject areas. In the early years, the focus seems to be solely on the personal. From the literacy perspective, this is problematic. There are instances in the early years where, with guidance from older peers or teachers, young children could access electronic sources of information as part of their work in Social Studies or Science.

Similarly, the standards imply that access to web tools and web authoring should not begin until students are in year 3. Students from an early age study factual topics and work with a range of texts and representations. With the support and guidance young children can create a simple multimedia presentation on a webpage to demonstrate their knowledge and understandings to peers in other schools. From a literacy perspective, if the content and processes are appropriate and important, it is the teacher's role to scaffold the processes of using the technology until the children begin to develop independence. This is the common approach with paper-based technologies. Parents move almost seamlessly from holding the books as they read to their very young child, to sharing the hold on the book, to allowing the child to hold and turn the pages as they decide when the pages have been read. The classroom teacher must recognise that the technology should be accessible to children of any age.

Although the standards refer to social and ethical use, there is limited reference to the sociocultural nature of the texts and the tools, particularly as these are cultural artefacts, which represent particular views and opinions dependent on the cultural background of the developers. Knowledge of the cultural aspects of texts can strengthen students' critical orientation to the use and reading of technology tools and their accompanying texts. There is also the need to situate the use of technology within a purposeful context and for a range of social purposes. It is not enough for students to use the Internet to access information on any topic of their choice. This will not provide them with a deeper understanding and greater knowledge. To change information into knowledge requires a purposeful context, where the texts that are being used, whatever the mode, are considered, critiqued and discussed. For example, in Australia, secondary students read texts about the Cold War that are written from an American perspective. Texts that convey a different perspective may be available to students through the Internet and active reading of the construction of these texts – Why were they written? Who wrote them? can provide students with alternative voices about an event, and skills to deconstruct other texts they are reading. However these are often 'read' as propaganda by the teacher, without considering their sociocultural construction. By having a clear purpose, embedding the use of technology in a topic, can provide students with deeper engagement with the text and provide the sociocultural and critical component lacking in the decontextualised use of technology.

The standards also need to recognise the diversity of the texts that make up the different technology tools. This includes the different genres and the demands on the user to read them, as well as recognising the different modes that information and the technology tools may employ – visual, aural, written, multimodal. The standards need to acknowledge the demands (literacy) of the different technology tools and their environments. For example, the literacy demands of reading from a computer screen are more complex than reading from a book. Layers of meaning (e.g. system level, browser level, site level) are stacked on top of each other with colour, position and perspective used to differentiate them; icons, symbols, labels play different and intersecting roles in providing access to the features and functions of the tool.

1.4 Literacies framework from a technology perspective

When reflecting on the multiliteracies framework from a technology perspective, a number of issues emerged, relating to the lack of attention to the diversity of tools and technologies implicit in the literacy processes. Other issues include the pedagogical demands on teachers when hierarchies of skills, knowledge and understandings are abandoned.

The model is silent in relation to the variety of technology tools and the need to select the appropriate tool according to the medium of construction and the mode of representation. Therefore, there is no rationale or description about how the tools are in fact linked to the purpose of the task, the curriculum content, or the use or creation of a text, and the needs of students. The framework needs to take into account the technology tools, and hence the ability to use them, so teachers may select the tools as well as the medium, mode and process to incorporate into their teaching. In doing this, the technologies and tools of the paper-based medium need to be articulated to sit alongside the newer digital technologies and other electronic technologies such as the television, the telephone, the video. By making explicit all information and communications technologies: those implicit in the traditional definitions of literacy; those that construct the field of study called 'media studies' and the newer digital technologies; the teacher is presented with a more integrated framework, where literacies and technologies meet.

The framework does not have an implicit hierarchy of skills or understandings. At the centre of the framework is 'the development and demonstration of understandings'. As teachers make decisions about the resources, experiences and activities, that they want their students to interact with and reflect upon, they identify the processes, mediums and modes of representation that the students will encounter. From this point they plan their literacy programme. It is an implicit expectation that teachers will draw upon the teaching strategies of teacher demonstrations; peer-supported, joint constructions (teacher-students, group work); and independent activity. It is only with a repertoire of strategies that teachers can free themselves from an hierarchical approach to skill development and use of technologies.

1.5 A redeveloped literacy curriculum framework

The redeveloped literacy curriculum framework makes explicit the diverse range of ICT that underlie the three media: paper-based, live, and electronic. In creating a field to record these technologies and their tools, the order of the concentric circles was re-organised to better reflect the natural progression of the elements of the framework. They are identification of: key concepts and understandings to be developed/demonstrated; key literacy processes used to demonstrate these, forms of representation, through the medium of these texts and specific technologies required. Figure 2 provides a visual representation of the revised framework.

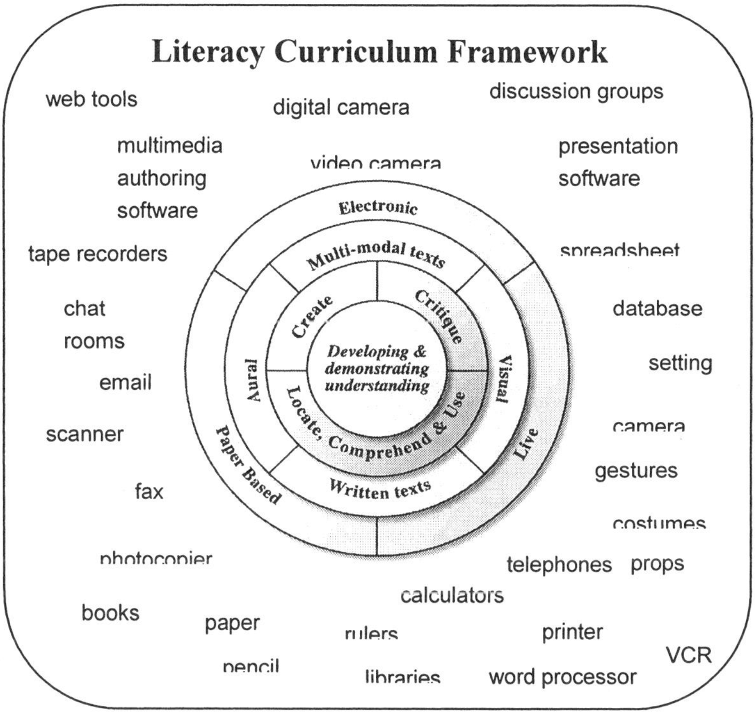

Figure 2. Revised Curriculum Framework

In this framework it is not the range of tools that are subject to a developmental scope and sequence as is the case in the ISTE (1999) technology standards and profiles. As technology is the tool, it should be integrated and selected according to the purpose and needs of the teacher and students. Hence, the tool is chosen to serve the literacy purposes or the teaching purposes. Selection of tools is not age or grade-specific nor dependent on technology skill level. If the necessary tool is too complex for independent use by the age group then skill development can be a whole class activity led by the teacher, a group activity led by peers with expertise or a paired activity where 'a driver' interprets the child's instructions so that the task in completed. In this framework what varies is the level of support, instruction and guidance, which will be related to the students' abilities and prior knowledge rather than just their age group.

2. CONCLUSION

We will be working in a number of classrooms of primary-aged children over the next twelve months. The feedback from the trial will be used to further modify the curriculum framework so teachers can use it in planning their integrated units of work. At the broader policy level, this mapping process and its outcome suggests that the approach of critiquing two frameworks against each other provides one way forward in the curriculum development process needed to increase the effective integration of the new ICTs into classroom learning. The advantage of the approach taken is that the two perspectives, the literacy and the technology perspective, can be accommodated within the one framework in a way that is useful and understandable to teachers.

REFERENCES

DfEE (Department of Education and Employment) (2000) *The Standards Site: Schemes of Work for Information Technology*. [http://www.standards.dfee.gov.uk/schemes/it/] 28.10.2000.

Downes, T., and Zammit, K. (2000, in print) New literacies for connected learning in global classrooms. A Framework for the Future. In *The Bookmark of the School of the Future. The Proceedings of the Conference of Working Group 3.1 of the International Federation of Information Processing*. P. Hogenbrik and H. Taylor (Eds.), Kluwer, New York.

ISTE (International Society for Technology in Education) (1999) *National Educational Technology Standards for Students*. [www.cnets.iste.org/intro_splash.htm]. 27.10.2000.

MCEETYA (Ministerial Council on Education, Employment, Training and Youth Affairs) (1999) *The Adelaide Declaration on National Goals for Schooling in the 21st Century*. Melbourne: MCEETYA.

BIOGRAPHY

Dr Toni Downes is an Associate Professor in educational computing; her research projects span from early childhood education to university education. Katina Zammit is a Lecturer in language and literacy; her research interests revolve around the analysis and use of multi-modal texts for literacy learning and teaching.

19

Encouraging Learners to Prepare Oral Presentations Using Computers

Erol Inelmen
Faculty of Education, Bogazici University, Turkey
inelmen@boun edu.tr

Keywords: collaborative learning, teacher education, secondary education

Abstract: One of the most important contributions of modern technology has been in improving communication between 'learning parties' during the educational process. Although the using computers to prepare presentations can be very rewarding, unfortunately many professionals are not well trained to make effective presentations. In this paper we share the experience gained with students from the faculty of education delivering *instructional material* on special topics of general interest. Presentation skills where enhanced when a creative and collaborative environment was created. It is hoped that the WCEE 2001 conference will provide 'learning parties' with a network where to share their gained experience.

1. INTRODUCTION

The Turkish Ministry of Education has for more than a decade now made great efforts to implement a 'computer based learning' scheme in the secondary schools (MEB 1997). Support from international banks and agencies have made it possible to provide secondary schools with the necessary hardware. Concurrently educational software has been developed with the contribution of the Turkish National Research Council (TUBITAK 1998). Recently the Turkish National Higher Education Council has mandated that graduate and undergraduate programs in computer education and educational technology be started in 14 of the 72 local universities (YOK 1999).

We can observe encouraging improvements in computer literacy performance of secondary school students now entering the universites. But we feel that there is still room for improvement in the method and content of teaching. Experience gained during the last five years in the university where the author is affiliated, highlights the need to develop professional skills way beyond the level of expertise the students are provided with. Given a specific topic, graduates should be able to work on a 'road-map' for a presentation and develop the material in an easy-to-follow format and include in the document information for further work.

This paper urges national and international educational parties to encourage the use of computers in the preparation of effective oral presentations in three main sections: a) needs for education reform, b) oral presentations and c) future work.

2. NEED FOR EDUCATION REFORM

Kant (1999) was one of the many thinkers that throughout the centuries were involved in the enhancement of education. In his view, the art of education brings human "nature one step nearer to perfection". He provided many recommendations for the physical, cultural, personal, moral and practical education of youth: "man can only become a man by education". We now wish to quote from the UNESCO report named, *Learning: The Treasure Within*, prepared by a Commission headed by Jacques Delors published in 1996:

> "There is, therefore, every reason to place renewed emphasis on the moral and cultural dimensions of education, enabling each person to grasp the individuality of other people and to understand the world's erratic progression towards a certain unity; but this process must begin with self-understanding through an inner voyage whose milestones are knowledge, meditation and the practice of self-criticism."

The report describes the four pillars of education – learning to know, learning to be, learning to do and learning to share – as a focus to improve the present conditions if we are looking for a better future in this our planet (UNESCO 1996). Unfortunately educational methods applying the traditional disciplinary boundaries are not adequate anymore to solve the expectations of today. Although universities – in order to cope with these changes – have created research centres that work with more interdisciplinary approaches, the discipline-oriented departmental system of education has survived. Pressure from existing budget regulations, established professional chambers, perceptions and expectations from the community prevents overturning 'the pseudo barriers' that exist between departments.

As the economic conditions in the world change, graduates find themselves coping with altogether foreign problems. Since future developments are unpredictable, continuous learning – a lifelong process – is the solution to the adaptability needed when new situations arise. While promoting teaching the art of applying various tools to problems that require the use of resources for the convenience of men, an education system should develop the ability of self learning in the suggested 'common fields of activities'. The fact that textbooks are written along disciplinary lines puts barriers between disciplines. When students are to be allowed to make their decisions regarding their education, fitting education to their abilities, counselling systems must be implemented (Yerlici 1987a).

Trying to make changes in education to cope with current developments by simply revising 'here and there' old methods of teaching is dangerous. Professionals, who are required to have the ability of communicating with others, are expected to find economical, practical, durable, innovative, aesthetic, safe clean solutions to human needs (Yerlici 1987b). Students must have experience in applying the basic principles to real problems, whatever these problems may be in the next decades. This requirement is at odds with the traditional education system that is based on formal lecturing. Radical changes are thus necessary: the assignment of projects can provide the proper environment for the students to develop the abilities to solve real problems (Yerlici 1989).

As a measure for reform, it is proposed that higher education should a) improve the ability to question and seek for answers, b) sharpen the vision of details, and c) refine the mind for greater sophistication at interpreting data and encourage independent thinking by allowing students observe masters doing their research work (Yerlici 1991, Yerlici 1992). While providing the basic knowledge, good teachers should stimulate the minds of their students towards critical thinking and creativity. Research activities, vital for raising funds and building public image that will attract better students, should not hinder the efficiency of teaching activities (Yerlici 1993).

3. ORAL PRESENTATIONS

Conventional 'Technological Mediated Learning' (TML) educational material emulates classical teaching techniques that have been implemented over the centuries. No matter how fancy TML is made by using sophisticated multimedia techniques, the students are expected to follow the guidelines given as passive agents. This situation leads inevitably to the same boring environment that lectures and textbooks are always blamed for. The following case study shows that by encouraging students to prepare the own educational material, a creative environment where the learner takes a fully active role and make learning fun is created. A holistic framework is suggested as a general educational program, which includes Social, Economic, Political, Legal, Spiritual, Ecological, Technological, Medical, Cultural and Educational fields of knowledge.

The author implemented a novel program of education during the spring semester of the 1999-2000 academic year at his university. A group of 38 university students from the Faculty of Education participated in the 'Introduction to Computers' course, designed to develop the basic communication skills required today in daily life using emerging technologies. The method adopted there was the result of many years of experience gained by the author while using computers as tools for learning.

Ideology
Secularism (mutlu)
Republicanism (bulut)
Nationalism (oksuz)
Estatisme (kapucu)
Revolutionism (gonullu)
Reforms
Hat (gunoz)
Constitution (yazlik)
Democracy (arin)
Language (akbay)
Early (yilmaz)
Amasya (bayhan)
Erzurum (degirmenci)
sivas (bayraktar)
Caliphate (ozturk)
March 31st (gocmen)
1950 (yucel)

Relations
Germany (evci)
Japan (sendogan)
URSS (recepoglu)
Pacts
Capitulations (kirbi)
Lausanne (yasar)
Nato (hocaoglu)
Conflicts
Canakkale (ozcelik)
Sakarya (baltali)
WW-II (baltali)
People
Enver (akpinar)
Inonu (ince)
Groups
New-Osman (uyrum)
Jon-Turk (kunduz)

Figure 1. Topics covered by 'Introduction to Computers Course'

Turkish History during the period between 1860 and 1960 was selected as the class general topic, each student sharing a unique subject matter. The objective was to encourage students to develop their own learning material following a weekly schedule which included the description of the keywords, the design of a roadmap of the presentation and the preparation of the presentation material using animation techniques. In Figure 1 we can see the classification of topics covered in the course.

The students prepared drafts on paper for the presentation slides and then transferred the approved material on the computer followed whenever possible by oral presentations. Make-ups were not allowed and grades points were deducted for the late of the presentations.

The standard grading system generally accepted was adopted as the basis for final assessment. Students not familiar with this 'project centred learning' approach, had difficulties adapting during the first weeks. Nevertheless performance improved as pride on the work accomplished became – without the pressure of grading – the main concern.

Although collaboration between students was not encouraged, in some cases it was inevitable. For the sake of checking the authenticity of the work, short examinations were given whenever possible. By the end of the semester students were requested to make one peer-evaluation and prepared the final own examination questions. There is no doubt that, although puzzled with the educational method adopted by the instructor, students enjoyed in most cases with this new learning approach. All the documents can be seen in web page folder (BU 1999).

Results obtained at the end of the semester were very encouraging. Students in many cases confessed that they were completely unfamiliar with some the themes of their own history. Presenting their contributions in class demanded effort to develop both written and oral presentation skills. This experience showed the need for a publication that would give learners a step by step method in public presentation. Such a document can now be found in the files *car.ppt* and *mpp00.ppt* in the new web page hamlin.cc.boun.edu.tr/~inelmen.

Curiously enough the author was involved another project that started at the same time for students in the areas affected by the recent earthquake in Turkey. A mobile bus furnished with 18 personal computers made visits to schools in the area. Here primary and secondary students got hands-on experience in the use of modern technology.

4. FUTURE WORK

Modern technology can provide efficient tools for communication that would eventually enhance the dialogue between cultures and lead hopefully towards world peace. There are some good examples available.

One good example is the implementation in Scotland as the home to Britain's first 'cyber school' which is in operation since August 2000. Up to

60 pupils were connected at the wired academy (BBC 1999). The WorLD project, implementing modern educational technologies in emerging areas, is being now sponsored by the World Bank (WB 1999).

The British Broadcasting Corporation (BBC), well known for offering reliable world news, has included the graphically three dimensional interactive presentation of Bury St. Edmunds Cathedral in the United Kingdom (BBC 2000). Very attractive web sites give comprehensive information about cultural life in Australia (1999), including the charming Salamanca Market in Hobart located in the island of Tasmania (1999).

5. CONCLUSION

Recent economic and social developments in the world require that education be re-engineered to deal with the life-long requirements of all the citizens in the community. Developing the necessary skills for self-learning is the only way to cope with these changes. Learners should be able to present their ideas orally to different groups by the effective use of modern technologies.

As a concluding note we wish to recall the story of a traveller that amazed with the beauties he saw in the construction site of a new building he was visiting for the first time, asked an artisan what he was doing. The artisan answered reluctantly that he was putting bricks one on top of the other. The traveller moved on and asked a second artisan the same question. This time the artisan answered by explaining that he was building the wall of the government's new headquarters. Satisfied with the second answer, the traveller repeated exactly the same question to a seemingly more experienced artisan. The third artisan answered enthusiastically: "I am proud of working on the wall of a building that will be in the future the pride of our citizens".

This paper gives evidence that students have pride in and enjoy learning if an environment that will encourage creative and collaborative work is provided. Vertical and horizontal integration in education will create the holistic educational approach that is needed in the information age.

ACKNOWLEDGMENTS

The inspirations of Prof. Avadis Hacinliyan and the financial support of the Research Fund of Bogazici University are acknowledged, as well as the dedication of the 38 students that prepared remarkable presentations.

REFERENCES

Australia (1999) [www.csu.edu.au/australia/culture.html].
BBC (1999) [news.bbc.co.uk/hi/english/uk/scotland/newsid_683000/683098.stm].
BBC (2000) [www.bbc.co.uk/history/programmes/cathedral/abbey2/abbey_inside.wrl].
BU (1999) [www.yeditepe.edu.tr/~eor/ders].
Kant, I. (1999) *Education*. The University of Michigan, Michigan, p. 6.
MEB (1997) Turkish Ministry of Education startegies web site [www.meb.gov.tr/index2.htm].
Tasmania (2000) [203.16.7.7/guidcity/salamanc.htm].
TUBITAK (1998) Turkish National Research Council web site [www.bilten.metu.edu.tr].
UNESCO (1996) *Learning: The Treasure Within*. UNESCO Publication, Paris, p. 15.
WB (1999) [www.worldbank.org/worldlinks/english/index.html].
Yerlici, V. (1987a) An Interdisciplinary Approach to Engineering Curriculum. In *Proceedings of the 16th International Symposium,* International Society for Engineering Education, Leuchtturm-Verlag, Alsbach, pp. 512-516.
Yerlici, V. (1987b) The Same Degree for All Engineering Students. In *Proceeding of the European Society of Engineering Education Conference 1987*, Helsinki, pp. 365-370.
Yerlici, V. (1989) A Different Approach to Formal Engineering Education. In *Proceedings of the 18th International Symposium,* International Society for Engineering Education, Leuchtturm-Verlag, Alsbach, pp. 130-133.
Yerlici, V. (1991) New Approaches in Engineering Education. In *Proceedings of the East-West Congress on Engineering Education,* The Australasian Association for Engineering Education, Cracow, pp. 300-303.
Yerlici, V. (1992) Open Engineering Schools for the Developing Countries. In *Proceedings of the 21th International Symposium,* International Society for Engineering Education, Leuchtturm-Verlag, Alsbach, pp. 612-616.
Yerlici, V. (1993) The Place of Teaching and Research in Engineering Education. In *Ingenieur Pedagogik Brücke Zwischen Lehre and Forshung*, A. Melezinek and G. Kurz (eds.), International Society for Engineering Education, Leuchtturm-Verlag, Alsbach, pp 297-300.
YOK (1999) Turkish National Higher Education Council web site [www.yok.gov.tr].

BIOGRAPHY

Erol Inelmen graduated from the American Robert College in Istanbul, Turkey in 1963 as a mechanical engineer. After ten years in industry as a project engineer he joined Bogazici University in 1982. In 1992 he gained his PhD in engineering management from the Marmara University in Istanbul, Turkey. He is now Assistant Professor in the Faculty of Education and is involved in subjects related to project management, computer-aided design/learning and engineering education.

20

Scaffolding or Skeleton

Software Supports Student Multimedia Development Activities

Anne McDougall and Martin Boyle
Department of Science and Mathematics Education, University of Melbourne, Victoria, Australia
a.mcdougall@edfac.unimelb.edu.au

Keywords: learner-centred learning, multimedia, research, teaching methods, case study

Abstract: A study investigated the use of software scaffolding for student design and construction of multimedia environments as a cross-curricular learning activity. The students (11 to 13 years) in a Melbourne, Australia, girls' school, worked in a technologically enriched learning environment and were experienced multimedia developers. The girls were provided with a pre-prepared scaffolding software package intended to challenge, stretch and support their learning. The scaffolding consisted of four aspects of Ancient Egyptian Mathematics: multiplication, The Horus-eye fractions, a hieroglyphic quiz and a potentially rich problem from the Rhind Papyrus. The girls were expected to take this scaffolding as a starting point and develop their own software package from it.

1. INTRODUCTION AND DEFINITIONS

This paper reports a study investigating the use of software scaffolding for student design and construction of multimedia environments as a cross-curricular learning activity. The subjects were students aged 11 to 13 years in a Melbourne, Australia, girls' school. The subjects developed multimedia software to teach students in the grade below them about aspects of Ancient Egyptian Mathematics. They were in a technologically enriched learning environment and were all experienced computer users. Each girl had her own notebook computer with the software necessary to produce multimedia packages.

Scaffolding is "a means of providing a framework which challenges and stretches learners beyond their actual development" (Vygotsky 1978, p. 86) but which also "refers to the practice of providing just enough assistance (not too much, not too little) to help students succeed" (Meichenbaum 1998, p. 141). We consider the practice of scaffolding is especially useful in the context of computer use in learning environments. It must not be too clever, indeed it is often better for it to be unattractive for students, to build confidence and encourage the desire to improve, or even discard, the provided scaffolding.

The use of scaffolding for learning is not a new issue (Bruner 1982, Kaye 1982). Successful classroom teachers have used scaffolding techniques since there were classrooms. Scaffolding can be as simple and effective as encouraging words, through to the use of significant physical scaffolding described in the next section. Roehler and Cantlan (1997) emphasise the wide range of effective types and characteristics of scaffolding.

2. SETTING THE SCENE FOR THE STUDY

The work reported here forms part of a wider study of boys and girls in Melbourne schools as they develop multimedia software to illustrate various aspects of their curriculum. The software was developed in the Visual Basic programming environment. Other supporting software including graphics packages, image editors and linking support to the Internet, provided rich sources of visual and audio effects.

Working in such complex environments runs risks for the learner, and without support the inexperienced are soon lost. This is especially so for young learners in a professional programming area like Visual Basic, as opposed to more protected environments such as MicroWorlds where striking, if cognitively shallow, effects are easily achieved with the manipulative interface as opposed to developing projects under program code control.

2.1 The scaffolding software described

The project involved the students in the production of a multimedia software package, which would be used as a curriculum resource to introduce students in the grade below them to Ancient Egyptian mathematics. The subjects were provided with a pre-produced Visual Basic Project to scaffold their learning of both the production environment and the mathematical content, and a workbook with relevant information in which results could also be recorded.

The scaffolding has been designed with an awareness that the level of support offered was crucial; it is vital that the complexity or cognitive demands of the task should not be reduced by the offered assistance. The scaffolding was menu driven and consisted of four main parts. Students were free to tackle the topics in any order they wished

2.2 The nature of the topics

The Ancient Egyptian multiplication algorithm. The multiplication algorithm (Figure 1) was included to provide a step-by-step mathematical process, offering the student the possibility of success merely by providing an explanation of the algorithm. It was of interest though to see whether the subjects would develop the Visual Basic form to incorporate their own presentational advances. It was not anticipated that the mathematical substance would be further developed, though the subjects were offered an avenue of expansion into binary number systems.

Horus-eye fractions. The Horus-eye fractions (Figure 2) were included to encourage the students to research the culture of Ancient Egypt beyond the mathematics. A mythical adventure underpins the fractions and the scaffolding was designed to encourage subjects to use various resources in exploring the implications of the myth for the ancient society and incorporate some of this information into their software.

A hieroglyph number quiz. The hieroglyph number quiz was designed to be the easiest of the activities to implement in an interest catching and dynamic environment. The students were encouraged to explore the number system of the Egyptians. Interest for the end users and the potential for interaction and dynamism in quizzing were also emphasised.

Powers of Seven. The most interesting of the mathematical content was to be found, well disguised, in the Powers of Seven section. Problem 79 of the British Museum's Rhind Mathematical Papyrus was introduced through the English 'Mother Goose' riddle 'On the way to St Ives'. This offered possibilities of expansion into international culture and also into a significant branch of modern mathematics.

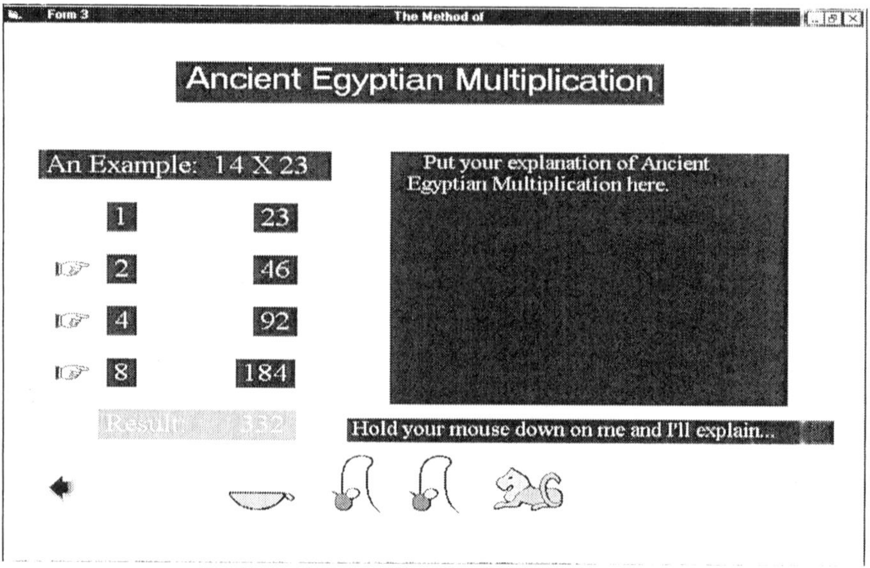

Figure 1. Ancient Egyptian Multiplication

Figure 2. Horus-eye Fractions

3. METHODOLOGY

The seven subjects were provided with copies of the scaffolding software and the workbook on Ancient Egyptian mathematics. They were to develop their own projects over six one-hour sessions. Their use of the scaffolding software was tracked for the first three sessions. The researcher maintained an observational log, and interviewed each of the subjects about using the scaffolding software and the workbook. The combination of this data for four students is reported.

4. RESULTS

4.1 Cherry's Story, Grade 5, 11 years old.

First session:
R: I see you're changing fonts.
Cherry: I don't want the same size! I want to do all my own thing!
R: What do you think of the scaffolding software?
C: I like it because it gives us an example and you can see what you want to do. You see it would take me ages to set this up. But maybe I don't like it because if we didn't have the software we wouldn't have this stuck in our minds forcing us really to do it this way.
Here we have a possible disadvantage of scaffolding. Cherry is reporting an over-influencing effect, feeling forced by the scaffolding to do things in a particular way.
Second session:
Whatever her concerns, Cherry was far from inhibited...
R: You've made big changes.
C: I'm doing the multiplication page first. And I want to get it completely finished. Look it's totally different to yours. The way you work the multiplication is the same of course, but as soon as I'd learnt how to do that from yours I changed it all so that it would be my own work.
Third session:
By this session Cherry was completely in charge of what she wanted from her software...
R: You've changed the whole Horus-eye page?
C: Yes, I wanted to set the graphics out in a completely different way.
R: That didn't confuse you in working out the coordinates?
C: No. It's all the same anyway, in the working out.

From the outset Cherry was confident that she understood what was required and was happy to make substantial changes to establish her own interface.

4.2 Eunice's Story, Grade 6, 12 years old

First session:
R: What do you think of the scaffolding software?
Eunice: It's OK...But maybe it's too much...it sort of says that I've got to do four things and maybe I'd do more or less. It will depend on what I want to do with the project. So this sort of makes me do what it wants. But it's OK. At least I know what to do, so I suppose I can do it in my own way later.
Again the scaffolding is considered too constraining at the start.
Second session:
E: I've worked on the multiplication page. After I figured out how to do the multiplication from yours I changed it all. Now I think it looks real cool. See.
Now Eunice is confident that she can cope with the content of the software and she is ready to break free from the scaffolding.
Now I'm working on the Horus-eye fractions. I've taken your graphic of the eye and divided it up into its six different parts and I've put them on different parts of the page. Now I've got to figure out what to do next to make it interesting.
Third session:
By the start of this session Eunice had worked through all four activities, making substantial changes to their appearance. There was also substantial change in the underlying code for all four even though the mathematics had not yet been done for two of them.
R: You're happy doing all these changes even before you have explained all of the maths?
E: Yes. I know what I have to do so I'd rather just get on with it.
Eunice was very cautious at the start but when she found her feet she flew.

4.3 Frances' Story, Grade 7, 13 years old

First session:
R: What do you think of the scaffolding software?
Francis: It's cool because I know what to do right from the start. I don't think I could have done this from the workbook because I wouldn't have known how to set up the pages to go from one to another. I'll learn, but it's good to get straight into the work without having to worry.
Frances immediately saw the complexity of this programming environment. She appreciated freedom to ignore the technical details, which would have taken the whole session to master unsupported.

Second session:
F: I've worked on the multiplication. As soon as I understood what to do I made up my own example and put it in place of yours.
R: I see you've left the screen more or less the same. It's your multiplication, but laid out much the same.
F: Yes. Your one's OK. I want to keep it so that I can concentrate on making sure that I explain the multiplication well. I'd rather put the time into making sure that people will understand.
An example of the developer putting the user first! Frances was determined to make sure the software worked well for her users and was happy to retain the example given in the scaffolding and devote her time to explanation.
Third session:
F: After what you said last time I've made so many changes to the Horus-eye page that I'm completely lost. See, I even change the picture so it's no longer a Horus-eye. I don't know what to do? Would it be possible to start again...but I've done my multiplication and I want to keep that.
R: What we can do is delete just the Horus-eye page and then I can give you only that page from the scaffolding.
F: Yes please!
Frances started in her own cautious style but picked up erroneously from the researcher that she was expected to do more exciting things which she equated to making changes to the scaffolding. The subsequent departure from her normal work style could only be repaired to her satisfaction by starting again with the original software pages.

4.4 Gale's Story, Grade 7, 13 Years old

First session:
R: What do you think of the scaffolding software?
Gale: I don't really know. Some things I like and some things I don't. It's not really our work. It's what you did. I would have to change all of it so that I can say that it's mine.
Gale is another student who need ownership of the software.
Second session:
G: I've done the multiplication. See, the screen is completely different to yours. I'm really happy to have my own version. Now I can tell people that it's my work. Of course I made sure I understood the multiplication you did before I changed it, but then I did my own one. Actually I did lots of examples to get a good one and I needed to get some extra graphics as mine is longer than yours.
Gale has not been able to wait to change the look of the software. She is much happier and more productive now that the software is hers.
R: What's this you're doing now?

G: I'm working on the Horus-eye fractions. I've taken the eye graphic and put it in its own image box. I think I want to move it around the screen, but I haven't done that yet.

Gale has decided on a complex area of development but she runs the risk of not being able to use the scaffolding code directly.

Third session:

Gale has replaced the Horus-eye graphic in its original position!

G: I see now why you gave us the scaffolding. I could never have worked out the coordinates for the Horus-eye fractions if I had to set up the whole thing myself. I've got it all working but now I want to animate the last part. Do you think that's a good idea?

Finally, Gale took a very 'common sense' approach of making sure she fully understood before making alterations or enhancements.

5. CONCLUSIONS

Though the scaffolding software was developed in the style of an individual it was quickly adapted by the subjects to use in their own learning style. The subjects soon realised that the process of personalising another developer's work was a learning experience in its own right.

It should be noted, though, that other than a page for recording coordinates, little or no use was made of the printed scaffolding workbook. The subjects became immediately engaged with the software.

The seven girls approached the scaffolding in quite different ways. For some it provided an initial framework which the girls extended, changed, and in some cases almost discarded as they developed their multimedia projects. For others it was more like a skeleton for their work, enabling various approaches to 'fleshing out' their projects, but providing a fundamental and lasting support structure around which they developed their own versions of the software.

The objections to the scaffolding were that the subjects did not feel initially that they were doing their own work and that the scaffolding in some way forced the subjects to work in a certain style.

The main advantages of the scaffolding were in providing inspiration for the subjects and, most importantly, providing time. The subjects had time to concentrate on the content of the project sure in the knowledge that the technical aspects of multi-media development were covered.

This small study supports the view that software scaffolding can be a valuable strategy for supporting learning in student multi-media development activates. The wider study, of which this work has been part, will investigate in more detail strategies for development of software scaffolding to cater for differences in student approaches to its use. Figures 3 and 4 below illustrate the girls' work. A typical re-working of the Horus-eye screen. The cursor is on the complex hieroglyph for 1/8 at the top. Clickingon the black box leads to an informative Internet site

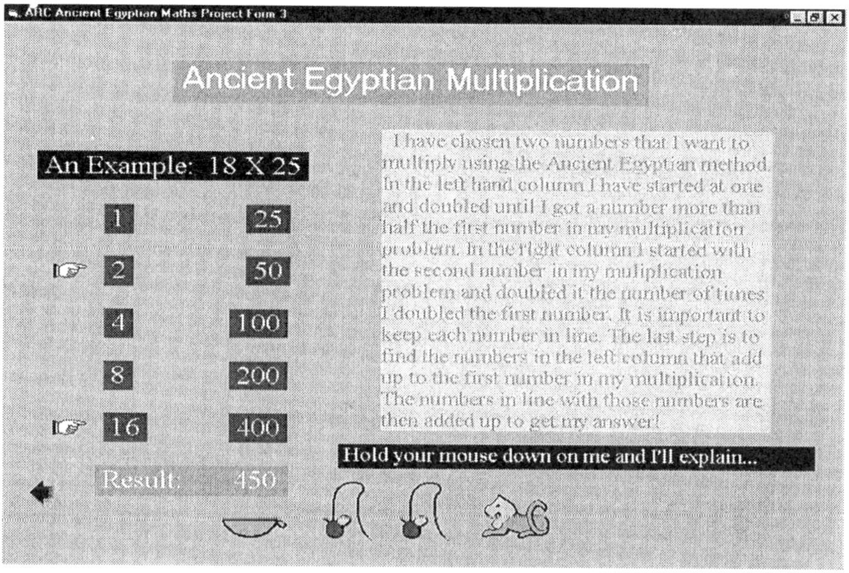

Figure 3. A Typical re-worked multiplication screen.

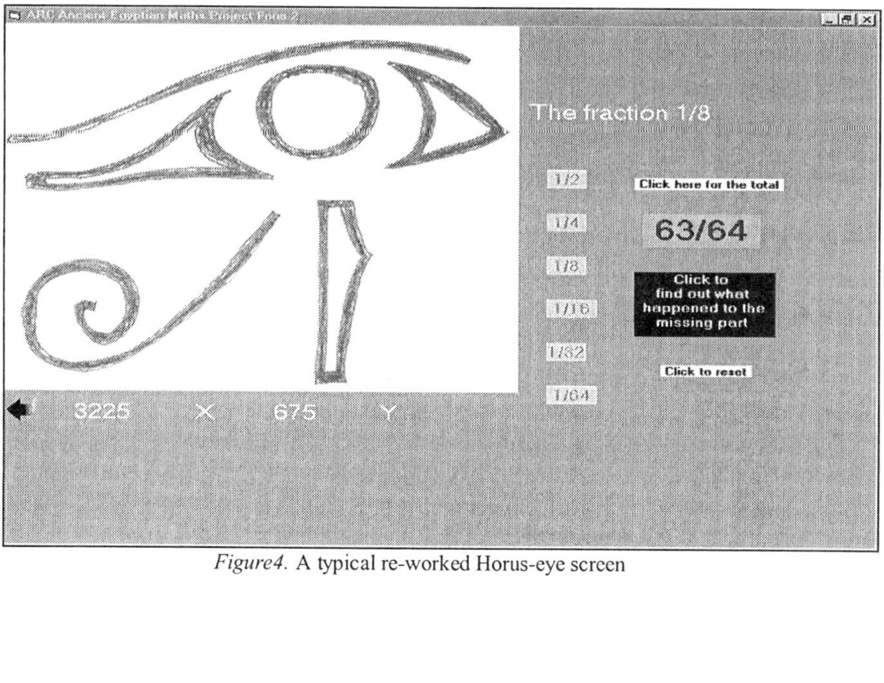

Figure4. A typical re-worked Horus-eye screen

REFERENCES

Bruner, J. (1982) The Organisation of Action and the Nature of Adult-Infant Transaction. In *The Analysis of Action*, M. von Cranch and R. Harre (eds.), Cambridge University Press, Cambridge, UK, pp. 313-328.

Kaye, K. (1982) Organism, Apprentice and Person. In *Social Interchange in Infancy*, E. Tronick (ed.), University Park Press, Baltimore, MY, pp. 183-196.

Meichenbaum, D. and Biemiller, A. (1998) *Nurturing Independent Learners*. Brookline Books Cambridge, MA.

Roehler, L. and Cantlan, D. (1997) Scaffolding: A Powerful Tool in Social Constructivist Classrooms. In *Scaffolding Student Learning: Instructional Approaches and Issues*, K. Hogan and M. Pressley (eds.), Brookline Books, Cambridge, MA.

Vygotsky, L. (1978) *Mind in Society (Ed. M. Cole).* Harvard University Press, Cambridge, MA.

BIOGRAPHY

Martin Boyle was educated in the UK and Australia and after extensive school teaching experience has spent the last five hears in teacher education. His research interests include developing learning environments to assist students who are failing in normal school mathematics.

21

Machine Interviewing for Assessing Student Learning

Automatic Interviewer and Past Recorder Technology

Marie K. Iding, Thomas W. Speitel and Martha E. Crosby
University of Hawaii at Manoa, Honolulu, HI 96822 USA
miding@hawaii.edu

Keywords: assessment, evaluation, classroom teaching, multimedia

Abstract: This paper describes how computer-based machine interviewing and recording devices can be used as formative and summative assessment tools in schools, in the context of electronic portfolios. We describe demonstration prototype instructional and assessment systems that have been developed at the University of Hawaii, including the Automatic Interviewer and Past Recorder. Instructional applications and future directions are described.

1. INTRODUCTION

This paper explores ways that computer-based machine interviewing and recording devices can be used as formative and summative assessment tools for learning science, especially in the context of electronic portfolios. These devices, which can be utilised by individual teachers as stand-alone devices on individual computers, or as networked tools on the World Wide Web, allow teachers to capture and track students' original conceptions or preconceptions in preparation for science (or other subject matter) instruction. They also act as formative assessments to allow teachers to evaluate and remediate possible misconceptions early in the instruction process, and as summative assessments that show teachers, parents, the students themselves, and others, what students have learned.

Machine interviewing and recording devices enable students whose strengths may not be in traditional writing skills to express their learning in other formats that could more intrinsically motivating for them and less restrictive. The richness of individual differences, including cultural, ability, and linguistic diversity can add to the varieties of expression possible in these forums. Additionally, students with disabilities can find modes of expression and note-taking that capitalise upon their strengths and circumvent possible limitations. Machine interviewing and recording devices are consistent with current instructional movements toward non-traditional assessments, such as portfolios, dynamic assessments, and performance assessments. Constructivist teaching practices, project learning and inquiry, and World Wide Web based instruction, and other kinds of distance education, all lend themselves ideally to the incorporation of machine interviewing and recording devices.

Finally, we describe demonstration prototype instructional and assessment systems that are being researched and developed at the Curriculum Research Development Group at the University of Hawaii. These tools are being developed to demonstrate the advantages of employing a distributed computing approach in education and training environments. The devices described and their uses are not an exhaustive list, but serve as the focus of this discussion because of their direct utility as learning and assessment devices in classrooms. The following are being researched, designed, prototyped, and tested: human interaction with machine interviewing, human interactions with past-recording prototype devices, and human interaction with electronic portfolio prototypes. Below, we briefly describe the tools, then we provide research highlights.

1.1 Automatic interviewer

Automatic Interviewer software facilitates machine mediated digital-video interviews with immediate opportunities for self-improvement. The Interviewer serves as a mechanism for teachers to present questions or topics. Students respond to a computer that video-digitises their responses. Students may delete and re-record their own responses until they are satisfied with their own performance. The Automatic Interviewer may be used as a stand-alone application or incorporated into the electronic portfolio by the teacher. Automatic Interviewing is ideally suited to performance assessments and the current movements toward standards-based performance assessments.

1.2 Past recorder

Past Recorder allows selective recording of not only the present, but also the past. Past Recording places audio and, potentially, video events in a small random access memory buffer that is constantly being overwritten. The time duration of the buffer (typically 10 seconds) allows the user to 'reach back into the past' when they start a recording process that also includes the 'present.' For example, an individual using the Past Recorder in a lecture would have the software constantly audio-recording and overwriting audio in a 10 second buffer. When she hears something important that she would like to retain, she presses the record button and the Past Recorder immediately begins recording, while at the same time retaining the previous 10 seconds that would have been erased.

The advantage is clear – by the time an individual makes a determination that something is important and would start recording on a typical tape recorder or other recording device, a major part of the utterance would have been lost. This technology was developed because we assume that no one intends to record all human and natural events at any specific meeting or classroom lecture (Speitel and Iding 1997). The Past Recorder, like the Automatic Interviewer, can be used as part of the electronic portfolio, or as a stand-alone device.

1.3 Electronic portfolio

The computer-aided electronic portfolio prototype tools were developed for education and training purposes. The portfolio serves as a mechanism for students to demonstrate and record what they know and can do in a way that instructors can categorise, assess and provide critical feedback on an individual or class basis. The systems enable rapid incorporation of classroom, multimedia data and text. The Past Recorder and the Automatic Interviewer can be used as stand-alone devices or incorporated into electronic portfolios, the portfolio is described. Extensive educational research addresses topics relevant to electronic portfolios in general; therefore, only issues related to machine interviewing and recording will be addressed in this paper.

Below, we describe highlights from actual classroom applications and research employing Past Recording and machine interviewing.

2. RESEARCH ON MACHINE INTERVIEWING

Machine interviewing has been employed in several educational contexts, with diverse populations. First, we describe some of the actual contexts or cases in which the Automatic Interviewer was employed then we describe general conclusions and observations that have emerged through our research and development.

2.1 Preservice teachers practice responding to job interview questions

An early implementation involved testing the Automatic Interviewer with preservice teachers in one of their regular classes. Students responded to typical job interview questions posed by the Automatic Interviewer, such as requests to introduce themselves and to describe their teaching philosophies. Student feedback indicated that seeing themselves responding to the interview questions was valuable feedback, as was the opportunity to practice responding to questions by repeatedly recording themselves until they felt completely comfortable with their answers. The Automatic Interviewer was set up in a room away from the rest of the class to provide privacy and quiet while students interviewed. Half of the students were left to work with the computer alone, and the other half were assisted by one of the experimenters, an education professor. Students were more likely to rerecord in the unattended condition.

2.2 Middle school students respond to pre- and post-questions in science

A. University of Hawaii Laboratory School science teacher piloted the use of many of these devices in her science classes. In one of the implementations (also described in Iding, Crosby, Speitel, Shimabuku and Nguyen 2001), the teacher used the Automatic Interviewer to have students describe their initial preconceptions and final conceptions about the relationship of light and heat. After lessons and experiments on the subject, their post-conceptions were recorded. The teacher also used the played the results of pre- and post-instruction to parents at an open house as a continuous video. This provided a clear indication for parents of how students' conceptions changed as a result of instruction.

2.3 Special education students use the automatic interviewer at a science camp

An example of how machine interviewing was used in a special education environment was provided at camp sponsored in part by a grant from the National Science Foundation to the Oceans of Potentiality Project, 'Camp Waianae' in Hawaii. The purpose of this camp was to provide special education students with a chance to learn science in a camp-like setting. As soon as the students arrived at 'Camp Waianae,' they used the Automatic Interviewer to introduce themselves. The interviews were stored on the computer so that the next day the campers could hear and see their interviews and add or delete information. As the camp progressed, they added more information to their initial interviews. One of the activities that used the Automatic Interviewer involved having the students take apart a computer and listen to a talk on how parts of the computer functioned. This process gave the students an opportunity, during the interview, to explain the functionality of the computer components. Since this information was saved in the computer, instructors could later play the interviews to learn about any student misconceptions.

3. RESPONSES TO MACHINE INTERVIEWING: MOTIVATIONAL AND COGNITIVE ASPECTS

Our research suggests students in high school and college may improve their self-perception and delivery mode when given machine digital-video interviews with immediate opportunity for self-improvement. For example, the majority of high school students responded very positively. When assisted by an adult, a few sometimes appeared self-conscious and concerned about whether their peers were watching them and how their peers might have reacted (typical concerns of adolescents). We concluded that it might be advantageous to provide opportunities for machine interview where students of this age are physically separated from peers (or outside hearing range). From our observations, students seemed more likely to re-record when left to machine interview without an adult or other assistant present.

Students in the special education camp were especially enthusiastic about using the Automatic Interviewer and other technologies. As one of the co-authors who was also present at the camp commented, "The students loved talking to the computer. They especially liked the fact that the software let them immediately see a movie of their interview and remake any portion of it." When asked if the students were open to a machine and under what circumstances, she added, "These students were definitely open to the machine. The hearing-impaired students particularly liked being able to sign their interview and have it recorded in the movie. The translators provided a voice over the movie so that people not able to understand the American Sign Language (ASL) signs could still understand the interview."

From a cognitive perspective, a number of benefits can emerge from the use of machine interviewing technologies like the Automatic Interviewer. First, students can actually see and improve their own performances. This often iterative process includes metacognitive aspects of seeing and self-evaluating one's own level of understanding as well as one's own effectiveness in communicating that level of understanding. Also, being able to 'erase' and re-record performances allows students to practice their responses and even try different presentation strategies without the pressure of having to produce a single, perfect, final product.

The benefits of machine interviewing devices are consonant with other cognitive, socio-cultural and distributed cognition frameworks and perspectives, depending upon how the instructor structures the learning situation. For example, having students explain or teach other students could be structured to include some of the aspects of Palinscar and Brown's (1984) 'reciprocal teaching,' in which students gradually learned to be more effective teachers and readers.

Additionally, the benefits of students' seeing and explaining their levels of scientific understanding pre- and post-instruction is consistent with constructivist approaches in science education that aim at uncovering and remediating students preconceptions or scientific misconceptions. An effective example was employed by a high school science teacher who had students describe their original conceptions and make predictions about a scientific phenomenon covered in the curriculum via automatic Interviewer ('pretest'); and later their final conceptions and how they have changed. This was originally designed to correspond with Champagne, Gunstone and Klopfer's (1985) description of 'ideational confrontation' (i.e., making predictions about a phenomenon, creating theoretical explanation, doing a demonstration, reconciling original predictions with outcomes of demonstrations).

Clearly, there are other practices consistent with current educational perspectives and practices that could easily be exemplified in the Automatic Interviewer. For example, students' levels of understanding could be 'scaffolded' by the teacher's placement of progressively more difficult or comprehensive questions in the Interviewer. In that sense, the Interviewer could be considered to provide a form of dynamic assessment. Similarly, tasks or questions could be linked to performance standards for students and even for teachers to address in their own instruction.

4. RESEARCH ON PAST RECORDING

Part of the machine-interviewing system involves past recording. This past recording will also be used for more open-ended evaluation procedures to capture and gauge human performance, and for note-taking and general recording purposes.

4.1 Note-taking for high school students

Speitel and Iding (1997) worked with high school sophomores to compare the efficacy of studying science with Past Record versus listening, normal recording, or paper and pencil note-taking. Past Record students averaged more correct responses on a recall test than their peers in the other conditions. Furthermore all information recorded by Past Record students consisted of complete utterances, whereas their 'normal recording' peers were able to only record complete utterances 40% of the time. A Past Record student commented, “I think this is an excellent way of studying. Not only do you record what sounds good, but if you like what you heard previously, you can record that as well. It really helped me in getting the information I wanted to review” (Speitel and Iding 1997, p. 345). Another student said, “Well I think that past recording is very interesting. I think it is better than writing down notes or listening or memorising. Recording is such an easy method because you can listen to what the person is saying and then record it and then go back to it. And you can hear it word for word. Plus you can get a lot more notes on it” (Speitel and Iding 1997, p. 346).

4.2 Peer teaching for high school students

Past Record can also be useful for teaching and performance situations such as the one described by the high school science teacher in which she used the Past Recorder with her ninth grade science students. The students were presenting 'Teacher for a Day' projects. As the teacher explained, “In this project each student group is presenting a different invertebrate phylum. The past recorder enables me to show evidence of each groups' presentation. As I evaluate each group I am able to record important segments of the presentation. I can then play back the recording for the student and use it as a coaching tool. This will be helpful for many reasons; one, the students can learn from their 'mistakes' and because they are able to hear portions of their presentation it allows for reflection. Second, it gives me specific examples as to why the student earned a certain grade for the presentation (example if the student is reading from a paper or if the student is able to present without the use of note-cards). These examples also give the student a chance to hear things that they may have missed during the presentation.”

5. RESPONSES TO PAST RECORDING

Speitel and Iding (1997) described some of the difficulties associated with regular note-taking practices, including short term memory limitations for speech processing (Simon 1974), and lack of completeness of student notes (King 1995). Past recording can be an efficient solution although it might be most beneficial for college-level students who generally do take notes, or as part of an instructional unit on note-taking as a study strategy for high school level students.

In previous research (Speitel, Iding, Crosby and Shimabuku 1999), we described other possible uses for Past Record, including for persons with visual, auditory and other motor impairments that would affect notetaking skills. We also noted that Past Record could be useful for ESL and foreign language teachers and students, and for speech pathologists and linguists interested in recording utterances. We have not yet fully investigated its usefulness for other performance situations besides teaching, although we speculate that this technology would be valuable for those practicing artistic or musical performances, speeches, and story-telling.

6. FUTURE DIRECTIONS

Machine interviewing technologies like the Past Recorder and Automatic Interviewer have great potential as formative and summative assessment tools for students in all content areas, especially when linked to electronic portfolios and even to content performance standards. These technologies are particularly appealing for recording changes in individuals' understandings over time, and for capturing important verbal interchanges and performances that might not as easily be expressed in written form.

Issues that remain to be addressed by future research, especially in instructional contexts, include problems that may be associated with the use of portfolios generally. For example, portfolios (both electronic and paper-based) can be relegated to simple repositories of material unless the selection of materials is done in a thoughtful, reflective, and planned fashion, with clear instructional goals in mind throughout the process. Length of video clips in portfolios is also an important consideration, as very short clips may not adequately capture and convey sufficient information.

Other issues that remain to be addressed with respect to automatic interviewing can include simple aspects of classroom management and noise levels as teachers determine how to most effectively implement activities where many students might be talking simultaneously. Finally, as students articulate their understandings about scientific phenomena, teachers need to carefully monitor students' descriptions, in order to detect and prevent possible misconceptions from becoming deeply entrenched.

Despite these issues, machine interviewing can help organise students' recordings in ways that are meaningful to students and teachers. In conclusion, these tools are beneficial to all students, particularly those with disabilities.

ACKNOWLEDGMENTS

This work was supported in part by ONR grant no. N00014970578 to the third author and DARPA Space and Naval Warfare Systems via ONR grant no. N660019818911.

REFERENCES

Champagne, A. B., Gunstone, R. F. and Klopfer, L. E. (1985) Effecting changes in cognitive structures among physics students. In *Cognitive structure and conceptual change*, H. T. West and A. L. Pines (Eds.), Academic Press, Orlando, FL.

Iding, M., Crosby, M., Speitel, T., Shimabuku, T. and Nguyen, T. (2001) Cooperative and collaborative learning in computer-based science instruction. *HICSS34 Conference Proceedings*.

King, A. (1995) Cognitive strategies for learning from direct teaching. In *Cognitive Strategy Instruction for Middle and High Schools*, E. Wood, V. Woloshyn, and T. Willoughby (Eds.), Brookline, Cambridge, MA, pp. 18-65.

Palinscar, A. S. and Brown, A. L. (1984) Reciprocal teaching of comprehension-fostering and comprehension-monitoring activities. *Cognition and Instruction*, 1, pp. 117-175.

Simon, H. A. (1974) How big is a chunk? *Science*, 183, pp. 482-488.

Speitel, T. and Iding, M. (1997) Audio past recording software for computer-assisted learning. *Computer Assisted Language Learning*, 10 (4), pp. 339-347.

Speitel, T., Iding, M., Crosby, M. and Shimabuku, T. (1999, October) Computer-aided learner electronic portfolio software development. In *Conference Proceedings for WEBNET 99 World Conference on the WWW and Internet.*

BIOGRAPHY

Dr. Marie K. Iding is an Associate Professor in the Educational Psychology Department at the University of Hawaii. Her research interests include scientific visualisation and text processing with multimedia systems. She teaches courses in learning and cognition. Dr. Thomas W. Speitel is a Professor at the Curriculum Research and Development Group at the University of Hawaii. His research interests include teaching and learning of science materials. Dr. Martha E. Crosby is a Professor in the Department of Information and Computer Sciences at the University of Hawaii. She teaches courses in human-computer interaction, cognitive science and adaptive systems.

22

Visual Perception in Design Education

Aysu Sagun
Department of Interior Architecture and Environmental Design, Bilkent University, Ankara, Turkey
saysu@bilkent.edu.tr

Keywords: case study, modelling, virtual reality

Abstract: The recent developments in computer and information technology enable traditional Computer Aided Design (CAD) and Virtual Reality (VR) programs to be used as alternative tools for design education. However, visual perception from two-dimensional representation in traditional CAD programs is quite difficult. Immersion, presence, interactivity and dynamism in virtual environments are facilitating communication and visual perception of complex concepts and information and motivating students to participate in design process, by increasing data awareness. Related to these concepts, a case study was conducted at Bilkent University with freshmen interior design students, taking scale, shape, color and texture as independent variables, to compare visual perception in VR and traditional computer presentations, using traditional computer program, AutoCad and VR computer program, Virtus. The results indicate that the hypothesis, which states that use of VR programs provides a more accurate visual perception than traditional computer drawing programs, is not rejected except for scale and shape.

1. INTRODUCTION

Drawing is a type of modeling that is vital for the designers since it assists the externalisation and development of mental concepts (Donath 1996). The spatial information given in the architectural design drawings allows the designer to understand the space being designed and helps them for the next steps in the improvement of the project (Badler 1995). There are a wide variety of media or rendering techniques in drawing. Orthographic drawings such as plan, section and elevation are the two dimensional abstractions that force the observer to construct the design model in their mind. Axonometric and perspective drawings are the other techniques to present the design data, two-dimensional images representing the third dimension. Besides there are computer modeling and interactive computer generated worlds-Virtual Environments (VE). Both the computer modeling and VE give you the experience of building in the same way it would be if the building were constructed. Then, the question arises: How does VE differ from traditional computer drawings?

Perception is a matter of data input to the mind from the environment so we need more and more input to the senses to observe the sense of real. Visual experience is the result of data input to our mind through our eyes. The visual world is formed with information about scale, shape, color and texture. Continuous changes in the structure of visual world are projected to retina (Coyne 1994). A primary goal in examining an image is recognising and understanding the features and objects within the image (Hende and Wells 1997). Traditional computer graphics allows the observer to look through a restricted window to perceive the space designed since the observer is limited to a single viewpoint each time. Architecture is a static entity. Its dynamics come from the aspects of moving through the space (Emmett 1992). Thus, the perception of form in VE is much greater than it is in traditional computer drawings because of flexibility of movement of the viewpoint through the environment (Brill 1993). Virtual worlds can provide a better understanding of the image of the space since they are multi-dimensional, interactive computer generated environments, which enable people to act in and upon a space with varying degrees of time. Thus, virtual environments let us leap through the restricted window to experience the space. In other words, the observer can directly access and manipulate the data in VE. Due to the interactive movement, more cues about scale can be captured and used in virtual worlds. Color and texture, on the other hand are enhancing the perception with the help of interaction.

The ability to control a viewpoint of two-dimensional moving image and the ability for the observer to access and manipulate data, including representation choice, increase the experimental understanding. Although the observers cannot physically move their body, they are given the possibility to control a viewpoint that can be manipulated by keyboard or mouse movements. In this way, the observer can control the sequence of events that is being observed (Van Dam 1993). Simply, we can say that a universal field of sensory input is provided by VE since the idea of virtual reality relies on concepts of perception and representation. The components of VE for interaction include a means to display visual information, a means of 3D location of viewpoint and a means of manipulating the environment.

Moreover, there are research studies on the perception of VE however they are based upon the equipments such as head mounted displays and data gloves, used in more developed virtual reality systems. They include not only the visual perception, but also the perception of other senses such as hearing, smelling and touching.

2. RESEARCH DEFINITION

In this research, the aim is to investigate how VE differ from traditional computer drawings in terms of visual perception. The question has arrived from the discussion on computer aided architectural design education tools. The hypothesis is that using computer programs that generate VE provides a more accurate visual perception than the traditional Computer Aided Design (CAD) programs in architectural design education. In this study, the traditional experimental method is used to test the effectiveness of VE. A traditional computer program (AutoCad 14) and a virtual reality program (Virtus 1.0) are compared to test the hypothesis. Visual perception is the dependent variable that is being studied. Shape, scale, texture and color are chosen as the independent variables since visual perception is a combination of these properties in human brain.

The solid that creates the structure and void is called *shape*. It is a medium used by architects since interplay and changes in form and shape are observed while moving in the architectural space. Simply, we can say that it makes up everything that can be seen and touched. The second independent variable, scale contributes to the understanding of the architecture. It provides a close estimation of size of the objects and elements by a visual comparison. There are three types of scale, physical scale (direct size relationship of one form to another one), human scale (relationship of the size of human being to the architectural elements) and proportional scale (relationship of forms within the set of objects (Zobel 1995). In this research, the relationship of forms within the set of objects, in other words, the proportional scale is used to enable the subjects to roughly measure the visual field. The other two independent variables, texture and color give clues for understanding the size, shape and depth of architectural forms (Zobel 1995). Texture is related to the materials of the objects. Color is the property of an object carried to the photoreceptors of the eyes by light. It provides distinctions or similarities between objects or spaces. When it is mixed with surface textures, it revels the basic quality and composition of the object, such as purity and material (Zobel 1995).

Research Framework For this study, two groups of twelve participants (totally twenty-four subjects) were chosen randomly from the Department of

Interior Architecture and Environmental Design at Bilkent University. All of the subjects were at the same education level, freshman students who have almost the same experience in architectural design and no computer experience in drawing. Two different tasks are used for comparison. One of them is a traditional computer program-AutoCad 14 and the other one is Virtual Reality Program- Virtus 1.0. The same interior space with abstract forms is drawn on computer using both programs (see Figure 1).

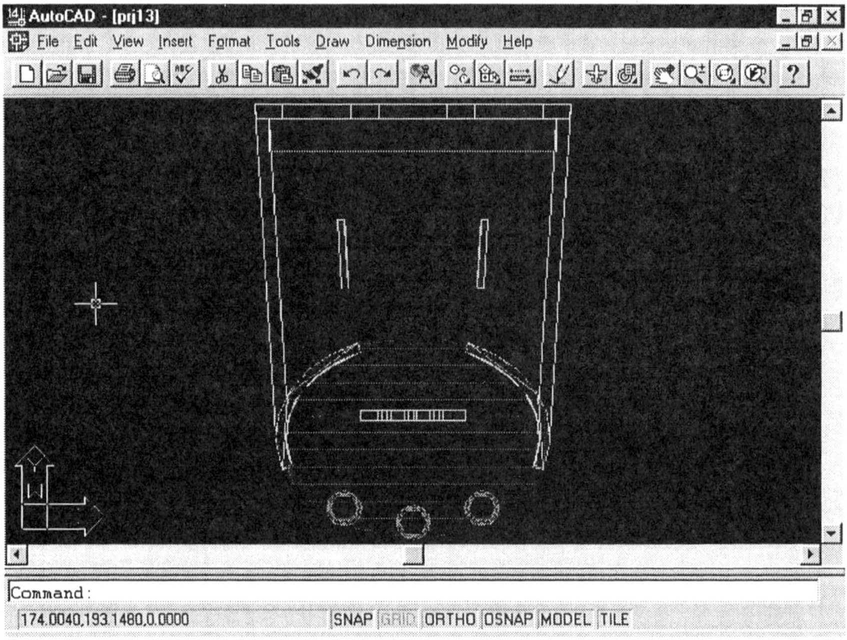

Figure 1: Top view of the abstract space

Abstract forms are preferred in order to avoid assumptions that can appear related to the observer's experience. For instance, if a chair was used as an object in the project, the observer may want to use its size as a criterion for proportion. In Figure 1, the top view of the abstract space can be seen however the participants did not observe this view. The views observed by the subjects can be seen in Figures 2 and 3. Finally, a questionnaire was developed to be given to both of the group of subjects including twenty questions about shape, scale, texture and color, consisting of five questions for each.

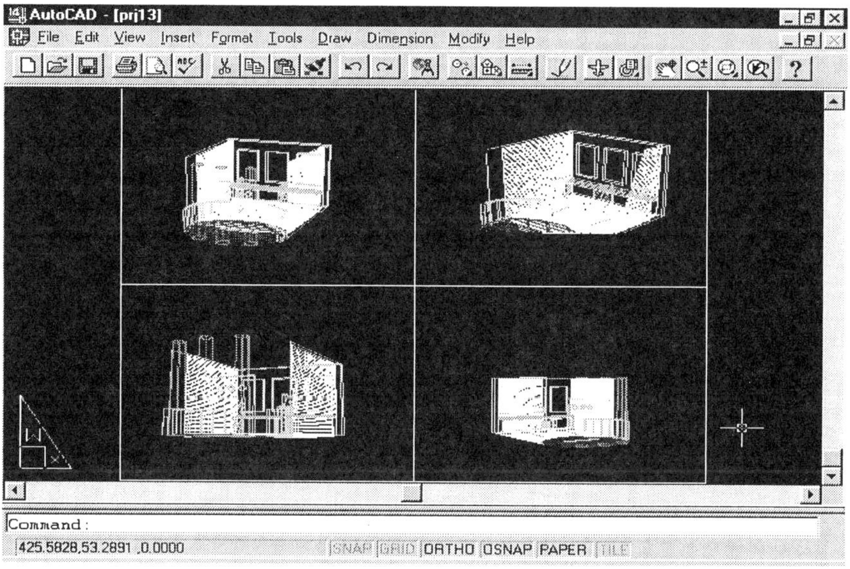

Figure 2: The four perspective views of the abstract space created in AutoCad

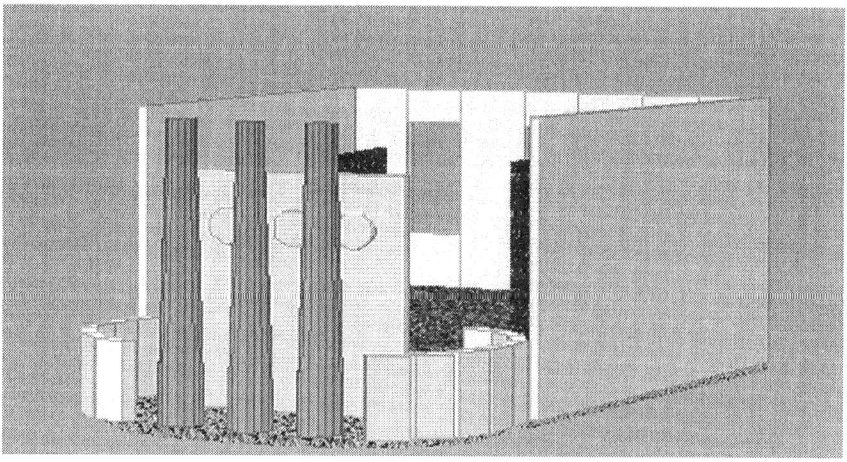

Figure 3: A view from the abstract space created in Virtus VE

The two groups of samples were allowed to observe the same four 3D perspective views – created from four different viewpoints – presented in AutoCad drawing and experience the 3D virtual world constructed using Virtus, one by one. The first group of twelve subjects was asked to observe AutoCad presentation. Since it is impossible to manipulate data on computer in AutoCad, they were allowed to zoom in and out to view the details in the perspective views only. The second group of twelve subjects experienced

VE created by Virtus and were able to move through and around the space using mouse only. After each observation, the questionnaire was given to the subject respectively and asked to answer the twenty related questions. There was no time constraint. It took each sample about 15 to 20 minutes to observe and complete the questionnaire.

Questionnaire The questionnaire was composed of four parts about scale, shape, color and texture. First part, scale, included questions about the relationship of height of the elements, such as parapet and columns, with the room and questions that compare length and width of the space and openings. Descriptive questions were asked in the second part, to understand how the shape and form of the room and elements in the room is perceived. The third part, color, involves two approaches in which relative questions about the color of the surfaces and objects were investigated and descriptive questions in which color chips were used. Finally, the last part, texture, included descriptive questions in which texture and material of the surfaces were asked to be defined from the verbally or visually given choices.

Measurement The results of the questionnaire were analysed by using statistical methods, because statistical methods represent the summary and analysis procedures for determining group performance, more precisely and conveniently than visual inspection of raw data. Since the number of subjects used in a group in this study was small (less than 30), non-parametric statistics was used.

Statistical Analysis Non-parametric method of analysis offers alternative procedures. It is used in case of normal distributions such as small sample size. Non-parametric method of analysis are descriptive, they are based upon statistical models for data. They require fewer assumptions to be built into the model (Cooper and Weeks 1983). They have generally higher variance than distributional statistics. Comparison is made between parameters. In this study, we tested our hypothesis by using Mann-Whitney Test, which is a non-parametric method of analysis. In this test, the focus is on the median as the measure of location or central tendency. When the objective is to test for a significance difference between two locations statistics computed from two independent samples, Mann-Whitney Test is usually used (Daniel and Terell 1995). Mann-Whitney Test is preferred for this study since the sample size is small (less than 30) in our case. The raw data can be seen in Table 1.

Table 1: Raw Data (the correct answers given to the 20 question. P1 is the population for AutoCad and P2 is the population for Virtus)

	1	2	3	4	5	6	7	8	9	10	11	12	13	14	15	16	17	18	19	20
P1	11	5	6	12	9	6	2	8	1	7	4	9	5	1	7	9	1	5	3	5
P2	11	4	9	8	9	9	6	9	2	7	8	9	10	12	11	12	9	11	9	11

The null hypothesis is that the medians of two populations are equal. The alternative hypothesis is that the median of the population using AutoCad is less than the one using Virtus. Minitab is used to apply the Mann-Whitney Test and the results were as follows:

```
MTB>Mann-Whitney 95.0 c2 c1;
SUB> Alternative -1
Mann-Whitney Confidence Interval and Test
C2      N=20      Median= 5.500
C1      N=20      Median= 9.000
Post Estimate for ETA1-ETA2 is -3.000
95.0 pct c.i. for ETA1-ETA2 is (-4.999, -1.000)
W=302.0
Test for ETA1=ETA2 vs. ETA1 l.t. ETA2 is significant at 0.0018
The test is significant at 0.0016 (adjusted for ties)
```

Figure 4: Computer Results

Calculations for each variable are given in the Figures 5, 6, 7 and 8:

```
MTB>Mann-Whitney 95.0 c1 c2;
SUB> Alternative -1
Mann-Whitney Confidence Interval and Test
c2      N=5      Median= 9.000
c1      N=5      Median= 9.000
Post Estimate for ETA1-ETA2 is  1.000
95.0 pct c.i. for ETA1-ETA2 is (-4.001, 5.002)
W=29.5
Test for ETA1=ETA2 vs. ETA1 l.t. ETA2.
Cannot reject since W is g.t. 27.5
```

Figure 5: Calculations for Scale

```
MTB>Mann-Whitney 95.0 c3 c4;
SUB> Alternative -1
Mann-Whitney Confidence Interval and Test
c3      N=5      Median= 6.000
c4      N=5      Median= 7.000
Post Estimate for ETA1-ETA2 is -1.000
96.3 pct c.i. for ETA1-ETA2 is (-6.999, 4.001)
W=22.5
Test for ETA1=ETA2 vs. ETA1 l.t. ETA2 is significant at 0.1736
The test is significant at 0.1706 (adjusted for ties)
Cannot reject at alpha=0.05
```

Figure 6: Calculations for Shape

```
MTB>Mann-Whitney 95.0 c3 c4;
SUB> Alternative -1
Mann-Whitney Confidence Interval and Test
C5      N=5      Median= 5.500
C6      N=5      Median= 9.000
```

```
Post Estimate for ETA1-ETA2 is -3.000
96.3 pct c.i. for ETA1-ETA2 is (-7..998, -0.000)
W=18.0
Test for ETA1=ETA2 vs. ETA1 l.t. ETA2 is significant at 0.0301
The test is significant at 0.0289 (adjusted for ties)
```

Figure 7: Calculations for Color

```
MTB>Mann-Whitney 95.0 c3 c4;
SUB> Alternative -1
Mann-Whitney Confidence Interval and Test
C7        N=5        Median= 5.000
C8        N=5        Median= 11.000
Post Estimate for ETA1-ETA2 is -6.000
95.0 pct c.i. for ETA1-ETA2 is (-9.999, -2.000)
W=16
Test for ETA1=ETA2 vs. ETA1 l.t. ETA2 is significant at 0.0108
The test is significant at 0.0096 (adjusted for ties)
```

Figure 8: Calculations for Texture

Evaluation Of Statistical Analysis According to the calculations done with a computer, the results of the Mann-Whitney Test, for total 20 questions, indicated that null hypothesis iwa rejected. The alternative sub-command (less than, <) was used to do a one-sided test, for specifying the level of confidence desired for interval estimate. The confidence interval for point estimate went from -4.999 to -1.000. This meant that the medians of correct answers using AutoCad program was 1 to 5 less than the Virtus. The chance of observing two samples when in fact the populations have the same median was 0.0018. The p value, in other words the probability of committing error was 0.05 since the degree of confidence is 95%. When we look at the table of Mann-Whitney Test Statistics, quartiles (lower critical value for test statistics) at 0.05 is 139. Since the critical value for test statistics is less than the calculated value W (139<301), the null hypothesis was rejected. When we evaluated each variable, scale, shape, color and texture individually in the same logic (see Figures 5-8), the null hypothesis was rejected for color and texture. However, the null hypothesis could not be rejected in scale and shape at probability of committing error of 0.05, since the critical values for the test statistics was greater than the calculated values.

3. DISCUSSION

In this study, in order to examine which computer application would be more productive in architectural design education, freshman students without any experience in computer drawing was preferred. As we can see from the results, our hypothesis, which stated that usage of virtual reality computer programs provided a more accurate visual perception than traditional computer drawing programs, was not rejected except for the scale and shape. The null hypothesis for scale and shape can be rejected, however the medians of the scale and shape data of two computer programs were quite close to each other (see Figures 5-6). Since it was a small sample test, we can say that, it supported the idea that using virtual environments in architectural design practice is better than traditional computer drawing programs for a more accurate visual perception.

As it was stated before, the movement, interactivity and flexibility in VE enables the observer to visually perceive the data of projects more accurately. Thus, the design concepts, examples and projects can be presented to the design students in VE as well as students can work on their own design projects in VE. The feedback, crits, provided to students about architectural design projects would be more reliable if a model is constructed and observed in a VE since it is possible to perceive the space designed as a whole with all the clues needed to understand a space.

Moreover use of VE is spreading in many design institutes throughout the world, using other advantages of VE other than visual perception, such as collaborative design studios or multimedia applications. The reliability of VE in architectural design education can be studied in further research, improving the study in this case with more subjects and more developed tools to produce solutions to the problems in VE.

REFERENCES

Badler, N., Dorsey, J., Nimeroff, J. and Simoncelli, E. (1995) Rendering Spaces for Architectural Environments. *Presence: Teleoperators and Virtual Reality*. April, pp. 286-296.

Brill, M. L. (1993) Kicking the Tires of Virtual Reality Software. *Computer Graphic World*, June, pp. 40-53.

Cooper, R. A. and Weekes, J. (1983) *Data Models and Statistical Analysis*. Barnes and Noble Books, New Jersey.

Coyne, R. (1994) Heidegger and Virtual Reality: The Implications of Heidegger's Thinking for Computer Representations. *Leonardo*, 17, pp. 65-73.

Daniel, W. and Terrell, J. (1995) *Business Statistics for Management and Economics*. Houghton Mifflin Company, Boston.

Donath, D. and Regenbrecht, H. (1996) Using Virtual Reality Aided Design Techniques for Three-dimensional Architectural Sketching. *Acadia*, pp. 201-212.

Emmett, A. (1992) New Dynamism. *Computer Graphics World*, June, pp. 30-38.

Hende, W. R. and Wells, P. T. (1997) *The Perception of Visual Information*. Springer, New York.

Van Dam, A. (1993) VR as a Forcing Function: Software Implications of a New Paradigm. In *IEEE 1993 Symposium on Research Frontiers in Virtual Reality*, California, October, pp. 5-7.

Zobel, R. W. (1995) The Representation of Experience in Architectural Design. *Presence: Teleoperators and Virtual Reality*, 4, pp. 254-265.

BIOGRAPHY

Aysu Sagun, MFA, is PhD student at Bilkent University. She is an interior architect and has been working as a teaching assistant in the Department of Interior Architecture and Environmental Design since 1998. Her interests include virtual reality and web-based design education. She has an M.F.A degree about the use of virtual environments in design education and Virtual Reality Modeling Language (VRML). She is broadening her research studies to the field of Universal Design Education through the use of new computer technology in her PhD study.

23

Portable Computing and the Networked Learner

Wireless is nearly a Total Solution

C. Paul Newhouse

School of Education, Edith Cowan University, Perth, Western Australia

p.newhouse@cowan.edu.au

Keywords: laptop, networks, barriers, classroom teaching/practice

Abstract: The use of wireless networking with the latest portable computers may provide the solution to many technical and logistical problems faced by schools in facilitating the use of computers by students. This paper reports on an ethnographic action research study with the aim to investigate the potential of wireless networking in primary (elementary) schools. Data was collected about students, teachers and technology using formal interviews, observations of lessons, questionnaires, and informal discussions with teachers. The technology was successfully implemented with no significant technical problems supported by a mentoring approach to the professional development of teachers.

1. INTRODUCTION

The 'Holy Grail' in educational computing has been to provide access to adequate computer processing to support the learning of students wherever they are, whenever they need it and for whatever task it is needed. The reality now is that there are few technical barriers to these requirements (Becker, Ravitz and Wong 1999). The range of software available to support learning is vast and improving in quality to support almost any task we can imagine. The availability of sophisticated networking and powerful desktop and portable computers have provided the means of organising access to computer processing for students whenever it is needed. Finally, wireless networking has set the computer free to roam wherever it is needed by students.

For at least two decades many researchers and national projects have investigated the use of computers in schools (e.g. Collis 1994, Gardner, Morrison, Jarman, Reilly and McNally 1994, Mandinach and Cline 1996). Educators have increasingly proclaimed the potential of computers in education to fulfil many of our aspirations. Consistently the finding has been that computer technologies have had little impact on schooling (Plomp and Pelgrum 1992). However, reports over the past few years appear to indicate that this situation is starting to change (Becker et al. 1999). To be realised critical changes will be required in curriculum, schools and classroom learning environments. Will these changes precipitate from the avalanche of computers into schools, particularly through schemes to provide one computer per student or must these changes occur before embarking on such schemes? While it is relatively safe to contend that most students in the future will have some form of portable computer processing, given the historically robust nature of schools it is difficult to predict in practice what impact this will have on schooling and the curriculum. Longitudinal research needs to be conducted at many school sites before any reasonable predictions can be made.

2. FINDINGS FROM MY EARLIER RESEARCH

The researcher was invited by the Principal of a secondary school to conduct an independent evaluation of the implementation of an initiative designed to encourage every student to have and use a portable computer to enhance their learning. As a result the researcher became immersed in the school community for a period of three years and collected a wide variety of data from students, teachers and the administrative records of the school. Four years later the researcher returned to collect follow-up data. Overall data were collected from over 60 teachers, 350 students (three cohorts of secondary students) and the observation of a large number of lessons (71 were analysed). Only a few of the findings of this large study can be alluded to in this paper.

2.1 The adequacy and applications of the technology

The Macintosh notebook-style computers appeared to be well matched to the needs of the students in terms of operation and portability, but not physical reliability. Although most models of computer used did not appear to be sufficiently robust, this in itself was not an inhibiting factor for either students or teachers. Students were inhibited by some features such as short battery life, perceived heaviness (if books required as well), and inadequate processing power and memory for some tasks. It was difficult to get access to the school's network and thereby the internet, since classrooms had at most one access point. Students had to connect via one of a handful of access points in the library or use a desktop computer. In the final year of secondary school about 50% of the students still had their portable computer (half of these boarded at the school).

Apart from in specialised computing classes, the computers were mainly used as writing tools (word processor) and for game playing. This concurs with the findings of many other researchers (e.g. Ainley, Bourke, Chatfield, Hillman and Watkins 2000). Occasionally subject specific applications such as Math Master® or MacGlobe® were used. In computing classes, students used a wider range of applications from databases and spreadsheets to Hypercard® and web-page production. In Year Eight (13 year old) the computers were typically used for about 3 hours per week at home and initially between 2 and 5 hours per week at school with an average of 8.4 hours per week in 1999. Year Twelve students (17 year old) estimated a mean of 3.7 hours per week using computers at home and almost none at school. For about 90% of these students only the word-processor and perhaps internet applications were used. In 1999 many Year Eight students mentioned applications such as spreadsheets for graphing, draw packages for graphics, internet applications and some multimedia presentation applications.

2.2 Students' skills and attitudes

One of the school's major aims was to increase the computer literacy of all students, common to many such programmes (e.g. Ainley et al. 2000). While to a large extent this was realised, most students developed skills in a haphazard way, relying on information gleaned from computer support teachers and other students, particularly those in computing classes. Students still required and expected more guidance and instruction in the efficient use of the machines and a better understanding of the underlying concepts. Irrespective of how well the programme was implemented it was likely that about 5% of the student population would have negative attitudes towards either the computers or their own competence in using the computers. Generally students were positive about the programme although many felt that teachers needed to facilitate more use of the computers. While there were increasingly positive outcomes for Year Eight students, particularly for those who were boarders, the experiences of many older students where the computers were rarely used, put them off using computers altogether.

Year Twelve students perceived the main benefit of having the computers to be the development of computer literacy for future work requirements and that this had largely occurred in Years Seven and Eight. They did not perceive the computers being a useful learning tool but felt that they needed to use the computers at home for word processing assignments, particularly for English. Over 90% indicated a reasonable level of computer literacy, 69% indicated they couldn't do without computers and 72% felt the programme had been a success. These perceptions should be very disturbing for the school since a computer literacy based on experiences four years previous is clearly inadequate and the relegation of such a powerful tool to typing up assignments and occasionally finding information on web-pages would seem extremely wasteful.

In 1999 the programme was seen as successful by all Year Eight students, even those who didn't like using the computers. The main benefits concerned the development of computer literacy and the easier and neater production of work. Most students used a commercial 'book on CDROM' for mathematics that they liked because it saved carrying the book around. There was still little if any mention of the computers being a useful learning tool but it was seen as a useful production tool and by some for accessing information. Some students felt that some of their classes had changed because they used their computers for 'everything'. The major problems were still the weight of carrying the computers and the high level of breakdowns. A number of students felt that they needed more systematic instruction on using their computers.

2.3 The curriculum, teachers and learning environments

Students were more likely to use the computers for classes associated with subjects such as English and social studies in which teachers required a substantial amount of document production. The computers were less likely to be used in classes with older, higher ability students than younger and/or lower ability students. This seemed to result from teachers' perceptions of the requirements of preparing students for tertiary entrance examinations. These examinations dominated the curriculum for most teachers and students, even in the lower secondary school. It was perceived that students needed to practice handwritten work in all subject areas to be prepared for these examinations. While there was little that could be done about the examinations themselves, further investigation should be conducted on the perceived link between using computers within the curriculum over the five years of secondary schooling and the performance of students in examinations.

In responding to the presence of the portable computers in a class, a teacher's actions could be classified into three broad types:

a) actively facilitates the use of the computers (*Active*),

b) permits the use of the computers by those students choosing to do so (*Passive*), or
c) unconsciously or otherwise discourages the use of the computers (*Negative*).

Most teachers in 1995 typically responded in either *Negative* or *Passive* ways which limited the use of the computers. Only a few (about eight) usually responded in *Active* ways which is consistent with Becker's (1994) finding that only 5% of computer-using teachers are exemplary. His definition of such teachers would classify them as responding in an *Active* manner.

Many teachers were interested in facilitating the use of the computers but were not sure how to go about doing so with their classes. They did not want to be forced to use them but rather felt that they needed more examples of computer use applied to their area of the curriculum. Others did not see the computers as relevant to either their curriculum or their preferred teaching strategies. While many indicated a good level of computer literacy, a lack of operational knowledge of computers was still perceived by many as inhibiting their ability to facilitate students' use of the computers. The computers were not perceived as a necessary, or even critically useful, technology by almost all teachers. Clearly to support more than minimal use of the computers teachers need up to five years of experience in using computers in their learning programmes (Becker 1994),

Because of the minimal and limited use of the computers very few classes were observed in which the use of the computers made any sustained or major impact on the learning environment. Only those teachers who aimed to create classroom learning environments which promoted student-centred learning (refer to Brady 1985) tended to regularly facilitate the use of the portable computers with their classes. Where teachers employed an instructivist pedagogy (refer to Reeves 1993), students were either required to use computers for only the limited role of a writing machine or were rarely required to use the computers at all. Some students left their computer at home when they did not think it would be needed. Research is increasingly supporting the notion that if computers are to be of significant value in classrooms, their introduction must be accompanied by a shift towards more student-centred teaching strategies (Dwyer, Ringstaff and Sandholtz 1991, Fishman and Duffy 1994, Hannafin and Savenye 1993)

3. CURRENT RESEARCH

Considering the results from these earlier studies the researcher decided to consider ways of addressing the technical, curriculum and pedagogical obstacles to using portable computers to support learning. Most of the curriculum obstacles concerned the rigidity of the curriculum and the dominance of the tertiary entrance exam. Therefore I decided to work within a government primary school where neither of these would be a factor. Secondly to overcome the pedagogical obstacles I decided to work with enthusiastic volunteers who were happy to utilise me as a mentor. Finally, to overcome the technical obstacles of weight, battery time, start-up time and network access I decided to work with Apple iBook computers with wireless networking.

The school had a class set (15) iBook portable computers with an AirPort Base Station. All classrooms had one or two ethernet port connections to the school's network which had internet connection. The AirPort Base Station may be plugged into the ethernet port in a classroom to provide network access for all the iBooks provided they are within about a 50 metre radius. The iBooks were kept in a specially designed trolley where they could be recharged while not in use (refer to Figure 1). All students had a workspace folder on the main network server which was password protected.

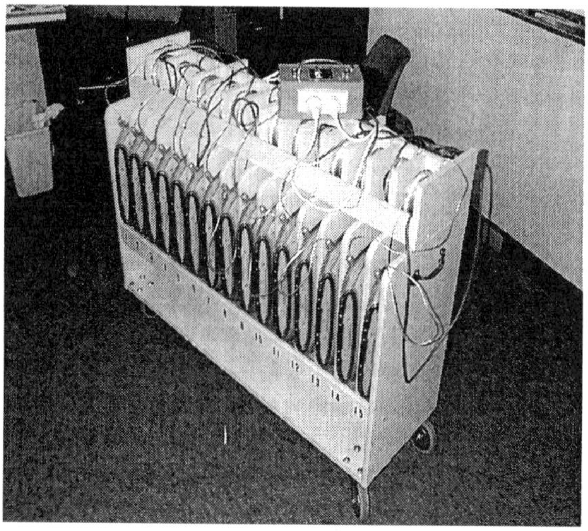

Figure 1. Purpose designed trolley with the iBooks ready to be charged.

During the year 2000 I conducted action research with two Year Seven classes and their teachers to investigate the use of wireless networking to support the use of computers in schools. This involved discussions with the teachers, observing the class, conducting a number of lessons and using questionnaires to conduct student surveys. In this paper I will briefly outline the first project on which the students worked with me as part of their drug education programme.

The project aimed to get the students, working in pairs, to collect and present information about one of the drugs: cannabis, tobacco, caffeine, or alcohol. The end result would be the creation of a slideshow presentation of their information which would be viewed by the other students and parents. Initially the students collected information from the library or from the internet, recording the information on a pre-designed A3 note-taking sheet under specific headings. In a number of sessions the students used the iBooks to access teacher-supplied web-sites. The students were shown how to save web-pages and graphic images from web-pages to their workspaces on the network server. At the same time the issues of copyright and referencing were addressed.

The teachers had not created slideshows before and therefore the I took on the task of showing the students how to use Microsoft Powerpoint to create slideshows and at the same time showing the teachers. In two1 hour lessons the researcher worked with the students to create the slideshows. In the first lesson the students created slides, entered text into the outline, and selected a main slide design. I used the school's large monitor to demonstrate the features of a slideshow using one I had designed. In the second session the students inserted graphics and clip-art, and added transitions and effects. In a later lesson the students saved their slideshows as HTML, placed the folders into a common directory on the server which then acted as an intranet server (using the web-sharing MacOS facility). The students worked enthusiastically with each pair completing a slideshow. Towards the end of the project students started to consider questions of design and the implications of the information they had assembled.

To assist in focussing on the content the students had been asked to add a 'Questions' slide at the end of their slideshow to contain five questions to be answered by those who viewed their work. A week after the slideshows had been completed the students were required to view each others work and complete a content evaluation form which included answering the questions as well as a technical quality evaluation form for each presentation they viewed. After the completed evaluation forms had been viewed by the teacher they were returned to the designer of each presentation as feedback to allow for improvements to be made. The following week parents were invited to come in and view the presentations. There were some restrictions on when the students could use the computers because the lead teacher had many responsibilities in the school that meant he was not with his class (at least half of the time). Other teachers who took over the class were not involved with using the computers and did not feel confident enough to do so.

From classroom observation it was found that all students were able to complete all the required tasks such as accessing a particular internet site, conducting a search, taking notes, saving web-pages and graphics, creating a slideshow and evaluating the work of other students. There were almost no technical problems with the computers and none with the access to networking via the AirPort wireless technology. Some students had explored extra features such as animations and it was clear from similarities in the final products that students often learned from each other.

The students indicated in a questionnaire that they were enthusiastic about using the computers and found the computers helped them. About 50% felt they had learned lots about drugs with all but one student indicating that they had learned some things about the drugs. About half preferred to work individually rather than in pairs but only 3 complained about sharing the computers. They found the computers most useful in creating the report, collecting the information and presenting the work to their teacher.

The teachers were enthusiastic about the results of the project and were keen to show off the work at the parents' night. They recognised that they had relied on the researcher for application ideas and skills in implementing those ideas. However, they felt confident enough to work with other teachers in the school on similar projects and began to do so. They began to think about what projects they could apply the computers to during the rest of the year. The relatively unrestricted curriculum of primary school education in Western Australia afforded them this luxury.

4. CONCLUSIONS

In my mind it is certain that in the near future most students in Australian schools will have access to some type of portable computing device (other than a calculator) most of the time. This will afford them access to a range of powerful applications, including networking applications. However, despite the removal of many of the technical barriers to provide this 'when and where needed' access it is still likely that there will be little impact on the learning experiences of most students. There remain many barriers to be overcome associated with school organisation, teacher skill, curriculum and pedagogy.

My research has found problems to overcome associated with the limited expertise and experience of most teachers and restrictions imposed by the curriculum and pedagogic organisation of the school. When the restrictions are removed and there is sufficient support for the teachers portable computers with wireless networking can readily support the constructivist learning environments many of us are striving to provide for students.

Initially teachers need support in developing application ideas and skills in implementing those ideas. It is likely that a mentoring approach will be the most successful strategy to rapidly develop the necessary level of expertise and experience. These teachers may then become mentors for other teachers. The successful implementation of computers to support learning is now fundamentally dependent on teacher beliefs, attitudes, perceptions, experiences and skills rather than hardware and software characteristics.

REFERENCES

Ainley, M., Bourke, V., Chatfield, R., Hillman, K. and Watkins, I. (2000) *Computers, Laptops and Tools*. Australian Council for Educational Research, Melbourne.

Becker, H. J. (1994) How exemplary computer-using teachers differ from other teachers: Implications for realizing the potential of computers in schools. *Journal of Research on Computing in Education, 26* (3), pp.291-321.

Becker, H. J., Ravitz, J. L. and Wong, Y. T. (1999) *Teacher and Teacher-Directed Student Use of Computers and Software.* (Teaching, Learning, and Computing: 1998 National Survey. No. 3). Center for Research on Information Technology and Organizations, University of California, Irvine, California.

Brady, L. (1985) *Models and methods of teaching*. Prentice-Hall, Sydney.

Collis, B. (1994) Triple innovation in the Netherlands. *The Computing Teacher, 22* (2), pp. 23-26.

Dwyer, D. C., Ringstaff, C. and Sandholtz, J. H. (1991) Changes in teachers' beliefs and practices in technology-rich classrooms. *Educational Leadership, 48* (8), pp. 45-52.

Fishman, B. J. and Duffy, T. M. (1994) Classroom restructuring: What do teachers really need? *Education Technology Research and Development, 40* (3), pp. 95-111.

Gardner, J., Morrison, H., Jarman, R., Reilly, C. and McNally, H. (1994). *Personal portable computers and the curriculum.* (Practitioner Minipaper No. 13). Scottish Council for Research in Education, Glasgow.

Hannafin, R. D. and Savenye, W. C. (1993). Technology in the classroom: The teacher's new role and resistance to it. *Educational Technology, 33* (6), pp. 26-31.

Mandinach, E. B. and Cline, H. F. (1996) Classroom dynamics: the impact of a technology-based curriculum innovation on teaching and learning. *Journal of Educational Computing Research, 14* (1), pp. 83-102.

Plomp, T. and Pelgrum, W. J. (1992). Restructuring of schools as a consequence of computers. *International Journal of Educational Research, 19*, pp. 185-195.

Reeves, T. C. (1993) Interactive learning systems as mind tools. *Viewpoints, 2*, pp. 2-11.

BIOGRAPHY

For nine years Paul Newhouse taught in an innovative state secondary school in Western Australia working with pre-service and practising teachers in two universities. He is currently a lecturer at the School of Education at Edith Cowan University, Western Australia.

24

Teaching and Learning through Technology-mediated Interaction

Ruth Geer and Alan Barnes
University of South Australia, Adelaide, Australia
ruth.geer@unisa.edu.au

Keywords: collaborative learning, communication, interactive, Internet, open flexible learning

Abstract: In response to the increasing complexity of online environments, educators are seeking ways to utilise evolving technologies for effective teaching and learning. This paper introduces a framework for technology-mediated interaction that attempts to conceptualise the relationship between types of interaction and the suitability of various technologies to support quality learning outcomes. The seven-level model has collaboration as the highest level of meaningful interaction with social interaction, as the foundation level. The quality of learning outcomes at various levels finds their basis in theories of cognitive development and behavioural and social interdependence. The paper provides a guide to sampling such interaction and evidencing quality learning outcomes.

1. INTRODUCTION

Currently there is accelerated growth in online course delivery and a rapid evolution of Internet based technologies. Foremost among these technologies are those that enable interaction among students and their educators. Establishing a presence in the online education market is a major focus for many universities. With the rollout of Internet technologies into the K-12 sector, online education may become broadly established across all of education.

Extensive research in the previous decade has shown the capability of computer-mediated communications to engender quality learning (Henri 1991, Newman et al. 1997, Gunawadena et al. 1997). A major thrust of that research was to provide an analysis of the content of the textual discourse and the interactions of the participants; and to identify indicators of cognitive and metacognitive learning that demonstrated the presence of quality learning. With the advent of the World Wide Web, the rise of non-textual interactions and the explosive development of online learning, the major issues have shifted to developing the teaching and learning approaches that can best deploy the new range of technologies in the pursuit of quality learning.

Many factors, such as cultural variables, student characteristics and informal socialising impact on successful teaching and learning through online interactions. A framework is needed that encompasses all these factors, including particularly current and future technologies, and that supports the reflective development of teaching and learning in an online form. Such a framework should not only assist in developing more effective teaching and learning approaches but should enable better evaluation of those approaches. In an effort towards the development of such a framework this paper introduces a model for online interactions and develops techniques for more rapid assessment of the quality of learning generated. These techniques are tested in the context of a current online course.

2. THE MODEL

There are a number of factors that influence an effective teaching and learning environment. Interaction and collaboration have been recognised as desirable ingredients in the learning process where students are not only active and supportive, but also interactive (Hiltz 1998, King and Doerfert, 1996). Three essential attributes, which have been identified in an effective learning community, are active learning in the construction of knowledge, positive interpersonal relationships and rich discourse. In collaborative learning communities, students are actively engaged in supporting each other in the development of higher level reasoning strategies, critical thinking, hypothesis formation and reflection. Computer technologies are used to support collaborative and discursive interaction, and build relationships by providing the opportunity to connect and engage learners from many diverse backgrounds. A number of theoretical perspectives, with their foundations in cognitive developmental, behavioural and social interdependence theories (Johnson and Johnson 1996) are guiding the design of courses and our understanding of how students learn.

Each of the factors or drivers that impact on the effectiveness of the learning environment must be considered and where appropriate, deliberately designed into the instructional program (Berge 1999, King and Doerfert 1996). These drivers, which include cultural variables, student characteristics, informal socialising, prior knowledge, assessment, available technologies and the lecturer's role, impact in varying ways on the types of interaction and associated learning outcomes. One of the difficulties associated with this literature is, that at the time of its writing, many of the contemporary technologies that mediate these interactions, were not in use, and particularly in relation to the web, were not yet conceived. Indeed much of the literature has been concerned with text only communications. There is a need for a new model to help conceptualise how contemporary Internet technologies can promote deep learning and critical thinking resulting in improved learning outcomes.

The following model (Figure 1) of Technology-Mediated Interaction (TMI) incorporates hierarchies of interaction, technologies and learning outcomes together with their influential drivers. It is represented in the shape of a pyramid comprising seven levels. The assumption is, that the higher the level, the greater the quality and frequency of interaction and the higher the learning outcomes that will be achieved. Each level denotes a type of interaction that might be expected in relation to specific teaching and learning approaches. In some approaches students might only move through levels of social interaction, general discussion and topic focussed activities throughout the duration of a course. In other approaches students might be required to reach higher levels, such as cooperative or collaborative levels. In the model the term 'technology-mediated' has been used to characterise interaction through the use of contemporary and future Internet technologies.

Collaboration is surmised as providing the highest level of meaningful interaction and engagement through the use of sophisticated and often specialised multimedia communication tools. It implies working together, yet challenging each other through continual interaction to create meaning, explore topics, construct shared understanding and knowledge, accept group accountability and through a combination of efforts achieve the group goal. Cooperation also implies teamwork and task distribution, but is seen as one step lower down the pyramid where the end result is an aggregation of efforts and individuals are held more accountable. At both levels students work together to support each other. Underlying the ability to cooperate, and ultimately to collaborate, is the ability to show understanding, trust and respect of other learners.

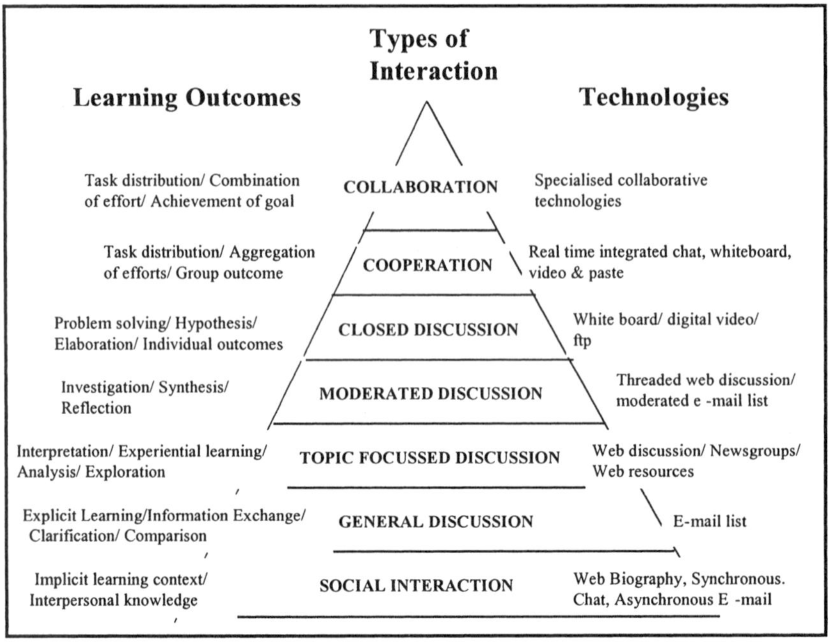

Figure 1. Model of Technology-Mediated Interaction

Interactivity can be defined both in terms of social and content interaction. Social interaction, which forms the foundation on which all levels of interactivity are dependent, is critical in the building of a collaborative learning environment (Jonassen et al. 1999, Hughes and Hewson 1998). It helps students overcome some of their reticence in the exchange of ideas. Interpersonal knowledge helps to create solidarity and commitment and develop standards of conduct for performing group tasks. Web biographies, synchronous chat and asynchronous email can be used to provide opportunities for self-disclosure, an appreciation of social behaviours and the capacity for mutual consideration. The subtleties and specifications of the various levels of interactivity suggest opportunities for varied levels of engagement through the use of appropriate technologies that impact on the learning outcomes.

3. DILEMMA OF AN ABUNDANCE OF DISCOURSE

The rise of TMI brings with it a dilemma. Face-to-face conversations have been replaced with interactive digital discourse. Even though these *conversations* are generally less rich and less frequent than their face-to-face counterparts, they exist in overwhelming abundance and are stored permanently by computer systems. What do educators do with this abundance of digital discourse? For educators this dilemma is particularly acute as the discourse calls for educational evaluation. The amount of discourse generated can be overwhelming. The collection of 27 students in this study yielded over 160 postings, many of considerable complexity, in an 8-week term. While many tools exist for the detailed analysis of this discourse, this is impractical for all but the best-resourced educators. The concerned educator needs to find ways to get a sense of the educational quality of the discourse and to be able to intervene strategically and appropriately in the interactions.

A framework for education with TMI needs to be buttressed by effective content sampling that can give confidence that quality learning is occurring. The literature on computer mediated communication indicates that such an analysis (Henri 1991) requires treatment of the participative, social, interactive, cognitive and metacognitive dimensions. It must also be able to identify indicators at the individual and the group level (Gunawardena et al 1997). Table 1, column 1, below, shows a schema of indicators relevant to quality learning, based on the work of Gunawardena and Henri. Sections I and G of the schema have been utilised in the work of Sringam and Geer (2000) to analyse student-led discussion. Section S adds social indicators that are relevant to the pyramid model (Figure 1). Various indicators of this schema will differentially appear in the discourse at various levels of the pyramid model.

Table 1 A Schema for Social Behaviour, Cognitive Development and Interactive Analysis with frequency results of indicators in the discourse

	Indicator (f)	Section (f)
S. Participation and social behaviour		
S1 Individual disclosure		
S1-a Basic introduction	12	
S1-b Extended revelation	9	
S1-c Self evaluation	11	32
S2 Social behaviour		
S2-a Courtesy	54	
S2-b Level of dominance/authority	0	
S2-c Seeking help	14	
S2-d Willingness to initiate	12	80
S3 Mutual Consideration		
S3-a Identifying mutual interest	8	
S3-b Willingness to exchange	23	
S3-c Valuing others' views	29	60
Section S Total		**172**

I. Cognitive behaviour analysis at individual level:		
I1 Elementary clarification		
I1-a Observing/studying a problem	5	
I1-b Identifying its elements	25	
I1-c Observing/studying their linkages	4	34
I2 In-depth clarification		
I2-a Analysing a problem	7	
I2-b Identifying assumptions	0	
I2-c Establishing referential criteria	0	
I2-d Seeking out specialised information	0	7
I3 Synthesis and application		
I3-a Drawing primary conclusions	2	
I3-b Proposing an idea based on links and relevant information	24	
I3-c Value judgement on relevant solutions	0	
I3-d Making final decisions and deciding on the action to be taken	0	26
Section I Total		**67**
G. Interactive behaviour analysis at group level:		
G1 Planning		
G1-a Organising work/planning group work/setting shared tasks	0	
G1-b Initiating activities/setting up activities for group work	0	0
G2 Sharing/comparing/contributing of information		
G2-a Defining and identifying a problem	7	
G2-b Stating opinions regarding the problem	24	
G2-c Asking and answering questions to clarify details of statements	16	
G2-d Sharing and exchanging knowledge, resources and information	49	
G2-e Corroborating examples provided by one or more participants	0	
G2-f Challenging others to engage in group discussion	2	
G2-g Help and feedback giving	5	103
G3 Inconsistency of ideas, concepts or statements		
G3-a Identifying and stating areas of disagreement	1	
G3-b Asking and answering questions to clarify the source and extend of disagreement	0	
G3-c Restating the participants' position and advancing arguments or considerations supported by references	0	1
G4 Negotiation of meaning/co-construction of knowledge		
G4-a Negotiating or clarifying the meaning of terms, areas of agreement and disagreement	0	
G4-b Proposing new statements embodying compromise and co-construction	0	
G4-c Integrating or accommodating metaphors or analogies	0	0
G5 Testing and modification of proposed synthesis or co-construction of knowledge		
G5-a Testing against existing knowledge and information	0	
G5-b Testing against personal experience	0	
G5-c Testing against formal data collected	0	0
G6 Agreement statement(s) and application of newly constructed knowledge		

G6-a Summarisation of agreement(s)	0	
G6-b Application of new knowledge	0	0
Section G Total		**104**
Total number of classified utterances		**343**
Total number of posts		**168**
Number of students		**27**

3.1 The social and participative dimension

Social exchanges have the potential to alleviate misunderstandings and misinterpretations that can occur through a lack of social cues and face-to-face interaction. The social community that is created during the learning process can impact on the nature of the learning activities and the learning outcomes (McLoughlin 1999). While an examination of the participative and social dimension does not add directly to an assessment of quality learning it underpins to varying extents cognitive, and metacognitive processes. Clearly the degree of participation in the discourse can be gleaned from direct inspection of the TMI record. Non-participating students deserve and may need considerable individual attention from the diligent educator. In the study described below reasons for non-participation were mostly structural (e.g. email does not work).

Individual disclosure is often needed to underpin stronger relationships of exchange and mutual consideration. A basic introduction (name, professional interests, background, etc.) provides a basis for discourse. Extended revelation (preferences, feelings, likes, dislikes, etc.) becomes important in sustaining discussion of ideas that begins in the *Topic Focussed Level* and is more pervasive in the *Moderated Discussion Level*. The capacity for self-evaluation becomes important as students become more reflective through the *Moderated and Closed Discussion Levels*. However, it is more critical to task distribution and cooperation on tasks at the *Cooperation Level*. The extent of revelation and self-evaluation is strongly impacted by cultural and individual characteristics.

Certain social behaviours impact on the types of communications that can be expected in TMI. Courtesy or netiquette is widely recognised as a necessary concomitant of mutually valued discussion (Curtis 1998). Small courtesies lubricate the reciprocal exchange of resources and information starting at the *Topic Focussed Discussion Level*. The dynamics of dominance and the perceptions of authority come into play in the more complex exchanges of the *Moderated Discussion Level* and above. These dynamics become critical where there are disagreements over task allocation at the *Cooperation Level* and where the development of competing ideas is critical to goal achievement especially at the *Collaboration Level*. Authority issues do not arise as much in homogeneous student groups but variegated knowledge, professional experience or status may have communication consequences for some groups. The cultural make-up of a group is also important. For example, the educator may become a highly impacting authority figure in groups of Chinese students. While authority is a socially ascribed quality, dominance/submissiveness may be an individual characteristic of some consequence.

Another important social behaviour indicator is the willingness to seek help and the willingness to initiate. Seeking help becomes first evident in general discussion level as the students come to understand the explicit learning context. It is also important, as the technologies become more complex at the *Cooperation* and *Collaboration Levels*. The amount of help sought should be seen as a positive indicator of the clarification of learning goals and processes. The willingness to initiate new ideas, to question and to provoke is increasingly important from the *Closed Discussion Level* upwards. At these levels lack of willingness to initiate can have educational consequences for individuals. Both indicators are strongly impacted by individual and cultural characteristics.

Mutual consideration is an important reinforcer of the free flow of ideas and criticism, and is characteristic of *Closed Discussion Levels* and above. The development of mutual consideration can begin at the *Social* and *General Discussion Level* through identifying mutual interests and dispositions. The willingness to exchange information is evident at the general discussion level and generally speaking its absence has a strong impact on the lack of exchange of opinions, ideas and inventions at higher levels. The capacity for valuing the views of others becomes important in the *Cooperative Level* but is critical to successful collaboration.

3.2 Mapping indicators to levels of interaction

In the spirit of providing for more rapid evaluation of student discourse a map of cognitive, social and behavioural indicators to levels of TMI is presented below. It is convenient to consider the level of interaction at which the indicator is first and most naturally likely to appear. It is instructive to consider where an indicator is a critical condition for a certain interactive type.

Column three can be used as a guide to quick investigation of the discourse. The absence of the indicators in column four in the discourse may signal that educational intervention is necessary.

Table 2. Sampling Guide for types of interactivity

Pyramid Level	Type of Interactivity	Likely First Instance of Indicator	Critical Indicator for Interactive Type
Level 7	Collaboration	G1b, G5a-c, G6a-b	S3c, G1b, G2e-f, G3a-c, G4a-b, G6a
Level 6	Cooperation	I3d, G1a, G2e-f, G3a-c, G4a-c	S1c, S2b, I2c, I2d, I3d, G1a, G2a-d
Level 5	Closed Discussion	I2c, I2d, G2a-d	S2c, S2d, I3a I3c
Level 4	Moderated Discussion	I1c, I2b, I3a, I3c	I1c, I2b
Level 3	Topic Focussed Discussion	I1a, I1b, I2a, I3b, G2g	S2a, I1a, I1b, I2a, I3b
Level 2	General Discussion	S2b, S2c, S3b, S3c	S3b
Level 1	Social Interaction	S1a, S2a, S3a	S1a

3.3 The study

Two groups of students taking the Internet in Education course in the Graduate Certificate in Educational Computing (University of South Australia) were the subjects of this study. The groups were chosen at random from the 4 groups taking the course. The expected sequence of interaction types in this subject were Social Interaction in week 1, General Discussion in week 2-4, Topic Focussed Discussion in week 3-8. The technologies used were email list, threaded web discussion and web resources. Students identified a topic of interest concerning the use of the Internet in education and posted a brief outline of its educational merits. In addition students were required to post peer critiques of the outlines to the discussion group. The manipulation of the assessment driver introduced an element of cooperative input in the preparation of final papers for assessment.

Table 1 shows the instances of occurrences of indicators in the aggregated discourse generated by the two groups. Generally the frequency of indicators was consistent with the occurrence identified in the Table 2 above. The indicators in G2 were prevalent in the discourse due to the use of the assessment as a driver to establish an element of cooperation.

4. CONCLUSION

A pyramid model for Technology-Mediated Interaction has been presented which together with the major drivers and 'rapid' evaluative mechanisms provides a tentative framework for developing and for informing teaching and learning in an online context. While the impact of the assessment driver, within the given teaching and learning approach is evident from the case study, much more needs to be done to characterise this and other drivers. A 'rapid' evaluation mechanism that can provide greater confidence in the quality of learning has been presented. The extent to which such confidence can be quantified will be examined in a forthcoming paper. Evaluation of non-text interactions will be the subject of future research.

REFERENCES

Berge, Z. (1999) Interaction in post secondary web-based learning. *Educational Technology*, 39 (1), pp. 5-11.

Curtis, D. D. (1998) *Guidelines for online interactions.* [http://www.roma.unisa.edu.au/11565/onlineinteract.htm] 28.6.1998.

Gunawardena, C. N., Lowe, C. A., and Anderson, T. (1997) Analysis of a global online debate and the development of interaction analysis model for examining social construction of knowledge in computer conferencing. *Journal of Educational Computing Research*, 17 (4), pp. 397-431.

Henry, F. (1991) Computer conferencing and content analysis. In *Collaborative Learning through Computer Conferencing*, A. R. Kaye (ed), Springer-Verlag, Heidelberg.

Hiltz, S. R. (1998) *Collaborative learning in Asynchronous Learning Networks: Building learning communities.* [http://eies.njit.edu/~hiltz/collaborative_learning_in_asynch.htm] 24.8.1999.

Hughes, C. and Hewson, L. (1998) Online Interactions: Developing a neglected aspect of the virtual classroom. *Educational Technology*, vol. July-August, pp. 48-55.

Johnson, D. W. and Johnson, R. T. (1996) Cooperation and the use of technology. In *Handbook of Research for Educational Communication and Technology*, D. Jonassen (ed), Macmillan Library Reference, New York, USA, pp. 1017-1044.

Jonassen, D. H., Peck, K. L. and Wilson, B. G. (1999) *Learning with Technology: A Constructivist Perspective*, Merrill, Upper Saddle River, New Jersey.

King, J. L. and Doerfert, D. L. (1996) *Interaction in the distance education setting.* [http://www.ssu.missouri.edu/ssu/Aged/NAERM/s-e-4.htm] 7.9.1999.

McLoughlin, C. (1999) Culturally responsive technology use: developing an on-line community of learners. *British Journal of Educational Technology*, 30 (3), pp. 231-243.

Newman, D., Johnson, C., Webb, B. and Cochrane, C. (1997) Evaluating the quality of learning in computer supported co-operative learning. *Journal of the American Society for Information Science*, 48 (6), pp. 484-495.

Sringam, C. and Geer, R. (2000) An Investigation of an instrument for analysis of student-led electronic discussions. In *Learning to Choose*, ASCILITE 2000 Conference Proceedings, Coffs Harbour, NSW, Dec. 2000, pp. 81-91.

BIOGRAPHY

Ruth Geer is a lecturer in educational computing; her research focuses on drivers of collaborative interactivity in internet-based courses and their learning outcomes. Dr. Alan Barnes is a senior lecturer in the School of Education (Magill), with an extensive research background in use of ICT.

25

Perceptions and Uses of Technology among Adolescent Boys and Girls

Alice A. Christie
Arizona State University West, PO Box 37100 MC 3151, Phoenix, AZ 85069-7100, USA
alice.christie@asu.edu

Keywords: barriers, collaborative learning, culture, learner-centered learning, research

Abstract: In this study, I used interpretive methods in an open-ended computer environment to study and explain gender diversity in middle school computer classrooms. Through observations and a series of focus groups, I found that adolescent boys and girls view and use computers differently. Each gender seems to accept this as a natural part of their culture, and, in general, are accepting of each other's visions and uses. Turkle and Papert called for a new social construction of the computer to contribute to our understanding of the ways males and females think about and use computers. This paper answers that call. It breaks ground for future studies to create, and simultaneously study, computer cultures which honour female and male ways of knowing and which allow the research community to begin to break down gender stereotypes and the idea of one privileged – usually male – way of thinking about computers.

1. INTRODUCTION

Both the popular and academic press point to a gender gap in computer use, computer competency, computer attitudes, and in the ways men and women view the computer. However, some question this commonly held belief. Turkle and Papert (1990) call for the development of a new computer culture which "would require a new social construction of the computer" (p. 133), which is, in turn, more inclusive than the existing male-dominated culture. They cite the work of feminist scholar, Gilligan (1982), who questions the "idea of one privileged, mature way of thinking" (p. 123) as parallel to their view of "the computer as a projective screen for different approaches to knowledge" (p. 134).

Morse and Daiute (1992) identified a need for "more research on computing activities which are not related to mathematics or programming activities and which look at what women and girls do like about computers" (p. i). They believe that most research to date is quantitative and has "short-changed girls and women in documenting the computer gender gap" (p. 1). They state that Likert scale questionnaires are an especially inaccurate "way to measure female responses to computing" (p. 5) They state the need for more research using interpretive methods in open-ended computer environments so that we might better study and explain gender diversity in our computer classrooms.

In this study I seek to answer this call for a new kind of research. I assume, as does Gilligan (1982), that the way people talk and write about their lives is significant, that the language they use and the connections they make reveal the world as they see it.

In this study, I used interpretive methods in an open-ended computer environment so that I might better study and explain gender diversity in middle school computer classrooms. I hoped to gain insight into *how* girls and boys conceptualised and used computers – not just *if* there were differences in how boys and girls used and felt toward computers. By focusing particularly though not exclusively on girls, who historically are either left out or underrepresented in studies of technology, I hope to shed light on how girls view their experiences with technology. Gilligan (1982) recounts how she used "the group left out in the construction of theory to call attention to what is missing in its account" (p. 4). I hope this study of what is often missing will allow us to abandon our previous understandings of how humanity views technology (which were based on a predominantly male view) and adopt a more encompassing view of all people and technology.

2. THEORETICAL STANCE

Theoretically, I view both gender and the computer as social and cultural constructions. Gender is assumed to be constructed within a culture and not genetically inherent in an individual (i.e., gender is not something we are, but something we do) (West and Zimmerman 1987). Doing gender is unavoidable; one can never 'not do' gender. Technologies do not exist in a vacuum – with no history and no social implications or connections. Technologies exist only in social contexts, and as such, exist in a gendered world. And as Benston (1985) stated so succinctly, technology is gendered and its gender is male. I also view the classroom as a community of learners where power is shared and where participatory, democratic processes help learners develop independence. This classroom is collaborative, co-operative and interactive. It is an active classroom where risk-taking is encouraged, where intellectual excitement abounds and where power is viewed as energy, capacity, and potential rather than domination.

3. LITERATURE REVIEW

A review of several hundred empirical studies on gender and computers conducted between 1984 and the present paints an overall picture of male dominance. Males used computers more than females, especially for programming and game playing. This tendency begins in elementary school where boys tended to dominate computer use and often 'crowded girls out'. In addition, three times as many boys as girls participated in summer computer camps, and parents were more likely to purchase computers, computer software and peripherals for boys than for girls. By high school, the gender gap in computer use was even more pronounced. Boys were more likely to own a computer, understand the electronic operations of computers and be part of extracurricular computer classes. The trend continued at the college level where, in an introductory computer course, more than half the males used the computer lab after hours while almost none of the females took advantage of this opportunity. At all levels, boys were more likely to be chosen to assist the teacher with technology than were girls (Sanders 1990). Christie (1995) observed that girls generally enjoyed computing less than boys because most available software appeals to boys rather than to girls; the software uses gaming formats which are competitive and often violent and which pit two players against each other or one player against the computer. And finally, male teachers used computers more than female teachers at the elementary, secondary, and university levels (Hattie and Fitzgerald 1987). Therefore students lacked female role models in this domain.

Gender stereotyping attitudes were more decisive. When surveying 1,600 Kindergarten through grade 12 students, Wilder, Mackie and Cooper (1985) found that both boys and girls considered computers as more appropriate for males than females. When asked to draw a computer user, both boys and girls were more likely to draw boys in this role (Martin, Heller and Mahmoud 1992). Gender stereotypes, such as these, were reinforced by parents, peers, and the educational system (Walkerdine 1990).

4. DESCRIPTION OF THE STUDY

The focus in my study is not to further investigate the perceived gender gap in terms of technology, but rather to address the meanings that adolescents assign to computers as they interact with them more and more in today's world. West and Fenstermaker (1993) believe that gender is "a mechanism whereby situated social action contributes to the reproduction of social structure in which people *do* gender; and men and women do it differently" (p.158). In a similar vein, objects, such as computers, take on meanings constructed by individuals as they interact with these objects. People negotiate and renegotiate meaning as they personally interact with objects, thereby constructing a social order as well as a personal meaning. Within this perspective, computers are social constructions that vary from person to person. This research delves into these personal meanings.

In my role of teacher/researcher, I co-taught a technology-rich social science unit to 250 middle school students. My team-mate and I worked with each group of 25-30 students for approximately eight to ten hours in four separate sessions. Data sources included:

- Open-ended student surveys about their uses of and attitudes toward technology
- Open-ended parent surveys about their uses of and attitudes toward technology
- Field notes and observational data
- Documents data
- Structured focus groups data.

As this study is still ongoing, this paper includes only data from nineteen structured focus groups with 94 students. Each focus group included four to six middle school students. I conducted focus groups at eight schools with the configurations listed below:

School	Number of Students	Gender Configuration
School 1	4 students	All Boys
Three Focus Groups	5 students	2 Boys and 3 Girls
	5 students	All Girls
School 2	5 students	2 Boys and 3 Girls
Two Focus Groups	6 students	All Girls
School 3	6 students	All Boys
Two Focus Groups	5 students	All Girls
School 4	6 students	All Girls
Two Focus Groups	5 students	All Boys
School 5	4 students	1 Boy and 3 Girls

School	Number of Students	Gender Configuration
Two Focus Groups	4 students	All Girls
School 6	4 students	2 Boys and 2 Girls
Three Focus Groups	5 students	All Girls
	5 students	1 Boy and 4 Girls
School 7	4 students	All Boys
Three Focus Groups	5 students	All Girls
	5 students	All Girls
School 8	5 students	All Girls
Two Focus Groups	6 students	3 Boys and 3 Girls

4.1 Girls' definitions of computer

The following lists reflects the major definitions seventh and eighth grade girls gave to the construct *computer*:

- I don't know how to define a computer technically
- Something to keep you connected to your friends
- It helps you communicate with others
- A machine that does things that you tell it to do
- A lot of stuff combined into one thing to make life easier
- A gateway to information
- It can substitute for a book because it contains so much information
- It organises and stores your thoughts
- It's a resource tool for learning things
- It can communicate, it can do problems in math and it can write
- It improves your everyday life
- A tool that makes your work look neater and more professional
- A tool that helps you work quicker
- It's whatever you want it to be.

4.2 Girls' uses of computers

Girls used computers in a number of ways. The following list summarises uses identified by seventh and eighth grade girls:

- Word processing for homework and research
- Word processing for writing process to easily do lots of drafts
- PowerPoint presentations for classes
- Email to talk to friends both locally and at a distance
- Chat rooms to keep in touch with friends and make new friends
- Instant messaging to talk to classmates

- Email to talk to guys and flirt with guys
- Games to play if I'm really, really bored, like PacMan or Solitaire
- Definitely NOT for games
- The Internet to shop or 'window shop'.

4.3 Boys' definitions of computer

The following lists reflects the major definitions seventh and eighth grade boys gave to the construct *computer*:

- A machine with a CPU and a motherboard and circuits
- A high tech calculator, a giant calculator
- A machine that does what you program it to do
- A machine that thinks for you
- A machine that processes information and stores it
- A toy for people to have for entertainment
- A machine that does things faster than a human can
- A machine that allows you to look up stuff
- It let's you do things quicker and easier.

4.4 Boys' uses of computers

Boys used computers in a number of ways. The following list summarises uses identified by seventh and eighth grade boys:

- Mainly for fun, maybe some homework now and then
- To play games (Solitaire, casino games, sporting games, logic games, simulations where you kill people, war games)
- Entertainment 24 hours a day
- The Internet for information to do homework
- The Internet for Nintendo codes
- Run an FTP from my computer that's up 24 hours a day.

5. INTERPRETATIONS

All of the adolescent boys and girls in this study were competent, confident and frequent users of computers, computer software, and the Internet. Despite their equivalent competence, confidence and frequency of use, girls and boys view and use computers differently.

In terms of definitions, girls saw the computer as much more multi-dimensional then did boys. The phrase *it's whatever you want it to be* best captures this understanding. Girls defined computers as multi-use tools that facilitate connecting with friends, doing homework and research, gathering information, solving math problems, organising ideas and information, producing more professional products, and accomplishing a multitude of tasks in a quicker, easier way. Boys, on the other hand, had a more narrow view of computers. Boys identified computers as machines, toys, or high tech calculators that let you do things quicker and easier. It is interesting that no girls used the terms *machine* or *toy* in defining the computer. Rather, they focused on what the computer allowed them to accomplish. The major foci for girls, in order of importance, were computer as communication tool, computer as productivity tool, and computer as multi-purpose tool. The major foci for boys, in order of importance, were a machine for entertainment and gaming, a thinking machine, and an information machine.

In terms of general use, girls used computers to *connect* with others, and boys used computers to *compete* with others. Girls' most predominant uses centred around communication: emailing friends and family, chatting with friends, making new friends, using instant messaging to communicate daily with classmates, and connecting and flirting with guys. Boys' most predominant uses centred on competitive, often violent, gaming activities such as war games and killing-people simulations, and sporting games. In terms of school-related use, girls focused on the numerous ways they used computers, including word processing, creating multimedia presentations, writing multiple drafts of papers, and producing neat, professional looking work. Boys, however, mentioned that they used computers for homework and schoolwork only now and then, and the only tool they mentioned was the Internet.

In terms of Internet use, each gender identified several uses not mentioned by the other gender. Girls said they used the Internet to shop or browse for fashion ideas. They also focused on using the Internet to flirt with guys or see pictures of 'handsome hunks.' Boys mentioned using the Internet to look up codes for various games that would allow them to move to the next level of the game. And several boys mentioned their sophisticated use of computers to create FTP sites for other gamers to find codes and secrets for popular software and Internet games. Interestingly, the only critical note of the focus group sessions was several groups of girls saying that they played computer games not at all or only when they were very, very bored. They then elaborated that they thought computers games were bad influences on their male classmates because gaming made the boys into anti-social couch potatoes who didn't know how to communicate with their female classmates.

An interesting and unexpected trend that I discovered when analysing data was that girls used more *exact language* to describe computer use than did boys. For example, boys said the used computers for homework; girls specified that that used word processing, *PowerPoint* and the Internet to do homework. Boys called the computer a *machine that allows you to look up stuff*, while girls said it *was a resource tool for learning things*. Boys were less specific about their uses than girls. For example, boys never mentioned how they did homework, while girls mentioned how they used word processors to do multiple drafts and how using the computer made their work look neater and more professional. And even though both boys and girls mentioned the convenience of computers, they chose different language to express this idea. Boys used the generic it when they said *it let's you do things quicker and easier*; girls identified the computer as a tool when they said it's *a tool that helps you work quicker*.

6. CONCLUSION

Adolescent boys and girls view and use computers differently. Each gender seems to accept this as a natural part of their culture, and, in general, are accepting of each other's visions and uses. Turkle and Papert (1990) called for a new social construction of the computer to contribute to our understanding of the ways males and females think about and use computers. This paper answers that call. It breaks ground for future studies to create, and simultaneously study, computer cultures which honour female and male ways of knowing and which allow the research community to begin to break down gender stereotypes and the idea of one privileged (usually male) way of thinking about computers.

REFERENCES

Benston, M. L. (1985) The myth of computer literacy. *Canadian Women's Studies*, 5, pp. 20-22.

Christie, A. A. (1995) *No chips on their shoulders: Girls, boys and telecommunications.* (Doctoral dissertation, Arizona State University, 1995). Dissertation Abstracts International, 56 (11A), 96-08340.

Gilligan, C. (1982) *In a different voice: Psychological theory and women's development.* Harvard University Press, Cambridge.

Hattie, J. and Fitzgerald, D. (1987) Sex differences in attitudes, achievement and use of computers. *Australian Journal of Education*, 31, pp. 3-26.

Martin, C. D., Heller, R. S. and Mahmoud, E. (1992) American and Soviet children's attitudes toward computers. *Journal of Educational Computing Research*, 8, pp. 155-186.

Morse, F. K. and Daiute, C. (1992, April) *I LIKE computers vs. I LIKERT computers: Rethinking methods for assessing the gender gap in computing* (Research Rep. No. ED 349 939). American Educational Research Association Conference, San Francisco.

Sanders, J. (1990, July) Computer equity for girls: What keeps it from happening. In *Fifth World Conference on Computers in Education in Sydney, Australia*, Amsterdam, Elsevier Science Publishing, pp. 181-185.
Turkle, S. and Papert, S. (1990) Epistemological pluralism: Styles and voices within the computer culture. *SIGNS Magazine*, 16(1), pp. 128-157.
Walkerdine, V. (1990) *Schoolgirl fictions*. Verso, London.
West, C. and Fenstermaker, S. (eds.) (1993) *Power, inequity and the accomplishment of gender: An ethnomethodological view*. Aldine, New York.
West, C. and Zimmerman, D. H. (1987) Doing gender. *Gender & Society*, 1(2), pp. 125-151.
Wilder, G., Mackie, D. and Cooper, J. (1985) Gender and computers: Two surveys of computer-related attitudes. *Sex Roles*, 13, pp. 215-228.

BIOGRAPHY

Dr. Alice Christie has been a teacher since 1967, serving in elementary and secondary schools and most recently at the university level. She received a B.A in English from Denison University, a M.Ed. in Reading Education from Boston University and a Ph.D. in Elementary Education with concentrations in Language and Literacy and Educational Technology from Arizona State University. She joined the ASU West Faculty in 1995 and currently serves as Associate Professor of Technology and Education.

Her research interests include gender and technology and literacy and technology. Her research focuses on ways in which females can become competent, confident and active users of technology as well as on ways technology can enhance literacy in elementary school children. www.west.asu.edu/achristie is her educational web-site.

26

Working with Dyslexic Learners

Authoring in a Multimedia Environment

Yota Dimitriadi
University of Reading, Flat 6, 4 Shinfield Road, Reading, RG2 7BW, UK
esr97pd@rdg.ac.uk

Keywords: pedagogical ICT facilitator, creativity, special needs

Abstract: The fundamental principles of the teaching methodology followed for dyslexic learners evolve around the need for a multisensory approach, which would advocate repetition of the learning tasks in an enjoyable way. The introduction of multimedia technologies in the field of education has supported the merging of new tools (digital camera, scanner) and techniques (sounds, graphics, animation) in a meaningful whole. Dyslexic learners are now given the opportunity to express their ideas using these alternative media and participate actively in the educational process. This paper discusses the preliminary findings of a single case study of two English monolingual dyslexic children working together to create an open-ended multimedia project on a laptop computer. The project aimed to examine whether and if the multimedia environment could enhance the dyslexic learners' skills in compositional. Analysis of the data has indicated that the technological facilities gave the children the opportunity to enhance the style and content of their work for a variety of audiences and to develop the responsibilities connected to authorship.

1. INTRODUCTION

This paper discusses the preliminary findings of a single case study designed to explore whether a multimedia authoring program, which supports a variety of notations (text, sounds, images, video clips), could become a 'functional learning environment' (Newman 1997) for the development of literacy skills in learners with dyslexia. The term 'functional' relates to activities purposeful from the point of view of the children (op. cit., 1997), and relevant to their experiences, interests and goals (Dewey 1938). Literacy is defined as 'a way of developing and communicating a child's thoughts, [extending] beyond simple manual encoding and decoding of text' (McFarlane 1997). Thus it is shifting the emphasis beyond the mechanics of spelling into an interest for content and style of information (Graves 1983) and respect towards the needs of an audience (Lachs 2000).

The focus of the project was twofold. Would the children's work be sporadic recordings of talk or whether there would be some of the linguistic features, connected to both structuralistic (spelling) and formalistic (fonts, layout) elements of writing, as identified in the National Curriculum. And whether the new technological environment would contribute to improving areas where the children underachieved.

2. BACKGROUND

Over the years the emphasis on dyslexia has shifted from the medical to the educational arena, concentrating mainly on poor reading and spelling performance. Recent research though, (Stackhouse and Wells 1997, Clayton 1999) has pointed to the idea that dyslexia probably has a neurological origin. This suggestion supports the notion that dyslexia is a syndrome, an umbrella term, for difficulties also connected with short-term memory, visual and auditory processing and recall. Apart from problems with literacy, dyslexia is connected to difficulties with mathematical and musical notation, sequencing and spatial awareness.

The introduction of computers in every day lives and activities has given dyslexic learners the possibility to approach information and scaffold their ideas in alternative ways. The notion of literacy has been redefined from a singular form noun and activity, involving mastering of writing, to a plural one, including the ability to express ideas in visual and auditory format. More specifically, the generic facilities of multimedia applications such as Talking Books, CD-ROMs, the Web allow the representation of information in a variety of symbolic systems. The on-screen product is a mixture of text, sounds, video clips, still or animated images and data can be organised in a non-linear sequence. Access to script for dyslexic learners whose decoding skills are not always fluent, is facilitated by alternative representations. Pictures and key words trigger users' attention and enable understanding of information.

The generic features of a multimedia program could allow literacy to be supported by oracy, and images to become an important operative medium of conveying a message. This interaction with various media can also become a dynamic creative tool in the use of authoring packages that support the construction of such multimedia applications. The constraints that typing and spell checking the information imposes on dyslexic learners can be replaced by the input of speech and images, signalling a meaningful use of notations (letters, sounds, images) in a context defined by the users' preferences. Similarly, writing is transformed from a motor skill to a complex cultural activity while higher levels of language-forming acts, such as, analysing, synthesising and combining, can be developed to negotiate meaning. The process could be compared to piano playing where moving on from 'finger dexterity' and ability 'to strike the keys while reading music, [one is being] involved in the essence of music itself' (Vygotsky 1978).

The generic facilities offered by a multimedia program could support the specialised teaching methodology followed for dyslexic learners. According to Hornsby and Shear (1993), Hickey (1977), and Miles (1990) teachers should encourage a multi-sensory approach for the development of skills. As dyslexic learners usually present qualitative and quantitative differences in their performance, the use of all the senses is advocated to support the stronger cognitive areas and assist the processing and retain of information (Pollock and Waller 1994).

According to the National Curriculum for English in Key Stage 2 (p.15) the process of writing involves: planning and drafting, composing, revising, proof-reading and presenting the ideas in a correct and clear final copy. "These processes cross over the oral/written divide" (Smith 1994). Multimedia authoring packages can bridge this gap and facilitate the creative process by harmonising the existence of oral speech, images and written text in the same environment. On the whole, these five stages can be then grouped into three broader areas:

- Exploring topic and creative media (Planning and Drafting)
- Composing the task (Composing; Presenting)
- Assessing and evaluating the product and the process (Reflecting; Proof-reading).

Looking at the development of the writing workshops organised by Graves (1983) and Calkins (1983) each of the five stages in compositional writing can be further analysed into the understanding and skills associated with their development.

The diagnostic assessments dyslexic learners undertake emphasise the difficulties they face in each of the writing stages. The language parts of the screening tests include spelling, reading, free-writing tasks and most dyslexic learners score very poorly in all three of them. Working in a multimedia authoring package can promote writing as a dialogic and multisensory process.

3. THE PROJECT

The project was organised in a single case study over a period of 12 weeks with two 50 minute-meetings per week. Two siblings, a boy (D, aged 8) and a girl (C, aged 10), of English monolingual background, helped with the empirical part of the project. The work took place at the children's home. It was hoped that this would give them more flexibility to concentrate on the project and not to see it as extra schoolwork.

The researcher took on the role of the teacher, introduced the program to the children and supported them in scaffolding their ideas, as conferencing with the children (Graves 1983) has been described as one of the most important elements in developing writing skills.

Assessment of their reading, spelling and mathematical skills (Table 1) indicated weaknesses and a discrepancy between their general abilities and their academic performance, which was further supported by their class teachers. Both children were confident in their alphabet skills and they knew the short and long vowel sounds. Their ability in recognising initial and final blends was also average. They indicated though poor concentration span, weaknesses in their organisational and spatial awareness skills, untidy handwriting, limited sight vocabulary, weaknesses in auditory processing and recall, together with a lack of knowledge of basic spelling rules of the English language.

Table 1. The children's educational profiling

C.		D.	
C.A.	10 yrs:0 mths	C.A.	8 yrs:2 mths
R.A.	7 yrs:0 mths	R.A.	6 yrs:0 mths
S.A.	8 yrs:0 mths	S.A.	7 yrs:0 mths
M.A.	1 0yrs:0 mths	M.A.	8 yrs:9 mths

C.A.: Chron/ical Age
R.A.: Reading Age
S.A.: Spelling Age
M.A.: Maths Age

'Hyperstudio' was selected as the multimedia-authoring program for the project. It has a user-friendly interface, a content-free setting where the user can combine text, graphics, animation, sound and video clips in a series of cards called 'stacks', a working template which resembles that of a children's drawing package, and big comprehensive icons on the toolbars. It was also considered more elaborate that generic programs such as *PowerPoint* and less complicated that other professional packages such as *Macromedia Director*. Visible and invisible 'buttons' can be set up as 'hot links' to enable transition through the cards. All the functions of the application are in drop-down menus; two of the most basic menus: 'Tools' and 'Colours' come in separate toolbars. There is a spell checker and storyboard to assist the users in visually mapping the whole project.

4. DISCUSSION

The preliminary findings from the empirical data have been classified into the three broader areas identified above, and analysed against the stages identified by the National Curriculum for English and the difficulties that the children's profile had shown. The results so far have indicated that the children's work included all the elements and the responsibilities involved in authorship.

4.1 Exploring topic and creative media

4.1.1 Planning and drafting

- *Knowledge and understanding*. The children were introduced to the idea of multimedia by exploring two professional CD-ROMs and a multimedia project completed by other children during the first two sessions. The discussions on the format of the presented topics led to the formulation of a working definition of what multimedia is in order to create a framework for their own project.
- *Language and communication*. A notebook was used for the children to make notes, draft their ideas and keep a diary of each session. In these the children wrote down their spoken versions of text to rehearse it before they recorded it. They decided to incorporate sound and text on each card 'for people who cannot read or see'. Pictures were also important media 'so people from China can understand' what the passages were all about.
- *Skills and processes*. The program did not seem to have been conceptually difficult for the children as they learnt easily how to use advanced techniques such as creating their own animated graphics. But the multi-sensory construction of the program might have contributed to a better understanding of its features. The children's response to it was positive from the start. They were excited to use it as firstly they did not have much access at school and secondly because it reminded them of games and having fun. There did not seem to be any negative associations connected to the use of the computer as there were with using a pencil. Typing can be considered a laborious task; the children did not seem to mind.

4.2 Composing the task

4.2.1 Composing

- *Knowledge and understanding.* The children explored the features of the program to produce their desired effects. When they were not able to create what they had in mind, they negotiated alternative ways of presenting the message; they never gave up.
- *Language and communication.* The whole project is in dialectic form. The children communicate to an audience: they give instructions of what to do in the card; they give factual information to the user about each sport; they take on the role of the sports commentator and describe highlights of games.
- *Skills and processes.* The children seemed to enjoy the sessions, which sometimes lasted for more than an hour. They were motivated to discuss spelling patterns introduced during the sessions and revisit their cards to improve content and layout. So their sight vocabulary also increased. They became more comfortable with navigating through the program and reading the menus. They also learnt technical terms such as 'animation', and appropriate vocabulary such as 'instruments' and setting'.

4.3 Presenting

- *Knowledge and understanding.* The children talked about the main idea of the project and realised that their emphasis had been on sports rather than on dinosaurs. They identified elements they should have included if they wanted to talk about dinosaurs (names and information about different species). The allusions to computer games described by the children could have instigated the creation of an action story. Instead they decided to present a virtual picture of life where real life sports take place in 'realistic' settings with 'realistic' rules. The photographs of the players scanned in and used in the 'Football' card, a comment on "too many clouds in the sky pattern", may indicate their need for 'reality' in their designs.
- *Language and communication.* A month after the project the children seemed to have maintained ownership of the work. They were still able to discuss the content of the project, justify their choices, revise the spelling patterns presented during the sessions and map out the structure and the content of each card.
- *Skills and processes.* The final product follows the classical structure of a book, with a title page-card followed by a content page-card. It has a

horizontal structure with things appearing at the click of buttons, rather than interrelating with other cards. The children indicated preference in developing the content of each card as much as they could before moving on to the next one. With more time, it would be interesting to see if more elaborate interconnections would have been created.

4.4 Assessing and evaluating the product and the process

4.4.1 Revising and proof reading

- *Knowledge and understanding.* Although an initial look at the product indicated that the children's preferred media were the drawing tools and the speech recorder, a closer examination of it alongside the transcripts which decode the process, indicate that written language was evident in almost all their cards. The templates they developed for their cards show consistency in the choice of media: text.; the 'Back' button, leading to the 'Contents' card, is always at the top right corner of the card and the font size, type and colour are the result of long discussions and trials. When sound was selected as the presentational mode of the information, the children prepared the passage in their notebook and rehearsed it before the actual recording. The researcher then discussed spelling points in the children's texts. When the children felt motivated to construct their thoughts in written format the researcher did not interrupt their flow of ideas and discussed spelling, syntactic or grammatical points later. This gave another opportunity to revise the form and the content of the passages. The immediate feedback (an application could be visualised immediately) and the visual structure of some of the program features ('Tools', 'Colours') gave the users autonomy and confidence in the process.
- *Language and communication.* The children were in charge of checking whether the links between cards worked and whether they were set up as they wanted them. The children mentioned the spell checker as an advantage, even though they never used it. preferring to ask the teacher-researcher. Feeling more relaxed about correcting the script, C, who had been described by her teacher as a girl who dislikes writing, composed a passage on football on her own in less than five minutes. Equally important, she agreed to go back and improve both the layout as well as the spelling and punctuation in various other sessions. The children worked together on most of the ideas but not to the extent that it was expected. The girl being older tended to overpower the process. She wanted to do most of the writings and the drawings, even though she had

more problems in spelling and writing than her brother. The boy went along, letting his sister lead the process. At some points though he performed probably in order to be in the centre of attention. He always carried an object with him so he could have the opportunity to talk about it or made noises and gestures. At those points, C was asked to talk the boy through the processes he missed by being far from the screen. D was willing to ask C questions about the project.

- *Skills and processes.* Repetition of techniques became meaningful as the children moved back and forth in the cards trying out sounds and animated graphics. At the same time they saw the information written there and read the labels of the buttons. Drill and practice of the constructed tasks was initiated by the children themselves, sometimes to the objection of the researcher who insisted on moving on with the project rather than trying out all the links they had made. Luckily the children did not always agree. The initial screening of the children's literacy skills indicated reluctance to reading and writing tasks. Both children developed initiatives in reading out the information they composed. C, described by her teacher as a reluctant reader, took ownership of her passage, reading it so often that she learnt it by heart.

As the sessions developed the children had to read the menu options and decide whether they were relevant (defining size of the card, saving the stack, moving back and forth). Each time they added a button on one of their cards. A series of questions concerning the things to do, places to go and the transition to the other card, came in menu boxes and the children had to make their choices before proceeding. Though at first it was difficult for them to read all the words on the tool bar they began to access the information more easily, and they developed a functional sight vocabulary which was tested at the end of the project with the use of out-of-context cards.

The children did not look at other resources even though two children's booklets were provided, one on dinosaurs and one on sports. The researcher did not expect the children to use them because their reading accuracy age was quite low, even though the books were for young children, and also because the whole project was perceived as an after school activity that did not necessitate any extra preparation. Both children were happy to explore the facilities offered by the program during the sessions.

5. CONCLUSION

The study focused on structure, form and content as integral parts of authorship and tried to see how the children explored these elements. It also wanted to investigate whether the new technological environment provided an enjoyable setting for the development of areas where the children underachieved, but also an alternative platform for them to negotiate their ideas and for others to evaluate their potential in the authoring process.

Empirical work in this field is important to support children with learning differences by introducing alternative ways of using their creative skills. The package, even though it realises the basic methodological principles advocated for the education of dyslexic learners, does not stick to the 'basics', in the sense that it does not necessitate the teaching of phonemes as a prerequisite in the constructive process.

The preliminary findings have indicated that the children's work included all the elements and the responsibilities involved in authorship. They took ownership of the product, and they negotiated meaning. The effect of mastery in the use of the tool led on from a sensory-motor activity to a conscious and structured task where respect towards varied needs of different types of audience became part of the context. One of the children's responses to those needs was to create a guessing 'Game' card as the people who were going to use the project 'must have fun'.

As indicated by their teachers and samples of their schoolwork, the children demonstrated an active role in the process quite different to their previous authoring attempts with more traditional media. They were willing to revisit their work and redraft it, discuss the choice of language, the style and content of their presentations.

The discourse recorded on the videotapes, the product itself, as well as a post-project assessment have also pointed out that the learners showed improvement in sporadic spelling patterns identified during the project. They were also able to identify and read fluently words that were introduced during the project and passages they themselves composed.

In summary, by focusing upon the needs of two individual children, this work does not claim to be generally applicable but the findings may provide the basis for further experimentation into the children's own perceptions of literacy through the medium of multimedia technology.

ACKNOWLEDGEMENTS

The author would like to acknowledge the support of the Foundation of National Scholarships (IKY) and of the British Computer Society. Thanks also to Sue Flohr from the British Dyslexia Association, to the children who participated in the project and to their families.

REFERENCES

Calkins, L. McCormick (1983) *Lessons from a Child.*

Clayton, J. (1999) Lost for Words. *New Scientist,* 24th April, No 2183, pp. 26-30.

Dewey, J (1938) Experience and Education. Collier Books, New York. In: Newman, D. (1997) Functional Environments for Microcomputers in Education. In *Mind, Culture and Activity. Seminal Papers from the Laboratory of Comparative Human Condition,* M. Cole, Y. Engstrom and O. Vasquez (eds.), Cambridge University Press, Cambridge.

Graves, D. (1983) *Writing.*

Hornsby, B. and Shear, F. (1993) *Alpha to Omega. The A-Z of Teaching Reading, Writing and Spelling.* 4th Edition, Heinemann Educational, Oxford.

Lachs, V. (2000) *Making Multimedia in the Classroom: A teacher's guide.* Routledge, London.

McFarlane, A. (ed.) (1997) *Information Technology & Authentic Learning.* Routledge, London.

Miles, E. (1990) Principles of Teaching Students with SpLD. In: *Meeting Points in Dyslexia,* G. Hale, M. Hales, T. Miles and A. Summerfield (eds.), BDA, Reading.

Newman, D. (1997) Functional Environments for Microcomputers in Education. In *Mind, Culture and Activity Seminal Papers from the Laboratory of Comparative Human Condition,* M. Cole, Y. Engstrom and O. Vasques (eds.), Cambridge University Press, Cambridge.

Pollock, J. and Waller, E. (1994) *Day-to-Day Dyslexia in the Classroom.* Routledge,.London.

Stackhouse, J. and Wells, B. (1997) *Children's Speech and Literacy Difficulties. A Psycholinguistic Framework.* Whurr Publishers Ltd., London.

Vygotsky, L. S. (1978) *Mind in Society. The Development of Higher Psychological Processes.* Harvard University Press,.Cambridge, Mass.

BIOGRAPHY

Yota Dimitriadi is a specialist teacher and assessor for dyslexic learners. She works for the British Dyslexia Association providing advice at the National Helpline. She is also involved with the New Opportunities Fund teacher training programme on ICT and SEN (Special Educational Needs) at the Institute of Education, University of London.

27

Researching Agent Technologies in the Electronic Classroom

Carolyn Dowling
Australian Catholic University, 115 Victoria Parade, Fitzroy, Victoria 3065, Australia
c.dowling@patrick.acu.edu au

Keywords: research, innovation, lifelong learning/education, distance learning, computer assisted instruction

Abstract: Designers of online education are increasingly making use of the Internet not just to enable students to access information, but to provide opportunities for communication between the various participants in the learning process. These frequently include a range of more or less personified and 'intelligent' computer programs generally referred to as 'agents', many of which are designed to play a key role in the social interactions that mediate learning. Through discussion of a selection of current implementations of agent technology within educational contexts, this paper highlights some key directions for ongoing research and evaluation.

1. INTRODUCTION

An important consequence of the increased rate of technological and social change that is being experienced in most parts of the world is the formal recognition by government, industry and educational institutions, of the need for increased flexibility in the provision of opportunities for learning. Computer based learning environments, particularly those that are Internet based, are one obvious vehicle for achieving such flexibility. Online education is becoming an increasingly popular alternative to traditional face to face modes of teaching at all levels, from elementary education to tertiary institutions and on-the-job technical or professional training. Within these contexts the Internet not only enables students to access information but, in keeping with current emphases on the importance of social interaction in the construction of knowledge, it also provides opportunities for communication between the different participants in the learning process.

Within a number of online educational environments we are now witnessing the emergence of a new participant in the social interactions that mediate learning. The substitution of 'agents', computer programs possessed of varying degrees of intelligence, autonomy and 'personality', for different aspects of human presence in the classroom, raises a number of issues in relation to the processes through which knowledge is constructed, and the qualities which permit successful participation in those processes.

Software agents are already a familiar part of our computing experience, from the anonymous programs that scurry about the Internet locating information for search engines to the cheerful little characters that pop up on our screens offering assistance with tasks ranging from formatting a date to constructing a complex audio-visual presentation. We may even have interacted with software 'characters' in 'chat' environments without realising they were not in fact human.

An early but still useful conception of a software agent with which many educators would be familiar is, "A character, enacted by the computer, who acts on behalf of the user in a virtual environment", useful in mediating " ... a relationship between the labyrinthine precision of computers and the fuzzy complexity of man" (Laurel 1990, p.355). The practical implementation of this concept has resulted in a range of more functional definitions such as, "An agent can be viewed as an object which has a goal and autonomously solves problems through interaction, such as collaboration, competition, negotiation and so on" (Kinoshita and Sugawara 1995).

Summarising the writings of a number of researchers, Aroyo and Kommers (1999, p.237) identify four major characteristics of agents as being autonomy, responsiveness or reactiveness, pro-activeness and social ability. Other qualities frequently proposed, but not supported by all researchers or indeed by all users, include the ability to learn from experience and consequently to respond in flexible and possibly unforeseen ways to particular situations, and the possession of a believable 'character' or personality as a basis for social interaction.

As is the case with agents in the physical world, there are many possible roles for software agents. They may represent the interests of individuals as would a trustworthy personal servant. They may be modelled on the personal qualities and preferences of a person, and so function as a type of electronic 'clone' within electronic environments where the user is not able to be present 'in person', or they might fulfil more complex roles in which they represent the interests of more than one person and act as 'brokers' of deals.

They may present themselves to us openly, or function in the background, somewhat in the manner of a 'secret agent' in the physical world. According to the complexity and sophistication of their programming they may have a greater or lesser degree of independence of action, and a more or less developed 'character'.

2. AGENTS IN THE ELECTRONIC CLASSROOM

Agents within educational contexts are designed to fulfil a range of purposes. Types of agents currently implemented in projects around the world include record keepers, information seekers, testers, facilitators of collaboration, tutors or instructors, fellow learners and tutees. Some operate behind the scenes entailing minimal interaction with students. These are of only marginal relevance to the main focus of this paper. Others either wholly or partly substitute for human-to-human interaction. In terms of our current understandings of the extent to which knowledge is socially constructed, this is for many people the most valued and pedagogically important aspect of the face to face classroom. Indeed it might be argued that unless it can be demonstrated that the social interactions that mediate face to face learning have a digital equivalent, online courses will inevitably be regarded by most educators as 'second best'.

The 'social' role of instructor or tutor has of course long been associated with educational uses of computers, albeit in forms now generally regarded poorly by most educators. Other socially interactive roles such as that of 'fellow learner' are more obviously innovative, and suggest the possibility of a far richer and more complex interactivity within electronic educational environments than that to which we are accustomed. Each role raises special challenges, not simply in relation to the technical capabilities of the software, but in terms of our understanding of the nature of both teaching and learning.

While research undertaken from an AI perspective necessarily focuses on the technical capabilities of agents, research within the special context of education needs to place greater emphasis on matching the capacities of the software with current understandings of pedagogical theory. How effectively does engagement with a software agent substitute for the various dimensions of human to human pedagogical interactions? Further, do such interactions incorporate the potential to extend our existing understandings of what constitutes an effective learning environment?

Johnson (1998) has proposed the following definition the role of a pedagogical agent:

"Pedagogical agents are autonomous agents that support human learning, by interacting with students in the context of interactive learning environments. They extend and improve upon previous work on intelligent tutoring systems in a number of ways. They adapt their behaviour to the dynamic state of the learning environment, taking advantage of learning opportunities as they arise. They can support collaborative learning as well as individualised learning, because multiple students and agents can interact in a shared environment. Given a suitably rich user interface, pedagogical agents are capable of a wide spectrum of instructionally effective interactions with students, including multimodal dialog. Animated pedagogical agents can promote student motivation and engagement, and engender affective as well as cognitive responses" (Johnson 1998, p.13).

This is a comprehensive and optimistic vision, incorporating a number of possible roles for software agents within educational environments. Many of these have already been implemented in various contexts. In evaluating the success of existing implementations and in considering future directions, several issues stand out as necessitating further research in relation to their implications for learning.

3. RESEARCH ISSUES

One of the key issues for developers of software agents is the degree to which these programs should appear to the user to be 'human'. In the electronic classroom this question clearly relates more to the socially interactive agents than to those performing more tool-like functions, which arguably would require a less developed 'personality'. There are strong arguments that a degree of personification of computer interfaces is inevitable. As Shirk put it:

"Although there is some dispute among software critics concerning the advisability of having 'personalities' in computer programs, their presence seems unavoidable. Any time there is communication between a computer and a human, the information presented by the computer has a certain style, diction, and tone of voice which impact upon the human's attitude and response toward the software" (Shirk 1988, p.320).

Further, our current understandings of learning depend very much on an acceptance of the role of the social construction of knowledge. It is in this regard that online interactions of a 'social' nature with a significantly personified entity can be perceived as adding value to educational activities

However the degree to which personification should be deliberately fostered is not entirely clear. While we might intuitively assume that computer users would prefer a highly personified interface, some research suggests that the reality is less straightforward. For instance, users react badly if a software 'personality' represented on the screen by an extremely realistic video image is unable to support its appearance with an appropriately high level of knowledge and understanding. As Masterton, puts it, "A common problem with AI programs that interact with humans is that they must present themselves in a way that reflects their ability. Where there is a conflict between the ability of the system and the users' perception of that ability a breakdown occurs and users may either fail to exploit its full potential or become frustrated with its shortcomings" (Masterton 1998, p.215). He goes on to suggest the implementation of a degree of anthropomorphism intended to convey qualities such as friendliness and usefulness, without the implication of possession of full human capabilities (Masterton 1998, p.211).

Some developers have addressed this issue through creating 'characters' that are more sketchily represented, for instance through cartoon-like graphics. This is a delicate and complex matter however, as some users also react badly to being given instructions or correction by an entity which they would normally regard as inferior to them – such as the animated paper clip familiar to users of Microsoft Office. Within some existing electronic learning environments for young students, the problem is cleverly addressed through the use of agents presented in the guise of various types of animals. Examples of this are the 'learning companions' developed by Chan (Chan 1996, Chan 1998).

In educational contexts this is an extremely complex issue, in view of the nature of the relationship between knowledge and authority or power in the classroom setting. It can be complicated still further within electronic environments by the special expectations students of different cultures might have in regard to how they interact with teachers as well as with fellow learners. Further, it is likely that optimal degrees and styles of personification might differ in accordance with the ages of students. This is certainly an aspect of the implementation of pedagogical agents which require considerable research

Another important issue in the development of educational software agents is their degree of autonomy or independence of action. Autonomy in the context of agents, is generally understood as meaning that they have the ability to make certain 'decisions' in the course of undertaking an activity, without the need for constant monitoring and intervention. Implicit in the recognition of the need for a capacity to exercise initiative is an acknowledgement that some outcomes of agent activity may not be easily predictable. This could pose certain difficulties for both teachers and students. From an educational point of view, the strong tendency in contemporary thinking to give more, rather than less control to the learner, suggests that limits should perhaps be placed on the capacity of educational agents to act independently. While they may be programmed so as to exercise considerable control over the learner, they may also be configured so as to be more sensitive to individualised user models, and more responsive to instruction from the student. However, while in the latter case the agent would have a greater degree of responsibility towards the perceived needs and wishes of learner, this may be contrary to the pedagogical goals of the teacher. The balance of freedom and control inherent in the structures and processes of more traditional learning environments depends to a significant extent on the ability of human teachers to sensitively modify their roles in response to the immediate situation. The ability of agents to achieve this is necessarily limited by the range of possibilities envisaged by their programmers. This is another aspect of pedagogical agents requiring further exploration by researchers.

A further concern in regard to the autonomy of pedagogical agents relates to the issue of intervention in the learning process. Despite the finding of Aroyo and Commers (1999, p.237) that pro-activity is a quality frequently sought after in agents, there is an important issue of balance to be addressed in relation to the educational process. It is well accepted that a high degree of unsought assistance whether from a human teacher or an excessively diligent and proactive agent can be quite detrimental, in particular to the metacognitive aspects of learning. Of course this is also an issue for teachers and learners in face-to-face educational contexts!

Closely associated with our ambivalence towards agent autonomy is the issue of trust. Teachers are generally accepted as being among the most trusted members of our community, both in relation to their responsibilities towards their students and also in broader terms. How do we decide whether to invest similar 'trust' in a software agent? While to an extent we can judge the competency, even the 'good intentions' of an agent through the outcomes of its actions, if we have had no hand in its programming we have little insight into its capabilities and limitations, even into what we might describe as its 'motivations'. Even if we are prepared to trust the agents with whom we deal directly, a further question remains as to how agents might reasonably 'decide' how to trust one another. In a number of fields, agents already have the capacity to interact with other agents emanating from different systems, and the exploration of such possibilities is very much a part of some research agendas in education. This another area in which extensive dialogue between educators and researchers would seem to be desirable.

The whole notion of an agent as a participant in the social construction of knowledge raises issues regarding whether or not computer programs can be said to 'learn' in a sense equivalent to that of human beings. If not, can they usefully participate in this aspect of a learning environment? The belief that they can do so is central to the thinking of many theorists and developers. Sheremetov and Nunez (1999), for example, whose work derives overtly from the theoretical frameworks of Piaget and Vygotsky, argue that:

"The design of learning environments, virtual or not, aims to promote productive interactions. In this type of learning a student changes from being a passive information receiver to an active collaborator, interacting with the tutors and colleagues in the learning process. Learning does not only result from acquiring knowledge, solving problems or using tools, but also from interacting about these on-going activities with persons and agents" (Sheremetov and Nunez 1999, p.305-306).

In relation to their specific project they write: "Our emphasis lies in the role of interactions in an artificial learning community as a group of real and artificial learners, tutors, and facilitators, working, supporting and learning from each other" (Sheremetov and Nunez 1999, p.306).

On the other hand it has been argued quite extensively that even the most heavily personified and autonomous of computer programs suffer from an intrinsic lack of ability to participate in the metacognitive aspects of learning. Pufall (1988), for instance, expresses a strong belief that a computer program is unable at any level commensurate with human capacities to modify its own knowledge structures or cognitive processes, and so cannot be regarded as a co-constructor of knowledge in a meaningful sense. While this might well have been the case in relation to earlier computer based learning environments, can we continue to make the same claims with confidence today or in the future? The capacity of software to 'learn' and adapt to experience through the incorporation of new information, the appropriate modification of its representation of the context in which it functions (its 'world'), and of its inference mechanisms, is undoubtedly increasing. This suggests that, whatever the differences in the underlying learning mechanisms, it might be possible to program agents that are able to convince their human companions that they are 'fellow learners'. Whether this is sufficient to enhance the learning experiences of students is another area requiring investigation.

At the core of the implementation of agent technologies in any context is the assumption that the range of tasks undertaken by single human being in a particular role can be effectively enacted by a multiplicity of agents. These should ideally be capable of interacting not only with the user but also with one another, and increasingly with agents associated with other programs. Within the electronic classroom the individual purposes of such entities derive from theoretical analyses of the component tasks and activities that are included in the larger scale pedagogical interactions of human beings. As educators, and indeed as students, we may simultaneously enact a range of roles in the classroom. The apparently unitary activity of 'teaching' involves such elements as demonstrating, guiding, telling, questioning, explaining, testing, motivating, criticising – even learning! Once identified, the assumption is that these diverse functions can be separated out and ultimately enacted through different configurations of agents working in relationships ranging from collaboration to competition. In keeping with the 'social' roles enacted by many of these agents, a metaphor commonly employed in conceptualising their aggregation is that of a 'society'.

Strategies for combining the activities of multiple agents already occupy a significant part of the research agenda in this area, and must continue to do so. However, while on the one hand the variety of functions enacted within a multi-agent environment is a clear attempt to realise the type of rich user interface described by Johnson (1998), some educators and researchers question the assumptions underlying these practices, arguing that they are underpinned by a reductionist rather than a holistic understanding of the processes and relationships involved in teaching and learning. In separating out the different components of pedagogical interactions, are we enabling each part to be realised more effectively, or are we failing to acknowledge that the global act of human teaching may in fact be more than the sum of its component parts? This is a research issue of a broader dimension than those concerned with issues of implementation.

4. CONCLUSION

In considering both actual and potential implementations of agent technology within the electronic classroom, it is clear that there is a pressing need for research not simply into the means of achieving the desired functionality, but also into the more complex question of the extent to which software entities are able to substitute for the delicate and subtle network of interactions and relationships which constitutes the social dimension of face-to-face pedagogy. To the extent that this can be realised, there is a further issue which must be addressed, namely the possibility that these technologies might have the potential to extent our understanding of the role of social relationships and interactions in the learning process.

REFERENCES

Aroyo, L and Kommers, P. (1999) Preface – intelligent agents for educational computer-aided systems. *Journal of Interactive Learning Research*, 10 (3/4), pp.235-243.

Chan, T.-W. (1996) Learning companion systems, social learning systems, and the global social learning club. *Journal of AI in Education* 7 (2).

Chan, T.-W. (1998) *The past, present, and future of educational agents*. [www.apc.src.ncu.edu.tw/apc/ppt_chan.html] 3.2.2000.

Johnson, W. L. (1998) Pedagogical agents. In *Proceedings of the Sixth International Conference on Computers in Education (ICCE '98)*, T.-W. Chan, A. Collins and J. Lin (eds.), Beijing, October. pp.13-22.

Kinoshita, T. and Sugawara, K. (1995) *Agent oriented computing*. Soft Research Center, Tokyo.

Laurel, B. (1990) Interface agents: metaphors with character. In *The Art of Human-Computer Interface Design*, B. Laurel (ed.), Addison-Wesley, Reading, Massachusetts, pp. 355-367.

Masterton, S. (1998) Computer support for learners using intelligent educational agents: the way forward. In *Proceedings of the Sixth International Conference on Computers in Education (ICCE '98)*, T.-W. Chan, A. Collins and J. Lin (eds.), Beijing, October, pp. 211-219.

Pufall, P. (1988) Function in Piaget's system: some notes for constructors of microworlds. In *Constructivism in the Computer Age*, G. Forman and P. Pufall (eds.), Lawrence Erlbaum Associates, Hillsdale, New Jersey.

Sheremetov, L. and Nunez, G. (1999) Multi-agent framework for virtual learning spaces. *Journal of Interactive Learning Research*, 10 (3/4), pp. 235-243.

Shirk, H. N. (1988) Technical writers as computer scientists: the challenges of online documentation. In *Text, Context and Hypertext: writing with and for the computer*, E. Barrett (ed.), MIT Press, Cambridge, Massachusetts.

BIOGRAPHY

Carolyn Dowling is an Associate Professor and Head of the School of Arts and Sciences (Victoria) of Australian Catholic University. Her research interests include computer mediated writing, virtual reality in education and training contexts, social and ethical aspects of computing, software agents, and academic usage of the Internet.

PART THREE

NEW PEDAGOGIC IDEAS

28

Teacher Scaffolding: An Exploration of Exemplary Practice

Jennifer Masters and Nicola Yelland
Faculty of Education, Queensland University of Technology, Brisbane, Australia
j.masters@qut.edu.au

Keywords: classroom teaching/practice, integration of ICT, primary education

Abstract While computers have increasingly been used in classroom over the last twenty years, their application has often been mundane; being merely used to reinforce existing educational practices rather than as a catalyst for educational innovation. An effective way to bring about change may be to identify instances of best practice and then study associated strategies that may be useful for teachers trying to use computers in new and meaningful ways. This study investigates strategies used by a teacher deemed to be exemplary at using computers and associated technology in her classroom. It involved observing and recording teaching sessions conducted by the teacher. This paper discusses the learning task, the children's progression through the task and the teaching strategies used. In particular, it looks for instances of teacher scaffolding as a strategy for supporting children working with computers.

1. BACKGROUND

One of the most significant directions evident in education in recent times has been the restructuring of education catalysed by technological innovation. An integral and core part of the restructuring process is a change to instructional practices. New models for teaching and learning incorporate a focus on problem-solving, collaborative learning, real purpose tasks and transformed teacher roles (e.g. Jonassen 1996). As teachers are expected to adopt new models, they also need to reassess their approach towards educational processes and the integration of technology tools (Bork 2000). It seemed that the advent of technology-based school reform demanded new attitudes from teachers, different strategies and even that teachers adopt a new teaching paradigm.

Even though policy was requiring a new approach to teaching with computers, research indicated that resistance to change was still an impediment. While transformation in practice was demanded, it seems that teachers were finding it difficult to make the adjustments required. Sandholtz, Ringstaff and Dwyer (1997) suggested that rather than blame teachers for their reluctance to use technology in new ways, the problem should considered from the teachers' perspectives. Teachers have a responsibility to foster learning for their students and they need to be reassured that using computers in constructive ways will promote positive learning outcomes. Research from the Apple Classroom of Tomorrow (ACOT) project (Sandholtz et al. 1997) found that although teachers initially relied on traditional teaching strategies when using computers, over time, with supportive teacher development, they did adapt to more constructivist approaches.

Campoy (1993) suggested that the use of computers and especially software that promotes constructivist learning might actually be a catalyst to encouraging teachers to teach in more constructivist ways. This was supported by Hannafin and Savenye (1993) who felt that the show-casing of success stories of teachers using computers in meaningful ways would encourage others to try new methods. Additionally, in a report on the use of technology (President's Committee of Advisors on Science and Technology 1997) it was identified that teachers need to be provided with pedagogical support, including opportunities to observe within the classrooms of successful technology-using teachers.

A major component in the attempt to bring about effective computer use in schools is the type of activity that teachers are initiating in their classrooms. Research over the last twenty years has shown that using computers for traditional educational tasks, in traditional teaching styles has not significantly changed educational outcomes (Jones, Valdez and Nowakowski 1995). Instead, effective computer implementation is hinged on new learning tasks that promote "engaged, meaningful learning and collaboration involving challenging and real-life tasks, with technology as a tool for learning, communication and collaboration" (p. 1). Therefore, when examining teaching practices, we must also be cognisant of the type of activity that the children are engaged with. In particular we need to seek 'rich tasks', i.e. tasks that are designed to engage children with "knowledges, fields and paradigms that have power and salience in researching, analysing and interpreting the world" (Education Queensland 2000).

In previous research (Yelland and Masters 1999) we have identified that teacher scaffolding is a key aspect of effective computer use by children. The term 'scaffolding' was first described by Wood, Bruner and Ross (1976), who defined it as "a process that enables a child or novice to solve a problem, carry out a task or achieve a goal which would be beyond his unassisted efforts (p. 90)". The concept arose out of a consideration of Vygotsky's theories in which he hypothesised that guided interactions with an adult or a more capable peer could assist children to develop at a higher level of operation. Vygotsky suggested that this support allowed a child to extend through the Zone of Proximal Development. Consequently, when scaffolding is provided, a child may not only accomplish the task at a higher level but also internalise the thinking, strategy or mechanisms used to be able to approach similar tasks. (Rogoff 1990).

Research has shown that although the nature of the scaffolding is dynamic and must be modified according to the task and the learner, several key characteristics of scaffolding can be identified (Beeds, Hawkins and Roller 1991). First, the interaction must be collaborative, with the learner's own intentions being the aim of the process (Searle 1984). Second, the scaffolding must operate within the learner's zone of proximal development. Rather than simply ensuring the task is completed, the scaffolder must access the learner's level of comprehension and then work at a slightly beyond that level, drawing the learning into new areas of exploration (Rogoff 1990). The third characteristic of scaffolding is that the scaffold is gradually withdrawn, as the learner becomes more competent. Palincsar (1986) suggests that this notion re-inforces the metaphor of a scaffold as used when constructing buildings in that the means of support is both adjustable and temporary.

In our own research (Yelland and Masters 1999) we have identified that scaffolding with computers can also be classified into categories. In addition to *cognitive* scaffolding where a teacher can support children when constructing understanding, we also found that scaffolding may be *affective*, with the teacher supporting the children emotionally, and *strategic*, in which the teacher can provide task management support. A final category that is especially pertinent to using computers and associated technology is *technical* scaffolding. In this situation the teacher facilitates the operation of both the hardware and the software, in order for the students to focus on the learning aspects involved.

2. THE SETTING

The classroom chosen for this investigation was somewhat special. The research school was designed to be a state-of-the-art technology institution and was purpose built with facilities to support the integration of information and communication technologies in the classrooms. The infrastructure of the school incorporated at least four networked multimedia computers in each classroom with ceiling wiring to enable them to be situated in central hubs. Each double classroom also had a large screen monitor on a movable trolley that could be connected to any of the computers. Additionally, the students had access to peripherals such as still and movie digital cameras and scanners. A full time technology co-ordinator supports classroom teachers at the school.

Woodcrest College opened in 1998 as a primary campus and in 2000 extended its scope to incorporate a P-12 curriculum over a lead-in period, which will reach capacity in 2004. Another feature of the school is the Teacher Development Centre, which provides professional development for teachers in effectively using technology in classroom teaching practice. The centre runs a program in which teachers from other schools can visit to observe the teachers using technology with students and to participate in discussions about staff development, and school change. The stated learning outcomes of the project are that participants are presented opportunities to develop an understanding of:

- Constructivist classroom practice
- The role of educational technology in supporting effective learning and teaching
- Strategies to integrate educational technology into classroom practice
- A range of applications of educational technology to support a student centred constructivist approach to learning and teaching.

The class we observed in this study was a double year two/three group, with 52 children aged between 6 and 9 years. The group occupied two large adjoining rooms, separated by a sliding panel that could be closed or opened as required. The setting had been arranged so one room served as an activity area with very little furniture, while the other was used for seated activities, with tables for groups of children. There were eight computers located in pairs across both rooms, with four moveable workstations in the activity area to allow for maximum adaptability.

There were two teachers with the class who had both been teaching at the school since it was opened (3 years). One teacher, Angela was a graduate when appointed, while the other, Gillian, had previous teaching experience and was completing a Masters degree specialising in computers in education. Both teachers were recognised as having expertise with integrating computers into classroom activity and both regularly hosted visitors from the teacher development program.

3. THE ACTIVITY

The class had been investigating 'mini-beasts'. This topic had been integrated across the curriculum and the children had been examining the lifestyle and habits of various mini animals such as insects, arachnids and small reptiles, e.g. geckos. The culminating activity for the theme was for the children to work in groups of five or six and use the computer to produce a modelling clay animation (a quick-time movie) depicting a sequence in the life of a chosen mini-beast. In the animation they needed to illustrate the mini-beast's home, the food source and its mechanism for movement. In order to conceptualise their animation, the children had examined a 'Wallace and Grommit' movie, a popular children's series that uses a modelling clay technique to produce animation.

Figure 1. Bee set with bee, hive and flower

The activity was broken down into a number of tasks:

- Decide on the mini-beast and define the home, food and movement for that beast.
- Use a storyboard to plan the sequence. The sequence should include at least six stages.
- Design and produce the props. Produce a mini-beast using modelling clay and develop the set for the movie. This will include a backdrop, a foreground and any objects on the set.
- Film the sequence. Assemble the set and set up the digital camera on a tripod. Take a series of still shots of the mini-beast on the set in order to develop the animation.

- Take the disk/s with the still shots to a computer and load them into the quick-time software.
- Create a movie. Edit the still shots to make the animation sequence. This includes sequencing the shots and removing any unwanted files. An option may be to add a music sound track.
- Share your movie with the class and reflect on the processes you used and the decisions you made.

4. RESEARCH FOCUS

While this activity provides a number of opportunities for research, particularly in relation to 'rich tasks', the focus that we had during this study related to the ways in which the teacher scaffolded the children during the task, and particularly while using the technology in steps four to seven. The task was one of several on-going projects happening in the classroom during the week of our visit. During this time, both teachers worked with all groups within the class on a needs basis. In order to isolate the task in the milieu of classroom practice, we video-recorded the progress of two groups through the 'mini-beast movie' production over several consecutive days. In these sessions, the more experienced teacher, Gillian, supported the 'bee' group and the 'spider' group in their work with the technology.

5. PROCEDURE

Before the children began any work with technology, the technical processes of the task were explained to the class during a mat session in the activity room. The large monitor was used for this session and both teachers and all the children were present. While the children had had previous experience with both the digital camera and the editing software, Gillian explained and demonstrated each step of the process in the context of the new task. In this situation, the other teacher, Angela, adopted a secondary role which involved asking guiding questions and reinforcing the processes described by Gillian. After this briefing, the groups were allowed to move to the technical aspects of the task when they were ready for stage 4 or if it was their turn. It should be noted too, that this procedure was reinforced in a de-briefing session at the end of activities for the day. In a half-hour mat session, the groups were asked to briefly share their progress for the day, any problems they encountered and any strategies that they used to solve those problems. This meant that children who had not yet attempted the animation task could benefit from the experiences and advice of others.

When the children in the groups worked on the production, it seemed they had plenty of previous experience with working with technology in this mode. In general the children appeared to be confident with the equipment (digital camera and editing software) and also the animation process. They also managed turn taking and assignment of roles within the task, although this was one of the aspects that needing scaffolding from Gillian (especially with the bee group). During this time Gillian remained within range of the students, in order to help or contribute when necessary.

Figure 2. The animation process

The reflection stage consisted of a mat session with the large monitor for display. Each group nominated a spokesperson and another person to operate the computer. The presentation was not rehearsed, rather Gillian choreographed the process through directed questioning. The structure tended to be a brief introduction on the content, a presentation of the product and then a reflection on decisions and problem solving that occurred during the process. During the presentation the class members were prompted to ask questions and the spokesperson was encouraged to call on members of the team in order to respond thoroughly.

6. SCAFFOLDING STRATEGIES

On first impressions it seemed that Gillian had a passive role and during much of the activity monitored without comment, sometimes from the other side of the room. However when reviewing the process, it was obvious that she was actually providing scaffolding throughout the whole task. During the production of resource she implemented a number of scaffolding strategies that can be summarised as:

6.1 Cognitive strategies

Gillian systematically monitored the concept development in the group activity. This incorporated steering the children through decision making to reach their goal product. This included:

- Task reinforcement – "Now, what is it exactly that you need to do?"
- Seeding ideas during group discussions – In response to a spinning bee problem -"What about if you use two pieces of thread instead of one to suspend your bee?"
- Reviewing progress – "OK, where are we up to? What is next?"
- Conceptualisation reinforcement – "So where does the bee have to go next?"
- Narrowing choices – "Well you could make the spider eat the fly now or you could wait until it gets back to the web. What do you think?"

6.2 Strategic

Group management was a key factor during the task, especially as a group of six children was fairly large. Gillian supported the group dynamic, when necessary, by:

- Defining roles – "Now, you need two people holding the spider and the camera person needs to be here"
- Recruiting – "Sam, why don't you come and have a go at taking a picture?"
- Time management – "We have about 5 minutes left. What are the tasks left to do?"

6.3 Affective

The groups that were engaged in the task during our observations were remarkably confident and supportive of each other. It is likely that for this reason we saw little in terms of affective scaffolding. The affective scaffolding that we observed included:

- Granting permission – "Can we turn the bee so the camera is looking at this side?" – "Yes of course you can, that will be great."
- Reassurance – "You're going really well. Just a few more shots and you will be finished."

6.4 Technical

In terms of technical competence, the children obviously had experience using computers and were not afraid to try new options. It is probable too that the prior instruction session prepared the children effectively for their technical tasks. The technical scaffolding that we observed included.

- Technical instruction – When the children were taking pictures – "You need to squeeze the button slowly and keep pressing until it goes click. It is different to a normal camera".
- Technical recovery – If the children did make a technical mistake or something went wrong with the equipment, Gillian increased the amount of intervention considerably. This may have incorporated prompts or guiding questions – "Lets look through the menu and see if we can find an option that will help" or even physical intervention – "Hang on, I'll just get that back for you".

7. DISCUSSION

The support that Gillian provided for the children is perhaps typical teacher activity in any primary classroom. However by analysing this activity we can begin to tease out strategies that can be suggested to other teachers for computer implementation in their classrooms. In particular we would like to identify whether this activity can be considered as scaffolding, in which the interaction is collaborative, with the learners' intentions as a focus, where the learners are crossing their own zones of proximal development and the scaffolding is being progressively withdrawn. While the aspect of a teacher scaffolding a group of children simultaneously is somewhat complex, there is evidence to suggest that Gillian was scaffolding during the task.

The first aspect is to establish whether Gillian worked in a collaborative mode with the children, with their intentions as the goal. The fact that the children were working in a group meant that individuals needed to negotiate in terms of their own intentions. However, the nature of the task did ensure that the goal was actually determined by the students. In this sense, the teacher's intentions (that is, the objectives of the task) 'faded' to groups intentions in that teacher direction did not dominate and the children had a great deal of control.

Possibly the most difficult aspect of scaffolding to conceptualise is the notion of crossing the Zone of Proximal Development. Even with an individual child in a one to one scaffolding situation, it could be difficult to ascertain understanding levels and consequential shifts. The concept of promoting equivalent learning with six children at once is quite unrealistic. This inequity in achievement was especially apparent with the bee group, which had several group members off-task and uninvolved, while two members dominated the activity. Nevertheless, it was also evident that with both groups, some participants seemed to be gaining key concepts and making significant shifts in understanding. This observation was reinforced when the children were able to reflect on their processes and achievements.

Given the small window of time in which we observed the class, it would be inappropriate to make sweeping claims about Gillian applying scaffolding and then withdrawing the scaffolds as the children adopted new concepts. However, an interesting observation was that Gillian implemented quite different amounts of scaffolding for the two groups. While both groups we given the opportunity to experiment with both the technology and the task, Gillian used far less intervention with the spider group. It is possible that the spider group was at a different stage of development to the bee group and that some early scaffolding had already been withdrawn. Our initial observation that Gillian had a relatively passive role in the group work may also contribute to this theory. It is likely that much of the scaffolding that supported the children when they initially started using the digital camera and the computer had been withdrawn as the children became more comfortable with its use.

8. CONCLUSION

This exploratory investigation of strategies used by an experienced teacher has provided some interesting insights into how a teacher might scaffold when children are using technology. We have found that an experienced teacher constantly monitors children's progress and contributes in a number of different ways during a task. The teacher must also know when to withdraw support in order to allow children to explore and construct new understandings. Further research in this area will investigate the role teacher scaffolding plays in an individual child's learning while using computers. It will also examine a teacher's management of their class activity and especially how a teacher can scaffold each class member while they use computers for learning goals.

REFERENCES

Becker, H. J. (1994) How exemplary computer-using teachers differ from other teachers: Implications for realizing the potential of computers in schools. *Journal of Research on Computing in Education*, 26 (2), pp. 291-321.

Beed, P., Hawkins, M. and Roller, C. (1991) Moving learners towards independence: The power of scaffolded instruction. *The Reading Teacher*, 44 (9), pp. 648-655.

Bork, A. (2000) Learning technology. *EDUCAUSE Review,* January/February, 1.

Campoy, R. (1992) The role of technology in the school reform movement. *Educational Technology*, 32(8), pp. 17-22.

Education Queensland (2000) *New Basics Project Technical Paper.* [http://education.qld.gov.au/corporate/newbasics/html/tnbf.html] 4/8/2000.

Hannafin, R. and Savenye, W. (1993) Technology in the classroom: The teacher's new role and resistance to it. *Educational Technology*, 33(6), pp. 26-31.

Jones, B., Valdez, G., Nowakowski, J. and Rasmussen, C. (1995) New times demand new ways of learning. *Plugging In: Choosing and Using Educational Technology,* Council for Educational Development & Research, North Central Regional Education Laboratory, Washington, D.C. [http://www.ncrel.org/sdrs/edtalk/newtimes.htm].

Jonassen, D. (1996) *Computers in the classroom: Mindtools for critical thinking.* Prentice-Hall, Englewood Cliffs, N J.

Palincsar, A. S. (1986) The role of dialogue in providing scaffolded instruction. *Educational Psychologist*, 21(1 & 2), pp. 73-98.

President's Committee of Advisors on Science and Technology (1997) *Report to the president on the use of technology to strengthen K-12 education in the United States.* pp. 1-66. [http://www.whitehouse.gov/WH/EOP/OSTP/NSTC/PCAST/k-12ed.html] 3/2/2000.

Rogoff, B. (1990) *Apprenticeship in thinking: Cognitive development in social context.* Oxford University Press, New York.

Sandholtz, J., Ringstaff, C. and Dwyer, D. (1996) *Teaching with technology: Creating student centred classrooms.* Teachers College Press, New York.

Searle, D. (1984) Scaffolding: Who's building whose building? 61(5), pp. 480-483.

Wood, D., Bruner, J. and Ross, G. (1976) The role of tutoring in problem solving. *Journal of Child Psychology and Psychiatry,* 17, pp. 89-100.

Yelland, N. and Masters, J. (1999) New ways of learning with technology: Scaffolding children learning and understanding. *Advanced Research in Computers and Communications in Education: New Abilities for the Networked Society*, Proceedings of ICCE'99, IOS Press, Chiba, Japan, pp. 499-506.

BIOGRAPHY

Jennifer Masters is a lecturer in Technology Education at Queensland University of Technology. She has taught at both Early Childhood and Primary levels and currently specialises in the integration of computing in Early childhood and Primary curriculum. Some specific interest areas include discovery learning and constructivism, using computers for 'real' purposes, publishing and presenting with computers and computer-based problem-solving opportunities – including LOGO. She is currently enrolled in a Ph. D course and has research interests relate to young children using computers, with particular focus at present on how teachers can 'scaffold' or support children working with computers.

29

Show What You Can Do with Media

The Media Literacy Portfolio

Annemarie Hauf-Tulodziecki and Wolfgang Weber
Landesinstitut für Schule und Weiterbildung, Paradieser Weg 64, D-59494 Soest, Germany
anna-marie.hauf-tulodziecki@mail.lsw.nrw.de

Keywords: catalyst for adaptation, competencies, evaluation, lifelong learning, self-assessment

Abstract: By media literacy we understand a wide range of abilities, which are not taught as an individual subject but which are, in principle, included in all subjects at all levels of teaching and in all types of schools. The difficulty of such 'cross-sectional tasks' is that quality and quantity of engagement with them is nowhere explicitly documented and assessed. The development of the portfolio was initially motivated by the wish to provide pupils with a possibility to document their individual achievements in a suitable way. This instrument can play an important role in the development of teaching media literacy within schools because a vital prerequisite for an attractive portfolio are interesting school activities.

1. INTRODUCTION

Teachers as well as representatives from the fields of business and politics are of the opinion that media literacy is an indispensable qualification which is vital for coping with the demands of the information and media society. However, when you talk to them individually, the term 'media literacy' often means completely different things to them.

At present, promoting media literacy is probably one of the most frequently cited educational goals throughout the Federal Republic of Germany. It is precisely the comprehensive initiatives to equip all schools with multimedia computers and internet connections which are committed to meeting this pedagogical goal.

Within the foreseeable future, when the schools are adequately equipped, and advanced teacher training is sufficiently effective for the use of the New Media, in particular, to be gaining in importance across a broad spectrum, the question is also going to be asked: How media-competent are our pupils?

Formal proof of the standard methods of grading and certification is not possible. In North-Rhine-Westphalia there is not a separate subject which is aimed at teaching media literacy. As a result, it is not possible to award a grade which provides information about the pupils' achievements in this subject. Instead, the recommendation is to see the subject matter of media training, i.e. all teaching aimed at promoting media competence, as being, as a matter of principle, the task of all types of schools, age-ranges and subjects.

However, if, ideally, inter-related media topics are regularly taught at a school and relate to different subjects, these still do not lead to a grade: the success or failure of the efforts, the commitment shown, the knowledge and methods which have been acquired, are, to a certain extent, reflected in the subject grades and consequently in the school reports, and perhaps the school report can include an additional comment. Nevertheless, it is true that outsiders will not be able to ascertain the degree of existing media literacy.

An additional problem of 'proof' arises as a result of the fact that apart from lessons or voluntary school events there are other opportunities for pupils to acquire and deepen their media competence. This may be in the form of practical training, or courses which they can attend outside school, or – as quite frequently happens – taking an active interest in a topic or subject during their leisure time.

It is by introducing a portfolio in media literacy that we see a good opportunity to provide information about the media literacy which pupils have acquired.

2. FROM A PEDAGOGICAL VIEWPOINT

The term 'portfolio' generally refers to a 'structured file of documents' which can be 'presented' on specific occasions. The term is frequently used in the world of finance where, for example, shareholders list document stocks and shares in a portfolio. However, artists also combine some of their selected works into a portfolio in order to demonstrate the breadth of their artistic abilities. Our concept of a portfolio in media literacy is based on just such an artist's portfolio, in that pupils should be able to show interested parties which media they have prepared themselves or to what extent they were involved in the preparation of these.

Yet simply compiling a list of their own results is insufficient when it comes to documenting something as complex as media literacy. And the concept of a portfolio also includes additional pedagogical possibilities which we wished to take into account in what we were developing. Two of our examples will show that portfolios can be more than mere files.

2.1 Example 1: The European portfolio for languages

How should language skills be documented so that they can be understood throughout Europe, and so that they can also be comparable? Experts on the European Council have been working on this since the beginning of the 1990s. It did not prove possible to create the required transparency in respect of school reports and grades, firstly because the grades and the way they are interpreted differ from one country to another, and secondly because grades also only relate to aspects which are taught or tested as part of the teaching process. Skills which have been acquired outside school, for example within the family, during practical courses, or during stays abroad, as well as intercultural experiences, were not recorded.

The European Portfolio for Languages, which was presented for the first time in 1997, was intended to create this transparency. Following an initial evaluation phase, the portfolio (in the version used in North-Rhine-Westphalia) consists of 3 parts:

- The *language passport* contains the documentation of language competency at the end of a course of training in secondary level I or II.
- In the *language biography* the pupils themselves describe an individual assessment of their abilities and intercultural experiences.
- In the *dossier* they collect examples of their own personal achievements, e.g. especially successful class-papers and class-work.

One important element which describes achievements in the field of languages is the six levels of competency which have been agreed throughout Europe as frames of reference. On the basis of this frame, the teachers assess the pupils' performance at pre-determined times (Christ 1997).

In addition to the practical importance of the portfolio, especially as documentation – agreed upon throughout Europe – of language knowledge and skills, it is the pedagogical functions of the portfolio which are seen as being of special importance, for instance:

- the portfolio for languages is increasingly seen as an instrument which motivates both young and adult learners to orientate themselves towards several languages, and to learn foreign languages throughout and as part of their lives.

- by means of the portfolio, learners are motivated to follow their own learning processes and to become aware of the progress they are making before they document this progress.
- reflecting on their own learning increases the learners' independence and self-responsibility.

The developers are assuming that the portfolio can serve as a tool for quality development and quality assurance provided that at regular intervals it forms a part of lessons (Gerling and Thümann 1998).

2.2 Example 2: The portfolio as an alternative to grades

No grades are awarded in the 'Bielefelder Oberstufenkolleg'. Instead, the collegiates can provide proof of their achievements in their courses. At the end of the course, it is only a matter of deciding between 'passed' or 'not passed'. Within the framework of a competition called 'Qualität schulische Arbeit' (= quality of schoolwork), the aim is to introduce experiences by including portfolios in the marking of work. In those portfolio courses which have already been set up, the collegiates document not only proof of their achievements, they also record brief self-evaluations and the comments of those who teach them. 'Achievement files' are introduced which overlap courses, and in the final stage, each collegiate is responsible for keeping an overall performance file.

The portfolio concept is considered to have a great deal of potential, for example when it comes to a changed, democratic approach to pupils' performance. It is precisely in schools which practise open, differentiated teaching, during which individual profiles can be built up, that assessment of performance using the portfolio system can provide the necessary flexibility. On the one hand the learner has a wider choice of material from which to learn, and on the other, there are the learner's own checks and assessment of his or her learning progress which act as a correcting influence, as well as an obligation to meet certain standard requirements. This encourages a positive attitude towards achievement (Oberstufenkolleg Bielefeld 2000).

Just as in the example of the language portfolio, the 'achievement portfolio' also offers advantages such as:

- communication between teacher and learner about achievement is simplified
- the pupil's own reflection on learning and achievement is stimulated
- the pupil has a better awareness of his or her own abilities, deficits and development
- the files make the course more easily comprehensible and easier to reflect on, and further steps can be planned on this basis.

Although the kinds of motivation to make use of portfolios are so different, they also show how the wide spectrum of pedagogical possibilities makes the development of a portfolio in media literacy worthwhile.

3. A PORTFOLIO IN MEDIA LITERACY

The initiators of the portfolio in media literacy were the principals – one female, one male – at two high schools in which 'media' is included as an important aspect of their school programme. It was their idea to develop a portfolio by means of which their pupils could demonstrate their specific skills. The Bertelsmann Foundation, which sponsors media activities in one of the schools, was just as interested as the Ministry for Schools, Science and Research, which commissioned the State Institute for Schools and Further Education to participate in developing the portfolio. The advantages of development a portfolio to prove media literacy were immediately obvious, but it was the details which were the problem:

3.1 Defining the term 'media literacy'

The term 'media literacy' is often used in a variety of ways, and so it was first necessary to define it. Only when that had been done was it necessary to define competencies.

- Which basic abilities, skills, knowledge, methods form part of media literacy?
- Which media are involved?
- How is it possible to establish whether pupils have these competencies?

The first step was to set up an orientation framework as a general system of reference; this framework consists of five areas of responsibility. These include both forms of activity-orientated analysis of media:

1. the selection and use of what the media have to offer
2. designing your own media work.

In terms of content, both forms include knowledge and analytical abilities in connection

3. with the creative opportunities on which the various kinds of media are based,
4. with the pre-conditions for use and the effects of media, and
5. with economic, social, technical, political conditions which are connected with the production and dissemination of media.

In practical schoolwork, an experiment has already produced positive results with this orientation framework (MSWWF des Landes NRW 1998, Tulodziecki et al. 1995). Instead of proof of appropriate competencies on the part of the learners, the first stage is for them to list the (media) events in which they have taken part.

3.2 Agreeing on minimum requirements

Media literacy is not taught as a subject, there are no specified inner structures, catalogues of content, or any procedure which is built up in important sectors. Knowledge relating to media education can be developed using different media and topics and then transferred to other subject matters.

- How is it possible to ensure that, in spite of a lack of obligatory content material in lessons in respect of media, a wide range of content is offered and different methods of dealing with content in lessons are employed or are expressed in the documented proof?
- How is it possible to ensure that all the knowledge and achievements relevant for media literacy which are demonstrated in the portfolio make themselves felt?

The orientation framework presented above can be used in a flexible fashion: unnecessary restrictions are avoided, and instead relevant knowledge can be classified according to the five areas of responsibility. What is being called for as proof of media literacy is that all areas of responsibility must be dealt with in the course of time, and that this takes place using the example of different kinds of media. In this meaning, subjects offered at school are to be documented by the teachers in the form of brief descriptions which allow for classification.

3.3 Planning flexible design

There is a wide range of opportunities for pupils to acquire media literacy. These may be available in compulsory school courses, but also in elective courses or voluntary study-groups. In addition, it should be possible to document extra-curricular activities in the portfolio, whether these activities are 'organised' in external courses or carried out on the learners' own initiative, such as the self-guided learning of a computer programming language in order to solve a specific problem.

- How can extra-curricular opportunities and the results of the learners' own initiative be appropriately documented?

These project forms are also to be used by so-called 'external suppliers'. Pupils, too, should be able to fill in a project form by themselves if they have acquired relevant skills by themselves.

3.4 Ensuring that individual work is recognised

Media education should be taught in an activity-orientated way. This means that media work both in and out of school must be more project-related than other lessons. Pupils will frequently meet in groups and carry out different partial tasks in order to find the solution to a more complex task; in doing this, they will deal more intensively with individual problems than their fellow students, use special tools, or design a specific medium. Increasingly, they will first organise the tasks by themselves so that the organisation itself only provides a framework, and the important learning processes each take place in the groups with the setting of different, individual emphases.

- How is it possible to ensure that the individual contributions of the learners – often produced with a great deal of commitment – are suitably documented?

The learners will prepare their own results forms for the individual project descriptions, and they will use these forms – with reference to the official description – to describe their own personal contribution within the framework of the project. They should collect those results which they have come to, or to which they have made a major contribution, in their file.

3.5 Assessing technical abilities and skills

In order to work with media, to prepare your own media or to make use of media-supported methods, you need technical abilities, skills in dealing with equipment and technical systems, hardware and software or computer-supported tools. Although from a pedagogical point of view media education is less a matter of detailed technical knowledge which can be used at once (in any case, technical knowledge is soon out of date), such knowledge can be very interesting and helpful for outsiders, for example those companies which offer apprenticeships. They provide information on whether the owner of a portfolio is accustomed to using more complex technical systems, whether he has worked with certain types of software, and how intensively he has worked with these

- Which technical skills and knowledge of the use of media are important for thorough media literacy and should be listed specifically?
- How can this knowledge be assessed?
- Who is responsible for carrying out the assessments?

Within the framework of their personal project documentation, the learners should also state how intensively they have worked with technical media. In doing this, they should grade themselves according to a four-level scale with the grades of 'observer', 'beginner', 'advanced' or 'professional' and record this in the documentation. The learners will be given brief texts to help them assess themselves according to these levels. The learners' own description of their work on the project, and their own assessment can be read by the teacher or supervisor, and added to if necessary.

3.6 Ensuring comprehensibility and readability

The portfolio becomes the property of the pupils, and should be binding. For outsiders the details should be comprehensible, interesting, meaningful and reliable. It should be possible to understand the important information quickly.

- What must the documentation look like so that it is easily comprehensible, easy to read, and informative for third parties who were not involved in the preparation process?
- Should the portfolio provide for additional comments on the owner's work, achievement and social behaviour?
- Should a summary of the assessment be provided?

The individual project reports with the relevant individual results forms are again condensed down to the important details: the first overview contains what has been dealt with, in each case with the topic, reference to the range of tasks, types of media, and individual points of emphasis; the second contains a list of the technical media and the details of which levels of literacy were achieved in which projects.

A further summary of the assessment is not carried out. Any special efforts or commitment can be seen by means of additional information in the first overview relating to whether the projects in which the learners took part involved in-school, extra-curricular, compulsory or voluntary work. However, the descriptions provided by the learners themselves, or additional comments by the instructors, should provide evidence of competencies such as reliability and the ability to cooperate.

3.7 Avoiding unnecessary additional work

The preparation and keeping of the portfolio is not intend to be an unnecessary burden on the pupils, or the teachers or 'suppliers'.

- How can the amount of work involved in the use of the portfolio be kept within limits?

Using a standardised design for the documents, with many opportunities to tick off possible answers, is intended to reduce amount of work involved. However, only an evaluation process will produce reliable information on whether these measures are sufficient.

4. THE CONSTITUENT PARTS OF THE MEDIA LITERACY PORTFOLIO

Taking all these considerations into account, the media literacy portfolio consists of the following constituent parts:

1. Information for the pupils in the form of a booklet with information on what the portfolio is intended to achieve, and how they can use it.
2. Information for the teachers, on a separate DIN A4 leaflet, explaining the general purpose of the portfolio and the specific details of the project.
3. Several project forms which are filled in by the in-school or external suppliers with the official details of the relevant project.
4. Several results forms in which the learners describe their individual results in respect of the relevant project and also provide their own assessment of their knowledge and skills with reference to the technical media which they have used.
5. An overview of all projects (activities) in which the learners have taken part; this is added to each time a project is completed.
6. An overview of the results with a list of possible technical media from the fields of photography, audio, video and computers, as well as different software and computer programming systems. This is where details of the levels of literacy which have been achieved, and the numbers of the projects in which they were acquired, are entered. However, it is also possible to designate other systems and to record the results which have been achieved.
7. A file for storing the project and results forms, but also any certificates which may have been acquired.
8. The media box for the collecting of personal results. The owner decides which products are shown here.

4.1 Additional expectations

The aim of the test is to optimise as quickly as possible this draft of the portfolio of media literacy for pupils at secondary levels I and II and to make it 'ready for use'. The focus is on aspects such as comprehensibility, content, extent, design, and ease of use. If the portfolio is well-received in principle, we expect impulses for media education in school on all levels.

We believe that it is an attractive tool with which pupils can present the results of their own work and their own media literacy, can design their own paths of learning and plan specific further steps, can talk about their achievements and assess these, and can also demonstrate increased willingness to achieve results.Teachers can feel motivated by the portfolio to reflect on what they are doing about media education and how to extend this.

Schools may conclude that they need qualified, comprehensive teaching, not only to improve the pupils' opportunities to produce a comprehensive portfolio but also because it can have a positive effect on the quality of schoolwork and the attractiveness of the school. There are opportunities to support media education in schools through advanced teacher training and via the field of media education on the NRW education server learn:line.

REFERENCES

Christ, I. (1997) Europäisches Portfolio für Sprachen – Eine Initiative des Europarats. In *Wege zur Mehrsprachigkeit. Informationen zu Projekten des sprachlichen und interkulturellen Lernens 2*, LSW, Verlag für Schule und Weiterbildung, Bönen, pp. 5-11.

Gerling, U. and Thürmann, E. (1998) Portfolio – ein Beitrag zur Qualitätssicherung – und noch mehr. *Schulverwaltung (NRW)*, 3, pp. 69-71.

MSWWF des Landes NRW (1998*) Rahmen für die Medienerziehung in der Sekundarstufe I. Ergebnisse des Modellversuchs 'Differenzierte Medienerziehung als Element allgemeiner Bildung'*, Düsseldorf.

Oberstufenkolleg Bielefeld (2000*) Alternativen zur Zensurengebung (2) Portfolios – Leistungsmappen.* [http://pluto.osk.uni-bielefeld.de/leistung/f2b.htm] 09.2000.

Tulodziecki, G. et al. (1995) *Handlungsorientierte Medienerziehung in Beispielen. Projekte und Unterrichtseinheiten für Grundschulen und weiterführende Schulen.* Klinkhardt, Bad Heilbrunn.

BIOGRAPHIES

Annemarie Hauf-Tulodziecki works in the State Institute for Schools and Further Education of North-Rhine-Westfalia in curriculum development and projects concerned with computer literacy and media literacy in school.

Wolfgang Weber is head of the Advisory Centre for New Technologies, State Institute for Schools and Further Education of Nortth-Rhine-Westfalia, Germany.

30

A Psycho-Pedagogical Model for ICT Use in the Educational Process

Yaacov J. Katz
School of Education, Bar-Ilan University, Ramat-Gan 52900, Israel
katzya@mail.biu.ac.il

Keywords: ICT methodologies, instruction and learning, psycho-pedagogical attitudes

Abstract: Empirical studies have indicated that the existence of certain psycho-pedagogical attitudes is important for the facilitation of positive ICT utilisation by both teachers and students. In addition, research findings clearly indicate that certain psycho-pedagogical attitudes of students and teachers can significantly facilitate the implementation and enhancement of preferred ICT methodologies. The present paper suggests the adoption of a psycho-pedagogical model which graphically presents those psycho-pedagogical attitudes that, according to both teachers and students, facilitate the implementation of ICT as well as intrinsically enhance the quality of learning and instruction in the school classroom. The implementation of this model could improve the utilisation of ICT methodologies in learning and instruction by providing a flexible and positive psycho-pedagogical environment in the classroom. This could well lead to positive educational developments in the digital age and facilitate an improvement in the educational process when utilising sophisticated technologies for learning and instruction.

1. INTRODUCTION

Since the 1960s when the first attempts were made to introduce Information and Communication Technology (ICT) into the school classroom as both instructional and learning aids, much experience has been gained although, at the same time, much frustration has been generated. The dream of achieving radical change and improvement in the educational system through the use of ICT has only partially been fulfilled. The major reason for the lack of significant success regarding the use of ICT in education thus far may be attributed to the complicated nature of the educational environment in which a multitude of psycho-pedagogical variables interact with cognitive constructs and needs and possibly interfere with the utilisation of ICT in the school classroom. Thus it is clear that there is an urgent need for a model that will pinpoint as many relevant psycho-pedagogical factors as possible that affect teaching and learning through the medium of ICT that need to be taken into account when introducing ICT into the educational setting.

In order to define any type of educational model, it is imperative to clearly describe the basic goals to be facilitated by the model. Thus a model, which will represent the facilitation of ICT educational methodologies in the school environment, should emphasise those psycho-pedagogical variables that contribute to the utilisation of ICT utilisation in education. Ongoing research, designed to identify a workable psycho-pedagogical model of teacher and student attitudes towards ICT utilisation in the learning and instructional process, has indicated how certain psycho-pedagogical attitudes held by teachers and students have a significant bearing on the application of different ICT methodologies in the educational process and the importance of addressing these attitudes in the classroom situation.

2. ICT METHODOLOGIES

Before examining the psycho-pedagogical issues that are significantly related to the use of ICT learning and instructional methodologies, it is necessary to briefly describe the different ICT methodologies presently used in the classroom situation at all levels in the educational system. Offir, Katz and Passing (1994) described the historical development of ICT use in the educational process and indicated that, since the introduction of ICT into educational settings, the 'traditional – open' courseware continuum succinctly and accurately depicts the progress made in the use of ICT for learning and instruction. The 'traditional – open' continuum provides an insight as to how ICT methodologies evolved and developed as educational media since the early 1960s up till the present time. Offir, Golub and Friedel (1993) reported that in the early days of ICT use in the school classroom, traditional CAL (computer assisted learning) and CAI (computer assisted instruction), based on rigid and 'closed' drill and practice, were the dominant ICT methodologies. When poignant questions were raised regarding the relative advantages and effectiveness of drill and practice over more traditional learning and instruction methodologies, more flexible and 'open' learning and instruction programs were developed and introduced into the educational system. These included the development of the use of ICT based spreadsheets (Dreyfus, Einstein and Talmon 1997), which contribute to the enhancement of learner independence and creativity and provide students with sophisticated graphic assistance that promote the understanding of complicated subject matter. The use of databases which were also developed and incorporated in this stage of ICT development (Appelberg 1997) provide students with the opportunity of enriching their knowledge and comprehension of subject matter by facilitating the ability to conduct comprehensive searches for sources hitherto available only in libraries and museums. The introduction of the use of ICT based spreadsheets and databases in the educational process contributed to the promotion of improved learning and instruction and increased effectiveness in the educational process.

During the next stage of development, simulation described by Offir and Katz (1994) as a sophisticated, progressive and improved ICT methodology, designed to simulate situations that exist in reality, was introduced into learning and instruction. Through the methodology of simulation, teachers are able to provide their students with realistic models of subject matter as experienced in real life situations thereby facilitating students' understanding and mastery of the learning situation. Thus simulation enhances ICT mediated learning by providing an added dimension that closes the gap between theoretical subject matter and the applications of knowledge to real life situations.

In the present stage of ICT based educational developments, multimedia methodology has become an important component of the ICT based educational process. Passing and Levin (2000) provided an in-depth analysis of multimedia packages suitable for the educational process and stated that when utilising multimedia methodologies in learning the student does not only study the subject matter, but also learns how to deal with the synthetically programmed environment. The ease of use and the uniformity of the multimedia interface have significant implications for both teacher and student, since they provide a platform for a higher level of motivation, concentration, and understanding of the content being studied. The design of multimedia educational packages attempts to provide a clear, consistent and attractive ICT platform, which contributes towards the ability of teachers and students to reach excellence through user-friendly instruction and learning methodologies.

Distance learning methodologies are additional up-to-date sophisticated ICT means available in the present stage of ICT development produced to enhance the performance of both teachers and students in the classroom situation. Katz (1998 and 2000) described sophisticated third generation distance learning systems that include synchronous interactive video, email, Internet, and Intranet technologies that can be utilised in the educational process. According to Katz learning and instruction through the medium of synchronous distance learning methodologies has been redefined to include and focus on teacher-student interaction. Interactive video-conferencing, and interaction through the medium of Internet or Intranet and email, offer one-to-many or one-to-one tuition in which teachers and students are able to communicate on-line thereby solving cardinal instructional and learning problems in real time. Third generation distance learning methodologies are characterised by their flexibility and allow teachers to continuously monitor overall progress of students. These methodologies also permit tutors to modify, reinforce and model educational processes, thereby fulfilling the cognitive needs and requirements of students. Interactivity available in third generation Distance Learning methodologies promotes active engagement of students in the learning process and leads to improved academic achievement. The implementation of multimedia and distance learning technologies at different educational levels (elementary school, high school, college) has been found to promote enhanced learning and instruction (Katz 1998, Katz 2000).

3. PSYCHO-PEDAGOGICAL VARIABLES

In a series of studies Chandra, Bliss and Cox (1988), Katz and Offir (1990), and Offir and Katz (1990), as well as numerous others, testified to the existence of psycho-pedagogical attitudes held by teachers and students at all educational levels (elementary, secondary and college) that contribute to the efficient utilisation of different ICT methodologies such as drill & practice, the use of spreadsheets, and databases in learning and instruction. In instruction using the above-mentioned ICT methodologies, psycho-pedagogical attitudinal constructs such as independence, creativity, tough-mindedness, sociability, risk-taking, stimulus seeking and sensation seeking are factors connected with efficient ICT use. Teachers characterised by the above psycho-pedagogical attitudes have been shown in research studies to hold more positive attitudes toward the use of the different ICT methodologies in classroom instruction than teachers not typified by the same variables.

In additional studies designed to examine student attitudes towards ICT use in learning, Dunn and Ridgway (1991), Katz (1993), and Katz and Offir (1991) indicated that students at different levels in the educational system (elementary, secondary and college) whose personalities were characterised by certain psycho-pedagogical attitudes, were favourable towards ICT use in the learning situation. Students typified by attitudes such as self-image, social-image, self-confidence, internal locus of control, learning satisfaction, and motivation for study were more positive towards the utilisation of the different ICT modes and methodologies such as drill & practice, the use of spreadsheets and databases in the learning process than students not typified by the same attitudinal traits.

Offir, Golub and Friedel (1993) demonstrated that students using simulation methodologies in the learning process were more highly motivated in their studies than students studying the same content matter without utilising simulation technologies. Passig and Levin (2000) indicated that in schools where sophisticated multimedia learning and instructional packages were introduced into the school curriculum, student and teacher interest in the educational process was increased, and student achievement was enhanced. Katz (1998 and 2000) confirmed that psycho-pedagogical attitudes such as satisfaction of students, control of the learning process, and self-confidence in learning are significantly enhanced when distance learning methodologies are used in the educational process at the college level.

The evidence regarding the relationship between psycho-pedagogical attitudes of both students and teachers on the one hand and the utilisation of different ICT methodologies, from very basic drill and practice through the use of spreadsheets and databases, and culminating in the use of more advanced and sophisticated simulations, multimedia packages and ICT distance learning methodologies on the other, indicates a clearly significant and positive connection between the two areas. It is apparent that positive psycho-pedagogical attitudes contribute to a favourable standpoint of both teachers and students towards the use of ICT methodologies in instruction and learning. ICT use, in turn, enhances students' and teachers' attitudes towards learning and instruction, which in itself is an important goal of the educational process.

4. PSYCHO-PEDAGOGICAL MODEL

After reviewing the literature dealing with different aspects of ICT utilisation in the educational process, a psycho-pedagogical model that encompasses some of the key teacher-based as well as student-based psycho-pedagogical attitudes which apparently contribute to efficient ICT use in instruction and learning clearly emerges. In this model there are three major parallel structures. The first structure includes the psycho-pedagogical attitudes that contribute to the promotion of positive and effective ICT utilisation in instruction and learning, pinpointing the key psycho-pedagogical attitudes of teachers that promote the use of ICT in the educational process. Attitudes such as independence, creativity, tough-mindedness, sociability, risk-taking, and stimulus seeking are those, which contribute to teachers' willingness to adopt the use of different and varied ICT methodologies in the instructional process.

The second structure presents the different commonly used ICT methodologies, namely drill & practice, spreadsheets, databases, simulation, multimedia, and distance learning methodologies, which are affected by the relevant psycho-pedagogical attitudes of teachers and students. The third structure presents the psycho-pedagogical attitudes of students that contribute to the enhancement of positive utilisation of different ICT methodologies in the learning process. Student attitudes such as self-image, social-image, self-confidence, internal locus of control, satisfaction, and motivation are those, which lay the foundation and contribute towards the willingness of students to use ICT methodologies in learning and instruction.

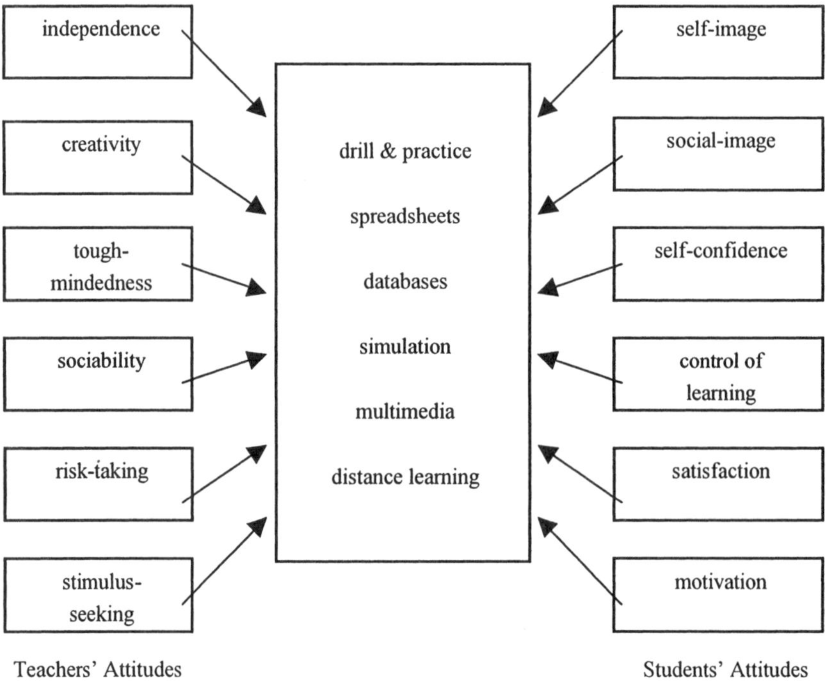

Figure 1. Relationship between ICT methodologies and psycho-pedagogical attitudes of teachers and students

5. IMPLEMENTATION OF THE MODEL

A number of psycho-pedagogical attitudes have been empirically shown to be related to the utilisation of ICT by students and teachers in the learning and instruction processes. The psycho-pedagogical model described above indicates the relationship between ICT and psycho-pedagogical attitudes that enhance and promote positive utilisation of ICT methodologies in learning and instruction. Psycho-pedagogical attitudes, adopted by teachers, such as independence, creativity, tough-mindedness, sociability, risk-taking, and stimulus-seeking, as well as psycho-pedagogical variables held by students, such as self-image, social-image, self-confidence, internal locus of control, satisfaction, and motivation for study have been shown to make a positive impact on both teachers and students in their willingness to use ICT in learning and instruction. It is evident from the empirical evidence quoted above that these psycho-pedagogical attitudes of teachers and students are vital to positively enhanced ICT utilisation that conceivably leads to an improvement in the educational process.

Now that headway has been made on the long road to the charting of a psycho-pedagogical model that describes attitudes which promote potentially improved willingness to use ICT in the educational system, further studies should be designed to pinpoint more exactly the relative contribution of the psycho-pedagogical attitudes of teachers and students towards the learning and instruction processes. When conducted these future studies could conceivably add to the reliability and validity of predictors and indicators of enhanced ICT utilisation in instruction and learning in the digital age.

REFERENCES

Appelberg, L. (1997) Communication-learning-information technology applied examples. In *Information technology: supporting change through teacher education,* D. Passey and B. Samways (eds.), Chapman & Hall, London, pp. 216-221.

Chandra, P., Bliss, J. and Cox, M. (1988) Introducing computers into a school-management issue. *Computers and Education*, 12(1), pp. 57-61.

Dreyfus, A., Feinstein, B. and Talmon, J. (1997) The electronic spreadsheet and cognitive skills in inquiry oriented biology. In *Information technology: supporting change through teacher education,* D. Passey and B. Samways (eds.) Chapman & Hall, London, pp. 278-284.

Dunn, S. and Ridgway, J. (1991) Computer use during primary school teaching practice: a survey. *Journal of Computer Assisted Learning*, 7, pp. 7-17.

Katz, Y. J. (1993) Achievement level, affective attributes and computer oriented attitudes: a profile of a successful end-user. In *Informatics and changes in learning,* A. Knierzinger and M. Moser (eds.), IST Press, Linz, Austria, pp. 13-15, (Section VII).

Katz, Y. J. (1998) The relationship between distance learning methods and satisfaction and achievement of college students. In *Teleteaching '98: distance learning, training and education,* G. Davies (ed.), Austrian Computer Society (OCG) and IFIP, Vienna, pp. 569-578.
Katz, Y. J. (1999) Kindergarten teacher training through virtual reality three-dimensional simulation methodology. *Education Media International,* 36 (2), pp. 151-156.
Katz, Y. J. (2000) The comparative suitability of three ICT distance learning methodologies for college level instruction. *Educational Media International*, 37 (1), pp. 25-30.
Katz, Y. J. and Offir, B. (1990) Computer assisted instruction and students' social orientations. In *Proceedings of 5th Jerusalem Conference on Information Technology,* IEEE Computer Society Press, Los Alamitos, CA, pp. 660-664.
Katz, Y. J. and Offir, B. (1991) The relationship between personality and computer related attitudes of Israeli teachers. *Education and Computing*, 7, pp. 249-252.
Offir, B., Golub, M. and Friedel, S. (1993) Attitudes toward courseware as a function of high school students' creativity level. In *Informatics and changes in learning,* A. Knierzinger and M. Moser (eds.), IST Press, Linz, Austria, pp. 17-19 (Section VII).
Offir, B. and Katz, Y. J. (1990) Computer oriented attitudes as a function of risk-taking among Israeli elementary school teachers. *Journal of Computer Assisted Learning*, 6 (1-2), pp. 168-173.
Offir, B. and Katz, Y. J. (1994) The computer as an instructional aid for studying the humanities. In *Applications and impacts: information processing '94 (volume II),* K. Brunnstein and E. Raubold (eds.), Elsevier Science Publishers, Amsterdam, pp. 660-665.
Offir, B., Katz, Y. J. and Passig, D. (1994) The utilization of 'open' courseware for developing an inquiry approach in the study of non-scientific subjects. In *Exploring a new partnership: children, teachers and technology,* D. Benzies and J. Wright (eds.), Elsevier Science Publishers, Amsterdam, pp. 97-101.
Passig, D. and Levin, H. (2000) Gender differences of favoured multimedia learning interfaces. *Journal of Computer Assisted Learning*, 16, pp. 64-71.

BIOGRAPHY

Professor Yaacov Katz serves as the Director of the School of Education and the Head of the Institute for Community Education and Research at the Bar-Ilan University. He specializes in the study of values and attitudes of teachers and students towards learning and instruction in general and towards the use of ICT in the educational process in particular. Professor Katz has published numerous scholarly works and papers on the above topics.

31

The WebQuest Model for Inquiry-based Learning Using the Resources of the World Wide Web

Harriet G. Taylor
Dept. of Educational Leadership, Research, and Counseling, Louisiana State University, Baton Rouge, LA 70803, USA
taylor@lsu.edu

Keywords: learner-centred learning, teacher education

Abstract: The WebQuest model of organising classroom learning inquiries involving resources on the Internet has become an important component of technology teacher education at one university. Educators create realistic, challenging learning environments that are related to their own curriculum and students. Through WebQuests, they practice guiding and directing learning rather than prescribing it. The WebQuest model has flexibility as well as structure. It allows for diversity and co-operation as well as creativity. As a result of the WebQuest development activity, educators are empowered and connected with each other and turned on to active learning that is facilitated by technology.

1. INTRODUCTION

The World Wide Web has opened up a global classroom full of resources and challenges for students and educators. Many educators are quick to recognise the potential of the Web but are equally quick to realise the complexity of the Web and its resources. Educators must learn to structure classroom activities that include Web investigations so that students can use online time wisely and productively. At the same time, many Web-oriented projects must be defined in such a way as to allow for great diversity in learners and in learning outcomes so that all students can benefit from Web-based activities.

One method of organising classroom activities is through WebQuests, inquiry-based learning activities in which some or all of the information that students interact with comes from the Internet. WebQuests can involve short-term, three or fewer class periods, of work or be more extensive. They often involve collaboration and are multidisciplinary.

2. THE WEBQUEST MODEL

The concept of WebQuests was introduced by Bernie Dodge of San Diego State University in 1995 (Schrock 2000). According to Dodge, "A WebQuest is an inquiry-oriented activity in which some or all of the information that learners interact with comes from resources on the Internet" (Dodge 1998). A WebQuest includes a specific, clear task or quest for students often working collaboratively. The WebQuest itself is organised through the development of a Web site with teacher and student pages. Each page contains the six main WebQuest components needed to introduce, organise, and direct the inquiry. These include an introduction, the task, the process, the information sources, evaluation, and conclusion (Dodge 1998, Mautner 1997). WebQuests are usually inquiry-oriented and involve student products demonstrating synthesis of concepts or other representations that illustrate higher-order thinking skills and learning.

The Web contains a number of excellent resources on the development of WebQuests as well as example quests. Bernie Dodge's WebQuest site (Dodge 2000) contains a wealth of resources. These include samples organised by discipline (Dodge 2000), sample templates for quest construction, sample rubrics for evaluation (Dodge 1999a), and discourse on the nature of the model itself (Dodge 1997, Dodge 1998). In fact, he uses his own model to teach about WebQuests by providing a *WebQuest on WebQuests* at the site. Kathleen Schrock (Schrock 2000) maintains an excellent teacher resource page with WebQuest links, including a link to a *PowerPoint* presentation on the WebQuest model. Tom March, who was also involved in the development of the model and many of the early examples, provides an online work (March 2000) which discusses the rationale of the model as well as pointers for those starting to develop WebQuests.

WebQuests provide an outstanding way of organising a learning activity. Sites such as those described above provide resources to help in the development of WebQuest learning activities. They also contain a wealth of proven, effective WebQuest activities allowing educators to share their work and expertise around the world.

3. USE IN TEACHER EDUCATION

WebQuests have been used effectively in both pre-service and in-service teacher education at Louisiana State University. Prospective teachers are introduced to technology applications and technology supported learning via participation in collaborative WebQuests related to their curricular areas. Graduate education students, all experienced teachers, participate in WebQuests as well, but many also use the model for developing their own instructional units.

3.1 Prospective teachers and WebQuests

At Louisiana State University, groups of education students who are preparing to be teachers are introduced to the Web and technology-supported learning with WebQuests. For example, in March of 1999, a group of pre-service mathematics and science teachers were introduced to Web-based learning during a five-hour session. In the morning, the educators were introduced the WebQuest model and to *Power Point.* They previewed samples of real quests and student products done by others. They were presented with a Rainforest WebQuest and told that they should organise themselves into teams of four to carry out the quest in the afternoon. At noon the students were united in their protests of unfairness. They had been given an unreasonable task that they would not be able to complete due to their limited technology skills and limited time to complete the project.

That afternoon, the students began work despite their reservations. Soon most were no longer upset but were excited and motivated. They were amazed at the wealth of resources on the Web and the amount that they learned about the rainforest. They worked together to produce masterpiece *PowerPoint* presentations incorporating information, graphics, and sounds from the Web. During the final part of the session, the students proudly shared their presentations with each other and they were truly impressed with themselves and what they had accomplished. They were confident that they could use WebQuest lessons that were developed effectively and they also began to brainstorm about ideas for their own WebQuests. They fully understood the benefits and power of technology-supported, collaborative learning and the teacher preparation that was needed to do it effectively.

3.2 Graduate educators develop WebQuests

WebQuests have proven to be exciting and useful alternatives to the traditional lesson plan approach to instructional organisation. Graduate education students at Louisiana State University have developed a collection of WebQuests that are now in use many places around the world. These can be found at the *LSU WebQuest* site (Taylor 1999). WebQuest development usually takes place over a six to seven week period. Students must follow a prescribed timeline of activities including topic and resource selection, page development, peer assessment and revision, and production of sample or actual student projects.

3.2.1 Topic selection and resource identification

The students are introduced to the WebQuest model. This includes presentation by the instructor and some sample WebQuests and student products. The students then do an abbreviated form of the *WebQuest on WebQuests* (Dodge 1999c) for their grade level. This exercise helps them identify the elements of good WebQuests and understand the importance of selecting appropriate curricular topics and resources for WebQuests

They then study the model and examples found at the WebQuest Page (Dodge 1999b, Dodge 2000) appropriate for their own content areas. Students discuss topics that would and would not make good WebQuests and brainstorm on ideas. Then students work in teams to determine the topic and goals of the quests they will develop. They search to be sure that a WebQuest on the same topic does not already exist. They are encouraged to develop quests of particular value to them as educators. That is, they should think about their curriculum and units that their students study and develop a theme that they can use with their classes.

Once they have identified one or more potential topics, the students then need to locate and examine resources. Often this is the point at which the critical decisions are made about the actual topic that will be developed. Students quickly find that some topics have many more Web resources than other topics and learn to identify areas that are and are not best served by Web research. They must the e-mail the professor within one week with a proposal of a topic. The professor then corresponds with them about their proposal until then have a plan that reasonably fits the WebQuest model.

3.2.2 Development of WebQuest materials

The students are instructed to submit a proposal for a short WebQuest, one that the target student population can complete in three class periods. In addition to developing the WebQuest, they must also develop sample student products or test the WebQuest with students and submit the actual student products. They are told that the time is critical. Once the proposal is accepted, the students have two weeks to develop the teacher page of the WebQuest on which they define all of the WebQuest components including the goals and products to be expected. The Dodge WebQuest model includes both a teacher page and a page just for the students. Often these are very similar with a little less formal information on the student page. The LSU students are given some flexibility on this. If they feel their teacher page is sufficient for students, they do not have to make a separate student page.

3.2.3 Peer evaluation

During class two weeks later, the students work in teams to review the quests of each other. They use a modified version of the draft rubric (Dodge 1999a) for evaluating WebQuests. This proceeds in two or more cycles depending on the size of the class. They first work with their own team to evaluate the quest of another group. Then at least one member of the team returns to their site to receive feedback and the others give feedback to the group that they reviewed. In the next cycle, students are paired with others who are not on their team, all following a prearranged rotation schedule developed by the professor. This has proven to be one of the most valuable components of the activity. Students get insights into their own work by critically looking at the work of others and they also benefit from discussing the merits of certain approaches with others not on their team. They must deal with knowing that things that seem very clear to them are confusing to others and make value judgements when they receive conflicting information from different review teams. Students are encouraged to continue the peer review informally as they refine their WebQuests so that their end product is educator and student friendly as well as substantive in content and scope.

3.2.4 Sharing WebQuests and student products

Two to three weeks later, the final WebQuests and student products are due. Students present their work and display their sample products. The depth of their work and learning is obvious and the scope and quality of the work is appreciated by all. Many students have said that the WebQuest sharing is one of the most valuable learning experiences they have ever had. They learn about many curricular areas, approaches to learning, and innovation. Frequently, topics that seem blatantly mundane and unexciting become magical when viewed with the student products. For instance, a middle school mathematics teacher and school counsellor developed a WebQuest on hurricanes (Birke and Pitchford 1998). The basic premise of the quest was fairly straightforward with a student product that described certain qualities of hurricanes. The middle school students decided to develop their own unique representation of their learning in a slide show presentation of a diary of a hurricane. It included birth, getting a name, growing up, teenage dreams of grandeur, and finally immortality. It displayed a grasp of the concepts in an engaging, almost humorous way, and brought immediate respect to two students who had been struggling in the class.

3.2.5 Collection in a common site

The final WebQuests are then collected on-line in a common site (Taylor 1999). Most are put on-line in temporary testing locations prior to completion as well. The students provide short blurbs for the listing and quests are grouped according to grade level.

4. EXAMPLES

The WebQuest model is one that is best appreciated by examples and practical experiences. Students can look at the examples the Dodge site (Dodge 1999b) or read about real examples in Maureen Yoder's article (Yoder 1999). It is important that teachers see the wide range of topics, tasks, and student products that can be included in WebQuests. This is illustrated by several examples developed at Louisiana State University.

Sadako and the Thousand Paper Cranes. This WebQuest for students in grades 3-5 is based on a well-known book by the same name and uses many Web sites devoted to Sadako, Japan, and the war. Students do a variety of interdisciplinary activities, including timelines, origami, writing based on research, map exploration, and cultural comparisons.

Life in Rural America During the 1800s. Middle school students investigate how people lived in the 1800s. They rewrite a modern story as if it took place in the 1800s using historically correct terms. They make PowerPoint presentations including music and graphics that depict the times.

The Titanic. Secondary students use an excellent Australian database to verify the reliability of two seemingly conflicting quotes about the Titanic disaster. They develop spreadsheet charts that illustrate their finds as well as presentations and written explanation of their charts.

5. RESULTS

The WebQuest model has proven to be an exciting and challenging part of the education curriculum at LSU. Educators have found the model and the development of effective WebQuests to be difficult but rewarding. In constructing their own WebQuests they have experienced the same joy in taking charge of their learning that their students do. They approach WebQuest development with far more enthusiasm than a traditional lesson plan assignment. Most are also eager to implement their products with real students and incorporate their WebQuests into their teaching.

The education students' WebQuest development activity is a structured learning activity. It includes several stages and checks. It includes instructor and peer feedback, design and investigation, and production and evaluation. In addition to producing the WebQuest, the students must also produce sample student products, similar to those that they might expect from the WebQuest, or they can field test the WebQuest with a group of students and turn in results and actual products.

The WebQuests that have been developed are archived at a single Web site (Taylor 1999) and reached through the San Diego State site. This has led to many interesting encounters with others around the world. Some of the LSU WebQuests been used for professional development workshops around the nation and have been well acclaimed by others. Thus the WebQuest development activity has enriched the professional lives of the education students in ways that were unimaginable to most of them.

6. ELEMENTS OF GOOD WEBQUESTS

Repeated experience as well as research of others had led to an appreciation of several critical elements that are needed for successful WebQuest lessons. These include:

1. **Simplicity**. Often educators tend to get too involved in using many technologies, sites, and resources. A simple, doable approach that can be achieved by most educators is best.
2. **Design**. WebQuests are implemented as live Web sites. Attractive sites that are easily navigated and current are essential.
3. **Resources**. The heart of the WebQuest is the resources. Thus educators developing WebQuests must locate excellent resources from reliable sources which have a high potential to remain online over time.
4. **Organisation**. WebQuests must follow a set pattern, but they still must be well organised. Activities must be clear and simply stated.
5. **Visualisation**. The first comment often heard when educators evaluate good WebQuests is "I can see the kids doing that!" Educators need to be able to visualise the activities and products before using the WebQuest.
6. **Diversity**. WebQuests should allow for creativity and diversity in students and student products. This often comes in the form of describing quest teams where each student has a role or in the form of identifying a range of possible student products.

7. **Quest element**. WebQuests are effective when they actually are presented more as quests than simple chore lists. It is often better to leave some things to student imagination and creativity rather than being too prescriptive about products and assessment.
8. **Curricular link**. WebQuests are designed for real students and teachers. The topics must be aligned with curricular goals and outcomes that teachers identify and value.

Developing a good WebQuest is an involved process. It requires knowledge of classroom practice, student abilities, and content as well as technology tools.

7. PROBLEMS AND ISSUES

Development of sound WebQuests is not a simple process. WebQuests are always works in progress that need care, maintenance, and updating over time. Several problem areas or issues have evolved.:

1. **Maintenance of site**. The students develop the WebQuests as part of a course. Some take ownership of their work and responsibility for updating links and maintaining their sites after the class. There are issues with the ownership of the work and mechanisms to ensure the continued maintenance of the quests on our local site.
2. **Central location for quests**. Web space for the quests is an issue that has been addressed several ways at LSU. A central WebQuest page has been developed with links to all the sites. At one time, all the quests were housed in a common space. Now students store their quests in their own assigned space that they manage. Each method has merits and drawbacks. No real ideal solution has been found.
3. **Field testing/validation**. Testing and validation, particularly of the educational value of the products is an important component of WebQuest development. When possible, the educators who develop the WebQuests test them with their students. The feedback received from actual use is different that of peer review. Often developers substantially revise their work to have much more realistic tasks and simple, clear directions when field-testing is involved. Continuous testing and validation during development is essential to the development process.
4. **Student products.** A WebQuest must have some expectations of students as a result of the quest. This is usually a product of some type, often collaboratively developed, which reflects synthesis of concepts and ideas. The product may or may not involve technology, but often does involve the use of technology and sharing the findings with other audiences. It is essential that the developers also deal with the student product issue. That

is, the developers must also produce or see actual products representative of their students and determine how to assess these products. The student product component is easily the most provocative and rewarding part of the experience for most students.

5. **Development time**. One could take a WebQuest template and type in some information in a very short time. WebQuest development is not a simple task and takes a great deal of time for critical thought and evaluation. Students will perceive them as the instructor perceives and presents them. That is, they will give a WebQuest time and energy based on the importance placed on it by the professor in terms of time and interaction. Thus, others planning WebQuest development activities must carefully structure the activity and allow time for the WebQuest to evolve and flourish with the students.
6. **Lesson plan versus WebQuest**. In the course, students preview countless sites that provide well-organised lesson plans. For most of the students, WebQuests are different. There is a sense of adventure in writing the WebQuest so that it encourages and invites exploration or learning rather than dictates it. The professor has rarely seen a student become excited over developing a lesson plan. She has seen students totally consumed with their WebQuests and has found it to energise many educators as they accomplish goals well beyond their imagination.

8. CONCLUSIONS

The WebQuest model has proven to be an excellent organisational model for teacher education at one university. Students preparing to be teachers participate in collaborative WebQuests as a way of learning about inquiry-oriented learning and technology applications. Experienced educators practice their skills at guiding or directing learning rather than prescribing it. The WebQuest model is one that has great potential for teachers and teacher educators. It is a proven model that has flexibility as well as structure. It allows for diversity and co-operation, structure and imagination. WebQuests represent one of the many ways in which we must restructure learning and the teacher education process if we are to prepare educators to meet the challenges of the technology-rich, connected classrooms that will characterise education in the very near future.

REFERENCES

Birke, M. and Pitchford, T. (1998) *Hurricane WebQuest.* [asterix.ednet.lsu.edu/~edtech/webquest/canequest.htm] 15.8.2000.
Dodge, B. (1997) *Some Thoughts About WebQuests.* [edweb.sdsu.edu/courses/edtec596/about_webquests.html] 15.8.2000.
Dodge, B. (1998) *WebQuests: A Strategy for Scaffolding Higher Level Learning.* [edweb.sdsu.edu/webquest/necc98.htm] 15.8.2000.
Dodge, B. (1999a) *A Draft Rubric for Evaluating WebQuests.* [edweb.sdsu.edu/webquest/webquestrubric.html] 15.8.2000.
Dodge, B. (1999b) *Matrix of Examples.* [edweb.sdsu.edu/webquest/matrix.html] 15.8.2000.
Dodge, B. (1999c) *WebQuest about WebQuests.* [edweb.sdsu.edu/webquest/webquestwebquest.html] 15.8.2000.
Dodge, B. (2000) *The WebQuest Page.* [edweb.sdsu.edu/webquest/overview.htm] 15.8.2000.
March, T. (2000) *WebQuests & more.* [www.ozline.com/learning/index.htm] 15.8.2000.
Mautner, C. (1997) Using WebQuests in the K-12 Classroom. *School Web Page Design Guide*, Classroom Connect, Inc., Lancaster, PA, pp. 13-16.
Schrock, K. (2000) *WebQuests in Our Future: The Teacher's Role in Cyberspace.* [discoveryschool.com/schrockguide/webquest/webquest.html] 15.8.2000.
Taylor, H. (1999). *LSU WebQuests.* [asterix.ednet.lsu.edu/~edtech/webquest] 15.8.2000.
Yoder, M. (1999) The student WebQuest. *Learning and Leading with Technology*, 26(7), pp. 6-9, 52-53.

BIOGRAPHY

Harriet G. Taylor is professor of education at Louisiana State University. Her research interests include telecommunications and distance education, human factors, retraining programs, technology integration into K-12 classrooms, technology supported mathematical models, computer science curricula, programming languages, teaching methodology, technology standards and accreditation, publishing on the World Wide Web.

32

Searching Using 'Microsoft® Encarta™'

A Study of Cognitive Style Effects on Secondary Students' Strategies

Helen Drenoyianni, Ian Selwood[1] and Richard Riding[1]
Aristotle University of Thessaloniki, School of Education, Arch. Mouseiou 29, 546 40, Thessaloniki, Greece
edren@eled.auth.gr
The University of Birmingham, School of Education, Edgbaston, Birmingham, UK[1]

Keywords: multimedia, interactive, research, learning models, secondary education

Abstract: This paper reports on a study of the effects that cognitive style may exercise on information retrieval strategies. The background to the research project, the nature of cognitive style and the ways in which it may influence the learning process are discussed. Analysis of research data revealed that students' lack of information retrieval skills disallowed wide differences to emerge in terms of searching strategies. Some interesting tendencies and consistent preferences were identified with respect to the Wholist-Analytic style. The paper concludes by considering the possible existence of a searching style and discussing its interpretation.

1. BACKGROUND

A fundamental issue for education is the influence that learners' individual differences may exercise on the efficiency and effectiveness of the learning process. A student's prior knowledge base, gender, intelligence, preferences and cognitive style form the student's learning agenda and determine what will be selected as information from the environment, how this information will be encoded and how it will be retrieved or recalled.

It has frequently been suggested that the educational system should provide for the needs of individuals, by achieving an appropriate match between the functional characteristics of learners and the teaching methods and materials used (Messick 1985, 1995, Moran 1991). This implies changes in teaching and learning practices and places emphasis on the utilisation of flexible self-instructional materials suited to a range of learners.

Interactive multimedia applications with an encyclopaedic format, apart from having the significant advantage of presenting information in a range of different ways, empowers users "to interact with the material and influence the course of presentation" (Tannenbaum 1998). Information in these systems are not connected and presented in a linear manner but through linking words or ideas, and access to these information sources can be achieved through a range of different and sophisticated information retrieval techniques. Indeed, the searching system of a multimedia encyclopaedia permits users to interrogate entries not only by using the traditional Index, but also through the utilisation of a multitude of searching strategies. Keyword searching, which entails the use of logical operators and Boolean logic, as well as searching by topic, place, time, media, etc. are generally available.

Essentially, the existence of a variety of access routes provides a flexible method of information retrieval, which can be strongly associated with individualised learning. It also follows from this that if these kinds of applications can truly "suit a variety of learning styles" (Perzylo 1993), then different types of learner will follow different routes while using these systems. Indeed, several researchers and theorists have suggested that learning styles may influence the ways in which multimedia applications are used (Heller 1990, Riding and Chambers 1992).

The implications of the above for research into interactive multimedia applications are that individual attributes that a learner brings to the learning situation, implications of the characteristics of the use demonstrated, and the design of the multimedia application, must be considered. This approach was adopted in this particular research, which sought to examine the effects that cognitive style may exercise on students' actual use of and attitudes towards the searching system of an interactive multimedia encyclopaedia.

2. COGNITIVE STYLES

Cognitive styles have been perceived and defined as consistent individual differences in the ways of constructing and processing information and experience (Messick 1976). They can be seen as "stable, traitlike consistencies in one's approach to attending, thinking and perceiving" (Schmeck 1988) which are independent of general ability and "reflect the fundamental make up of a person and have a physical basis" (Riding 1996). Numerous attempts have been made to identify cognitive style and describe its nature and implications for learning, and as long ago as 1986, Child (1986) suggested there was a growing need for rationalisation.

Riding and Cheema (1991) after conducting a survey of cognitive style labels suggested that these could be assigned into two principal, and independent from each other, cognitive style dimensions.

- The Wholist-Analytic style, is an individual's inclination to process information as a whole or in parts, and
- The Verbal-Imagery style, is concerned with an individual's tendency to represent information in memory verbally or as mental images.

Recognising the fact that the usefulness and validity of the cognitive style dimensions proposed are highly dependent on how clearly defined, assessed and distinguished they are from other important constructs a computerised test, the Cognitive Styles Analysis (CSA) that assessed an individual's position on each cognitive style dimensions was developed (Riding 1991). Through the administration of this test, Riding and his associates, offered empirical evidence which supported the independence of cognitive style from gender, ability, and other personality attributes (Riding and Caine 1993, Riding and Pearson 1994, Riding 1997, Riding and Rayner 1998). Nevertheless, cognitive style's independence from other significant constructs was not enough in educational settings and it was recognised that it should have implications for teaching and learning and in this respect it should also be related to observed behaviours.

Considering the Wholist-Analytic dimension. Analytics perceive situations as collections of different parts. They approach learning in an analytical fashion and consequently they may appear quite successful in tasks requiring comparison, differentiation and analysis. A negative aspect of the Analytic style is that it may not enable comprehension of a "balanced view of the whole" (Riding 1996). By contrast Wholists are global in their information processing approaches. They can perform quite well on tasks needing an overall perspective, while they may have a foggy picture of the parts that make up a problem or a situation (Riding and Sadler-Smith 1992, Riding 1997, Riding and Rayner 1998).

The Verbal-Imagery style, may influence an individual's preferred mode of presentation, in the sense that Verbalisers are inclined to memorise information through 'word-like' propositions or codes, whereas Imagers tend to use analogical or 'pictorial' representations. As such, Verbalisers may often learn better by processing verbal information while Imagers prefer processing images or diagrammatic information (Riding and Cheema 1991, Riding and Rayner 1998)

A significant number of early studies that investigated the effects of cognitive style on learning appear to support these theoretical assumptions. In summary, research evidence suggests that cognitive style differences exist among learners, and these affect students' learning preferences and academic performance. In the case of Wholist-Analytic style these differences may be associated with the structure of the information presented (Riding and Sadler-Smith 1992, Douglas and Riding 1993, Riding and Rayner 1998). While the Verbal-Imagery style, could be related to the mode or form within which information is presented (Riding and Douglas 1993, Riding and Sadler-Smith 1992).

However, most of these studies concentrated on differences in students' recall rather than the process through which students managed to achieve a particular outcome. As a result, the differences identified could not be directly associated with behaviours that would explain the product achieved. Moreover, prior research relating to the effects of cognitive style on students' information seeking strategies is non-existent. Thus, nothing could be assumed concerning cognitive style effects in this study, which examines the individual preferences of, and the procedures through which, students retrieve information from a CD-ROM encyclopaedia.

3. METHODS-PROCEDURE

Considering the methodological shortcomings of past cognitive style research and bearing in mind that the current project might result in 'spying out lands' never actually met before, a decision was made to follow a flexible, exploratory, and semi-experimental research design that would reflect the problem under investigation. In particular, it was hypothesised that if the use of encyclopaedic CD-ROMs truly suits a variety of individual preferences related to cognitive style, then these preferences would be mirrored in students' chosen and applied information seeking strategies.

Setting up an experimental situation, in which students could be asked about their searching preferences and be systematically observed using an electronic encyclopaedia on a standard set of tasks, would enable cognitive style groups to be compared. A set of seven discrete and differentiated, in terms of searching demands, activities were therefore devised to act as stimuli for engaging the students in information seeking procedures Furthermore, a structured schedule/instrument was devised for systematically observing the students. This instrument provided a record of the students' actions when using 'Microsoft® Encarta™', which due to its popularity and regular utilisation in educational settings became the target application of this study (NCET 1994, Sparrowhawk 1995). Further, a list of discussion topics and questions to be asked in the course of interviewing the students was constructed.

Each student was observed individually for about an hour interacting with 'Encarta' in a quite classroom of the school in which s(he) was being educated. At the start of these sessions each participant was given the set of the questions and asked to answer them using the information provided by the encyclopaedia. At the end of the observational session, each student was asked whether s(he) would like to talk about the encyclopaedia. If a positive answer was obtained then interviewing would take place immediately or shortly after. After the observations and the interviews had been conducted, the identification of students' cognitive style was accomplished through the administration of the CSA test (Riding 1991).

3.1 The sample

The population participating in the observational phase of the research consisted of 88 secondary school students, 36 were also interviewed. All of the students were of above average ability and of similar age (Year 9: 13-14 year olds), and all had prior experience of using 'Encarta'. However, in order to make sure that the students' level and quality of experience in using the encyclopaedia would not differ widely, a training session was given in the use and the features of 'Encarta'. These training sessions took place approximately 2 weeks before testing started.

The results of the CSA test were initially in the form of ratios. However, for the purposes of statistical analysis all 88 students were grouped into equal divisions on the basis of their ratios on each cognitive style dimension.

4. THE RESULTS

This section concentrates on analysing and discussing the across-activities findings with respect to the cognitive style effects on students' information retrieval strategies by considering students' searching preferences and the quantity of searching performed. Nevertheless, in order that this description is meaningful to the reader, the first part of this section will consider briefly the general findings about information seeking regardless of cognitive style.

4.1 General findings regarding information seeking

The rate of success in answering the set questions was very high. With rare exceptions almost all the students managed to retrieve the specified information in each of the given tasks. It would appear from this finding that in general the students found it easy to retrieve information.

Indeed. when interviewed, approximately half the students (53%) pointed out that they found it easy to find information. However, the other half expressed their reservations regarding the ease of information retrieval. In some of the interviews concerns were expressed regarding the multiplicity of searching methods available, and to the task specific aspect of the ease of searching.

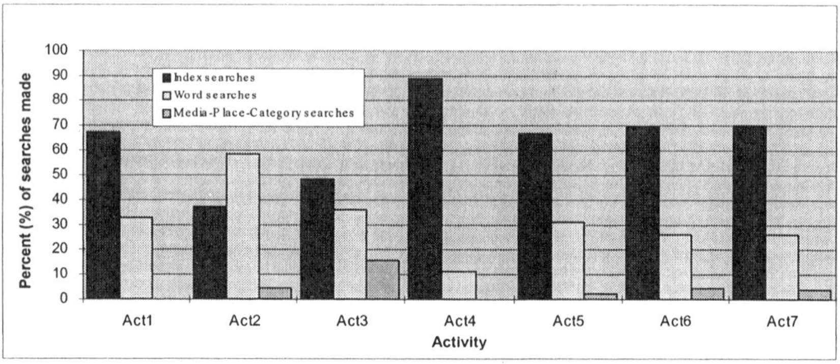

Figure 1. Frequencies of types of searches used

Inspection of the types of searches that students chose to utilise across activities offered a reasonable interpretation of these findings. As Figure 1 illustrates, students' most preferred and most used searching strategy was the Index/Title search. Yet, the decision to use the Index/Title search was not always the most appropriate. The predominance of the Index search over any other kind of search suggests that in general this is the strategy that students habitually utilise for retrieving information in school or at home. This was endorsed by the interview data collected, with 45% reporting that they only used Index/Title search, while 19% stated that they mainly used the Index and sometimes they might utilise keyword searching. In search for an explanation, it was found that students' persistence in the use of the Index was related to their past experiences. Of the students interviewed, 80.6% pointed out that their participation in this research project was a learning experience in the sense that they found out a lot about 'Encarta's' searches in the training session.

4.2 Information seeking and cognitive style effects

The findings presented above illustrate students' inefficient searching strategies and have implications not only for teaching and learning, but also for emanating cognitive style effects. Students' lack of information skills was expected to disallow extensive variations to be exhibited in students' information seeking tactics. Obviously, a preference in searching strategy cannot emerge when almost all individuals are aware of only one strategy. Thus, it was anticipated that cognitive style effects observed would be minimal.

To some extent this proved true. Statistical analysis of the total time students spent on searching, the total number of searches performed and the searching choices students made, showed that no statistically significant differences existed among students of differing cognitive style. However, some consistent, meaningful tendencies were identified indicative of how cognitive style may effect searching preferences.

As regards the Wholist-Analytic style dimension, diverse inclinations were identified between the searching preferences of Wholists and Analytics. The majority of students insisted on using an Index search for finding the information required. There was however a number of students who actually preferred the use of keyword searching (Word search). Across all 7 activities, the students that used Word search tended to have a common position in the Wholist-Analytic continuum of style (Figures 2 & 3, Table 1).

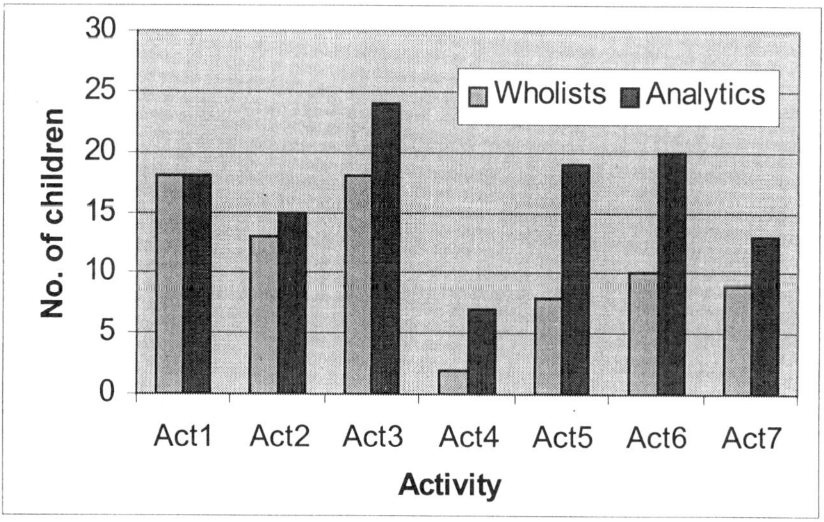

Figure 2. Cognitive style and children using word search

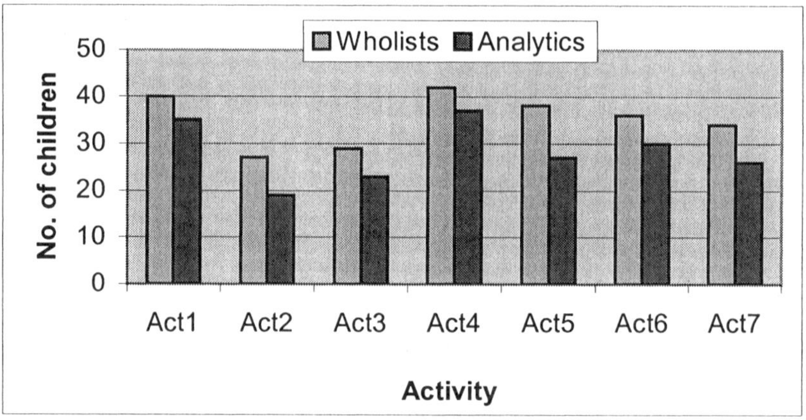

Figure 3. Cognitive style of children using index search

Table 1. Statistical significance of the group differences shown in Figures 2 & 3

	Act.1	Act.2	Act.3	Act.4	Act.5	Act.6	Act.7
Test	Anova	χ^2	χ^2	χ^2	χ^2	χ^2	χ^2
Significance	$P<0.05$	NS	NS	NS	$p<0.01$	$p<0.05$	$p<0.05$

Inspection of the above figures and table, indicates that across all the tasks, a consistently higher number of Wholists used the Index search to retrieve the information needed, while many more Analytics used the Word search. This was also evident in the average total number of Index and Word searches (Table 2).

Table 2. Cognitive style and mean total number of searches

	Wholists	Analytics
Index Searches	9	7.1
Word Searches	3.8	5.8

On average, Wholists made two more Index searches than Analytics, whereas the latter made two more Word searches. Furthermore, Wholists' preference towards Index search and Analytics' tendency to utilise keyword searching was also manifest in the interview data collected. When questioned regarding the type of search habitually utilised when looking for information in 'Encarta', a significantly higher number of Wholists referred to the use of Index search. Adversely, most Analytics claimed they use Word search or that they combine different searches (see Table 3).

Table 3. Cognitive style and types of searches reported as commonly used (Chi-quare=7.734, df=2, p<0.05)

	Wholists	Analytics	Total
Index Search	11	5	16
Word Search	1	7	8
Combination of searches	4	8	12
Total	16	20	36

These findings appear to point to the possible existence of a searching style or a preference related to the Wholist-Analytic style. Even though not always significant in statistical terms, Wholists and Analytics tended to differ in the information seeking strategies they followed. The activities set differed substantially in their optimal searching requirements. For some tasks the Word search was most appropriate, in others the Index, and elsewhere both were needed. Many Wholists and Analytics remained fairly consistent in their searching preferences regardless of suitability for the task in hand. Undoubtedly this finding gives credence to the viewpoint that cognitive style is actually independent of general ability and its effect on performance may be positive or negative depending on the task (Riding 1996, Riding 1997, Riding and Pearson 1994). Consequently, Wholists' and Analytics' diverse searching tendencies may actually represent a practical application of cognitive style in information handling situations. Since no literature exists concerned with the effects of the Wholist-Analytic style on information seeking strategies, comparisons with earlier research is impossible. In all likelihood, the searching styles illustrated are related to the disparate ways in which Wholists and Analytics process information and necessarily they may be interpreted through cognitive style theory.

Probably, Wholists' tendency to appreciate the overall context of a situation is associated with the holistic point of view that a summarising title may entail. By using Index/Title search, Wholists demonstrated that what they comprehended from a particular question is that they have to search for specific information regarding a broad topic or a theme. Resultantly, they looked for a source that would have an entry titled as this theme. By contrast, Analytics may have perceived the same question as an accumulation of different concepts. Consequently, they felt the need to search for sources that would contain or refer simultaneously to these concepts and for this purpose the use of keyword searching might better represent their understanding of the question.

The effects of the Verbal-Imagery style were not so explicitly evidenced by the analysis of the data collected. In most of the activities, no consistent influences were illustrated on the part of this style dimension. Verbalisers and Imagers selected and followed similar information seeking strategies to find the sources needed, and the quantity of searching they performed was relatively similar. This lack of statistically significant effects was also demonstrated in the total number of searches students performed, the total time taken on searching and the overall number of Index, Word and other (Media/Category) types of searches used.

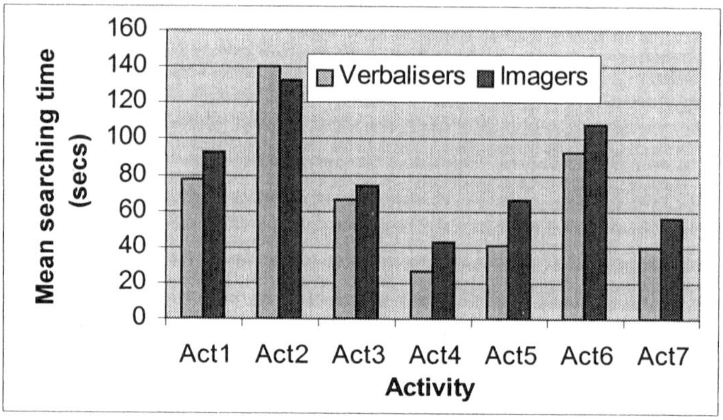

Figure 4. Cognitive style and searching time spent across activities

Yet, some consistent, but not statistically significant, differences were identified on the searching times across the 7 tasks. The statistical tests performed did not support the idea that the differences in time between these two groups of learners were wide enough so as not to be an outcome of pure chance. However, this finding may gain in significance through its repeated occurrence across the tasks posed (see Figure 4 and Table 4).

Table 4. Cognitive style and mean number of searches across activities

	Verbalisers	**Imagers**
Activity 1	2.5	2.6
Activity 2	2.4	2.6
Activity 3	1.5	1.7
Activity 4	1.0	1.0
Activity 5	1.2	1.6
Activity 6	2.8	2.8
Activity 7	1.1	1.3
Total	13.0	13.9

Even though Imagers and Verbalisers made about the same number of searches for retrieving the information required, Imagers in almost all of the activities appear to have spent more time looking for this information. It follows from this, that Imagers may have found it more difficult than Verbalisers to construct and phrase their searches.

The non-existence of studies concerned with the searching behaviour of these cognitive style groups does not enable comparison of this finding with earlier research. Necessarily, the only, if not the most possible, interpretation to it can be derived by theory regarding the ways in which Imagers and Verbalisers process information. In general terms, Verbalisers are superior when working with verbal versions of information and Imagers when learning from pictorial modes of presentation (Riding and Ashmore 1980, Riding and Douglas 1993). Resultantly, it may well follow that Imagers took longer than Verbalisers to comprehend the questions asked and transform the information contained in them into searching descriptors recognisable by the database. In conclusion, however, it is worth noting that the time differences between Imagers and Verbalisers were not significantly different and necessarily further research is needed to support these findings and comment on possible explanations.

5. CONCLUSIONS

As with much research, the present study generated more questions than those that it attempted to answer. One of the most significant and unexpected findings was students' extensive lack of information retrieval skills and the subsequent and unavoidable effects that this had on cognitive style influences, which were the main interest of this study. Students' ignorance of 'Encarta's' search engines did not allow the emergence of extreme variations in searching strategies. Minor and insignificant differences were found between the times that Imagers and Verbalisers spent on searching for information, and the tendencies identified on the part of the Wholist-Analytic style were not always statistically significant.

Nevertheless, it is still notable that even under those unpropitious circumstances some sort of searching style occurred which was consistent in its appearance. Wholists used, and stated that they often used, the alphabetical Index for finding information, while Analytics showed an inclination towards keyword searching. Yet, any attempt to interpret this finding appears to be a difficult task, especially if one considers that no literature exists with direct relevance to it. It is possible that Wholists' propensity to process information in wholes (Riding 1996, Riding 1997, Riding and Rayner 1998) may be related to their preference for a summarising title, whereas Analytics' inclination to 'break' information into their constituent parts, encourages them to search for the occurrence of multiple keywords.

Yet, regardless of the potential explanations, it seems appropriate to suggest that only further research can identify the reliability of these inclinations. Meanwhile, one could suggest that the present study has supported cognitive styles' independence from ability and pointed at interesting and practical applications of the Wholist-Analytic style in the educational context, which can be either eliminated or exacerbated as students' experience in using interactive multimedia applications increases.

REFERENCES

Child, D. (1986) Cognitive Styles: Some Recent Ideas of Relevance to Teachers. In *Personality, Cognition and values*, C. Bagley and Gajendra K. Verma (eds.), The Macmillan Press Ltd, London.

Douglas, G. and Riding, R. J. (1993) The effect of pupils cognitive style and position of prose passage title on recall. *Educational Psychology*, 13, pp. 385-393.

Heller, R. (1990) The role of hypermedia in education: A look at the research issues. *Journal of Research on Computing in Education*, 22 (4), pp.431-441.

Messick, S. and associates (1976) *Individuality in Learning*. San Francisco: Jossey-Bass.

Messick, S. (1985) Style in the Interplay of Structure and Process. In *New directions in educational psychology: 1. Learning and Teaching*, N. Entwistle (ed.), The Falmer Press, London.

Messick, S. (1995) Cognitive Styles and Learning. In *International Encyclopedia of Teaching and Teacher Education*, 2nd Ed, L. W. Anderson (ed.), Elsevier Science Ltd, Oxford.

Moran, A. (1991) What can Learning Styles Research Learn from Cognitive Psychology? *Educational Psychology*, 11 (3 &4), pp. 239-245.

NCET (1994) *CD-ROM in Education: CD-ROM in Primary Schools, Initiative 1994, CD-ROM Titles Review*. NCET, Coventry.

Perzylo, L. (1993) The application of Multimedia CD-ROMs in schools. *British Journal of Educational Technology*, 24 (3), pp. 191-197.

Riding, R. J. (1991) *Cognitive Styles Analysis*. Learning and Training Technology, Birmingham.

Riding, R. J. (1996) *Learning Styles and Technology-Based Training*. DFEE, Education and Training Technologies, Sheffield.

Riding, R. J. (1997) On the Nature of Cognitive Style. *Educational Psychology*, 17 (1&2), pp. 29-49.

Riding, R. J. and Ashmore, J. (1980) Verbaliser-Imager learning style and children's recall of information presented in pictorial versus written form. *Educational Studies*, 6, pp. 141-145.

Riding, R. J. and Caine, T. (1993) Cognitive Style and GCSE performance in mathematics, English Language and French. *Educational Psychology*, 13, pp. 59-67.

Riding, R. J. and Chambers, P. (1992) CD-ROM versus Textbook: A comparison of the use of two learning media by Higher Education Students. *Educational Training and Technology International*, 29 (4), pp. 342-349.

Riding, R. J. and Cheema, I. (1991) Cognitive Styles – an overview and integration. *Educational Psychology*, 11 (3&4), pp. 193-215.

Riding, R. J., and Douglas, G. (1993) The effect of cognitive style and mode of presentation on learning performance. *British Journal of Educational Psychology*, 63, pp. 297-307.

Riding, R. J. and Pearson, F. (1994) The relationship between cognitive style and intelligence. *Educational Psychology*, 14, pp. 413-425.

Riding, R. J. and Rayner, S. (1998) *Cognitive Styles and learning Strategies: understanding style differences*. David Fulton, London.

Riding, R. J. and Sadler-Smith, E. (1992) Type of Instructional Material, Cognitive Style and Learning Performance. *Educational Studies*, 18, pp. 323-340.
Schmeck, R. R. (1988) An Introduction to Strategies and Styles of Learning. In *Learning Strategies and Learning Styles*, R. R. Schmeck (ed.), Plenum, New York.
Sparrowhawk, A. (1995) Report on initial findings from schools in the primary CD-ROM initiative and visited during the Autumn term. *MICRO-SCOPE*, 45 (Summer 1995), pp. 9-12.
Tannenbaum, R. S. (1998) *Theoretical Foundations of Multimedia.* Computer Science Press, W. H. Freeman and Company, New York.

BIOGRAPHY

Helen Drenoyianni is a lecturer in IT in Education. Her current research interests concern information and society, information handling skills and the role of IT in trans-disciplinary curricula.

Ian Selwood is a lecturer in IT in Education. His current research interests are ITEM, managing IT in schools, IT and teacher education.

Richard Riding is a reader in educational psychology, and Director of the Assessment Research Unit, at The University of Birmingham. His research interest is concerned with Individual Differences and Learning.

33

Walking with Woodlice

Biodiversity On-line and in the Field

Roy Hawkey
The Natural History Museum, London, UK
r.hawkey@nhm.ac.uk

Keywords: case study, experiment, hypermedia, innovation, website

Abstract: This paper describes the development and implementation of a web-based project that encourages and enables first-hand encounters with the biodiversity of the natural world. Aimed at 7 to 14 year-olds, the project was designed to raise awareness of biodiversity by involving students actively in biological research. The paper explores their use of identification keys and investigates the potential of the Internet as a mechanism for sharing and distributing biodiversity data. The identification tools and the processes of data submission and analysis are described and sample results presented. The paper concludes with a preliminary evaluation of the project's findings.

1. BACKGROUND

The Natural History Museum's website was launched in 1994. From the outset, it was seen as a potentially excellent vehicle for conveying ideas about the life and earth sciences to a much larger and more diverse audience. As with many museum sites, the early content was principally visitor information – about opening times, entrance fees and bus routes – but included something of the nature and scope of both collections and exhibitions (Shaw 1995).

In addition to general improvements in graphic design and enhanced functionality, subsequent elements have increasingly featured active involvement by the virtual visitor. These interactive materials include *Science casebook*, dinosaur datafiles, *The voyage of the* Endeavour and *QUEST*.

The Museum's *QUEST* project – 'Questioning, Understanding and Exploring Simulated Things' (www.nhm.ac.uk/education/quest) – has been described in detail elsewhere (Hawkey 1999, Hawkey 2000). Put simply, virtual visitors use virtual tools to investigate virtual objects, to discover what they can about them, in the manner of a research scientist. Its innovative approach to learning from objects on-line significantly changes the relationship between expert and learner. Critical to its success are the high level of learner choice and decision-making, opportunities to 'engage, explore and build' and for 'scaffolded reflection' (Wild and Quinn 1998). Most innovative is the on-line notebook, where learners can share thoughts and exchange ideas. The positive reception of *QUEST* within the education community encouraged the development of further projects in which the learner engages directly with the scientific research process.

2. RATIONALE, AIMS AND OBJECTIVES

Taxonomy is the science of naming and classifying fossil and living organisms. Systematics goes beyond taxonomy in also working out their evolutionary relationships (UK Systematics Forum 1998). Together they underpin our understanding of biodiversity – the variety of genes, species and ecosystems. While many people recognise this as a 'good thing' globally, there is little understanding of its importance in the local environment. The principal association of biodiversity in the public mind is with tropical rain forests and other distant and exotic habitats. But the UK has biodiversity too, and it extends to every kind of organism. Projects involving members of the public in the collection, interpretation and communication of biodiversity data could make a significant contribution to promoting understanding of biodiversity by concentrating on the local environment. Such projects could also help to compensate for the tendency of the formal science curriculum to reduce – or, even, to omit altogether – the study of taxonomy and systematics.

Walking with woodlice (www.nhm.ac.uk/woodlice) was originally conceived early in 1996, at a time when Internet usage in UK homes and, especially, schools was really quite limited. Development and implementation were therefore delayed for several years until the potential audience was adjudged to be sufficiently large, as reflected in feedback from teachers at the annual meeting of the Association for Science Education. Its launch was finally facilitated by a timely request from the BA's creatingSPARKS festival for an 'on-line biodiversity project'.

The project identified a number of major aims (for the Museum) and intended learning outcomes (for the on-line learner). These are indicated in Table 1.

Table 1. Project aims and intended learning outcomes

	Biodiversity	ICT
The Natural History Museum aims to...	raise people's awareness of UK biodiversity; explore issues of protocol and standardisation relating to the collection, interpretation and communication of biodiversity data	develop interactive science education activities on the Internet; pilot the design of network parataxonomy tools; pilot the use of volunteer recorders in supplying biodiversity data on-line
Learners can...	develop taxonomic skills (use a dichotomous key); appreciate the significance of biodiversity in the UK	use the Internet to exchange data and to communicate with each other and with professional scientists; manipulate and interpret data presented in tables, maps and graphs on-line

In addition to the immediate feedback on the habitats and distribution of the specific organisms under investigation, it was hoped that the project would act as a pilot experiment in exploring and resolving a number of key issues relating to the collection and exchange of biodiversity data. The project would therefore act as a prototype for a potentially much broader application, in which a greater variety of people, be they members of wildlife trusts or other interested non-specialists, will become involved in collecting and recording data about a much larger range of UK species. This aim is reflected in the establishment of the National Biodiversity Network (www.nbn.org.uk), in which The Natural History Museum is playing a major role.

Woodlice were chosen as the group for this experimental project for a number of reasons. They are common and widespread and easily observed, and are not subject to significant seasonal variation. They are readily recognised as a group, but people are not generally aware that there are a number of different species – thirty-seven native to the UK. Woodlice vary little within each species, but display fairly easily identified differences between species – at least for the most common types. In pragmatic terms, woodlice are more inherently dynamic than less active organisms yet easy to locate and catch. They are not easily harmed nor do they evoke phobias!

3. DEVELOPING THE SITE

Having established the fundamental ideas, development was required on three complementary fronts:

- background material of scientific integrity
- interpretation / explanation of this material in ways accessible to the target audience
- the web-site itself.

In addition, promotion of the site to students, teachers and the general public would be essential if sufficient worthwhile data were to be generated, as anomalies in distribution data caused by a limited number of enthusiasts with a restricted geographical range are well known.

Experts in isopod crustaceans in general and woodlice in particular, both within and beyond the Museum, were consulted. In particular, Stephen Hopkin gave advice on possible approaches to adapting his standard key (Hopkin 1991) for this project's particular purposes.

Background information – on biodiversity, taxonomy and systematics in general and on woodlice in particular – was provided in a lively format, together with additional supporting material for teachers, to enable ready linkage with the school curriculum. In addition to promotion on the Museum's own web-site, information about the project was carried in the promotional materials for the British Association's creatingSPARKS festival and in the national press. With the support of the Association for Science Education, a simple poster was distributed to teachers of science.

4. KEY TO SUCCESS?

The dichotomous key is a standard tool in the life sciences. In principle, its very nature – the binary tree – should make its representation by computer very simple. (Indeed, one of the best of the early science software products for primary schools was *Branch*, which enabled young learners to construct and use their own keys.) There are, however, a number of difficulties that have to be overcome in producing a key for on-line use by students or others outside the expert taxonomic community.

The keys that taxonomists use are founded, as far as is possible, on natural groupings and sub-groupings. Each step of the identification process utilises a feature that is present (or of a particular quantity or quality) in one group but absent from the other (or of a different quantity or quality). This has clear scientific advantages, in that each sub-category has integrity, but often leads to the use of features for identification that are very difficult for the non-specialist to interpret. (Such keys also tend to use complex technical terminology to make fine distinctions. For example, the standard key to UK woodlice (Hopkin 1991) begins, not with the more obvious body shape – cylindrical or flattened? – nor with the ability to roll up into a ball, but with detailed differences in the segmentation of the antennae.)

In developing keys for wider use, it is generally desirable to take a para-taxonomic approach. This is not concerned with the integrity of sub-groups and can therefore use more readily accessible features en route to the identification. A further advantage of the para-taxonomic key is that it does not need to try to include every single species, however rare it may be. Thirty-seven species of woodlice have been recorded in the UK, but fewer than ten of these can be regarded as common. A relatively simple key is likely to be sufficient in the vast majority of cases.

In an earlier study, Tardivel and Morse (1998) compared the performance of undergraduate biology students in using a key to woodlice presented in different formats. They found that user confidence was highest for the computer-based version, but that the results were actually more accurate when using a paper version. This probably relates to a false sense of confidence and greater ease of use, especially given that the full Hopkin (1991) key was used.

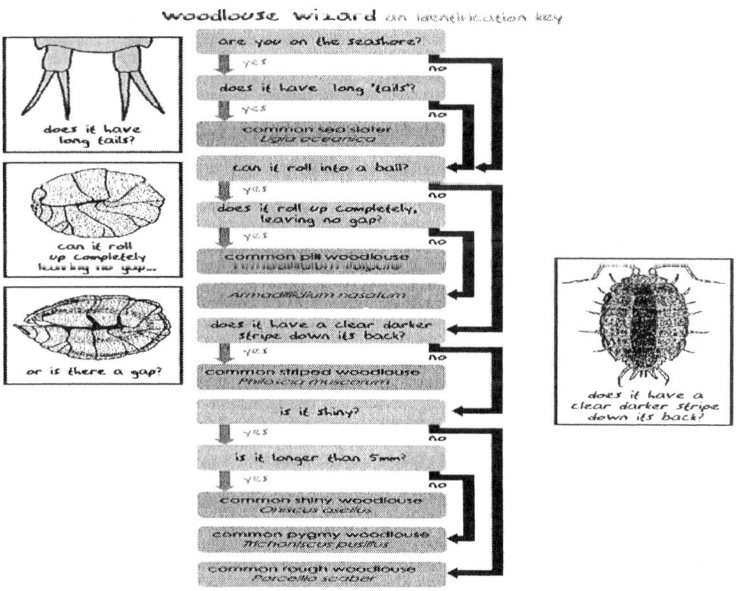

Figure 1. Woodlouse wizard: a simple dichotomous key

An earlier Museum project had developed a simple paper-based key to eight species of woodlice (Education Unit 1997). This formed the basis for the *Walking with woodlice* key, but the new version (Figure 1) was modified with the addition of one species and the removal of two others. Such findings and other considerations – including the need for a paper version to use in the field, limitations on budget and on the ready availability of technical support – suggested that a compromise approach would be likely to be most successful in the context of the project. Presented as part of the web-site, the key to the 'top level' seven species was produced in two versions. The first has interactive links to further details – both text and high quality colour photographs. The second is a greyscale.gif file (Figure 2), easily printed out for use out of doors. Details of the next most common set of nine species were made available through hypertext links. For the remaining (rare and/or unusual) species learners were referred to Hopkin's (1991) guide.

5. DATA COLLECTION, SUBMISSION AND INTERPRETATION

There is a tendency to assume that the use of web-based learning material is somehow an alternative to real learning. One of the features of *Walking with woodlice* is that it promotes learning not only in the real (but artificial) world of the classroom or teaching laboratory but also in the real (and natural) world of the biotic environment. The promotion of fieldwork and its interaction – through data recording and analysis – with the electronic realm is a key element of the project.

A simple form was provided on the web-site for recording details of species, habitat and geographical (post-code) information. This was then sent by email directly to the project co-ordinator. Because much of the data was collated into sets by a teacher, student representative or family member it is not possible to exactly quantify the number of individual learners participating in the project. However, over two thousand sets of data were received, the majority of useable quality. As this was a pilot project, each item of data was examined, simple checks made on its veracity and then incorporated into a database from which the distribution maps and other data displays were generated. Only the presence or absence of species in particular locations was required, so duplicates from the same post-code area were disregarded in the data presentation and analysis.

Data was initially analysed and presented as...

- species maps, by postcode (Figure 2)
- species lists, by habitat (Table 2); this 'raw' data facilitates further manipulation and analysis by learners

- species biodiversity (richness), by habitat (barchart and piechart).

For comparison, both in terms of the nature of the data collecting process and to explore changes over time, data from earlier scientific surveys (Harding and Sutton 1985) was added to the site. Finally, learners' comments, observations and questions were posted.

Table 2. Frequency of woodlouse species by location (percent)

Species \ Location	Building	Coast	Garden	Grassland	Playground	Waste ground	Woodland	Other
Androniscus dentiger	0.08		0.32			0.08		0.08
Armadillidium depressum			0.16	0.08				
Armadillidium nasatum	0.32		4.21	1.78	0.08	0.40	2.51	0.24
Armadillidium vulgare	1.05		8.66	2.10	0.16	0.49	2.83	0.73
Cyclisticus convexus			0.08	0.08				
Ligia oceanica	0.08	0.16	0.24	0.08	0.08			
Ligidium hypnorum				0.08		0.24	0.24	
Oniscus asellus	0.49		9.63	2.91	0.08	0.49	3.88	0.89
Philoscia muscorum	1.05		11.57	3.64	0.24	0.06	4.45	0.97
Platyarthus hoffmannseggi			0.08					
Porcellio dilatatus			0.08	0.01				
Porcellio nidespruinosus							0.08	
Porcellio scaber	0.81		12.86	2.99	0.16	0.65	3.56	1.38
Porcellio spinicornis			0.08				0.16	
Trachelipus rathkei			0.08	0.16			0.24	
Trichoniscus pusillus	0.32		4.53	0.40	0.16	0.32	1.86	0.24

6. ENGAGING AND EMPOWERING LEARNERS

In recent years there has been a marked shift of emphasis in the informal learning of science (in museums, science centres and elsewhere) towards engaging and empowering learners (Hawkey 2001). This has already begun to supplement – and may ultimately supplant – the more traditional didactic, fact-laden approaches that are also being questioned in our schools.

Although *Walking with woodlice* can call upon the leading experts in the field, it is less concerned with approving and validating the findings than with encouraging participants, having submitted their own data, to join in analysing and commenting on the results. The project's next step, therefore, was to prepare a series of prompts to stimulate further minds-on participation to complement and extend the earlier hands-on involvement.

They include...

- Which are the most/least common species?

- Can we 'trust' these results? Or any scientific results?'
- What did the survey not find out? What else would it be useful to find out?
- Where were no results recorded? Does this mean there are no woodlice there?
- What are the limitations of the survey? What could be done next?

It appears, however, that learners are initially less confident in making comments on the data than they were in submitting it. This may be natural reticence, or it may be a reflection on the presumed hegemony of experts.

7. EVALUATION

The nature of the UK climate (and the distribution of daylight hours) means that both woodlice and learners are much more active in the environment from April to October. The organisation of the academic year (September to July) means that work begun in the summer is unlikely to be followed up in the autumn. Feedback from teachers suggests, however, that repeating the project will bring an increased rate of response and continuing engagement, as the previous year's data will be available from the outset.

Some indication of the level of awareness of biodiversity (both in general and with specific reference to woodlice and the use of keys) emerges from the nature of the observations submitted in response to the on-line invitation to comment on the survey results – and from the results themselves. While this is not direct evidence of the effect of *Walking with woodlice*, it will form a useful baseline for future work. More immediately useful material comes from unsolicited feedback, which provides helpful pointers, even though it is not necessarily representative.

Use of the keys under supervision, for example within the Museum's *Investigate* gallery, has borne out their general effectiveness. The level of public participation has confirmed the worthwhile nature of the project and has encouraged the Museum to extend the exercise.

There is, inevitably, some doubt as to both the validity and reliability of the data on species distribution. Broadly, however, the results are as might be expected, and concur with expert opinion. A cursory glance at the results, however, can be misleading and certainly raises questions for further investigation:

- Why are there no records at all from certain parts of the UK?
- Are the six most commonly identified species really more common? (Table 2) Or are they more frequently identified because of their location in the top-level key?

- Is Armadillidium nasatum extending its northerly range, as some experts have suggested? (Figure 2)
- Does the location data tell us more about woodlice or learners? Is it of any value?

Figure 2. Distribution of *Armadillidium nasatum*. (Note the records from NE England, not found in previous surveys.)

8. FUTURE DEVELOPMENTS

Three areas are under active consideration as the project evolves. One concerns the nature and presentation of the identification key. Opportunities will be taken to develop further, more dynamic versions of the on-line keys and also to explore approaches other than the basic dichotomous model, such as Karnough mapping. The second area relates to technical matters and the need for an automated system to generate tables, graphs and maps directly – and, preferably, in real time – from the data. The third concerns the possible application of similar approaches to different organisms, and, if so, which group. Ladybirds, bumblebees and butterflies are the groups most frequently suggested. Any of them could build upon the initial success of *Walking with woodlice* in exploring biodiversity on-line, but none has all of the advantages of the terrestrial crustaceans.

ACKNOWLEDGEMENTS

The Natural History Museum is grateful to the British Association's 'creatingSPARKS' festival and to GlaxoWellcome for making possible the development of *Walking with woodlice*, to Publitek New Media for technical implementation and to Dr. Stephen Hopkin for advice and encouragement.

REFERENCES

Education Unit (1997) *Kaleidoscope of life*. Activity guide, The Natural History Museum, London.

Harding, P. T. and Sutton, S. L. (1985) *Woodlice in Britain and Ireland: distribution and habitat.* Institute of Terrestrial Ecology, Huntingdon.

Hawkey, R. (1999) Learning from objects on-line: virtue and reality. *British Journal of Educational Technology*, 30 (1), pp. 73-77.

Hawkey, R. (2000) Real education from virtual objects: active learning in science on-line. In *Proceedings of M/SET 2000,* R. Robson (ed.), San Diego, February. pp. 202-206.

Hawkey, R. (2001) Science beyond school: representation or re-presentation? In *ICT, Pedagogy and the Curriculum: Subject to Change*, A. Loveless and V. Ellis (eds.), Routledge Falmer, London, pp. 107-124.

Hopkin, S. (1991) *A Key to the Woodlice of Britain and Ireland.* Field Studies Council, Shrewsbury. (Reprinted from *Field Studies*, 7 (4), pp. 1-52.)

Shaw, M. (1995) *Highways for learning: an introduction to the Internet for schools and colleges.* National Council for Educational Technology, Coventry.

Tardivel, G. M. and Morse, D. R. (1998) The role of the user in computer-based species identification. In *Information technology, plant pathology and biodiversity,* P. Bridge, P. Jeffries, D. R. Morse and P. R. Scott (eds.), CAB International, Wallingford, pp. 247-259.

UK Systematics Forum (1998) *The web of life: a strategy for systematic biology in the United Kingdom.* UK Systematics Forum, London.

Wild, M. and Quinn, C. (1998) Implications of educational theory for the design of instructional multimedia. *British Journal of Educational Technology*, 29 (1), pp. 73-82.

BIOGRAPHY

Roy Hawkey was a science teacher and university lecturer in science education before becoming Head of Education at The Natural History Museum, where he has been responsible for a number of innovations such as *QUEST* and *Investigate*. Roy has published widely on science education and given conference papers and presentations on a variety of topics, although his principal interests are the development of resources for independent and constructivist learning, the role of ICT in science education and the public understanding of science. He is currently a Visiting Research Fellow in the School of Education at the University of Brighton.

34

Evaluating Usability of SAGRES Virtual Museum
Considering Ergonomics Aspects and Virtual Guides

Márcia Cristina Moraes, Ana Carolina Bertoletti and Antônio C. Rocha Costa
PPGC/UFRGS, FACIN/PUCRS, Av. Ipiranga, 6681 - prédio 30, POA, RS, Brazil
mmoraes@inf.ufrgs.br
MCT/PUCRS Av. Ipiranga, 6681 - prédio 40, POA, RS, Brazil
ESIN/UCPEL, Félix da Cunha, 412, Pelotas, Brazil

Keywords: home learning, internet, hypermedia, World Wide Web

Abstract: The SAGRES Virtual Museum is an educational environment built on the Web that facilitates the organisation of visits to museums, presenting museums' information bases in a way adapted to the user's characteristics. SAGRES incorporates personal assistants to help the user during the navigation and operation of the system. As an educational environment it is important to evaluate the usability of SAGRES, because products with low usability are generally responsible for frustration, anxiety and low productivity, and they can allow the learner to arrive at mistaken or erroneous conclusions. So we developed some validations. We adopted two methods: tests with users and usability inspection. With these validations we identify some positive and negative characteristics of the system, considering the usability and ergonomics aspects of the interface.

1. INTRODUCTION

Most of the virtual museums on the Web are sites that offer on-line learning resources, inviting the visitor to investigate and to explore the information available. SAGRES is a virtual museum that seeks a cooperation between museums and schools, in order to create a new educational environment that provides continuous education, allowing access to information about the museum to the community in general. SAGRES facilitates the organisation of visits to museums, presenting museums' information bases in a way adapted to the user's characteristics (capacities and preferences). The system determines the group of links appropriate to the users, showing them in a subsequent HTML page (Bertoletti and Costa 1999).

There is a module in SAGRES, the agent's module, responsible for overcoming some limitations of hypermedia systems, such as the lack of initial training and the possibility of the user getting lost during navigation, due to the large amount of links available. This module uses software agents to overcome these limitations. Thus, software agents are used as virtual guides and they have the responsibility to assist the learner during an interaction with the system. These guides are represented by animated characters. According to Hayes-Roth and Doyle (1998) the introduction of characters on the Internet could bring the sensation that people are interacting with 'real characters' in virtual worlds. This sensation is intensified because characters simulate verbal and physical behaviour, similar to the humans, such as happiness, satisfaction and greeting. As people are social beings and interact instinctively with each other, the user's interaction with the interface should become friendlier.

As an educational environment is important to evaluate the usability of SAGRES, because products with low usability are generally responsible for frustration, anxiety and low productivity and they can allow the learner to come to mistaken or erroneous conclusions. This paper presents some validations applied to the SAGRES. According to Nielsen and Mack (1994) it is important to make more than one kind of analysis to validate software. So, we adopted two methods – tests with users and a usability inspection. For the first method, we produced a questionnaire based on the principles of the ISO 9241-10, and for the second we used a ckecklist, ErgoList, developed by the Usability Lab at UFSC in Brazil.

We developed another questionnaire in order to confirm the benefits of personal assistance provided for users and to show that interface personification through animated characters is attractive to users, facilitates the navigation, motivates the accomplishment of tasks and provides a personalised assistance and presentation of information. This questionnaire was based on the criteria presented by Hayes-Roth and Doyle (1998) to validate specifically software agents represented by animated characters.

2. THE SAGRES VIRTUAL MUSEUM

SAGRES is designed for three kinds of users: visitor, teacher and learner. The visitor is responsible for building and managing their visit to the museum. Visitors choose the subjects they are going to study and which activities they are going to do. The teacher is responsible for building a visit about some subject and makes this available for groups of students. The learner is able to execute a visit previous planned by their teacher.

The agent's module is responsible for generating and managing virtual guides. These guides assist users helping them in navigation and the operation of the system, discarding the need of an initial training and being useful in the analysis and monitoring of the users' actions. The guides are represented by animated characters that use the directed improvisation paradigm (Moraes et al. 1999) to interact with the user. In directed improvisation, animated characters can decide what to do and how to behave during their interaction with the user. To do this they execute instructions that can be in pre-conceived scripts and at the same time they improvise behaviours that are in agreement with the context of the interaction with the user. These behaviours include verbal and physical behaviours, that are similar to those of humans, like vibration and greeting, and can be expressed in different ways (as movement, gestures and conversation). With this representation we intend to provide a friendly interface for the users.

To support the independence between the module agents and SAGRES, the development model was developed in three layers: presentation, business and data. The layers of data and business meet in the server. The data layer stores the SAGRES databases and information related to the agents. The business layer implements the agents' functionality. The presentation layer is located in the client and contains the SAGRES HTML pages and agent's pages. The layers can be seen in Figure 1.

3. CLASSIFYING SAGRES AS EDUCATIONAL SOFTWARE

We found in the literature different forms for classifying educational software. Gamez (1998) presents the following taxonomy.

- *Exercise and Practice*, which has the objective to exercise contents or abilities already known by the learner.
- *Tutorial*, which is responsible for the presentation of contents, using animations, sounds and control of the learner' performance.

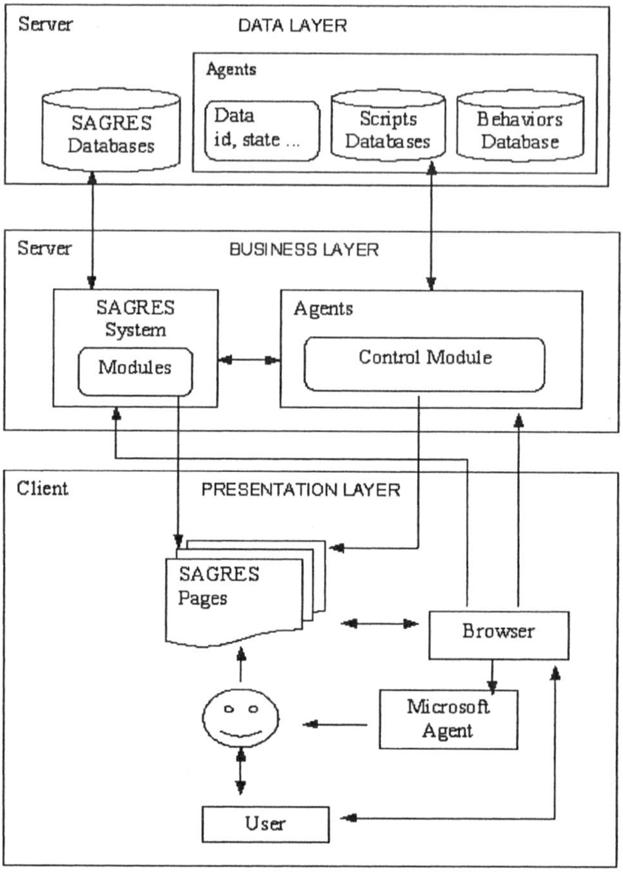

Figure 1. SAGRES Tree Layers Model

- *Intelligent Tutorial System*, which has the objective to consider the knowledge and previous abilities of the learner to choose strategies of learning more adapted for each one.
- *Simulation*, which has the objective to represent or to model parts of the real world as objects, systems and events.
- *Educational Game*, which provides learning trough entertainment;
- *Informative*, which seeks to present information in the form of texts, graphs or tables.

- *Hypertext /Hypermedia*, which is commonly defined as a non lineal form to store and to recover information. The hypertext and the hypermedia can be used as adapted tools to the learning process.

Based on the taxonomy described in Gamez (1998) we can verify that SAGRES can be classified as hypertext/hypermedia, because it is a system developed to the Internet. In this way, it inherits the natural characteristics of the hypermedia. The system also supplies for the teacher, the possibility of elaborating exercises. So, the learner can also do exercises that are additional material. The system also has some characteristics of educational software classified as exercise and practice.

4. USABILITY EVALUATION OF SAGRES AS AN EDUCATIONAL SOFTWARE

For some systems succeed, it is necessary for four characteristics to be present the ability to be useful for a certain public, the ability to be easy to learn, the ability to be easy to manipulate, and the ability to have an attractive interface to get the user's attention. In this sense, the usability evaluation of interfaces is an important stage in the system's life cycle. The main objective of evaluation is to identify problems that can link the user's interaction with the interface. This kind of evaluation is particularly important in the analysis of educational software, because products with low usability are generally responsible for frustration, anxiety and low productivity, and they can allow the learner to come to mistaken or erroneous conclusions.

There are several methods for usability evaluation. These methods are classified as usability inspection methods and empirical tests with the users. Some authors point out that more than one method can be applied to the same interface (Nielsen and Mack 1994, Winckler et al. 2000). We applied two techniques for SAGRES analysis: tests with users through questionnaires, and usability inspection using ErgoList, a specific checklist for ergonomic inspection developed by the Usability Lab at UFSC.

4.1 Tests with users

Medeiros and Cybis (2000) made a study of different ways to do usability evaluation and they verified that one way is through the identification of the users' satisfaction degree, considering the dialogue principles in the part 10 of the ISO 9241 norm.

In order to verify the satisfaction degree and usability of SAGRES, we developed a questionnaire with questions organised into seven categories: suitability for task, self-descriptiveness, controllability, conformity with user expectations, error tolerance, suitability for customisation, suitability for learning (Blanchard 1997). To reduce the time for filling the questionnaire, for each category we defined the maximum of 5 questions. Each question had four options for answers: bad, regular, good and very good, with an associated weighting of one to four.

It is important to note that the objective of the questionnaire was to provide a complete evaluation of the system and each category included certain characteristics of the system. The characteristics related to the virtual guide are present in the suitability for learning and self-descriptiveness. However, this paper also intends to provide a specific evaluation of the virtual guide, in order to verify the learner acceptance and improvements related to its inclusion in the system.

We researched about evaluation approaches for intelligent agents. Hayes-Roth and Doyle (1998) point out that work on intelligent agents inherited the evaluation approaches of Artificial Intelligence and other fields of Computer Science, such as Human-Computer Interfaces. These approaches defined the desirable qualities of systems. However, as virtual guides intend to be more similar to people, traditional approaches need to be adapted or modified. Hayes-Roth and Doyle (1998) present an adaptation of some important categories for the evaluation of animated characters. As virtual guides are represented through animated characters, we could apply these modifications: reliable become variable, predictable becomes idiosyncratic; correct becomes appropriate; complete becomes effective; efficient becomes interesting, and optimal becomes distinctively individual.

Following the ideas presented by Hayes-Roth and Doyle, we also developed a questionnaire to evaluate characteristics related to the agents. Some questions were: Did the guide present appropriated behaviour to each task? Did the guide help you in a personalised way and did he encourage you to do your tasks? Did the guide help you to concentrate on relevant information? Did the information presented by the guide are easy to understand? And, in the future, if you can choose the presentation with or without the guide, which one you choose?

4.2 Usability evaluation

The tool used for the usability evaluation was ErgoList. This tool provides a way to evaluate the facility of use of interactive software. The ergonomic evaluation is accomplished through checklists. Each one is specialised in one aspect or approach that determines the ergonomics of a human-computer interaction (Project ErgoList 2000). The tool is composed of 18 checklists that seek to evaluate the following characteristics: readiness, grouping for location, grouping for format, feedback, legibility, conciseness, minimum actions, density of information, explicit actions, user's control, flexibility, user's experience, error protection, error message, error correction, consistency, meaning and compatibility. Each one of these checklists comprises of three to twenty-seven subjects, that seek to test the applicability and the conformity, or not, with ergonomic approaches.

4.3 Users identification

The tests were applied to learners from fundamental, medium and superior levels that are partners of the Computer Club at Museum of Sciences and Technology at PUCRS. This selection was made random, and the learners involved are of both genders, with different ability levels and knowledge, all being assiduous users of the system.

4.4 Analysis of the results

The current phase of the research has completed all the usability evaluation tests applied to the visitor module (user's tests and inspection). The usability inspection has been completed for all modules, including teacher and learner modules. And although the tests with users are not fully completed, the data obtained supplies very important information about the usability of the system.

In the data obtained through the tests with users, considering the dialog principles, we verified that some categories have a larger rate: suitability for learning, with average 3,68; self-descriptiveness, with average 3,635; controllability, with average 3,5. Although the other categories have obtained superior average to the good concept, the analysis of the results indicates that some aspects of the system can be improved.

- *Error tolerance*, with average 3,22: the learner should be supplied with immediate feedback. As this system was developed in the Web, the time of request can vary due to the net traffic and the system doesn't inform that a request is being processed.
- *Suitability of task*, with average 3,33: the options vocabulary should be improved, because learner at the fundamental level had difficulties to identify task related to options.
- *Conformity with user expectations*, with average 3,375: a larger information base should be available, including other areas of knowledge.
- *Suitability for customisation*, with average 3,4: it should be clear the available options to adapt the system.

In the analysis of the virtual guide, the average obtained in the questionnaire was 3,68. We verified that users favour the guides' behaviours during the execution of tasks, obtaining an average 3,875. It is important to say that the other aspects obtained averages superior to 3,6. So, the guide successfully reached the approaches proposed by Hayes-Roth and Doyle, displaying normal variability in their choice and manner of executing behaviours, being attractive and interesting to users. Besides, the guide treats the learner in a personalised way, aiding and motivating him to accomplish tasks.

Considering the variables for suitability for learning and self-descriptiveness included the virtual guide reached the most average in previous questionnaire, we can conclude that the learner shows satisfaction with using the guides. This satisfaction is explicit, because all the learner answer ‘with’ to the question ‘In the future, if you can choose the presentation with or without the guide, which one you choose?’ In this way we verify that the virtual guide is an important aid to the learner during the operation of the system, executing its main functionality and serving as incentive for future access to the system.

The data obtained through the inspection test, with ErgoList, shows the percentage of conformity, or not, with certain characteristics in the system. Figure 2 shows that most of the applicable approaches obtained percentage of conformity higher than 50%. The best categories are: minimum actions (100%), grouping for location (81,8%), density of information (77,7%) and grouping for format (64,7%). In contrast, error protection and user's experience are the worst categories, because they are not in conformity with ErgoList. This is because certain characteristics are not present in SAGRES such as: confirmation of destructive actions, existence of buttons to undo destructive actions, and existence of dialogues compatible with the users' abilities.

Indeed, several of the approaches are not applicable, because ErgoList is not a checklist developed for Web evaluation. So, the approaches of error correction, user's control, flexibility and explicit actions have questions that do not match with characteristics of Web systems.

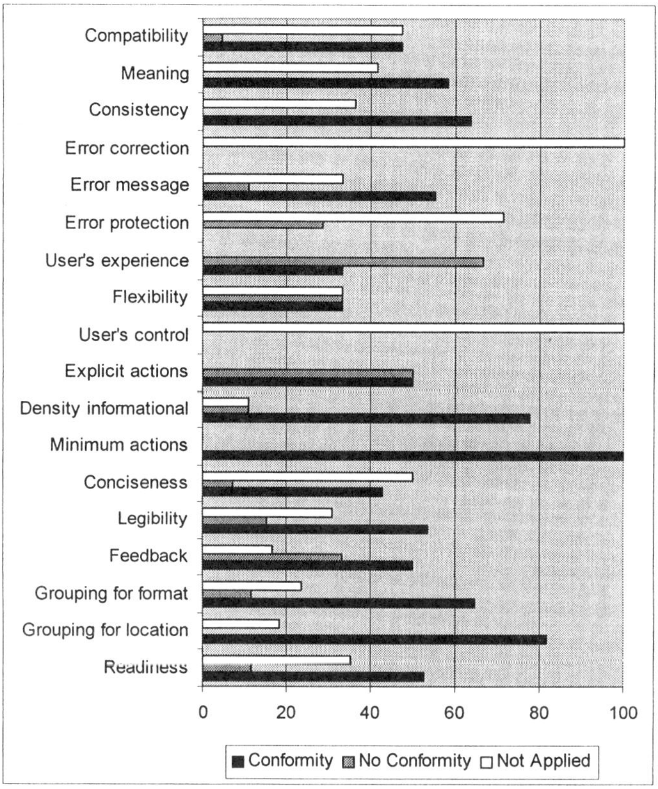

Figure 2. Percentage of Conformity

5. CONCLUSIONS

The evaluation phase presented in this paper presents a usability and practice framework for collecting the degree of users satisfaction, to identify positive and negative points that must be revised and improved, and to validate the satisfaction of users in relation to the virtual guide.

Both methods, tests with users and inspections with ErgoList, show equivalents results, indicating that the ergonomics' aspects of the interface really influence the usability of the system. Considering that error correction, error message and error protection of Ergolist, can be compared to error tolerance in ISO 9241-10, we verify that both present the lowest degree of satisfaction, and must be revised. Additionally, the user's experience of ErgoList, and suitability of tasks of ISO 9241-10, reflect the need to adapt, not only the information presented, but also the dialogues (menus, error messages and help) within the system. The questionnaire used to probe use of the virtual guide demonstrates that users like the virtual guide. We believe it can facilitate navigation, offering personalised help and demonstrating interesting ways to interact with users, thus achieving its initial goal.

REFERENCES

Bertoletti, A. C. and Costa, A. C. R. (1999) SAGRES – A Virtual Museum. In *Museums and The Web 1999 Conference,* D. Bearman and J. Trant (eds.), New Orleans, Louisiana, March.

Blanchard, H. E. (1997) Standards: User Interface Standards in the ISO Ergonomics Technical Committee. *SIGCHI Bulletin*, vol. 29, n. 1, January.

Gamez, L. (1998) *Ticese: Técnica de Inspeção de Conformidades Ergonômicas em Software Educacional.* MD thesis, Universidade de Minho.

Hayes-Roth, B. and Doyle, P. (1998) *Animate Characters. Autonomous Agents and Multi-Agent Systems.* 1, 195-230, Kluwer Academic Publishers.

Medeiros, M. A. and Cybis, W. A. (2000) Método de Avaliação de usabilidade de *software* a partir da satisfação de usuários e da aplicação de quesitos da norma ISO 9241. In *IHC'2000 – III Workshop sobre Fatores Humanos em Sistemas de Computação,* pp. 93-101.

Moraes, M. C., Bertoletti, A. C. and Costa, A. C. R. (1999) Virtual Guides to Assist Visitors in the SAGRES Virtual Museum. In *International Conference of the Chilean Computer Science Society – SCCC'99*, IEEE Press, Chile.

Mulken, S., André, E. and Müller, J. (1998) The Persona Effect: How Substantial is it? In *XIII Proceedings of the HCI'98,* Berlin, pp. 53-66.

Nielsen, J. and Mack, R. (1994) *Usability Inspection Methods*. John Wiley & Sons, Inc. 413p.

Projeto ErgoList (2000). [www.labiutil.inf.ufsc.br/ergolist/check.htm] 20.10.2000.

Winckler, M., Nemetz, F. and Lima, V. (2000) Interação entre Aprendiz e Computador: Métodos para Desenvolvimento e Avaliação de Interfaces. In *Tecnologia Digital na Educação,* Editora da UFRGS, pp. 7-33.

BIOGRAPHY

Márcia Cristina Moraes, a PhD student in Computer Science at UFRGS, is a professor in the FACIN/PUCRS. Her current research interests are Distributed Artificial Intelligence and Human-Computer Interaction.

Ana Carolina Bertoletti is the Coordinator of Multimedia and Internet Division at MCT/PUCRS. Her current research interests are Computers in Education and Virtual Museum. She has master degree in Computer Science.

Antonio Carlos da Rocha Costa has a Ph.D. in Computer Science and is a lecturer at the ESIN/UCPel. His interest areas are Computers in Education, Distributed Artificial Intelligence, and Theoretical Computer Science.

35

Web-based Exploratory Cross-curricular Learning Contexts

The Case Studies of IRIS and GAIA Environments

Yannis Kotsanis, Anna Chronaki, Demetrios Sampson and Nikos Dapontes
Doukas School, Messogion 151, Maroussi GR-151 25, Greece and Pliroforiki Technognosia Ltd, Konitsis 11B, Maroussi, GR-151 25, Greece
kotsanis@doukas.gr
Open University, Walton Hall, Mitlon Keynes, MK7 6AA, United Kingdom
Informatics and Telematics Institute, Kyvernidou 1, Thessaloniki 54639, Greece
Directorate of Secondary Education of Hellenic Ministry of Education, Greece

Keywords: secondary education, interdisciplinary, collaborative learning, multimedia

Abstract: The pedagogic implementation of web-based exploratory learning contexts through the examples of the IRIS and GAIA educational software is discussed. IRIS and GAIA are two learning environments based on multiple representations addressing the teaching of subjects such as physics, mathematics, geography and visual arts through a cross-curricular and project oriented approach. The pedagogic and methodological principles that guide the design of these environments is being outlined followed by examples of the ways in which experimentation and construction can facilitate the learning in different subjects.

1. INTRODUCTION

The implementation and use of interactive technology tools introduces new habits and roles in the didactic practice (Chronaki 2000). Students and teachers come to relate in different ways not only with the tools but also amongst themselves. Specifically, such tools promote users' direct manipulation of information and their active engagement with the content represented in the software. As a result, the pedagogic context of such a tool is rooted in the design principles, but also in the way of its implementation by teachers and students in the classroom. The focus of this paper is to highlight some pedagogic implementation of web based exploratory learning contexts through the examples of the IRIS and GAIA educational software.

2. DESIGNING EXPLORATORY LEARNING ENVIRONMENTS

The design of IRIS and GAIA exploratory software is based on pedagogic principles rooted in the theories of constructivism and socioculturalism (Papert 1991, Resnick 1995). These pedagogic principles have emerged through a methodology involving a dialogue between theory and teaching practice. This dialogue was materialised in two levels. First, the design team was interdisciplinary, involving people with different expertise and experiences (i.e. subject teachers, educationists and software designers). Second, there was a close co-operation between the team members and classroom teachers. This meant that any original idea concerning design could be discussed from both theoretical and practical viewpoints but also such ideas could be tested in real conditions that would enable to get feedback from teachers and students. The pedagogic principles can be summarised in the following five basic guidelines for the design and implementation of the educational software.

Approaching concept learning through problem-solving in authentic situations The basic idea in both environments of IRIS and GAIA is that the didactic treatment of concepts in specific subjects should emerge through the solving of problems arising in authentic situations. Such situations are closely connected with situations we are faced in real life (e.g. the construction of a town square in IRIS, the trip around the Earth in GAIA) and which mostly have a cross-curricular character. Through such open contexts, subject specific questions can be posed. For example, questions such as: "what is vector and how can be measured?", "how we measure the sides of a triangle?", "what is area and how can be measured?", "what might be a good form for decorating the floor of the square?" address the subjects of physics, maths and visual arts.

Use of experimentation and constructions Whilst working with specific tasks in the IRIS and GAIA environments, teachers and students can experiment with either real situations (i.e. in the case of IRIS) or simulations of real situations (i.e. in the case of GAIA). Experimentation allows the users to approach a problem from a variety of viewpoints and moreover encourage them to try out their own envisaged solutions (e.g. simulate trips on the surface and on the atmosphere, in GAIA, construct linear, free forms and create mosaics and decorative motives, in IRIS). Experimentation and construction takes place in a specially designed web space, called the 'activities centre'.

Systematic use of information and communication In both environments users are encouraged to utilise systematically information. Especially, two centres have been designed to encourage users towards searching, discussing and reflecting about information. These web-based centres are called the 'information centre' and the 'communication centre'. The 'information centre' consists an interactive database that includes information in the form of multimedia. This information is relevant to the suggested tasks and aims to assist learners in their work through projects and worksheets. The 'communication centre' enables learners and teachers to actively interact and discuss online aspects concerning their involvement with the tasks.

Promotion of collaborative learning and teaching The learning environments of IRIS and GAIA require students and teachers to collaborate at many different levels. First, students should collaborate whilst working in small groups of two or three in their worksheets. Second, teachers and students collaborate in the classroom whilst experimenting and reflecting on their work through specific tasks. Finally, online distance collaboration amongst students and teachers who work on same topics (through specifically designed tasks) but in other schools is also encouraged. For example, the measurement of the Earth's radius necessitates the collaboration between two schools, as well as the exploration of ultimate forms in constructing and designing the town square encourages interaction amongst students and teachers who live in very different locations.

Promotion of critical, political and aesthetic thinking The topics and especially the questions found in the proposed tasks aim to promote students' critical, political and aesthetic thinking over situations. For example, questions about decision making concerning issues of design, construction and the economy of a particular space such as the town square are closely related with people's political and critical thought in a community where they share activity and life. Choosing one solution over another means that these people have treated aspects of the problem not only rationally, but also critically, politically and aesthetically.

3. ELABORATING EXPERIMENTATION AND CONSTRUCTION

Viewing the development of learning as an active endeavour of students necessitates that the pedagogic design of a didactic situation encourages participants in 'doing' and 'trying out' their ideas. Both GAIA and IRIS offer specially designed tools that can be used for *experimentation* and *construction* in particular tasks. Such tools promote specific activities (i.e. through visualisation, simulation, direct manipulation and multiple representations) that enable users' exploration and work in experiments and constructions.

Multiple representations (Van Someren et al. 1998), in particular, are based on the idea that exploratory learning can be achieved when students move from one representation to another in a way that is meaningful for the purpose of their activities. The use of multiple representations is strongly exploited when the parameters of interactivity, that modify the working area, act as multiple inputs. In other words, one can move the explorer around the globe and/or the world map by clicking and dragging on it and/or changing the value of longitude and latitude.

3.1 Examples from GAIA

GAIA is realised through seven microworlds, covering a different thematic areas related to Earth (the Greek word GAIA is a synonym of the word Earth). Each microworld is equipped with a number of tools, interaction items and representations that are integrated with the correct educational material in order to support different educational scenarios (Kotsanis et al. 2000).

One of the most well specified scenarios is the one that helps students understand the concepts of geographical longitude and latitude, in the *Jason microworld.* The users have at their disposal an 'explorer', for example a plane or a helicopter, that is shown and can be visually manipulated (Lemeignan et al. 1996) in the following four representations (see Figure 1).

Planet Earth shows a three-dimensional sphere with earth's image that the students can rotate eastwards or westwards. Choosing a point on the sphere's surface allows the user to designate the explorer's position, which corresponds to a longitude and a latitude value-pair that are represented, in turn, by a meridian and a parallel respectively. *World Map* shows the explorer's position on the earth's map. Using direct manipulation the students can change its location. *Sections* consists of two hemispheres. The South hemisphere is used to show the longitude on the surface that corresponds to the equator, via an indicator that moves in a circle scaled from 180 to 180 degrees. A vertical hemisphere is used to show the latitude on the surface that corresponds to a meridian, via an indicator that moves in a semicircle scaled from 90 to 90 degrees. The explorer's attributes, such as location, velocity and distance can be manipulated through the *Flight Deck. Flight Deck* consists of many controls and instruments representing a variety of attributes related to the microworld.

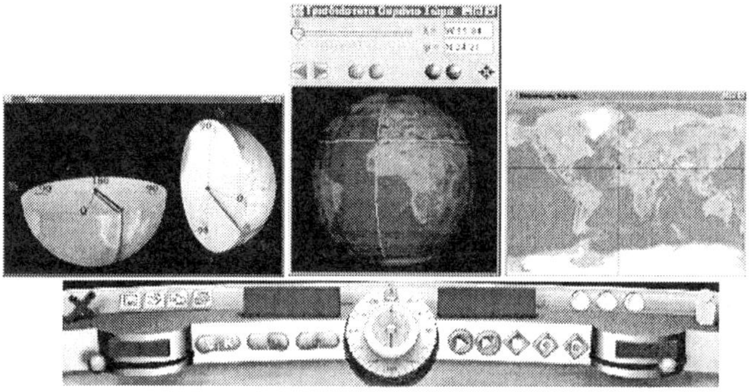

Figure 1. Sections, Planet Earth, World Map and Flight Deck representations

Students can change the explorer's location in four different ways: (1) with direct manipulation of the explorer, either on Planet Earth, or on the World Map; (2) with rotation of the wheel, or change the position on the Flight Deck; (3) with the change of the arithmetic value (in degrees) of longitude and/or latitude, either on Planet Earth, or the Flight Deck; and (4) with direct manipulation of the three-dimensional representations of longitude and latitude in Sections. Any of the above changes triggers a simultaneous update of all the representations depicting the explorer's location.

In addition to Jason, GAIA supports six other microworlds (Newton, Gilbert, Eratosthenes, Torricelli, Egkelados and Aristarchos) that enable students to:

- Observe satellite orbits around any planet of the solar system, and solve problems related to the velocity and type of orbit;
- Study earth's geomagnetic field, the characteristics of the magnetic needle and the effects of mineral deposits on magnetometers;
- Calculate earth's radius, following the procedure used by the Greek mathematician Eratosthenes before 2300 years;
- Measure the pressure and temperature of the earth's atmosphere, to study levity and to simulate free fall;
- 'Travel' inside esoteric part (crust, mantle, core) and study it through a simplified model of seismographers; and
- Study the orbits of the planets in a model of earth's solar system or even in an imaginary solar system that users can construct by choosing planets with different characteristics.

It should be noted that an explorer is used in all microworlds. However, depending on the microworld, the explorer that is represented by a different object and therefore image. For example, in Jason microworld students can choose between an airplane, a helicopter or a ship, in Gilbert a magnetic needle or a magnetometer, and in Torricelli a balloon, an airplane, or a parachutist.

3.2 Examples from IRIS

The constructions and experiments in the local environment of IRIS, occur through three tools (see Figure 2): two *Unit Constructors* for vectors and bitmaps and a *Motif Generator* (Kotsanis et al. 1999). Along with the two *Unit Constructors*, the user creates either vector designs or graphics and images in bitmap format. Both constructors provide the basic geometric shapes (point, segment, open polygon line, closed polygon line, square, rectangle, circle, arc, regular polygon) with the possibility of either colouring the line and filling the shape, as well as a set of mathematical transformations such as symmetry, rotations, displacement, stretch and resizing. The function that differentiates the two constructors, beyond the format of the design is the selection of a grid. In the first (which resembles the simplified Geometric Sketchpad) (Rowling 1997), the grid is made up of dots on which the shapes can be constructed. In the second (which resembles Windows Paint), the grid is made up of a rectangular area, which can be filed with colour.

The *Motif Generator* repeats the simple or complex units made by the unit constructors as motifs, in a rectangular area, with horizontal and vertical sizes that can be modified. One to four units can be placed (only one or two horizontally or two vertically or four adjoin units) in each of which we can use the function: flip horizontal/vertical and rotation, to construct a motif.

The above development of these tools is not based on the approach of multiple representations and direct manipulation. The user exploits the tools independently either through file management or by just taking advantage of copy/paste functions. In the new (under development) version of Iris, the approach of multiple inputs through four representations is being used. The first three include the functions for the construction of a *unit*, a *motif* (which is made up of one to four units), and a *mosaic,* which repeats the current motif. Through the fourth representation, the *sketch deck*, the user can interact directly to each and every one of the parameters of the other representations. The result appears directly in one of the other representations and concurrently have the result projected in the other two. For example, the user can: change the current colour or shape of the unit to a series of other colours and shapes, modify one of the units using the flip horizontal/vertical and rotation functions, and change the number/size of repeated motifs (see Figure 3).

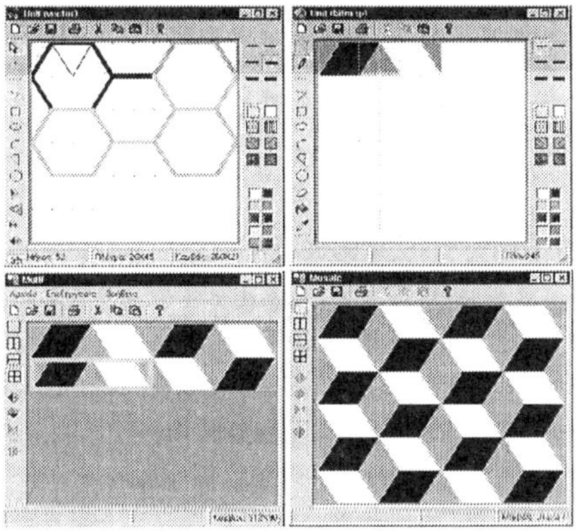

Figure 2. The Unit Constructors and Motif Generator tools

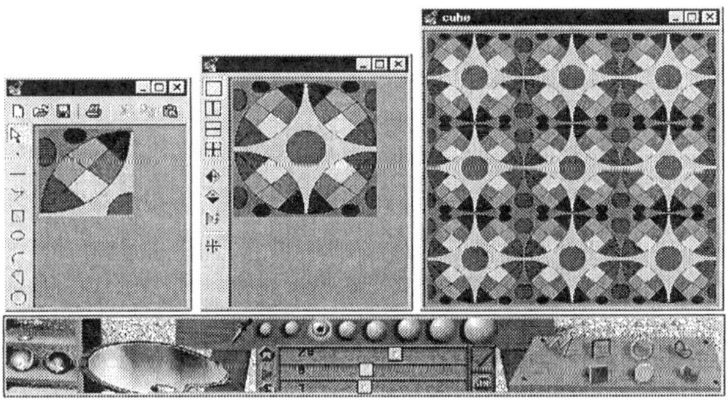

Figure 3. Unit, Motif, Mosaic and Sketch Deck representations

4. CONSTRUCTIVE USE OF WEB TOOLS

An important element of the design considerations for both educational software case studies, is the provision of web-based facilities which allow the building of a 'network learning community' around these educational applications and their school use for connected classrooms.

Hence, both GAIA and IRIS are designed such as to provide access to a web-based Learning Community Centre (LCC). This is not a static information retrieval focal point on the web, but it serves as the enabling platform for the community members to organise their activities. Therefore, the Learning Community Centre is constantly being constructed by its users. We consider this as an integral part of the educational software itself, and moreover, as an important element of the internet-based constructionist aspect of the connected classroom use of the software.

Constructionism (Papert 1991) involves claims that learning is an active process, in which people actively construct knowledge from their experiences in the world. Recently, the term 'distributed constructivism' (Resnick 1995) is introduced, to describe how the basic constructionist thesis can be enhanced by an emphasis on the social dimension of such activities when shared among many participants.

This is the rational based on which the concept of Network Learning Community Centre is developed. The main objective of the web-based LCC is not to create a fully self-sufficient information web site for users to enjoy, but to provide the basic framework and facilities towards building communities of learners engaged in collaborative activities that involve not only the exchange of information but also collective construction of personally meaningful activities and knowledge accumulation. As a result, both educational software case studies presented in this paper are supported on-line with a web-based Network Learning Community Centre consisting of the following three centres (Sampson 1999).

Figure 4. List of Images from the Information Centre

The *Information* centre provides user-friendly access to databases of educational material and content (in various forms, such as, text, images, graphs, video and web-links, e.g. Figure 4). Although, a seed material is pre-stored in these databases, all registered users (learning community members) are given the privileges to upload new material from emerging collaborative project activities.

The *Communication* centre provides the necessary tools to enable communication via Internet, facilitating the exchange of ideas and collaboration between on-line community members.

The *Activities* centre provides the workplace and the tools for the on-line activities experimentation. Exploiting the facilities of both the Information centre (for example work sheets or relevant stored activity material) and the Communication centre (for example discussions between community members) the community members can construct their own project activities. The Activities centre gives them, also, the opportunity to experience, criticise and eventually learn from the constructions of others. This enhances the potential of the exploratory educational software in use from an environment of personal expression to a learning environment through which the individual learner encounters and interprets a symbolic representation embodying the ideas of others.

5. CONCLUSIONS

Tasks in the proposed exploratory environments address topics that cover the curriculum in several secondary subjects such as science, geography, maths and visual arts. They provide tools for the teaching of these curriculum subjects through tasks and activities that promote open and exploratory learning. This pedagogic context is based on the use of simulations, experimentation and constructions as well as the communicative and collaborative interactions achieved amongst participants either face to face or online. Current piloting of the implementation of these learning environments in classroom conditions provides very optimistic results and feedback on the success of such contexts as far as it concerns the learning development and conceptual change for both teachers and learners.

Note: The first phase of GAIA and IRIS was developed on the frame of the SIRINES and NAUSICA projects, while the second phase of GAIA is currently being developed on the frame of the PENELOPE (EPEAEK projects funded by the Hellenic Ministry of Education, Greece, under the co-ordination of the Computer Technology Institute – CTI).

REFERENCES

Chronaki, A. (2000) Computers in Classrooms: learners and teachers in new roles. In *International Companion in Education,* B. Moon, S. Brown, and M. Ben-Peretz (eds.), Routledge, London.

Kotsanis Y., Chronaki, A., Taliadorou L. et al. (1999) *Technical Annex*, IRIS: The Art of Mathematics and the Mathematics of Art, EPEAEK/NAYSIKA Project. [http://www.compupress.gr/iris].

Kotsanis Y., Dapontes N., Karastathis V., Sampson D. et al (2000) *Technical Annex*, GAIA II: Educational Multimedia Microworlds for Cross-Curriculum Earth Navigation, EPEAEK/PINELOPI Project. [http:// gaia.compulink.gr].

Lemeignan G. and Weil-Barais (1996) *Construire Des Concepts En Physique. L' Einseignement de la Mecanique*, Paris.

Papert, Seymour (1991) Situating Constructionism. In *Constructionism,* Idit Harel and Seymour Papert (Eds.), Norwood, NJ: Ablex Publishing, 1991.

Resnick M. (1995) New Paradigms for Computing, New Paradigms for Thinking, Computers and Exploratory Learning. In A. diSessa, C. Hoyles and R. Noss (eds.), *Computers and Exploratory Learning*, Springer Verlag NATO ASI Series, pp. 31-44.

Rowling, Dawn (1997) *Introducing The Geometer's Sketchpad to the Classroom.* The Global Schoolhouse.

Sampson D. (1999) Collaborative Learning in School Education via the World Wide Web: The NETLogo Project. *European Multimedia, Embedded Systems and Electronic Commerce Conference*, EMMSEC'99, June 1999, Stockholm, Sweden, pp. 21-23.

Van Someren, M., Reimann, P., Boshuzen, P. and De Jong, T. (1998) *Learning with Multiple Representations*, Pergamon.

BIOGRAPHY

Yannis Kotsanis (PhD in Software Engineering) is the Head of Information Technology Dept. at Doukas School and Senior Researcher at Pliroforiki Technognosia Ltd. He has worked as trainer, software designer and project manager in numerous educational research projects.

Anna Chronaki (PhD in Mathematics Education) is an Assistant Professor at the University of Thessaly, Greece. She has been a Researcher and Lecturer at the University of Bath and the Open University, U.K., in the areas of technology, educational ethnography and learning environments design.

Demetrios Sampson (PhD in Electronic Systems Engineering) is the Head of the Advanced Electronic Services at ITI/CERTH. He has professional experience in design, development and management of international and national projects in the areas of informatics and telematics.

Nikos Dapontes (PhD in Educational Technology) is currently Head of the Information Society Dept. at Hellenic Ministry of Education. His current interests are open learning environments, simulations, modelling, problem solving, science and teacher education.

36

Critical Evaluation of Scientific Websites by High School Students

Marie Iding, Robert E. Landsman and ThanhTruc T. Nguyen
Educational Psychology Department, University of Hawaii, Honolulu, Hawaii, USA
miding@hawaii.edu
ANOVA Science Education Consulting, Honolulu, Hawaii, USA
Curriculum Research and Development Group, University of Hawaii, Honolulu, Hawaii, USA

Keywords: internet, secondary teaching, classroom teaching/practice, critical evaluation

Abstract: This study describes an instructional intervention in which high school biology students learned to develop criteria for critically evaluating science Websites and scientific information contained in them. Results indicated that the *process* of learning to critically evaluate Websites was what was most valuable to them. Students' lists of criteria for critically evaluating Websites were more extensive after instruction. Furthermore, the majority of students reported learning something new, indicated that they would spend more time evaluating scientific information on Websites, and reported increased confidence in their ability to evaluate scientific information on the Web.

1. INTRODUCTION

The question of the validity or credibility of information on the World Wide Web is a growing concern to educators, parents, students, and others. As students are encouraged to engage in project-based research, more of their information is from the Web where anyone can publish anything at anytime. Teachers frequently assume that students have learned how to critically evaluate Website information sources and that it is the responsibility of *other* teachers (most often English teachers) to have covered this topic (Nguyen 2000). This often inaccurate assumption underscores the need for students to learn to evaluate information sources, and for teachers to learn to carry out instruction that effectively facilitates this process in all content areas.

This concern is especially important in the area of science learning because students as beginning scientific researchers, or at the very least, lifelong consumers of scientific information, must be able to adequately assess claims and make judgments about scientific information in general, not just information on the World Wide Web. This aspect of scientific literacy is deemed to be essential by the American Association for the Advancement of Science in *Benchmarks for Science Literacy* (1993):

> "In everyday life, people are bombarded with claims – claims about products, about how nature or social systems or devices work, about their health and welfare, about what happened in the past and what will occur in the future. These claims are put forth by experts (including scientists) and nonexperts (including scientists), by honest people and charlatans. In response to this barrage, trying to separate sense from nonsense, knowledge helps." (p. 298)

Learning to critically assess information is important in part because of the proliferation of non-refereed material on the Internet. It is also imperative due to the movement away from single-textbook-based science teaching where judgments of accuracy of information were outside the purview of teachers and students, and in the hands of textbook writers and editors. Accuracy judgments have been placed into the hands of individual students and teachers who are very likely to have not experienced instruction in how to effectively make those judgements. Therefore, in this paper we examine work that provides a needed foundational research base for students' critical evaluation of Web-based scientific information, then we describe a study in which we worked with high school students to facilitate their development of individual and group criteria to evaluate scientific information on Websites.

Prior work in this area includes research that develops criteria for evaluating Websites or, frequently, software and/or multimedia in general (e.g., Chen 1995, Sherry 1998, Nguyen 2000). Chen (1995) for example, provided an interesting approach that evaluated the pedagogical techniques employed by software, according to learning theories. Sherry (1998) described an exercise in which she had students develop a "multimedia matrix" for developing their own multimedia. Although this approach was employed at the graduate level, her suggestions for student personalization of the matrix could well be adapted for students at other levels evaluating Websites.

An innovative approach was developed by Nguyen (2000) where high school students in three different subject areas, including science, created an evaluation tool called *OASIS* to use in selecting appropriate resources from the World Wide Web. Teachers surveyed in Nguyen's study also indicated that they allow Web resources for student research more than other multimedia resources such as CD-ROMs, videotapes, audiotapes, and television shows. Though these latter four multimedia resources usually have editing and review bodies, it is the resources from the Web that are most accepted by teachers (Nguyen 2000).

Other research examined ways that scientists and others evaluate the credibility of information sources generally (e.g., Klemm, Iding and Speitel, in press). In that research, Klemm, Iding, and Speitel (in press) found that preservice elementary and secondary science teachers and scientists rated the credibility of many science information sources differently, with scientists ascribing less credibility to most sources listed, with the exceptions of PBS television (public television) and a scientist researching a question, which they rated as more credible. Interestingly, elementary teachers rated popular investigative weekly television newsmagazines like 20/20 as among the highest in credibility, while scientists rated them as among the lowest. This research underscores the need for developing critical judgement skills in the general population.

In addition to this research, there are a number of Websites that present criteria for evaluating Websites and the information contained in them. Two such Websites are the Internet Detective (*http://sosig.ac.uk/desire/internet-detective.html*) by the Desire Project and ICYouSee: T is for Thinking (*http://www.ithaca.edu/library/Training/hott.html*) by Henderson of Ithaca College Library. Also, Dr. T. Matthew Ciolek, in conjunction with the World Wide Web Consortium, maintains a Website entitled Information Quality WWW Virtual Library (*http://www.ciolek.com/WWWVL-InfoQuality.html*) dedicated to keeping track of online resources relevant for evaluation, development and administration of high quality factual/scholarly networked information systems. However, many of the lists of criteria on the Web are unaccompanied by actual research.

To address the lack of extensive research in this area, the present project was undertaken. The current work was carried out in two sections of an inquiry-, project-based high school biology classes. In this class, students learn how to approach scientific problems and how to solve problems experimentally using scientific methodology. Students also learn how to apply probability theory to decision making through the use of statistics, design and carry out their own experiments, and communicate about their studies through APA style written and oral reports.

One of the central features of this endeavor is actual library and Web research. In conjunction with the actual gathering of appropriate resources, students make assessments about the validity of material. As a result, the authors were interested in providing students with the opportunity to examine and further develop their own criteria for the assessing information from the Web. It was hoped that students would understand the importance of critically evaluating scientific Websites and the information contained in them. In the rest of the paper, we explain how the process was facilitated and evaluated, and discuss the impact of the process on the students.

2. METHOD

2.1 Participants

Participants were students in two senior biology classes at the University of Hawaii Laboratory School. The students are from diverse ethnic, ability, and socioeconomic backgrounds reflective of Hawaii's population. The ethnic breakdown consists of approximately 38% mixed ethnicity (including part-Hawaiian), 18% Caucasian, 18% Filipino, 16% Japanese and 10% other (including Asian, Pacific Islanders, African-American). In the first class, participants included 10 boys and 10 girls. In the second class, participants included 9 boys and 10 girls.

2.2 Procedure and materials

This workshop on scientific Website evaluation took place in the students' regular biology classes, over the course of four days. The three authors, their regular biology instructor (a scientist and curriculum developer), an educational technology specialist, and an educational psychology professor co-facilitated the workshop. Below, we briefly describe the sequence of events and the materials that were used.

On the first day, students answered two pretest questions that required that they list and describe what they consider first, when deciding to use a Website in general; and, secondly, what they consider when evaluating the scientific information on the Website. They ranked the items in their lists. Then, the educational technology specialist provided a brief description of the terms Internet, World Wide Web, Websites, and individual Web pages. She also provided a general introduction to three areas to consider when evaluating Websites and the scientific information on them: *credibility* of authors and institutions, *validity* or accuracy of the information contained in Websites, and the *presentation* aspects or organisation of the Website and its information (e.g., layout, graphics). This characterisation of Websites is derived from Farah (1995) and Rader (1998) and adapted in the research of Nguyen (2000).

On the second day, students engaged in actual Website evaluations to gain experience in the critical evaluation process. They carried out written evaluations of two Websites containing scientific information about a disease. One was accurate and credible while the other contained deliberate errors and invalid information. These websites were created for educational exercises of this sort. Students compared the Websites in terms of reliability, credibility, and presentation. Then, students evaluated a third Website containing information about frogs and learning. They listed pros and cons of using the Website to look for scientific information in general, and for using information from the Website for their scientific research or scientific research papers.

On the third day, teams of 5 students developed collaborative lists containing characteristics that they determined would be important for themselves or other students like them to use in evaluating scientific information on Websites. In the second part of the class, their teacher and the educational psychology professor facilitated the development of whole-class lists on the board, via whole-class discussion of characteristics from the collaborative lists. The purpose of this activity was to facilitate students' deeper processing and refinement of their criteria.

On the fourth day, summative evaluation took place. First, using the same two questions that were used in the pretest, students created individual lists for evaluating scientific Websites generally then for determining whether to use scientific information from Websites. These items were ranked. The instructions were the same as those given for the pretest. Next, students filled out follow-up questionnaires consisting of 12 items assessing whether their views of how to evaluate scientific information on Websites had changed and how, whether their confidence in their abilities to evaluate Websites had improved, what the most important things were that they had learned, and their general suggestions and comments regarding the activities.

3. RESULTS AND DISCUSSION

3.1 Did criteria for evaluating change?

The items from the pre- and post-Website evaluation program student-generated lists used to evaluate scientific Websites and the science information on Websites were categorised by the experimenters into the categories validity, credibility, or presentation. The pre- and post-education program data for the three categories were then summarised as percent of total (Tables 1 and 2) and means (Figures 1 and 2).

Table 1. The number (in parentheses) of student-generated items used to evaluate scientific Websites generally categorised as validity, credibility, or presentation and expressed as pre- and post-education program percent of totals and change in percent of totals

	Validity	Credibility	Presentation	Total
Pre	51% (80)	40% (63)	9% (15)	100% (158)
Post	45% (116)	32% (83)	23% (59)	100% (258)
Change	-6% (+36)	-8% (+20)	+14% (+44)	

Table 2. The number (in parentheses) of student-generated items used to evaluate scientific information on Websites categorized as validity, credibility, or presentation and expressed as pre- and post- Website evaluation program percent of totals and change in percent of totals

	Validity	Credibility	Presentation	Total
Pre	63% (79)	27% (33)	10% (10)	100% (158)
Post	52% (136)	27% (69)	21% (55)	100% (258)
Change	-11% (+57)	0% (+36)	+11% (+45)	

As can be seen in Tables 1 and 2, for both the Website and information on the Website, the percent of total was the highest for validity-related items, followed by credibility-related items and then presentation-related items. Analyses of variance indicated that when the number of items for the three categories were combined, students generated significantly more evaluative items for both scientific Website and for scientific information on Website evaluation after participation in the Website evaluation program [Pre vs Post mean ± S.E.M.: 1.32 ± .121 vs 2.15 ± .168, $F\ (1,119) = 19.7, p < 0.00003$; 1.03 ± .109 vs 2.17 ± .209, $F\ (1,119) = 37.0, p < 0.00000002$, respectively]. Although the number of student-generated items appeared to be greater following participation in the Website evaluation program, the percent of totals changed in the positive direction only for presentation-related items (Tables 1 and 2). This indicates that the web evaluation program may have had the most impact on student awareness of the presentation aspects of scientific Website and information evaluation.

Figures 1 and 2 present the mean number of student-generated items for the three categories before (Pre) and after (Post) the web evaluation program.

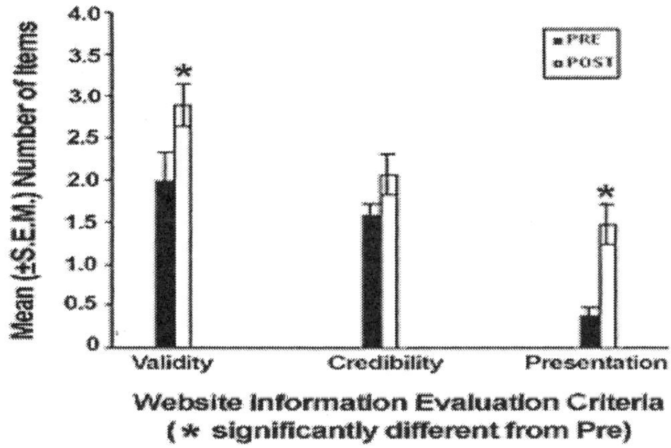

Figure 1. Means for general Website evaluation criteria

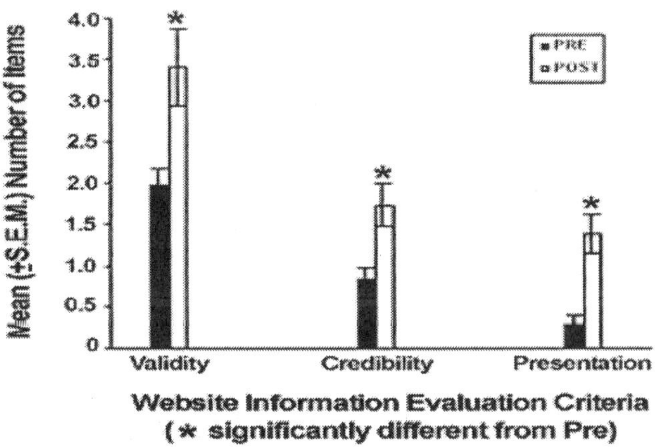

Figure 2. Means for scientific information criteria

For both scientific Websites (Figure 1) and scientific information found on Websites (Figure 2), the number of student-generated items was significantly higher following the Website evaluation program for validity [t(df=39)=-2.05, $p < 0.05$ and t(df=39)=-3.29, $p<0.003$, respectively] and presentation [t(df=39)=-4.70, $p = 0.0001$ and t(df=39)=-4.51, $p=0.0001$, respectively]. The number of student-generated credibility-related items following the Website evaluation program was significantly greater for scientific information found on Websites than before the program [t(df=39)=-3.40, p<0.002]. However, the Website evaluation program did not significantly effect the number of student-generated credibility-related items used for evaluating scientific Websites [see Figure 1, t(df=39)=-1.90, p>0.05].

3.2 Had students' evaluation processes changed ?

On a scale ranging from 'not at all' (0mm) to 'moderately' (7.4 mm) to 'very much' (14.8mm) on the post-program evaluation questionnaire, students indicated that the Website evaluation program moderately (mean=7.94 mm) changed their views of how they should evaluate scientific information on a Website. According to 80% of the students, this change in view was due to the *process* of creating and discussing their lists of items; 20% attributed the change in view to the actual lists that they created. One student wrote, "I think that what changed my views was the exercise in general, bringing attention to the problem of false Websites." Ninety-percent of the students indicated that, in the future, they will spend more time evaluating scientific Websites before using the information.

The majority of students (75%) involved in the Website evaluation program claimed they had learned something new about evaluating scientific information on Websites. Comments from student's about specific ways their views of how to evaluate scientific information changed included validity, credibility, and presentation characteristics. For example, "There are phony Websites and checking a Website is important when researching a specific topic, especially when you want to use the information as a source for your scientific paper", "I learned to always check an author's credentials before using his/her information," and "The way a site looks. Is it organized, readable, eye-catching, pictures, diagrams, etc?"

Students also indicated that they realised that presentation in itself does not justify believing the information presented in a Website: "A nice looking Website does not mean it's credible. There are many more ways of determining if a Website is good enough for use or consideration. My view is that evaluating scientific information is a little more important than I thought," and "Read carefully, don't automatically assume information is accurate if presented nicely."

When students were asked to rate the importance of the *process* of learning to critically evaluate information on scientific Websites (1=not at all important, 2=of little importance, 3=important, 4=very important, and 5=absolutely necessary), the mean rank (3.8) indicated they considered this process of learning to be between important and very important. Student ranks about the process were significantly related to their level of confidence in their ability to evaluate scientific information on Websites [$r(N=40)=.60$, $p<0.005$, $r^2=.36$]. Ninety-five percent of the students felt that their confidence about their ability to evaluate scientific information on Websites improved as a result of this Website evaluation program.

4. CONCLUSION

Clearly, educational activities facilitating students' critical evaluation of scientific information on Websites and the Websites themselves can be effective. In the present research, students indicated that the *process* of learning to critically evaluate Websites was what was most valuable to them. Additionally, students' lists of criteria for critically evaluating Websites were more extensive after instruction, and included more presentation-related criteria. The majority of students in this study reported learning something new, agreed that they would spend more time evaluating scientific information on Websites, and reported that their confidence in their ability to evaluate scientific information of the Web had increased.

The ability to critically evaluate scientific information, such as the information on Websites, is consistent with the American Association for the Advancement of Science (1993) description of scientific literacy, and is necessary as more and more scientific information is disseminated on the World Wide Web and referenced by students for research projects. This is, in turn, important as these students disseminate their own scientific research reports and contribute to scientific and educational databases on the Web. As future directions for educational programs and/or research endeavours, we recommend working with students at all levels and in all content areas to facilitate their critical Website and information evaluation skills.

REFERENCES

American Association for the Advancement of Science (1993) *Benchmarks for Scientific Literacy: Project 2061*. Oxford University Press, New York.

Chen, M. (1995) A methodology for characterizing computer-based learning environments. *Instructional Science*, 23, pp. 183-220.

Farah, B. (1995) Information literacy: retooling evaluation skills in the electronic information environment. *Journal of Educational Technology Systems*, 24 (2), p. 127.

Klemm, E. B., Iding, M. and Speitel, T. (in press) Do scientists and teachers agree on the credibility of media information sources? *International Journal of Instructional Media,* 28 (1).

Nguyen, T. T. (2000) *OASIS: Student Evaluation Methods for World Wide Web Resources.* Unpublished master's thesis, University of Hawai`i, Honolulu, Hawaii, U.S.A.
Rader, H. (1998) Library Instruction and Information Literacy. *Reference Service Review,* 26 (3/4), p. 143.
Sherry, A. C. (1998) Evaluation of multimedia authoring instruction based in a behaviorist-cognitive-constructivist continuum. *International Journal of Instructional Media*, 25(2), pp. 201-216.

BIOGRAPHY

Dr. Marie Iding is an Associate Professor in the Educational Psychology Department at the University of Hawaii. Her research interests include scientific visualisation and text processing with multimedia systems. She teaches courses in learning and cognition.

Dr. Robert Landsman is a neuroscientist whose scientific research focuses on neuroendocrinology and psychoneuroimmunology. He recently founded ANOVA Science Education Consulting (5223A Kalanianaole Highway, Honolulu, HI. 96821, anovaone@aol.com) where he is a science research education consultant. Dr. Landsman is interested in science education reform through the integration of scientific research into high school science curricula.

Miss ThanhTruc Nguyen is an Instructional Designer with the Curriculum Research and Development Group at the University of Hawaii. Her research interests include marine science education, technology integration in non-traditional settings, and the development of Web use standards for middle school and high school students.

37

Beware of the Web

Thao Lê and Quynh Lê
Faculty of Education, University of Tasmania, Australia
T.Le@utas.edu.au
University Department of Rural Health, University of Tasmania, Australia

Keywords: internet, critical discourse, flexible learning, virtual learning, web-based learning

Abstract: The contribution of the Web to society and education, particularly its contribution to on-line teaching and learning, are often discussed. Its usefulness, impact and power have been recognised. How neutral is the Web? Is the Web value-free from an ideology-loaded discourse? Questions such as these need to be addressed if we wish to take Web-based education seriously. The discussion examines some concepts and issues in Critical Discourse Analysis and relate them to the positive and negative influences that the Web can exert in education and intercultural interaction.

1. INTRODUCTION

Beware of the wolf! This popular message in fairy tales and fables for young children reminds children of dangers that a wolf can cause. Though the image of a bad wolf is no longer relevant, there are many dangers we need to be aware of with the permeation of computer technology in society. The Web is a fascinating phenomenon in terms of social impact. It has shortened space and time and has brought different peoples and cultures together in a virtual reality as well as in the real world. As the Web cannot be divorced from its social context, one cannot just evaluate the role of the Web entirely in terms of computer technology. The Web and its impacts in society and culture should be critical examined. This is where Critical Discourse Analysis (CDA) could provide some insights.

2. THE WEB IN DISCOURSE ANALYSIS

What is Critical Discourse Analysis (CDA)? According to Fairclough and Wodak (1997), the following key ideas are dealt with in CDA.

- CDA addresses social problems
- Power relations are discursive
- Discourse Constitutes Society and Culture
- Discourse does ideological work
- Discourse is historical
- The link between text and society is mediated
- Discourse analysis is interpretative and explanatory
- Discourse is a form of social action.

CDA is concerned with social power, which is normally manifested in terms of social control of groups or institutions. This ability presupposes a power base of (privileged access to) scarce social resources, such as force, money, status, fame, knowledge, information, 'culture' or various forms of public discourse and communication. In any social discourse, one can find mixture of enthusiasm, desperation, information, misinformation, use, abuse, advertisement and propaganda; our existence can be enhanced or threatened by different paradigms. We are consciously or unconsciously participants in a discourse which cannot be value-free, being a family, university, health organisation or member of a small remote and isolated village. Some people are victims or fortunate inheritors due to the discourse in which they are brought up and become discourse members. Concepts such as revolution, paradigm, enlightenment, and empowerment are often used to describe the changes from one system into another. Paradigm shift refers to a meaningful change from one alternative to another. The Web could be a tool or a force which creates a paradigm shift. Thus, the Web is seen by many as a powerful tool for teaching and learning.

How innocent is the Web, ideologically? Is the Web value-free from an ideology-loaded discourse? The answer could be 'no' or 'yes', or a mixture of both. Many of us would agree that the Web is only a tool. It is a physical entity, which is subjected to good use or abuse by human beings. Simply, the Web is morally innocent and ideologically neutral. However, the Web is a product of a system or regime, which cannot be divorced from its historical background and functioning. It is 'there' for a social function. It was invented and has been maintained by a professional group or elite for serving their growing needs and reinforcing their images and metaphors of their worldviews. The Web is 'there' because it serves a purpose such as supporting an enterprise or maintaining a system. It carries social norms, expectations and exerts some impacts socially and culturally on the Web discourse, locally and internationally.

Recently, Critical Discourse Analysis has emerged to argue strongly that a discourse can enhance some people and discriminate against others. CDA is a type of discourse analytical research that primarily studies the way social power abuse, dominance and inequality are enacted, reproduced and resisted by text and talk in the social and political context. Thus, CDA advocates take explicit position, and want to understand, expose and ultimately to resist social inequality. The Web is not seen by them as 'innocent'. Its role in a Web discourse is closely tied to a social discourse within a culture or inter-culturally. The concept of emancipation is fundamental to CDA, particularly when one considers the kind of society in which great social imbalance exists: the ruling class, the elite, the oppressor, the powerful and the underdog, the oppressed, the disadvantaged. The three terms 'emancipation, enlightenment and empowerment' are used frequently in CDA to examine critically the power relationship among discourse members.

It is normally accepted that the power of the Internet has increased so rapidly. It is powerful as it can perform huge tasks with its speed. The newly introduced prefix e- such as e-mail, e-commerce, e-trade, e-banking shows clearly the impact of the Internet in modern society. It empowers many institutions to revolutionise their old practices. The Internet and globalisation walk merrily together. However, this is not the way emancipation is perceived from the CDA perspective. It can be seen in terms of disempowerment as the Internet could signal a division between the e-people and those who cannot afford the Internet or those whose culture does not accept or worship the virtual reality. When a highway runs across a village, its culture and environment are no longer the same. Metaphorically, this could apply well to the Internet as a superhighway.

Indoctrination is to fill in the mind of someone with particular ideas or beliefs with uncritical acceptance. It is not always easy to draw a line between indoctrination and education. In a dictatorship country, education is in essence indoctrination as learners are presented with knowledge from only one perspective that is expected to be accepted as 'universal truth'. In a meaningful learning discourse, academic slavery is a hindrance to intellectual development as it reinforces a closed mind rather than an open mind. However, can education be free from coercion and indoctrination?

The challenge by Critical Discourse Analysis to the educational establishment is important for educators because it raises crucial questions regarding certain hegemonic aspects of modernism and by implication how these have affected the meaning and dynamics of present-day teaching and learning. Education is not the process of acquiring new knowledge but fundamentally to make sense of knowledge and even to challenge it. CDA advocates encourage learners to question how the master narratives become constructed and how they influence their views and living experiences. In addition, the regime of knowledge should be challenged as it is 'there' in the curriculum because it is part of power. Power, content, expression and knowledge cannot be easily separated in an educational discourse, as social structures and processes are organised through institutions and practices such as the law, the political system, the church, the family, the education system and the media, each of which is located in and structured by a particular discussive field. Discussive fields consist of competing ways of giving meaning to the world and of organising social institutions and processes. They offer the individual a range of modes of subjectivity. Within a discussive field, for instance, that of law or the family, not all discourses will carry equal weight or power. Some will account for and justify the appropriateness of the status quo. Others will give rise to challenge to existing practices from within or will contest the very basis of current organisation and the selective interests which it represents. Education is about the learners and their internal and external worlds. If education is liberating the learners from fear and dogmatism, the notion of power can be seen as against education. Power is therefore important in conditioning and training because in conditioning and training there is a hierarchy of power relationship between the teacher and the learner. It is fair to say that there has been good progress in changing the power relationship between teachers and learners in education. For example, teaching is no longer passing knowledge from the teacher to the learner. In other words, the transmission model of learning in which teachers are the source of knowledge and learners are its receiver has been challenged by critical thinkers. Constructivism encourages learners to challenge knowledge and treat it as a means for the mind to explore not as the end of learning. Similarly, we have raised issues against establishments. The paradigm shift from instructivism to constructivism has become a great achievement from primary education to tertiary education. However, constructivism is not enough as the task of creating a critical discourse does not lie squarely with teachers and learners.

The Web has provided learners and teachers with an extremely powerful tool for sharing information in courseware. It also brings along problems in a human context. Like any discourses, one can question the value of globalisation of education in which the Web plays an important role. Perelman (1992) expressed a similar sentiment in his book with a provocative title *School's out: Hyperlearning, the new technology, and the end of education*. Postman (1995) demands redefining the value of school in a computer-based education. Clark takes a strong view against multimedia, arguing that media will never influence learning. Like face-to-face teaching, virtual classroom teaching in intercultural education needs to be culturally sensitive as it may create cultural conflicts between course designers, teachers and learners (Mester and Krumm 1999). Factors such as cultural stereotyping, cultural norms in social interaction, learning styles and cultural attitudes to education need to be taken into consideration. Otherwise the superhighway can lead to educational conflict, particularly when the cultural gap between the educational provider and the receiver is very wide. The importance of personal knowledge of the people involved in any open, distance and flexible learning is sometimes lost in a context of 'globalisation' trends and a techno-idolatry often associated with it. And yet all education is a moral activity. It is concerned with people significantly affecting the lives of others and educators have a moral obligation to consider how their individual actions in the teaching/learning nexus might significantly affect the lives of those immersed in it (Davison 1997)

CDA takes seriously the notion of power, or abuse of power, in a discourse, whether it is a school, or a virtual reality environment. One would consider the ways in which Internet power could be abused to affect people's beliefs and actions in the interest of dominant groups, and against the best interests or the will of the others. The abuse can be in different forms such as promotion of violence and norm-violation that hurts others. In this way, dominance of the Web could lead to the illegitimate exercise of power. Recently, we have witnessed demonstrations against 'globalisation' associated with the power control of economic forces.

Different cultures see issues differently and people engage in discussing those issues are culturally constrained. In one culture, talking about sexual behaviour is encouraged in education while in other cultures it is censored or totally banned. A 'virtual classroom' in one cultural context may become a villainous classroom in another. There is a strong belief in Web-based education that teaching is not the process of acquiring new knowledge but fundamentally to make sense of knowledge and even to challenge it. Postmodernism encourages learners to question how the master narratives become constructed and how they influence their thinking and living experience. In addition the regime of knowledge should be challenged as it is 'there' in the curriculum because it is part of power. Social structures and processes are organised through institutions and practices such as the law, the political system, the church, the family, the education system and the media, each of which is located in and structured by a particular discursive field. If all those issues are ignored due to financially driven principles and pure excitement with the magic of the Web, the culturally ill-perceived educational superhighway could lead to ideology imposition and cultural conflicts. It is not always easy to draw a line between imperialism and education.

Due to the enormous popularity of the Web in general and educational Websites in particular, it is important to help students to make appropriate evaluation of the usefulness of the Websites that they encounter in their exploration of the virtual world. Criteria and guidelines based on educational philosophies and screen design principles should be introduced to assist students in their use of Websites. As the Web has gradually permeated education at all levels, students particularly those in primary and secondary education, should be helped to be critical of the Web in their lives. Metaphorically, they should be aware of 'bad wolf' in the virtual reality.

3. CONCLUSION

Power is integrated in 'hegemony'. Class domination, sexism and racism are manifestations of such hegemony, in which the Web demonstrates its magical power. One should not treat the Web as a bad wolf whom we should avoid at any cost: it can be tamed. However, the Web should be closely watched as it can 'misbehave' when it travels across territories, carrying with it hidden traces of hegemony.

REFERENCES

Davison, T. (1997) Creating Moral Dilemmas in Open, distance and Flexible Learning. In *Open, flexible and Distance Learning: Education and Training in the 21 Century*, J. Osborne, D. Roberts and J. Walker (eds.), University of Tasmania, Launceston.

Fairclough, N. L. and Wodak, R. (1997) Critical discourse analysis. In *Discourse As Social Interaction*, T. A. van Dijk (ed.), Sage, London, pp. 258-284.

Mester, A. and Krumm, H. (1999) Culture On-line: Development of a Culturally Supportive Web Environment for Indigenous Australian Students. In *Proceedings of Ed-Media 99,* T. Ottmann and I. Tomek (eds.), Association for the Advancement of Computing in Education Charlotteville, Va, pp. 287-292.

Perelman, L. J. (1992) *School's out: Hyperlearning, the new technology, and the end of education*. William Morrow, New York.

Postman, N. (1995) *The End of Education: Redefining the Value of School.* Alfred A. Knopf, New York.

BIOGRAPHY

Quynh Lê and Thao Lê have undertaken a number of research projects about courseware development, on-line teaching and evaluation of the role of the Web in education. They have developed courseware to support teaching at undergraduate and postgraduate levels. They are the editors of the Internet Journal *Language, Society and Culture.*

38

Activity Theory to Investigate the Implementation of ICTE

Geoff Romeo and Ian Walker
Faculty of Education, Monash University, PO Box 527 Frankston 3199, Australia
geoff.romeo@education.monash.edu.au

Keywords: integration of ICT, primary, research, in-service training, management

Abstract: The purpose of this pilot study was to examine how one primary school implements Information and Communication Technologies in Education (ICTE). The principal, IT coordinator and two class teachers were interviewed to determine their views of how ICTE was being implemented. Activity theory was used as a means of analysing the data. The findings suggest a range of views about ICTE existed within the school. The implications suggest it is important for schools to recognise the different views of ICTE existing in their communities and to take cognisance of this when, for example, planning professional development. The study also suggests that more sensitive analytical approaches need to be developed to enable more critical evaluations of ICTE's implementation within schools to be made.

1. INTRODUCTION

Computers have been with us for just over fifty years and what has emerged in that time is a number of different, yet interrelated, perspectives on the use of information and communication technologies in education (Roblyer and Edwards 2000). Two of these perspectives in particular are worth highlighting in this discussion. The first perspective focuses on the computer as a mechanism by which to deliver information. This view is very much influenced by behaviourist learning theories and has led, for example, to the development of computer-assisted instruction (CAI), computer-based training (CBT) and technology training. The second and contrasting perspective focuses on the use of computers as a system to enhance teaching and learning. This view, often referred to as computers in education, very much influenced by the ideas of constructivism, is about exploiting technology's versatility and uniqueness to help the teacher establish powerful environments for children's learning across the curriculum. In the Australian context the latter view has tended to predominate, with the development of computer literacy and awareness as a subordinate objective. In most cases it is not until the latter years of high school that more formal information technology subjects are introduced.

During the 1990s significant events happened that further influenced how educators viewed the use of computers in the classroom. Two of these events in particular relate to Victorian schools. The first was the development of Intranets and the Internet, especially the World Wide Web (WWW), which allowed users to view multimedia via a browser such as Netscape or Internet Explorer. The second event was the commitment, by successive governments, to the development of technology in schools for administrative and curriculum purposes. This commitment has resulted in the expenditure of millions of dollars and the development of an astonishing array of projects and initiatives. This systemic commitment to the development of technology for administrative and curriculum purposes has had an enormous impact on schools. The use of computers in education or what is now more commonly referred to as information and communication technologies in education (ICTE) is now recognised as a critical aspect of a schools' teaching and learning program and consumes a considerable slice of a school's budget.

Increasingly, teachers, administrators, parents, education departments and governments are asking whether the return on the investment has been worthwhile. Searching for the answer to this question is difficult. The difficulty lies in how to judge the effectiveness of computer use in schools. A response to the question, favoured by some, is to count things (see for example the Department of Education, Employment and Training in Victoria 2000). But does this give a clear enough picture of what is actually happening in classrooms and does it reflect the reality of teacher attitudes towards the technology? For a deeper, more meaningful depiction of the current scene, further analysis is needed and powerful analytical tools must be employed. The purpose of this study was to investigate the potential of such a tool.

2. ACTIVITY THEORY AS AN ANALYTICAL TOOL

One way of understanding the introduction, development and maintenance of ICTE is to see it as a socially constructed practice in much the same way as researchers and practitioners view other educational concepts. The effect of seeing ICTE in this way is that it enables us to consider how those involved in the implementation process construe the activity. A way of doing this was to capture, through interviews, how those working in the same school viewed their own and others' positions relative to the development of ICTE.

We sought a theoretical perspective that would help us in our analysis of people's comments and, for this purpose, selected an approach that is referred to as activity theory. It is necessary to note that this choice was made to assist us in analysing the interview data we had planned to obtain rather than providing us with any meta-theory with explanative or predictive capabilities (see also Nardi 1996). In this way ICTE implementation in a school can be treated as a human endeavour that, in a Vygotskian sense, is mediated by social-cultural-historical tools and practices (Vygotsky 1978). The work of Engestrom in particular was taken as a useful means of applying the notion of activity theory to our investigation (see Engestrom et al. 1999, Engestrom 1993). Our choice of activity theory as an analytical device provides us with a holistic and systemic view of human engagement, in this case in ICTE implementation.

3. METHODOLOGY

The school used in this study is one of the largest government primary schools in the state of Victoria with over 800 pupils and 40 staff. This school was selected because of its reputation for innovative use of ICTE. On the surface it would appear to meet many of the criteria identified in, for example, EkinSmyth (1998) in order to determine effective ICTE implementation. We intended to seek volunteers to participate in this pilot study. The principal, however, selected three staff members: the current IT coordinator, a reluctant teacher, and a recent graduate, as well as himself to participate. Each interview, lasting approximately forty minutes, was audio taped.

4. ANALYSIS

The major elements of activity theory – subject, instruments, object and outcome, rules, community, and division of labour – were used to organise the interview data. This organisation was then used to identify major commonalities and contradictions amongst participants' perceptions of ICTE in their school. In order to preserve a sense of character in the analysis we present it in terms of how each participant saw ICTE being implemented.

We summarise each participant's views in diagrams (after Engestrom 1987) accompanied by a brief discussion of the major aspects of how he or she constructs ICTE.

4.1 Kevin: the principal

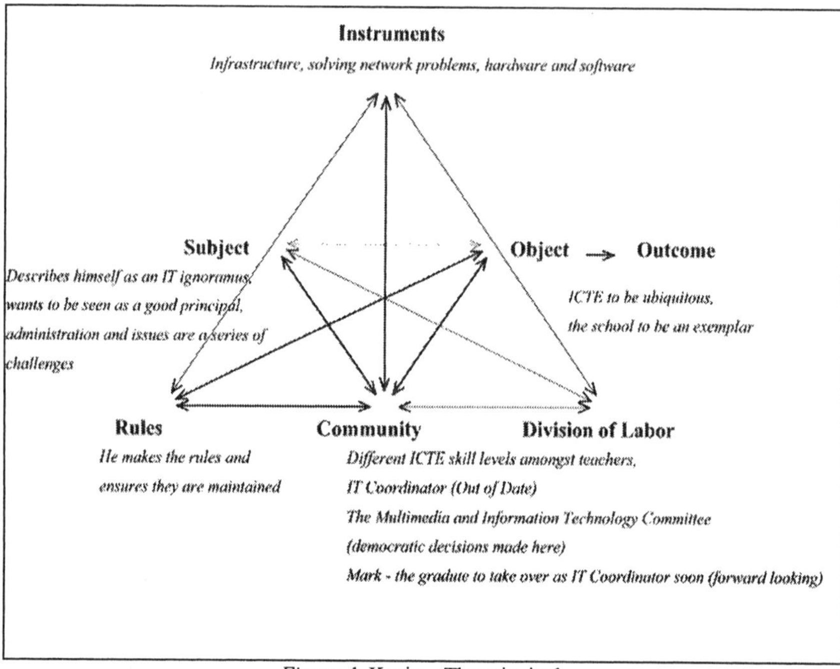

Figure 1. Kevin – The principal

Kevin is the inaugural principal of the school who describes himself as an "IT ignoramus". His comments about himself merge very quickly into how he saw the school's mission as essentially one of serving the wider community. The word "challenge" appears frequently in his description where, for example, the implementation of ICTE is seen merely as one of a number of competing challenges facing a principal of a large school. Kevin also frequently talks about these challenges in terms of how others, and in particular, the community, judge the school and, perhaps more importantly, himself.

The main object that Kevin identifies for ICTE is that it should be considered, among other things, as being embedded within normal classroom activities; " we don't see IT as a separate entity, we want it to be used right through the eight KLAs" [Key Learning Areas]. For Kevin the ideal classroom is one where the teacher "is flexible enough to work on many different things [including IT activities] at any given time, so the computers in the room would be ticking away...". To achieve this object Kevin, despite obviously being aware of computer software and the notion of computers being integrated across the curriculum, focuses on getting the infrastructure and related hardware working. This is illustrated, for example, in his final words about the school's intranet.

> "...not working all the time (and) I've got to get the technician to a point where the whole thing is compatible and it works... once these problems are solved and this new magic, super duper file server is in place, if we can speed up the system...then that's terrific, so that's what we want, ease of use...but from an administrative point of view it doesn't work as well as 300,000 dollars worth of equipment should work, by my way of thinking".

Given that it would appear the school was misled a number of years ago about appropriate network architecture for its computers, the emphasis by the principal on infrastructure difficulties is not surprising.

When asked about the members of the school community who were involved with ICTE, Kevin highlights, as did all participants, the different level of ICTE skills held by teachers including some of the key players. He provides this, along with infrastructure difficulties, as an explanation of why ICTE has not gone as far as it might have in the school. As far as the principal is concerned, for example, the current IT coordinator is out-of-date, the graduate teacher is more au fait with current technology and in a better position to move ICTE in the school forward.

Another community element recognised by all participants in the implementation of ICTE is the Multimedia Information and Technology Committee (MMIT). Listening to Kevin one would think that this committee provides a democratic opportunity for staff to be involved in the decision-making processes regarding ICTE. Subsequent interviews suggest that others do not share this view.

The rules by which an organisation such as a school goes about its work is a further revealing feature of an analysis based on activity theory. It is in the principal's comments about the roles and responsibilities of his staff in terms of ICTE that insight into the rules governing work in the school become most apparent. As with other issues facing the school, the development of ICTE is very much under the control of one person – the principal. Kevin, for example, comments: "I sort of insist on software being purchased across the various KLAs and at the moment I've got the brakes on the system". The other participants reinforce this view of the principal's control over the school's activity in ICTE, and other areas.

4.2 Peg: the *reluctant* teacher

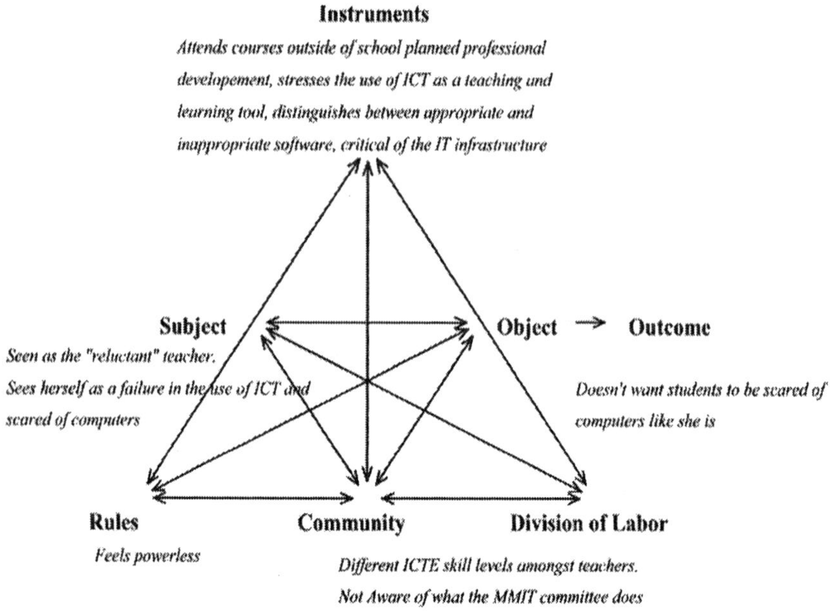

Figure 2. Peg – The 'reluctant' teacher

Early in her interview Peg, a current year 4 teacher, remarks that the principal had construed her as "the reluctant staff member". As the interview progressed, however, it becomes apparent that this is an incorrect assessment. Peg consistently describes herself as being "basically scared of computers", something she traces to a lack of the technology in her background. However what emerges is that this fear, rather than acting as a deterrent to her engaging with computers, acts as a very strong motivator. It accounts for her pursuit of knowledge about information technology through attendance at a number of short courses offered by both private companies and TAFE (Technical and Further Education) colleges; something one is not likely to find in a *reluctant* teacher. What is particularly significant here is that Peg chooses to go outside of the school and its professional development agenda to gain this experience. Peg's declared fear of computers also leads her to be especially cognisant of the needs of the children she teaches. For example:

"I think I'm basically scared of computers and because I'm scared of them I don't want them [the children] to be like that because they are going to be much more into the use of computer technology in their lives than what I am".

In terms of the mediating instruments on which Peg focuses her comments, there is an interesting contrast between these and comments made by both the principal and the IT coordinator. Whereas these two participants highlight the infrastructure in the development of ICTE, Peg stresses the use of technology as a tool for teaching and learning. This represents an important difference in how participants think about ICTE: whether the focus is on the technology itself or on its application in a teaching and learning environment. Peg, for example, acknowledges the need for professional development but considers that what the school currently offers is not related to teaching and learning and not sufficiently practical. Peg also believes that much of the software used by children is inappropriate in that it does not enable them to easily obtain information for specific projects. Clearly Peg is judging the instruments in this activity differently to the principal (and to the IT coordinator).

The interview shows Peg to be someone who is easily frustrated by what appears to be an unstable infrastructure. She is repeatedly critical of the system: "our computer lab is less than efficient and often the computers don't work or one half works and the other half doesn't work, so it becomes a very frustrating exercise". It may well be these criticisms that lead Kevin, who wants his school to be judged as successful, to see her as 'reluctant'.

This interview reveals much of the complexity of how individuals see themselves and others in relation to developments, such as ICTE, occurring within their school.

4.3 John: the IT coordinator

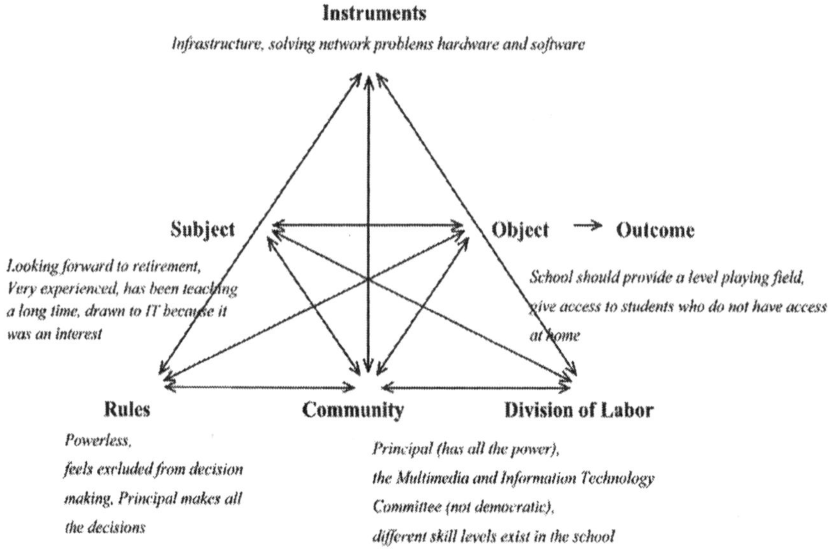

Figure 3. John – The IT coordinator

John, who has been teaching for over 30 years and is looking forward to his retirement next year, is the IT coordinator at the school. His role in this position is seemingly one based on “just an interest that I have picked up” and John has not considered it necessary to pursue formal qualifications specific to ICTE. Whereas Peg saw the importance of ICTE as ensuring that children feel unthreatened by computers, John sees ICTE more in terms of creating a level playing field so that children without computer access at home are not disadvantaged.

Like the principal, John focuses much of his discussion on the infrastructure in the school highlighting the fact that it is not working efficiently. Throughout John's interview there appears to be a note of disenchantment with many aspects of ICTE in the school and a feeling of helplessness in terms of his involvement in the decision-making process. John, for example, cites the MMIT committee as a means by which the administration establishes what appears to be a democratic process on the one hand, while effectively controlling the important decisions on the other. He is keen to pass blame for the system not working, therefore, to a principal who is keen to control, but who “really doesn't understand computers and doesn't use them”.

Although John is the designated IT coordinator it would seem that many decisions about computers are being made by the principal, without his input. We picked up a sense that both John and, indeed, the principal are waiting for John's retirement. In fact, during our interview with the principal, it was clear that he had already decided on John's replacement – Mark, "a promising young teacher".

4.4 Mark: the recent graduate

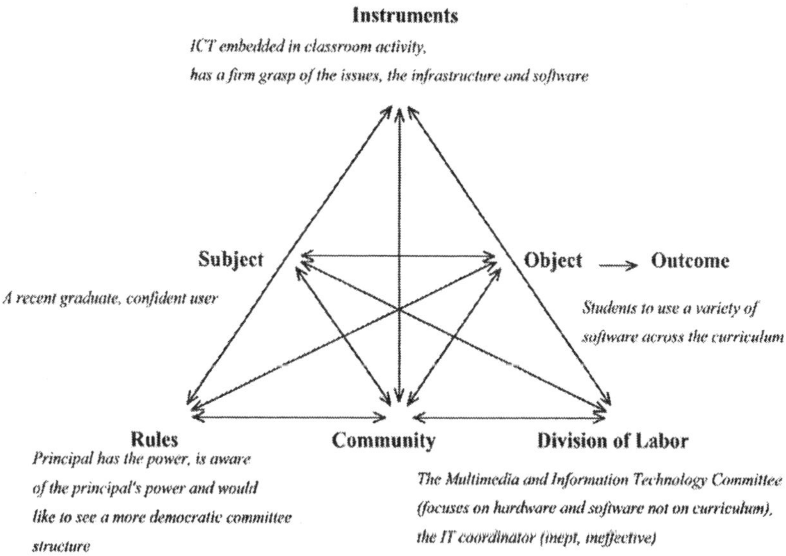

Figure 4. Mark – The recent graduate

Mark is a recent graduate who has been teaching at the school for over two years. He is currently teaching children in their first year of schooling. Unlike Peg, Mark has no fear of computers. He has not completed any formal courses in information technology; other than as components of his journalism and teaching qualifications, but computers have always been a part of his life. "In primary school we had the old Commodore 64s and…I've never been afraid of them and I know where they're coming from in a lot of ways". Like Peg, Mark sees ICTE best being embedded within classroom activities thereby enabling children to use it for a variety of purposes across the curriculum. For these reasons Mark is happy to experiment with new software. At the same time he believes he has a grasp of the infrastructure and hardware issues in the school and feels confident in talking about them.

During a discussion of the MMIT committee Mark's comments resonate with those made by both Peg and John regarding this committee's focus on hardware. He also talks about the lack of genuine engagement many teachers like Peg have with the committee. Whereas John attributes this lack of engagement to the principal's control and lack of knowledge, Mark sees the disengagement more in terms of the fact that the committee focuses on the wrong issues: "...a lot of the meeting is devoted to the technology that is coming in or the hardware rather than the programs that are being done...a lot of teachers don't know enough about the hardware".

5. CONCLUSIONS

From the analysis it is clear that there is not a shared vision about how ICTE should be implemented in the school used in the study. For Kevin and John the focus of their thinking is extensively about cables, servers and boxes on desks. For Peg and, to a lesser extent Mark, it is about teaching and learning. As the four people interviewed for this project are key players in the implementation of ICTE in this school, one could assume that the lack of a shared vision is indicative of the staff's mindset. This lack of a shared view of what ICTE should be is problematic: without consensus on the key issues stagnation and waste are likely and, according to Kevin, a reality – "we haven't got our 300000 dollars worth".

The two major factors impeding the development of a shared vision about ICTE for this school are: the decision-making process and, how this in turn is tied to ownership of ICTE and its implementation. It is worth briefly examining each of these factors.

Throughout each interview, the principal's effective control of all of the school's activities, including ICTE, is apparent. Although it is understandable that a school principal takes ultimate responsibility for these activities, in many schools and in many areas of activity such responsibility is delegated to other members of the school community. In the case of ICTE in this school, however, it would seem that the delegation is superficial and the principal effectively maintains complete control of the important decisions that need to be made regarding its implementation. There is, for example, a designated IT coordinator and a committee (MMIT) seemingly established to encourage communication among teachers regarding decisions about ICTE. However, it is clearly the principal who controls the MMIT committee and has managed to marginalise the current IT coordinator by denying him serious budgetary responsibility, a point reinforced by Mark.

The strength of the principal's control over the decision-making process contributes to a lack of shared ownership of the ICTE process in the school.

For John this results in cynicism, resentment and resignation. For Peg it results in disengagement and for Mark in opportunity. It would seem that the machinations of the MMIT committee also contribute to a sense of alienation. Teachers like Peg are disenfranchised from the workings and discussions of the MMIT; they do not know what the committee discusses, what its role is, they never get any feedback about its decisions and they are not asked to contribute to the committee's deliberations.

6. IMPLICATIONS

A number of implications emerge from this pilot study. First, in an attempt to appreciate how a school goes about implementing policies such as ICTE, it is useful to locate the implementation within the broader milieu of the school and, in particular, the way decisions are made. Second, it is important for schools to recognise and cater for the range of views of ICTE held by members of its community. As there is a variety of ways teachers, for example, construct information technology and its relation to children's learning, it is necessary, for effective implementation to occur, to know what these constructions highlight – whether, for example, is it computer infrastructure or its application to teaching and learning that most interests individuals. Schools need to consider the different constructions of ICTE when planning effective professional development activities.

Thirdly, the criteria commonly used to evaluate the level of ICTE implementation taking place within a school need to be developed, so that they become more sensitive to the subtleties of policy and program implementation and to people's attitudes towards it. Our pilot study, for instance, shows that although one school would satisfy a number of indicators suggested in the literature as a means of determining the extent to which ICTE is being effectively implemented, closer examination reveals greater complexity and contradiction.

Finally, it has been stated throughout this paper that this was a pilot study. We have found both the means of obtaining data and its analysis used in the study to be valuable in uncovering something of the richness of life in a school: in this case, the implementation of ICTE. We recommend, therefore, that larger studies be undertaken in a variety of educational settings to obtain a greater sense of how different schools are implementing ICTE and the factors that account for its success or failure.

REFERENCES

Department of Employment, Education and Training, Victoria (2000) *Learning Technologies Projects, Products and Services.* [http://www.sofweb.vic.edu.au/itb/]16.10.00.

(DEET) Department of Employment, Education and Training (1988) *Teachers Learning: Improving Australian Schools Through Inservice Teacher Training and Development.* Australian Government Publishing Service, Canberra, Australia.

EkinSmyth, C. (ed) (1998) *Rethinking Learning and Teaching: The Navigator Schools' Experience.* Report 1, July 1998, Melbourne, Community Information Service, Department of Education, Victoria.

Engestrom, Y. et al. (1999) *Perspectives on Activity Theory.* Cambridge, UK, Cambridge University Press.

Engestrom, Y. (1993) Developmental Studies of Work as a Test Bench of Activity Theory: The case of primary medical care practice. In *Understanding Practice*, S. Chaiklin and J. Lave (eds.), Cambridge, UK, Cambridge University Press.

Engestrom, Y. (1987) *Learning by Expanding: An Activity-Theoretical Approach to developmental Research*, Helsinki, Orieta-Konsultit.

Fullan, M. and Hargreaves, A. (1990) *What's Worth Fighting For? Working Together For Your School.* Australian Council for Educational Administration Inc. Hawthorn, Victoria, Australia.

Nardi, B. (1996) *Context and Consciousness: Activity Theory and Human – Computer Interaction.* Cambridge, Massachusetts, MIT Press.

Roblyer, M. D. and Edwards J. (2000) *Integrating educational technology into teaching.* Upper Saddle River, N. J. Merrill.

Vygotsky, L. (1978) *Mind in Society: The Development of Higher Psychological Processes.* Cambridge, Massachusetts, Harvard University Press.

BIOGRAPHY

Geoff Romeo and Ian Walker are teacher educators and researchers working at Monash University. Dr Walker's research interests include parental involvement; children's literacy; literacy practices in the workplace; teaching practicum and more recently the use of technology in schools. Dr Romeo's research interests include the use of information and communication technology in education to improve teaching and learning, the development of primary curriculum, action research and primary education in general. Dr Romeo is president of the *Computing in Education Group of Victoria* and a board member of the *Australian Council for Computers in Education*.

PART FOUR

TEACHING MATHS

39

SelMa – New Perspectives for Self-guided Learning in Teaching Mathematics at Senior High School Level

Wolfgang Weber and Kristine Fankhänel
Landesinstitut für Schule und Weiterbildung, Paradieser Weg 64, D-59494 Soest, Germany
wolfgang.weber@mail.lsw.nrw.de

Keywords: classroom teaching, curriculum change, learner-centred learning, open flexible learning, secondary education

Abstract: How can new media make the teaching and learning of mathematics more exciting? How can school prepare for lifelong, self-guided learning? It is questions like these that the project 'SelMa – Selbstlernen in der gymnasialen Oberstufe – Mathematik', which is supported by the Federal Republic of Germany and the state of North Rhine-Westphalia, addresses. The aim of the project is to show ideas and possibilities for the ways in which mathematics can be taught if student activity and self-guided learning are supported, and how the idea of self-guided learning in general can be integrated into daily school routine. SelMa is run in close co-operation with schools.

1. GENERAL INFORMATION

The pilot project 'Selbstlernen in der gymnasialen Oberstufe – Mathematik' (SelMa) is one of 25 pilot projects taking place in Germany within the framework of 'Systematic Incorporation of Media, Information and Communications Technologies in Teaching and Learning Processes' (SEMIK). The aim of the SEMIK programme is to support the permanent integration of new media in all types of schools and at all levels. SEMIK includes various projects that make use of new information and communications technology. New media are to be integrated in teaching and learning processes and to help to put into practice innovative concepts of teaching. The main focus is upon problem-orientated, self-guided and co-operative learning.

The four-year SelMa project, which is funded by the federal government and by the state of North-Rhine-Westphalia, started on February 1, 1999.

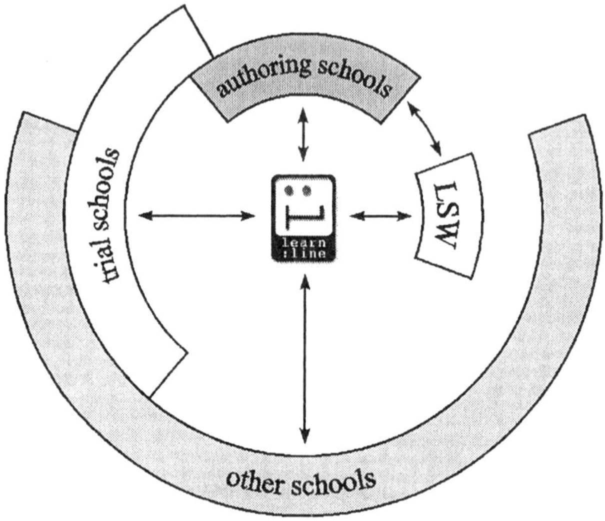

Figure 1. The SelMa structure

SelMa is monitored by the LSW (State Institute for School and Further Education). The aim of the pilot project is to show what teaching mathematics at senior high school level can look like if self-guided learning and activities are supported by the use of new media. Special importance is placed on integrating aspects of self-guided learning in everyday teaching.

Learning, mathematics and the use of new media – these are the pillars on which SelMa stands. Special emphasis is placed on the delivery of the new curriculum for mathematics, which focuses upon aspects of self-guided learning and must be integrated in everyday school life. The purpose of SelMa is to give teachers orientation and impulses for their own teaching.

Scenarios and materials for self-guided learning phases in teaching mathematics at senior high school level are being developed in five ‘authoring schools’. These learning arrangements are accessible for teachers for trial purposes on the North-Rhine-Westphalian web-site ‘learn:line’. learn:line provides an information, communication and co-operation environment for this purpose. Pupils can contact a ‘teacher on demand’. learn:line also encourages the exchange of information and experiences between teachers, and initiates discussions with experts.

The development of materials by the authoring schools is to take place in an 'open workshop', so that other schools can also try out them at an early stage and regularly report on their own experiences. A special role is played by ten 'trial schools' which systematically try out and evaluate the materials which have been developed to see whether they work in everyday usage. Their feedback will be incorporated in the on-going development of materials.

Furthermore, authoring and trial schools are to disseminate their practice so that networks of schools can be created in the different regions and the materials on learn:line can be further developed. In this way the scenarios will be used in an increasing number of schools. Publishers are to be included at an early stage. This is expected to lead to high-quality (offline and online) media which will support phases of self-guided learning in teaching mathematics.

2. IMPORTANT ISSUES

Based on the focus upon learning, mathematics and use of media, the pilot project addresses various issues. The work of the authoring schools is monitored by academics and experts. Some of the aspects of methodology that are pertinent to learning/self-guided learning are:

- Which topics are suitable for phases of self-guided learning?
- How must the topics be presented?
- What different kinds of support do teachers need?
- What different kinds of support do pupils need?
- How can progress in learning be monitored?
- How do pupils acquire and use their knowledge?
- How can knowledge be consolidated by means of intelligent practice?
- How are media used by pupils?
- How does the use of media improve the quality of learning?
- What off-line and on-line materials must be provided?
- How can communication between the pupils be encouraged?
- What kinds of support are requested?
- What role does a 'teacher on demand' play?
- What opportunities for co-operation exist?

These questions show the broad range of issues the SelMa pilot project addresses. The measures taken to qualify teachers so that they can profitably incorporate both the individual learning process and the use of new media in their teaching should not be forgotten, either.

3. WEB-SITE

The current state of affairs can be viewed on-line on the NRW educational web-site learn:line (http://www.learn-line.nrw.de/angebote/selma/index.htm). The web-site offers a wide range of opportunities for information, communication and co-operation in the fields of self-guided learning, mathematics and use of media.

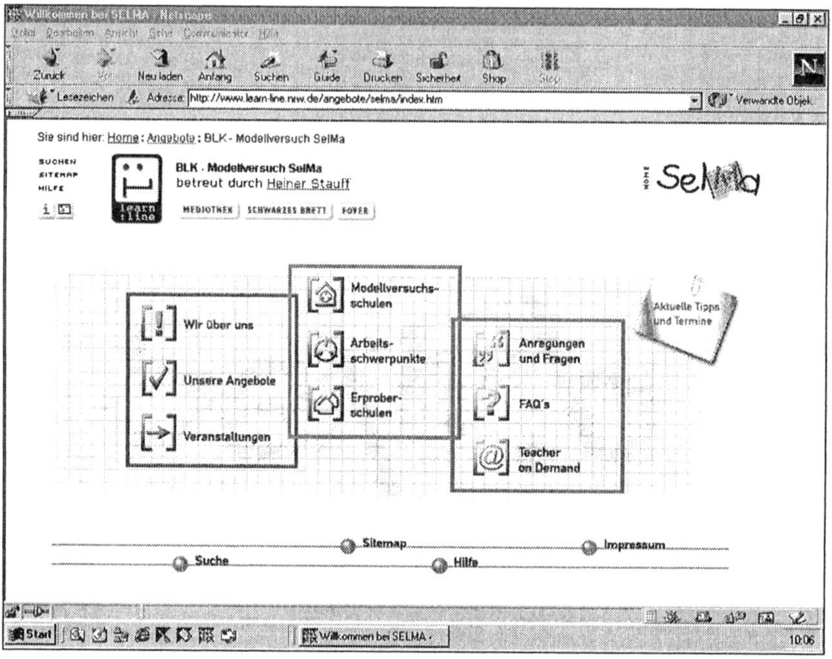

Figure 2. Home page of the SelMa web-site

The contents of the SelMa web-site are arranged in three blocks which are marked in different colours.

The left-hand 'red block' contains information which the SelMa-LSW team has compiled. This is where general information can be found on the pilot project as well as material on the topics of self-guided learning, mathematics, use of media. In addition to transcripts of talks, this section also offers references to literature, software and internet addresses.

The right-hand 'green block' offers a wide range of opportunities for communication which are supported by the 'teacher on demand'. For questions and suggestions relating to mathematics and self-guided learning users can have a look at the FAQ section. Of course, users can also leave their own messages on a message board.

The 'blue block' in the centre is linked to information about and from SelMa schools. This is where the pilot schools present information on themselves and their projects. Up to now five authoring schools have developed projects for Year 11, and additional projects will be following soon.

4. PROJECTS

The self-guided learning scenarios and materials which are being developed by the authoring schools are at the core of the SelMa. Various models of self-guided learning have been used as a basis. Materials for use in self-guided learning centres, collections of exercises for use in everyday teaching, and suggestions and materials for learning at stations using different approaches are included. Each project is accompanied by a project description.

4.1 Materials for the independent learning centre

The work of a SelMa authoring team is closely related to further developments in their school. In an independent learning centre, pupils work on their own, on mathematical topics specified in the curriculum for Years 11 and 12. The material which is prepared for the independent learning centre consists of courses on the one hand and of collections of problems on the other. Graded aids for learning relating to the pupils' existing knowledge provide both food for thought and initial approaches towards solving the problems. Suggested solutions to the problems allow the learners to check the progress they are making. The computer provides opportunities for simulation and visualisation of mathematics.

Pupils normally meet in groups of two or three in the independent learning centre and discuss individual problems. The aim is for the individual pupil to establish as precisely as possible those areas where practice is most necessary. Under no circumstances must the pupil's personal speed of learning suffer from group pressure.

In practice it has been found that pupils can contribute a lot of help and suggestions when it comes to designing the materials. In further projects, pupils who are already experienced in using the materials should be involved even more closely as co-designers.

4.2 Group jigsaw puzzle

At one of the other authoring schools, a teaching unit on optimisation has been developed and tested. It focuses on mathematical modelling and working on problems involving extreme values. The teaching unit is divided into the following phases:

- Instructory phase
- First independent learning phase: partner work
- Second independent learning phase: learning by teaching (group jigsaw puzzle)
- Presentation and reflection phase.

What is particularly interesting is the approach of using group jigsaw puzzles for independent learning. The first phase involves individual familiarity with the mathematical problems, as far as possible. In subsequent phases, it is up to each individual pupil to pass on their knowledge and, on the other hand, the group aim is to ensure that at the end of the process all pupils involved have acquired the relevant knowledge.

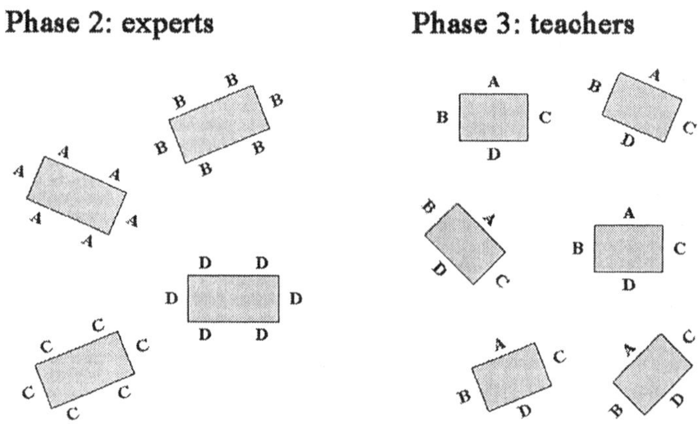

Figure 3. Phases 2 and 3 of the group jigsaw puzzle

In an initial phase, pupils work on the topic on an individual basis. In the second phase, a group of experts is set up. Any matters which are unclear are discussed and clarified. This is how the transfer of the knowledge is prepared. In the third phase, new groups are formed. Each pupil now teaches the topic which he or she has prepared. A computer algebra system allows pupils to work on new fields of teaching mathematics, whether in groups or with a partner. The work rate varies from one group of partners to another. The lessons plan has been designed for Year 11.

It has been shown that the teacher's main function is to initiate the individual learning process, to explain what needs to be done, to organise the formation of groups and to ensure that the time schedule is kept to. The degree of teacher control is reduced increasingly, and the pupils take on responsibility for their own learning process.

4.3 The collection of exercises

Another authoring team has developed a 'linear optimisation' learning plan for co-ordinate geometry. Through the learning plan pupils study a mathematical optimisation procedure and at the same time revise the concept of linear functions they were taught at lower secondary level. The learning plan links new material with what the pupils already know in order to guide them step by step towards assuming responsibility for their own learning. It is important that the problems dealt with are relevant to real life situations in order to emphasise the relevance of mathematics in general to real life situation.

In this project, the interests, speed of work and the different learning paths of the pupils are accommodated. Pupils are not told to work through the materials in a given way. They practise the meaningful use of graph plotters and computer algebra systems, which visualise mathematical concepts. It has become clear that the use of computer algebra systems does not always have the desired effect, especially in the case of the weaker pupils, i.e. supporting their confidence in their own solutions and calculations through graphic representation and through easy ways of checking their own work. It has been found, in particular, that many pupils have very little experience with more open and complex problems when they first enter the senior high school level. They seem to have rarely been working on mathematics problems in groups. Obviously, in the past, they have hardly given any thought at all to their own learning strategies, to how they take in knowledge and solve problems.

4.4 Learning at stations

The project 'Learning stations: higher order quadratic functions' focuses on the revision and development of aspects of co-ordinate geometry, and pupils also study new subject matter individually. Here, too, the importance of problems relevant to real life situation is stressed. In this project, individual learning is particularly supported by having pupils study materials at different learning stations. The complete learning circle consists of 21 stations, which are assigned to four thematic areas. The stations are set up in such a way that different background levels of learning, different speeds of learning and working, and different needs in terms of working individually, in pairs or in groups, are accommodated.

There are compulsory and optional stations. To help pupils find their way, they are given a 'docket' which lists all the stations (number; title; topic; compulsory or additional station; individual, pair or group work). Different media are used at different stations, e.g. the Derive computer algebra system, or the TI-89 calculator (which can show graphs), but also worksheets or index cards. The tasks are usually activity-orientated, such as a jigsaw puzzle or a physics experiment. Teaching covers 6 to 8 hours, which take place at the stations using different media. The main function of the teacher here is that of an advisor and co-ordinator. The authoring team has found that the opportunity for and necessity of pupils checking their own work and taking their own decisions as to which station to use has increased the responsibility they take for their own learning and their awareness of their own strengths and weaknesses. The difficulties which have been found to occur, when this type of teaching was used more frequently, lie in the extremely time-consuming setting up of the individual stations and the organisational problem of setting up a suitable room in the school for a longer period of time. However, putting up the problems in HTML form may have solved the first problem to a great extent.

5. LEARNING DIARIES

In the pilot project pupils gain experience with keeping diaries. One authoring school has already gained experiences with regard to the use of personal learning diaries as a supplementary method in teaching mathematics at senior high school level. Compared with team-related learning diary, this type has demonstrated two strengths. On the one hand, pupils continuously reflect on their progress in terms of the subject matter, and on the other hand, this method allows very personal diary entries about the pupil's progress in learning – provided the learning diary is read only by the teacher.

In an introductory session, during which the pupils were also given a corresponding leaflet, it was explained to them that the learning diary should contain all the important aspects of the lessons in condensed form and, in each case, the pupil's reflections on his or her own learning process. After each three-months period, the learning diary was assessed by the teacher and formed part of the general assessment of the pupil's performance in class. During the first semester of the school year the keeping of the diary was compulsory, in the second semester it was voluntary. Almost half of the class made use of this method in order to monitor their own progress. The web-site within learn:line presents and documents 25 exemplars from diaries in the six fields of reflections on lessons, aha-effects, individual explanations, self-assessment, analyses of mistakes, and further issues.

So far experiences have shown that the keeping of a learning diary has a permanent and positive effect on the learning process in mathematics at senior high school level if pupils accept this method. We therefore recommend leaving the decision to the pupils. The pupils clearly pay more attention to the learning process, try to answer questions immediately (rather than waiting until the last possible minute before the test), and are far more aware of their own strengths and weaknesses when studying mathematics.

The personal learning diary encourages pupils to reflect more on their own learning strategies. Without exception, pupils who had been using this method for some time gradually displayed more stable and better performance in mathematics compared to that at the beginning of the school year. The learning diary supports comprehending and solving mathematical problems. It increases medium and long-term retention and can relatively easily be incorporated in normal everyday teaching.

6. SYSTEMATIC TRIAL AND EVALUATION

Experiences from SelMa so far have been based primarily on the work done by the authoring schools. Teachers who have developed the methods and materials have tried them out in their own lessons, as well as other teachers in the same schools have been used them in other courses.

One aspect of particular interest to the pilot project is how the knowledge and experiences from the authoring schools can be disseminated to other schools. The results have therefore been documented and made available to all schools via the SelMa web-site within learn:line. In this way, schools that are interested can profit immediately from the work that has been done. Furthermore, it is one objective of the pilot project to identify the pre-conditions for effective dissemination.

Therefore trial schools have been included in the pilot project. It is their task to try out and evaluate systematically the methods and materials that have been developed. The knowledge and experiences gained from these trials will be incorporated in subsequent developments. The trial schools exchange information with the authoring schools.

In-service teacher training has already been recognised as one major factor. On the one hand, teacher training takes place 'face to face' in meetings, and on the other hand, issues of whether or how in-service training can be supported by ICT, in particular by the NRW web-site learn:line, are also addressed within the pilot project.

7. FUTURE PROSPECTS

Initial projects for Year 11 have now been developed. All the schools involved are highly interested in further exemplars and materials – in particular with regard to topics which have been newly included in the senior high school curriculum. It is here, in particular, that they see a good opportunity to include new methods and materials. The pilot project must address the issue of how other schools can be integrated. The experiences made with the trial schools are pertinent to this in particular. One has to think about how the present groups of schools can be developed into larger networks of schools and how such networks can be supported both effectively and efficiently. Another issue that needs to be addressed is how the prototypes of off-line media and on-line materials developed within the pilot project can be made available to schools outside the project. The aim is to co-operate closely with producers and publishers of media. It is hoped that thus the prototypes can be developed and distributed further in a more efficient and effective way.

REFERENCES

Mandl, H. et al. (1998) *Gutachten zum BLK-Programm: Systematische Einbeziehung von Medien, Informations- und Kommunikationstechnologien.* Forschungsbericht Nr. 93, Ludwig-Maximilians-Universität, München.

BIOGRAPHIES

Since 1990 Wolfgang Weber has been working in the Advisory Centre for New Technologies at the State Institute for Schools and Further Education of North-Rhine-Westfalia, Germany, as a manager of several projects in the field of new media in education, and Head of Centre.

Kristine Fankhänel has been working in the fields CBT, authoring systems, hypermedia and multimedia, and the internet. Since 1999 she has been working at the State Institute for Schools and Further Education of North-Rhine-Westfalia, Germany, and coordinates the project 'Self-guided Learning in Teaching Mathematics at Senior High School Level' (SelMa).

Networking the Learner in Professional Development

A Study of Teachers' Use of math•ed•ology™

Gary G. Bitter and Brandt W. Pryor
Educational Technology, Arizona State University, Tempe, AZ 85287-0908, US
bitter@asu.edu
Educational Leadership, Lamar University, Beaumont, TX, 77710, US

Keywords: distance learning, teaching methods, teacher training, multimedia, research

Abstract The 25-module math•ed•ology™ program was created to help primary (grades K-5) teachers in the United States learn and implement the teaching standards of the National Council of Teachers of Mathematics. This study of teachers' use of the program's first completed module suggests that an important amount of learning can occur in just under four hours of program use. Teachers gained knowledge of the teaching standards, and ability to implement them. Differences between elementary and secondary teachers' responses were noticeable, although less than expected, suggesting that the K-5 program offers a useful base for a similar program for secondary teachers (grades 6-12).

1. GOALS

This mixed method study had two goals: (a) summatively evaluate a program for helping primary teachers understand and implement national teaching standards K-12, and (b) formatively investigate ways in which the program should be changed to accommodate the preferences of secondary teachers, for a similar program to be developed for their grade levels. Building on an earlier investigation of teacher use of the program's pilot (Bitter and Pryor 1999) this exploratory study examined use of an interactive multimedia program, with video of classroom instruction, by 39 in-service teachers (K-12).

2. BACKGROUND TO STUDY

There is evidence that the U.S. National Council of Teachers of Mathematics (NCTM) standards for teaching are not being implemented (Ball 1993), and that typical in-service is ineffective at long term change of teaching behaviour (Ball 1996, Darling-Hammond 1994, Lieberman 1995). In-service teachers in the U.S. value opportunities to observe other teachers in practice, even more so than formal coursework (Sowell et al. 1995). But there are numerous limitations to observation, including the lack of easily available models of standards-based instruction (Ball 1990). Videotape offers a more feasible alternative without loss of effectiveness (Winitzky and Arends 1991), but Goldman and Barron (1990) found its linearity too inflexible for instruction. Interactive multimedia that includes video of standards-based classroom instruction, presents numerous advantages over these other means of observing, and studies have shown the effectiveness of interactive video in teacher education (e.g., Bitter 1993). The National Science Foundation funded the development of math•ed•ology™, an interactive multimedia program for professional development in mathematics education, currently available on the web or on CD-ROM [http://www.thejournal.com].

3. METHOD

3.1 Subjects

Subjects were 39 in-service teachers from the Phoenix, Arizona Metropolitan area, who were enrolled in two graduate classes at Northern Arizona University (NAU), ECI 675 Curriculum and Instruction, and EDF 670 Philosophy of Education. (NAU offers graduate coursework state-wide.) Subjects used the program over a four-hour period, as a part of class requirements. They represented all grades, K-12, and ranged from 1 to 17 years of teaching experience (mean = 5.9, median = 5 years). Their previous experience in using CD-ROM technology was higher than expected: On a 7-point scale (from 7 = high to 1 = low), subjects ranged from 7 to 1, with a mean of 5.26.

3.2 Apparatus

The module's software was programmed in Authorware, allowing use on Macintosh or Windows computers. The software used allows for expeditious exploration, and review of the many program components. The entire program comprises 25 different modules, each of which includes edited full-motion video of an primary grade, NCTM standards-based mathematics lesson, supported by such materials as lesson overview, commentary, lesson plans, lesson concepts, and focus questions. An electronic notebook can be launched in the program, as an aid to reflection on the strategies being applied in the lesson. An assessment area allows users to gauge their increased understanding, and staff developers to assign school district credit for use.

3.3 Procedure

Subjects signed a registration sheet at the beginning of each NAU course to visit the study site for either a morning (8am-noon) or afternoon (1-6pm) session. Two subjects typically were in each session, along with an investigator. Each study session began with a brief welcome, explanation of procedures, opportunity for questions, and an introduction to the module. Subjects were asked to follow the suggested user path through the module for the first few sections. After they had attained sufficient familiarity with the module (typically about an hour), they were asked to choose their own paths through it.

3.3.1 Data sources

An observer took notes throughout the session and provided guidance as needed. At critical points in module use, the observer stopped the subjects to ask, and record on audiotape, their thoughts about the sections they had just been through. At the end of module use, the subjects were again interviewed and a questionnaire was administered. Subjects were assigned – by their NAU professor, Dr. C. R. Wactler – to write four lesson plans in which they were to demonstrate their understanding of the teaching standards studied with the module. The analysis of these lesson plans is not yet complete (Pryor 2000).

3.3.2 Data analysis

Quantitative data consisted mainly of 7-point bipolar evaluative and probability scales measuring variables that previous studies (Pryor and Bitter 1998) have shown to be important in the evaluation of interactive multimedia. (Open-ended items in the questionnaire allowed for the entry of new variables, as did the interviews.) These data were analysed using descriptive statistics, as well as chi-square, and *t*-test. These data, especially those on knowledge gained from using the module, will be triangulated with data from interviews and the analyses of lesson plans (Wactler 1999).

4. RESULTS AND DISCUSSION

4.1 Overall

Overall responses to the module were quite positive, and most important, teachers learned from using it. Knowledge gain, in four areas, was assessed: (a) teaching standards, (b) ability to implement the standards, (c) ability to reflect on practice, and (d) ESL strategies. Scores on the two most critical areas are reported in Table 1.

Table 1. Mean Scores on Knowledge and Ability: Pre- and Post-use

	Pre-use (n=39)	Post-use (n=39
Knowledge of NCTM teaching standards	2.6	5.4**
Ability to promote classroom discourse	5.1	6.2**

Note. Mean scores on 7-point scales scored from 7 to 1, through a neutral mid-point of 4. ** p.<.01

On 7-point bipolar probability and evaluative scales (scored from -3 to +3 through a neutral midpoint of zero), subjects rated the module on key variables, including the module's perceived utility, attitude toward the module, and ease of use, as reported in Table 2. The module's utility for learning the teaching standards was rated as 2.0 ('quite good'), attitude was 1.8 (nearly 'quite favourable'), and ease of use was 1.9. The interview data suggest that nearly all subjects learned from the module. Given this satisfactory summative conclusion about the module, the focus of the study moved to the investigation of any changes that might need to be made in the module (besides grade level of the lesson), to make it as well received by secondary level teachers as by primary teachers.

Table 2. Mean Responses on Major Variables

Variable	$\bar{X}$
Intention to use other modules	0.8
Subjective norm	1.3
Experience using module technology	1.3
Attitude to use other modules	1.4

Variable	$\bar{X}$
District support of NCTM standards	1.7
Attitude towards module	1.8
Ease of use	1.9
Utility of module	2.0
NCTM teaching standards increase students' achievement	2.2
Years of teaching experience	5.9
Knowledge of NCTM standards	5.4

Note. Mean scores on 7-point bipolar scales scored from +3 to -3, through a neutral mid-point of zero with the exception of 'years of teaching experience', and 'knowledge of NCTM standards'.

4.2 Primary-secondary differences

To accomplish this second study goal, the responses of K-6 teachers were separated from those of middle and secondary teachers (hereinafter referred to as 'secondary'), and are reported in Table 3. This beginning of the summative program evaluation found responses from primary subjects generally more positive than those of secondary subjects. The beginning of the formative evaluation for the secondary application, found those subjects less positive generally, in many cases due to curriculum differences at the different grade levels.

Table 3. Mean Responses to Major Variables: Primary vs. Secondary Teachers

Variable	Primary (n=23)	Secondary[a] (n=16)
Knowledge of NCTM discourse standards before	-1.0	-2.0*
Knowledge of NCTM discourse standards now	1.6	1.2
Understanding of ESL strategies before	0.2	-0.4
Understanding of ESL strategies now	1.7	1.7
Ability to reflect on teaching before	1.3	2.0*
Ability to reflect on teaching now	2.2	2.5
Ability to promote classroom discourse before	1.0	1.1
Ability to promote classroom discourse now	2.3	2.1
Value of Watching:		
Classroom observation	2.6	2.4
Video tape of a teacher teaching	1.3	1.8
Module-based video of a teacher teaching	2.3	1.9
Module more valuable than traditional in-service	1.6	0.8

Variable	Primary (n=23)	Secondary[a] (n=16)
Attitude toward the module	2.0	1.5
Attitude toward using other modules in program	2.0	0.4**
Utility of module for learning standards	2.4	1.3**
Intention to use other modules in program	1.6	-0.4**
Ease of use	2.0	1.7
Subjective norm	2.0	0.1**
District support of NCTM teaching standards	2.0	1.4
NCTM standards increase students' achievement	2.4	2.0
Experience using module technology	1.0	1.7
Years of teaching experience	5.6	6.4

Note. Mean scores on 7-point bipolar scales scored from +3 to -3, through a neutral mid-point of zero with the exception of 'years of teaching experience,' and 'knowledge of NCTM standards.

[a] 'Secondary' column includes scores of middle school teachers as well as high school teachers.

* $p<.05$

** $p<.01$

For example, as reported in Table 2, ratings on attitude toward the module, utility, and ease of use were quite positive, but as reported in Table 3, ratings were more favourable from primary subjects. The fact that the video showed a third grade lesson might have been influential in these differences.

Differences between the groups in knowledge and ability gain were also investigated. As illustrated in Tables 3 and 4, differences between primary and secondary subjects were dramatic. Primary subjects began module use with significantly higher ($p<.05$) levels of understanding of the standards, but secondary subjects ended with understanding that was not significantly lower than that of primary subjects. In their ability to implement the standards, primary subjects began module use not significantly lower than secondary subjects, but ended more highly, achieving more gain. Perhaps these differences are due to the different weight primary and secondary teachers attach to pedagogy and content.

Table 4. Mean Ratings of Module Components: Primary vs. Secondary Teachers

Module Components	Primary (n=17)	Secondary (n=11)	Overall (n=28)
Supplementary Material			
Introduction	1.4	1.2	1.3
NCTM Standards	2.5	1.4*	2.1
Bilingual/ESL	2.4	1.7	2.1
The Lesson			
Overview			
Setting & context	2.2	0.7*	1.6
Lesson Plan	2.4	1.3*	2.0
Mathematical concepts/animation	1.9	1.5	1.8
Language environment	1.9	1.2	1.7
Teacher interviews	2.4	1.2	1.9
Video of complete lesson	2.4	2.2	2.3
Lesson Parts			
Lesson part video with transcript	2.6	-0.2**	1.6
Teacher's commentary	2.1	1.3	1.8
Mathematics educator's commentary	1.8	1.0	1.5
Language specialist's commentary	1.8	1.5	1.7
Mathematician's commentary	1.2	0.9	1.1
Discourse standards	2.8	1.8*	2.4
Curriculum standards	2.5	1.7*	2.2
Bilingual/ESL	2.5	1.6	2.1
Student work	1.0	0.5	0.8
Focus questions	1.8	0.5	1.2
Assessment			
Reflect	1.3	0.8	1.1
Identify	1.5	0.8	1.4
Extend	1.6	1.0	1.4
Apply	1.9	1.2	1.6

Note. Mean scores on single-item scales scored from +3 to -3, through a neutral mid-point of zero.
* p.<.05
** p.<.01

Another aspect of this study goal was comparison of the two groups' ratings on the module's 23 components. Significant differences were found on five items within The Lesson component: Setting and context, Lesson plan, Lesson part video with transcript, Discourse standards, and Curriculum standards (see Table 4).

Table 5 illustrates changes in the value in-service teachers place on three methods of classroom observation, after using the module. An interesting change in value occurred. Teachers perceived a higher value in watching a module-based video after only four hours of use. We found this result encouraging and anticipate further investigation into teachers' beliefs.

Table 5. Mean Responses to the Value of Three Learning Experiences on their Value for Learning

	Pretest (n=17)	Posttest (n=17)	Posttest (all) (n=39)
Classroom observation of a teacher teaching	2.5	2.6	2.5
Watching a video tape of a teacher teaching	0.9	0.9	1.5
Watching a module-based video of a teacher teaching	0.6	1.9*	2.1**

Note. Mean scores on 7-point bipolar scales scored from +3 to -3, through a neutral mid-point of zero. The pretest was implemented mid-way during the study, in response to comments made by subjects during the interviews.

* $p < .05$
** $p < .01$

5. CONCLUSION

This study of teachers' use of the program's first completed module of math•ed•ology™ suggests that an important amount of learning can occur in just under four hours of module use. Teachers made gains in knowledge of the teaching standards, and ability to implement the standards.

Differences between primary and secondary teachers' gains in knowledge and ability following use of the module were also investigated. Differences between the groups were dramatic. Primary subjects began module use with significantly higher levels of understanding of the standards, but secondary subjects began with significantly lower levels than those of primary subjects. In their ability to implement the standards, primary subjects began not significantly lower than secondary subjects, but ended higher, achieving more gain.

When the two groups' ratings of the module's 23 components were compared, primary teachers' ratings were higher than secondary teachers' in every case, although differences were significant on only 6 of the 23 components: Background on NCTM standards, and five components within The Lesson section. It seems likely that secondary teachers' ratings were lower because they perceived the third grade lesson as irrelevant to their practice. The lack of major differences between the groups, however suggests that the structure and tools in the program designed for primary teachers will prove a useful base for development of a program for secondary teachers. The findings of this study concerning the module's efficacy have been echoed recently by other studies of interactive video in teacher education (e.g. Al-Mekhlafi 2000, Markel 1999).

REFERENCES

Al-Mekhlafi. A. (2000) Instructional media for teachers' preparation. *International Journal of Instructional Media*, 28 (2), pp. 202-219.

Ball, D. L. (1990) Breaking with experience in learning to teach mathematics: The role of a preservice methods course. *For the Learning of Mathematics – An International Journal of Mathematics Education,* 10(2), pp. 10-16.

Ball, D. L. (1993) With an eye on the mathematical horizon: Dilemmas of teaching elementary school mathematics. *The Elementary School Journal*, 93(4), pp. 373-397.

Ball, D. L. (1996) Teacher learning and the mathematics reforms: What we think we know and what we need to learn. *Phi Delta Kappan*, 76 (7), pp. 500-508.

Bitter, G. G. (1993) *Teaching mathematics methods using interactive videodisc: The TMMUIV research results*. Monograph Series of Technology Based Learning and Research, 5.

Bitter, G. G., and Pryor, B. W. (1999, April) *Multiple perspectives from four stakeholder: groups on interactive multimedia*. Paper presented at the meeting of the American Educational Research Association, Montreal.

Darling-Hammond, L. (Ed.). (1994) *Professional development schools: Schools for developing a profession.* New York, Teacher's College Press.

Goldman, E. S. and Barron, L. C. (1990) Using hypermedia to improve the preparation of elementary teachers. *Journal of Teacher Education*, 41 (3), pp. 21-31.

Lieberman, A. (1995) Practices that support teacher development: Transforming conceptions of professional learning. *Phi Delta Kappan*, 76 (8), pp. 591-96.

Markel, S. L. (1999, March) *Conversations of community: Dynamics of discourse and change in an on-line virtual conference, multi-media math seminar course*. Paper presented at the International Conference on Mathematics/Science Education and Technology, San Antonio, Texas.

Pryor, C. R. (2000, February) *Teachers' applications of the NCTM discourse standards: Using math•ed•ology™ for K-12 curriculum development.* Paper presented at the meeting of the Association of Teacher Educators, Orlando, Florida.

Pryor, B. W. and Bitter, G. G. (1998, November) *Investigating the relative Utility of Data Collection by Electronic and Traditional Means.* Paper presented at the meeting of the American Evaluation Association, Chicago.

Sowell, E. J., Buss, R. R., Fedock, P. M., Johnson, G., Pryor, B. W., Wetzel, K. and Zambo, R. (1995, August) *K-12 mathematics and science education in Arizona: A status report.* Tempe, AZ, Arizona State University, Eisenhower Mathematics and Science Program, Arizona Board of Regents.

Winitzky, N. and Arends, R. (1991) Translating research into practice: The effects of various forms of training and clinical experience on preservice students' knowledge, skill, and reflectiveness. *Journal of Teacher Education*, 42 (1), pp. 52-65.

BIOGRAPHIES

Gary G. Bitter is Professor of Educational Technology, and Executive Director, Technology Based Learning and Research, both at Arizona State University. He has published widely in the areas of educational technology, mathematics education, and the professional development of teachers. He has developed several interactive multimedia programs for the professional development of teachers, including *Understanding Teaching* and math•ed•ology™

Brandt W. Pryor is Associate Professor of Educational Leadership, Lamar University. He was the Co-principal Investigator on the Math Discourse Project which developed the math•ed•ology™ program at Arizona State University. His primary research interest is the application of attitude theory to understanding educational decision-making. He is currently studying teachers' decisions about integrating technology into their instruction.

41

Dynamic Geometry Software and Mechanical Linkages

A Visually Rich Environment for Geometric Reasoning

Jill Vincent
Melbourne Girls Grammar School, 22 Gardenia Street, Blackburn, 3130 Victoria, Australia
Jill.Vincent@mggs.vic.edu.au

Keywords: dynamic geometry software, mathematics, geometry, mathematical proof, mechanical linkages, constructivist learning

Abstract: Widespread interest has arisen in the use of dynamic geometry software as a constructivist learning tool. However, the software has been accused of contributing to an empirical, data-collecting approach to geometry, where students have little or no understanding of deductive reasoning. Mechanical linkages which occur in many common household items, as well as in 'mathematical machines' from the past, offer a wealth of geometry appropriate for secondary school mathematics. Dynamic geometry models of these linkages form an interface between the concrete and the theoretical, and create a visually rich environment for students to explore, conjecture and construct geometric proofs.

1. INTRODUCTION

The unique design features of the class of software known as dynamic geometry, for example, Cabri Geometry™ and Geometer's Sketchpad™, have created widespread interest in the software as a constructivist learning tool. Screen drawings in this software can be purely visual or they can be constructed using in-built tools based on Euclidean geometry, such as parallel or perpendicular lines, angle bisectors or perpendicular bisectors. Segments or angles can be constructed precisely, accurate measurements can be made and the loci of points traced. The 'drag' facility distinguishes dynamic geometry software from other computer drawing software, since only those features based on appropriate geometric constructions, such as parallel or perpendicular lines, will remain invariant when a screen drawing is dragged.

Recent decades have seen a general decline in Euclidean geometry in school mathematics curricula, with the geometry which remains becoming largely empirical and students having little idea of the significance of proof. With the facility to measure angles and distances, and the ability to obtain multiple screen images by dragging, dynamic geometry software has been accused of contributing to a 'data-gathering' empirical approach and the removal of students' need for geometric proof as verification. Noss and Hoyles (1996) express concern that in the UK there is little evidence of the powerful new ways of approaching geometry offered by dynamic geometry software. Instead, geometry is being reduced to pattern-spotting by dragging screen drawings, with little or no emphasis on theoretical geometry or deductive reasoning. Healy and Hoyles (1999), reporting on the project, Justifying and Proving in School Mathematics, note that the National Curriculum in the UK

> "...prescribes an approach to proving... in which the introduction of formal proofs is reserved for 'exceptional performance', and thus delayed until after students have progressed through early stages of reasoning empirically and explaining their conjectures. Most of the requirements to explain and justify take place within investigations driven by numerical data."

De Villiers (1998) has criticised the emphasis on the *verification* aspect of proof in school mathematics, arguing that in a traditional approach to the teaching of proofs, illustrations of pattern failure, optical illusions and false conclusions are used to create doubt in the minds of students in order to justify and motivate the need for proof. He asserts that in a dynamic geometry environment, the focus should move to proof as *explanation* rather than *verification*. While some students may have a cognitive need for proof as conviction, many see little point in proving something which they already 'know' to be true. Hofstadter (1997) argues that the certainty given by dragging a dynamic geometry construction is more convincing for him than a proof: 'it's not a proof, of course, but in some sense, I would argue, this kind of direct contact with the phenomenon is even more convincing than a proof, because you really see it all happening right before your eyes'.

Reflecting the revival of interest in proof in school mathematics, much of the recent dynamic geometry research has focused on the role of the software as an environment for conjecturing and deductive reasoning. Hoyles (1998) cautions against the assumption that the computer will "help to build bridges between the empirical and the deductive", noting that "there remains the question of how to develop a 'need for proof'". She asserts that links between empirical verification and deductive proof should be developed at each level of school mathematics to establish 'a culture of proving':

> "....we need to design *new* learning contexts which require the use of clearly formulated statements and definitions and agreed procedures of deduction but which also allow opportunities for their *connection* with empirical justification and the conviction this engenders."

The question, then, is how to exploit the rich visual environment of dynamic geometry software to engage students in deductive reasoning and proof. Healy (2000) and Arzarello, Micheletti, Olivero, Robutti and Paola (1998) describe teaching experiments involving geometry problem-solving, where the loci obtained by purposeful dragging provided the data for students' conjecturing and proof construction. Scher (1999) asserts that the software can influence the style of experimentation and reasoning so that 'the boundary between deductive reasoning and dynamic geometry becomes blurred: the software finds its way into the proof process'. He notes, however, the frequent situation where, 'having used the software to convince themselves of a theorem's plausibility, mathematics classes turn to the traditional paper-and-pencil medium to ponder a proof. In the process, they create a boundary between the computer and deductive reasoning'. Scher uses the example of the modelling of the pantograph of Sylvester to illustrate how feedback from dragging the screen construction can contribute to the conjecturing and proof processes. Through an interplay between experimentation and deductive reasoning, 'dynamic geometry can provide not only *data* to feed a conjecture, but tools to jump-start *ideas* and feed a proof'.

2. MODELLING MECHANICAL LINKAGES

Mechanical linkages, or systems of hinged bars (Cundy and Rollett 1981, Bolt 1991), are found in many common household items as well as in 'mathematical machines' from the past, and offer a wealth of geometry appropriate for secondary school mathematics. Many of these linkages are based on the simple geometry of similar figures, isosceles triangles, parallelograms or kites, providing a motivating environment in which to introduce students to conjecturing and proof. With the emphasis on the underlying geometry, dynamic geometry software models of linkages which simulate the action of the actual linkages form an interface between the concrete and the theoretical, enabling students to visualise the linkages as geometric figures. In this visually rich environment students can explore, conjecture and construct geometric proofs: Why does the cage of an elevated work platform remain vertical when it is raised or lowered? Why are rhombus linkages so widely used? How is a pantograph designed to produce an image with a particular enlargement factor? The accurate measurements, animation and tracing of loci which are possible with the software contribute to a conjecturing environment where proof assumes the multiple roles of *verification*, for example, that apparent invariants are in fact invariant, *understanding* of geometric relationships, and *explanation*, that is, giving an insight into *why* the linkage works the way it does.

In the simple linkage of a folding table (Figure 1), for example, why does the top stay parallel to the floor as the table is raised or lowered? The proof, based on two similar, isosceles triangles, draws on familiar geometry and provides an appropriate introduction to formal proof construction. Could the requirement that the top remains parallel to the floor be achieved if the legs AB and CD were of unequal lengths? Under what circumstances are triangles APC and BPD congruent?

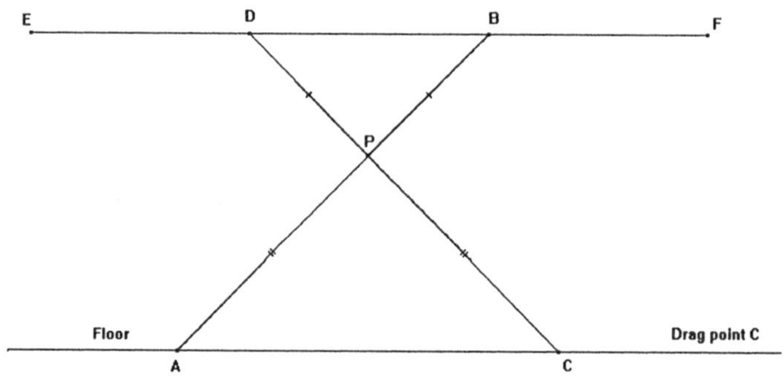

Figure 1. Folding table linkage

The elevated work-platform, commonly known as a 'cherry-picker' (Figure 2), contains two parallelogram linkages, ACED and EFGH. A dynamic geometry model of the linkages demonstrates clearly how the rigid structures ABC and DEF ensure that GH remains perpendicular to AB and hence that the cage remains in a vertical position. The relationship between ∠BAC and ∠DEF is shown in Figure 2b. Similar linkages are to be found in wall-mounting brackets for equipment such as medical instruments, desk lights and computer monitors.

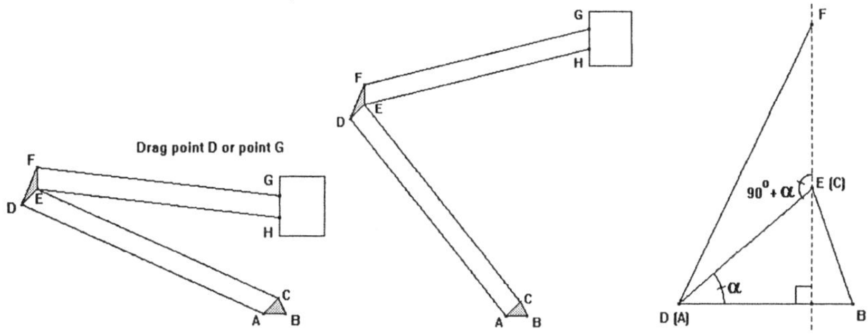

(a) (b)

Figure 2. Modelling the parallelogram linkages of a 'cherry picker'

The expanding toolbox (Figure 3) has two parallelogram linkages, ABDC and EFHG. BD and FH are attached along a straight line parallel to the base to ensure that the trays remain parallel to the base as they move. The loci of AC and EG demonstrate the significance of the parallelogram linkages to the design of the toolbox. Would the toolbox still function if the links were attached so that ABDC and EFHG were rectangles when the toolbox was in its closed position? What would happen if the links formed trapezia rather than parallelograms?

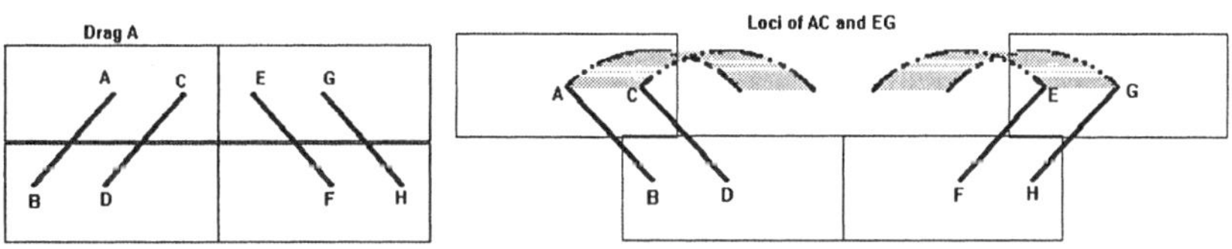

Figure 3. Parallelogram linkages of an expanding toolbox

Rhombus linkages are widely used in the elevated work platforms known as 'scissor lifts', as well as in expanding trellises and barriers, riveting tools and corkscrews. Figure 4a shows the application of the rhombus linkage in a car jack. Why is the locus of B perpendicular to AP? What is the significance of this for the operation of the jack? An alternative design of car jack (Figure 4b) is based on an isosceles triangle where the arm PB is extended by an equal amount BC, so that AB = PB = BC. The conjecture, that ∠CAP is a right angle, can be proved readily by students using the properties of isosceles triangles. How would the locus of C be influenced if the extension BC were not equal to PB? Could this different linkage design have any useful applications?

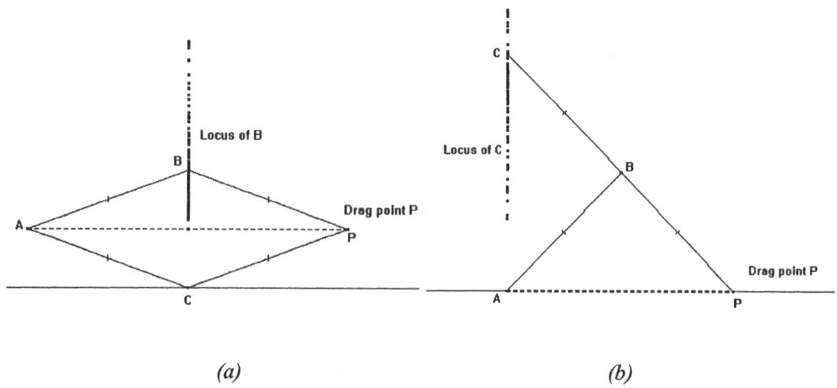

Figure 4. Rhombus and extended isosceles triangle linkages

Pascal's angle trisector (Figure 5) is based on two isosceles triangles, with AB = BC = CD. As the rod AF is rotated, D slides along AF and C slides along AE. Measurement of angles in the dynamic geometry construction and observation of the changes as AF is rotated should lead students to the conjecture that the measure of ∠DCE is three times that of ∠FAE. Can students prove their conjecture? What if further links are added? What determines how many more links are possible? What is the relationship to ∠FAE each time another link is added to create a new angle?

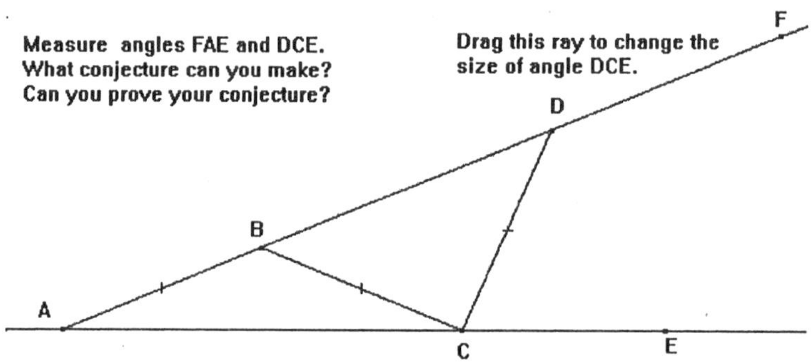

Figure 5. Pascal's angle trisector

The flourishing of mechanical invention which occurred as a result of the industrial revolution led to the development of a number of linkages for converting circular motion into linear motion. Tchebycheff's linkage (Figure 6), for example, provides an opportunity to introduce students to the need for proof. The linkage consists of a crossed quadrilateral ABCD where A and B are fixed, AB = 4 units, CD = 2 units and AC = BD = 5 units. It can be shown that P is exactly 4 units above the line AB when CD is horizontal or in either of its two vertical positions.

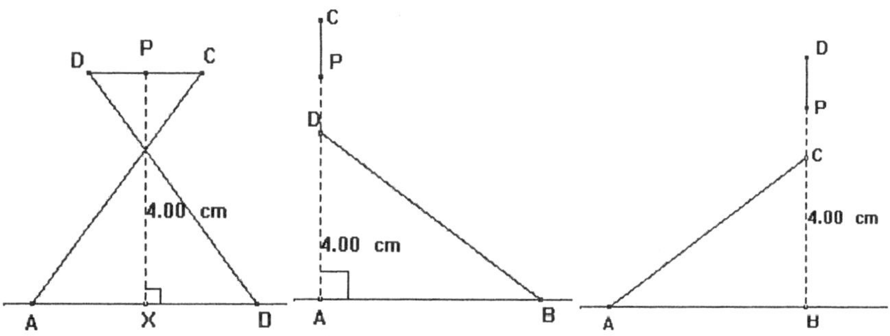

Figure 6. Tchebycheff's linkage

In other configurations, it may appear at first that the locus of P is linear (Figure 7a). However, further tracing of the locus of P and measuring the distance of P from AB with the maximum number of decimal places (Figure 7b) soon reveals that the locus of P is a good approximation of linear motion. The linkage provides an opportunity for introducing the need for proof as verification and also the role of counter-examples.

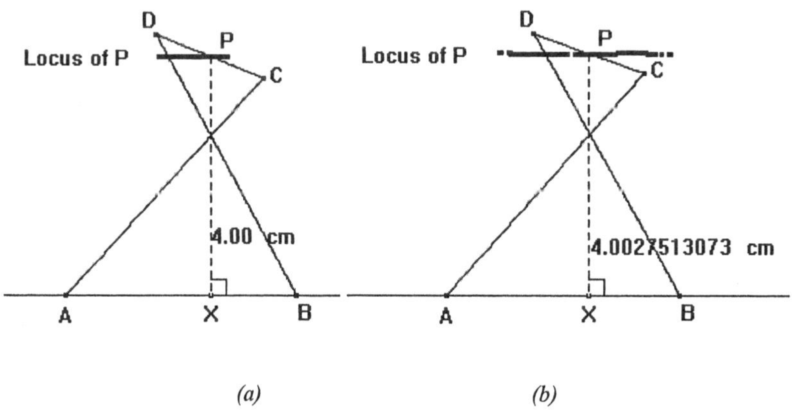

Figure 7. Tracing the locus of P in Tchebycheff's linkage

Many of the linkages for converting circular to rectilinear motion are based on kites or parallelograms, and their computer models provide a rich source of geometry for students to explore, conjecture and construct proofs. Sylvester's linkage (Figure 8) is based on two similar kites, AEDC and DCBF, with O and F fixed so that OABF is a parallelogram. As point B is dragged, the locus of E appears to be a straight line through F, while measurement of angles suggests that ∠OFE is a right-angle. The challenge for students is to *prove* the conjecture that E moves along a linear path perpendicular to OF.

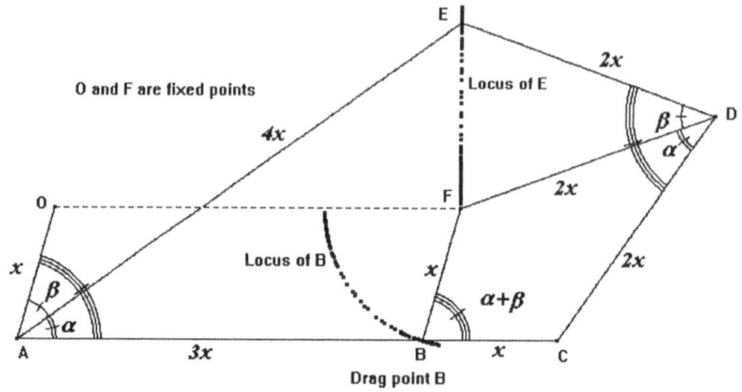

Figure 8. Dynamic geometry model of Sylvester's linkage

Pantographs, mechanical devices originally used for copying or enlarging drawings, are another source of interesting geometry. Although pantographs are no longer used as drawing tools, computer-controlled versions are now used as precision cutting tools. The pantograph of Sylvester (Figure 9) consists of a parallelogram OABC and two links, AP and CP', where AP = CP' = OC and ∠BAP = ∠BCP' = α, a fixed angle.

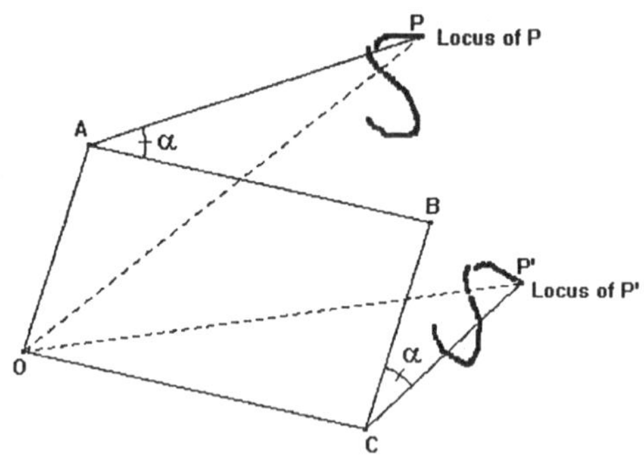

Figure 9. Pantograph of Sylvester

Tracing the paths of P and P' as P is dragged, demonstrates to students that P' traces out a rotated image of the path of P. Feedback from dragging the dynamic geometry model and measurement of OP, OP' and ∠POP' should lead students to the conjectures that OP = OP' and ∠POP' = α. Proof of these conjectures, based on congruent triangles OAP and OBP', then confirms why the movement of P' is an image of the movement of P, rotated through an angle equal to α. The geometry of the linkage poses many questions: Do the lengths of the links AP and CP' influence the image? Are the lengths of the parallelogram links significant? What if OABC were a rhombus?

The pantograph shown in Figure 10, in which ABDC is a parallelogram, points O, C and E are collinear and O is fixed, can be used for enlarging or reducing. By tracing the locus of points C and E students can compare the sizes of the loci and construct a proof based on the conjecture that ΔOAC, ΔOBE and ΔCDE are similar. How would you design a pantograph with a given enlargement factor?

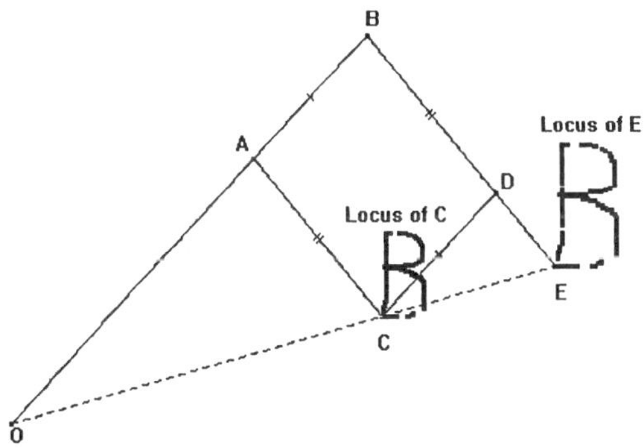

Figure 10. Enlarging or reducing pantograph

As a consequence of the hierarchical dependence of points in dynamic geometry software, it is not always possible to construct linkages which can operate by dragging more than one point. An actual pantograph, for example, may be operated by fixing either of two points and moving the other, whereas the computer model may allow movement of only one point. It is important, however, to note the emphasis here is on the *geometry* of the linkages. While there are certain restrictions imposed on modelling with dynamic geometry software and constructions of many linkages may prove too difficult for the majority of students, these limitations do not diminish the usefulness of the computer models in exploring geometric properties and relationships. Whether the students construct the computer models of the linkages themselves or are provided with constructions, the unique features of dynamic geometry software and the curiosity aroused by the operation of the linkages create a visually rich and motivating environment for students to explore, conjecture and construct geometric proofs.

REFERENCES

Arzarello, F., Micheletti, C., Olivero, F., Robutti, O. and Paola, D. (1998) A model for analysing the transition to formal proofs in geometry. In *Proceedings of the 22nd Psychology of Mathematics Education Conference*, A. Olivier and K. Newstead (Eds.), 2, Stellenbosch, Programme Committee of the 22nd PME Conference, South Africa, pp. 24-31.

Bolt, B. (1991) *Mathematics meets technology*. Cambridge University Press, Cambridge, UK.

Cundy, H. M. and Rollett, A. P. (1981) *Mathematical models*. Tarquin Publications, Norfolk, England.

De Villiers, M. (1998) An alternative approach to proof in dynamic geometry. In *Designing learning environments for developing understanding of geometry and space*, R. Lehrer and D. Chazan (Eds.), Lawrence Erlbaum, Hillsdale, NJ, pp. 369-393.

Healy, L. (2000) Identifying and explaining geometrical relationship: Interactions with robust and soft Cabri constructions. In *Proceedings of the 24th Conference of the International Group for the Psychology of Mathematics Education*, T. Nakahara and M. Koyama (Eds.), 1, University of Hiroshima, Hiroshima, pp. 103-117.

Healy, L. and Hoyles, C. (1999) *Justifying and proving in school mathematics: Technical report on the nationwide survey*. Institute of Education, University of London, London.

Hofstadter, D. (1997) Discovery and dissection of a geometric gem. In *Geometry turned on: Dynamic software in learning, teaching, and research,* J. King and D. Schattschneider (Eds.), MAA Notes 41, Mathematical Association of America, Washington, DC.

Hoyles, C. (1998) A culture of proving in school mathematics. In *Information and communication technologies in school mathematics*, J. Tinsley and D. Johnson (Eds.), Chapman Hall, London, pp. 169-181.

Noss, R. and Hoyles, C. (1996) *Windows on mathematical meanings: Learning cultures and computers*. Mathematics Education Library, Vol. 17, Kluwer Academic Press, Dordrecht, The Netherlands.

Scher, D. (1999) Problem solving and proof in the age of dynamic geometry. *Micromath*, 15 (1), pp. 24-30.

BIOGRAPHY

Jill Vincent has taught Mathematics at Melbourne Girls Grammar School for the past ten years. The school is a 'laptop' school, where all students from Years 5-12 have their own laptop computers. Jill uses computer technology extensively in her mathematics teaching and is currently researching the role of dynamic geometry software in Year 8 students' approach to geometric proof as part of her PhD studies at The University of Melbourne.

42

User Centred Design in a Learning Environment Based on a Computer Algebra System

Dominique Lenne and Jean-Michel Gélis
Institut National de Recherche Pédagogique, 91, rue Gabriel Péri, Montrouge, France
dominique.lenne@inrp.fr

Keywords: user interface, didactics, open learning systems, integration of ICT, problem solving

Abstract: Though they have not been designed for this usage, computer algebra systems are increasingly used in learning situations. In order to improve their didactic capabilities we study the possibility to graft mathematics interactive learning environments onto them. We present in this paper our design approach that relies on Human Computer Interaction methods and integrates mathematics learning knowledge. This approach has been applied to design a learning environment, called Limites, that helps students to study, work out and justify limits of rational functions. We present the main features of this environment, focusing on three points: algebraic expressions manipulation, conjectures and proofs.

1. INTRODUCTION

Though they have not been designed for this usage, professional software packages are often used in learning and training situations (Cheikes et al. 1998). That is the case with Computer Algebra Systems (CAS), such as Maple, Derive or Mathematica, which are increasingly used in mathematics teaching and learning.

Students are special users of these software packages because their goal in using them is not only to solve a problem but also to improve their knowledge. Unlike professional users, they often have a very partial, but strongly evolving knowledge of the domain covered by the software.

Moreover, professional tools are generally complex and the time needed to master them is often too long in comparison with the short time during which students will have to use them.

Taking into account these problems, we study the possibility to graft (Pachet et al. 1994) learning environments onto those tools. To design these environments we adopt user centred methods inspired of the Human Computer Interaction domain (Norman 1986), considering two types of users: students and teachers.

In this paper, we describe our approach and we show how it has been applied to Limites, a learning environment based on the Maple computer algebra system and centred on problem solving in the limits domain. This environment provides students with tools to study, work out and justify limits of numerical functions and provides teachers with tools to parameter and to adapt it.

2. CAS-BASED ENVIRONMENTS

Much research work have been done about the integration of CAS in mathematics education. In the eighties, artificial intelligence research tried to integrate them in problem solving systems and to construct explanations using solutions produced by these systems (Vivet 1984). In the nineties, when CAS became usable on microcomputers and on handheld calculators, mathematics education researchers (Artigue and Lagrange 1998, Trouche 1996) analysed the conditions of their integration in education. They showed that this integration was not as easy as one could firstly think and stressed the importance of the learning situation. Following cognitive ergonomics works (Rabardel 1995), they particularly focused on the instrumentation process and on the identification of students action schemes.

Our approach consists in designing, on the top of a CAS, environments that facilitate learning in specific mathematical domains, and reduce the complexity of action schemes observed in existing CAS.

3. USER CENTERED DESIGN

We present below some key points of our approach that relies on one hand on a study of CAS utility and usability in mathematics learning and on the other hand on an analysis of students problem solving activity. It takes into account didactic goals and allows teachers to tailor the environment to their needs.

3.1 Utility and usability of CAS in mathematics learning

Computer Algebra Systems are powerful that can make most of the calculations (numeric or symbolic) needed at different levels (secondary schools or university). Moreover they have extended capacities in graphical representation and animation.

However, the integration of CAS in mathematics' teaching raises many questions (Lagrange 2000), particularly relating to the relationship between conceptual and technical aspects. For the most part, the existing CAS have been developed for research and industry and not for learning. Above all designed in order to be efficient, they use complex algorithms that do not match the methods taught to the students. They do not follow the principle of 'cognitive fidelity' (Beeson 1998, Nicaud et al. 1999) needed in a learning environment.

CAS have many flaws regarding their interface and help capabilities (Lenne and Gélis 1998).

- The great number of functions they propose (more than 2700 for Maple)
- The unsuited power of some functions (automatic simplifications, integration of several calculus steps in one function)
- Conversely, the impossibility to perform other simple functions (unneeded in a powerful software)
- The difficulty to take into account definition domains
- The resolution of equations in the complex numbers set, which leads to results difficult to understand for some students
- Many ergonomic flaws such as the difficulty to visualise the state of variables and functions and to spread a modification.

Some of these flaws lead to usability problems related to the interface, others to utility problems related to the functional kernel that are more difficult to deal with.

Note that most of these flaws are seen, conversely, as advantages in professional situations.

3.2 Students' activity analysis

In order to conceive a learning environment in the limits domain, we analysed students' activity relying on their paper and pencil work and on their work with the aid of a classic CAS. Their foreseeable future activity in the learning environment is based on this analysis, but it is also guided by learning goals defined by the teachers and mathematics' teaching specialists involved in our project.

3.2.1 Paper and pencil activity

In a paper-and-pencil context, working on limits implies carrying out two different tasks. The first one consists in applying theorems and properties in order to calculate the limit. The second one allows applying some transformations when the limit evaluation leads to an indeterminate form (such as $0 \times \infty$ or $+\infty - \infty$).

Teachers note many difficulties when students carry out these tasks, such as misapplication of theorems or calculus errors when transforming expressions. Moreover, students often manage to fit in both of these tasks, which leads to some confusion. In Limites, the learning environment we designed, these two tasks have been clearly separated, and the calculations are made by CAS.

3.2.2 CAS-aided problem solving activity

With a classical CAS, the student's task consists in finding a sequence of commands or functions leading to a 'good' expression, i.e. an expression that can be used to calculate the limit (if it exists). When executing this task, students encounter the above mentioned CAS utilisation problems. Among them, the major problem is that available functions are often too powerful because they have not been designed to facilitate learning but in order to be efficient.

Moreover, a CAS provides calculus functions but it is helpless in producing proofs. For example, the value of a limit can be calculated but there are no means (e.g. reference limits, theorems) to prove it.

3.3 Didactic goals

To experiment with this approach, we chose the domain of numerical functions' limits at a high school level. This domain is interesting from several viewpoints: it implies to work on algebraic expressions and on their syntactical structure, it implies the use of theorems and reference limits to prove a result and it allows one to tackle the analysis domain by using inequalities to evaluate some particular limits. Moreover conjectures can be obtained by numerical or graphical means.

3.3.1 Learning the limit concept

To identify the difficulties encountered by high school students in limits learning, we carried out a preliminary pilot study. Students had to solve limits problems in a paper-and-pencil mode. The observed difficulties concerned the three following main points.

- *Manipulation of expressions*: many difficulties appear when students try to apply transformations on expressions. They sometimes have difficulties in identifying sub-expressions and they often choose complicated or inappropriate transformations in order to obtain an expression with which the limit can be calculated; moreover they make many calculation errors in applying them.
- *Proof*: students often have many difficulties in justifying their results. They use incorrect operations involving $+\infty$ or $-\infty$, abusively generalise some theorems (for example, they use the limit of the higher degree term for a non-polynomial expression) and often have little knowledge on reference limits.
- *Conjectures*: when the limit does not exist or when it is uneasy to calculate, students do not always think to make conjectures by using numerical or graphical means. Moreover, they do not always know the difference between a conjecture and a proof.

3.3.2 The learning situation

The learning situation we propose in the Limites environment aims at taking into account these difficulties. It puts the emphasis on the students activity by providing them with relevant calculus, conjecture and proof tools.

Furthermore, we aim at encouraging links between numeric, graphic and symbolic registers, in order to facilitate conjectures (Artigue and Lagrange 1998), specially in situations where students are stuck.

Lastly, didactic goals change while students knowledge evolves. For example, when the limit concept has just been introduced, students only know elementary theorems and few reference limits. They have to justify each step of reasoning. When the notion begins to be mastered, they can use more powerful theorems and do not have to justify all the elementary steps of reasoning.

3.4 Teachers' viewpoint

The learning situations we consider involve teachers. Therefore, we have to analyse their tasks and to take into account their needs. We note other authors (Van Labeke et al. 1999) that have stressed the importance of integrating teachers in the design process.

In our project a key issue has been to give teachers means to tailor the environment to the students level and to the kind of justifications they expect. As a pilot study we undertook has shown, the expected justifications vary not only according to the teaching level but also to the teacher himself.

4. THE LIMITES LEARNING ENVIRONMENT

The Limites learning environment has been designed in accordance to the above didactic goals and in order to reduce difficulties that students encounter both in paper-and-pencil and in CAS context. We describe below its architecture and its main features, focusing on three points: algebraic expressions' manipulation, conjectures and proofs.

4.1 Architecture

Limites is composed of two main units, the first one taking in charge the interaction with the student and the second one the adaptation of its requests to the CAS (see Figure 1). These two units have been written in Delphi (Pascal Object) and the CAS we used is Maple. Relating to the previous section, the adaptation unit takes charge of CAS utility problems while the interaction unit takes charge of usability problems.

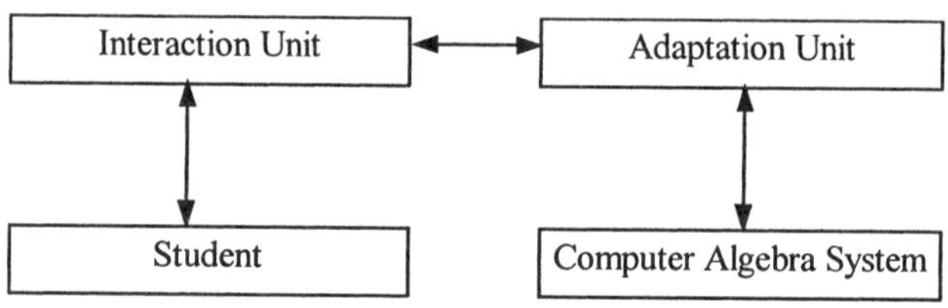

Figure 1. Architecture of Limites

In addition, the adaptation unit makes the interaction unit independent from the CAS by including a representation of its expected capacities.

4.2 Manipulation of expressions

Manipulation of expressions can be divided into at least three tasks: entering an expression, selecting a sub-expression and applying a transformation.

4.2.1 Entering an expression

In the current version of the environment, students have to enter an expression under its linear form. It is then parsed and displayed in its two-dimensional form. Starting from this representation, expressions or sub-expressions can directly be selected in order to calculate a limit or to apply a transformation.

We plan to add later a mixed expression entry mode, allowing the student to use both of these representations. Both of them can indeed be useful to lead to a better understanding of expressions structures.

4.2.2 Selecting a sub-expression

In order to transform an expression, students have to recognise and to work on its sub-expressions. This task is sometimes difficult for students in paper and pencil mode and it is even more complicated with a CAS. Limites helps students in this task by allowing them to visualise the expression or sub-expression they can select. When moving the mouse over the expression, different moving frames are drawn, showing sub-expressions that can be selected by clicking (Figure 2).

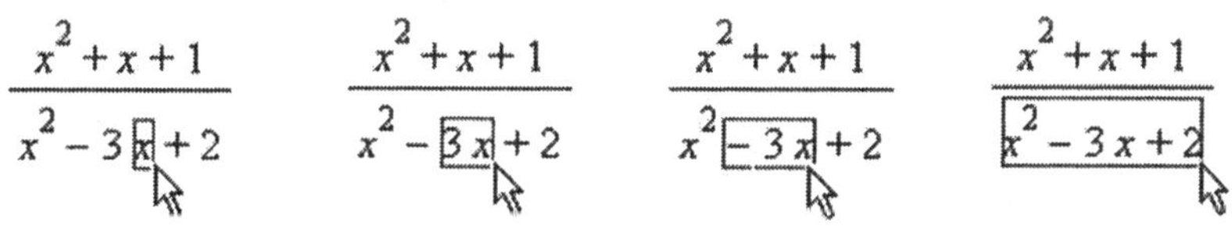

Figure 2. Visualisation of sub-expressions

4.2.3 Applying transformations

In order to calculate limits, students often have to perform transformations (e.g. expand, factor, simplify), particularly when the current expression leads to an indeterminate limit. In Limites, to achieve this task, they have (1) to select a sub-expression (2) to choose a transformation in a list. Some transformations are always available in the list, others vary according to the expression type. The chosen transformation is applied to the expression by the system.

For example, to study the limit of x^2-3x+2 when x tends towards infinity, students who do not know that the limit of a polynomial, function when x tends towards infinity, is the same as its higher degree term limit have to solve the non-determination by using the 'factor' transformation leading to $x^2(1-3/x+2/x^2)$.

4.3 Conjectures

Students have to be able to make conjectures either on the value of a limit or on its non-existence (e.g. for some trigonometric functions when the variable tends towards infinity). Numerical and graphical tools can help them in Limites. They look like other tools in classical CAS, but in addition, non-linear scales that can give a better but unusual insight of the behaviour of a function are provided.

Conjecture tools are available at the same level as proof tools and a clear difference is made between these two types of tools.

4.4 Proof

The limit concept is studied at different teaching levels. Teachers justification requirements vary depending on the teaching level. At an early stage, each step has to be justified, while later some evident results can be omitted. An important feature of a learning environment is therefore to provide several levels.

By now, we have implemented three levels (these levels can easily be adapted and more levels can be considered).

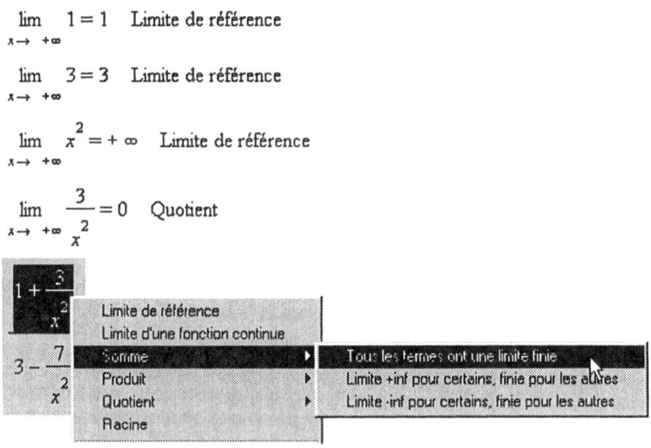

Figure 3. A limit calculus at the first level

At the first level (Figure 3), the proof has to be stated step by step with elementary theorems. At the upper levels, some justifications can be implicitly admitted and more powerful theorems become available. In our example, at the second level the number of justification steps needed is reduced to two. At the third level, a new theorem relating to the limit of a polynomial function when the variable tends towards infinity allows the student to perform the calculus in only one step.

5. CONCLUSION AND FUTURE WORK

In this paper, we presented the learning environment Limites which is based on a CAS. We showed how the design process has been centred on the users of this environment. On one hand students tasks and activities with and without the CAS have been precisely analysed. On the other hand teachers' needs and requirements and didactic goals have been taken into account. The expected outcome is a better integration of this environment in classroom situations.

A prototype of this environment is fully functional and could be used as is in high school classrooms. We are evaluating this prototype with students and teachers, both from a pedagogical and from a HCI point of view. The first results showed the great ease of use of the environment. We now try to observe the mathematical work of students with the environment and to see to what extent it helps them in constructing the limit concept.

Our future work will concern the extension of the mathematical domain by allowing students to calculate limits thanks to relevant inequalities.

REFERENCES

Artigue, M. and Lagrange, J. B. (1998) Instrumentation et écologie didactique de calculatrices complexes: éléments d'analyse à partir d'expérimentations en classe de première S. *Actes du colloque "Calculatices symboliques et géométriques dans l'enseignement des mathématiques"*, IREM de Montpellier, pp. 15-38.

Beeson, M. (1998) Design Principles of Mathpert: software to support education in algebra and calculus. In *Computer Human Interaction in Scientific Computation*, N. Kajler (ed.), Springer-Verlag, pp. 89-114.

Cheikes, B., Geier, M., Hyland, R., Linton F., Rodi, L. and Schaefer, H. P. (1998) Embedded Training for Complex Information Systems. *ITS'98, 4th International Conference on Intelligent Tutoring Systems*, San Antonio, TX, Springer, pp. 36-45.

Lagrange, J. B. (2000) *Approches didactique et cognitive d'un instrument technologique dans l'enseignement. Le cas du calcul formel en lycée.* Mémoire d'Habilitation à Diriger les Recherches. Université Paris VII.

Lenne, D. and Gélis, J. M. (1998) Integration of Learning Capabilities into a CAS: the SUITES Environment Example. In *Proceedings of 4th International Conference On Computer Aided Learning and Instruction In Science and Engineering*, C. Alvegard (ed), Chalmers University, Göteborg, pp. 342-349.

Nicaud, J. F., Bouhineau, D., Varlet, C. and Nguyen-Xuan, A. (1999) Towards a product for teaching formal algebra. In *Proceedings of Artificial Intelligence in Education*, S. P. Lajoie and M. Vivet (eds.), IOS Press, pp. 207-214.

Norman, D. (1986) *User Centered System Design*. Lawrence Erlbaum Associates.

Pachet, F., Giroux, S. and Paquette, G. (1994) Pluggable Advisors as Epiphyte Systems. In *Proceedings of CALISCE'94, International Conference On Computer Aided Learning and Instruction In Science and Engineering*, Telecom, Paris.

Rabardel, P. (1995) *Les hommes et les technologies: une approche cognitive des instruments contemporains*. Paris, A. Colin.

Trouche, L. (1996) *Etude des rapports entre processus de conceptualisation et processus d'instrumentation*. Thèse de doctorat, Université de Montpellier.

Van Labeke, N., Aiken, R., Morinet-Lambert, J. and Grandbastien, M. (1999) IF "What is the core of AI & Education ?" is the Question THEN "Teaching Knowledge" is the Answer. In *Artificial Intelligence in Education*, S. P. Lajoie and M. Vivet (eds.), IOS Press, pp. 241-248.

Vivet, M. (1984) *Expertise mathématique et informatique: CAMELIA, un logiciel pour raisonner et calculer*. Thèse d'état, Université Paris VI.

BIOGRAPHY

Dominique Lenne is in charge of research in the 'New Technologies and Education' (TECNE) department of the French institute of pedagogical research (INRP). His current research interests are centred on the design and evaluation of computer algebra learning environments.

Jean-Michel Gélis is senior lecturer at the teacher training institute of Versailles. The work reported in this paper has been carried out with helpful contribution of Hervé Hamon and Michel Enjalbert, qualified high-school mathematics teachers.

43

Teaching of Discrete Mathematics

Using Functional Languages in Computer Science Courses

Simone C. Mendes, Tiarajú A. Diverio and Dalcidio M. Claudio

Instituto de Informática e PPGC da UFRGS, C.P. 15064, 91501-970 Porto Alegre, Brazil

diverio@inf.ufrgs.br

Keywords: computing, algorithms, higher education, programming

Abstract: This paper presents an alternative methodology of development for the discipline of Discrete Mathematics offered to courses in the area of computation. It explores the availability of new teaching tools and programming languages. This way, we try to stimulate and provide students with an environment in which they can reach better results in order that it can contribute in the creative and constructive application of their knowledge.

1. INTRODUCTION

The constant development of technology has unleashed new challenges in education. Its use has been seen as a strong element for knowledge construction support. This makes it possible for the teacher to adopt a new role, as a mediator and facilitator of the student's learning.

Some parts of mathematics disciplines have found difficulties in using computational tools in the development of their concepts and the performance rate in these disciplines have not been satisfactory. One such case is Discrete Mathematics, which is essential to the formation of the courses in the area of Computer Science, as seen in universities of Rio Grande do Sul State (Menezes et al. 2000).

An alternative methodology is desired for the development of the Discrete Mathematics discipline, offered to courses in the area of computation, by exploring the availability of new teaching tools and programming languages. Thus, we try to stimulate and provide students with an environment in which they can achieve better results and contribute to a creative and constructive application of their knowledge.

2. MATHEMATICS AND COMPUTATION

The development of computation creates a propitious environment for the launching of new educational technologies. Such tools end up giving value to the process of the student's learning and renew the didactic methods used by the teacher.

The integration of technology with education has taken place in different periods in the most distinctive areas. The Mathematics teaching, specially the Discrete Mathematics for graduation courses of the computational area in Brazil, has not found yet a way to incorporate computational tools to the development of very important concepts for the formation of the student in this area. It is very common for students to study the disciplines in a forced way, as an obligation they must fulfill. They do not see direct or indirect application of the contents in their future professional life, and even less they do not see it as a necessary and essential knowledge for the rest of the course.

It is very common for them to study the disciplines of the mathematical area as if they were independent of the rest of the course, without having the opportunity to experience learning in which the intrinsic relation between mathematics and programming is explained.

Mathematics is very used in several areas of Computing Science, in applications that include the specification of programs, data structures, analysis and implementation of algorithms and correctness. The use of computers, however, can help making mathematics easier to be understood and used, by turning mathematical terms executable and abstract concepts more concrete, all through the use of computational tools such as mathematical proof verifier.

Mathematics provides fundamental tools to any scientific discipline, which is essential to programming because it helps the student to rationalise the implementation of the programs. And the programming, on the other hand, has been utilised since its beginning for the resolution of mathematical problems. However, nowadays the courses on mathematics are delivered in a separate way from the programming courses, and they make very little use of the second one to re-enforce and stimulate the learning of mathematical concepts.

The solutions for the mathematical problems can be drawn and implemented in the computer, as if it were the pencil and the paper traditionally used for this very purpose. This new way to reach the solution modifies the procedure as a whole, but without depriving it of its characteristics. The traditional process, according to Rosa and Cirigliano (1999), is one that creates a mathematical model, starting from the problem, and then creating a transformed model that will conduct it to the solution, upon which the proof will be carried out in order that the solved problem can be finally obtained. When integrating the programming to this model, we have a new process in which the mathematical model is implemented by reaching the solution through the computer. To assure the validity of this solution we must then demonstrate the equivalence between the models, which guarantees that the solution obtained by the program is correct. This new model, through which it is, illustrated the process of resolution of problems under the algorithm approach of the mathematical concepts and the approach on the functional characteristics of a programming language is represented in Figure 1.

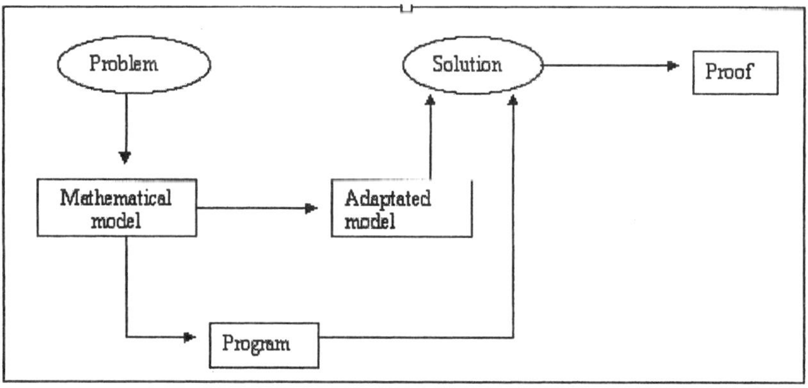

Figure 1. Process of resolution of a problem through the implementering in a programming language

It is important for the student to acquire, from the beginning of the course, a habit of specifying, solving problems and try to solve them by using the computer and a mathematical method to reason about them. Students can have a vision of the integrated process represented in Figure 1 through the methodology of the application of a language as formalism, in which the solutions for certain problems are programmed.

3. STATE OF ART OF THE DISCRETE MATHEMATICS DISCIPLINE

The discipline of Discrete Mathematics is present in the courses of the Computer Science area according to the Policy Laws and Bases of the Education and Culture Ministry of Brazil (MEC 2000). According to this document, the discipline is a fundamental pre-requisite for several other disciplines that follow in the posterior semesters, such as programming, computation and algorithms, computer architecture, compilers, database and artificial intelligence. Such evidence re-enforces the fact that their contents must be worked out in a general and ample way, in order to develop the pertinent reasoning, so that students can have a strong base for the moment they start studying the other disciplines of the course.

Although the discipline is essential for the rest of the course, nowadays it is not obtaining the desired success. The approval rates verified in the two principal universities of Rio Grande do Sul, during the between 1998 and 2000, are considered unsatisfactory due to its importance. The data below demonstrate the performance of the students that attended this discipline in the mentioned universities.

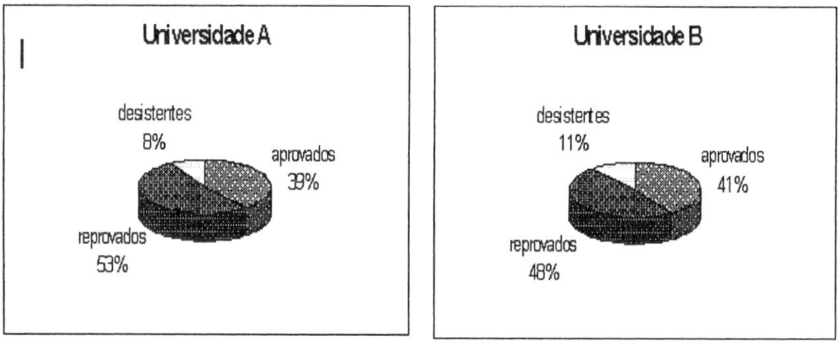

Figure 2. Performance of students in discrete Mathematics, period 1998-2000

This discipline is delivered today in a traditional manner, through theoretical-expositive classes and through realisation of works and written exams. We can notice, thus, the necessity to search in the programming paradigms an alternative, through the utilisation of a functional language.

4. UTILISATION OF A FUNCTIONAL LANGUAGE

The utilisation of a functional language as a supportive tool to the development of discrete mathematical contents makes it possible to naturally express the mathematical language, to easily prove the properties about the programs and to prove the equivalence between the model and the implementation.

The functional language holds reasoning similar to the one necessary for the development of discrete mathematical contents. That is, it is very similar to the one used in the mathematical formalisms. This fact allows the utilised language to be introduced in the course in a natural way, without requiring extra efforts from the students to learn other programming syntax.

For example, let be the theorem P ∧ Q→ P. its proof can be carried out in a traditional manner by using a functional language. The traditional manner to prove it is through the utilisation of the inference rules of the propositional logic, by structuring it in a tree form, as it can be observed in Figure 3.

1. Rule 1: $\wedge EL$: elimination of "e" (∧) to the left
1. Rule 2: $\rightarrow I$: Introduction of the implication (→)
    1. $\underline{P \wedge Q}\ \{\wedge E_L\}$
    1. $\underline{\quad P \quad}\ \{\rightarrow I\}$
    1. $P \wedge Q \rightarrow P$

Figure 3. Theorem proof through the traditional manner

The proof carried out by using the functional programming language (for example, the Haskell language), allows the student to apply the same necessary rules for the proof demonstrated in the previous figure at the same time it works on the functional programming concepts. This way, it accomplishes the integration between the concepts developed in classroom and the programming. The proof of the same Theorem using a functional language for this purpose is represented in Figure 4.

```
prova Regra :: Prova
provaRegra =
ImpI
        (AndEL
              (Assume (And P Q))
               P),
        (Imp (And P Q) P)
```

Figure 4. Theorem proof by using the alternative methodology

Based on these facts, and through a master's thesis, an alternative methodology for the teaching of Discrete Mathematics that aims at utilising a functional language in the development of the discipline's concepts has been developed and proposed. The work is based on a prototype in which libraries using the Haskell language were worked out, which implement some theorem proofs, mathematical recursion and induction, having as a model the proposal of Hall and O'Donnell (2000). The work set results in the proposition of a new methodology that culminates in the restructuring of the discipline as a whole and its reflects on the discipline itself and the other disciplines of the graduation course.

Through the utilisation of theorem prover, for example, the student develops several parallel skills. Besides needing knowledge of the propositional logic rules, students must know how to apply them in order to carry out the correct implementation of the proof, while they develop programming skills in a language very similar to the one used in the proof. Figure 5 illustrates some of the skills developed simultaneously when the programming is utilised as a tool in the assistance to the learning of mathematical concepts.

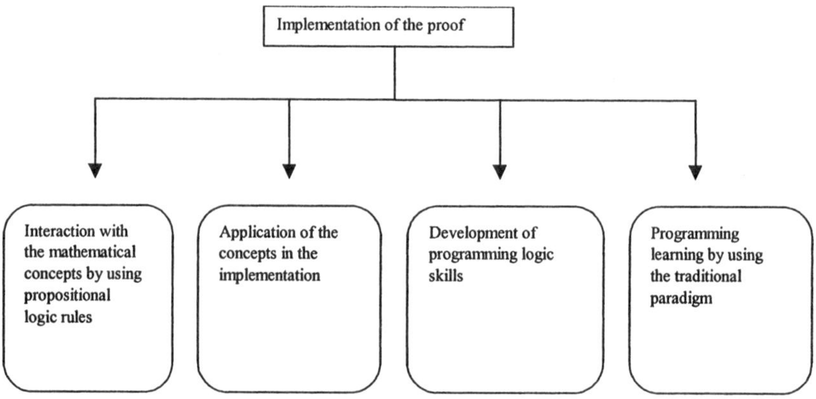

Figure 5. Skills developed during the implementering of proof

When programming and the model of resolution of a problem are integrated, instead of just one process being used, no matter the theorem proof, several parallel processes are developed, important and necessary skills to the students of the computational courses. Without the integration, a basic process takes place, which is the interaction of the student with the mathematical concepts, as demonstrated in the examples of Figures 3 and 4, through the utilisation of the propositional logic rules in order to carry out the traditional proof of the theorem.

The integration of the programming the proof of the Theorem develops three new skills, which added to the one described in the traditional process, are the following:

Interaction with the concepts of the discipline: the student performs learning of fundamental concepts of the discipline.

Application of logic concepts in the implementation: to implement the solution of the proof, the student must have the knowledge of the concept (1) and, then, apply them in the implementation of the proof;

Development of programming logic skills: at the same time it is thought about a solution to carry out an implementation of the proof, it performs logical reasoning activities necessary to the programming;

Learning of the programming by using the functional paradigm: due to the fact that the syntax of the functional language is similar to the mathematical language, the student learns to program by using the functional paradigm without too many difficulties.

The skills created when using the alternative methodology are illustrated in Figure 5.

5. FUNCTIONAL LANGUAGE AS FIRST LANGUAGE

The first language taught in the courses of the Computer Science area in the main universities of Rio Grande do Sul that is a procedimental language. Its characteristics do not allow logic concepts, theory of the sets and demonstrations to be worked out with the same facility that a functional language, for example, does.

The functional languages, like the Haskell language, have as a principal characteristic the reproduction of a mathematical language because in this paradigm the programs are formed exclusively by functions, which justify its denomination. The principal program is a function that receives entry parameters and produces a result, in the same way the student reasons mathematically when he is solving a problem on the paper.

The teaching of a functional language in the first semester of the course helps the learning process of the concepts of discrete mathematics, mainly because these two languages have the same syntax used in Mathematics.

This way, we could have the teaching situation represented by Figure 6. The figure illustrates the skills developed in each one of the methodologies, the utilised languages as first language of the course and de performance obtained and/or expected from the students.

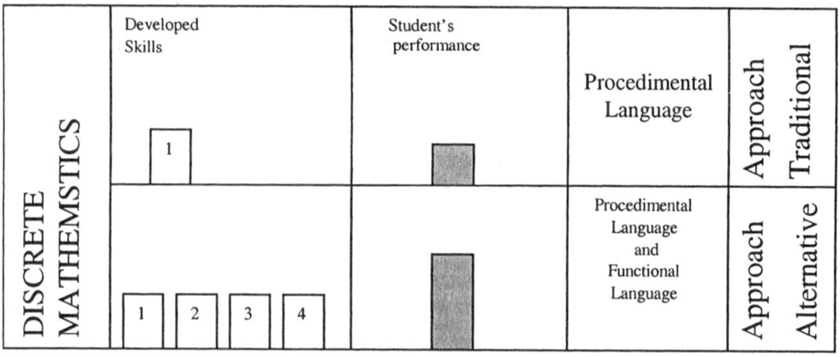

Figure 6. Utilisation of the alternative methodology: functional language also as first language

6. FINAL COMMENTS

The utilisation of a functional programming language in the discipline of Discrete Mathematics, offered in the first semester, is an alternative methodology of teaching. This methodology allows the student to apply and construct in a creative way, interaction skills with the concepts of the discipline, their application in the implementation, development of programming logic skills and learning of the programming with focus on the functional paradigm, as demonstrated in Figure 6.

The mathematical union with the functional programming paradigm also makes possible for students to develop concepts of discrete mathematics, which are very important for their development, without them noticing it. At the same time, they are developing functional programming concepts, with are only worked in more advanced semesters of the course.

The utilisation of the functional programming as a tool for the constructive and applied development of the theoretical concepts, does not require extra efforts for the comprehension of its programming syntax, as its programs are formed exclusively by functions. Thus, the necessary reasoning for both activities are similar, which provides a friendly integration of the discrete mathematics with the functional programming.

Finally, all the educational technology available to provide students with a learning environment that keeps them away from the hard classes, and apparently with no application for their professional future, must be used. It is necessary, then to allow students to make use of all their potential and enthusiasm in the activities that have as a principal objective the students' learning.

REFERENCES

MEC (2000) *Diretrizes curriculares das áreas de computação e informática*. Brasília. [www.mec.gov.br/Sesu/diretriz.shtm] 12.06.2000.

Rosa, S. and Cirigliano, G. (1999) Ensayo sobre Matemática aplicada a Computación. In *VII Congresso Iberoamericano de Educación Superior en Computación*, 1999, Asuncíon, Paraguay, Anais, Asunción, p. 141.

Hall, C. and O'donnell, J. (2000) *Discrete mathematics using a computer*. 1ª ed., Springer.

Menezes, P.B. et al. (2000) Proposta de plano pedagógico para matéria Matemática. In *Congresso da Sociedade Brasileira de Computação*, Curitiba, PR.

BIOGRAPHY

Simone C. Mendes has a Masters in Science Computer and Mathematics at PPGC-UFRGS. Her areas of interests are Informatics in Education and Computational Mathematics.

Tiarajú A. Diverio graduated in Mathematics for the UFRGS, and has Masters and Doctorate in Computer Science to the CPGCC (1986 and 1995). He is Professor and Researcher of the Institute Computer Science at UFRGS. His areas of interest are Processing of High Performance (Processing Vectorial, Parallel and Distributed and Parallel Mathematical Algorithms) and Informatics in Education (Educational Development of Software for Mathematics).

Dalcidio M. Claudio has a Doctorate in Computer Science from Karlsruhe. He is a researcher of the Institute Computer Science at UFRGS and Professor at CPGCC in PUCRS. His areas of interest are Interval Mathematics, Scientific Computation and Informatics in Education (Educational Development of Software for Mathematics).

44

Automatic Differentiation in Intelligent Tutoring Systems

Vladislav Katkov and Ada Novosselova
Institute of Engineering Cybernetics, National Academy of Sciences, 6 Surganov Street, Minsk 220012, Belarus
katkov@newman.bas-net.by
Byelorussian State University, 4 Scorina Avenue, Minsk 220050, Belarus

Keywords: learning environments, intelligent tutoring systems, automatic differentiation

Abstract: The automatic differentiation is widely used with the decision of a wide class of problems. The expansion of languages C/C++, Fortran-77 and Pascal for these purposes and its realisation as system Diff are described. The application of the offered approach is shown by development several tutoring systems: Graph – for drawing of the graphs, Autopracticum – for automation tutoring works on numerical analysis and mathematical modelling and data analysis. The system Diff is realised on IBM PCs under supervising of Windows 95/97/98.

1. INTRODUCTION

Use of the computer for calculation of the value of function given by the formula has been known for a long time – from the moment of the computer's appearance. In many tasks along with value of function it is often required to know its derivatives. The existing practice of such tasks is that all analytical manipulations are carried out manually beforehand, for stages of algorithm development, and then the program is written and executed. This approach has three problems. First, the analytical manipulations can appear rather labour consuming and, as they are carried out by the person, the probability of mistakes is high. Second, these mistakes are in the program and in practice they cannot be discovered except by programmer's methods. Consequently the process of program debugging becomes longer. Third, with change of initial functions it is necessary to repeat the calculations anew and to correct the program; in many cases new mistakes penetrate into the program and it will require the repeated debugging.

As the process of differentiation is strictly formalised, it can be automated with the help of the computer. Attempts to make it were undertaken repeatedly. Apparently, Kahrimanian (1953) and Nolan (1953) were the first. The Kantorovich's article (Kantorovich 1957) provided the determining influence on works on the analytical calculation. The formalism for representation of any expression as a sequence of tetrads consisting of operands, binary and monadic operations were offered in it. The program CODEX and its further modification SUPER-CODEX intended for automatic differentiation on a Fortran were developed at the University of Wisconsin-Madison (USA) under a management of Reiter (Rall 1981) in mid-sixties. The procedures of differentiation were included in standard library of compiler; as a result the applied program practically did not require preliminary processing and at once passed on compilation and execution. In 1992 at Argonne National Laboratory and Rice University (USA) the system ADIFOR for automatic differentiation on Fortran-77 was developed under approximately the same scheme that was used in CODEX and SUPER-CODEX (Bischof et al. 1992).

The *Diff* system developed in the Institute of Engineering Cybernetics, National Academy of Sciences, Belarus, (Katkov 2000a) calculates the partial and total derivatives, derivatives of implicit functions, derivatives of functions given by sequence of formulas, Jacobian, Hessian matrix (matrix from second order derivatives), and Taylor's series etc. For inclusion of differentiation in C-programs the language was extended by the description of functions and was complemented by corresponding library of procedures for calculation of derivative, Jacobian, expansion in Taylor's series and other means.

Recently there was a new application of differentiation connected with sensitivity analysis of numerical solution to the errors or uncertainties in the input data and parameters (Dongming et al. 1997). If the solution is calculated by finite-difference methods it results in necessity of analytical calculation and numeric estimation of several millions derivatives already for grids of the order 50 x 50 nodes. Manually it's practically impossible to fulfil this work. This problem is easily resolved using automatic differentiation systems.

2. AUTOMATIC DIFFERENTIATION IN MATHMATICS COURSES

This technique is widely applied in the educational process. For example, with study of Newton's method for minimization of multivariable function student can investigate speed of convergence for different input functions, different initial approximations, and different conditions of the iterative loop termination. We list some other themes in which the automatic differentiation is effectively used.

- Calculation of a root of the equation by Newton's method – use second derivative for choice of initial approximation and first derivative with calculation of next iteration.
- Drawing of the graph of function – calculation of first derivative for finding of minimum/maximum of function and second derivative for calculation of points of inflection, areas of convexity/concavity of function, finding asymptotes.
- Calculation of limits with use of l'Hospitale's rule.
- The calculation of integral with an estimation of the remainder term – for example, in Simpson's method is required to know fourth derivative.
- The solution of the differential equation by expansion in Taylor's series.
- The calculation of numerical values of Lipschitz's constant with an estimation of the differential equation solution.
- The investigatio of the singular points of the differential equation $y' = P(x,y)/Q(x,y)$ – expansion of P and Q in Taylor's series.
- The construction of tangents to a curve, calculation of radius of curvature, length of a curve, evolute and evolvent.
- The summation of functional series with an estimation of the remainder term.
- The calculation of integral by a method of differentiation on parameter etc.

3. AN EXAMPLE OF *DIFF* SYSTEM USE

Suppose it is required to calculate a minimum of function of two variables by Newton's method. The method has a square-law speed of convergence, but its use in practice demands hand-operated differentiation with all negative consequences.. As rule, the user is compelled to use other, less effective algorithms.

Algorithm. Let (x_0, y_0) is an initial approximation to a point of minimum. The next approximation is calculated under the formulas

$$x_{k+1} = x_k - (h_{2,2}fx_k - h_{1,2}fy_k)/\det(h), \quad y_{k+1} = y_k - (-h_{2,1}fx_k + h_{1,1}fy_k)/\det(h),$$

where $\{fx, fy\}'$ is gradient of function $f(x,y)$, $\{h_{i,j}\}$ is Hessian matrix: $h_{1,1} = f_{xx}$, $h_{1,2} = h_{2,1} = f_{xy}$, $h_{2,2} = f_{yy}$, and det (h) is determinant of a matrix h. The calculations are performed by iterations so long as two consecutive approximations will differ less than on ε.

The program for function $f(x,y) = 100(y-x^2)^2 + (1-x)^2$ can be written down in the following form:

```
// Standard introduction to the program
$func_i f(x,y) = 100*(y-x^2)^2 + (1-x)^2;
$func_i fx(x,y) = $diff(f,x);      // Gradient of f(x,y)
$func_i fy(x,y) = $diff(f,y);
$func_i H11(x,y) = $diff(fx,x);  // Hessian matrix
$func_i H12(x,y) = $diff(fx,y);
$func_i H22(x,y) = $diff(fy,y);

void Minimum()              // Main program
{ const double eps=1e-6;    // Error
  double x0=-1.2, y0=1.0;   // Initial approximation
  double h11, h12, h22, det; // Hessian matrix h and its determinant
  double fx, fy, dx, dy;    // Gradient of f(x,y)
  int iter = 0;             // Iteration counter
  do
   { iter++; h11=H11_c(x0,y0); h12=H12_c(x0,y0);
    h22=H22_c(x0,y0); fx=fx_c(x0,y0); fy=fy_c(x0,y0);
    det=h11*h22-h12*h12;
    dx=(h22*fx-h12*fy)/det; dy=(h11*fy-h12*fx)/det;
    x0-=dx; y0-=dy;
    printf(/* iter=..., x=..., y=..., f(x,y)=...*/);
   } while (sqrt(dx*dx+dy*dy)>=eps;
   return;
}
```

Let us make some explanation. A line '$func_i f(x,y)=100*(y-x^2)^2 +(1-x)^2;' describes the function: its name (f), arguments names (x, y) and expression. In a line '$func_i fx(x,y)=$diff(f,x);' one more function (derivative $\partial f/\partial x$) is defined; the differentiation operation '$diff(...)' is used for it. To carry out the computation it is necessary to transform the function definition '$func_i ...' into C-text. Just it also is done by a description '$func_i fx(x, y) = ...', which translates the announcement 'fx' into the function's definition 'fx_c ...' in C-language and inserts it into the program, adding suffix 'c' to name 'fx'. In result the standard call 'fx_c(...)' in the C-program may be used. For example, for 'fx_c' the next text will be generated

```
double fx_c(double x, double y)
{ return (-400.0*(y-x*x)*x-2.0*(1.0-x)); }
```

The following results will be printed after program updating by the *Diff* system, compilation and execution:

```
iter = 1   x = -1.17...     y =  1.3...       f(x,y) =     4.7...
iter = 2   x =  0.7631...   y = -3.1...       f(x,y) = 1411.8...
iter = 3   x =  0.7634...   y =  0.58...      f(x,y) =     0.05...
iter = 4   x =  0.9999953   y =  0.94...      f(x,y) =     0.31...
iter = 5   x =  0.9999957   y =  0.9999914    f(x,y) =     0.0000000
iter = 6   x =  1.0000000   y =  1.0000000    f(x,y) =     0.0000000
iter = 7   x =  1.0000000   y =  1.0000000    f(x,y) =     0.0000000
```

If there is a need to solve the same task by another method that is not requiring differentiation, for example, by Nelder-Mead algorithm (Himmelblau 1972) with the same initial data, 179 iterations will be required. As we see, the application of automatic differentiation allows giving 'a second life' to such powerful method, as Newton's one.

4. *GRAPH*: INTELLIGENT TUTORING SYSTEM FOR GRAPH DRAWING

The function graph is powerful and convenient tool for the research of functional dependencies in mathematics and applications. Graph drawing is widely used in various activities at schools, colleges, universities, R&D institutes, in business, in a science, and in industry. This activity is realised in many applied programs, for example, in universal systems of numerical and analytical manipulations *Mathematica* and MATLAB. The universality and the multipurpose of such systems means that the user is compelled in the beginning to study them, and only after that they be able to modest solve the simple task – to draw the graph relevant to their function. For example, the *Mathematica* user's guide occupies 1400 pages.

The purpose of our work – to propose the simple and effective system for graph drawing not requiring any appreciable efforts in mastering it by the novice (Katkov 2000b). At the same time for the experienced user there are a additional possibilities allowing users to build and analyse the complex graphs of functions and to represent the result in a convenient form. It is permitted to make some transformations over graph for the reception of the required image or analysis of function. The system was developed in two variants: *School*, for the beginners, and *Basic*, in which all facilities of the system are accessible. The *Graph* system works in a semi-automatic mode and provides help for the user in inconvenient settings. Basically it works through updating of the singular points and work to infinity.

The system has the built-in library of the most widespread functions, in which for each function will be given its formula, graph with some typical values of parameters and brief explanation. The library consists of two parts: libraries of school functions (algebraic functions, trigonometrical functions and inverse to them, exponent, logarithm, power, hyperbolic and other functions) and basic library (special functions).

The *Graph* system has the interconnected set of help and demonstration examples. There are rich means of polygraphic representation of the graphs for the most popular textual and graphic editors.

4.1 Construction of Function Graph

The process of graph drawing consists from the following steps:

- To determine domain of function definition.
- To calculate the singular points, points of maximum and minimum, points of inflection and points of function discontinuity.
- To calculate asymptotes vertical, horizontal and sloping. To find limits of function in the chosen points, including indefinites of a kind $0/0$, ∞/∞, $0\cdot\infty$, $\infty-\infty$, 1^{∞}, 0^{0}, ∞^{0}.
- To set the sizes of the graphs, to draw axes to put inscriptions.
- To draw the graph of function.
- To edit a figure before printing or insert in the document.

The domain of definition. The *Graph* system calculates the domain of definition for what writes out restrictions on argument of function: the denominator is not equal to zero, the argument of the 'log' function is positive, the subradical expression for a root of an even degree is non-negative etc.

The singular points and function breaks points, points of maximum and minimum, points of inflection and points of function discontinuity are defined. The points of a maximum and minimum, and also point of inflection are calculated with use of the first and second derivatives.

The calculation of asymptotes vertical, horizontal and sloping. The parameters k and b of sloping asymptote $y = k{\cdot}x + b$ calculated on well-known formulas. The uncovering of indefinitesses $0/0$, ∞/∞ and others with use of l'Hospitale's rule is made up in a semi-automatic mode, when the user can see intermediate result and to operate the analytical calculations.

The setting of the graph sizes, drawing of coordinate axes and inscriptions. Before drawing of the graph it is necessary to specify its sizes, to draw axes of coordinates, to choose types of scales for axes of coordinates (usual, logarithmic, half-logarithmic), to superscribe numbers on them, to set drawing a coordinate grid, if it is necessary. The graph can be supplied with inscriptions and explanatory text.

Drawing of the graphs. The *Graph* system works in a dialogue mode and can simultaneously build the graphs of two functions $f(x)$ and $g(x)$ in two different windows or in one window by superposition. The graphs are drawn in Cartesian coordinates. The function can contain no more than one parameter. The *Graph* system can build family of the graphs with various values of parameters. Each graph is represented by a curve, at which the color, thickness and type of a line (from an offered set) are easy selected.

The function is set analytically in one of the following forms:

a) Explicitly, as $y = f(x)$, $a \leq x \leq b$.
b) Parametric, as $x = X(t)$, $y = Y(t)$, $a \leq t \leq b$.
c) Implicitly, as $f(x, y) = 0$, $a \leq x \leq b$ or $c \leq y \leq d$.

Edition of a figure for printing or insert in the document. The user can transform a figure to a textual or graphic file of the appropriate textual or graphic editor. It is supposed to use such formats, as .doc, .rtf, .pdf, .bmp, html, .pcx, .gif, .jpg. It is possible also to convert symbolic expression for function and its derivatives into a textual file for WinWord, Adobe Acrobat etc. The *Graph* system can translate the function definition and its derivatives in languages C/C++, Fortran, and Pascal.

5. *AUTOPRACTICUM*: INTELLIGENT TUTORING SYSTEM

The intelligent system of automation of learning process in mathematics should have the following minimal features (Katkov and Novosselova 1997).

- Symbols manipulations: automatic differentiation, simplification of expressions, reduction of similar terms and so on.
- Drawing of the graphs of functions.
- Friendly interface: the native language, dialogue menu, convenient features of the definition of input parameters and presentations of results, and help.
- Ergonomics requirements: minimisation of number of control keys, colour, sound and so on.

Proposed below is a model of an integrated approach to the process of automated teaching (training). The model includes: (1) maximal use of computer for routine work; (2) some popular symbolic manipulations; (3) broad use of textual and graphic help menus for topics under study; (4) use of ergonomic means for control of the teaching system (colour, sound, dynamic pictures, light buttons/keys, menus); (5) presentation of results in an easy way (graphs, diagrams, tables, pictograms).

The *Autopracticum* system provides an approach which makes the system carry out all the routine while leaving the intellectual part for the student (well-grounded selection of the numerical method, examination of its properties and peculiarities, analysis of results). The system is programmed to keep up basic didactic principles: problem-oriented education, use of visual aids, activity and consciousness, simplicity, systematic approach and consistency, sound knowledge and recurrence.

The *Autopracticum* system has the following sections that calculate roots of non-linear equations, calculate integral values, draw function graphs, and carry out mathematical modelling and data analysis.

The system is intended for the students 2-4 courses and is used in educational process of the Byelorussian state university. Use of *Autopracticum* raises efficiency of educational process in 3-5 times.

5.1 Method of practical work in numerical analysis

When assigned problems to get roots of non-linear equations, the student, using the *Autopracticum* system, can: (1) view the function's graph to visually define the segment where the root is located; (2) choose the appropriate method using a concise help menu in the form of static or motion pictures (Newton's method, for example); (3) enter the initial data: function $f(x)$, segment $[a, b]$, and the error of calculation; (4) run the calculation with the system automatically calculating the $f'(x)$ and $f''(x)$ derivatives in the analytic form, selecting a or b as the initial x_0 approximation by $f'(x_0) \cdot f''(x_0)$ sign, creating the calculation formula $x_{n+1} = x_n - f(x_n)/f'(x_n)$, making the calculations and producing the result – the root value and the number of iterations; (5) store the results of calculations and print them as a report at the end of the work.

With the results derived by different methods for different initial data at hand, the student can assess the advantages and disadvantages of the examined algorithms.

6. CONCLUSION

As well as for any other tool of programming, the area of its real application depends on needs and ingenuity of the user. We propose that the automatic differentiation technique will allow the wider application of mathematical methods in the most various applied areas alongside with the numerical analysis.

REFERENCES

Bischof, C., Carle, A., Corliss, G., Griewank, A. and Hovland, P. (1992) ADIFOR – Generating Derivative Codes from Fortran Programs. *Scientific Programming*, Vol. 1, pp. 11-29.

Dongming, H., Byun, D.W. and Odman, M.T. (1997) An automatic differentiation technique for sensitivity analysis of numerical advection schemes in air quality model. *Atmospheric Environment*, Vol. 31, # 6, pp. 879-888.

Himmelblau, D.M. (1972) *Applied Nonlinear Programming*. McGraw-Hill Book Company.

Kahrimanian, H.G. (1953) *Analytical Differentiation by a Digit Computer*. M. A. Thesis, Temple Univ, Philadelphia.

Kantorovich, L.V. (1957) About mathematical symbolics convenient for performance of machine calculations. *Doklady Akademii Nauk SSSR*, 11, pp. 738-741 (in Russian).

Katkov, V.L. (2000a) Automatic differentiation and its applications. *Vesti National Academy of Sciences*, Belarus, 1, pp. 68-75 (in Russian).

Katkov, V.L. (2000b) The Graph system for function graph construction. In *Proceedings of Conference on Educational Uses of Information and Communication Technologies*. 16th World Computer Congress 2000, Beijing, August, p. 240.

Katkov, V.L. and Novosselova A.N. (1997) Intelligent Tutoring in Numerical Methods. In *Proc. of AI-ED World Conference on Artificial Intelligence in Education*, Kobe, Japan, August, pp. 607-608.

Nolan, J. (1953) *Analytical Differentiation by a Digit Computer*. M. A. Thesis, M. A. MIT, Cambridge.

Rall, L. B. (1981) *Automatic Differentiation: Techniques and Applications*. Lectures Notes in Computer Science, Vol. 120. Springer-Verlag, Berlin Heidelberg New York, pp. 1-160.

BIOGRAPHIES

Professor Vladislav Katkov is a head of laboratory and works in the field of computer algebraic systems and automation of educational process in a higher school. Under his management some systems symbol manipulations and development of the computer programs by a top down method were created. Recently his interests have been concentrated on writing of the electronic textbooks on computer science.

Ada Novosselova is lecturer, she has developed intelligent tutoring system *Autopracticum* for automation of laboratory works on numerical methods, mathematical modeling and analysis of the data. Further work on the development of the system is being undertaken.

PART FIVE

TEACHING COMPUTER SCIENCE

45

PC Interfacing by Example

John Fulcher
School of Information Technology and Computer Science, University of Wollongong, Northfields Ave, Wollongong NSW 2522, Australia
john@uow.edu.au

Keywords: control technology, experimental, problem solving, programming, user interface

Abstract: A laboratory environment for the teaching of microcomputer interfacing and real time computing is described. An Integrated Development Environment (IDE) running on the host PC facilitates the writing of software for a target 68HC12 microcontroller, which connects to host via the latter's serial port. Students are encouraged to learn by doing, including learning from their mistakes – hence necessitating good debugging facilities within the IDE. This approach is in keeping with that of situated learning (Lave and Wenger 1991). To put it another way, knowledge as such is not *taught*, but rather imparted through a process of apprenticeship. In this context, the role of the educator is primarily to provide a nurturing environment in which students are able to get their hands dirty and attempt to interface to real-world peripheral devices. Lecturing staff are used as consultants or last resort trouble-shooters, with students encouraged to perform the bulk of their own software development and debugging. Experience has shown that students respond admirably to such an approach, commonly experiencing the subject as "it's a lot of work, but very enjoyable – I learnt a lot".

1. INTRODUCTION

We have a tradition at the University of Wollongong of designing our undergraduate subjects to be very much laboratory-based. This is particularly the case with the Microcomputer Interfacing and Real-Time Computing subject which students can elect to undertake during their third and final year of their Bachelor of Computer Science study. We believe students learn by doing, *especially* by getting their hands dirty and learning from their own mistakes (Fulcher 1990). Furthermore, they best learn underlying principles by having to apply these to real-world problems (Fulcher 1991).

Another emphasis – in both subjects – is the exposure of students to what lies under the hood of the computer. In other words, they gain an appreciation of what is contained within this black box called a computer.

Introductory subjects in computer architecture, computer systems and/or assembly language programming tend to use simulators (e.g. Gray 1987, Patterson and Hennessy 1994). By contrast, we have recently shifted the focus of our introductory computer systems subject to that of PCs in general, and the Pentium processor in particular (Duntemann 2000) – one reason for this, by the way, is that this is the first time the author has encountered PC assembly language programming covered not only from a DOS perspective, but also for Linux.

The shareware assembler `NASM` forms the common link between DOS and Linux in the PC environment (an entire NASM-IDE in the case of the former). The inbuilt (16-bit) `debug` is used in the DOS environment, whereas the (32-bit) `gcc` debug tool – `gdb` – is used under Linux (which causes a slight trauma in students migrating from the Intel-style syntax of `debug` to the AT&T syntax used in the `gcc` tool suite!). Furthermore, reliance on BIOS software routines under DOS shifts to standard C library function calls under Linux.

The PC emphasis of the earlier Introduction to Computer Systems subject is expanded upon in the third-year Microcomputer Interfacing and Real-Time Computing subject. In the latter, students are given ample opportunity to control real-world devices (not just *simulations* thereof). Feedback from students is invariably positive – they typically cite this subject as one of the best they undertake during their entire 3 years Bachelor of Computer Science degree studies.

Enrolment numbers are typically between 30 and 40, compared with 120 to 150 in the first-year Introduction to Computer Systems subject.

2. LABORATORY SETUP

Previous incarnations of the Microcomputer Interfacing Laboratory were based around the 8-bit Motorola MC6800 (via Heathkit ET3400 trainers – Fulcher 1989a), and the 16/32-bit MC68000 (via firstly Motorola's Educational Computer Board, thence the Applix 1616 – Fulcher 1989b,

Fulcher 1990, Fulcher 1991). In each case, the basic microcomputer trainer interfaced to individual experiment pods via in-house expansion circuitry.

In choosing individual (plug-in) experiment pods, we were conscious of making the laboratory assignment work both interesting and accessible to the students. Typical experiments include:

1. LCD/Dot Matrix displays
2. timer/music
3. serial communications
4. bar code reader
5. x-y drill positioner
6. slot car controller
7. model train scheduler, and
8. turtle robot controller.

In each case, heavy emphasis is placed on students writing their own (rudimentary) software drivers for the hardware controllers provided. To quote from the preface of an earlier accompanying textbook (Fulcher 1989a): "Interfacing peripheral devices to a microcomputer involves three important factors. *Firstly*, we need to know the basic operating principles of the peripheral device we're attempting to interface to the computer. *Secondly*, we need to know the characteristics of the particular peripheral support chip we're using for this task. *Thirdly*, we need to write the control software."

The immediate feedback provided to students by having LEDs flash on/(off), interrupts being generated, and the actual movement of real world devices greatly assists students in their learning experience.

A few years ago we decided to migrate our existing (MC68000-based) experiment pods to a PC platform. One motivation behind this decision was to impart skills to students which they would be able to take *beyond* the classroom laboratory setting and into the real world following completion of their formal studies.

In order to ease the transition to a PC environment, we developed an in-house ISA expansion card, which allowed direct connection to our pre-existing (MC68000) range of experiment pods. The following year saw these older experiment pods replaced by a single development platform based around a Motorola MC68HC12 microcomputer.

3. LABORATORY ASSIGNMENTS

The first PC-based laboratory assignments were undertaken on the PC itself, using the Open Source DJGPP C/C++ Compiler (in fact a complete Integrated Development Environment – http://www.delorie.com/djgpp).

Open Source software was chosen rather than commercial, in order to kept costs low (e.g. Microsoft Visual C++ – Buchanan 1996).

Extensive use is made of interrupts – both hardware (from external peripherals) and software. The latter focuses on BIOS library function calls, with which students become familiar during the (first-year) Introduction to Computer Systems subject. It is only in the later-year subject however that the separation of functions contained within the *highly integrated* PC support chips becomes clear. Indeed, a complete system can be constructed using just three (highly integrated) peripheral support chips:

1. i82439 System Controller (DRAM, SRAM/cache, ECC),
2. i82371 PCI/ISA Xcelerator (IDE, PCI-ISA bridge, Priority Interrupt Controller, timers, plug-and-play, mice, USB root hub), and
3. i82091 Advanced Interface to Peripherals (2 serial, 1 parallel, FDD).

In the later-year subject, interfacing is approached from a *functional* perspective, but again with a focus on interrupt-driven IO and buffering.

The mode of operation of the laboratory equipment was subsequently changed from code development on the target machine (i.e. the PC itself), to a PC host/68HC12 target configuration. A locally developed 68HC12 Monitor-in-RAM provides students with rudimentary functionality, although not as comprehensive as that contained within the PC BIOS:

D<from, nbytes>	-	Display memory
F<from, nbytes, data>	-	Fill memory
T<from, nbytes>	-	Test memory
G[addr]	-	Go from address (i.e. start executing from)
L	-	Load record (i.e. *.S19 executable file)
H	-	Help (i.e. list of available commands)

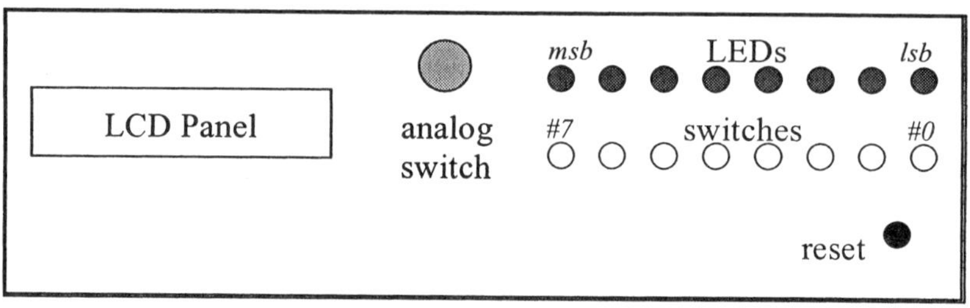

Figure 1. MC68HC12 Target Microcontroller Front Panel

The 68HC12-based microcontroller is shown in Figure 1. It cost around $600 per unit to produce, and incorporates the following peripherals (with associated 68HC12 ports – see Figure 2):

1. 8 switches Data Register=Port-D 0x05 Data Direction Reg-D=0x07

2. 8 LEDs Port-J 0x28 DDRJ 0x29
3. (2-line*8-digit) LCD Panel *Data:* Port-H 0x24 DDRH 0x25
   Control: Port-T 0xAE DDRT 0xAF
4. 5 timer channels (3-7) Port-T 0xAE DDRT 0xAF
5. Serial Interfaces (2 asynchronous SC0(1) + 1 synchronous SP0)
   SC0(1): 0xC0-C7(0xC8-CF) SP0: 0xD0-D5
6. 8-channel (8-bit) Analog-to-Digital Converter Port-AD 0x70-7E
7. USB interface *(under development)*

The HC12 interfaces to the PC via the latter's RS232 serial port (an upgrade to USB is currently underway).

The 68HC12 microcontroller cross development platform takes the form of the ImageCraft C-compiler – ICC12. As with the DJGPP C/C++ Compiler, the Integrated Development Environment adopts the usual Borland style (i.e. integrated editor, compiler, linker and debugger, all accessible from the same Graphical User Interface).

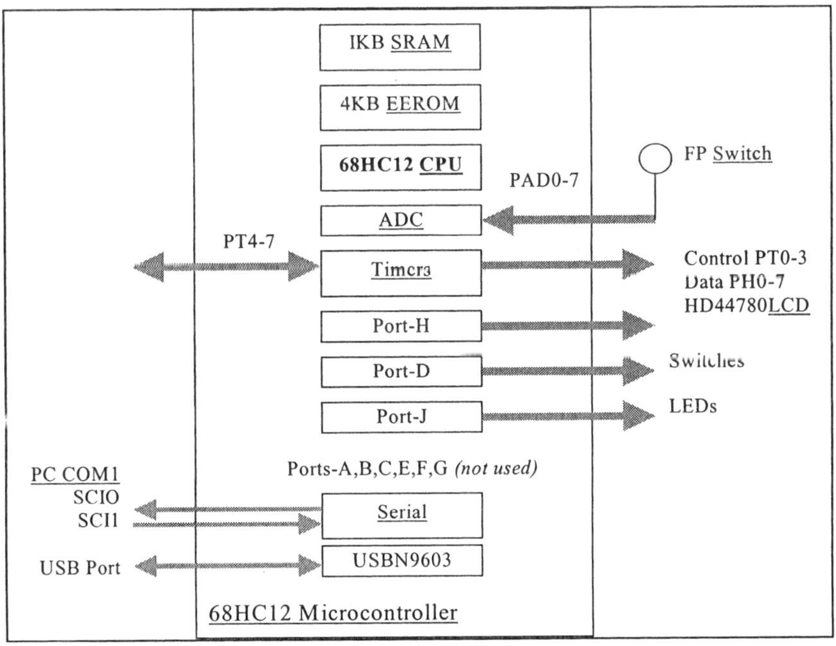

Figure 2. Motorola 68HC12 Microcontroller

Typical assignment tasks include the following:

1. Simple IO (switch input; LCD output):
   – activation of least significant (software debounced) switch(#0) → print name on LCD

- switch#1 ➔ flash student_number @ 1-second rate
- switch#2 ➔ scroll (pre-buffered) message R➔L on LCD
- switch#3 ➔ start LEDs counting (up if switch#4 = 0; down if 1)
- switch#5 ➔ LEDs chaser + increment through printable ASCII character set and/or own characters on second line of LCD
- switch#6 ➔ reflect switch setting as an ASCII character on LCD
- switch#7 ➔ terminate (exit to 68HC12 Monitor program)

2. Stopwatch/Clock, based on inbuilt 68HC12 programmable timer (channel):
   - switch#0 ➔ Clock mode: display HOURS:MINS:SECS:TENTHS + increment LED count
   - switch#1 ➔ preset Clock setting (via PC keyboard)
   - switch#2 ➔ reset Clock
   - switch#3 ➔ start LEDs counting (up if switch#4 = 0; down if 1)
   - switch#4 ➔ reset the Stopwatch (back to zero)
   - switch#5 ➔ stop the Stopwatch (temporarily)
   - switch#6 ➔ (re)start the Stopwatch + display LEDs chaser (or bouncing ping pong ball)
   - switch#7 ➔ place program in Stopwatch mode
3. Serial IO, based on inbuilt 68HC12 asynchronous serial communications:
   a) reflect characters typed in ICC12 Terminal Window to PC HyperTerminal Window, & vice versa (Xon/Xoff flow control, modulo-n circular buffers, X-modem)
   b) implement a rudimentary (interrupt-driven) Kermit protocol to communicate with PC (HyperTerm) – i.e. send/receive text/binary files only
4. Pre-emptive (Real Time process) Scheduler, which co-ordinates the following (*concurrent*) tasks:
   a) display a rotating graphical symbol on LCD Panel,
   b) display a LED chaser/binary up(down) counter on the LEDs,
   c) display a Clock/Stopwatch in a HyperTerminal Window, using the 4 remaining switches,
   d) echo (short) messages typed on the PC keyboard to the 68HC12 Trainer LCD.

The assignments build progressively, from simple polled programs to interrupt-driven ones. By the end of the last assignment, students have gained practical skills, which they can transfer to Real-Time software development in the *real world*.

A critical aspect to this laboratory assignment work is that students learn RT programming skills by interfacing to real-world devices. Central to this process is making mistakes and learning from these. This is consistent with a situated learning approach (Lave and Wenger 1991). More specifically, knowledge as such cannot be taught, but is imparted via apprenticeship – learning by doing. Situations are thus viewed as co-producing knowledge through activity (Brown et al. 1989).

Program design can become quite sophisticated toward the latter part of the course (e.g. the use of state diagrams in the Kermit and Scheduler assignments – (iii) and (iv), respectively). Students necessarily spend a large proportion of their time not only on program design, but especially on testing and debugging of non- (or partially) functioning programs. The rudimentary debugging capabilities of the ICC12 Monitor are indispensable in this regard. These low-level tools nicely complement the usual debugging facilities, which come as part of the ICC12 IDE (such as source level debugging and program list files).

4. CONCLUSION

Our experience confirms the notion that students learn best by doing (Fulcher 2000). We further observe that students become highly motivated by having to interact with real-world devices (as opposed to *simulated* peripherals), which does not abate even when they make mistakes with their code. Making mistakes, debugging their programs, and learning from these mistakes form key aspects of students learning microcomputer interfacing and real time programming. To paraphrase past student experience "it's lot of work, but very enjoyable – I learnt a lot". What is particularly gratifying from an educators perspective is to observe individual students come good, as it were, during the semester – more specifically, from taking a flying leap at the problem at the start of semester to adopting a methodical, structured, modular approach by semester's end. Furthermore, they have come to this point from their *own* endeavours.

ACKNOWLEDGEMENTS

Financial assistance was gratefully received from both the School of Information Technology and Computer Science, and the Institute for Mathematical & Computer Modelling at the University of Wollongong (Intelligent Systems Research Group). Thanks are due to Michael Milway for the development of the MC68HC12 microcontroller used in the third-year Microcomputer Interfacing and Real Time Computing Laboratory.

REFERENCES

Brown, J. S., Collins, A. and Duguid, S. (1989) Situated Cognition and the Culture of learning. *Educational Researcher*, 18 (1), pp. 34-42.

Buchanan, W. (1996) *Applied PC Interfacing, Graphics and Interrupts.* Addison Wesley, Reading, MA.

Duntemann, J. (2000) *Assembly Language Step-by-Step.* 2nd ed., Wiley, New York.

Fulcher, J. A. (1989a) *An Introduction to Microcomputer Systems: Architecture and Interfacing.* Addison Wesley, Reading, MA.

Fulcher, J. A. (1989b) The Development of a Microcomputer Laboratory for the Teaching of Real Time Computing. *Journal of Electrical & Electronics Engineering, Australia,* 8 (3), pp. 159-167.

Fulcher, J. A. (1990) On the *Best* Way to teach Computer Interfacing. In *Proceedings of 5th IFIP World Conference on Computers in Education – WCCE'90*, Sydney 9-13 July, pp. 100-101.

Fulcher, J. A. (1991) Fun and Games and Microcomputer Interfacing. *Micro,* 11 (1), pp. 18-78.

Fulcher, J. A. (2000) Teaching Course on Artificial Neural Networks. In *Innovative Teaching Methods in Artificial Intelligence, Neural Networks, Fuzzy Systems and Evolutionary Computing*, L. Jain (ed.), Physica Verlag, Berlin.

Gray, N. A. B. (1987) *An Introduction to Computer Systems.* Prentice Hall, Englewood Cliffs, NJ.

Imagecraft (1999) *ICC12: Imagecraft C Compiler and development Environment for Motorola HC12 V.6.* [http://www.magecraft.com].

Lave, J. and Wenger, E. (1991) *Situated Learning: Legitimate Peripheral Participation.* Cambridge University Press, Cambridge, UK.

Patterson, D. A. and Hennessy, J. L. (1994) *Computer Organization and Design: the Hardware/Software Interface.* Morgan Kaufmann, San Mateo, CA.

BIOGRAPHY

John Fulcher is currently an Associate Professor in the School of Information Technology and Computer Science, University of Wollongong, Australia, as well as a member of the Institute for Mathematical Modelling and Computation. John researches into neural networks, computer standards and interfaces. John's teaching responsibilities include computer systems and microcomputer interfacing at the undergraduate level, and neural networks, data mining and parallel computing at the graduate level.

46

Didactic System for Object-oriented Modelling

Torsten Brinda and Sigrid E. Schubert
Didactics of Informatics, University of Dortmund, D-44221 Dortmund, Germany
brinda@ls12.cs.uni-dortmund.de

Keywords: didactics, knowledge representation, learning systems, modelling, secondary education

Abstract: The authors introduce a didactic system for object-oriented modelling (OOM) as a new and flexible learning concept for informatics education and outline a development methodology which is in evaluation. With the aim to improve the quality and individualization of lessons the following components of a didactic system have been identified so far: and-or-graphs for the representation of the knowledge structures within the subjects of OOM, classes of new exercises, which allow to apply and consolidate different modelling techniques and interactive visualisation modules for selected contents in order to support the initial contact with the contents and to illustrate underlying principles.

1. MOTIVATION

'At present, the educational aims are completely changing from programming of small imperative solutions to modelling, construction and deconstruction of complex and object oriented systems of informatics. But there is a big gap between the didactical needs of the subject informatics at schools and the finished research results in this field. (Magenheim and Schubert 2000). This new orientation has essentially been influenced by Schwill and Hubwieser, which described a well-founded suggestion for informatics education based on fundamental ideas and modelling techniques (Schwill 1997, Hubwieser and Broy 1999). 'Informatics modelling opens up a general educational method of access to the understanding of informatics systems.' (Schubert 2000), (see Figure 1).

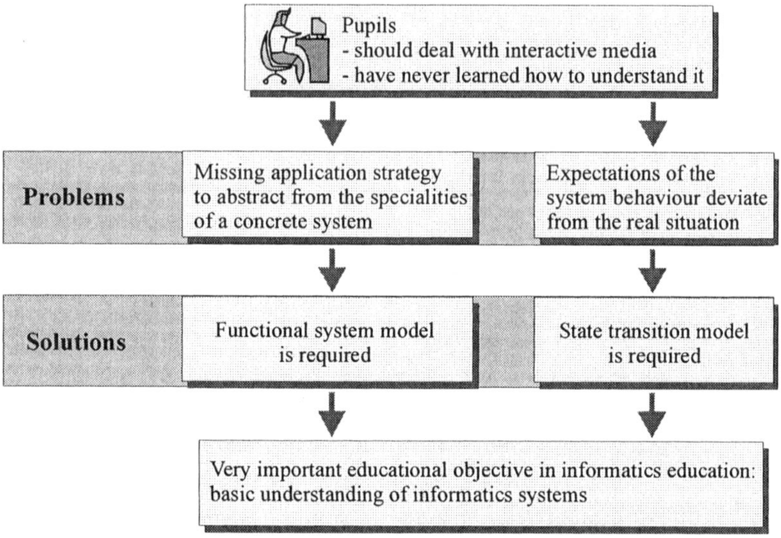

Figure 1. Informatics models in general education

'And a new Informatics Literacy, based on Discipline Integrated Informatics, will emerge.' (van Weert 1995). Independent of this conceptional change the object-oriented attempt has steadily gained importance in informatics education. In 1995 Schwill gave reasons for starting informatics education with the object-oriented approach: informatic-oriented demands for up-to-date education with powerful concepts, like extendability, encapsulation, evolutionary software development and others can be fulfilled and the didactic principle of continuation according to a spiral curriculum can be used. He emphasized furthermore that the object-oriented view gets very close to the natural manner as people are aware of their environment. Today object-oriented programming (OOP) has been established in German informatics teaching curricula, but the conceptional change has reached only a few informatics lessons yet. It is often still the implementation, now in an object-oriented packing, that dominates the lessons and the value of object-oriented modelling (OOM) does not become clear enough.

The great popularity of the object-oriented programming language Java and the learners' motivation and interest gained from its wide use in distributed systems also intensifies this problem. A flexible concept, supported by informatics modules, for learning and teaching OOM in informatics lessons, which supports experimenting with and exploring of object-oriented concepts while forcing back the dominance of programming languages in opening new learning by doing oriented possibilities, is missing.

2. RESULTS OF RESEARCH

The approach of the didactic system for OOM is developed in the following. A didactic system is understood here as the mapping of a didactic concept to a learning supporting series of informatics modules with recommendations of application in informatics education. These informatics modules can either be exercises or so called exploration modules (see below). It is the aim of the concept to support learners and teachers in studying and teaching the basics of object-oriented modelling and also to build up a bridge between traditional and computer supported learning and teaching or, more precisely, informatics system supported learning and teaching. At least the following components belong to a didactic system for OOM.

2.1 Structuring of subject contents

Technical terms, methods and concepts of OOM are presented as nodes of a directed graph. The edges between these nodes represent an 'is-required'– or 'is-helpful-for'-relation, that structure the contents for learners and teachers in order to clarify, which contents are needed or helpful as pre-knowledge for other contents. The purpose is primarily the clear and compact illustration of how the subject contents are based on each other and also to give a brief view of the order in which contents should be studied or where can be continued due to a given pre-knowledge. Moreover it shall be clarified, which components from algorithms and data structures are inalienable for OOM and where they should be included within a course 'OOM from the beginning'. For learners this structuring can be useful for the organization of individual study phases or for the repetition of lessons. Summing up this structuring shall work as a tool in a scientific-oriented teaching and learning process. Within the design process of the didactic system the structuring will also be used for constructing a series of so called exploration modules (see below) for the object-oriented basics. This series of modules shall also reflect the structuring. In didactic publications concept maps are often used for the structuring of knowledge and for the representation of multiple relations between concepts, but they do not make any boolish combination of relation couples possible, though. This is required here to be able to express that of a choice of contents either only one or all can be needed as pre-knowledge for a higher content. And-or-trees, which have their origin in the discussion of optimal strategies in game theory, contain such combinations already as integral components. For the given purpose a tree structure is impractical since different contents often require the same entry knowledge. To avoid repeating sub trees the and-or-tree is extended to an acyclic and-or-graph. The and-or-graph has successfully been used by the authors to structure contents of OOM, e. g. see Figure 2.

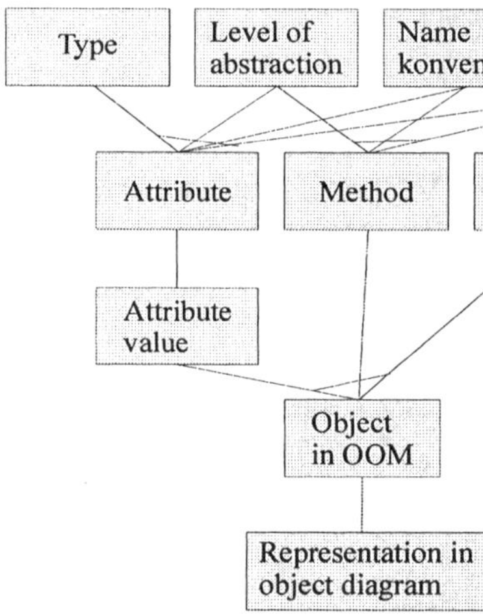

Figure 2. Example of an and-or-graph with OOM-content

2.2 Hierarchy of exercise classes

An essential constituent of a concept for learning and teaching OOM are exercise examples which allow to use and consolidate different modelling techniques. Within the teaching and learning process new contents are worked out on problems from the learners' reality to bring about a motivating learning process for them. Advanced exercises must contribute to various learning objectives, such as saving well known contents as well as acquiring new ones. With the aim to provide a construction methodology for exercises to OOM already published exercises (e.g. Rumbaugh et al. 1991) have been analysed. The transformation and selection of examples, which have not been constructed for informatics education at school but for higher education, need the following quality criteria (Brinda 2000):

- *Emphasis of the modelling*: It is the aim of the examples, that learners get to know and use different modelling techniques, in order to be able to structure and formally describe reality sections and to transform these models iterative-incrementally in a form processible on a computer.
- *Language independence*: Only examples are selected, that avoid focussing on syntax details of a certain modelling or programming language and that stress the underlying concepts instead.
- *Complexity*: For the teaching and learning process exercises of various size are needed, beginning with small tasks to practice a single modelling step and ending at complex and multilayered modelling tasks. This complete range must be covered. The size of the exercises is restricted though. The complexity of the examples must follow the intellectual abilities of the learners. According to the given learning objectives the complexity of an exercise is limited. If it is the aim to develop certain new strategies, an adequate complexity of the exercises is required for increasing of motivation status and for developing the learner's skills (Vygotsky 1978).

If the selected concrete exercises are condensed to abstract exercise framework classes by separating them from their example context, they can be ordered hierarchically in accordance with the learning objectives and later be easily selected and combined for a concrete informatics lesson. Using the criteria mentioned above the exercise classes shown in Figure 3 have been identified for constructing a static object-oriented model.

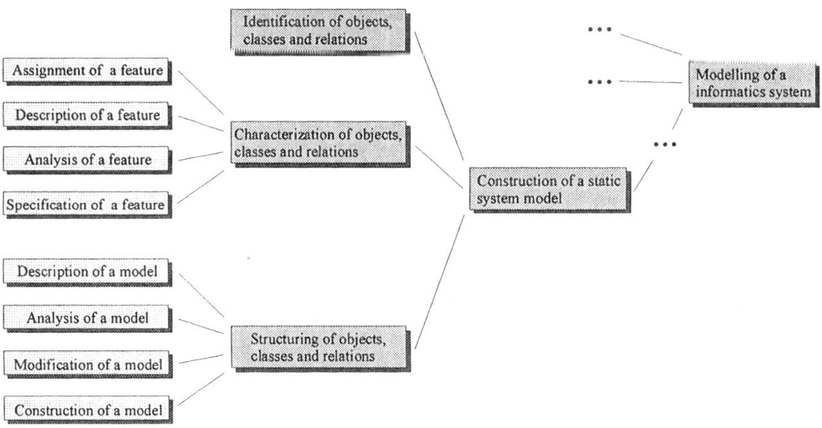

Figure 3. Hierarchy of exercise classes for constructing a static object-oriented model

Besides the hierarchy a catalogue of example contexts must be built up to instantiate exercises from the abstract classes. Especially the following criteria qualify a suitable context:

- *Suitability for OOM*: An object-oriented procedure should be suggested by the example context and not been enforced by the teacher.
- *Experience reference*: For didactic reasons learners should know an example context with its various connections from their daily own experience.
- *Easy changeability and extendability*: Structuring techniques, like class hierarchies, abstract classes etc. show their quality only, if existing structures are changed or enlarged. So an open example context is required, in which expansions and modifications of the model structure are possible.

With the exercise classes hierarchy and the catalogue of example contexts a systematic problem-oriented entry to OOM will be opened.

2.3 Exploration modules

At first new contents shall be discovered individually and explored in a learning by doing oriented manner. Therefore interactive exploration modules must be provided for selected contents in order to support the initial contact with the contents and also to illustrate underlying principles. The question of the architecture and the offered functionality of such modules is of great importance here. The following criteria are of great meaning for the construction of an architecture concept for exploration modules:

- *Size:* It is the purpose of every single module to experiment with some few concepts of OOM in a 'learning by doing' oriented manner. The main advantage of a series of small modules is their flexible and selective usability. Moreover small modules can be handled with less training.
- *Combinability:* The architecture of the modules shall be constructed in a way that data interchange is made possible between the different modules.
- *Relation to an example context*: From this aspect two different kinds of modules can be distinguished.
    1. *Modules which are bound to the semantics of a special example context:* Changes in the model are shown in a separate window, that illustrates the changes in the semantics of the underlying example context. The main disadvantage is that one can only experiment with models from one example context.

2. *Modules which are independent of the semantics of a special example context:* These can be used for arbitrary models but they are less illustrative.

With the concept of the exploration modules a learning by doing oriented approach will be established for contents, which have often been worked out in the course of the programming.

2.4 Concept of application

The concept of application describes, how the components mentioned before are linked together in the teaching and learning process in a productive way. The main difficulty is, that learners must acquire knowledge in object-oriented basic principles, object-oriented system design and an object-oriented programming language at the same time to be able to individually construct object-oriented models. It is the aim of the concept to work out concepts and techniques of OOM with the learners systematically. The structuring of the subject contents gives well-founded suggestions about the order of the acquirements. The traversation of the content graph results in a possible structuring for a series of lessons. At first new object-oriented basic principles shall be studied experimentally with exploration modules. At the beginning of the teaching and learning process such modules can be of great value because learners do not have any own design competence at this stage of their informatics education. Linked with this phase a series of exercises with growing complexity can be used for practising and consolidating contents learned before. The hierarchy of the exercise classes promotes the structuring of exercise phases according to content. While the exercises serve to use and to deepen contents, the exploration modules shall help learners to acquire new knowledge and to build up hypotheses on the contents. By working with the modules and exercises knowledge and abilities in software development methods and an object-oriented programming language will be built up.

3. DEVELOPMENT OF A DIDACTIC SYSTEM

For the design of complex software systems design patterns (Gamma 1995) have been established as a successful tool since about 1995. In the context of software technology design patterns describe "cooperating objects and classes which are customized to solve a general design problems in a certain context". Design patterns represent template-like solutions for abstract design problems which are characterized by the four basic constituents pattern name, problem, solution and consequence section. Since the design of a didactic system is also a difficult and extensive task, it shall be tried to identify patterns for the design of didactic systems, to simplify and to make possible the construction of further didactic systems. It particularly is not the aim to force creative processes of lesson design into rigid schemes here. However, design patterns can contribute to a definition of quality standards in the Didactics of Informatics and can also simplify the comparability of informatics lessons.

With help of patterns the structuring of subject contents and the construction of exercises can be simplified. The idea shall be illustrated by a simple pattern. The similarity pattern can be used, if a new content shows a structural and / or semantic similarity with already known contents. This can be the case, if a concept of the (real) world is transferred to informatics, as it the case e. g. with the description of objects in the real world and in object-oriented models. The similar concept also can originate another, necessarily known, science area. Even a reference to a similar concept within informatics is possible (e. g. abstract data type and class). Given a structural similarity of the concepts involved the elements of the known concept form as entry knowledge the prerequisites for the corresponding elements of the new concept. A reference to known concepts can make learning easier, if the complete group of learners has the required pre-knowledge. Such a procedure is not suitable if the known concept is not familiar to the complete studying group. Moreover it can be possible, that certain ideas of the basic concept can be cognitive barriers for the new concept.

The idea of the design patterns can also be illustrated at the exercise examples. Here one can find the correspondences between the terminology of design patterns and didactics shown in Table 1.

Table 1. Correspondences between the terminology of design patterns and didactics

Design patterns	**Didactics**
Problem section	Learning objective(s)
Solution section	Abstract exercise(s), recommendation(s) for example context(s)
Consequence section	Reaching of learning objective(s) and increasing of competences or not

For the identification of design patterns for didactic systems sources from different areas must be consulted:

- *Technical sources*: Different authors have their own view on a science part, they structure and justify it correspondingly. Technical sources on OOM concentrate in general on an object-oriented programming language or on analysis and design. To structure contents of OOM for informatics lessons it is necessary to also take into account components from algorithms and data structures (variable concept, parameter concept, algorithms etc.).

- *Didactics of Informatics sources*: Theoretical concepts, lesson series and exercise examples already consider the specific target group, give well-founded suggestions which contents should be taken into account and which not. It is often the problem of these sources in OOM, that for secondary education they are not age adequate because of a too low cognitive level, and that they do not correspond to the educational principle of scientificity since the meaning of the modelling remains unclear.
- *General didactic sources*: General didactic sources suggest certain structurings of learning and teaching processes, others are indicated as avoidable.

If one abstracts these representations, then design patterns for the construction of above described components of a didactic system can be identified.

4. STRATEGY OF EVALUATION

The theoretical concept was empirically examined in discussions with school heads and teachers, performance tests, by interviewing pupils and the video recording of lessons. In 1998/99 and 1999/2000 lessons at school were visited for the exploration and description of the traditional informatics lesson with main focus on OOM. Parallelly a research report on analysis of teaching and learning concepts for OOM was worked out in the winter term 1999/2000. So the necessity of a concept for didactic systems was established. The theoretical conception for didactic systems was carried out under application and further development of technical and didactic foundations in the summer term 2000. On the basis of this concept there will be a first implementation in the study year 2000/2001. The concept will be enriched with recommendations for education and with teaching and learning materials. Informatics modules are designed and implemented. A process accompanying evaluation takes place in the field of teacher education with first tests of application in informatics lessons in order to receive a design feedback. In the school year 2001/2002 the main emphasis is on the qualitative and quantitative evaluation of the concept and the design methodology of a didactic system with informatics teachers. The results flow into the revision and improvement of the didactic system for OOM.

REFERENCES

Brinda, T. (2000) Sammlung und Strukturierung von Übungsaufgaben zum objektorientierten Modellieren im Informatikunterricht. *LOGIN*, 5, pp. 39-49.

Gamma, E., Helm, R., Johnson, R. and Vlissides, J. (1995) *Design Patterns*. Addison-Wesley Longman, New York.

Hubwieser, P. and Broy, M. (1999) Educating Surfers or Craftsmen: Introducing an ICT Curriculum for the 21st Century. ComNEd – Communication and Networking in Education in a Networked Society. In *Proceedings of the IFIP Open Conference*, Aulanko – Hämeenlinna, June, pp. 163-170.

Magenheim, J. and Schubert, S. (2000) Evaluation of teacher education in informatics. 16th World Computer Congress 2000. In *Proceedings of Conference on Educational Uses of Information and Communication Technologies,* D. Benzie and D. Passey (eds.), Beijing, August, pp. 181-184.

Rumbaugh, J., Blaha, M., Premerlani, W., Eddy, F. and Lorensen, W. (1991) *Object-Oriented Modeling and Design*. Prentice-Hall, New York.

Schubert, S. (2000) The impact of modelling in informatics education on collaborative learning with school Intranets. In *The Bookmark to the School of the Future*, P. Hogenbirk, and H. G. Taylor (eds.), Kluwer Academic Publishers, Boston, pp. 247-258.

Schwill, A. (1997) Computer Science Education based on Fundamental Ideas. In *Information Technology. Supporting change through teacher education*, D. Passey and B. Samways (eds.), Chapman & Hall, London, pp. 285-291.

van Weert, T. (1995) Integration of informatics into education. In *Integrating Information Technology into Education*, D. Tinsley and D. Watson (eds.), Chapman & Hall, London, pp. 101-110.

Vygotsky, L. S. (1978) *Mind in Society*. Harvard University Press, London.

BIOGRAPHY

Torsten Brinda received his diploma in computer science from the University of Dortmund (Germany) in 1998. In 1998 he became assistant professor in didactics of informatics at the University of Dortmund. From 1999 to 2001 he was manager of a multimedia project in teacher education. His research interests are concepts for learning and teaching object-oriented modelling in secondary and higher education.

Sigrid Schubert received her diploma in physics from the University of Dresden (Germany) in 1972 and her doctoral degree in didactics of informatics from the University of Chemnitz in 1988. Since 1972 she has been teaching informatics in secondary and vocational education. In 1998 she became professor in didactics of informatics at the University of Dortmund. Her research interests are: informatics at secondary schools, collaborative learning, multimedia evaluation in teacher education. She is chairman of the Department on Informatics Education of the German Informatics society (GI).

47

Simulators: Tools for Teaching Theory of Computation

Tiarajú A. Diverio, Ingrid V. Mito, Thiago F. Moesch and Luis F. R. Lima
Instituto de Informática e PPGC da UFRGS, C.P. 15064, 91501-970 Porto Alegre, BRAZIL
diverio@inf.ufrgs.br

Keywords: higher education, computation, simulation, distance learning, tutor

Abstract: This paper describes simulators, which are programming tools that make available the following formalisms: Turing Machine, Register Machine and Post Machine. With these simulators it is possible to teach Theory of Computation in a new way, where students may visualise numerical computed functions and check language recognition, including, therefore, the chapters of computability and universal machines. These simulators are part of the project Theory of Computation Laboratory. Also, this project consists of a set of educational software simulators built to improve teaching with quality and provide tools for the remote teaching project. The objective of this research is to develop software that gives more flexibility for its users in editing and creating abstract machines, by providing a friendly user interface, large set of operations, and knowledge base of these machines. This is the foundation for an integrated teaching environment on the Web.

1. INTRODUCTION

The motivation for this work was the lack of educational software for teaching theoretical computations, and also the importance of generating qualified human resources to work in the several computer graduation courses existent in Brazil. This work is meant to help students, through simulated programs, to understand the computational formality studies in the Theory of Computation subject including the Turing Machine, Finite Automatons, Post Machine, Norma Machine, and Lambda Calculus. Through simulators we can create and carry out programs related to the desired machine in a fast, simple and intuitive way. The system aims to help not only students in understanding the content, but also teachers, who will have in their hands a powerful tool for creating exercises, their correction and demonstrating examples in classrooms. This paper proposes that simulators are important tools for teaching in general.

2. SIMULATORS

Simulators are instructional packages that make available the visualisation of formalisms or theoretical machines such as: Turing Machine, Norma Machine, Finite Automatons with Stacks, and Post Machine (Diverio and Franciosi 1996, Mito and Diverio 2001, Moesch et al. 1998).

The objectives of these simulators are the development of a laboratory environment for the students that are Bachelors in Computer Science of the Federal University of Rio Grande do Sul (UFRGS). Here students can develop programs in different machines, run programs step by step for learning and correction, solve exercises, and provide assistance for teachers in the working out and correction of exams.

The idea of the simulators arose during a practical task carried out in the discipline of Theory of Computation. Due to the good quality of the works presented, it was decided to develop a project to make instructional packages available in a local environment (the laboratories of the Computer Science Institute of UFRGS). So some alterations were necessary in order to transform the different prototypes into a unique environment. The alterations aim at standardisation and unification of the interface and uniformity in the computational environment (language and computer). For standardisation the following is defined.

- The simulators are developed in *Delphi* through the Pascal language Oriented to Object. The system's operation platform is based on PC's with operational system *Windows*.
- All simulators create files that can be saved on disk for further reading. All files are saved in ASCII format, using a simple structure making them portable to any architecture and accessible to other modules.
- The simulators have a standard installer interface of the programs compatible with Windows. In this case, it was used the *InstallShield*™ as an installer software, which will copy the files and offer a help system.

- The Execution can present the final result of the computation, and also the possibility of carrying out the computation process step by step, so that the user can interpret the results in due time. Two ways of running have been defined: *Uninterrupted* (the alterations performed at each step of the computation are showed, but the execution only stops when it is finished), and *Step-by-Step* (the execution stops at each step of the computation, and waits until the user authorises the continuation of the process).
- The simulators count on a help system that assists the user during the utilisation of the software. In this system it is also included the idea of tutor, which gives concepts about the simulator in use.

Three simulators developed are described in the next sections.

3. TURING MACHINE SIMULATOR

Among all the universal machines studied, the Turing Machine is notably the most important because it is simple and powerful. The Turing Machine consists basically of a one-side infinite tape, a tape head and a program. The tape head has the capacity of reading and writing a symbol on the tape and, after that, according to the program's specification, moving a cell to the left or a cell to the right. A complete definition of the Turing Machine can be found in Diverio et al. (2000).

The Simulator of the Turing Machine is composed of four modules: tutor, program editor, program emulator through graphs, and program emulator through functions. The Tutor is composed of the basis of knowledge about the chapter on computability through Turing Machines, which can be accessed in an electronic book or help format. In the current stage, the Tutor is not equipped with intelligence, but studies are being developed with this purpose in mind.

3.1 Program emulator through Graphs

The emulator programs through Graphs allow the definition of programs by a state machine. Among the available functions in this tool we have the definition of a Turing Machine (in which the entry alphabet, state set, auxiliary alphabet, final state sets, initial state and program are introduced), editing of machine already defined, saving of machine in file and running of a program. For the definition there are available tools such as editing, state creation, indicator of the initial and final states, editions of transitions. In Figure 1 we showed a transition form, where p is the concurrent state, q is the new state, a_n is the read symbol, a_v is the writing symbol, and 'm' the movement of the head, which can be to the left or to the right.

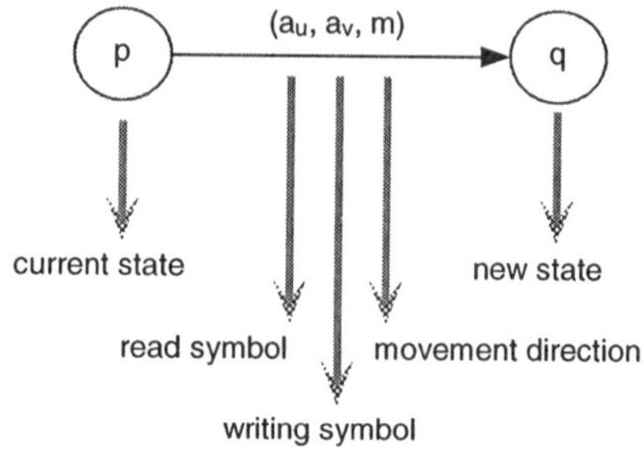

Figure 1. Definition of transition through graphs

For the edition of a transition, the program offers a window (Figure 2) with the pre-defined values. Operations with states and transitions are available; states and transitions can be removed. The interface offers a tool bar that is activated by the T icon. The graph can be easily re-ordained when moving the states. At the end of the edition we can save, create an image of the graph and insert this image in other file.

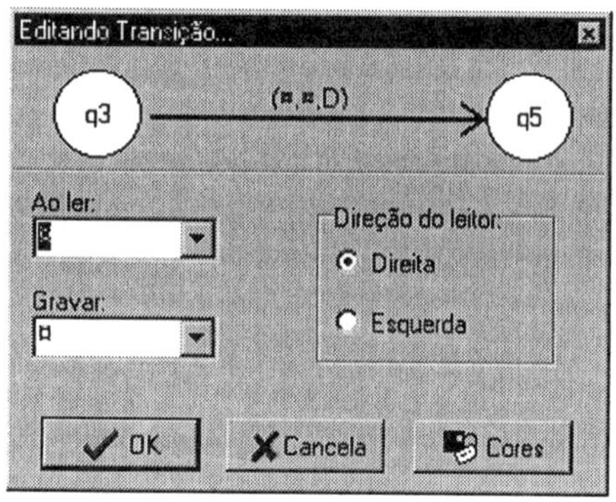

Figure 2. Edition Screen

Once the consistence of the program is achieved, we can execute it by clicking the execution icon. The tape will appear all filled in by the special symbol on a white character (β) and also a window to introduce the entry. The execution can be done in the two formats: step by step or uninterrupted. In both cases the current position in the tape and the current state will be displayed as they are coloured. Figure 3 shows the screen of the program emulator through graph. The graph showed in that figure performs the parenthesis evaluation.

So, to sum up, this module describes the program as a graph in which the vertices represent the states and transitions, which may involve change of symbol, displacement and move of state. It is characterised by the creation of automatons in a fast and intuitive way. Therefore, the user is provided with a tool bar with simple functions such as create a state, create a transition, edit a transition and other functions.

The states can be positioned on the screen according to the user's preferences, by just moving it with the mouse. It allows the re-drawing of the transitions, considering their new positions. The alteration of the states can be given through the tool bar or through a click on the right button of the mouse. The transitions also can be modified in a very simple way, and just two clicks are necessary on the desired transition.

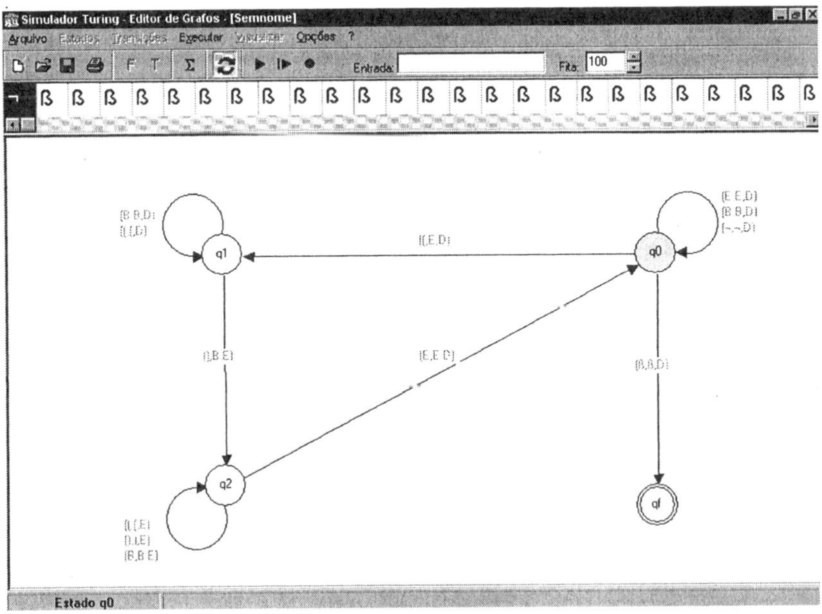

Figure 3. Program Emulator through graph'S screen

3.2 Program emulator trough transition functions

The program emulator through transition functions implements the definition that uses a matrix of two states in order to represent the program, and offers resources such as copy and paste. In Figure 4, the same example of the Turing Machine is presented, which performs the parenthesis evaluation. We can notice in Figure 4 that, during the execution, the current symbol of the tape is selected, as well as the matrix field that is being analysed. The software allows the user to dimension again the size of the lines and columns of the matrix, as well as alter its style and its font size.

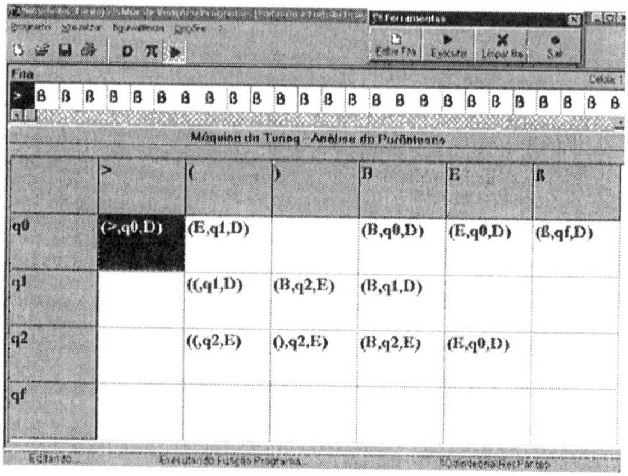

Figure 4. Turing Machine that evaluates parenthesis

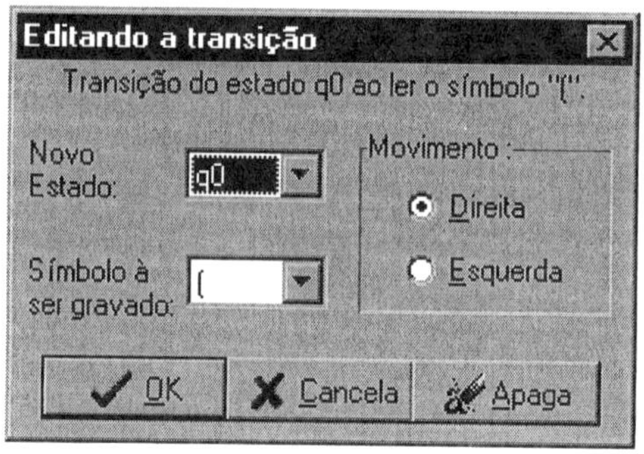

Figure 5. Editing Screen

This module is divided basically into three parts: machine definition, editing of the transition matrix (program) and execution. We can define the machine by introducing its symbol alphabets (entries and auxiliaries) in its states. The programming is achieved by editing the transitions as a matrix element. It is carried out by clicking the desired position (state x symbol) and by filling in all the necessary fields, as showed in Figure 5. Finally, there is the program's execution window, in which the user can enter the tape and execute his program, either through the step by step or through the uninterrupted form.

The actual state of the program and the position of the tape reader are represented by selecting the correspondent cell. There are options to be chosen, so that during the execution the simulator is able to show the last states of the tape, as well as to save in one file all the tape's contents that were created during each step of the computation.

The Editor module, with capacity to convert types, is the module that offers program editor facilities in both types of programs and allows the conversion of a program through graphs in a program through transition functions and vice-versa. It allows the editing of programs simultaneously in the two formats; that is, it makes the compatibility and the translation between formats and programs.

4. NORMA REGISTER MACHINE SIMULATOR

Norma (Number Theoretic Register Machine) is a universal machine defined by Bird (Bird 1976). The memory is composed of infinite registers and the entry and exit sets are non-null integers. The operations and tests defined by Norma are the most natural ones: to add and subtract a unit to the register and verify whether a register is zero. We can notice that in the definition of the subtraction over the A register, it is supposed that, when the A register is already null, the null value remains in A.

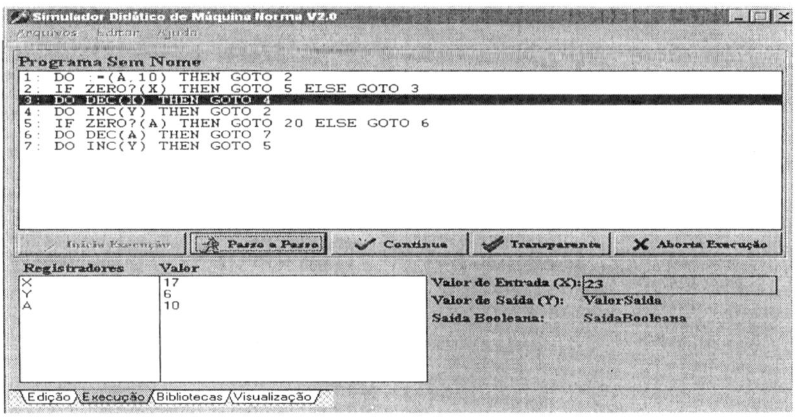

Figure 6. Norma program Editor

The registers X and Y have special treatments. The entry function of Norma loads the X register with the entry number and starts all the other registers with zero. The Norma exit function withdraws the final content of the Y register as exit. Norma processes programs in a flowchart, showed as labelled instructions.

The simulator of the Norma register machine was developed in such a way that not only we can verify the functioning of Norma and the characteristics above, but we can also learn them with the assistance of tutorials and helps. The principal characteristics are as follows.

Registers. In order that we may simulate the functioning of this machine it has been defined that all registers will have a representation of 128 decimal digits, which implies the restriction that the major number is 10^{128};

Instructions format. To facilitate the implementation of the simulator, it has been defined that the instructions (operations and macros) would be represented in the following way: *name* $(OP_1, OP_2, ..., OP_n)$, where *name* is any word set of symbols (not containing numbers) and $OP_1,.., OP_n$ are the registers involved. The basic operations are defined, respectively, as INC(A), DEC(A), ZERO?(A), to any A register.

Data entry. The data entry can be done in two ways: through flowcharts (written in a text box in the editing screen) or through the X entry value (which is introduced through a n editing box in the editing screen).

Macros. The macros are created in order to facilitate the development of programs. On the macro manipulation screen, all the information related to them must be defined. The previously defined macros can be re-utilised or consulted during the edition of a diagram, through boxes on the editing screen that contain the macros and their description.

Tutorial. The tutorial is divided into two parts: one part contains all the information about the NORMA register machine, and the other part contains all the information about the utilization of the simulator.

Conversion. It is possible to make the conversion of flowcharts into labeled instructions and vice-versa.

5. POST MACHINE SIMULATOR

Inside the context of the Theory of Computability, the formalism of the Post Machine (developed by the mathematician Emil Leon Post in 1936) is very important due to its equivalence to the most known Universal Machines (such as the Turing Machine). One of its main applications was the recognition of languages, necessary for the understanding and construction of a compiler.

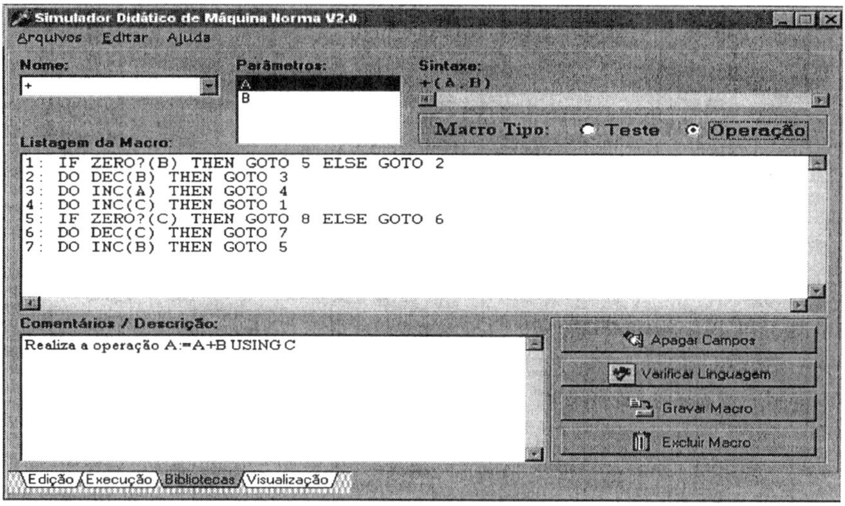

Figure 7. Macro Editors

The Post Machine is characterised by having a unique entry, exit and work memory structure, the *queue* type. It consists of two parts.

X variable. The mentioned structure, queue type, is used as memory, entry and exit. This variable does not have fixed size, or a limit. Its length is the length of a word stored in the time instant. In case the X does not have symbols, the entry is called *empty* and is represented by ε.

Program. It is a finite sequence of instructions, represented by diagram of flow, in which each vertices is an instruction.

The Simulator has two work environments: the editing environment and the executing environment. The editing environment is used for the definition of symbols to be used and for the entry of the function program in the form of a diagram composed of labels linked through transitions, in the same functions distinguished in the formal definition.

In the execution environment the editing screen is disabled and the computation of the word is made following the transitions connections with the respective label operations. The algorithm used is simple: from the first transition (start label) follow the transitions, and they carry out the operations indicated by the subsequent labels (attribution and test), until it finds a stop label (accepted/rejected). The computation, in this case, stops accepting or rejecting the entry word.

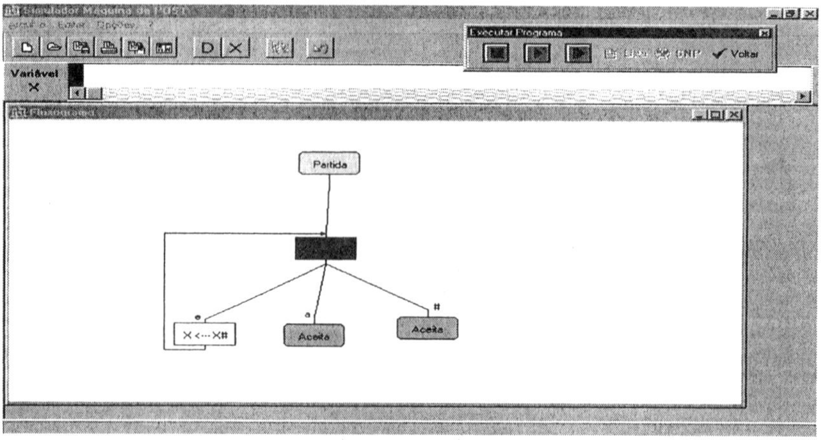

Figure 8. Execution Environment of the Post Simulator Machine

This tool is important mainly because of its pedagogical character, which helps in the comprehension of the concepts offered during the classes, providing teacher and students with a visual and interactive resource to work with this knowledge. Because it is small and portable software, the teaching resource can be used outside classroom, especially in the performance of exercises and works applied by the teacher.

6. FINAL COMMENTS

The simulator embraces two emphasis of the Turing Machine: one recognises words (Menezes 2000) and the other calculate functions (Diverio et al. 2000). The first one has in its definition two final states, which indicate whether the word has been accepted or rejected. The second one however has only one final state, which indicates whether the function's calculation has been successful or not. In both cases, if the machine stops in a state that is not defined as final, an error message is presented, and the execution is interrupted.

The simulators were initially developed with the purpose of being used in local environment, in which the software would be available in the laboratories of the Computer Science Institute. It aimed to stimulate the theoretical Computing teaching. However, they are being proposed as one of the modules of the remote teaching environment, which has been integrating teachers and students from the groups of Mathematics of Computation and High Performance Processing, Information Systems and Artificial Intelligence.

REFERENCES

Bird, R. (1976) *Programs and Machines – an introduction to the theory of computation.* John-Wiley, London.

Diverio, T. A. and Francisco, B. R. T. (1996) Experiência do GMC no desenvolvimento de software Instrucional. In: *Conferência Latinoamericana de Informática, XXII Clei 96,* Santafé de Bogotá: CLEI, junho, pp.1003-1012, v.2.

Diverio, T. A., Tiarajú A. and Menezes P. F. B. (2000) *Teoria da Computação: Máquinas Universais e Computabilidade.* Sagra-Luzzato, Inst. Informática UFRGS, Porto Alegre.

Menezes, P. F. B. (2000) *Linguagens Formais e Autômatos Finitos.* Sagra-Luzzatto, Porto Alegre.

Moesch, T. F., Grandi, R. H., Lutz, F. and Diverio, T. A. (1998) Ferramentas de Apoio ao Ensino de Teoria da Computação. In: *Conferencia Latino-Americana de Informática, Clei 98,* Quito, Equador: CLEI, outubro. Vol. 1, pp. 13-24.

Mito, I. V. and Diverio, T. A. (2001) Foundations for Virtual Environment to Support Theory of Computation Teaching. In *International Conference Intelligent Multimedia and Distance Education, ICIMADE '01,* Fargo, USA, 1-3, June, 2001.

BIOGRAPHY

Tiarajú A. Diverio graduated in Mathematics for the UFRGS, and a Masters and Doctorate in Computer Science to the CPGCC (1986 and 1995). He is Professor and researcher of the Institute Computer Science at UFRGS. His areas of interest: include Processing of High Performance (Processing Vectorial, Parallel and Distributed and Parallel Mathematical Algorithms) and Informatics in Education (Educational Development of Software for Mathematics).

Ingrid de Vargas Mito graduated in Science Computer at UFRGS and is doing a Masters in Computer Science to the PPGC-UFRGS. Her areas of Interests are Artificial Intelligent, Agents and Informatics in Education.

Thiago Fernandes Moesch and Luis Franscisco Ramos Lima are graduates in Science Computer at UFRGS, with interests in Informatics in Education and E-Commerce.

48

Simulation of Real-world Development Processes in Computer Science Classes

Paula Gabbert and Kevin Treu
Department of Computer Science, Furman University, Greenville, S,C USA
pgabbert@furman.edu

Keywords: simulation, classroom teaching/practice, collaborative learning, learner-centred learning, pedagogy

Abstract: Educators have long recognised that learning takes place most effectively in an environment in which the student is engaged in the process of their own education. One method for doing so is to put more control over the teaching and learning of course material into the hands of the students themselves. This paper describes an approach to learner-centred learning that involves the simulation of industrial software development practices as the central teaching technique. Our initial experiences with two courses – Web programming and systems analysis – are discussed in this paper.

1. INTRODUCTION

Engaged learning, inquiry-based learning, learner-centred teaching and other similar terms have gained prominence in recent years as educators strive to get students to take a greater role in their own learning process (Abernethy, Gabbert and Treu 1998, Jackson, Manaris, and McCauley 1997, Leasure 1998, Walker 1997). The lecture-based method of teaching has fallen into disfavour to some extent as teachers attempt to be 'guides on the side' rather than 'sages on a stage'.

Though we are not prepared to sound the death knell of the traditional lecture style of teaching, we have had success with an approach to teaching certain computer science topics that de-emphasises lecturing on the part of the professor. In this paper we describe this simulation-based approach and the courses in which we have applied it.

What we have attempted to do is to simulate real-world industrial development environments as closely as possible within the constraints applied by the academic model. Significant elements of this approach include:

- Real projects and deadlines
- Goal-oriented study and research
- Student ownership of projects
- Teamwork with clear divisions of responsibility
- Progress and summary reports.

Though lecturing is still a part of the process, lectures are delivered primarily by the students themselves. Their study is demand-driven – motivated by the need to learn the concepts and skills required to complete a project. They are required to learn these by any of various available resources, and are expected to instruct fellow classmates in what they have learned.

The teacher in this model has considerably less responsibility for writing lecture material, but more responsibility in terms of organising available resources, making them available, and guiding students in the appropriate directions. They must also be prepared to be flexible, as students choose to explore different concepts or skills than those anticipated.

We have applied this approach to two different courses: Web-Based Application Design and Systems Analysis. In this paper, we discuss our approach to teaching these subjects, the various implementation decisions that were made, and the results observed.

2. APPLICATIONS OF SIMULATION-BASED LEARNING

Our interest in teaching using simulation of real-world work environments was a natural outgrowth of our interest in simply teaching these subjects effectively. In essence, the course material required that something other than a lecture-based approach be taken. For the Web programming course, the sheer volume of available information and its changing nature made a traditional approach not feasible. For the systems analysis course, we found that it is far more effective to simulate a business environment so that students could observe the interconnections between modelling tools from CS and project management techniques from business.

2.1 Web-based application design

The basic objective of this course is to build a foundation for understanding some of the leading technologies that contribute to the power of the Web. In addition, students learn what is required to build state-of-the-art interactive Web sites.

The same explosive growth that makes the Web so important and interesting as a subject of study also presents significant challenges in the design of a course such as this. Covering all of the various Web technologies in detail would require multiple academic terms.

Also, the strong appeal of Web programming makes it a subject for many enthusiastic hobbyists outside the academic realm. Thus it is expected that there is expertise to be found among the collective participants in the class that would be difficult to find in any one person. In other words, it is likely that for any given topic, there is at least one student whose expertise exceeds that of the professor. Our experience suggests that this is a somewhat unique situation, but one that presents interesting opportunities.

2.1.1 Basic course organisation

These observations point the way to the use of the simulation-based format. In fact, they essentially demand it. The basic principle of the class is that all class participants (not just the professor) are responsible for learning certain topics and teaching them to the rest of the group. The course work is driven by a series of four case studies, real problems with real clients to which appropriate solutions are applied. In a sense, the participants in the course act as a fledgling Web design company (with the professor as CEO) which has deadlines, teamwork, performance reviews, and a vested interest in making sure that everyone has learned the technology.

The basic topics covered include:

- Dynamic HTML (HTML augmented with client-side scripting)
- Active Server Pages (server-side scripting and database interface)
- Database implementation
- Macromedia Flash animation
- Server maintenance and security.

The class is divided into four working teams. For each of the four case studies there is a Design Team, an ASP Team, a Database Team and a User Interface Team. The Maintenance Team is made up of members from the other four teams. The teams rotate from topic to topic with each case study, so every student has a chance to work in each area. Each team is responsible for doing the following for each case study:

- Writing a design document at the outset of the work

- Preparing and delivering a lecture on the technology used
- Installation and testing of the team's portion of the site on the server.

There is a project manager designated for each case study. Simulating as closely as possible the duties of a corporate manager, this person is responsible for:

- Scheduling and holding team meetings
- Meeting weekly with the professor and the other managers
- Maintaining a journal of team activities
- Preparing brief written and oral progress reports
- Assigning tasks to team members
- Co-ordinating the development of the team's design document and lecture
- Reviewing the work of the team members.

Development of each case study follows a three-week schedule. The class as a whole initially meets with the client to determine the requirements of the project. Each team subsequently drafts a design document for their area, which is refined in the first manager meeting and then distributed to all teams.

During this process, the teams are responsible for learning the basic tools of their area. An extensive online resource list is provided for this purpose. In addition, as the course progresses from case study to case study, previous work is available as a guide.

In the second week, teams are expected to make concrete progress towards implementing the designs. The manager meeting focuses on progress reports and the resolution of any design conflicts that arise.

During the third week, work is completed on each component of the case study and the site is uploaded and tested. Each team then delivers its final report. These lectures build upon previous presentations, so they do not all cover the same ground.

In class, time is devoted to the various stages of this process – design, implementation, troubleshooting, and various oral reports. In addition, special topics are introduced, by the professor, guest speakers and preferably students in the class. Topics covered during the most recent offering included Java servlets, JDBC, XML, COM objects, VRML and Cold Fusion. Though students are not able to get hands-on experience with all of these topics, exposure to them helps expand the base of knowledge that is being constructed.

2.1.2 Grading

Assigning grades to the students is a difficult challenge for a course organised in this fashion. In an effort to remain true to the notion of simulating an industrial environment, each student was primarily evaluated based on the quality of work produced, rather than exam results.

That decision raises the concern about whether or not students – who do not in reality face the prospect of being 'fired' for poor effort – are actually doing their share of the work. We attempt to assess this via written peer evaluations. At the conclusion of each case study, students are required to evaluate the work of their team-mates. These peer reviews factor into the grade each student receives for a case study, with the manager's review being weighted more heavily.

It is important, of course, to ensure that students are actually learning the course material appropriately. To assess this in the absence of written exams, the students are encouraged to take active roles in the class through several incentives that earn them points towards a higher grade, rather than higher pay. Included among these incentives are taking on the role of project manager or maintenance team member, taking an active part in the final lectures, preparing and delivering lectures or tutorials on one of the special topics and discovering or reviewing new tutorials. A high level of participation in these activities beyond the project work makes it easy to confirm that a student is assimilating the material.

2.1.3 Results

The course has, by all indications, been successful. Not only in terms of student enthusiasm but also in terms of student effort and quality of work produced. Quantitative information about the success of the class has been gathered via student surveys. A sampling of the results paints a positive picture. The average response to the question "How much did you learn in this class?" was 4.5, where a response of 1 indicated 'Nothing', 3 indicated 'An average amount' and 5 'A great deal'. 12 of 16 students responded to the anonymous survey.

The average response to the question "How effective was the case study approach in helping you learn the basic course material?" was 4.33, where 1 indicated 'Ineffective', 3 'Reasonably effective' and 5 'Very effective'.

The students were also asked this question: "Would you consider it to be a good idea for the class to be made more professor-focused (e.g., based more on professor-delivered lectures)?" Potential responses to this question ranged from 1 meaning 'Strongly disagree', to 3 'Neutral', to 5 'Strongly agree'. The average response was 2.33. The comments of those who responded with a 3 or 4 (there were no 5's) expressed frustration with some of the student lectures that were ineffective. Our conclusion is that the students are generally receptive to the idea of taking more control over their own learning, but that more must be done to ensure quality work on the parts of their classmates.

The anecdotal results were also favourable. Students in the class maintained a high level of enthusiasm and clearly learned the material even in the absence of the threat of an exam. From a teaching perspective, it has been energising to be in the position of learning alongside the students.

The results of the case study work for this course, along with additional information about course organisation and grading, can be found on the Web at *http://s9000.furman.edu/~treu/cs95/*.

2.2 Systems analysis

The Systems Analysis course is a project-based course that focuses on the analysis and design of large information systems. The projects used in the course are much larger in scope than those typically found in introductory level courses so that students will see the benefit of using the systems modelling tools that are developed in the course. A goal of the course is to engage the students in an interactive learning environment so that they experience the information system development process first hand.

The course also focuses on the skills necessary for the management of large projects including cost benefit analysis, project scheduling, and group management. Communication skills for meeting management and presentations are also developed. Many students have the opportunity to participate in internship experiences outside of the classroom at some point in their academic career, but rarely in these internships are they given leadership roles in the development of a project. These additional opportunities are becoming more important within the CS curriculum (Little et al. 1999).

2.2.1 Basic course organisation

In the last two offerings of our *Systems Analysis* course, the classroom was transformed into an IS development company with the professor as the CEO (Abernethy et al. 1998). The class was broken into 5-6 development teams where each team was responsible for their own information system. The classroom is our meeting room where members of the development teams discuss important issues relating to the projects, disseminate related material to the members of the team, and support each other in their efforts to learn and employ new technologies and techniques. The class attempted to involve all of the students in each of these activities. Central to this effort was a class web site that was designed and maintained by members of the class. The web site was used as a vehicle for disseminating appropriate technical information, communicating with members in the class, and organising meeting materials.

Each class meeting had a facilitator who organised the meeting agenda, posted the agenda on the web one day before the class meeting, and then ran the meeting. If a student wanted to make a presentation on a topic, they contacted the facilitator who then put them on the agenda. In addition, there was a meeting secretary who took minutes for the meeting and distributed those minutes on the web. Students were encouraged to prepare appropriate material to contribute to the class meetings, but no official assignments were given. Possible course material included answers to questions found at the end of chapters in the textbook, reviews of journal articles, descriptions of job interviews for analysis positions, or any other pertinent information.

Course material was also presented by the instructor, but students were expected to reference the agenda and read the related chapters before the class meeting. Students were encouraged to present the review problems to start the meeting discussions. The instructor was responsible for facilitating discussions on the topics and providing additional materials on the analysis and design tools. These 'lectures' were developed on the spot based on the needs arising from the discussions. In addition, there were weekly case studies to provide students with larger applications for the tools and techniques being studied.

2.2.2 Grading

Student participation in all of the class and web site activities was encouraged by the requirement to earn a certain number of 'participation points' during the term. Participation points were awarded when activities were completed and a given number of points had to be earned during each half of the course, primarily so that students did not wait until the last week of the course. Students were required to explore a variety of activities by limiting the number of points allowed for each one. For example, students could only earn points for facilitating one class during the term, five review questions, 2 article reviews, etc.

Another component to the course grade was the team project. All members of the team were awarded the same grade for the project. In order to ensure fairness among the group, peer evaluations were used to determine whether all members were supporting the team effort. In addition, the professor observed group dynamics during the weekly laboratory when groups met to work on their projects. Although not all of the project work was completed during these two hours, it was clear from these observations who was contributing to the group effort and who was not.

Finally, this course also lent itself to a midterm and a final exam to determine if the students were understanding the tools from the course. The course coverage is separated into two distinct sections, one for analysis and one for design. Hence, the midterm covered the analysis concepts and the final covered the design concepts.

2.2.3 Results

Student response to the first offering of this course was initially very tentative. They appeared to be confused and apprehensive about the expectations of the class participation. But as more students made presentations and updated the Web site, interest increased. It appeared that they simply needed someone to 'start the ball rolling'. Soon after the midterm point, all the meeting facilitator and secretary slots had been taken. The Web site was fully functional by then as well and had a variety of pages to help organise the class material. More exciting was the number of students offering to make contributions to the class that had not been originally suggested. The students seem to appreciate the chance to learn from each other and try to find new and interesting ways to accomplish the goals of the class. In the second offering of the course, the students became engaged much quicker as 'word was out' about the expectations of the class and the benefits of the classroom environment.

3. CONCLUSION

Simulation of real world processes is an important application of computer science. Accordingly, it seems natural for practical, applied CS concepts such as Web programming and systems analysis to be taught by simulating the environments in which professionals practice them. Though this idea is not unique, we are not aware of the use of such simulation-based learning as the organising principle of an entire course. In this paper we have described experiments with two courses that are designed to use this approach.

Numerous benefits have accrued. First, both courses are solid examples of engaged learning (learner-centred) principles. Rather than being the central focus of a student's attention, the professor becomes more of an organiser and guide while a student learns by exploration. This is meant to mirror the process by which a corporate project leader 'teaches' – he or she makes the objectives clear, makes the resources available, and provides guidance as the team member learns what is necessary.

Second, student enthusiasm for both courses is very high, as indicated by both quantitative and anecdotal results. The information to be learned is not viewed as being tedious or boring when it is leading to a product that will actually be used, and when there are team-mates relying on you to learn it.

Third, students have a sense of ownership of the information when they were primarily responsible for learning it. The pride that they feel in accomplishing their goals is a tremendous motivating force.

Finally, we have observed that experiences such as these in the undergraduate curriculum serve students extremely well in their professional pursuits after graduation. In the short time that these courses have been taught with the simulation-based approach, many graduates have reported that they were among the most useful and relevant of all their college courses.

REFERENCES

Abernethy, K., Gabbert, P. and Treu, K. (1998) Inquiry-Based Computer Science Instruction: Some Initial Experiences. *6th Annual Conference on the Teaching of Computing and 3rd Annual Conference on Integrating Technology into Computer Science*, August.

Jackson, U., Manaris, B. and McCauley, R. (1997) Strategies for Effective Integration of Software Engineering Concepts and Techniques into the Undergraduate Computer Science Curriculum. *ACM SIGCSE Bulletin*, Vol. 29, No. 1.

Leasure, D. (1998) Improving Student Learning Through Real-World Internet Projects. *The Journal of Computing in Small Colleges*, Vol. 14, No. 1.

Little, J. C., Granger, M. J. (co-chairs), Boyle, R., Gerhardt-Powals, J., Impagliazzo, J. Janik, C., Kubilus, N. J., Lippert, S. K., McCracken, W. M., Paliwoda, G. and Soja, P. (1999) Integrating Professionalism and Workplace Issues into the Computing and Information Technology Curriculum. *ACM SIGCSE Bulletin*, Vol. 31, No. 4.

Walker, H. (1997) Collaborative Learning: A Case Study for CS1 at Grinnell College and University of Texas-Austin. *ACM SIGCSE Bulletin*, Vol. 29, No. 1.

BIOGRAPHY

Paula Gabbert is an Associate Professor of Computer Science at Furman University. She has done extensive development of new educational methodologies in the CS curriculum including foreign study programs, simulation, and peer review.

Kevin Treu is an Associate Professor of Computer Science at Furman University. His professional interests include Web programming, interactive Web environments, and innovation in computer science pedagogy.

49

How to Educate Students to be Future Systems Engineers?

Mikihiko Ohnari
Department of Management Science, Faculty of Engineering, Science University of Tokyo, 1-3 Kagurazaka, Shinjuku-ku, Tokyo, 162-8601, JAPAN
ohnari@ms.kagu.sut.ac.jp

Keywords: learner-centred learning, problem solving, thinking, creativity, case studies

Abstract: Companies require new employees who can create a business chance and utilise information technology. For future systems engineers we have to teach students fundamental methods of systems engineering for development of information system or systems thinking. Teachers need an information environment and useful application software for students to freely use computers for their interesting field and chances to cultivate their abilities. As a result these environments strengthen their insights into issues, users' requirements and selection of software in views of problem solving and raise the level of their abilities dealing with information technology.

1. INTRODUCTION

Now in the era of information technology (IT), many computers are used in various fields in business. Companies are continuing to invest computer powers in their offices and works to improve their efficiency in management. For these investments, many systems engineers are required not only in information companies, but also in other types of companies. In Japan, many graduates get their jobs in the companies related to the IT industries and also in information processing sections in the conventional companies not related to the IT industries. Companies eagerly require new employees who can utilise computers. This implies that undergraduate students should have acquired some abilities of systems engineering or systems thinking in order to get jobs with companies.

2. RESPONDING TO REQUIREMENTS FOR NEW EMPLOYEES IN JAPAN

In education in universities in Japan, especially in technological faculty, computer literacy is a graduation requirement. In almost all faculties of engineering in universities and colleges in Japan, students can use fundamental functions of personal computers as tools for preparing papers, presentations, emails and Internet surfing.

In our Department of Management Science, Faculty of Engineering, Science University of Tokyo, the main objectives of teaching are: (1) computer, (2) technologies for utilising a computer, such as mathematics for analysis, modelling and simulation, and (3) management in social, economical and industrial fields. Computer education in our department focuses on teaching about 100 students in each grade of the first and second undergraduate the fundamental knowledge of computer: literacy, how to use Internet and a computer language. In the fourth grade and the second grade in a Master course, 80 percent of students apply for jobs with IT industries or IT related sections in companies and as systems engineers.

Social or company requirements for abilities of new employees are (1) creation of a business chance for a company, and (2) utilisation of IT in various fields of management. The abilities are cultivated by applying so-called systems thinking to a target issue. Systems thinking always grasps the target issue in a normative fashion or in top-down viewpoints. In other words companies require of employees some of the abilities of systems engineers. The roles of systems engineers are to set up the objectives of the target issue, to discover problems against the objectives and to apply IT to various fields of management. Systems thinking are key abilities for every systems engineer. Fundamental education of systems engineering is vital for students aiming to be future systems engineers.

In our department, we intend to teach students how to utilise computers. In the ways of computer utilisation, there are two directions: enhancement of application technology and adapting application software to user's requirements. The role of systems engineer is important for the latter case. In introducing IT, it is difficult for company managers as users to make clear their requirements for IT, compared with an introduction of a manufacturing machine in a plant, because a manager cannot estimate the performance per cost of IT. To make clear what types of hardware and software should be introduced in the site is one of the main roles of systems engineer.

Conventionally Japanese education focused on teaching "How to do ---?" but society outside of schools requires employees to think about "What to do ---?"

For developing future systems engineers we have to teach our students methods of system development and systems thinking, especially methods of requirement analysis: declaring target issues, proposing alternatives of ideas solving the issues and their evaluation. In a process of system development, systems thinking plays a very important role in selecting one of alternatives or in decision-making.

3. ENFORCEMENT OF ICT WITH SYSTEMS ENGINEERING IN EDUCATION AND TRAINING

Among lectures related to ICT (information and communication technologies), I give two lectures for the third grade students as shown in Table 1. One is 'information system engineering' and the other is 'theory of simulation' (Ohnari 1998).

Table 1. Education for 3rd & 4th Grade Students

3rd grade				
	April	July	Sept	Jan
Lecturer	Information System Engineering		Theory of Simulation	
	100 students		50 students	
Seminar	Training of Systems Engineering		Training of Modelling	
4th grade				
	April	July	Sept	Jan
Tutorial		Research for Graduation Theme		
		5 to 14 students		
Students	Job-hunting.			

In the lecture of information system engineering, I teach informatics combining with essence of systems engineering (Ohnari 1994). Systems engineering teach us a normative thinking, in other words, top-down thinking. System is defined as that it has objectives and contains many elements, and elements are organically combined each other. A system is usually too complex to understand because there are many elements in it. So relations of elements should be visually described in normative fashion by using an objective tree for example. In my classroom I teach normative expression, objective trees, evaluation and selection of alternatives by use of relevance matrix. I assign students some homework to find a problem occurring for each student, to make clear the problem with the aid of some tools used in systems engineering, to search alternative solutions as many as possible, to evaluate the alternatives by the relevance matrix, and to select the best one among the alternatives or rank them. Students are also requested to write their thinking processes visually. Lastly each student has to compare the selected result with their intuitive hypothesis. If a result differs from the intuitive evaluation, the student is asked to review the difference between the result and their hypothesis or intuition. I give students advice on how to make much of personal intuition, by introducing an episode of intuition power which professional players of GO or SYOGI have. In the course of lecture of Shannon's information theory, I ask students to draw the theory visually in order to learn the comprehensiveness of drawings at a glance.

A result of the questionnaire taken from students reviewing the lecture of systems engineering reveals its effectiveness for them as shown in Table 2.

Table 2. Results of Questionnaire (20 students)

Q1: What kinds of impression do you have in education of systems engineering?			
	Yes	Medium	No
Fresh, stimulative	7	3	
Useful, may be useful	10		1
Hard to understand	5		
Not able to understand	2		
Q2: Systematic or visual expression of issue around you			
	Yes	Medium	No
Interesting exercise	8	1	
Enjoyed	2	2	2
Hard to describe	14	1	
Useful, may be useful	5		
Not able to understand	1		
Q3: Systematic or visual expression			
	Yes	Medium	No
Interesting exercise	7		1
Enjoyed	1	3	3
Hard to describe	14	1	
Useful, may be useful	13		1
Not able to understand		1	

In the lecture of theory of simulation, I lay emphasis on how to build a model from gathered data by the method of multiple regression analysis that is selected as the simplest modelling method (Ohnari 1997). For preparing to teach regression analysis, the sweep-out method for solving simultaneous equations is demonstrated in order to show how to implement it on a spreadsheet software Excel in personal computer. Every student implements an example of the sweep-out method for solving two-elements-simultaneous linear equations on each personal computer. While in implementation, a value in cell is obtained by dividing some value by a value of pivot cell. In this division, conversion of pivot cell address in a relative expression (e.g. A1) to in an absolute expression (A1) is an important point to learn. After mastering Excel and implementation of the sweep-out method, students are guided to build up a procedure of a multiple regression analysis by applying the sweep-out method to a given set of data on each personal computer. This guidance is aided by a sheet of computer printout, which shows calculation process and results of multiple regression analysis for the given data of two independent variables and a dependent variable.

Two types of homework are given to students: compulsory problem and free problem. The compulsory problem offers students a problem of regression analysis with a set of data. Through this problem, students learn how to draw scatter map, and slopes intuitively in it, and select independent variables by the step-wise regression method.

For the free problem, students have to gather data and analyse it and build a model by the regression analysis. In the course of modelling some students encounter the problem of multicollinearity. When some students meet with it, I explain its reason.

4. HOW TO BUILD AN INFORMATION SYSTEM: A KEY ISSUE OF SYSTEMS ENGINEER EDUCATION

For training future systems engineers, it is effective to encourage them to build a small information system by themselves from the start of selecting and finding their themes to the final step of evaluating the outcomes of their developments. Building even a small information system inevitably contains an engineering process as shown in Figure 1, including many problems which systems engineers has to deal with.

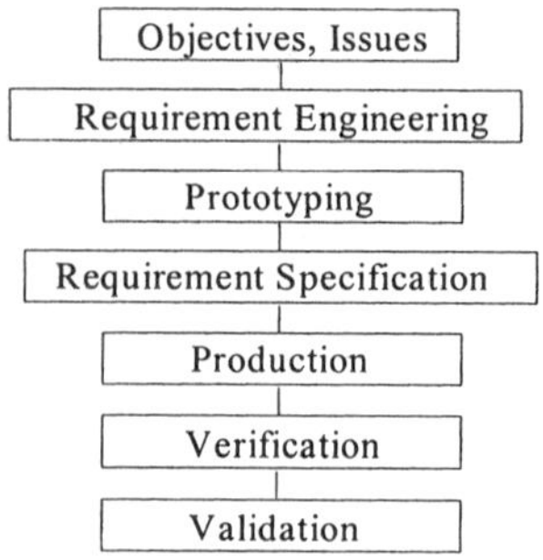

Figure 1. Flow of Information System Development

In Japan, many students in the forth grade in the faculty of engineering are assigned to a research laboratory and have a chance to receive a graduation tutorial from their teacher for making a graduation thesis. Each teacher has a speciality in technology or academic field. Many teachers naturally guide each student to select a theme among their specialities for a graduation thesis or give them a concrete theme.

As I have experienced in building models in various fields when I engaged in research laboratories of a manufacturing company, I have not given students any concrete theme. I intend to give each student a chance to find a theme by themselves. Finding a theme has various risks and issues for students to learn and experience. Every student in my laboratory has to select a field and find an issue with which they can deal as a theme for the graduation thesis. Some students in my laboratory find analysis problems as their themes. For preparing graduation theses in the forth grade, the third grade students are trained in each laboratory beforehand.

5. TRAINING STUDENTS FOR BUILDING AN INFORMATION OR ANALYSIS SYSTEM

For preparing the themes for graduation theses, each teacher in our department gives seminars to the future applicants to their laboratory among the third grade students. I also open two seminars sequentially in a year for them: one for training them how to practice systems engineering in the preceding term and the other for reinforcing the abilities of them in modelling in the last term.

For training a group of the third grade students who are interested in systems engineering, I give them chances to practice requirement analysis because it is important for systems engineer to find issue and problem. In order to solve the issue, systems engineer usually analyse user's requirements and propose a configuration of hardware and software, algorithms and tools for solving the problem.

Each student is required to find an issue of a personal matter and consider it as a problem of system construction. After doing this problem for homework, each student presents a report including their theme, objectives, issue, alternatives of solving, selection of the best solution, and evaluation of his or her thinking process.

I ask them, in the meantime, to describe some specifications of their handicrafts, handiwork, dishes and so on, which they made in their younger ages. These days many students have rare chance to build something by themselves, so it is important to teach them the process of design and manufacturing in a primitive form.

For training students in modelling and simulation techniques, I give students an exercise of making a polynomial model of t values with the significant level of 0.05 by using the data shown in t distribution table attached to a book of statistics with the aid of regression analysis. Another modelling exercise is to generate a set of data by using a cubic curve and adding random number, to select several subsets of the data, and to make several types of polynomial models depending on the subset. Students understand the effects of data selection by this exercise.

In order to build up an information system, builders use several types of software. Students who are going to build some computer system have to select some software for use beforehand. So I give them advice of acquiring the knowledge of application software needed for the system construction. Students in my laboratory have utilised several types of application software such as Visual basic or VBA for making graphical user interface, relational database management system Access for unitary management of data, animation software Macromedia director and Poser 3, and statistical software packages for the regression analysis and economical time-series analysis.

6. GRADUATION TUTORIAL AND THESIS

The fourth grade students attached to my laboratory have to find their themes for graduation theses. Finding a theme means to choose a field and select some methodology to handle the theme in a computer. It takes many months to determine concrete themes, partly because students are very busy for applying for jobs or the entrance examination of master grade from spring to early summer. During job hunting, students learn many types of company activities and social problems including etiquette. After the summer vacation, students begin to think about their graduation theses in earnest. I give advice to students in my laboratory to select an acquainted field such as circle activities in university, part-time jobs, family business or jobs of parents, and hobbies in families. If a student knows well the field, they can play both roles of user and maker of an application system in computer in finding issues and problems, gathering and devising many alternatives of solutions.

During eight years I have been engaged in the university as a professor, several dozen of students graduated from my laboratory. Almost all students selected their graduation thesis by themselves.

Typical fields of graduation theses are sports of baseball, golf, ski, snowboard, boat, yacht and scuba diving, culture lessons of KIMONO dressing, tee ceremony and tole painting, part-time jobs of pizza delivery shop, Japanese pub, KARAOKE shop, VCR rental shop and hotel cloakroom, and small companies managed by parents of resort hotel, clothing shop, fruit & vegetable retailer and connector manufacturer.

Typical theses are listed in Table 3 by categorised them by themes.

Table 3. Typical Graduation Theses

Sports training
Development of educational software for alpine ski technique (Odaka and Ohnari 1999)
Development of pitching behaviour simulator for baseball training (Mori et al. 2001)
Prototyping of self-learning system of strategy and tactics in yacht races
Development of scuba diving training system
Development of learning system of golf putting with the aid of animation
Supporting of culture lesson
Development of learning system how to dress KIMONO (Kawabe and Ohnari 1999)
Development of system for communing with tee ceremony
Development of educational software for tole painting technique (Yuguchi and Ohnari 2001)
Analysing some business segments of companies students were hired as part-timers
Analysis of posting effects on pizza delivery shop depending on the delivery areas
Construction of models for prediction of sales amounts and required man-hour in Japanese pub by economical time-series analysis
Prediction of the number of baggage to be kept in the custody of floor cloakroom in a hotel
Analysis and estimation of sale amounts in KARAOKE shop by economical time-series analysis
Supporting small companies managed by one of their parents
Management Improvement of a small size overseas resort hotel with the aid of information technologies
Construction of an Intranet preparing for e-business in a small-size manufacturer of electric connectors
Development of system for sending and receiving orders in fruit and vegetable retailer
Sales support systems for small clothing shops

7. EVALUATION

Results of selecting an acquainted field for each student reveal that: (1) a student can decide the ways in their research alone, because they have a measure of value in the selected field. Therefore they can tackle their issues without doubt, (2) in the themes of analysis problem, if a student selects a theme related to their part-time job, they can easily gather data in their working site and devise a new method of gathering or arrangement of field data, (3) in the case of selecting a tool, they can select an appropriate tool to their issue, because they can decide or review the tool in view of a critic or user. Therefore they can concentrate on the theme by using the tool with confidence.

In the course of research for graduation, although various unknown matters burden students, they challenge and gradually overcome these matters, gain new knowledge, and cultivate their abilities. Many graduates of my laboratory express their impression that my teaching and training process are effectiveness when they joined in companies and engaged in systems engineering. They say that education of systems engineering and thinking is useful especially in information companies. I myself evaluate that my teaching philosophy and training practices satisfy the requirements of today's company.

8. CONCLUSION

After being engaged in laboratories of a manufacturing company in Japan, I have been a professor teaching information system engineering and simulation engineering. In the classrooms and seminars, I tried to guide students to think and build something they have interested in.

Education of the computer is usually aimed to make students able to use computers up to a limited level. The theme of this conference is "Computers in Education". I think this theme urges teachers to create an environment to students who freely use computers for their interesting field and chances to cultivate their abilities of finding issues and solving problems by computers. For these purposes it is important to maintain computer environments and to prepare useful application software for their use. As a result these environments strengthen their insights into issues, user's requirements and selection of software in views of problem solving and raise the level of their abilities for IT.

REFERENCES

Kawabe, M. and Ohnari, M. (1999) Development of learning system how to dress KIMONO (in Japanese). *J. of Japanese Society for Information and Systems in Education*, Vol. 15, No. 4, pp. 188-192.

Mori, J., Ohno, N. and Ohnari, M. (2001) Development of pitching behaviour simulator for baseball training (in Japanese). *J. of Japanese Society for Information and Systems in Education* (to be published).

Odaka, N. and Ohnari, M. (1999) Development of educational software for alpine ski technique (in Japanese). *J. of Japanese Society for Information and Systems in Education*, Vol. 15, No. 4, pp. 182-187.

Ohnari, M. (1994) Education of Computer and Information Science with Systems Thinking (in Japanese). *JCET*, pp. 77-80.

Ohnari, M. (1997) Education Method of Regression Analysis for Teaching a Modelling Technology and Practice (in Japanese), *J. of Japanese Society for Information and Systems in Education*, vol. 14, No. 4, pp. 171-176.

Ohnari, M. (1998) *Simulation Engineering*. Ohmsha and IOS Press.

Yuguchi, R. and Ohnari, M. (2001) Development of educational software for tole painting technique (in Japanese), *J. of Japanese Society for Information and Systems in Education* (to be published).

BIOGRAPHY

Mikihiko Ohnari has experience of system developments especially in installing control computers into industrial or social plants, such as rolling mill plants, municipal water supply plants. In these system developments in Hitachi, Ltd., he encountered issues in extracting users' requirement and describing requirement specification, verification and validation. Now he is Professor of Science at the University of Tokyo and teaching students who will be future system engineers through lectures, such as information systems, and the theory of simulation.

50

A Study Program is more than a Set of Courses

About Designing a Program Environment

France Henri and Sylvie Doré
Télé-université du Québec, 4750, Henri-Julien, Montréal, H2T 3E4, Canada
fhenri@teluq.uquebec.ca
École de technologie supérieure, Université du Québec, Montréal, H3C 1K3

Keywords: distance learning, pedagogical design, development, support services, web-site

Abstract Realising that a program is much more than a series of courses, we set out to create a space, over and above the courses, where students can interact with the program's human and material resources. We call this space the *program environment*. Conceptually, a program environment is closer to the notion of *gateway* or *Learning Service Provider* than to that of a web-based course. Whereas an instructional designer has a plethora of course design and delivery platforms to choose from, the same cannot be said for the design and delivery of a program environment. Most commercial gateways are programmed from scratch. This reinforced our feeling that the project requested a strong methodological framework. We make use of the *MISA* pedagogical engineering method, and its companion modelling tool, *MOT*. Our modelling approach starts by representing scenarios students will adopt to fulfil their needs within the environment. Scenarios of the other actors will be derived from the student's scenarios. By doing so, we ensure that the environment is truly student centred.

1. CONTEXT

To face challenges brought about by the information age, more and more educational institutions are joining forces to create new learning opportunities. In 1996, four institutions of the Université du Québec network, Télé-université (Téluq), École de technologie supérieure (ÉTS), Institut national de recherche scientifique – Telecommunication section (INSR-Telecom) – and Université du Québec à Montréal (UQÀM), created the École de technologie de l'information (ÉTI) (Information Technology School). Its mission is to ensure training, research and university-industry transfer activities in the field of information technology. Training activities are geared to develop higher-level knowledge and skills in information processing systems engineering as well as in the management of technological change and it's the evaluation of its organisational impact. The students of the new school are graduates in the fields of engineering, applied and computer sciences, administration or management.

ÉTI offers two graduate programs: a 30 credit Graduate Diploma and a 45 credit Master's degree which were created by assembling courses extracted from existing programs offered by the four partners. While Téluq's courses are offered in distance-learning mode, the other courses are campus-based.

Aiming to better cater to the needs of students who complete their studies while working part or full time, and eventually to offer the program in all French speaking regions of the world, the institution decided to increase the number of web-based courses offered. By the end of 2001, it is anticipated that a student enrolled in one of ÉTI's programs will be able to complete all the required coursework in distance learning mode. In order to achieve this goal, the *AMÉTIST* project (Multimedia access to information technology studies – A techno-pedagogical strategy) pursues two objectives: to develop seven ÉTI web-based courses and to create a virtual community at the program level. This paper presents the conceptual framework and methodological approaches adopted to fulfil this second objective.

2. A SOLUTION: FROM THE STUDENT'S POINT OF VIEW

For ÉTI, a networked virtual institution, the main challenges are to:

- fulfil its mission despite a multiplicity of partners, a decentralised structure and a distributed campus, both physically and virtually – with three campuses spread out within a few kilometres of downtown Montreal, an information web-site and web-sites for each distance learning course
- create unity and ensure coherent programs which are derived from existing ones offered by partner institutions
- attain the highest graduation rate possible
- make the students feel that they belong to *one* school, not that they are spread out among the different campuses, isolated, without a home-base.

These challenges could have been addressed by ÉTI through a series of administrative decisions but instead, *AMÉTIST* proposes to embrace the students' point of view and formulates a single question. How can we foster student success throughout his/her program?

The solution we propose to encourage the success of each student enrolled in a virtual institution is to create a space, a place, a location, over and above the courses, where they can interact with the program's human and material resources. We have called this space the *program environment.*

To develop this environment we make use of the following three models.

1. The virtual campus conceptual model developed by LICEF Research Centre (Paquette et al. 1997) which establishes:
   - a network of five types of actors: learner, designer, information provider, trainer and manager
   - five virtual spaces: information, production, communication and collaboration, assistance and management spaces.
2. The student support model developed by Begin and Palkiewicz (1998) which considers two mutually inclusive axes of the students' life:
   - the critical moments: the onset of the studies and its continuation
   - the dynamics of student interactions with: the institution, his/her personal life, the program, the courses, teachers and research director, academic disciplines and content, tasks and situations related to learning and intellectual work.
3. The persistence model (Chenard and Ringuette 1998, Pageau 2000) which identifies a series of factors facilitating student enrolment and graduation.

Pageau found that for students studying full time, obtaining the diploma is influenced most by the intention of graduating and by passing all first semester courses. While the intention of graduating is also very important for part-time students, the desire not to interrupt the course of their studies and knowledge of the program and career prospects are almost as important.

The objectives we set for the program environment are based on the student support and persistence models. Through this environment, we wish that students will:

- *Progress optimally within the program.* At first glance, this may seem as a trivial goal. But realising that a large portion of ÉTI's clientele is made-up of part-time or full-time workers and knowing what influence knowledge of the program has on this student population increases its significance. Furthermore, one must realise that, at the onset of the program, the student population is far from homogeneous. Yet at its completion, all must have developed engineering as well as management skills. The progression within the program must therefore take into account the background preparation and level of expertise in information technology of each student at the beginning of his/her study course.

- *Learn to study at a distance.* Learning at a distance is an experience completely different from that of attending a campus-based lecture. New skills are required, new aptitudes must be acquired. As professors and program administrators we cannot expect the students to automatically adapt to this new way of learning. Moreover, few will challenge the statement that the adaptation from college to graduate school is as great as the one from high school to college. A student must therefore learn the skills expected of him/her as a graduate student. Here also, students must be supported in the development of a new proficiency.
- *Maintain the desire to graduate.* Except for a minority of students that enrol in the Graduate Diploma program to polish up their knowledge in the field of information technology and register to a few courses only, most students intend to graduate at the inception of the program. Through a series of activities, we must help them keep this dream alive, we must cherish the flame.

With these student objectives in mind, as designers of the program environment, we aim at helping student to:

- find information
- get advice and orientation
- develop a coherent and well integrated understanding of the program
- assess career prospects
- obtain various types of support:
  - conative persevaration
  - methodological assistance to pursue intellectual work
  - strategies to manage distance learning
  - technological help
  - etc.

3. DEVELOPMENT METHODOLOGIES

Two methodologies are used to develop the program environment. The first one is a pedagogical engineering method and the second is a modelling method.

3.1 Pedagogical engineering method

The development of a program environment aiming at the objectives identified previously is a complex process for many reasons:

- it has to deal, at a distance, with each student's individual case
- it must take into consideration cognitive, metacognitive and conative dimensions

- it must provide a wide range of information, resources and tools
- it should support acquisition, not of only academic knowledge, but of knowledge about the program and the process of going through the program.

Possibly our greatest challenge stems from the absence of similar models as we have found no other accounts of a similar endeavour.

To tackle such a task we required a solid and proven method. Since there exists no method to develop program environments, but because such an environment involves an important learning component, we can selected a pedagogical engineering method, *MISA* (Paquette et al. 1997). MISA not only includes classical ADDIE phases of instructional design (Analysis, Design, Development, Implementation and Evaluation) but it also permits a global and concurrent planning of four models using an object-oriented modelling approach. These models are: the *knowledge model* which specifies the types of knowledge objects and their relationships in the learning system; the *pedagogical model* which shapes up scenarios and identifies all resources required by the learner; the *media model* which defines the types and format of the various material components; and the *delivery model* which specifies the technological and organisational infrastructures required for distributing the learning system.

3.2 Modeling method

While developing a number of computerised learning environment, we found MOT, an object-oriented modelling method and its associated tool, to be extremely valuable. We decided to use it in the development of the program environment. MOT is a companion of MISA. It is intended to assist designers with no computing background to construct learning systems. MOT enables designers to represent schematically all components of the environment, especially the four models proposed by the MISA method and the various scenarios of all the actors of the program: students, teachers, counsellors/advisors and managers.

Our modelling approach starts by representing scenarios students will adopt to fulfil their needs within the environment. Examples of such scenarios include how to locate information, to ask for advice, to request assistance, to get to know other students enrolled in the program, to become skilled at learning at a distance, etc. Scenarios of the other actors will be derived from the student's scenarios. In that way we ensure that the environment is truly student centred.

4. TECHNOLOGICAL CHOICES

Originally, one of Teluq's contribution to ÉTI was to host all web-based distance learning courses. However, teachers from partner institutions whose courses are in the process of being transformed from face-to-face campus delivery mode to web-based distance learning mode prefer hosting the courses within their own institutions. This choice is primarily motivated by a greater ease of in-house course material maintenance. One consequence of this choice is that ÉTI, and AMÉTIST, now have to deal with a number of different course delivery platforms (in-house programmed web sites, WebCT, Learning Space, etc.). AMÉTIST commissioned a study in order to establish the technical compatibility of the delivery platforms and to identify the challenges that their multiplicity creates on the institution, its teachers and its students. The study revealed no particular technological barrier to their integration within a program environment.

Conceptually, a program environment is closer to the notion of 'gateway' or 'Learning Service Provider', a new phenomenon in the world of education, than to that of a web-based course. Whereas an instructional designer has a plethora of course design and delivery platforms to choose from, the same cannot be said for the design and delivery of a program environment. Most commercial gateways are programmed from scratch (Lamontagne 2000). We based the selection of the program environment delivery tool, namely Explor@ (Paquette 2000) on the following criteria:

- a neutrality as large as possible with regard to a particular pedagogical model
- a system with which to manage the different objects composing the environment
- a system capable of easily communicating with other systems.

Explor@ was also developed by LICEF Research Centre and is commercialised by Technologies Cogigraph inc. Explor@ is a system which centrally manages the resources used by the actors as modelled by the LICEF virtual campus. Interestingly, Explor@ is configurable in the sense that the resources available can be made to vary from one actor to another. Because it is centrally managed, it can act on a set of courses, resources and actors. Furthermore, contrarily to most design and delivery platforms which double as authoring tools, Explor@ integrates web sites which will have been authored elsewhere. This insures neutrality with respect to pedagogical choices.

5. CONCLUSION

The program environment is still under development. We are currently defining its main concept and the orientations of the four models (knowledge, pedagogical, media and delivery). The environment will present itself as a one-stop tutoring centre. In addition to the tools and information required to fulfil the objectives defined earlier, each student will dispose of a personal space where all information and data on his study course, marks, records of personal notes, trace of all transactions and interactions will be centralised. Before implementation, a prototype will be tested in a natural setting.

The originality of our project lies in:

- The development of an environment on top and above the courses. Although universities are more and more preoccupied with escorting their students throughout their program, to diagnose students problem, to depict and prevent the risk of drop-out, none or few of them have be involved in the development of an environment to offer this type of service in a virtual mode. We are conscious that the existence of virtual program environment will place a demand for program resources available to the students. Teachers, advisors, counsellors will have to become involved.
- Our approach suggesting that going through a program not only involves a process of acquiring academic knowledge but that learning about the program and how to get through the program is as important. This type of knowledge is not formally stated when a student enrols in a program although it is most often taken care of implicitly. The fact that an effort is made to highlight this aspect of student life and to systematically try to take care of this situation by adequate support might have an impact on his/her success.
- Our will to formally tackle the question of offering students systematic and rationally developed support and assistance lead us to use a pedagogical engineering method. Geared at developing learning environments, we soon realised that it requires adaptation to cover all aspects of the program environment, especially those dealing with the conative dimension.

REFERENCES

Begin, C. and Palkiewicz, N. (1998) *Modèle pour une approche globale et intégrée de l'encadrement. Document d'animation et de diagnostic.* [http://www.unites.uqam.ca/depc/grandoss/encad_modele.htm]

Chenard, P. and Ringuette, M. (1998) Entrée, intégration et persévérance aux études. Ouvrir nos portes aux étudiants. *Réseau*, Avril.

Pageau, D. (2000) Les clés du succès: volonté et engagement! *ACPRI Annual meeting*, Saskatoon.

Paquette, G., Ricciardi-Rigault, C., de la Teja, I. and Paquin, C. (1997) Le Campus virtuel: Un réseau d'acteurs et de ressources. *Revue de l'éducation à distance,* XII, *1*/2.

Paquette, G., Crevier, F. and Aubin, C. (1997) Méthode d'ingénierie d'un système d'apprentissage (MISA). *Revue Informations In Cognito*, 8.

Paquette, G. (2000) *Explo@ – the virtual learning center.* [http://www.licef.teluq.uquebec.ca/gp/htmlang/prodexpl.htm]

BIOGRAPHIES

France Henri is professor at Télé-université (distance learning institution of the Université du Québec network). She has a Ph.D. in educational technology. As a member of the LICEF research centre, she has been conducting work in the design of learning environments for some twenty years. Her main interests also include collaborative learning.

Sylvie Doré is professor in mechanical engineering at École de technologie supérieure affiliated to the same university network. She has been involved in distance education since 1998.

They are co-responsible of the AMÉTIST project, which aims at the development of a program environment and distance education courses for ÉTI (higher education school in information technology).

51

Recent Experience with the Computer Science Accreditation Process

Chao Lu, Doris K. Lidtke, Charles Dierbach, and Gabriele Meiselwitz
Department of Computer and Information Sciences, Towson University, Towson, Maryland 21252 USA
cdierbach@towson.edu

Keywords: accreditation, assessment, competencies, curriculum policies

Abstract: Accreditation of programs in Computer Science in the USA began in 1986. There are now over 150 accredited programs and the number is increasing each year (CSAB 1997). There is significant international interest in the mutual recognition and coordination of accreditation of computer science academic programs. The B.S. of Computer Science program at the Department of Computer & Information Sciences, Towson University received the Computing Sciences Accreditation Board (CSAB) initial accreditation in 1994, and has just gone through a reaccreditation visit during the Fall 1999. In this paper, we would share our experiences of the computer science accreditation process; lessons learned, and present our curriculum as one example of the accredited computer science programs in USA.

1. BACKGROUND AND DEFINITION

Accreditation of programs in Computer Science in the USA began in 1986. There are now over 150 accredited programs and the number is increasing each year (CSAB 1997). An accredited program is one that has been reviewed by qualified, trained visitors and meets the Criteria established Computer Science Accreditation Commission (CSAC) and approved by the CSAB. Only programs that are in institutions that have regional accreditation can be considered. This means that the evaluators visiting the institution are assured that the institution has in place the necessary infrastructure to offer programs leading to the degrees they offer, particularly on the undergraduate (baccalaureate) level. The accreditation process is nearly two years long and involves a self study by the program requesting accreditation, a visit by three qualified evaluators, formal analysis of the program, and finally a vote by the CSAC at their annual meeting. Accreditation of a program is for 6 or 3 years. A three year accreditation is for programs which are deemed to have some issues regarding stability of the program, for example, many recent, substantive changes in the institution, many significant changes in the curriculum that may not be fully implemented, or a history of difficulty with keeping faculty.

2. THE PROCESS

The first important step in considering accreditation is to see if the program meets the CSAC/CSAB Criteria. If a program needs help or guidance, the department may hire a consultant, who is experienced with CSAC accreditation, or may send an observer to a CSAB session on training for Program Evaluators, where the observer will learn more about the process, particularly how Criteria are interpreted and applied.

Once the department feels that their program will probably meet the Criteria, they begin to prepare the self-study and to collect course materials, about a year prior to the visit. This is a good time to discuss the process with the administration of the institution to be certain that they are supportive of the process and willing to provide the money for the fees. By January 31 of the year the program is to be visited, the institution needs to submit a Request for Evaluation form. By June 1 of the same year the institution must pay the fee for the accreditation visit. In late Spring the institution will be sent a list of Program Evaluators (PEs) and Team Chairpersons (TCs). The institution is asked to cross off any PEs or TCs that they choose not to have as visitors. Those excluded should include recent former faculty, consultants, graduates, and anyone who may have a conflict of interest concerning the program.

The self-study must be submitted to CSAC by July 1 of the year of the visit. This two volume document is key to the accreditation process. In preparing this self-study the faculty of the program must critically analyse their program in all its aspects. The self-study by the program includes detailed documentation of the curriculum, the students, the faculty and the environment in which the program is delivered. The forms for the self-study are available on the web at www.csab. Detail required includes all courses in computer science that count toward the major. syllabi for all courses and details about the material covered in each course, faculty vitas, and information about students in the program.

In July, using the list of visitors acceptable to the institution and eliminating all PEs and TCs who live in the same or an adjacent state, CSAC will pick a TC for each institution to be visited in the fall. The TC will be given the names of at least two possible PEs to try to form a team. Once the TC has formed a team, they will contact the institutional contact person and agree the exact dates and schedule for the visit.

During the two-day, on campus visit, the team will talk with students, faculty and the leading administrators. The team will also examine course displays, which include the syllabus, a copy of the textbook, all handouts supplied to the students, and samples of graded student work from homework, tests, projects and examinations. These samples must include both work of excellent students, but also work representative of average and poor students. The three people who visit the institution to evaluate the program comprise a team. There are two Program Evaluators (PEs) and a Team Chair (TC). The program evaluators are nominated by the societies, which established CSAB, the Association of Computing Machinery (ACM) and the IEEE Computer Society (IEEE-CS). The TC will have served on several previous visits as a PE. Each TC is asked to evaluate the PEs on the team and based upon their evaluation and the evaluation by the institution itself. Several Program Evaluators are invited each year to become Team Chairs in the coming year. There is an effort made to have at least one industry representative on each team.

3. CRITERIA FOR PROGRAM EVALUATION

A program should be designed to provide a broad general education at the baccalaureate level so that they can function effectively in the profession. 'Programs designed to prepare graduates for supporting roles, for example technician, are not eligible, nor are programs that fail to provide an adequate base for the application of concepts fundamental to the discipline (CSAB 1997)' Although special circumstances, such as evening or cooperative baccalaureate programs and distance education, are not specifically addressed, these programs are eligible for consideration. 'The criteria are intended to assure an adequate foundation in science, mathematics, the humanities and social sciences, and computer science fundamentals, and to assure appropriate preparation in advanced computer science. They are designed to be flexible enough to permit the expression of an institution's individual qualities and ideals. [They] are intended to encourage and stimulate creative and imaginative programs (CSAB 1997)'. Nothing should be interpreted as constraining an institution in the development of its educational programs.

The criteria are divided into five major categories: Faculty, Curriculum, Laboratory and Computing Resources, Students and Institutional Support. The self-study and the team visit examine each of the criteria in detail. The original Criteria which was used for the first CSAC visits was modelled after the ABET Criteria for accrediting programs in engineering. The only category, which differed to any large extent, was the section on curriculum. Over the years the self-study documents have evolved in each organisation and are somewhat different.

4. WHO BENEFITS FROM ACCREDITATION?

Many groups benefit from accreditation, including students, employers, the public, and the institution, department and the program. The students benefit by being assured that they are being taught what they need to know to prepare them to function as a professional in the computer science field. They are able to choose to go to a university which has shown that it provides the type of education which is deemed necessary by CSAB and the professional societies which support CSAB, ACM and IEEE-CS. The students' parents have the assurance that they are paying for an education which will adequately prepare their son or daughter to enter the workforce or go on to graduate studies in the field.

Employers value accreditation because it insures a minimum level of preparation for the students they hire. Accreditation provides the employer with a workforce which has acquired a certain level of ability in the field. Employers are encouraged to have their personnel participate in the accreditation process, specifically by commenting on changes in the Criteria and serving as Program Evaluators and Team Chairs. As business, industry, government and individuals rely increasingly on computers and software, it is vital that minimum standards of preparation of workers be set in place. Accreditation is one way to assure minimum preparation of people entering the field. As more computer systems can impact the life, health and safety of people, it is important that computer professionals be adequately prepared for their work.

The institution, the department and the program that is accredited also benefit. The reputation of the institution is enhanced when the program is recognised as having met the standards of accreditation. The department benefits by having a recognised program as they recruit students and try to attract and retain faculty. The program benefits by being constantly reviewed and improved.

5. PREPARATION FOR ACCREDITATION

Preparation for accreditation requires considerable effort; a program may need to spend several years studying the Criteria and seeing how close their program is to meeting each criterion. For accredited programs, the re-accreditation process requires a minimum of 20 months, though two years is generally recommended. The formal process begins with the submission of a Request for Evaluation by January of the year prior to the visit by the evaluators. For the process to go smoothly, the program should be continuously reviewed, updated and care taken to be sure that all of the criteria continue to be followed. The collection of current syllabi, handouts and graded student work needs to be done a year prior to the visit.. Every member of the program should be involved in the process. Motivating all faculty members and students to participate and getting all course materials collected are not trivial tasks, especially if the program has a large number of majors. First, an internal team consisting of two or three experienced faculty and the department chair is formed. Each member of the internal accreditation team should be assigned specific tasks with deadlines. Assigned time should be given to these members for their work. The team should meet regularly to update each other on progress and to discuss and address any problems.

The self-study, Questionnaire for Review of the Computer Science Program, needs to be prepared and sent to CSAB by July prior to the visit. Both academic and administrative issues are addressed. The program will be initially evaluated on the basis of the data provided in the self-study. Programs without an adequate self-study within the time will not be considered. Collecting data and preparation is the most important first step of initial accreditation, as well as for re-accreditation.

The Administration should be informed of each step in the process and receive a copy of the self-study when completed. Since the University senior managemenet will be involved, co-ordination with their offices is necessary. Scheduling is crucial since the accreditation visit involves so many university administrators, all the faculty members in the department, some faculty members from other related departments, staff members from library and other units in the university.

The accreditation visit is usually scheduled in the Fall. Prior to the visit, all the course material and textbooks should be set up for display in a conference room. All faculty and staff should be available during the on-site visit; on the first day the team chair interviews all the administrators then other related staff while the other two team members interview all the faculty members and students. On the second day the team meets to discuss the visit among themselves, then the team debriefs the Chair, then the

President. These exit meetings with the team are an opportunity to correct any errors in fact that the team may have, and to provide missing information. Also in the exit interviews the team will point out any deficiencies in the program and any concerns they have. Any program that has a deficiency by the time of the Annual Meeting of CSAC will not be accredited. So if the team points out a deficiency, the faculty should begin work immediately to change things so that the deficiency no longer exists. Concerns should also be addressed.

During the ten days following the visit the institution and program may submit any evidence to the team to show that a deficiency has been remedied. Information submitted within the ten days accepted. In Spring the institution will receive a Preliminary Statement from CSAC detailing the findings of the visiting team and listing explicitly any deficiencies and concerns. The institution has 30 days to reply to this statement. This is time to provide proof that deficiencies have been eliminated and concerns addressed. Then before the annual meeting of CSAC, the institution may still submit any supplemental information to the Commission for consideration of the evaluation team's report.

Program accreditation assists in quality assurance and enhances opportunities for international interchange. Towson University has a large computer science graduate program with many international students. It would be helpful to identify students coming from accredited institutions at admission at both the graduate and undergraduate levels.

6. CHANGES IN CRITERIA

In 2000 the Criteria for Accrediting Programs in the United States (CSAB 2000) was revised. This new Criteria has the same goals as the previous criteria; most programs meeting the previous criteria would meet the new. One area that is markedly different is on Objectives and Assessments. Here the intent is that 'The program has documented objectives, including expected outcomes for graduates. The program regularly assesses its progress against its objectives and uses the results of the assessments to identify program improvements and to modify the program's objectives.' Thus the goal of accreditation is quality assurance.

7. INTERNATIONAL ACTIVITIES AND IMPLICATIONS

For a number of years CSAC/CSAB has been interested in developing mutual recognition of accredited programs with other countries, granting substantial equivalence to programs outside the USA, and assisting in the development of their own accreditation process. Dr. Willis King, University of Houston, Texas, has been a leader in this activity (IWCSEA 1996). He was convener of the National Science Foundation supported International Workshop on Computer Science and Engineering Accreditation in Salt Lake City, Utah, in 1996. He is also the Principal Investigator for a joint project between the USA and the European Union to investigate the possibility of mutual recognition of programs in computer science. This project attempts to promote student exchange, 'to exchange ideas and experiences in curriculum development, and to stimulate collaboration and harmonisation of degree programs in computer science. ... The ultimate goal of the project is to promote mutual recognition of academic degrees in computer science. In these days, when more and more governments are advocating the licensing of practitioners of computing sciences, it will be beneficial to our graduates if their degrees are recognised internationally.' (Willis 1999) The three courses which were developed as a part of this project were presented at the Frontiers in Education (FIE'99) in November 1999 in San Juan, Puerto Rico. (Clements 1999, Lidtke 1999, Oswald 1999).

8. AN EXAMPLE CURRICULUM

We present here our current curriculum as an example of accredited programs (TU 1999).

A. Title of degree – Major: Computer Science. Diploma Bachelor of Science

B. Credit Hour Definition: One semester hour normally represents one class hour or three laboratory hours per week. One academic year normally represents at least 28 weeks of classes exclusive of final examinations. But the COSC 236, Introduction to Computer Science I, has a two-hour lab that counts as one hour of course credit. Three additional hours of lecture account for the total of four credit hours. Students have two hours of closed lab, and must spend additional time in open lab. Numbers represent credit hours

Computer Science Curriculum

Core courses:

COSC 236 Introduction to Computer Science I (4)
COSC 237 Introduction to Computer Science II (4)
COSC 280 Assembly Language/ Computer Architecture (3)
COSC 336 Data and File Structures (4)

COSC 338 Computer Organisation and Architecture (4)
MATH 263 Discrete Mathematics (3)
MATH 273 Calculus I (4)
MATH 274 Calculus II (4)
MATH 330 Introduction to Statistical Methods (4)
Lab Science I (Lab science – 1st of sequence) (4)
Lab Science II (Lab science – 2nd of sequence) (4)
Science Elective (Science required by respective major)
Science Elective (Science required by respective major)

Total credits: 46-48

Advanced courses:

COSC 439 Operating Systems (3)
COSC 455 Programming Languages: Design + Implementation (3)
COSC 457 Database Management Systems (3)
COSC xxx Category A Elective (3)
COSC xxx Category A Elective (3)
COSC xxx Category B Elective (3)
COSC xxx Category B Elective (3)
MATH xxx Upper Level Math Elective (3-4)
COSC 480 Senior Seminar (1)

Total credits: 27-28

Computer Science Elective Categories:

Category A: Theory-Related Electives

COSC 367 - Discrete Structures (3)
COSC 415 - Compiler Design (3)
COSC 417 - Theory of Computing (3)
COSC 441 - Performance Evaluation (3)
COSC 459 - Simulation and Modelling (3)
COSC 461 - Artificial Intelligence (3)
COSC 483 - Design and Analysis of Algorithms (3)

Category B: - Application Related Electives

COSC 350 - Data Communications and Networking (3)
COSC 412 - Software Engineering (3)
COSC 431 - Selected Topics (3)
COSC 438 - Parallel/Vector Computing (3)
COSC 471 - Computer Graphics (3)

D. Overall Accreditation Curriculum Requirements

The minimum curriculum requirements established by CSAB for program accreditation:

Total amount of computer science. The program must have at least one and one-third years of computer science topics (at least 40 semester hours).

Core courses. The computer science segment of the curriculum must have a broad-based core consisting of the equivalent of 16 semester hours. (Basic coverage of algorithms, data structures, software design, concepts of programming languages, and computer organisation and architecture).

Theoretical foundations. At least the equivalent of three semester hours of theoretical material in the required core courses.

Mathematics requirement. The curriculum must include at least one-half year (at least 15 semester hours) of mathematics.

Science requirement. The curriculum must include at least two-fifths (the equivalent of 12 semester hours) of a year of science, accepted in that major. In addition, two courses must form a sequence.

Overall mathematics/Science requirement.

CSAB criteria require that the combined total of all required mathematics and science courses be at least one year of study (equivalent to 30 semester hours).

General education courses. CSAB criteria require that there be at least one full year of courses from the following areas: Humanities, social sciences, arts, and other disciplines that serve to broaden the background of the student.

Other. It is also required that students be trained in two other areas: Oral and communication skills, and ethical and societal implications of computing.

Programs are expected to meet the above minimum requirements in order to receive accreditation.

9. CONCLUSIONS

The curriculum presented here integrates technical requirements with general education requirements and electives to prepare students for a professional career in the computer science field. While some of our graduates go on to graduate education, a large majority of our graduates go to work in industry and government agencies. Our program stresses two important components: a broad-based theoretical foundation, and the latest development of computer technology. The core provides basic coverage of algorithms, data structures, software design, concepts of program languages, and computer organisation and architectures. Closed laboratories (i.e., laboratory time with instructor) are used in Computer Science I (COSC236) and Computer Organisation (COSC338). Electives provide area-specific topics of computer science, with COS431 Special Topics in Computer Science dealing with topics of the latest technology. Given the fast changes in the computing field, the curriculum needs to be continuously reviewed and updated while making sure that all the regulations of accreditation are followed.

Program accreditation not only assists in quality assurance, but also greatly enhances opportunities for international interchange. Towson University has a large computer science graduate program with many international students, and therefore identifying students coming from accredited institutions during the admission process would be of great benefit.

REFERENCES

Clements, A. (1999) Towards A Modern Computer Architecture Curriculum. In *Proceedings of Frontiers in Education Conference,* A. Clements, A. Shvartsman, W. King, C. Lu, and D. Dupont (eds.), (FIE '99, November 10-14 1999), San Juan, Puerto Rico, pp. 11b8-4-9.

CSAB (Computer Science Accreditation Commission) (1997) Evaluative Criteria. *1997 Annual Report*, 34-35, Computing Sciences Accreditation Board, Inc.

CSAB (Computer Science Accreditation Commission) (2000) *Criteria for Accrediting Programs in Computer Science in the United States*. January 2000, version 1.0. [www.csab.org/criteria2k_v10.html].

IWCSEA (1996) *International Workshop on Computer Science and Engineering Accreditation.* Salt Lake City, Utah, USA, Nov. 10-11, 1996.

Lidtke, D. (1999) Professionalism and Social Issues in Informatics: An International, collaborative Curriculum Development Project. In *Proceedings of Frontiers in Education Conference,* D. K. Lidtke, M. Israel, G. L. Engel, E. L. Leiss, and D. Waetjen (eds.), (FIE '99, November 10-14, 1999), San Juan, Puerto Rico, pp. 11b8-10-13.

Oswald, A. (1999) An International Common Project Model. In *Proceedings of Frontiers in Education Conference,* A. Oswald, S. Azadegan, M. Aiguier, D. Smarkusky, S. Huang and J. Spiess (eds.) (FIE '99, November 10-14, 1999), San Juan, Puerto Rico, pp. 11b8-14-17.

TU (Towson University) (1999) *Questionnaire for Review of the Computer Science Program to the Computer Science Accreditation Commission for the 1999-2000 accreditation cycle.* Volume II, Department of Computer and Information Sciences, Towson University.

Willis, K. et al. (1999) Towards a common computer science curriculum and mutual degree recognition – An Intercontinental Project. In *Proceedings of Frontiers in Education Conference*, W. K. King and M. Israel (FIE '99, November 10-14, 1999), San Juan, Puerto Rico, pp. 11b8-1-3.

BIOGRAPHY

Chao Lu is chair of the department, Doris Lidtke is professor in the department and active in computer science curriculum development both nationally and internationally, Charles Dierbach is Associate Professor and has been involved in introductory computer science course development, and Gabriele Meiselwitz is active in course science course development for non-majors.

52

A Lifelong Learning Course Based on Learning Objectives

Robert Aiken and Cheryl Sandås
Temple University, Computer and Information Sciences Department, 038-24, Philadelphia, PA 19122, USA
aiken@joda.cis.temple.edu

Keywords: lifelong learning/education, pedagogy, collaborative learning, fluency in information technology

Abstract: This paper describes our approach for developing a second level course that provides a strong foundation in information technology. The course was designed as a follow-up course to one often described as Computer Literacy. The course focuses on a hands-on-use of the technology in different complex, research and information-rich environments for students who are not computer and information science majors. In this paper we discuss how the course was developed after the authors carefully delineated the pedagogical goals they wanted to achieve. Both the advantages and disadvantages of organising a course in this manner are discussed.

1. INTRODUCTION

Information Technology (IT) is central to modern society (Toffler and Toffler 1995). Learning to use IT effectively in individual and organisational domain-specific processes cannot be done in a single step. Such learning requires appropriate introductory concepts, experiences, and motivations, and a life-long commitment to learning.

Courses that introduce IT generally fall into one of the following categories: 'computer literacy', 'programming', 'great ideas of computer science', and 'computer and society'. Such courses seldom combine the following elements: understanding of IT ideas and instruments, understanding of IT's role in framing and solving specific problems in various disciplines, and the ability to actually use IT to solve these problems. Students who are interested in specific themes and subject domains, such as chemistry, sociology, or anthropology need to understand IT from the perspective of these domains.

The question we address is how to bring students to the level beyond the introductory course. At this new level students should be able to integrate IT into the problem-solving logic and operation of their specific disciplines. We propose a new course to achieve this transformation. It will demonstrate through complex case studies the power of IT integration. We propose in-depth case studies as the best approximation to apprenticeship learning. Additional details on the case study approach and framework can be found in Aiken et al. (2000).

We should note here that the planning for this project has been underway for several years and was independent of the 'Being Fluent with Information Technology' report that was written by a Committee on Information Technology Literacy and published by the National Academy Press (1999). However, in many ways our ideas and concerns are similar. What we discuss is one specific way to address the concerns addressed in this report of how to make a larger number of college/university students fluent in technology and life long users of IT.

Principal objectives of our proposal also include establishing a framework to develop portable case studies, assessing the effectiveness of the course in achieving its stated goals, and disseminating our results as widely as possible. This is certainly consistent with the above mentioned report which states, "In summary, FIT individuals, those who know a starter set of IT skills, who understand the basic concepts on which IT is founded, and who have engaged in the higher-level thinking embodied in the intellectual capabilities, should use information technology confidently, should come to work ready to learn new business systems quickly and use them effectively, should be able to apply IT to personally relevant problems, and should be able to adapt to the inevitable change as IT evolves over their lifetime."

2. PEDAGOGICAL OBJECTIVES

In designing this course we decided to proceed from a set of pedagogical objectives that are consistent with standards in general use (International Society for Technology in Education 1998).

The following six objectives were the ones chosen to provide the backbone for the course:

Basic operations and concept

- Students demonstrate a sound understanding of the nature and operation of technology systems.
- Students are proficient in the use of technology.

Social, ethical, and human issues

- Students understand the ethical, cultural, and societal issues related to technology.
- Students practice responsible use of technology systems, information, and software.

Technology productivity tools

- Students use technology tools to enhance learning, increase productivity, and promote creativity.
- Students use productivity tools to collaborate in constructing technology-enhanced models, preparing publications, and producing other creative works.

Expressive and collaborative communication

- Students use IT to collaborate, and interact with peers and other audiences.
- Students use a variety of media and formats to communicate information and ideas effectively to multiple audiences.

Technology research tools

- Students use technology to locate, evaluate, and collect information from a variety of sources.
- Students use technology tools to process data and report results.
- Students evaluate and select new information resources and technological innovations based on the appropriateness to specific tasks.

Technology problem-solving and decision-making tools

- Students use technology resources for solving problems and making informed decisions.
- Students employ technology in the development of strategies for solving problems in the real world.

These were the primary objectives that we wanted to emphasise in the course. In order to better understand how these objectives helped influence the design of the course we will discuss topics that were covered under one of these objectives and describe how they assisted us in developing the course and presenting the material.

2.1 Social, ethical and human issues

The first author developed most of the material for this objective. Our overarching goal with this objective was that students understand the ethical, cultural, and societal issues related to technology. The crucial point is that technology, though by itself neutral, can have wide reaching and potentially harmful effects. So the question becomes not so much, "Can we do it?", but " Should we do it?". This topic was presented in week 11 of the course after a number of technical subjects had previously been covered. Students were asked to read a paper, which discusses the role of ethics in the development of Artificial Intelligence systems of the future; with particular emphasis on educational applications (Aiken and Epstein 2000).

This paper built on previous class discussions, which focused on articles that students had collected in a previous assignment regarding controversial uses of computers in society. The next lecture was devoted to exploring in some detail three (out of more than 40) scenarios on the web that paint a rather grim picture of what the future might become if we allow computers to become too intelligent and subsequently rely on them too much. (see www.cs.wcupa.edu/~epstein/AIStories.html.) In order to anchor this material we found it useful to use articles and stories to facilitate class discussion about ramifications of the material presented. Also students were required to write a three-page paper analysing one of the three scenarios.

2.2 Expressive and collaborative communication

In addition to promoting class discussion by designing participatory exercises and open-ended discussion questions, we required the students to either choose a project from the ones we offer or design and develop their own web-based project. Our goal was to have them use tools similar to those they had explored during the semester and to acquire greater facility with all the methodologies we had presented for building web-based material. The web is a media for disseminating information to and interacting with a wide spread population at minimal cost. Thus, we felt that it was essential that students master the skill of rendering information in an organised and appealing way on the web. Each group of two students was required to present their results to the class on the last day of class in addition to turning in a written report. One of our objectives was to work with them on collaboration strategies as well as provide them an opportunity (challenge) to demonstrate their project and give an oral presentation.

2.3 Pedagogical objectives in the lab

The lab portion of the class provides an environment for the concepts presented in lecture to be implemented and to address many of the pedagogical objectives. We accomplish this through various hands-on exercises and projects that support the material covered in the lectures.

Among the pedagogical objectives covered in the lab are basic operations and concepts, technology productivity tools, expressive and collaborative communication, technology problem-solving and decision-making tools. A few of these objectives will be discussed in detail and compared to the approach of Snyder and his colleagues at the University of Washington who take a project and programming based approach in their Fluency with IT course (www.cs.washington.edu/education/courses/100/99au).

Our main objective in the lab is to focus on the concepts presented in lectures using IT. We do not focus on basic computer skills because all of the students have taken a 'Computer Literacy' course where these skills are provided. However, basic operations and concepts of IT are covered as we utilise a variety of software applications such as Excel, Idrisi (a geographic information system), Alchemy (molecular modelling software), FrontPage, Word, Netscape/Explorer, Intelligent Tutoring Systems, and multimedia software. During the course students must demonstrate their knowledge of IT by creating and maintaining web pages, by completing analytical exercises and by presenting results using different software such as Idrisi, Alchemy, and Microsoft Excel.

Since a wide variety of software is used ranging from the basic to the very complex, we are presented with certain opportunities and challenges. The opportunities are that by teaching the students how to use new software we can provide in-depth comparisons between many different software applications as well as review some of the basic computer skills that the students acquired in the 'Computer Literacy' course. In this way, we can cover the concepts of files, help, features and error recovery in addition to mentioning these concepts while students use the software applications and navigate the web. The main challenge is to teach the students enough of the software that they can perform some of the analyses that are presented in lecture and lab plus learn enough of the key concepts to interpret the results.

In order to meet this challenge, three case study lecturers (colleagues from Anthropology, Chemistry and Sociology) first take the students through a sample exercise in the lab so the students can ask questions and get a sense of the process the researcher follows to analyse their models. In the labs associated with all the lectures, multimedia tutorials that we have created, class presentations, and written instructions are used to teach new software. On-line help is also available.

Snyder and his colleagues use Notepad, Word, and Netscape to create and view web pages, Access, and Visual Basic. By focusing on fewer software applications, they are able to cover each in more depth thus allowing them to develop more complex projects. Using Visual Basic gives the instructors the flexibility to address a wide array of topics ranging from computer modelling to algorithmic thinking. However, it does require students to learn a programming language – something that we wanted to avoid in our course. We did not want the students to spend time acquiring basic programming skills at the expense of utilising a wide range and variety of application software.

The pedagogical objective of appropriately using IT to solve problems is primarily met through the lab exercises associated with the case studies. In lecture, the case study lecturers discuss their motivation, model and methodology for examining the problems that they present, and in the lab, they lead the students through a series of exercises to solve these problems. The students are then given an assignment that necessitates using this software to solve a problem related to the one that was presented. The exercises provide the students with examples of how IT is used in different disciplines to solve complex problems and the challenges involved in using IT in this manner. The challenges include selecting the appropriate IT for solving the problem and verifying the accuracy of the results.

In most cases, the case study lecturers have chosen the IT they use from several alternatives. Some of the IT are domain specific while others are not. In the case where the IT selected is not domain specific we discuss why the lecturer thought it would work in their domain. The process of making this decision is also discussed briefly with the students. Since most complex problems are solved in multiple stages, potentially using different software at each stage, the lecturers discuss the problem solving process with students from beginning to end. Through these discussions in the lab and the lecture, students obtain a better understanding of the procedures researchers follow to solve problems. In this way we believe that students will have 'role models' – people from various disciplines who demonstrate how technology has, and continues to, effect how they think and work.

The FIT course at the University of Washington also addresses this objective with their modelling project. In one modelling assignment they use Visual Basic to simulate the falling of raindrops on pavement. The students are asked to embellish and experiment with it in order to see how computers are used to model the world, experiment with a model to observe how its different characteristics affect the result, and understand how the simplifying assumptions of the model affect the answers. We address the same issues that they do, however, we also address IT choice and research motivation, which is a component that a case study approach can add.

3. CONCLUSIONS

Students enjoy using a variety of tools to solve different problems but there is a question of how to maintain coherence in the course across topics.

Our solution in part has been to try and develop some common themes or threads throughout the course such as examining different problems using a similar systems design approach.

Lecturers were given the flexibility and responsibility for designing the lab assignments that accompanied their lectures. This helped integrate the lectures and labs for the individual instructors But their lecture styles differed considerably so the composition and form of the labs varied as well. Our solution was to have the graduate assistant assume responsibility for running all the labs with the goal of making the work across the labs more consistent.

Having lecturers from different disciplines provides a successful, interdisciplinary flavor to the course but trying to determine how to provide 'credit' to each person is very difficult. Our solution was made easier by the fact that a grant to fund the development of the course permitted us to pay the lecturers for some of their time.

This course provides schools a solution as to how to go beyond a typical Computer Literacy course for non-computer science majors but that raises the question of how to staff the course. This is especially critical since most computer and information science departments do not have sufficient resources to even teach all the courses for their own students. Our solution was to not include programming and design the course so someone who was not a computer scientist, but who was knowledgeable about computing could teach it.

In general we feel that the course has met our most important objective – that of providing the students with sophisticated computing skills and the knowledge that it will be necessary for them to continually hone these skills. As each generation becomes more computing proficient the need for such a course will be obviated. But in the meantime this course provides a foundation to not only make students computer fluent, but to impress upon them the importance of staying abreast of technological developments.

ACKNOWLEDGEMENTS

The development of this course is in part funded by a grant from the National Science Foundation, DUE 9951418. The authors would like to thank Professors N. Kock and M. Mandviwalla for their participation in the development and teaching of the course and to Professors D. Dalton, D. Elesh and A. Ranere for both their design of the case studies, and their teaching of them.

REFERENCES

Aiken, R., Mandviwalla, M., Kock N. and Sandås C. (2000) Life Long Learning: Reaching out to Non-CIS Majors. In *Proceedings of IFIP 16th World Computer Congress 2000*, Publishing House of Electronics Industry, Beijing, August 2000, pp. 100-106.

Aiken, R. and Epstein R. G. (2000) Ethical Guidelines for AI in Education: Starting a Conversation. *Journal of Artificial Intelligence in Education*, 11, No. 2, pp. 163-176.

Committee on Information Technology Literacy (1999) *Being Fluent with Information Technology*. National Academy Press, Washington, D.C.

International Society for Technology in Education (ISTE) – National Educational Technology Standards (NETS) Project (1998) *Technology Foundation Standards for All Students*. [http://cnets.iste.org/sfors.htm] 5.5.2001.

Toffler, A. and Toffler, H. (1995) *Creating a New Civilization: The Politics of the Third Wave*. Turner Publications, New York.

BIOGRAPHY

Robert Aiken is a Professor in the Computer and Information Sciences Department. His primary research areas are applying Artificial Intelligence tools and techniques to Collaborative Learning Environments, and issues related to making effective use of technology in teaching and learning.

Cheryl Sandås is a graduate student at Temple University. She is interested in the impact of technology on education.

53

Designing an IT College

Peter J. Denning, Ravi Athale, Nada Dabbagh, Daniel Menascé, Jeff Offutt, Mark Pullen, Steve Ruth and Ravi Sandhu
George Mason University, Fairfax, VA 22030 USA
pjd@gmu.edu

Keywords: information technology school, core curriculum, progressive competence, assessment, professional education

Abstract: The University of the United Arab Emirates (UAEU) commissioned an international panel of experts to devise a model curriculum for their new College of Information Technology. The model has a university core in the freshman year, an IT core in the second year, and a professional concentration in one of seven degree programs in the third and fourth year. The seven degrees are computer science, computer systems engineering, software engineering, information systems, network engineering, information security, e-commerce, and educational technology. The curriculum is structured around a progressive-competence model, whose graduates meet recognised standards for entry-level professionals.

1. THE GROWING DEMAND FOR IT COLLEGES

The first academic departments of computing, computer science, computer engineering, and infomatics were organised in the 1960s. Their number has multiplied world-wide: more than 180 PhD-granting departments exist in North America alone. Departments offering Information Systems degrees have multiplied likewise. Software Engineering shows every sign of following the same path. In the 1990s Information Technology (IT) came to pervade the university: many departments are setting up IT groups, requiring IT fluency of all undergraduate students (National Research Council 2000), and encouraging students to take IT minors. The

ACM and IEEE Computer Society have completed work on a new core curriculum for computer science and engineering, emphasising the need for the core to serve CS and other IT disciplines as well (2001), a departure from the tradition of a core for CS&E alone (ACM 1991, ACM 1997, Denning et al. 1989). Meanwhile, a large network of over 1500 corporate universities offers on-the-job IT training for hundreds of thousands of people each year (Corporate University Xchange 2000).

Computing is no longer simply a discipline, but is part of a large emerging profession with already over three dozen organised specialities (Denning 1998, 2001a, 2001b). Education of IT professionals can no longer be the responsibility of a single university department or degree program. IT curricula must include a professional body of knowledge complementing the intellectual body of knowledge. Many universities are seriously investigating whether and how to consolidate several computing-related departments or degree programs within a single academic unit. The design of curricula for these new schools is a growing concern (Tsichritzis 1999).

The pioneers of IT colleges in the USA are the School of Information Technology and Engineering at George Mason University (1985), the School of Computer Science at Carnegie-Mellon University (1988), the College of Computing at Georgia Tech (1991), the School of Information Science and Technology at University of Nebraska Omaha (1996), and the School of Informatics at Indiana University (2000). The University of Nebraska Omaha published a curriculum for an IT school (Lidtke et al. 1999). Tony Greening assembled a collection of proposals for IT curricula (Greening 2000). In Fall 1999, the Chancellor of the University of the United Arab Emirates commissioned a panel of experts well versed in the above trends to design a model curriculum for their newly formed IT College. The remainder of this paper will present the model and discuss its innovations. The model is designed to help any other university organise a coherent IT curriculum in a single academic unit. A full copy of the panel report is on a website (Denning et al. 2000).

1.1 The IT Field

The IT field has been maturing rapidly from a set of narrowly focused, autonomous disciplines into a broad profession (Denning 1998, 2001a). The IT profession comprises all the professionals who make a living helping other people with their IT concerns, breakdowns, and opportunities. The forty or so concentrations of the profession fall into three groups: the *IT specialities* are concerned with information technology itself; the *IT-intensive disciplines* pursue other concerns with a heavy dependence and investment in IT; and the *IT infrastructure* areas are professionals who implement, maintain, operate, and repair IT.

Table 1. The Information Technology Field

IT Specialities	**IT-Intensive Disciplines**	**IT Infrastructure**
Artificial intelligence	Banking and Financial	Computer technician
Computer science	Bioinformatics	Help desk technician
Computer engineering	Cognitive science	Network technician
Computational science	Digital library science	Professional IT trainer
Database engineering	E-commerce	Security Specialist
Graphics	Genetic engineering	System administrator
Human computer interaction	Information science	Web services designer
Network engineering	Information systems	Web identity designer
Operating systems	InfoSec and Privacy	
Performance engineering	Instructional design	
Robotics	Knowledge engineering	
Scientific computing	Mgt information systems	
Software architecture	Multimedia design	
Software engineering	Telecommunications	
System security	Transportation	

The IT field is thus much more complex than computer science and presents major new challenges to educators. A single university department cannot serve it. The smallest organisational unit that can is a school. But an IT school cannot be neatly segregated into autonomous departments like many other schools because the professional areas share significant bodies of knowledge. The degree programs offered by the school are best designed through a co-ordinated effort.

Because the IT field is dominated by professional specialities, not just intellectual disciplines, its students need to be immersed in practice as much as in a study of concepts and principles. They need to learn to be professionals, which means they need to learn and embody their speciality's body of knowledge, its standards of practice, and its ethical codes of conduct.

Designing a curriculum for a set of related IT professional degrees is not the only challenge. Because the half-life of technical knowledge is so short – and with 'Internet time' continues to get shorter – an IT school must pay special attention to fostering in its graduates the ability to continue learning both new technologies and new practices throughout their careers. The curriculum must present students with many opportunities to practice mobilising their resources and creativity – including negatives such as incompletely specified projects, fickle and demanding customers for project teams, and midstream changes of direction. Students need to develop a tolerance for uncertainty and a facility to recover from breakdowns.

In addition to being fast-paced, the IT market features a model of innovation that is quite different from the research model cherished in universities (Tsichritzis 1997). The market model emphases fast time-to-market; it funds projects with venture capital; it fosters innovation by rewarding entrepreneurs who specialise in transforming people's practices to become more productive with the help of new technology. The university research model emphasises careful development of ideas and principles; it funds projects by federal and state grants; it achieves innovation only after ideas have gone through a long 'pipeline' that distils out the best and brings them into practice (over 15-20 years). The dichotomy between market and idea-pipeline models presents great challenges to educators. Graduates of IT programs need to understand the market model as well as the idea-pipeline model. Most faculty have not experienced the market model first hand. Intensive market involvement of undergraduates can be accomplished by involving them in industry through internship programs and by offering training in the skills of entrepreneurship.

In summary, the design of an IT curriculum is complicated by factors in the IT market and by the complex structure of the IT profession.

2. A MODEL CURRICULUM

2.1 Degree programs

Our model for the IT school curriculum encompasses seven degree programs and one certificate program, all based on a common IT core curriculum. The Computer Science (CS) Curriculum is consistent with the principles of the new ACM/IEEE Computing Curriculum (ACM and IEEE-CS 2001). The Information Systems (IS) Curriculum is based on the ACM IS'97 model with updates (1997). The Computer Systems Engineering (CSE) Curriculum is a variation of Computer Engineering, embodying a modern mix of signals, circuits, and software. The other four degree programs – Software Engineering (SWE), Network Engineering (NE), Information Security (SEC), and Electronic Commerce (EC) – are the first (or are among a very few) rigorously technical undergraduate programs anywhere in the world. The Educational Technology (ET) certificate can be offered to students outside the IT school. The curricula for these programs, along with a catalogue of their 135 courses, a matrix representation of the IT body of knowledge, and an IT core curriculum can be found on report website (Denning et al. 2000)

2.2 The body of knowledge

The body of knowledge consists of two parts. The intellectual body sets forth the knowledge areas with subdivisions into theory, abstraction, design, and technology. The professional practices body sets forth levels of competence that exist in every speciality.

Intellectual Body. Following the model of the ACM/IEEE-CS report, *Computing as a Discipline* (Denning et al. 1989), we specified a body of intellectual IT knowledge as a matrix with rows corresponding to knowledge areas and columns for theory, abstraction, design, and technology. (The technology column is new.) Whereas the computing body of knowledge contained 10 knowledge areas in 1989, the IT body contains 48 areas today. Examples of IT knowledge areas are architecture, digital devices, software design, network protocols, cryptographic protocols, business systems and processes, management information systems, and instructional design. The granularity of these areas is just broad enough to correspond to professional specialities that have their own identity, recognised literature, and communities of practice. Each area hosts one or more courses in the curriculum. Except for survey courses, no course cuts through multiple areas.

Professional Body. Professionals progress in competence over time through six levels whose standards of performance are set by the community:

- Beginner
- Advanced beginner
- Entry-level professional
- Proficient professional
- Expert
- Virtuoso
- Master

These are levels of embodied competence – i.e., performance in action. It takes time, practice, and experience for a person to attain a level. One's professional career can be interpreted as a journey on a path to mastery.

Our model delivers entry-level professional competence, a challenge not often met by IT undergraduate programs.

Students at the Beginner Level (sophomore year) are aware of the structure of the IT field and the nature of the work in the various specialities; they able to develop algorithms, data structures, and simple circuits to solve well-defined problems; they are able to program and test their algorithms and circuits. While not expected to see the connections and interrelations among the components of typical computing systems, they are expected to understand the purpose of each component.

Students are the Advanced Beginner Level (junior year) are familiar with the terminology and concepts of the speciality; they see many connections among components of computing systems; they are able to design algorithms (and possibly circuits) of moderate complexity (several dozen modules), program them, and test them. They are able to carry out tasks for a customer but need supervision to avoid common pitfalls and breakdowns. They are able to communicate effectively in speaking and in writing.

Students at the Entry-level Professional Level (senior year) are thoroughly familiar with the speciality; they understand systems and can diagnose system problems; they are able to design systems of moderately large complexity (hundreds of modules), program them, test them, document them, and present them. They can carry out standard professional tasks for customers in application domains without supervision. They practice professional ethics.

2.3 Exhibitions and their management

Our model is designed to lead students to the entry-level professional level at graduation. Each year concludes with an exhibition, a major milestone at which students perform tasks demonstrating knowledge. Not only are exhibitions a valuable experience for students, they are the primary assessment tool for measuring whether a student has attained a level of competence.

We do not recommend using exhibitions as gateways between stages. That would create a significant management overhead to provide non-passing students with additional practice and an opportunity to retake the exhibition. We do recommend that faculty advisors work closely with students who do not pass exhibitions to help them prepare for the courses in the next year of study.

Exhibitions are an uncommon practice within a university. Their management challenges should not be a reason to abandon them. They program must be carefully planned and executed.

Exhibitions can be packaged as regular courses. Each section can contain 30 students, organised by the instructor into 3-person teams. The instructor's time will be devoted primarily to managing the teams through weekly progress reports and individual team meetings. A few all-hands meetings will be required; in them, the instructor can review common rules, constraints, and knowledge, and have the students perform dry runs of their project presentations. At the end of the exhibition course, all the teams will present their projects in a final exposition. An Exhibition Week can be reserved late in the spring semester to enable all students and faculty to attend exhibitions and to celebrate the completion of the academic year.

Staff support will be needed to help link student teams with industry customers, place the students into sections according to common themes, obtain the meeting and exhibition space, and otherwise to manage the exhibition program.

2.4 The IT core

The UAEU has a standard freshman year for all students covering 26 hours of language, culture, humanities, mathematics, and technology. The professional degrees each need a total of 132 credit hours for graduation. Of the remaining 106 credit hours, we allocated 42 for the IT core (sophomore year including summer) and 33 hours each for the junior and senior years including their exhibitions.

One of the novel aspects of our model is its IT core curriculum. The core consists of 42 credit hours concentrated mostly in the sophomore year as shown in Table 2. IT majors substitute the first course in programming for the freshman 'computer literacy' course. Except for the Professional Responsibility Workshops, all courses are 3 credit hours.

Instead of one 3-credit ethics and professionalism course that will soon be forgotten, we recommend three one-credit professional responsibility workshops conducted 1 hour per week for one semester in each of the sophomore, junior and senior years. We also recommend a course on speaking and writing in the junior year; this course can be taught by a humanities' department after the IT College has approved its content. A more advanced programming course, not part of core, is available for some of the majors.

In addition to the 132 credit hours to attain a professional IT degree, we recommend that each student be required to participate in an industry internship for one semester (15 credit hours). This work is best done in one or more of the summers.

Our full report addresses operational issues that must be taken care of if the IT College is to succeed. These include: managing exhibitions schoolwide, course websites as part of the corporate memory of the curriculum, recruitment of good faculty, training of faculty, facilities management, distance instruction, team teaching, and accreditation. We recommend that the dean appoint a chief academic officer for the school to co-ordinate these aspects and maintain the curriculum's quality, currency, and integrity.

Table 2. Overview of the IT Core Curriculum

AREA	F	SOPHOMORE			J & S
Math		Calculus concepts (derivative, integral, simple diff eq, linear algebra)	Probability and statistics	Discrete math	
Systems		Digital hardware and communication	Computing Systems (OS, networks, architecture)	Information Systems (Web, database, security)	
Programming	Prog I	Prog II			(Prog III)
Business			Business basics	Enterprise basics	
Science			Biology Concepts	Physics Concepts	
Communication					Speaking and writing
Professional responsibility		Sophomore Professional responsibility workshop			J & S Professional responsibility workshops
Exhibition				Core exhibition	

3. SUMMARY

Our curriculum recommendation is attuned to the structure of the emerging IT profession and is designed to help graduates be effective as IT professionals. The model has a common IT core to be used in the second (sophomore) year by all majors, followed by two years in the respective majors. Students progress through the curriculum by a progressive-competence model, not simply by accumulating course hours. At the end of each year, students demonstrate their knowledge through an exhibition. The three exhibitions represent three major milestones, certifying that students have attained beginner, then advanced beginner, and finally entry-level professional competence in their chosen degree field. Within this structure, we have offered a rigorous curriculum that emphasises math, science, humanities, and technology in each of the degree programs.

In addition to the exhibitions, the model contains several innovations. The IT Core (sophomore year) is shared among all the degree programs of the College. Three programs – E-Commerce, Network Engineering, and Information Security – may be the first-ever rigorously technical undergraduate programs. The Software Engineering program is one of a few specified for undergraduates. The Educational Technologies certificate may be the first program of its kind outside a college of education that enables technologists to assist other educators design and deliver high quality educational materials. A strong theme of business and entrepreneurship pervades the curriculum, starting with the core business requirements and including a semester of industry experience. There is also a strong emphasis on systems thinking through the curriculum – specification, integration, measurement, testing, modelling, and evaluation.

REFERENCES

ACM (1991) *Curriculum 91, Recommendations for undergraduate computer science degree programs*. ACM Inc., 1515 Broadway, 17th Floor, NY, NY 10036. [www.acm.org] 5.1.2001.

ACM (1997) *Curriculum IS'97: Recommendations for undergraduate information systems degree programs*. ACM Inc., 1515 Broadway, 17th Floor, NY, NY 10036. [www.acm.org] 5.1.2001.

ACM and IEEE-CS (2001) *Computing Curriculum 2001: Draft recommendations for new undergraduate computer science and engineering degree programs*. [www.acm.org/sigcse/cc2001] 5.1.2001.

Corporate University Xchange (2000) *An organization of 1500 corporate universities*. [www.corpu.com] 5.1.2001.

Denning, P., Comer, D., Gries, D., Mulder, M., Tucker, A., Turner, J. and Young P. (1989) Computing as a discipline. *Communications of ACM 32*, 1, pp. 9-23. A condensed version was published in *IEEE Computer*, February 1989.

Denning, P (1998) Computing the profession. *Educom Review 33* (Nov-Dec), pp. 26-30 and 46-59.

Denning, P., Athale, R., Dabbagh, N., Menascé, D., Offutt, J., Pullen, M., Ruth, S. and Sandhu, R. (2000) *A Model Curriculum for the United Arab Emirates University*. [cne.gmu.edu/pjd/UAE] 5.1.2001.

Denning, P. (2001a) Who Are We? *ACM Communications,* 44, 2 (February), pp. 15-19.

Denning, P. (2001b) Crossing the Chasm. *ACM Communications*, 44, 4 (April), pp. 21-25.

Lidtke, D., Stokes, G. and Haines, J. (1999) *ISCC'99: Information Science-Centric Curriculum*. [www.iscc.unomaha.edu/] 5.1.2001.

Greening, T. (2000) *Computer Science Education in the 21st Century*. Springer-Verlag.

National Research Council (2000) *Becoming Fluent in Information Technology*. A panel report from the Computer Science and Technology Board. [books.nap.edu/catalog/6482.html] 5.1.2001.

Tsichritzis, D. (1999) Reengineering the university. *Communications of ACM 42*, 6, pp. 93-100.

Tsichritzis, D. (1997) The Dynamics of Innovation. In *Beyond Calculation: The Next Fifty Years of Computing,* P. Denning (Ed.). Copernicus Books.

BIOGRAPHIES

Peter J. Denning is Professor of Computer Science at George Mason University. He was founding director of the Research Institute for Advanced Computer Science (RIACS) at NASA Ames Research Centre. He was President of ACM (1980-82) and is currently chair of the ACM Education Board. His co-authors, Ravi Athale – Associate Professor in the Electrical and Computer Engineering Department; Nada Dabbagh – Assistant Professor in the Instructional Technology program, Daniel A. Menascé – Professor of Computer Science and the co-director of the E-Center of Excellence in Research and Education in E-Business, A. Jefferson Offutt – Associate Professor in the Department of Information and Software Engineering, J. Mark Pullen – Associate Professor of Computer Science and a member of the C3I Center, Stephen R. Ruth – Professor of Technology Management in the School of Public Policy, and Ravi Sandhu – Professor of Information and Software Engineering and Director of the Laboratory for Information Security Technology, all work at George Mason University.

PART SIX

FORMS OF ASSESSMENT

54

Chat as Media in Exams

Claus Witfelt, Poul Erik Philipsen and Birte Kaiser
Danish University of Education, Emdrupvej 101, DK-2400 NV, Denmark
clw@dpu.dk
CVU-Vest, Hammerum Hovedgade 7, DK-7400 Herning, Denmark
CVU-Vest, Skolebakken 171, DK-6505 Esbjerg S, Denmark

Keywords: distance learning, further education, assessment, open flexible learning

Abstract: The paper reportsdocuments our experiences using chat as a medium for exams in a so-called flexible education. The type of education is adult learning and planning of education. The experiences show some interesting results. It is a very different way of communicating, which leaves a new level of initiative and control to the student. A new way of assessment has qualified the study process, and this work has examined one way to do virtual assessment.

1. INTRODUCTION

The Voksplan education is a flexible version of the Danish diploma-degree in adult learning and educational planning. By flexible we mean delivered with ordinary teaching sessions combined with learning via the Internet and electronic conferences. ICT should be a predominant and natural part of the education. Accordingly, we wanted to investigate how exams could also be held via ICT.

To many people, chatting suggests the notion of non-serious, very light discussions, often without deeper meaning. However, our experiences as teachers from other flexible courses and education was that chat can be used for discussing serious issues as well – with very good results. But in order to turn chat into a valuable tool, the users need to develop a special language, as is the case with any other media. We wanted to stimulate the students to do this and to test chat as a media for serious discussions by using chat as a media for exams. This paper documents our experiences with this experiment.The development of this special version of the diploma-education has been supported by CTU Denmark's National Information Centre for Technology Supported Learning. The Voksplan education itself has earlier been documented in a series of papers [http://www.dpu.dk/voksplan]. The authors are both the developers of the curriulum and the teachers.

2. THE HISTORY OF CHAT AS MEDIA IN EXAMS

On several earlier occasions, we found that the students made good use of the chat functions in electronic conferencing environments like FirstClass and Webboard. They typically used chat when the normal, asynchronous conferencing facilities got too tedious. When arrangements about when to meet face-to-face, were to be made, chat was used. On the LINK-course, featured chats were arranged where the participants could chat with the authors and speakers about certain topics, for instance organisational change. We were inspired by the media, but felt that it could be used and exploited further.

The whole development of the flexible version of the traditional diploma-education was already in process, but still it had to be approved by the board in charge of the adult teaching in the Danish University of Education. But as chat has a non-serious reputation, this was not an easy quest. Could serious discussions be held via chat? Could we be sure that there was only one present in the room, when the students were examined? Were we sure that it was the actual person we were chatting with? In the official description of the education, we had to change the word 'chat' into synchronous Internet-based communication, in order to have it approved.

We did not intend to force anyone to graduate using this media, if they did not want to do it, but the majority of the students chose to participate in the experiment. Almost all of the students were teachers themselves, and they found it interesting to participate.

Immediately after the first exam, several of the students claimed that they did not want to participate. Some argued that they could not see the difference, whether you discussed live or via chat. Some did not see the point in examining via chat, and others presented arguments which could hide fear for not being able to get good grades via this new kind of exam. However as time passed and the students practised with the chat and got used to the idea, most of the students decided to take part in the experiment.

The majority of the students were very enthusiastic about the idea of chat-exams, as it fits a flexible course. The seminars take place in Herning, about 400 kilometres from Copenhagen. Many of the students found that it was a good thing not to have to take the trip all the way to Herning, 'just' to pass an exam. Another argument was that if chat-exams constituted a new way to graduate students, they better try it as students, so they could use it themselves in their own courses. 9 chose to try the chat-exam; 5 chose the traditional exam. The chat-exam came out with grades on the same level as the traditional versions of the module in this diploma-education, between 7 and 11. (In the Danish grade-system, 00 is lowest, 13 is highest, so 7 is average as 11 very good).

3. WRITTEN OR ORAL MEDIA?

Is chat an oral or written media? Are chat-exams written exams or oral? The word chat suggests something oral, but you communicate with the keyboard, so seen from a technical point of view it is a written media. Seen as a genre, chat is most definitely an oral media. You use quick, very simple sentences and often smileys and abbreviations, for instance, the characteristic acronyms (BTW, LOL). The turn taking is quick too. But, chats do not have to be held in the genre you find in the big, public chatrooms. You can indeed have serious discussions, but our experiences as teachers (we have also used chat for teacher co-operation) are that it takes time to develop a language for this specific media. Our conception of chat is that it is a hybrid between written and oral media. The students as well have to develop a way to use it. However, we realised how difficult this may be; we have decided, however difficult this may be for us, to ignore spelling errors, bad language.

One of the problems that teachers as well as students must face, and find solutions to, is pauses. Are the students expecting anything? Are the teachers? Will the student come up with more or is it time to pose a new question? Another problem is the role of the teacher; should they take the initiative during the exam or should the students? What happens in case of technical problems?

4. ABOUT THE CHAT

We used the chat function, which is built into the conference-system that is used as standard on the Danish University of Education, that is a version of O'Reilly's Webboard. This chat is very similar to other chat-functions, for instance in FirstClass. This chat is not very advanced, but it works. The major disadvantage is that it is not possible to make postings of more than 500 characters. As a backup against system-breakdowns, we also supplied a small web-based chat, based on Info-Chat.

All the way through their education, the students have been stimulated to use chat. They were taught the functions of the system and some students have used it a lot. On their own initiative, they held exams in order to practice using this media. Some groups have not used the chat, some have not even used the conference, but all tried during the second module to chat, so as to gain experiences with the chat in order to be able to pass an exam.

Because it was a development process it was decided that both the examiners, internal and external, should sit in the same room in the location in Herning, so they could discuss face-to-face and use a high-capacity connection to the Internet. The chat was to be held on basis of a synopsis, a written essay of a maximum of 20 pages. The students developed the work in teams, but wrote their own synopses. Both the external and internal examiner received the synopsis in time for reading.

5. A LANGUAGE FOR THE CHAT-MEDIA

We believe that for every media you need to develop a special language. This is also our experience with chat. You can only develop this special language by practising, i.e. by chatting. Both teachers and students need to use the media in order to experience possibilities and drawbacks with the media and find solutions to the problems. An example of such a problem is the 500 character limitation. Chat is normally only used for one-line comments, but in our case we needed also to use the compose function that allows the chatters to compose messages of up to 500 characters. This helps, but even 500 characters are not enough, if you want to get into depth with something – as in our exams.

The students who had chatted a lot had already developed solutions to some of the problems, for instance the question of more text being on the way. If nothing was done, the examiner posed new questions, which resulted in several questions being 'in the air' at one time.

We wish to share what we have learnt by studying the behaviour and habits of experienced chatters in the large, public chatpools

6. TO BE ICT-LITERATE OR NOT...

It is not necessary to be ICT literate when you start the Voksplan education. On the contrary we use a lot of energy in training the students to get them well off the ground with the technology. All the same, they must develop their ICT-skills during the education, in order to be able to fulfil the goals of the education. To avoid very ICT literates having an advantage over non-ICT literates, we made the exam non-mandatory.

Already in the initial seminar we use a whole day to introduce the students to the Voksplan website, how to work in conferences and to moderate conferences, how to chat. All these competences that we consider a natural part of ICT-literacy. Accordingly the students should have equal terms for passing this exam. It was quite evident however, that those students who had practised a lot with chatting and used it in their everyday studies and even had made exams were much better than those, that had not done so. An interesting question is, what would have happened, if chat-exams were used as a media with youngsters, that have used chat the way adults have used the phone? Other investigations have to uncover this.

7. THE EXPERIENCES

We experienced, that the groups that had used the chat a lot and made test chat-exams behaved more naturally in the chat environment. To many of our students, the Voksplan education was their first chat-experience. Therefore, it could be interesting to carry through a chat exam with children who are very used to chatting everyday.

Obviously, it is much slower to write than to talk, but the examiner had plenty of time, whereas the students felt an extreme time pressure. As one student put it: “You have so very little time. Chat-exams must simply take more time than normal exams”. An answer that takes 10 minutes to compose, can be read in 10 seconds, so the examiner/censor will have to be patient.

Body language does not exist in chat-exams. This is a two-edged sword. It is nice, because the examiner cannot see the student, and grades are given alone on basis of the synopsis and what is written in the chat, but from a communicative point of view much is lacking. Another problem is the small ansynchonicity. Chat is a synchronous media, but since it takes longer to write than to discuss orally, two questions can be discussed at the same time, but which can raise the stress level.

After the chat-exam, we asked the students about their experiences with chat-exam in the conference-system. The following all originates from these interviews.

Some find that the fear of exams has gone, because you are at home, less stressed and you do not have to think about your body-language. However, there are also drawbacks. The feeling of closeness has gone and at times, there is more than one question at a time, which increases the stress-level. One of the students reported that it was a huge advantage to have tried to be 'chat-examiner' before being examined, because you recognize the problems and know how short of time you feel you have.

Is this kind of exam really well suited for an education like Voksplan, where there are no correct answers, but instead discussions of attitudes, values and aesthetic learning processes? At first you might think that this was the case, since chat is normally used for discussions, but both the examiners and the students report problems with getting into depth with the issues discussed (Kaiser and Philipsen 2000). Our data is too limited for us to conclude upon this, but it seems as if chat could be used better with exams in more factual themes. One student report: “It is difficult to get dialogue at a higher level than ‘teacher asks – student answers’. It was also difficult to get into more theoretical issues”.

Both internal examiners told us that they had initially discussed with the students how many items to discuss and that they would tell the students, when they changed subject. This was a way to ensure that there was time enough to get into depth with the issues raised.

8. INITIATIVE AND CONTROL

When using chat as teacher-communication media, the teacher-group itself experienced that chat is much slower than ordinary dialogue or video-conferencing. Furthermore we found out that it is more difficult to locate where the dialogue is heading and to get into depth with the issues discussed. To help the students overcome these problems we decided that the examiner should lead the dialogue. In this way we hoped that the control of understanding could be better. Furthermore it was an advantage that the students were examined in a synopsis, a short 10 pages of text. This limited the amount of topics.

The question about who is taking the initiative in the dialogue is interesting. The students possess a lot of possibilities for controlling the exam, that do not exist in normal exams. As one on the examiners put it “The students are more in control. You cannot as easily interrupt in the dialogue” (Kaiser and Philipsen 2000). Another examiner felt that (s)he should interrupt and have control. Therefore he has typed some questions in a file, in order to easily pose the questions. This helped the examiner to control the exam and avoid the more chatting-style communication.

Both the examiners and students that have tried out the testexams report back, that it is very much the students, who have the initiative. One examinator reported "I had to be extremely well prepared, if I wanted to gain control over the exam" (Kaiser 2000). A student reported "As the student, that is examined, the codewords are: Fire at will."

9. CONCLUSION

There are many things at stake, when one decides to use chat as media in exams. We have chosen to discuss 2 issues. Is this a new future form for exam? Can this new, radically different way of doing exams teach us something about the normal way we do exams?

9.1 Chat-exams – the exam form of the future?

Our data are too sparse to conclude, whether this is a new way of carrying out exams, but our students were very enthusiastic about this form. We think it was a good experience and we intend to offer future classes the possibility of doing chat-exams, in order to learn more about it. But much more, we want to gain experience about a very different way to do exams to tell us something about our normal of doing exams.

There are a lot of unsolved questions, like what happens, if the system breaks down under the exam? Are the students allowed to pass another then? We need to develop new ways to do exams in flexible environments. It has been interesting to test new forms of exams, especially as in this case, where some of the power is moved from the examiner to the student. We need to know a lot more about it, for instance how to train the students better towards developing a language for interacting in the chatroom.

Furthermore it has been interesting to work with a form that creates a more fluent study form and a greater coherence between form of study and form of examination. We hope that this idea could inspire more course and educational designers.

9.2 Chat-exams and traditional exams

Doing the chat-exam forced us to pose the fundamental question: What is basically an exam? Is an exam solely an evaluation or should it rather be an experience, where experts from outside the institution give their comments on the work done? Is it just the 20 last minutes of a project or an integrated part of a longer competence-development.

We find that the most important answer to this is that by making exams and study-forms more equal, we approach the last goal. We force the students to develop the study competences (chat) by making it mandatory in the end. When we are working in a flexible learning environment, we also test the student's study-competence when using chat-exams.

We have experienced and the students report back that they find it difficult to act convincingly, but this might, after all, just be a question of gaining enough experience with the chat.

9.3 Future chat-exams

The next class has not yet reached the 2nd module, where the chat-exam is a possibility, but we have emphasised chat much more in the initial seminar, where the students get a whole day introduction to the electronic conferences, chat etc. These students use chat much more to discuss, than ordinary electronic conferences, which are mostly used as a virtual library. In the first class, the students used the conferences very actively as discussion media and only a few of the groups chatted regularly. To us, this is a very important reason why one should consider doing exams via the chat: Approaching the exam form in the way the students study, forces the student to work with the media. The exam helped them qualify their study process.

REFERENCES

Kaiser, B (2000) Evaluation note about testexam by Birthe Kaiser, teacher, Esbjerg.

Kaiser, B. and Jørgensen, B. (2000) *Mennesket er ikke et æsel* (Man is not a donkey). DPU, Esbjerg.

Kaiser, B. and Philipsen, P. E. (2000) Interview with Birte Kaiser and Poul Erik Philipsen, August 8th,unpublished, Herning.

BIOGRAPHIES

Claus Witfelt, a researcher at the Danish University of Education, Institute for Curriculum Research, works with flexible learning. Poul Erik Philipsen is a leader of the centre for adult education in CVU Vest, Herning. Birte Kaiser is a teacher and doctoral student at CVU-Vest, Esbjerg.

55

Assessment of Performance Quality

Metrics for Process rather than Result

Peter Summons

Information Systems Group, School of Management, The University of Newcastle, Callaghan NSW 2308, Australia

mgpfs@cc.newcastle.edu.au

Keywords: assessment, basic skills, competencies, computing

Abstract: Assessment grades provide a final result typically regarded as an indicator of how well a student has mastered the concepts underlying assessment tasks. Student knowledge is normally derived from a dimension whose metric is the amount of correctly completed tasks. This result is outcome-based and indicative of *what* was done, without consideration of *how* it was done. This paper proposes that a complete assessment requires more ; that information regarding how students attempt assessment tasks is also necessary to provide a feedback mechanism for future assessment and teaching content. This paper presents a proposed research direction for an ongoing Australian project.

1. INTRODUCTION: HISTORICAL FOUNDATIONS

Studies by D'Ambra (1991) and Ablong (1991) support that knowledge of results can enhance learning and performance outcomes. Well-designed assessment can also be regarded as a learning a learning tool for students 'Quality assessment tasks also provide clues to students about what is important for them to learn' (McIntosh 1996). A practical implementation of these principles is provided by the utilisation of practice assessment tasks in conjunction with detailed feedback of assessment results. The assessment tasks can show an aspect of a course objective and thus can provide incentive and direction (Summons et al. 1997a, 1997b).

Not only can assessment and feedback benefit students but it can also be used as a feedback mechanism for educators, providing insight as to the quality of teaching, the merit of the assessment material, and also providing direction for future teaching content and delivery. This is the proposal for future direction of the Automated Assessment Management Project (AAMP), being conducted at The University of Newcastle and Deakin University, Australia.

The use of computer software applications is taught in similar introductory subjects at Newcastle and Deakin Universities. At Newcastle, INFO101 is taught across two campuses and averages more than 1300 students per year. Deakin University offers a similar subject to more than 750 students per year. It is also taught across multiple campuses as well as being offered in an external, off-campus mode. Each subject incorporates a practical course content where students learn Microsoft Word, Excel and Access on IBM PCs. In line with the view that the '...best way to learn is by doing' (Ablong 1991) assessment of the application software component in both subjects uses skill-based, hands-on, practical tests conducted during students normal tutorials.

The Automated Assessment Management Project was started to provide a mechanism to solve the logistic and human difficulties of assessment in large classes (1000 plus), involving both on-campus and off-campus delivery. An instrument and a methodology to assess computer literacy skills (specifically Spreadsheet) were developed and have been used extensively in the last few years (Summons et al. 1997a, 1997b, 1998). To date approximately 6000 students have been tested with this instrument at Newcastle alone. We have utilised on-line, interactive real-time assessment and marking of students as well as asynchronous testing and marking.

The instrument and methodology we use reflects the initial aims of the project, many of which have been achieved (Summons et al. 1997a, 1997b). These involve both educational and logistic goals that utilise the assessment instrument to:

- Standardise marking and eliminate bias in marking individuals within groups, involving both inter- marker (different concepts) and intra-marker (moods over time) bias
- Rationalise Course Logistics & Cost enabling
- Enable cost reductions through rationalisation of staff numbers and staff time spent in Marking
- Facilitate easy Articulation and Post-testing of students
- Implement fast Turnaround of results to students
- Act as a Learning Tool through the use of Practice Tasks where students learn by doing with practice assessment tasks
- Provide comprehensive, individual feedback is provided to students
- Change the role of the tutor to the guiding expert for remediation
- Show students realistic course expectations

- Reduce student advantage gained from 'cheating'.

The project has been supported by internal teaching grants from The University of Newcastle and an Australian National Teaching Grant (Summons et al. 1997c) between the University of Newcastle and Deakin University, with Newcastle taking the overall coordinating role.

The computer program used in the AAMP is not meant to cater for every possible variation of student answer. The intention is that, although it will handle the vast majority of student responses, there will always be a need for human intervention with the ability to override or modify the software-generated score in specific circumstances. Experience has shown that this may account for one or two cases per thousand in each assessment. An implicit goal in this approach is that the overriding power resides with one person only – the course co-ordinator. The approach has been successful in eliminating past scenarios, where many independent and uncoordinated spur-of-the-minute marking decisions were made by individual tutors (Summons et al. 1998b).

Often in subjects with very large student numbers the tutor has more intimate knowledge of the potential ability or capability of the student than the central course co-ordinator. This results from the closer relationship involving more personal contact between the tutor and student. The tutor is aware of the student as a person, as opposed to the central course co-ordinator who may be only aware of the student by name, or by number, as one of the individuals making up a class of more than six to seven hundred students. The tutor is therefore in a better position to act as a local expert and mentor for the student than the course co-ordinator.

The assessment results and the individual feedback to the student outline what the student did incorrectly. The tutor may then work in conjunction with the student, using the assessment result to try and establish what the student should do to correct future work. This may be simple correction advice or it may be a set of remedial activities.

Note that at this point there is no presumption that the tutor has to be involved in this sort of remedial activity. Certainly with the pressure of significant course content it may have to be initiated by the student. Even if a student does initiate a request for clarification of an incorrect result, there is more chance that a tutor will show the student the correct method rather than try to establish *why* the individual student was incorrect. There is certainly no formal expectation that knowledge gained by the tutor in student remediation will be passed on to the course co-ordinator, apart from exceptional circumstances. This would, of course, be expected to occur if the tutor noticed a majority of students with a common misconception or complaint, indicating the possibility of an incomplete learning outcome in the former or a mistake in the marking guide/program for the later. If a small number of individuals in each tutorial group suffered the effects of either of these problems then it might possibly remain unreported, as individual tutors would probably not notice the accumulation of case evidence unless they were teaching in multiple tutorials.

Initial surveys of the AAMP indicated a problem with the tutors acting in the role of mentor in conjunction with the automated assessment (Summons et al 1998). They showed that tutors were ineffective as remediators when they took a totally passive part in the marking process. The simple remedy of ensuring tutors had a detailed copy of the marking scheme quickly overcame this problem. However, this break in the assumed continuity of lecturer/tutor/student knowledge highlighted the potential problem described earlier; that the knowledge of how students were interpreting a question and why they were answering things incorrectly, might possibly stop at the level of the tutor. This would be important feedback to provide to the lecturer to enable modification of the content or the style of presentation of course material. Unfortunately, the assessment task results available to the central course co-ordinator merely indicates student outcomes, even if they are expressed in reasonable detail. How could we capture this additional knowledge? That answer forms the basis for the proposed and ongoing research presented in this paper.

2. THE PROPOSED RESEARCH: HOW VERSUS WHAT

Quite often we only see the results of a question and we interpret these to suit our purposes. We see *what* the student has produced, that is the outcome, but not *how* it was produced.

AAMP application testing is accomplished under the control of a computer program interacting with the student in real-time. The assessment program initiates the application and accesses both the test questions and the application data required for the assessment task, and also directs the storage of the completed student answer. It controls a student's ability to redo a question anew and governs the storage of the replacement answer. It also controls a student's ability to modify completed sections within the duration of the assessment time.

The interactive assessment program incorporates a marker function. This either marks at the end of the assessment period, or during it as the student moves from question to question. The marking function stores individual student's results and marks for each answer and for the overall test. In addition to the present creation and storage of marks as outcomes of the student's competency, the automated assessment instrument can easily incorporate technical details regarding a student's performance.

It is intended to extend the present functionality of the assessment program and marking function to include the collection and storage of such information. This new information is specific to a student's performance for each question and also to their performance in the overall test. It consists of details such as the:

- The test
- Time spent per question
- Time spent on subsequent returns to a question
- Number of returns to specific questions
- Number of new attempts at specific questions, where a previously attempted answer is abandoned
- Number of 'modified' answers, where a previous attempt is retained but modified
- Sequence of correct and incorrect attempts for specific questions.

Other indicators could be aggregated but would require more implementation complexity. Examples of these include recording:

- Events, such as the use of 'undo', 'delete' and 'backspace' that may be applicable to specific applications at the task level
- The mouse clicks per question. These can also be associated with screen position but this would not be useful on a first-cut pilot study.

The indicators above can be matched with traditional outcome-based performance measures reflecting success, such as the student's final score on completion of a question. The combined data could indicate parameters, specific to the assessment task population that refer to the degree of difficulty experienced by students in completing particular questions.

Measures of the temporal difficulty experienced by students in answering questions coupled with indicators of student achievement, for example the percentage of correct responses to the question, can give an insight to the real complexity of the question. The temporal distribution of students who answer a question correctly (or incorrectly) adds additional information to our interpretation of the relevance and complexity of the question. As a simple example, if a question is answered correctly by the majority of the class and is finished quickly then it may represent an easy task or a well-understood concept. The reasons for poor temporal performance could be investigated and this may help future teaching. It should be noted that there could be many reasons for poor performance specific to the topic, to the course facilities, or to student demographics. Examples include a difficult concept being assessed, a poorly presented concept, or a poor or ambiguous assessment question.

Comparison of actual student answer-time versus the assessor's expected time for answering a question provides another dimension to the interpretation of how well a concept has been learned by students. Additional information is also provided when examining the results of groups of students who have answered a question in a similar time. This allows a finer granularity of student classification by creating an extra dimension of comparison. If individual student identification was supported then commonalities of students forming temporally similar groups could be investigated in a similar manner to the present capability for finding commonalities of students with similar achievement levels. This information could then be used demographically to identify advantages or disadvantages of specific tutorial groups.

Performance data can therefore be beneficial by providing extra clues for tutors regarding the most appropriate remedial activities for individual students. Traditionally, students only tend to request remedial help for questions that were answered incorrectly. If a tutor instigates remedial feedback, the fact that a student answered a question correctly may mean that the concept in the question is not included as a remedial activity as it is assumed that the student knows the concept. However, if the student took a long time answering a question, even though it was eventually answered correctly, this may indicate potential difficulty with that question concept. If students return to the same question many times, even if they do not change their (correct) answer, this may also indicate that they are unsure of the question concept. Likewise, if a student changes their answer before settling on the final correct answer, then it may indicate uncertainty of the question concept. When questions are answered incorrectly, temporal information is also useful, but this is probably not as important from a remedial viewpoint as the question concept is likely to be included in the set of remedial concepts for the student.

For the moment however, the proposed performance data to be gathered at The University of Newcastle is only intended to serve as an aggregated indicator of trends and unusual performance for the central co-ordinator. Ethical considerations constrain the gathering of performance data in that the ability of the central co-ordinator to obtain individual identification of performance indicators other than question marks will be suppressed. At the moment the assessment program identifies individual students by their system log-in identifiers, which reflects their unique student number.

To satisfy ethics requirements for gathering data at The University of Newcastle, students will have the option of choosing not to have performance data gathered about them. This will be in the form of a check box on the assessment that they can select if they wish to stop data gathering. The students doing the test will be notified that the purpose of the data gathering is to refine future assessment tasks and evaluate the presentation of course content. They will also be advised of the anonymity of the performance data in respect to student identity. This will be done both within the assessment instrument and as prior notification within tutorials.

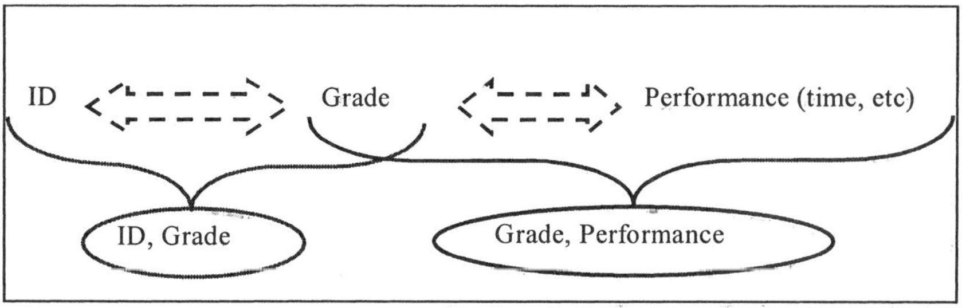

Figure 1. Data Set Collection

The assessment program will provide two sets of collection instruments, as depicted in Figure 1. One will collect details of Student ID and Grade, as is done at present. The other will collect details of grade and performance parameters, but will not have student identification incorporated. Whilst theoretically, individual identification from a statistical collection such as the later data set is still possible, the data set will only be available to authorised personnel interested in aggregated data indicators rather than specifics.

3. CONCLUSION

The incorporation of performance parameters provides additional temporal and sequence information regarding how a student performs in a test, rather than the traditional outcome-based parameter which simply indicates what they have done. This additional information allows us to form a more complete picture of the assessment and the assessed course content. It can help to indicate individual student weakness areas and also identify student groups with a finer granularity than is possible with outcome-based indicators alone.

Even though restrictions to the use of the performance parameters will apply at The University of Newcastle, the performance metrics will help provide a mechanism to add to our knowledge of how well concepts are taught and learned by students, and how appropriate our assessment is. It should also be noted that it is possible to use the technique in other, simpler forms of assessment carried out on computers, such as the multiple-choice style of testing.

This paper has described work-in-progress to provide additional performance metrics for the traditional outcome-based, practical assessment of computer applications. It has identified performance parameters that can be gathered and it has indicated how these measures can provide a richer understanding of the assessment outcomes, both for remedial activities for students and as feedback for future course direction.

REFERENCES

Ablong, A. P. (1991) Theories of Learning and Their Application to Prototyping. In *Proceedings of the International Working Conference on Shaping Organisations Shaping Technology*, Adelaide, South Australia, Oct., pp. 1-11.

D'Ambra, J. (1991) Computer Literacy – No Longer an Option. In *Proceedings of the Australian Computer Conference ACC'91 MOSAIC*, Adelaide, South Australia, Oct., pp. 111-122.

McIntosh, W. J. (1996) Assessment in Higher Education. *Journal of College Science Teaching*, Vol. 26, Sept./Oct., p. 52-53.

Summons, P. F., Coldwell, J., Henskens, F. and Bruff, C. (1997a) Automating Assessment and Marking of Spreadsheet Concepts. In *ACSE'97: the 2nd Australasian Computer Science Education Conference*, Melbourne, July, p. 178-184.

Summons, P. F., Coldwell, J., Henskens, F. and Bruff, C. (1997b) Automated Evaluation of Spreadsheet Concepts – Excel in Action. In *SITIS'97 Proceedings of the Second NSW Symposium on Information Technology and Information Systems*, Sydney, Feb., pp. 87-93.

Summons, P. F., Coldwell, J. and Bruff, C. (1997c) 1998 Australian National Teaching Development Grant – Individual. *Automated Assessment and Marking Management Package*, the Committee for University Teaching and Staff Development [http://services.canberra.edu.au/CUTSD/announce/1998Indv.html#Newcastle].

Summons, P. F., Bruff, C., Simon and Coldwell, J. (1998) Automated Assessment and Management Project. In *CATE'98 IASTED International Conference on Computers and Advanced Technology in Education*, Cancun, Mexico, May, pp. 181-184.

Summons, P. F. and Simon (1999) Authentication Strategies for Online Assessments. In *ACSE'98 the 3rd Australasian Conference on Computer Science Education*, Brisbane, July, pp. 101-105.

BIOGRAPHY

Peter Summons is a lecturer in Information Systems at The University of Newcastle, Australia. He is currently doing a PhD in Knowledge Acquisition for Medical Decision Support Systems. He has worked as a Systems Engineer and a consultant in industry. He is currently teaching information management and supervising MIT information systems projects.

56

ICT Support for Electronic Portfolios and Alternative Assessment

The State of the Art

Helen C. Barrett
School of Education, University of Alaska Anchorage, 3211 Providence Dr., Anchorage, AK 99508, USA
afhcb@uaa.alaska.edu

Keywords: self-assessment, empowering, catalyst for change, learner-centred learning, multimedia

Abstract: This paper covers the use of technology to support three aspects of Alternative Assessment: Observations of Student Learning, Performance Assessments, and Electronic Portfolios. Discussion includes the differences between Performance Assessments and Portfolios, definition of electronic portfolios, the benefits of electronic portfolios, along with the author's five-stage and five-level electronic portfolio development process. Technology tools to support electronic or digital portfolios are outlined, including proprietary software and the use off-the-shelf multimedia development software. Significant research in electronic portfolio development will be discussed along with examples from the USA and international examples with corresponding web sites.

1. OVERVIEW

This paper covers the use of ICT to support three different aspects of Alternative Assessment: Observations of Student Learning in the Classroom, Performance Assessments, and Electronic Portfolios. A discussion of these strategies will be included, with a perspective on the present international state of the art.

2. ALTERNATIVE ASSESSMENT

The terms alternative assessment, authentic assessment, or performance-based assessment are often used synonymously "to mean variants of performance assessments that require students to generate rather than choose a response" (Herman, Aschbacher and Winters 1992, p. 2). The characteristics of this type of assessment are: the student is involved in meaningful performance tasks; there are clear standards and criteria for excellence; there is an emphasis on metacognition and self-evaluation; the student produces quality products and performances; there is a positive interaction between assessor and assessee (Burke 1999). There are two central features to alternative assessments: "First, all are viewed as *alternatives* to traditional multiple-choice, standardised achievement tests; second, all refer to direct examination of student performance on significant tasks that are relevant to life outside of school" (Worthen 1993, p. 445).

Burke (1999) and Fogarty (1998) advocate a balanced approach to assessment, with a focus on three components:

- Traditional Assessment, with a focus on grades and rankings, knowledge, curriculum, and skills, implemented through classroom assessments (tests, quizzes, homework assignments), and standardised tests (either norm-referenced or criterion-referenced)
- Performance Assessment, with a focus on observable results and standards, application and transfer, implemented through standards, tasks, criteria and scoring rubrics.
- Portfolio Assessment, with a focus on growth and development over time, implemented through selection, reflection and inspection of classwork, along with goal-setting and self-evaluation

2.1 Performance assessment

"Performance assessment focuses on the direct observation of a student's performance" (Fogarty 1998, p.10). Students create projects or perform tasks based on predetermined standards, criteria, and indicators, which are evaluated by scoring rubrics. Teachers have always observed student learning in the classroom. However, until recently documenting these observations has been difficult and time-consuming. In the early 1990s, several tools were developed to collect and organise these observational data; the Greater Victoria (B.C., Canada) School District developed a system using bar codes to record student classroom activities. Subsequently, the software was published by Sunburst as *Learner Profile*, and moved from using bar code readers, to using Apple's Newton and now Palm hand-held devices to collect data in the classroom. The most promising application of the Palm involves linking data collection to generic database applications, such as *FileMaker Pro*, to allow more flexible use of observational data.

There is a new program developed that supports the performance assessment process. Educational Testing Service and Grant Wiggins' re: Learning have developed *Assessment Wizard*, a professional development tool for designing and sharing student assessments (http://www.teachingandlearning.org). The program includes a master file of sample assessments and associated rubrics or scoring guides indexed by subject, topic, and grade level, and linked to both generic and state-specific standards.

There are significant differences between Performance Assessments and Portfolios. A portfolio is a container that holds examples of student or teacher work (the 'artefacts') and reflections on that work that transforms the artefacts into 'evidence' of achievement. Many of those artefacts could be the results of performance assessments with associated evaluations and reflections. A standards-based portfolio creates linkages between student tasks and performance assessments, with their associated scoring guides, and the standards that they are designed to demonstrate. The reflections of the portfolio developer create the rationale or argument for converting these artefacts into evidence.

2.2 Portfolio assessment

Portfolios have been used for years by professionals in the graphic arts field, to demonstrate the quality of their work often for marketing purposes. A financial portfolio documents the accumulation of fiscal capital or monetary assets; an educational portfolio documents the development of human capital or intellectual assets. Educators began adopting the portfolio in the early 1990s as a means for determining grades and reporting student progress to parents (Linn and Gronlund 2000). More recently, portfolios have become powerful tools for teacher professional development (Wolf 1999, Burke 1997) and documenting pre-service teacher education (Campbell, Melenyzer, Nettles and Wyman 2000). Wilcox and Tomei (1999) propose to extend the possibilities for the portfolio in education "by going beyond assessment, learning and professional development to the use of the portfolio as a living history of a teaching-learning life" (p.5).

Educators in the Pacific Northwest (Northwest Evaluation Association, 1990), developed the following definition of portfolio:

> "A portfolio is a purposeful collection of student work that exhibits the student's efforts, progress, and achievements in one or more areas. The collection must include student participation in selecting contents, the

criteria for selection; the criteria for judging merit, and evidence of student self-reflection."

Portfolios give a richer picture of student work than can be gained from more traditional, objective forms of assessment. Traditionally, portfolios have been stored in three-ring binders or folders with physical dividers between sections. Students place work on paper media presenting text and images and sometimes include an analog videotape. In a standard paper-based portfolio, matching specific artefacts or evidence to desired learning standards or outcomes is dependent on the organisational structure imposed by the linear medium of paper, and very problematic when attempting to find specific clips on a video tape.

2.3 Types of evidence in portfolios

Barton and Collins (1997) have identified four types of evidence that can be placed in a portfolio:

- Artefacts: documents produced during normal academic work
- Reproductions: documents of student work outside the classroom
- Attestations: documentation generated about student's academic progress
- Productions: documents prepared just for the portfolio, such as:
  - Goal Statements: student's personal interpretations of each specific purpose for the portfolios
  - Reflective Statements: students write as they review and organize the evidence in their portfolios
  - Captions: Statement attached to each piece of portfolio evidence, articulating what it is, why it is evidence, and of what it is evidence.

2.4 Electronic portfolios

An electronic portfolio includes technologies that allow the portfolio developer to collect and organise artefacts in many media types (audio, video, graphics, and text). A standards-based electronic portfolio uses hypertext links to organise the material, connecting artefacts to appropriate goals or standards. Often, the terms 'electronic portfolio' and 'digital portfolio' are used interchangeably. However, this author makes a distinction: an electronic portfolio contains artefacts that may be in analogue (e.g., videotape) or computer-readable form. In a digital portfolio, all artefacts have been transformed into computer-readable form. (Barrett 2000)

The benefits of developing electronic portfolios for either students or teachers includes: minimal storage space, easy to create back-up files, portability, long shelf life, learner-centred, increases technology skills, meeting standards through hypertext links, and accessibility (especially web portfolios) (Kankaanranta, Barrett and Hartnell-Young 2000)

3. ELECTRONIC PORTFOLIO DEVELOPMENT PROCESS

Creating an electronic portfolio should be viewed as a series of stages, each with its own goals and activities, and requiring different types of software. The author has derived a framework for electronic portfolio development from two bodies of literature: portfolio development in K-12 education and the multimedia or instructional design process. These complimentary processes are both essential for effective electronic portfolio development. Understanding how these processes fit together and how standards or goals contribute to electronic portfolio development, teachers gain a powerful tool for demonstrating growth over time.

From a discussion of both the Multimedia Development Process and the Portfolio Development Process, five stages of Electronic Portfolio Development emerge:

1. Defining the Portfolio Context & Goals (Purpose and Audience)
2. The Working Portfolio (Archive Creation/Digital Conversion)
3. The Reflective Portfolio (asking questions: What? So what? Now what?)
4. The Connected Portfolio (using the capability of the computer to create hypertext links between reflections and portfolio artefacts)
5. The Presentation Portfolio (publishing on WWW, CD-ROM, videotape)

In addition to the stages of portfolio development, there appear to be at least five levels of electronic portfolio development, each with its own levels of expectation and suggested software strategies at each stage depending on technology skills of the student or teacher portfolio developer (Barrett 2000). These levels are roughly related to 'ease of use:' from Word processing documents, PowerPoint or database files or hypermedia stacks, Adobe Acrobat (plus digital audio and/or video files), HTML – Web pages, to Multimedia authoring (i.e., Macromedia Director)

3.1 Reasons for developing electronic portfolios

There are many reasons to move from paper-based to digital portfolios, According to Sheingold (1992), by using technology to store student portfolios, we can make their work portable, accessible, and more easily and widely distributed. We can also replay performance works anytime. This author's assumptions (Barrett 1998) include:

- Today, many documents placed in a traditional portfolio are initially created with a computer, and then printed to paper
- The use of hypertext links allows clear connections between standards and portfolio artifacts
- There is emerging evidence that creating an electronic portfolio can develop skills in using multimedia technology
- A teacher who models the development of an electronic portfolio may be more likely to have students who value the use of this tool to support and document their own learning
- It may also be more motivating and easier to manage the portfolio development process!

3.2 Electronic portfolio development strategies

There are many strategies for developing electronic portfolios, and they appear to fall under two general approaches: the generic tools approach or using off-the-shelf software, and the customised systems approach which involves designing a networked system or buying a proprietary software package.

3.2.1 Generic tools approach

Portfolios are developed with reflections and artefacts that more closely emulate the traditional 3-ring binder. The portfolio's structure is imposed by the learner or the software for maximum flexibility and creativity. There is a relatively low cost for equipment or software, but there may be a higher cost for training. Students can continue developing their portfolios once out of the educational system. There are some good commercial electronic portfolio programs on the market, although they often reflect the developer's style or are constrained by the limits of the software structure. Many educators who want to develop electronic portfolios in the classroom tend to design their own, using off-the-shelf software, or generic strategies. There is a variety of off-the-shelf multimedia development software that have be adapted for the purpose of electronic portfolios, including relational databases, hypermedia card formats, Network-compatible hypermedia, and multimedia authoring software.

3.2.2 Customised systems approach

Portfolios are also developed as online record-keeping systems that can be used to collect reflections and artifacts. They are usually highly structured using an online database, leaving the learner with limited flexibility and creativity. There is a high cost for equipment, network server and software development. There may be a lower cost for training, depending on system design. One concern is whether the students can continue developing the portfolio once they are out of the educational system.

Software packages to support these types of electronic or digital portfolios are varied and the titles are growing yearly. The current trend in electronic portfolio development is to make them web-accessible (often using the customised systems approach). The most common choice is developing portfolios as static web pages. However, an emerging trend is to develop dynamic web pages supported by a server-based relational database.

3.3 Examples from U.S.A.

Some other examples from around the USA that can be found on the World Wide Web include:

- Alaska, USA: Mt. Edgecumb's electronic student portfolios digital learning portfolio research. Many examples of student portfolios from Alaska's boarding school for rural high school students – http://www.mehs.educ.state.ak.us/portfolios/portfolio.html
- Colorado: Teachers at Peakview Elementary School have developed a strategy for developing electronic portfolios using *HyperStudio* which, once organised on the computer, are recorded to video tape for sharing with parents. Their program is being marketed through Forest Technologies as the as *Designer Software Electronic Portfolio Toolkit.*
- California: An early project at Bell High School created video portfolios, digitised and written to CD-ROM. Initially a project of the Advanced Technology Group of Apple Computer, this project is one of the earliest illustrations of the use of digital video in portfolios.
- Susan Silverman's web site is one of the few sites on the Internet with electronic portfolios for early elementary students – http://kids-learn.org

3.4 Examples from around the world

There are several significant projects conducted internationally that illustrate the world-wide interest in this topic.

Women @ the cutting edge is a small team based at RMIT University in Australia. It originated from a group of women teachers, determined to show that women can lead the development and implementation of technology (http://www.results.aust.com) This project began as a response to the growing need to record learning and achievements, and to reflect on them for performance review, recruitment and certification. Two of the team members, Elizabeth Hartnell-Young and Maureen Morriss, recently published a book through Skylight Professional Development, which outlines the results of their work. Currently in the state of Victoria, over 12,000 school teachers now have laptop computers leased from the government, and as a condition of the lease they are required to complete professional development activities. Web-based multimedia portfolios are being developed which reflect the linkage of two trends, ICT and professional portfolios. These authors believed that teachers who engage in developing multimedia portfolios will increase skills in technology, enhance self-knowledge, gain in self-esteem and present a forward-thinking image to their employers. (Kankaanranta, Barrett and Hartnell-Young 2000)

The CATO project conducted by the Institute for Educational Research at the University of Jyväskylä, Finland, presents an action research study, in which digital school portfolios are used interactively as a means for teachers to collaboratively display and assess the pedagogical practices of kindergartens and primary schools (http://www.pedanet.jyu.fi/cato/ or http://www.pedanet.jyu.fi/portfolio/). This research project was designed to enhance mutual collaboration and understanding between kindergartens and schools. The development work is made visible, followed and assessed through the research network by means of digital portfolios. In this study there is an emphasis on teacher support in the form of teacher training in educational technology.

A very innovative web site is the Portfolio Info Site at the Amsterdam Faculty of Education: http://www.efa.nl/publicaties/english.html. This web site was developed by the Educative Faculty of the Netherlands as an experimental project in portfolio development. The site was custom-designed to their specifications, and has both public and restricted access.

The Ministry of Education in Singapore has begun a research project on implementing electronic portfolios with teachers and students. In October, 2000, the author trained over 40 Senior IT Trainers on developing professional portfolios. In the next year, electronic portfolios will be implemented in two elementary schools and a high school, to assess the impact of this strategy on student learning.

All of these examples, and many more, can be found on the author's internationally-known web site on this topic: http://www.electronicportfolios.com/portfolios.html. The web site is always under development, new additions are welcome, and educators from around the world are encouraged to share their experiences with electronic portfolios and other forms of ICT support for alternative, authentic or performance-based assessment. The author maintains a listserv on electronic portfolios that has members throughout the world, to continue the dialogue on this emerging method of documenting, assessing, and storing the results of student learning and teacher profession development.

4. CONCLUSIONS

With the widespread dissemination of ICT in homes and schools, and the many software tools available to support development, the electronic portfolio is becoming a viable option for dynamically documenting learning and reflection across the lifespan. Young children, with the assistance of older students or parents, can learn to digitise samples of their work and reflect either in writing, or using the power of the technology, to record reflections on their learning in audio or video clips. Older students and adult learners can prepare digital portfolios for employment to further their professional advancement. Teachers can develop electronic portfolios to document their own professional development or achieve advanced certificates. It is the author's wish that electronic portfolios become dynamic celebrations of learning across the lifespan.

REFERENCES

Barrett, H. (1998, June) Presentation at National Educational Computing Conference, San Diego, California.

Barrett, H. (2000, April) Create Your Own Electronic Portfolio. *Learning & Leading with Technology,* 27 (7), pp. 14-21.

Barton, J. and Angelo C. (1997) *Portfolio Assessment: A Handbook for Educators*. Dale Seymour Publications.

Burke, K. (1999) *How to Assess Authentic Learning*. Arlington Heights, IL: Skylight Professional Development.

Burke, K. (1997) *Designing Professional Portfolios for Change*. Palatine, Illinois. IRI/SkyLight Training & Publishing.

Campbell, D. M., Melenyzer, B. J., Nettles, D. H. and Wyman, R. M. Jr. (2000) *Portfolio and Performance Assessment in Teacher Education*. Allyn & Bacon, Boston.

Fogarty, R. (1998) *Balanced Assessment.* Arlington Heights, IL: Skylight Professional Development.

Hartnell-Young, E. and Morriss, M. (1999) *Digital Professional Portfolios for Change.* Arlington Heights: Skylight Professional Development.

Herman, J. L., Aschbacher, P.R. and Winters, L. (1992) *A practical guide to alternative assessment.* Alexandria, VA: Association for Supervision and Curriculum Development.

Kankaanranta, M., Barrett, H. and Hartnell-Young, E. (2000) *Exploring the use of electronic portfolios in international contexts*. Paper submitted to Ed-Media Conference.

Linn, R. L. and Gronlund, N. E. (2000) *Measurement and Assessment in Teaching*. Upper Saddle River, NJ: Merrill.

Sheingold, K. (1992, June) *Technology and assessment.* Paper presented at Technology & School Reform Conference, Dallas, TX.

Wilcox, B. L. and Tomei, 1. (1999) *Professional Portfolios for Teachers.* Christopher-Gordon Publishers.

Wolf, K. (1999) *Leading the Professional Portfolio Process for Change*. Arlington Heights, IL: Skylight Professional Development.

Worthen, B. R. (1993) Critical issues that will determine the future of alternative assessment. *Phi Delta Kappan*, February, pp. 444-456.

BIOGRAPHY

Helen Barrett is on the faculty of the School of Education at the University of Alaska Anchorage. She has been researching electronic portfolios since 1991, publishing a website on Technology and Alternative Assessment since 1995 (http://electronicportfolios.com) and is the Assessment Coordinator for the International Society for Technology in Education's (ISTE) National Educational Technology Standards for Teachers (NETS•T).

57

Developing Generic Capabilities through Web-based Student Profiling

Wendy Fountain and Janelle Allison
Faculty of Built Environment & Engineering, Queensland University of Technology, Brisbane, Australia
w.fountain@qut.edu.au
School of Design & Built Environment, Queensland University of Technology, Brisbaen, Australia

Keywords: higher education, integration of ICT, World Wide Web, curriculum changes, assessment

Abstract: This paper reports on the development of the web-based Student Capability Profile (SCP) that is one institution's response to the increasingly complex professional, cultural, economic and social demands upon today's university graduates. This flexible and portable student profile facilitates and records students' generic capability or key skill development throughout the duration of study, anchored in core curriculum activity and drawing from other life experiences. Particular attention is given to the interdependence of the profiling process, its pedagogical framework, and the web and database technology that underpin the system. The implications and anticipated outcomes of the SCP's introduction are discussed and the SCP is finally considered as a catalyst for change impacting upon teaching practice and graduates' interface with society.

1. INTRODUCTION

With integration of information and communication technology (ICT), and namely the World Wide Web, frequently directed toward the delivery and support of courses and subjects in higher education, this paper describes an innovative application of web and database technology that transcends subjects, years and even entire courses. The emerging area of web-enabled student profiling for the purposes of facilitating and documenting the long-term development of generic capabilities or key skills is gaining momentum. The specific case of the Student Capability Profile (SCP) currently in development at Queensland University of Technology (QUT), Brisbane, Australia is a fusion of flexible learning and reflective practice principles, structured curriculum integration and the many opportunities afforded by the web medium's properties.

Profiling engages the student in a continuous monitored process of personal development facilitated by the web-based system and its human collaborators. Retained in possession of the individual, the capability profile is a documented attainment of capability synthesised from recordings and reflections of student experiences in all spheres of life, and tracked over the duration of study. As a process embodying the student's total experience, the SCP represents a major catalyst for change as graduates will begin to emerge from the institution with a more inherently connected range of disciplinary, technical and generic skills and knowledge.

The Student Capability Profile is a work-in-progress closely related to sister projects in three other Australian universities also in the membership of the Australian Technology Network (ATN). Planned for eventual implementation at institution level, two pilots are to extend from February to June, 2001 in the Faculty of Built Environment and Engineering. The background to the profile's development is presented below, followed by explanation of the relationship between the profiling process, its pedagogical framework and the properties of the web medium. The implications and anticipated outcomes of the profile's integration are then summarised.

2. BACKGROUND

An explanation of the perceived need for a student profile and its purpose reinforces the topical themes that are manifested within the concept of a student profile: graduate attributes, lifelong learning, integration of ICT to assist learning, and generic capabilities. Supporting students' personal development in the latter forms the central objective of the SCP. Generic capabilities may alternatively be termed 'key skills', 'generic skills' or 'transferable skills' in the literature, however distinctions are debated. These terms are all suggestive of the kinds of skill and knowledge identified by Ramsden (1992), the Dearing Report (1997) and Bowden and Marton (1998) among others, as extending beyond a discipline or subject area and which are applicable to all spheres of life. In the absence of a definitive list, such skills might include communication, interpersonal, and problem-solving skills;

information, technological and critical literacies; and community, cultural and environmental consciousness.

The impetus for the development of student profiling in the Australian setting emerged from several quarters. Prominent among these was the AC Nielsen project (1999) that involved surveying employers to establish desired generic capabilities, and determining to what extent hired graduates displayed those capabilities. In short, the results revealed a sizable deficit in graduates' generic skills compared with their technical skills. Prior to this research, professional organisations such as the Institution of Engineers Australia (1996) became active in requiring universities to demonstrate how generic and technical skills were being cultivated. A further initiative that heavily informed the development of the SCP was the widely disseminated report prepared by the Australian Technology Network (ATN) entitled 'Generic Capabilities of ATN University Graduates' (1999). This report outlines a framework for generic capability development through curriculum integration and teaching practice, case studies of which are examined. Extending on the work of Bowden and Marton (1998), the report also raises critical distinctions in levels of generic capability attainment relative to their application in different contexts.

Examples of student profiling can also be found further afield. Of particular interest to the early stages of the QUT project, was the Universities of Liverpool, Manchester and Leeds' 'LUSID' project. Its aim was '...to implement a World Wide Web based system to reflect upon and record the outcomes of learning in a variety of contexts, including academic and non-academic activities'. The philosophy is further shared in the mission 'to reflect upon and record key skills development' in the undergraduate population (LUSID 2000). It contrasts most with SCP in its introduction as an optional tool outside of core curriculum activity, and its starting focus on capability rather than experiences that yield capability development. A further PC-based profiling approach is in use at Thames Valley University (1998) with emphasis on career planning in addition to key skill development.

3. THE INTERDEPENDENCE OF PROCESS, PEDAGOGY AND MEDIUM

The capability profiling process involves student interactions within a database-supported web environment, the pedagogical framework of which allows sufficient scope and flexibility for the teacher to customise and adapt system functions to achieve integration with core curriculum. This includes the creation of tasks, insertion of media and examples, linking of resources and exemplars, and the provision of access to appropriate mentors, guides and peers who also interact with students within the web environment.

In an orientation to the SCP students are prompted to undertake a 'self-audit', rating themselves through reflection upon a range of life experiences. This self-assessment is made relative to the set of generic capabilities that are described and illustrated through exemplars in the system. Students are then assisted to identify areas in need of development, and opportunities for such development within core curriculum activities. Action then becomes explicit through the fundamental cyclical process of auditing, reflecting, and assessing. Students can also elect to release their profile to others within the system environment such as peers, mentors or tutors for the purposes of assessment, seeking feedback or collaborating.

It is envisaged that teachers would provide a greater degree of task structure for students early in the undergraduate time line, compared with third or fourth year students advanced in the creation of their capability profile. The notion that latter year students will utilise the profile more independently was supported in a recent focus group session with third year students. The important principle here is that regardless of year level, students can seek to demonstrate and record their attainment of a given generic capability at any point. The concern highlighted in the ATN Report (1999) is for the *context* in which the capability is to be demonstrated rather than any objectified 'satisfactory' level of capability. This factor recognises the diversity of background and prior learning students possess when embarking upon an academic program. Additionally, students are encouraged to support their profile with recognition of achievement in the community, the workplace or in study-related activities such as camps, school visits and special programs.

The resultant Student Capability Profile that augments a student's academic transcript upon graduation, is an extract of demonstrated generic capability attainment in the different contexts posed by course progression. In its attachment to the individual, the capability profile can flexibly accommodate changes of academic program, periods of overseas study, or be resumed after a deferment.

4. PEDAGOGICAL PRINCIPLES AND IDEALS

Several key pedagogical principles underpin the profiling process described above and have directed the way in which the web medium has been harnessed:

- Prompting individuals' consideration of their *total* engagement with the world, profiling promotes 'wholeness' i.e. a consciousness of the validity and value of all experiences and transfer of new skills to subsequent experiences

- Self-paced and personally constructed, students own both their learning process and the resultant capability profile, through which they are encouraged to develop a self-directed orientation to lifelong learning
- The system does not prescribe a path to a 'correct' end. Students are prompted to create unique paths based on their own experiences, and appreciate that the tutors, mentors and peers whom they encounter through the profile represent multiple perspectives
- While students interact with the system environment, their monitored actions are guided by human interventions that unfold as dialogue within the profile. This functions in the manner of Laurillard's (1993) rhetorical 'extrinsic feedback' upon which the student acts
- Recording and reflecting are central iterative processes that seek direct application in the context of curriculum objectives and activities, again conferring with Laurillard's learning schema (1993)
- Integration of the web-based profiling system is in itself conducive to the meta-cognitive development of a range of generic capabilities, especially in respect to technological and information literacies. Oliver and McLoughlin (1999) have raised this characteristic of web technology through their attempts to develop key skills over recent years. Supportive development of these highly transferable capabilities can contribute greatly to a student's ability to negotiate higher learning.

5. PROPERTIES OF THE WEB MEDIUM

Profiling in itself is not an innovation as the now dating texts describing paper-based approaches attest. What is exciting and compelling about the combined web and database medium is its conduciveness toward the pedagogical principles described above and to achieving a flexible framework. The major supportive properties include:

- Continuous access and functionality irrespective of time and location. Presuming web access, students and collaborators can log on 24 hours in principle, mindful that technical hitches will inevitably apply
- Database capabilities enable the recording, revisiting, organising and extraction of qualitative text input
- Levels of security allow students to activate the release of selected parts of their profile for task submission and additionally as desired, otherwise input remains personal and exploration need not be limited by scrutiny

- In combination, secured access and the recording function allow authorised collaborators to generate an asynchronous text-based dialogue with students in support of a timely formative feedback turnaround
- References to shared events that occur *outside* the system in face-to-face scenarios, but are recorded *inside* the system by a tutor or peer, remain visible to reinforce the linkages between the curriculum activity and the related profile task
- The sophistication of current web authoring and graphics tools supports the creation of intuitive interfaces, a narrative graphic language and alternative prompt options that acknowledge diversity in learning and thinking styles, and an identifiable web environment with which students become familiar
- Ease of content exchange creates a responsiveness to changing emphases outside the system that demand particular skills e.g. a focus on flexible work practices within the new knowledge economy
- As a network node, the system makes explicit and meaningful connections between existing institution-based resources (such as online tutorials and guides that support information and technological literacy) that are otherwise passive and risk obscurity
- Viewing the network globally, the system acts as a gateway to a host of other web-based interactions and experiences that can be subject to meaning-making and testing upon return to the profile environment.

A further set of web medium properties converges with selected key 'learning paradigm' characteristics that MacFarlane (1997) regards as having superseded a passive, unidirectional and location-specific 'instructional paradigm':

- Interactivity is evoked by both system elements such as exemplars that may be activated, along with the input of human collaborators as action provokes response and feedback loops are generated
- In-built system support and examples of use are continuously available to avoid impeded progress reliant on human intervention
- Realistic bandwidth/file size solutions for dynamic media such as animation, audio and video are approaching and will result in more compelling exemplars, and concept mapping with minimised reliance on screen-based text.

Acceptance of the web medium's great opportunities as a platform in support of SCP cannot go unquestioned without examining some of its considerable challenges. Major implications are discussed below.

6. IMPLICATIONS OF SCP INTEGRATION

As the web becomes an increasingly prevalent part of life it is easy to overlook that the Internet still poses some weighty equity issues for students. These include access for those with impairments, the inadequacy of on-campus computer facilities, the costs of online time and hardware for off-campus access, and deficits in the fundamental technical skills that allow participation. The integration of SCP with any student cohort demands a pre-study to first guarantee a realistic and equitable level of access and address alternatives if this cannot be achieved.

As suggested in discussion of the web medium's properties, there is potential for the SCP to become a more compelling experience through the integration of dynamic media. As web development in both the commercial sector and in education are beginning to address accessibility and usability, the conflict between providing high-end web applications and maintaining accessibility for the impaired user becomes very great. At a future point the institution will possibly have to consider the development of an alternative profile that seeks to meet all accessibility requirements while offering equivalent learning opportunities.

The objective to integrate the SCP institution-wide is an ambitious one, demanding something of a cultural revolution. Quite apart from huge resource and infrastructure implications, it asserts a new paradigm where the minimum standard of teaching includes rigorous integration of generic capabilities into core curriculum, and teaching with ICT, in addition to the previously accepted expertise in disciplinary knowledge and technical skills. This will clearly necessitate a lengthy process in which small scale integrations will gradually permeate outward. Such a shift will result as much from visionary leadership as policy, and specialised, dedicated educational development support. To complement this there will need to be equivalent infrastructure support for an eventually monstrous system with thousands of user accounts, and vast data management and archiving.

As the paradigm shift above suggests, there are many dimensions to the staff development that SCP will necessitate that extend far beyond learning to use and administrate the system. Negotiating the tension between what many see as achieving generic capability development at the cost of 'content' and vice versa, suggests that staff need assistance in reconceptualising these as being enmeshed in an interdependent whole. Once teaching with SCP, there will be the need to optimise one's approaches to moderating, mediating and providing meaningful feedback. Perhaps the most difficult concept with which the SCP developers and the institution still need to grapple is the substantive basis upon which students are verified as having attained levels of generic capabilities.

In the expectation that employers, recruiters and professional bodies will understand, value and promote the SCP, they need to be regarded as part of a collaborative network and continue to inform the profile's iterative development. Workplaces will also form the sites of long-term evaluation when the first graduates who emerge with a SCP take up positions and research is conducted in how these graduates interface with professional workplaces.

Development and implementation of the SCP institution-wide is obviously a resource intensive endeavour. In the current climate of resource scarcity in higher education, commercialisation of the SCP has already been mooted to recoup costs and capitalise on the investment made in its development. The development of LUSID (2000) was coupled by a similar intention to make the system available to other institutions, and more lately the focus has turned to small to medium enterprises without personnel or staff development units. At QUT, alumni have been identified as a potential 'market' but all such pursuits under the model of economic rationalism require vigilance to avoid the day when the SCP becomes a product rather than a scholarly approach to teaching and learning.

7. ANTICIPATED OUTCOMES

In the first instance students will come to understand the limitations of discipline-only knowledge and technical skills, and appreciate the significance and value of generic capabilities. Students will also:

- Come to conceptualise the interdependence of all life experiences
- Consciously identify their own needs and make explicit the development they derive from curriculum and other activities
- Develop the skills to engage in effective peer mentoring of students in earlier stages of development
- Move from being supported to taking responsibility for their own long-term development
- Make connections between bodies of knowledge that were previously viewed in isolation, and understand the multidisciplinary nature of professional activity
- Participate in and adapt to changing economic and social conditions, and be equipped for multiple career paths and complex cross-cultural interactions.

Aside of the inherent challenges, positive outcomes are also anticipated for staff. It is an unrealistic expectation that all staff will represent a consistently high level across a diverse spectrum of generic capabilities. The SCP integration presents the opportunity for concurrent personal development and knowledge sharing through the formation of complementary 'skill teams'. The SCP will likely represent an initial foray into teaching with ICT for many staff. Favourably this will occur with formal support at institution level, and from an increasing collegial support network as the integration permeates. There will also be the opportunity to keep pace with advances in web and database technology as it is appropriated into the system.

8. CONCLUSION

Integration of the SCP at QUT is a catalyst for change at many levels. In the student experience it will result in improved outcomes for learning, personal growth and development; while in the staff experience it will also redefine teaching practice and priorities. It will also challenge and advance curriculum design and integration, and through this process advance the scholarship of teaching. Simultaneously the SCP will reveal and make common the experience of teaching with ICT in contrast to the relatively isolated pockets of ICT application that exist today. As an integration of ICT into higher education, the SCP is a multi-faceted catalyst for change in its relationship to students, staff and the institution.

REFERENCES

Nielsen AC (1999) *Employer satisfaction with graduate skills: research report.* [www.detya.gov.au/highered/eippubs/EIP99-7/execsum99_7.htm] 24.10.2000.

Bowden, J., Hart, G., King, B., Trigwell, K. and Watts, O. (1999) *Generic capabilities of ATN university graduates.* [www.clt.uts.edu.au/ATN.grad.cap.project.index.html] 24.10.2000.

Bowden, J. and Marton, F. (1998) *The University of Learning. Beyond Quality and Competence.* Kogan Page, London.

Dearing Report (1997) *Higher Education in the Learning Society.* HMSO, London.

Institution of Engineers Australia (1996) *Changing the culture: Engineering education into the future.* Institution of Engineers Australia, 21 Bedford Street, North Melbourne, Australia, 3051.

Laurillard, D. (1993) *Rethinking University Teaching: A Framework for the Effective Use of Educational Technology.* Routledge, London.

LUSID (2000) *LUSID final report, May 2000 – Lessons learned and future activity.* [http://lusid.liv.ac.uk/public/report2000/lessons.html] 18.10.2000.

MacFarlane, A. G. W. (1997) New learning paradigm: Changes in pedagogy. In *Towards a learning strategy for the University of the Highlands and Islands*, L. Broumley, ed. [www.uhi.ac.uk/LET_Report.html#chapter2] 17.10.2000.

Oliver, R. and McLoughlin, C. (1999) Using web and problem-based learning environments to support the development of key skills. In *Proceedings of the Conference of the Australasian Society for Computers in Learning in Tertiary Education*, J. Winn (ed.), Brisbane, December. pp.249-256.

Ramsden, P. (1992) *Learning to Teach in Higher Education*, Routledge, London.
Thames Valley University (1998) *Profiling User Guide*, Thames Valley University, London.

ACKNOWLEDGEMENTS

Great thanks to Martin Murray, Doug Hargreaves, Jill Franz, Anne-Marie McArdle, Gail Hart, Halima Goss and SMILE, Weilin Chang and the QUT students of Civil Engineering and Interior Design.

BIOGRAPHY

Wendy Fountain is an educational designer and is currently coordinating the redevelopment of a faculty web environment. She has taught in the vocational, corporate and higher education sectors in Australia and Sweden, and has researched the experience of students and staff within ICT integration. Her current research interests are the qualitative aspects of online learning environments and web usability in respect to cognition and learning.

Janelle Allison is currently Interim Head of the new School of Design and Built Environment. Her research and teaching interests focus on regional planning and local economic development, and she has received both grants and consultancies on the role of local government in local economic development, community development, and industry clusters and networks. Her recent work has focussed on a new innovative learning communities approach to community development strategies.

PART SEVEN

MANAGEMENT AND RESOURCE

Comparative Evaluation of the Implementation of Computerised School Management Systems
– in Hong Kong, The Netherlands and England

Alex Fung[1], Adrie Visscher[2], Debbie Smith[3] and Phil Wild[3]
1) Department of Education Studies, Hong Kong Baptist University, Kowloon, Hong Kong SAR, China
alexfung@hkbu.edu.hk
2) Faculty of Educational Science and Technology, University of Twente, Enschede, The Netherlands
3) Department of Education, Loughborough University, Loughborough, United Kingdom

Keywords: school information systems, usability, effectiveness, school management, evaluation

Abstract: The paper describes the results of a study to assess the implementation of computerised school management systems used in secondary schools in Hong Kong, the Netherlands, and the UK. Large scale surveys were carried out in all three countries and from the results we evaluated system-usage and the implementation promoting factors.

1. INTRODUCTION

Over the last decade schools in Hong Kong, the Netherlands and the United Kingdom have experienced much organisational change. There has been a tendency toward devolution of financial and managerial responsibility away from central government into local government and/or schools. Computerised school administration systems have been introduced into schools to contribute to such local management.

In 1993 the Hong Kong government invested 70 million US dollars in the development of an integrated computer network, linking the Education Department and all government and aided sector primary and secondary schools. This included the implementation of a centrally developed and standardised School Administration and Management System, SAMS, in all public-sector schools.

In the Netherlands there has been no centrally led initiative providing school information system (SIS) software. Three SIS's emerged over the last decade as market leaders in the secondary education marketplace, School+, Scholis and Schoolfact. These three systems were investigated in the Netherlands study.

In 1989 the UK government made available £325million to provide computer systems to schools in an enterprise that was administered by Local Education Authorities. SIMS™ (Capita Software) the most widely used software was the focus of the UK study.

The SISs investigated were modular in architecture. The SAMS in Hong Kong consisted of 12 core applications and 4 supporting applications handling student, staff and organisational information in many different contexts. In the Netherlands School+, Scholis and Schoolfact consist of around 20 main modules with similar functionality. SIMS in the UK comprises 28 different modules.

This comparative study used a similar questionnaire in all three countries to investigate issues in this diverse range of SIS implementations. In 1996 in Hong Kong, questionnaires were distributed to 641 schools using SAMS with a reply rate of 56%. The schools included government, private and subsidised primary, secondary and special schools. In the Netherlands (1997) questionnaires were sent to 498 secondary schools with a return rate of approximately 13% (63 schools). In the UK (1999) questionnaires were sent to a sample of 962 English secondary schools with a return rate of 47%. Although the UK study was carried out respectively three and two years later than the Hong Kong and Dutch study we do not think the situation in those two countries has changed much.

2. RESEARCH QUESTIONS, FRAMEWORK AND DATA ANALYSIS

The following questions were addressed:

1. The extent to and ways in which SISs are used in schools
2. The user opinion on system-quality
3. Users' views on the nature and quality of the implementation process
4. Factors affecting the degree of SIS-usage.

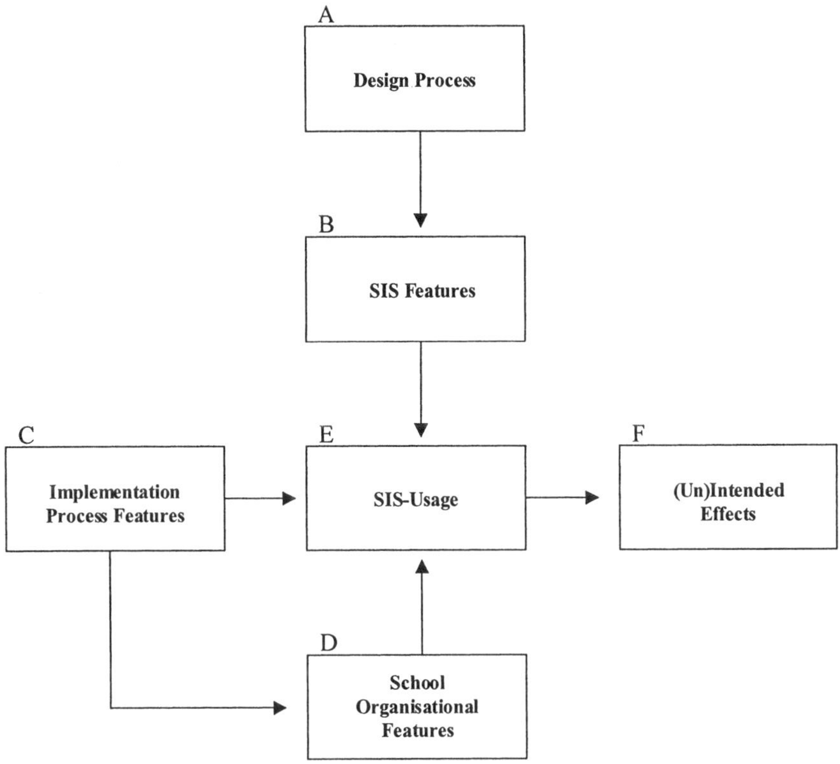

Figure 1. The variable groups influencing SIS-usage and its effects (source: Visscher 1996)

The variables relating to the above issues that were investigated in this study fell into five distinct categories according to Visscher's model (Visscher, 1996; see figure 1 above): features of the SIS, system-usage, the implementation process, school organisation, and the intended/unintended effects. The studies assumed possible interrelationships between all these variable groups. System-usage is expected to be more intense if users' evaluations of the qualities of the SIS, the implementation process and the school organisation are more positive. More intense SIS-use is expected to lead to more (un)intended effects.

Descriptive statistics were computed for all variables studied (frequencies and cross-tabulations). A limited number of variables were selected since they were considered as the most promising predictors of system-usage. They were entered into a stepwise regression analysis to determine which variables influence SIS-usage.

3. RESULTS

3.1 System-usage

The extent and type of SIS-module usage varied quite widely in the different countries. In Hong Kong schools the amount of module use varied from one school to another, and only a small number of schools were found to be using all the SAMS modules. Overall, the most widely used modules were the Housekeeping and Security, Student, and Staff modules.

In the Netherlands the amount of module usage also varied widely between schools. The most frequently used modules overall are Student Test Scores, Final Examination Registration and Financial and Student Data modules. A little less common was the use of the modules Attendance Registration and Timetabling.

SIMS in the UK had the widest variety of modules of the three countries. Of these the most frequently used modules were Student Data, the Information Manager and Timetabling followed by Financial Management and Student Attendance.

3.2 Direct and indirect system-usage

Module usage varied with the users roles within the school. Usage was categorised into 'direct use' by those who had hands-on use of the system and 'indirect use' by those who used printouts supplied by other staff.

In Hong Kong 57% of the respondents were direct SAMS users (50% of these were SAMS administrators). Principals tended to be indirect users, mainly using reports from the system for routine administrative tasks. Teachers used SAMS least, over 80% for less than one hour a month (directly and indirectly). Only SAMS administrators used the system for a substantial number of hours per month (40% direct use 11-30 hours). Clerks or secretaries tended to use SAMS less than 10 hours per month, only 18% used it directly for over 11 hours. Overall, the degree of SAMS use was low.

In the Netherlands 76% of the sample were direct users and 24% indirect users. There was limited system use by teachers together with relatively intense use by clerks and SIS administrators, which was consistent with expectation, as was the limited direct use by principals. Among 60% of principals SIS-usage was limited to 4 or less hours per month. This is much lower than that in the UK study. However 25% of principals and SIS administrators used the system indirectly for 5-10 hours per month, which is similar to UK findings.

In the UK a different pattern was observed. On average across the whole school, direct use was 5-10 hours per week and indirect use 1-4 hours. This was much higher than in either of the other two studies. Only 1% of the sample were never direct SIS users. Clerical staff and office managers worked the longest hours using the system directly, followed by SIMS administrators and teachers. Heads and deputy heads used the system least. However the amount of time spent on indirect use was similar across all roles.

3.3 Modules used in making management decisions

The Hong Kong study showed that for managerial purposes, the most frequently used information was on Student Achievement. Student Attainment and Annual Score statistics, Class Overall Score List, Score Statistics and School and Class Structure Lists were the printouts most commonly used by principals in making managerial decisions, but there was no evidence to show that a large majority used these modules over others.

In the Netherlands the analysis showed that considerable numbers of printouts that were supposed to have a management support capacity were not used by principals. The printouts used most commonly concerned student results and administrative printouts (e.g. student counts).

In the UK, the modules used for managerial purposes were financial management and information analysis, followed by timetabling, attendance and personnel, assessment and cover (teaching duties) modules.

Modules such as financial and personnel reports in which relationships between data are portrayed, or in which patterns in the data are analysed in support of school policy-making were not used much in the three studies. Hence it is probable that management support, if it exists, is of an administrative type while higher order forms of management support are largely under utilised.

3.4 Perceived quality of the SISs

The perceived quality of the SISs compared with manual/previous systems used was assessed for direct users only (Table 1).

Table 1. Average overall level of satisfaction compared to previous system

	HK (secondary)	Netherlands	UK
Much Worse/worse	2%	7%	4%
Same/ Satisfactory	20%	22%	14%
Better/much better	57%	71%	64%
Don't Know/Missing	21%		18%

The following aspects of SIS-quality were compared to the previous system: data input, data accuracy, data relevance, data currency, information completeness, management support capacity, system performance evaluation and ease of information availability.

The Dutch and UK results were broadly similar to the majority of users preferring the current system to any previous. The results for Hong Kong however suggested that a slightly smaller number of users evaluated the system as (much) better.

3.5 The implementation process

In Hong Kong about 60% and 40% of users had received external and internal training respectively. The rest had not been trained at all. The training hours varied among the four respondent groups, administrators being trained the most: 40% for 1-30 hours, 60% for more hours. Around half of the users were neutral on the quantity and quality of the external and internal training received. Around one third of them were (very) happy and one fifth (very) unhappy.

About 60% of Dutch users had had external training and only about 30% had internal training, much lower numbers than in the UK. As with the UK study, the amount of training they received was very dependent on the role of the user, for example the majority of clerical staff had received 11-30 hours training.

In the UK 91% of the sample received some external training. Of these 80% were trained externally by the Local Education Authority (LEA). Internal training was received by 90% of the respondents. There has not been much internal training in the UK, the majority of users having experienced little or none. The majority was happy with the quality of the training but not so happy with the quantity.

The emphasis in the balance of training was slightly different between the UK and the Netherlands with more technical and practical training in the Netherlands. Table 2 shows how users evaluate the content of the training, when they have to choose between two extremes.

Table 2. Balance of training*

	Hong Kong	Netherlands	UK
Technical system aspects – How to use system	20% v 60%	50% v 15%	14% v 43%
Practical system use – Theoretical use	65% v 10%	37% v 20%	45% v 11%
Administrative work – Managerial functions	30% v 45%	36% v 28%	21% v 25%
Retrieving data – Inputting data	NA	37% v 13%	18% v 17%
Printing out data – Interpreting and using data	50% v 20%	37% v 23%	35% v 16%
Printing self-defined reports – Printing standard reports	10% v 60%	28% v 27%	14% v 36%

* Extremes only shown, central values not included

3.6 Access to help outside or within school

In Hong Kong, if users experience a problem with SAMS, 40% were (very) happy about the ease of getting help from school, 30% neutral and 30% (very) unhappy. As far as external help was concerned, only 48% were (very) happy. Sources of help being used were the SAMS-hotline of the Education Department, the SAMS administrator in school, help from a colleague, and the user manual.

In the Netherlands 44% of the users were (very) satisfied with the ease of getting internal help when they experienced a problem with their SIS. About 30% were (very) satisfied with the ease of getting external support, 30% of the users were unsatisfied.

When users had a problem, 77% of them frequently worked this out themselves, 50% often consulted the system administrator. A hot line, colleagues within school, and the system manual were each used frequently by 20-30% of the direct users. Colleagues outside the school were seldom a source for problem solving.

In the UK similar results were obtained. 48% found it (very) easy to get help within the school and 37% found it (very) easy to get help outside the school. The majority of these (85%) often or very frequently solved problems themselves. Of the users 46% said that SIMS administrators often solved problems and 40% indicated that they successfully used the SIMS/LEA hotline. Only 18% used on-line help.

3.7 Levels of user satisfaction

When average variable scores were investigated a number fell below neutral on a 1-5 normalised scale (5 being the most positive user response, 1 the least).

In Hong Kong users were mostly dissatisfied with the quality of SAMS. The results below neutral value were: the extent of user training, the quality and quantity of both internal and external training which was also perceived to be unsatisfactory, previous computer knowledge, perceived quality of information about SAMS, and the perceived clarity of the goals of the innovation process.

In the Netherlands the variables below neutral value were: the extent of external and internal training, ease of getting external help, extent of hot line support, satisfaction with the innovation pace, help from internal colleagues, external colleagues, and from the user manual.

In the UK below neutral scores were obtained for working environment, training (internal and external), problem solving, user interface issues, system quality, planning and communication, the amount of time spent on the system, and the users computing experience.

3.8 Predictors of SIS-usage

In addition to the descriptive results presented so far regression analyses were carried out to find out which variables explained most variance in SIS use. Put differently, the goal was to determine which variables seem to be associated most with the extent of system-usage. Fourteen variables were entered into the analyses because they were expected to be the best predictors of SIS-usage. Table 3 shows which variables indeed proved to predict SIS-usage in one or more of the studies.

Table 3. Predictors of System-usage

	Hong Kong	**Netherlands**	**United Kingdom**
Start motivation	x		x
Computer experience	x		x
Internal training	x	x	
External training	x	x	x
SIS quality	x		
SIS data quality	x		x
Clarity innovation goals	x		
Clarity innovation means	x	x	
Ease internal help	x		x

Five variables did not have a significant relationship with SIS-usage: ease of external help, encouragement from principal, encouragement from SIS-administrator, satisfaction with training, the length of the SIS in operation.

Table 3 clearly shows the importance of the implementation process. Training is the most relevant variable, possibly because it can be used to motivate the target group to use the system and clarify the goals and methods of the innovation process. The perceived quality of the SIS and the data it produces also appeared as significant predictors of system-usage.

Also found to be important are the amount of computer experience users already have, and the ease with which they can get internal help if the experience problems with SIS-usage. The data show that the quality of the design activities, the resulting SIS, and the data it produces are crucial.

4. CONCLUSION

Summarising, the meta-analysis showed that:

- SIS-usage varies considerably between the schools in the same country
- The basic administrative SIS modules prove to be used most for routine tasks (e.g. financial and student administration)
- There is little support of higher order school management activities which could lead to better school policies and improved school functioning
- Few schools use all modules of the SIS they possess
- Direct system-usage varies across the three countries between 60% and 100% of the respondents and is dominated by clerical staff and SIS administrators
- Principals use SISs mainly indirectly
- Across the three countries about 60-70% of respondents think the SIS is (much) better than their previous system; according to 20-30% the SIS is no improvement (2-4% even considers it a deterioration)
- About 30% of users are unhappy with the ease of getting support in solving problems with SIS use
- Users on average also seem to be dissatisfied with the quality of the SIS and the training (e.g. too technical), the innovation clarity, and the support received during the change process
- Most predictors of SIS-usage prove to be aspects of the implementation process.

Overall, the research indicates that although there is room for improvement SISs are a useful, if not indispensable tool for school administration. However, school staff should benefit much more from the possibilities of SISs to support their higher order management work. To achieve the latter we first of all need better SISs, systems that have been designed from the perspective of school management work. The results clearly highlight the impact of the implementation process, particularly the role played by training. This has provided an impetus for further research on how carefully designed training can help in promoting managerial SIS use. For example, Visscher and Branderhorst (2001) are currently involved in a quasi-experimental study, in which a school management training course has been designed to take account of the professional experience of school managers, their characteristics as adults, the factors motivating them for change, the ideal mix of instructional strategies, and the potential barriers for change. From this further research we hope to be able to refine our insights into how training can help in adding value to the management and functioning of schools.

REFERENCES

Visscher, A. J. (ed.) (1996) Information Technology in Educational Management. *International Journal of Educational Research*, 25(4), pp. 289-390.

Visscher, A. J. and Branderhorst, E. M. (2001) How should school managers be trained for managerial school information system-usage? In *Pathways to Institutional Improvement with Information Technology in Educational Management,* P. Nolan, A. C. W. Fung and M. Brown (eds.), Kluwer, London.

BIOGRAPHY

Alex Fung is an associate professor in the Department of Education Studies, and Director of the School Administration & Management System Training and Research Unit, at the Hong Kong Baptist University. He teaches and researches in ICT in Education, particularly in educational management with a focus on managing change.

Adrie Visscher is an associate professor in the Faculty of Educational Science and Technology at the University of Twente in the Netherlands. His research focuses on the organisational and information technological prerequisites for quality assurance in schools.

Debbi Smith is currently a researcher at the Centre for Research on Social Policy at Loughborough University working on IT in educational management and the impact of new technologies in schools.

Phil Wild is Head of the Department of Education at Loughborough University. He works on the evaluation and implementation of IT to support the administration and management of schools.

59

Knowledge Management and Resources Planning

Using Enterprise Portal in Higher Academic Institutions

Mohd Syazwan Abdullah and Zulkifli Mohamed Udin
University Utara Malaysia, School of Information Technology, 06010 Sintok, Kedah, Malaysa
pathma@webmail.uum.edu.my

Keywords: internet, intranet, administration, integration of ICT, world wide web/website

Abstract: Planning and managing resources in efficient and effective ways will contribute to the higher productivity of the organisation leading to a gain in competitiveness. With the emergence of the Internet technology, the manager can use it to plan and manage resources in their organisation. One technology that uses Internet, Intranet and Extranet capability is Portal technology. Portal technology was developed to enable users to easily access the database, work collaboratively and have the information at their fingertips to organise, personalise and publish what is needed. Furthermore, by applying Portal technology, it can improve the business processes where the information does not need to flow from one level to another. This paper introduces the concept of enterprise portal technology, with an example on how it works. This is compared with the traditional way of managing resources. Finally the integration of enterprise portal technology in knowledge management and resource planning is shown in detail together with a list of portal benefits.

1. INTRODUCTION

The enterprise portal is the concept of centralisation and categorisation of information in an organisation, which can be accessed through a web browser. The utilisation of ICT – internet, intranet and extranet in businesses – are an important factor in improving organisations' competitiveness in the networked economy. The objectives for implementing an enterprise portal in an organisation are to improve worker productivity, lower operational cost, save the time needed in acquiring data, report preparation and knowledge management (CTRC 2000). It is predicted that by 2001, nearly 50 percent of all businesses will be using enterprise portal (CTRC 2000). Enterprise portal will play an important role in an organisation by increasing the quality of decisions made, aiding an organisation's strategic planning process, managing worker's knowledge and enterprise level resources planning.

In achieving a world-class organisation standard, the ability to plan, acquire and manage the organisation's resources and knowledge are the critical success factors. Resource planning means the ability to manage all the resources in the organisation that will be used in producing products and services, including how the organisation can manage the resources for input, process and output life cycle. Capital, raw materials, human, machinery and equipment, procedures, are the resources for an organisation.

Knowledge management within an organisation is also crucial. According to Malhorta (1998, in McCampbell, Clare and Gitters 2000), 'Knowledge management caters to the critical issues of organisational adaptation, survival and competence in face of increasingly discontinuous environmental change. ...Essentially, it embodies organisational processes that seek synergistic combination of data and information processing capacity of information technologies, and the creative and innovative capacity of human beings'. There are two kind of knowledge an organisation needs to manage. One is explicit knowledge, information and data in the form of computer printouts and files, and written down. The other is tacit knowledge, 'know-tos' of knowledge that resides in workers of the organisation. "Knowledge management is an application of enterprise information portals and intranets that uses ICT tools to organise, manage and share diverse forms of business information created by individuals and teams in an organisation. These form of stored information help creates a knowledge base or organisational memory of strategic business information to be shared within the organisation" (O'Brian 2001).

Organisations can not only save the cost of production by utilising these knowledge and resources in an effective and efficient way, but also increase the quality of products or services. This will lead to an improvement in the organisations competitiveness.

2. ENTERPRISE PORTAL

'An enterprise portal is a web page from which work begins. It combines access to all significant information on the corporate network into a gateway. Enterprise portal facilitate shifting through the complex, previously overwhelming maze of networks and documents by bringing all relevant information together in a single place' (CTRC 2000).

Enterprise portal is the place where employees of one organisation can organise, personalise and publish information through web browser. This helps them reduce the amount of time spent on searching for data. It also enables the employees to work in a collaborative manner, sharing enterprise information needed in their project. Enterprise portal encompasses the concept of knowledge management, implementing and utilising the Business Intelligence concept and intranet applications. From the users' perspective, the added value of Portal technology comes from the information that it contains. Enterprise portal provides users with easy-access to internal and external information relevant to their role and job function.

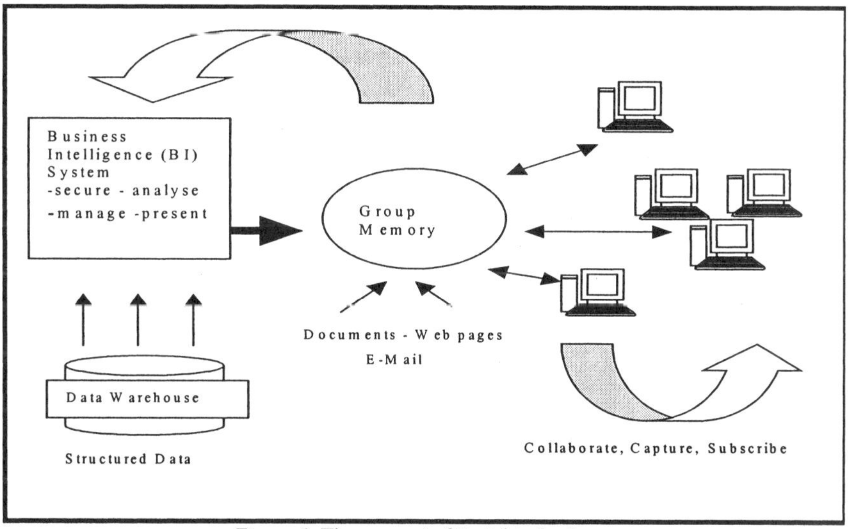

Figure 1. The concept of Portal technology

Portal technology also offers several other attractive capabilities such as tailored to individual executives needs, extract, filters, compress and track critical data, provide online status access, trend analysis, exception reporting and drill-down, user-friendly and requires little or no training to use and has the capability to present graphical, tabular and/or textual information. This concept can be viewed in Figure 1 as proposed by Intraspect (CTRC 2000)

3. MANAGING RESOURCES IN HIGHER ACADEMIC INSTITUTIONS

Planning and managing resources in higher academic institutions is a critical task for management. Knowledge resources such as academic, administrative and support staffs, and students, together with other physical and logical resources like lecture halls/theatres, tutorial/class rooms, class schedule, accommodations, and libraries are the elements to be managed effectively in order to produce high quality students and graduates.

In larger academic institutions such as universities, the top management or board of directors needs information about all the resources available to plan and develop strategies. In traditional practices, the information will only be sent to the top management from departments if there is any demand or request for information from them. Every time particular information is needed, the top management has to call people in a department to get it. This prolongs the time to acquire the information, as the department needs to search, compile and arrange the information before delivering it. The information has to be updated and validated regularly. Most information is available in the operational database; it will change from time to time. Thus the process of getting information to top management is time consuming.

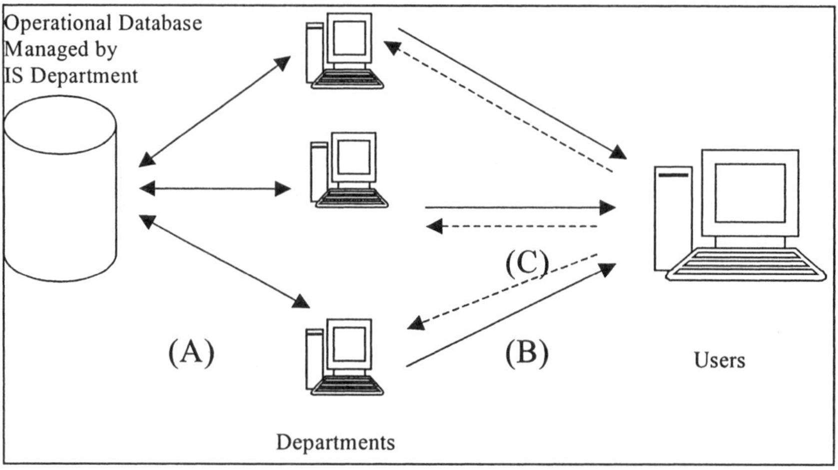

Figure 2. Gathering knowledge the traditional way:
(A) - data operator from respective departments
- key-in operational data
- search, compile & arrange information for top management
(B) - requested information send to the top management
(C) - request information from department

Another problem in this process is managing the knowledge. Information will be used by management to make decisions, chart out a course of action, and implement solutions to problems. Any outcome is actually considered as knowledge by the workers' for the institution. Most of this knowledge is kept as hardcopy reports or computer files in personal computers or notebooks. What happens when a particular member of the management team leaves the institution? Reports and computer files will leave the organisation too. It is also difficult to identify where this knowledge is kept in the organisation even if the person leaves it behind. Figure 2 shows the process of getting information in a traditional way.

The traditional way of performing the above tasks can be done in a better and efficient way by applying the portal technology.

4. APPLYING PORTAL TECHNOLOGY

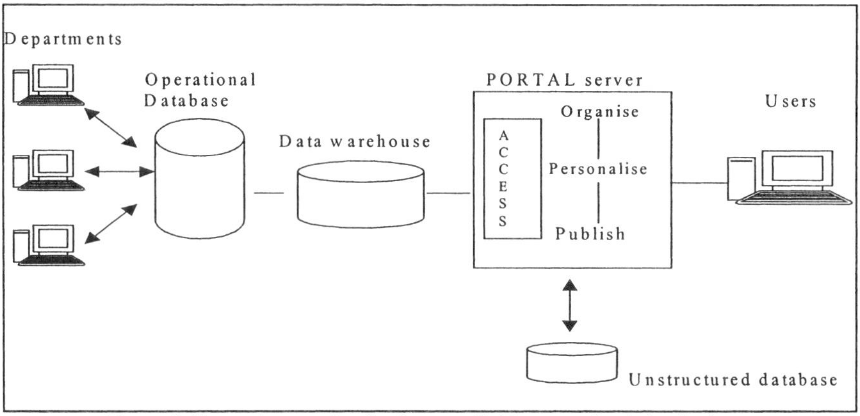

Figure 3. Enterprise portal technology applied in an academic institution

By applying Portal technology, the information needed by top management is at their fingertips through an attractive and easy-to-use interface. In higher academic institutions such as universities, planning and managing resources and knowledge are very complex processes. Adding to this complexity is that the usage of technology is not at an optimum level. By adopting of Portal technology managers can access information easily, in a short time period and presented in the attractive way. The outcome of the their decisions can be well documented, organised and stored for future usage.

Based on Figure 3, we can see how the information from departments regarding students profile, staff profile, inventories, library, financial and information about its customers, supplier, stakeholder and even competitor that are stored operationally, is pumped into data warehouse before it sent to the top level managers. Data warehouse is a database design for analytical task using data from multiple applications in the institution. It contains current and historical data to provide a historical perspective of information and is periodically updated. From the data warehouse, the Portal server will access all the data to organise, personalise and publish it according to users' needs. All information will be in the web page format and can be accessed through Internet or intranet. The user can access all the data by clicking the icon or the hypertext to link it to the required application.

In a university environment, top management can easily access the summarised information that can be used for decision-making process. For example, Vice-Chancellors may want to know about how many classes should be opened to accommodate students with a given number of lecturers and lecture halls. By using the Portal, they can get this information spontaneously without having to get it from the respective departments. This information can be viewed through textual or graphical or even in video format. They also can make a projection about how many classrooms should be made in the next five years based on the projection of students' numbers. The projection or decisions made can be kept in the any unstructured database attached to the portal server as a tool to manage knowledge.

By utilising Portal technology in resource planning, the business process of the organisation can be improved. The information that is needed by top management, need not to flow from one level to another in the traditional way. Users can directly access the information they need with some authorisation. Furthermore, Portal technology helps to reduce the number of intermediate steps in these business processes that will allow the task to access the information can be accomplished more independently and easily.

5. CONCLUSION

In the era of knowledge power, organisations that have knowledge and know how to use them effectively and efficiently will gain the competitive advantage and will lead the market. In order to have information or knowledge just right at the fingertip, Portal technology is one of the solutions. In this paper, we proposed a conceptual framework that is based on the generic Enterprise Portal framework that produced by CTRC. As discussed earlier there are many benefit of this technology to user.

Table 1. Summary of Enterprise Portal Benefits

Portal Benefits	Description
Aggregation of information sources	Combines ➢ Personalised interfaces ➢ All pertinent corporate information ➢ Access to news and web information ➢ E-commerce potential
Business intelligence	➢ Provides ideal interface for application ➢ Real-time information and data from sources

	➢ Basic component of all enterprise portals
Real-time visibility	➢ Leverages corporate information assets ➢ Gives effortless visibility of corporate sources
Simplified complexity	➢ Evaluates and presents new product data ➢ Minimise search for pertinent information ➢ Organise existing information sources
Competitive advantage	➢ Combines and integrates pertinent information ➢ Enhance corporate work performance ➢ Improves access to existing information
Return on investment	➢ Offers advantages of off-the-shelf solutions ➢ Increases choice of portal software products ➢ Provides specialised portal products opportunities
Cost reductions	Takes advantage of ➢ Operating resources saving potential ➢ Supply chain economies of scale
Potential to generate revenue	➢ Offers virtual corporation operations potential ➢ Creates new revenue sources ➢ Tests new products ➢ Establishes ready management system for new operations
Sharing corporate resources	Provides ➢ Universal access to corporate information ➢ Facility for control and organisation ➢ Agglomerated information for creating knowledge
Increased productivity	➢ Supplies individual tools for each employee ➢ Reduce unproductive search time ➢ Accelerates product/service cycle times
Enhance decision-making process	➢ Encourages more decisive employee behavior ➢ Enables faster and consistent communications ➢ Assists in selling and customer service decisions
Enhance effectiveness	➢ Provides access to new information sources ➢ Focuses in information on specific tasks ➢ Develops more knowledgeable and effective employee
Lower cost of information	➢ Automates character searching ➢ Provides significant advantage over private solution ➢ Lowers cost of information delivery
Organised and searchable corporate information	➢ Affords common view of corporate information ➢ Impacts upon new employee integration ➢ Encourages consistent view of enterprise worldwide ➢ Assists in collaboration processes
Employee collaboration	➢ Promotes collaborative employee environment ➢ Presents common objectives clearly ➢ Alleviates corporate fragmentation issues
Advertising advantage	➢ Eliminates unwanted online advertising ➢ Reduces employee distractions ➢ Allows corporate control of online advertising ➢ Creates potential for advertising revenues

The benefits are users can have more timely and accurate information; greater access to timely data, more concise and relevant information, new or additional information, better knowledge management within the organisation, faster access to information and reduced paper costs. Portal technology also can improve users job performance abilities and productivity. Furthermore it can give greater support for users specifically top-level manager to plan and manage their resources and knowledge in decision-making process.

Finally, though this technology can contribute the effective way in managing resources through the information available, it is also important that some issues related to humans should be considered, such privacy, culture, and managing change. Based on our proposed conceptual framework, it is believed that the planning and managing of resources and knowledge in an higher academic institutions can be done more effective and efficient. This will contribute to higher productivity in the organisation.

REFERENCES

Armistead, C. (1999) Knowledge management and process performance. *Journal of Knowledge Management,* 3 (2), pp. 143-154.

Chan, S. L. (2000) Information technology in business processes. *Business Process Management Journal,* 6 (3), pp. 224-237.

Chung, S. H and Snyder, C. A. (2000) ERP adoption: a technological evolution approach. *International Journal of Agile Management Systems,* 2.

CTRC (Computer Technology Research Corporation) (2000) *Implementing Enterprise Portal: Integration Strategies for Intranet, Extranet and Internet.*

McCampbell, A. S., Clare, L. M. and Gitters, S. H. (2000) Knowledge Management: The new Challenges for the 21st Century. *Journal of Knowledge Management,* 3 (3), pp. 172-179.

O'Brian, J. A. (2001) *Introduction to Information Systems: Essentials for the International Internetworked E-Business Enterprise.* 10th ed., McGraw-Hill, New York

BIBLIOGRAPHY

Mohd Syazwan Abdullah @ Pathmanathan is a faculty member of the School of Information Technology at Universiti Utara Malaysia. His area of research interest is in knowledge management in academic institution and legal issues of information technology in the knowledge economy.

Zulkifli Mohamed Udin is a faculty member of the School of Information Technology at Universiti Utara Malaysia. His area of research interest is in supply chain management, knowledge management and computer support collaborative work.

60

Computer-supported Workplace Learning

Bente Elkjaer
Department of Informatics, Copenhagen Business School, Howitzvej 60, DK-2000 Frederiksberg, Denmark
elkjaer@cbs.dk

Keywords: in-service training, lifelong learning education, vocational education

Abstract: This paper deals with the following conceptual issues: What is workplace or organisational learning? What is learning? What is computer-supported learning? And what is computer-supported organisational learning? The grounds for dealing with these issues are an empirical study on the organisation of IT-supported workplace learning. This study shows that there are many ways of organising IT-supported education in organisations ranging from IT-training to training that results in different kinds of certificates to highly specialised university degrees via distance learning. In conclusion, the paper suggests that there is a need to develop new models for computer-supported workplace learning based on the concrete organisational work practices and the information systems employed by the organisation.

1. INTRODUCTION

Results of surveys show a gradual increase in the use of information technology (IT) for educational purposes in Danish private enterprises (IFKA 1996-2000). Thus, in 1995 a third (32%) of Danish enterprises applied IT for educational purposes, while the number in 1999 included more than half the enterprises (55%). The surveys were ordered by the Centre for Technology-Supported Education (CTU), a Danish organisation to further computer-supported education. For five years, CTU employed a consulting firm, Institute for Konjunktur-Analyse (IFKA), to make the surveys. The objectives were to find out how many enterprises applied IT for educational purposes, why and for what specific purposes. The surveys were based upon 600 telephone interviews with the persons in charge of education and training in a representative sample of Danish private enterprises.

Private Danish enterprises apply IT for educational purposes to enhance the general level of IT competencies, to save time and money and to improve flexibility in time and space regarding education and competence development. Thus, computer-supported education has mainly focused on IT itself, and in 1999 more than half the enterprises used their computer-supported education on PC driver's licenses and other computer training courses. The surveys do not indicate how the enterprises *organise* their computer-supported education and what sort of *workplace learning* computer-supported workplace education provides.

The lack of information about the organisation of computer-supported workplace education and the actual learning outcome was the reason why I contacted CTU and proposed a collaborative project on computer-supported workplace learning. The method implied that IFKA should ask some of the enterprises that in 1999 applied IT for educational purposes to participate in an interview conducted by me. The enterprises should have less than 100 employees and be situated in Zealand or in the Greater Copenhagen area. Apparently, this was not an easy delimitation as I had enterprises with several thousands employees on my list.

In this paper, I report on the study making tentative conclusions and suggesting further research based on the study itself, but also on the theoretical landscape of the domain, computer-supported workplace learning. As the domain has yet to be defined, I include theories on the workplace as a context for learning in addition to general theories on learning, computer-supported learning and computer-supported organisational learning. In conclusion, I suggest that more studies need to be made on workplaces where computer-supported workplace learning is viewed in light of the overall learning activities in an organisation, including the information systems applied to share knowledge. The latter is included to ensure that unintentional learning in workplaces is considered and viewed as part of the overall organisational learning.

2. RESEARCH AND RESULTS

79 enterprises met the criteria established by me, but only 18 wanted to participate in the study (Elkjær and Olsen 2001a, Elkjær and Olsen 2001b). The reason why only about 25% of the contacted enterprises wanted to participate is unclear, but probably Danish enterprises get a great many calls asking them to participate in different surveys, etc. I contacted the persons in

charge of education and training in the enterprises – the same persons that IFKA had contacted previously. In 3 out of the 18 enterprises, I was already told on the phone that they did not apply IT for educational purposes (maybe because I used the term "computer-supported learning" rather than "application of IT for educational purposes"). In another enterprise, the contact person had changed to another job, and finally I included one large enterprise that was not part of the original sample. All in all, I interviewed 15 people in 15 enterprises. In the interviews, I asked them about the organisation and the content of their computer-supported workplace education. I also asked them to assess the benefits and problems related to learning in connection with computer-supported education in the workplace.

Out of the 15 interviewed enterprises, 7 did not apply computers for *intentional* educational activities. The other half of the enterprises (8) had either organised the education as individual home-based learning, with or without an on-line tutor or teacher, or as work-based learning. The work-based computer-supported education was either organised as individual learning in a separate room, learning from the employees' own work-stations or teaching in groups or classes with live or on-line access to a teacher and peers.

On the one hand, the content of the computer-supported education aimed at providing identical training for the great majority. For example, training resulting in a PC driver's license and other kinds of certificates. The latter was the case in large industries (and groups) with many specific quality standards, e.g. enterprises that were part of a group or industry such as the pharmaceutical industry, in which many conventions in research and production must be followed according to agreement. These enterprises are large enough or may co-operate within their industry to develop computer-supported educational programs, which, in turn, enable many employees to obtain specific certificates through the use of jointly developed CD-ROMs or Internet-based Computer-Based Training (CBT). On the other hand, the Internet provides a huge market for specialist education in demand by enterprises that survive on their competitiveness to be innovative. Such enterprises can e.g. be found within tele-communication. These two extremes within computer-supported education may exist within the same enterprise, but they have different employees as target groups. Thus, enterprises working in very competitive environments see the Internet as a huge market place where their demand for highly specialised competencies can be met and where they can procure highly qualified education for their professionals. In other words, computer-supported education is a way in which to provide both certificates for the great majority and specialised education for the few.

There was a certain apprehension about whether learning benefits could be derived from applying computer-supported education in introductory teaching. It was, for example, difficult to learn programs (e.g. the modules in the PC driver's license) that the learner had never used before. This was the reason why computer-supported education was not used in introductory education within for example quality. Another problematic aspect of computer-supported education was the lack of personal contact to a teacher or tutor. Individually based computer-supported education without contact to a teacher or co-learners require a great deal of self-discipline regardless of whether the training takes place at home or in the office. An advantage in computer-supported education was the 'private' learning-room around the computer. It appeared to have a beneficial effect on employees who were not so school-minded as it allowed them to operate in a room of learning without being subject to (negative) judgments. This assessment was based on class-room teaching with access to a teacher.

On the one hand, organising computer-supported education as individual learning seems to be faced with problems of a motivational nature. On the other hand, the individual learning space around the computer seems to be beneficial in class-room organised computer-supported education. In this setting, the learner can ask a teacher without being subject to the social sanctions of a public learning space. The content of the computer-supported education was also mixed. It comprised both mass-produced and modulated CD-ROMs or Internet-based CBTs, including highly specialised education programs from the market selling teaching-programs.

The study was designed to provide an overview of the different ways in which computer-supported workplace education can be organised and to point out the benefits and problems in connection with such education. I believe, however, that it is necessary to adopt a broader perspective to see computer-supported workplace learning in the light of its venue, the workplace, and its tools, the organisational information systems. This is the background for including the following conceptual issue, the workplace as a context for learning, in addition to learning theories and theories of computer-supported learning and computer-supported organisational learning.

3. THE WORKPLACE AS A VENUE FOR LEARNING

In 1988, Zuboff coined the phrase "learning as the new form of labour" (Zuboff 1988, p. 395) based on knowledge as a prime asset in enterprises that employ IT beyond automation. Behind Zuboff's phrase is the contention that highly skilled computerised workplaces will require continuous organisational learning (see also Elkjaer 2000). Today, organisational learning is a notion that is widely accepted although there is no agreement on its meaning, which depends on the understanding of learning and organisational life and changes (Argyris and Schön 1996, Easterby-Smith 1997). Likewise, the term "workplace learning" is making its way into the domain of learning in organisations (Boud and Garrick 1999). An understanding of workplace or organisational learning (terms that I use indiscriminately) involves recognition of its complexities, its competing interests and the personal, political and institutional influences that affect it. In addition, it involves recognition of workplace or organisational learning as an issue between, on the one hand, organisation and management studies, and, on the other, educational studies and adult education (see also Tight 2000). This means that workplace learning draws upon very different academic fields and practical solutions.

A definition of workplace or organisational learning might be to view the workplace or organisation as a specific context. The workplace as a context sets some conditions for workplace learning. Furthermore, workplace learning is always directly or indirectly connected to the workplace practices, including the employees and the management who perform the work. Therefore, the activities around which learning unfolds are either an integral part of the work practices, of which the daily work consists, or they involve teaching, instruction or training that point towards these practices. In other words, workplace learning may be unintentional processes of learning in connection with work performance, but it may also be formally organised activities with explicit intentions to produce learning outcome. Following the attempt to define the context of computer-supported workplace learning, the next issue is to look at what learning is and what computer-supported learning may be as well as what it is.

4. COMPUTER-SUPPORTED LEARNING

The theoretical landscape of computer-supported learning reflects the general development of the dominant learning theories during the 20th century. It may be described as a development from behaviourism focusing on the demands of an environment with fixed structures to cognitivism focusing on an organism's mental structures as fixed. The latter approach involves learning to solve problems by acquiring good reasoning methods through mental representations. The most recent paradigm within learning is a situated learning perspective or a transactional concept of learning that actually dates back to the work of John Dewey (1859-1952) (Bredo 1997,

Dewey 1916, c.1966). In a transactional notion of learning, there are no fixed structures, and, thus, no boundary between organism and environment. Both organism and environment play a functional part in an activity. Thus, learning implies the creation of environments that can stimulate people to think and act 'mindfully' to solve relevant problems by way of experimenting. The focus of transactional learning comprises the whole life including feelings and emotions as opposed to the sole focus on cognition or behaviour. Transactional learning views learning as a social activity that takes place in communities, which implies that learning is relational and collaborative.

This development of learning theories can also be found in Koschman's (1996) overview of the paradigmatic development of computer-supported learning. Koschman identifies three past paradigms and one future paradigm for the instructional use of IT. The past paradigms are termed Computer-Assisted Instruction (CAI), Intelligent Tutoring Systems (ITSs), and Logo-as-Latin Paradigm. Computer Supported Collaborative Learning, CSCL, may be the future paradigm for computer-supported learning. In the CAI paradigm, learning is viewed as the acquisition of a body of knowledge. The teacher's role is to find efficient ways of sharing knowledge and determine whether students have learned what they were taught. Instruction is a process of transmission or delivery. The strategy of CAI applications is to identify a specific set of learning goals, decompose the goals into a set of simpler component tasks and, finally, develop a sequence of activities designed to eventually achieve the original learning objectives. Although CAI is the oldest paradigm for computer application in education, it is by no means abandoned. The PC driver's license is an example of a CAI application.

The next paradigm, Intelligent Tutoring Systems (ITSs), was a direct result of an immigration of workers from the field of Artificial Intelligence (AI) into the educational area. The ITSs paradigm is based upon the Information Processing Theory in which problem solving is viewed as a process defining the representation of a problem space consisting of an initial state, a goal state, and a set of operations enabling movement from one state to another. Learning, in this light, is the process by which the problem solver acquires a proper representation of a problem space. Instruction consists of activities designed to facilitate the learner's acquisition of such a representation. The role of technology in the process is really not very different from the role it plays in the CAI paradigm. The differences are more in degree than in kind. In both cases, the designed application serves instruction by posing problems and providing the learner with feed-back. The difference is that ITSs aspire to employ a more interactive approach involving a more complex set of skills.

The Logo-as-Latin paradigm originates in an epistemological perspective that looks at knowledge as acquired through a process of subjective construction on the part of the experiencing organism. This view of learning is referred to as constructivism and proposes that learning occurs through personal inquiry and discovery. Seymour Papert (1980), who argues that the activity of programming computers can play an important role in learning, provides an example of constructivism in computer-supported education. The construction of computer programs is particularly interesting in terms of learning because they can be executed. The assumption is that by engaging in the activities of programming, the learner acquires cognitive benefits that extend beyond simply learning to code in a particular language. A great deal of research within this paradigm involves learning to program in Logo, a powerful language designed in the mid-1960's for young children. Koschman has termed the paradigm the Logo-as-Latin Paradigm because it focuses on learning how to program in the service of more general educational objectives.

The central issue in constructivist research is cognitive self-organisation. It views the mind as a phenomenon residing within the head of the individual. CSCL is founded upon social constructivism that regards knowledge construction as an essentially social process in which learning is viewed as a process of entering into a community of practice (Lave and Wenger 1991). As an instructional technology, CSCL introduces a shift in reference leading to a foregrounding of the social and cultural context as the object of study. The model of instruction involved in CSCL is collaborative learning, i.e. learners are engaged in joint processes of learning. Technological applications to support collaborative learning are manifold and include all kinds of connecting technologies such as network, mediational and communication tools, tools for storage and for the support of co-operative knowledge construction.

When computer-supported learning enters the organisational world and becomes computer-supported organisational learning, it is often related to information processing and decision-making and as such becomes a matter of the organisational flow of information and knowledge. In literature on computer-supported organisational learning, learning tends to be viewed as comprising problem-solving, knowledge acquisition (or construction), distribution and application (Goodman and Darr 1998, Pentland, 1995). Computer-supported systems aimed to enhance organisational learning share features with traditional e-mail systems as e.g. the ability to bridge time and space. But they also differ by having a memory function and search facilities. The organisational memory is important in working with computer-supported organisational learning. It includes a joint understanding of an organisation's identity, the mental models that represent the organisational theories-in-use in addition to the cognitive and behavioural routines (Robey et al. 2000).

Using Koschman's paradigms, computer-supported organisational learning is grounded in the paradigm of ITSs and the Information Processing Theory. Computer-supported organisational learning seems to draw on learning as a process that constructs the representation of a problem space to solve organisational problems efficiently and to contribute to the organisational memory. It involves learning that relies on the organisational members' ability to apply replicable reasoning methods. In working with computer-supported organisational learning, the workplace is seldom viewed as a conflictual political scene. More often, the workplace is viewed as a fairly abstract entity consisting of streams of information and knowledge as well as mental representations in the minds of the organisational members.

5. FURTHER RESEARCH

I believe there is a need to develop new models for computer-supported workplace learning based on the concrete organisational work practices and the information systems applied in an organisation. This will imply a study of computer-supported workplace learning that is not based on an understanding of organisations as flows of information and knowledge, but on organisational members' use of the information systems at hand for their various needs. I also believe that to assess the benefits of computer-supported education, it is necessary to view the learning as part of the whole organisational learning environment and not as isolated attempts to acquire specific skills and knowledge. This means that there is a need to study organisations as cases for workplace learning where computer-supported learning is seen as part of the overall learning activities, but also as part of the IT application as such in organisations. The latter includes the unintentional learning that is part of information sharing while working in and on the organisational work practices.

REFERENCES

Argyris, C. and Schön, D. A. (1996) *Organizational Learning II. Theory, Method, and Practice*. Addison-Wesley Publishing Company, Reading.

Boud, D. and Garrick, J. (eds.) (1999) *Understanding Learning at Work*. Routledge, London.

Bredo, E. (1997) The Social Construction of Learning. In *Handbook of Academic Learning. Construction of Knowledge*, G. P. Phye (ed.), San Diego, Academic Press, pp. 3-43.

Dewey, J. (1916, c. 1966) *Democracy and Education. An Introduction to the Philosophy of Education*. The Free Press, New York.

Easterby-Smith, M. (1997) Disciplines of Organizational Learning: Contributions and Critiques. *Human Relations*, 50 (9), pp. 1085-1113.

Elkjaer, B. (2000) Learning and getting to know: the case of knowledge workers. *Human Resource Development International*, 3 (3), pp. 343-359.

Elkjær, B. and Olsen, M. (2001a) *Virksomheders anvendelse af IT-støttet uddannelse – muligheder og problemer (Enterprises' application of IT-supported education – possibilities and constraints)*. Department of Informatics, Copenhagen Business School and Learning Lab Denmark. [http://www.ctu.dk/ctu/ctuwebsi.nsf/2c81d99d07e66774c12565e6003d89c4/fbe6101ecdad5e75c12569de003cf3ab!OpenDocument].

Elkjær, B. and Olsen, M. (2001b) *Virksomheders anvendelse af IT-støttet uddannelse – muligheder og problemer. Kommenteret bibliografi*. Department of Informatics, Copenhagen Business School and Learning Lab Denmark. The bibliography (in Danish) can be downloaded here: [http://www.ctu.dk/ctu/ctuwebsi.nsf/2c81d99d07e66774c12565e6003d89c4/7038d1dced8ff473c12569ec003b56a3/$FILE/Bibliografi.pdf].

Goodman, P. S. and Darr, E. D. (1998) Computer-aided Systems and Communities: Mechanisms for Organizational Learning in Distributed Environment. *MIS Quarterly*, 22 (4), pp. 417-440.

IFKA (1996, 1997, 1998, 1999 and 2000) *Informationsteknologi til uddannelse i private virksomheder (Information technology for educational purposes in private enterprises)*. [The reports can be found at CTU's home page: www.ctu.dk].

Koschman, T. (1996) Paradigm Shifts and Instructional Technology: An Introduction. In *CSCL: Theory and Practice of an Emerging Paradigm*, T. Koschmann (ed.) Lawrence Erlbaum Associates, Mahwah, NJ, pp. 1-23.

Lave, J. and Wenger, E. (1991) *Situated Learning. Legitimate Peripheral Participation*. Cambridge University Press, Cambridge.

Papert, S. (1980) *Mindstorms*. Basic Books, New York.

Pentland, B. T. (1995) Information Systems and Organizational Learning: The social epistemology of organizational knowledge systems. *Accounting, Management and Information Technology*, 5 (1), pp. 1-21.

Robey, D., Boudreau, M.-C. and Rose, G. M. (2000) Information Technology and Organizational Learning: A Review and Assessment of Research. *Accounting, Management and Information Technologies*, 10 (2), pp. 125-155.

Tight, M. (2000) Critical Perspectives on Management Learning. A View from Adult/Continuing/Lifelong Education. *Management Learning*, 31 (1), pp. 103-119.

Zuboff, S. (1988) *In The Age of the Smart Machine. The Future of Work and Power*. Heinemann, New York.

BIOGRAPHY

Bente Elkjaer is an associate professor and the current Head of Department in the Department of Informatics at the Copenhagen Business School. She takes a special interest in computer-supported workplace learning from the perspective of both workplaces, and designers and suppliers of e-learning.

61

Developing Courseware for Higher Education
Reflections on the Role of Evaluation

Wendy Doube[1], David Kennedy[2] and Juhani Tuovinen[2]
[1]Faculty of Information Technology / [2]Centre for Learning and Teaching Support, Monash University, Churchill, VIC 3842, Australia
Wendy.Doubé@infotech.monash.edu.au

Keywords: computer assisted instruction, courseware, evaluation, higher education, quality

Abstract: In CFL development, relationships can be established between development team organisational maturity, selection of an iterative development methodology, and effective use of evaluation in a pedagogical as well as a technological domain, as guides to successful project outcomes. A large, higher education multimedia CFL product was developed as two projects (two years apart) by multidisciplinary teams. The first project was developed using a linear-sequential methodology. Significant technical evaluation took place but only minimal pedagogical evaluation was undertaken, mainly after alpha testing. The second project used an iterative approach to development and incorporated formative pedagogical evaluation as part of the development methodology. Resource wastage was considerably reduced and student learning requirements were better realised.

1. INTRODUCTION

The development of academic courses that use computer-based technologies in higher education has increased markedly in recent times. The use of computer-facilitated learning (CFL), particularly the development of web-based courses, is increasing as the nature of higher education itself is changing (Australian Vice Chancellors' Committee 1996). The process of developing CFL courseware, web-based courses and computer-mediated communication (CMC) has now become an institutional point of focus rather than the domain of innovators and enthusiasts.

As CFL has moved from the fringes of higher education to being a core component of course materials, issues of software quality, student learning outcomes and integration of CFL modules within the entire curriculum, have become paramount (McNaught et al. 2000).

1.1 Evaluation in higher education

In higher education, despite summative and formative evaluation procedures being mandated as desired practice, rarely does evaluation take place during the materials development phase. The evaluation process usually concentrates on affective issues of learning – the appropriateness of teaching materials, feedback provided by the teacher, and access to resources. Formative evaluation (e.g. focus groups, peer assessment) of traditional learning activities (e.g. lecture, laboratory, class) is rarely undertaken. Only after course delivery, are assignment and exam grade distributions analysed, and student and/or peer feedback examined, so that subsequent course offerings can be amended and fine-tuned.

2. QUALITY SOFTWARE

In the IEEE Glossary of Software Engineering Terminology, software quality is defined as 'the degree to which a system, component or process meets customer or user needs or expectations'. In actual practice, software quality means different things to different stakeholders in a software development project. The International Standards Organisation has defined characteristics of quality software in ISO9126. Project documentation in the form of a Software Quality Assurance Plan describes processes for assessing the quality of the software being developed, (e.g. inspections, walkthroughs, and code evaluations). ISO has also produced standards that address not only the quality of a product but also the quality of the processes in the development process. The Capability Maturity Model (CMM) (Humphrey 1995) is one of several models which prescribe a number of steps to continuously improve software development processes.

3. QUALITY HIGHER EDUCATION SOFTWARE

3.1 A pedagogical perspective

Strong support for the use of a constructivist perspective can be found in the literature of CFL development (Duffy and Jonassen 1991, Reeves 1997). These perspectives require that students actively interact with materials in ways that require reflection. They need to make decisions in their work which clearly reveal their own knowledge constructions. However constructivism, as an underlying pedagogy for developing courseware has been seen as problematic (cf. Merrill 1991, Anderson, Reder and Simon1997). Dills and Romiszowski (1997) suggest that these divisions are not useful in courseware development, and regardless of the pedagogical paradigm, evaluation remains a key issue.

3.2 A development perspective

> "Originally....software engineering was approached as a linear activity in which a series of sequential steps were applied in order to solve problems. Yet, linear approaches to software development run counter to the way in which most systems are actually built. In reality, complex systems evolve iteratively, even incrementally. It is for this reason that a large segment of the software engineering community is moving towards evolutionary models of software development." (Pressman 1997, p. 832)

> "In an ideal project most participants would be software engineers." (Johnson 1997).

These statements represent opposing views of software development. While Johnson's assertion may be perceived as naïve, it is not uncommon amongst software developers and can impact on CFL quality.

3.2.1 Identifying users and their needs

In order to meet software quality criteria, users and their needs should be defined. When the software to be developed is CFL, the wide range of possible pedagogical approaches, the lack of teacher autonomy, technical constraints and the differing requirements of stakeholders, make the definition of user needs and expectations an extremely problematic process.

Users of the final product can fall into several classifications, each with a separate set of needs to be considered. Students with more diverse backgrounds, interests and motivation now undertake tertiary studies (Australian Vice Chancellors' Committee 1996, Bates 1997, Laurillard and Margetson 1997). Not only should the variety of learning styles displayed by students be considered, but also a variety of teaching styles. But teaching style can be very personal, and the investment cannot usually be justified unless the teacher's peers are comfortable using the product. If the product is sufficiently generic, peers and students outside the institution may wish to use it and may require additional consideration.

If we assume that the fundamental user need in CFL is learning, then specifying user needs is equivalent to specifying learning outcomes, course content, and processes which will assist students to engage effectively with the content. According to a constructivist perspective, an optimum specification will describe processes in which students will interact with the content in such a way that they will be able to construct their own meaning from it, assisted by dialogue closely resembling their face-to-face communication with a teacher.

However, developing CFL may be a new experience for the teacher who may also be ignorant of the most suitable pedagogical approach. The teacher may be unable to even visualise the final product. In this case, the specification documentation may be inadequate, and also could be subject to misinterpretation by developers. Many factors in the CFL development process, without pedagogical quality assurance, can dilute that vital teacher-student communication. Glossy, robust materials that meet software quality criteria, may be the result, but whether or not they promote learning, may be a moot point.

In order to focus on student needs and guarantee software quality criteria, appropriate formative evaluation procedures should be incorporated into the courseware specification process.

3.2.2 Selecting a model of software engineering for CFL

Most models of software engineering (SE) include similar stages, each producing similar outputs. The major differences between models lie in the order and emphasis placed on each stage, which in turn affects the iterative processes within the SE life cycle. Table 1 summarises five major SE models and some of their benefits in courseware development.

Table 1. Summary of software engineering models and their application to courseware

SE model	Benefits for courseware development
Linear-sequential (waterfall)	Strong emphasis in developing documentation which provides a point of reference and a deliverable for each stage. Requirements are documented early in the life cycle leaving developers to produce systems efficiently without interruption

SE model	Benefits for courseware development
Incremental	Educational designers and teachers gain realistic expectations of technical constraints
	Decreases risk of unexpected (unwanted) development outcomes.
Spiral	The specification negotiation processes of the Win Win model may be useful in large projects with many defined stakeholders.
Prototyping	Teachers do not need to specify all of the courseware requirements prior to commencement of the programming.
Evolutionary Throwaway	Specific interactions in the CFL have the opportunity of student and peer evaluation.
	Iterative design procedures can result in a better quality product
Evolutionary	Teachers can specify gradually as they become better acquainted with the system.
Rapid Application Development (RAD)	Can take advantage of the academic year by using non-teaching weeks for workshops.
	Includes the advantages of prototyping.
	Supports team understanding of the multiple perspectives held by different stakeholders.
Object-oriented	As per incremental development.

3.3 Testing and the software life cycle

> "The essential feature in successful life-cycle models is quantitative forms of feedback, which make it possible for a software process to evolve, to adapt to changing environments and technologies, and to achieve the optimising level in the CMM." (Peters and Pedrycz 2000)

Verification and validation techniques are available for each stage of the lifecycle. Testing activities are planned and documented and IEEE standards can be followed in detail. Testing in the early stages has been shown to be of the greatest benefit to a project.

One of the key features of the linear-sequential model is the provision for feedback from one stage to the previous one. In practice, this is difficult to achieve. In iterative life-cycles, feedback from testing can continue to improve a stage or set of stages until they are working well enough for the next stage to proceed.

3.4 Pedagogical evaluation

Production of traditional print-based learning materials usually follows a linear path, from teacher/author, to production, to the student, with iterations involving editing and proof-reading generally confined to the initial development process. In contrast, the development of educationally effective CFL requires a wider range of specialist skills imparted by multi-disciplinary teams including content experts, educational designers, programmers and graphic artists (Fraser 1997). A good team dynamic with congruence of understanding of the design and development process, and good communication channels, can result in higher quality outcomes.

Other stakeholders may be even further removed from the actual teaching process. The development team may be reporting to a manager, who in turn must justify expenditure to funding bodies, either internal or external to the institution. In large teams, communication lines lengthen and the fundamental student-teacher relationship can be diluted. Responsibility for evaluation may no longer rest with the teacher. In practice, evaluation of the courseware may be neglected, often leading to less than optimal courseware development (Alexander, McKenzie and Geissinger 1998). The teacher responsible for developing the materials may move to other courses and never see the materials in use. The normal refinement processes which take place during and after course delivery may never happen.

Hedberg and Alexander (1994) have developed a model for formative and summative evaluation that addresses interface issues and student learning outcomes in the development of CFL. They argue that early formative evaluation with the target group will alleviate many potential design problems. Formative evaluation can be fundamental in CFL development if a quality product is to be delivered (Burkhardt 1992). Moonen and Schoenmaker (1992) also state that in higher education the interaction of the user with the problem is often very difficult to specify precisely, and an early prototype 'almost always elicits comments and suggestions for alterations'.

4. DRAWING ON EXPERIENCE

4.1 The first project

Two university departments – the materials development centre and the Faculty of Information Technology – received funding to develop CD-ROM based multimedia learning modules for five introductory IT subjects. An experienced multimedia project manager was employed by the materials development centre. He assembled a development team and implemented a range of formal processes within a linear-sequential development methodology. One module was produced first, and used as an example for the others, which were developed in parallel. Each module was developed in a linear-sequential life-cycle. One educational designer conducted initial student evaluations, three other educational designers worked with content experts on the modules, and another prepared an evaluation plan to be implemented during alpha testing. The development team worked happily together in one laboratory. Content experts and educational designers regularly consulted with the team in the laboratory in an ad-hoc manner. Five modules were produced and proved popular with students. The project was cited as an example of best practice by the funding body.

However, much of the first module had to be completely redesigned and redeveloped. Two entire sub-modules were designed but never developed, while a fourth sub-module was discarded after substantial development because it failed to meet content expert expectations. After release, multiple content errors were discovered in a fifth module.

Results of the first evaluation were not translated into the design of the modules although they did influence the overall look and feel of the product. The final evaluation was never performed because of schedule over-run. After release, some ad-hoc evaluations were performed by teachers but never documented or used to improve the product.

The developers' perspective of the first product varied markedly from that of the other stakeholders. They viewed the modules that were developed with minimal academic and educational designer intervention as the most successful, even though these were the modules which required the most alteration after development or were discarded.

4.2 The second project

Two years after the first grant, a second project received funding to extend the original product. A content expert (first author) who had been involved with three of the original five modules was appointed as academic project leader. Two educational designers, new to the project, worked on the project, one to supervise design, the other evaluation. By now, the original technical development team was busy with other projects and had reached a control and co-ordination level of maturity. It could no longer function effectively with the constant interruptions of unscheduled visitors and implemented firmer standards and controls, including time logs, in order to manage multiple projects simultaneously.

The academic project leader felt that the problems with the first module of the first project were the result of the content expert being divorced from the development process between design and delivery. She had therefore work-shopped with the development team throughout the life cycle of other modules. In the second project it was felt that the development team was not equipped to deal with a prototyping methodology, and a single additional iteration was introduced into the development life cycle. A 'broad design' stage, which produced user interfaces and non-standard interactions to assist content experts define their needs, preceded a 'detailed design stage' from which the final product would result.

The educational designers drew up an evaluation plan which was integrated into the development methodology. Task analysis, and overall course perspectives were obtained from students before the project started and fed into the broad design. Peers and students evaluated storyboards, the implementations of first the broad and then the detailed design which was edited and then released. On-going evaluation was planned post-release.

In the second project, all designed modules were fully developed. Academics were more satisfied with the application of the pedagogical design perspective in the resultant specifications. However, the development team's new procedures assumed linear-sequential development and required initial detailed user specifications to remain largely static throughout the life cycle. Formal communication procedures impeded the clarification resulting from informal contact between technical developers and other team members during the broad design stage. Some conflict was inevitable. In compensation, weekly multidisciplinary workshops were scheduled for the detailed design.

4.3 Technical vs. learning evaluation

Both project teams included experienced educational designers, well versed in evaluating the effect of materials on *learning*. They also included academics, used to continually refining their materials in response to qualitative and quantitative student feedback.

However, in the first project, when new to CFL, academics and educational designers had less influence on evaluation processes:

- following the traditional waterfall model of software development, learning evaluation was scheduled after development, during software testing
- the focus of this evaluation became software validation and verification, rather than learning.
- the impact of the user interface on learning was still being explored. Issues such as the impact of spatial arrangements and navigation on learning were addressed in the only educational design evaluation actually executed
- any post-development educational design changes resulting from evaluation would have been too costly to implement. In any case, by that time, all project funds were spent.
- any post-development evaluation would only impact on future products and therefore was perceived as a reduced priority. After release of the

product, academics responsible for it had moved on. Often evaluation didn't take place at all.

In summary, we could infer that in the first project, evaluation was driven by more *technological* rather than learning requirements. The scant pedagogical evaluation concentrated on interface and navigation issues.

In the second project:

- students and academics had become more familiar with the CFL interfaces which became less of an evaluation priority
- content experts and educational designers were more involved in determining the development process which promoted the evaluation of learning
- the value of iterative software development methodologies for CFL was now apparent. These methodologies created more opportunities for evaluation during the lifecycle
- storyboarding and scripting techniques had become sophisticated enough to be able to provide a good indication of the final product. Some evaluation was able to take place before development

In summary, we could infer that as CFL became more widespread, and as the project team gained a greater understanding of courseware development processes, evaluation concentrated more on *learning* and less on technological issues.

5. CONCLUSION

The experience of these two large CFL development projects highlighted the importance of selection of an iterative model of software engineering for courseware development. In the first project, a linear-sequential model reduced the impact of pedagogical evaluation on the specification of user requirements, except in issues of interface design. The major focus of evaluation was linked to software testing by which time it was too late to change the specifications. As a result, design and development effort was wasted on modules that did not meet user requirements. A more iterative model of SE was adopted in the second project, where formative peer and student evaluations were integrated into the SE life cycle. Very little effort was wasted and the product was more congruent with the educational intentions of its authors.

Inferences may be made that CFL development will be enhanced by

- development team maturity,
- selection of an iterative SE model
- equal emphasis on learning and technical quality control

- continuous involvement of content experts and instructional designers throughout the life-cycle.

REFERENCES

Alexander, S., McKenzie, J. and Geissinger, H. (1998) *An evaluation of information technology projects for university learning: Executive summary*, Report, Committee for University Teaching and Staff Development (CUTSD). [http://www.autc.gov.au/in/in_pu_cu_ex.htm] 26.10.2000.

Anderson, J. R., Reder, L. M. and Simon, H. A. (1997) *Applications and misinterpretations of cognitive psychology to mathematics education*. [http://act.psy.cmu.edu/ACT/papers/misapplied-abs-ja.html] 1998, February.

Australian Vice Chancellors' Committee (1996, 9 October) *Exploiting information technology in higher education: An issues paper.* [http://www.avcc.edu.au/avcc/pubs/eitihe.htm] 10.02.1997.

Bates, T. (1997, 18-20 June) Restructuring the university for technological change. In *Carnegie Foundation for the Advancement of Teaching: What kind of university?* Proceeding of the Carnegie Foundation for the Advancement of Teaching Conference, London, pp. 1-23.

Burkhardt, H. (1992) Classroom observation in courseware development. *International Journal of Educational Research*, 17, pp. 87-98.

Dills, C. R. and Romiszowski, A. J. (1997) The instructional development paradigm: An introduction. In *Instructional Development Paradigms*, C. R. Dills and A. J. Romiszowski (eds), Educational Technology Publications, Englewood Cliffs, New Jersey, pp. ix-xxx1.

Duffy, T. M. and Jonassen, D. H. (1991) Constuctivism: New implications for instructional technology? *Educational Technology,* 31 (5), pp. 7-12.

Fraser, K. (1997) Academic developers. Enhancing the pedagogical value of multimedia products developed by higher education learning environments. *International Journal of Academic Development.*

Hedberg, J. and Alexander, S. (1994, 28 June – 2 July) Implementation and evaluation: The forgotten end of interactive multimedia development. In *APITITE. 94*, M. Ryan (ed), Proceedings of the Asia Pacific Information Technology in Training and Education Conference and Exhibition, APITITE 94 Council, Brisbane.

Humphrey, W. S. (1995) *The systems engineering Capability Maturity Model: A discipline for software engineering*. Addison-Wesley.

Johnson, L. (1997) *Software Engineering 3A, 433-341: First Semester Handbook and Notes.* The University of Melbourne Department of Computer Science.

Kennedy, D. M., Fritze, P. and McTigue, P. (1997, December 7-10) An interactive graphing tool: The meeting of pedagogy and technology. In *What works and why, ASCILITE'97*, R. Kevill, R. Oliver and R. Phillips (eds.), Proceedings of the Australian Society for Computers in Learning in Tertiary Education, Perth, pp. 331-337.

Laurillard, D. and Margetson, D. (1997) *Introducing a flexible learning methodology: Discussion paper (7).* Griffith University, Brisbane.

McNaught, C., Phillips, R., Rossiter, D. and Winn, J. (2000) *Developing a Framework for a Useable and Useful Inventory of Computer-facilitated Learning and Support Materials in Australian Universities*, (DETYA No 6472 HERCOA), Canberra.

Merrill, D. M. (1991) Constructivism and instructional design. *Educational Technology*, 31 (9), pp. 45-53.

Moonen, J. and Schoenmaker, J. (1992) Evolution of courseware development methodology: Recent issues. *International Journal of Educational Research*, 17, pp. 109-121.

Peters, J. and Pedrycz, W. (2000) *Software Engineering: An Engineering Approach*. Wiley, New York.

Pressman, R. S. (1997) *Software engineering: A practitioner's approach*. 4th ed., McGraw-Hill, New York.

Reeves, T. C. (1997) Established and emerging evaluation paradigms for instructional design. In *Instructional Development Paradigms*, C. R. Dills and A. J. Romiszowski (eds.), Educational Technology Publications, Englewood Cliffs, New Jersey, pp. 163-178.

Robertson, L. A. (2000) *Simple Program Design*. 3rd ed., Nelson, Australia.

BIOGRAPHY

Wendy Doubé has taught computer programming, software engineering and computer graphics to both on and off-campus students, producing course materials in a wide range of media, including the multimedia modules discussed in this paper and chapters on object-oriented design in the textbook, 'Simple Program Design' (Robertson 2000). Her publications have explored the impact of distance and media on teaching and learning computing. She is currently investigating the motivational impact of multimedia interactions in learning.

David Kennedy is an educational designer who works with academic staff across the university to develop more flexible learning environments that require the appropriate use of technology.

Dr. Juhani Tuovinen is the Senior Research Fellow in Interactive Multimedia at Monash University's Centre for Learning and Teaching Support. He has been a secondary school teacher and a university lecturer in education. His expertise is in distance education, the use of computer and communications technology in education and cognitive science. His current research interests include the application of cognitive principles to distance and flexible learning and the use of modern technology in university education.

62

A System of Reciprocity

Empowering Stakeholders to Do More with Less in Educational Technology

Catherine P. Fulford and Ariana Eichelberger
Educational Technology, University of Hawaii, Honolulu, Hawaii, 96822, USA
fulford@hawaii.edu

Keywords: higher education, empowering, teacher education, teacher training, tutor

Abstract: A System of Reciprocity is a way of thinking and working within an existing system to generate resources or services that one does not have, in return for giving resources or services that one does have. A System of Reciprocity has been employed to create mutual benefit for students, faculty, the department, the college, and the university. A key element is that those involved in the system are aware of their involvement and how it directly benefits them. The synergy created by this faculty-student effort allows both to accomplish far more than either could accomplish alone.

1. INTRODUCTION

The pace of changing technology has created a climate of frenzy in many institutions. With changes in hardware, upgrades in software, and new inventions occurring daily, it is impossible to keep up. Budgets have shifted to accommodate purchases while technology training needs are frequently overlooked. Systems are short of the human resources required to accommodate growing needs in professional development. Pressure is put on educational technology programs to provide solutions to these growing needs. Often, these programs lack the resources to keep up themselves, much less accommodate everyone else's needs.

A shift in thinking may be required to help solve these complex problems. The systems approach is commonly taught in educational technology programs, but how often is it used to redesign, recreate, and improve the program itself? Harris (1972) said that general systems theory is used as a tool by social scientists "for understanding human behaviour and for increasing the ability of individuals to work creatively and productively with one another" (p. 1). He noted that "an important advantage of a systems approach is flexibility. You can arrange and rearrange the environment any way you want which is consistent with the school's purpose" (p. 7).

In the Educational Technology (ETEC) Program at the University of Hawaii (UH), one faculty member introduced what she termed a System of Reciprocity as a way to empower the department to do more with less. The System of Reciprocity is a way of thinking and working within an existing system to generate resources or services that one does not have, in return for giving resources or services that one does have. This type of system is an example of a Win/Win situation described by Covey (1994). "Win/Win means that agreements or solutions are mutually beneficial, mutually satisfying. With a Win/Win solution, all parties feel good about the decision and feel committed to the action plan" (p.117). This concept should work equally well in a university, government agency, or business. The System of Reciprocity has been employed by ETEC to create a mutually beneficial situation for its students, faculty, the department, the college, and the university.

2. HISTORY

The system was originally developed in 1988 by an ETEC faculty member when she had worked as a training manager in a government setting. The agency had 6000 employees who needed services, yet there was no budget and the secretary was shared with five units. When brought in to develop the district training program, the training manager applied her experience in instructional systems and team-building. It was in this challenging environment that the System of Reciprocity was originated (see Figure 1). The concept was that when services were rendered, the recipient would provide resources to the system, which in turn would allow more services to be provided. Payment for services was not possible, so a subtle system of barter was created. The key to making the system work was to consistently act upon this concept and inform those requiring services of their role in the system.

Concepts were used from research on change theory to create a conducive environment. Havelock (1973) emphasised the importance of involving stakeholders, that is, people in system that have an interest in the outcome. In this case, the orientation for new employees and management training were used as an opportunity to positively market the training department. The training manager used the idea of the primacy effect and the recency effect (Dawson and Medler 1997) to help employees remember her. These mean that the first thing and the last thing one does are remembered best. The training manager personally handled the orientation, and the beginning and ending management training sessions, and sought to make them memorable experiences. She made a point of acquainting herself with the new employees and management staff, alerting them to her services, and assuring them they could ask for assistance.

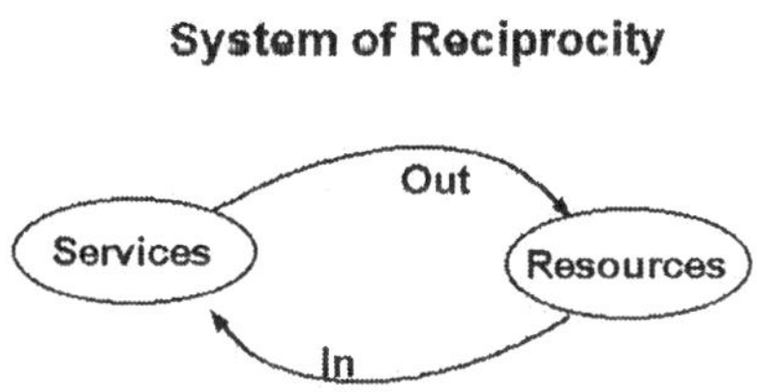

Figure 1. Original System of Reciprocity

Another group of stakeholders was the trainers hired to meet specific unit needs. These people operated independently and in isolation. The training manager created events to organise them. This empowered the trainers by giving them an identity and making them an integral part of the training system. They gained a support system and professional development. With this strategy the training manager expanded her sphere of influence and gained access to a pool of qualified trainers.

A key element of a functional System of Reciprocity is that those involved in the system are aware of their involvement and how it benefits them. When the training manager was asked for services, she would give clients a diagram of the system and explain it (see Figure 2). For example, consultation was provided to employees who needed it. In exchange for the *consulting*, recipients were asked to verbally *support* the training department by saying positive things about the training department's services to fellow employees. When people heard good things about the department, they came to her for *technical assistance*. The training manager would explain that if the employee's department purchased the materials and the excess *supplies* where kept in the training department, supplies would be available for continued media support for all departments.

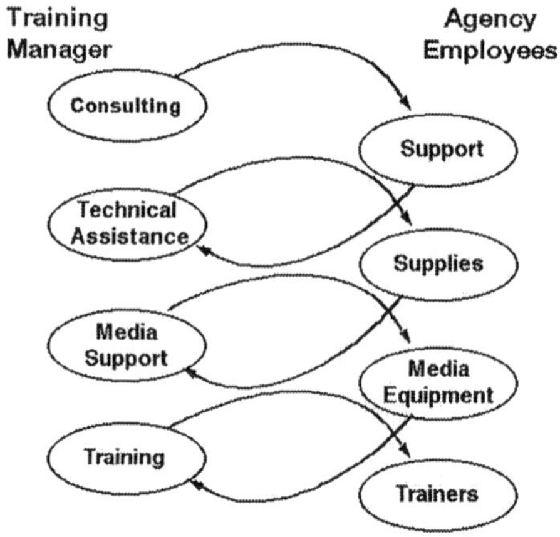

Figure 2. Government agency – System of Reciprocity

When providing employees with *media* support, they were asked to remember the training department at the end of the year when they had their budget surplus to spend. This money provided *media equipment* and training materials for the system. With more resources the department was better able to meet the needs of the agency in its primary function – training. In a district of 6000 employees, one person could not meet the demand for general training. When managers asked for *training* for their department, she would in turn ask if they or someone in their department might be a good trainer. In the training sessions, the training manager would be keenly aware of the people who caught on quickly and were self-assured. She would also recruit these people to conduct training sessions. In this way, she created a network of available *trainers*. Through this process, with no budget and one-fifth of a secretary, the training manager was able to get supplies and equipment and spread her services further than she could do alone. Everyone benefited.

3. EDUCATIONAL TECHNOLOGY DEPARTMENT

The System of Reciprocity has now been successfully transferred to the Educational Technology Department at the University of Hawaii. When the training manager became a professor, she found that the System of Reciprocity worked equally as well in an academic environment The System of Reciprocity started in the department as a means to help individual faculty members. Since the department had no graduate assistantships to help faculty with research and teaching, the department was convinced to allow the independent-study course and the required internship as a way to recruit help. Previously, the independent-study course generally benefited one student while increasing the workload of the faculty member. Internships were primarily sought outside of the department. The emphases of these courses were changed to allow faculty to recruit and handpick students as teaching and research assistants. The students in turn were allowed to count these credits toward their degree program. ETEC faculty have provided many collaborative and authentic projects for their students. One of the most valuable has been involving students in research, publication, and grant writing. The students receive special attention and mentoring through the process, and most importantly use their newly learned skills to work on real projects or practice teaching. In this Win/Win situation students provide their time and effort to faculty who need publications and good teaching evaluations for tenure and promotion (see Figure 3).

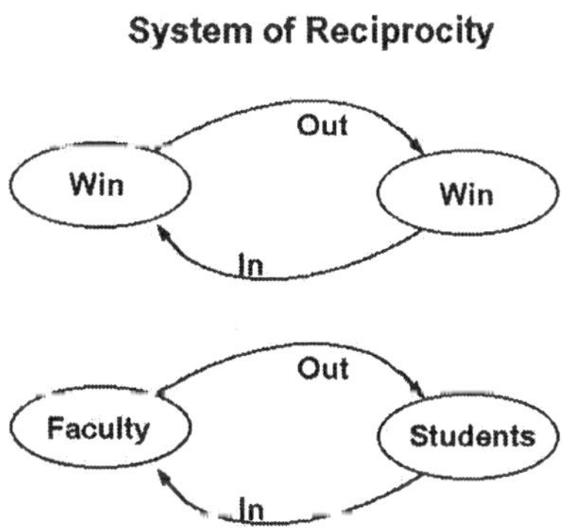

Figure 3. Department of Educational Technology System of Reciprocity

The key to making this work is having the student and faculty member ask themselves "what's in it for me?" (WIIFM). Then, the student and faculty member negotiate a plan that is mutually beneficial. As seen in Figure 4, the department provides the *opportunity*; the students supply the *time*. The department gives the student credit and the students gain *expertise*. While the department receives *help*, the students gain *real-world experience*. The faculty members receive *recognition* and entries on their vitas for work accomplished, as does the student in improving their *resumes and portfolios*.

Knowing this help is available, faculty have sought numerous opportunities to obtain grants providing the additional benefit to students of paid positions. The department now has the equivalent of graduate assistantships without having the budget for them. The professor who introduced the System of Reciprocity has benefited from 22 teaching assistantships, 25 research assistantships, and 45 paid employees for a total of 92 collaborators over a ten-year period.

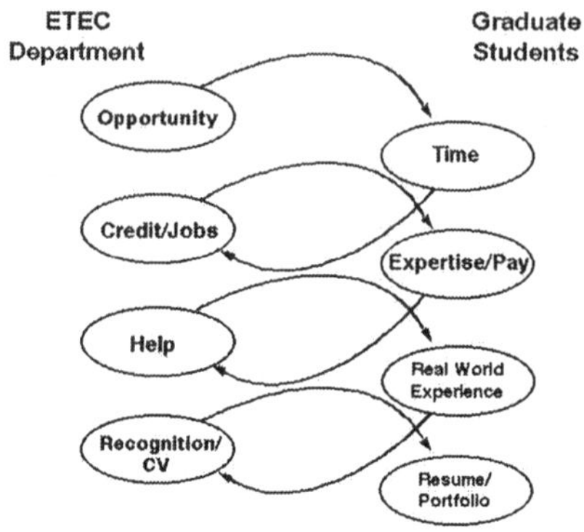

Figure 4. ETEC Department – Expanded System of Reciprocity

In addition to helping individual faculty, the System of Reciprocity is also at work on the departmental level. As in the government setting, a yearly orientation and renewal session is provided to instil an environment of co-operation and promote opportunities for working on various projects. As a result, many students choose course and master's projects to develop course materials, create databases, and conduct needs assessments, and research that benefit the department. Students are not required to do these projects, but many find value in projects that have a direct, real-world use.

The System of Reciprocity also contributes much to departmental grant projects. Students' willingness to participate in the system has resulted in ETEC faculty being awarded 5 grants for over $2.7 million to support technology integration in College of Education (COE) courses. Since the department has not been allotted any graduate assistantships, one of the most important outcomes of grant funding has been to provide relevant employment for ETEC master's students. The recognition and jobs available help a great deal in recruiting additional and quality graduate students into the program. The department through its grant efforts has been able to hire 38 students over the last five years for this project. With the assistance of the students, the faculty and staff are able to stretch their time and get more done. As the department is able to do more, it receives recognition, which enhances relationships with the college, university, funding agencies, and professional organisations.

4. EDUCATIONAL TECHNOLOGY COURSES

For a number of years the university has been experiencing the most severe budget crisis in its history. While the COE is committed to using technology in the teaching and learning process there were very few technology resources or training sessions made available to students and faculty through university funding. Because of the Educational Technology faculty's technical expertise, the department was often asked to fill this gap by providing informal training and technical assistance to other faculty in the college. While the department provided this help, it took time from the faculty members' already busy schedules and did not provide them with many rewards. At that point, the system was non-reciprocal. The ETEC faculty provided valuable services to the college beyond their job descriptions, and yet they themselves did not directly benefit from it.

Again, the ETEC faculty member who had developed the System of Reciprocity applied it to an ETEC course to reduce the pressure on the department for technology training. A Win/Win situation was created through a required practicum course in which graduate students are provided an authentic setting to apply their new skills by designing and conducting technology workshops for COE faculty. In their first year, students learn to analyse instructional systems, develop needs assessments, apply change theory, design instruction, develop various media, and make high-tech presentations. As a way to apply these skills, ETEC practicum courses are offered every fall to advanced students. They use current needs assessments as a guide to inform them of the topics faculty are interested in learning. They also consider their own WIIFMs in choosing topics. Based on this knowledge, the students develop a semester-long series of technology workshops for the COE faculty. Students handle all aspects of each workshop including design, delivery, advertising, registration, and evaluation. Past workshops have covered such topics as using layers in Photoshop, online collaboration with Web CT, electronic portfolios in Powerpoint, and editing digital video with imovie2.

The System of Reciprocity in this context works by the instructor first offering the *opportunity* to the ETEC students through teaching the course (see Figure 5). In exchange for the opportunity to take the course, the students give their *time* to create the workshops. They receive *credit* for the course in exchange for *expertise*. ETEC students come from a variety of backgrounds and bring in a multitude of skills Due to the success of the course the department has received grant *funding* to support the course and its efforts. This funding helps the practicum students buy supplies they need to produce professional quality materials and provide refreshments to workshop participants. The instructor benefits by increasing the overall *technology proficiency* of COE faculty. The students benefit from a *real-world experience* that provides them with design experience and presentation skills. They are empowered through the role reversal of becoming mentors to the faculty. Every year students have chosen to continue this project. Their reflections of the course in their final report show they value the experience (Fulford and Eichelberger, 2000).

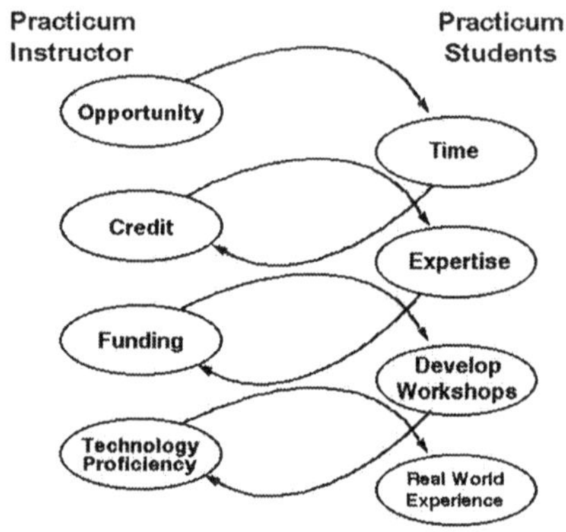

Figure 5. Practicum Course – Expanded System of Reciprocity

Other course instructors have followed this model. For example, in one course students were involved in developing the Technology Learning Center. They wrote letters to vendors requesting software and hardware donations, organised a database, and set up a computer as a software viewing station. The outcome of this project was a corporate gift that funded graduate students as workers to run the system and the purchase of additional hardware and software. Another course created a photographic database on CD-ROM so that students and faculty could have access to copyright-free local images. The video design course has created several instructional videos used in other ETEC courses.

5. THE COLLEGE AND UNIVERSITY

Once students were willing participants, the System of Reciprocity was expanded to include both the College of Education and the University of Hawaii faculty through grant funding. Again, a Win/Win situation was created to be able to recruit faculty to participate in the grant projects (see Figure 6). The technology workshops developed by the ETEC practicum courses provide *technology training* for the COE/UH faculty. The *attendance and time* spent by the faculty in the workshops allows the department a venue for grant funding. The COE/UH faculty recruited from the workshops agree to participate in the grant project. Their *participation* provides them with *incentives* such as equipment and software to *redesign their courses* to integrate technology. To help them in this process, the most valuable resource provided is one-on-one technology *mentoring* by ETEC graduate students. In turn, the COE/UH faculty's efforts provide the necessary *outcome* of technology integrated courses required by the grant and enhances possibilities for continued grant funding. In this way everyone wins.

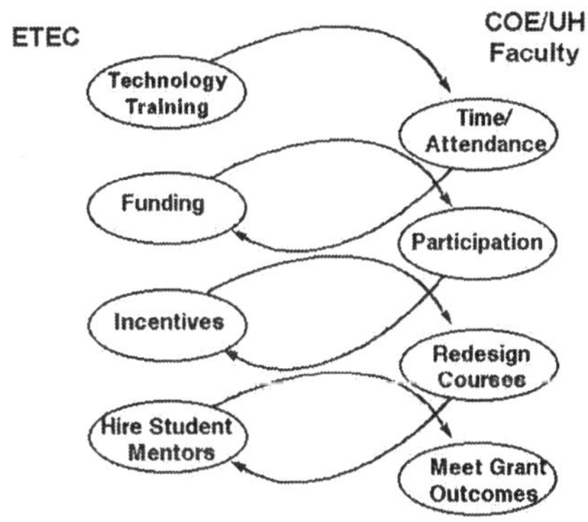

Figure 6. College/University Expanded System of Reciprocity

The $2.7 million in funding has enabled the department to hire a staff of 21 including two new faculty members and enhance the Technology Learning Centre that circulates high-tech equipment for faculty and student use. Through these efforts, ETEC graduate students have assisted faculty in revising more than 50 COE and UH courses to be Technology Intensive. From a philosophical or pedagogical perspective, this Win/Win relationship empowers the stakeholders – ETEC, COE/UH faculty and students – with more options for effective, innovative, and relevant teaching.

REFERENCES

Covey, S. R. (1994) *Daily reflections for highly effective people*. Fireside – Simon and Schuster, New York.

Dawson, M. and Medler, D. (1997) *The University of Alberta's Cognitive Science Dictionary*. [http://web.psych.ualberta.ca/~mike/Pearl_Street/Dictionary/dictionary.html] 10.15.2000.

Harris, T. (1972) *The application of general systems theory to instructional development.* US Office of Education, Bureau of Libraries and Educational Technology and National Special Media Institute.

Havelock, R. (1973) *A change agents guide to innovation.* Educational Technology Publications, Englewood Cliffs, New Jersey.

Fulford, C. P. and Eichelberger, E. (2000) Win-Win: Students using instructional design skills to teach faculty to integrate technology in teacher education. *22nd Annual Proceedings of Selected Research and Development Presentations of the 2000 National Convention for the Association for Educational Communications and Technology,* October, Denver.

BIOGRAPHY

Catherine P. Fulford is an Associate Professor in the Department of Educational Technology at the University of Hawaii at Manoa. She has been co-principal investigator and has received significant grant funding on the Technology Intensive Project for four years. Ariana Eichelberger is the Grants Manager. She oversees work on the United States Department of Education (USDOE) Preparing Tomorrow's Teacher's to Use Technology grant entitled LEI Aloha (Learning Enhancement through Innovations).

63

Technology Education for the 21st Century in Australia?

Investigating Effective Practice in Schools

C. Paul Newhouse
School of Education, Edith Cowan University, Perth, Western Australia
p.newhouse@cowan.edu.au

Keywords: computing, curriculum changes, curriculum policies.

Abstract: This paper reports on recent research to investigate effective practice and develop a definition of quality technology education in Australian primary and secondary schools. In Australia technology education encompasses a range of practical subject disciplines including working with materials, fabrics, food and media, and the provision of computer (ICT) education. The study developed a theoretical model of quality and effective practice that was used to describe the technology education provided by a selection of leading schools. A number of major issues were identified and recommendations were developed. In particular, many schools needed substantially more equipment, materials and teacher training and the 'optional' status of technology education in the compulsory years of education needed to be removed.

1. INTRODUCTION

During the late 1990s technology education policy and practice in Australian school systems has been undergoing a gradual revolution. In policy documents technology education has been recognised as an important area of learning in the same way that mathematics and language are so recognised. At the same time it has been recognised that the types of experiences students need are different to those of students in the 1950s and 1960s, the era from which traditional technology education courses have emanated. There is a need to clearly define quality technology education and suggest strategies to encourage effective practice in schools.

This paper reports on the outcomes of a component of a study that aimed to analyse effective practice and develop a definition of quality technology education in Australian primary and secondary schools.

2. METHODOLOGY

The component study employed two main methodologies. The first was a literature search to develop a model for a definition of quality technology education and effective practice in schools. The second used a series of case studies of leading sites throughout Australia to verifying and modify the model. The review of literature continued throughout the project but was particularly intense at the beginning.

It was planned to have at least three leading sites in each state to cover primary and secondary schools, regional schools, government and non-government schools. Each leading site was visited by a researcher for at least one day in order to collect data that included observation of facilities, interviews with school personnel, and questionnaires for samples of students and teachers. The observational schedule focused on whole school-level rather than classroom level features and was concerned with curriculum implementation and support at a school site. The interview schedules focused on classroom level features and was concerned with the implemented curriculum and teacher attitudes, understandings and beliefs.

3. THEORETICAL MODEL

The theoretical model of quality and effective practice in technology education was based on literature, particularly from Europe (principally United Kingdom), the United States of America, New Zealand and Australia. It was presented as a concept map (this may be accessed at http://edresearch.ed.ac.cowan.edu.au/paul/technology/) with a discussion paper outlining the features on the concept map. At the centre of the model are the concepts "Quality Technology Education" and "Effective Practice".

Quality Technology Education in a school is fundamentally represented by the learning outcomes achieved by the school's programmes. Quality is based on the attainment of valued outcomes with students that in technology education will concern technological capability. Kimbell (1994) and others see the concept of "active technological capability" as the fundamental goal of technology in schools" (p. 1). The concept concerns students doing rather than simply knowing about. It encompasses a view of the world that perceives technology as a means of transforming the natural world to satisfy some human need. In outcomes-based education assessment of technological capability will be based on the judgements made by teachers. However, clearly this will also be evidenced by the perceptions of students. The project did not attempt to measure learning outcomes, rather they were implied within the definition of effective practice expounded within the model.

Effective Practice contributes to Quality Technology Education and is evidenced by features of a number of aspects of the school's programmes. Effective practice as filtered by pedagogical philosophy will be evidenced by a number of constructs associated with schooling. These constructs, based on the findings of relevant international research, were represented in the concept diagram: the intended curriculum, the implemented curriculum, instructional methodology, assessment practices, and the facilities and equipment available. Each of these constructs is supported by a number of observable features also represented in the concept diagram. These observable features are discussed below and formed the basic framework for reporting on data collected from schools.

3.1 Judgements of teachers

Assessment under an outcomes-based system is dependent on teachers making judgements about the level of a student's technological capability based on what students do and say. This is stated in most Australian system curriculum statements and will involve making judgements about students' understanding of concepts, their level of technology skill (e.g. process skills, manipulative skills), and their attitudes towards technology. Unfortunately the limited conception of technology and the lack of understanding, knowledge and confidence of primary school teachers in the area of technology education (Australian Science Technology and Engineering Council 1997) will make it difficult for them to make these judgements.

3.2 Perceptions and conceptions of students

Students perceptions and conceptions of technology have a major impact on their technological practice, perhaps even more than teaching strategies (Jones 1997). Typically students while having a positive attitude have a limited concept of technology. Broader views of technology allow students to undertake activities in a holistic fashion in terms of the processes they use (Jones 1997). Clearly for older students their perceptions of the role of technology in the workplace, particularly as related to potential careers is important. However, for all students the perception of personal use of technology will influence their attitude towards learning activities at school. This has been particularly relevant for computer technology.

3.3 The intended curriculum

The intended curriculum is that laid down by educational systems or authorities to which teachers must adhere. Typically this is defined formally in documents variously labelled curriculum frameworks and syllabus statements. These are often supported by resource materials and informal understandings communicated through policy or practice forums. In Australia a national curriculum framework was developed in the early 1990s (Curriculum Corporation 1994). Most states also have a comprehensive curriculum framework such as that in place in Western Australia (Curriculum Council of Western Australia 1998). These frameworks support the importance of technology education and support its proper implementation.

3.4 The implemented curriculum

The implemented curriculum is that instituted within a school by teachers for students based on the intended curriculum. A recent Australian study found a disparity between the official support for technology education and "that which occurs in practice" (Australian Science Technology and Engineering Council 1997, p. 1) with particularly little emphasis at the primary school level. If the implemented curriculum is to provide opportunities for the development of technological capability then it will need to provide appropriate activities with supporting facilities and equipment, consider equity and progression, and provide a breadth of technological activity.

Students should actively work with a range of technologies (Todd 1997) that are appropriate to their present and perceived future needs and to support their interests. There is a danger that in an attempt to provide the infrastructure to support a range of technologies within budget limitations that schools provide facilities and equipment which do not allow for authentic contexts for activities.

The curriculum must make provision for equity and progression. All students should also be provided with a technology education that allows for a progression of experience and is integrated with the rest of their curriculum. Central to learning are the experiences or activities that students engage with. These must challenge and interest them while being realistic contexts(Jones 1997). Kimbell (1996) suggests that contexts of tasks need to be real and that students be provided with activities that vary in their entry points from highly contextualised to highly particularised.

3.5 Instructional methodology

Technology education fundamentally concerns the application of process with the development of conceptual knowledge (McCormick 1996). It involves processes of design, problem-solving and investigation in the application of independent bodies of knowledge and skills to holistic activities (Jones 1997).

The technology process involves students in investigating, designing, making, and evaluating products, processes, systems, environments and services. The aim is to meet human need through enhancing the environment. The central processes involve design and problem-solving. The process of technology is not a rigid set of specific tasks (McCormick 1996), but varies depending on the nature of the activity, the prior experience of the students, and the outcome goals the teacher would like the students to achieve.

Problem-solving is defined by Todd (1997) as "a structured component within a general investigative approach to learning" (p. 207) and it implies that there is a problem to solve. While much of the conceptual knowledge base required by students relies on other curriculum areas technology education should contribute to the development of such conceptual knowledge. This can be accomplished by allowing students to generalise through working in a number of different contexts. Specific knowledge is developed on a need to know basis (McCormick 1996).

Students work independently and in shared situations at various stages in the technology process. It is important for students to regularly experience collaborative work in technology activity both from the point of view of promoting learning and to replicate workplace requirements (McCormick 1996). Students need to experience working with each other with technology, not just on isolated group-work activities, but as part of many parts of the Technology Process such that they share goal-setting, creating designs and the production of technologies.

The role of performance on skills in technological capability is a contentious issue that has normally focused on assessment of practical skills (Lewis 1999). The Technology Process approach requires students to develop skills in critical thinking, decision-making, information processing, modelling and general problem-solving (Levande et al. 1998). As they encounter a range of technologies students will need to develop skills in their use and application when they are needed within activities.

3.6 Assessment practices

Many authors and reports link the technological literacy rationale with a need for standards and assessment. It is argued that these will raise the low status of the area by establishing high expectations and provide an impetus for improvement of teachers and learning environments (International Technology Education Association 1996). Where there is an emphasis on summative assessment students are likely to devalue the processes and principles involved in their activities (Jones 1997). Assessment should be used by teachers, administrators and educational leaders to plan future programmes. Assessment activity in technology education must encompass a full view of the principles, particularly associated with the Technology Process, which lends itself to portfolio assessment (Levande et al. 1998).

4. ISSUES ARISING

The following issues arose from an analysis of the data collected from the leading sites (schools). Specific data can't be provided due to confidentiality requirements.

4.1 The low status of technology education

While it is clear that in the eyes of teachers and school administrators technology education is being afforded the status of a learning area separate from science or mathematics it still has to fight to be treated as being of relatively equal importance. Typically technology education has been an 'elective' area in secondary schools and a 'new' area or a peripheral area to science in primary schools. One of the primary school principals commented that a problem was the "weak perceptions held by parents of the Learning Area – apparently there exists the view that Technology is 'play' and not serious education." In addition there is little requirement for study in technology education for post-secondary destinations, and there is no clear definition or requirement for technological literacy. Even in primary/early childhood environments it is often viewed as a luxury as compared with central importance of numeracy and language literacy.

Strong support from the Principal is required to implement an effective technology education programme. To change the perceived low status of the area typically requires specific initiatives that have serious budgetary and policy implications and therefore require the support of the Principal. In most leading sites the Principal not only supported the learning area but was able to clearly explain the nature and aims of the area. Principals often provide support for the professional development of teachers if they possess an understanding and empathy for the learning area.

4.2 The balance between vocational and general educational aims

Traditionally the aims of technology education have mainly focussed on developing skills for the workplace or more recently home living requirements, vocational aims. During the past decade the curriculum emphasis has moved towards the more general educational aims concerning the development of awareness, conceptual understanding, and considering the broader issues of using technology in society. This balance between vocational and general educational aims tends to be mirrored in the balance between product and process with vocational aims associated with concentration on the development of skills in high quality production. The balance between these two sets of aims has implications for the range of technologies made available and the type and quality of equipment and materials provided in secondary schools.

A number of the selected schools had developed an approach to technology education which used it as the vehicle for broader aims of curriculum integration and/or the introduction of an outcomes-based approach to education. This improved the status of the area and encouraged teachers to invest in the implementation of technology education and, at the secondary level, move away from the traditional vocational-product approach to technology. Many of the selected schools found that concentrating on a new area such as technology education which was well suited to an outcomes-based approach helped induct teachers and school communities into the approach.

4.3 Providing a range of technologies and materials

The range of technologies and materials available for students at a school, particularly primary school, depended a lot on the expertise and enthusiasm of teachers and the costs of providing adequate access. All schools had increased their provision for computer technology. Leading secondary sites tended to aim to provide a range of technologies which focussed more on newer or 'lighter' technologies such as microwave food technology, power-tools for wood and metal, multimedia and control technologies. In primary schools there was an enthusiasm for introducing as wide a range of technologies as possible, often starting with computer-related technologies and then wood-related technologies (typically hand-tools and some power-tools).

Since much of technology education provides new content for Primary programmes few schools have the resources to provide adequate experience for students other than with craft type materials. A limitation for most schools is the lack of adequate room-space to conduct production with equipment needing to be taken into cluttered regular classrooms giving rise to safety concerns. A further problem in primary schools was the lack of experience and training in the area of most teachers (predominantly female). They lack competence and confidence in using basic hand and power tools used with materials such as wood, metals, electronics and plastics. As schools purchase such equipment it will either be used inefficiently or dangerously. There is a need for primary schools to have a designated co-ordinator for technology education to encourage progression of learning experiences.

Most components of technology education at all levels of schooling suffer from a lack of technical support persons with teachers being required to complete many maintenance and installation procedures. Given the equipment and materials intensity of the learning area it is difficult, particularly in secondary schools, to comprehend this when compared with the support traditionally given to the science learning area. This was a problem for most government school leading sites and some non-government schools.

4.4 The place of computing (IT)

There has been increased confusion concerning the role of computing in technology education since the term 'learning technologies' has become almost synonymous with using computers to support learning. The complexity of the relationship between technology education and the use of computers has led to serious levels of confusion among teachers, parents and educational leaders. There are extreme attitudes from "computers are not a part of technology education" through to an equation between computers and technology education. In many schools (including some of the leading sites) the leader of computing is also the leader for learning technologies which adds to this confusion. Within technology education it is legitimate to focus on computers as an area of study where students will learn about computer technologies, how to use them and their place within society. Computers may also be used as a learning tool but this is a different issue. All the leading sites had developed significant computing resources and most provided comprehensive learning programmes in computer technology. Computers were also used to support many technology processes and were used as learning technologies in many learning areas, including technology education.

5. CONCLUSIONS

The study generated a number of recommendations. Primary schools needed substantially more equipment, materials and teacher training to provide effective technology education. The 'optional' status of technology education in the compulsory years of secondary education needed to be removed and replaced with a minimum requirement such as that which exists for mathematics, English language and science. The Universities needed to be encouraged to free up rules for entry and accept studies in technology. The leadership roles in schools for Technology Education needed to be separated from that of Learning Technologies. All schools needed to be provided with adequate technical support for the range of technologies made available to students. Primary school facilities needed upgrading to include a purpose-built area for technology with appropriate equipment, storage and professional development for teachers. Clearly there is still much to be done to provide all Australian children with a high quality technology education.

REFERENCES

Australian Science Technology and Engineering Council (1997) *Foundations for Australia's Future: Science and Technology in Primary Schools.* Report, Department of Industry, Science and Tourism,Canberra.

Curriculum Corporation (1994) *A statement on technology for Australian schools.* Carlton: Curriculum Corporation.

Curriculum Council of Western Australia (1998) *Curriculum Framework for Kindergarten to Year 12 Education in Western Australia.* Curriculum Council of Western Australia, Perth

International Technology Education Association (1996) *Technology for All Americans: A Rationale and Structure for the Study of Technology.* Report, International Technology Education Association, Reston, Virginia.

Jones, A. (1997) Recent research in learning technological concepts and processes. *International Journal of Technology and Design Education*, 7, pp. 83-96.

Kimbell, R. (1994) Technological capability and its assessment in the UK National Curriculum. In *Australian Council for Education through Technology*, Hobart, Tasmania.

Kimbell, R. (1996) Technology tasks and pupils' learning. In *Technology Education for Teachers*, J. Williams and A. Williams (Eds.), MacMillan Education Australia Pty Ltd., Melbourne, pp. 93-110.

Levande, J. S., Glaser, R., Henrion, A., Kruyer, R., Schmitt, L. and Woodman, D. (1998, April) *Technology education initiatives and statewide curriculum integration in Michigan.* Paper presented at the Annual Meeting of the International Technology Education Association, Fort Worth, Texas.

Lewis, T. (1999) Research in technology education – some areas of need. *Journal of Technology Education*, 10 (2).

McCormick, R. (1996) Instructional methodology. In *Technology Education for Teachers*, J. Williams and A. Williams (Eds.), MacMillan Education Australia Pty Ltd., Melbourne, pp. 63-92.

Todd, R. D. (Ed.) (1997) *A new paradigm for schooling.* (46 ed.), McGraw-Hill, New York.

BIOGRAPHY

I have always considered myself to be both an educator and learner in all aspects of my life. For nine years this was largely realised in an innovative state secondary school in Western Australia where I had the opportunity to put into practice a range of philosophically based programmes and strategies in teaching across the curriculum. Since then I have had the privilege of sharing my experiences with pre-service and practicing teachers for over ten years in two universities. My current appointment is as a lecturer with the School of Education at Edith Cowan University.

64

Visions About Mobile Technologies in Elementary Education

Harri Ketamo, Jarkko Alajääski and Jari Multisilta
Pori School of Technology and Economics, Tampere University of Technology, Po.Box 300, 28101 Pori, Finland
harri.ketamo@pori.tut.fi
Department of Teacher Education in Rauma, University of Turku, 26100 Rauma, Finland
Pori School of Technology and Economics, Tampere University of Technology, Po.Box 300, 28101 Pori, Finland

Keywords: learning environments, mobile communication, future visions, elementary education

Abstract Mobile and wireless communication technologies are developing rapidly. These technologies could be used to support a pedagogical meaningful, place-and-time independent learning process. At the Pori School of Technology and Economics, Finland, we have started a research and development project in wireless communication's capabilities in primary and early childhood education. In this paper we present a scenario for a problem-based learning in the wireless environment. The mobile devices may become a major communication devices within all kinds of electronic communication and they might displace traditional computer networks in some areas of learning. These technologies have to evaluate today in order to implement the next generation mobile eLearning.

1. INTRODUCTION

One of the most rapidly developing areas in the field of technology is wireless communication (WCT) and especially mobile phone communication (MCT) (Räihä et al. 1999). The technological breakthroughs in this area, as well as in information technology (IT), will give totally new alternatives for school education, including primary and early childhood education. According to the National Strategy of the Finnish Ministry of Education (1995), it is the school's task to give for every boy and girl the necessary skills of information retrieval and knowledge acquisition needed in information. Thus, it is important to find out how the children use WCT/MCT and how they experience it (Laurel 1995, Downes 1995, Downes 1999).

In Finland the children and young people have grown up into a culture of mobile communication; 70% out of the students in lower secondary schools, 90% of those in upper secondary schools and 95% out of the university level students owns a mobile phone. Approximately the same number of the students at the different levels of education use their mobile phones daily both for taking care of their 'businesses' and for other communication with their friends (Ketamo and Multisilta 2001). With modern mobile communication technologies it is possible to support the studying and learning process. For instance, current technology makes it possible to browse the examination calendar, to enter to an examination and to get the examination results by way of a simple WAP-based mobile phone. It's also possible to construct a simple WAP-based learning game (Keiho, Lahti and Multisilta 2000). In addition to learning questionnaires basing on traditional pen and paper-method, also WAP-based learning questionnaires can be utilised. In order to implement a www-like open learning environment utilising mobile technology, radical improvements in performance are needed. Especially, the screen size, cpu-power and data transfer capacity set limitations for the use of current mobile devices as a technique of learning environments. The mobile learning environment may be based on the same general principles as the www-based learning environments. The carefully developed mobile learning environment can make the place-and-time-independent studying possible on contrary with the www-learning environments which are bound to physical network connections and to workstations located in certain classrooms.

2. THE WIRELESS COMMUNICATION IN LEARNING-PROJECT

At the Pori School of Technology and Economics and the Department of Teacher Education in Rauma, Finland, we have started a research and development project in wireless communication's capabilities in primary and early childhood education. The project is multi-scientific and in it WCT is studied from two points of view: 1) WCT as a subject in education, 2) WCT as a means of education. The starting points of the study are the following.

Wirelessness. No one can still exactly foresee the technological solutions of the mobile learning environments of the future. Like www-techniques, also WAP-techniques serve frames for the environments. However, the WAP-techniques are still quite undeveloped and they cannot yet be utilised as the techniques of a learning environment. Also, the costs of data transfer are still quite high. The disadvantages of wireless PC-techniques include the quite limited operational range and the fairly large size of the mobile computers. However, the costs of data transfer are minor and the performances of the devices can be adjusted to sufficient level for the requirements of a learning environment.

Teaching/instruction. A starting point for instruction is the use of wireless communication in situations where some additional value is to be achieved from it to the teaching. The technology is not used just for itself (technological imperative), but it is tried to be used to support problem-based and/or co-operative learning (Hakkarainen, Lonka and Lipponen 1999).

Communication is restricted to interpersonal communication; the man-machine communication is excluded in the context of learning. Thus, technology is regarded only as a tool with which a mobile learning environment applying to and effectively maintaining social knowledge construction (Bereiter and Scardamalia 1993) is made possible.

3. REQUIREMENTS OF A GOOD LEARNING ENVIRONMENT

On the basis of learning theories, the following properties are required from a good computer based learning environment: 1) The environment has to support the constructivist point of view on learning and thus it has to counsel the learner to active working. 2) The environment has to support social interaction in order to maintain co-operative or problem-based learning tasks. 3) Delivering information, tasks and objectives should be possible in the environment. 4) Arranging tests and examinations should be possible in the same environment. 5) The environment should support giving feedback. 6) There should be the possibility to extend the environment and openness of the environment. It should be able to bring other teaching materials, documents and tasks to the environment (Ruokamo and Pohjolainen 1998, McGee and Howard 1998, Hopper 1998, Multisilta 1999).

In designing a learning environment especially the users' needs should be taken into account which often differ from the views of the programmer (Häkkinen 1996). A good user-interface is based on the users' images of the functions, and performs whole tasks at a time, and the user does not need to be trained to use of the tool first. Also, the instructions for the users have to be planned and accomplished carefully as unclear instructions lead attention away from the essentials.

The purpose of the learning environment in this paper is to emphasise Vygotsky's idea about children learning from each other. A portable mobile learning environment makes possible many different forms of communication with which the children can discuss learning problems or tasks even without seeing each other. The communication may be delivered for instance as traditional phone calls, image calls, literal text-messages, on-line chat boards or off-line message boards. All these forms can be carried out between two or more partners. It is also possible to arrange for each learner a personal working area where the others can send messages and the learner can respond to them in a way they prefer. In this way, it is possible to arrange the learner a chance for asking for advice from a teacher without the other participants even knowing it. This kind of 'facelessness' has been reported to have enhanced university students' argumentation (Marttunen 1997). The traditional teacher-centred instruction is also possible in the mobile learning environment of this study, but it is assumed that the learning will be self-directed to social inter-student knowledge construction.

4. SCENARIO – A 5TH GRADE BIOLOGY EXERCISE

Problem-based learning is very suitable method to elementary school science lessons. Often, when complex exercises are done outside the classroom, teachers work becomes quite hard; the teacher must instruct and control every pupil. When pupils are around the schoolyard, it becomes almost impossible. Also, when doing out-of-class exercises, the need of instructions arises heavily. It is also common, that completed exercises don't reach the aims of the planned exercise because of the lack of the instruction.

This scenario focuses on 5th grade biology exercise, where pupils have to observe how different trees grow. According to their observations, they should draw illustrations on different growing styles and write short explanations to the illustrations. An exercise begins with short introduction in classroom. Each pupil and the teacher get their mobile-pc and after that children spread around the schoolyard.

The wireless network reach pupils, when they are in schoolyard (circle-plots in Figure 1). If there is a connection between the server and the workstation, the teacher knows that pupil (or at least the machine) is in the schoolyard. Pupils can individually walk around the schoolyard and same time stay socially connected as in the classroom. In fact, there are even more versatile possibilities to communicate to each other than in normal classroom. When doing the exercise, pupil 1 faces difficulties. Normally, she must search the teacher, but in this case she just sends some kind of message to the teacher and the teacher answers in one way or another. In case the instructions were poor, the teacher can give information to all pupils or just answer individually.

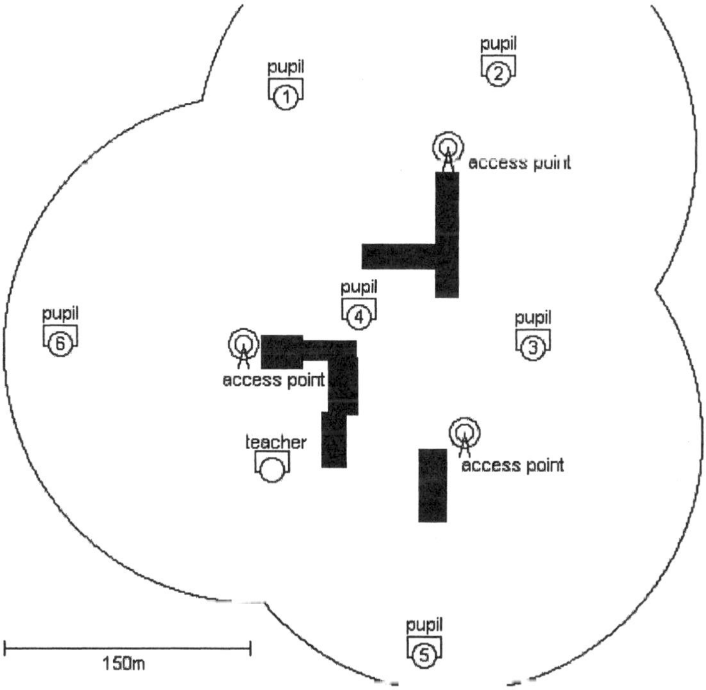

Figure 1. WLAN and pupils in the schoolyard.

A more common case, when pupil 2 want to ask advice from another pupil she can send some individual question and nobody else need to know that. If pupil 2 wants to ask a common question, she can do that also by sending message or by using videoconference to all. When time is up, the teacher can inform everyone by any kind of messages, or even by closing the pupil's workspace.

In this scenario the wireless network is build by using WLAN technology. WLAN is based on access points, which transports the signal between the laptops. There must also be a WLAN pc-card in the laptop. If the WLAN is planned to be just an intranet, the server can be one of the laptops. If connection to the internet is needed, server or access point must have a cable connection to the internet. Nowadays a maximum WLAN range between access point and workstation is approximately 300 meters in the open air; in this scenario the range is thought to be smaller because of different blocks in the schoolyard. The total area of scenarios WLAN is reached by using several access points, which reach each other.

In the future, when fast mobile solutions (GPRS/UMTS) are in use, building this kind of network becomes redundant. With those solutions the access points are not needed and specific servers can be replaced by one server, which handles all communication. Also, there would be no limitations in network range. With GPS tracing-systems in future mobile networks, teacher could control the position of pupil quite correctly without seeing the pupil.

In this scenario, learning is seen as a result of social interaction. Technology is seen as a tool for making more versatile communication possibilities and different learning opportunities for different learners. When learning opportunities becomes more versatile, there is more space for different learning styles, and that way the technology might be a good motivation element for learners. Technology is also seen as teacher's assistant, which allows teacher to focus on guiding pupils instead of routine work, like controlling pupils.

5. DISCUSSION

Communication technology is rapidly developing and some day the new products with new powerful preferences will be in common use. It is quite possible that internet services (www, email, news etc.) will become available to mobile devices in a few years, and for taking a full advantage from the new solutions, we should study the possibilities of those applications beforehand. In these studies we should focus on the content of the use, not to the usage of the technology. When there is a need to learn the usage of the technology, pupils will manage it easily. On the other hand, using (and learning to use) the mobile devices, pupils and students prefer to ask help from their friends than using any other sources (Ketamo and Multisilta 2001). Accordingly, the teaching of the usage of device could be quite unnecessary, in fact the device should be implemented so that anyone can easily recognise its usage.

The new mobile technology might displace traditional computer networks in some areas of learning support. Mobile devices might, for example, become a major communication devices within all kinds of electronic communication. The role of the computer might become exactly a workstation in the meaning of work, not meaning the overall-environment. After all the pc-technology is not disappearing, because of its power in certain areas of learning, but its supremacy in the field of learning environments is certainly over.

REFERENCES

Bereiter, C. and Scardamalia, M. (1993) *Surpassing ourselves. An inquiry into the nature and implications of expertice.* Chigago, IL, Open Court.

Downes T. (1995) Children and Electronic Media: The Home-school Connection. In *World Conference on Computers in Education VI. WCCE '95 Liberating the Learner*, J. David Tinsley and Tom J. Van Weert (eds.), Chapman & Hall, London, pp. 543-552.

Downes T. (1999) Playing with Computing Technologies in the Home. *Education and Information Technologies*, Vol 4, No 1, pp. 65-79.

Finnish Ministry of Education (1995) *Koulutuksen ja tutkimuksen tietostrategia*. Helsinki, Opetusministeriö, [Information strategy in education and research. Helsinki, Finnish Ministry of Education].

Hakkarainen, K., Lonka, K. and Lipponen, L. (1999) *Tutkiva oppiminen: Älykkään toiminnan rajat ja niiden ylittäminen.* Wsoy, Porvoo, [Explorative learning: The limits of intelligent activity and surpassing them].

Hopper, M. (1998) Assessment in www-based learning systems: Opportunities and challenges. *Journal of Universal Computer Science*, Vol 4. [http://www.iicm.edu/jucs_4_4/assasment_in_www_based/paper.html].

Häkkinen, P. (1996) *Design, Take into Use and Effects of Computer-Based Learning Environments – Designer's, Teacher's and Student's Interpretation.* University of Joensuu. Publications in Education, No 34.

Keiho, H., Lahti, J. and Multisilta, J. (2000) Teaching WAP Technology as a Part of Multimedia Course. In *Proceedings of IFIP World Computer Congress*, (eds.), Beijing, China, pp. -.

Ketamo H. and Multisilta, J. (in press) *Lapset, Nuoret ja matkaviestintä.* [Child, youth and mobile communication] Publications of Pori School of Technology and Economics 34/2001, Pori, Finland.

Laurel B. (1995) The Nature of Computing. *Educom Review*, Vol 30, Issue 4. pp. 36-42.

Marttunen, M. (1997) Electronical mail as a pedagogical delivery system: An analysis of the learning of argumentation. *Research in Higher Education*, Vol 38, No 3, pp. 345-363.

McGee, S. and Howard, B. (1998) Evaluating educational multimedia in the context of use. *Journal of Universal Computer Science*, vol 4, [http://www.iicm.edu/jucs_4_3/evaluating_educational_multimedia_in /paper.html].

Multisilta, J. (1999) Open learning environments – Old wine in new wineskins? In *Proceedings of AI-ED, What do we know of open learning environments?*, J. Multisilta (ed.), LeMans, France.

Najjar, L. J. (1995) *A review of the fundamental effects of multimedia information presentation on learning,* [http://www.cc.gatech.edu/gvu/reports/TechReports95.html].

Ruokamo, H. and Pohjolainen, S. (1998) Pedagogical principles for evaluation of hypermedia-based learning environments in matematics. *Journal of Universal Computer Science*, vol 4. [http://www.iicm.edu/jucs_4_3/pedagogical_principles_for_evaluation/paper.html].

Räihä, K-J., Jääskeläinen, K. and Oesch, K. (1999) *Uusi käyttäjäkeskeinen tietotekniikka. Digitaalisen median raportti* 5/99, Esiselvitysraportti. Helsinki, TEKES. [New user-centered information technology. Report of digital media 5/99].

BIOGRAPHY

Harri Ketamo is a researcher at the Pori School of Technology and Economics, Tampere University of Technology, Finland. He has focused on digital learning environments in elementary and higher education and mobile communications among children and youth.

Jarkko Alajääski is a senior lecturer of mathematics at the University of Turku, Department of Teacher Education in Rauma. He has over 50 publications about science education.

Jari Multisilta is the Professor of multimedia at the Pori School of Technology and Economics, Tampere University of Technology, Finland. Prof. Multisilta has published over 50 articles in international conferences and journals. His research interests include applications of multimedia, distance learning and mobile internet technologies.

65

Assessing Internet Resources for Early Childhood Education

Leonie Arthur, Bronwyn Beecher and Toni Downes
School of Education and Early Childhood Studies, University of Western Sydney, Penrith South 1797, Australia
l.arthur@uws.edu.au

Keywords: elementary education, evaluation, integration of ICT, internet, research

Abstract: Educators and parents must make sound educational decisions about of digital resources for use with young children. This paper reports on a project which evaluated current online resources for children eight years and younger. Over sixty sites were evaluated. Analysis examined the availability and quality of the sites and suitability for two groups: under fives and over fives. Many sites were difficult for young children to use independently and demanded expertise with literacy processes beyond the level of children in this age group.

1. INTRODUCTION

For many young Australian children desktop computers, DVDs, game-boys and mobile phones are a familiar aspect of their home and community environments. In many of these homes the computer is connected to the Internet. The Australian Bureau of Statistics (ABS) estimates that over 60% of Australian households with children have computers. For households with younger children, the percentages are slightly lower, with 48% of households with children aged between birth and four years and 54% of households with children aged between five and nine years having computers (ABS 1998). The picture with regard to the Internet also reveals significant access by young children. In 1998 approximately a third of a million households with young children had Internet connections (ABS

1998). Between 1996 and 1998 the rate of Internet access increased four-fold (ABS 1998). Given these accelerated rates of Internet connections to homes, the 1998 figures are likely to be quite conservative. It would be reasonable to estimate that in 2000 over half of preschool age children in Australia have access to a computer in their home, and two thirds of these also have Internet access.

Many families in Australia are mindful that their children learn through interactions with digital resources. Families of preschool aged children in a large project that mapped early literacy practices in New South Wales Australia noted that their children learnt literacy early and fast and in enjoyable ways through technology (Makin, Hayden, Holland, Arthur, Beecher, Jones Diaz and McNaught 1999). Most parents interviewed (71%) identified technology as important to their child's literacy learning especially for bilingual children. Similarly in the United States, families from a range of socio-economic backgrounds with children aged 2 to17 years regarded Internet use as beneficial for children and very useful within the family for communicating and learning (National Schools Board Foundation 2000). In this study, families who connected to the Internet to support education found that their children's learning with the Internet went beyond schoolwork and that their attitude to educational settings improved. In addition, rather than interrupting children's healthy activities the Internet often actually promoted less television watching and encouraged more interests, increasing time playing outdoors as well as involvement in creative arts. The Internet was also seen as promoting communication between families, children and others. Families viewed the Internet as providing potentials for improved communication with their child's teacher and educational setting about their child's learning as well as better access to management processes.

In general, these positive attitudes and patterns of access to computers and the Internet do not flow over to early childhood settings. Currently in day care centres and preschools in Australia there are low levels of computer use and almost no Internet use (Makin et al. 1999). While there are a range of complex factors that help explain such low use, educators' attitudes and perceptions about the appropriateness of access to and use of computers and the Internet play a significant part (Dockett, Perry and Nanlohy 1999).

Amongst early childhood educators there is much debate about the appropriateness of access to and use of the Internet with young children under eight. Educators are often resistant to incorporating technology in early childhood programs (McNaught, Clugston, Arthur, Beecher, Ashton, Hayden and Makin 2000). The language that many early childhood educators use about computers indicates that they have constructed 'using the computer' as an activity separate from and in opposition to social interaction and appropriate play experiences. It is as if the spectre of 'solo, intense computer game-playing' over-rides all other possibilities in the minds of the educators.

These prevailing negative attitudes are often difficult to change even with the evidence of long term research related to the beneficial effects of developmentally appropriate computer use as well as parents' anecdotal evidence of children's learning at home with computers. Appropriate professional development can assist in the process of attitudinal change and thus changes in practices (McNaught et al. 2000).

However, professional development while necessary is not sufficient. Early childhood educators need access to appropriate quality digital resources. This includes reliable hardware, quality software, relatively cheap and fast access to the Internet and quality online resources. Furthermore they need an understandable framework from which they can generate learning activities using these quality digital resources.

One way of framing the pedagogy and curriculum around use of digital resources is to consider these resources in parallel to other resources already found in early childhood settings, such as paint, blocks, books and sand pits (Downes, Beecher and Arthur 2000). The task of the early childhood educator, then, becomes one of structuring learning environments in which young children use digital media and tools to express and represent their thoughts, understandings and feelings as they make sense of their worlds – just as they would with traditional media (paper, sand, blocks) and tools (brushes and spades). All these resources offer children alternate ways to play, interact with others, investigate their environments, to solve problems and to be creative.

Positive learning outcomes require educators to make pedagogically sound decisions about the nature of the learning experience and the appropriateness of the digital resource. Teachers and parents need to pay attention to evaluating digital resources in the same way as they would for other learning resources. This paper reports on a project where current online resources were evaluated for use with young children.

2. OVERVIEW OF PROJECT

The project reported upon in this paper was conducted in 1999. It focused on the use of digital resources, particularly the Internet, with children eight years and under. Participants in the study represented the stakeholders in early childhood education across day care, preschool and early years of school: educators, systems representatives, academics, researchers, policy makers and advisers, parents and children. They were asked to reflect on their beliefs and practices with digital technologies and to suggest ways in which Internet sites could be better designed and used to support children's learning.

Data concerning the participants' views and current practices involving digital resources were collected in a range of ways. Methods included: a one day national workshop for early childhood educators and researchers from around Australia; telephone interviews with early childhood educators; focus group discussions with parents and with children; observations of children interacting with online resources; and evaluation of online educational and recreational sites. Early childhood teacher education students identified and evaluated appropriate educational, recreational and popular culture sites relevant and appropriate for young children in the age groups birth to five and five to eight and they identified key elements in the nature and provision of Internet sites for young children.

Children's sites on the Internet were judged according to the nature, safety, portability and the overall quality of the site with consideration given to the site's purpose. Quality was defined in terms of content and design.

2.1 Content

Five key criteria were used to assess quality.

2.1.1 Open-ended experiences

Resources that are open-ended enable children to respond and interact in their individual ways, at their own pace, and to explore their own interests. Thus children can investigate, problem solve and jointly construct with others as they pose questions and share findings. In doing so, children often discover new unintended uses for resources and become highly engaged in their investigations.

2.1.2 Appropriate challenges

Online resources for young children need to respond to what children can do independently as well as what children can do with assistance from peers and adults. The nature of complexities inherent in the resource needs to be appropriate to the child in addition to being culturally relevant and of personal interest. Appropriate resources move with the child's changing competencies and learnings (NAEYC 1998) and can thus be used repeatedly by the child (Mamamedia 1998).

2.1.3 Opportunities for collaboration

Useful online resources for young children promote social interactions, contributing to increased levels of co-operation and assistance. Children prefer to collaborate with one or two other children to working alone (NAEYC 1998). Associated with this collaboration is often language learning as children discuss ideas, take turns and negotiate. The Internet also provides children with opportunities for collaboration with others beyond the setting and so broadens a narrow, local or ethnocentric view of people and the world.

2.1.4 Quality of information and experiences

Children benefit from access to sites that offer an expansive range of information and experiences that are relevant to their own lives and interests as well as to the curricula of the first years of school. The information needs to be accurate and current and to be organised and presented in ways that reflect various mixes and levels of challenge of aural, visual and written texts.

2.1.5 Ability to cater for diversity and challenge stereotypes

All resources convey explicit and implicit messages about people to children. Each child's uniqueness should be acknowledged and supported by positive sounds, images and texts about cultures, languages, lifestyles, families and differing abilities (NAEYC 1998). In addition, opportunities to challenge and critique prevailing assumptions and stereotypes are important for children from the dominant culture as well as for those from minorities.

2.2 Design

Four key criteria were used to assess the quality of design.

2.2.1 Integration of sound, text, graphics and animation

Sites attractive to young children appeal to their senses, since this is how children explore and learn about their environment. Children want to investigate and seek to explore objects that respond in some way to their actions. Therefore appearance, sound and animation are significant aspects to consider when evaluating the suitability of a resource. Integrated sound, graphics, animation and text are necessary within resources, especially for under fives (Mamamedia 1998, De Voogd and Kritt 1997).

2.2.2 Ease of navigation

Sites need to be easy to access and to use. Navigation within the site and between the various activities needs to be obviously different to that which takes the child into and out of the site, or from the activities to the marketing areas. Consistency in layout promotes children's successful navigation (El-Tigi 1996).

2.2.3 Efficient technology

Children want resources to respond quickly to their actions, continue the interactions and propose some form of feedback. Sites need to be stable, consistently available and load with ease. Young children's requirements for resources offering quality graphics, sound, text and speed contradict what technology can presently supply. The purpose of these features needs to be assessed by educators when making judgements about efficient technology of resources.

2.2.4 Safety

Safety is of prime importance as children's contact with Internet resources increases and commercial sites multiply. Families express concerns about children being targeted and used for commercial purposes and seek security assurances. Current debates include claims of deceptive online marketing where children are targeted by advertisers, where content and advertising are integrated and where characters promote products (see http://www.cme.org). Implications for judging sites include:

- Checking that there is a clear distinction between advertising and editorial focus;
- Ensuring that the family need to give permission before information is collected from children; and
- Checking that the privacy policy declares if collected information is sold to unknown parties (Mamamedia 1998).

3. FINDINGS

The analysis of current online resources for young children identified a growing number of sites that were labelled as children's sites. Over sixty sites for young children were located and evaluated. Children's sites on the Internet can be grouped into four types based on the nature of the activity undertaken. There were design and make sites, work and play sites (including activity and game, explore and investigate, and information sites), communicate and share sites, and online project sites. While these groups are not mutually exclusive, they provide a useful way of thinking about the nature and quality of Internet sites for young children.

3.1 Analysis of online resources

There was significant variation in the number and quality of sites suitable for different age groups. Similarly, there were variations, in number and quality of the various types of sites. Each of these differences will be discussed below.

3.1.1 Sites for the under fives and over fives

Overall the range and quality of resources for independent use by children under five were poor. Currently the higher quality digital resources that are appropriate for independent use by children of this age group already exist as CD-ROM based software. Many Internet sites required physical manipulation that meant it was difficult for children under five to navigate their way around. The sites were also heavily reliant on print text to make meaning. Most Internet experiences for this age group will continue to be useful in the short to medium term, when they are mediated, if only in part, by older peers, parents and educators. Communication and sharing sites, in particular, will remain joint activities until voice recognition and transmission are better-developed technologies.

For the five to eight year olds, the quality and range of resources were patchy, yet there were sufficient sites of quality to enable educators working in the early years of school to effectively integrate digital resources from the Internet into their curriculum. Of uniform quality were the online project sites, both in terms of the range of sites offered and the quality of the actual projects. Design and make sites could not compete with their CD-ROM counterparts. Appropriate work and play sites, particularly information sites, while patchy in quality, existed in sufficient numbers to make a validated collected of quality sites viable and extremely useful to educators. Communicate and share sites may continue to have little place in educational settings for their roles are already fulfilled by email and online project sites.

3.1.2 Availability and quality of different types of sites

There were few design and make sites which offered children the opportunity to create, make, design or build. The few sites for under fives reflected closed experiences, such as puzzles and colouring in, whilst sites for five to eight year olds offered more active and open-ended experiences such as making postcards and writing letters. However, these experiences demanded expertise with literacy processes beyond the level of many children in this age group.

Three types of work and play sites emerged:

- *Activity and game sites*: Many of these offered closed and trivial experiences which provided limited opportunities for making meaning and developing understandings. However, children often found these sites interesting and used them at home as they linked to information sites about popular culture characters.
- *Investigating sites:* There were very few sites offering investigative experiences. No such sites were found for children under five and few for five to eight year olds. The sites that were available, such as 'educational' sites provided by museums, more often than not provided closed experiences such as colouring.
- *Information sites:* The Internet provides easy access to information in relation to leisure activities and for school-related purposes. It was found that information sites abound for school curriculum areas and topics but rarely did these collections provide pointers to sites for under fives nor did similar validated collections of information sites exist for the under fives. Some sites appeared at first to be appropriate for under fives although the actual information the children were taken to was more appropriate for older children. The content of the information sites evaluated, however, would be valuable as resources for adult-directed or scaffolded use.

The Internet was seen by parents who participated in the consultation to be most useful as a tool for communicating with others although early childhood educators rarely spoke of using the Internet for themselves or with children in this way. As well the basic functions such as e-mail, the Internet provides a range of sites where children can chat with each other in a 'safe environment' and where they can publish their writings and artwork. However these sites seemed more appropriate for home than for educational settings, in the sense that e-mail (to known recipients) and communication and sharing through online projects already provide these facilities for educational settings.

Online project sites were mostly provided by educational authorities or organisations and included a range of high quality projects in which early childhood educators and young children could participate. The projects were aimed at the early years of school, although they could be adapted for use with younger children. While the projects tended to be structured, they encouraged high degrees of sharing and included possibilities for open-ended experiences. However, these sites were not generally used by early childhood educators.

4. CONCLUSIONS

Overall, the quality of sites that would be appropriate for young children to use independently was poor or patchy, with a better range being available for the five to eight year olds. However, many of the quality sites that had content suitable for younger children but required the reading of text would be appropriate for young children with adult assistance.

In terms of quality across various types of sites, the findings were mixed. The commercial activity and games sites, while well-designed, offered limited opportunity for making meaning or being creative. Most of the activities on work and play sites were closed and trivial. Greater potential for appropriate open-ended activities lies with the communicate-and-share sites and the specially designed online project sites. However, these types of sites were rarely accessed from home (where connection to the Internet was more common) or the early childhood centres. It would be fair to say that in general the CD-ROM based software currently offers the wider range of high quality open-ended learning environments for young children to use independently.

However, given the rapid expansion of the Internet in terms of access and the increase in the number and quality of sites, parents, educators, curriculum and policy makers need to become more aware of the potential of quality sites to enhance recreational and educational activities for young children, and to use these sites as they become more readily accessible.

REFERENCES

ABS (Australian Bureau of Statistics) (1998) *Household use of information technology* (Australian Catalogue No 8146.0). Commonwealth of Australia, Canberra.

Clements, D. (1999) Young children and technology. In *Dialogue on early childhood science, mathematics and technology education*, G. D. Nelson (Ed.), pp. 92-105. American Association for the Advancement of Science, Washington, DC.

DeVoogd, G. and Kritt, D. (1997) Computer mediated instruction for young children: Teachers and software missing the zone. *Site 97–Young children*. University of New Orleans, New Orleans.

Dockett, S., Perry, B. and Nanlohy, P. (1999) Computers in early childhood services: A part of the educational program or less time to play? *ARECE 99 Computers in Early Childhood Services*.

Downes, T., Beecher, B. and Arthur. L. (2000) *Effective learning environments for young children using digital resources: An Australian perspective*. A paper presented at the

World Congress on Computers in Beijing, China, August 2000 (contact t.downes@uws.edu.au for a copy of the paper).

El-Tigi, M. A. (1996) *Perception of elementary students of visuals on the web. VisionQuest: Journeys towards visual literacy.* Selected readings from the annual conference of the International Visual Literacy Association.

Mamamedia. (1998) What makes a good kids' website? [http://mamamedia.com/area/grownups/newhome.html].

Makin, L., Hayden, J., Holland, A., Arthur, L., Beecher, B., Jones Diaz, C. and McNaught, M. (1999) *Mapping literacy practices in early childhood settings.* 2nd edition, NSW Department of Community Services and NSW Department of Education and Training,Sydney.

McNaught, M., Clugston, L., Arthur, L., Beecher, B., Ashton, J., Hayden, J. and Makin. L. (2000) *The early literacy and social justice project: Final report.* NSW Department of Education and Training and NSW Department of Community Services, Sydney.

NAEYC (National Association for the Education of Young Children) (1998) *Position Statement on Technology and Young Children* [http://www.naeyc.org/about/position/pstech98.htm]

National Schools Board Foundation (2000) *Safe and smart: Research guidelines for children's use of the internet.* [http://www.nsbf.org/safe-smart/full-report.htm].

Roberts, D. F., Foehr, U. G., Rideout, V. J. and Brodie, M. (1999) *Kids and media @ the new millennium.* A Kaiser Family Foundation Report.

BIOGRAPHY

Leonie Arthur lectures in early childhood education; her research and teaching interests are in the areas of children's literacy including the role of play in literacy learning and multiple literacies. Bronwyn Beecher lectures in early literacy learning; her main research and teaching areas include links between prior to school and school settings, the role of technologies in literacy learning and literacy play. Toni Downes is an Associate Professor in educational computing; her current research projects span from early childhood education to university education.

PART EIGHT

TEACHER EDUCATION

66

Email Reducing Stress for Student Teachers

Bruce White and Rosie Le Cornu
School of Education, University of South Australia, Adelaide, Australia
Bruce.White@unisa.edu.au

Keywords: teacher education, electronic communication, research

Abstract: This paper reports on one aspect of a study which investigated the use of email between student teachers and university lecturers during the final practicum experience in a four year Bachelor of Education pre-service primary teaching course. The paper explores how the nature of electronic communication, together with the students' perceptions of 'university supervision' and their place in the school setting, affected the level of stress experienced by the student teachers in their placements. Student teacher stress has been reported in the literature as one factor which impedes student teacher learning during the practicum (Zeichner 1980). We argue that ICT has the potential to maximise student teachers' learning outcomes in the practicum by giving them more control over the learning process, reducing their stress, and enabling them to manage their practicum experience more effectively.

1. INTRODUCTION

The current context of higher education in Australia is characterised by reduction in government funding, strong competition amongst universities for students, and high staff-student ratios within many university programs. In addition, universities are being called to account for ensuring high levels of student learning outcomes while at the same time being asked to do so in increasingly more cost effective ways. These trends impact on the field-based components of pre-service teacher education programs (practicum), which traditionally have been costly in both time and money, but, as widely reported in the literature (Britzman 1991) seen by both students and educators as playing a critical role in pre-service teacher education.

Within this context, there has, at the same time, been an increasing focus on the use of ICT within the higher education sector. Much of this focus has been to support subject delivery for campus based courses and much has been written about the challenge of academics teaching 'on-line'. However, there has been much less written in regard to the practicum and ICT. It is only very recently that we are starting to read descriptions of its use, discussions about its value in the practicum and research into aspects of its application (Schlagal, Trathen and Blanton 1996, Wentworth, Monroe, Orme and Lynes 1999).

This paper reports on a study that investigated the use of email between student teachers and university lecturers during the final practicum experience in a four year Bachelor of Education pre-service primary teaching course.

2. BACKGROUND

The students involved in this study were enrolled in their final practicum subject, during which time the students had an on-campus component for ten weeks followed by a four weeks practicum. Each university lecturer teaching in the subject had a workshop group of about 27 students, with whom they worked in the structured on-campus program and then were responsible for them when they went into the practicum. The university lecturer's role was to support the student teachers in their schools via email and to support the mentors (supervising teachers) in schools via phone contact. The mentor's role was to facilitate their student teacher's professional growth. We encouraged a 'collaborative mentoring' approach that involved the following practices: systematic reflection, focused sharing, collaborative planning, negotiated observations, constructive feedback and learning conversations (McCann and Radford 1993). The emphasis in the final practicum subject was on the student teachers having increased autonomy and responsibility and so their role required them to be actively involved in their own learning.

The study investigated student teachers' experiences with 'email supervision'. This model of supervision required the student teachers to email their university lecturer twice throughout the practicum and make weekly contact with a peer, known as a 'critical friend'. This innovation was made possible because of two changed conditions. Firstly, the students were competent users of email, having had prior exposure to email though a core subject in the first year of their degree. In this subject students were taught how to use the University computer systems, email, discussion lists and netiquette. In addition to this subject, students were then expected to communicate with their lecturers and tutors via email throughout the remainder of their course. Secondly, schools in South Australia had recently been connected to the Internet in a systematic way that provided World Wide Web (WWW) and email access to all teachers and students.

The wide range of skill and comfort levels within the teaching population, together with access problems in the past, has meant that we are only now trailing email communication with the teachers. This paper therefore focuses only on student teachers' and university lecturers' experiences with email.

3. METHODOLOGY

The study had two stages. In 1999 a pilot study was conducted with twenty students, involving the use of focus groups. The focus groups were conducted several months after the students had completed their practicum and revolved around questions which explored student teachers' experiences with ICT in the practicum, what helped and what hindered and their perceptions of using email as a form of communication in the practicum. The focus group data were analysed and key issues were identified.

The second stage of the study focused on the 2000 cohort of 124 students who went to 84 schools for the practicum. A questionnaire, based on the issues highlighted from the focus groups and the literature, was administered to the students on completion of their practicum. The data from the questionnaires were then entered and analysed using SPSS.

4. RESULTS AND DISCUSSION

In the results ninety-three (76.2%) of the student teachers surveyed regarded 'email supervision' as appropriate for the final practicum. When the reasons for this were analysed, reduction of stress was one of the key findings. It is this particular finding which is the focus of this paper. The factors that were perceived as reducing stress will be discussed under the following headings.

- Structural and cultural conditions of practicum
- Nature of electronic communication.

4.1 Structural and cultural conditions of practicum

The traditional practicum experience, where student teachers spend time observing and teaching in one classroom, has been criticised in the literature, for not optimising student teacher learning (Martinez 1990, Zeichner 1980). In the past decade, many teacher educators have been involved in reconceptualising the practicum around the concepts of reflection, partnerships and collaboration. It is recognised that for practicum reform to be effective there must be a focus on both structural changes, referring to the changes to roles and responsibilities of the various participants in the practicum and cultural changes, or changes to the shared beliefs, customs, attitudes and expectations (Hargreaves 1994, Le Cornu 1999).

In this study, changes to the structural and cultural conditions of practicum were enabled by the use of electronic communications. The structural changes can best be exemplified by highlighting the perceived less threatening supervision experienced by some of the student teachers. The cultural changes can be exemplified by a perceived change in status in the school setting experienced by some of the student teachers. Each will now be briefly discussed.

4.1.1 Less threatening than traditional university supervision

Many of the student teachers found the 'email supervision' model utilised in the program, less threatening than the supervision they had been used to. They compared how they felt emailing their university lecturer, with their previous 'face to face' visits, where in many instances, they were observed in the classroom. The following quotes depict the anxiety associated with these visits:

> "It wasn't as threatening experience as personal contact i.e. Uni. supervisors breathing down your neck."

> "It was a lot more comfortable than having a Uni. supervisor 'watching' our lessons."

This finding is consistent with the claim in the literature that it is the 'act of being supervised' that causes stress (Calderhead 1988). Even with changes which have been made to supervision, from traditional models based on classroom observation to more facilitatory models which aim to develop the reflective capabilities of prospective teachers (Martinez 1990), university supervision, which requires face to face communication, continues to be problematic. Amidst the current climate of reduction in government funding, higher student-staff ratios and increased expectations and demands on academics' time, school visits by university staff are becoming increasingly difficult to maintain. Even when students are seen in their school by a university lecturer, conversations are often short and usually focus on immediate classroom practices and events of the day (Wentworth et al. 1999). Moreover, school environments are becoming increasingly 'busy places' and so people feel under pressure to make time available within school time, to meet. Similarly, student teachers are leading increasingly busier, more complicated lives, with many of them often juggling part-time work commitments alongside their practicum commitments. As one student described the benefits of the email process:

> "Easy, quick. We had a lot to do. This was 'low stress' which was great."

The flexibility of emailing, together with the reduced stress of a face to face visit, were seen by many of the student teachers to contribute to the ease of managing their practicum. The role of student teacher as 'manager', of both the personal and professional dimensions of being a 'student teacher', is increasingly, a more demanding role. Student teachers need to be able to manage the demands of 'learning to teach' as well as their own energy and stress levels. Emailing their university lecturer, in this study, was seen to enable this process.

4.1.2 Perceived changed status within the school setting

Some of the student teachers in this study clearly perceived a change in status, for themselves within the school setting. Rather than seeing themselves as 'only student teachers', they saw themselves as emerging professionals. They interpreted the use of electronic communication as a way of supporting their level of maturity in the course. This point is depicted in the following:

> "We are about to enter the teaching profession so it was good that we were treated that way."

> "Shows we can be trusted. It was made our responsibility."

Not only did the student teachers perceive themselves differently, but a number reported a different relationship they experienced with their mentor and other school staff, as they too perceived them differently. Several student teachers reported examples where they had been publicly cited as 'colleagues', particularly where they had been seen to make a contribution to the school environment. A relevant example of this was related to the students' competency in the use of technology, where they were able to provide assistance and in-service training on the use of ICT. This perceived change in status is important, given what we know about the micro-politics of the practicum, where issues of status and power impact on both student teacher learning and their stress levels (Groundwater-Smith 1993).

While student teachers will always encounter a range of confusing and often contradictory messages about their position in a school, how we, as university teacher educators interact with our students 'in the field', can affect the level of stress experienced by them.

4.2 Nature of electronic communication

Much has been reported in the literature about the benefits of asynchronous electronic communication (Everett and Ahern 1994, Jonassen 1996) and this was also evident in the data collected in this study. Email enabled both lecturer and student teacher to contribute to professional discussions at various times convenient to them. Some student teachers were able to utilise non-teaching time in schools to access a computer and email their university lecturer, while others chose to do it from home after the school day had finished. In terms of access almost half of the students (45.1%) used email from home, with 31.1% accessing from their school setting, with the remainder of the students accessing from other unnamed locations. Access was rated as 'easy' or 'very easy' by 88.9% of the students with only five students (4.3%) rating it as 'very difficult'.

> "The flexibility and ease of access afforded by the use of email is reflected in the following:"
>
> "It is often difficult to arrange a time to meet people while teaching at school. It is much easier to email."

The students had varying perceptions of the emailing process with the majority of students identifying it as a written communication (65.8%), and more than half the students (71.3%) proof reading their email before they sent it. The comments indicated that these students saw it more as a formal 'professional' process and allowed them time to construct their response. For example:

> "Writing is different to speaking. Good to have 'professional' and 'independent' dialogue."
>
> "I was able to sit down on the weekend and really think about what I would write rather than just babble on the phone. It was useful for me to reflect on the week and be quite open about what I wrote. I definitely prefer written contact than oral/verbal."

However a small number likened email to the spoken word and regarded it as a much less formal process. This was exemplified in the following:

> "Email is a verbal form of communication, and it was like speaking personally of successes and failures. It was less formal than a written response, which allowed honesty and reflection."

> "As I saw it as a verbal mode of communication, I was able to really engage."

From these results it can be seen that regardless of the students' perception of the nature of email, they were able to engage with the medium.

In the second stage of the study guiding questions were provided to the student teachers to assist them when communicating with their lecturers. This overcame a concern that had emerged in the stage 1 focus groups in regard to what to write in their emails. The results showed that 90% of the students found these questions very useful in structuring their email responses. Their written comments supported this finding, as exemplified by:

> "It encouraged me to identify areas of significance, and critically reflect on these."

This is consistent with the work of Geer and Au (1998) who also found that while email has the potential to increase interaction and encourage a deeper understanding of the subject matter it needs to be supported.

Engaging in 'learning conversations' has been found to be of use both in the learning to teach process, and in ongoing teacher development (McLaughlin 1997). Opportunities for these conversations were structured into the design of the email supervision process described in this paper. The students were asked to rate the effectiveness of the dialogue with their mentor, critical friend and the university lecturer, on a scale of 1 to 5 where 1 was 'ineffective' and 5 was 'very effective'.

Table 1. Dialogue Effectiveness

	Mean	Std. Deviation
Dialogue with my mentor	4.5084	.7421
Dialogue with my critical friend	4.1780	.8611
Email dialogue with my workshop lecturer	3.9957	1.0245

From Table 1 it can be seen that students found all three sources of dialogue useful in terms of their learning. The most useful dialogue identified by the students was not surprisingly with their mentor, but the level of satisfaction with both their critical friend and their university lecturer was still very high.

5. CONCLUSION

While we are not advocating 'email supervision' for all students in all practicums, this study has shown that email can be used effectively by university teacher educators to facilitate less stressful practicum experiences for student teachers. There will always be an element of stress for student teachers in relation to the practicum because of its very nature, however ICT has the potential to give more control over the learning process to the student teachers and therefore enable them to manage their practicum experience more effectively.

The students in this study clearly valued the email dialogue they had with their university lecturer during the practicum. This confirms the importance of the university lecturer's role in practicum, but at the same time challenges the established and often romanticised views of the value of face-to-face university supervision which, of economic necessity as mentioned earlier, has decreased in frequency and quality over the last years.

REFERENCES

Britzman, D. P. (1991) *Practice makes practice: A critical study of learning to teach*. State University of New York Press, Albany NY.

Calderhead, J. (1988) The Contribution of Field Experiences to Student Primary Teachers' Professional Learning. *Research in Education*, 40, pp. 33-49.

Everett, D. R. and Ahern, T. C. (1994) Computer-mediated communication as a teaching tool: A case study. *Journal of Research on Computing in Education,* 26 (3), pp. 356-357.

Geer, R. and Au, W. (1998) Electronic mail and student learning. In *Where is IT & T at? ACEC 98 Refereed Conference Proceedings,* CEGSA, Adelaide, pp. 76-81.

Groundwater-Smith, S. (1993) The micro-politics of the practicum: A critical issue. In *Learning in the Field: The Current Face of Practical Experiences in Professional Preparation,* Post Conference Publication of the 5th National Practicum Conference, Macquarie University, Sydney.

Hargreaves, A. (1994) Restructuring – beyond collaboration. In *Changing Teachers, Changing Times: Teachers' Work and Culture in the Postmodern Age*, Cassell, London.

Jonassen, D. H. (1996) *Computers in the classroom: Mindtools for critical thinking*. Prentice Hall, New Jersey.

Le Cornu, R. (1999) Remapping the Practicum in Teacher Education. *Waikato Journal of Education*, 5, pp. 121-132.

Martinez, K. (1990) Critical Reflections on Critical Reflection in Teacher Education. *The Journal of Teaching Practice,* 10 (2), pp. 20-28.

McCann, I. and Radford, R. (1993) Mentoring for Teachers: the collaborative approach. In *The Return of the Mentor*, B. Caldwell and E. Carter (eds.), Falmer Press, London, pp. 25-43.

McLaughlin, M. (1997) Rebuilding Teacher Professionalism in the United States. In *Beyond Educational Reform: Bringing Teachers Back In*, A. Hargreaves and R. Evans (eds.), Open University Press, Buckingham.

Schlagal, B., Trathen, W. and Blanton, W. (1996) Structuring telecommunications to create instructional conversations about student teaching. *Journal of Teacher Education*, 47 (3), pp. 175-183.

Wentworth, N., Monroe, E., Orme, M. and Lynes, B. (1999) Enriching Preservice Field Experience through Email Mentoring. In *Society of Information Technology in Teacher Education*, Conference Proceedings.

Zeichner, K. (1980) Myths and Realities: Field Experiences in Preservice Teacher Education. *Journal of Teacher Education*, 31 (6), pp. 45-55.

BIOGRAPHY

Bruce White and Rosie Le Cornu are lecturers at the University of South Australia, involved in preservice K-12 teacher education. Their current research includes ways that ICT can be used to develop a learning community to support student in the practicum.

67

Using IT to Support Authentic Tasks in Teacher Education

Dianne Chambers and Martin Boyle
Science & Mathematics Education, Faculty of Education, The University of Melbourne, VIC 3010 Australia
d.chambers@unimelb.edu.au

Keywords: teacher education, case studies, teamwork, innovation

Abstract: Preparing teachers, who will be teaching until perhaps 2040, for classrooms and schools whose technology we can barely imagine is a daunting task. At the Department of Science & Mathematics Education at the University of Melbourne, Australia, a number of projects have been undertaken to allow undergraduate education students to engage in tasks and situations that will foreshadow their experiences as teachers. Online and multimedia resources have been developed that allow students to be projected into their future role as a teacher and it has been found that students respond well to this style of teaching. Observation of student work using these resources shows deeper thinking and enhanced reflective practices in considering how classrooms can be managed and in working as a team.

1. INTRODUCTION

Education students have been observed to respond well to tasks for which they can see relevance in their future role as teachers. To enhance the learning of students the staff of the Department of Science and Mathematics Education (DSME) at the University of Melbourne, Australia, have developed resources that project undergraduate students into their future role as teachers by setting up authentic tasks and scenarios utilising multimedia. This paper will discuss some of the multimedia resources and a subject developed at the University of Melbourne for use in teacher education in the

Bachelor of Education (Primary) course. [It should be noted that a number of multimedia resources for authentic tasks have also been developed in the area of mathematics education within DSME – see Chambers and Stacey, (1999) for descriptions.]

The Bachelor of Education (Primary) degree is a four year course of study and is the principal vehicle for the training of primary (elementary/K-6) teachers at the University of Melbourne. In 1995 the degree was restructured and updated extensively. This restructuring was accompanied by a substantial reassessment of the direction of the course and of the priorities for competing areas. Furthermore, budget constraints imposed a rethinking of delivery of the course and of the ways in which students undertake practical experience in schools. From the end of 1996, a reduction of 20% was made in the number of days of supervised practical work in schools ('teaching rounds'). It was therefore an ideal time to invest in revising course delivery in the Bachelor of Education (Primary) degree. Multimedia has the potential to make experience with children a well-integrated part of the university course. In this paper two recent projects in the area of information technology (IT) in education are described. We highlight the ways students engage actively with multimedia resources and the authentic tasks that have been designed to give students 'experiences', skill development, and knowledge about being effective users of IT as a classroom teacher and in being a decision-maker about IT issues in a school. [The term 'student' is used throughout this paper to mean a student in a teacher education course.]

2. USING MULTIMEDIA IN TEACHER EDUCATION

2.1 Computers and the K-6 classroom: Kids can do!

For the compulsory second year undergraduate subject 'Computers in the Primary Classroom' a resource entitled *Computers and the K-6 Classroom: Kids Can Do!* (Chambers and Dobbins 1997) was developed in 1996-97 with version 1 being launched late in 1997 (version 2 was released in early 1999, and version 3 is projected for release in 2002). This resource contains lecture notes and workshop activities, over 100 articles about using computers in K-6 classrooms, demonstration versions of educational software for children, examples of teachers' and children's classroom work with computers, and the *Virtual Classroom* resource. *Kids Can Do!* is used as a resource to support traditional 'face to face' teaching with a weekly lecture and workshop over an academic year.

The *Virtual Classroom* was developed using Macromedia's *Director* program and contains QuickTime VR with embedded video clips of three local classrooms that allows students to view a class in action, and includes interviews with the three classroom teachers (Figure 1). The three classroom models illustrated are: a classroom with two computers; a computer laboratory; and a 'mixed model' of classroom computers plus access to a computer laboratory. Each teacher has a different view on why their style of using computers works for them and for the children in their class. The inclusion of a range of, sometimes contradictory, opinions was deliberate so that our students could see that there are many ways of using computers and associated technologies effectively in classrooms. That is, the effectiveness of the use of computers was dependent not on the number of computers available or the layout of the computers in the room, but rather on how a teacher uses the resources and manages their classroom.

Figure 1. A 'flattened' image from one of the QuickTimeVR photographs from the Virtual Classrooms from 'Computers and the K-6 Classroom: Kids Can Do!' CD-ROM

The *Virtual Classroom* resource is quite different from many commercially available resources, such as 'Learning about Teaching' (Mousley, Sullivan and Mousley 1996) that shows lessons or lesson segments. The *Virtual Classroom* resource illustrates classroom activities, as it presents a snapshot in time of all that is going on in a busy classroom. As our students 'move' around the room they can see what each group of children is doing and how the teacher is managing the classroom.

2.2 Analysing classroom interactions and classroom management

In the *Virtual Classrooms* resource our students explore the classrooms of teachers at three schools. The classrooms and teachers were selected as each is using computers effectively across the curriculum, yet there are major differences in how the computers are used and how they are set up in (and out of) the classrooms. The observation of classrooms and their workings by our students is made considerably easier through the use of multimedia, as it allows all students to observe exemplary practice in the uses of computers in the classroom. This is something not all students have an opportunity of observing during their time in school experience ('teaching rounds') and the same experience is shared by all classmates. In addition, students can visit and revisit the *Virtual Classroom* and as their own experience grows they extract new significance from the interactions they observe.

Students investigate aspects of the room in a QuickTimeVR environment and by clicking on 'hotspots' a video clip of an interaction is played. Our second year teacher education students analyse the classrooms in the *Virtual Classrooms* resource to investigate the interactions and to identify the key issues in classroom management in using computers effectively that are illustrated in the video clips. Students work in pairs for this activity and they engage in thoughtful discussions. Their responses indicate deep reflection on the layout and activities in the classrooms – the level of reflection and focus on the task is often greater than during other activities with these students. Below is an example of a second year undergraduate student's response to an aspect of this task. It indicates both detailed observation and identification of the key issues illustrated in one video clip.

> "The classroom was well set-up with different activity tables relating to the same theme. This scene showed how organised the boys were when they had finished their computer task. They immediately went straight to the roster chart, marked it off and checked which activity they had to move to next. It showed them working co-operatively, and they were not distracted as they knew exactly where they had to go next. The roster was placed strategically near the teacher so that she could also keep an eye on who should be where and when. All computers were placed against the back wall, with their wires placed at the back of the tables."

3. USING PBL AND A SUBJECT WEBSITE FOR LEARNING ABOUT SCHOOL-WIDE IT ISSUES

During the third and fourth years of the Bachelor of Education (Primary) degree students select one optional subject each year. This allows students flexibility to strengthen an area of interest at an advanced level or to broaden their knowledge in a chosen area. An option that is available in either third or fourth year is the subject 'IT in Primary Schools'. This subject runs over 18 weeks in a weekly two hour block. The subject employs the problem based learning [PBL] approach (see Stover 1998, Stepien and Gallagher, 1993) and each problem is explored in a three week cycle (Table 1).

Table 1. Activities during the three week cycle of each problem in the subject 'IT in Primary Schools'

Week 1 (of 3 week cycle)
• 1h introduction that raises general issues that may be useful when approaching the problem – Supported by materials available on subject website including many links to useful sites
• 1h workshop where the problem is introduced – Supporting artefacts, including a rich description of the fictional school and its staff, to support the problem are available on the subject website
Week 2 (of 3 week cycle)
• 2h workshop session for teams to work on the problem with staff available to mentor the teams.
• Experts (principals, teachers, and others) are available (via email) to team leaders to gather further information about the problem and solutions/suggestions/ideas. This will provide students with a range of views on the problem and will require development and refinement of questions to ask and interpretation of responses.
Week 3 (of 3 week cycle)
• 2h workshop where teams present to the group their recommendations, the style of meeting is similar to a school council meeting.
• Students critique and discuss the recommendations of each team.
• The teams submit a 'Recommendations' document in a format suitable to send to school council members or the principal.

In this subject the students work in teams of five students and tackle five problems involving IT in a primary school over the course of the academic year. The scenario presented to teams is that of committees that are established to respond to a brief developed by the school principal. The team leader is in the role of committee chair and team members as committee members. Teams meet in scheduled class times once each week and are expected to confer – either electronically or in person – outside class time in addition to during class.

The problems include: allocating a budget for IT needs of the school; developing an IT professional development plan for the staff; integrating IT into the curriculum; and, designing the physical layout of a classroom that is about to have IT infrastructure installed. Teams are supplied with a rich description of the (fictional) school and artefacts (such as budget documents, IT skills profiles of staff members, community responses about internet use for children, *etc.*). These allow them to explore the context of the problem and to tease out aspects of the problem they need to explore and consider. These materials are available to students through the subject's website and may be text, video, or images of 'school documents' as appropriate. In addition to the artefacts, 'experts' are made available for each problem for the team leaders to communicate with via email. These experts are teachers, principals or other experts that have some knowledge of some aspects of the problem and experience in how their school has approached a similar problem. They are drawn from the Australian educational community and are experienced educators who have been invited to work with our students to develop their skills and to mentor the students through the problem. In keeping with the problem based learning approach, problems are not so tightly defined that there is a simple answer, and there is no single 'right' answer. It is expected that students will develop recommendations that differ vastly from team to team and that students will learn much from considering and critiquing the recommendations of other teams.

Each team develops recommendations that they present to other teams and to academic staff members in a 'School Council' style of meeting and prepare as a written recommendations, documents for submission. Students take on the role of team leader on a rotating basis and this is where responsibility for compiling and submitting the report and the presentation rests. All students contribute to the team's report of recommendations for all problems (as in the role of committee members). This allows students to have experience in working as a team and in leading a team to meet a deadline. These are highly valued skills for students to develop in addition to the content knowledge developed through exploring each of the problems.

3.1 Why problem based learning for learning about IT in schools?

Finkle and Torp (1995) described problem based learning (PBL) as "a curriculum development and instructional system that simultaneously develops both problem solving strategies and disciplinary knowledge bases and skills by placing students in the active role of problem solvers confronted with an ill-structured problem that mirrors real-world problems". This approach for the subject was considered when new graduates (first year teachers) informed us that they were members of the Information Technology Committee (or equivalent) at their school. This is a large role for a new teacher and one for which little of their university studies had prepared them. In response to this need, the subject was developed to give to students experiences in tackling the kinds of IT issues that they may encounter when a teacher, and to experience the role of committee member and chair of a committee with responsibilities for developing a report with recommendations for a school council or principal.

Other powerful learning experiences to support the PBL approach are the individual reflections that each student prepares in the week following the conclusion of each problem. In this document the student reflects on their role in the task and the team process, the activities that facilitated or blocked their learning, and their overall response to the learning experience the problem gave them. Following is part of a reflection from the problem about integrating IT into the curriculum, and illustrates the rich experience that can be gained using this approach in teacher education.

> "Having to participate in this problem in the hypothetical role of a teacher gave me great insight into my own thoughts and feelings about teaching and learning. I had never consciously applied a teaching philosophy in any of my own work nor assigned a certain style of learning for students to use. Working through this problem enabled me to think about the sort of teacher that I want to be and how I would like my students to learn. Constructivism and PBL model effective teaching practice about teaching and learning."

3.2 Why use IT to support a PBL subject?

All subjects taught by the Computers in Education group of the Department of Science and Mathematics Education have a website, including undergraduate subjects (all of which are taught on campus in the 'face to face' mode). The subject web sites are routinely used by students for accessing course materials, including lecture and workshop notes. It was thus natural that materials to support this subject would be delivered online as part of the subject website and the technology allows us to include audio and video and to host electronic discussions to support the problems. Making artefacts that support the problems available through the subject's website also allows us the opportunity to model to our students some ways of using technology to support teaching and learning.

4. CONCLUSIONS

The resources that have been developed for undergraduate teacher education studies at the University of Melbourne allow our students to have experiences where they can see exemplary practice in a classroom or investigate how authentic problem involving IT in a school may be solved.

Our experience to date has been that multimedia used in educationally appropriate ways has enhanced our teacher education courses. Using technology in these ways has allowed our students to 'experience' classroom situations where technology is being used in exemplary ways to support children's learning and to analyse situations at a school level and consider alternative solutions or paths of action while working in a team.

In both of these examples, common elements that strongly influence students' experience and learning are that: (i) students have the opportunity to hear the opinions of practising teachers; (ii) students do not work on these materials alone, but rather must discuss their findings with colleagues; and (iii) that students are given opportunities to reflect on teaching and on their own learning. Connecting with the experiences of exemplary teachers, reflecting on observations and experiences, sharing with others and developing the skills required in being a successful team member will serve our students well in the rapidly changing environment of schools of the twenty first century.

REFERENCES

Chambers, D. P. and Dobbins, M. (1997) *Computers and the K-6 Classroom: Kids Can Do!* (CD-ROM) Department of Science and Mathematics Education, University of Melbourne, Parkville, Victoria, Australia.

Chambers, D. P. and Stacey, K. (1999) *Technically simple and educationally rich multimedia to support authentic tasks in teacher education.* International Conference on Computers in Education (ICCE99). Kisarazu, Chiba, Japan.

Finkle, S. L., and Torp, L. L. (1995) *Introductory Documents*. Illinois Math and Science Academy. Aurora, Illinois.

Mousley, J., Sullivan, P. and Mousley, P. (1996). *Learning About Teaching*. Australian Association of Mathematics Teachers, Adelaide.

Stepien, W. and Gallagher, S. (1993) Problem-based learning: as authentic as it gets. *Educational Leadership,* April 1993 v50 n7 p. 25(4)

Stover, D. (1998) Problem-Based Learning: Redefining Self-Directed Instruction and Learning. *The Forum*, Fall 1998, vol. 7, Issue 1. [http://www.mcli.dist.maricopa.edu/labyforum/Fall98/forum7.html] October 2000.

BIOGRAPHY

Martin Boyle was educated in the UK and Australia, and after extensive school teaching experience has spent the last five years in teacher education. His research interests include developing learning environments to assist students who are failing in normal school mathematics.

68

Preparing Teachers to Teach Science and Mathematics with Technology

Margaret L. Niess
Science and Mathematics Education, Oregon State University, Corvallis, OR, USA
niessm@ucs.orst.edu

Keywords: teacher education, teaching methods, integration of ICT, secondary education, pedagogy

Abstract: Oregon State University has developed a teacher preparation model for preparing teachers to teach with technology. Student teachers develop extensive plans for implementing hands-on technology activities integrated with teaching science or math content. Following instruction, their reflections are directed toward student learning of science and math with technology. Does the technology support or hinder conceptual development? Ultimately, they recognise enhanced instructional outcomes related to the science and/or math of the technology. Recognition of this key factor enhances their understanding of integrating technology in a manner that extends student learning beyond traditional science or math outcomes.

1. INTRODUCTION

Emergence into the 21st century features tools that are different, communication that is different, information that is different, and work that is different. Education proposes to provide the avenue for success in an increasingly globally competitive marketplace. Teachers are asked to prepare students 'to live, learn, and work successfully in an increasingly complex and information-rich society' (ISTE 2000). This growing recognition highlights that learning must be different incorporating computer-based, electronic technologies, and that learning to use these technologies must not be separated from learning and communicating in the context of the academic subject areas. Given this perspective, how teachers have learned their content is not necessarily the way the topics should be taught in the 21st century.

New, ambitious mathematics and science standards propose a scientifically and mathematically rich curriculum where technology is an essential component of the learning environment, not only in the curriculum but also in the instruction. Similarly, new technology standards for students and teachers challenge educators to integrate technology throughout their instruction. The direction of these standards emphasises that electronic technologies are "an integral component or tool for learning and communications within the context of academic subject areas" such as mathematics and science.

The question remains: how are teacher preparation programs integrating technology into their courses and program outcomes to prepare teachers at a time when electronic technologies will significantly impact and change teaching and learning in K-12 science and mathematics classrooms? Recent calls have identified not only the need for research on inserting technology as a viable and integral part of the general education curriculum, but also for research to identify essential professional development for teachers to make this shift. These efforts underscore the need for identifying, testing and sharing different models that prepare teachers to teach with technology as an integral tool in teaching and learning.

2. THEORETICAL BACKGROUND

Numerous studies have yielded consistent findings on the difference in the thoughts and instructional practices of expert and novice teachers (Borko and Livingston 1989, Leinhardt 1989). As novices, pre-service teachers are involved in integrating new knowledge into their prior understandings for teaching the subject. From a constructivist perspective, as novices, their actions largely stem from personal experiences, an understanding largely based on having been taught their subject in particular ways. With teacher preparation program experiences and instructional practice, their beliefs, knowledge and thinking mature. Comprehensive reviews of research on teachers thought processes related to instructional practice have identified three important components: *planning* during the pre-active (prior to teaching) stage (Clark and Yinger 1979); *monitoring and regulating* during the interactive (teaching) stage (Fogarty et al. 1983); and *assessing and revising* in the post-active (after teaching) stage (Ross 1989). However, the development of an integrated knowledge structure more typical of expert teachers requires experiences focused on an integration of these stages. Pre-service teachers need experiences that specifically relate to or interconnect with their thinking in these three stages; the additional experiences provide critical actions in support of the growth and maturation of the pre-service teachers' decision making and thinking skills and abilities (Shavelson 1986).

With respect to teaching with technology, teacher preparation programs typically provide a course about technology perhaps with a unit or discussion on teaching with technology and a requirement that students design lessons to teach with the technologies. However, experiences that require the integration of the three stages of decision-making and thinking are typically missing. The purpose of this paper is to investigate a new model for preparing teachers to integrate teaching with technology within the context of teaching of science and mathematics. This exploratory study examines a model that emphasises the interaction of the three stages of decision-making to support connections more typical of the thinking processes of expert teachers when thinking about integrating technology in teaching science and mathematics. Two questions guided this research.

1. What are the key characteristics of the model of a preservice teacher preparation program focused on integrating teaching with technology in teaching science and mathematics?

2. What are the characteristics that describe successful preservice teachers in planning, implementing, and reflecting on instruction integrating technology in teaching science/mathematics?

To explore these questions, 22 students (admitted as a cohort group July 1999-June 2000) participated in the graduate level, subject specific (mathematics/science) teacher preparation program. For admission, students had earned a Bachelor's degree with the equivalent of a major in the teaching area (e.g. biology). Once admitted to the program, students were referred to as 'interns' because of the extensive internship requirements in the program.

3. THE PROGRAM

Oregon State University offers a one-year, 54-quarter hour, graduate level, subject-specific science and mathematics teacher preparation program for grades 3-12 focused on the integration of technology throughout the year. The overall conceptual framework of the program emphasises the development of an integrated knowledge structure of the various domains of knowledge critical for effective teaching, a framework described as Knowledge Growth in Teaching (Shulman 1986). With an emphasis on the integration of six domains of knowledge (subject matter, learners, schools, curriculum, pedagogy, and pedagogical content), the program supports the professional development of teachers in preparation to address and confront the multiplicity of decisions required during the preactive, interactive and post-active phases of teaching. Within this framework, key themes are emphasised in specific courses and practical experiences: (1) researched-based teaching and learning; (2) technology integration; (3) pedagogical content knowledge (PCK) development; and (4) instructional practice integrated with campus-based coursework.

The research-based teaching and learning theme is emphasised primarily in the Methods sequence and the Analysis of Classrooms sequence. The summer Methods course introduces interns to writing lesson plans that demonstrate a clear introduction, body or development, closure with estimated times, the content main points, planned key questions with expected answers, plans for explicit student involvement, instructional logistics, plans for extra time and early finishers, and plans for evaluation and homework. The subsequent Methods courses emphasise research-based instructional methods/modes, contemporary mathematics/science curriculum goals, classroom management instructional planning, and assessment of student achievement. The Analysis of Classrooms sequence applies observational techniques and effective teaching research to enhance interns' understandings of the complexities of classrooms and the school culture.

The technology integration theme emphasises preparing interns with skills in using electronic technologies, while also preparing them to engage their students in learning using appropriate computer-based technologies that support the development of science and mathematics knowledge. The Technology courses are focused around the pre-active, interactive, and post-active stages of teaching to provide interns with methods, abilities, and skills in teaching with technologies, preparing them to make informed decisions about which technologies to use for teaching specific topics in the curriculum. They receive direct instruction in the use of technologies in teaching mathematics and science over the four terms. The instruction models teaching specific science or mathematics concepts with technology. In the Technology and Pedagogy I course, interns are required to develop plans to teach with technology in a sequence of lessons (3-5 instructional days to be taught during their full-time internship). Real-time data collection devices are required as the technology. Since not all classrooms have access to such equipment, a classroom set is available. Interns are expected to prepare a planning notebook describing their proposed plans for teaching with the technology; the plans contain the rationale for teaching the particular lessons, goals/objectives, calendar, materials, detailed instructional plans, and evaluation plans. The plans must involve a pre-lab that includes a demonstration preparing students for working with the technology, a hands-on lab where students in groups collect data for investigating specific math/science concepts or problems, and a debrief or closure to the activity with some evaluation of the students' progress in meeting the objectives of the lessons. Faculty provide extensive reviews of the lessons and determine each intern's preparation to teach with technology. Interns are expected to make adjustments as recommended and have their university supervisor and mentor teacher review their work before actually teaching during their full-time internship (or student teaching). After teaching the technology sequence, interns are expected to revise and expand the planning notebook to reflect the actual teaching experience, adding their daily reflections on the lessons and an extensive analysis of teaching/learning. In this final section, the interns prepare an analysis of: (1) each student's understanding of the concept with the use of the technology in assisting in learning the concept, (2) the success of the integration of the technology in the lessons (overall as well as recommendations for changes), and (3) their own teaching while integrating technology. This final notebook is submitted in the Technology and Pedagogy II class, a class to extend the notion of teaching with technologies, particularly focusing on pedagogical concerns identified during the full-time internship. More specifically, this course highlights PCK aspects of teaching with technology. Concerns are presented about the misconceptions students may gain as a result of learning specific concepts with technology.

The theme of PCK is evident in more than the technology courses. Two classes, one prior the full-time internship and one following, focuses on PCK specifically related to teaching science and mathematics. Interns develop and analyse a variety of representations of subject matter within specific instructional contexts appropriate for different grade levels, different science/math content levels, and different student ability levels. These analytic experiences provide them with additional integrative experiences in the pre-active stage of teaching.

In support of the instructional practice theme, internships are integrated with the campus-based instruction, extending the opportunities to apply their knowledge about teaching, to critically observe classroom instruction, and to reflect on their experiences and developing integrated knowledge base. The interns are expected to plan, teach, and reflect on lessons integrating technology through a variety of instructional practice experiences interspersed throughout the other courses in the program. In the microteaching course, the interns plan and teach lessons, practising specific strategies (inductive, deductive, hands-on/lab, demonstration); one of the four lessons must include teaching with technology. Interns must reflect on the teaching experiences; and after submitting their reflection considering ways to improve the lesson and their own teaching, they are provided with the instructor's evaluations of the lesson plan and the teaching of that lesson.

These micro-teaching experiences focus the interns on the interactive phase of teaching providing both monitoring and regulating assistance; additionally, the reflective expectations are designed to continually interconnect their thinking in the three stages, preactive, interactive and post-active.

The school-based experiences focus on the preparation of lesson and unit plans, implementation of those plans, active interaction with students, implementation of management strategies, reflection on and revision of instruction, professional communication, and demonstration of content and pedagogical knowledge. The full-time internship (student teaching) takes place over Winter and Spring terms (12 weeks of teaching). During this full-time experience, the interns teach in multiple courses. Supervisors and mentors are asked to review all plans before teaching, complete weekly clinical supervision visits providing systematic feedback to monitor the interns' progress in teaching. Similarly, mentors and supervisors work with the interns with their technology sequence. Interns are required to reflect in writing following the teaching of each lesson taught.

This pre-service teacher preparation program differs from the traditional model with three, key ways.

1. Instruction with different technologies is specific to learning science/math, a subject specific teacher preparation. Problem-based activities are used to instruct the pre-service teachers in learning about the technology, teaching/learning with the technology, and teaching/learning the specific science/math topic.

2. Assignments and expectations for learning to teach science/math with technology are interwoven among all courses. All faculty members have responsibility to present technology as an integral component for teaching and learning science/math.

3. Interns are required to actually plan, teach, and reflect upon sequences of lessons that involve their students in hands-on work with technology during their full-time internship. Interns are supported by activities that require them to integrate their thinking and decision-making interrelating the pre-active, interactive and post-active stages of teaching.

4. INTEGRATING TECHNOLOGY IN TEACHING: KEY FACTORS

To investigate the model for preparing to integrate technology in this teacher preparation program, systematic course observations were supported with informal interviews and formal meetings with supervisors, faculty, and interns. Collection and analysis of all coursework and assignments provided the basis for the previous description of the program identifying the key characteristics of the model. To identify the characteristics of successful interns in teaching with technology, analysis of the data occurred at two stages: (1) the completion of the first six months of the program immediately prior to the full-time internship and (2) the completion of the entire pre-service program (in June).

At each stage, the interns' success and preparation for integrating technology in teaching science/mathematics were assessed. During the first stage, success was determined in terms of the demonstration of the ability to think carefully through the multitude of issues that might arise in teaching with technology. This ability was assessed primarily from the interns' planning notebooks. Interns were provided with extensive feedback on their plans for teaching with technology. In describing the preparation of the intern's for teaching with technology, three areas (knowledge of content, knowledge of technology, knowledge of teaching with technology) were rated using a three point scale: Good, Adequate, or Inadequate. A rating of Good (indicating good preparation for teaching with technology) required a rating of Good in all three areas. The rating of Adequate meant that the ratings in each of the three areas were at least Adequate. The Inadequate rating indicated that at least one of the areas had received an Inadequate rating. The ratings were determined by assessing their plans prior to the full-time internship and on their revised plans, observations of their teaching, and the interns' reflections on teaching. Comparison of the plans prior to teaching, work during teaching, and the intern's reflective analysis provided the major data source for the second stage. The primary data source for the determination was the final technology experience notebook using similar ratings as with the prior notebook.

At the end of the program, of the 22 interns, 14 were identified as demonstrating good content knowledge in math/science, with technology, and in the integration of technology in teaching math/science; while six were identified as being adequately prepared while two interns were considered as inadequately prepared for teaching with technology. Key factors in the interns' decision making in the pre-active stage included recognition of the time requirement in preparation for teaching with technology in a laboratory setting. For a successful experience, interns needed to attend to the relevance of the lab work, the structure involved in the activities, the methods by which students record and report data, classroom management and evaluation of student work. Time and good organisational skills were essential for designing the hands-on activities, preparing materials with detailed instructions, thoroughly testing all the equipment and the lab details. Decisions in the interactive stage depended upon careful pre-active stage planning. Without the extensive planning, the interns were focused on classroom management and troubleshooting with the equipment rather than engaging student thought during the interactive stage. The post-active stage provided the interns with the greatest learning opportunity – thinking back over their planning and the results of their plans. Work during this stage focused on student learning with the technology, whether the technology supported or hindered concept development. At this point, successful interns recognised the importance of an additional set of outcomes when using the technology – outcomes related to the science and/or math of the technology. Recognition of this key factor focused their thoughts on integrating technology in a manner that enhanced student learning beyond the traditional science or math outcomes. Successful interns were able to integrate technology in their lessons in such as manner as to encourage students to explore science or mathematics in more depth and in ways that involved the theoretical basis of the technology.

5. SUMMARY

Teacher preparation programs preparing teachers to teach with technology must focus on the development and enhancement of three key domains of knowledge: knowledge of the subject matter – science or mathematics; knowledge of the technology, including an in depth understanding of the science and/or mathematics embodied in the technology; and knowledge of pedagogy – an understanding of teaching and learning. The one-year graduate program provides a model focused on an integration of these domains of knowledge to support the development of teachers to address and confront the multiplicity of decisions required during the three stages of teaching. Ultimately, the program focused the interns' thought processes on the development of pedagogical content knowledge required in teaching science/mathematics with technology. This highlights key factors for successful experiences: importance of extensive planning and preparation with concern for the content to be taught, the technology to be used, and teaching the content within a technology context (considering learner experiences, needs and skills, curriculum development, and instruction considering classroom implementation and management). Requiring pre-service teachers to actually teach a sequence of lessons provides them with opportunities for reflection that integrate their thinking and decision-making interrelating the pre-active, interactive and post-active stages of teaching, leading to an integrated knowledge structure with respect to teaching their content with technology. Thus, they naturally consider technology as they think about teaching mathematics or science. In one intern's words, "It is clear to me that even if the class did not use the technology to learn the topics ... they still would have learned the information. However, by using the technology the students were able to cover some objectives that wouldn't be so easily or quickly met without the use of technology."

REFERENCES

Borko, H. and Livingston, C. (1989) Cognition and Improvisation: Differences in Mathematics Instruction by Expert and Novice teachers. *American Educational Research Journal* 26 (4), pp. 473-498.

Clark, C. M. and Yinger, R. J. (1979) Teachers' Thinking. In *Research on Teaching,* P. L. Peterson and H. J. Walberg (eds.) Berkeley, CA: McCutchan, pp. 231-263.

Fogarty, J., Wang, M., and Creek, R. (1983) A Descriptive Study of Experienced and Novice Teachers' Interactive Instructional Thoughts and Actions. *Journal of Educational Research,* 77, pp. 22-32.

International Society for Technology in Education (2000) *National Educational Technology Standards for Teachers*. Eugene, OR: Author.

Leinhardt, G. (1989) Math Lessons: A Contrast of Novice and Expert Competence. *Journal for Research in Mathematics Education.* 20 (1), pp. 52-75.

Ross, D. D. (1989) First Steps in Developing a Reflective Approach. *Journal of Teacher Education,* 40 (2), pp. 22-30.

Shavelson, R. J. (1986) *Interactive Decision Making: Some Thoughts on Teacher Cognition.* Invited address, I. Congreso Internacional, "Pensamientos de los Profesores Y Toma deDecisiones," Seville, Spain.

Shulman, L. S. (1986) Those Who Understand: Knowledge Growth in Teaching. *Educational Researcher*, 15, pp. 4-14.

BIOGRAPHY

Margaret Niess is Professor of science and mathematics education and Director of science and mathematics teacher preparation. She has focused on the integration of instructional technology in teaching science and mathematics over the past 20 years and has led the integration of technology in graduate level, preservice teacher preparation (K-12) and in-service teacher preparation under given support from the US West Foundation. She is co-editor of *School Science and Mathematics* and mathematics section editor of *Learning and Leading with Technology.*

69

Multimedia and Online Video Case Studies for Preservice Teacher Preparation

Terence R. Cannings and Sue Talley
Graduate School of Education and Psychology, Pepperdine University, 400 Corporate Pointe, Culver City, CA, 90230, USA
cannings@pepperdine.edu

Keywords: case studies, teacher education, distance learning, multimedia, world wide web/website

Abstract: Case studies have been used successfully as a part of teacher education. There are many possibilities in extending the impact of case studies through the use of technology. Video and the Internet could enable demonstration of more examples, dissemination beyond the walls of the classroom, and discussion between geographically dispersed preservice teachers. Several projects are now investigating the possible ways that technology might enhance or extend text case studies. After exploring four existing products, four essential elements for video case studies are proposed. As video case studies move to the Internet, additional issues arise and these are also explored.

1. SCENARIO

Joe has the opportunity to use technology in his Math methods course. One of the demonstrations he sees in his face to face course is done by Paula Howe, a master teacher from a local school district who has actively worked to integrate appropriate technology with a very strong mathematics curriculum. Several other demonstrations are given by Dr. Lamp, the course instructor. Dr. Lamp also actively models the use of technology in the instruction of the course itself by appropriately using multimedia presentations. In addition, Joe uses many online resources to explore other possible technology resources that he can use in an elementary classroom.

These resources include several video case studies that encourage students to explore and discuss the infusion of technology into learning. Joe also creates lessons that infuse the technology and uses them as part of his student teaching experience.

All of these technology resources represent current thinking about best practices and are correlated to the appropriate state and national curriculum standards and frameworks. To make this particularly easy to see, the materials are indexed according to elements of the curriculum as well as subject levels. Joe is able to indicate specific areas of interest, just as he might on an e-commerce site for purchasing books. This will tell him of any new resources that have been added that might be of interest.

It is difficult for a novice teacher to enter any classroom and feel comfortable with the demands placed on them. In addition to the demands expected of a novice in the more traditional curriculum areas, Joe is expected to integrate technology tools to improve student achievement, as exemplified in the above scenario extract. Teacher educators continue to search for effective strategies that will enhance the use of technology tools in the preservice program and ultimately in the novice teacher's classroom. Unfortunately, "despite increasing demand for technology use in the classroom, many teachers still feel they are ill-prepared to integrate these tools into the classroom" (Sprague et al. 1998, p.25).

When faced with the challenge of developing more teachers and making certain that these teachers are prepared to infuse technology into their classroom learning strategies, new ways of preparing preservice teachers are clearly needed. This paper will describe one such strategy, development and use of multimedia and online video case studies in teacher preparation programs.

2. CASE STUDIES AND TEACHER EDUCATION

Traditionally, text-based case studies such as those developed by Judith Shulman (1992) and Rita Silverman (1996) enable preservice teachers to reflect upon descriptive scenarios on teaching and learning within a given context. These case studies have emerged as a powerful tool for bringing the complexities of classroom activities into focus and supporting preservice teachers in connecting theory and practice. Lee Shulman (1992) recommended the case study methodology as an effective tool to create a bridge between principle and practice in an "engaging, more demanding, more intellectually exciting and stimulating..." way (Shulman 1992, p. 16).

Similarly, Wasserman (1994), Silverman, Welty and Lyon (1996) and Merseth (1994) advocate case study methodology as an appropriate pedagogical technique for teacher education. As Merseth (1994) stated, a case study is "...a descriptive research document, often presented in narrative form, that is based on a real-life situation or event. It attempts to convey a balanced, multi-dimensional representation of the content, participants and reality of the situation" (p. 16). The scenarios presented within the case studies are essentially a tool for discussion and interpretation for users with differing perspectives. The case studies can be viewed in different ways, "Case [study] purpose falls into three categories: (a) cases as exemplars; (b) cases as opportunities to practice analysis, the assimilation of differing perspectives, and the contemplation of action; and (c) cases as stimulants for personal reflection" (Merseth 1994, p. 18). Adoption of these three categories, as shown later in the paper, presents developers of future case studies with interesting challenges.

Implicit in studying such cases is the understanding that there are no clear-cut, simple answers to the complex issues teachers face on an hourly or daily basis. These cases describe nettlesome dilemmas, which are the stuff of daily classroom life. Effective text-based case studies demand active student engagement and promote the preservice teacher's ability to discern the essential learning and teaching elements in a given situation, and to analyse and interpret data to inform an action.

According to Wasserman (1994), five basic principles guide the construction and use of text-based case studies for use in teacher preparation:

1. Cases are well written, 'pack a wallop', do not end with a resolution and help explain the relationship between the big ideas in the case and the preservice course. Cases that end with a dilemma encourage open debate.
2. Appended to each case is a list of study questions, which call for thorough examination of important issues raised by the case.
3. The small group's work ideas are discussed and tried out in the safest context.
4. Debriefing a case places great skill on the way the instructor interacts with the students.
5. In follow-up sessions, effective case method teaching allows students to grow away from a desperate quest for right answers and solutions. (p. 16)

With increased Internet bandwidth, preservice students can now view video segments simply by accessing a website. That is, they can watch the action rather than just read about it. They can see and hear the teacher and students as they interact in the classroom. But do the same principles for designing and using text-based case studies apply to the online video version?

3. MULTIMEDIA AND ONLINE VIDEO CASE STUDIES

Emerging technologies, such as digital video and editing, more powerful CPUs, and DSL and cable delivery services, have now made available new instructional possibilities and multiple ways of presenting video case studies. Video, with graphic and text-based support, can capture the complexity of classroom interactions enabling preservice teachers to view the 'real' teaching and learning strategies utilised by the teacher. This video allows a group of students to share a common experience and review, perhaps over several sessions, important or critical teaching strategies missed in earlier viewings. As Barron and Goldman (1994) suggest, "from our own experience in using integrated media with preservice teachers, and from similar research and development efforts at other institutions, we are encouraged about the use and potential of such materials in preparing teachers for the challenges of the classroom" (pp. 104-105). But technology tools and delivery systems have changed greatly since 1994 with the Internet now the predominant delivery system.

According to Perry (2000), "the Internet and multimedia, which includes the non-linear integration of video, audio, graphics, and text, can provide a rich environment for case studies that promote the construction of knowledge about integrating technology into the curriculum in a learning community of peers and faculty facilitators" (p. 4). With advancements in web delivery, this environment can be accessed anytime and anywhere in a convenient and cost-effective way. Lindeman et al. (1995) support this claim by arguing that the web provides a new vehicle for delivering video cases to learners with the ability to transmit text, graphics, sound, short video clips, and hypertext. In addition, Kovalchick, Hrabe, Julian and Kinzie (1999) suggest that the web provides "three significant capabilities for the delivery of case studies: (a) the ability to simulate real-world complexities, (b) the ability to use multiple media in case presentations, and (c) the ability to use hyperlink/hypertext navigation features" (p. 145).

At two recent symposiums (AERA, New Orleans and US Department of Education, Atlanta, 2000) that focused on the development of online video case studies, several questions were raised as to the optimal use of this strategy: Do we show best practices or teaching dilemmas? Are the videos real or staged? Do the videos include single incidents or composite incidents? How should an instructor best use online discussion with video case studies? What are the intellectual property issues? Can we include children in online video case studies? How can we avoid surface mimicking and promote learning of best practices? See Online Video Case Study Conference Web site references:

New Orleans:
http://www.intime.uni.edu/ovcs/pedagogy/discussion1.htm
and Atlanta:
http://www.intime.edu/ovce/the_conference/atlantaconference.htm

These discussions indicate that while video case studies have the potential to be an effective instructional tool for preservice teacher education there is still no definitive understanding of how best to use these technologies for optimal teaching and learning practices. In an attempt to create a list of essential multimedia and online video characteristics a brief review of four selected products is presented.

4. CURRENT MULTIMEDIA AND ONLINE PRODUCTS

In this section, three multimedia (CD-ROM) and two online video case studies are reviewed. For each example, a brief description of the case study, its use, and distinguishing features is given. Screen shots are included as appropriate.

a. *Understanding Teaching*: Association for Supervision and Curriculum Development (ASCD) and Arizona State University (1997).

"Understanding Teaching: Implementing the NCTM Professional Standards for Teaching Mathematics" provides firsthand observational experience that models the National Council of Teachers of Mathematics (NCTM) Professional Teaching Standards. The program incorporates a natural interface that situates learners in a real-world classroom environment. Four CD-ROMs utilise hours of classroom video, expert audio commentary, and 3-D graphics and animations that model math instruction. The program can be used as a stand-alone tool but it is suggested that two people or a community of practice (CoP) use the program to increase interaction and facilitate learning (see Figure 1). Several features are particularly worthy of note. There is a notebook option that can be used to archive the CoP's reflections. The product consists of 46 video vignettes and animations that model NCTM Teaching Standards. There are also 8 videos available for evaluating the CoP's ability to identify which NCTM standards they see in the videos.

In essence, this product is designed to help pre-K-6 teachers recognise, understand, and explain the NCTM Professional Standards for Teaching Mathematics.

Figure 1. A 'Teachable Moment'

b. Making Weighty Decisions: Syracuse University, New York (1999). This video case study was designed to help preservice teachers understand the complexity of the classroom, become better observers of classroom interactions, and learn to reflect on their own developing practice. This case study can provide a common context within which interesting aspects of an eighth-grade mathematics lesson implemented in a real classroom can be discussed, analysed, and understood in terms of the preservice teacher's developing practices. The facilitator of this case study can use this multimedia case to develop themes or highlight incidents that are of interest in the professional growth and development of preservice teachers (see Figure 2).

The classroom video consists of about 40 minutes of edited video for each day of the four one-day lesson sequences. Additional materials are included such as the seating chart, teacher reflections, and lesson plans. In essence, the video case study has organised the issues of teaching and learning mathematics that can be explored in four categories: lesson planning, facilitating classroom interaction, understanding student thinking, and mathematical content and context.

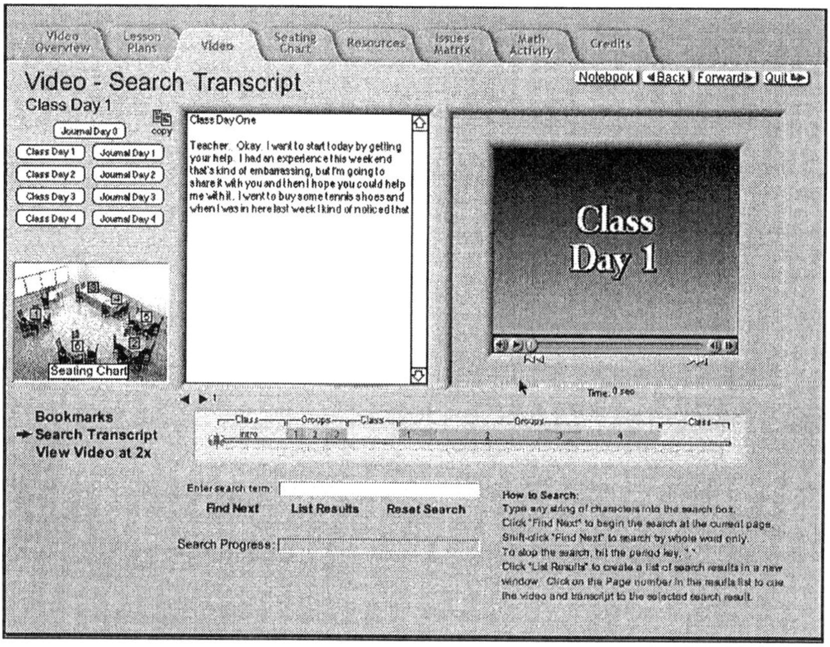

Figure 2. Video transcript search

c. A Classroom View: Austin Independent School District and the University of Texas, Austin (1999).

This product is an interactive multimedia program for educators. The CD-ROM contains more than 150 video vignettes of authentic pre-K-12 classroom environments with ready-to-use Units of Practice, teacher-created templates, and an extensive explanation about the district's Stages of Technology (SoT) integration. Using the word processing application as the focus, users are lead through the identified SoT (Integrating Change, Taking Control, Extending Your Reach, and Creating New Worlds) at a chosen grade or academic level.

Video vignettes from 16 host classrooms representing all academic levels are included, representing four stages of integration. 32 Units of Practice (applied ACOT research) are demonstrated for teachers to adapt for their own use.

An observation is coupled with a video segment to facilitate the user in identifying the NCTM Teaching Standard illustrated in the video segment.

The video screen has room for a text display of comments as well as video of the classroom interactions. The Search function allows the user to search for specific items within the transcript and the corresponding video clips of classroom interaction. In addition, a small version of the visual seating chart allows the user to more easily follow student interaction in the video.

d. InTime (Integrating New Technologies Into the Methods of Education): University of Northern Iowa (2000).

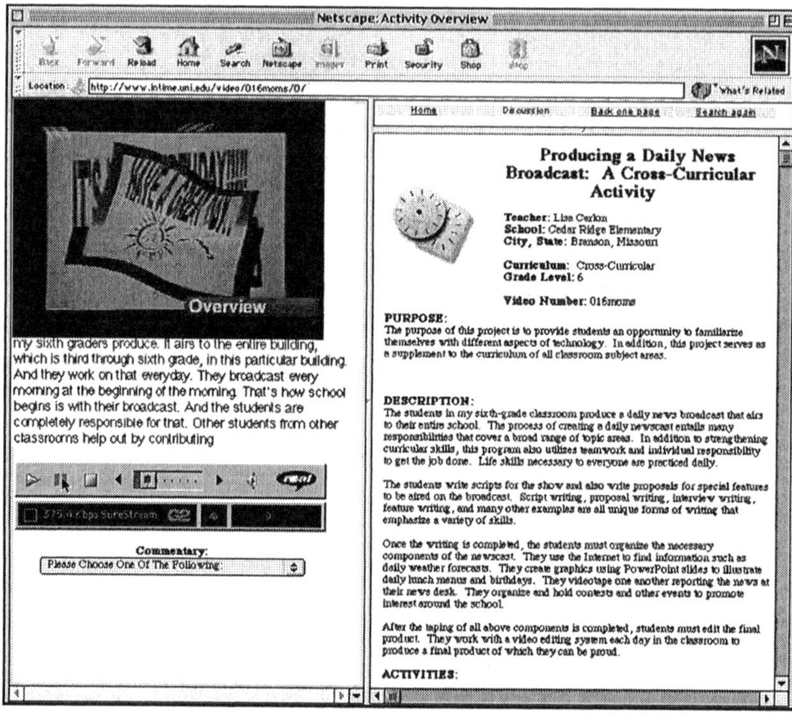

Figure 3. Activity overview.

The purpose of InTime is to provide the resources for methods faculty to use in revising their courses, modelling technology integration, and assisting preservice teachers to integrate technology into their lesson units (http://www.intime.uni.edu/about/about.html). The InTime project includes the development of video scenarios of pre-K-12 teachers effectively integrating technology, along with components of quality education, in a variety of grade levels and content areas. Faculty uses the video scenarios and online discussion forum to model technology integration (see Figure 3).

A wide variety of classroom videos in related content areas are shown along with rolling text aligned with the audio. The entire approach is based on a model of 'Technology as Facilitator of Quality Education.'

5. ESSENTIAL ELEMENTS FOR CREATING MULTIMEDIA/ONLINE VIDEO CASE STUDIES

A review of the previously mentioned products, projects and research suggests that some elements are effective in video case study development.

1. *An engaging tool interface.* The tools available to encourage ongoing observation, dialogue and reflection should include, but not be limited to, teacher reflection on lesson planning and delivery, audio or video contextual clues, asynchronous and synchronous discussion, a user journal reflection tool, and access to additional resources such as web sites and content experts discussing the case study.
2. *An ongoing communication system.* Preservice teachers, through their community of practice, require asynchronous tools such as a threaded discussion to engage in reflective dialog. Preferably, a synchronous chat room should be present which will enable facilitators to further engage the preservice teachers in real-time dialog on the case study. These tools may require partnerships with other organisations which have developed exemplary models in this area.
3. *Contextual clues for viewing.* The inclusion of the teacher's voice reflecting on planning the actual lesson and the lesson itself with background data on the school, students, and classroom activities provides the user with contextual clues within which the video case study is viewed. These contextual clues can be presented in text-based, graphic, audio or video formats.
4. *Access to additional resources.* Web-based programs enable the frequent update of relevant resource material aligned to video case studies. Preservice students can access articles, references, and commentaries related to the teaching and learning process as well as the content areas.

InTime models various ways for preservice teachers to integrate technology. In this activity overview, the user is able to see a full text description of the activity details along with video and a rolling transcript of the audio.

6. ISSUES IN THE DEVELOPMENT OF ONLINE VIDEO CASE STUDIES

Many of the products reviewed above were produced in a CD ROM format. As these products move to the web, additional issues arise.

1. *Philosophical approach to development.* Three different approaches can be taken: (a) 'best' or 'exemplary' practice illustrating the practices to

which a preservice teacher should aspire; (b) a dilemma asking the users to create strategies to answer the dilemma; (c) an approach like that used in the medical field, similar to that experienced in an Emergency Room, where users can manipulate different factors within the environment. The larger issue with online video case studies is the impact of the video on contextualising the practice. Is it possible that the video provides too much context, making the example too specific?

2. *Length of video segments*. Although no empirical study has been conducted, many of the current projects use 3 minute up to 8 minute video clips illustrating parts of a connected lesson or clips of selected concepts. These numbers reflect current bandwidth constraints. It is still unclear whether there should be even shorter videos (1 minute or less) supplemented with other materials or whether the videos must be even longer than 8 minutes.
3. *Online bandwidth requirements*. Bandwidth obviously impacts download capabilities of video, which can be accessed through progressive download or streaming. What technology takes best advantage of the bandwidth available? What techniques should be used to allow for the range of bandwidths from 56K through DSL and cable?
4. *Real or staged videos*? Capturing the action in a real classroom can present an audio challenge. While the video is important, recording good audio is critical. This factor alone may necessitate video case studies of staged classrooms. How much of the video can be staged and still capture the realities of the classroom?
5. *Appropriate video production*. Standard video production technologies must be adapted for web use. Large group shots, zooming and camera sweeps of classrooms don't present well on the web. Of greater importance is the availability of good quality audio recording of interactions between students and teacher and student-student interaction. What techniques work best for the web?
6. *Role of facilitator*. Although the video case studies can be used as stand-alone materials, online facilitation, in our opinion, is critical to optimal impact of this approach. What are the expectations for the role of this facilitator?

7. SUMMARY

In summary, multimedia and online video case studies enable preservice teachers to reflect on classroom practice that they might otherwise not experience. Preservice students can view complex, interactive situations that are in a constant state of flux and can begin to acquire pedagogical tools for situations in which there are no easy, clear-cut answers. Ongoing development and analysis of multimedia and online video case study projects will enhance efforts to provide preservice teacher educators with additional tools and strategies for integrating technology into pre-K-12 classrooms.

REFERENCES

Barron, L. C. and Goldman, E. S. (1994) Integrating technology with teacher preparation. In *Technology and education reform: The reality behind the promise,* B. Means (ed.), Jossey-Bass, San Francisco, pp. 81-110.

Kovalchick, A. M., Hrabe, E., Julian, M. F. and Kinzie, M. B. (1999) ID case studies via the World Wide Web. In *The ID casebook: Case studies in instructional design*, P. A. Ertmer and J. Quinn (eds.), Merrill, Prentice Hall, New Jersey, pp. 141-148.

Lindeman, B., Kent, T., Kinzie, M., Larsen, V., Ashmore, L. and Becker, F. (1995) *Exploring cases on-line with virtual environments*. Curry School of Education, University of Virginia. [http://www.csc195.indiana.edu/csc195/-lindeman.html] 5.21.2000.

Madfes, T. J. and Shulman, J. H. (2000) *Dilemmas in professional development: A case-based approach to improving practice*. McGraw-Hill, New York.

Merseth, K. (1994) *Cases, case methods, and the professional development of educators*. (digest ED401272), ERIC Digest Number: 95-5.

Perry, G. (2000) *Video case studies and teacher education: A new tool for preservice education*. Unpublished manuscript, Pepperdine University, Culver City, CA.

Shulman, J. H. (1992) *Case methods for teacher education*. Teachers College Press, New York.

Shulman, L. (1992) Toward a pedagogy of cases. In *Case methods in teacher education*, J. H. Shulman (ed.), Teachers College Press, New York, pp. 1-30.

Silverman, R., Welty, W. M. and Lyon, S. (1996) *Case studies for teacher problem solving*. 2nd ed., McGraw-Hill, New York.

Spiro, R. J. et al. (1988) Cognitive flexibility theory: Advanced knowledge acquisition in ill-structured domains. *Tenth Annual Conference of the Cognitive Science Society*. Hillsdale, Erlbaum, NJ.

Sprague, D., Kopfman, K. and de Levante Dorsey, S. (1998) Faculty development in the integration of technology in teacher education courses. *Journal of Computing in Teacher Education*, 14 (2), pp. 24-28.

Wasserman, S. (1994) *Introduction to case methods teaching*. Teachers College Press, New York.

BIOGRAPHY

Terence Cannings currently serves as Associate Dean of Education at the Graduate School of Education and Psychology (GSEP) at Pepperdine University. Under his leadership the Education Division received a Catalyst Grant from the U.S. Department of Education for Pre-service Teacher

Education & Technology Preparation. His current research interests are in distance learning and technology use in teacher education. Recent activities have included presentation to The Glenn Commission in Washington D. C. and a month in China as part of the People to People Ambassador Program in teacher education.

70

School-based Teacher Education with IT as a Tool

Palle Bendsen
Copenhagen Day and Evening College, Ejbyvej 25, 2740 Skovlunde, Denmark
palle.bendsen@skolekom.dk

Keywords: teacher education, tele-teaching, collaborative learning, curriculum changes, innovation

Abstract: In this study we used virtual tutoring and collaborative learning in a normal class of students in a Danish College of Education. Electronic guidance was established as an addition to traditional teaching. All students and teachers had a computer with Internet connection to an electronic conference system. Our experiences are that electronics increase the possibilities of collaboration, and electronic communication has an encouraging effect on learning and acquisition. The electronic tutorial style must be discussed with the students before and during the period of work. Electronic communication gives new possibilities for co-ordination of the teacher's mutual collaboration. Electronic communication leads to far more social and professional contacts among the participants than is the case in the usual student environment.

1. VIRTUAL TUTORING AND COLLABORATIVE LEARNING

Electronically tutoring (Veen et al. 1994, Collis 1994) is a useful and effective tool in the education of teachers because it is collective, open and in writing. Our experiences from four years of innovation experiments in teacher education (Bendsen et al. 1997) show the following:

- Electronics increase the possibilities of collaboration, because all students in a class can follow the professional communication at the same time.

- Electronic communication has an encouraging effect on learning and acquisition because the students have to formulate their thoughts regarding professional and educational subjects.
- Telecommunication, combined with oral tutoring, will strengthen problem– and process-centred tutoring.
- The tele-tutorial, which is extremely quick, minimises time waste. It will be possible to work with clearly marked deadlines through an open control of the stages of the process.
- The electronic tutorial style has to be discussed thoroughly with the students before and during the period of work, because it may seem overwhelming far-reaching concrete and authoritative.
- Electronic communication gives new possibilities for co-ordinating teacher's mutual collaboration, as well as collaboration with the students.
- Electronic communication leads to more social and professional contacts among the participants than is the case in the usual student environment.

It is difficult to evaluate the importance of these different facts as a whole, but we think it improves social life and may increase the professional quality of the work.

2. A REACTION TO THE CRITICISM OF DANISH TEACHER TRAINING

It was, among other things, the Danish media's continuous criticism of the Folkeskole (municipal primary and lower secondary school) and the teacher education, which caused the Copenhagen Day and Evening College to establish a project supported economically by the CTU (Denmark's National Information Centre for Technology Supported Learning). The title of the project contains the two elements which form part of the purpose of the project: 'School-based Teacher Training with IT as a Tool' (Bendsen et al. 1997). With the use of the word 'school-based', we expressed our wish for a closer connection between theory and practice (Bendsen 1996) and 'IT as a tool' signals that the possibilities in IT could be exploited during the course at the same time. The intention was to look for new answers to the didactic and pedagogical problems that are presented in the education of teachers, both during the 6 weeks demonstration in a school (Bendsen 1996) and in the course itself. In addition, the students and we gained experience with the methodical and didactic application of IT.

The technical conditions were simple, as students and teachers were to have access at home to a PC and a modem. Those chosen were a group of students who had enrolled with the idea of working with IT related subjects during their education. But at the same time the group would meet with the teachers of different subjects every week according to a traditional timetable. This is not distance teaching.

The students' computer screen contained four different open tele-conferences and a personal e-mail mailbox. The new concepts are as follows.

The Open conference system: - a forum which allows one-to-one or one-to-many communication. In particular, this provides the possibility for group communication or many-to-many debates. Everybody can make themselves heard and the writing (electronic mail) becomes the means of expression in a process which supplements and to a certain degree replaces the face-to-face communication (Dam1996).

The Tele-dialogue: - is the debates all students participate in. They are highly structured professional and pedagogical conferences, controlled by the teacher. They are based on practical problems that the students write about, during their meeting with the Folkeskolens' everyday life. We include some trainee teachers' participation in the tele-dialogue, citing their experiences of what we called: 'This weeks tele-theme'.

Collaborative learning (Sorensen 1996): - The thing that distinguishes collaborative communities from most other communities is a desire to construct new meanings about the world through interaction with others. The collaborative communities become a medium for both self-knowledge and self-expression. The collaborative situation is about how to be able to create new acquisition/learning jointly through their own experiences and arguments through confrontation with other people's opinions and attitudes.

3. TUTORING IN VIRTUAL SPACE

During a co-operation project called School and Society, the electronic tutoring was tested. As a starting point we agreed on the following:

- A set time frame.
- Method of work: a group-based project with the teachers as tutors and educators. The method of work contained the formulation of a problem with a delimited subject, a purpose, division of work, timing etc., plus the choice of method and arranged presentation for the whole class, all put down in a written report.
- All students could ask for a face-to-face tutorial with their teacher, but usually the teacher gave written response in the virtual conference.
- The application of collaborative learning was a process in which all student groups mailed their provisional theme problem, at the same time, to the common professional and pedagogical conference.

Our intention in creating this comprehensive scope, including the teachers′ co-ordinated response, was that the collaborative learning described should contribute something new, something different, and enable broader learning through a common construction of knowledge and inspiration in relation to the theme, School and Society. The subsequent exchange of experiences was an element of the collaborative learning, in the sense that it is interesting and exciting for the motivated student and teacher to follow the professional dialogue between teachers and the student groups and among the students themselves. Naturally, the individual student could also suggest his own professional related contribution, which also happened. This suggests an openness and use of insight which does not usually occur in a course. The whole innovation has taken place as a cross-curricular sequence with the participation of the following subjects: Danish language, psychology, pedagogy, social science, arts and religious instruction.

REFERENCES

Bendsen, P. et al. (1997) *Skolebaseret læreruddannelse med ikt som arbejdsredskab*. Rapport nr. 1 and 2, Copenhagen Day and Evening College, Copenhagen.

Dam, E. (1996) *Moderator eller ordstyrer*. Copenhagen Day and Evening College, Copenhagen.

Veen, W. et al. (1994) Tele-tutoring in Teacher Education. *Journal of Information Technology and Teacher Education.*

Collis B. (1994) *New Possibilities for Teacher Education Through Computer-Based Communication Technologies*. University of Twente, The Netherlands.

Bendsen P. (1996) Hvad lærer de studerende i praktikken ? – refleksion som metode. *Kalejdoskop,* Copenhagen Day and Evening College, Copenhagen.

Sorensen, E. K. (1996) *Kommunikation og læring i den virtuelle skole*. Manus, Aarhus University.

BIOGRAPHY

Palle Bendsen is a specialist in pedagogical psychology and has participated in several research and evaluation projects. He was the leader of the first IT-classes in the Danish teacher training classes in the College of Education: Copenhagen Teacher Training College.

71

Mapping New Territories

ICT Integration Across the Bachelor of Education Program

Mitchell Parkes, Chris Reading and Jo-Anne Reid
School of Curriculum Studies, University of New England, Armidale, NSW, Australia
mparkes2@metz.une.edu.au

Keywords: integration of IT, teacher education, teamwork, pedagogical ICT facilitator

Abstract: This paper describes the integration of Information and Communication Technologies (ICT) skills and practices across the Bachelor of Education (Primary) program at the University of New England, Armidale. The program was reviewed and modified in the light of ICT competencies specified by the NSW Government. The aim was to ensure that all students gained experience in these competencies throughout their pre-service teacher training. It was necessary to improve staff ICT competencies. Members of the Information Technology teaching team helped design activities and team taught with other staff members. Reflections and feedback from staff indicated that the exercise increased staff and student ICT awareness and expertise and offered enhanced opportunities for students to gain ICT in authentic teaching/learning contexts.

1. INTRODUCTION

In 1997, the New South Wales Ministerial Advisory Council on the Quality of Teaching (MACQT) released the report *Computer Proficiency for Teachers*. In this document the Council, whose task is to provide the NSW Government with advice on teacher education issues from initial teacher education to ongoing professional development, stated the following:

> "All people employed as classroom teachers need to develop the skills which will enable them to maximise the use of the computer as a teaching resource to enhance student learning and to prepare students to master a high technology society in which lifestyles, attitudes and skills are challenged daily. For this to be accomplished, teacher education programs

and professional development programs for practising teachers will need to focus on the provision of an understanding of the application of computer knowledge, and of both the basic and more sophisticated skills associated with computer proficiency" (MACQT 1997).

In support of this statement, a list of computer competencies for beginning teachers was developed. These competencies can be viewed at: http://www.det.nsw.edu.au/publications/minister/teacher1.htm
The competencies fall into five broad areas: basic operations, use of information technology, evaluation of software, teaching practice, consideration of pedagogical issues and awareness of values and ethics related to Information Technology in education. To ensure these standards were met, it was mandated that from 2000 onwards all beginning teachers would need to demonstrate these competencies in order to be eligible for employment in N.S.W. Government schools. In response to this Government directive, the University of New England's main pre-service teaching program, the Bachelor of Education (Primary) was examined to determine the extent to which it would provide students with the necessary ICT competencies required for employment. This analysis showed that a number of modifications would have to be made to the program in order for students to meet the government's requirements. This paper describes a project managed by teaching staff of the Faculty of Health, Education and Professional Studies which modified the Bachelor of Education (Primary) by integrating the teaching and development of these ICT competencies across all of the compulsory pre-service teacher education units of the program.

2. BACKGROUND

The Bachelor of Education (Primary) is a four year, professionally orientated degree, initiated in 1998 and offered on-campus at the University of New England in the rural town of Armidale in New South Wales, Australia. As well as gaining generalist training in infants and primary education, students have the opportunity to focus their study in specific Key Learning Areas or in specialist fields of professional practice which include Aboriginal Studies, Languages Other Than English (LOTE), Special Needs and Technology in Education. Although largely taught by staff in the Faculty of Education, Health and Professional Studies, the program has been designed with the assistance of members of the teaching profession and provides students with the opportunity to develop knowledge, skills and attitudes to become successful beginning teachers in the Australian context.

The course consists of three strands: a curriculum strand, a professional strand and a personal studies strand. The curriculum strand provides the necessary background knowledge of the school syllabus, teaching methodology and programming for the six primary school subjects (or Key Learning Areas). The professional strand provides the necessary background in the foundational and theoretical aspects of teacher education. The personal studies strand provides for a number of aspects of teacher education and includes an opportunity for students to develop their personal background in subject disciplines necessary for primary school teachers.

It was the aim of the Faculty to integrate the teaching of Information and Communication Technologies (ICT) across all of the compulsory units of the four-year program. Students, instead of learning an isolated or arbitrary set of skills, would learn ICT skills and practices in a meaningful context within the framework of their pre-service teacher education units. It was felt that such levels of sustained practice and consolidation of these competencies in authentic teaching/learning situations would lead to deeper and richer forms of understanding and greater mastery of ICT skills. As a result, newly trained teachers would be more likely to use ICT in their own teaching.

3. IMPLEMENTATION OF THE PROJECT

At the core of the project was the development of the B. Ed (Primary) unit *Foundation Studies* (CSST 192). This unit was the organising framework upon which was based the integration of ICT skills and practices into other units. CSST 192 was set within the context of the *Computing Competencies for Beginning Teachers* (MACQT 1997) and provided student teachers with an introduction to each of the five areas of ICT competence. CSST192 covers all of these competencies, with the majority of practical activities being designed to deliver the computing skills required for success in other first year units.

CSST192 operates during first semester as a one semester unit, in conjunction with three year-long core units. For second semester, students then undertake the unit CSST 193 *Reading in the Primary Curriculum*, along with the three year-long core units. All of these are compulsory units, and comprise the first year of the B. Ed (Primary) program. A reciprocal relationship has been forged between CSST 192 and the other first year units. The other units are encouraged to make use of the computer competencies taught in CSST 192, while academic literacies from these units such as: summarising, paraphrasing and creating concept maps have been integrated into pedagogical tasks for CSST 192.

From a practical perspective, the task of integrating ICT competencies across the entire B. Ed. (Primary) program was approached at two levels. Firstly, working within the Faculty to increase staff awareness of and expertise in the use ICT *across* the whole 4-year program. Secondly, working *within* the program to develop staff expertise and student understanding ICT in relation to specific curriculum areas.

In order to increase staff awareness and expertise in the use of ICT across the B. Ed. (Primary) program, two members of the Information Technology (IT) Team, Chris Reading and Mitchell Parkes worked with staff reviewing individual units. This was undertaken in order to determine the extent to which units addressed the ICT competencies and built upon the foundations of ICT competence laid for students in CSST192. This work was allied to an ongoing program of *Advancing Academic Literacies* within the Bachelor of Education (Primary) program, in which all staff working within the first year units had collaboratively mapped and shared the 'literacy' demands of their disciplines and pedagogy. Incorporating ICT into this expanded view of 'l(IT)eracy' was the next logical step. During the consultation process, advice was provided about effective ways of incorporating ICT into existing pedagogy within units. Care was taken to ensure that any ICT activities added were driven by the curriculum needs of the unit and not as a means of simply covering a competency.

The result of these consultations was the creation of a map showing the coverage of ICT competencies across all units taught in the B. Ed. (Primary) program. The resulting map is a representation of the program at one point in time – a standard against which comparisons can be made towards the goal of achieving integrated l(IT)eracy experience and practice for students. The map itself shows clearly those areas: Basic Operations, Information Technology And Evaluation of Software, where the program is adequately providing the teaching and learning experience expected. It also highlights those areas: Pedagogical Issues and Values and Ethics, where students need to be offered greater learning opportunities. Information gathered from the mapping exercise will form the basis for further sessions where staff can collaboratively aim to fill the gaps, in the most meaningful ways.

Once the ICT competencies had been mapped onto individual units, the next stage involved working with individual staff members to help improve their own ICT skills and practices within their particular curriculum areas. Time was provided for members of the Information Technology team to work with staff developing practical activities. When necessary, members of the Information Technology team taught with staff members and provided assistance and technical support. Examples of activities included: working with the Literacy team reviewing electronic texts; working with members of the Science team collating and analysing data using a spreadsheet for a pendulum experiment and creating and manipulating digital images with a member of the Art team.

These activities proved to be extremely successful and popular with staff and students. From a professional development perspective, many staff members reported increases in computing skill and confidence in using the technology in their teaching. Some reflections by staff members involved in these activities are given below.

> "As a member of the English teaching team, I found these sessions particularly useful. I believe that team teaching situations are educationally valuable. I think that it enhanced the sessions greatly. Even though I was not uncomfortable with the technology, I can always learn something from the person with expertise" (Paul Muirhead 2000).

> "As part of our Science methods unit with first-year pre-service primary students, four weeks was set aside for students to learn how to incorporate computer technologies into their teaching. Students were expected to undertake a number of activities culminating in a computer portfolio and reflection as an assignment. While I feel competent with word processing, using the Internet, and working with spreadsheets, this has always involved just me and my computer. It is quite a different game when there are thirty eager (and sometimes not so eager) faces all wanting computer help. The benefits of working with someone who is competent in the area enabled students to gain the help they needed quickly and accurately so that the time spent during the workshops was seen to be effective. For myself, I gained confidence in dealing with large groups of students on the computers and insight having learned a number of skills I did not possess previously. The other advantage with this type of collaboration is that students see the integration between the various components or units they are studying. They also are able to observe various 'experts' in their own fields working together to enhance student learning. This professionalism may be discussed during lectures but seeing it in action has a much greater impact. I believe that this was an extremely valuable experience for our students!" (Debra Panizzon 2000).

> "Over a two-week period, my visual arts classes for first year B. Ed. students were all conducted in the computer lab. Mitchell Parkes kindly agreed to come to all seven of these classes to teach the students how to use Adobe PhotoShop software to manipulate photos that had been taken earlier with a digital camera. I found that the exercise was a huge success and both the students and I benefited greatly. The students are immensely proud of their efforts and have asked me about the possibility of doing further computer art exercises similar to this one in other art education electives next year. It has helped me expand our use of technology in

generating art images within this unit and I can now see a number of ways in which this can be expanded even further over the next few years. I am confident that I could lead these sessions in future without support and I have also used my new skills in other ways since our lab workshops. Many of these new skills have been incredibly useful to me while I was recently preparing an on line art exhibition of students' work for one of the external units that I teach". (Frances Alter 2000).

4. FUTURE DIRECTIONS

The mapping activity has already provided new directions and challenges. One example is the unit CSST193 *Reading in the Primary Curriculum*. This unit focused on instruction for children learning to read at all levels of the primary school. As well as attention to beginning reading, the unit also covered content area reading and reading for information. The challenge for the unit is in relation to multi-literacies, and dealing with expanded notions of literacy and text. As a response to the ICT competencies related to pedagogical issues, this unit was expanded and now attempts to assist student teachers to understand how computer technology can enhance student learning, and how to manage classroom environments and school resources most effectively. In the redevelopment of the unit it was found that models for teaching comprehension using traditional print-based materials were inadequate when applied to electronic text. As a consequence, a new model for the analysis of electronic texts was sought (Reid, Reading and Parkes, under review).

5. CONCLUSION

The ICT competency map represents a snap shot of where the BEd. (Primary) program is at present. Such a map is not something that remains fixed in time but must be dynamic, responding to the professional and educational needs of staff and students. We are just at the beginning of our journey and although we may have mapped new territories, our map is far from complete and our journey is far from over.

REFERENCES

MACQT (1997) *Computer Proficiencies for Teachers.* [http://www.det.nsw.edu.au/publications/minister/teacher1.htm] 26.10.2000.

Reid, J., Reading, C. and Parkes, M. (under review) *Changing Gear.* Paper submitted to the *Australian Journal of Teacher Education.*

BIOGRAPHY

Mitchell Parkes is a lecturer in Information Technology, whose current research interests are online learning, information literacy and technology related professional development for teachers.

Chris Reading is a lecturer in Information Technology, whose current research interests are electronic learning networks, information literacy and students' understanding of statistics.

Jo-Anne Reid is a lecturer in Primary English Curriculum, whose current research interests are English literacy and connections between existing literacies and those required in new learning situations.

Pre-service Teachers' Teaching with Computers

Some Factors Influencing Pre-service Teachers' Self-efficacy

Peter Albion
University of Southern Queensland, Toowoomba Q 4350, Australia
albion@usq.edu.au

Keywords: teacher education, integration of ICT, research, evaluation

Abstract Although computers are widely available in schools and their use is supported by public policy, their uptake by teachers is not universal. There is evidence that, even where teachers have access and essential skills, they lack confidence in their ability to integrate computers in their teaching. Multimedia cases have been developed for the purpose of increasing teachers' self-efficacy beliefs (confidence) for teaching with computers (SETWC). It was important to understand what factors might influence SETWC. This paper reports the results of a study which examined the effect of several variables on SETWC. The most significant influence on SETWC was levels of comfort with using computers

1. INTRODUCTION

In Queensland, Australia, as in other parts of the industrialised world, computers have become widely available in schools. Whether the equipment is located in laboratories or classrooms, the vast majority of teachers have some access to computers for use in support of teaching and learning. Policy makers, school administrators and the community support and encourage the use of computers at all levels of schooling. In Queensland, the government has provided financial support for Schooling 2001, a policy framework which includes as goals the use of computers "in every subject area at every level of education" and the connection of every classroom to the Internet by 2001 (Education Queensland 1998).

Nevertheless, not all teachers have adopted the use of computers as an integral part of their professional practice. Although there are instances of exemplary practice, the overall situation has been described as "patchy" (Galligan, Buchanan and Muller 1999). Recent discussions among pre-service teachers returning from teaching practice have included comments about the limited use being made of computers in some classrooms. However, students observed that even teachers who did not use computers in their teaching expressed belief in the importance of computers for education.

There is unlikely to be a single, simple explanation for the apparent reluctance of some teachers to embrace information and communication technologies (ICT). Teachers appear to share the broad community enthusiasm for ICT in education and see it as a 'good thing'. However, they report a lack of confidence in their ability to use ICT effectively for teaching and often attribute this to inadequate preparation (Albion 1996, Handler 1993).

In a previous paper (Albion 1999) research about the preparation of teachers for working with ICT was reviewed and an argument was developed in support of teacher beliefs as an important issue to be addressed in seeking to extend the use of ICT in teaching. Self-efficacy for teaching with computers (SETWC) was identified as an area of belief which was related to teacher behaviour in the longer term, was measurable using existing scales and was capable of being influenced by teacher educators in the context of pre-service and in-service courses. Multimedia cases designed using a problem-based learning framework have been proposed for this purpose (Albion and Gibson 1998).

As part of the evaluation of the multimedia materials (Gibson and Albion 1999), it was proposed to examine the effects of the materials on pre-service teachers' SETWC as measured before and after working with the materials. Teachers' beliefs and behaviours in respect of computers are unlikely to stand in isolation from their other beliefs (Albion 1999). Hence it was decided to obtain measures of some other variables which might be associated with SETWC in order to control for the effects of those other variables in the study. This paper presents the results obtained for the additional variables and their association with SETWC and discusses the implications of the relationships for future work on increasing pre-service teachers' SETWC.

2. FACTORS EXAMINED

The Microcomputer Utilisation in Teaching Efficacy Beliefs Instrument (MUTEBI) was initially developed and used in the context of science teaching (Enochs, Riggs and Ellis 1993) but it is not specific to that context. It comprises two sub-scales corresponding to the two components of the self-efficacy construct identified by Bandura (1977), namely efficacy expectations, which was labelled by Enochs et al. as self-efficacy (SE), and outcome expectations, labelled as outcome expectancy (OE).

It seems reasonable to assume that positive attitudes towards computers and strong self-efficacy for computer use would be prior conditions for positive self-efficacy for teaching with computers. Scales for the measurement of attitudes towards computers and self-efficacy for computer use have been developed and used with teacher education students (Kinzie, Delcourt and Powers 1994). The Attitudes towards Computer Technologies (ACT) instrument comprises two scales, one of 8 items measuring Comfort/Anxiety related to computers and the other of 11 items measuring Usefulness of computers. The Self-efficacy for Computer Technologies (SCT) instrument was developed and later modified to assess self-efficacy with different types of computer technologies (Kinzie et al. 1994). Form B of the instrument, as described by Kinzie et al., comprised 46 items measuring perceived self-efficacy for word processing (10 items), electronic mail (9), searching CD-ROM databases (6), use of spreadsheets (7), creation and management of databases (7) and use of statistical packages (7). A more recent study conducted with pre-service teachers (Albion, in press) reported on the development of a slightly modified version of the SCT. The modification consisted of replacing the sub-scale relating to statistical software with sub-scales related to operating systems and the Internet. The scales used in this study were the original ACT and the modified version of the SCT.

Various studies have suggested a relationship between teachers' use of ICTs and approaches to classroom management. Pupil control ideology (Graham, Benson and Henry 1985) is a uni-dimensional construct which locates attitudes towards pupil control along a continuum between custodial and student-centred orientations. The 10 items instrument described by Graham et al. was used in this study.

There have been many studies of the construct variously referred to as teacher efficacy or self-efficacy for teaching. In a study of the construct dimensions of teacher efficacy, Guskey and Passaro (1994) modified the items used in previously published versions of the instrument to remove what they saw as anomalies in the wording of the items. Their instrument included 21 items which resolved into two dimensions. The first, the *internal* sub-scale, appears to represent perceptions of personal influence in teaching and learning. The second, the *external* sub-scale, appears to represent the influence of elements beyond the direct control of the teacher. Because it seemed likely that SETWC might be related to more general self-efficacy for teaching the Guskey and Passaro (1994) instrument was included in the battery for this study.

A study involving 170 practising teachers and 167 pre-service teachers in the USA found that innovativeness was a significant predictor of computer use for the practising teachers (Marcinkiewicz 1994). Hence innovativeness was of interest in this study and was measured using the 10 items version of the scale (Hurt, Joseph and Cook 1977).

All instruments used in this study were derived from previously published studies. The body of the questionnaire comprised 134 items representing 15 scales and sub-scales as described above. For consistency and ease of use, all scales were presented as a four point Likert items ranging from strongly disagree to strongly agree. Scale scores were computed as the mean of item scores on each scale in order to facilitate comparisons among the scales.

3. RESULTS

The questionnaire was administered during a mass lecture in the first week of semester to students enrolled in a final year subject required for all students in the Bachelor of Education programs. A total of 178 responses was collected.

Most (62%) of the respondents were pre-service Primary teachers enrolled in the four year undergraduate (55%) or two year graduate entry (7%) degrees. A further 26% were enrolled in Early Childhood undergraduate (25%) or graduate entry (1%) degrees and the remainder (12%) were pre-service Secondary teachers.

The majority of the respondents were female (82%). Most (75%) reported their age as less than 25 years, with 35% aged less than 21 years and 40% between 21 and 25 years. A further 10% were aged from 26 to 30 years with the remainder (15%) aged more than 30 years. The high proportion aged less than 25 years suggests that most were traditional students who had entered their university course directly from secondary school.

For most of the respondents (74%), the only computer-related subject studied at university was a compulsory unit usually taken in first year, although some (14%) reported that they had studied five or more computer related subjects. Almost all respondents (92%) reported having access to a computer at their residence during semester; 72% reported Windows and 20% Macintosh systems. In a previous study conducted with the same cohort of students during their first year at university (Albion, in press), analysis of posttest data (N = 110) found that 78% had access to a computer at their residence during semester; 54% Windows and 16% Macintosh. That study reported that there had been an increase in access (from 58% to 78%) over the first year of university study. Data from the current study suggest that the proportion of students with home access has continued to increase.

Computer use in a typical week was reported as: less than one hour (12%), 1 to 5 hours (46%), 6 to 10 hours (26%) and more than 10 hours (16%). The comparable values from the previous study (Albion, in press) were: less than one hour (21%), 1 to 5 hours (43%), 6 to 10 hours (22%) and more than 10 hours (14%). That study reported a significant increase in hours of computer use during the first semester of study and that increased level appears to have remained stable over three years.

Table 1 lists the Cronbach's alpha reliability coefficients, means and standard deviations calculated for the Likert scale data. The maximum possible score for each scale was 4.0. As described previously (Albion, in press), scores on the sub-scales of the SCT were combined to form a composite measure of self-efficacy for computer use which was used in subsequent analysis.

Table 1. Alpha reliability, mean and SD of scores (N = 178)

Instrument	Sub-scale	Reliability (alpha)	Mean	SD
MUTEBI	Outcome expectancy (OE)	.74	2.66	.40
	Self-efficacy (SE)	.88	3.00	.45
ACT	Comfort/Anxiety	.89	2.98	.65
	Usefulness	.76	3.36	.42
SCT	E-mail	.98	3.31	.83
	Internet	.94	3.02	.88
	Word processing	.94	3.67	.49
	Operating system	.91	3.26	.72
	Spreadsheet	.96	3.22	.85
	Database	.98	2.98	.94
	CD-ROM	.96	2.65	.93
	SCT composite	.98	3.20	.63
PCI		.66	2.09	.37
Teacher Efficacy	External	.74	2.21	.37
	Internal	.75	2.87	.32
Innovativeness		.85	3.11	.43

Because the study sought to investigate any relationships among the variables, especially any possible effect on the SE scale of the MUTEBI, Pearson product moment correlation coefficients were computed for pairs of measures. The results are shown in Table 2.

Table 2. Correlation coefficients for pairs of variables (N = 178)

	Comf.	Usef.	SCT	PCI	OE	SE	Ext.	Int.
Usef.	.50 ***							
SCT	.70 ***	.46 ***						
PCI	-.15 *	-.35 ***	-.07					
OE	.12	-.02	.18 *	.21 **				
SE	.64 ***	.60 ***	.56 ***	-.23 **	.14			
Ext.	-.07	-.33 ***	-.03	.39 ***	.09	-.39 ***		
Int.	.13	.09	.22 **	.00	.43 ***	.26 **	-.13	
Innov.	.22 **	.37 ***	.20 **	-.38 ***	.07	.45 ***	-.52 ***	.16 *

* p < .05 ** p < .01 *** p < .001 (2-tailed)

It is evident from Table 2 that there are several significant correlations. For the purposes of this study, the correlations involving the SE sub-scale of the MUTEBI are of primary interest. SE was significantly correlated with each of the other variables except OE. Moreover, many of those variables were significantly correlated with each other. The potential influences of other variables on SE were important in study of the effects of the multimedia materials since, if SE were to be strongly influenced by relatively stable factors, there might be less potential for the materials to effect changes in SE.

In order to clarify the relative predictive influence of other variables on SE, backward multiple regression was applied. SE was entered as the dependent variable. SCT, both sub-scales of the ACT, PCI, Innovativeness, the two sub-scales of teacher efficacy, age, gender, number of university computer subjects studied and weekly hours of computer use were entered as independent variables and backward regression analysis was applied. Six variables were retained by the analysis in a model which accounted for 61% of the variance ($R^2 = .61$, $F [6, 161] = 42.24$, $p < .00005$).

Table 3 shows the results for the final regression model. Of the six variables remaining in the model, scores on the ACT and SCT sub-scales have been previously found to be positively associated with computer use (Albion, in press). Any gains in those scores as a result of working with the multimedia materials might be expected to contribute to an increase in SE. Although there is no evidence that Teacher Efficacy or Innovativeness would be affected by working with the materials, it is conceivable that exposure to successful exemplars of innovative teaching practice might impact positively on users' attitudes. Thus, there is no reason to consider that any of these predictors of SE should impact negatively on the effects of the multimedia intervention.

Table 3. Final regression model for SE sub-scale of MUTEBI

		B	SE B	Beta	T	Sig T
ACT	Comf.	.239	.051	.341	4.72	.0000
	Usef.	.238	.069	.219	3.45	.0007
SCT		.112	.051	.156	2.19	.0303
Teacher efficacy	Ext.	-.265	.074	-.211	-3.60	.0004
	Int.	.152	.071	.108	2.13	.0347
Innov.		.148	.062	.142	2.39	.0178
(Constant)		.810	.395		2.05	.0420

4. DISCUSSION

Of the six variables in the final regression model, the most significant effect was for the comfort/anxiety sub-scale of the ACT. It would be surprising if being comfortable about using computers were not associated with, or probably a precondition for, being more confident about using them for teaching. There is a clear implication here for teacher education programs that seek to prepare teachers for teaching with ICT. Previous research (Albion, in press) found that experience with computers was the principal influence on the level of comfort with computers among pre-service teachers at the commencement of their studies. Teacher education courses should be structured so as to encourage pre-service teachers to make frequent use of computers for meaningful tasks.

The second strongest predictor of SE in the regression model was the external sub-scale of the teacher efficacy scale. The internal sub-scale of the teacher efficacy scale was also in the final regression model, although it was the weakest predictor of SE remaining in the final model. Considering both the external and internal factors of teacher efficacy, the implication is that the more confident pre-service teachers are about their capacity to teach, the more likely they are to be confident about teaching with computers. One implication of this finding is that teacher education programs that include activities designed to increase pre-service teachers' self-efficacy beliefs for teaching should also result in increased self-efficacy for teaching with computers.

The usefulness sub-scale of the ACT was the third strongest predictor in the regression model. In principle, it might be possible to believe in the educational usefulness of computers and still lack confidence for using computers in the classroom. However, in practice, such belief is likely to either result from experience with computers or to encourage such experience. In either case, an increase in confidence for teaching with computers might be a logical consequence. Teacher education programs that encourage frequent and varied use of ICT to accomplish tasks that pre-service teachers perceive as relevant and important are likely to encourage beliefs in the usefulness of ICT and may indirectly increase pre-service teachers' self-efficacy for teaching with ICT.

Self-competence for computer use and Innovativeness have been found to predict computer use for teaching (Marcinkiewicz 1994). The final regression model obtained in this study included Innovativeness and self-efficacy for computer technologies (SCT) as, respectively, the fifth and sixth strongest predictors of SE. Innovativeness is associated with a positive attitude towards change and it is understandable that higher scores on the Innovativeness scale might be associated with willingness to adopt new approaches to teaching involving ICT as measured by SE. The association of higher scores on SCT with SE is explicable in terms of teachers with higher levels of self-efficacy for using computers in other settings being more prepared to use them in class. In a period of rapid social change such as the present time, openness to change is an important quality, which should be encouraged in teacher preparation programs. Where they succeed, there may be positive implications for self-efficacy for teaching with ICT. In previous research (Albion, in press), the only consistent predictor found for higher scores on SCT was greater computer use. Teacher education courses seeking to prepare teachers to teach with ICTs should adopt practices which encourage consistent use of ICT for relevant tasks.

Higher scores on the PCI scale represent a more custodial orientation. Hence the negative correlation between PCI and SE implies that pre-service teachers with less custodial orientations towards classroom management are more likely to have higher SE. This is consistent with studies that have found use of ICT in teaching to be associated with more student-centred approaches to management. PCI was very significantly correlated ($p < .001$) with usefulness, Innovativeness and the external factor of teacher efficacy, each of which was more strongly correlated with SE than was PCI. Hence, it was eliminated from the regression analysis model and the other variables were retained.

There are implications in these relationships for the potential effectiveness of an intervention such as multimedia materials that seek to increase users' self-efficacy for teaching with computers. Were SE to be significantly dependent upon one or more factors that would not be affected by the intervention, then the effectiveness of the multimedia, for at least some users, might be reduced. Among the significant predictors of SE identified above, attitudes towards computer technologies (comfort/anxiety and usefulness) and self-efficacy for computer technologies might be expected to be positively affected by working with the multimedia materials. These relationships increase the likelihood that working with appropriate multimedia materials (Gibson and Albion 1999) will have the desired effect upon pre-service teachers' self-efficacy for teaching with computers and their subsequent inclination to integrate ICT into their teaching.

REFERENCES

Albion, P. R. (1996) Student-teachers' use of computers during teaching practice in primary classrooms. *Asia-Pacific Journal of Teacher Education, 24* (1), pp. 63-73.

Albion, P. R. and Gibson, I. W. (1998) Designing problem-based learning multimedia for teacher education. In *Technology and teacher education annual 1998*, S. McNeil, J. D. Price, S. Boger-Mehall, B. Robin and J. Willis (Eds.), Association for the Advancement of Computing in Education, Charlottesville, VA, pp. 1240-1244.

Albion, P. R. (1999) Self-efficacy beliefs as an indicator of teachers' preparedness for teaching with technology. In *Technology and teacher education annual 1999*, J. D. Price, J. Willis, D. A. Willis, M. Jost and S. Boger-Mehall (Eds.), Association for the Advancement of Computing in Education, Charlottesville, VA, pp. 1602-1608.

Albion, P. R. (in press) Some factors in the development of self-efficacy beliefs for computer use among teacher education students. *Journal of Technology and Teacher Education.*

Bandura, A. (1977) Self-efficacy: Toward a unifying theory of behavioural change. *Psychological Review*, 84 (2), pp. 191-215.

Education Queensland (1998) *Schooling 2001 – Aims*. Education Queensland, Brisbane.

Enochs, L. G., Riggs, I. M. and Ellis, J. D. (1993) The development and partial validation of microcomputer utilization in teaching efficacy beliefs instrument in a science setting. *School Science and Mathematics*, 93 (5), pp. 257-263.

Galligan, J., Buchanan, P. and Muller, M. (1999) *Application of new technologies to enhance learning outcomes for students*. Education Queensland, Brisbane.

Gibson, I. and Albion, P. (1999) *Integrating information technology into teaching* [Multimedia CD-ROM]. University of Southern Queensland, Toowoomba, Australia.

Graham, S., Benson, J. and Henry, N. (1985) An analysis of the dimensionality of the pupil control ideology scale. *Educational and Psychological Measurement*, 45 (4), pp. 889-896.

Guskey, T. R. and Passaro, P. D. (1994) Teacher efficacy: A study of construct dimensions. *American Educational Research Journal*, 31 (3), pp. 627-643.

Handler, M. G. (1993) Preparing new teachers to use computer technology: Perceptions and suggestions for teacher educators. *Computers & Education*, 20 (2), pp. 147-156.

Hurt, H. T., Joseph, K. and Cook, C. D. (1977) Scales for the measurement of innovativeness. *Human Communication Research*, 4(1), pp. 58-65.

Kinzie, M. B., Delcourt, M. A. B. and Powers, S. M. (1994) Computer technologies: Attitudes and self-efficacy across undergraduate disciplines. *Research in Higher Education*, 35 (6), pp. 745-768.

Marcinkiewicz, H. R. (1994) Computers and teachers: Factors influencing computer use in the classroom. *Journal of Research on Computing in Education*, 26 (2), pp. 220-237.

BIOGRAPHY

Peter Albion was a teacher of mathematics, science and computing in Queensland secondary schools for seventeen years before joining the University of Southern Queensland in 1991. He is currently Senior Lecturer in Educational Computing. His research interests include the development of teachers' self-efficacy integration of ICT into teaching and the application of problem-based learning to the design of multimedia and online education.

73

Training Kindergarten Teachers with Virtual Reality

David Passig and Tali Noyman
School of Education, Bar Ilan University, Ramat-Gan 52900, Israel
passig@mail.biu.ac.il

Keywords: virtual reality, teacher training, simulation

Abstract: In this study we used Virtual Reality to simulate a toddler's first few days' experiences in kindergarten and test whether we can improve the teacher's understanding of a toddler's feelings. The virtual worlds were developed in accordance with the toddler's way of emotional, cognitive and visual thinking. The participants in this study were 40 teachers who work with infants aged 6 months to 4 years old. The findings indicate that experiencing a virtual world that reflects the real world of children improves the teacher's awareness to the emotional experiences that a toddler undergoes in her/his first days in day-care or kindergarten.

1. INTRODUCTION

The emotional competencies of the child are very different from those of an adult. These competencies affect the way the toddler cope with the new environment. Erickson (1950) describes eight stages in the emotional development of a child. The first stage is the development of trust and confidence. In this stage the child will express trust in his caregivers if his needs will be fulfilled, such as warmth, love, and nourishment. On the other hand, the child will express mistrust if those needs will not be provided. The level of trust depends on the maternal attitude that he will receive. The parents should represent for the child a deep belief that there is a meaning to what ever they are doing for him (Erickson 1950).

Srof, Kooper and Dehart (1998) introduced a different emotional aspect that develops with toddlers. When a toddler starts recognising people as well as various items and develop expectation the child begins experiencing negative attitudes toward strangers (7-10 months). This fear from strangers might stretch a few months that can be prolonged to the second year. Therefore, when the toddler enters the day-care at that stage they will probably develop anxiousness to the new faces around (Shechter and McKolic 1989, Tal 1991).

Moreover, toddler's abilities to think and perceive are different from those of an adult, thus influencing the way in which they will adjust to a new place. The toddler's world outlook is absolute. Infants mix their 'self' with the world, and only later do they distinguish between their private point of view and that of other individuals. Toddlers believes that they are the centre of everything that takes place, and that things always remain as they sees them (Piaget 1967). Even when their thought progresses to the pre-operational stage (from 2 to 7 years), it is with difficulty that the toddler learns to see from someone else's viewpoint. Their thought is concrete – things are as they seem from their direct and egocentric perception, and unsubstantial phenomena appear to them as tangible (dreams, thoughts) (Flavell 1970).

Toddlers egocentricity leads to Magi-like thoughts. They believe that their wishes, thoughts, and the words they emit from their mouth are the tools of their super-powers. When toddlers are at the stage at which they believe that they are omnipotent, and that it is within their power to sway their influence over every object in their environment, their entrance into a new framework shakes this belief: Suddenly events are out of their control, they do not understand them, and they are not sure that their needs will be met; feelings of fear and anxiety are awoken in them.

The assumption at the basis of this study, therefore, was that the caregiver does not possess enough awareness of the influence that the separation from parents has over a toddler's behaviour at the beginning of the year in the kindergarten.

By using 3D VR worlds that simulate mental aspects unique to toddlers, this study investigated whether it is possible to increase the teacher's awareness to the toddler's emotional experiences in their first days at the kindergarten. To the best of our knowledge, this is the first time that VR technology has been used in training toddlers' teachers, and in simulating toddlers' emotional experiences.

VR is defined as a computer-based immersive environment with a high level of interactivity (Pantelidis 1994). For this research, an experiment was carried out with the help of a virtual world that acted according to the rules of toddlers' cognitive and emotional development, and simulated toddlers' worlds for the caregiver. Studies carried out in other fields have indicated that the use of simulation can help to improve comprehension in various areas (Psotka 1995, Cass and Roblyer 1999).

We designed 3D VR worlds, in which we embedded cognitive and emotional elements from toddlers' experiences, based on Piaget's theories. The following is a description of the worlds, with an ascription of the various images to the emotional and cognitive aspects upon which they were based. These VR worlds can be accessed through the Internet with a free downloadable VR plugin (Viscape) at http://faculty.biu.ac.il/~passig/vrprojects.html (look for VR KINDERGARTEN).

1.1 Object constancy

The caregiver (in this case female)) enters a forest. Before her, she sees paths leading to further paths that lead to a house. After a few moments, different objects connected to the child's world start to fly past at speed. The objects swiftly and randomly approach and disappear. In the background, unclear sounds can be heard, interspersed with a number of clear words. From time to time, the user sees bodily parts approach and then recede. The user moves, and sees everything from the height of a child. The participant has to reach the house. She is not given any instructions. She needs to experience it on her own. If she finds herself unsuccessful, she must conclude that she needs to ask for assistance.

According to Piaget, the appearing and disappearing objects and voices reflect the developmental element of object constancy. According to Piaget (1967), up until the age of 8 months, infants think that if a certain object disappears from sight then it no longer exists. Only when infants are about one year old do they start to look for hidden objects, but even then they will look in the first place that the object was hidden. Only as toddlers reach the age of two years old do they learn that objects that cannot be seen still continue to exist. As a result, toddlers feel a sense of instability, living as they does in a world in which objects and people appear and disappear, and it is not clear what is going on around them. They live with a feeling that they lack control over their environment. Searching for the house via the paths represents the way the infant experiences things and learns – by trial and error (Flavell 1970).

Figure 1. A picture from the virtual world – the house in the forest that the user must reach

1.2 Trial and error

Upon reaching the house, the caregiver enters a room. The room is a playroom in a kindergarten. Once more, the participant sees everything from the toddler's perspective. In the centre of the room a maze appears. The participant must pass along all of the maze's paths until she reaches the exit. She must knock over the cones that she encounters along the way. Because of the change in perspective, each time the user touches a cone, it changes shape. This also relates to the element of spatial perspective (objects) – the child perceives the object differently from each angle. When the teacher participant leaves the maze, she sees a door in front of her. She must touch the door, and move in to the next room. The attempt to find the way through the maze reflects the way the infant experiences things and learns – by trial and error (Flavell 1970).

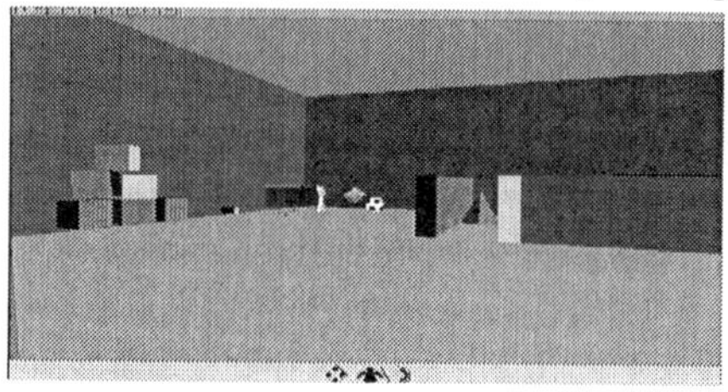

Figure 2. The maze in the virtual world's playroom as seen from outside

1.3 Spatial perspective – height and objects

The second room is designed like a playground. The participant can see a slide ahead of her. She is not given any instructions, and she must try to work out what to do alone, or ask for assistance. The participant must climb the ladder and slide down the slide. When she looks at the slide she can only see certain parts of the people and objects around her – she cannot see them in their entirety. After sliding down the slide, the participant will see big balls. She will struggle to catch them. The balls will roll away from her, until they disappear from her field of view, as if they no longer exist. After a number of attempts, a door will once more appear on the other side of the playground. The participant must touch the door and enter the next room. The teacher's attempts at catching the elusive balls once more reflect the element of trial and error. The rolling balls, escaping and disappearing from the user's field of vision, represent the developmental element of object constancy.

Figure 3. Part of the slide's ladder in the playground in the virtual world – view from below

1.4 Imagination and reality

In the third room, the participant can see a rug with toys on it, a vacuum cleaner and a drill. For the whole length of this room's experience, the sound of the drill can be heard. The teacher looks around her and sees the drill in action, rotating, making an exaggerated noise, and making enormous holes. When the drill ceases to work, the vacuum cleaner comes on. At this moment its dimensions enlarge and expand, it makes noise, and sucks up every object in its path.

This experience represents the toddler's inability to fully distinguish between imagination and reality. According to Piaget (1967), the infant tends to attribute Magic importance to his/her thoughts. The infant thinks they can change reality with a word or a look, and also attributes human characteristics to inanimate objects. The vacuum cleaner, for instance, can 'eat' everything – objects and people (Piaget 1967).

Figure 4: The drill in action in the virtual world's third room

1.5 Egocentricity

While experiencing the virtual world, the participant wears a Head Mounted Display (HMD) and enters another world – the world of children. Throughout the experience, an effort is made to give the user the feeling that she is the centre of this virtual world – everything happens around her. She is required to activate the virtual world, otherwise, nothing happens; there are no people there other than her. Everything happens only to her and not to anyone else. The participant does not receive a description of what will happen to her during the experiment, but only a general explanation, and that in order to create a feeling of expectation, curiosity, and impatience to reach the next stage. This represents the infant's egocentricity. According to Piaget (1967), toddlers feel as if everything that happens is centred on them, and that they are at the centre of the world. They cannot see from another's point of view, and finds it hard to delay satisfaction (Piaget 1967).

2. THE RESEARCH

2.1 Participants

The sample included 40 female teachers (Table 1.). The term 'teacher' relates to baby-minders and caregivers who work with infants aged 6 months to 4 years old in different private kindergartens under the supervision of the Ministry of Education..

Table 1. The sample of participants

Age	**20-28** ***(n=12)***	**29-41** ***(n=14)***	**42-58** ***(n=14)***	***Total*** **(n=40)**
Education	6 did not finish high school	14 completed 12 years of K12 education	19 studied between 13-17 years	1 did not respond

2.2 Design

After the VR worlds had been built, the researchers scheduled personal meetings at the caregivers' convenience. The meetings usually took place in the afternoon when the caregiver had finished work. Two to four caregivers participated in each meeting, each of which lasted between 2 and 3 hours. The researchers brought the hardware and software needed to run the virtual worlds to the kindergarten.

The research design included a pre-test, an experience in the VR worlds and a post-test. The researchers did not believe that a comparison with a control group that learned the cognitive state of mind, say through videotape, would be credible.

2.3 Pre-experiment questionnaire

Each participant received a short written explanation of what was about to happen. Each teacher was interviewed (questions 1 - 4 in Table 2), and was asked about her opinions as to ways in which infants cope with their entrance into a new environment, and their reactions to it. Through the interview, the caregiver's level of awareness as to the effect of the toddler's separation from his parents on his behaviour before intervention was also tested.

Table 2. Pre-experiment interview

1. What situations, in your opinion, can cause a child to be irritable, and not calm?
2. A child is not without his comfort blanket and dummy for a week at the beginning of the term. How would you react? Why?
3. A child chooses to sleep all the time. What would you do? Why?
4. About a month after the beginning of the year, a child still regularly bursts out crying. What should be done? Why?

Additionally, each caregiver was asked to fill out a questionnaire (Table 3, questions 5-14). The caregiver was asked to react to a variety of situations. The questionnaires of this study were comprised with the help of infants' experts from the Baker Centre, Bar-Ilan University, Israel, since no adequate questionnaires were found to meet the purpose of this research. The experts from the Baker Centre who specialize in infants' development found this questionnaire suitable to the aims and procedures of this study.

Table 3. Pre-experiment questionnaire

5. An irritated child that cries frequently. How would you address him/her?
6. A child holds a blanket that he brought from home and does not want to separate from it. Should you do something? If yes, what would you do? Why is he behaving that way, in your opinion?
7. A child prefers to sleep during the activity times? Should you react? If yes, how?
8. A child starts crying whenever someone approaches him? What should you do? Why is he behaving that way, in your opinion?
9. A child does not want to leave his bottle? Should you react? If yes, what in your opinion you should do during the day-care time and at home?
10. A child sits in the corner and watches the activity with a serious look. Should you do something? If yes, what would you do?
11. A child throws items all over the room. What would you do? Why is he behaving like that, in your opinion?
12. A child prefers playing solo, and doesn't want to join others. Should you do something? If yes, what can you do?
13. A child holds on one of the caregivers and doesn't want to leave her and play around. How would you react, and what can be done?
14. A child hits and bites other kids in his surrounding. Should you react? If yes, what should you do?

2.4 Virtual experience

After completing the questionnaire, the researchers formed two groups of caregivers. One group experienced the virtual worlds without any emotional mediation, i.e., the researchers explained to each caregiver that she is about to enter a child's world, that no explanations or instructions will be given during the experiment, and that if she wants to know what to do, she must ask for help (Figure 5). This kind of introduction was given to just 20 (n=40) of the participating caregivers. The other group was introduced to the experiment with emotional assistance. The researchers used a process of emotional mediation towards this group when after the caregiver put the helmet on, the researches reflected her feelings of helplessness in the VR children world. They emphasized their empathy with her difficulties, and finally offered her assistance. The researchers told the caregiver that she could ask for any kind of assistance whenever she likes to.

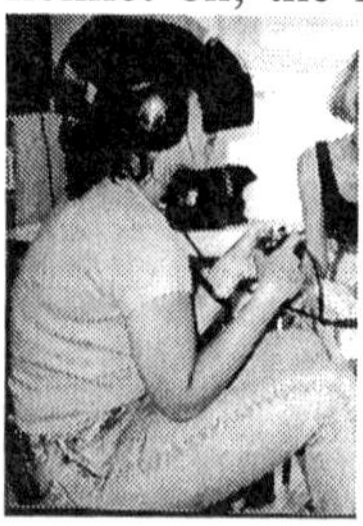

Figure 5. A participant wearing the Head Mounted Display (HMD) and using the joystick whilst experiencing the virtual world

Each experience took about ten minutes. Many of the caregivers struggled to get by in the virtual world using the joystick. Very few asked for help, even when they did not ask what to do in each room in the virtual world the researchers assisted in their navigation and provided guidance.

2.5 Post-experiment interview

After the experiment, the caregivers were interviewed. They were asked about their feelings during and following their experience. The aim was to verify whether the caregiver experienced anxiety, frustration and the need for help during the experiment. Another objective was to verify whether the experience would affect her attitude towards a newcomer infant to her day-care.

Table 4. Post-experiment interview

You have just had an experience that you have never had before. With the help of the HMD, you entered a children's world inside a computer. You were asked to do various activities. Tell us how you felt?

15. What did feel while putting on the HMD?
16. How did you feel when you were asked to climb the ladder and slide?
17. How is the feeling of viewing the world from a toddler's point of view?
18. What did you feel when the experience was over?

After undergoing this new experience, how do you think you will plan the intake of a new child into the kindergarten? How will you help him to settle in and adjust?

2.6 Post-experiment questionnaire

After the caregivers went through the VR experience, they were asked the same questions they have been asked before the experiment (Table 3). In addition, each caregiver was asked to answer the following question: How would you address differently a new infant in your day-care after going this experience.

3. RESULTS

3.1 Emotional awareness

We assumed that caregivers are not aware sufficiently to the difficulties a child goes through the separation from his parents in his first days at the kindergarten. We have tested this assumption with the direct question, which has been asked following the VR experience: what would be your attitude to a new child attending your kindergarten now that you have experienced the VR worlds?

The answers of the 40 participants indicated that:

25 of them (62.5%) reported some type of change in their attitude towards a new child attending kindergarten. This result was found to be significant $t=(8.0, 39), p< 0.001$

12 out of these 25 (48%) pointed to changes that correspond to emotional aspects (3 of them related to just emotional aspects and 9 to both emotional and cognitive aspects).

This assumption was fortified by the direct question; meaning that the VR experience improved the awareness of the caregivers to the toddlers' emotional experiences in the first days in kindergarten.

3.2 Emotional awareness with and without emotional mediation

However, the other objective of this study was to test whether experiencing VR with emotional mediation will improve the caregiver awareness to the feelings of anxiety, frustration, and need for help. The assumption was that a VR experience coupled with emotional mediation will better improve (Table 5) the emotional awareness of the caregivers to the toddler's first day's feelings in kindergarten.

Table 5. Change in attitude

	Experiencing feelings of fear, frustration and need for help during the VR experiment	
	R	
Change in attitude towards a newcomer infant to the kindergarten	Caregivers that received emotional mediation (n=20)	-0.602*
	Caregivers that did not receive emotional mediation (n=20)	-0.101

*p < 0.01

Among the group that received emotional mediation we found a higher correlation (0-fear, anxiety, need for help; 1- other feelings) between those that reported feelings during the VR experience and those that reported a change in attitude towards a newcomer infant to their day-care (1 – reported change in attitude; 0 – reported no-change) r=-0.602<0.01.

On the other hand, among the group that did not receive any emotional mediation, we did not find a correlation between those that reported feelings during the VR experience and those that reported a change in attitude towards a newcomer infant to their day-care.

Thus, the results clearly indicate that experiencing VR toddler's worlds with emotional mediation improved the awareness of the caregiver to the feelings that a toddler go through in his first days in kindergarten.

4. DISCUSSION

The purpose of this research was to test whether using a cutting edge technology – Virtual Reality – to train teachers would make an impression on the teacher, and influence her future behaviour with toddlers. The research aimed to test whether a very small investment in time (10 minutes in a toddler's simulated virtual world) would produce significant training results for the teachers.

To the best of our knowledge, this is the first research project to report positive results for such a hypothesis. Many other studies have proved the effectiveness of Virtual Reality in other training situations, but our review of the literature did not reveal any use of VR with cognitive and emotional aspects related to toddlers.

The literature offers examples of users of Virtual Reality who reported similar feelings who were influenced by the sensation of 3D immersive VR (Bricken and Byrne 1992, Shapiro and McDonald 1992). However, no report has been published demonstrating a simulated infant cognitive state of mind and its impact on adults.

No reliable tool was found in the literature in order to carry on this research. Therefore, different 'childhood experts' were asked to draft a list of questions that will represent (somehow) the toddlers' cognitive and emotional way of thinking. It was quite an experience to draft this list. The 'experts' (faculty members of the Baker Centre for Early Childhood Education, School of Education, Bar-Ilan University http://www.biu.ac.il) recommended a short list that would be simple enough for the participants to follow. This seems satisfactory as an initial attempt to simulate the emotional state of a toddler and test its efficiency. If not to clearly indicate the efficiency of the VR technology to enhance the awareness of the caregivers to the toddlers' emotional experience, then at least at observing evidence that count for a trend.

Following the exercise in the virtual worlds, the most noteworthy improvement in the caregivers' awareness was in relation to the fact that with some kind of emotional mediation the VR experience better improved the caregivers' awareness to the emotional state of the ttoddlers in the first days in kindergarten.

It could be that this kind of improvement stems from the caregiver's feeling as she enters the virtual world, in which she is by herself, with everything happening around her. She had to activate this virtual world, to operate and manipulate objects. It could well be that during an experience, in which everything that happens is dependent only on her, help (emotional mediation) that she is receiving emphasises her awareness to others' emotional needs.

The results of this research are by no means final, since without VR we would have had no means at all of getting the material across to the caregivers, apart from the conventional, lengthy, wearisome and expensive way – with words. This type of research opens a new path into uncharted territories – worlds that we could not easily and quickly touch and demonstrate. As opposed to other research projects using Virtual Reality, this research did not simulate situations or worlds familiar to us, but rather created abstract scenarios from a human brain, and tested the efficiency of another person's interaction with it. This study tested the immediate change in the caregivers' attitude. Further research should be conducted to test the long-range effect of VR on their behaviour. Nonetheless, this research offers tools and hope for educators that they may be able to understand what is happening in the worlds of those children under their responsibility.

REFERENCES

Bricken, M. and Byrne, C. M. (1992) *Summer students in virtual reality: a pilot study on educational application of virtual reality technology*. University of Washington. Seattle, WA. [http://www.hitl.washington.edu/projects/education].

Cass, M. D. and Roblyer, M. D. (1999) A review of experimental research on virtual reality in special education: the status of the dream. *VR in the Schools*, 4. [http://150.216.8.1/vr/vrel.htm].

Erickson, A. (1950) *Childhood and Society*. Hapoalim Press, Tel Aviv, Israel (in Hebrew).

Flavell, J. H. (1970) *The developmental psychology of Jean Piaget.* Otsar Hamoreh, Tel Aviv (in Hebrew).

Pantelidis, V. S. (1994) Virtual Reality in the classroom. *Computers in Education*, 30 pp. 3-13, Tel Aviv (in Hebrew).

Piaget, J. (1967) *The world representation of the child.* Hakibutz Haarzi Publication, Tel Aviv (in Hebrew).

Psotka, J. (1995) *Immersive-tutoring systems: virtual reality and education and training.* US Army Research Institute, U.S.A, Alexandria, VA.

Shapiro, M. A. and MacDonald, D. G. (1992) I am not a real doctor, but I play one in virtual reality: implication of virtual reality for judgments about reality. *Journal of Communication*, 42, pp. 94-114.

Shechter, R. and McKoli, K. S. (1989) *When Your Children are Afraid.* Hadar, Tel Aviv (in Hebrew).

Srof, A., Kooper, R. and Dehart, G. (1998) *Child Development: nature and course.* Open University, Tel Aviv (in Hebrew).

Tal, K. (1991) *Struggle with Fears in Early Childhood.* Sara Batz Publication, Tel Aviv (in Hebrew).

BIOGRAPHY

David Passig is a faculty member at the Bar-Ilan University. He teaches Future Methodologies and Systems Theory, and is heading the Virtual Reality Laboratory at the graduate program of Technology & Communication at the School of Education. His current research endeavours are: Future learning technologies and their cognitive impact, MM and VR learning interface, future cognitive and learning skills (www.passig.com). Tali Noyman is a researcher at the Virtual Reality Laboratory.

74

Design Elements for a CSCL Environment in a Teacher Training Programme

Ditte Lockhorst[1], Wilfried Admiraal[1], Albert Pilot[1] and Wim Veen[2]
[1)] Institute of Education, Utrecht University, PO Box 80127, 3508 TC Utrecht, The Netherlands
d.lockhorst@ivlos.uu.nl
[2)] Faculty of Technology, Policy and Managment, Delft University of Technology, Jaffalaan 5, 2628 BX Delft, The Netherlands

Keywords: collaborative learning, electronic communication, teacher education, didactics, research

Abstract: In the design of a Telematic Learning Environment (TLE) in which student teachers learn collaboratively, we consider three clusters of design elements as important: the Telematic Work Environment, the guidance of the instructor and the task instruction. We will have a look at the way group and task behaviour, triggered by these design elements influence the collaborative outcomes. Experiments have revealed that the technical environment is not as important as we had expected beforehand. This research shows that the task instruction (pre-imposed structure, role taking and intrinsic motivation for the task) and the group process itself have far more impact on the online collaborative work of the student teachers.

1. INTRODUCTION

Computer Supported Collaborative Learning (CSCL) is receiving considerable attention in contemporary educational research. (Kagan 1994) stresses the need for co-operative learning because "increasingly, the workplace consists of interdependent teams working on complex problems which no individual alone can solve" (p. 2:1). In addition, both schools and universities show a growing attention for co-operative learning and the use of new media and Telematic environments.

The purpose of our study was to examine the elements involved in designing a training environment in which student teachers effectively learn to cooperate by means of Telematics. In this paper, we will describe these design elements and emphasise the task instruction, based on a literature study and expert interviews (Lockhorst 1999). In addition, we will also discuss the student teachers' evaluation of their co-operative processes in two studies involving different Telematic Learning Environments (TLE's).

These studies have taken place in the framework of our larger research project at IVLOS, the Institute of Education of the Utrecht University in the Netherlands, in which different TLE's have been designed, implemented and evaluated. The first study described in this paper was our first TLE, which we based on a preliminary theoretical orientation. The second TLE we will discuss was based on the results of the first study.

2. CSCL AND THE DESIGN OF TLE'S

Studies show that it is difficult in TLE's to have a meaningful discussion showing elaboration, explanation, and reciprocal exchange. In fact, sometimes there is no discussion at all.

There are several variations on the group- and task arrangements that influence the interaction in a group and that are relevant to our study. Positive interdependence, which can be reached by goal- and resource interdependence, can stimulate effective group behaviour (Johnson and Johnson, 1994). We assume that individual accountability, in many cases translated in reward interdependence (e.g. Johnson and Johnson 1994), is an important factor for creating effective groups, but we are sceptical about the use of rewards in adult education. Another way to create individual accountability could be the evaluation of the individual's role during the process (Strom and Strom 1996). According to Cohen (1994), interdependency should be fostered by presenting challenging tasks and stimulating learner's intrinsic motivation and collaborative skills.

The task arrangement influences the interaction as well. Cohen (1994) states that a strong structuring of the work process hampers the collaborative process, particularly when adult learners are presented with ill-structured problems. The use of roles is questionable, as studies disagree on the effect of role taking on the interaction.

The number of participants in a group and their background (ability, race, gender, age, etc.) influence the co-operative learning process as well. Groups of four seem to diminish the chance of the free-rider or sucker effect (Cohen 1994). Groups with learners who have different frames of reference can stimulate the discussion and the exchange of information, as the group members are mutually dependent with regards to information resources and skills. Miller and Harrington (1992) indicate personalisation as an important factor for working efficiently, as it overrides participants' initial categorisation and leads to shared responsibility. The experts interviewed have indicated that, in an on-line environment, personalisation is even more important and preferably done in face-to-face (F2F) meetings.

On the basis of expert interviews and the literature search on CSCL and TLE's in general, we distinguish three clusters of design elements: the Telematic work environment, the task instruction and the teachers' guidance. In addition, the context, including the student characteristics as well as all preconditions of the educational context in which the students and teachers worked (such as the technical conditions of the students at home), also play an important role. The design cluster 'Telematic work environment' refers to the functionalities of the website and programme used, the navigation and the structure. With the 'task instruction' we mean characteristics of the task, such as role taking, pre-imposed structure, task specialisation, type of task, and the training of students. It relates to the instruction the students receive before the co-operative task begins. The 'teachers educators' guidance' refers to the teachers' instruction and communication during the on-line task.

3. RESEARCH METHOD

In both studies, data was gathered through individual and group interviews with student teachers and teacher educators, semi-structured questionnaires for student teachers, electronic logfiles, and the storage of electronic communication of all groups.

The results of the two studies described here are based on an analysis of the student teachers' questionnaires and the electronic communications. Social Network Analysis (SNA) has been used to quantify and visualise the amount and type of interactions.

The pre-structured questions were measured on a 5-point Likert scale. The response rate was 100%. Descriptive statistics will be presented and student response to the essay questions are summarised and included in the results. In the presentation we will focus on the task instruction. In our studies, we observed that this aspect had more influence on collaboration than both the teachers' guidance or the features of the Telematic work environment.

4. STUDY 1: HISTORY TEACHING METHODS

4.1 Design of TLE

The first study to be described is a teacher-training course on history teaching methods, attended by 15 student teachers and run in the second half of 1999. Objectives of the course were to increase students' knowledge and experience with teaching methods, with the use of ICT and with co-operative learning. The students worked on four on-line assignments in groups of three to four using the TLE for communication and document exchange. The students worked in heterogeneous groups based on training background (fulltime, in-service, international students) aiming that students could take advantage of each others' knowledge and experiences because of the various frames of reference of the group participants. In this way we tried to stimulate reciprocal interdependence. The students had a F2F meeting every other week at the institute in which they presented their group outcomes and talked about additional assignments. They did not receive any grades for their assignment, but had to include the end products and a reflection on the collaboration process in their portfolios. The students received a low pre-imposed structure of the task: they had to plan the assignment and divide the tasks among themselves on-line. Only manuals with directions for group behaviour were provided on-line.

The TLE included information about the course, manuals on how to work with Internet, groupware and directions co-operative learning, a diary inlcuding all deadlines and milestones, hyperlinks to educational resources, the assignments and an expert (experienced history teacher educator) for feedback on individual teaching experiences and group assignments. Groupware was attached to the TLE. Bscw (http://bscw.gmd.de) as workspace for the groupwork, and Webboard (http://webboard.com) as social platform. The students received a training on how to use the website and exchange messages and files during the first face-to-face meeting.

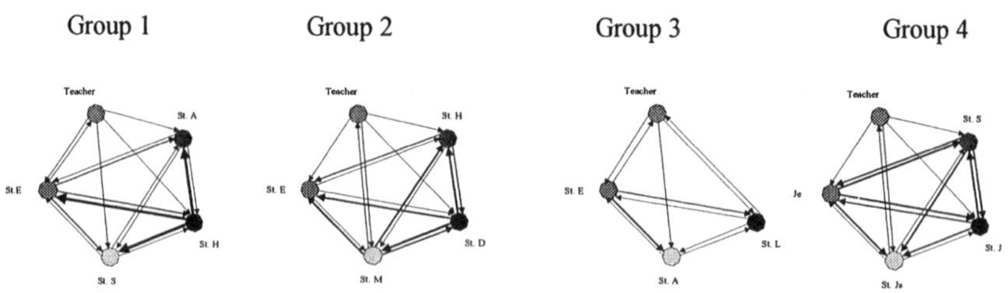

Figure 1. Interaction patterns of 4 groups

4.2 Results

Figures 1 shows the interactions patterns of the four heterogeneous groups. The thickness of the arrows represent the amount of messages sent.

In three groups, the frequency of communication was low, while in group two the frequency of communication was relatively high and equally divided. A satisfying co-operative learning process should have been one where students participated equally and actively by reading and commenting on the work of group mates while also contributing their own work. On the whole, there was little on-line discussion as the students tended to go over to task specialisation. Individual contributions were compiled at the end without further consideration. Most communication referred to organisational and procedural matters and document exchange.

Although the groups did not work as was planned, the students experienced positive outcomes. Twelve students indicated that their knowledge of the use of ICT had increased and that they have learned to co-operate with their peers. Fifty percent of the students thought the on-line work had helped them to increase their knowledge of subject teaching methods. However, almost all students felt that they would have increased their knowledge more if the assignments had been done F2F. Striking is the fact that the students did not appreciate the social function of the TLE. From many other studies (e.g. McIntyre and Tlusty 1995) we know that most student teachers experience the social function (exchange of experiences, emotional and motivational support) as an important outcome. Social contact in our TLE was less important to the students because they did not know each other very well, and because they already had social contact in other training groups.

Although the students found the groupware to be complex, they thought the programme was fairly easy to use. However, problems with Internet connections or the absence of a computer at home delayed work and de-motivated the students.

4.2.1 Task instruction

Several aspects of the task instruction may have had a restrictive influence on the on-line discussion. Firstly, most students found the heterogeneous groups to be unpleasant. Differences between the types of students were more profound then expected and the students were not open to feedback from other types of students. Only the students of group two were positive about the mixed group composition and this helped their discussion to be productive.

Secondly, the groups experienced low personalisation. The students did not know each other beforehand and although team building was a focus during the first F2F meetings, this was only done in the whole group and not in the subgroups of four. This resulted in the students' lack of responsibility for the group work and negative personal relationships.

A third reason could be the fact that the students were not motivated for the assignments. In spite of the use of ill-structured problems, the students thought the assignments were not challenging enough as they focussed on theoretical rather than practical topics. In addition, some students indicated that the structure of the assignments triggered task specialisation. This task specialisation, combined with the lack of criticism from the teachers on the incoherent end products, resulted in limited on-line discussions. The use of a portfolio as a single assessment tool does not seem to encourage students to discuss the content on-line.

Finally, the time period in which the students had to work on the assignments was too short (2 to 4 weeks). Setting up a lively discussion takes more time, especially when some students only have access to an on-line connection once a week.

The lack of on-line discussion about the content led the teachers to give the groups time during the F2F meetings to plan their work at the start of each assignment period. Together with an interim evaluation, this stimulated the team feeling. The agreements made on planning and procedures in the F2F setting stimulated students' responsibility towards the group assignments.

5. STUDY 2: INTERNATIONAL TEACHER EDUCATION PROGRAMME

5.1 Design of TLE

This study was implemented in the first half of 2000 as part of IVLOS's international teacher training programme. Seventeen Dutch students, located all over the world, participated during their overseas teaching practice period. Objectives of this TLE were to train the students in teaching strategies, to continue units of study that started at the institute, to guide the students while they were abroad, and to keep the students in contact with each other and the training institute. The students worked, in different groups on four on-line assignments, which were running parallel during a period of four months. One of these (called TIE) was the focus of the second study. Its design was based on the results of the first experiment on history teaching methods. The students had to design, revise and actually give a lesson in a second-language class with the help of their group mates. In this study, we decide to use a pre-imposed structure; in contrast to the first study which was marked by a limited on-line discussion, task specialisation and the assembly of individual end-products. The groups received a week to week prescribing procedure, specifying who had to do what aspect of the task and when. In addition, the roles were strictly defined: each role and its corresponding task was described in detail.

The second TLE differed on other aspects of the design. There were no F2F meetings, the guidance of the students was completely on-line except for one visit of a teacher per country and the groups consisted of three students, located in different countries. Another difference with the first experiment is the groupware used. Because the communication in Bscw quickly becomes unorganised, we decided to use Webct (http://www.webct.com/wyw) in this study.

5.2 Results

The logfiles of WebCT show that the students have used the website intensively, particularly the Bulletin Board. Again the functionality and usability of the groupware was not a restrictive factor. WebCT generated no problems.

Figure 2 shows the amount of messages read and posted by the students. The social discussion forum in particular was used frequently and very long discussion threads were produced. The students made it very clear that they appreciated the social function of the TLE: it kept the group together. This is

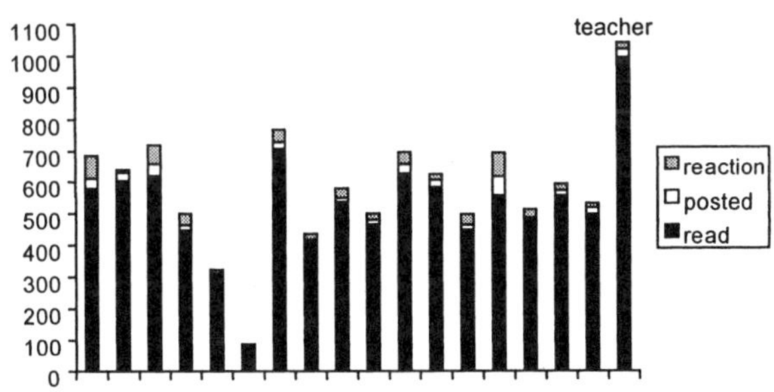

Figure 2. Number of messages read and written

not surprising, because the group knew each other very well before their work in the TLE and they were physically separated for some month's.

Figure 3 shows the interaction patterns of two of the TIE groups, which are representative for all TIE groups. The figures show that there was an equal interaction pattern, implying that the three group members were involved in the on-line discussion with the same frequency.

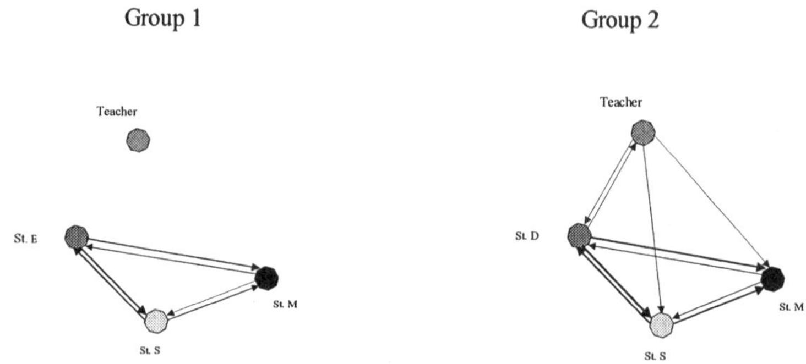

Figure 3. Interaction patterns of two TIE groups

5.2.1 Task instruction

Most groups did work out the assignment on a satisfactory level. However, the majority of students felt that the TIE assignment was useless (94.1%). They used terms like: artificial, time-consuming, not related to the things they were doing, did not see the goal. Their motivation to do the assignment was very low, and they felt working on it as an obligation. The absence of assessment and feedback from the teacher educator increased their feelings of uselessness of the assignment. However, the pre-imposed structure and role taking offered them a framework to work in. A similar result has been found in another of our experiments, in which students did little work on the assignment for the first three months until the teacher gave them a very strict pre-imposed structure, after which all the work was completed in just one month (Lockhorst 2000).

The students did not like the TIE assignment, and did it perfunctorily, contrary to other assignments in this TLE, in which they had to make their own planning and procedures. Three groups used the TLE voluntarily to complete one of these assignments. Notable is that in their discussion forums the largest amount of messages were exchanged. The students clearly saw the usefulness of the TLE for their co-operation and this resulted in an extensive discussion and information exchange. This shows that intrinsic motivation is important in on-line co-operative learning. Nevertheless, when students have to complete assignments for which they are less motivated, a pre-imposed structure and role taking could help them to carry out the assignment (extrinsic motivation).

6. CONCLUSION AND DISCUSSION

Three clusters of design elements have been presented. The results of the two studies described implicate that the influence, of these clusters on the group and task behaviour, differ.

Both studies show the importance of the task instruction. The impact of the use of a pre-imposed structure, role taking and intrinsic motivation has been substantial in both studies. In the first study, a minimal pre-imposed structure and lack of motivation for the task resulted in very limited on-line discussion and co-operation. The second study shows that, although students were not motivated for the assignment, the pre-imposed structure and role taking stimulated them to co-operate on the task. In our opinion there is much attention in the field of CSCL for outcomes and the cognitive learning process, while less attention is paid to the influence of the task instruction. This seems strange in some sense, because in research on co-operative learning, the importance of task instruction is recognised.

The fact that the students of the second study knew each other very well and had no F2F contact, motivated them to work on-line. In contrast, the students of the first experiment mentioned that lack of personalisation, the atmosphere in the groups, the lack of shared interests, concerns and feelings of responsibility for the group as well as the product, had a negative effect on their group behaviour. The heterogeneous grouping on the basis of training background thus frustrated the co-operative learning process. In future research on CSCL, more attention should be paid to the group process (including student characteristics) and the influence of this on the outcomes.

Both studies do reveal that the technical environment did not have a great impact on the outcomes. We used different groupware and although there were some dissimilarities in user-friendless and functionalities, the programmes were useful for the tasks. The technical context of the students at home and their technical skills did have a great impact on their role in the group process. Cautiously, we dare to say that, considering its limited impact, the technical environment should not receive so much attention in CSCL research. Many researchers work on the development of new programmes for CSCL, with special and more and more advanced functionalities. This is undoubtedly useful, but to study the influence of these new programmes on the outcome of CSCL without considering the influence of the task instruction, the teachers' role and group dynamics, is not doing justice to the latter.

REFERENCES

Cohen, E. G. (1994) Restructuring the Classroom: Conditions for Productive Small Groups. *Review of Educational Research,* 64 (1), pp. 1-35.

Johnson, D. W. and Johnson, R. T. (1994) Learning Together. In *Handbook of Co-operative learning methods*, S. Sharan (ed.), CT: Greenwood press, Westport, pp. 51-65.

Kagan, S. (1994) *Co-operative Learning*. Moore Data management services, San Diego.

Lockhorst, D. (1999) Summary of the interviews. Internal report. IVLOS/Utrecht University, Utrecht, The Netherlands.

Lockhorst, D. (2000) *Evaluatie Teleleren ICLON: project Vuistregels.* (Evaluation Telelearning at ICLON: project Rules of Thumb) IVLOS/Utrecht University, Utrecht, The Netherlands.

McIntyre, S. R. and Tlusty, R. H. (1995) *Computer-mediated discourse: electronic dialogue journaling and reflective practice.* Paper presented at the AERA, San Fransisco.

Miller, N. and Harrington, H. J. (1992) Social categorization and intergroup acceptance: Principles for the design and development of cooperative learning teams. In *Interaction in cooperative groups, the theoretical anatomy of group learning*, R. Hertz-Lazarowitz and N. Miller (eds.), Cambridge University Press, Cambridge, pp. 203-225.

Strom, R. and Strom, P. (1996) Student Evaluation of Social Skills. *Journal of Instructional Psychlogy,* 23 (2), pp. 111-117.

BIOGRAPHY

Ditte Lockhorst has worked for more than ten years as a consultant on ICT in education. From multi-media developer, she co-ordinated of the EU REFLECT project and also worked in the EU T3 Project (Telematics for Teacher Training). Wilfried Admiraal is educational researcher. His research is focused on how to include peer students into university teaching and learning in order trigger effective and efficient learning processes, with or without the use of electronic learning environments. Albert Pilot is full professor of curriculum development in IVLOS Institute of Education at Utrecht University an in 1998 also as professor of Chemistry Education in the Department of Chemistry of that university. Wim Veen is head of the Centre of Educational Innovation and Technology at Delft University of Technology. This centre provides training and consultancy services for educational change and curriculum development for faculties, professional development of university teachers, and teacher training for secondary education.

PART NINE

NATIONAL INITIATIVES

75

Historical Overview of Computer Use in Brazilian Teaching

Márcia R. Notare, Simone C. Mendes, Ingrid V. Mito and Tiarajú A. Diverio
Instituto de Informática e PPGC da UFRGS, C.P. 15064, 91501-970 Porto Alegre, Brazil
notare@inf.ufrgs.br

Keywords: developing countries, national programme

Abstract: This paper presents a historical overview of the use of information technology in the Brazilian Education. It identifies the main phases of the process of computer usage in education. It offers a general view of the main Brazilian Educational Projects that support the process of introducing computers in schools all over the country. Computer usage phases in Brazilian education are also descrobed. The evolution of resources used by the teachers are analysed. Finally, tools for planning, creating and maintaining educational environments are described, and some distance teaching environments available in the Web are characterised, according to their functionality and applicability.

1. INTRODUCTION

Nowadays, computers are no longer 'specialised products'; they have to be considered now as 'household appliances'. Their sales are not restricted to specialised computer stores anymore; now these machines can be acquired in department stores and supermarkets. Another change that came along with the computerisation and the 'popularisation of the machine' is the fact that computer is now common equipment for most of the Brazilian middle-class houses. And almost all of them can be connected to the Internet. In the same way technology has been improved through the introduction and development of informatics, so education must present the same evolution characteristics. This is the very aspect of interest to this study.

Some time ago, when we thought about education we would think about a classroom in which a teacher, students, blackboard and schoolbook would form a picture of tradition and good results. The answers to the questions bellow compose a timeline in which we can observe the adaptation phases of education to the new technologies that are capable of assisting and modifying this process.

How has this evolution happened?

How was the reaction and adaptation of education in the beginning of computerisation?

What is the actual reality of education in this aspect? Has there been any advancement?

This paper presents an analysis of the principal phases of the evolution process of computer usage in education in Brazilian Educational Institutions (Moraes 1997). The evolution of the process will be presented based on the reality of some of the main Brazilian Universities involved with Informatics in Education.

2. SOME BRAZILIAN EDUCATIONAL PROJECTS

The first governmental initiatives for an incentive to the introduction of informatics in Brazilian Education were taken around 1981 through the *EDUCOM Project*. This project had its origins in the 'I Seminário Nacional de Informática na Educação' (1st National Seminar on Informatics in Education) held in Brasilia the same year. The project aimed at implementing pilot-centres in which the formation of professionals capable of using the new technologies in classroom would be available. Finally, in 1983 the *EDUCOM Project* document was introduced as an interdisciplinary proposal, with the implementation of pilot-centres with infrastructure meant to provide capable professionals for further implementation at schools.

The *FORMAR Project* was implemented in 1987, through two courses about specialisation of informatics in education, at an ungraduate level, held at UNICAMP University (University of Campinas, SP). The project was meant to give capability to teachers from public schools. The capability of the teachers of this project came from pilot-centres of the *EDUCOM Project*. The graduate teachers would design and implement, together with their Education Secretariat, a CIEd – Educational Informatics Centre, with technical and financial support from the Education Ministry. After the accomplishment of the *FORMAR Project*, 17 CIEd's were introduced, one at each Brazilian State.

The National Program of Educational Informatics – *PRONINFE*, of 1989, aimed at developing the educational informatics in Brazil. The program was developed through projects and activities, on solid and updated pedagogical fundamentals, in order to guarantee the vital scientific, technical and political unity to the success of the efforts and investment involved. The program also intended, among other things, to give support to the development and utilisation of Computer Science in the 1st, 2nd and 3rd degrees and special education; to promote the infrastructure of support related to the creation of several centres spread all the country, by means of consolidating and integrating researches; to produce qualified human resources and to produce, acquire, adapt and evaluate educational software.

Finally, the *PROINFO* – National Program on Informatics in Education – was launched (MEC/SEED/PROINFO 1999). The *PROINFO* had main initial targets to finance the introduction of the information technology and telecommunications in the Fundamental and Middle public education and to initiate the universalisation process of the use of new technologies into the educational public system. The program's main purposes were to improve quality on the teaching-learning process and at the same time to make possible the creation of a new cognitive pedagogy in the schools environments through adequate incorporation of the new information technologies throughout the schools. All these would offer an education turned to the scientific and technological development. The *PROINFO*, by the time it was launched, anticipated some target actions such as the preparation and support of state projects on computers in education; planning the school's computerisation; support to school's projects; qualification of human resources; introduction of educational technology centres; definition of the technical specifications; and the follow-up and support to projects.

Nowadays, the Brazilian Education is divided into Fundamental Teaching, Middle Teaching and Superior Teaching. One of the government's actual concerns is the *TV-School Program*, which is a television channel via satellite exclusively dedicated to education. The main objectives of this program are the qualification of teachers from the public schools of Fundamental and Middle Teaching, as well as the enrichment of the teaching-learning process. And further, it aims at providing populations residing in the far-away areas of the country, such as Amazonian, with proper education.

3. PHASES OF THE COMPUTER USAGE IN EDUCATION

In this section, two subjects are discussed on the use of technologies in the classroom. The first concerns the use of the computer as a tool for helping students to develop reasoning an intelligence. The second shows the evolution of the use of the technologies by the teacher during the planning and presentation of their teaching.

3.1 The computer in the teaching-learning process

The first way computer was used in education, and the most diffused one in terms of quantity, was Computer Assisted Instruction (CAI), also known as Programmed Instruction. Programmed Instruction is composed, briefly, of repetitive exercises for fixing, tutorials and demonstrations. The most utilised ones are the repetitive exercises. They are programs that make the student to perform a sequence of exercises ordained by the degree of difficulty.

The tutorials are supposed to make the computer instruct the students, in the same way a teacher would do in individual contact with them. Usually, the tutorial provides the student with some information, followed by related questions, in which possible answers are foreseen by the system. The quality of the tutorial is measured by the capacity of the group that developed it in foreseeing all the possible entries, including and mainly the wrong ones.

Finally, we have demonstrations. The computer can give demonstrations in a classroom to a highly sophisticated degree. Graphic, sound and chromatic resources can be utilised and, consequently, the overhead projector and transparencies are gradually replaced. Undoubtedly, the computer's potential is demonstrated trough the facility with which the variables can be manipulated and through the instantaneous feedback it provides.

However, Programmed Instruction, despite being more diffused, is not the only way of computer usage in teaching. Simulations and educational games are very important and have great pedagogical value. A simulation is a model that tries to imitate a real or imaginary system, based on an operation theory of this same system. Through the use of simulated programs the student can easily test complex hypothesis, manipulate variables and verify the model's behaviour under varied conditions and situations.

Pedagogical games are those that differ from the others by its purpose, which is explicitly to promote learning. Nevertheless, like all the other games, the pedagogical games are intended to be entertaining. There are games that require from the student the application of logic and obviousness rules. This makes the student face thought, logic and language very seriously. The student learns to process information, make logical inferences and test conjectures.

Among the programming languages constructed for education, we have the LOGO language, which is the oldest and most diffused one. It is an extremely interactive and friendly language, which emphasises self-learning and which has rapidly become the most used one in the educational fields. Several studies have showed that learning through discovering, exploration, investigation and search not only have a special significance for the development of the cognitive structures (because it consists of high-significant learning for the student), but it is also retained for a longer period.

It is important to mention the use of application packages in education, such as the text editors, electronic spreadsheet, database managers and others. Such software can have a high practical and pedagogical potential.

However, during recent years, the STI's (Intelligent Tutorial Systems) have arisen. They are an evolution of the CAI's, used in the Programmed Instruction. STI's are computer programs that make use of the Artificial Intelligence in order to represent knowledge and provide the student with a better interaction with it. The main objective of the STI's is to make the computer adopt an intelligent conduct that allows it to control the acquisition process of knowledge and that provides the student with an adapted Instruction. Figure 1 graphically explains the phases approached in the text.

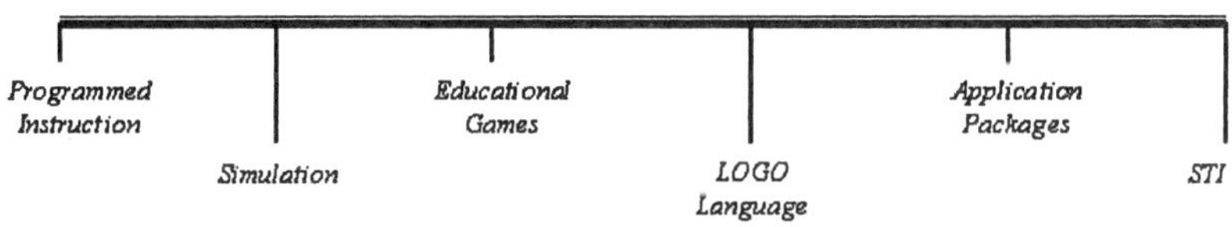

Figure 1. Ways of computer usage in the teaching-learning process

3.2 The evolution of pedagogical resources

Traditionally, classes were ministered with the help of books. With the introduction of the overhead projectors in the schools, teachers started to use hand-written transparencies. With the personal computers, the transparencies became more developed and printed, which produced a breakthrough in terms of visual quality.

Afterwards, came the tools to implement more creative classes, like the Microsoft Power Point – and the whole package Microsoft Office. Since then, the content of the classes could be presented through transparencies with larger and better resolution. Its major advantage was the pre-format of transparencies provided by the tool.

The next step was the use of the World Wide Web. This way, teachers were able to update their contents and look for the latest researches in the Internet. And mainly, they could create their own pages using poor Html editors, which did not allow them to improve the environment from the graphic perspective.

Soon afterwards further tools arose, like the FrontPage, a Web manager. From then on, came the constructions of the first Web environments destined to be educational supports, and the first trials of virtual classes.

In the next phase, the Microsoft Office, and specially the PowerPoint, turned to be totally integrated with the Web. Documents created in these tools started to have the possibility to be saved in the Web's standard format, html. The last and big phase of this process is being initiated with the new version of this package, where we can have the total integration of the machine with the Web.

The computer usage evolution in teaching has been a gradual process. The insertion of technology in any area of education has followed the same sequence of steps. It is important to emphasise that the evolution has not necessarily passed through all the presented phases, but probably just a few of them occurred in a different way from the one presented in Figure 2. Besides this, the timeline illustrates a process that was initiated in main research centres, such as the universities. In those centres, this process has not been completed in all courses yet. We can notice a major development and utilisation of these resources in courses linked to the Exact Sciences, such as Engineering and Computer Science. In the other areas this process seems to be slower.

To most of the Fundamental and Middle education schools this is still a reality that is being implemented, or analysed by its educational professionals. The Figure 2 shows the timeline of the pedagogical tools used by the teacher.

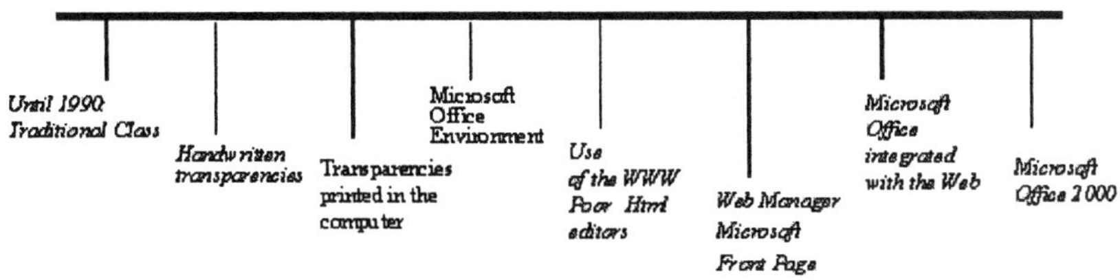

Figure 2. The evolution of pedagogical tools

4. TOOLS AND ENVIRONMENTS FOR DISTANCE TEACHING

This section is dedicated to comments on tools and distance teaching environments considered important (Saba 1999).

4.1 Tools

There are several tools that help the implementation of EaD environments. A site can be composed of various resources that, when united, transform it into a consistent educational material/environment. Among them, we can list the following:

Discussion Classrooms: Allow communication 'in real time' among people through the textual language. They can be used for clarification of doubts, debates and discussions.

Search Engine: Searching sites used in order to locate sites' addresses of a specific subject in the Internet. Distance teaching environments usually have links available for the main sites that do this type of search.

Discussion Lists: Students and teachers broach questions for discussion. In this list, through the E-mail, all participant teachers and students have access to the sent messages. It is an asynchronous communication channel.

Electronic Book: Contains the contents treated in the virtual classes available in the sites. They can be transparencies of the disciplines, files with the contents, the very content available on the page or generated through finite automatons.

Online Exercises: Exercises created by the teacher and that may complement the learning, serve as access authorisation to the next content or evaluate the student. Their most common forms are questions of multiple choice and questions of true or false.

Videoconference: Synchronous meetings that utilise audio and video resources through a camera installed in the machine of each participant and through assistance of a videoconference tool.

Teleconference: Videos or previously recorded classes can be utilised and they are transmitted via satellite or via computer network to the receiver locations.

Nowadays we can find other resources in the web, such as: *pools*, which are tools that give support to, for instance, voted questions in classrooms and discussion lists; *vault*, which are special locations in which important questions or experiences are stored in order to be used in the future, where all have access to store or consult information; *threads*, which are tools that allow the visualisation of the directions that a certain message took, making possible the monitoring of discussions; *find*, which are search and consult engine that permit to locate a specific topic or word in a text.

For the construction of the site, the Html editors are used. The sites can be improved with visual resources in order to call the student's attention, such as flashes or pictures in motion.

4.2 Environment classification proposal

In this section we introduce some tools and EaD environments. The environments and tools have been classified according to their functionality and applicability. Depending on the point of view at the moment of the environment analysis and the considered aspects, they can be classified in more than one category.

4.2.1 Management systems for distance teaching

The Management Systems for Distance Teaching are tools that make possible the creation, administration and maintenance of virtual courses via Internet. The communication services offered by the tools are the electronic mail, chats, discussion lists, debates, news, and others. For administration, they usually have notice board, appointment, schedule, news.

4.2.2 Projects in Brazil

With the development of Distance Education via Internet in Brazil several projects started. Most are developed in universities, with the purpose of promote research in each area, publicise projects, articles, events and results and integrate the EaD community of the country. Some offer complete 'remote' courses, while others have just an informative character, and offer collection of texts and articles of the area, specialists' reports or tips of links. Projects include:

- *Kidlink* Brazil (http://venus.rdc.puc-rio.br/kids/kdlinkv1.0)
- LUAR Project – Leading the University to the Distance Learning (http://penta.ufrgs.br/edu/telelab/luar.htm)
- Aprendiz Project (http://www.uol.com.br/aprendiz/)
- LED – Distance Teaching Laboratory (http://www.led.ufsc.br)
- S.A.B.E.R. Centre – Support to Learning Based on Remote Education (http://www.centrodesaber.com.br/)
- Telecourse 2000, http://www.bibvirt.futuro.usp.br/acervo/matdidat/tc2000/tc2000.html
- Campus Global – PUCRS (http://terra.cglobal.pucrs.br/).

4.2.3 Courses via Internet

The remote courses offered in the Internet are completely remote. In order to participate in these courses students need to register; access is through a password. Not all courses offered in the Internet are free. The students' frequency is controlled. Communication between student and teachers is via E-mail, lists or chats. Not all have synchronous communication or student classes and they have a specific period to start.

Evaluation is based on the student's performance during the exercises and tasks required during the course and final exams. All offer certificates when the course's requirements are fulfilled. The following are examples of virtual courses in Brazil: Virtual Centre of Classic Studies (http://www.centrovirtual.org/ entrada.htm), English Course – World On-line (http://www.cultural.org.br/wol/), *Surfing & Learning* (http://cogeae.uol.com.br/sal/) and e-Courses on Movie Scripts (http://www. conexao.net/).

4.2.4 Virtual libraries

Virtual Libraries are characterised by the heavy quantity of information they offer in remote areas. They are composed of collections of articles and texts, links, books and manuals, magazines and newspapers, reports, events, projects, organisations, tools, remote courses, educational and research institutions, theses and essays, tutorials. They also have discussion lists, visiting register book and chat rooms. A search service is also offered, in order to facilitate the user's consultation.

5. FINAL COMMENTS

This paper reviewed the evolution and actual situation of computer usage in the Brazilian Education. We considered some historical aspects of technology, governmental policies that supported the introduction of computers in the schools and the evolution of the distance teaching. With the identification of the phases of computer usage in education we can notice that there are in Brazil schools in all levels of evolution, in other words, there are schools that have not started the use of computer not even in their administrative activities and, at the same time, there are schools that use the Internet in order to promote research, communication and cooperative work among students.

It is known that the computerisation process of education is slow compared to computerisation in other activity areas. This is because it involves a change of mind concerning the society's concepts and values, as new ways of thinking and acting emerge.

REFERENCES

MEC/SEED/PROINFO (1999) *História da Informática Educativa no Brasil.* [www.edutecnet.com.br/edprhist.htm] 14.10.1999.

Moraes, M. C. (1997) *Informática Educativa no Brasil: uma História Vivida, Algumas Lições Aprendidas.* [www.edutecnet.com.br/edmcand.htm] 15.10.1999.

Saba, H. (1999) *Distance Education: An Introduction.* [www.distance-educator.com/portals/06researchers.html] 14.10.1999.

BIOGRAPHY

Tiarajú Diverio is Professor and researcher of the Institute Computer Science at UFRGS. His areas of interest include Processing of High Performance and Informatics in Education.

Marcia Notare, Simone Mendes and Ingrid de Vargas Mito are graduates in Science Computer or in Mathematics at UFRGS and doing a Masters in Computer Science to the PPGC-UFRGS. Areas of interest include Artificial Intelligent, Agents, and Informatics in Education.

76

An Italian National Curriculum on ICT for Schools

Giuseppe Callegarin and Agostino Cortesi
Istituto Regionale di Ricerca Educativa del Veneto, Mestre-Venezia, Italy
g.callegarin@irrsae.veneto.it
Dipartimento di Informatica, Università Ca' Foscari di Venezia, Mestre-Venezia, Italy

Keywords: primary education, secondary education, computer science, didactics

Abstract: This paper reports a contribution towards the definition of a new ICT National Italian Curriculum for both Primary and Secondary Schools. A method is proposed that supports the generation of the ICT Curriculum for each year or stage, with a convincing solid theoretical and pragmatic foundation. The key idea is to iterate progressively around some general operations on information: searching, analysing, structuring, processing, presenting and communicating. At each iteration, we suggest some contents, abilities and tools. Preliminary experimental results on the application of this method have been very promising, giving evidence of its effectiveness.

1. INTRODUCTION

Designing an ICT National Curriculum is a challenging task for several including the rapid evolution of hardware and software, because ICT is not yet accepted by many teachers as a discipline, and because of the required teacher competence. Moreover, some possible negative consequences of ICT on education and public investment (Stoll 1999) must be taken into account. Italy, along with many other countries, has been facing this challenge.

Italy is going to take a critical step as part of its reform of the whole School System. A recent law (Italian Parliament 2000) established that Primary School, called 'scuola di base', will cover 7 years (including Elementary School) and Secondary School will cover 5 years. The curriculum of the Secondary School will be divided into four main areas: Classic-Humanistic, Scientific, Technical and Technological, Artistic and Musical. The first two years of each area should provide some common background.

This reform is intended to enable people to find a job more quickly after compulsory school, and follows the example of many European countries. This reform also provides a chance critically redefine the aims of education, the need and role of traditional subjects, and the growth of new subjects.

A key concept that has been clearly identified is that any person after the Secondary School should possess certain skills. A skill is a suitable set of knowledge and abilities over a field (e.g. economics, foreign languages.) which enables a person to be 'competent' in some field regardless of the context in which they will work.

ICT skill has been considered relevant since the first analysis: basic education cannot ignore the new ways of building, communicating and presenting information. In this regard, Italy seems to be late compared with other countries that have had an ICT National Curriculum for several years, e.g. the UK (1999). Some critical decisions have then to be made in 2001/2002 in order to establish an ICT National Curriculum for Italy.

Until now, ICT has been taught as a subject for study only in a few Technical Secondary Schools. Some aspects of ICT have also been taught in almost every school (typically within Mathematics and Physics in the age range 14-15), with a variety of results.

This paper reports a contribution to help the task force called to propose the new ICT National Curriculum for both Primary and Secondary Schools (Infant School will also be closely involved). The aim is the definition of a method capable of 'generating' the ICT Curriculum for each year or stage in some detail and with a convincing solid theoretical and pragmatic foundation. With regard to the 'state of the art' on ICT, our main reference is the Computing Curricula 2001, jointly proposed by IEEE and ACM (IEEE-ACM 2000), the two biggest professional associations in the field.

The key idea of our proposal is to iterate progressively around some general operations on information: *searching*, *analysing*, *structuring*, *processing*, *presenting* and *communicating*. At each iteration we suggest some contents, abilities and tools. In this way, we aim at covering the basic aspects of four main ICT areas: data, programming, systems and languages.

The rest of this paper is structured as follows. The next section will describe the constraints to be overcome for the establishment of an Italian ICT National Curriculum for the compulsory school to be effective. In the subsequent section our model is introduced. Then a case study is discussed, that describes the application of our model for generating the curriculum of the first years of the Secondary School (age 13-14). Finally we will mention a didactic experience in a Primary School following the proposed model.

2. CONSTRAINTS

In this section, we briefly discuss the main constraints any curriculum proposal for Primary and Secondary Italian schools have to take into account in order to be effective.

How many years of school? In the new setting, Infant, Primary and Secondary schools will be organised into three cycles: 3 to 5 years, 6 to 13, and 13 to 18. Even though some very preliminary idea can be experimented in the first cycle, our proposal focuses just on the second and third cycles, covering the 12 years of compulsory school.

How many hours per year? We assume that between 30 and 40 hours will be assigned to ICT strongly related activities.

Which kind of teachers are available? Unfortunately, at the moment many teachers enrolled have a poor, if any, background in Computer Science. Therefore, this proposal needs to be shared, understood and appreciate by all of them first, otherwise it will result in something totally useless.

Which kind of tools are currently available in the schools? Computer systems change rapidly and quickly become obsolete. this is a serious problem, and often results in poor investment policies (and a museum of obsolete laboratories that in many cases have rarely been used). The best way to tackle this problem is to maintain very small computer laboratories. In addition, incentives for families to buy computers, mostly as an educational tool, should be included in any sensible public policy. In our proposal, we make very little assumptions about the tools available, and we believe that it is part of a teacher's duties to translate contents and methodologies in the particular school context.

What is the expected background of the pupils? Computers are mostly seen either as a support for video-games, or a way to access the Internet. However, pupils are totally unaware of its relevance, and in most cases we can assume basic abilities (e.g. interacting by properly using keyboard and mouse commands) that may often even precede and overrule reading and writing abilities.

Which are the peculiarities of the Italian education system? The Italian education system, like the economics and social systems, is anything but homogeneous. One of the main roles of the compulsory school is to promote a common background, in order to give all children the same cultural chances. On the other hand, any proposal has to take into account these differences, and flexibility is a key issue in this respect.

3. A SPIRAL MODEL

Speaking about ICT instead of 'Computer Science' is not just a matter of fashion. The emphasis is on the keywords 'information' and 'communication'. The reason for teaching, to the next generation, methodologies and tools coming from research in Computer Science, is not only demanded by the impact of new technologies on our daily life, but also by the intuition that technologies have a deep impact on the way pupils look at the world around them, a world where information is becoming crucial. Moreover, the *way* information is searched, analysed, structured, processed, presented and communicated is a valuable information.

The activities just mentioned are the keywords of our proposal. This leads to a spiral process as depicted in Figure 1, where the three iterations roughly correspond to the three main steps (Primary School, the 2 years stage of Secondary School, and finally the 3 years stage of Secondary School). Each cycle is followed by two crucial steps: verification with respect to the initial aims, and planning, to adapt the next cycle iteration to the specific class.

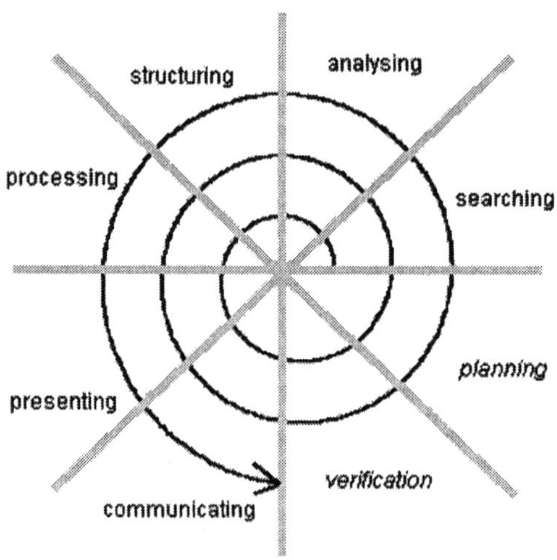

Figure 1. The spiral model

Let us present in some detail the six phases of each iteration.

Searching. Questions like "what kind of information is available?" and "what I'm really looking for?" can be considered as starting points. In Primary School, these questions would lead to activities that emphasise the crucial role of selecting research keys, and of verifying the matching between aims and results. Then, in the following years, they move to the introduction of basic ideas about the different ways a database may be structured, in order to design and tune effective queries. At a further step, useful ideas on searching techniques in semi-structured databases, like the web, must be introduced in the Secondary School.

Analysing. Analysis means interpreting, i.e. getting to the semantics. The basic step here is decoding the information from its source, and navigating the information space looking at the contents more than on the syntactical aspects.

Structuring. Information structuring includes several aspects: data presentation, motivations for using tables, functional lists, spreadsheets, whether data oriented or event oriented. The concepts of information hiding and other data abstraction processes are also included here.

Processing. Design and Programming are the main skills that are considered here. The main problem-solving strategies can be introduced at different depth levels. The idea of procedural abstraction can be gradually introduced, focusing on generalisation and specialisation methodologies. Basic algorithms can be presented and discussed with respect to correctness, efficiency, termination, usability, etc., by emphasising the independence of the design with respect to specific programming language issues. Then, the importance of expressing the solution of a problem (the algorithm) through the choice of a suitable (high or low) level programming language will be considered.

Presenting. The same effort that is necessary when analysing information (interpreting a message from its support) has to be put into the opposite direction, when choosing the way information has to be presented in order to be well understood. The key issue, in this respect, is the notion of interface.

Communicating. The last step is about how to share information with other people. Effective communication depends both on the quality of the information that is shared, and on the choice and correct use of communication tools. Security issues can also be taken into account.

The validation of the syllabus relies on the analysis of the way it covers the main Computer Science research areas, as depicted in the ACM-IEEE Computer Curricula 2001 (the draft version currently available), focusing in particular on the following areas.

- *Data Representation and Management*: hierarchical, relational and object oriented approaches to data representation organisation and retrieval;

- *Algorithms*: problem solving – basic algorithmic strategies and complexity issues;
- *Systems*: system architectures – networks;
- *Languages*: syntax and semantics issues.

4. A CASE STUDY: GENERATING AN ICT CURRICULUM FOR THE 13-14 YEAR STAGE

Let us show an application of the method outlined in the previous section to 'generate' a curriculum valid for a central period of the school age: 13-14 years, i.e. the first two years of the Secondary School according to the new Italian system. This stage will act as a bridge between the Primary School and the final 3-year stage, to be chosen from among four areas.

Because of the variety of approaches and of the teachers' training, we need to verify the basic ICT competence that pupils get from the Primary School. At the same time, we have to improve the quality of their knowledge and introduce new concepts, abilities and tools. We can summarise the special constraints for this period as follows.

- To assess and consolidate the basic ICT competence that pupils get from Primary School;
- To cover each operation about information in a significant way;
- To ensure the ICT competence required to support documentation and communication in all subjects of the final 3-year stage;
- To cover the four main cross-ICT areas in a way that pupils can recognise ICT both as a Science and a Technology (this can help them in choosing the subsequent area and sub-area of study).

A solution satisfying all these constraints is reported in Tables 1 and 2. For each operation on information, the first table reports also an estimate percentage of all the time devoted to ICT. Decisions on how to build educational modules/units, or what to assign to the first or second year, could be postponed till a further refinement or decided by each school in the context of the autonomy the law now gives to each school.

Table 1. Contents and abilities

OPERATION	CONTENTS	ABILITIES
Searching (~ 10%)	Data accessing modes: sequential, direct, content driven.	*Accessing a database table by means of the three access modes.* *Proper use of search engines.*
Analysing (~ 15%)	Syntax and semantics concepts. The HTML case. The image file case.	*Deciding the syntax correctness of a text on the basis of a simple grammar (e.g. a subset of the HTML grammar).* *Reading an HTML page at several abstraction levels. Getting a picture from a scanner and converting it into several standard formats.*
Structuring (~ 15%)	Hypertext/hypermedia, tables – spreadsheets, trees, hierarchical classification.	*Building hypertexts or hypermedia from conceptual maps.* *Basic uses of a spreadsheet.* *Recognising the tree structure of some information.*
Processing (~ 30%)	The concepts of process, processor, algorithm, program. The "what/how-to" distinction. Storing, processing and communicating functions of a hardware or software component. Basics on Operating Systems.	*Attempting to solve problems by means of simple procedural and/or declarative programming techniques.* *Recognising the basic function of a computer component or system.*
Presenting (~ 10%)	Text formatting. Slide presentation. Binary number representation. Coding/decoding. Data reports. Charts.	*Using a word processor.* *Building a slide presentation.* *Converting binary to decimal and vice-versa.* *Using ICT presentation tools and techniques for document and communication purposes.*
Communicating (~ 20%)	The concept of information as knowledge increase. Messages, protocols, communication problems (reliability, security, …). The client-server paradigm: -the e-mail case study; -the web case study.	*Using standard communication tools (e-mail, chat, forum).* *Configuring an e-mail client.* *Configuring a web browser.* *Recognising standard communication failure messages.*

Table 2. Tools and ICT areas

OPERATION	TOOLS	ICT Areas
Searching	Tape-readers, CD/DVD readers. Simple databases. WEB.	***Data, Systems***
Analysing	'Ad hoc' tools for illustrating the syntax analysis process of a freely chosen grammar. Text editor, web browser, binary editor. Scanner + image processor.	***Languages***
Structuring	Hypertext/hypermedia developer. Spreadsheet processor. 'Ad hoc' classifier. File system of an operating system.	***Data***
Processing	Computer components. 'Ad hoc' simple CPU simulators. Developing environments for educational programming languages. 'Ad hoc' software for testing simple declarative solutions.	***Programming, Systems***
Presenting	Word processor. Slide developer. Spreadsheet processor.	***Data***
Communicating	Internet communication tools. A net game (e.g. based on chatting) for consolidating the information concept. 'Ad hoc' software for illustrating the protocol and communication failure concepts and messages.	***Data, Systems, Languages***

Of course, programming is not intended as just 'coding': it is problem solving, algorithm discovering/choosing/adapting. The language used in the laboratory should have some educational features which make it clear, attractive and friendly for this age; currently adopted languages do not belong to this category.

Some declarative tools and techniques should be considered in order to apply the 'what/how-to' distinction. An 'always terminating' language – hence not Turing-complete (Rogers 1967) – such as SQL or QBE – can be adopted if this can simplify the task.

The 'net-centric' new point of view of ICT has been considered in the Communicating operation; the client/server paradigm is introduced and investigated under two well-known cases: e-mail and http.

In the following three remaining years, time and attention will be given to some operation instead of others depending on the area and sub-area of the Secondary School.

5. A FIRST EXPERIENCE AND CONCLUSIONS

The method has recently been applied to generate a curriculum and a detailed activity plan for all years of the new Primary School (Taffurelli 2001). The initial part of the plan has also been applied and tested with encouraging results in the 'G. Gallina' Elementary School in Venice, under the supervision of Pietro Tonegato, a teacher involved in a project promoted by *IRRE del Veneto*, a regional educational research institute.

The test was done in October 2000 with pupils of the first level (i.e. 6 years old) and was mainly based on the use of traditional tools, like boxes and coloured paper shapes. Ad hoc software has also been used just as self-assessment tools and to further motivate the pupils. More information (in Italian) on this experience and the software tools used can be found on the *IRRE del Veneto* web site [http://www.irre.veneto.it/informatica].

The aim of the test was not to follow the hype of introducing computers in the schools and using them in almost any subject. Instead, it was giving strength to the idea that it possible to view ICT as a subject for study with a solid foundation even from the beginning of the Compulsory School.

A first version of this paper has already influenced a proposal for an Italian National Curriculum of Technological Education for the new Primary School. Of course, much work needs to be done to make it effective and shared by all the teachers involved.

Nobody knows weather or when this will happen. We don't know how the new Italian government will continue to effect the School System Reform and the ICT education challenge. Nonetheless, we claim the method here outlined permits to design an ICT National Curricula for all countries with reasonable and useful compromises between the Scientific and Technological views of ICT.

REFERENCES

IEEE-ACM (2000) The Joint Task Force on Computing Curricula (IEEE Computer Society Association For Computing Machinery). *Computing Curricula 2001*, (draft). [http://www.computer.org/education/cc2001/report/cc2001-draft.pdf]

Italian Parliament (2000) Legge-quadro in materia di riordino dei cicli dell'istruzione (Re-organization of Education System Act). *Gazzetta Ufficiale* n. 44, 23 February 2000, pp. 3-9. Also available at: [http://www.istruzione.it/news/2000/testo_rifcicli.htm].

Rogers, H. (1967) *Theory of Recursive Functions and Effective Computability*. McGraw-Hill, New York.

Stoll, C. (1999) *High-Tech Heretic: Why Computers Don't Belong in the Classroom and Other Reflections by a Computer Contrarian*. Bantam Doubleday Dell, New York.

Taffurelli, E. (2001) *Il Curriculum di Informatica nella Nuova Scuola di Base*. Tesi di Laurea, Università Ca' Foscari di Venezia.

UK (1999) *The ICT National Curriculum for England.* [http://www.nc.uk.net/download/cICT.pdf] 8.5.2001

BIOGRAPHY

Giuseppe Callegarin received a Laurea in Scienze dell'Informazione at the University of Pisa in 1978. He started to teach Informatics in 1980 writing several high school textbooks on this discipline. He has been involved in several national projects on ICT education as a commission member and/or as a teacher trainer. Since 1996 he extended the teaching experience both to elementary and university levels. His current research activities at IRRE del Veneto are mainly concerned with distance teacher training, educational programming languages design and ICT curriculum development.

Agostino Cortesi received a Laurea in Mathematics at the University of Padova in 1986, and a PhD in Applied Mathematics and Computer Science in 1992 at the same University. In 1992/93 he was a post-doc research associate at the Dep. of Computer Science at Brown University (USA). In 1994 he joined the Dept. of Computer Science at Ca' Foscari University, Venice (Italy) where he is now appointed as Associate Professor. Currently, he gives classes on Programming and Software Engineering. His main research interests concern programming languages theory and static analysis techniques.

77

Concept, Realisation, and Evaluation of SEMIK

Jan Hense, Heinz Mandl, Katja Kruppa and Cornelia Gräsel
Education and Educational Psychology, Ludwigs-Maximilian-Universität München, Leopoldstr. 13, 80802 München, Germany
hense@emp.paed.uni-muenchen.de

Keywords: integration of ICT, national programme, evaluation, catalyst for adaption/changes

Abstract: The programme SEMIK comprises 25 different projects in all parts of Germany. Its main goals are: implementing new media in all grades and kinds of schools in a sustainable way, applying innovative methods of teaching and learning, promoting students' media literacy, and advancing school development. To ensure the quality of the programme and to assess its outcomes, measures of formative, summative, and self-evaluation have been combined. Early results of the evaluation process are reported and general consequences for the sustainable implementation of new media and ICT in schools are discussed. It is argued that a systemic perspective and provision of new concepts for learning and teaching are mandatory for the success of similar programmes.

1. THE PROGRAMME SEMIK

New media and the closely interrelated possibilities of information and communication technologies have a growing impact on our professional and private everyday lives. One of the central tasks of today's schools therefore is to enable students to use these new techniques in an active and at the same time reflective way. The national programme 'Systematic Integration of Media, Information and Communication Technologies in Teaching and Learning' (SEMIK), which is jointly funded by the German government and the 16 federal states, aims at contributing a solution to this task.

This paper will describe the concept and realisation of the programme, illustrate the function of its scientific consultation, evaluation and self-evaluation, report first results, and discuss necessary consequences.

1.1 Goals of the programme

The central guiding principles of the programme are built around a conceptual framework (Mandl, Reinmann-Rothmeier and Gräsel 1998): A superior goal of education is the necessity for lifelong learning in a knowledge society which gives rise to additional demands for their members. It is mandatory to create conditions for this kind of learning in schools. The didactical guiding principle of problem oriented learning, which is inspired by moderate constructivist models of learning research, is appropriate for these needs (e.g. Cognition and Technology Group at Vanderbilt 1997). Additionally, it is believed that in the end a change of the learning culture in schools is needed to bring this guiding principle into action.

The main goal of SEMIK and each of its projects is to implement media in all grades and all kinds of schools in a sustainable way. The main focus is on projects using new media and information and communication techniques (ICT). New media are to be embedded in processes of learning and teaching, and are to serve the realisation of innovative concepts of teaching. The main emphasis is on problem oriented, self-directed, and cooperative learning. Reception as well as production of media is meant to foster students' media literacy, i.e. reflection and responsibility in using media. Processes of school development are a precondition for sustainable progress, for without changing or at least considering the framework of schools, changing of schools and teaching beyond the duration of projects seems unachievable.

1.2 Scientific consultation

The role of the central scientific consultation of SEMIK is to support projects in fulfilling the intended goals. Besides evaluation, which is to be described in a section of its own, this involves the following tasks:

1. Scientific consultation and support for the projects. This includes consulting projects in translating the programme's principles into action, supplying theoretical and practical input, consulting projects in commissioning additional scientific services, and advising the programme coordination in commissioning additional external services.
2. Promotion of cooperation and creation of networks. Necessary steps to enable synergy effects among the different projects include the installation of a central infrastructure for communication and cooperation,

organisation of central workshops and encouragement of cooperation between projects and with external partners.

3. Documentation and reporting. To set out the results of the programme in writing in a systematic way, guidelines for documentations and reports had to be devised.

2. REALISATION AND MAIN FOCUSES OF THE PROGRAMME

The programme SEMIK has started in September 1998 and will last for five years. It comprises 25 different projects in all of the 16 federal German states. Each of the 25 projects is concerned with one or more of five main focuses, which will be described in detail.

2.1 Development of new concepts of teaching

The new media offer a huge potential for applying new instructional methods, for the use of new media should never be a purpose of its own. Much more important than supplying technical equipment is to answer the question which problems are to be solved better with new media than with conventional means. Therefore we need concepts that reveal how the potential for innovation inherent to new media can be used to support new forms of teaching and learning. Traditional structures of teaching often restrict or even inhibit constructivist activities, self-regulation, reflection, and cooperation of learners. Therefore new media should be used to create learning environments following the principle of problem orientation, thus favouring a balance between instruction and construction (Grasel 1997).

2.2 Teacher education and further education

Teachers have a key role in changing education by the use of new media. Teachers have to know how to use new media as a tool in lessons, they have to be able to judge the impact of new media on students, they have to look out for equal opportunities in accessing new media, and they have to use new media for their own learning in- and outside of official further education. Since only some of today's teachers are able to meet these demands, this cannot be confined to teacher education, but must include further education. It seems most appropriate to enhance traditional further education by school internal training. The possibility of implementing new ideas and knowledge more directly than in traditional seminars prevents the production of 'inert knowledge' (Renkl 1996).

2.3 School development

Systematic integration of new media in schools is expected to cause far reaching structural changes. On the other hand, to attain sustainability it depends on a systematic change inside of schools. This refers to flexibility in temporal, spatial, and subject-related structures, as well as to personnel and budget planning. School itself has to become a learning organisation. One of the central measures to set off this process is to develop school programmes and profiles that are tailored to the potential and context of a specific school.

2.4 Development of technical tools

Availability and access to media have often been found to be a particular weakness for using the potentials of ICT in an optimal way. Therefore development and provision of technical tools has become another main focus of the programme. This includes technical equipment (hardware, software, networks) as a mandatory precondition, tools for editing and presentation of contents, tools for interactive cooperation and communication, and finally access to digitised media for learning and teaching. Since plenty of tools are already available, it is more important to work out and show ways of making these more accessible to learners and teachers, and how they are to be integrated into everyday school.

2.5 Curricula development

Learning and teaching are dependent on content. It is expected that significant changes will have to be made in curricula to adequately use the potential for innovation inherent to new media. The subject, defining a topical and temporal systematic and possessing its own pedagogical-didactical logic, has a central role in our schools. Two tasks for curricula development evolve. First, the strict boundaries between subjects have to be torn down to enable interdisciplinary learning. The subsequent emphasis on complex and authentic problems enforces the reduction of the contents of curricula (Cognition and Technology Group at Vanderbilt 1997). Second, we need curricular concepts that coordinate the didactical use of new media with the requirements of specific subjects.

3. EVALUATION

Evaluation is taking place on the levels of single schools, on the level of each single project, and on the level of the overall programme. The evaluation of SEMIK is aimed at two major goals.

1. Ensuring quality by formative evaluation. By taking accompanying measures of evaluation, improvements are planned to be initiated while the programme is still running. This is accomplished by giving feedback to the projects on the results of the evaluation, by offering support on problematic areas, and by identifying best practice models among the participating projects.
2. Assessing success by summative evaluation. By reviewing the outcomes of the programme in its end, its achievements are to be documented for its employers and the interested public.

3.1 Dimensions of evaluation

The evaluation of SEMIK is concerned with four central topics, which are to be described in detail in the following sections.

3.1.1 Potential for innovation inherent to the systematic use of new media and ICT

The term 'potential for innovation' includes all questions concerning the degree to which change in schools is supported by the use of media. Three areas of interest have been found to be particularly central in regard to the potential for innovation of the use of media. Each area is given with an exemplary question.

1. Learning culture; e.g. what kinds of teaching and learning methods are most effective in integrating new media and ICT?
2. School development; e.g. which technical and organisational conditions promote or inhibit the course of the project?
3. Competencies and learning success; e.g. do uses of new media enable learning outcomes that would not have been possible or as effective without it?

3.1.2 Cooperation within the programme and with external partners

One of the central goals of the programme is to encourage the creation of networks between projects. Therefore this is also a question of interest for evaluation.

- Do projects cooperate with other projects within or outside of the programme or with external partners?
- Which factors do promote or inhibit cooperation of projects?
- Have there been steps to improve possibilities of communication? Which role did ICT play?

3.1.3 Transferability of results

Even while the projects are still running, one can observe to what degree results and products are apt to be transferred to other projects. The following questions are central.

- Have there been steps to make the results of the projects available and usable for other schools, projects, or federal states?
- Are conditions for success of a project identifiable that might be of interest for others?
- Are the results usable in different frames of conditions?

3.1.4 Sustainability of effects

An important criterion of success for projects concerned with promoting innovation is the sustainability of changes that have been initiated. The following questions are of interest.

- Which media are used? Which is the role of ICT?
- Which changes in structure and which measures of school development ensure the broad use of media and ICT in school even after the project has ended?
- Which steps have been taken to use the results of the project after the termination of funding?

3.2 The process of evaluation

A broad spectrum of different instruments and measures has been developed, tested, and partly revised to evaluate the SEMIK projects.

Questionnaires for students and teachers exist in online and paper-pencil versions. The main evaluative phase of SEMIK gathers data on participants' views on topics such as usage, acceptance, motivation, and attitudes concerning new media and new concepts of teaching, changes in learning and teaching, and context conditions.

Structured interviews with participants have been taking place since shortly after the beginning of the programme. The data has been summarised and commented on, to be able to give projects appropriate feedback on their progress.

Schemes for the documentation of lessons/trainings and schemes for participant observation of lessons are used to gain insight into what is actually happening in classrooms. Data collected by using them adds to the picture gained by questionnaires and interviews.

3.3 Self-evaluation

The major goal of self-evaluation in SEMIK is to enhance the quality of the participating projects' work on a personal level. Teachers use the results of self-evaluation to reflect on their professional behaviour and improve it subsequently (Buhren, Killus and Müller 1998). The results of those four projects that take intensified measures of self-evaluation are made available for the whole programme by delivering reports of their experiences. All measures of self-evaluation are closely linked with the external evaluation.

Instruments of self-evaluation have been developed in close cooperation with participating teachers. This included clarifying teachers' specific goals, finding indicators for the achievement of these goals, devising instruments to measure these goals, testing the instruments, and discussing their outcomes. Typical instruments that have been developed this way are pedagogical diaries, guidelines for interviews with students, questionnaires, observation schemes, checklists, and schemes for documentation of lessons.

4. RESULTS

Although the SEMIK programme is still far from termination, results from the early phases of the evaluation process are already available. At the moment, their function is on one hand to be used as a means of feedback and correction for the programme, and on the other hand to reveal important consequences for the general introduction of new media in schools.

4.1 Uses of new media

New media have been used in a variety of different ways and applications in the context of the individual SEMIK-projects' goals.

1. In regular lessons, e.g. as a tool to present the results of students' assignments or as a means of seeking information.
2. As a medium of communication and cooperation to facilitate exchange in schools and between schools and other institutions.
3. As basis for phases of self-regulated learning.

4. As subject-matter, e.g. to promote media literacy or method competencies.

4.2 Innovative concepts of learning and teaching

Many of the projects have taken significant steps towards a central goal of the SEMIK programme: the realisation and testing of innovative concepts of learning and teaching in school as well as in further training of teachers. Some basic conditions have been identified that determine the success of these innovative concepts: One recurrent obstacle was insufficient technical equipment in some of the projects. So the need for a proper setting was identified as one essential precondition.

Another basic condition concerned the varying need of the programme's participants for further training in topics such as 'innovative concepts of teaching' or 'project management'. Many of the participating projects provided evidence that changing teachers' roles from facilitators of knowledge to moderators of learning processes is a goal not easily reached. Therefore further training dealing with these pedagogic-didactic topics for participating teachers has been a measure applied more often than initially intended. The exchange of best practice models in intra-school trainings proved to be a particularly effective measure.

4.3 School development

To realise the systematic implementation of media thoroughly and effectively it is necessary to clearly codify this goal in a school's programme. Those schools and projects that explicitly put down the use of media in their school programmes already show sustainable changes in structure at this moment, since support of most of the school's teachers is thus ensured.

Tendencies like these are not only to be recognised in projects belonging to the programmes' main focus 'school development' but also in other SEMIK-projects. Similar statements can be made for the main focus 'teacher education and further education'. Cooperation within schools' staffs, e g. by team teaching, by mutual support in further training, or by exchange of experiences has been identified as an integral part of processes of school development

4.4 Conclusion

The overall balance that can be struck of the SEMIK programme at the time of writing shows a positive picture. A number of developments have been initiated that implement new media in schools on a pedagogical basis. Nevertheless, it has become clear to what degree the success of this process of implementation depends on certain basic conditions, in particular technical and personal set-up, curricula, and opportunities for further education. Up to now, at least four goals have been reached within the programme:

1. All participants succeeded in enhancing their competencies necessary for the implementation of new media in processes of learning and teaching significantly. This increase in qualification is an important foundation for further efforts.
2. Participants' reluctance concerning the use of new media in education has been reduced in a number of projects. This is an essential condition for the sustainable implementation of new media.
3. Cooperation between teachers has been intensified significantly by participation in the projects.
4. Important effects of synergy have been accomplished by cooperation of projects with each other.

5. CONSEQUENCES

At the moment, two basic consequences for the sustainable implementation of new media and ICT in schools seem inevitable when taking into account the experiences made in the programme SEMIK based on the first results of evaluation.

1. The introduction of new media cannot be confined to enriching conventional methods of instruction with new technologies. It rather has to be accompanied by measures on all levels that are relevant for school life. From a systemic point of view, this must include the revision of curricula, the adjustment of teacher education, the promotion of school development, as well as changes in methods of teaching and learning.
2. The introduction of new media depends on supplying new concepts for teaching and learning. Teachers cannot be expected to develop completely new lessons and projects from scratch as an additional effort. To reduce this deficit seems to be an important challenge for future research.

REFERENCES

Buhren, C. G., Killus, D. and Müller, S. (1998) *Wege und Methoden der Selbstevaluation. Ein praktischer Leitfaden für Schulen*. IFS-Verlag, Dortmund.

Cognition and Technology Group at Vanderbilt (1997) *The Jasper Project: Lessons in curriculum, instruction, assessment, and professional development*. Erlbaum, Mahwah.

Dubs, R. (1998) *Qualitätsmanagement für Schulen*. Institut für Wirtschaftspädagogik, St. Gallen.

Gräsel, C. (1997) *Problemorientiertes Lernen. Strategieanwendung und Gestaltungsmöglichkeiten*. Hogrefe, Göttingen.

Mandl, H. and Reinmann-Rothmeier, G. (1995) *Unterrichten und Lernumgebungen gestalten*. Forschungsbericht Nr. 60, Ludwig-Maximilians-Universität, Institut für Pädagogische Psychologie und Empirische Pädagogik, München.

Mandl, H., Reinmann-Rothmeier, G. and Gräsel, C. (1998) *Gutachten zur Vorbereitung des Programms 'Systematische Einbeziehung von Medien, Informations- und Kommunikationstechnologien in Lehr- und Lernprozesse*. Bund-Länder-Kommission für Bildungsplanung und Forschungsförderung, Bonn.

Renkl, A. (1996) Träges Wissen: Wenn Erlerntes nicht genutzt wird. *Psychologische Rundschau*, 47, pp. 78-92.

Resnick, L. B. and Wiliams Hall, M. (1998) Learning organizations for sustainable education reform. *Daedalus*, 127 (4), pp. 89-118.

BIOGRAPHY

Jan Hense is school psychologist and works as scientific employee at the university of Munich, Germany. He is mainly concerned with the scientific consultation and evaluation of SEMIK, and with advising projects in planning and realising their self-evaluation. His research topics include the use of new media in teaching and learning, evaluation of ICT, and self-evaluation.

Heinz Mandl is Professor of Education and Educational Psychology at the Ludwig-Maximilian-University of Munich. His main research areas are knowledge management, acquisition and use of knowledge, net-based knowledge communication, and design of virtual learning environments. He is initiator of several research programmes of Deutsche Forschungsgemeinschaft (DGF) in Knowledge Psychology, Knowledge and Action, Teaching-Learning-Processes in Initial Business Education, and Netbased Cooperation in Groups. He carried out applied research and development projects with Siemens AG, Andersen Consulting, BMW, and Telekom.

Katja Kruppa is educationist and works as scientific employee at the university of Munich, Germany. She is concerned with the scientific consultation and evaluation of SEMIK. Her research topics include the implementation and use of new media in teaching and learning and evaluation of ICT and problem-based learning environments.

78

Information Technology Training in Developing Countries

A Case Study in Jamaica

Ken Abernethy, Paula Gabbert and Han Reichgelt
Computer Science Department, Furman University, Greenville, SC, USA 29613
Department of Mathematical Sciences, University of the West Indies, Mona, 5 Kingston, Jamaica, W.I
ken.abernethy@furman.edu

Keywords: developing countries, catalyst for change, case studies, economy, vocational education

Abstract: It is well known and well documented that there is a severe shortage of information technology professionals around the world. In an approach to address this shortage, Furman University in Greenville, South Carolina and the University of the West Indies in Kingston, Jamaica have developed a training program to help produce and sustain an information technology workforce in Jamaica. This paper describes the Caribbean Institute of Technology (CIT), a software training institute that was started in Jamaica in 1999. The institute consists of a main centre in Montego Bay and several satellite centres distributed across the island of Jamaica. These centres provide an intense ten-month training program for up to 100 Jamaicans at each site every year. The paper describes the organisation of the centres, the curriculum of the program, the co-operative efforts between Furman University and the University of the West Indies, and the future direction of CIT. Although this paper describes a case study within Jamaica, such an institute might well be duplicated in other developing countries.

1. BACKGROUND

An acute shortage of information technology (IT) workers is hampering the ability of companies to reach their potential in an information-based economy. For example, a recent survey indicates that almost 20 percent of top U.S. executives cite the lack of skilled IT personnel as *the* most serious constraint on the growth of their business. In a 1997 report (U.S. Commerce 1997), the U.S. Department of Commerce projected that more than one million new information technology workers will be needed in the U.S. by the year 2005. A 1998 survey (ITAA 1998) by the Information Technology Association of America and Virginia Polytechnic University concluded that there were at that time more than 300,000 unfilled information technology jobs in large and mid-sized corporations in the U.S. today. Similar shortages in information technology workers have also been reported internationally (OECD 2000).

Further, the demand for IT workers appears to be mushrooming. In a more recent report released June 30, 1999 (U.S. Commerce 1999) on the challenges to expanding the IT work force, it is projected that 1.4 million more computer programmers, computer scientists, and engineers will be needed in the U.S. by *2003*. In the same report, it is estimated that information technology accounted for 35 percent of U.S. economic growth in 1998.

The studies cited narrowly define the term information worker to include only programmers, systems analysts, and software engineers. When Web page designers, electronic commerce developers, database administrators, computer support specialists, and others are added to the list, the shortages are considerably higher.

There are at least three major factors contributing to the global shortage of IT workers:

- the rapid rate at which information technology changes and is integrated within business processes;
- the inability of colleges and universities to produce adequate numbers of educated IT workers; and
- the exclusion of a large segment of the global population from opportunities to fully participate in an information society.

Clearly the first factor is something over which we have little or no control. With regard to the second of these factors, all U.S. colleges and universities are producing only 25,000 computer science and information science baccalaureate graduates a year. Universities and colleges are simply not able to re-engineer themselves at the pace needed by corporations hiring new college graduates, meaning that this factor will not be an easy one to overcome. Indeed, we argue that addressing the information technology worker shortage will require fundamental changes in our approach to information technology education. The case study presented here describes one experiment of how this could be done. The focus of the approach described addresses the third of the above factors.

It seems natural that the identification and cultivation of new sources of human capital will assume an important role as we attempt to address the information worker shortage. Indeed, the combination of the importance of information technology to corporations competing in a knowledge-based economy and the severity of the shortage of information technology workers injects a crucial new parameter for economic development. In particular, those geographic regions that can produce and retain a supply of well-trained information technology workers will gain a competitive advantage over those that come up short in this important area.

Given the shortages described above, many major U.S. corporations have already looked offshore to India, the Philippines, and other locations to find scarce software development resources. Indeed, many have argued that the new information and communication technologies provide important opportunities for the developing world (e.g. Talero and Gaudette 1996). We agree that the magnitude of the global shortage of IT workers presents opportunities for other developing countries to establish IT industries, *provided* they can train an adequate number of high-quality IT workers. The case study we present focuses on a training program to produce such workers in Jamaica, but we believe the concept we have implemented will find usefulness in a number of additional locations.

2. A SOFTWARE TRAINING CENTER IN JAMAICA

Jamaica boasts a literate and conscientious workforce and the country has demonstrated its ability to adapt readily to modern industrial technologies. The Jamaica Digiport International (JDI), a joint venture between AT&T, Cable and Wireless, and Telecommunications of Jamaica, established Jamaica as the most sophisticated telecommunications market in the Caribbean, boasting a 100% digital network. With 2.5 million citizens, Jamaica is the largest English-speaking country in the Caribbean. When an excellent telecommunications infrastructure and a literate and large English-speaking population are combined with its proximity to the U.S. and a shared time zone with the U.S. East Coast, Jamaica offers a promising location for the development of an offshore software industry to serve U.S. markets.

However, there is one crucial factor missing. Jamaica does not have an adequate supply of trained software developers, nor a system for producing such a supply. A robust software industry requires a reasonably large number of well-trained IT workers (Reichgelt 2000). The traditional route to producing such a workforce is through tertiary education. We have already remarked on the difficulty of producing the required numbers of these workers through the traditional tertiary educational system in the U.S. This approach will be markedly more difficult in developing countries where resources for tertiary education are more limited and access to tertiary education is far less widespread.

In Jamaica, for example, the graduation rate for tertiary education is 5% of the eligible population. This can be compared with 43% in the U.S. and 35% in Canada and the United Kingdom (World Bank 2000). Even if developing countries could mount efforts to increase the overall tertiary graduation rates, increasing the number of students graduating with credentials in software development is yet another challenge.

In this paper we describe a non-traditional program to complement the traditional tertiary educational system. This program is the outcome of a unique international university partnership between Furman University (Greenville, SC, USA) and the University of the West Indies (Kingston, Jamaica) to help establish and nurture an IT training center, called the Caribbean Institute of Technology (CIT), in Jamaica (Abernethy and Reichgelt 2000a). The primary rationale for such a center is to create a critical mass of trained software developers and put in place a system for producing larger numbers of such workers to fuel the growth of a software industry in Jamaica.

As mentioned earlier, a commonly held view has been that at least a bachelor's degree in computing is a necessary prerequisite for a career in software development. The concept of CIT is based on a different assumption. CIT enrolls talented secondary graduates into an intensive full-time (40+ hours per week) software development training program. The training offered is focused entirely on software development concepts, methods, and skills. There is no pretense to offer a broad or liberal educational experience (Abernethy and Reichgelt 2000b). Admittedly, this approach has drawbacks, but it may be the only way developing countries can attain the numbers of trained IT workers to enable a chance of success in the evolving global IT market.

2.1 The CIT curriculum

The planning and development of the CIT curriculum was coordinated by Furman University and the University of the West Indies. The two universities also took the lead in the interviewing and testing process for selecting students for CIT acceptance. Finally, the universities also helped in recruiting instructors for CIT and developed and delivered training sessions for these new instructors.

As noted in the previous section, the program of instruction at CIT is non-traditional. Of course, this calls for a new curricular approach. The curriculum designed and implemented by Furman University and the University of the West Indies focuses on client/server computing. It consists of a 15-week Core Curriculum, followed by two 8-week modules chosen from several different focus areas. The Core Curriculum emphasizes pseudocode and algorithm design, object-oriented principles, programming in C and C++, database concepts and SQL, and Web authoring with HTML and DHTML. Focus areas are chosen from (currently) one of four areas: Advanced C++ Programming, Visual Basic Programming, Database Design and Advanced SQL, and Java Programming. The entire CIT curriculum will be online by the spring of 2001 to facilitate its use in additional training centers in Jamaica (see the section *Future Development of CIT* below).

The curriculum is delivered with an emphasis on hands-on laboratory experiences. A typical 8-hour instructional day would be broken into 3 hours of lectures and 5 hours of laboratory work and programming projects. In addition to the formal instructional component, students are expected to complete a significant 'real-world' project near the end of the rigorous ten-month program. After graduation, the students are prepared for entry-level programming positions.

2.2 Increasing university co-operation

Starting in January 2001, co-operation between University of the West Indies and Furman University expanded when a group of 10 Furman students and 2 Furman faculty spent 6 1/2 weeks in Jamaica, as part of a study abroad program focusing on the impact of technology on globalisation in developing countries. One interesting aspect of the globalisation of business is the increasing integration of developing nations into the global business arena either through competition or co-operation. Information technology is a tremendous driver and facilitator of this globalisation. In keeping with the current emphasis on experiential learning at Furman University, one way to enhance student's understanding of globalisation is to enable them to visit business and technology centres in a foreign location. Not only are they able to experience a different culture but they can also observe first-hand the influence of culture and national development on information technology and business, both locally and globally.

Students participating in the study abroad program were enrolled in two courses through Furman University: Issues in Global Business and Issues in Information Technology and Globalisation. Two Furman faculty members taught these courses using visits to businesses and technology centres in Montego Bay to facilitate discussions within both courses. Related lectures, readings, and discussions addressed issues of business development and investment in developing countries and how selected technologies have enabled the globalisation of the economy. The material utilised provided general coverage of concepts with the use of specific examples within Jamaica.

In addition to the coursework, Furman students were required to spend 20 hours a week at the CIT training centre engaging in service learning activities. The students interacted with the Jamaican students, leading small group projects, mentoring the Jamaican students, and facilitating lab activities. In some cases, the Furman students led the instructional activities in areas where particular students had significant expertise. Small group activities with the Jamaican students focused on research projects about various globalisation topics and firms who operate globally. The groups then developed web sites about their findings. These types of projects provided learning opportunities for the Jamaican and Furman students as they explored issues of globalisation within information technology and software development and also gave the Jamaican students an opportunity to practice their web publishing skills.

Furman students also made presentations to CIT and the University of the West Indies students about their personal internship and job experiences within the United States. Other interactions with the students were less formal through social gatherings, classroom visits at the University of the West Indies, and on-line interaction with other Furman students still in the US. In addition, Furman students spent several days shadowing a number of the Jamaican programmers who completed the CIT program last year.

The benefits to this component of the CIT program are numerous for both the Jamaican students and the Furman students. The Jamaican students benefited from learning about international businesses and expectations of those businesses. This information will become important when they eventually deal with clients from the US and around the world. They also benefited from the technology expertise that the Furman students brought to the CIT program. The Furman students benefited from these interactions by getting a better appreciation for the lives of computer professionals in a developing country. They also had the opportunity to observe an off-shore training and programming site in operation. Opportunities in these types of training centres will become more prevalent as more developing nations try similar programs.

3. FUTURE DEVELOPMENT OF CIT

The initial phase of the CIT project established a productive working relationship among the project partners and created and implemented a 'proof-of-concept' training program in Montego Bay. On February 8, 1999, 57 students enrolled in the new CIT in Montego Bay, Jamaica. Forty-three of these students graduated 10 months later and were offered employment in a new software development centre operated by one of the project partners, Indusa Global, LLC, in Montego Bay, Jamaica. On November 10, 2000, the second CIT class of just under 100 students graduated. These students have found employment with a number of different software development companies seeking to locate offshore centres in Jamaica. On January 4, 2001, 103 students enrolled in the third class of CIT in Montego Bay.

In October 2000, the first CIT satellite centre opened in Kingston, Jamaica, with 50 students enrolled. An additional centre opened in Janaury of 2001. CIT satellite centres will use the CIT curriculum in an instructional program modeled closely after the original CIT program in Montego Bay. An additional 6 satellite centres are planned to open by the end of 2001. By June 2002, it is expected that CIT will have trained more than 400 programmers.

Because there is a shortage of available computer professionals and instructors in Jamaica, instructors for the pilot program were brought from India and the U.S. A vigorous recruiting effort is underway to staff the CIT satellite with Jamaican instructors where possible. The instructional staff and professors at Furman University and the University of the West Indies will conduct orientation and training sessions for all new instructors.

4. EVALUATING THE PROJECT

The ultimate test for CIT will be the performance of its graduates as software developers. Although CIT is still too young to permit a comprehensive assessment of its graduates, early anecdotal evidence is encouraging. We mentioned above that the 43 graduates from 1999 were hired by Indusa Global, an offshore provider based in Montego Bay. Almost a year later, all but three of the graduates are still employed at Indusa Global and their work has been judged excellent by Indusa Global's managers. Of course, more data will be required before CIT can be declared a success, and follow-on evaluation of the quality of their work will be conducted as a part of the ongoing assessment of the CIT project.

REFERENCES

Abernethy, K. and Reichgelt, H. (2000a) *Linking with Others: Experiences with the Caribbean Institute of Technology.* Panel presentation to ALO/USAID Synergy 2000 Conference, Washington, DC.

Abernethy, K. and Reichgelt, H. (2000b) *A Software Development Training Program for Jamaica*, Presentation to ALO/USAID Synergy 2000 Conference, Washington, DC.

ITAA (1998) *Help Wanted 1998: A Call for Collaborative Action for the New Millennium.* Report of study conducted by the Information Technology Association of America and Virginia Tech.

OECD (2000) *OECD Information Technology Outlook 2000.* Report form the Organisation for Economic Cooperation and Development.

Reichgelt, H. (2000) Software Engineering Services for Export and Small Developing Countries. To appear in *Information Technology for Development.*

Talero, E. and Gaudette, Ph. (1996) *Harnessing Information Technology for Development: A Proposal for a World Bank Group Strategy.* The World Bank, Washington, D.C.

U.S. Commerce (1998) *America's New Deficit: The Shortage Of Information Technology Workers.* U.S. Department of Commerce.

U.S. Commerce (1999) *The Digital Workforce: Building Infotech Skills At The Speed Of Innovation.* U.S. Department of Commerce.

World Bank (2000) *Higher Education in Developing Countries: Peril and Promise.* The World Bank, Washington, D.C.

BIOGRAPHY

Dr. Ken Abernethy is Professor and formerly Chair of Computer Science at Furman University. Dr. Abernethy is currently Director of the Center for Advanced Technology at Furman University. He has been involved in the development of the Caribbean Institute of Technology from its inception and serves on the Institute's Board of Directors. He has assumed primary responsibility with Dr. Han Reichgelt for the development of the Institute's curriculum and instructor training programs.

Dr. Paula Gabbert is Associate Professor of Computer Science at Furman University. She is the co-organiser of a study abroad program for Furman students that is focused on the role information technology plays in economic development in the developing world. She led the first such six-week study abroad trip conducted in Jamaica during the winter of 2000.

Dr. Han Reichgelt is Associate Professor in the newly formed School of Information Technology at Georgia Southern University. He was formerly Professor and Chair of Computer Science at the University of the West Indies, Mona, Jamaica. With Dr. Ken Abernethy, he has assumed a primary role in developing the curriculum and training instructors for the Caribbean Institute of Technology.

79

Teacher Training in Sub-Sahara Africa

The Imfundo Initiative

Michelle Selinger
Cisco Systems, 9 New Square Park, Bedfont Lakes, Feltham, TW14 8HA, UK
mselinge@cisco.com

Keywords: developing countries, distance learning, in-service training, integration of ICT, teacher education

Abstract: Imfundo was set up in May to consider ways in which ICT could be used in education, particularly teacher education, in developing countries with a focus on sub-Saharan Africa. It has three objectives. First, the establishment of pilot initiatives to find out what the main issues are in using ICT for teacher training in the developing world. Then development of a ResourceBank, a repository for private sector commitment of project management skills and resources in kind or at cost; and the KnowledgeBank, a web site of information and discussion about ICT use in education in developing countries.

1. BACKGROUND TO THE IMFUNDO INITIATIVE

The Imfundo initiative was set up in May 2000 in response to the UK Prime Minister's millennium initiative for education. Based in the Department of International Development (DFID) in London, Imfundo's remit was to consider ways in which ICT could be used in education in developing countries with a focus on teacher education, thus providing one way for the UK to support the International Development Targets for universal primary education by 2015. The main focus was to be in sub-Saharan Africa, which had some of the worst statistics on basic education. The initiative team hsd six months to explore and report on this objective; they had to identify and develop a small number of pilot initiatives and to conduct a feasibility study into how this initiative could be taken forward.

They also had to consider the involvement of the private sector, and from the outset included three secondees from industry on the seven-strong initiative team. Imfundo is currently developing five pilot initiatives in three countries.

Imfundo was also asked to consider sustainability with a focus on involving the private sector and developing public-private partnerships. Many companies are keen to contribute to development initiatives, yet in order to avoid a plethora of well-intentioned projects that are unconnected and divorced from Government policy, it is important to co-ordinate efforts into a sector wide strategy. Imfundo can identify and scope such initiatives in liaison with DFID and other donor agencies, and then draw in private sector support as appropriate. To this end the team have developed the ResourceBank, a repository of private sector commitment from which to draw down resources for initiatives. The nature of this support will be in the form of project management expertise, hardware, software, technical expertise and other resources. It is not the intention to ask companies for donations: expertise and resources are what is required. The involvement of local private sector is as important as involving international companies, and indeed, could be crucial to ensure that initiatives are sustainable beyond the initial funding stage.

At the start of the initiative it was important to understand and have information about the use of ICT in education and in teacher training; the current infrastructure in countries, including access and costs of telecommunications, information technology and power; and background to the reasons why children did not go to school. Gathering such information takes time. Therefore a KnowledgeBank was established and published on the Imfundo web site (www.imfundo.org) to provide a central repository to inform the team and others, thus helping anyone involved in related initiatives. An electronic forum in which participants are encouraged to comment on KnowledgeBank papers, and share insights and information has supplemented this knowledge sharing. Currently over 200 participants world-wide are taking part in this active forum.

2. TRAINING TEACHERS: THE ISSUES

HIV/AIDS and civil war have decimated the teaching population in many countries in sub-Sahara Africa. There is little capacity to train the increasing number of teachers needed. 113 million children are currently out of school, 97 per cent of them in the less developed regions of the world and 60 per cent of them girls (UNESCO 2000). An international development target is to to achieve universal primary education by 2015, and to eliminate the gender disparity in primary and secondary education by 2005.

While some regions, notably Latin America, the Caribbean and East Asia, are on course to achieving universal access to primary education, others are slipping behind. The problem is particularly marked in sub-Saharan Africa, where the number of children not in school is increasing. Of the 113 million children out of school in 1998, 42 million lived in sub-Saharan Africa; of these, 56% were girls. When children do go to school, the quality of education is poor as many teachers have received inadequate training and class sizes are large. The pupil teacher ratio varies considerably across sub-Saharan Africa, and exceeds 50 in many countries. In Central and West Africa, the median class size is 52.

International development targets mention the quality of education, but do not give it sufficient emphasis. Nearly two thirds of children who go to school in sub-Saharan Africa leave school illiterate. About half of teachers in developing countries are unqualified in terms of their own country's formal standards for teachers' education. Teaching methods are often antiquated with a focus on rote learning and little opportunity to try new teaching strategies with group work or learner-centred approaches. Many countries in provide little or no in-service professional development support for teachers.

3. A CASE STUDY

In one country ravaged by civil war, the shortfall of teachers was made up by a large number of unqualified teachers mostly comprising people who have no more than secondary education themselves, and a few not having even completed that. An emergency short training programme on teaching methodologies was mounted in programmes of up to five days, but this was inadequate to meet their full training needs. This measure was less than sufficient for teachers to gain appropriate skills, but it was all that was possible when the priority was to rehabilitate and refurbish schools so that children could return to school with sufficient teachers to teach them.

Therefore there was a pressing need to develop both content knowledge and professional capability. In addition the number of secondary schools is rapidly increasing. Class size is usually around 40-50 but in some schools it can be nearer 70. 16% of children go to secondary school and this number is intended to rise to 20%. Teachers cannot be taken out of school in large numbers for the extensive training programme that is required. In reality this should be, a three year, full-time training programme and equivalent to a pre-service programme in both subject knowledge and pedagogy. Removing teachers from the classroom for this length of time is unworkable. Teacher training institutions would have neither the physical capacity nor the human resources to train such large numbers. So distance education is the only feasible alternative, with teachers training while still teaching. The benefits would be to keep them in classrooms while undergoing training so school attendance targets could be maintained, allowing teachers to put new ideas into practice so integrating theory and practice. A lesser issue, was the relative costs of distance training.

Research on distance education in developed countries is extensive, but there is relatively little covering the developing world. Hilary Perraton comments on distance education in developing countries, including the relative costs of distance education and classroom based teaching.

> "Distance education has particular strengths where it is used to support extension agents so that a multiplier effect comes into play. Education out of school, whether for adults or through alternative secondary schools, has lower costs than conventional education and would probably not exist unless it did so. In many cases its modest costs are matched by modest success; poor completion and pass rates mean that its costs per successful student tend to compare much less favourably with conventional alternatives. Teacher education has a potential multiplier effect and high motivation levels, for teachers expecting promotion, and has brought high success rates with competitive costs per graduate." (Perraton 2000, p1)

Butcher (2000) also considers the financial issues, but additionally cites the top down approach of initiatives being a cause of failure. Ensuring buy-in from those who will have to implement and use the systems is paramount. Despite a number of issues in developing distance learning programmes, there is evidence that a number of models are being used across the developing world, many with older technologies like radio and video as well as some trialling new technologies (Capper 2000, Fontaine 2000).

In this country there were problems with part-time learning. Historically teachers were paid for attending training courses, but the country is now unable to afford any extra payments; teachers will receive training free of charge, but with no funds to help them to attend. With so many teachers requiring this training, it is hoped that for several years there will be a steady stream of teachers willing to support themselves, with the only reward being higher salaries on completion. A number of initiatives including visits to head teachers and local education officers, and identification of training centres in regional centres that had telephone access and an adequate power supply. There are plans to staff these centres with a well-qualified teacher as a tutor supported by an administrative assistant.

Head teachers have been made aware of the need to give teachers undergoing the training extra time to study by, for example, allocating them smaller workloads, exempting them from evening and weekend duties, and granting loans to purchase transport (bicycles or motorcycles) to support their travel to training centres. Part-time study for further qualification is becoming an accepted aspect of further education in this country so there is a firm belief that there will be heavy demand for these courses.

Another problem the country faces is the capacity to develop distance learning resources. The initial costs of setting up such programmes are high compared to traditional courses, and there is lack of expertise in developing distance learning materials. This problem has been solved through donor funding to bring in distance learning expertise and a number of subject experts from other countries for a fixed time period to develop the materials and to train existing staff at the teacher training institution.

As in many developing countries the costs of books and other resources is high, and maintaining up to date libraries is expensive. Postal deliveries are unreliable or take a long time, so the exchange of assignments and materials would be slow and would also make student progress slow. Tutors based in regional centres would have to be expert in all secondary subject areas if they were required to support all students, and any extra support from the central teacher training institution would be restricted to phone calls and post. Telephone lines are limited with very few lines available outside thc country's capital.

3.1 ICT as a solution

A range of new and old technologies could help. Internet connectivity in cach of the regional centres would provide teachers in training and the regional tutors with fast access to the central teacher training institution. Here subject specialists could respond in electronic discussion forums to questions posted by tutors or trainees; extra materials could bc supplied digitally for printing at the local centre; and some interactive internet based resources could also be accessed by teachers after school and weekends, at times to suit them. Video materials could be sent via a satellite link or on videocassette; and up to date resources could also be accessed through the Internet.

The successful use of the Internet is teacher training is reported in a number of international initiatives (see Perraton 2000). In Africa it has been tried successfully in townships in South Africa through the ShoMa initiative in South Africa ((ShoMa undated). Together with the National and Provincial Education Departments ShoMa has developed a professional development curriculum for teachers. Multimedia materials are delivered digitally via satellite. ShoMa involves a three stage process in a three hour weekly course. In the first part of the process, teachers are actively engaged in learning about various aspects of the new outcomes based education programme that has been recently introduced into South African schools. Short video excerpts are downloaded via satellite and viewed followed by a discussion that is prompted and guided through the questions posed on screen. The second stage involves the Internet in which teachers individually explore the concepts discussed in the video. Through this ShoMa staff believe teachers are able to determine their own needs in terms of theory and interest. Relevant aspects of the video have been digitised to support the written component and to integrate the learning experience.

Teachers interact with the Internet based materials and the data they enter is kept on a database that can be printed out later and added to the teacher's portfolio as evidence of their developing understanding and for assessment purposes. The final stage is considered to be the most important aspect of the learning experience. In this stage teachers work collaboratively in groups of approximately six to develop their lesson plans for the following week. By making use of facilitators from the Education Department or a 'leader' educator, ShoMa helps teachers to share experiences and develop lesson ideas through the application of their new knowledge.

3.2 Details of the training

It is planned to integrate a modified version of the ShoMa materials into the programme, and Imfundo have facilitated personnel from ShoMa to work with the teacher training institution. The training will start at diploma level and develop to degree level as resources become available and teachers become accustomed to improving their skills through distance learning. Modules will develop knowledge in two subjects and in pedagogical skills, and will be based on the new four year full- time initial teacher training course that is currently in its third year of operation at the teacher training institution.

The original plan was to train 1000 students per year over 5 years but after further discussions it has been decided to roll out the programme more slowly opening two centres in 2001, training between 50 and 100 teachers in each location. The training centres will come on stream in a phased progression and will be open six days a week, and there will be organised weekend and evening sessions as well as opportunities for teachers to drop in and use the facilities. Residential summer schools will be run of approximately two to three weeks duration in four identified secondary school locations in each region.

3.3 Sustainability

Technology is expensive but in developed countries the cost of maintaining and updating ICT is also of major concern. Parts as well as PCs carry high tariff charges. In developing countries issues of sustainability have to be addressed, not only in terms of the maintenance and renewal of equipment, but also in the provision of spare parts, qualified engineers and trained personnel to troubleshoot minor issues and train users. Many development initiatives have failed once funding has ceased because long term sustainability was not taken into account. The ResourceBank is one way in which sustainability can be addressed. The international private sector are being asked to give support in terms of reduced costs for or donations of equipment, software etc, or to provide personnel to train local people or to initiative manage the establishment of the centres. Local private companies have been invited to make use of the spare capacity of teacher training centres to run basic ICT skills and adult literacy courses, and small businesses are to be encouraged to make use of the facilities for their own work at a small charge. In other words these teacher training centres will aim to double up as multi-purpose community centres.

4. IS ICT APPROPRIATE?

There is not a straight choice between using new and old technologies in distance education. For example, where teachers are supported through resource centres, it would be possible to use radio and text for much the content, with other resource centres to provide opportunities for interaction and support. Radio is pervasive in developing countries. In their research Imfundo did not uncover any teacher education programme that combined new and old technology.

Distance education, whether or not technology enhanced, is cost effective only if it is on a reasonably large scale. Thus while it may be cost effective in Nigeria or South Africa, it may not be in smaller countries such as Gambia. Therefore Imfundo intends to undertake further work on the opportunities for regional initiatives to share technology, curriculum and infrastructure across countries. For example, it is cheaper to adapt curriculum material made in a neighbouring country than it is to start from scratch; the adaptation of the ShoMa materials is one model being trialled.

5. THE FUTURE OF IMFUNDO

Imfundo has reached the end of its first phase. The second phase started January 2001, is a five year initiative to work in at least five more countries in sub-Sahara Africa with a new team leader and two advisers in place. They will be supported by DFID reporting to the Africa Economic and Policy Development Unit, and working closely with country desks and the education department. The new team will continue to maintain the focus on teacher training and professional development, and on educational management issues. Imfundo are currently in negotiation with other donors who are also focused on ICT in education, and thus continuing to ensure that development initiatives are coordinated and sustainable.

REFERENCES

Butcher, N. (2000) Distance education in developing countries. *The Imfundo KnowledgeBank* [http://www.imfundo.org/butcherthree/contents.htm] 5.8.2001

Capper, J. (2000) Teacher training and technology: an overview of case studies and lessons learned. *TechKnowLogia*, 2 (6), pp. 17-19 [www.techknowlogia.org].

Fontaine, M. (2000) Teacher training with technology: Experience in five country programs. *TechKnowLogia,* 2 (6), pp. 69-71 [www.techknowlogia.org].

Perraton, H. (2000) Teaching the teachers. The Imfundo KnowledgeBank. [http://www.imfundo.org/Hilaryfive/contents.htm] 5.8.2001.

ShoMa (undated) *ShoMa Education Foundation: professional development initiative.* [http://www.shoma.org.za] 5.8.2001.

UNESCO (2000) *Education for all 2000 Assessment: Statistical document.* [http://www2.unesco.org/wef/en-docs/findings/efastatdoc.pdf] 5.8.2001.

BIOGRAPHY

Michelle Selinger is an Education Specialist at Cisco Systems and Senior Visiting Research Fellow at the Open University's Institute of Educational Technology. Her current research interests are in elearning and changing pedagogies in ICT environments.

80

Workflow Embedded Training in the IT Sector[1]

Matthias Rohs
Fraunhofer Insitute for Software and Systems Engineering (ISST), Mollstrasse 1, D-10178 Berlin, Germiny
matthias.rohs@isst.fhg.de

Keywords: government, didactics, further education, catalyst for changes, in-service training

Abstract On the one hand, the rapid innovation cycles lead to a considerable lack of IT-specialists. On the other hand, there are more than 32,000 unemployed IT-specialists and 60,000 unemployed engineers in Germany. These trends can also be ascribed to a quasi non-existent concept of IT-Training. To solve these problems and close the gap caused by the lack of IT-specialist an association of representatives of employers and unions ('Bündnis für Arbeit') have initiated a re-structuring of advenced vocational training for the IT-sector. The Fraunhofer ISST has been commissioned to develop a concept for putting this system into practice. Under the title 'Further Professional Education based on Working Processes' (APO 2001), a concept which is work-integrated and based on business processes is to be developed in collaboration with industrial partners and educational institutes.

1. INTRODUCTION

Rapid technological development in the IT-sector leads to a considerable shortage of qualified IT-specialists. Currently, there is a lack of 70,000 IT-experts in Germany. According to experts, there will be a demand of 1.1 million experts in the field of IT-related technology till the year 2010. With

[1] This research was supported by the German ministry of research and technology (bmb+f) as part of the research project 'APO' (2001).

existing 800,000 specialists in mind, 50,000 qualified IT-experts p. a. will be needed (Petersen and Wehmeyer 2000).

But there are only 5,000 to 8,000 graduates from universities and technical colleges p. a. and there will be 60,000 graduates from IT-related vocational training courses by the year 2003. So Germany has – according to a survey (Bitkom 2001) – the largest need of IT experts as compared to all other Western European countries.

This lack cannot be solved in the long run, even with the 20,000 'Green Card specialists' from abroad (currently 5,000).

One reason for that dilemma is that there is no real system for IT-qualification apart from university (Figure 1). Universities are not able to cope with the need for IT-specialists and there are no other high-quality courses in addition to IT-vocational training.

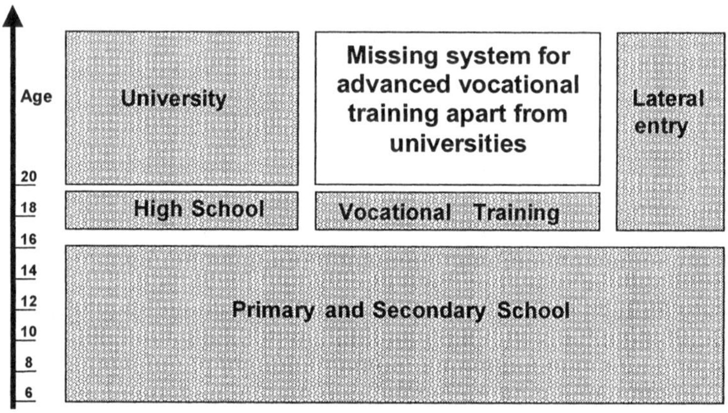

Figure 1. German system of vocational and further vocational education in the sector of IT

In order to solve this problem in the medium-term, the German Federal Ministry for Education and Research (BMB+F) has initiated the set-up of a Regulation Procedure for structuring the further education system. This procedure is carried out by the German Federal Institute for Vocational Training (BiBB). In collaboration with IT-experts, quality standards will be conceived which are aligned to the requirements of the industry. Graduates from IT-related training courses, university dropouts and unemployed IT-specialist are the target groups. They will be offered new carrier prospects by means of further education. (Grunwald and Rohs 2000).

2. THE NEW GERMAN STRUCTURE OF FURTHER VOCATIONAL TRAINING IN THE IT SECTOR

As a first result of the Regulation a structure was developed. In this structure about 30 profiles on three levels are defined: specialists, e.g. network administrators, operative professionals and strategic professional profiles (Figure 2). While doing so, several qualification profiles are each summed up and merged with the respective higher level. Degrees on the level of the operative professionals are thought to be comparable with a Bachelor degree, strategic professionals have a qualification similar to a Master degree.

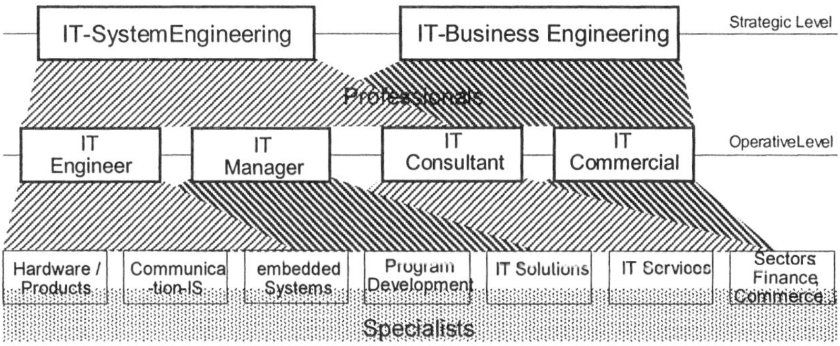

Figure 2. New Structure for Advanced Vocational Training in the Sector of IT in Germany

The Fraunhofer Institute for Software and System Engineering (ISST) has been commissioned by the German Federal Ministry for Education and Research (BMB+F) to develop a concept for the realisation of this structure. This project is called APO (2001): Arbeitsprozessorientierte Weiterbildung (Workflow Embedded Training); it should develop a didactic base as a guideline for workflow embedded training courses in the IT sector.

3. DIDACTIC CONCEPT

The basis of the didactic concept are the requirements of the IT-branch and the recommendations of the association of representatives of employer and unions. The goal is to develop a workplace-oriented concept for IT-training.

3.1 Requirements

The basic requirements of a didactic model for further education also result from the requirements of the IT-sector. So the IT-specialists must cope with changed objectives and different working environments. They work in interdisciplinary teams and increasingly customer-oriented. Therefore it is necessary for them to:

- Improve their professional skills
- Strengthen their social capabilities
- Develop auto-didactic capabilities.

Moreover, IT-specialists are urgently needed experts who can only rarely be taken out of the production process. However, the need for advanced vocational training is very high to special skills for information technology. Therefore advanced vocational training must take place in the working process through learning-by-doing. Thus acquired knowledge is mostly product- and project-oriented. These learning strategies are common because they comply with the demands of the IT branch. We intend to integrate them in a didactic concept. Furthermore, the basic concept has to pay attention to developing self-learning strategies and to impart the fundamentals of information technology. With these capabilities an IT specialist will be able to keep up with the technical progress. As a result the educational concept has to be

- Embedded in the companies' workflow
- Oriented on the practice
- Adapted to the individual skills
- Oriented on competencies.

3.2 Workflow orientation

The goal of the APO (2001) Project is to embed vocational training within the workflow and to consider individual learning efforts as a part of learning organisation (Dehnbostel 2000, Albrecht 1999). IT-technicians will be trained *on-the-job* and *on-demand* in a *project-like manner.*

Within the working process learning is always stimulated when employees are confronted with new or difficult tasks. But those informal learning processes occur unsystematically and without any outward signs (Livingstone 1999, Kirchhöfer 2000). In contrary to this, curricular vocational training-measures are more structured and transparent but they do not correspond with the tasks and demands of the processes.

3.3 Reference projects

A workflow-embedded approach relies on objectives that are based on practical experience. Therefore fundamentals of our concept are real-work assignments. But these practice projects are very different so that there is no quality standard for the qualification as a whole.

That's why the key element of our concept is so-called *reference projects*. They represent typical and ideal work processes of a professional profile. In cooperation with well-known IT-enterprises we identify and analyse suitable projects. For example: the basis of the reference project for a software developer was the development of an e-commerce system carried out by *Software AG* (Tübingen).

Projects are suitable when they are up-to-date, documented, complete, typical and instructive. It is also possible to combine parts of different projects, e.g. the processes 'change management' and 'performance management' for a network administrator. The reference project is not a case study but a generic scheme of a professional and thus a profound basis for workflow embedded training.

The reference project has at least three functions:

- It enables the assignment of knowledge to a certain professional field
- It serves as a model to apply tools and methods and carries out own projects and
- It serves as a quality standard for vocational training by means of a certain profile.

The reference project has the task to close the gap in the workflow between the work assignment and the requirements of advanced vocational training. This allows the adaptation of the individual learning assignments but will also lead all participants to a homogeneous competence level (Figure 3).

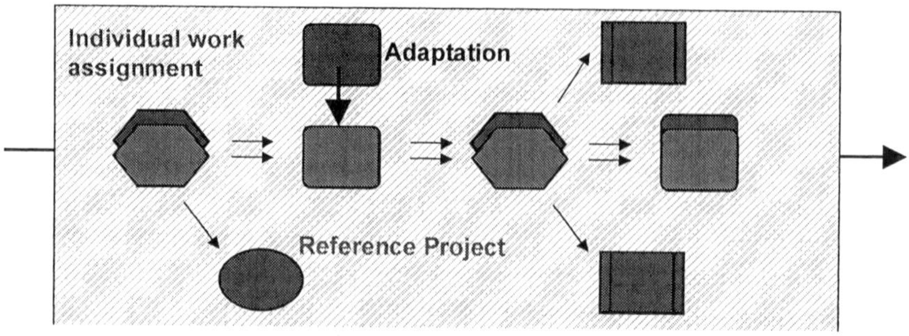

Figure 3. Adaptation of individual work assignments

4. IMPLEMENTATION

The strong focus on the practice-oriented tasks requires a basic concept of instruction and assistance. Major problems are the different general conditions for its realisation between companies, e.g. the learning culture and the size of an enterprise, the number of participants, the possibilities to support the learner, suitable work assignments and many more. Thus an important attribute of the concept is flexibility to suit for different general conditions.

4.1 Learning arrangement

The arrangement of the implementation is oriented on the decentralised human resources development approach (Staudt and Kriegesmann 1999). Superiors are the key figures. They are interested in well-qualified staff, know individual abilities and are able to provide the conditions for learning on the workplace. But in most cases the superiors aren't able to manage further education by themselves. Participants need help for special questions and support for the organisation of the learning process. That's why specialists, mentors and trainers support the learner together.

In this way the resources of an enterprise can better be used for its own human resource development. Therefore the APO-concept is not only a contribution to a learning organisation but also support and an incentive.

But these model can not be achieved in all cases because there is either no qualified staff to give the learner sufficient feedback or the organisation of the learning process is inappropriate. If so, external specialists can attend to these part(s). For small enterprises it could be useful to build (specific) networks to support one another. In this way one trainer or one specialist can instruct participants of different enterprises. Special internet tools can support communication and collaboration.

4.2 Informal and self-oriented learning

The aim is to coach and accompany the participants in their learning processes rather than to teach them detailed information. Most of them are highly experienced. What they lack is a certification of their qualification. The practice and the reflection of this experience are the basis for the instruction of theoretical complexes. That's why a revision of experience and reflection is the basis for the learning process.

The teaching of fundamental knowledge for certain qualifications is conducted by short courses and specifically supported by teaching adequate knowledge.

The adaptation of these general qualifications to the specific requirements of the respective company are done by a mentor. This procedure supports both the participant's active competence and the transfer of the skills into the daily working routine.

4.3 Media resources

Even though instruction remains obligatory in APO-oriented vocational training, conventional instructional resources like books, manuals and static web sites become more and more obsolete.

- Content is getting more unique and very specific; instructional resources to guide and support the learning process should also be conceived that way.
- Learning environments are proprietary, much information needed to transform knowledge from theory into practice is company-specific and only destined for internal use. Instructional resources that may accelerate this knowledge transfer must include domain-specific and company-specific knowledge.
- Real-world problems must be solved within reasonable time; e.g. a network administrator must be able to reconfigure a router in a short time. Instructional resources that enable an IT technician to learn about router configuration on-the-job must be made available within hours or even minutes.

These requirements cause a demand for instructional resources that are highly adaptive, highly integrative and can be produced on-demand. Recent approaches which support the on-demand selection and sequencing of modular learning resources (e.g. Caumanns 2000) seem to be suited well to provide the flexibility needed for this new kind of instructional material.

5. SUSTAINABILITY

Because of the rapid development in the IT-sector, sustainability is a central issue for instructional quality. Therefore it is not only instruction but also the suggestion that self-learning competencies to update knowledge effectively on the job is the primary aim of the concept.

It is necessary to find a way to merge informal learning processes and instructive elements.

5.1 Fading

The ultimate goal is to support the participants in the process of developing auto-didactic skills and not to suppose that they are a given fact. To achieve this, media, methods and the organisational structure of the qualification process are increasingly adapted to authentic working conditions. That means that the trainer who teaches basic knowledge at the beginning gradually supervises and assists the learning process on demand. Participants should successively organise their own comprehension processes, practice their own skills and use tools, e.g. search engines instead of didactically prepared teaching material (Figure 4). This method is part of a basic approach thought to develop skills and is oriented to the basic approach of 'Cognitive Apprenticeship' (Brown, Collins and Duguid 1998).

Figure 4. Fading

6. PERSPECTIVE

Our didactical concept is adapted to certain professional profiles within the IT-branch. Along with special recommendations for its realisation this draft is documented in a manual. This manual is thought to be the basis for the implementation of future training courses. The recommendations in the manuals allows companies to train IT-specialists independent from producers and saving quality standards.

A first course based on APO (2001) will be carried out by German Telekom AG in the Summer 2001. About 15 employees will qualify to network administrators by training them individually and on the job.

REFERENCES

APO (2001) [http://www.apo-it.de].

Albrecht, G. (1999) *Personenqualifizierung im Kontext neuer Lernwelten*. Bertelsmann-Verlag, Bielefeld.

Bitkom (2001) *Kein Ende des Mangels an IT- und E-Business-Spezialisten absehbar*. Press Release. [http://www.bitkom.net/presse/presseinformationen/060301.html] 3.05.2001.

Brown, J. S., Collins A. and Duguid P. (1998) Situated Cognition and the Culture of Learning. *Educational Researcher*, Issue 1, pp. 32-43.

Bundesanstalt für Arbeit und Sozialordnung – BAM (2001) *Informationen zum Fachkräftebedarf in Deutschland*. [http://www.bma.de/de/aktuell/thema/it1.htm] 3.05.2001.

Caumanns, J. (2000) *Bottom-Up Generation of Hypermedia Documents. Multimedia Tools and Applications*. Vol. 12, November, Issue 2/3, pp. 109-128, Kluwer Academic Publishers.

Dehnbostel, P. (2000) Erfahrungslernen in der beruflichen Bildung: Ansatzpunkte für eine neue Lernkultur? In *Arbeits- und erfahrungsorientierte Lernkonzepte*, P. Dehnbostel and H. Novak (eds.), Bertelsmann, Bielefeld.

Garrik, J. (1998) *Informal Learning in the Workplace: Unmasking Human Ressource Development*.

Grunwald, S. and Rohs M. (2000) Arbeitsprozessorientierung in der IT-Weiterbildung. *Berufsbildung in Wissenschaft und Praxis*, Heft 6, pp. 22-24.

Kirchhöfer, D. (2000) *Informelles Lernen in alltäglichen Lebensführungen*. QUEM-report, Issue 66.

Livingstone, D. W. (1999) Informelles Lernen in der Wissensgesellschaft: Erste kanadische Erhebung über informelles Lernverhalten. In *Quem-report: Kompetenz für Europa: Wandel durch Lernen – Lernen durch Wandel*, Heft 60, pp. 65-91.

Marsick, V. J. and Watkins, K. E. (1990) *Informal and incidental learning in the workplace*. Routledge, London.

Petersen, A. W. and Wehmeyer, C. (2000) Die neuen IT-Berufe auf dem Prüfstand: Erste Ergebnisse der bundesweiten IT-Studie. *Berufsbildung in Wissenschaft und Praxis*, 29 (6), pp. 7-12.

Staudt, E. and Kriegesmann, B. (1999) Weiterbildung: Ein Mythos zerbricht. In *Arbeitsgemeinschaft Qualifikations-Entwicklungs-Management. Kompetenzentwicklung '99*, QUEM (eds.), Waxmann Verlag, pp. 17-60.

BIOGRAPHY

Matthias Rohs studied pedagogy, sociology and psychology with an emphasis on media psychology and media didactics at Freie Universität Berlin. Parallel to this he has worked as an assistant at the Department of Mathematics and Computer Science in the field of multimedia. His diploma thesis was in the field of learning software for vocational training. Since 2000 he has been a member of the scientific staff at the Fraunhofer Institute for Software and Systems Engineering and has been responsible for designing didactic concepts.

81

Students' IT Confidence and Skills

The Affects of an Information Systems Approach, The Oman Experience

Syed J. Naqvi
Department of Information Systems, College of Commerce and Economics, Sultan Qaboos University, Al-Khoud, Sultanate of Oman
cce3249@squ.edu.om

Keywords: basic IT skills, competencies, higher education, students, databases

Abstract: This paper addresses the affects of Information Systems Approach on students' IT confidence and their IT skills in comparison to a more Traditional Approach. The data was collected using questionnaires on IT skills, confidence and attitudes and analysed using Sign test and comparing the simple means of responses using pretest, posttest control group. design. The study found that the group following the Information Systems Approach were generally more confident and acquired more IT skills than the groups followed the Traditional Approach. The study suggest that the business students should be introduced IT following the Information Systems Approach in preference to the Traditional Approach.

1. INTRODUCTION

This study is an attempt to improve the quality of education and better prepare the students of the College of Commerce and Economics in Oman, where this research was conducted, to be more IT literate specially in business applications. It is in line with the objective of the college to impart IT skills to students to match the changing needs of the local business organisations, which offer jobs to graduates of the college.

There are several possible approaches for delivering IT skills including Word-processing First Approach, which is also known as the Traditional Approach (TA), the Spreadsheet First Approach (SFA) and the Database

First Approach, known as Information Systems Approach (ISA). The most common one is the Traditional Approach. This approach after introducing some computer concepts, begins with word-processing and students enhance their IT skills most in this, many researchers believe, and less in other follow-up IT applications such as spreadsheets, graphics and databases (Naqvi 2001). By contrast, the ISA as proposed by Freeman & Rowley, after introducing the computer concepts and IT applications used in business, begins with databases followed by spreadsheets, graphics and word-processing (Freeman et al. 1995).

This approach offers a more realistic perspective on the contribution, which IT can make to the effective operation of business activities. This approach encourages students to consider information first, and then to progress to tools for its analysis and presentation. This is more in keeping with developing an appreciation of the way in which information systems are used in business. The SFA starts with spreadsheets and graphics, followed often by word-processing and then students will usually, but not always are introduced to databases and database software (Freeman et al. 1995). This approach is not commonly practiced, as it alone is restricted to handling quantitative data skills.

There is hardly any literature on the empirical study of these approaches. This has therefore led to this present study in the College of Commerce and Economics in Oman. The purpose of this research study, as highlighted earlier, is to investigate the students' IT confidence and the acquisition of their IT skills by two comparable groups, one following the Information Systems Approach and known as the ISA group and the other group following the Traditional Approach, called the TA group. The focus is on whether the ISA is more effective on issues, such as IT confidence and IT skills, in comparison to the TA.

This research was based on a longitudinal study to increase the validity and reliability of the results, comprising a Phase I study followed by Phase II and Phase III in the sub sequent semesters. In a study of this nature pretest data needed to be collected to assess the initial IT abilities of students and posttest data for comparison, to see the effectiveness of the approaches followed. For this purpose a pretest-posttest control group research design was selected and mainly questionnaires were used as data collection tools to assess the merits of the proposed ISA on IT confidence and IT skills issues in comparison to the TA.

2. METHODOLOGY

Questionnaire: A questionnaire was developed and used to collect initial and final data on students IT confidence and their skills. The questions were grouped on these issues. The questions on IT skills were general and related to word-processing, spreadsheets/graphics and databases. The responses to each item was based on a Likert scale ranging from 1 to 5, where 1 = Unable, 2 = Slightly Able, 3 = Uncertain, 4 = Able and 5 = Strongly Able.

Sample: Data were collected from nearly 150 students in all the six groups with similar academic standards. All these groups were drawn from the College of Commerce and Economics, where this research was conducted, where two groups were randomly selected for each phase of study.

Procedures: An identical questionnaire was used to collect data from the groups. The questionnaires were administered during normal classroom lesson time by the researcher. For Phase I, one group was introduced IT through the ISA, while the other group used the TA. The data collection process was repeated in similar fashion for Phase II and III taking two groups at a time in each phase.

The initial data was collected in two stages prior to the course, called as 'Prior' and in retrospect, conducted at the end of the course and called 'Retro'. The Retro was planned to validate the initial IT abilities, assuming that the Prior and Retro will stay the same, if not, then either the students overestimated or underestimated their IT abilities at the Prior stage. The final IT abilities were also assessed through the questionnaire at the end of the course.

The initial IT abilities of both the groups were compared to assess the similarity between them. The comparisons of the groups were on two major issues, namely, IT confidence and IT skills. If the two groups were similar in their initial abilities then the final abilities of the two groups were considered. Otherwise, these initial IT abilities were then compared with their final IT abilities.

Statistical tests were used to analyse the data including the 'Sign Test' to compare the positive and negative responses and using simple group means to assess the size of change in the ISA and the TA groups. The results of these statistical tests were incorporated to examine the merits of the ISA in comparison to the TA.

3. SUMMARY OF THE FINDINGS

The results indicated that the groups were not exactly similar in their initial IT confidence and IT skills either at Prior or Retro stages. To see the effectiveness of the ISA, 'Sign Test' was used to compare the number of positive and negative responses like Prior-with-After and Retro-with-After stages. These results are summarised in Table 1 and Table 2 and graphically presented the After stage results in Figure 1 and Figure 2.

3.1 IT confidence

Phase I. The results of the ISA group indicated more positive responses than the TA group when compared Prior and After responses. The size of change of the ISA was much higher than the TA corresponding to 1.72 versus 0.72. The results appeared similar, when compared the Retro and After responses, the size of change of the ISA group was 1.69 corresponding to 1.40 of the TA group. These results suggest that the ISA seems more effective in building IT confidence in comparison to the TA.

Phase II. The overall trend of the result of the Phase II appeared similar, though these changes were not so high compared with Phase I. The ISA group responded more positive corresponding to the TA and the size of change from Prior to After was corresponding to 1.06 versus 0.87. When compared Retro and After responses the size of change of the ISA was 1.63 corresponding to 1.27 of the TA. The ISA seems more effective in enhancing the students IT confidence.

Phase III. In general, the students of both groups agreed with the statements and clearly indicated a great deal of improvement in their IT confidence at the end of the course compared to before the course. The size of change for the ISA group was much higher than the TA group either in comparison with Prior-versus-After or Retro-versus-After. This change from Prior to After responses of the ISA group was 1.56 corresponding to 1.05 in the TA and Retro to After was 2.03 versus 1.25 (see Table 1). The trend of these results is similar to the Phase I and II results, rather higher.

There is consistency in the results of Phase I, II and III. It appears that the ISA is effective in enhancing more students' IT confidence than the TA as shown in Figure 1.

Table 1. IT Confidence Group Mean Responses

Groups	Prior	Retro	After	Difference = After – Prior	Difference = After – Retro
TA (Phase I)	3.21	2.53	3.93	0.72	1.40
ISA (Phase I)	2.54	2.57	4.26	1.72	1.69
TA (Phase II)	3.28	2.88	4.15	0.87	1.27
ISA (Phase II)	3.18	2.61	4.24	1.06	1.63
TA (Phase III)	2.83	2.64	3.88	1.05	1.25
ISA (Phase III)	3.07	2.60	4.63	1.56	2.03

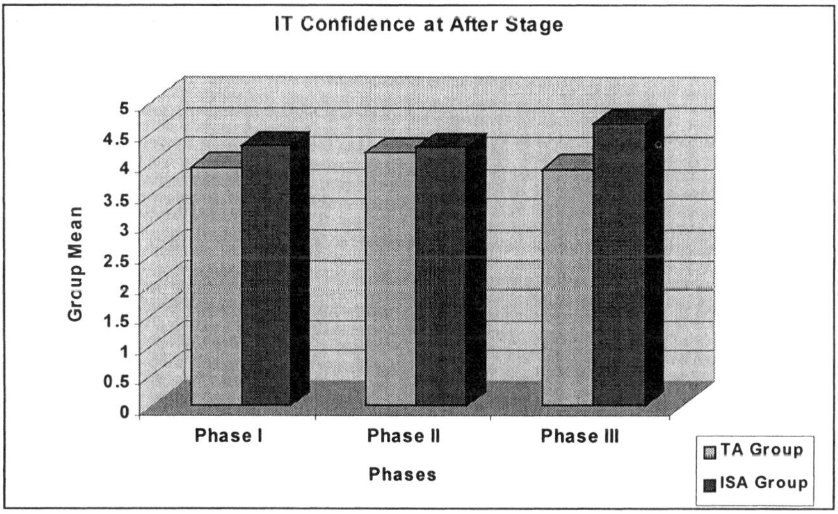

Figure 1.

3.2 IT Skills

Likewise, the ISA had made a significant effect on the acquisition of IT skills in all the modules presented including databases, spreadsheets/graphics and word-processing. The size of change in IT skills from Prior-to-After and Retro-to-After stages of both groups are presented in Table 2 and the comparison of After stage results are graphically presented in Figure 2.

Phase I. The ISA group responded far more positive than the TA group. The size of change from Prior-to-After stage of the ISA was 2.75 corresponding to 1.09 of the TA group. Similarly the change from Retro-to-After was 2.88 of the ISA versus 1.75 of the TA. This indicated that the students in both the groups improved their IT skills, but this improvement appears far more in the ISA group.

Phase II. A similar result appeared in Phase II, the students of the ISA group had given more positive responses and the size of change from Prior-to-After of the ISA group was high, compared to the TA corresponding to 2.04 versus 1.39 and from Retro-to-After were corresponding to 2.60 versus 1.92. These results lead to similar findings that the ISA appears more effective in developing IT skills than the TA.

Phase III. Likewise, the results of Phase I and II, Phase III had shown far greater improvement in students' IT skills as compared to the TA group. The size of change from Prior-to-After in the ISA group was 2.50 versus 1.72 in the TA and the Retro-to-After was 2.61 versus 1.71.

The results of Phase I, II and III are consistent and indicated that the ISA made a significant effect in bringing about positive change in developing more IT skills than the TA. This can also be seen in Figure 2.

Table 2. IT Skills Group Mean Responses

Groups	Prior	Retro	After	Change = After – Prior	Change = After – Retro
TA (Phase I)	2.70	2.07	3.79	1.09	1.72
ISA (Phase I)	1.85	1.72	4.60	2.75	2.88
TA (Phase II)	2.54	2.01	3.93	1.39	1.92
ISA (Phase II)	2.41	1.85	4.45	2.04	2.60
TA (Phase III)	1.89	1.90	3.61	1.72	1.71
ISA (Phase III)	2.09	1.98	4.59	2.50	2.61

Overall, it seems that the ISA has made a significant affect not only on students' IT confidence but also on their IT skills.

4. CONCLUSION

A number of preliminary conclusion emerged from consideration of the research question posed in the study. The findings of this study suggest that the students in the ISA group demonstrated more IT confidence and consequently more IT skills in support of business activities as compared to the TA. These findings are in line with Freeman and Rowley's view on the ISA (Freeman et al. 1995).

This finding is also supported by the relationships diagram as shown in Figure 3 between IT conceptual understanding, IT usage, IT attitudes, IT confidence and IT competence (Naqvi 2000).

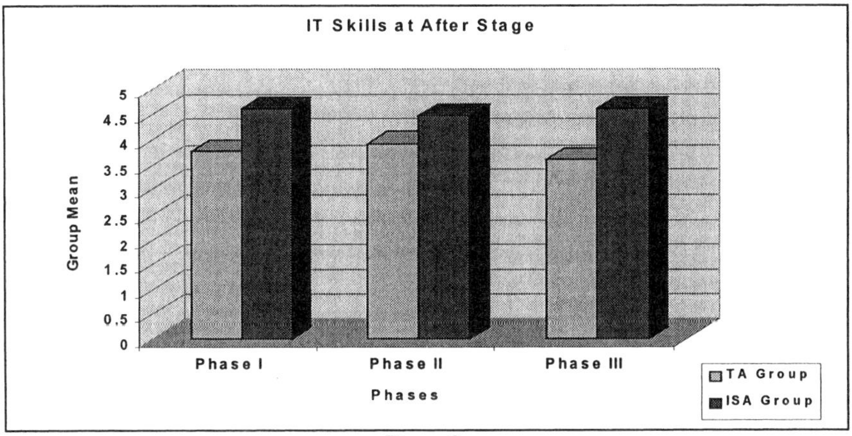

Figure 2.

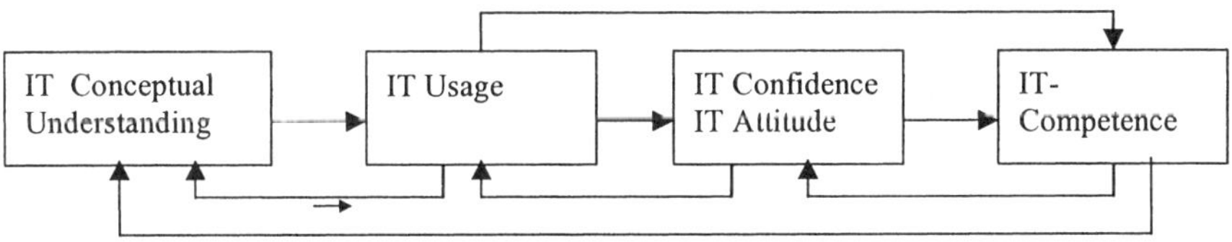

Figur 3. IT concepts, usage, confidence and competence relationship diagram

Greater conceptual understanding motivates the students to use IT more and more use brings about more IT confidence and competence. The findings of this study suggest that since the ISA puts more emphasis on information literacy and on IT applications in business, the business students in the ISA group could relate their class work to the IT applications used in business organisations. The students felt the immediate usefulness of the material learnt in class, which brought them closer to the IT to use it more with enthusiasm.

The findings of this study are in line with several others findings (Hunt et al. 1993, Kohang 1989, Soule 1995), as these findings lead us to believe that more use of IT, especially in the direction of its intended use, bring about more positive attitudes and hence give more confidence to the users. This enhanced confidence turns students to use IT more often and so paved the way for higher IT skills.

The findings of this study also support that the groups with more positive attitudes towards IT is generally expected to be more confident in IT, in turn enhances IT skills (Buckland 1995, Leavenworth 1994, Zoraini 1995).

Another interesting finding of this study supports that the groups, which started with word-processing and followed the Traditional Approach gained more skills in word-processing and not so much in other applications of IT such as the follow-up modules, spreadsheets and databases (Freeman et al. 1995).

With the proliferation of powerful PCs and the availability of more user-friendly business software packages, however, most business organisations are looking for skills in information handling and not merely in word-processing. Many business organisations use databases and spreadsheets/graphics programs for their data processing needs and use word-processing for data presentations. At present the clerks and secretarial staff use word-processing but for business information and for decision-making the popular packages used in businesses are databases and spreadsheets software.

Since the ISA appears more effective in developing IT skills, it could be followed in any institute of higher learning in their introductory IT course, to acquire more information handling skills and not merely word-processing. In addition, the scope of the ISA needed to be extended to cover also the topics, such as the Internet, e-Mail, a World Wide Web (WWW) of computers and on line information searching techniques to meet the changing needs of IT in businesses.

Though there are many merits of ISA, still learning IT through the ISA would not make the students fully conversant with all of the IT applications used in businesses, but it may help to form a firm foundation on which to explore advanced techniques of IT.

REFERENCES

Buckland, B. K. (1995) *Testing the role of knowledge barriers in the diffusion of information technology within and among small businesses.* Thesis, University of Colorado at Boulder, USA.

Freeman, M. and Rowley, J. (1995) An Information Systems Approach to Teaching IT Skills. *Computer Education*, 80, pp. 5-7.

Hunt, N. P. and Bohlin, R. M. (1993) Teacher education students' attitudes towards using computers. *Journal of Research on Computing in Education*, Vol. 25 (4), pp. 487-497.

Koohang, A. A. (1989) A study of attitudes toward computers: Anxiety, confidence, liking and perception of usefulness. *Journal of Research on Computing in education*, Vol. 22(2), pp. 137-50.

Leavenworth, S. L. (1994) *Identification and Validation of Computer Competencies Needed by Nurses.* Thesis, East Texas State University.

Naqvi, S. J. (2000) An Information Systems Approach for Teaching Basic IT Skills used in Business. *Computer Education*, 95, pp. 23-28.

Naqvi, S. J. (2001) A Study of Various Approaches to the Development of IT Skills Used in Business. In *Proceedings of the International Conference on Millennium Dawn in Training & Continuing Education*, University of Bahrain, Bahrain, April, pp. 69-74.
Soule, H. (1995) *Administrative Utilization of And Attitudes Toward Microcomputers in the Public Schools of Mississippi.* Thesis, The University of Southern Mississippi.
Zoraini, W. A. (1995) Attitudes Towards Using Computers Among Malaysian Teachers Education Students. In *Proceedings of the sixth IFIP World Conference on Computers in Education*, Chapman & Hall, London, July, pp. 154-162.

BIOGRAPHY

Syed Naqvi is presently teaching Computer and Information Systems courses at Sultan Qaboos University, Oman. Besides teaching, he is actively involved in research on computer education, delivering IT skills to business students, multimedia and e-commerce.

82

Giving IT a KICT

Successful Professional Development Models in Small, Semi Rural Schools

Martin James and Kay Rye
Paihia School, School Road, Paihia 0252, New Zealand
miha@voyager.co.nz

Keywords: primary education, catalyst for change, case studies, teacher education, transfer

Abstract: Interactive Education: An Information and Communication Technologies (ICT) Strategy for Schools was launched by the New Zealand Government in October 1998. The strategy is a concerted effort by the government at a national level to integrate ICT into teaching and learning programmes in primary and secondary schools. One strand of the strategy was the establishment of 23 ICT Lead Schools. This paper examines the work of Paihia School, one of the 23. The school underpinned its professional development programme with characteristics that research indicated promoted sustainable change in curriculum development when applied to school based professional development models

1. INTRODUCTION

Co-ordination of ICT use in New Zealand schools began to evolve in the early 1990's with the publication of the Consultel Report: "*The use of telecommunication technologies for the enhancement of educational services*". It warned against uncoordinated and unsupported implementation of new technologies into learning environments stressed the need for educators using the technology to be adequately trained and called for implementation to be well coordinated and funded.

Harris (2000) stated that a common theme amongst those interviewed by the authors of the Consultel Report was that technology in itself was not the answer. The technology was described as a tool, that had to be matched to educational methods in a way that 'augmented' or added value to learning to be successful.

It maintained that, "new technologies are teaching and learning tools. They do not substitute for teachers but technology developments provide an additional means by which learning can take place."

This study was primarily concerned with open learning and distance education, but its findings apply equally to all educational areas. While there were a range of initiatives involving ICT in the mid-1990's involving both business and the Ministry of Education it wasn't until 1998 that much of the work came together under a new strategy.

Interactive Education: An Information and Communication Technologies (ICT) Strategy for Schools was launched by the New Zealand Government in October 1998 (M.O.E. 1998). It was supported with a budget of $14.5 million over three years. The strategy is a concerted effort by the government at a national level to integrate ICT into teaching and learning programmes in primary and secondary schools. One strand of the strategy was the establishment of 23 ICT Lead Schools, who work with approximately 300 cluster schools developing professional development models and supporting them in the integration of ICT into their schools over a three-year period. Paihia School is one of the 23 Lead Schools working with sixteen schools in the Far North region of New Zealand, they have developed a professional development model that effectively supports small, rural, semi isolated schools. This paper explores the foundations the model is built on, how it is being implemented and what impact the model is having on three of the schools involved. It indicates that there are common characteristics that exist in schools adopting ICT integration, where there was previously little or no expertise in this area.

2. SETTING

The Far North District, New Zealand

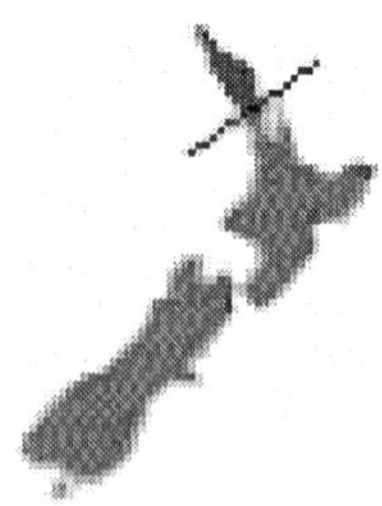

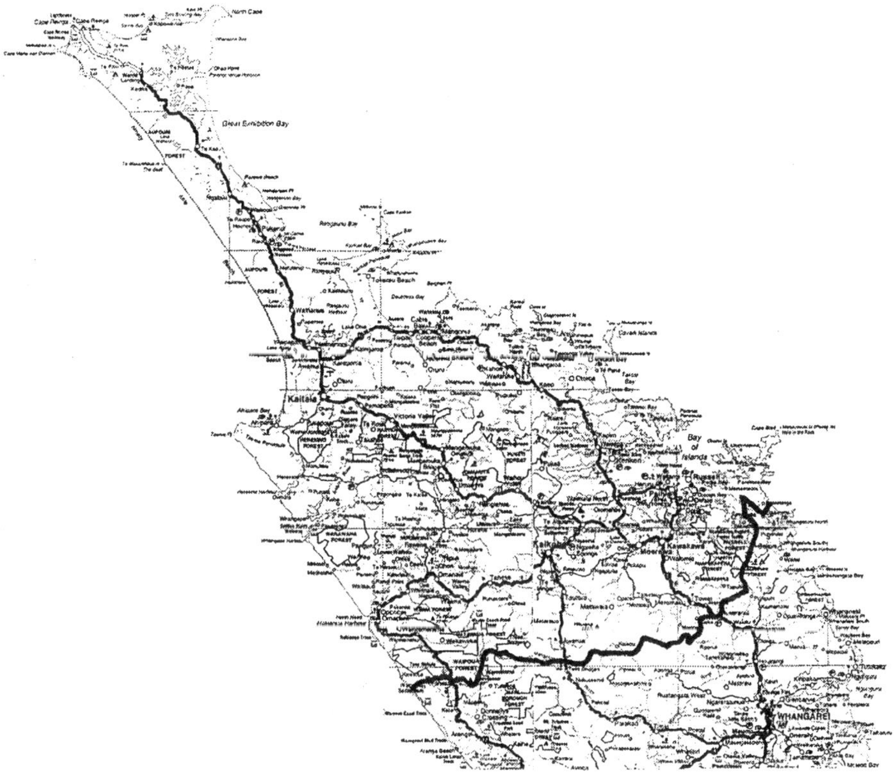

To understand the application of this professional development model and how the applied theory is put into practice one must first understand the social context of the schools in which the model is being applied. An Education Review Office (ERO 1998) report on Schooling in the Far North stated that, "A high proportion of students in the Far North can be classified as *at risk* as a result of their family and social circumstances". This statement was determined by OECD (1995). Family and social factors, which predict *at risk* status are:

- A background of poverty
- Ethnic minority status
- Fatures of family arrangements, such as single parent status
- Community factors such as poor housing
- Poor knowledge of the language of instruction.

The Far North population has a number of features which distinguish it from the rest of New Zealand.

- There is a significantly higher Mäori population. Almost half of the Far North population (45.5 percent) identify as Mäori, compared with 15.1 percent in the whole of New Zealand.
- There is a greater proportion of older people and children. Compared to the New Zealand population as a whole, there are more young people aged 15 to 29, more children aged 0 to 15 and more older people aged 50 to 69.
- There is a lower level of educational attainment. In the Far North 43.8 percent of people aged over 15 have no formal qualifications, compared with 34.8 percent in the whole of New Zealand.
- There are more single parent families. One parent with child(ren) comprises 22.3 percent of families compared with 17.7 percent for New Zealand as a whole.
- There is a higher rate of unemployment. The unemployment rate is 12.9 percent compared with 7.7 percent in New Zealand.
- Income levels are lower. In the Far North 71.9 percent of people aged over 15 have an annual income of $20,000 or less and 3.8 percent have an annual income of over $50,000. The comparable figures for New Zealand as a whole are 58.6 percent and 7.3 percent. 31.1 percent of the Far North population aged over 15 receive a government benefit compared with 19.6 percent for New Zealand as a whole.

The Paihia School Cluster is made up of: 1 College (Years 9-13), 1 Area School (Years 1-13), 1 Intermediate (Years 7-8), 2 Kura Kaupapa Maori (Years 1-8 schools with instruction in Maori), and 12 Primary Schools (Years 1-8). These schools are spread throughout the Northland region across a longitudinal distance of 200 kms and with a travelling time of two and a half-hours between the furthermost schools. All schools have:

- phone lines which allowed modem connections between 9600 and 28800 bps depending upon line quality
- electrical power supply of varying quality
- some form of computer technology varying in age from new to five years old.

3. THE MODEL

Underwood (1996) reported that the World Conference on Computers and Education Working Group concluded that there was a Cycle of Ignorance that had been created in the use of ICT, due largely to the rapidity of the IT innovation cycle, resulting in ineffective training and support in the use of IT for teachers. A strategy to break the cycle of ignorance consists of:

- Providing effective role models of good practice

- Personal IT skills are a prerequisite to pedagogic change
- The process of self development needs to be repeated with our students
- Identifying factors that support effective transfer into the classroom is essential.

Our professional development programme is built upon these recommendations. At the heart of our model is the belief that in order to effectively integrate ICT into teaching and learning an examination of the teaching paradigms that exist within schools is necessary. The term 'authentic pedagogy' is used to describe the teaching and learning conditions we want schools to create. Our model provides teachers and principals in participating schools with opportunities to develop effective use and integration of ICT into their schools through:

- Exposing teachers and principals to models of best practice
- Supporting the development of their personal ICT skills
- Empowering students to develop innovative use of ICT
- Creating characteristics of successful change models in our cluster schools

Readings we explored on School Based Professional Development Models included the ACCO Model of Change, Robertson (1991) and subsequent evaluations by Hall, Casey and Robertson (1995). These, along with other evaluations of schools-based projects by Ramsey et al. (1990), Stringfield et al. (1991) and Poskitt (1992) indicated that, "in spite of numerous findings of international literature in this area, once a sound pattern of curriculum development is set in place, it is likely to be sustained providing that certain conditions are in existence". These conditions included:

- Teachers being involved in setting priorities for change with the time frame for change of sufficient duration
- School-wide change requires targeting whole staff development but also identifies key individuals to co-ordinate improvement
- Teachers must 'own' the change process by, becoming familiar with research that relates to effective practice, assessing current practices and setting performance goals
- An outside agent or facilitator is crucial in identifying needs, developing strategies and plans, as well as setting deadlines
- Ensuring that leadership develops a clear sense of direction and vision, which is agreed to by teachers
- Involving school communities in the development.

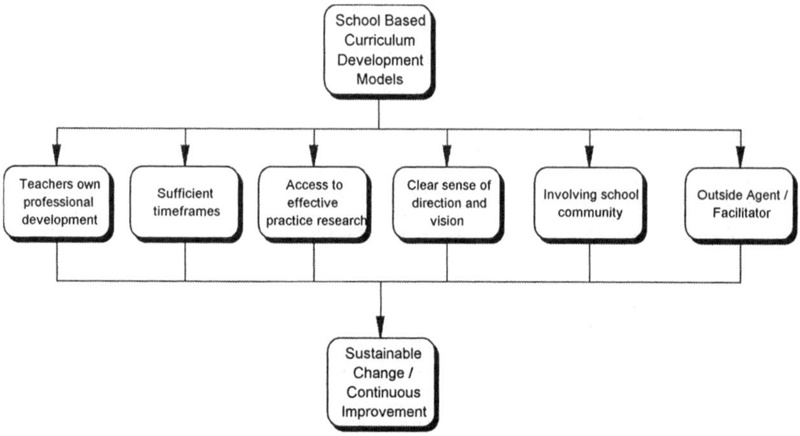

Figure 1. Conditions required for sustainable change

The model we developed encapsulates all these characteristics in some shape or form. The model has a two-strand approach. One strand targets principals and Boards of Trustees. The focus is to support them in developing appropriate policies and sustainable development plans for ICT in their schools, that look at infrastructure, teacher capability and application. This involves working directly with principals and board members in their schools. The second strand provides direct support to teachers in the classroom through the establishment of Key Information and Communication Teachers (KICTs) in all participating schools. The role of the KICT is to be actively involved in professional development focusing on:

- Personal ICT Skills
- ICT application in teaching and learning
- Learning Theory
- Developing PD Programmes for other staff members.

The goal is to create autonomy for schools in relation to ICT professional development and the development of an authentic pedagogy that effectively integrates ICT into teaching and learning programmes.

This is achieved through the creation of a sustainable resource in the KICT, who can support the schools professional needs. As the school evolves in developing its infrastructure and programmes it looks to its' KICT for direction and support in applying ICT to teaching and learning programmes.

Substantial research, based on the work of Fullan (1991), has shown that a change in pedagogical practice not only depends upon the willingness of the individual teacher but on policies and practices of the institution as a whole and of the culture within the institution. This research supports our two strand approach. One must also understand that the majority of New Zealand schools, because of their size, (average school size is less than 200 pupils) have teaching principals. Principals who are actively involved in teaching allow the two strands to entwine more readily, as small school principals maintain their role as curriculum leader, as opposed to some of the larger schools where the principals' administrative demands often mean curriculum leadership is delegated.

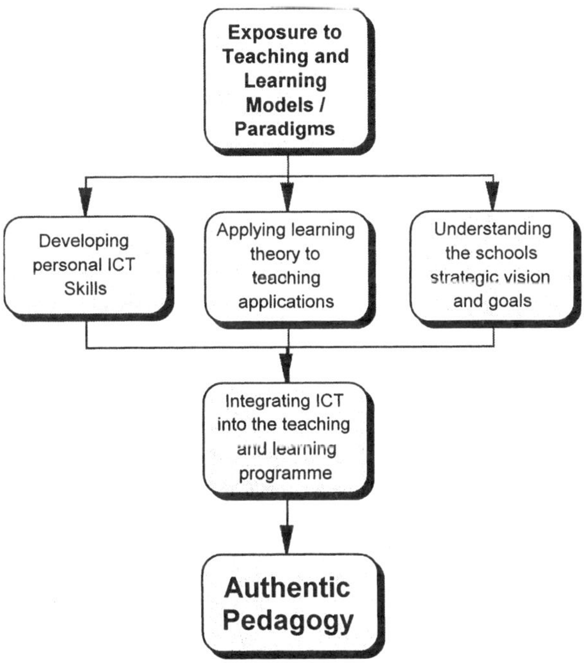

Figure 2. Conditions for creating authentic pedagogy

4. CASE STUDIES

The model we proposed for all schools is developmental in nature. The first step is working with schools in developing Key ICT teachers while at the same time working with principals developing strategic documentation. Each school is at a different place along the development continuum, depending upon previous professional development experiences. Some schools have pockets of ICT innovation occurring. None of the 16 schools at the beginning of the contract had school-wide ICT PD programmes. Although a number of the schools included ICT equipment replacement as part of their strategic plans, there was no evidence of ICT professional development programmes with an ICT focus.

4.1 School 1

A bi-lingual full primary sited in a small town. It is the largest of the cluster primary schools with a teaching staff of 16. In response to the large number of Maori pupils enrolled, the school operates a parallel stream of four classrooms for Year 1-8 students, in which the language of instruction is Te Reo Maori. Teachers, aides and students must speak Maori at all times, although the students write in English and use English texts.

The Principal, is an active user and supportive in the provision of ICT equipment. However there is little technical expertise within the staff and no apparent planned ICT strategy.

Elements identified that support ICT development

- Stable staff
- Principal active user
- Key teachers were in positions where they would be able to effect change.

The identified key teachers were the deputy principal and the most competent ICT user in the immersion classes. Both carried a full teaching load as well as administrative responsibilities. In order for them to engage with enthusiasm, it was essential that the professional development enhanced their current classroom practice rather than created another job. This requirement has determined the direction of ICT integration throughout the school. ICT must be used in authentic contexts and in the most appropriate way. There will be very few contrived student uses of ICT in this school. The immersion teacher had a further particular need – how to effectively use ICT to promoting exemplary models of Te Reo Maori.

During 1999, both teachers received 8 in-school visits. Four visits were to teach skills needed to pass on to their students. The balance of visits were professional discussions – the rationale of ICT use, management and organisation issues and programme planning.

In the second year, 2000, the two KICT's and the external facilitator delivered a similar professional development programme after-school to 6 more teachers. The teachers were then expected to pass their skills on to their students. In the third year, the 6 teachers will work with team members to pass on their skills while the KICT's will receive further individual skills training to start the cycle again.

4.2 School 2

A 3 teacher full primary school sited 8 kilometres from their nearest shop and 17 kilometres from their nearest high school. School 2 is typical of many New Zealand rural primary schools. Virtually all their students are bussed to school from the surrounding farms and the staff live nearby, but not necessarily within the school community.

Elements identified that support ICT development

- Stable staff who all planned ICT use for their students
- All three staff were users of ICT
- Key teacher was positive towards change
- High computer/student ratio – (1:5).

Whilst the principal and school secretary worked within the network of learning principals to develop ICT use in their administrative processes, the KICT worked with the external facilitator.

In the first year, 1999, the immediate need was to develop some management strategy which would allow her Year 1 to 3 students to independently access the word processor to complete language tasks. The KICT learned how to write macros that delivered the required document to the desktop setout with the desired font, style, and student cues.

This successful strategy allowed the KICT and facilitator to explore other ICT tools in the school. By the end of the year, her students had all used the fax, the speakerphone and digital camera successfully and understood how each tool empowered them. In the second year, the staff identified their individual ICT needs, which were then addressed by the KICT and external facilitator in a series of after school workshops. Two final staff meetings with the facilitator helped the staff clarify their school's ICT philosophy and rationale of use.

4.3 School 3

The school already had a teacher who was effectively integrating ICT into teaching programmes. The principal was already using effective professional development models for change in other curriculum areas. There were coordinated efforts to improve access to ICT for all students. The principal also possessed strong personal ICT skills.

Elements identified that supported ICT development.

- Stable staff

- Key teacher technically capable and innovative user and supporter of other staff
- Principal supportive and active user
- Effective professional development model already existed.

As the school had an infrastructure that was already place, the school was already providing staff training sessions both at syndicate and whole school level on using computers. The entry point for the outside facilitators was further along the continuum than at other contract schools because of this. The school was also able to manage minor technical issues. In the first year facilitators worked with the principal on developing an ICT strategic plan as well as providing personal ICT skills. The principal was prepared to apply these new skills and was seen by staff as an active user of ICT in teaching programmes. The Key ICT teacher was supported in the classroom in developing student mentors who could work alongside students from other classrooms. The second year saw the school move to a whole school development model where the key teacher was released to provide professional support for other teaching staff. The programme evolved to where staff were setting performance goals in the use of ICT. They were supported in the classroom by the key teacher. The model worked where by time was spent on both personal IT skills and the application of these skills into teaching programmes. The contract was able to support the school in funding some of the release time necessary for the key teacher to work in this way. The external facilitator worked with support staff rather than teachers on personal ICT skill development, as the internal release time was unable to be extended to pick up these staff members. While in most instances, the need for an external change agent is required through the change process, the school in this case was able to pick up much of this person's role. In 2001 the key teacher will be released to apply this model of professional development in other small Northland schools.

5. SUMMARY

Creating a network of learners suggests some form of link. The link that binds each network, each learning community or each school in this instance is ICT. Creating a consistent group of characteristics that are proven to support school based curriculum development initiatives has been critical to the success of the programme to date. The developmental nature of the programme and the varying degrees in which individual schools enter this continuum of development has allowed us to predict future directions for many of the schools. In schools where these characteristics are strong, one can see a growing autonomy, schools becoming less dependent upon outside agents and taking greater responsibility for ICT integration. Once organisations begin to develop this autonomy, they then become more aware of it interdependence on other learning networks, other links to support their own understanding and use of ICT in teaching and learning. Inter-school / organisational interactions at regional, national and international levels increase as the level of autonomy increases. The establishment of a national education portal (www.tki.org.nz) supports such interactions in New Zealand. The challenge for schools is to ensure that, as they adapt to include ICT into their teaching and learning programmes, more and more time needs to be spent examining the teaching paradigms that ICT is built on. While this model to date is producing more innovative use of ICT in authentic learning contexts, we must continue to examine the authenticity of the activities we expose our learners to. They must be imbedded in sound learning theory with technology that allows learners to do things in new ways, or ways in which traditional learning tools do not allow. Creating a critical mass of teachers who operate in this form of paradigm will ensure effective models of ICT integration are sustainable and on going.

REFERENCES

ERO (1998) *Schooling in the Far North.* [http://www.ero.govt.nz/Publications/eers1998/far_north/farnorth1.htm].

Fullan, M. (1991) *The New Meaning of Educational Change*. Teachers College Press, New York.

Hall, A., Caesy, G. and Robertson, J. (1995) *A resounding ACCO*. Educational Leadership Centre, University of Waikato, Hamilton, New Zealand.

Harris, D. (2000) *Information and Communication Technology in the New Zealand Educational Context.* NZCER. [http://www.minedu.govt.nz/Schools/ITinSchools/].

M.O.E (1998) *Interactive Education: An Information and Communication Technologies (ICT) Strategy for Schools*. Ministry of Education, Wellington.

Poskitt, J. M. (1992) *Report on the ACCO Teacher Development Contracts*. Educational Research and Development Centre, Massey University, Palmerston North.

Robertson, J. (1991) *ACCO: Achieving Charter Curriculum Objectives*. Final Report TD 90/1, The University of Waikato, Hamilton, New Zealand.

Stringfield, S., Billing, S. and Davis, A. (1991) Implementing a Research-based Model of Chapter 1 Programme Improvement. *Phi Delta Kappan*, April, pp. 600-606.

Underwood, J. D. M (1996) *Breaking the Cycle of Ignorance: Information Technology and the Professional Development of Teachers*. Chapman and Hall, London.

BIOGRAPHY

Martin James and Kay Rye have worked on a range of collaborative ICT related projects over the last eight years in their varying roles as teachers, principals and advisers. Much of this work has been in small, rural primary schools. Kay has been involved with the Te Kite Ipurangi Reference Group while Martin has been part of the reference group developing the new government ICT strategy.

83

ICT and the Development of a Cross-national Curriculum

Don Passey and Petra Hobrecht
Department of Educational Research, Lancaster University, Lancaster LA1 4YL, UK
d.passey@lancaster.ac.uk
Landesinstitut für Schule und Weiterbildung, Paradieserweg 64, 59494 Soest, North-Rhine Westphalia, Germany

Keywords: communication, culture, distance learning, literacy, primary education

Abstract: The width of uses of ICT in education, society and in the workplace means that the development of basic skills needs to be considered within a multimedia as well as in a paper-based environment. ICT use is being considered a basic core skill. ICT provides opportunities for teachers and pupils to develop on-line projects, across national boundaries, raising issues about skills such as literacy and numeracy. This paper explores this, considers the implications of on-line cross-national project work, and concludes that overarching policies may be needed to shape and support such practices if pupils are to gain effectively in learning terms.

1. INTRODUCTION

In the past teaching and learning for life has always been based upon a range of knowledge areas in a set of curriculum guidelines or perhaps a national curriculum. However different the knowledge that was deemed necessary for life in different societies, curriculum guidelines or national curricula have always focused universally on basic skills such as literacy and numeracy. Education for all has meant teaching every child to read and write as well as using basic mental arithmetic techniques. At the same time education has long been associated with periods of attendance at certain institutions at certain times in a lifetime, or events at various stages of an educational or training period. Attendance has often been seen as statutory school attendance or attendance of specific courses at irregular times.

Both of these patterns are shifting because of the influence of communication technologies. Basic skills need to be reconsidered in terms of what constitutes such skills within a multimedia environment just as much as in a paper-based environment. Attendance needs to be reconsidered in terms of on-line access as much as that based in a particular institution, and also in terms of growing needs for lifelong learning strategies. This paper focuses mainly on shifts over basic skills, which are brought about by the advent of ICT, but also looks at lifelong learning needs where useful and appropriate.

2. SHIFTS IN TEACHING AND LEARNING

On the one hand education has always been strongly associated with the mastery of the three R's – reading, writing, arithmetic. On the other hand, it has always had much to do with the acquisition and memorisation of factual knowledge. However, it often seemed that the two things had little to do with one another. Children were taught to read, but not necessarily, it seemed, to enable them to read in order to take in more factual knowledge. Knowledge was delivered by a teacher to an individual or a group of learners.

The rapid expansion of world knowledge and the advent of ICT, which has led to an equally rapid dissemination and easy accessibility of this knowledge, makes it necessary to reconsider curriculum guidelines and national curricula. This has in some countries brought about a shift from a syllabus of knowledge to a syllabus focusing on basic skills. ICT is now placed in some countries as a core curriculum subject or skill (see the National Curriculum 2000 in the UK (Department for Education and Employment 2000), for example, or the subject curricula for upper-secondary education in Germany (Ministerium für Schule und Weiterbildung, Wissenschaft und Forschung des Landes Nordrhein-Westfalen (1999)). The need for pupils to be able to handle ICT from a very early age is seen more and more strongly, but what does that mean with regard to the basic skills they need? What exactly are the effects on skills such as literacy and numeracy that have traditionally been seen as vital and therefore basic? What does literacy, for example, mean in ICT terms?

ICT provides a medium where literacy is perhaps involved in a wider range of ways than might be the case with a paper medium. From a literacy viewpoint ICT as a medium can

- enable the development of traditional forms of reading and writing, and support the development of reading and writing in enhanced ways, and in a variety of locations,

- provide a range of sources of literacy materials,
- support a range of new forms of literacy techniques,
- help to assess certain achievements in writing.

But new forms of literacy abilities are demanded in order to access and use the medium fully and adequately in the variety of ways and locations possible. These abilities must be understood if on-line projects, particularly cross-national projects, are to be successful.

A further consideration is that the ICT medium itself should provide for enhanced learning outcomes. Traditional literacy arenas such as writing a letter, a story, or a poem can be developed on the ICT medium, just as it is possible to read a story from the ICT medium. Authors such as Scrimshaw (1993), Jessel (1997), Passey et al. (1999), Passey and Hobrecht (2001) argue that the use of ICT can be used to enhance traditional approaches. However, a range of emergent literacy abilities are developing through the use of the ICT. Writing emails can mean the same as writing letters, but writers of email are also enabled to 'talk' to each other as replies can be interspersed with originating text. The use of the internet certainly demands an understanding of iconography that goes beyond the realms of traditional texts, and an understanding of the relationship between images and text in a more profound way than that associated with traditional paper media. The fact that ICT now enables learners to develop traditional literacy in places other than classrooms adds a further dimension for redefinition.

3. IMPLICATIONS IN TERMS OF LITERACY

So what are the implications of using the communication potential of the ICT medium in on-line projects with young learners in terms of literacy and the teaching of basic skills?

Communication through email, searching the WWW for information, publishing one's own ideas and work outcomes all require basic skills such as reading and writing. However, with regard to ICT, literacy no longer only means reading and writing in terms of putting letters together to form words and from there sentences to convey meaning. In terms of multimedia literacy, aspects such as the understanding and use of iconography, integration of imagery in still and animated form, presentational techniques, use of sounds and music, and a fine focus upon audience and purpose are all brought forward in terms of their importance. No longer is the written text the prominent or dominant feature of the medium. The other aspects of sounds, imagery and presentation are as important – indeed, some multimedia authors would say that they are more important. So the teaching of literacy abilities needs to address these aspects, too.

When on-line projects are developed, the range of issues that arise and are concerned with the direct use of the on-line environment fall into three different types – accessing ideas or information, handling information or data, and presenting outcomes or information. In terms of access, one of the issues arising is the vast amount of information in many different languages accessible through the WWW. Pupils and teachers need to develop efficient search strategies to find the information they are looking for. Once they have found possible sources, they have to separate the 'wheat from the chaff'. Traditionally, pupils would read through all the documents word by word. The internet, however, forces them to develop scanning and skimming techniques at an early stage in their literacy development. Furthermore, handbooks about what is good web authoring generally emphasise the fact that on-line readers do not have much time and want to gather all the important facts at one glance. So many on-line documents use very short and precise language, add graphics or sounds to convey parts of the meaning, and spread information across a number of web pages. On-line readers, have to take in all the different elements of a web document, decode the 'shorthand' used, and gather all the different parts that constitute the whole set of information. So pupils need abilities including having and using visual understanding to abstract information.

In terms of handling information or data, the collecting of information demands that pupils have both effective search skills and selection skills, alongside literacy skills, and other skills. For example, pupils may be asked to gather data about shopping habits in order to have a perspective on a local, regional or national basis, which can then be compared to the findings of other pupils. Here the need for and nature of data gathering techniques include issues of statistics and probability, and a consideration of the reliability of the data gathered. Since resources can now be created in multimedia forms, the synthesising of information gathered from different types of multimedia also demands a greater understanding of how these multimedia forms can be used and interpreted. The use of the medium to question and to gather information by questioning, requires a consideration of how email can be used to elicit pertinent information. Another question illustrating the wider range of skills is when considering comparisons such as local or national traditions such as Christmas, in different countries. In such a case, pupils need to discuss whether a particular form of statistical data gathering is needed and how much statistical data is needed in order to make any general assumption at a local, regional or national level. Pupils need information handling skills such as those needed to reorder information for particular purposes, or relating to short term experiences for wide publication.

In terms of presenting information or outcomes, ICT provides the opportunity and possibility for pupils to create outcomes in suitable presentational forms for web publication. This means, however, that pupils need to be aware of their audience and the fact that this audience may be found far beyond the classroom. So pupils need to consider the message and the style of their documents much more carefully, and they also need to think about ways of enhancing the effect of their writing, for instance by integrating images and sound. This then means that they must analyse the way in which text and images and sound work together and the implications of that for the document's effect on the audience.

4. ON-LINE PROJECTS AND CROSS-NATIONAL COLLABORATION

Communication facilities now enable teachers and learners to share and express their ideas at a distance, sometimes within the same nation country, but also across national boundaries. On a European level particularly, the need to do this is widely recognised. In 'Learning in the Information Society: Action Plan for a European Education Initiative (1996-98)', the European Commission (1995) states that

> "Europeans will have to learn to use the new information and communication tools from an early age if they are to find a place for themselves in an increasingly knowledge-based society. Upon this will depend their employment prospects and their future as indicated in the *European confidence pact for employment*".

However, there are certain considerations in terms of the effects that communication technologies have on basic skills when pupils and teachers are linked across school boundaries, or even across national boundaries. The most obvious implication, of course, is that teachers and pupils may be faced with the challenge of having to read material in another language. The European Commission (1995) puts forward the view that

> "Difficulties arising from communication in different languages should neither be ignored nor overestimated: indeed, schools benefit from a privileged environment for the learning of languages, and multimedia provides a versatile means of communication using sound and image which can greatly facilitate mutual understanding."

The difficulties that arise from cross-national projects, in particular at primary level, were addressed at the EUROPRIM 2000 conference held in Soest, Germany, in October 2000 (see http://www.europrim.de). More than

60 teachers from 14 European countries had been invited to this conference to discuss criteria for the success of on-line projects and to develop and put into practice cross-national on-line projects for primary school pupils.

The outcomes of this conference showed that most projects that were suggested strongly relied on the communication potential of sound and image. Only in some cases was the use of language or languages seriously considered as a vital part of the project, which is not difficult to explain. Although in many European countries education policies today emphasise the need for early foreign language learning, the reality is often quite different. Most pupils still do not really start learning a foreign language until they are ten years of age or older. So without a common language to use, communication in a traditional way is very difficult. However, the ICT medium offers new possibilities for sharing thoughts and ideas through sound and image. And it also enables distance communication at a rapid speed. It does not take a great deal of time to send a sound file or even a video file attached to an email, given sufficient bandwidth access.

Children who are just learning to read and write their own language can use the ICT medium and share their thoughts and ideas in multimedia form. In projects from Denmark, which were presented at the EUROPRIM 2000 conference, primary pupils were involved in expressing their ideas without using words. They were able to use a multimedia environment, creating moving images as well as using sounds. In one of the projects the pupils needed to describe in visual forms 'The Story of the Creation'. Pupils in another class wrote their own 'Scary Story' using similar activities. In a collaborative project, within or across national boundaries, one could imagine, for example, pupils showing their understanding of a written story by turning it into a multimedia presentation using sound and image only, while another group would show their understanding of this presentation by writing down in text form the story it tells them. And if pupils at a very young age are already able to express their ideas in picture form, why should they not be able to communicate with children of their age in another country in the same way?

5. NEED FOR A CROSS-NATIONAL CURRICULUM

It became apparent during EUROPRIM 2000 how much the uses of ICT within schools at a national level differ across Europe. The focus of uses of ICT and their prominence in curriculum guidelines or in the national curricula differs considerably in terms of ICT as an individual subject or ICT skills embedded in other subject areas. If schools in different countries are to develop cross-national on-line projects, then the issues concerned with how these projects can be enabled and supported through the curricular guidelines or the national curricula should be addressed and explored at a cross-national level in both general terms and with a particular focus on the demands for literacy abilities.

Schools and teachers involved will need support in a range of areas. Teachers, and also pupils, need appropriate on-line literacy skills to understand the contents of diverse web-sites, which may also be in other languages. They must be aware of social and cultural aspects when considering the information and its possible uses. Certainly teachers and pupils need to understand the importance of focusing on the audience even more strongly than that required at a national level. Schools involved in cross-national projects need to consider audience with regard to social and cultural issues, and the differences that audiences make at a local, national, or cross-national level. Schools also need to consider the literacy skills required by this form of project within a wider social and cultural understanding. Part of this requirement might be the need for relating native literacy skills to imagery arising in one or more country. Developing projects where common imagery can form a cross-national basis for agreed working certainly appears to be a positive way forward, but ways need to be sought also for creating resources accessible in other languages. Schools should be encouraged to think about different forms of strategy to address the issues arising, including the consideration of how access through other languages might be accommodated by pupils themselves.

Curricular guidelines or national curricula should embrace an agreed cross-national curriculum which offers a set of guidelines to facilitate teachers setting up on-line cross-national projects. So the possible content or features that should be contained in that cross-national curriculum or set of guidelines need to be discussed at a European level, and, furthermore, the implications for curriculum and policy for age ranges beyond the primary phase must be addressed.

Setting up on-line cross-national projects places high demands upon teachers, and these demands are likely to need to be supported at a national level, but further support is required at a cross-national level if teachers are both to value and to be able to create effective on-line projects. A cross-national curriculum or set of guidelines should consider:

- issues of language, both from an access and a creation viewpoint,
- the ways in which information is handled when collected from diverse sources,
- the information handling skills required by pupils,
- the literacy abilities required in terms of other areas of cultural, social or statistical understanding,

- the ways in which resources are created and designed from a presentational and audience viewpoint,
- the uses of ICT facilities to support and enhance learning effectiveness,
- the equipment and facilities needed and available in different countries,
- the relationship of thinking skills to literacy skills and ICT,
- the planning and pedagogical issues involved when establishing on-line cross-national projects.

Whilst the development of such curriculum policy or guidelines would help to highlight issues and enable primary schools to address these issues, there are consequences also for schools that take pupils on beyond this phase of education. The question of how secondary schools will face this emerging dilemma remains to be considered in future work.

REFERENCES

Department for Education and Employment (2000) *The National Curriculum*. DfEE, London.

European Commission (1995) *Learning in the Information Society: Action Plan for a European Educational Initiative (1996-98).* EC, Brussels.

Jessel, J. (1997) Children writing words and building thoughts: does the word processor really help? In *Using Information Technology Effectively in Teaching and Learning,* Routledge, London.

Ministerium für Schule und Weiterbildung, Wissenschaft und Forschung des Landes Nordrhein-Westfalen (1999). *Richtlinien und Lehrpläne für die Sekundarstufe II – Gymnasium/Gesamtschule in Nordrhein-Westfalen*. Ritterbach Verlag GmbH, Frechen.

Passey, D., Forsyth, K., Hutchison, D., Lever, R., Scott, A. (1999). *Anytime, Anywhere Learning Pilot Programme: A Microsoft UK Supported Programme in 28 Pilot Schools End of First Year Implementation Summary Report*. Microsoft, UK.

Passey, D. and Hobrecht, P. (2001) On-line resources and effective teaching and learning. *Education,* 3-13. 29, 1, pp. 3-8.

Scrimshaw, P. (1993) Teachers, learners and computers. In *Language, classrooms and computers,* P. Scrimshaw (ed.), Routledge, London. [http://www.europrim.de].

BIOGRAPHY

Don Passey is a Senior Research Fellow in the Department of Educational Research at Lancaster University. He has wide experience with evaluation of technological innovation and research as policy and practice.

Petra Hobrecht has taught English and mathematics at secondary schools in Germany, and has been seconded to work in the Advisory Centre for New Technologies at the State Institute for School and Adult Education (Landesinstitut fur Schule und Weiterbildung) in Soest, Germany for the Ministry of Education in the State of North-Rhine Westphalia.

84

Action Research in the ICT Strategy for New Zealand Schools

Margaret Lamont
EdCom Network, MultiServe Education Trust, PO Box 19059, Wellington, New Zealand
margaret@edcom.co.nz

Keywords: classroom teaching/practice, curriculum changes, integration of ICT, learner-centred learning, pedagogy

Abstract Governments, schools and teachers worldwide are investing in the ICT challenge – the challenge of making effective use of ICT to support teaching and learning. Government initiatives are providing funds for hardware, software, professional development, on-line resources, technical support and research initiatives. The challenge for educators is to explore and exploit the full potential of ICT to support teaching and learning outcomes; to explore the possibilities ICT offers, and to investigate ways in which ICT can provide an environment which will "engage and facilitate critical thinking and higher order learning" (Jonassen 2000).

1. INTRODUCTION

'These are fantastic times...... we are about to see a decade of change, the like of which we won't see again this century' (Heppell 2000).

A few years ago, we marvelled at the Information Technology tools, which supported teaching and learning: the word processor, database, spreadsheet, Logo and simulations. Teachers used such tools and integrated them into the curriculum. The capacity for storing and organising information; modelling structures and environments, and manipulating text and images, freed students from laborious time consuming tasks, facilitated higher order problem solving and investigations, and enabled students to produce publications to professional standards.

Now the challenge is greater. With a focus now on the communication element within ICT, whole new learning communities are emerging, allowing synchronous and asynchronous contribution and participation; new channels for creative expression; easy and instant access to information. We have moved beyond the *integration* of ICT tools into the curriculum; we must now look to how ICT can best be used to support learning experiences, which are challenging, engaging, participative and rewarding, and how ICT can support meaningful learning:

'Mindtools are computer based tools and learning environments that have been adapted or developed to function as intellectual partners with the learner in order to engage and facilitate critical thinking and higher order learning' (Jonassen 2000). If we do not rise to this challenge, there is a danger that the richest learning experiences for students will be those outside of the education system. We must design a system, which will nurture the 'creative, collaborative and productive cyber athlete, rather than the passive, consuming and predictable cyber couch potato' (Heppell 2000).

We are in a time of accelerating change and ICT will change both the teaching and learning practices in education. We can either choose to go forward with the knowledge that the changes are sound and well implemented or we can drag the chain using ICT in a mediocre way and miss the chances ICT offers to make a real difference to how teaching and learning occurs in schools. 'We've gone past the rhetoric of computers making a difference in schools. Now a clear view is emerging that you can get (ICT in education) wrong, or you can get it right. We are in the opportunity stage where we are asking what is the right thing to do' (Heppell, 2000).

There are many teachers who are successfully incorporating ICT into teaching and learning within the New Zealand Curriculum Framework. What is required now, however, is to identify the ways in which those technologies can empower students and teachers so they can participate fully in the technological society of the future. ICT can, and must, bring about curriculum innovation that will provide for critical technological literacy. Educators must 'think outside the square' and identify those empowering elements. We must now look beyond the confines of the schools and institutions, and identify the ways in which the use of ICT is challenging students; providing new and exciting learning environments; providing a real focus for communication and expression; changing the expectations of students in terms of the nature and context of learning. The curriculum, and the role of the teacher must evolve to meet the changing needs and expectations of our students.

2. ICT STRATEGY FOR NEW ZEALAND SCHOOLS

In October 1998, the New Zealand Ministry of Education launched its ICT Strategy (Ministry of Education, 1998) with a number of initiatives. One initiative, designed to establish and maintain an ICT infrastructure, is the development of a central on-line resource centre, launched this year. Te Kete Ipurangi (www.tki.org.nz) is a web site for New Zealand teachers and students. Two other initiatives were designed to support ICT professional development in schools. The ITPD project, started in 1998, has funded more than 1,000 schools in organising and managing their own professional development. Each school has to set clear objectives and develop an operational plan, upon which they received funding for a period of one year for their own in-house professional development.

Another development saw 23 clusters of schools throughout New Zealand receive funding over a three-year period to provide professional development and resources. With a final year to run for these 23 cluster schools, the Ministry has announced another 25 clusters for a three-year period beginning in January 2001. Information on the cluster schools, and resource materials produced by them can be found on www.tki.org.nz.

3. ACTION RESEARCH APPROACH

A cluster of four secondary schools in the Wellington area are embarking upon a three year action research project, to identify the ways ICT can enhance, extend and innovate the curriculum, and explore means of supporting teachers and educators in reflecting on their own practice in their uses of ICT to support teaching and learning. The proposed cluster of secondary schools has been based on the diversity in size and culture that each of the schools offers. Two schools are well down the road in providing ICT professional development based around the secondary school curriculum, and senior management has actively supported this professional development. Another school taking part in a separate teaching and learning project, wishes to expand what has been achieved in this to teaching and learning specifically using ICT.

The cluster schools also have an interest in ensuring their student population are not disadvantaged by lack of access to ICT, and are keen to explore the ways in which ICT can support their Te Reo Maori programmes. In addition, the Lead School has made structural changes to the junior school regarding ICT and needs to find some way to evaluate the effectiveness of those changes in improving the teaching and learning outcomes for both staff and students. The Lead School needs to go forward confidently in their decisions. This project will enable a group of schools to support each other, and to enable evaluation and feedback.

One of the goals of the project is to 'support individuals, departments and whole schools in developing the necessary skills for effective implementation of ICT in teaching and learning'. The main challenge, is to meet such a diverse range of needs within the scope of this project. The project proposes a innovative approach, to adopt an action research model as an umbrella for a variety of activities across the cluster.

In initial discussions with the principals from the cluster schools, it was noted that all were very keen to develop an action research element. The action research model will ensure a clear focus for each area of development. Each participating individual, or group of individuals, will be encouraged and supported in the study of their own teaching and educational practice. Through support materials and appropriate scaffolding, areas of interest will be clearly identified; steps will be taken towards finding a solution or bringing about improvement; relevant evidence will be gathered to enable a judgement to be made; research will be validated by sharing findings with others throughout the cluster.

The action research model will provide scope for development in a number of different areas. One of the needs, common to all schools in the cluster, is the identification of ways in which ICT can be used to enhance, extend and innovate teaching and learning within the New Zealand Curriculum Framework, and the development of individual ICT capabilities of staff through the use of personal profiling and goal setting. These will be ongoing throughout the project. Other areas for investigation are the:

- Development and implementation of school ICT strategies and policies
- profiling of student ICT capabilities
- Identification and implementation of professional development strategies to support teachers in using ICT effectively within teaching and learning
- Impact of ICT on students' research, communication, presentation, metacognition
- Identification of successful management strategies to achieve optimum use of ICT by teachers and students
- Development and monitoring of on-line learning communities within and beyond the cluster
- Investigation of the impact of ICT on the educational issues surrounding culture, gender and special needs.

The action research model allows development to be supported at different levels, and within a variety of areas of interest, therefore addressing the diversity of school and individual needs within the cluster. The examples above are only possibilities at this stage, and it is understood that only a limited number of initiatives will take place at any given time over the three-year duration of the project.

Key Project Personnel

The *project director* will liaise with the lead school and the cluster; promoting leadership support and direction; providing on-going professional guidance, support and resources; supporting and encouraging publication of research findings.

The *facilitators* will take responsibility for extending their knowledge and skills in innovative uses of ICT in teaching and learning, by participating in negotiated professional development and action research initiatives, and supporting focus groups, across the cluster, in using ICT effectively within teaching and learning.

The *key staff* will facilitate access to hardware and software, and provide on-site technical and professional support for facilitators and focus groups.

The *focus groups* will take responsibility for extending their knowledge and skills in innovative uses of ICT in teaching and learning, and work alongside the key staff to take increased responsibility for providing on-site support for other staff.

The *advisory group* will liaise with the project director and senior management to review progress and further development, and advise the cluster with regard to any other relevant developments and publications.

A crucial element of the project will be the regular sharing of information and relevant ongoing professional development within schools and across cluster. By necessity, the facilitators will change as initiatives roll over. Focus groups will be groups of interested parties across the cluster, such as departmental staff, senior management, and library staff. The focus groups will also change according to the progression of the project. Where appropriate, information will be shared with whole staff groups, although it is recognised that most initiatives may be of interest initially to a particular focus group. The advisory group will include a representative from New Zealand Council for Educational Research, and facilitators/directors from some of the current ICT contract holders. This group will contribute by means of e-mail and electronic conferencing and discussions.

4. PROFESSIONAL DEVELOPMENT

In a secondary school, separation into curriculum areas is quite marked and the lead school has found that the most successful way to approach ICT-related professional development is within curriculum or learning areas. This approach ensures that professional development activities and contexts are relevant to the needs of particular staff. The lead school, having participated in the Ministry's ITPD funding initiative, have found that the following factors contribute to the effectiveness of professional development in supporting the use of ICT in teaching and learning:

Professional development needs to be ongoing – one off demonstrations whet the appetite, but don't ensure that techniques / skills are developed, expanded and incorporated into programmes.

Train the trainers – recruit people who are sound, innovative practitioners; who can model good practice in the incorporation of ICT into teaching and learning programmes within their own curricular area or area of interest. A partnership is needed between the ICT specialist who can be an effective facilitator and the curriculum specialist who can demonstrate enthusiasm and the particular relevance of ICT to their own practice.

The process has to be developmental rather than 'the big hit'. Professional development should be planned over a period of time to allow for training, trial, evaluation, adaptation and implementation.

Drip feed approach is best – frequent, relevant workshops with individuals and small groups are more effective in providing 'just in time' support.

Professional development must meet individual needs – all staff are at different stages in their readiness to implement ICT effectively in their teaching programmes. Support should reflect these differences.

Professional development in ICT must address pedagogical and professional elements as well as practical skills, and in doing so, should relate closely to the New Zealand Curriculum documents.

A range of professional development strategies can be employed in order to satisfy individual, departmental and institutional needs. These strategies could include: one-to-one support, visits to other schools to see examples of good practice and new ideas, group workshops, in-class support, team teaching / peer support, whole-staff sessions to share information and foster a shared vision, attendance at seminars / conferences, and keeping up-to-date with current developments in ICT in education, nationally and internationally.

Two of the schools have made significant progress to date with their ICT Strategic Plans. One of the main factors contributing to this success has been the support and involvement of senior management. Therefore it is crucial that senior management are not only kept informed, but are also supportive of the project and provide leadership in the initiatives.

One study of ICT professional development for teachers was the INTENT Project (Somekh 1993) in the UK. Two of the four aims of the INTENT project were to 'develop management strategies to support developments in ICT' and 'monitor the process of institutional change'. In pursuit of these aims, Somekh, Whitty and Coveney (Somekh and Davis

1997) found that the direct involvement of senior management within a staff development strategy was very effective, as it 'put into place supportive structures, to allocate essential resources, and highlighted the importance of the initiative to the institution as a whole'.
They also noted that the partnership between 'coal face and senior management always uncovers surprising misconceptions on both sides', and that 'this new mutual understanding of the perspectives of them and us can reduce tensions and enable a genuine cross-fertilisation of ideas'.

It is also pertinent to recognise that, in secondary schools more particularly, there are real barriers to effective change in ICT across whole institutions. Somekh, Whitty and Coveney identify four main reasons why institutions such as secondary schools find it difficult to implement change in ICT across the whole institution.

Cultural alienation and stereotyping – culturally constructed conceptions about people who use computers; engineering culture vs. literature, history, arts; threat to culture and values – dehumanised element; complications of gender issues.

Compartmentalisation – history of introduction of computers into schools by Maths or Science departments; separate computer studies departments with 'control' of the computer 'laboratory'; computers established as a specialist discipline rather than a general tool; difficulty of implementing cross-curricular initiatives within departmental structure.

Equitable allocation of resources – difficulties in allocating 'fair' distribution of budgets for computer resources; difficulties of ensuring equal and adequate access to ICTs for all.

Responsibility without power – those people delegated responsibility for bringing about change don't always have the power to make decisions or allocate resources; difficulties faced by the ICT co-ordinator in influencing all colleagues across all departments.

It important, therefore, to take these factors into consideration, to recognise the barriers that may exist, and to be aware of a range of possible solutions and strategies that can be put into place in order that each school achieves the optimum benefit from this programme.

The lead school has already identified that there are diverse needs from Computing, Text and Information Management and other Curricular areas, all making demands on a expensive and scarce resource. Many teachers have been forced to join the ICT bandwagon without careful and well-researched reasons. Schools are under pressure from parents, industry, and ICT companies all pushing for ICT in schools, each for their own reasons, and these may not necessarily be the reason teachers, as educators, should be implementing the new technologies.

In order to address these issues, the management and staff at the lead school have made some structural decision. They now wish to analyse, observe and adjust these from the perspective of knowing they are on a sound educational footing. The school has a philosophy based around personal responsibility for behaviour and learning, and they are basing their ICT learning programmes around this. Various strategies are in place to integrate ICT into the fabric of the school's learning environment.

'The true challenge to the teaching role comes not from the official curriculum developers, but from the children themselves. It is here that teachers and curriculum developers will learn the most creative uses of the computer for educational purposes; if only they will watch, and listen, and explore the cues provided by learners themselves' (Schostak 1988). The action research approach will encourage experimentation and creativity, at a time when the teachers themselves are still learning to cope with ICT and finding out what it has to offer. There has to be a climate where teachers are prepared to take calculated risks, to experiment along with their students, and to become confident that they can use ICT to support meaningful learning, which will engage their students in a challenging and stimulating environment.

REFERENCES

Jonassen, D. H. (2000) *Computers as Mindtools for Schools* (p. 1-20) Prentice-Hall, NJ.
Heppell, S. (2000) *ACEC 2000 Conference*, Melbourne, Australia.
Ministry of Education (1998) *Interactive Education – An Information and Communication Technologies Strategy for Schools Ministry of Education*, New Zealand.
Somekh, B. (1993) *Project INTENT 1990-92: Final Report*. National Council for Educational Technology Coventry.
Somekh, B. and Davis (1997) *Using Information Technology Effectively in Teaching and Learning*. Routledge.
Schostak, J. F. (1988) *Breaking into the Curriculum – the impact of Information Technology on schooling*.

BIOGRAPHY

Margaret Lamont has been involved in teacher education and ICT in Scotland and New Zealand. She is currently supporting the action research initiative being conducted by some of the schools funded within the NZ ICT Strategy for Schools.

PART X

PROFESSIONAL GROUPS

85

Social, Ethical and Cognitive Issues of Informatics and ICT

Working Group 3.1

Chair: Sigrid Schubert (DE)
Rapporteur: Robert Munro (UK)
Participants: Valentina Dagiene (LI), Michael Hammond (UK), Alti Hardarson (IS), Raul Wazlawick (BR), Wolfgang Weber (DE)

Keywords: basic skills, computer science, secondary education, social, ethical issues

Abstract: The group members, drawn from countries with very different educational systems, were all concerned with teaching informatics courses, developing information/computer science curricula or promoting the integration of ICT in schools and higher education. Concern that pupils leave education with a limited understanding of basic concepts of informatics/ICT led to the identification of key actions to resolve this problem. Exploration of social and ethical issues associated with ICT development brought a plea for fresh and exciting curriculum content. After addressing the difficult area of the relationship between informatics and other subjects the group proposed the creation of new, ICT-rich, learning environments.

1. INTRODUCTION

During the course of their deliberations the group addressed a great number of topics and issues related to social, ethical and cognitive issues in informatics/ICT. All members were concerned that, although the impact of informatics/ICT is so profound and so pervasive in society, many young people – and indeed a large percentage of their teachers – have only a superficial understanding of both the basic concepts of informatics/ICT and of the social and ethical issues involved in this rapidly developing area. At all times their discussions attempted to identify reasons for what they regarded as a regrettable situation and suggest possible remedial action.

2. CONCEPTS OF INFORMATICS

The group unanimously supported the assertion that too many pupils currently leave the education process with an imperfect understanding of the basic concepts of informatics/ICT – concepts which fall into four principal categories: computer architecture and operation, changes in informatics/ICT and in society, developing informatics/ICT skills, and information handling concepts.

Most of their informatics/ICT experiences in school or college are concerned with 'doing' – usually what they have been told to do – rather than thoughtfully or critically selecting informatics/ICT resources and deploying them for purposeful activity. Normally their task has not been fully explained to them and they frequently do not appreciate or understand why informatics and ICT is being chosen over other options. Thus much of their educational experience of informatics/ICT is concerned with brief encounters with, or excursions into, different software applications – often only one application rather than the judicious use of a number of complementary applications – with little consideration of how the software operations are performed or indeed why they are necessary and no appreciation of the specific advantages which accrue from their selection and use.

Equally, many teachers, particularly those who have had little or no education in informatics or computer science, lack understanding of these basic informatics/ICT concepts. Many teachers who use informatics/ICT in their classrooms are self-taught or have attended short in-service courses and then refined the ideas, concepts and skills which these courses have covered so that they can make use of the new technology resources which are available in their schools. Even teachers who have been able to get some training find they are unable to bring informatics/ICT into their teaching and learning as effectively as they would wish as hardware and software supplied is inappropriate and they are not afforded time to reflect on the training and develop their new found skills. In the past, though less so now, training has been technical in orientation and has ignored pedagogic applications.

In addition the group were concerned that too often teachers turn to the informatics/ICT expert in school to solve all of their problems and make unrealistic demands on the time/resources of these individuals.

The group were clearly of the opinion that pupils and teachers need to be introduced to a set of basic concepts of informatics in a structured way and that they should fully understand these concepts so that they can make the best and most effective application of the technology which is and will increasingly be in their classrooms. Teachers already in post need to be offered appropriate training which should include consideration of how best to establish these concepts with pupils in different classroom contexts. They will also need time to consider these concepts and create classroom opportunities for coverage in their curriculum.

Student teachers in teacher education institutions need to be introduced to the concepts. These should permeate the teacher education experience and the students should be led and supported by teacher trainers who model good practice. The training programme should offer opportunities to introduce informatics/ICT into their classroom experience and students should be assessed in their mastery and understanding of informatics/ICT concepts.

Pupils in school should be involved in a curriculum which is rich in appropriate informatics/ICT experiences. The group appreciated that there is tremendous diversity in the opportunities which are currently offered to students, in the demands of the tasks they should complete and in the standards they are expected to achieve. This diversity was clearly demonstrated at WCCE 2001. Additionally there is much debate as to whether or not pupils should be examined in and gain accreditation for their mastery of informatics/ICT concepts and abilities. The group consider that pupils who are grounded in informatics/ICT concepts will be better able to make judicious selection of informatics/ICT tools for particular tasks and will also be better equipped to transfer skills from one application, or one generation of application, to another.

The group realises that pupils acquire and understand the aforementioned basic concepts at widely different ages and stages. There should not only be an attempt to map concepts to ages and stages which would give form to their curricular introduction and development but there would be considerable educational benefits if these concepts were visited and progressively refined through the delivery of a spiral curriculum model. In considering the mapping and delivery of these basic concepts in curricular programmes it is important to remember that new developments add to or introduce new concepts and this should be built into the planning.

3. SOCIAL AND ETHICAL ISSUES

Many aspects of informatics/ICT have ethical implications and all of them generate social implications. A great number of these aspects and applications have already exercised a profound impact on society. Teachers must become conversant with the field of social and ethical issues that result from the use and development of new technologies and should be able to guide their pupils/students to appreciate and understand them.

The group discussion on social and ethical issues was triggered by a comment on plagiarism. This sparked wide ranging discussion over a host of topics which were seen not only as presenting problems which had to be urgently addressed, but also opening up new challenges and possibilities for education to respond to and exploit. The topics included copyright; the changing forms, flows and patterns of communication; pornography; racism and discrimination; the need to respect cultural differences and linguistic diversity; the globalisation of legal systems; security and privacy.

The group appreciated that social and ethical issues are often dealt with last in any courses/curricula in schools and that the topics that are addressed – which really could be made relevant and fascinating to pupils – are all too often presented in a sterile and uninteresting way. These are topics and issues that it is very important to explore and discuss with pupils as they will increasingly impact on their day-to-day life. We must try to ensure coverage within the curriculum, ensure they are addressed in an interesting and motivating way and that pupils are encouraged to reflect quite deeply on these topics and issues and on their implications for our global society.

Different group members offered fresh ways in which topics and issues might be explored – issues of copyright might be considered through reference to music-CD and DVD piracy (even piracy of pupil compositions) – sexuality through an examination of chatroom behaviour and discussion of Web content and access compared to paper content and access – security issues through on-line shopping and a review of the strengths and weaknesses of financial organisations' protocols – discrimination through evaluation of relevant Web-content and examination of authorship.

An important conclusion which emerged was the need to involve and motivate pupils to examine ICT sources, particularly those on the Web, very carefully and critically – to try to establish the veracity of content and to develop skills which will help identify discriminatory, biased or propaganda material.

As the flow and volume of data/information which is accessible through the spread of ICT increases, teachers should help pupils to become more critical of the materials they are exposed to. Alongside the development of critical thinking skills many of the group members saw opportunities for promoting values education and moral education through the use of ICT.

Another interesting area that might be developed is the exploration of games/simulation software which illustrates how past civilisations were organised and operated or which presents and invites consideration of different ethical perspectives. Pupils might valuably engage in constructing scenarios and other games/simulations that could explain or illustrate their interpretation of social and ethical issues.

The group appreciate that responding effectively to the many socio-ethical problems and issues posed by ICT will be difficult but it is a challenge educators must address.

Many aspects of informatics hold ethical implications and all hold social implications. Many applications have already exercised an extremely profound impact on society. Teachers must be conversant with the field of social and ethical issues which result from the use and development of new technologies and should be able to guide their pupils to appreciate them.

4. RELATIONSHIPS BETWEEN INFORMATICS AND OTHER SUBJECTS

The world of our pupils is increasingly dominated by an ever more sophisticated technology. It is the pervasiveness of this technology that makes it essential that an integrated view of ICT is presented to every pupil.

This highlights a major problem in many schools in most countries at present. The group was unaware of any comprehensive course on informatics which is offered to all pupils. They quoted examples where courses tend to be delivered to the older students (often the able student who may also be studying mathematics or science subjects) usually after they have had many experiences with computers/software across the curriculum.

In secondary schools it is common that teachers of subjects other than computer science only superficially address and establish basic concepts of informatics/ICT. Rather they encourage pupils to see computers and the new media resources they can be interfaced to as 'black boxes' which should be intelligent enough to meet all of their demands and solve all of their problems. They want to use the technology to illustrate concepts in subjects ranging from geography to art and music or to find, manipulate and present subject-oriented information. However, many subject teachers tend to make limited use of ICT in their teaching and learning – all to often because they have few models of good practice to build on and have had too little time to consider how they might deploy ICT in their classrooms – always supposing they have access to resources and a supportive school administration which promotes use.

It is time for teachers of many subjects to see the informatics teacher, not simply as a hardware provider and technical trouble-shooter but as a colleague who can make a valuable input to the skills and concepts which children should experience across the curriculum. The group did not see the responsibility for creating curricular resources to help establish basic concepts or developing opportunities for discussion and evaluation of issues resting solely with teachers of informatics/computer science. This is a whole school problem. Curriculum change and resource development must be discussed at relevant times by various members of staff. All staff should be involved and school management should coordinate the experiences throughout the curriculum to ensure coverage is interesting, stimulating and provocative to enthuse pupils.

All subject teachers should regularly appraise their curriculum to reflect the impact ICT has on their teaching and learning.

The group noted that there are a number of problems associated with different cultures which have not yet been fully considered in schools and proposed that interdisciplinary projects could promote co-operation and collaboration. Collaborative development focused on language could stimulate writing, thinking and promote evaluation of information sources. If such collaboration will be extended to involve pupils of different nationalities it would force pupils to consider different cultures and different linguistic features.

5. A NEW LEARNING ENVIRONMENT – NEW TEACHER EDUCATION

It is vitally important, but has so far proved to be extremely difficult, to create an ICT-rich environment in schools and persuade all teachers to integrate ICT into their teaching and learning. It has also been difficult to persuade teachers of many subjects to build on informatics concepts established by their colleagues.

Various conference presenters at WCCE 2001 spoke most forcefully on this subject – one contributor outlining five criteria which must be satisfied before successful advancement of pupil knowledge can be realised. Presenters and the SECIII group raised the importance of defining what an appropriate learning environment comprises. It is clear that we do not, as yet, have a clear vision of this environment. We have yet to determine its technological demands or provisions. We simply know it will be more ICT-rich than we have today and trust it will be more educationally stimulating and effective.

Certainly the curriculum which is studied, the delivery effected by the teachers and the interaction between the teachers and the pupils will be different. To date the changes have been mainly to the hardware and infrastructure with less impact on curriculum transformation and alternative teacher delivery.

It has also been difficult to persuade teachers of many subjects to build on the informatics/ICT concepts established by their colleagues. The group are convinced that in-school relationships need to be improved and that senior management must become more involved in managing and engineering staff interaction to ensure that all pupils have equitable access to opportunities where they can acquire and reflect on the basic concepts and the examples or issues which are focused on.

The group appreciate that different countries have adopted different policies, plans and strategies concerned with the integration of Informatics concepts and ICT integration in the curriculum – most expensive – most unsuccessful. Indeed, within many countries a number of responses and emphases exist. The group suggests that, while a convergence of thinking on basic concepts and on ICT integration into the curriculum is welcome, any policy formulation and determination of a national framework should respect and support cultural and linguistic diversity.

Perhaps most hope for success in this field rests with the new generations of teachers who will have had a lifetime of experience of ICT. They will be conversant and comfortable with the technology and will feel free to address the issues associated with the technology's introduction.

6. CONCLUSION

The SECIII group* found the professional group task they were set at WCCE 2001 extremely challenging but most absorbing. The diverse nature of the backgrounds of the group members ensured a wide cross-section of topics and issues were explored. The group thought it important that they formulated a number of responses and recommendations to address these issues and there was great unanimity in determining these. They were particularly concerned that a major problem exists and that educators need to try to resolve it as soon as possible.

*SECIII – Social, Ethical and Cognitive Issues in Informatics and ICT, IFIP Open Conference, Dortmund, GE, 22-26 July 2002

86

Schools of the Future

Working Group 3.1

Chair: Pieter Hogenbirk (NL)
Rapporteur: Anna Kristjánsdóttir (IS)
Participants: Henk Arangies (ZA), Crilles Bacher (DK), Douglas Butler (UK), Roger N. Carlsen (US), Gil Hunter (NZ), Vivi Lachs (UK), Paul Madsen (NZ), Ann O'Callaghan (AU), Lisa O'Connor (AU), Marcos Clayton Pessoa (BR), Sanya G. Pedersen (DK), Lori N. Rounds (US), Lee Sansom (AU), Carmel Wikman (AU), Katina Zammit (AU)

Keywords: catalyst for changes, empowering, future, learner-centred-learning, teacher

Abstract: The School of the Future will be formed during the next 5-10 years. The discussion focused on important changes related to the Learning Processes and New Learning Environments when integration of IT evolves. The present teacher role was analysed in order to discuss and foresee the future role of the teacher. The third aspect of integration of IT into schools is a holistic school perspective concerning the whole organisation.

1. INTRODUCTION

This professional group discussed different aspects of the 'school of the future'. This included different aspects of changes in education and paid obviously attention to the role of ICT within these changes (ICT in the broadest meaning and in every variety that occurs or may occur in the future). From the discussion it was considered useful to make some preliminary remarks.

First of all *the* School of the Future does not exist. The educational environment may have many forms: formal, informal, physical, virtual, public, private, commercialised etc., and all kinds of combinations of these forms. The group focused on different aspects which could be characteristic of *a* school of the future, whereas a *school* is defined as a learning environment where assessment on learning takes place and credits are given for positive learning results.

We decided to take a 5 to 10 year perspective; far enough in the future to emerge from our present status and close enough to use the same words and stay realistic. In this respect one can distinguish four phases of development: emerging, applying, integrating and transforming (van Weert 2001). We agreed to examine an educational environment in a transformed stage.

Finally we did not elaborate on the why question: why should education change? We just assume that societal, cultural, technological changes and new scientific concepts will enforce change whatsoever.

The theme Schools of the Future was elaborated on at the WG3.1 conference in Chile 2000 (Taylor and Hogenbirk 2001) where four different aspects were identified. We discuss in this report the following three aspects, integrating at the same time the issues of 'connectivity' or 'networking' in all three. Each one starts with an opening from the briefing document before the report from the professional group.

2. THE LEARNING PROCESSES AND NEW LEARNING ENVIRONMENTS

ICT already provides us with new opportunities in education, particularly for teaching and learning. Traditional models of classroom practice may not be appropriate for an information rich environment. Equally, it may be that the only access to this potential environment comes through the use of ICT. This aspect addresses the following questions.

- What will be the context of the new learning environment in the School of the Future?
- What will this new learning environment look like?

In a school of the future the learning environment and the context within which learning takes place will have changed. We assume that the learning environment is a connected environment with access to the World Wide Web and other tools and technology. In this context, we will need to rethink the curriculum and the roles of both students and teachers.

In relation to curriculum, there will be a shift to more flexibility in the curriculum and a decrease in the amount of material taught by a teacher. The core curriculum will be reduced, with fuzzier boundaries across subjects. This will allow students to make more decisions and determine more of the tasks they will complete to achieve the outcomes or objectives of the system.

As a result of this greater flexibility of the curriculum there will be a shift in the balance of power relationships within the learning environment from the teacher to the learner. Students will be a part of the process of deciding how to achieve the standards or objectives and the curriculum will no longer be 'secret teacher's business'. The teachers' role will be to guide, facilitate, advise, challenge and intervene when and where they believe it is necessary or when approached by their students.

The new roles of teachers and students will affect the environment and we need to consider what learners will be doing and how ICT can empower the learner to achieve their outcomes. There will be multiple learning environments and multiple possibilities. Although we do not yet know what new technologies will be available and used in the future, we do know that they will play an increasing role in the way students obtain information and the speed with which this information can be acquired.

Among significant technology developments that we can foresee over the next 5-10 years are those having the effect making use of technology totally seamless and totally portable. The notion of 'taking the group to the lab' will disappear and teachers can use traditional methods and technology as it seems appropriate, allowing a variety of approaches. This is due to several developments. Large screens that are at present not generally affordable will be so as the development of light emitting polymer screens promises to make a large screen in every classroom a reality. This is also due to radio networking that will enable wireless communication with all devices, clearing the learning space from all trip-wires. And finally is the battery technology that will soon enable all portable devices to last easily the whole day. Pupils will then have small, light-weight, radio connected devices, capable of performing all the tasks of the teacher's devices.

Students will be interacting with the global environment not just a local one. They need to learn the social and cultural ramifications of this.

As learners take control of their own learning, they need to learn how to learn. This will entail learning about their own learning style. The teacher will need to guide the student to get to know this and the range of possibilities. The student will also need to learn how to learn in other less preferred ways in order to be prepared for diverse learning contexts.

Students will choose whether to work as an individual or collaboratively with others. Intervention by the teacher occurs when and where necessary, and is still part of the learning environment; Explicit teaching or assistance still occurs at the point of need for the student or students. ICT will enhance the quality of the teaching but the use of ICT does not necessary ensure quality teaching in itself.

3. CHANGING THE ROLE OF THE TEACHER

Currently teachers play the most significant role in shaping the learning environment for pupils. Politicians might claim that ICT can take over some of the teachers role while others believe that ICT can only realise its full potential to enhance the learning process if teachers are empowered to play their full part in an ICT rich environment. This aspect addresses the following questions:

- How will the role of the teacher change in schools of the future?
- How can ICT support this new role of the teacher?

In discussion about a changing role of teachers it seems necessary to analyse what that role has included and see how different parts of it may become or have already been influenced by ICT. The job of teachers has partly been directed by decisions from outside, for instance about the syllabus, partly by making decisions through own professional knowledge, and it has partly been about presenting to students but also about interacting, reflecting on and carefully laying foundations for a community of learners. The teacher's job has partly been that of a stimulator and supporter but also an evaluator of progress toward competency. Important decisions in the students' process of learning that have been taken by teachers have frequently been without much collaboration and co-deciding with other professionals.

Which parts of a teacher's job are already influenced by ICT, which can be and which will be, supposing that there will always be teachers because they as human beings have an important role in the life of young people? If teachers will in the future meet students regularly as a group, how will ICT affect the initiating phase of work that earlier has been a presentation by the teacher. How does a powerful learning environment affect the work of students and what kind of interaction, intervening, challenging and orchestrating, will be valuable contributions by the teacher? How does the teacher deal with the managerial role that goes with making use of a rich and powerful learning environment that is not limited with a school as a building?

One question is analysing a teacher's role with respect to future development. Another one is to find how necessary changes can take place. Shortage of qualified teachers in many areas is a threat to schools and ways of acting on new situations by all teachers require breaking the isolation of each classroom as a working space.

Teachers will in the future provide modules of learning to provide a more ICT flexible learning – arranged by projects and results based upon individual and team needs. They will also make an effort to help their students in constructing a coherent and for them an easily attainable personal knowledge.

Various learning immersion patterns will be visible. Students can work for 3-4 days solidly on a project which will call upon a shift-work pattern for teachers to support students with help of ICT.

The role of teacher as facilitator of learning will continue to advance as content becomes more available through an increasing range of ICT resources. This enhanced role of the teacher as guide of learning process will enable teachers to focus on the individual needs of the learner rather than be content deliverers. The increased range of available resources to match the variety of learning styles will enable teachers to scaffold student learning in more meaningful ways.

Connectivity will enable teachers to collaborate on a wider scale thus improving opportunities for critical reflection in a peer-supported environment in order to improve the teaching/learning process. These enhanced communication and information retrieval facilities will also support teachers as life-long learners with a range of professional development opportunities available for 'just-in-time' learning. The variety of roles performed by teachers will further be able to be streamlined by the use of ICT so as to enable teacher time to be focused on student learning rather than on some of the current administrative tasks.

Teachers and pupils will make increasing use of institutional intranet systems for storing resources, which will be shared throughout the greater school community (including pupils' homes). Entire courses will be stored here for on line use. And broadband internet will continue to evolve and offer quality educational resources, which will become more and more interactive.

Within schools of the future there will be a movement towards more types of professionals than is the general situation now, as experts from industries will be found working with teachers. Teachers will be able to work in different schools at the same time, to work only for a short period or part-time and have flexible timetable. Older students will also be found mentoring younger students.

Lifelong professional learning will be of paramount importance for teachers. They will be able to access own learning modules online as required, and as at present will make profession use of email and video-conferencing to share ideas and resources with other teachers in other institutions.

4. CHANGING SCHOOL CULTURE AND THE ORGANISATION OF THE SCHOOL

At the IFIP World Conference on Computers in Education (WCCE) in 1990, Seymour Papert commented that unlike other professions, a teacher from 100 years ago would still feel familiar in the classroom of today. One might argue that this is still true, but increasingly challenges are being made to the structure of the curriculum and the classroom environment.

This aspect addresses the following questions:

- What might the classroom of tomorrow look like? Will there be a classroom?
- How will the infrastructure of the school and the possibilities offered by ICT, support the changes foreseen?

Countries differ culturally, economically and socially. Additionally within countries there are issues around class, race and culture. These issues will influence what a school or classroom of the future will look like.

ITC in education will provide the opportunity to totally reinvent learning as we know it today. An ITC classroom of tomorrow will be an open learning community, and could exist either with or without physical boundaries. ITC will have the capability to provide increased access to learning without regard to time and place. Through ITC integration, boundaries between subject areas, schools, nations and even businesses will begin to dissolve, leaving teachers and individual schools less isolated. Management of the learning environment will be the responsibility of the teacher and the student, with the student able to self-assess their work. Parents would have access to their own children's electronic portfolios and up to the minute progress reports could be generated at will.

The learning communities could be world-wide, with the capability of providing 7day x 24hour access for students, parents, and teachers. There will be many different types of learning spaces available for people of all ages to access resources, support, guidance, and feedback. Collaborative learning will become standard, both face-to-face locally and through video ITC, on a national and international basis. Businesses will become part of the learning community as well, providing learning partnerships. Schools will remain the main source of education, yet partnerships with business and industry will provide real-life learning for students.

Call Centres located world-wide could be accessed and Chat type technology would be essential to support flexible learning. ITC tools will be ubiquitous and multi-sensory, thus providing open flexible learning for all learners regardless of ability, skill level, or special needs. These tools will provide support in the management of the learning community as well.

Teachers, through ITC tools, will have the opportunity to receive the professional development needed to be effective in the educational ITC environment. Traditional teacher training and individual teaching methods will evolve to compliment ITC technology. ITC in education has become the catalyst for change, empowering teachers, students, parents and businesses with new learning opportunities, providing them with a new, open flexible and global learning environment.

REFERENCE

Taylor, H. and Hogenbirk, P. (eds.) (2001) *Bookmark of the School of the Future*. Kluwer, Chile.

van Weert, T. (ed.) (2001) *Information and communication technology in secondary education, a curriculum for schools*. Updated 2000 version, UNESCO.

87

Reality and Virtuality in Schools

Working Group 3.1

Chair: Yvonne Buettner (CH)
Rapporteur: Paul Nicholson (AU)
Participants: Kerry Dollman (AU), Francesco van Ferd (NZ), Cecilie Stranger-Thorsen (NO)

Keywords: virtual reality, students, teachers, building design, electronic education

Abstract: The increasing use of virtual environments in education raises many issues and challenges for educators. Teachers and students need to develop critical understandings about its nature and use. Teachers need to develop skills in creating new kinds of learning experiences for students, and to explore new forms of pedagogy. There is also a need to develop an increased awareness of ethical issues and social concerns with this medium. VR can extend and enhance teaching and learning through multi-sensory experiences that can support role-playing and simulation in which the participant is an active element.

1. REALITY AND VIRTUALITY

In any discussion about the nature and use of virtual learning environments in education, there is a need to consider the nature of those environments, their relationship to 'reality', and the socio-cultural and critical frameworks that inform their development and use in particular social and cultural contexts. In this report, we suggest some areas that need further detailed consideration by educators and developers in order to develop a situated understanding of the principles and issues that form the basis of the development and use of virtual learning environments.

The use of the terms 'reality' and 'virtuality' in relationship to ICT is problematic, in that there is a long-standing philosophical debate about their fundamental nature and relationship. However, in this report, we take a focus on the implementation of virtuality in education settings. I doing this, we adopt the framework in Figure 1, which posits that there is a continuum of experience from reality (face-to-face classroom environments) to complete immersive virtual-reality environments.

a) Virtual reality is a way for humans to visualise, manipulate and interact through computer generated objects and environment and with people.

– *Adapted from " Silicon Mirage: The Art and Science oj Virtual Reality. Steve Aukstakalnis and David Blastner "*

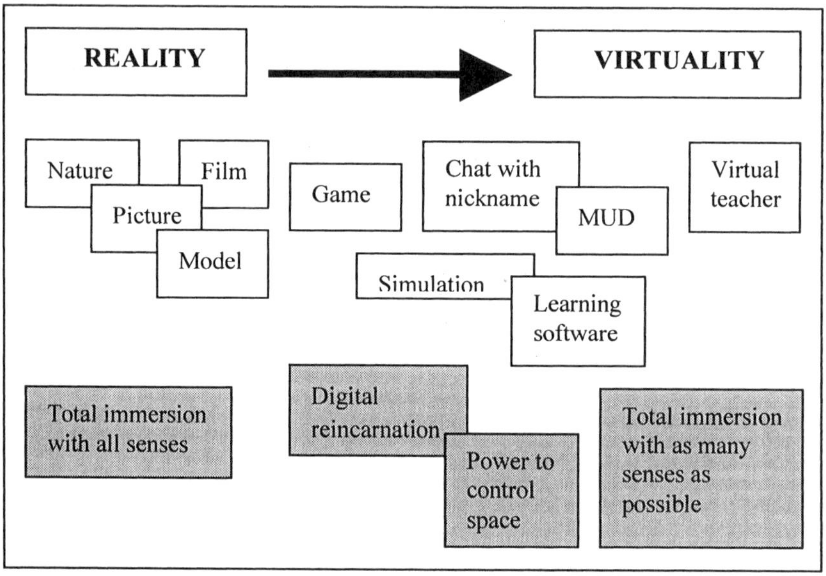

Figure 1: Framework for considering the reality – virtuality continuum

This framework is not meant to be a definitive model, but rather, an aid to considering the relationship between reality and virtuality, and the kinds of educational experiences and learning environments that might be employed for particular educational contexts. This professional group spent considerable time in debating many aspects of this framework, and the philosophical and educational issues that it is embedded in. In the remainder of this paper, we discuss a number of key issues, and elaborate on aspects of them that need further detailed consideration by students and educators of virtual learning environments.

2. CLASSROOM ENVIRONMENTS

While Virtual Reality (VR) supports the visualisation of events, objects etc. that are usually inaccessible, it also supports new forms of interaction, engagement, and pedagogy. If we see VR as a fundamentally new way of teaching, we might see the virtual existence of students as a threat to old methods of teaching. However, it is possible to see VR as a logical extension of modern pedagogical methods. The potentially wide range of sensory inputs that VR supports allows for more and complex and authentic experiences. For example, VR could give a common experience to a class in a short period of time, and allow for individual students to explore a subject both individually and with other members of the group (including the teachers) so that the experience is both personal and social. It also allows for new kinds of exploration of the classroom in which students interact virtually with people and events from other places and times. In this way, VR allows teachers to spend less time delivering facts and more time at discussion challenging (scaffolding) pupils.

However, we still have to be critical about its use and purpose because sometimes the use of film or discussion may be a better approach to achieve the desired goals. This means that we really have to think very carefully about the goals of using VR, and why we want to use it instead of other media. In addition students need to be trained in its nature and use and to be made aware of possible dangers to be found in some VR environments. They also need to develop an understanding of the appropriate etiquette of behaviour and communication in VR environments, and how to use it and why.

3. THE ROLE OF TEACHERS

The role of teachers in regard to virtual environments is the same as in 'normal' classroom environments – to scaffold and guide the students' development within the applicable curriculum structures. However, they also have to help students to understand their experiences – to develop ethical behaviour (in these environments), to help develop their skills in analysis and critique so that they can interpret their experiences in some rational manner. Perhaps when the technology becomes more empowering students will be able to construct their own VR materials/environments, developing a literacy of the new medium that empowers them to fully comprehend its power and limitations, and embedded notions of manipulation and control of the medium by designers and developers.

There is also a strong need to educators to define models of good practice with VR in regard to instructional design, pedagogy, and the evaluation of learning outcomes. Is it, for example, easy (or appropriate) to translate existing 'good teaching' models from the classroom into a VR equivalent, or does the use of multi-sensory media demand new pedagogical models? In this regard, the professional group agreed that the focus of the educational use of VR should be on providing students with a broader range of developmental experiences, or applying existing knowledge to new contexts, rather that on using it as a medium for delivering 'routine' content i.e., the medium should be used for its power as a multi-sensory medium to enhance the curriculum, rather than replace existing media forms such as film and textbooks.

The question is then how will teachers develop the knowledge and skills to be able to do these things? How will teacher training have to adapt to this challenge? Currently, Teacher Education is having great difficulty addressing related issues from 'basic' forms of ICT, such as multimedia and online environments. Virtual reality environments present a further level of concern because they are not yet routinely used in education, and especially not in Teacher Education, yet are increasingly being used in a variety of applications outside of Education – such as in Museums. Given the reluctance of many educators to develop extensive ICT competencies, there may be a need to explicitly include material on virtual learning environment design (including VR) in Teacher Education programmes. There is a clear need for teachers to understand the technology they work with in order to make effective educational use of it – Shulman's notion of Knowledge Bases for Teaching provide a clear rationale for such an approach. Similarly, recent work on teacher cognition has demonstrated its situated and contextual nature, and implies that teachers need a diverse range of knowledge from different domains in order to be effective teachers. Further support for this position comes from the 'out of field' problem experienced by teachers – where they are least effective teachers in areas with which they are least familiar (such as the use of technology, and its educational application). It is therefore important for teacher educators to explicitly scaffold the development of teachers' understandings of the relationships between pedagogy and technology. And in particular the development of pedagogical content knowledge that bridges both domains, so that teachers can both understand, and make effective use of, technology for a diverse range of educational purposes.

4. CONCERNS

One potential concern held by the group is that the large investment needed to make quality VR might lead to the selective representation of ideas and understandings through the wide scale dissemination of commercial products, rather than a representative sampling such as might be produced by educators. It was felt that more empowering technology, when it emerges, might help to address this issue. There is, however, considerable concern that the high quality of commercial products might be difficult for educators to match, and given the sensory nature of VR, might lead to products that children would find unappealing.

An additional concern may be that children become confused about the blurred boundaries of reality and VR. However this might serve as a starting point for a critical discussion on representations of reality in general: how real or objective are the news programs we are exposed to, and the implicit manipulation of all media forms.

88

Needed: New Indicators of Success
Working Group 3.1

Chair: Doug Brown (UK)
Rapporteur: Mike Kendall (UK)
Participants: Tim Denning (UK), Jenny Filsell (AU), Michelle Selinger (UK)

Keywords: economy, government, national programmes, policy, standards

Abstract: Current indicators of success for ICT tend to focus on hardware, infrastructure and traditional measures of performance, linked to literacy and numeracy. The success of public ICT investment by government utilises such measures. Globally, current evidence does not suggest a significant impact. If investment is to continue, new indicators of success need to be realised, drawing upon new understandings of learning and what constitutes basic literacy and competence. IFIP could play a significant role in such developments.

1. NEW EDUCATIONAL VALUES

Government investment in educational ICT has been increased over the last few years in many parts of the world. This investment is based on the belief that 'computers are a good thing' and will increase the success of individual students and whole education systems, contributing to overall economic and social successes. This investment is bringing with it increasing challenges to demonstrate a clear return on the investment when budgets and politicians are subject to many competing demands, and the evidence of impact upon the traditional indicators of success is not readily available. If this is the case, are the indicators measuring the right things, and would they be the same across nations? The diversity of nations in itself provides a greater challenge, and impetus to reach consensus on indicators of success, identifying valid measures. The indicators should be appropriate for the information economy and the knowledge society. Are the current indicators and measures appropriate, and if not what else should be considered and are they enough to cover all cultural contexts? Should the measures be based on an agreed framework of skills, understanding and knowledge that is right for the individual and collectively by societies? Should they be based on a broader framework of indicators of success for the impact of ICT on learning, building on the ideas of the four pillars of education proposed by the Delors Commission for UNESCO (UNESCO 1996)

The political, economic, cultural and educational values and context of the state, community and individuals impact significantly on the development of indicators of success. Within the UK, the heavy emphasis on standards requires indicators to be validated by national tests and quantitative data; qualitative data is less influential. For other countries this may not be a requirement. A UK Department for Education report (DfES 2000) used data from the external inspection reports of schools to provide evidence illustrating a significant impact on the results in national tests for 11 year old students when the ICT resources and teaching were of high quality. In Chile ICT is a key part of broadly based educational reform inculcating creative thinking and problem solving (Luz 2000) with overall social cohesion and development objectives. Clearly, the impact on an industrial economy will be different to the impact on an agricultural or knowledge economy. For each of these there may be differing indicators of success. Nonetheless, in confronting the diverse challenges of each and every society and its economy, learning with and through ICT has the potential to increase access to learning, to accelerate progression with learning and to create new learning opportunities.

Learning is being transformed in the context of a changing world. ICT is a catalyst and provides different, varied and new building blocks for scaffolding learning. Unfortunately current international indicators tend to measure infrastructure. For example, OECD reports compare countries by numbers of computers and Internet connections for schools. Although they continue to provide contributory or proxy indicators, such as levels of collective and individual access to a range of ICT in and out of school for students, staff and the wider community. Indicators of success need to move from solely referencing the provision of the technology infrastructure itself. A key task for school systems is to realise a range of indicators of success and progress within generic frameworks, such as the UNESCO/IFIP publication *Information and Communications Technology in Secondary Education, A curriculum for Schools* (2000).

2. THE FOUR PILLARS OF EDUCATION

The UNESCO (1996) report of the International (Delors) Commission on Education for the Twenty-first Century *Learning, the Treasure Within*, identified "... learning throughout life [as] the heartbeat of life..." as one keys of the twenty-first century. The Four Pillars of Education are the basis of the whole report, learning to know, learning to do, learning to live together and learning to be. The existence of such widely reported and acknowledged principles for learning offers a basis on which to build a series of indicators of success for the impact of ICT on learning and the management of learning.

> Learning to know, by combining a sufficiently broad general knowledge with the opportunity to work in depth on a small number of subjects. This also means learning to learn, so as to benefit from the opportunities education provides throughout life.
>
> Learning to do, in order to acquire not only an occupational skill but also, more broadly, the competence to deal with many situations and work in teams. It also means learning to do in the context of young peoples' various social and work experiences which may be informal, as a result of the local or national context, or formal, involving courses, alternating study and work.
>
> Learning to live together, by developing an understanding of other people and an appreciation of interdependence – carrying out joint projects and learning to manage conflicts – in a spirit of respect for the values of pluralism, mutual understanding and peace.
>
> Learning to be, so as better to develop one's personality and be able to act with ever greater autonomy, judgment and personal responsibility. In that connection, education must not disregard any aspect of a person's potential: memory, reasoning, aesthetic sense, physical capacities and communication skills.

3. NEW INDICATORS OF SUCCESS ARE NEEDED

Formal education systems tend to emphasise the acquisition of knowledge to the detriment of other types of learning; but it is vital now to conceive education in a more encompassing fashion. Such a vision should inform and guide future educational reforms and policy, in relation both to contents and to methods." (UNESCO, 1996)

The framework of the four pillars of education provides an opportunity to move from narrow 'learning to do' indicators to a recognition of broadening perspectives on competencies. The information economy and knowledge society requires digital, informational and critical literacy, building upon traditional literacy and numeracy and extending these indicators as they may currently be constraining rather than enabling change.

The requirements of industry and commerce go beyond basic ICT skills; they demand a number of 'soft competences' or behavioural skills such as being analytical, creative, and flexible. Employers look for leadership qualities, communication, planning and organisational skills, a commitment to excellence, an ability to work collaboratively and a strong professional attitude, which includes a willingness, and ability to continue to learn. Schools need to start to prepare students, so that at each stage of education and at entry to the workplace these skills are established making students employable and able to contribute effectively to society from the outset of their careers.

Additionally curricula need to adjust to the Information and Knowledge Economy. Indicators that this is not happening are witnessed in the ICT skills industry where there is an international skills shortage and in response vendor programmes are entering into the upper secondary and vocational educational sectors. The Cisco Networking Academy programme is one example of this. Students work on an instructor led e-learning curriculum with hands on practical sessions to teach them how to install, maintain and troubleshoot computer networks. The programme is taught in over 120 countries world-wide and involves over 200,000 students

The challenge will be to develop new approaches to assessment that are sensitive to the needs of lifelong learners and employment in the 21st century and that recognise and reward progress in learning. The work of Nicholson and White (2001) identifies the requirement to design learning environments such that the learner develops the ability to handle 'fuzzy' contexts "...those which do not have a well articulated knowledge base, a clear solution, a best strategy or a readily available basis for decision making." As Delors identified, "...it is vital now to conceive education in a more encompassing fashion." The future success of societies will depend on levering the intellectual capital of its people, which of course you can do without ICT. Hence we need to identify indicators of success that identify the contribution of ICT. Such indicators will ask questions of the contribution of ICT as a catalyst to assist acceleration, freeing teachers and learners from a focus on lower order skills. Students and school staff will require the tools and environment for learning.

So the need is to address both the learner and the teacher.

Little research has yet been done:

- On the influence of new information and communication technologies on learning
- And more specifically on the support they provide to teaching and the teacher
- And on the assistance they provide to a student in the learning situation.

It could be interesting to raise some questions about the nature and the extent of technological change on the subject one is teaching, on the primacy of methods over content, of the real implications of technology on pedagogy. Developing research on these questions appears urgent, especially the consequences of technological change on knowledge acquisition.

Traditionally assigned the task of transmitting knowledge, teachers who are deeply committed to the technological revolution are today faced with more and more wide ranging demands; they must or should be able to:

- Have knowledge at their fingertips
- Create their own professional approach
- Be capable of consulting research
- Awaken a critical sense
- Complete and sometimes replace the parental role
- Guarantee equity within the education system
- Transmit social values
- Supervise student projects
- Contribute to the production of tools, reports
- Contribute to the training of colleagues
- Be capable of doing original research
- Be open to permanent self-improvement (UNESCO 2001).

One of the indicators of a successful teacher would be a teacher who could incorporate the above in their work.

Our current challenge is to ensure we have success indicators for the more recently valued learning's such as collaborative learning, self-managed learning and meta-cognitive reflection; abilities such as problem solving, and developing concentration and memory skills and the ability to think; dispositions such as interdependence and global identity. Research such as that of Cuttance, AU, developing tools to examine cognitive and affective learning outcomes in technology rich and constructivist classrooms needs to underpin such indicators for success.

When considering the above, the group were conscious that we were quite small and only represented two countries. However we do feel that we have identified some key issues for further debate. IFIP could play a key part in this debate and should look to their current working group structure to support this. We would propose that each working group considers the indicators of success when discussing other topics and prepares one paragraph per conference, which can be collected, for producing a larger report in the future. Thus the Open IFIP Conference on Social, Ethical and Cognitive Issues of Informatics and ICT should identify how we would judge if ICT has been beneficial in this area and produce a brief summary statement on this. Previous work by IFIP produced 'success stories' which demonstrate effective practice. The evidence gathering proposed above could lead to a similar publication to reach a wide-ranging audience.

What is also clear is that public schools systems will become even more accountable and – partly because of the necessary high investment – ICT will be under scrutiny more than most. We need to have evidence of success to persuade the policy makers that what often currently is a 'leap of faith' is worth continued investment and political commitment because ICT really is a 'good thing'.

REFERENCE

DfES (2000) *A Preliminary Report for the DfEE on the Relationship Between ICT and Primary School Standards*. London.

Nicholson, P. and White, G. (2001) *Teaching for Quality Learning Online: A layered design model for higher-order thinking*. Paper at WCCE2001, Copenhagen, Denmark.

Luz, S. M. (2000) *Chilean Experience – Overview*. Paper Chile 2000, The Bookmark of the School of the Future.

UNESCO (1996) *Learning: The Treasure Within (Delores Report)*. Geneva.

UNESCO (2000) *Information and Communications Technology in Secondary Education, A curriculum for Schools*. IFIP TC3, Geneva.

UNESCO (2001) *Winds of change in the teaching profession*. French National Commission for UNESCO, Geneva.

89

Distributed Expertise in Teaching

Working Group 3.2

Chair: Lillian Cassel (US)
Rapporteur: Deepak Kumar (US)
Participants: Anneke E. N. Hacquebard (NL), Richard J. LeBlanc (US), Jacob-Steen Madsen (DK), Claus Poulsen (DK), Joseph Regev (IL)

Keywords: teacher collaboration, creativity, teaching materials, website

Abstract: Given the rapid advances in various disciplines it is sometimes difficult for faculty who regularly teach core courses to stay up-to-date and to effectively incorporate the recent advances into a course curriculum. Sometimes faculty are required to teach courses outside of their area of expertise especially computer science. The paper discusses how distributed resources can be set up for teachers using website portals. Updated textbooks or web-based text resources are very useful as well as tutorials, exercises, suggestions for further reading, notes on learning styles and educational organisations. A special added value is a list of available experts wish can be contacted, an electronic forum for further talk and discussion. Big questions are who will contribute to expert portals? Are teachers interested in co-operation?

1. INTRODUCTION

Given the rapid advances in various disciplines it is sometimes difficult for faculty who regularly teach core courses to stay up-to-date and to effectively incorporate the recent advances into a course curriculum. In most instances it is to be assumed that faculty expertise will not cover all topics that form the core of a course. In fact, in a number of institutions, it is typically the case that faculty are required to teach courses outside of their area of expertise. This has especially been true for a number of computer science courses where faculty often are required to teach courses outside of their area of research.

In such instances faculty tend to rely on available texts and the course is defined by the content and organisation of the text. Consequently, the success of the course is mostly dependent on the quality of the text and the ability of the instructor to effectively teach from it. Considering the time required to produce and distribute a textbook, it is not surprising that many texts are hopelessly outdated. Moreover, faculty who rely heavily on a text may be hesitant to abandon it, however old.

Modern communication and resource sharing mechanisms make possible new ways of assuring high quality education at locations where faculty expertise does not cover all topics appropriate to core courses. This professional group will explore the possibilities of distributed expertise applied in support of high quality course offerings. For example, in the case where the course is of a traditional format, local faculty with complete control over the content of the course, assignments, and expected performance will benefit from the availability of materials developed by others and from the support of experts in topic areas of the course.

2. WHAT IS DISTRIBUTED EXPERTISE?

We define distributed expertise to be a resource for teachers in a particular subject area that can be used to provide high quality education. We envision such a resource to be accessible via a web portal that provides an entry into pedagogical materials that may be of use to various teachers. While the entry point to this resource is a web site, we envision it to contain at least the following components.

- Tutorials on topics related to the subject.
- A repository of teaching materials appropriate for each topic, to include lecture notes, illustrated examples, exercises, suggestions for further reading, possible examination questions.
- Strategies for addressing learning styles, classroom formats, educational organisation.
- A list of suitable texts for each topic.
- A list of available experts who would be willing to consult on a given topic.
- A forum for continuing discussion
- A search facility for locating specific materials at the portal and beyond.
- Links to related information.

In short, a distributed expertise resource helps connect faculty with usable content, teaching methodologies, and contact with experts in the field. It is important to emphasise that providing a distributed resource may not be just a matter of providing adequate content knowledge. It is equally important to provide guidelines for presentation and various ways to organise learning experiences in the context of a specific topic.

3. ORGANISING DISTRIBUTED EXPERTISE

Creating a distributed expertise resource should necessarily follow a thoughtful process that clearly identifies the structure of the main portal and how it incorporates the above facilities. There already exist several web sites that provide content that would fall in any of the above categories, it should be noted that the primary goal here is to provide support for teachers. Hence, such a resource would inherently differ from the now prevalent distance learning portals. We do recognise that there will be some overlaps and in some cases distributed expertise portals may very well serve the same role as distance-learning sites. However, the primary targets for delivery of distributed expertise portals will be teachers.

One could begin creating a distributed expertise portal by planning an exhaustive coverage on a particular subject. However, our experience suggests that teachers will be better served if such portals focussed on immediate needs. In researching this issue for the case of a core computer science course (Computer Organisation and Architecture), we have discovered that such a resource should begin by performing a study of the prevailing practice and identifying the burning pedagogical issues. Providing distributed expertise in support of the identified weakness should be the top priority though gradually, it would inevitably be the case that such a resource would grow to incorporate a nearly complete coverage of the field of study.

A survey of the prevailing practise also yields a lot of useful information about the subject that should be incorporated in the portal. This provides a teacher, perusing the portal, with a good sense of the state-of-the-art in addition to what may already be available. For instance, by conducting a survey of Computer Organisation and Architecture course, we were able to gather information about various texts, teaching environments, available software, lab toolkits, etc. These will naturally form an integral component of the portal.

3.1 Enlisting (distributed) experts

We recognise that the key component of the proposed portal is the availability of subject experts. Experts will be needed to provide tutorials and related content. Experts may also volunteer to be available to teachers (via e-mail or other means of communication) for assistance. Experts may also be required to maintain parts of the course content and to keep them updated.

Experts may not be restricted to subject matter experts. We recognise that other faculty colleagues could play the role of an expert. Such colleagues may be locally available, in some instances, or accessible via electronic communication. experts.

3.2 Distributed expertise and textbooks

Most textbooks do a decent job of presenting most of the content well. By creating a distributed expertise portal, we are not necessarily discounting the usefulness and value of available texts. However, given the long production cycle of texts, it is to be expected that, in rapidly advancing fields, texts will be unable to provide an up-to-date coverage. Yet, we suggest that, in order to address this issue, authors of texts rethink of new ways of supporting their texts that could be facilitated by the creation of a distributed expertise resource.

How to get the true experts to participate? Can we ask people to give us their educational material as is and we put it on the web and make it available to others? This could provide inspiration as well as real use. But what about intellectual property rights? Within the university, faculty protect their property. How do we deal with conflicting opinions among experts; recognise minority opinions in particular? We need to list of different practices, not best practices because you cannot say what is best. There is not likely to be one way that is best in all contexts.

Is the subject topic the problem or is it how to present and organise the learning experience? When we talk of resources, we must include other dimensions besides content. Points of discussion included:

- What is distributed expertise?
- Web-based resource that reaches out to real people. Contact with experts.
- How is this organised?
- Content or teaching methods?
- Start with weak areas through maybe several experts contributing.

Before starting, what sort of educational organisation are we supporting – traditional classrooms; competence based environments; teacher as guide or coach? One guide is probably not enough; could distributed expertise can help in that sort of situation? Subject, methodology, educational organisation dimensions are all relevant.

An instructor who is not an expert will find a book or approach from someone they know; take some as given and fill in as they can. With supplemental resources that provided experiences, projects, etc. To produce useful things, someone must provide an architecture for a course. Education is now very fractionalised. We propose a learning process not having one teacher, but *a lot of experts* connected to the students more directly. For instance in a four-campus university, all the faculty are there and are qualified, but have to deliver courses or parts of courses to various campuses. Someone locally oversees the overall course, and is repsonsible for assessment, but the experts write the exam questions.

3.3 Other dimensions besides content

More collaborative way of learning and teaching also must be part of our work. How to support the authors of text books? What other materials should there be to help teachers that may feel uncomfortable with the topic areas? Is the subject topic the problem or is it how to present and organise the learning experience? When we talk of resources, we must include other dimensions besides content.

The key may be in Web pages. Can we persuade different experts who have web pages to list where questions can be posted? There could be question/answer sections, and room for evolving discussion. But would this need a moderator to be sure that the questions get answers, and must there be control the number of people who have access? Would an expert be able to give enough time?

3.4 The community is the expert

Perhaps we should explore the open source model as an example. The community is the 'expert' which smoothes out the load. Can we formulate the questions well enough to use this model? Experts are responsible for maintaining their own area of expertise. An open source community is focused on some artefact. There are usually some reasonably small group of people who moderate the contributions and form groups around a very identifiable topic, with branches out of the centre for sub topics.

There are professional societies, such as IFIP. for the various parts of the discipline. They hold educational seminars as well as conferences. The people who primarily teach are not always connected to the people who do research in the topic. Workshops and tutorials are held at the research conference where the people who teach and need more content help are often not present.

There are international and national teacher support organisations, such as IFIP TC3, ACM SIGs, IEEE TCs, AAAI. Teachers need an interchange of experiences related to how to conduct classes and use learning styles in the classroom. There needs to be more communication between local teachers who are working on similar things but not talking to each other. If local groups do not function, the bigger scale will not. Would people use distributed expertise?

4. ARE TEACHERS INTERESTED?

Who will benefit? Different teachers in different countries have a range of concerns In Denmark and the Netherlands, teachers at high school are subject trained, but not taught teaching. Would such a resource lead to one way communication.? Is there a lack of interest in new ways of doing things? Do older teachers have problems while newer ones have more requirements. In Israel, teachers in remote places may know very little about the subject and need help to get onto their feet. There is a global shortage of teachers in many fields. Trying to keep up with a changing field when teachers are already very busy is hard.

How can an open community be organised? Will 20% of the people (experts?) provide 80% of the answers?

90

Factors Influencing Implementation of ICT in Higher Education

Working Group 3.2

Chair: Matti Sinko (FI)
Rapporteur: Peter J. Dekker (NL)
Participants: Palle Bendsen (DK), Jan Cern (CA), Bas Cordewener (NL), Halfdan Eika (DK), Ulla Klimt (DK), Rolf Larsen (NO), Jane Murmann (DK), Pia Thomsen (DK)

Keywords: implementation, higher education, scaling up, support, standardisation

Abstract: This report describes first the factors, which have an influence on the implementation of ICT in higher education (HE). We clustered them in four groups: global challenges, technological promises and imperatives; pedagogical and subject specific factors; obstacles and restrictions of using ICT; and motivational and political issues. Then we identified five means to implement ICT. These are: demystification of ICT, its role and benefits in education; project management issues; standardisation; institutional commitment and support; and scaling up new enhanced ICT supported practices developed in pilot projects or in research experiments.

1. FACTORS THAT INFLUENCE IMPLEMENTATION

It is a challenge for HE to make teaching and learning meet the growing demands that are placed by global as well as local developments. There is the challenge in meeting the needs, desires and aspirations of our students to be able to educate themselves to become professionals capable of facing the challenges of tomorrow's world. There are also justified needs identified and policies developed by national authorities, education institutions to provide more effective, efficient, and appropriate education based on new research findings and developments. We strongly believe that new technologies will open new avenues to better learning, necessary for overcoming these challenges. But we also recognise that it is an unsurpassed call for our professional communities to develop concepts, models and applications that will fully exploit these potentials.

In the group introductory notes, from Matti Sinko and Petra Fisser, a number of factors were listed that may impact on the use of ICT in HE (Sinko and Lehtinen 1999, Sinko 2001).

1.1 Global challenges, technological promises and imperatives

There are a number of global factors, which go beyond any single institute or university to influence. Global trends underpin and influence the strategic choices all HE institutions are currently facing. These may also be used as arguments to pursue other agendas. Nevertheless global developments cannot or should not be overlooked when analysing the factors influencing the uptake of new technologies in HE.

The following issues among others were addressed when discussing and designing successful implementation of ICT in HE education. These were: increasing complexity of issues HE is facing; the need for improved pedagogy enhanced with the use of ICT to cope with the complex learning challenges; increased demands of efficiency and effectiveness; the need to serve a larger number of students with varying needs; the general impact of proliferation and penetration of ICT throughout society; and the potential and problems of improved access to education resources for enhancing democracy, strengthening sound social fabric and ethical conduct in increasingly complex societies.

Undoubtedly new technologies themselves bring enormous challenges to HE in providing new exciting opportunities to address in new ways pertinent challenges of teaching and learning. Technology in itself poses a tremendous challenge to educational institutions in how to learn to master and develop the technological domain itself. We should pay attention to issues like: the role of ICT literacy in the curriculum; the role of new technologies in the strategies and policies of HE institutions; and the commitments of HE institutions in providing ICT literate graduates in general and in teacher education in particular.

1.2 Motivational and political issues

Motivational issues need to be looked at from a number of viewpoints of various interest groups. The motives of institutions include: economic factors; striving for excellence, improved competitiveness and better service for students; changing political demands, policy requirements, new agendas and preferences expressed by various external stakeholders; improving collaboration and networking with working life and the surrounding community for the institutional needs as well as for student carriers enhancement; and internal expectations of students and staff. The motives of staff to start using ICT include: a desire for professional development, to perform better, and for better instructional environment; institutional policy decisions from management; requests from students; encouragement and support by or pressures from colleagues; and fears of becoming unpopular or even redundant. The motives of students include; improved employability; increased value to learning processes; added value to competence; a need for flexibility and efficiency; and a desire for getting the cutting edge education.

1.3 Pedagogical and subject specific factors

Choosing technologies to support teaching and learning should be determined by their appropriateness, which may vary according to the needs of teachers, learners and the subjects respectively. We have to consider carefully why, when, where and how to put ICT in place; to analyse, what is proper ICT support in each subject domain in each historic situation; to analyse and understand customer needs e.g. on going virtual, providing courses at distance; and to understand the impact of intensified use of ICT in research on the increased need for using ICT in teaching and learning of those areas of research.

1.4 Obstacles and restrictions of using ICT

Here are listed some of the obstacles making the use of ICT difficult or inappropriate: a lack of support to staff or students, of time (of staff and students), of competence among staff, of appropriate technology, hardware and software, lack of funding, and of collaboration among staff and between departments. Further obstacles include:: reluctance of staff or students towards using ICT; fear of increasing workload; inappropriate physical surroundings for new uses; legal restrictions, e.g. in applying new pedagogically more relevant types of assessing student performance; unsolved copyrights; text-based ICT compared to more familiar oral communication; and poorly implemented accountability towards society, policy makers and students.

2. MEANS TO INFLUENCE IMPLEMENTATION

Five means that could be beneficial to take into account, when implementing ICT in HE were identified.

2.1 Demystifying ICT

Putting ICT in place in any organisation means always uncertainty or crisis within the organisation. Thus there are often unjustified promises. Educational institutions are no exception. ICT is supposed to make teaching or learning easier and more effective. There is however little evidence that applications of ICT are easy solutions for learning, or that using them would lead to lighter workloads for staff or students.

Many projects fail because staff have not been properly prepared to accept changes. Careful attention needs to be paid to 'selling' new ICT based systems and practices to staff. The argument often used, increased efficiency, is seldom true in a short run. Another expectation is greater effectiveness, which also may be true only in the longer term. Users may be easily misled to anticipate unjustified short-term benefits such as their work made easier, quicker, and more attractive. Much effort is put in implementing ICT because it is generally – and rightly so – believed that education can be improved through elaborated use of educational ICT tools. This means that the underlying rationale in implementing ICT should have focus on making teaching and learning more effective.

Suggestions:

- Promises should be realistic and truthful – do not feed the myth that ICT makes teaching or learning easier or cheaper.
- Efforts (time, energy, money) invested are probably not validated by rapidly improved results, but the alternative (doing nothing) might cost even more, if the competitive edge will be lost.
- The idea is that ICT in education makes the students – and for that matter the teachers as well – more employable.

2.2 Project management

Projects are perhaps the most typical way of implementing change in education. There is a rich literature on project management issues. Yet we felt it useful to emphasise the importance of good project management as a success factor in either designing new applications or implementing new practices. There is some evidence that neither teaching staff nor managerial people of an educational institution are best to implement ICT development. Teachers have little project managerial expertise. And project management has to be clearly separated from normal institutional management. This is difficult to achieve, if the stakeholders are running the project. Stakeholders should some say in developing their own working environment, but it calls for a clear definition of responsibilities and roles.

Suggestions:

- The project manager should not personally be a stakeholder or have potentially conflicting interests with the possible outcomes of the project. The project manager should be accountable for the professional project management only.
- The educational and technical expertise for running faculty projects should be separated from the project management role.
- The success criteria for the project should from the first include a sustainability model and an exploitation plan ensuring scaling up the results.
- Top-down approach has its strengths, one being the commitment of the policymakers, and the management level. It works if everyone from the beginning shares the need for change.
- Bottom-up approach, however, often yields better results in capitalising the personal motivation of all involved and thus resulting in better commitment in results as well.
- Most probably mixing both approaches is necessary. Furthemore using a network-based collaborative approach does not limit the resources to existing organisational hierarchies.
- Put effort into project visibility with good publicity. This makes participants proud of participating, with a positive impact on the project, their self-esteem and professional development.

2.3 Standardisation

Networking is both a means for development and implementation as well as for normal, daily operational procedures. One hindrance of fully capitalising the potential of networking is the lack of standards enabling smooth flow and use of resources accumulated in the nodes and niches of the net. The education sector in general and academia in particular has been reluctant to respond positively to addressing the complex issues of standardisation. If the academic community does not commit itself on all levels in harmonising its way of describing, defining and presenting data, it will exclude itself from fully exploiting the potential of networking.

There is some consensus on standards on hardware and networks. Standardisation of presenting data, including indexing educational content, needs more attention. One problem is their rapidly becoming outdated and needing to be updated before they have been consolidated.

Suggestions:

- More resources and higher priority for standardisation in educational policy making on national and on institutional level, and in professional communities, like IFIP TC3.
- Stimulate and encourage organisations to use and comply with the standards when ever available.
- Designers of ICT-based learning materials should commit to comply with standards.
- When working on innovative projects, encourage such projects to keep in mind the need standardisation for a successful scaling-up.

2.4 Institutional commitment and support

When implementing ICT, organising the support of the people who are going to use ICT is important. Implementing ICT is in a way organising the support. And this support has to be functioning during the implementation period, and afterwards when the implementation has been incorporated into normal life. Without sufficient support it is likely that the use of ICT will decrease. Two areas are important: the support itself and the organisation of the support.

The organisation should provide a certain level of technical support for teachers using ICT; teachers are not technicians, and lack of technical support will diminish their confidence with the hardware.

Suggestions:

- The management has to allocate sufficient time for project participants. Projects should not be done on extra hours; the results become dependent on the efforts of only enthusiastic staff.
- The management has to provide technical and methodological support, at initial and in-depth levels. Resource allocation between institutional level and departmental level should be balanced.
- Teachers need training in using ICT. Training should be differentiated according to the needs and skills level of users.
- When offering training, the staff development policy of the institution should be kept in mind. Training should be supported by incentives and should be part of a personal development plan.
- Using a top-down approach (everyone has to meet the formulated goal) is an effective form of implementation Resistance is likely to occur. But there is growing support for the top-down approach because of the need for strong leadership; sometimes things have to be changed in spite of the feelings of the people involved.

2.5 Scaling up new enhanced ICT supported practice

Consolidating and scaling up new enhanced ICT supported practices developed in pilot projects or in research experiments has a growing importance as it has become clear that the record of successful educational ICT projects is not outstanding. Indeed few projects can be considered successful if evaluated by criteria measuring consolidation and measuring the success of being disseminated to other institutions. ICT implementations often have an impact on many processes within the organisation. Therefore changes in all the processes should be anticipated and incorporated in the implementation plan. ICT projects have the tendency to gradually or drastically change the culture of an organisation.

Conditions for scaling up are better if ICT projects are undertaken in collaboration with other organisations. Problems and solutions may be shared in the network of collaborative partners, sharing already being part of scaling up process itself. Workshops, presentations etc. are an often-used ways of scaling up the results of project (teachers telling each other their experiences). There is, however, experience that the effect of this type of scaling up will level out. It is also agreed that is difficult to transfer project findings from one situation to another. But this should not be as big a problem for projects that focus on developing content that can be used independently. It is found, however, that adopting new practices developed elsewhere is not easy, because of the 'not-invented-here' syndrome. This could be an indication that running projects should not be the only way of trying to implement ICT.

Collis and Moonen (2001) have developed a model which describes factors that predict whether an individual teacher will start using ICT in a new situation. The so-called *4-E model* hypothesises that an individual likelihood of using application can be described by four variables.

- Environment: the institution's profile with respect to technology use
- Education effectiveness: gaining from the technology use
- Ease of use: ease of difficulty in making use of technology
- Engagement: personal engagement about technology use for learning-related purposes.

According to the model these features are expressed as vectors. The sum of these vectors – education effectiveness, ease of use, and engagement – can be interpreted as the likelihood-of-use vector. When this hypothetical vector sum is high enough, then the individual is likely to make use of the network application in his or her own situation. The height of the threshold is critical; environmental conditions can lower it.

Suggestions:

- Collaboration only starts when all parties involved need to have the means and the reasons to collaborate. To share content is not enough of a reason.
- For scaling up successfully all suggestions mentioned earlier (regarding project management, standardisation, institutional commitment) apply. Scaling up adds complexity to both co-ordination and collaboration by implementation process partners.
- Consider establishing an umbrella organisation on a national level, steered by, and working for, all HE institutes, aiming at successful ICT infrastructure and implementation of ICT. This organisation should encourage collaboration, standardisation and managerial professionalism. It may be positioned as a catalysing force for knowledge sharing and innovation on a super-institutional level.

REFERENCES

Collis, B. and Moonen, J. (2001) *Flexible learning in a digital world: Experiences and expectations*. Kogan Page Limited, London.

Sinko, M. (2001) Implications of 'going virtual' to higher education. In *Desafios 2001. Actas da II conferéncia international de technologies da informacão e comunicacão na educacão. Centro de competéncia nónio século XXI da Universidade do Minho*, Portugal, pp. 87-94.

Sinko, M. and Lehtinen, E. (1999) *The Challenges of ICT in Finnish Education*. Atena Kustannus, Juva. [http://www.sitra.fi/english/index_publications.html].

91

Authoring Pedagogically Meaningful Content for Networked Learning

Working Group 3.3

Chair: Jari Multisilta (FI)
Rapporteur: Pentti Hietala (FI)
Participants: Ole Djurhuus (DK), Bernie Dodge (US), Tony Fisher (UK), Birthe Gawinski (DK), Ole Jorn (DK), Harri Ketamo (FI), Jens Paludan Melson (DK), John C. Miller (US), Preben Nielsen (DK), Alfonso Quarati (I), Ruth Reiz (IL), Deonne Smith (AU), Inge Sonne (DK)

Keywords: learning materials, interactive, learner-centred learning, distance learning, pedagogy

Abstract: This professional group set out to approach this topic from three perspectives: from underlying pedagogical principles, from design models for the designer, and from the tools and platforms that the designer had available for the implementation. The group as a whole concluded that although the design process should be theory informed, there is no one theory, no one process model, or no one implementation platform inherently better than others. Finally, the group identified several qualities for the design process and implementation tools.

1. BACKGROUND

Networked learning environments are widely considered to be a sophisticated and effective way to distribute distance learning. They may replace not just traditional modes of distance education, but also courses previously offered primarily face to face. The importance of network-based learning has dramatically increased as life-long learning and learning at the workplace has become as important as formal education within school institutions. This places new demands for the design of networked learning environments.

However, research has shown that a much instructional design practice has evolved as a procedural and media-production craft rather than a process grounded in pedagogical theories. This trend seems to continue to be the case in networked learning. Many of the Internet-based learning environments have been designed and implemented ignoring well-known pedagogical approaches facilitating effective teaching and learning.

Lack of appropriate tools for a non-professional in computing was long a major problem for the design of Internet-based learning environments. Now, there is commercially available software to support the implementation of online courses, many in the public domain. Some of these are so called integrated authoring tools that provide a large suite of pre-programmed facilities for the designer to choose from. In most cases, however, while such software provides support for the teaching process, that is, for the administration of the students and the courses, what is missing is the support for designing pedagogically meaningful content. The content may be created also using standard HTML Editors.

In this professional group we discussed the process of authoring online educational materials in an attempt to outline methods for designing and implementing pedagogically meaningful content for networked learning environments.

2. GROUP WORK

The group approached the topic from three perspectives. The first sub-group discussed the underlying theoretical principles: what does it mean if we have 'pedagogically meaningful learning content'? And what does this implicate for the design and implementation process? The second sub-group considered the issue of detailed design models for the preparation of instructional materials. Our third sub-group dealt with the implementation issues: the languages, tools and platforms that could be used in crafting the learning content onto the Web. The work of each sub-group was intertwined with the others, so after summing up and consolidating a common view on each issue emerged.

3. PEDAGOGICAL ISSUES AND BEST PRACTISES

We discussed best practices and the notion of 'pedagogically meaningful content'. Four important issues arose in the discussions.

The first was that all *learners* bring differing experiences, knowledge, skills and understanding to potential learning situations. They make sense of the things they learn through the filter of their current understandings of the world. They also have differing cognitive skills, learning styles, and focus of control preferences, i.e., some students learn best when the learning is scaffolded in a very logical and sequential manner and others learn best when they can have more control over how the information is accessed and engaged with.

An appropriate pedagogy provides multiple entry points to engage and challenge diverse groups of learners. The interactive didactic program with multiple entry-point-access in course A, must ensure the acquisition of common knowledge and skills (a shared repertoire) needed to create collaborative learning process in a course B, based on course A. A goal-free evaluation of course A must be developed to spot content-related knowledge and skills presupposed in course B. A theory of educative institutional frame is relevant to a pedagogical theory of learning-process. The institution must specify and implement its requirements for pedagogical progression in learning.

The second issue was that we need a *meta-pedagogical theoretical frame* incorporating the qualities of both the 'objectivist' and the 'constructivist' approach. Opposing objectivists and constructivists in a negative-positive polarised schema of summed combinations of qualities within a continuum is at its best a pedagogically simplified illustration. However, taken at face-value it leads, through its awe-inspiring terminology and authoritativeness, to a pseudo-theoretical discussion that reveals partisan intentions, thus biasing the debate on the relation between learning theory and best practices among experienced teachers, forcing them either to corral or bandwagon. Summing qualities in a non-ordered model illustrates the danger of proliferating relations that invalidates the model's controllability and applicability. The use of 'continuum' as a term illustrates the danger of an approximate terminology in the pedagogical discourse that might alienate an important part of the target group with most experience of systematic approach and logical analysis, i.e. the teachers of exact sciences, that should be able to integrate ICT in learning/teaching. Heuristic approaches functional to the specific strategy of introducing new (ICT-adequate) parameters in education should not overshadow the question of creating a theory of pedagogical best practices.

The third crucial issue is *interactivity*. All software is interactive at some level. Pedagogically meaningful software must be interactive at the very highest level, and in many different respects. Current technology can offer a remarkable degree of interactivity, but actually providing such support to learners, and assisting them in learning to avail themselves of it, makes preparation of highly interactive materials vastly more complicated and difficult than it would be otherwise. Depending always on the particular discipline, subject and pedagogical approach, the following types of interactive support should be more or less routinely available.

- Intelligent tutor emulation, with content reflecting the particular student's current status and apparent competence level
- Complete Internet access
- Access to peers, synchronous or asynchronous as practical
- Measures of both progress made and work remaining, both on the current topic or project and in the overall course or program
- Statements of, and/or relevant questions about, pertinent general principles, to help the student comprehend the big picture even when concentrating mainly on details
- Samples of good work of the current sort, correctly solved problems of the current general type, similar enough to be helpful without admitting direct copying
- Facilities for editing, reviewing, retracing and revising earlier work
- Access to appropriate tools, such as spelling and grammar checkers and calculators
- Access to low level help, such as keyboard and mouse practice, tutorials on how to save current work, and many others.

Students often do not 'discover' available interactive support facilities on their own. Pedagogically effective software should monitor each student's use of the interactive support facilities, and then help the student who appears unaware of their availability to learn to use them. The group were not aware of any Internet-based or computer-based instructional materials which can be cited 'fully interactive'. Programs must be designed in a way that creates a possibility to choose different ways to learn. For example, programs can use 3D-virtual reality simulated environments that students can be part of and involved in.

The fourth important issue is *collaboration*. Didactic principles for collaboration in learning communities are mutual engagement, shared repertoire and activity. These principles are a way to create efficient learning, to incorporate the principles of learning communities in all aspects and dimension of the design of computer supported collaborative learning. This includes the choice and design of technology, learning-/teaching-manner and the institutional frame. A design based on these principles can intensify the collaboration, thereby engaging and motivating the student to make and maintain a learning community.

4. PROCESS MODELS AND EXISTING METHODS

We discussed the process models and existing methods for instructional design. First, we identified a set of five assumptions.

1. Pedagogically meaningful knowledge is best achieved by a constructivist approach in most situations.
2. In designing an instructional design model to author meaningful content in a networked environment, we should not tie ourselves down to the present realities of lockstep-classes and standardised testing. We should assume that learning will be more individualised and asynchronous, and less place-bound.
3. Instructional design in the broadest sense needs to include the notion of students as designers of their own learning.
4. The network brings information to learners and can help to manage multiple paths to multiple learning goals.
5. A truly effective instructional design system works at the level of whole curricula, cutting across multiple disciplines and over several years of a learner's life.

To illustrate our view on instructional design, we outlined the following principles. The design process should begin with a tentative set of learning goals that are subject to change. The instructional design process has a sequence, but each step can be revisited and the results of each step are subject to change. The process should be collaborative, with learners as active participants and co-designers. Instructional design skills are best practiced in context, and the best designers are situated and experienced in that context and content. A good learning environment is anchored in an open-ended, constructivist approach and punctuated by direct instruction when appropriate. The core of a good lesson is an open-ended problem situation with direct instruction provided for just-in-time learning. Assessment of student learning should be based on a blend of quantitative and qualitative data with some emphasis on the latter.

We considered the WebQuest approach as one expression of the principles that are key to good instructional design. We also discussed the models presented by Willis, Jonassen, Dick & Carey and ones described by McManus. We concluded none of these fulfilled our criteria for a dynamic, holistic, forward-oriented instructional design process. The creation of an alternative instructional design model however was not possible during the work period of this professional group. We also recognised the tensions involved in providing in a model, a necessarily simplified description of a complex, recursive process.

Thus we expect networked learning to play a major, and increasing, role as the learner will influence a growing part of the instructional design process, and networking will be a key instrument of this influence.

5. LANGUAGES, TOOLS AND PLATFORMS

We discussed learning management systems, existing languages and platforms for authoring learning content. The discussion led us to define the concept of learning objects. Finally, we discussed XML as a future solution for standardising the learning content. When discussing general requirements of tools or platforms in educational use, we cannot avoid the fact that the needs of educational systems differ greatly. For example, in schools usage focuses on lessons, not in the time outside school; in universities administrative support plays a greater role. So, specific requirements for learning environments cannot be given.

The most useful recommendation might arise from modularity. When platforms are built from independent modules, whose interface is defined, authors can build the platform according to their needs, using the best platform and authoring tools. Learning Management Systems are practical for delivering content for networked learning, but most important is the quality of the content. Content should be developed to take advantage of the potentials of technology. Materials should differ from the traditional way of producing books and use the possibilities offered by the technology, for example hypermedia and multimedia. A promising solution to authoring learning materials is the notion of learning objects. When using learning objects, the learning material can be seen as a collection of the best possible objects. It is not necessary that authors of the material write all the material themselves. The objects can be obtained or bought from experts, who are specialised to certain areas.

The learning objects can be seen as normal objects, labelled with certain well defined inputs, it can do, execute or play one of the well defined tasks and finally it gives a well defined output i.e. the learning object should have well defined interfaces. With such a system we can separate the course and the content and one learning object can be used in many courses. For example, ideas about triangulation (defining a point in 3D-space) can be used in a mathematics course, in a geographic course, and particularly today in the course (learning material) on mobile networks as the background for localisation services.

The learning object can be designed and implemented by using any tool or language. The learning material that is calling the learning object is responsible for ensuring that the system can run (present) the object. For example, if the learning material is web-based and the learning object is an executable file, the learning material should decide how the object is used or whether is it used at all. This gives the experts and content producers more space to produce learning objects with the most suitable tools and with the most suitable methods. This also might raise the quality of learning materials, because the learning material can be collected from the set of the learning objects and one bad object can be easily replaced with another.

To be effective, the communication of the learning objects must be defined well, and standards are needed. When calling the object, the material should know something about the object. For example there could be two types of objects: note and tasks. Note can be a picture, animation, text, sound or whatever material that do not give evaluation or other feedback about its user. Task relates feedback to material, the task can be a test or a game, but in every case it gives some evaluation about user.

It is not always realistic or possible that the learning material is produced by the individual teacher. In those cases we suggest that support teams are established at local level to help teachers produce and publish their material. The support teams should be subsidised through public financing and grants from private companies and funds.

The improving role played by XML technology in the design and development of educational material and environments, is mainly due to its essential features: XML is a meta-language through which one can define structured or semi-structured information; de-coupling content by its many possible representations; so allowing the creation of, reusable content and its personalisation independently from platform and proprietary tools constraints (it is a standard). Though these are features that apply to other application sectors, lets´examine three possible scenarios into which XML reveals its usefulness for designing of pedagogically meaningful content.

The author/teacher/expert, is free to write the educational material with their preferred editor and then through the application of simple tools transform it into XML format. One further transformation step will permit the addition of other information such as for example information relating to students' profiles or layout style. Finally the use of different stylesheets will allow the publishing of the content in the most suitable format, for example html to deliver the content via the Web or pdf to print it.

XML allows us to realise learning paths (courses), based on a possibly wide collection of educational objects, which are structured and organised with respect to the actual pedagogical needs. In an XML file it is possible to identify: which learning objects are involved in a learning path; the ways in which they are organised; the relationships that exists between them; and the particular target to which they are devoted. Through this, it is possible to automatically obtain 'tools' such as index, guided maps, navigation buttons, which will allows instant delivery of a complete course to the web.

Through the use of XML-languages (such as MathML, OpenMath), and the emerging family of related graphical tools it is possible to realise and integrate information of different domains into one educational object.

6. CONCLUSIONS

We studied the process of authoring pedagogically meaningful online educational materials. From the pedagogical view-point the four important factors are heterogeneous students, interactivity, collaboration and an adaptation of the best of different learning theories. It is important that the design is informed and grounded by theory. There are many ways to ground design principles, none of which is inherently better than other approaches.

Pedagogically meaningful material must be highly interactive and support content and constructive student collaboration. Pedagogically meaningful materials should provide multiple entry points to engage and challenge diverse groups of learners. Programs must be designed in flexible ways for learners to choose different ways to interact with the materials. The instructional design system should be designed to support the authoring of meaningful pedagogical content in a networked environment. The core of an environment is open-ended, flexible problems with just-in-time instruction. A good learning management system is important for delivering content for network learning, and the quality of the content is essential. The role of standardisation and standardised languages, such as XML, becomes more important when learning systems become more modular. Standardisation would be one milestone when making more intelligent and pedagogically meaningful learning systems.

We decided to continue the work initiated in this professional group. An email discussion list will be established and this topic will be a stream at the IFIP Open Working Conference, eTrain 2003: E-Training Practices for Professional Organisations (7.-11.7.2003, Pori, Finland).

92

ICT Based Learning Environments: What Are The Current Research Streams?

Working Group 3.3

Chair: Rosa Maria Bottino (IT)
Rapporteur: Margaret Cox (UK)
Participants: Mette Andresen (DK), Ida Binderup (DK), Harald Bjar NO), Tom Dousma (NL), Dick Owusu-Darko (UK), Katharine Hayden (US), Pateep Methakunavudhi (TH), Philip Oppenheim (DK)

Keywords: research, integration of ICT, catalyst for change, teaching, learning

Abstract: The growing use of ICT materials and tools was considered by the group in relation to key issues about how the evolving ICT based learning can be effectively integrated into different learning environment and subject areas. Participants considered three metaphors which represent the evolution of ICT based learning environments; namely, transmission, learner centred and participation. The main issues emerging from the discussion were a change in the whole learning situation (i.e., the tool, teacher, curriculum objectives and organisation of the learning process) as well as the effects and implication of factors affecting the learning environments. All these offer great opportunities and challenges which we believe requires research to establish and create a forum for a proper debate to resolve the issues concerned.

1. ICT BASED LEARNING ENVIRONMENTS

The focus of the group was on teaching and learning, concentrating on the mediation which ICT based learning systems can provide to the teaching and learning processes in the learning environment.

The professional group's work was supported by a briefing paper on the aims of the group and a background paper on advanced learning environments (Bottino 2001). The interests of the members ranged from primary to higher education, from the development of computer-based training materials to teacher education, and from the integration of pedagogical practices to the future roles of the teacher in new learning environments. These different interests led to a discussion of the perceptions of ICT based learning environments from the perspectives of the different countries of the participants and the different levels of education in which the participants were working. The purpose of this discussion was to consider the advantages and disadvantages of different learning environments, synthesizing the evolution of ICT based learning relating to three main metaphors and trying to determine the main elements characterizing this evolution.

Three metaphors were presented as a starting point for eliciting ideas about crucial issues in ICT based learning environments. These metaphors were:

1. Transmission: drill and practice, programmed learning, some web-based courses, and some computer based training courses
2. Learner centred: programming, microworlds, modelling and simulations
3. Participation: situated multi-tool system (integration of tools for different cognitive functions such as exploration, representation and communication), e.g. ICT based learning tools involving socialisation of the learner.

These metaphors can apply to the same software, for example a situated multi-tool system (participation metaphor) may also include microworlds (learner centred) and drill and practice (transmission). The discussion revealed some main elements that characterised the evolution of ICT-based education and its evolution (e.g. technological evolution, changed cognitive and pedagogical frameworks, changed role assigned to ICT-based systems in education, etc.). Three main issues emerged concerning ICT based learning environments:

1. ICT tools can influence and transform learning by fundamentally changing the content of a subject and the way in which it could be taught and learnt. When considering the design and use of such environments we need to consider the whole learning situation, for example, not only the tool, but the teachers who will be using the software, the ways in which it will be used, the curriculum objectives, the social context and way in which the learning is organised. This means that consideration needs to be given not only to the software design but also the definition of the possible ways it might be used effectively.
2. Learning strategies can influence the effectiveness of ICT design and use. The contrast between the structure and design of the learning environment may conflict with or support the individual learning styles

of the learner. The ways in which the learning environment is used can change its original designers expectations; for example, there may be difficulties in accommodating different learning styles in the design of learning environments. Teachers can influence the learning strategies of the learner and thereby the ways in which ICT based learning environments are used.

3. Teaching and learning practices directly relate to the design and use of ICT based learning environments. We have to consider the fact that as ICT based learning environments change, the relationship between the factors above will also need to develop and change. For example, teachers might develop skills in organising individual use of ICT with their class of students, but when the opportunities increase for collaborative learning then the teacher will need to rethink the way in which he or she uses ICT within the subject and at a particular level.

2. CURRENT PERSPECTIVES

The main issues which the group considered to be important were identified according to new perspectives to be considered in the design of software based learning tools and the requirements from the teaching perspectives.

Requirements for the design of *software based learning tools*:

- The increasing scope for collaboration and communication needs to be considered when designing new software tools for subject based and cross-curricular based teaching;
- Software tools can be outside the conventional screen based applications and can be embedded in practical object based tasks, e.g. measurement and control;
- ICT tools should include where possible the facility for teachers to customize the learning activities according to the teaching and learning needs of their students;
- Software tools should include ideas about good pedagogical practice so that the user can make best use of the software;
- The design could be enhanced by examples of good pedagogical practices relating to learning theories and design principles, which could be used as guidelines for software development;
- Design of new tools should take into account of the value of non-text based activities. This means that not only should the software include, where appropriate, the use of pictures, figures, drawings, films and sound, but also it should enable the learners to interact with a variety of screen

based objects to enable them to access knowledge from a different and more constructive perspective;

- ICT based tools should support the student problem solving processes and provide them with the opportunity to carry out open-ended problems, that is problems which do not have a closed defined answer.
- There should be the possibility of using different types of computing devices for learning, according to different teaching and learning needs. For example, the opportunities of lap-top and palm computers were discussed, pointing out their low cost and flexibility of use, compared with standard desk top computers.

These recommendations were considered in relation to the wider context of the teaching and learning environments, i.e. the teaching perspectives.

Requirements from the *teaching perspectives*:

- The teaching support and ICT learning resources need to be organised to sustain the enthusiasm of teachers for using ICT effectively;
- The initial training of teachers should incorporate techniques to show new teachers how to integrate ICT into their subject/curriculum areas;
- ICT resources should include materials which show how the activities support the learners' other activities;
- Teachers need to develop their pedagogical competencies to use ICT effectively in support of the learning goals;
- Professional school administrators (Senior management staff) need to be trained in the use of ICT in order to support, model and assess teachers' use of ICT in the classroom;

The group also considered factors that prevented the majority of teachers using ICT in their curriculum. Examples where ICT is used willingly and appeared to motivate the teacher to integrate it into their teaching included:

- The use of the WWW to access information to support subject based work
- The use of specific tools for specific purposes; e.g. in medical education
- The use of Office based software because of its vocational skills value.

Each of the participants had different knowledge and experiences of the barriers to the uptake and use of ICT in teaching and learning. These barriers were often linked to specific policies and practices of teachers within various education systems.

The issues and requirements previously discussed led to the identification of a range of research challenges. The reasoning behind the research issues identified is based on our original metaphors relating to ICT based learning environments. For example, in the case of the transmission metaphor then the group considered the role of the teacher having an effect on drill and practice software being used, and how the teacher's role might affect its contribution to learning. For the learner centred metaphor, then the participants pointed out that such type of software requires a change in the role of the teacher and the way in which the learning is organised in the classroom. Therefore research needs to be done to investigate how the classroom settings need to be changed to make ICT based learning effective. For the participation metaphor, a range of research issues were identified which reflected the complex nature and balance of the different components of the learning environment and how these would affect pupils' learning.

3. RESEARCH CHALLENGES: TOWARDS A NEW VISION FOR LEARNING ENVIRONMENTS:

Research challenges which were identified relating to the three main issues previously discussed: i.e. ICT tools to transform learning; learning strategies, and teaching and learning practices are given below.

- What are the cognitive functions that need to be considered when investigating the impact of new learning environments on teaching and learning processes?
- Which kinds of tools need to be integrated in advanced ICT based systems to support such cognitive functions?
- What kinds of learning strategies and outcomes are promoted by the diverse types of user interfaces and knowledge representations?
- How does the concept of an ICT-based learning environment change according to the different metaphor considered?
- How can models of best practice be defined?
- What are the most appropriate and effective ways of evaluating learning environments?
- How do ICT based learning environments affect the learning through collaboration and communication?
- What barriers affect the delivery and implementation of ICT in the curriculum, and how are these affected by the changing technology?
- What positive factors motivate teachers to use ICT and what support mechanisms need to be in place?
- What new models of teacher training lead to the long-term integration and sustained use of ICT in teachers' practice?

REFERENCE

Bottino, R. M. (2001) Advanced Learning Environments: changed views and future perspectives. In *Computers and Education: towards an interconnected society*, M. Ortega and J. Bravo (eds.), Dordrect, Kluwer, The Netherlands (in press).

93

Use of Computer Based Concept Mapping Tools

Working Group 3.5

Chair: Eric Bruillard (FR)
Rapporteur: Lesley McCarthy (AU)
Participants: Maj-Britt Andreasen (DK), Sue Fewster (AU), Phil Nanholy (AU), Hajima Ohiwa (JP), Cynthia Sistek-Chandler (US)

Keywords: creativity, cognition, modelling, collaborative learning, assessment

Abstract: Concept mapping has been a subject of investigation especially since the introduction of computer based tools, which have simplified the creation and modification of concept maps. In education, concept maps can be used in many different ways: as planning tools, reflection support, creative support, assessment tool, teaching and learning tools. This professional group will identify and explore the range of applications for concept maps currently undertaken in the countries/systems/institutions of the participants and discuss issues surrounding the effective implementation of such strategies.

1. CONCEPT MAPS: WHAT IS IMPORTANT?

Concept mapping, the process of spatial representation of graphic and text based pieces of information and their links, has been a subject of investigation for many years but more so since the introduction of computer based tools, which have simplified the creation and modification of concept maps. Concept maps are used in many ways in education and also in other domains such as business and management. There are many definitions of concept maps, or knowledge representation strategies, in the literature beginning with Novak in 1976 (Novak 1990). According to Jonassen et al. (1993) concept maps are representations of concepts and their interrelationship that are intended to represent the knowledge structures that humans store in their minds. They are also, "spatial metaphors that indicate relationships among concepts in a node-link-node visual display" (Jonassen et al. 1993) Concept maps can be viewed as simplistic representations of what we know as humans. Data with labels is *Information*; information linked with other information is *Knowledge.* A concept map models those links. We can find many other definitions, many types of concept maps indicating that there are very general notions or objects.

In education, many authors have advocated the importance of concept maps (see review in Bruillard and Baron 2000). For example, Jacobi reported on the importance of concept maps in education as a means of presenting structure and an assessment tool, whilst McAleese (1994) commented on the process of creation. From a constructivist viewpoint, concept mapping aids the construction of meaning, organisation of ideas and information, creation and modification of links and relationships. But according to applications and contexts, what seems to be important may be different and sometimes almost opposite. For example, in the business community in Japan, the KJ method for concept map formation without crossed links is well known. This method was proposed in the 60's by an anthropologist Jiro Kawakita (1982) for creating new ideas from the scratch. KJ method is far more popular than Novak in Japanese schools (Ohiwa et al. 1990, Ohiwa et al. 1997). The method is widely accepted by business community in Japan because not only new idea generation but the method is extremely useful for consensus forming among the participants. If some map representation causes uneasy feelings among the participants, discussion starts and final map is formed through this discussion. Unease often comes for different interpretation of the word written in a box. After reaching a common understanding of the word, consensus for the map is easily reached. In the KJ method, important criteria for good map formation is that links must be formed among the adjacent boxes and links must not cross each other. The effort to realise these criteria requires a series of setting of the boxes and links. This forces participants to think deeply about the problem. The map Kawakita formed follows these criteria.

If we follow these criteria, we often have to give up and place either some boxes or links, for the clarity of the whole map. This may seem that an important part of the problem is discarded, but often our concept structure for the system is immature. Complex systems in the real world require simplicity and clearness if they have to work in the complex situation. In this example, the process of producing a map goes from the complex to the simple. But other examples suggest other methods. A reason for investigating the use and value of the cognitive tools known collectively as concept maps is their close association with the structure of hypermedia texts. These text types, with their characteristic structure of linked nodes, are becoming ubiquitous as the basis for the Web and widespread in other media types such as digital TV, electronic games and cellular phones. The influence of interactive screens and linked information nodes can even be seen in non-digital media such as cinema and popular magazine design.

From the most basic use as a graphical, perhaps linear, representation of knowledge to a complex web of spatially organised, interrelating concepts containing text, images, symbols and colours, concept maps are a very personal and individual expression of information. Here the process goes mainly from the simple to the complex. The more complex the concept map, the more profound the understanding of their producer. Another point is the evolution of a map and how to take into account this evolution. The requirements can be very different according to successive stages of learning

To summarise, a concept map is a trade-off between opposite constraints. In some situations, the nearness of concepts on the map may be more important than the existence of links, the spatial nature of the map allowing the expression fuzzy relationships, links expressing more formal ones. Placement is essential.

2. CONCEPT MAPS IN EDUCATION

In elementary schools, students and teachers alike take advantage of computer assisted concept maps. Teachers have utilised concept mapping software to: plan a unit of work linking outcomes/curriculum areas or themes; develop new concepts and relationships; map current knowledge or understandings; as a teaching tool to scaffold learning; demonstrate progression in concept development; assess student understanding; and plan for further research or investigation. Students use concept maps for: planning research tasks; literature reviews; record current knowledge, understandings and relationships; explore understandings of a concept; geographical maps; and planning or mapping web-sites or web presentations.

These lists have to be viewed as examples and are certainly far from being exhaustive. They give an idea of the wide range of applications we can imagine. Notice that behind all these examples, concept maps are a kind of external representation which can help to develop high order skills. Thus, as a brainstorming tool, concept maps can be used to help young children represent what they know about a subject. This can make more concrete the abstract and ephemeral ideas of 'thinking' and 'knowledge'. In this way concept maps can be a tool for children to move towards meta-cognition.

To draw a parallel with multimedia, concept maps can be seen as simplified representations of knowledge structures. A logical-hierarchical view of human knowledge creation and retention divides all that is known on a subject into a taxonomy of major ideas or all-embracing concepts which are defined more narrowly focused supporting concepts. So an example might be the idea of animals which different individuals would define with their own set of supporting concepts. Some of these would be logical (mammals, birds, reptiles etc) and some would be associative and possible social-emotional in nature (memories of the sight, touch, smell and feelings towards a pet). As a learning model it is suggested that humans compare each new piece of information with their growing stock of major concepts and accommodate the confirmation or contradiction the new brings to the store of experience. While such a view of learning and/or the structure of knowledge is simplistic it directly parallels with the structure and purposes of both concept maps on a micro scale and the Internet on a macro scale.

2.1 Computer based concept maps

The use of computer based concept maps has several advantages, mainly the ease of construction, the ease of revision, and the ability to customise maps in ways that are not possible when using paper and pencil. The ease of modification encourages effective learning through the creation of new schema (mind maps/knowledge maps) and the extension, modification and reconstruction of existing schema. The ease of input, the fluid nature of computer assisted concept mapping tools assist students to construct more detailed and complex concept maps with attractive visual representation. Computer assisted concept maps allow, assist and encourage development of higher order thinking skills, especially the analysis and synthesis of information and the delving deeper to extend/explore/create more complex understandings, links and interrelationships. They also assist in understanding and navigation of web design and the mapping through understanding of links that is inherent but not explicit in web construction.

Computer assisted concept maps are also used in collaborative group activities to develop shared understandings. Their use encourages greater exploration and in depth discussions, and the ease of manipulation of data, the modification of order, hierarchy, links and relationships ensures more time on thinking and less on the mechanics of producing the map.

The KJ method mentioned earlier, has been tried to be performed on the computer, and has been used for map forming in general. An important aspect of the computer support for map formation is the direct manipulation capability of software, because the forming process requires very hard concentration. If it requires, e.g. scroll bar operation, your concentration is damaged. Careful human interface design is essential for such software. One advantage of using the computer is re-trial of map forming is easy, the other is the process of the map formation can be recorded and replayed. This is useful for educational and research purposes of the human brain activities.

Concept maps are used in different contexts (education, business, personal development); references are accessible but very mixed (scientific books and papers, more ideological resources, commercial resources etc.) and may be contradictory. We have seen that requirements concerning concept maps can be very different, as the way of constructing them. Concerning one specific domain or phenomena, it is not possible to decide what can be the best concept map, even for a given purpose. We can only say when we are expert in a domain if a map is good or not. One key idea emerges is the idea of flexibility of such tools. In this context, the general question of interest of concept maps in education is meaningless. More practical questions are how these tools can be used in a powerful way in education. For that, good examples provide interesting hints.

3. EXAMPLES

As group participants, we shared some experiments showing very different uses of computer based concept mapping tools.

3.1 First example (thanks to Phil Nanholy)

This example of concept map usage describes their role as a support for research and for the creation of hypermedia texts in elementary school student's study of history. As the students prepared to research key historical figures in Australian history they used pencil and paper concept mapping to organise their brainstorming of areas to investigate. In one classroom small groups of students also created a wall display using string and file cards to publish their group maps for class discussion and comment. These same concept maps were later used to organise the structure of the hypermedia texts they created to report the findings of their research.

3.2 Second example (thanks to Sue Fewster)

Students aged 5-13 years use concept mapping (Inspiration) as a tool for constructing individual learning plans. Briefly each student chooses an issue of interest. They then set themselves a learning challenge in all areas of learning as described in the curriculum framework. These challenges are the first layer of their map. A next layer gives information about the resources they will access to find information and complete their learning challenges. Finally the students add a layer describing the way they intend to document their learning. Their concept map is then used to communicate and share their ideas with an adult during their Individual Learning Meeting. This takes place before they commence their challenges.

The concept map provides the adults, the student and their family with a means to reflect an existing knowledge, learning preferences and discuss the challenges. Inspiration ensures this collaborative construction is easy and stress free. There is no 'crossing out' of ideas as would occur on paper. Ideas can be altered, extended and regrouped as the learning conversation develops. During learning time the concept map forms the basis on which information can be added. For example, URLs are copied and pasted into notes that lay behind the resource bubble. Keywords, phrases and other relevant information can also be copied and pasted into notes the same way.

Some students/small groups may choose to use a concept map as a way of documenting their learning. For example, to communicate with others the factors affecting global warming, and the measures taken by governments as a way of dealing with the issue. Some also find concept maps useful for planning web pages, Hyperstudio stacks and imovies.

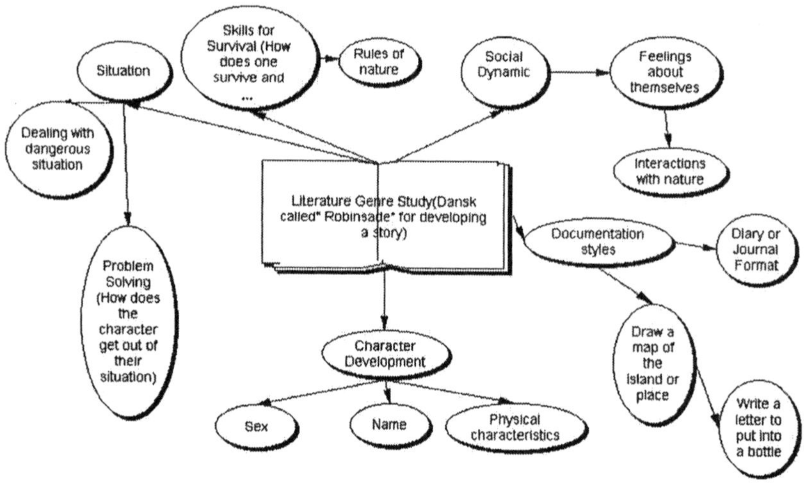

3.3 Third example (thanks to Maj-Britt Andreasen and Cynthia Sistek-Chandler)

In this example, concept maps are used for working with genres. One group member, discovering concept map for the first time, tried to prepare a classroom activity. She imagined that a concept-mapping tool might be applied to a 'Robisonade' project, already done with her class. The goal is for each student to write their own 'Robinsonade' in diary format. At the start the class will discuss 'Robinson Crusoe' by Defoe and other similar stories. Most students also know the TV-show 'Survivor'. By employing concept maps, several benefits are expected such as to get a better-structured Robinsonade, to help the students to see (literally), and remember, the individual parts that make up a Robinsonade, to evaluate more easily the project which can be more fun and instructive for the students.

Use of the Concept map in the 'Robinsonade' project could be implemented as follows (maps designed with the help of an expert in the use of concept mapping tools in school)

This map can be used in many different ways: as a tool for the teacher to organise the activity, as an assignment for the student, a reference for them, a template they have to complete etc. Another map shows an example of what a student could produce on the subject.

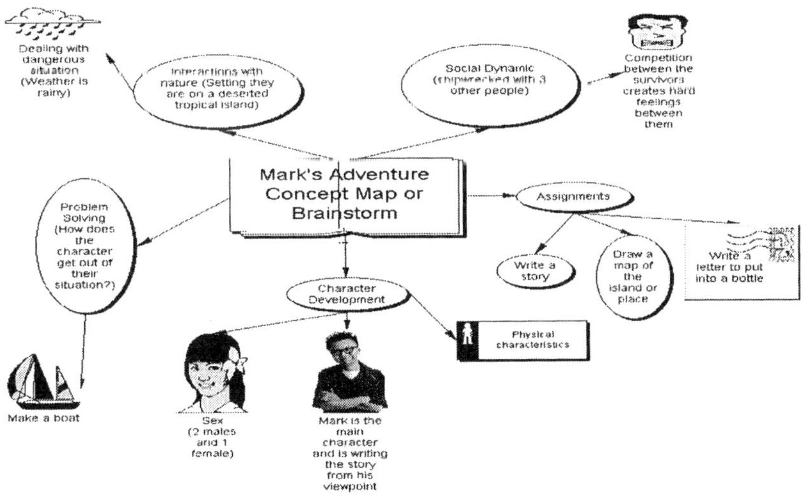

These three examples show uses of concept maps as brainstorming, organisational and planning tools.

4. SOME RESEARCH ISSUES

Many research questions emerged from the group discussion, at both a practical level and also a more theoretical one.

The main question is how to use computer based mapping tools in a fruitful way in education and how to take into account all kinds of students. The problem of culture and of learning styles appeared essential. According to various characterisations of learning styles (e.g. Lee's Learning Preference Scale, Gardner's Multiple Intelligences, and Kolb Learning Styles Inventory), which relations can be drawn with concept mapping (see for example Oughton and Reed 2000)?

In depth study about concept maps as organisational tools seems also important. As assessment devices, concept maps are to be considered. These cognitive tools are not only a better assessment strategy to assess explicit knowledge but also a method to give insights into the types of attribute that at present is not being assessed. Higher order skills and understandings need more subtle assessment strategies that give insights into the processes used to create a product. More theoretical problems could be investigated such as 3D (or more) representation of maps, the design of tools for comparing to maps (different persons or the same person at different stages), and the method for designing maps without crossings.

REFERENCES

Bruillard, E. and Baron, G.-L. (2000) Computer Based Concept Mapping a Cognitive Tool for Students: A review. In *IFIP World Conference, Beijing*, august 2000.

Jonassen, D., Beissner, K. and Yacci, M. (1993) *Structural knowledge: techniques for representing, conveying and acquiring structural knowledge*. Erlbaum, Hillsdale, N. J.

Kawakita, J. (1982) *The Original KJ Method*. Kawakita Research Institute, Tokyo.

McAleese R. (1994) A Theoretical view on concept mapping. *ALT*, 2, 2, pp. 38-48.

Novak, J. (1990) Concept mapping: a useful tool for science education. *Journal of Research in Science Teaching*, vol. 27, 10, 12/1990, pp. 937-950.

Ohiwa H., Tadeka, N., Kawai, K. and Shiomi, A. (1997) KJ editor: a card-handling tool for creative work support. *Knowledge-Based Systems*, 10, pp. 43-50.

Ohiwa, H., Kawai, K. and Koyama, M. (1990) Idea processor and the KJ method. *Journal of Information Processing*, vol. 13, pp. 44-48.

Oughton, J. M. and Reed W. M. (2000) The effect of hypermedia knowledge and learning style on student-centered concept maps about hypermedia. *Journal of Research on Computing in Education*, 32, 3, pp. 366-384.

94

Models of Teacher Development for the Integration of ICT in the Classroom

Working Group 3.5

Chair: Toni Downes (AU)
Rapporteur: Margaret Niess (US)
Participants: Peter Albion (AU), Karen Biering (DK), Pam Bishop (AU), Owen Burgan (AU), Terry Cannings (US), Martin James (NZ), Holly Jobe (US), Viki Lawrence (NZ), Avril Loweless (UK), Minttu Ollila (FI), Thea van Os (AU), Teresia Volotinen (FI), Dilanthe Withanage (Sri Lanka)

Keywords: in-service training, integration of ICT, teacher education, teaching/practice, teacher training

Abstract: This professional group explored a range of pre-service teacher education and continuing professional development strategies undertaken in the countries/systems/institutions of the members. No single strategy was identified as best, rather a variety of strategies were found to meet the varying needs. Issues during design, implementation and evaluation of strategies for the effective implementation include time, money, leadership development, alignment of the goals of assessment and professional development, lifelong learning, motivating teachers, rewards and incentives, language barriers.

1. INTRODUCTION

A number of national reports identify critical factors for a more comprehensive and effective integration of ICT into schools to respond to an information society curriculum. While each reports uses different language and frameworks, in all a set of inter-related factors need attention to ensure effective application of ICT in schools and effective teacher development. Teacher development is now the focus of many national strategies (APEC

1999). While much is known about effective teacher development (CERI 1998), implementation of effective strategies at the institutional and systemic level is often constrained by politics, finance and structures. Successful pre-service and in-service strategies may be transferable in certain situations. This report identifies some of these successful endeavours.

2. TEACHER DEVELOPMENT FRAMEWORKS

Models of teacher development vary across pre-service teacher education and continuing professional development. Group members provided a range of examples from their own institutions on the more common strategies. They noted the increasing use of online resources, learning environments, discussion groups in foundation and curriculum-focused subjects, and the growing use of video in online and CDRom based resources that bring classroom case studies into campus classrooms. Online interactions between student teachers and students in schools were the least common strategy.

Group members reported successful projects in the US and Australia in which pre-service teachers have acted as technology mentors for university faculty or classroom teachers. In these, skills and motivation of both mentor and mentee were increased. Partnerships between schools and pre-service education providers have been effective in the UK where there is collaboration and shared responsibility for planning, feedback and assessment. Partnerships included shared training for faculty and teachers in the development of ICT practice. Other elements included ready access by student teacher and teacher educators to equipment and networks, and the time and resources to undertake the necessary curriculum development.

The following tables resulted from discussion by group members of lists generated by an Australian Study (Department of Education, Training and Youth Affairs). Table 1 identifies the elements within pre-service teacher education programmes. Overall, elements A, B, C, F, H, I, K and L were seen by the group as the more critical components and element M as the critical success factor underpinning the success of all other elements. Table 2 lists both the CPD and Infrastructure strategic elements.

Table 1. Elements of models of ICT integration in pre-service teacher education programmes

A.	Separate compulsory ICT subjects — skill acquisition
B.	Separate compulsory ICT subjects — curriculum/pedagogy
C.	Diffusion — modelling and use across course (with integration across various subjects)
D.	ICT Electives — skill acquisition

E.	ICT Electives — curriculum/pedagogy
F.	Face-to-face use with children expected as part of learning experience or assessment tasks within particular subjects
G.	Online use with children expected as part of learning experience or assessment tasks within particular subjects
H.	Planning, teaching and evaluation of use of ICT for learning expected as part of professional experience requirement
I.	Modelling by classroom teacher expected as part of professional experience
J.	Online collaborative/team interactions with students in schools for projects/learning — virtual practicums
K.	Online interactions with teachers/professional communities as part of core learning experiences
L.	Partnerships with schools so that student teachers, classroom teachers and teacher educators engage in inquiry or development projects around the use of ICT for teaching and learning
M.	Faculty professional development
N.	Flexible delivery, student-centered approaches to teaching and learning
O.	Partnerships with industry: curriculum/software development programmes

Advantages such as 'being connected to the daily classroom work of teachers' or 'just-in-time assistance' were often juxtaposed against issues of time, cost and the increased workload of teachers. Using a mixture of elements maximised the advantages.

Members of the group provided some examples. At a national level, Sri Lanka has a national policy on IT (Withange 2001. The strategy aims to develop the human resource and physical infrastructure for teacher training through three levels – national, provincial and zonal – cascading out to each. From training lecturers at Universities and the National Colleges of Education, train the trainer programmes and out to the school level, all based on 10 intitial national trainers casacading their skills out to each level.

At the systemic level in several Pennsylvania (US) districts, groups of teachers worked designing technology-rich lessons for 'difficult to learn' maths concepts. Each teacher had a laptop, an email account and access to a

Table 2. Elements of models of continuing professional development programmes

Professional development strategies
A. Face-to-face single events within workplace
B. Face-to-face single events external to workplace
C. Face-to-face sequential multiple-event courses within workplace
D. Face-to-face sequential multiple-event courses external to workplace
E. University accredited courses

F.	Online single events
G.	Online sequential multiple-event courses
H.	Within workplace mentor programmes
I.	Online mentor programmes
J.	Teacher visits/exchanges
K.	Curriculum or materials development projects
L.	Collaborative topic-based teaching projects
M.	Professional learning community projects/study groups
N.	Sustained inquiry/action or teacher research projects
Infrastructure components	
A.	Funds for self-directed formal professional development
B.	Central and advisory services
C.	Teachers centres
O.	Navigator/Lighthouse schools offering mentoring, practicums, courses
P.	Allocation of specialist staff to schools – Professional Development Coordinator
D.	Development and provision of resources
E.	Provision and support for hardware etc. to teachers
Q.	Partnerships with teacher education institutions around practicum and induction of beginning teachers
F.	Partnerships with industry and other organisations
G.	Provision of teacher release
H.	Recognition and certification of learning/expertise
I.	Incentives and rewards for minimum standards
J.	Incentives and rewards for excellence/best practice

to a project listserv. Teachers met staff from their own and other school districts, tested their lessons with their students and another teacher, not in the project, tested the lesson design and materials. Another example is a group of Finnish teachers in the Netlibris Virtual Literature Circles project, part of the Virtual School project of the National Board of Education. A typical Netlibris teacher is primarily interested in literature; they meet, team-teach and support each other in a variety of ways. The new ICT component proceeds in small steps, the teachers working at first online in virtual literature circles 'as students', and then teaching collaboratively a mixed group of students. Team teaching and sharing students and responsibilities increases pedagogic awareness and commitment. A further example is the Teaching Futures project in Australia,. aiming to link school planning and pedagogy, which will incorporate ICT in new discussions towards a sense of shared leadership and a school wide pedagogy.

One example from the school level came from Victoria, Australia. One school used of 'in house' expertise and invited experts to conduct whole day and after school workshops on skill development, including ICT. Universities continue to provide CPD through postgraduate courses. Since the mid 1980's Faculties of Education in many countries, including ones like Sri Lanka, have offered postgraduate programmes in educational use of ICT.

3. ISSUES

Many issues are critical to sustaining effective teacher development.

3.1 Leadership development

Educational leaders need to foster a school culture conducive for teacher development. Key elements include distribution of resources, technical support and personnel to assist teachers in implementing what they have learned. A key strategy for supportive school cultures is the provision of parallel development/in-service opportunities for educational leaders. As one example, Pennsylvania, US, has initiated technology leadership academics for school superintendents, school boards and principals. These academies develop capacity to lead the implementation of technology-rich, learner-centred learning environments and to support ongoing teacher development.

3.2 Lack of time

Schools are constantly faced with a lack of time. New initiatives first add to existing workload due to unfamiliarity with new systems and processes. Some schools have worked to replace, rather than add to, teacher workload by restructuring curriculum delivery to an integrated format that meets many curriculum requirements simultaneously; restructuring assessments to include student self evaluation and multiple curriculum assessment tasks; using digital planning and assessment software to reduce duplication; and using ICT for administrative tasks so maximising meetings for CPD.

3.3 Motivation and life-long learning of the teacher

The issues of life long learning and motivating the reluctant teacher closely linked and interrelated. Those delivering CPD must find the key to excite and encourage teachers on their journey along the learning continuum. This key may appeal to teachers' professional lives through the subject matter or personal interest. Robert Kramer Rasmussen from LegoDacta, during his keynote address at WCCE 2001, emphasised that learning should be 'Hard Fun'. The learner should be presented with sufficient challenges to make the learning interesting and their skills develop; once in balance, the learner can enter a 'flow' of continuing learning. For this flow to occur a number of key features should be present.

- Multi-professional groups with various expertise join collaboratively to develop an environment – all support each other and share knowledge.
- Continuing dynamic dialogue between research and classroom practice and experiences of those involved in the collaborative group.
- Encouraging the culture of teacher as a reflective practitioner, who grows through experiences and taking risks. This can be done through dialogue, classroom experimentation coupled with self and group reflection.
- The professional digital portfolio can serve as an ideal forum to reflect, celebrate and share this learning.

3.4 Money

The CEO Forum on Education and Technology (1999) states that a minimum of 30% of a school's IT budget should be devoted to professional development. For a school this is reasonable if ICT use is successfully integrated; more is needed if not. But the figure is too low considering the cost of professional development courses and replacement costs for teachers. The problem is exacerbated in rural areas. A higher priority on the purchase of equipment often reduces funds for professional development. Some solutions to this dilemma could be student free days for whole staff training, clustering of schools and cost sharing, commercial or community partnerships, and online professional development.

3.5 Aligning goals of assessment and CPD

In the US and UK, the focus and motivation for teacher development is often related to perceived professional responsibilities and requirements. Many national assessment frameworks, 'high stakes' in expectations of teachers, do not require the integration of ICT to support learning and assessment objectives. Policies may request evidence that ICT is promoting achievement in traditional assessment objectives. Models for teacher professional development which are relevant and meaningful for teachers need to address how ICT developments relate to assessment frameworks for student and teacher performance, and which acknowledge issues of higher-order thinking, autonomy, collaboration, problem-solving and motivation.

Strategies at systemic and local levels could include acknowledgement and legitimation of the evaluation of alternative assessment practices.

3.6 Language barriers

For countries where English is not the mother language, the language of ICT is an issue. Most ICT education programs are in English; software and manuals are in English. This creates barriers for leaders, teachers and students in learning with ICT. More than 95% of teachers in Sri Lanka received their school education and/or university education in their mother language (Sinhala or Tamil). Considering the nature of the subject and global requirements, the national ICT education policy proposes that the medium of instruction for ICT education should be English with some support in the native language. Providing ICT training in English is identified as an essential, but a very complicated task to be achieved. A policy proposal is to have special programs called 'English for IT' on top of the ICT Programs. With most of technical terms in English (no appropriate useable words in the native languages), a special TV program called ' IT Power for Teachers' is to be offered to all teachers across the island.

3.7 Rewards and incentives

Educational systems world-wide are exploring opportunities to provide incentives to teachers to encourage their use of ICT in classrooms. These incentives, coupled with a reward system for early adopters, acknowledge the work of teachers and counterbalance the general feelings of uncertainty and exhaustive demands placed on teachers. These incentives and rewards may take the form of advance standing in the teaching or monetary rewards through salary increments. In addition, systems may foster teacher development through the provision of hardware or grants for further study.

As an alternate reward, the issue of micro-payments are beginning to emerge. Although not obviously related to professional development, the innovative teacher who develops new resources and strategies often does so through accessing the more flexible aspects of CPD (i.e. listservs, texts, web or online courses) resulting in learning objects and practices developed primarily in the teachers own time. Micro-payments may be presented in many formats and ways. Should they be introduced? Much debate should ensure that an equitable approach to them be achieved.

4. CONCLUSIONS

Even though the issues around teacher development and the integration of ICT in the classroom are challenging, there are numerous examples of solutions that have been designed and successfully implemented throughout the world. There is no one, short-term solution. There is a diversity of potential solutions for a diversity of needs, levels, and locations. The challenge is to learn from the diversity of the solutions. Pre-service teacher education and continuing professional development of all teachers as well as the educational leaders need on-going support at the highest levels.

REFERENCES

APEC (1999) *Integration of information and communication technologies through teacher professional development.* APEC workshop, December 1-3, Canada Forum, Toronto. [http://www.cmec.ca/international/forum].

CEO Forum on Education and Technology (1999) *Professional development: A link to better learning.* The CEO Forum on Education and Technology, Washington.

CERI (1998) *Staying ahead: In-service training and teacher professional development.* Centre for Educational Research and Innovation, Organisation for Economic Cooperation and Development.

Department of Education, Training and Youth Affairs (to be launched) *Models of teacher professional development for the integration of ICTs into classroom practice.* A Report to the Commonwealth Department of Education, Training and Youth Affairs. Commonwealth of Australia, Canberra. Further details can be obtained from Toni Downes: t.downes@uws.edu.au.

Withange, D. (2001) *National policy for IT education in Sri Lanka.* Ministry of Education. [http://www.moesl.org/Policy/ITPolicy].

95

Internet, Education and Culture: Should We Care?

Working Group 3.5

Chair: Anton Knierzinger (AT)
Rapporteur: Marta Turcsanyi-Szabo (HU)
Participants: Anne-Louise Agnew (AU), Bonnie Thurber (US), Christian Duckworth (UK), Ivan Kalas (SK), Odette Radi (AU), Rachel Cohen (FR), Roman Baranovic (SK)

Keywords: students, internet, culture, empowering, teacher education

Abstract: Internet, with its easy to use access to multimedia resources and linking tool has great impact on education and cultures. It is the way we use it that changes can be brought about and Webbing can be provided from small age, for minorities, disadvantaged, disabled, and different societies. Therefore one of the first steps in changes has to be made in teacher education itself.

1. EDUCATION

Internet provides the strings of togetherness; education is substantial in providing a meaningful life; culture with individual diversities colours our globe of life space. Why should we care? This report investigates issues in relation to the use of the Internet in education by proposing further questions.

To encompass a whole new way of learning with this new technology, we have to be aware that radical changes in our approaches to learning, classroom management, the role of the teacher and adequate change in teacher training is necessary.

1.1 What is the impact of Internet on education?

Concerns about Internet use show overuse or misuse might amplify problems, while actually radical changes are needed in pedagogy in order to benefit from use. Rather than just gathering information, the Internet should be used to construct knowledge, learning to learn, developing problem-solving skills, opening eyes to the realisation of other cultures and enrich lives.

Personal growth: The personal growth is a development of personality and soul. It can be an enhancement of knowledge, the ability to communicate or development of any competence found useful in life.

Education: Without doubt, the Internet today is widely recognised as a great tool for lifelong learning. For many, it is a tutor who helps increase the level of education. Many users appreciate the features the Internet offers – the availability of various teaching materials, the ability to be educated by top experts without necessity to travel or capability to time the education process to their busy schedule.

Opportunity to develop critical thinking: Internet is an endless source of information, which is easy to find and easy to produce. There is too much information on the Internet, so users need to develop skills to critically evaluate information and sources.

Development of social competencies: Internet helps to mature social competencies. Everyone can use the Internet to find friends and build relationships with people from all around the world.

1.2 In which way does Internet change education?

The Internet is a very powerful tool that removes the tyranny of distance between educational institutions within one nation and other nations. It is a useful tool, which allows easy access to a wide variety of educational information and resources. The Internet changes the way students conduct their research with the availability of combined text, voice, image, simulations and virtual reality and software tutorials enable students to play an interactive role in situations which otherwise require considerable exercise of imagination and discipline. However, the relationship between Internet accesses at home is distinctive to its use at school in its types and time of use.

The regular use of the Internet has implications on what the education systems aim to achieve. The Internet is a force for social and educational transformation, which implies changes to traditional learning.

The Internet is a great source of entertainment, especially for children. With proper supervision children can learn much by downloading desirable material.

In electronic communication, the printed text can often become 'ad-speak' and therefore unconventionally spelt. To what extent is cyber language changing the way we write? The Internet influences children's language and social outcomes. Because they are growing up with technology they can easily adapt, become self-educated and create their own digital communities.

1.3 From what age does Internet prove to be sensibly used and for what reasons?

Often it is believed that young children, particularly before age 6, should not and cannot use computers for any other activity than play.

Young children possess a fabulous mental potential, a great need to learn, and that mental development depends on the stimulation of the learning environment and the learning opportunities encountered by the learner. Recent research proves that young children can and enjoy use of the Internet, particularly activities based on collaborative work carried out with pals around the world.

These activities:

- Give the children a clear idea of what reading and writing is about: communicating with people who are not present
- Allow the children to get acquainted with children speaking a different language, having different habits of life but who have the same needs as themselves, which is an important beginning of education for international understanding
- Help the children and teachers to use technology in meaningful activities from the start
- Encourage children to express themselves, combining different means
- Allow the integration of children belonging to minorities and who are not fluent in the language taught in the class
- Enhance collaborative and interactive activities
- Help immensely the professional growth of the teachers.

In conclusion using Internet with young children for communication and collaborative activities shared with children from all over the world will create an international community of young children, oriented towards understanding and co-operation.

2. SOCIETY

2.1 Is filtering a solution for unwanted access?

If we structure the ethical aspects of the Internet, we might come up with the following:

- What is unwanted access?
- When and how is it possible?
- What might be its consequences? What are we afraid of?
- How can we eliminate, restrict or control it?
- What are possible solutions?
- What is a constructive and positive approach?

Unwanted access is the use of Internet resources which propagate or display violence, pornography, racial discrimination, terrorism etc., which we as educators find inappropriate for children. The situation may be, restricted or controlled by either software, hardware or educational means.

Internet is freedom and freedom is responsibility. It is real life and real society with all its good and bad, mixed and controversial influences. Education means preparing for real life. We have to talk to our students about the whole spectrum of possible gains and losses when working with the Internet. We have to make it clear to children that there are sources of information, which are appropriate or inappropriate, within the boundaries of culture. We have to help children live in the real life, not in the artificial greenhouse.

2.2 What is the impact of Internet on different societies?

The world in which we live is a rapidly changing one with many challenges for cultures and society as we have known it for many years. The challenge to educators today is to find ways of helping students to bridge the gaps between the cultures whilst at the same time enabling them to develop an awareness and pride in their own culture. By using the internet to bring students together, we can provide them with the facilities to celebrate cultures and the society in which they live, through the use of collaborative projects. The views expressed by students or reflected in the responses they give should come from their social experiences and the cultures that enrich this environment.

Although English is widely used on the Internet, it is imperative to provide the students with opportunities to work at their own level of learning in their native language. Collaborative projects done by students via the

Internet could be produced and published in their native language and also in other languages.

The Internet could enable students to discuss issues, to respond to questions and to provide a publishing space for work produced. It is a tool to enhance learning and to provide a means of fast, effective communication around the globe, developing an awareness, understanding and acceptance of the rich differences of cultures, without the constraints of borders and distance. It is also the first opportunity for many small, isolated communities to be present on a global scale.

2.3 How can minorities be involved and at the same time keep their own identities?

All countries have minority groups with distinct ethnic and cultural diversities. It is important for these groups to maintain their individuality. Some minority groups choose not to embrace technology because they are afraid of the changes which will be forced upon their culture.

For example, gypsies prefer to live an isolated life style to preserve their culture and traditions. They have their own history and are noted for their musical abilities such as singing. They have shared some of their music and history with people outside their community. How can technology be introduced in non-threatening ways to encourage these people to use it? The suggestion is that the gypsies could use technology to share their history and music with others.

A group of gypsy representatives could test new technologies, its value and find their own way of introducing it such that is relevant to their community. Whilst being trained, they would develop content about some aspect of their culture and spread the message amongst their society. Working with familiar content would help develop a comfort level while learning the new skills. Their own technology centres could be created to facilitate the learning of the new technologies to use in their everyday lives.

2.4 How should the disadvantaged be able to access resources?

Individual persons, minorities, remote communities, as well as whole countries could be in disadvantaged situation, not possessing the necessary infrastructure, knowledge, circumstance, or possibilities to access technology, tools and content. These individuals or communities are cast out from the privilege of knowledge, communication and global insight, which prohibits personal growth and job possibilities. In the long run this situation might well invite unlawful activities or the wish to leave the community.

Many countries, realising the burdens of disadvantaged, have shown good practices by establishing tele-huts, tele-houses to provide high technology and resources for all, bringing about changes in several ways:

- The ability to access infrastructure, tools, and resources gives an innovative aspect in viewing the future and provides self confidence through mastering technology
- Accessing the Internet provides a global view on the world, with freely available information sources, which demands selection and decision making
- The insight to differences and cultures around the world encourages the sense of self-respect and individual values to help preserve and inspire the willingness to express and publish self-identity, views, and culture – stepping forward from being just a consumer to a provider of information
- E-mailing facilities provide links and means for communication channels, where differences and circumstances diminish and only the ties become meaningful
- The bridging, through virtual strings, establishes bonds that form communities on different levels
- Distance, local and individual possibilities are over-ruled through the access to different telelearning and telementoring facilities, providing the chance for all to learn the most
- Personal growth opens new possibilities for jobs in virtual and real territories through teleworking channels.

These webbing possibilities, no matter how minute they might be, could make great differences to individuals and communities with respect to their view of the future and their role in society. Knowledge, respect and identity deletes internal need to override social rules or to flee from community.

2.5 What does Internet mean to the disabled?

A gateway to the world: Through virtual travel experiences of many kinds are facilitated. Also if travel is to be undertaken in reality the Internet can be used to research places and facilities to ensure easier mobility.

An educational tool: Learning packages can be devised for more formal learning and broken down into manageable sections suitable in length, frequency and intensity and presented at intervals suitable to the learner. Personal interests can be followed and a portfolio of skills acquired with consideration given to and adaptations made for special needs.

A means of conducting business: E-commerce, financial services, and shopping online all offer opportunities to those who would ordinarily have difficulty in going out to work or shop. A degree of independence can therefore be achieved.

An entertainment provider: Music, digital films, virtual art galleries and exhibitions on line can be visited and enjoyed regardless of disability.

A means of communication: For those who have speech, hearing or communication difficulties the computer and the Internet can offer the means to communicate with others through e-mail, or sending pictures, photographs or sound recordings. Opportunities to join in communities on the web, offer opinions, and most importantly, make a contribution to the world are available through forums, chat rooms etc.

Thus, the Internet offers the disabled equalities opportunities and empowerment.

2.6 How could we fight infrastructure constraints?

The fact that only a small minority of the Internet users is living in developing countries is mainly based on hardware constraints in these countries. For example Africa with 17% of the worlds population has less than 1% of the Internet users. This means that a majority of the people living on the earth is excluded from modern communication and information means.

What can be done to cope with infrastructure constraints? Even though financial support is a basic requirement to build-up a network infrastructure, there are some aspects to be taken into consideration to make support as effective as possible:

- In many cases it is the network infrastructure which is the most difficult part to be implemented. Large distances and the absence of any communication infrastructure, like telephone, makes it very difficult to provide internet access with the communication technology used in developed areas. It is necessary to use technologies that do not require cables to be laid. One can see satellite technology as a solution. It now offers the possibility to cover large areas with Internet access in a relatively inexpensive way, although mobile communication technology could also be a solution.
- There are successful projects undertaken in developing countries which combine the provision of different technologies like electricity and internet connection.
- When it is not possible to bring Internet access to every home, it should be offered in public areas. 'Telehouses' are a suitable and in many countries very successful concept to give the whole population access to electronic information and communication means. Giving this function to schools can be a very efficient solution.

Why should we care to broaden our circles? Internet allows all to join in; education assures the establishment of meaningful relations; the added colours of culture enrich the palette of wonders. Is it not worth caring?

96

Virtual Universities and Virtual Campuses
Working Group 3.6

Chair: Gordon Davies (UK), Bernard Levrat (CH)
Rapporteur: Tina Ebey (US)
Participants: Eric Bentzen (DK), Fred DeVries (NL), Esther Feffer (IL), Margareta Gisselberg (SE), Peter Holsoe (DK), Gunnar Johansen (DK), Stephen Kessell (AU), Lena Olsson (SE), Fred Mulder (NL), Neil Russell (AU), Tom Cato Seeberg (NO), Juhani Tuovinen (AU)

Keywords: open learning systems, distance education, higher education, economy, collaborative learning

Abstract: This report considers several issues that relate to virtual universities. Firstly a typology is considered to cover the main types of virtual university and their distinguishing features. One can distinguish several types of institutions: pure virtual universities, extension of current universities, outgrowth of current distance learning institutions, integrating the internet and purely commercial ventures. Following on from the typology, we consider how such universities are funded and how this might influence the curriculum. The curriculum is considered in a section on educational effectiveness, followed by issues related to accreditation and competitiveness. Finally, we comment on research in a virtual environment.

1. TYPOLOGY

We distinguish five dimensions for classifying virtual learning initiatives in higher education. The dimensions may have four discrete values or vary along a continuum. In all cases we use a scale of 1 to 4 along the dimension.

1. Method of funding:

Public:	government subsidy	1
	institutional budget	2
Private:	industrial financial support	3

corporate budget 4

They may combine in public-private partnerships.

2. Degree of collaboration, which may vary along a continuous scale from 1 to 4, meaning no collaboration at all (single organisation) through weak collaboration (e.g. project wise) to strong strategic alliances
3. Degree of virtuality in interaction, which may vary along a continuous scale from 1 to 4, meaning conventional face-to-face teaching to a wholly internet supported course, i.e. 100% virtual interaction
4. Degrec of virtuality in delivery, which varies along a continuous scale from 1 to 4, meaning conventional classroom delivery with supporting printed materials, to fully internet delivered materials with no direct teaching or supporting paper.
5. The variety of target populations:
   - 18-21 school leavers 1
   - life long learning
     a second chance university 2
     leisure learning 3
     professional development 4

1.1 Examples

The typology above is applied to several institutions around the world.

UK Open University and Dutch Open Universiteit

Funding	1, 2
Collaboration	2
Interaction	3
Delivery	3
Target	2, 3, 4

Dutch Digital Universiteit (consortium)

Funding	1, 2, 3
Collaboration	4
Interaction	4
Delivery	4
Target	1, 2, 3, 4

Swiss Virtual Campus

Funding	1, 2
Collaboration	2
Interaction	3
Delivery	4

Target 1

Phoenix University
Funding 4
Collaboration 1
Interaction 4
Delivery 4
Target 4

Curtin University Learning Technology Program
Funding 1, 2
Collaboration 2
Interaction 4
Delivery 4
Target 4

Monash University
Funding 1, 2
Collaboration 1
Interaction 1 - 4
Delivery 1 - 4
Target 1, 2, 4

It can be seen that there is a wide variation in the implementation of what is meant by a virtual university.

2. FUNDING

The various institutions and companies that offer on-line learning operate under very different financial regimes, according to whether they are privately or publicly funded (see typology).

Open universities are often national institutions and so are financed by the Government, thus covering most development costs and part of the tuition fees. The fees are set relatively high so that these institutions are able to cover their operating costs. In financial terms open universities have much in common with private companies and private universities except that the former don't have to concentrate (restrict themselves) to highly demanded courses and topics, such as those in the business and IT areas. The income of commercial, for profit, universities has to cover all costs, including both the development costs and the administration and running costs for web-based learning in the virtual classroom. The proportion of web-based courses and elements in ordinary courses is increasing and therefore it is expected that the need for funding for development costs will increase.

A true virtual 'higher education' institution will operate with net-based teaching and learning only. A virtual university has no need for lecture rooms and other infrastructure, thus reducing overheads. However, virtual universities have other high costs, namely those associated with the development of net-based modules from scratch. The traditional higher educational institutions offer face-to-face campus-based teaching and learning with add-on virtual support. There are lower costs for this wrap-around development.

In addition to the cost of developing coursework there is the cost of running and maintaining web-based modules sustained through ongoing changes in the curriculum, increases in the number of students and accordingly the tutoring costs. These factors render it necessary to plan the budget carefully, allowing for ongoing costs in addition to the initial production costs.

3. VIRTUALITY

3.1 Educational effectiveness

One of the key objectives of virtual universities is to improve educational effectiveness, where educational effectiveness in this context is taken to mean achieving the aims and objectives of educational programs.

It is considered that a key factor in achieving effectiveness in virtual universities is the strong support for the virtual operation by the institutional leadership. Without explicit strategic and financial support and institution is unlikely to be able switch substantially from a conventional mode institution to a virtual one.

In order to achieve educational improvements in virtual learning a certain amount of adaptation is required of all participants, both staff and students. New roles may have to be found for:

- Educational designers
- University lecturers
- University tutors
- Students
- Computers.

These new, emerging roles can be supported and enhanced by

- Preparation and maintenance of high quality learning materials, e.g. at minimum at least at the level of a standard textbook

- Improved delivery mechanisms
- Appropriate administrative structures, e.g. online enrolment
- Support structures, e.g. online library access
- Electronic collaboration mechanisms for student-student and student-university staff interaction
- Sustained training and professional development.

As a necessary prerequisite for the development of effective virtual learning is the need for student preparation for life long learning in virtual environments throughout their educational careers. One aspect of this is the development of independent learning skills, which need to be emphasised in virtual education, alongside social skills, e.g. the skills of virtual collaboration, to prepare self-motivated and independent students.

The scheduling and structuring of work task requirements in a virtual environment may need to be fitted to the independent learning capabilities of the students, e.g. students with minimal independent learning capacities may initially need a more comprehensive support structure which reduces with the student's maturity and development.

Students learn in a variety of ways so there should be a wide range of educational media and methods available in the virtual world, rather than assuming all virtual university activities must be solely conducted online.

To achieve these changes there needs to be more research on teaching and learning in virtual environments within the context of virtual universities.

4. COMPETITION

Educational institutions are now working in a competitive environment, which has changed over the recent years. They have become much more student centred; the student is the focus as a customer and this is expected to increase. Evolution will be demand-driven. The commercial influence will be strong as companies invest more in development work.

The traditional academic exam is still a yardstick for assessment, and will still be a necessity for first-degree students. For others, an exam becomes less important. Higher education, defined and created by faculties and institutions will be of less interest for the mature student. Adult students who constitute a major growth area will compose and define their own 'portfolios' of knowledge and training.

It is important that the meaning of 'quality' in higher education is clearly defined and described. Academic standards as regards subject knowledge must be maintained. New academic standards as regards form and delivery must be recognised and approved. Universities tend to offer education across a wide variety of subject areas; 'company education' and the commercial ed-market are often very specialised in a few subjects. Universities must keep up their academic standards and broad research-based education. But they must also realise that this is not enough in a competitive world. Didactic skills, based on research as well, must be developed and these include skills in ICT-based teaching and learning.

Currently, there are three different teaching scenarios, each with different aims and objectives: traditional classroom education, learning that is aided by a computer system and web-based education. Their existence and the movement between them must be recognised and adjusted to. In spite if the progress that has been made, there is a need for more effective learning systems. In ICT-based teaching/learning (t/l), a development in parallel streams can be observed. There is a pedagogic/didactic shift from computer-aided t/l to computer based t/l. A reverse shift can also be observed, when 100% net-based t/l reverses the trend and includes to an amount of classroom teaching. Also, there is the traditional, campus-based t/l. We believe that all these styles, or educational modes, must co-exist since they meet different student needs.

4.1 ACCREDITATION

Accreditation and credit transfer calls for international collaboration and national Cupertino. In order to meet the students' growing demands for international education, academic institutions must accept some adjustment for international standards and quality criteria, with respect to educational/didactic mode and delivery of each course on the market. Consumer information is important to the individual student as well as to institutions and employers. This can be developed and hopefully approved internationally. Quality criteria with respect to the content must still be an issue and responsibility for the institution and national boards.

Virtual universities, in the real sense, are universities operating together and pooling their limited resources, universities open to credit transfer among the member institutions above all, but also negotiating with institutions outside the consortium, the exchange of knowledge and experiences taking place within co-operating institutionally. Such virtual universities have no border limits and even fewer brick-and-mortar limits. Within the virtual universities, accreditation should be one of the most important assets in the competitive market.

5. EXCHANGE OF FREE COURSE MATERIALS

The workgroup on virtual universities and virtual campuses find that exchange of free course materials is an activity that deserves the full support of IFIP and that it should be actively encouraged and supported by IFIP and its local partners as well as by institutions of higher education world-wide.

The workgroup recommends the sharing of free course materials, meaning digital content presented in an educational context, and software licensed to be used free of charge for educational purposes.

Arguments for sharing are plenty: recycling materials reduces cost and time spent on developing courseware to the benefit of institutions and their lecturers, mutual inspiration, and supporting the development of content for the emerging virtual universities and virtual campuses world-wide.

The workgroup on virtual universities and virtual campuses recommend that an educational file- and courseware sharing (Napster-style) service and clearing house be initiated within the framework of IFIP, much along the guidelines employed by the open source community (http://www.opensource.org/). It is intended to use specifications on meta-data, content and structure representation as is currently worked out by organisations like: IMS (Instructional Management Systems), CEN-ISSS WS- LT (Council for European Norms / Information Society Standardisation System, Workshop on Learning Technologies) and the IEEE-LTSC.

In order for such a sharing scheme to be successful, the following recommendations and conditions are suggested:

1. Consideration of international and national copyright legislation
2. Easy-to-read student and peer rating of material/courses for quality control and for faster retrieval and overview
3. Material presented explaining its original educational context and with teacher guidelines
4. Acknowledgement of developer of course/courseware and copyright owner
5. Common guidelines for submitting materials (using meta-data etc.).

Other relevant factors include topics such as language and other cultural differences between learner communities, discount prices on commercial software packages for educational use, updating and maintaining shared courseware, and the work on international copyright issues carried out by WIPO.

6. RESEARCH IN VIRTUAL UNIVERSITIES

The issue of undertaking research in the Virtual University context is problematic. Most of the discussion so far has focused on teaching and learning. However, universities undertake research and the question arises whether it is possible to undertake research in such a virtual environment. It would seem important that research into virtual aspects of disciplines should be a characteristic activity of virtual universities, especially in virtual PhD programs. However, doubts exist about the desirability of implementing all of research training programs in virtual environments. The relationship between PhD supervisor and PhD student requires face-to-face contact.

It is considered that research programs in virtual universities should research how the various disciplines could be taught better in the virtual environments.

97

The Impact of ICT on Learning at a Distance

Working Group 3.6

Chair: Elizabeth Stacey (AU)
Rapporteur: Vicki Lowery (AU)
Participants: Jenny Arms (AU), Mark Beach (NZ), Charlotte Cederstrøm (DK), Erik Dam (DK), Lone Dirckinck-Holmfeld (DK), France Henri (CA), Petera Hudson (NZ), Soini Kari (DK), Ove Bardenfleth Nielsen(DK), Kim Fuglsang Østergaard (DK)

Keywords: culture, distance learning, electronic communication, pedagogy, teacher training

Abstract: Information and Communication technologies have helped to remove the isolation of learning at a distance and changed the nature of distance education. The discussion examined this change and how it has affected school, college and higher education students who have no choice but to learn at a distance as well as those who are choosing to use ICT for flexible access to online classes and resources. Four major themes emerged: Acculteration, Authentication and the flexibility of design of hardware and software, Support, management and professional development of distance education teachers and Flexibility of learning for adults through ICT. An over-riding theme was the effects of culture on the use of ICT for education.

1. INTRODUCTION

The advent of the Internet and the capability of a global network of computers have radically changed the nature of distance education. Learning at a distance was traditionally a response to barriers such as geographic remoteness or physical inability to participate in face-to-face classes and was particularly prevalent in countries where small pockets of the population was scattered over large distances such as in Australia and Canada. Distance learning has always been inextricably linked with technology from the use of early forms of text reproduction to use of telephone, radio and television to facilitate production, distribution and interaction. Countries with large, scattered populations were also able to use methods of distance learning to provide education more widely as technologies were developed. Countries such as China and Turkey have been able to use television as a means of reaching learning and distributing education.

However, none of these technologies have had the impact on distance learning that Information and Communication technologies, with the resultant networking of computers in every country of the world, has had on education today. Now every country is using distance education even if their learners are able to access traditional face to face education, as is often the case in parts of Europe and Scandinavia. All teachers are now having to learn effective strategies for distance learning and the concept of globally connected learners has resulted in global distance learning through virtual campuses that can enable access to any education institution in the world or exist only within the networked computers.

Such capabilities mean that learning by Internet-linked computers are seen by governments as a solution to their provision of education and by educational entrepreneurs as a way of providing international markets for education and training. This international distance education market is sought by both traditional institutions seeking students world-wide and by commercial institutions developed for the process of virtual learning. As all levels of education embrace distance education strategies, the impact of ICT use on this type of learning must be considered in all contexts.

Schools

- Teachers and students have had to learn new skills and work practices. Teachers have had to learn to deliver classes to students they could not see, creating new challenges for classroom management.
- Teachers also had to achieve skills in technology so that they had sufficient confidence to deliver their classes to their distant students.
- Students have had to learn a new range of communication skills using telephone, e-mail, video-conferencing and discussion forums.
- Combining face-to-face and distance education: It is easy for the teacher and class to forget the distant students just as it is difficult for distant students to keep their focus on a teacher/class they cannot see.

Vocational Education and Training

Introducing workplace training linked to programs taught from colleges of vocational education through ICT has opened up a range of issues about learning and learning support. Professional development of staff and development of students into self directed, independent learners who can engage with learning online is often a challenge particularly in practical vocational skills education. Institutes have needed to focus on digital network development, Web site development, professional development of staff -for teaching and student support, management systems for delivery, access and equity issues, and project co-ordination between workplaces and colleges.

Universities and Institutes of Higher Education

Principles of adult education and self directed, independent learning are again a feature of learning at a distance in higher education. Experiences of traditional institutions now entering this area as they provide programs online can be informed by the distance education universities and their adaptation to ICT over the past decades. Issues raised include:

- Collaborative learning and the development of a learning community at a distance is now possible with ICT and this has changed the way distance learners linked to universities now learn.
- The resource base now possible through databases and World Wide Web sites has also greatly changed their ability to research at a distance and libraries are now centres of ICT expertise and equipment.
- The support infrastructure required to provide quality higher education at a distance is of major importance to the success of virtual campuses.

The three issues for in the group discussion focused on:

- Removing isolation through use of ICT;
- Effects of change to distance leaning on both teachers and learners;
- Combination uses of ICT for on campus as well as distance students.

Participants were asked to consider the following factors in relation to each of the above and respond with reference to their country's perspective.

1. Development and delivery of distance learning: critical success factors.
2. Emerging technologies: what works, what has been trialled, what are the pitfalls?
3. Effectiveness of online learning: strategies that work – how to engage the learner?
4. Student and teacher perspectives on learning: examples of successes, failures, works-in-progress – both remotely and as a support to face-to-face classes.

The group was diverse, covering a range of educational backgrounds. While everyone's work revolves around a common theme of 'distance learning using ICT' there were several themes which participants were keen to explore further.

- *Acculturation* One group discussed the issue of 'culture' and the need to protect a culture and its language from the effects of globalisation. Participants in this group include a French speaking research director from Canada, a New Zealander involved in teacher professional development of Maori teachers and a Danish research professor who all agreed that there is a need to resist these negative influences.

- *Flexibility of learning for adults through ICT* In Denmark as in many European countries distance is not the issue but rather how to provide flexibility of access to all learners, no matter what their circumstances. This group included a program director for vocational education in Denmark and an IT co-ordinator for a teacher training institution in Denmark.
- *Authentication and the flexibility of design of hardware and software* Group members included a project manager with the Danish Standards Association, a system developer with the Danish defence department and a former teacher now developing educational software.
- *Support, management and professional development of distance education teachers* The members were the principal of the New Zealand Correspondence School and an Australian project officer managing the use of video conferencing in schools. Their focus was on reliable and appropriate technology suited to the content, support for teachers and students and the good management of the whole process.

The group facilitator teaches and researches professional educators online as well as teaching pre-service teachers the use of flexible delivery. The rapporteur develops and delivers professional development programs using a variety of ICTs to teachers in the school and technical education sectors.

While the themes appear disparate, participants agreed that their discussions emanated from their original talk on the impact of ICT on learning at a distance. Because of their varied backgrounds, skills and experiences, participants found it easier to break into groups to focus their discussions.

2. RESISTANCE AGAINST GLOBALISATION

As Mason (1998) explains, globalisation of education is taking place along with the globalisation of economy with all that the consequences that follow. Supported by the development of ICT, the globalisation movement in education could have strong positive effects: enriching learning environments, opening up classrooms an schools to the world, allowing global interaction among learners and among educators to share ideas and culture. For educational institutions, ICT offers interesting opportunities to develop new alliances, set up creative ways for the sharing of resources, and reduce costs. However, Mason also stresses that globalisation has negative effects by introducing the notion of education as a 'market', by imposing competition among institutions to gain more 'clients', and by carrying out usage of ICT as a sales gadget instead of an added value to learning.

Our reflection led us to insist on the necessity to become very much aware of the negative influence of ICT mainly because it is insidious, not easily observable. Technology is not neutral. Each tool, each system carries out values and a certain vision of man and of human activity that is not without influence on users and on the culture of the users. Since ways of knowing the world and learning about it is an intimate part of culture, we should be in control of it, and not let technology influence it without our consent. We want to prevent ICT tools, products and services threatening the education process by imposing unwanted transformations, by making it a prisoner of the 'screen culture', and by levelling and limiting our vision of the world to 'unique thinking', unique language and unique sets of value.

A prime example the invasion of computer positivist culture is given by the Maori learners in New Zealand who are expected to use the English version of computer applications to assist in the achievement of a learning outcome. However the medium of the screen culture is not adapted to their way of experiencing the world through their language. Work is being done in close association with Hawaiian colleagues, who are working on similar challenges. Associations with web browser and desktop publishing application publishers are being forget so that the 'faces' of applications are at least in the Maori language medium. But much more should be done.

Culture could be defined by the way of knowing and of communicating; it is not limited to ethnic differences. Our 'problematic' as educators, as technology users and as technology developers should be on a day-to-day basis to find ways and means to:

- Trace acculturation of the learning process generated by ICT
- Resist against the standardisation of learning suggested by ICT tools, products and services
- Maintain and promote the diversity of 'learning cultures'.

For that purpose, we should work towards the development of an acute and critical understanding of ICT in order to depict subliminal invasion of learning by undesirable values and ways of thinking embedded in ICT. Supportive professional development programmes could carry on such critical attitude towards technology as well as initial ICT curriculum for the training of computer specialist and computer users.

We should also urge technology developers to apply participative design methodology in order to involve ICT users in the creation of tools that are respectful of their culture and values. *Learn-Net* (Charlier and Peraya 2001) is a European project that gives an example of collaboration between technology developers and users to for the setting up of a virtual campus shared by X university from Y different country.

3. FLEXIBILITY OF LEARNING FOR ADULTS

In Denmark as in many European countries distance is not the issue but rather how to provide flexibility of access to all learners, no matter what their circumstances. In Denmark the possibilities of getting access to the Internet are very good. The following figures from "Danmarks Statistik" 7. May 2001, indicate the state.

Access to internet, either at work or home	Access to internet, either at work or home, family with children	PC at home	PC at home, family with children
72 %	80%	70 %	90 %

On the other hand are there some problems around high speed access, only 10% have more than 50 kbits lines.

When considering the issues above, we felt that it is important to look at the following key focus points for learning:

1. The process is more important than the outcome
2. Learning is always based on the experience, and is lifelong process
3. Learning is a conflict-filled process, challenging the individual's knowledge and experience
4. Learning must be a holistic and critical process, with feedback
5. Interaction between the learner and the environment is necessary for learning
6. Learning must have interaction between social knowledge (collective knowledge) and personal knowledge
7. Learning has to make sense
8. Learning needs motivation (wanting to)
9. Learning needs a loving and positive climate
10. The learning process has to be flexible, so the individual can learn in her own way and at times and places of his/her own choosing.

We outlined four main areas for work when doing an e-learning project:

1. Planning and developing an e-learning course
2. Quality assurance of your e-learning course project
3. Delivering and coaching your e-learning course
4. Evaluation programs/tools.

At Niels Brock Business College, Copenhagen, Denmark, a System Development course taught at undergraduate level used a problem based learning approach online with 50 students working in small groups on projects with real life application on corporate contexts. Student retention rate is usually only 50% when the course is taught face to face. During the course there are three face to face meetings for 1/2 a day at the beginning, half way and at a roundup point in the semester spaced. Between these meetings there is an online conferencing structured with collaborative groups with mature age female leaders. The assessment is both collaborative and individual with a final examination and a defence of the group report. There was a 10% better grade average than when run traditionally with only 2 students dropping out of the course.

It was successful because of student leadership, authentic tasks, and ongoing online communication throughout the semester. The quality of teaching rose with web based teaching as resources were developed for students in a public and accountable medium, and teaching online raised pedagogical reflection amongst teachers as they began teaching in a new environment.

At Deakin University, Australia, a detailed evaluation of the use of computer conferencing for units established in a Master of Professional Education and Training program was undertaken as part of a project, Learner Centred Evaluation of Computer Facilitated Learning Projects in Higher Education, which was funded by the Australian Commonwealth government Committee of University Teaching and Staff Development. The structuring of the units and their effects on interaction and learning online found:

- Student feedback supported the use of online conferencing in encouraging a learning community with teacher presence seen as central.
- Frequency analysis showed that required online involvement generated high frequency of messaging, a high teacher time requirement that needed more management with responsibility given to students. Patterns of communication showed that high teacher interaction encouraged high student response but in small groups this was devolved and required less teacher interactivity.
- Tasks designed for online discussion generated online interaction with a cognitive focus.
- Content analyses pointed to the importance of conferences for social interaction and administrative sharing as well as for a cognitive focus.
- Students perceived the value of considering other students' perspectives, ideas and resources as a component of their successful learning online.

4. AUTHENTICATION AND THE FLEXIBILITY

In the traditional way of teaching where the students show up in a classroom they can be recognised and identified by the teacher who generally has a reasonable idea of the abilities of the individual student. This is not the case when we speak of learning at a distance. In this case the teacher may never face the student and does not know very much about them. The teacher does not know if somebody else than the registered person is doing the training and taking the tests. An authentication process therefore needs to be put in place. The tests/examinations need to be electronically signed to prove that the right person was at least present at the test. This technical problem belongs to the generic design of the tools used. Systems with electronic signatures and certificates may solve the problem and ensure both the students and the teachers that the identification and credibility is present.

This is an important component of the design of an ICT application and is influential in ensuring the success of the ICT application. We are not able to start using ICT in any organisation without influencing the organisation and/or the goals of the organisation. We are not able to use ICT in any process without influencing the process and/or the goal or purpose of the process. We also need to consider whether ICT forces us to redefine what learning is? Many things we learn are outdated in a short period of time.

Leavitt (1965) developed a diamond model trying to show that changing any part (corner) of the system makes an impact on the other corners.

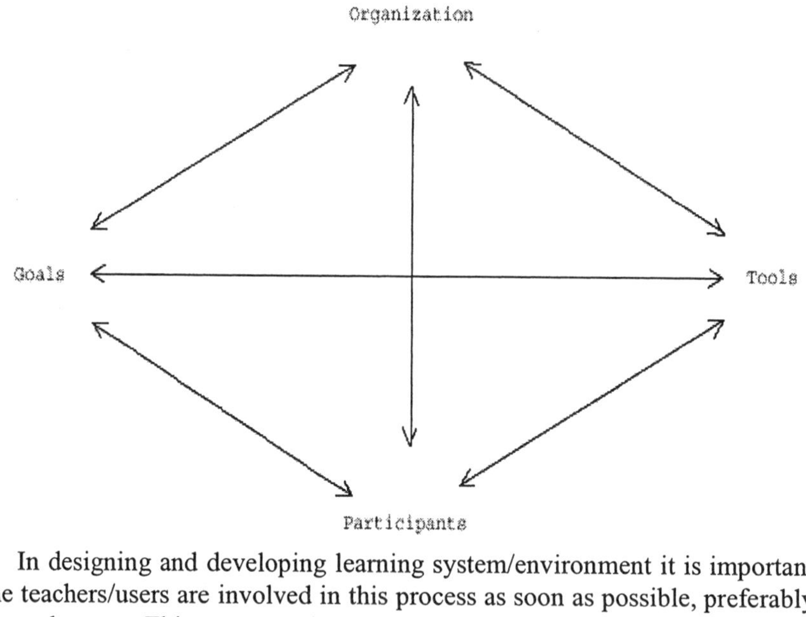

In designing and developing learning system/environment it is important the teachers/users are involved in this process as soon as possible, preferably from the start. This ensures a better integration within the organisation, and it makes the understanding of the necessity of the tools more obvious.

One of the important things to be aware of is the possibility to communicate within the system. This could be via e-mail, chat or some kind of conference or debate system. If implemented properly it can initiate discussions between colleagues and in the education give students the ability to argue any answer, question, solutions and suggestions in writing. The development of an asynchronous (teacher independent) communication for written argument and reflection between students provides an enhancement of the education. It puts a new perspective on the role of the teacher. It is also affected by and affects the culture of the learner depending on the communication medium used; chat, forum, e-mail, file sharing.

More and more people are involved in life long learning and increasingly post-school students access learning online. When you are involved in life long learning, you as 'teacher and student' should participate in the Life Long Design Process, particularly as teachers are no longer considered as the fount of all wisdom but are taking on the role of facilitator, guide and mentor. These roles are being well developed in the online environment, and as shown in the Danish case study above, often lead to greater student success rates.

5. PROFESSIONAL DEVELOPMENT

Core beliefs in learner centred learning acknowledge that learners have individual characteristics and learning styles, individual learning needs, and that learning often succeeds best in a collaborative environment. The digital world allows us to do new things in new ways. It imposes no limitations on the production, storage or access to material, opportunities for discourse, or time, manner and place of learning. We can be considered to be 'digitally minded' when we use synchronous and asynchronous tools to participate in co-operative and collaborative communities/relationships, re-examine the relationship between teacher and learner, and become more discerning and critically aware of information.

The major issues relating to using ICT for learning at a distance.

Technology Technology must be reliable and Helpdesk and Warranty covered. Technology must be available to anyone who wants it. Teachers and users need to be trained regularly as new hardware/software are released.

Support Teachers need time to write courses (perhaps training in multimedia), tools to write courses, to be valued for their contribution to the school, and need peer support (training, networks, attend conferences). Students need to be allowed to learn in chosen style, and appropriate technology tools.

Teaching and Learning Courses should reflect modern teaching and learning methods, including the use of appropriate technology (problem based, constructivist theory, project presentation). Courses need to promote innovation, and via ICT, courses should introduce experts, conduct regular classes, admin meetings, peer networks, conduct training.

Management Planning/negotiating curriculum between provider and student needs to be done centrally. Assessment needs to be decided centrally. Funding for technology/telecourses and course planning/implementation, should be available; evaluation must be done regularly.

6. CONCLUSIONS

In the final session, the group came together and agreed on a framework to encompass their discussions. The main focus was culture and how culture affected all aspects of the use of ICT, whether it referred to language, hardware, software or the view of the user. The major threads were:

- Culture of the hardware and software and the effect on users whose first language is not English
- Culture of the learner and the need to maintain indigenous and minority cultures and languages
- Support of the learner through mentoring, education and training
- Need for a learner-centred focus
- Communication and the interaction between teachers and students, students and students and teachers and teachers
- Collaboration and the balance with autonomous learning.

From these discussions the group concluded that we should be flexible in our use of IT in response to users, their culture, learning style and individual needs; we should plan course development with a view to quality and learning outcomes; and we should be respectful of the culture of learners in a global education market. We suggest that IFIP, backed by UNESCO, review ICT development from a cultural impact perspective.

REFERENCES

Charlier, B. and Peraya, D. (eds.) (2001, To be published) *Learn-Net.* Bruxelles, De Broeck.
Leavitt, (1965)
Mason, R. (1998) *Globalisation of Education.* London, Routledge.

PART XI

PANEL REPORTS

98

Provoking New Images of Research and Practice in Reformed Educational Spaces

Chair: Robert Aiken (US)
Panel: David Passig (IL), Matti Sinko (FI)

Keywords: research, classroom practice, innovation, social issues, methodologies

Question: Why are (many) teachers not using computers in the classroom?

Answer: Because we are using old methods of teaching which do not adapt well to the new technologies

Solution: Be forward looking and examine what teachers WANT and try to find ways to find ways to address these needs.

Matti Sinko used a series of tables from some recent Finnish studies that showed that while students are using computers more outside class, that many report not using them in class. And this is in a country where 81% of schools report using computers in classrooms for children from the ages of 10 -18! So there is a major 'disconnect' and that missing piece must be the teacher. As additional evidence Matti noted that most of the ICT teachers are also teachers of mathematics. Yet when they teach mathematics almost none of them use a computer in their classroom! Schizophrenic – maybe – but more to the point the computer is not providing them with a tool that they feel allows them to do something different or better or.... than their current practices.

David Passig picked up on this theme by declaring that we have not begun to tap the potential of the computer for education. And we won't unless we develop completely new approaches for providing teachers something that they really want. He reported on a survey in which he participated in this past year that asked a wide range of teachers in North America what they would like the computer to do for them. The answers were not at all what were expected. Rather than mentioning education aspects they focused on emotional, psychological and social issues. They wanted to be able to better understand the student's emotional level as clues to their way(s) of thinking and learning. They wanted the computer to assist them in developing more open social environments – and environments that would allow them to respond to the psychological needs of their students. In other words, they were interested in qualitative aspects that have rarely been studied or even sufficiently well understood.

David's message was clear. We need to undertake research that examines these issues or the technology will not have an impact on education! We must start this process now and we must take risks. As one example he discussed some of his own research that in part is based on constructing Virtual Reality (VR) environments. He pointed to the need for providing teacher scaffolding as a way to help them use computers to construct better environments for their students. As one example he briefly discussed a VR environment his research group has constructed that allows the user (teacher) to enter the world of a young child (5-6 years old) and 'feel' what the world looks like *from the perspective of the child.* Another example he discussed was how students are learning (and we are not studying) using hand held communication devices. There is an entire culture that has been created and is natural for young people to use, BUT there is little to no research on how we can/should incorporate such technology and ethos into the learning process.

So the message is clear: Change the way and types of research we are doing to explore what teachers really need and want or risk losing the opportunity which this technology provides!

99

Computing History of the Nordic Countries

Chair: Peter Bollerslev (DK)
Panel: Leo Højsholt-Poulsen (DK), John Impagliazzo (US), Jan Wibe (NO), Erling Schmidt (DK)

Keywords: computing history, languages, programming, informatics as a study topic

Peter Bollerslev, President of IFIP, stated that computing history is a rich area of academic and practical interest.

John Impagliazzo, Chair of IFIP WG9.7 (History of Computing), related how in Sweden Georg Scheutz built the first prototype of the Difference Engine in 1822 and the actual machine from 1840 to 1853. Willgodt Odhner designed the first commercial calculator in 1875, used for almost 100 years. Another, built by Carl Fridén in 1922, remained commercial until the 1970s. The Swedish government authorised the construction of first commercial computer, Binär Automatisk ReläKalulator (BARK), used from 1950 to 1955; from 1953 then developed the Binär Electronisk Sekvens-Kalulator (BESK) all-electronic computer that in 1954 was the fastest in the world. 12 BESK-type machines were made; one is quasi-operational at the University of Lund. In 1957 Facit designed EDB, the first Swedish commercial computer, while Saab designed the Saab Räkneautomat (SARA) for in-house calculations for aircraft. Datasaab (Saab) produced in 1962 the D21 computer, a commercial version. Ericsson, a force in communications since 1876, is today dominant in wireless communications and technology.

Erling Schmidt, of the School Authorities of Aalborg, highlighted achievements in Denmark, from the educational perspective. The development of Denmark's first computer – the Dansk Automatic Sekvens Kalkulator (DASK) – was an extension of the Swedish BESK after co-operation between Danish and Swedish scientists. Denmark's first educational computer was a binary-digital converter, introduced in Danish schools in 1968. By the early 1970s, it was clear that computers should be an integral part of education. In 1972, the Ministry of Education issued the so-called Johnsen-report, a plan for computers in the educational system at all levels. Although not implemented immediately, it generated much interest and spurred using computers in the school curriculum. The follow-up work by Bollerslev and others in 1982 and 1983, entitled *Datalære*, led to an infusion of computers in the Danish teacher education and school system.

Jan Wibe of Trondheim Universitet, the Norwegian University of Science and Technology, stated that Norway's early interest in computers was educational. The philosophy was to treat informatics as a subject area in its own right, to integrate computers in other subjects of learning, and to include computers as part of teacher education and training. From 1970 to 1983, all Norwegian schools offered an optional course in BASIC programming In 1983, the Minister of Education created a taskforce, Datasekretariatet, which fostered software development and projects in schools. All teachers had to have at least 40 hours of computer education in their training. By 1990, computers were integrated in all schools and a required component of all teacher education, which a further emphasis on training from 1990 to 1996. Between 1996 and 1999, a national four-year plan emphasised research, the development of learning resources, the use of computer projects in schools, and the deployment of distance education. Norway's new four-year plan (2000-2003) may be found at <http://www.dep.no/kuf/html/ikt/>.

Leo Højsholt-Poulsen of UNI-C in Århus, recalled his early days of computing – number crunching of mathematical equations. In the 1970s and the 1980s, in education the concentration was on programming and programming languages. ICT in schools was synonymous with programming, in BASIC. By 1980 the home-grown language of Comal became the language of choice in the school systems. Later, Pascal was used. In 1987, the Nordic countries developed Dataprogramgruppen, a consortium under the auspices of the Nordic Council of Ministers for the purpose of exchanging educational software between the Nordic countries. Between 1987 and 2000, this 'Baastad Model' encompassed over 250 educational programs that were part of the consortium pool. The model has helped the Nordic countries to stay abreast with ICT in schools and provided an avenue of leadership to explore new educational ideas in a technical society.

The audience, interested in this Nordic history, suggested that IFIP be more proactive in this area, possibility through a conference so it could be explored in greater depth.

100

Integrating Technology into Curriculum: Local Outcomes of a National Agenda

Chair: Bernard Cornu (FR)
Panel: David K. Stokes (US), Wanda Carrasquillo (US), Joyce Sibbett (US), Jeanette Jones (US), Wolfgang Weber (DE), Anne McDougall (AU)

Keywords: integration, curriculum development, national policies, teacher education, collaborative learning

The panel started with the presentation of a project by four colleagues from Westminster College (USA). This project was funded by the United States Department of Education within the pt3 programme: *Preparing Tomorrow's Teachers to use Technology.*

The U.S. Department of Education strongly wishes to overcome the digital divide and to have a population well versed in the use of computer based technology, and considers Teachers preparation as a major challenge in order to integrate information and communication technology into education. This is why the pt3 programme was launched in early 1999.

The School of education at Westminster College got an important funding in this project, and designed a strategy aimed at improving its preservice teachers' technology skills, attitude towards, and knowledge. For this, they radically revised their methods and core curriculum by integrating technology throughout.

The presentation showed the impact of this strategy at different level: impact on the school of education itself, its organisation, its methods and curriculum; impact on teacher trainers, and impact on the local schools and local teachers, with a particular emphasis on the role of school principals.

It increased team work, it helped changing the pedagogy and developing research.

Concrete examples were presented, such as the use of videoconferencing, and the changes in the methodology course. It was clearly shown how trainers start with fear, but take the challenge and go to success!

Positive effects were stated, such as the better level of reflection of the students involved in the project, particularly in the 'eBoard' experience, and also the commitment to life-long learning as a driving force to get involved in learning about technology applications in the trainers teaching and personal life.

But there are also difficulties, such as the differences in teachers skills, the aspects of the time it requires for learning new skills, maintaining and applying them, and also the difficulty of assessing the students' use of multimedia resources.

The discussion then went to an international exchange, initiated by Wolfgang Weber and Anne McDougall, and then involving the audience.

A national policy helps local actors to develop and integrate computer technology in education. But even if equipment is progressing quickly, it needs changes in the pedagogy and in the teacher preparation. There are more and more schools well equipped, but only few use new media consequently under pedagogical aspects in most of the subjects to increase the quality of learning. Redesigning methods and curriculum in teacher training institution is a very good opportunity for progressing. But we need trainers and teachers ready to change, we need teachers who dare and pupils who dare!

Teachers need time, teachers need help, and the idea appeared of a 'curriculum navigator' in order to support teachers better.

101

The Networking of School Systems: Can IT Improve Teaching and Learning?

Chair: Anne McDougall (AU)
Panel: Pam Bishop (AU), Lynne Schrum (US), Geoff Romeo (AU), Greg Baker (AU), Bert Moonen (NL)

Keywords: teaching methods, innovation, curriculum development, collaborative learning

Geoff Romeo described the support for ICT in schools in the state government school system in Victoria, Australia. A network, VicOne, links all government departments in the state; its largest user is the Department of Employment, Education and Training. Services provided by this network include an electronic mail system called EduMail; a very popular web site titled SofWeb which connects schools to global classroom projects, software and other resources, and discussion groups; professional development materials, and information from the state's so-called navigator schools where innovative activities involving learning technologies are undertaken.

Pam Bishop outlined features of the network CEVN, developed in Victoria for the Catholic education system in that state. This network was established late in 1998, and all the schools were connected by the end of 1999, with funding provided for a computing support staff member for each school. The aims of the project included provision of global communication and cheaper, faster and safer Internet access for students, development of a learning plan in each school, use of the local area network for classroom management, curriculum planning and development, and monitoring and reporting of student progress. A monthly newsletter is distributed to all schools. Ongoing financial support is needed for the project, and professional development for teachers, administrators, and principals is a critical issue to be addressed.

Greg Baker, also from Victoria, described initiatives being taken to build an on-line community associated with a non-government independent P-12 school. All the school's curriculum resources have been put onto an intranet available from both the school and the students' homes, with a view to encouraging home-school links and so-called anywhere anytime learning. Staff at the school is required to provide all curriculum materials – including homework, notices, etc. – on the intranet. Each staff member and each student has a personalised login to the system. Staff and senior students in the school are required to have portable notebook computers, and the school provides wireless networking for these machines as well as the regular backbone. The initiative is supported by a strong professional development program. Benefits of the project include improved access and better home-school links. Challenges have been associated with provision of technical support, security, system integration, and funding.

An international perspective was provided by Bert Moonen and Lynne Schrum. Bert Moonen described an Internet based wide area network or 'knowledge net' established in the Netherlands, a network to which all schools are to be connected by the end of 2001. The benefits include faster access, personal e-mail addresses for teachers and students, educational resources available on a supervised and secure part of the Internet, discussion groups, and connection for libraries, museums and publishers. The main problems were with reliability (early in the project) and the connection of local area networks to the wider area network.

Lynne Schrum at the University of Georgia is working with schools looking to use networking. Perceived benefits here include increased communication possibilities, relief from isolation, and enhanced professional development opportunities with on-line materials. The challenges faced have concerned security of information, privacy, the development of acceptable use policies, equity issues, and the problem of teachers being expected to be available 24 hours a day and 7 days a week.

102

Transatlantic Panel on Research and Implementation for eTraining and eLearning

Chair: Raymond Morel (CH)
Panel: John Cherniavsky (US), Harriet Taylor (US), Rick Adrian (US), Jens Christiansen (DK/EU), Jan Hylen (SE/EUN), Bernard Cornu (FR), Pieter Hogenbirk (NL), Doug Brown (UK)

Keywords: distance learning, research, learning models, collaboration and international cooperation, national programme

Following a brief overview of the different types of research and that the emphasis here would be on research which led to practical outcomes, the speakers – and the discussion which followed – covered a wide range of projects and proposals.

A number of joint ways of working are possible and indeed some current developments in the USA had potential for collaboration with activities in the EU. Three main themes emerged.

- Development of a learning grid (based on the experience from other domains but available for researchers and educators in both the USA, EU and elsewhere).
- Exchanges and visits to share and learn from each other.
- The provision of effective educational resources through the creation of artefact repositories.

The development of a learning grid is not in itself a new idea. The UK has their 'National Grid for Learning' and the EU has developed an educational portal for the exchange of ideas. However, the emphasis on research would lead this grid to offer something different. The idea of a community of learners was discussed and that the concept of collective intelligence underpinned this. The Internet allows for a new scale for addressing problems and for sharing ideas such as how ICT can make a difference to learning and student performance. The learning grid could support small research experiments in different countries and it could also support larger change. In the USA the average adult would now change jobs 6 times in their lifetime and there is a need to ensure the ability to continue learning if we are to be able to adapt to this environment. The challenge is to seek research which will lead to a revolutionary change rather than an evolutionary one.

There is already a formal agreement between the USA and the EU signed in December 1997. This determined to synchronise projects across the Atlantic, run joint seminars and arrange visits and exchanges. Joint programmes already exist – such as a project on the school of the future and the 'learning citizen'. There is a move towards increased cooperation in this area, with a desire to see exchanges of both researchers and students.

Work is currently underway in the USA on a digital library which will be operational by the latter part of 2002. The aim is to move from 'great piles of stuff 'to 'piles of great stuff'. This will be available to the international community and will seek to build on work in other areas. There is a desire to hear from others and collaborate on this work.

All these developments were generally welcomed by the group. New technology means new pedagogy, and this needs to reflect the shift from computer/informatics to communication and information in society. We need to practice what we preach, recognise that early adopters and innovators may provide and get a good personal feeling but we need to focus on the majority.

Being at the leading edge has a number of pitfalls but an EU seminar identified that governments' needed to a) move fast b) be bold and c) learn from each other. This collaboration across the Atlantic could be a key factor in enabling them to do this.

103

Experimentation in Telelearning Environments: 3 Case Studies

Chair: Robert Munro (UK)
Panel: Ken Eustace (AU), France Henri (CA), Wolfgang Weber (DE)

Keywords: distance learning, learning systems, collaborative learning, learning materials, management

This panel offered WCCE 2001 participants the opportunity to hear about and reflect on research conclusions associated with innovative practice in telelearning which aimed to promote a sense of community amongst participants.

While distance provision holds many attractions and resolves many educational problems, concern has focussed on the importance of creating rich learning environments and enhancing opportunities for group collaboration and co-operation.

The three presenters were keen to illustrate that learning is most effective when the learner is placed at the centre of the instructional model and value is derived from a greater community of learning. This panel attracted considerable interest – not least because of the experience in telelearning offered by the panel members but also because of the geographical perspective of these experiences.

Dr. Ken Eustace, director of the Research Unit for Telelearning Environments in the School of Information Studies at Charles Sturt University in Australia, works with various research groups and has considerable experience in installing, using and testing ICT tools. In exploring the added value of text-based synchronous workshop practice (ranging from raw telnet to full web interfaces) he has built up many effective learning communities on-line.

These have included Virtual Conferences, a Literature Circle Network linking primary schools in New South Wales and Tasmania, and the Executive meetings of National Societies such as the Australian School Libraries. All have demonstrated significant advantages over more conventional interactions.

Ken maintained it was vital that developers of virtual environments and learning communities made it simple to connect participants and provided adequate scaffolding and support for development and interaction. He considered it important that people were given time to explore the medium and develop/refine their skills in using ICT facilities. Ken envisaged three principal stages in a developing community – the initial socialisation period where introductions were made and stories and photographs might be swapped, an alliance building phase and finally the critical stage where participants worked as a team on project work.

He identified four main issues:

- Ensuring ethical use of computers by all
- Rights, responsibilities and behaviours for group protocol
- Intellectual property rights
- The shift in focus from instructor to learner with flatter hierarchical structures.

France Henri is a professor at the Télé-université of Montreal in Canada. This distance teaching university has more than 25,000 students and operates in many respects like the Open University in the United Kingdom. Teachers/professors at the University design and create learning environments for their courses/students and, once these are effected, students are free to interact and learn in the environments. There is no face-to-face teaching.

Five principal zones or spaces comprise the generic model for the construction of these learning environments:

- Information space which holds the content
- Management space which facilitates organisation and navigation
- Assistance space offering human or automated help systems
- Production space where development can take place
- Collaboration space.

Aided by a very comprehensive slide Ms. Henri illustrated the importance of the collaboration space. Here students develop their group identity – they bond and don't feel they are studying in isolation. The space offers resources and tools for sharing and for stimulating co-operation and collaboration and provides contacts to other students and a range of computer conferences.

In the Télé-université model on-line teaching has no place. The model is based on flexibility and autonomy – no professors or tutors tell the students what to do. Students are in control of, and are responsible for, their own learning. They study what they want when they want and at any depth. This approach neutralises the traditional model of learning employed in schools and promotes both individual and co-operative or collaborative approaches to learning – as and when necessary.

Wolfgang Weber is the Head of The Advisory Centre for New Technologies in The North Rhine Westphalian State Institute for School and Adult Education, Soest, Germany and their server provides learning environments for schools and colleges. Importantly, topic-oriented resources, detailed background information on a range of issues and lists of contacts are provided. Topics range from general information for primary school pupils to specific issues e.g. the environmental impact of air pollution/acid rain for College science courses. Message boards are accessible to participants who can interchange information and opinions. Mediators of these boards can select participants, restrict access and establish small group discussion areas. A media centre allows teachers and pupils to access different media resources and the 'Foyer' offers a publishing room. In addition 'workshop rooms' provide collaborative space where pupils from different schools can work on projects of communal interest. Audio conferencing, video-chat and white board communication workspace is available.

The system has been extensively tested in local primary and secondary schools. Institutions in North Rhine Westphalia and the Sud-Tirol area of Northern Italy have been linked. Teacher training and in-service courses are offered on how to use the system and materials development groups have been set up.

Some key considerations underpinned the design of the environment:

- Participants should have equal or similar rights of access
- They should preferably get to know each other face-to-face
- There must be structure to the planned work or co-operation.

The telelearning exemplars exhibited many similarities and addressed common issues of access, equity and collaboration. The presentations sparked a number of questions and particular interest was expressed in the importance of structure in designing the environments. The panel members stressed the importance of creating/choosing carefully structured tasks for participants and of designing the learning environment specifically and appropriately for the 'client group'. The better, more thoughtful, and more appropriate the design and structure then the more flowing the discussion and collaboration. Ken Eustace suggested that at the end of a course people wanted to meet to socialise and discuss. If they have faces to fit to writing styles this promotes both socialisation and discussion. France Henri and

Wolfgang Weber noted similar responses from users of their systems. The desire for socialisation is present no matter the age of participants.

All of the systems build in opportunities for co-operation and collaboration and this raised the question as to whether the problem-based work was largely individual or do the students genuinely co-operate? France Henri stressed that, while she always tried to build in a collaborative element, there must be a balance between individual and collaborative work. The Télé-université favoured a team or large group project set up early in the course. Wolfgang Weber said co-operation was an important consideration and was often related to the topic under investigation and the level at which students were exploring the material. With increased collaboration management issues became significant. Ken Eustace felt that the co-operative or collaborative element helped reduce feelings of isolation and built up self-esteem. As a result it was often difficult to close off the collaboration!

Following further detailed questioning the panel concluded that the telelearning community must urgently address cross-cultural issues, plagiarism and intellectual property/copyright matters.

104

The Next Generation of Programming

Programming as an Engineering Discipline

Chair: Juris Reinfelds (US)
Panel: Peter Van Royt (BE), Tiajaru Diverio (BR)

Keywords: programming, software engineering, computing

1. PROGRAMMING IS NOT TAUGHT IN THIS WAY

We define *programming* broadly as the step from specification to running program, which consists in designing the architecture and its abstractions and coding them into a programming language. Up to now, programming has been taught more as a craft than as an engineering discipline. Usually, programming is taught in the context of one (or a few) programming languages (e.g., Java, complemented with Haskell or Scheme). The historical accidents of the particular languages chosen are so closely interwoven with the fundamental concepts that the two cannot easily be separated. There is confusion between tools and concepts. This has led to different programming communities, based on different programming 'paradigms': object-oriented, logic, functional. The unity of programming as a single discipline has been lost. So programs often suffer from poor design. For instance, concurrency in Java is complex and expensive, so its use is discouraged. So Java taught programmers conclude that concurrency is *always* complex and expensive.

Program specifications are designed around concurrency restrictions, often in a contorted way. But such restrictions are not fundamental. There are forms of concurrency that are quite useful and yet as easy to program with as sequential programs. It is possible to implement threads almost as cheaply as procedure calls. If programmers were taught concurrency correctly, they could write specifications for and program in systems without concurrency restrictions, including improved implementations of Java.

2. THE KERNEL LANGUAGE APPROACH

Current languages, after five decades of language design, are capable of scaling to programs of millions of lines of code. This is not fortuitous, because they model essential aspects of how to construct complex programs. They are not just arbitrary constructions of the human mind; they merit scientific study. How can we separate the fundamental concepts in these languages from their historical accidents? The kernel language approach is one way. The full language is translated into a small *kernel language* that has a minimal number of *programmer-significant* elements, giving a student insight into what the language does. The kernel language has simple formal semantics, a foundation for the programmer's intuition and the programming techniques built on top of it. Reducing a complex phenomenon to its primitive elements is characteristic of scientific method. Earlier attempts to make programming an engineering discipline failed. The two approaches used to define languages precisely are foundational calculus and the virtual machine. A foundational calculus, like the λ–calculus or π-calculus, reduces programming to a minimal number of elements, regardless of whether these are relevant for practical programming – important for computation theory but largely irrelevant to programmers. A virtual machine, which defines a language in terms of implementation on an idealised machine, is useful for implementers, but concepts close to hardware are irrelevant to programmers.

3. A TEXTBOOK

Van Roy and Haridi's textbook based, on the kernel language approach,. organises programming at three levels: *Concepts* – compositionality, concurrency, encapsulation, lexical scoping, higherorder, dataflow, state, inheritance; *Techniques* – how to write programs with these concepts; and *Computation models ('paradigms')* – data entities, operations, and a kernel language. Often-used programming techniques are explained in terms of simple kernel languages, and introduced progressively, with complete and simple formal semantics. Programming paradigms emerge as a kind of epiphenomenon, depending concepts one used and which properties held. The textbook is being tested 2001-2002, in three universities (KTH in Stockholm, Sweden, UCL in Louvain-la-Neuve, Belgium, and NMSU in Las Cruces, NM, USA), The latest draft of the textbook is always available at [http://www.info.ucl.ac.be/people/PVR/book.html] complemented by a full-featured open-source software package, the Mozart Programming System [http://www.mozart-oz.org].

105

Robotics: An Agent of Change for ICT?

Chair: Erling Schmidt (DK)
Panel: Tom Lough (US), Cathy Fett (US)

Keywords: robotics, innovation, equality issues, collaborative learning, programming

This panel was designed to stimulate a discussion of robotics as an agent of change in education. The initial remarks by the panel were based on a survey mailed out to (US) schools early in 2001. The following questions were discussed. Do robotics activities affect male students differently than female students? What are some of the affective aspects of robotics activities? Do robotics in schools seem to have any impact on student career choices?

The 165 survey respondents were almost equally male and female, and were evenly distributed in teaching experience. The most common grades for robotics were in the middle school range.

The patterns for the responses describing male and female students were similar for several items. Male and female students were reported mainly 'quite often' for (a) demonstrates on-task focus of long duration, (b) collaborates with other students of the same gender, and (c) expresses interest and excitement. Male and female students were reported mainly 'somewhat often' for (a) demonstrates frequent and familiar use of robotics terms in operational vocabulary, (b) shows an emotional connection with robotics projects, (c) shows evidence of having discussed robotics with parents or other family members, (d) demonstrates uncommon persistence in the face of a daunting problem, and (e) participates in other technology-related programs (in school or outside of school).

Patterns for the responses describing male and females students were different for several items. Female students were described as having higher levels of the following activities than male students: collaborates with students of the opposite gender, accepts role willingly in teamwork situations, and shows a desire to work with others. Male students were described as having higher levels of the following activities than female students: tends to work by oneself, shows evidence of unprompted or non-required robotics work, spontaneously asks questions about other robotics applications, is willing to design and build a rough prototype that may or may not work, and comes to class on 'free time' to spend more time with robotics.

As observed by respondents, the vast majority of students want to participate in robotics activities, reporting for males very much 73% and somewhat 23%, and for females very much 36% and somewhat 41%. The responses suggest that female students are perceived to be more interested in collaboration and may be better team players than male students. Yet, male students seem to 'get into' robotics more than the female students.

Responses in the career-related items indicated little activity. Several of the items related more to students of high school age than to younger students.

Ideas and suggestions for teachers included (a) provide a combination of collaborative and competitive activities to appeal to both genders, (b) try different group combinations to adjust the social dynamics, (c) be aware of the attention given to the different groups, (d) make an effort to engage girls in the process so they participate more fully, and (e) allow some creative freedom in building and programming levels so all students can build and/or program to his or her highest level.

Panel attendance was satisfactory. A few questions were asked by members of the audience, and there were some interactions among audience members.

106

National Educational Technology Standards for Students and Teachers

Chair: Michelle Selinger (UK)
Panel: Helen Barrett (US), Bernard Cornu (FR), Pieter Hogenbirk (NL), Robert Munro (UK), Harriet Taylor (US)

Keywords: standards, integration of ICT, teacher education, collaborative learning, lifelong learning

In many countries in which ICT is becoming pervasive in schools, governments are developing a range of similar standards or benchmarks for both students and pre- and in-service teacher training. But are these the appropriate standards? Why should there be standards for the use of this tool? Developments in what it is we should be teaching, and what how knowledge is defined for the information age is also important, but not often recognised in these frameworks.

In addition it is recognised that teacher development in the integration of ICT goes through a number of stages from substitution through transition to transformation, but this is not reflected in the standards frameworks in many countries which assume some level of conformity. Setting levels in standards can provide a framework for both teacher training and for students but can also be an inhibitor. Levels can limit and constrain students and teachers aspirations for their students, and standards are too technical, therefore inhibiting the use of technology as teachers concerns focus on meeting the requirements. The real purpose is lost.

Perhaps we need educational standards rather than specific ICT standards, but which recognise the role ICT can have and lead to a change in the paradigm for learning.

These might include:

- Learning in co-operation

- Lifelong learning
- Learning in groups
- Learning to learn
- Learning about your own learning styles.

This might make sense if we consider the problems of setting standards; those we set today are not the standards that will be appropriate tomorrow. In addition the ability to reach a set of standards in schools will depend on the four 'pillars' that provide the foundations for effective integration of ICT. These are equipment, connectivity, curriculum and competence.

107

Rainforest Goes School

Chair: Helmut Stemmer (AT)
Panel: Michaela Picheler (AT), Ingrid Schwarz (AT)

Keywords: methodologies, curriculum development, teacher education, ethical and social issues, classroom practice

An important point was to see the rainforest project in relation to other papers compare findings, weaknesses, strengths, doubts, reflections, and so assess our project anew. This highlights the strength of this project, located in complexity and diversity of content, methods and media and reconfirmed that project is on the 'right path', despite of difficulties faced in the past. Concerning theories of learning and teaching, we have seen parallels to other presenters, that point to approaches that have been used successfully in the rainforest project and partly correspond to the methodology of the project taken from international development education called 'Global Learning'.

The paper from Bernard Cornu *Winds of change in the teaching profession* reflects the very complex role of teachers from today and tomorrow. These ideas describe the role that many teachers adopt in the rainforest project. Further, the demands that are put on the school from society (such as globalisation, democratisation and complexification), also mentioned by Cornu, meet the goals and means of the rainforest project.

The presentation from Lone Dirckinck-Holmfeld about *Conceptual design of a virtual learning environment based on problem oriented project pedagogy (POPP)* corresponds with the rainforest project in various ways:

- Learning to learn and to see problems and subject matters in a new way
- Critical information handling and teamwork
- Mutual responsibility for own and others learning.

The notion from the professional group about social and ethical issues that 'social and ethical issues are often purely presented to pupils in uninteresting ways', is a statement the Austrian rainforest project can respond to and offer a different position and experience. The project provides many possibilities and methodological approaches to learning about, and engaging pupils in, projects around social and ethical issues, which are not boring and uninteresting. It combines traditional methods plus ICT environment so the is enjoyable and interesting to students and teachers.

As often discussed at this conference, there is the difficulty that ICT without greater content is not very appealing to teachers and students. The rainforest project suggests and demonstrates that themes like globalisation, complexity, democratisation, equity and global citizenship can be discussed in schools successfully and combined well with the use of ICT. Students and teachers are interested and motivated to learn about the content and use ICT as medium to transport their messages to a bigger audience. ICT offers a range of methods to engage in these themes nationally and internationally.

Schools have either worked within specific subjects or have included the entire school in the rainforest project. It depends on the school culture, whether they put priority on project-oriented learning or not. In many countries these open learning spaces are barely available even when considered necessary. This ICT project can enhance open learning spaces, yet it also builds on pre-existing school-structures and will not offer miracles. Feedback appreciated that we verbalised that ICT does not save time, but enables better public visibility and offers more continuity.

Various participants have shown great interest in participating in this project and there might be a possibility of expanding it to countries such as Australia, New Zealand, Denmark, Germany, Slowenia and Mexico and thus allowing an international discussion between students about these crucial issues of rainforests and climate change. Some students in countries without rainforest, like Austria, are concerned that they should give advice on the situation of rainforests. "As this is not our intention and never has been, we really want to encourage, in this stage of the project process, students to discuss these issues world-wide, especially with kids and teachers living in or near a rainforest or generally in other countries, instead of proposing simple solutions. These complex problems and issues need a broad basis for discussion, reflection and action."

Another factor that has emerged was that the project bridges soft sciences and hard sciences, which many presenters and participants have asked for and considered as very important. It is an example of a content driven project that reaches out to use ICT as a tool to be more effective and more visible in the world.

108

Project PLANIT Findings for 1995-2001

Chair: Helmut Stemmer (AT)
Panel: Cesáro Morales (MX), Gerlad Knezek (US), Ronda Christensen (US), Bert Moonen (NL), Joke Voogt (NL), Charlotte Owens (US), Shafi Alamhaboub (KW), Dale Magoun (US)

Keywords: teacher education, equality, collaborative learning, integration of ICT, innovation

1. PROJECT FOR THE LONGITUDINAL ANALYSIS OF NEW INFORMATION

Technologies in education (PLANIT) was conceived during WCCE '95 with a goal of presenting five years of findings at the 2001 World Conference on Computers in Education. PLANIT requested participants to gather data from representative nations at least three times over a five-year period in the assessment of attitudes, skills, and level of technology utilisation for university faculty, K-12 teachers, preservice educators (university students), secondary students, or elementary school students.

Some results in detail:

1. Teachers' beliefs about the utility of ICT are surprising similar across nations and different levels of access/support
2. ICT student attitudes are gender-neutral at the early primary school level, may be slightly higher for females at the late elementary school level, and are definitely higher for males in secondary school
3. Students with home access to computers commonly have 2-10 times as much computer exposure at home as they do in school, and home access appears to positively impact school activities
4. Needs-based teacher education for classroom technology integration has a measurable positive impact on the attitudes of teachers and students; properly implemented classroom techniques impact student behaviour in

activities such as preference for using computers over watching television; and there is growing evidence that it has a positive impact on student achievement.

Last but not least two books were given to the auditorium:

Impact of New Technologies on Teaching and Learning (ISBN 968-5247-22-6; May 2000)

and a preversion of

Users Views of New Information Technologies in Education: Studies from Multiple Nations (July 2001)

2. SUMMARY

The goal of this international study about the use of ICT in education is to present five years of research and findings about attitudes, skills and level of technology utilisation in education. Special focus was given to gender issues. In some studies it was shown that women's attitude towards ICT improved, when their exposure to ICT is increased, such as through the on campus ICT program in Lousiana and other implemented projects. Generally it was noted that training of teachers is an important factor in the use of ICT in schools. Factors such as anxiety and avoidance can be changed to the better in that way.

109

Teacher Training for Networked Learning

Chair: Tom van Weert (NL)
Panel: Doug Brown (UK), Paul Nicholson (AU), Michelle Selinger (UK)

Keywords: teaching methods, pedagogy, collaborative learning, lifelong learning, teacher education

1. TOWARDS A NEW MODEL OF 'TEACHING'

Education is moving to a new 'teaching' model that implies learning in communities of students and teachers. In these networks learning is the central activity, not teaching. In these networked communities the teacher will be the expert learner, but sometimes a student will take this role or an outside expert. Those of the audience who took part in the discussions, were convinced developments in education go in this direction.

2. BRIDGING THE GAP BETWEEN TECHNOLOGY AND PEDAGOGY

But what about the teacher? If you make the above model the central part in your training, then experience shows that teachers will feel they have always done things in the wrong way and will feel inadequate. If, on the other hand, you make technology the central focus, it might well be that teachers use the technology for their own purposes, but not for teaching. A bridge should be built between technology and pedagogy. At the moment this bridge is many times lacking in initial and in-service teacher education.

2.1 A process of change

Introduction of computers in schools involves a process of change. New pedagogical situations have to be created that allow teachers to develop an understanding of what is needed to move from teaching situations towards learning situations supported by Information and Communication Technology (ICT). Teachers must feel safe both with ICT and with a changed role in the classroom.

2.2 Creating safe situations

Situations were discussed in which the teachers would feel safe to try on new ways of working with the students. A successful example of such a situation involved teacher training students in Australia. These students developed pedagogical situations and learning materials involving ICT for the teachers who supervised their training in school. As part of this training the new learning situations were tried out. In this way both the teacher training students and the supervising teachers got working examples of what it would be to use ICT in their classroom in a non-threatening way. Another example was from Sweden where students collaborated with teachers to develop or redesign study materials involving ICT.

Keyword index

Author index

IFIP – International Federation for Information Processing

The International Federation for Information Processing is a multinational federation of professional and technical organisations founded in 1960 under the auspices of UNESCO. IFIP is dedicated to improving worldwide communication and increased understanding among practitioners of all nations about the role information processing, or informatics, can play in all walks of life.

Organisation of IFIP

IFIP activities are organised around the Technical Committees (TCs). Each Technical Committee has a particular focus; education is the focus of Technical Committee 3. Work within a Technical Committee is done in their Working Groups (WGs) of specialists who are individually appointed by their peers, independent of nationality and government.

At the heart of Technical Committee 3 are the seven working groups.

IFIP Secretariat

IFIP Secretariat, Hofstrasse 3, A-2361 Laxenburg, Austria
Tel.: +43 2236 73616, Fax: +43 2236 73616 9,
e-mail: ifip@ifip.or.at, http://www.ifip.or.at